Asian Arts & Archaeology Series No-5

ICONOGRAPHIC DICTIONARY OF THE INDIAN RELIGIONS

HINDUISM – BUDDHISM – JAINISM

BY

GÖSTA LIEBERT
Professor of Sanskrit and Comparative Philology in the University of Gothenburg

SRI SATGURU PUBLICATIONS
DELHI, INDIA

Distributed by:-

INDIAN BOOKS CENTRE
Exportors of Indian Books
40/5, Shakti Nagar
DELHI-110007
(INDIA)

Published by:-

SRI SATGURU PUBLICATIONS
Indological & Oriental Publishers
40/5, Shakti Nagar
DELHI-110007
INDIA

First Edition: Leiden 1976
Second Edition: DELHI 1986

I.S.B.N. - 81-7030-098-3

Published with arrangement with E.J. Brill, Leiden

Printed in India at,
Chaman Offset Press,
DELHI-110006

EDITOR'S PREFACE

Ever since the publication of the first edition of Edward Moor's "The Hindu Pantheon" in 1810 iconography and mythology have been important branches of Indology. In numerous books and articles both received considerable attention in the past. In the course of time several works appeared in which the published material dealing with mythology was summarized in the form of dictionaries. So far, a similar manual for iconography was, however, not yet available. Professor Liebert's "Iconographic Dictionary of the Indian Religions", which brings together an enormous amount of material hidden away in countless books and articles, will therefore be welcomed warmly by many scholars working in this branch of Indology, for it fills a long-felt gap in the existing literature dealing with Indian iconography. In addition we owe the author a debt of gratitude for the numerous useful references to existing publications on specific subjects. The vastness of the area in which the influence of Indian religions was felt in Asia, as well as the nature of the subject, posed a number of technical problems and limitations which the author has tried to solve as efficiently as possible. Those intending to use this manual would therefore be well advised to read his Introduction carefully.

This book represents the result of many years of devoted hard work on the part of the author. He, as well as the other parties involved in its publication — Messrs. E. J. Brill and the Institute of South Asian Archaeology of the University of Amsterdam — are all three exceedingly grateful for the generous subvention from the *Swedish Humanistic Research Council* and to *Anna Ahrenberg's Foundation for Research and other Purposes*, Gothenburg, which made the appearance of this important manual possible.

University of Amsterdam, spring 1976 J. E. VAN LOHUIZEN-DE LEEUW

TABLE OF CONTENTS

INTRODUCTION

The origin of this "Iconographic dictionary of the Indian religions" stems from the lack of a work of reference, easy of access, and dealing with Indian iconographic terminology; it is intended primarily for readers who are interested in Indian iconography and the history of art and religion, but who are not trained in Sanskrit and other Indian languages. Since, however, much information concerning the iconographic details of the different deities is available, albeit in a piecemeal manner, experts may also find it useful.

The nearest equivalents among reference-works, such as DOWSON's *A classical dictionary of Hindu mythology and religion, geography, history and literature*, GARRETT's *A classical dictionary of India*, MOELLER's *Die Mythologie der vedischen Religion und des Hinduismus* (edited in Wörterbuch der Mythologie), are primarily concerned with the history of religion and deal only in a lesser degree with the iconography of the deities described. The same may be said of other works, such as WALKER's *Hindu world*, and MACDONELL and KEITH's *Vedic index of names and subjects*. It might therefore be valuable to give, in the brief and perspicuous form of a dictionary, on the one hand an account of the iconographic terms, their significance, and the deities to which they relate, and on the other, a brief description of these deities, with regard particularly to their iconographic characteristics.

This dictionary has been compiled from a selection of iconographic handbooks and from the literature of the history of art and religion. So as not to distort the balance of available space, particular descriptions of individual deities have not been given undue emphasis. Within this compass, however, as complete as possible a notation of the purely iconographic terminology has been aimed at, but I am fully aware of the fact that many more terms may be found in other works which I have not drawn upon. At the same time it seemed to me to some extent useful to give brief explanations, often mere translations, of those terms concerning rites, religious festivals, architecture, chronology, etc. which are often met with in iconographic literature. Philosophical and abstract terms are only exceptionally included.

As is clear from the title of this dictionary, it concerns the purely Indian religions (and thus not Islam and the like), and as regards its sphere of reference, since Hinduism has spread to Indo-China and Indonesia, and Buddhism has been carried to the whole of Eastern Asia, the line has been drawn at Sri Lanka, and Indonesia, Indo-China and the forms of Buddhism to be found to the east having been excluded; the Tibetan form of Buddhism, in its chief outlines, has however been included, owing to its close connection to Buddhism of North India, its symbolism and religious terminology being, to a great extent, dependant on Indian symbolism.

The iconographic terminology is drawn especially from Sanskrit, but partially also from Pāli and New Indian languages. In South India there is a rich terminology in Dravidian languages, especially Tamil, which is used either by itself or mixed up with Sanskrit terms which, besides, may be met with in a Tamilized form. To include all the Tamil terms would make excessive demands upon available space; it was necessary, therefore, to select only those terms of most general interest and those which, within the compass of the literature excerpted, are found together with Sanskrit terms.

A similar principle has been applied in the case of the Tibetan terms. Where parallel Sanskrit and Tibetan names occur, the Tibetan terms are generally left out, but if the Tibetan terms are generally adopted, or if Sanskrit equivalent words are lacking, they are included.

In the iconographic handbooks the chief interest of the authors is directed towards the description of the deities and their different attributes, and the purely iconographic terminology is therefore, as already been said above, dealt with too summarily. Terms are often used without any translation or explanation; terms in Sanskrit or in other Indian languages are used side by side with terms translated into European languages. The transliteration of Indian words is often unscholarly and inconsistent: words which should be printed with diacritical marks, are given without any such marks and are therefore sometimes indistinguishable to those who are not well versed in Sanskrit; if, e.g., Kālī and Kali, the names of two wholly different deities, are both rendered in print as Kali, this may confuse the reader. And if *ābhaṅga* ("bend") is given in the form *abhanga*, as it is usually met with, it might be wrongly interpreted as "not-bend"; cp. also the difference between *mala* and *mālā*. In this dictionary I have therefore sought to give a scientific transliteration of the terms in the main headwords, but many references to these main headwords are given in the divergent spellings to be found in iconographic literature.

It has not been possible to maintain strict consistency in the citing of the names of gods and the iconographic terms. All words the stems of which end in a vowel, such as Śiva, Viṣṇu, Agni, *śara*, are, of course, given in their stem forms, and all iconographers have stuck to this rule. Where the stem ends in a consonant, scholars have followed different rules. Brahmā, for exemple, is much more often cited in its nominative form (as here) than in its stem form Brahman, and, besides the nominative form Hanumān, this name is to be found, though rarely, either in its strong stem form Hanumant or in its weak stem form Hanumat, while, on the other hand, the stem form *arhat* is more frequently used than the nominative form *arhan*. The difficulty here was in deciding wether all names should be cited in their stem form, in which case readers accustomed to finding a name in a certain form, might be unfamiliar with another word-form, or, on the other hand, each name should be given in the word-form which is best known. After some hesitation I chose the latter method, and many writers on Indian iconography and history of religion have followed the same principle. The variant-forms are, however, given in brackets, and reference is made to the main headword, from which the variant form derives, if this, according to the lexical alphabetical order, is placed at some distance from the main headword.

Another difficulty is connected with the often numerous synonyms of the names of gods and the symbolic terms. The god of war, for instance, is by one author called Skanda, by another Kārttikeya, by a third Subrahmaṇya, even if these names do not signify different manifestations of the god; others again use these names indiscriminately and interchangeably. In such cases I have sought to normalize one name (in this case Skanda), while keeping the other names as epithets or as names of special manifestations of the god.

The same may be said of the terms for the symbols. For the attribute "arrow", for example, we find the synonymous words *bāṇa*, *iṣu*, *mārgaṇa*, *śara*, *uccaṇḍāstra* and *viśikha*, which may sometimes, perhaps, suggest some small differences in the shape of the object. This is generally of no iconographic significance, and usually originates in the abundance of synonyms in the Sanskrit language. Sometimes the meanings of such synonymous terms are briefly discussed in the handbooks (cp. Banerjea, B p. 272, noting of *vajraparyaṅka*, *baddhapadmāsana* and *vajrāsana* that they "all seem to denote the type of sitting attitude similar to *padmāsana*"), and scholars often disagree about the meaning of such terms (cp. s.v. *ālīḍhāsana* and *pratyālīḍha*). It is obviously impractical, in a dictionary, to mix up synonymous terms or terms with almost the same meaning. Here, therefore, the commonest or most convenient of such terms has been chosen as the headword and main term, which is then constantly used in the description of the iconographic accessories of the deities, the synonymous terms, with a description of their possibly divergent meanings, being given in their alphabetical order with a reference to the main headword, under which then all the synonymous terms are collected under the heading "Other n(ames)".

It was not possible, because of this principle, to avoid certain superficial inconsistencies in the terminology, since I did not wish to create new Sanskrit terms or to give preference to rare terms over those more commonly used. Various epithets are for instance used of many-headed deities to indicate the number of their heads, and the last member in these composite nouns of number may, for example, be *-śiras* (*-śīrṣan*) or *-mukha*. For "three-headed" the term *triśiras* is the one generally used, *trimukha* being a less frequent synonym; in the names for "four-headed" or "six-headed", on the other hand, we usually find the last word member *-mukha*: *caturmukha, ṣaṇmukha.* It is possible that there was, originally, a tendency to use *-śiras* in order to indicate several heads on one neck, the last member *-mukha* being preferred to signify several faces on one head, but even if this is so, the iconographers and the writers on history of art have mixed up these terms, and it has therefore not been possible to maintain, in this dictionary, a real distinction between these meanings, and to give different terms for the attributes "three-headed" (*triśiras*) and "three-faced" (*trimukha*), respectively. Therefore, it seemed to me misapplied zeal to create a uniform terminology with only *-mukha* in the main headwords.

Many deities in this dictionary are distinguished by a variety of attributes and other symbolic characteristics which can not all be said to characterize the god in any one representation, since they are drawn from different images or manifestations. It has, of course, not been possible to give a description of each representation individually here, as is done in the handbooks. It was thus inevitable that, in some instances, attributes conflicting among themselves are applied to a deity; when, e.g., Agni has the attributes both *dvimukha* "two-headed" and *triśiras* "three-headed", these naturally belong to different representations. It is frequently indicated which attributes are especially characteristic of a deity. On the other hand, references have not always been thought necessary to all those attitudes, *mudrās* and details of dress which are of a general nature and can not be considered typical of a certain divinity. It should also be added that, on account of the enormous variety of representations of deities existing in India, this dictionary does not provide an exhaustive account of all their peculiar characteristics; I nevertheless hope that it represents a good selection.

The reader who does not know Sanskrit may find it troublesome that the iconographic characteristics are always mentioned by their Indian names. Here the general practice in the specialist literature has been followed, and, the translation of terms often being unavoidably inexact and taking up a great deal of space, it is also for that reason to be preferred, at any rate so far as the more complicated symbols are concerned. The reader who looks for a certain symbol, but who does not know its Sanskrit name, can easily find it in the indices where the various terms are listed in sections according to their functions, and in which a brief translation of each term is given.

The articles have been made as brief as possible. Since practically all names and terms mentioned in the articles also occur as separate headwords, some degree of repetition in different articles was unavoidable. If, on the other hand, any article seems to provide insufficient information, reference should be made to all other names and terms mentioned in the article.

The references after each article to the specialist literature may sometimes seem unnecessarily numerous, but they are meant not only to indicate the source of the term and the literature on which the article is based, but also to make it possible for the reader who requires further information to choose between several works, easy of access, and, for the benefit of scholars in the history of art and museum personnel, to give references to as many illustrations as possible within the compass of a selected bibliography.

I owe a great debt of gratitude to the *Swedish Humanistic Research Council* and to *Anna Ahrenberg's Foundation for Research and other Purposes*, Gothenburg, who by very generous subsidies made the publication of this dictionary possible.

Finally, I am deeply grateful to the bishop emeritus of Tranquebar, the Rt. Rev. C.G. DIEHL; he has kindly done me the favour of reading my manuscript, made many corrections and given me valuable criticism and useful suggestions. I am also much obliged to my sister, Miss Svea LIEBERT, and to Mr Iain WHITE, Cambridge, for having read the manuscript and corrected my English. But it remains for me to emphasize that all errors and mistakes in this work are mine alone.

SELECTED BIBLIOGRAPHY AND ABBREVIATIONS

AA	Artibus Asiae. Ascona. Switzerland.
ACA	M. E. ADICEAM, Contribution à l'étude d'Aiyanār-Śāstā. Pondichéry 1967.
AFN	M. M. ANDERSON, The festivals of Nepal. London 1971.
AI	ALBERUNI'S, India. Ed. by E. C. SACHAU. (1-2. Reprint) Delhi etc. (1888) 1964.
AIM	W. G. ARCHER, Indian miniatures. London 1960.
AIP	The art of India and Pakistan, a commemorative catalogue of the exhibition held at the Royal academy of arts, London 1947-48. Ed. by L. ASHTON. Sculpture: K. DE B. CODRINGTON. Bronzes and textiles: J. IRWIN. Painting: B. GRAY. London (1950).
ASED	V. S. APTE'S, The practical Sanskrit-English dictionary. (Revised ed.) Vol. 1-3. Poona 1957-59.
AuA	J. AUBOYER, Les arts de l'Extrême-Orient. Paris 1949.
AuAS	——, Le trône et son symbolisme dans l'Inde ancienne. Paris 1949.
AuOW	The Oriental world. India and South-East Asia by J. AUBOYER, China, Korea and Japan by R. GOEPPER. London 1967. (Landmarks of the world's art).
B	J. N. BANERJEA, The development of Hindu iconography. 2. ed. Calcutta 1956.
BBh.	B. BHATTACHARYYA, The Indian Buddhist iconography. Mainly based on the Sādhanamālā and cognate Tāntric texts of rituals. (2. ed.) Calcutta 1958.
BECA	S. R. BALASUBRAHMANYAM, Early Chola art. P. 1. Bombay etc. 1966.
Bh.	J. B. BHUSHAN, The costumes and textiles of India. Bombay 1958.
BhIM	——, Indian metalware. Bombay 1961.
BKI	E. BAKTAY, Die Kunst Indiens. Berlin 1963.
BP	A. BONER, Principles of composition in Hindu sculpture. Leiden 1962.
BPR	K. W. BOLLE, The persistence of religion. An essay of Tantrism and Sri Aurobindo's philosophy. With a preface by M. Eliade. Leiden 1965.
BRI	See sub GoRI.
BS	D. BARRETT, Sculptures from Amaravati in the British Museum. London 1954.
BSA	T. BURCKHARDT, Sacred art in East and West. Its principles and methods. Transl. by NORTHBOURNE. London 1967.
CBC	A. K. COOMARASWAMY, Bronzes from Ceylon, chiefly in the Colombo Museum. Ceylon 1914. (Memoirs of the Colombo Museum, ed. by J. PEARSON. Series A No. 1)
CDS	——, The dance of Shiva. London 1958.
CEBI	——, Elements of Buddhist iconography. Cambridge, Mass. 1935.
ChI	J. CHARPENTIER, Indien. Historia, Religion, Kastväsen. Stockholm 1925.

CHIIA — A.K. Coomaraswamy, History of Indian and Indonesian Art. (New impression) New York (1927) 1965.

ChIMS — J. Charpentier, Indiska myter och sagor. Stockholm 1925.

CTLP — W. E. Clark, Two Lamaistic pantheons. Ed. with introduction and indexes. (Vol. 1-2). New York 1965 (Reprint. Originally published in 1937.). "pl." refers to Vol. 2.

D — J. Dowson, A classical dictionary of Hindu mythology and religion, geography, history and literature. London 1957 (reprint).

DCSS — D. T. Devendra, Classical Sinhalese sculpture c. 300 B.C. to A.D. 1000. London 1958.

DED — T. Burrow and M. B. Emeneau, A Dravidian etymological dictionary, Oxford 1961. Supplement. Oxford 1968.

DHP — A. Daniélou, Hindu polytheism. London 1964.

DIA — M.-M. Deneck, Indian art. London etc. 1967 (reprinted 1969).

DiCh. — C. G. Diehl, Church and shrine. Intermingling patterns of culture in the life of some Christian groups in South India. Uppsala 1965.

Diehl — Personally communicated by the Rt. Rev. C. G. Diehl.

DiIP — C. G. Diehl, Instrument and purpose. Studies on rites and rituals in South India. Lund 1956.

DKI — E. Diez, Die Kunst Indiens. (No year. Handbuch der Kunstwissenschaft. Ergänzungsband).

EB — F. Edgerton, Buddhist hybrid Sanskrit grammar and dictionary. Vol. 2: dictionary. New Haven 1953.

EGI — M. Edwardes, Illustrierte Geschichte Indiens von den Anfängen bis zur Gegenwart. München - Zürich 1960.

Enc. Brit. — Encyclopaedia Britannica (1964).

ET — V. Elwin, The tribal art of Middle India. London 1951.

FBKI — H. G. Franz, Buddhistische Kunst Indiens. Leipzig 1965. (Der indische Kunstkreis in Gesamtschau und Einzeldarstellungen).

FES — M.-P. Fouchet, The erotic sculpture of India. Transl. by B. Rhys. London 1959.

FHRI — See sub GoRI.

FK — W. und B. Forman, Kunst ferner Länder. Prag 1957.

FKR — J. Filliozat, Le Kumāratantra de Rāvaṇa et les textes parallèles indiens, tibétain, chinois, cambodgien et arabe. (Cahiers de la société asiatique… IV. Étude de démonologie indienne). Paris 1937.

G — A. K. Gordon, The iconography of Tibetan Lamaism. Revised ed. Tokyo 1959.

GBB — H. von Glasenapp, Brahma und Buddha. Die Religionen Indiens in ihrer geschichtlichen Entwickelung. Berlin 1926.

GBM — ——, Buddhistische Mysterien. Die geheimen Lehren und Riten des Diamant-Fahrzeugs. Stuttgart 1940.

GG — D. Greenlees, The gospel of the Guru-Granth Sahib. 3rd ed. The world gospel series 8. Madras, Wheaton, Ill., London 1968.

GH — H. von Glasenapp, Der Hinduismus. Religion und Gesellschaft im heutigen Indien. München 1922.

GI —, Indien. Der indische Kulturkreis in Einzeldarstellungen... B. 4. München 1925.

GJ A.K. COOMARASWAMY, Der Jainismus. Eine indische Erlösungsreligion. Hildesheim (Nachdruck) 1964 (1925).

GoRI Die Religionen Indiens. 1-2, by J. GONDA; 3, by A. BAREAU (= BRI), W. SCHUBRING (= SchRI), Ch. VON FÜRER-HAIMENDORF (= FHRI). Stuttgart 1960-64. (Die Religionen der Menschheit hrsg. von Chr. M. SCHRÖDER, Bd 11-13).

GOSA Orissan sculpture and architecture. Introduction and descriptive text by O.C. GANGOOLY. Surveyed and edited by A. GOSWAMI. Photographs by SUNIL JANAH, K.L. KOTHARI. Calcutta, New Delhi, Darjeeling 1956.

GrH B.Ph. GROSLIER, Hinterindien. Kunst im Schmeltztiegel der Rassen. Baden-Baden 1960. (Kunst der Welt).

GRI H. VON GLASENAPP, Die Religionen Indiens. Stuttgart 1955 (1943).

Gt J. GARRETT, A classical dictionary of India. (Reprinted) Graz 1971 (1871).

Gw. A. GRÜNWEDEL, Buddhistische Kunst in Indien. 2. Aufl. Berlin und Leipzig 1920. This edition contains more of iconographical interest than the later edition ("...neugestaltet von E. WALDSCHMIDT. T. 1. 1932).

Gz. H. GOETZ, Fünf Jahrtausende indischer Kunst. Baden-Baden 1959. (Kunst der Welt).

H M. HALLADE, Arts de l'Asie ancienne. Thèmes et motifs. 1. L'Inde. Paris 1954.

HAA T. HORVÁTH, The art of Asia. Budapest (2. [revised] ed., no year).

HAHI E.B. HAVELL, The art heritage of India, comprising Indian sculpture and painting and Ideals of Indian art. Revised ed. with notes by PRAMOD CHANDRA. Bombay 1964.

HIS H. HÄRTEL, Indische Skulpturen. 1. Die Werke der frühindischen, klassischen und frühmittelalterlichen Zeit. Unter Mitwirkung von E. WALDSCHMIDT. Berlin 1960. (Veröffentlichungen des Museums für Völkerkunde. Berlin. N.F. 2. Abt. Indien 1).

HM M. HERMANNS, Mythen und Mysterien, Magie und Religion der Tibeter. Köln 1956.

HRT S. HOFFMANN, Die Religionen Tibets. Freiburg/München 1956.

HS HARBANS SINGH, Guru Nanak and origins of the Sikh faith. Bombay etc. 1969.

HSIT J. HACKIN, La sculpture indienne et tibétaine au musée Guimet. Paris 1931.

HuET S. HUMMEL, Elemente der tibetischen Kunst. (Forschungen zur Völkerdynamik Zentral- und Ostasiens. H. 3). Leipzig 1949.

HuGT —, Geschichte der tibetischen Kunst. Leipzig 1953.

IA Indian art. Victoria and Albert museum. London 1952.

IC L'Inde classique. Manuel des études indiennes par L. RENOU et J. FILLIOZAT. 1-2. Paris 1947-1953.

IIM V. IONS, Indian mythology. London 1967.

IP Indische Plastik. Aufnahmen von W. DRÄYER. Nachwort von A. KESSER. München 1960.

JDI	G. Jouveau-Dubreuil, Iconography of Southern India. Transl. from the French by A. C. Martin. Paris 1937.
JMS	N. P. Joshi, Mathura sculptures (A hand book to appreciate sculptures in the Archaeological Museum, Mathura). Mathura 1966.
JSV	L. Jisl - V. Sís - J. Vaniš, Tibetische Kunst. Prag 1958.
JT	H. A. Jäschke, A Tibetan-English dictionary with special reference to the prevailing dialects. London 1881 (later reprints).
JTS	Journal of Tamil studies. Madras.
KBh.	W. Koppers, Die Bhil in Zentralindien. Horn-Wien 1948.
KiDG	W. Kirfel, Die dreiköpfige Gottheit. Bonn 1948.
KiH	Bilderatlas zur Religionsgeschichte. Lief. 18-20: Der Hinduismus von W. Kirfel. Leipzig 1934.
KiJ	Bilderatlas zur Religionsgeschichte. Lief. 12: Die Religion der Jaina's von W. Kirfel. Leipzig 1928.
KiK	W. Kirfel, Die Kosmographie der Inder nach Quellen dargestellt. (Nachdruck) Hildesheim 1967 (1920).
KIM	Ch. Kar, Indian metal sculpture. London 1952.
KiSB	W. Kirfel, Symbolik des Buddhismus. Stuttgart 1959. Symbolik der Religionen. 5.
KiSH	——, Symbolik des Hinduismus und des Jainismus. Stuttgart 1959. Symbolik der Religionen. 4.
KM	T. de Kleen, Mudrās. The ritual hand-poses of the Buddha priests and the Shiva priests of Bali. London 1924.
KrA	St. Kramrisch, The art of India. Traditions of Indian sculpture, painting and architecture. London 1954.
KrG	——, Grundzüge der indischen Kunst. Dresden 1924.
KrI	——, Indian sculpture in the Philadelphia museum of art. Philadelphia 1960.
KT	S. Konow and P. Tuxen, The religions of India. Copenhagen 1949.
LCD	K. Lal, The cult of desire. London 1966 (2. ed. 1967).
Mayrhofer, EWA	M. Mayrhofer, Kurzgefasstes etymologisches Wörterbuch des Altindischen. Bd 1 —. Heidelberg 1956 —.
MBPC	H. Mode, Die buddhistische Plastik auf Ceylon. Leipzig 1963. (Der indische Kunstkreis in Gesamtschau und Einzeldarstellungen [vol. 1]).
MD	Mousset et Dupuis, Dictionnaire Tamoul-Français. 3. éd. 1-2 Pondichéry 1938-1942.
MEIA	M.-Th. de Mallmann, Les enseignements iconographiques de l'Agnipurana. Paris 1963. Annales du Musée Guimet. Bibliothèque d'études. T. 67.
MG	E. O. Martin, The gods of India. London et Toronto 1914.
MH	R. J. Mehta, The handicrafts and industrial arts of India. Bombay 1960.
MKVI	A. A. Macdonell and A. B. Keith, Vedic index of names and subjects. Vol. 1-2. Delhi, Varanasi, Patna (3rd reprint) 1967 (1st ed. 1912).
MS	J. Marshall, A guide to Sāñchī. 3rd ed. Delhi 1955.
MSHP	E. Moor, The Hindu pantheon. A new ed. by W. O. Simpson. Madras (1864) reprinted 1897. (Good illustrations, but the text is out of date).

MW M. MONIER-WILLIAMS, A Sanskrit-English dictionary. New ed. Oxford 1899 (later reprints).

N NYANATILOKA, Buddhistisches Wörterbuch. Kurzgefasstes Handbuch der buddhistischen Lehren und Begriffe in alphabetischer Anordnung. Konstanz (1952).

NLEM New Larousse. Encyclopedia of Mythology. Introduction by R. GRAVES. London etc. 1959 (1968). The Indian section by P. MASSON-OURSEL and L. MORIN).

Or Suec. Orientalia Suecana (Uppsala).

P J. T. PLATTS, A dictionary of Urdū, classical Hindī, and English. Oxford 1884 (reprinted 1960).

pw O. BÖHTLINGK, Sanskrit-Wörterbuch in kürzerer Fassung. 1-7. St. Petersburg 1879-1889 (later reprint).

R T. A. G. RAO, Elements of Hindu iconography. 1-2. Madras 1914-1916 (later reprint).

RAAI B. ROWLAND, The art and architecture of India. Buddhist, Hindu, Jain. Melbourne, London, Baltimore 1953. (The Pelican history of art, ed. by N. PEVSNER, Z 2).

RhDS T. W. RHYS DAVIDS and W. STEDE, The Pali text society's Pali-English dictionary. London 1921 (later reprints).

RIS Ph. RAWSON, Indian sculpture. London and New York 1966.

RN T. N. RAMACHANDRAN, The Nāgapaṭṭiṇam and other Buddhist bronzes in the Madras Museum. Madras (1954, reprinted) 1965. (Bulletin of the Madras Government Museum. New series. General section. Vol. VII No. 1).

RV L. RENOU, Vocabulaire du rituel védique. Paris 1954. (Collection de vocabulaires techniques du sanskrit, dirigée par L. RENOU et J. FILLIOZAT. I).

SB P. R. SRINIVASAN, Bronzes of South India. Madras 1963. (Bulletin of the Madras Government Museum, ed. by the superintendent. New series. General section. Vol. VIII).

SchRI See sub GoRI.

SeKB D. SECKEL, Kunst des Buddhismus. Werden, Wanderung und Wandlung. Baden-Baden 1962. (Kunst der Welt).

Sh. I. SHEKHAR, Sanskrit drama: its origin and decline. Leiden 1960. (Orientalia Rheno-Traiectina. Vol. 7).

SIB C. SIVARAMAMURTI, Indian bronzes. Bombay 1962.

SKh. H. J. STOKE and K. KHANDAVALA, The laud ragamala miniatures. A study in painting and music. Oxford 1953.

SM E. D. SAUNDERS, Mudrā. A study of symbolic gestures in Japanese Buddhist sculpture. New York 1960. (Bollingen series 58. Pantheon books).

SMII C. SACHS, Die Musikinstrumente Indiens und Indonesiens. 2. Aufl. Berlin und Leipzig 1923.

SS S. K. SARASWATI, A survey of Indian sculpture. Calcutta 1957.

SSI H. K. SASTRI, South-Indian images of gods and goddesses. Madras 1916 (reprint 1974).

SSIP C. SIVARAMAMURTI, South Indian paintings. New Delhi 1968.

SSR J. SANDEGREN, Om Sydindiens rövarekaster och deras religiösa värld. Stockholm 1924.

STP	The ocean of story being C. H. TAWNEY's translation of Somadeva's Kathā sarit sāgara... ed. (2... ed. 1923-28). ... by N. M. PENZER. Vol. 1-10. (Reprint) Delhi-Patna-Varanasi 1968.
TDIL	R. L. TURNER, A comparative dictionary of the Indo-Aryan languages. London 1966. Indexes compiled by D. R. TURNER. London 1969.
Th.	D. R. THAPAR, Icons in bronze. An introduction to Indian metal images. London 1961.
TL	Tamil lexicon, published under the authority of the University of Madras. Vol. 1-6 and supplement. Madras 1924-1939.
W	W. J. WILKINS. Hindu mythology. Vedic and Purānic. Calcutta 1882.
WAA 25	Sh. L. WEINER, From Gupta to Pala sculpture. AA. Vol. 25 (1962), 167 ff.
WHW	B. WALKER, Hindu world. An encyclopedic survey of Hinduism. Vols. 1-2. London 1968.
WIA	M. WHEELER, Early India and Pakistan to Ashoka. London 1959. (Ancient peoples and places. 12).
WIC	——, The Indus civilization. 3. ed. Cambridge 1968. (The Cambridge history of India, supplementory vol.).
WM	Wörterbuch der Mythologie. Herausgegeben von H. W. HAUSSIG. I. Abteilung: Die alten Kulturvölker. Stuttgart 1966. (References are made to the vol.: Die Mythologie der vedischen Religion und des Hinduismus von V. MOELLER).
ZA	H. ZIMMER, The art of Indian Asia, its mythology and transformations. Completed and edited by J. CAMPBELL. 1-2. New York 1955. (Bollingen series 39. Pantheon books. References with only figures refer to pages of the first vol., with "pl." to the second vol.).
ZDMG	Zeitschrift der Deutschen Morgenländischen Gesellschaft. (Leipzig bzw. Wiesbaden).
ZM	H. ZIMMER, Mythen und Symbole in indischer Kunst und Kultur. Zürich 1951.

GENERAL ABBREVIATIONS [1]

a. pl. = and plate(s)
Arab. = Arabic
att. = attitude(s)
attr. = attribute(s)
Beng. = Bengalī
Buddh. = Buddhist, Buddhism
c. = century; circa
cc. = centuries
char. = characteristic(s)
Chin. = Chinese
cp. = compare
Drav. = Dravidian
Engl. = English
fem. = feminine
fig. = figure(s)
Hi. = Hindī
Hind. = Hinduism
ill. = illustration(s)
Ind. = Indian
Jain. = Jainism
Jap. = Japanese
k. (in the indices) = kind of
Kann. = Kannaḍa
lit. : = literally
Lit. : = Literature
Mal. = Malayalam
Mar. = Marāṭhī
masc. = masculine
M.Ind. = Middle Indian
Mong. = Mongolian
Mu. = *mudrā* (see this headword)
n. = name(s)
N.Ind. = New Indian
NP = nomen proprium
p. = page
Panj. = Panjābī
Pers. = Persian
Pkt = Prākrit
pl. = plate(s) (pl. indicates illustrations of all kinds)
plur. = plural
Port. = Portuguese
sing. = singular
Singh. = Singhaleṣe
Skt = Sanskrit
spec. = specially
sub = under
Sum. = Sumerian
s.v. = sub voce
Tam. = Tamil
Tel. = Telegu
Tib. = Tibetan
Vāh. = *vāhana* (see this headword)
< = is derived from
* after a word = see this headword
* before a word = indicates a hypothetical word-form

Repetions of the headword in the articles are indicated by its initial letter.

In the Literature references "p." for page(s) is usually omitted, and no indication is given as to whether the reference applies to more than one page.

The religion to which an article refers is generally indicated by "Hind.", "Buddh.", and "Jain.", respectively. If such an indication is not inserted, the religion in question is either understood to be Hind., or the article is of a common character.

The headwords are in Sanskrit unless otherwise indicated.

[1] Other generally-understood English abbreviations are also used.

TRANSLITERATION

The transliteration of the main headwords follows the generally adopted scientific methods of transcription of Sanskrit, the New Indian, Tamil and Tibetan languages. Many references are, however, also made to headwords with divergent spellings.

Among the particular phonetic signs may be noticed :

¯ over a vowel (e.g. ā) signifies a long vowel.

c is in Sanskrit, New Indian and Tibetan words the usual unvoiced palatal phoneme (as in English 'church'). In English this phoneme is very often written with ch; if, in this dictionary, a word is not found under ch, it should be looked for under c. – In Tamil words c is the usual (palatal) sibilant.

ch is the aspirated palatal phoneme (in English sometimes transliterated as chh).

ḍ is retroflex.

ḍh is the aspirated retroflex phoneme.

k̲h̲ (in Persian-Hindī words) is deeply guttural.

ḻ (in Tamil words) is a particular phoneme, something like Welsh ll.

ḷ is retroflex.

ṁ indicates a nasalization of the preceding vowel.

ṅ is guttural (or indicates, sometimes, a nasalization of the preceding vowel).

ṇ is retroflex.

ñ is palatal.

ṉ (in Tamil words) is alveolar.

ṛ is in Sanskrit words a vowel, usually pronounced ri, and in Hindī words a retroflex consonant.

ṟ (in Tamil words) is alveolar.

ś is palatal.

ṣ is retroflex (in English often transliterated as sh).

ṭ is retroflex.

ṭh is an aspirated ṭ.

A

A (Buddh.), a *siddha**, a kind of *yantra*. A graphical sign (in the *devanāgarī* script) used to represent either Ādibuddha as the primeval principle of all things, or Amitābha.

Lit.: SeKB 210, 278 (with ill.).

ābhaṅga "bend" (att.), n. of a *sthānaka*-posture "in which the plumb-line or the centre line, from the crown of the head to a point midway between the heels, passes slightly to the right of the navel" (TAGORE, see B), and which therefore shows a slight bend both in the upper and the lower halves of the body. – Cp. *bhaṅga*.

Lit.: B 265; MH 6; WM 89.

ābhāsvara ("shining"), n. of a group of 64 inferior deities.

Lit.: DHP 303.

abhaya(hasta)-mudrā "gesture of fearlessness, reassurance, safety" (Mu.), n. of a handpose which symbolizes "the assurance of fearlessness, tranquillity and protection given by the deity to his worshipper". In this Mu. (sometimes mentioned as a variety of the *patākāhasta**) the right (very seldom the left) hand, is displayed palm outward, turned towards the worshipper with the fingers raised. It is a Mu. common to all Indian religions, and most deities may show it.

It is possible that this handpose originates in the Middle East; it may be found in Roman art c. 200 A.D. and is also met with in Christian art as the "magna manus". In India it is among the *mudrās* which can be assigned earlier date (but cp. *añjali-mudrā*) and it is richly documented in Gandhāran art as char. of the Buddha. Here it seems to have indicated the "Preaching of the Law". Later it refers to the episode with the drunken elephant Malagiri* which provoked by Devadatta tried to kill the Buddha but was stopped by his displaying this handpose (SM). From this event its later symbolic meaning of protection seems to have developed.

A few other Buddhist images of whom this Mu. is char., may be mentioned here: Amoghapāśa, Āryajāṅgulī, Kanakamuni, Nāmasaṅgīti, Padmapāṇi, Śikhin, Sitātapatrā, Suparikīrtitanāmaśrī, Uṣṇīsavijayā, and many others.

In Hinduism *a.* is emblematic of Viṣṇu as the protector of the cosmic system (cp., e.g., Anantāśāyana), and also with Śiva Naṭarāja in the *ānandatāṇḍava*-dance and other danceforms it indicates the preservation or maintenance of the universe. In a narrower sense of protection and grace any god or goddess may show this Mu.; in an image of a woman (as distinct from a female divinity) it may symbolize that she represents a widow who as a *satī* let herself be burnt together with her husband on the funeral pile. It is further also char. of Jain *tīrthaṅkaras*.

This handpose may be regarded as the right hand gesture *par excellence*. Viṣṇu, the Buddha and the Jain *tīrthaṅkaras* are often denominated "right hand personages", and they may have received this appellation because they frequently display this Mu. Cp. *dakṣiṇa* and *śaṅkha*.

This Mu. may also be performed with both hands against the chest; in this form it is char. of Nāmasaṅgīti.

Other n.: *abhayandada-*, *abhayapradāna-*, *abhīti-*, *śāntida-*, *viśvābhaya-mudrā*.

Lit.: B 250; BBh. 432, see also 207 a.pl. 151 (performed with two hands); DHP 272; G 20 (ill.); GBM 97; GoRI 1:338; H pl. 5:42 b; HIS 43; KiSH 91; MH 7; R1:14 a.pl. 5:1-3; RAAI 271; SM 15, 43, 55; Th. 28; WHW 2:86; WM 98 a.fig. 14.

abhayandada "giving safety" (Mu.), see *abhayamudrā*.

Lit.: ZA 377.

abhayapradānamudrā "gesture of granting safety" (Mu.), see *abhayamudrā*.
Lit.: ZA 202.

Abheda ("without fracture"; Buddh.), n. of an *arhat*. Attr.: *caitya* (*stūpa*).
Lit.: G 12. 104.

abhicārika ("enchanting, exorcising"), n. of a kind of icon which is worshipped "for the purpose of inflicting defeat and death on enemies, is looked upon as inauspicious and is unfit to be set up for worship in temples built in towns and villages" (B). *a.* is therefore regarded as a terrific (*ugra*) aspect of a deity. – See also *dhruva*.
Lit.: B 399, 404, a.pl. 28:2; R 1:20, 79.

abhicārikāsanamūrti, n. of an *abhicārika*-variety of an *āsana*-posture of Viṣṇu (sitting, with two or four hands).
Lit.: R 1:90.

abhicārikaśayanamūrti, n. of an *abhicārika*-variety of a *śayana*-posture of Viṣṇu (lying, with two or four hands). – See also *Anantāśāyana*.
Lit.: R 1:95.

abhicārikasthānakamūrti, n. of an *abhicārika*-variety of a *sthānaka*-posture of Viṣṇu (standing, with two or four hands).
Lit.: B pl. 28:2; R 1:84.

Abhijit ("victorious"), n. of a *nakṣatra*.
Lit.: BBh. 382; IC 2:730.

Abhijñārāja ("king with the supernatural science or faculty of a *buddha*"; Buddh.), n. of a medicine-*buddha* (see Bhaiṣajyaguru). Char.: colour: red; Mu.: *dhyāna*-, *varada-mudrā*.
Lit.: G 56.

Abhimukhī ("friendly-disposed, facing the highest wisdom"; Buddh.), n. of a *bhūmi*. Char.: colour: yellow; attr.: *pustaka, vajra*.
Lit.: BBh. 335; GRI 255.

Abhinandana ("delighting, praising; joyful salutation"; Jain.), n. of the fourth *tīrthaṅkara*. Symbol: *vānara*.
Lit.: GJ 272; KiSH 142.

abhinīla "intensely blue or dark blue" (attr.; Buddh.), n. of a *mahāpuruṣalakṣaṇa* of the Buddha, signifying that his eye is very dark.
Lit.: KiSB 36.

abhiṣeka "consecration (by sprinkling water); religious bathing" of an image with water from a *śaṅkha*. See *pūjā*. – Another n.: *snāna*.
Lit.: DiIP 90, 118, 294; GBM 114; GoRI 2:35; HIS 57; JDI 15; MKVI 1:28; MW 71; RV 18; WHW 1:83.

abhiṣeka(na)mudrā "handpose of sprinkling (of water)" (Mu.; Buddh.). "Formed by placing the palms of the hands against each other, the fingers crossed and folded on the interior of the 'fist' thus formed; the thumbs and forefingers remain erect and touch at the tops". This Mu. is very like the *uttarabodhimudrā*. It indicates the ceremony of unction, the ritual consecration, and is performed by personages of an inferior order. – Cp. *kṣepaṇamudrā*.
Lit.: SM 111.

abhīti(mudrā) "fearlessness" (Mu.), see *abhayamudrā*.
Lit.: MEIA 323.

Ābhoga ("winding, curving"; attr.), n. of the *chattra* of Varuṇa. This *chattra* was, properly speaking, the expanded hood of a cobra used as an umbrella.
Lit.: MW 145.

abja "lotus (born in or produced from water)" (attr.), either a red lotus, see *padma*, or a blue lotus, see *nīlotpala*.
Lit.: BBh. 90; MEIA 262.

abjabhājana "lotus bowl" (attr.). Char. of Yogāmbara.
Lit.: BBh. 186.

Abjaja ("born in or from a lotus"), epithet of Brahmā who was born in a lotus which sprouted from the navel of Viṣṇu. – Another n.: Abjayoni; see also Kamalāsana.
Lit.: CEBI 17 a.pl. B; DHP 235; ZM 70.

Abjayoni, see Abjaja.

acala(mūrti) "not moving, immovable (image)" (attr.), n. of an immovable (i.e. not portable) image of stone. The *garbhagṛha*-image (*mūlabera*), for instance, is never moved.

Another n.: *dhruvamūrti*; cp. also *cala*.
Lit.: R 1:17; ZA 111.

Acala ("immovable"; Buddh.), n. of a *vidyārāja*. He is also regarded as the *dikpāla* of the north-east direction. Char.: colour: blue; attr.: *cintāmaṇi, khaḍga, padma, triśiras, vajra*. – Other n.: Trailokyavijaya, Vajrabhīṣaṇa. – See also Caṇḍaroṣaṇa.
Lit.: BBh. 155, 255; GBM 80 a.pl. facing p. 144; SeKB 236, 241 (ill.).

Acalā ("immovable"; Buddh.), n. of a *bhūmi*. Char.: colour: white; attr.: *vajra* on a *padma*.
Lit.: BBh. 336.

Acalaketu-Lokeśvara ("L. of the immovable sign, banner"; Buddh.), n. of a variety of Avalokiteśvara. Char.: att.: *samapādasthānaka*; Vāh.: *padma*; Mu.: *abhayamudrā*; attr.: *cāmara, pātra*.
Lit.: BBh. 429 a.pl. 79(A).

acalaliṅga "immovable *liṅga*", n. of a stone-*liṅga*. There are nine kinds of *a.*: *svāyambhuva-, pūrva-, daivata- (daivika-), gāṇapa(tya)-, asura-, sura-, ārṣa-, rākṣasa-, mānuṣa-* and *bāṇa-liṅga*. – Other n.: *sthira-, sthāvara-liṅga*.
Lit.: R 2:75.

acalamūrti, see *acala*.

Acala-Vajrapāṇi ("the immovable V."; Buddh.), in Lamaism, n. of a form of Vajrapāṇi. Char.: Vāh.: *rākṣasa*; attr.: *dharmapālābharaṇa, kapāla, khaḍga, pāśa, vajra*.
Lit.: G 63.

ācamana "the sipping of water from the palm of the hand (before religious ceremonies, before meals)", see *pūjā*.
Lit.: DiIP 72, 90; MW 131.

ācamanī "spoon" used by priests for sprinkling holy water and making oblations (attr.). Varieties: *laghu ā.*: "little offering spoon", *bṛhad ā.*: "large offering spoon". – Another n.: *kusi*.
Lit.: BhIM 35; KiH pl. 140:7 and 8.

ācārya "observing (the rules of his order)", n. of a teacher, a spiritual guide (esp. one who invests the student with the sacrificial thread, and instructs him in the Vedas etc.). Later also n. of a temple priest.
Lit.: DiIP 67; GoRI 2:17; MW 131; WHW 1:437.

Ācārya-Vajrapāṇi ("the teacher V."; Buddh.), n. of a variety of Vajrapāṇi. Char.: colour: blue; attr.: *dharmapālābharaṇa, pāśa, sarpamālā, trinayana, vajra*.
Lit.: G 62.

Acāta(?!)-Lokeśvara (Buddh.), n. of a variety of Avalokiteśvara. Char.: att.: *lalitāsana*; Vāh.: *padma*; Mu.: *abhaya-, varada-mudrā*; attr.: *dhanus, karttṛkā, khaḍga, śara*.
Lit.: BBh. 397 a.pl. 28(A).

Acchuptā ("untouched"; Jain.), n. of a *vidyādevī*.
Lit.: GJ 362.

Acyuta ("unfallen, the Never-falling"), n. of an aspect of Viṣṇu, see *caturviṁśatimūrti*. Śakti: Dayā; attr.: like Viṣṇu.
Lit.: D 2; KiSH 39; R 1:230.

Acyutā (Jain.), n. of a *śāsanadevatā* attending on the sixt *tīrthaṅkara*. Epithet: Śyāmā.
Lit.: GJ 362.

ādarśa "mirror" (attr.), see *darpaṇa*.
Lit.: GBM 105; SM 165.

Āḍavallār (Tam.), see Āṭavallār.

aḍḍhayoga (Pāli), n. of a so far unidentified kind of building.
Lit.: IC 2: 320.

adhama "lowest", as n. of a kind of image, see sub *dhruva(bera)*.

adharottara "upside down" (att.), n. of an inverted bodily position. Śiva Naṭarāja, e.g., is met with standing on one of his left hands on the belly of Apasmāra (lying on his back). Other char.: Mu.: *abhayamudrā*; attr.: *agni, ḍamaru*. – There are also inverted *yoga* postures.
Lit.: WHW 1:45; M. BUSSAGLI, La miniatura Indiana (Milano 1966) pl. 38.

adhidaivata "tutelary deity", n. of a group of 12 deities of the months, bearing names of Viṣṇu.
Lit.: IC 2: 320; MW 21.

adhijyakārmuka "bow having its bowstring stretched" (attr.), see *dhanus*.
Lit.: MEIA 145.

adhika(māsa) "additional month", see sub *candramāsa*.

Adhikāranandin ("Nandin of authority"), see Nandīśvara.
Lit.: B 534; R 2: 455 a.pl. 131; SB 351 a.pl. 331; SIB pl. 53.

Adhimukticaryā (Buddh.), n. of a *bhūmi*. Char.: colour: red; attr.: *padma* (red), *vajra*.
Lit.: BBh. 333.

Adhimuktivaśitā ("control of confidence"; Buddh.), n. of a *vaśitā*. Char.: colour: white; attr.: *priyaṅgukusumamañjarī*.
Lit.: BBh. 331.

adhiṣṭhāna "basis", the moulded pediment of a temple building. See also *upapīṭha*.
Lit.: BECA 1: 260, 270; ZA 270.

Adhokṣaja ("born under the axle; the Sphere of the Universe"), n. of an aspect of Viṣṇu, see *caturviṅśatimūrti*.
Lit.: B 411; DHP 154; KiH 14 a.pl. 33; KiSH 39; R 1: 230.

adhvaryu "officiating priest" in Vedic age.
Lit.: MKVI 1: 21; MW 24; RV 9.

āḍhyaliṅga ("the wealthy *liṅga*"), n. of a kind of *mānuṣaliṅga*.
Lit.: R 2: 90 a.pl. 6.

adhyayana "beginning of studying", n. of a ceremony which is performed when the pupil is received by a *guru*.
Lit.: GJ 414.

Ādibuddha ("the primeval *buddha*"; Buddh.).
1. N. of an original (divine) *buddha*, an All-*buddha*. He is the embodiment of *śūnya** and the primordial monotheistic god (BBh.). From him the five *dhyānibuddhas* (*tathāgatas*) originate. As identical with him are also regarded Vajradhara and sometimes Vajrasattva, Samantabhadra or Vajrapāṇi. Śakti: Ādidharmā or Tārā. – Epithets: Svabhāva, Svayambhū.
2. *Ādibuddhabimba* ("image of Ā."; attr.). The *dhyānibuddhas* and other deities are, as said above, regarded as emanations from Ā. This is symbolized by a little image of Ā., sitting in the *padmāsana*-att., on the crown or on the head or in one hand of an idol. This image is often mistaken for the *bimbas* of the *dhyānibuddhas* (see *Amitābhabimba* etc.), from whom many deities originate. The same image of Ā. is furthermore found in mixed Buddhist-Hindu representations, in which it characterizes the idol as a Lokeśvara, e.g. Viṣṇu-Lokeśvara, Bodhisattva-Lokeśvara, Śiva-Lokeśvara. – Cp. Yogāsana-Viṣṇu.
Lit.: B 547, 555; BBh. 42; FK pl. 152f.; G 49; GBM 85; H 32; KiSB 46.

Ādidharmā ("the primeval Law"; Buddh.), in Lamaism n. of the Śakti of Ādibuddha (i.e. as Vajradhara) in the *yab-yum*-att. with him. Attr.: *kapāla, karttṛkā*.
Lit.: G 50.

Ādi-Granth "the original scripture", n. of the Sikh canon, see also Guru-Grant.
Lit.: WHW 2: 398.

Ādimūrti ("the primeval personification"), n. of an aspect of Viṣṇu represented in an *āsana*-posture with four hands and accompanied by two wives. Char.: Vāh.: Ananta; att.: *lalitāsana*; attr.: like Viṣṇu.
Lit.: B 404, 407; GoRI 2: 117; R 1: 261 a.pl. 73; Th. 58.

Ādiśakti (Tam. Āticatti; "the primeval Śakti"), n. of "Śiva's concealed Energy..., one of *pañca-catti*" (TL). In R it is said that Durgā emanates from Ā.
Lit.: R 1: 342; TL 1: 228, 4: 2404.

Ādiśeṣa (Tam. Āti Cēṣaṉ; "the primeval Śeṣa"), see Ananta.
Lit.: B 404; R 1:261; TL 1:228.

Aditi ("boundless; the Primordial Vastness", DHP), NP of the mother of gods (*devamātā*), one of the wives of Kāśyapa or of Brahmā and the mother of the Ādityas (see also Dakṣa).
Lit.: D 3; DHP 112; Gt 8; IIM 94; WHW 1:2; WM 30.

Āditya ("descendant of Aditi"), n., or epithet, of several gods who are regarded as sun gods (sun genii); in later times Ā. is esp. epithet of Sūrya (as to Ā. as a planet, see Ravi). In Vedic times the number of Ā. was 6: Mitra, Aryaman, Bhaga, Varuṇa, Dakṣa and Aṅśa; later it was raised to 12

(according to one list): Dhātar, Mitra, Aryaman, Rudra, Varuṇa, Sūrya, Bhaga, Vivasvān, Pūṣan, Savitar, Tvaṣṭar, Viṣṇu (as to other lists, see MEIA), and, because of this number, *āditya* is also a symbolic n. of the number "12", see *saṅkhyā*. – Common char.: two or more *padmas*.
Lit.: B 428; BBh. 367; D 3; DHP 113; Gt 10, 765; IC 1:319; MEIA 76; R 1:299; WM 31.

ādityavāsara or *ādivā(sa)ra* "Sunday", see *ravivāra*.

Ādivarāha ("the Primeval Boar"), epithet of Viṣṇu in his *avatāra* as Varāhāvatāra, see Bhūvarāha.
Lit.: R 1:132; ZA 86 a.pl. 282.

ādivāsi "primitive", n. of primitive tribes. It usually refers to tribes in Orissa.
Lit.: GoRI 2:15.

ādyabīja ("Primordial-Seed"), also named *kālībija*, n. of a certain *bījamantra*. Form: *KRĪṀ*. "This *mantra* represents the power of time, the power of death, the destructive aspect of Śiva, and thus the goddess Kālī, the power of time".
Lit.: DHP 343.

āgama "tradition, a traditional doctrine, a collection of such doctrines" (attr.). As an attr. it has the form of a book and may therefore as a term also be covered by *pustaka*.
Lit.: DilP 43; IC 1:631; MW 129; R 2:507; WHW 1:10.

Agastya (interpreted as "the Mover-of-the-Mountains", DHP), NP of a *riṣi*, a son of Varuṇa and Urvaśī who is esp. related to South India. Char.: Mu.: *vyākhyānamudrā*; attr.: *ajina* (tigerskin), *akṣamālā*, *hukkā*, *tundila*, *yogapaṭṭa*.
Lit.: D 4; DHP 322; GH 96; Gt 12 a.Suppl. 3; IC 1:532; IIM 79; KiH 45 a.pl. 165; MKVI 1:6; NLEM 329; SSI 254 a.fig. 158; WHW 1:10; WM 32.

Aghora(mūrti) (lit. "not terrific", supposed to be a euphemistic title of Śiva (MW); the Tamilized word-form *akōram*, to which SSR refers, however means "violence, fierceness, cruelty"; cp. also Ghora); originally perhaps n. of a gracious representation of Śiva. In spite of the name, however, this is a n. of an *ugra*-aspect of Śiva. In this sense it is also included in the Mahādeva- and Sadāśiva-representations (here as n. of the head which is directed to the south). – A. may have 8 or even 10 arms (Daśabhuja-Aghoramūrti). Char.: Mu.: *abhaya-*, *jñāna-*, *kaṭi-*, *varada-mudrā*; attr.: *agni*, *akṣamālā*, *aṅkuśa*, *asthi*, *cakra*, *candra*, *caturmukha*, *ḍamaru*, *daṇḍa*, *ḍhakkā*, *dhanus*, *gadā*, *ghaṇṭā*, *kamaṇḍalu*, *kapāla*, *keyūra*, *khaḍga*, *khaḍgamālā*, *khaṭvāṅga*, *kheṭaka*, *kuṇḍa*, *mṛga*, *mudgara*, *nāga*, *padma*, *paraśu* (or *kuṭhāra*), *pāśa*, *pustaka*, *ratnas*, *śakti*, *ṭaṅka*, *triśūla*. It is also often said that the face of A. should be of 'terrific' aspect. – A. is further mentioned as one among the *ekādaśarudra*. – Another n.: Aghora-Bhairava; see also Pañcabrahmā and cp. Ghora.
Lit.: B 465, 478; DHP 212; KiSH 25; KrA pl. 101; MW 7; R 2:197, 376 a.pl. 48; SSI 148; SSR 152; Th. 85; ZM 205.

Aghora-Bhairava ("the Not-Terrific-Terrific"), see Aghora(mūrti).
Lit.: KrA 207 to pl. 101.

agni "fire, flame" (attr.). Above all the symbol of annihilation and destruction as a cosmic principle (of Śiva), besides having sometimes also the meaning of the annihilation of *avidyā* "ignorance", and, in consequence, also being a symbol of *jñāna* "knowledge". As an attr. it is described, now as a flame, now as a torch, and now (as an independant cult object) as a jar with flames. It can be carried in the left hand (cp. *vāma*) or may, as flaming hair, surround the head (cp. *keśamaṇḍala*). Char. of esp. Agni and Śiva as Aghora, Baṭuka, Bhairava, Naṭarāja (in different dance-forms), further of: Beg-tse, Bhadrakālī, the Buddha (on the head? But cp. *cintāmaṇi*), Hayagrīva, Kālacakra, Kālī, *kṣetrapālas*, Piṭāri, Rambhā, Śarabha. – Other n.: *jvāla*, *vahni*, (*kuṇḍa*). See also *cuṭar*.
a. is also n. of the sacrificial fires, of which

there are five (*pañcāgni*), viz. *gārhapatya*, *āhavanīya*, *dakṣiṇāgni* (these three being the most important of all domestic fires and known as *tretā* "triad [of fires]"; alluding to these three fires *a.* is also used as a symbolic n. of the number "3", see *saṅkhyā*), further *sabhya* and *āvasathya*. There are also other fires, not specifically mentioned here. – Another n.: *laukikāgni*.
Lit.: B 302; GH 46; GoRI 1:139; Gt 212; IIM 79; MEIA 241; R 1:7, 32 a.pl. 2:12-14; RV 1; SB 97, 107, 240; STP 2:256, 3:160; Th. 40 (ill.); WHW 1:358.

Agni, n. of the god of the (sacrificial) fire and the mediator between men and gods, who delivers the offerings to the gods.
1. (Hind.) A. is the son of Kāśyapa and Aditi, or (according to other sources) of Dyaus and Pṛthivī or of Aṅgiras. Wife: Svāhā (or Svadhā or Sāvitrī). Sometimes he is said to be the father of Skanda. In later Hinduism he is esp. worshipped as the *dikpāla* of the south-east direction (his *diggaja* is Puṇḍarīka). He is also the god of the month *jyaiṣṭha*. In his character of the god of destruction he is also regarded as an aspect of Śiva. – Char.: colour: red or dark; Vāh.: *aja* (or *meṣa*) or *ratha* drawn by red horses or by 4 *śukas* and having Vāyu as a driver; also *ardhacandrāsana*; Mu.: *abhaya-*, *varada-mudrā*; attr.: A. has 7 arms, *agni* (= 7 flames), *ajamastaka* or *dvimukha* (= either 2 goat-heads or human heads), *ājyapātra*, *akṣamālā*, *aṅkuśa*, 4 *dantas*, *dhūmaketu*, *kamaṇḍalu*, *késamaṇḍala*, *lekhanī*, *maṣībhājana*, *pāśa*, *śakti*, *(sapta)-jihva* (cp. *agni* above), 4 *śṛṅgas*, *sruk*, *sruva*, *tomara*, *trinayana*, *tripādaka*, *triśiras*, *triśūla*, *vajra*, *yajñopavīta*.
Lit.: B 524 a.pl. 45:4; D 6; DHP 63, 87, 195 a.pl. 6; GBB 128; GoRI 1:67, 229; GT 14 a.Suppl. 3; IC 1:325, 493; IIM 18 (ill.); IP pl. 27; JDI 106; KiH 10 (pl. 12); KiSH 55; MEIA 127; MG 31; R 2:521 a.pl. 152-153:2; SSI 240; Th. 110; W 18; WHW 1:12; WM 34.
2. (Buddh.) As *dikpāla*. Char.: colour: red; Vāh.: *aja*; attr.: *kamaṇḍalu*, *sruva*.
Lit.: BBh. 362 a.pl. 237.

Agni-Durgā, n. of a form of Durgā (8-armed). Char.: Mu.: *tarjanī-*, *varada-mudrā*; attr.: *aṅkuśa*, *cakra*, *khaḍga*, *kheṭaka*, *pāśa*, *śara*.
Lit.: R 1:343.

agnihotra "fire-sacrifice", n. of the daily fire-offering in Vedic age.
Lit.: KT 70; RV 4; WHW 1:13.

Agnijāta-Subrahmaṇya ("S., born by Agni"), n. of a form of Skanda as the son of Agni. Char.: Mu.: *svastika*; attr.: *ājyapātra*, *akṣamālā*, *dvimukha*, *khaḍga*, *kheṭaka*, *kukkuṭa*, *sruva*, *vajra*.
Lit.: R 2:441.

agnikumāra ("fire-prince"; Jain.), n. of a sort of *bhavanavāsī*.
Lit.: GJ 236.

agnikuṇḍa "sacrificial fire-pit" (attr.)
Lit.: R 1:370.

agniprajvālana ("the flaming, kindling of fire"; attr.), n. of a fire *mantra* with the purpose of "producing fire".
Lit.: DHP 347.

agnistambhana "fire-extinguishing" *mantra* intended "to render the body immune to fire" (attr.).
Lit.: DHP 347.

agrapūjā "the chief worship" (Jain.), n. of worship, consisting of the offering of fruit, rice, sweetmeats, lamps, incense, before the image of a saint.
Lit.: GJ 366.

āhavanīya "oblational (fire)" (attr.), n. of a domestic, sacred fire, taken from the *gārhapatya* and used for oblations to the gods. The offering is made in the easterly direction. See *agni*.
Lit.: GoRI 1:139; WHW 1:358.

ahi "serpent, dragon".
1. Vāh. of: Sitajambhala, Sitabrahmā, Vairocana.
2. (Attr.) see *nāga*. – *a.* is also a symbolic n. of the number "8", see *saṅkhyā*.
Lit.: G 85. 89; MEIA 216.

Ahirbudhnya ("the serpent of the deep"), NP of one among the group *ekādaśarudra*. Char.: Mu.: *tarjanīmudrā*; attr.: *akṣamālā*, *aṅkuśa*, *cakra*, *ḍamaru*, *gadā*, *ghaṭa*, *kapāla*,

kavaca, *khaḍga*, *mudgara*, *paraśu*, *paṭṭiśa*, *śakti*, *tomara*, *triśūla*.
Lit.: R 2; 389; WM 36.

Āhlādinī-Śakti ("Power-of-Enjoyment"), epithet of Pārvatī.
Lit.: DHP 264.

āhuti "offering of oblations with fire to the deities".
Lit.: DHP 125; MW 162; RV 33.

āhūyavarada(mudrā) "pose of inviting and gift" (Mu.), n. of a handpose which resembles the *kaṭakamudrā** but which, compared with that Mu., displays a quarter of the degree of turning shown therein so that the upper side of the hand is turned upwards. Thus it has much the same meaning as the *varadamudrā*, though not resembling that handpose. It is esp. found in South India. Char. of: the Buddha, Kevalamūrti, Naṭarāja, Varadarāja.
Lit.: BECA 1:260; SB 20 a.fig. 8 (left hand).

ahyaṅga "snake-limb" (?), n. of a kind of band (broad or narrow) or belt encircling the waist. The term may either be a corrupt form of *avyaṅga** or suggest that the girdle was made of a snake, cp. *udarabandha*.
Lit.: R 1:314.

Aihole, n. of a village in Central India, with temples from the Cāḷukya era.
Lit.: RAAI 133; ZA pl. 113 ff.

AIṀ a *bījamantra* named *vāgbīja* and representing Sarasvatī (attr.). Here *AI* represents Sarasvatī and the nasalization means the removing of pain. Its purpose is: "Acquiring knowledge and wisdom, mastery over words, and power of speech" (DHP). – In Jainism this is a *mantra* connected with the nose, see *śānti*.
Lit.: DHP 341; GJ 369; GoRI 2:35; WHW 2:104.

Aindrī ("the (Śakti) of Indra"), another n. of Indrāṇī as one of the *saptamātaras* or *aṣṭamātaras*. She symbolizes *krodha* ("anger, wrath") or *mātsarya* ("envy").
Lit.: KiSH 53; MEIA 150.

Airāvaṇa or Airāvata (derivative of *irā*[*vat*] as n. of the ocean, hence "arisen from the ocean"), NP of a white elephant, the Vāh. of Indra and Indrāṇī. Airāvata is also NP of the *diggaja* which accompanies Indra in his function as a *dikpāla*. The wife of this *diggaja* is named Abhramu. – A. came forth at the churning of the ocean of milk, see Kūrmāvatāra. Attr.: 4 *danta*s.
Lit.: DHP 109; KiSH 87; R 2:520; WHW 1:325; WM 36.

Aiyaṉār (Ayyanār, Ayenār; Tam. "Lord", said to be a corrupt form of Skt *ārya* "honourable"), NP of a saint or demigod (TL: "guardian deity of the village"), regarded as the son of Śiva and Mohinī (i.e. Viṣṇu in a female form). He is worshipped in South India, esp. in Malayālam, and he represents a fusion of the Śaivite and Vaiṣṇavite sects. Wives: Pūraṇai, Puṭkalai (or, possibly in addition, Madanā, Varṇanī). Char.: colour: black; Vāh.: *aśva* (black; or a white *gaja*, see Śāstā) or *padmapīṭha*; Mu.: *abhaya-*, *kaṭaka-*, *varada-mudrā*; attr.: *ceṇṭu*, *dhanus*, *dhvaja* with a *kukkuṭa*, *ikṣukodaṇḍa*, *jaṭābandha*, *khaḍga*, *kheṭaka*, *pallava*, *paraśu*, *pavitra*, *phala*, *śara*, *yajñopavīta* (white), *yogadaṇḍa*. – Epithets and varieties: Ayyappaṉ (? see this word), Cāttā, Hariharaputra, Nāyaṉār, Śāstā (Mahā-Śāstā).
Lit.: ACA 14; BECA 1:1; DiCh. 31; L. DUMONT, Une sous-caste de l'Inde du sud (Paris 1957), 314; FK 122; GH 111; GoRI 2:14; Gt Suppl. 13; IC 1:488; JDI 112; KIM pl. 37, 48; MG 196; R 2:485 a.pl. 139-140; SB 348 a.fig. 316; SIB pl. 34; SSI 229; SSR 142; Th. 99; TL 1:581; WHW 1:43; WM 36.

aja "he-goat, ram" (Vāh.). Char. of: Agni, Kubera, Maṅgala (Bhauma); symbol of Kunthu. – Another n.: *chāga*; cp. *meṣa*.
Lit.: GJ pl. 23:17; KiJ pl. 45; KiSH 87; MEIA 229; MKVI 1:12.

Aja ("goat" or "unborn"), n. of one among the group *ekādaśarudra*. He has 16 arms. Char.: Mu.: *tarjanīmudrā*; attr.: *akṣamālā*, *aṅkuśa*, *cakra* Sudarśana, *ḍamaru*, *gadā*, *ghaṇṭā*, *kamaṇḍalu*, *kapāla*, *khaṭvāṅga*, *mudgara*, *nāga*, *paraśu*, *paṭṭiśa*, *śakti*, *triśūla*. Besides, A. ("unborn") is also n. of Brahmā, Viṣṇu and Śiva.
Lit.: GT 19; R 2:386.

ajā "she-goat" (Vāh.). Char. of Īśāna.
Lit.: DHP 211.

Ajā ("she-goat" or "not born"), n. of an aspect of Pārvatī.
Lit.: DHP 286.

Ajagava (Ajagāva, Ājagava; the real meaning probably "made of goat- and cow-horn"; it is also interpreted as "the southern sun-path" (DHP); attr.), NP of a bow, see *dhanus*. Char. of: Śiva, Skanda, Durgā, Nandā.
Lit.: D 10; DHP 217; MW 9; WHW 1:56.

ajamastaka "goat-headed" (attr.). Char. of: Agni (1 or 2 goat-heads), Dakṣa, Naigameṣa, Naigameya, Revatī. – Another n.: *chāgavaktra*.

Ajaṇṭā, n. of a village in the province of Maharashtra with cave-temples (1st-7th cc.) chiefly famous for their paintings of the *jātaka*-stories.
Lit.: AuOW 42; FBKI 43; FES 24; GT 20; Indien. Bilder aus den Ajanta-Felsentempeln. (Also in English and French. Unesco. Paris 1954); Gz passim; RAAI 145; SeKB passim; WHW 1:17; ZA pl. 142 ff.

ājānulambabāhu (Mu.), n. of a variety of the *kaṭihastamudrā*, in which the arm is so long that "the hand reaches to the knee".
Lit.: B 258.

Ajayā ("unconquered, invincible"; Buddh.), NP of an inferior Mahāyāna goddess, attending on Buddhakapāla.
Lit.: BBh. 160.

ajina "skin" of an animal, usually an elephant, deer or tiger, worn on the body or, sometimes, held in one hand (attr.). Char. of: Amoghapāśa, Ardhanārīśvara, Beg-tse, Bhairava, Brahmaśiraśchedakamūrti, Cāmuṇḍā, Caṇḍaroṣaṇa, Candraśekhara, Dhvajāgrakeyūra, Durgā, *ekādaśarudra*, Ekajaṭā, Gajāsurasaṅhāramūrti, Hālāhala-lokeśvara, Hariharihariv āhanodbhava, Hayagrīva, Kālacakra, Kaṅkālamūrti, *kaṭisama*, Kṛṣṇa-Yamāri, Kṛśodarī, Kṛttivāsa, Liṅgodbhavamūrti, Mahābala, Mahācīnatārā, Mahākāla, Mahā-Sadāśiva, Mārīcī (in different forms), Māyājālakramakrodha-Lokeśvara, Mṛtyuñjaya, Nandīśa, Naṭarāja (in different forms), Nīlakaṇṭha-Avalokiteśvara, Paraśurāma, Parṇa-Śavarī, Samvara, Saptaśatika-Hayagrīva, Siṅhanāda, Śiva, Sukhāsanamūrti, Tārā, Uḍḍiyāna-Kurukullā, Vajracarcikā, Vajraśṛṅkhalā, Vana-Durgā, Vīṇādharadakṣiṇāmūrti, Virūḍhaka, Vyākhyānadakṣiṇāmūrti, Yamāntaka (Yamāri); also Śiva-worshippers. – Other n. and varieties: *carma*, *carmāmbara*, *gajacarma*, *kṛṣṇājina*, *kṛtti*, *vyāghracarma*, *vyāghrāmbara*.
Lit.: B 449, 559; DHP 216; HIS 21.

ajinayajñopavīta "sacred thread made of deer-skin" (attr.), see *yajñopavīta*.
Lit.: SIB 68.

Ajita ("unconquered").

1. (Buddh.) NP of a Lamaist *arhat*. Mu.: *dhyānamudrā*.
Lit.: G 104.

2. (Jain.) NP of the second *tīrthaṅkara*. Symbol: *gaja*.
Lit.: GJ 270; KiSH 142.

3. (Jain.) NP of a *yakṣa* attending on the 9th *tīrthaṅkara*. Symbol: *kūrma*.
Lit.: GJ 362 a.pl. 25:9; KiJ 11 a.pl. 28:9.

Ajitā ("unconquered").

1. (Hind.) NP of a female *dvārapālaka* of Gaurī.
Lit.: R 1:362.

2. (Jain.) NP of a *śāsanadevatā* (with the *digambaras*) attending on either the 9th or the 18th *tīrthaṅkara*. – Another n.: Mahākālī (?).
Lit.: GJ 362 a.pl. 26:18; KiJ 12 a.pl. 29:19.

Ajitabalā ("of unconquered power"; Jain.), NP of a *śāsanadevatā* attending on the second *tīrthaṅkara*.
Lit.: GJ 362.

ājīvika (*-aka*; properly "having a livelihood", i.e. following special rules with regard to livelihood), n. of a sect consisting of ascetics and forming a third assembly besides the Buddhists and the Jains. The founder of this sect was Maskarin Gośāla (M.Ind. Makkhali Gosāla), also named Maskariputra.
Lit.: GJ 29; GoRI 1:286; GRI 134; IC 2:631; MW 133; WHW 1:20.

ājya "melted or clarified butter, ghee" (attr.), see *ghṛta*.
Lit.: MEIA 243.

ājyakumbha "vessel with ghee" (attr.), see *ājyapātra*.
Lit.: RV 26.

ājyapātra "vessel with ghee" (attr.). Char. of: Agni, Agnijāta-Subrahmaṇya, Brahmā, Yajñamūrti. – Another n.: *ājyakumbha*, *-sthālī*; cp. *ghṛta*.
Lit.: B 302; MEIA 243; R 1:250, 2:441, 504; RV 26.

ājyasthālī "vessel with ghee" (attr.), see *ājyapātra*.
Lit.: MEIA 120; RV 27.

ākarṣaṇa "attraction" (Buddh.), n. of a rite (attraction of an absent person into one's presence by magic formulæ).
Lit.: BBh. 166; DiIP 269; MW 127.

Ākāśagañja ("treasury of ether"; Buddh.), NP of a *mānuṣibodhisattva* (= Gaganagañja?).
Lit.: BBh. 79.

Ākāśagarbha ("sky womb, essence of ether"; 'having space as a womb', "der den Raumäther als Mutterschoss hat" (GRI); Buddh.), NP of a Mahāyāna *(dhyāni)bodhisattva* who lives in the womb of the sky. Char.: colour: green; att.: *padmāsana* or *sthānaka*; Mu.: *(ratnasamyukta-)varada-*, *vyākhyāna-*, also *abhaya-mudrā*; attr.: *cintāmaṇi*, *padma* or *puṣpa*, *pustaka*, *sūrya*. – Another n.: Khagarbha.
Lit.: BBh. 85 a.pl. 52; CTLP pl. 8 f.; EB s.v.; G passim; GBM 80; GRI 257.

Ākāśagarbha-Lokeśvara ("L., the Sky womb"; Buddh.), n. of a variety of Avalokiteśvara. Char.: att.: *padmāsana*; Vāh.: *padma*; Mu.: *varadamudrā*; attr.: *padma*.
Lit.: BBh. p. 399 a.pl. 49(A).

ākhu "mouse, rat" (Vāh.). The symbolical meaning of this 'vehicle' lies in the reference to an animal which both forces its way through obstacles and which (by eating the products) is also connected with agriculture. Char. of: Gaṇeśa (Gaṇapati, Vināyaka), also of Śukra. – Other n.: *eli*, *mūṣa(ka)*. – See Gajamukhāsura.
Lit.: B 358; DHP 296; KiSH 88.

Ākhuratha ("having a rat as chariot, i.e. as Vāh."), epithet of Gaṇeśa.

akṣamālā (*-mālikā*, or shortly either *akṣa* or *mālā*) "rosary (or a string of beads)" (attr.; here used as a common n. of all kinds of rosaries). An *a.* is usually held in a hand or sometimes between the hands in the *añjalimudrā*. An *a.* may be composed of beads, pearls, bones and (in demon-rites) sometimes of skulls. Certain kinds of *a.* belong to particular sects; thus the *rudrākṣa* is char. of Śaivite worshippers, and the *tulasī** of Vaiṣṇavas. The number of beads of a Hindu *a.* is properly 50, corresponding to the number of characters of the alphabet beginning with *a* and ending with *kṣa* (hence symbollically *a-kṣa*, in spite of the fact that *akṣa* properly means "grain" of which the rosary is composed). Other numbers, however, often also occur, e.g. 81, 108. The Buddhist *a.* has often 108 beads; other numbers are: 9, 18, 21, 42 and 54 beads.

a. is char. of esp.: Brahmā, Sarasvatī, Śiva (in different forms), Avalokiteśvara (in different forms); further of: Agni, Agnijāta-Subrahmaṇya, Ahirbudhnya, Aja, Amoghapāśa, Aparājita, Ardhanārīśvara, Bahurūpa, Bālā, Bālā-Śakti, Balavikarṇikā, Bhadrā, Bhadrakālī, Bhṛkuṭī, Bhṛṅgin, Brahmacāriṇī, Brahmāṇī, Brahmaśāstā, Bṛhaspati, Budha, Caṇḍeśvara, Cundā, Dattātreya, Deśika-Subrahmaṇya, Dhanadā, Dharma, Ekajaṭā, Gaṇeśa, Hālāhala, Hariharamūrti, Harihariharivāhanodbhava, Hayagrīva, Hva-sang, Indra, Indrāṇī, Īśāna, Jayanta, Jñānadakṣiṇāmūrti, Kaṇṇappanāyaṇār, Kiraṇākṣa, Kṛṣṇā, Kurukullā, Lakulīśa, Mahākāla, Mahāsarasvatī, Mahāśītavatī, Māheśvarī, Maṅgalā, Mārttaṇḍa-Bhairava, Māyājālakrama-Kurukullā, Mṛtyuñjaya, *nāga(deva)*s, Nandīśvara, Pārvatī (Umā), Pāśupatamūrti, Prajñāpāramitā, Priyodbhava, Rambhā, Rati, Revata, *ṛṣi*s, Rudra, Ṣaḍakṣarī, Ṣaḍbhuja-Sitatārā, Sadyojāta, Sani, Sarvakāmika,

Sarvamaṅgalā, Sāvitrī, Siṁhanāda, Sitatārā, Skanda, Śukla-Kurukullā, Śukra, Sūrya, Tārakāri, Tatpuruṣa, Totalā, Trimūrti, Tripurā, Tryambaka, Vajradhātu, Vallīkalyāṇasundara, Vāmadeva, *vasus*, Vidyujjvālākarālī, Vijaya, Virūpakṣa, Viśvarūpa, Vyāghrapāda, Yajñabhadra, Yama. Other n.: *akṣasūtra*, *japamālā* (and *japya-*), *kamalākṣa*, *rudrākṣa*, *sūtra*. The *a.* belonging to Śiva is named *śivamālā*.

Lit.: B 303; BBh. 195, 432; BPR 56; G 16 (ill.); GJ 383; H pl. 6:55; MEIA 242; R 1:13 a.pl. 4:10; SIB pl. 53; SM 174; WM 108.

akṣara "imperishable; letter", as "a supreme creational principle", a term used equivalently to *bīja*.

Lit.: BPR 14, 20.

akṣasūtra "rosary" (attr.), see *akṣamālā*.

Lit.: BBh. passim.

akṣatapūjā "worship, consisting of an offering of uncrushed (seeds; especially rice)". Cp. *pūjā*.

Lit.: GJ 396.

Akṣayajñāna-Karmaṇḍā ("K. of undecaying knowledge"; Buddh.), n. of a *dhāriṇī*. Char.: colour: red; attr.: *karaṇḍa* with jewels, *viśvavajra*.

Lit.: BBh. 220, 341.

Akṣayamati ("indestructible mind"; Buddh.), NP of a *bodhisattva*. Char.: colour: yellow; Mu.: *abhaya-*, *varada-mudrā*.

Lit.: BBh. 83 a.pl. 49-50.

Akṣayamati-Lokeśvara ("L. of undecaying mind"; Buddh.), n. of a variety of Avalokiteśvara. Char.: att.: *padmāsana*; Vāh.: *padma*; attr.: *akṣamālā*, *kamaṇḍalu*, *padma*.

Lit.: BBh. 399 a.pl. 51(A).

akṣayavaṭa "the undecaying fig-tree" (attr.), see *vṛkṣa*.

Lit.: CEBI 7.

Akṣobhya ("imperturbable"; Buddh.).

1. NP of the second *dhyānibuddha**. He originates from the blue *bīja HŪṀ* and represents the *skandha vijñāna*. Śakti: Locanā (or Māmakī; BBh.). – Char.: colour: blue; direction: east (A. lives in the eastern paradise Abhirati); Vāh.: 2 *gajas*; Mu.: *bhūmisparśa-*, *dhyāna-mudrā*; attr.: *vajra*. In the *yi-dam*-form: char.: att.: *padmāsana* with *yab-yum*; attr.: esp. *ghaṇṭā*, *tricīvara*, *vajra*; further also: *cakra*, *cintāmaṇi*, *khaḍga*, *padma*.

As emanations of A. the *bodhisattvas* Mañjuśrī and Vajrapāṇi are esp. mentioned. Other emanations (as a rule of terrible appearance) are: Bhūtaḍāmara, Buddhakapāla, Caṇḍaroṣaṇa, Hayagrīva, Heruka, Hevajra, Jambhala, Kālacakra, Kṛṣṇayamāri, Mahāmāyā, Paramāśva, Raktayamāri, Samvara, Saptākṣara, Trailokyavijaya, Ucchuṣma-Jambhala, Vajrahūṅkāra, Vajrajvālānalārka, Vighnāntaka, Yogāmbara; the foremost of these is Heruka. Further female emanations are: Dhvajāgrakeyūrā, Ekajaṭā, Jāṅgulī, Jñānaḍākinī, Mahācīnatārā, Mahāmantrānusāriṇī, Mahāpratyaṅgirā, Nairātmā, Parṇa-Śavarī, Prajñāpāramitā, Vajracarcikā, Vajravidāraṇī, Vasudhārā, Vidyujjvālākarālī. Variety: Vajrāsana. As a *herukabuddha* A. is named Vajraheruka.

2. *Akṣobhyabimba* ("image of A."; attr.). An image of A. (cp. sub Ādibuddha) is carried by the emanations mentioned above.

Lit.: B 262; BBh. 154; BRI 152; G 32, 52; GBM 79; GI pl. 92; H 32; IC 2:570, 589; KiSB 43, 64.

Alakā ("curl lock"), n. of the capital of Kubera on Mount Meru.

Lit.: D 10; HM 84.

alaka-cūḍaka "crest of curls" (attr.), n. of a kind of hair-dress.

Lit.: B 286; R 1:30.

Alakṣmī ("bad luck"), n. of an *ugra*-aspect of Lakṣmī. Vāh.: *gardabha*.

Lit.: B 372; IC 1:536.

ālambana "base, support" of a *vedikā** (in architecture; Buddh.).

Lit.: ZA 233.

alapadmamudrā "sting-lotus-gesture" (Mu.), n. of a subvariety of the *saurapadmamudrā* with the difference: the thumb is straightened out. Signifies summer, 'hastening to the rendezvous,' sexual bliss.

Lit.: WHW 2:87.

alapallavamudrā "sting-sprout-, sting-bud-gesture" (Mu.), see *añcitamudrā*.
Lit.: R. 2:267.

ālīḍha(pada) (att.), see *ālīḍhāsana*.
Lit.: B 266; SB passim.

ālīḍha-cum-dvibhaṅga (att.), n. of the *ālīḍhāsana*-att. connected with *dvibhaṅga* of the body.
Lit.: SB 136.

ālīḍhāsana (or short *ālīḍha*) "jumping" ("das Springen" Gz; att.), n. of a *sthānaka*-posture. In B it is described thus: "…that particular mode of standing, usually sideways, in which the right knee is thrown to the front and the leg retracted and the left leg is diagonally stretched behind" (cp. MW; and MEIA: "la position inverse de celle du tireur à l'arc"). On the other hand G: "standing, stepping to left, right leg straight, left bent. 'Attitude of drawing the bow'." (Cp. BBh., WHW). A more neutral description is the following: "standing with body bent and swaying as in fight or duel" (RN). According to most scholars (except BBh. and RN) the att. *pratyālīḍhāsana* shows the opposite att. to *ā*; but cp. RN: "standing as in violent fight". These descriptions are, as may be seen, opposed to each other, but it appears that the real difference between these modes of standing lies not so much in whether the right or the left leg is bent or straight, as in the *force* of the att. Thus the *ā.* may signify a 'neutral' posture, the *pratyālīḍhāsana* a more violent one. This interpretation also takes into account the symbolism ascribed to the postures in RN, according to which *ā.* stands for "heroism" (and hence it may be symbolic for a warrior; it is also sometimes named "warrior pose"), *pratyālīḍhāsana* for "destruction and loathsomeness" (cp. however "die dämonische Gefährlichkeit" which Gz attributes to the *ā.*). – Since iconographers disagree about the forms of these attitudes, I have not made any distinction between them in this dictionary; therefore I use *ā.* as a synonym for both postures. – The foremost foot, or both feet, may be placed on the body (or on bodies) of a demon (demons). This term may also represent the running att. of Hanumān. – In Buddhism where this att. is esp. frequent, it is also often connected with *yab-yum*.

This att. is char. of: Aparājitā, Āryavajravārāhī, Bhūtaḍāmara, Caṇḍeśvarī, Caturbhujatārā, *ḍākinī*s, Dhvajāgrakeyūra, female *dvārapāla*s, the *gaurī*-group, Hanumān, Hayagrīva, *herukabuddha*s, Hevajra, Kālacakra, Kāladūtī, Kālikā, Kuliśeśvarī, Kurukullā, the *lāsyā*-group, Mahābala, Mahācīnatārā, Mahāmāyā, Mārīcī (in different forms), Māyājālakramakrodha-Lokeśvara, *navadurgā*s, Parṇa-Śavarī, Paramāśva, Prasannatārā, Saptākṣara, Tripurāntaka, Ucchuṣma, Vajragāndhārī, Vajrahūṅkāra, Vajrajvālānalārka, Vajrānaṅga, Vajravetālī, Vajravidāraṇī, Vighnāntaka, Yamadūtī, Yamāntaka (in different forms), *yi-dam*-deities.
Other n.: *ālīḍhapada*, *pratyālīḍhapada*, *pratyālīḍhāsana*; see also *niścalāsana*.
Lit.: B 266, 482 a.pl. 35:4; BBh. 432; G 24; Gz 101; KiDG 56; MEIA 218; MW 154; R 1:19; RN 31; SB passim; SSI pl. II:5-6; SSIP 88; WHM 1:74.

āliṅgahastamudrā "gesture of the embracing hand" (Mu.). Char. of: Āliṅganamūrti (Pradoṣamūrti), Mahākāla.
Lit.: Th. 28 (ill.).

Āliṅgana(-Candraśekhara)mūrti ("representation [of C.] in an embracing att.", n. of a variety of Candraśekharamūrti in a *sthānaka*-posture in which Śiva embraces his wife Pārvatī (Mu.: *āliṅgahastamudrā*). – Variety: Pradoṣamūrti.
Lit.: B 464, 466 a.pl. 38:3; R 2:120 a.pl. 18-20; Th. 80 a.pl. 42.

ā̠lvār (Tam., "absorbed in meditation on the attributes of the Supreme Being, lost in god"), title of a *vaiṣṇavabhakta*. The *ā.* are traditionally 10 or 12 in number. See also *bhakta*.
Lit.: B 302; DiIP 147; GoRI 2:125; SSI 259; TL 1:253; WHW 1:32.

AṀ, a *bījamantra* (attr.).

1. (Hind.) *AṀ* represents the *pāśa*.

Lit.: DHP 343.

2. (Buddh.) A mystical syllable. From the knowledge of this syllable Prajñāpāramitā has arisen.

Lit.: KiSB 92.

āmalaka (-ī) "(fruit of) Emblic Myrobalan" (attr.; Buddh.). Char. of: sMan-bla, Bhaiṣajyaguru. – *ā.* is also a "crowning lotiform member of *śikhara* temple". – Another n.: *dhātrī*.

Lit.: CHIIA 77; DKI 43; G 16 (ill.); IC 1:537; RAAI 271; W 392.

āmalasāra ("pure core", "der reine Kern"), n. of a part of the *śikhara* tower.

Lit.: DKI 43.

amānta "ending with the new moon", see sub *candramāsa*. Another n.: *śuklādi*.

Amarāvatī, n. of a town in Berar, a flourishing art-centre between the 2nd-4th cc. A.D. – See Āndhra.

Lit.: FBKI 149; SeKB passim; ZA pl. 38, 86 ff.

amastaka "headless" (attr.). Char. of: Rāhu, Vajrayoginī.

Lit.: KiSH 63, 107.

Ambā ("mother"), n. of an aspect of Pārvatī or Durgā as mother goddess. Char.: *abhayamudrā*; attr.: *bāla*, *kamaṇḍalu*, *padma*, *pāśa*. – Cp. Ambikā.

Lit.: B 191; D 12; SS pl. 31:139.

ambāṣṭaka "the group of eight mothers", see *aṣṭamātaras*.

Lit.: MEIA 153.

ambhoja ("water-born"; attr.), see *padma*.

Lit.: BBh. 97; MEIA 263.

Ambikā (or Amvikā, "mother").

1. (Hind.) NP of a goddess. She is often identified with Ambā*, but a distinction is made by R between these goddesses. Therefore Ambikā: Together with Pārvatī, Durgā and Kālī she forms the central object of the *śākta*-cult. Char.: Vāh.: *siṅha*; Mu.: *varadamudrā*; attr.: (*bāla*?), *darpaṇa*, *khaḍga*, *kheṭaka*.

Lit.: B 491; DHP 287; GJ 410; GoRI 1:259; JMS pl. 98; R 1:358; ZA 102.

2. (Jain.) NP of a *śāsanadevatā* attending on the 22nd *tīrthaṅkara*; she was the wife of Gomedha. Attr.: *bimba* of the said *tīrthaṅkara* on the hair-crown.

Lit.: B 563; GJ 362; SB 322 a.fig. 247.

Amida, Japanese for Amitābha.

Amitābha ("of unmeasured splendour"; Buddh.).

1. NP of the fourth *dhyānibuddha* who resides in the paradise Sukhāvatī. He originates from the red syllable *HRĪḤ*, and represents the *skandha sañjñā*. It is supposed, on the basis of his red colour that the concept of A. has been influenced by an Iranian light-religion. – Sakti: Pāṇḍarā. Char.: colour: red; direction: west (A. lives in the western paradise Sukhāvatī); Vāh.: 2 *mayūra*s (or *haṅsa*s); att.: *padmāsana*; Mu.: *dhyānamudrā* (both hands); attr.: *cūḍā*, *kamaṇḍalu* (*pātra*), *padma*, *saṅghāti*. – In the *yi-dam*-form: char.: att.: *padmāsana* and *yab-yum*; attr.: *cintāmaṇi*, *ghaṇṭā*, *tricīvara*. – As a *herukabuddha* he is named: Padmaheruka. – Emanations of A. are the *dhyānibodhisattva*s Padmapāṇi (Avalokiteśvara) and Mañjuśrī and many other Mahāyāna deities.

Amitāyus is often regarded as identical with A.; iconographically the distinction is made between them that A. is represented without a crown and Amitāyus with crown and *bodhisattvābharaṇa*. – Epithet: Vajradharma.

Lit.: BBh. 48 a.pl. 19; BRI 151; CEBI pl. 11:34; EB 63; G 32, 52, 86; GBB 245; GRI 258; H 32; HuGT 21; IC 2:569, 589; KiSB 43, 58, 64; ZA 204 a.pl. B9.

2. *Amitābhabimba* "image of A." (attr.). This image is carried on the hair(crown) or in the hands and signifies that the image is an emanation of A. (cp. *Ādibuddhabimba*). Thus esp. Avalokiteśvara (in different forms), e.g. on top of the elevenheaded Avalokiteśvara (named Nīlakaṇṭhāryāvalokiteśvara). This attr. is further char. of: Bhṛkuṭī, Dharmadhātuvāgīśvara, Ekajaṭā, Hayagrīva, Kurukullā (in different

forms), Lokanātha, Mahābala, Mahāśītavatī, Padmanarteśvaṛa, Samantaprabhā, Saptaśatika-Hayagrīva.
Lit.: B 547, 555; KiDG 53 (ill.).

Amitābha-Lokeśvara (Buddh.), n. of a variety of Avalokiteśvara. Char.: att.: *samapādasthānaka*; Vāh.: *padma*; attr.: *cakra, cāmara*.
Lit.: BBh. 429 a.pl. 87(A).

Amitābha-Mañjuśrī, see Mañjuśrī.
Lit.: BBh. 102.

Amitaprabha ("boundless light"; Buddh.), NP of a *bodhisattva*. Char.: colour: white or red; attr.: *kamaṇḍalu* (with *amṛta*), *mahāmbuja*. – Another n.: Amṛtaprabha.
Lit.: BBh. 90 a.pl. 61.

Amitāyus ("of unmeasured life"; Buddh.).

1. A. is sometimes counted among the *dhyānibuddhas* and regarded as identical with Amitābha (said to be a variety of this god). According to others (on account of his dress) he is a *(dhyāni)bodhisattva*. – No wife of A. is mentioned Char.: att.: *padmāsana* (sometimes also *sthānaka*); Mu.: *dhyānamudrā* (both hands); attr.: *bodhisattvābharaṇa, kamaṇḍalu* (in his hands in the Mu. mentioned above).
Lit.: EB 63; G 14, 32, 52; GRI 258; HSIT 18 a.pl. 45; JSV pl. 31, 71; ZA 206.

2. *Amitāyur(-Buddha)-bimba* "image of A." (attr.). Char. of Āyurvaśitā.
Lit.: BBh. 329.

'amle Oṛisā, n. of an era used in Orissa and beginning in A.D. 592. It differs only slightly from *vilāyatī**.
Lit.: IC 2:737.

Amma (Tam. *ammai, ammaṉ* < *ambā* "mother"), in South India n. of the tutelary deity of a village, see Mātā.
Lit.: GoRI 2:7; MG 245.

Ammaiappaṉ (Tam. "mother-father"), see Ardhanārī.
Lit.: SB 69.

Ammaṉ (Tam. "mother"), see **Amma**. A. without further epithets usually means Māriyammaṉ.
Lit.: DiCh. 15.

Amogha ("unfailing"), n. of a *śara* (attr.). Char. of Caṇḍeśvara.
Lit.: R 2:468.

Amoghadarśin ("of an unfailing look"; Buddh.), NP of a *bodhisattva*. Char.: colour: yellow; attr.: *padma*.
Lit.: BBh. 83.

Amoghapāśa ("whose *pāśa* is unfailing, i.e. binds firmly"; Buddh.), n. of a variety of Avalokiteśvara. He is represented in two forms: as one-headed with 6 (8) hands, or with 20 hands. Char.: Mu.: *añjali-, abhayamudrā*; attr.: *ajina* (tiger- or antelopeskin), *akṣamālā, cakra, ghaṇṭā, kamaṇḍalu, padma, pāśa, pustaka, sūrya, triśūla, vajra*.
Lit.: G 16, 65.

Amoghapāśa-Lokeśvara (Buddh.), n. of a variety of Avalokitésvara. Char.: att.: *samapādasthānaka*; Vāh.: *padma*; attr.: *aṅkuśa, caturmukha, dhanus, ghaṇṭā, khaḍga, pāśa, śara, tridaṇḍī, vajra*.
Lit.: BBh. 428 a.pl. 71(A).

Amoghasiddhi ("infallible power; whose fulfilment or succes is unfailing"; Buddh.).

1. NP of the fifth *dhyānibuddha*. He originates from the green *bīja KHAṀ* and represents the *skandha saṅskāra*. Śakti: Āryatārā (Tārā). Char.: colour: green; direction: north; Vāh.: 2 Garuḍas or *vāmana*; Mu.: *abhaya-, dhyāna-mudrā*; attr.: esp. *viśvavajra*, sometimes a seven-headed *nāga*. – In *yi-dam*-form: att.: *padmāsana* and *yab-yum*; attr.: *ghaṇṭā, khaḍga, tricīvara, viśvavajra*. – As a *herukabuddha* he is named: Karmaheruka. – As an emanation of him esp. the *(dhyāni)-bodhisattva* Viśvapāṇi should be mentioned; see below.

2. *Amoghasiddhibimba* "image of A." (attr.). This image, carried on the hair-crown or in the hands, signifies an emanation of A. (cp. sub Ādibuddha). Char. of: Āryatārā, Dhanadā, Dhanada-Tārā, Khadiravaṇī-Tārā, Mahāmāyūrī, Mahāśri-Tārā, Parṇa-Śavarī, Ṣaḍbhuja-Sitatārā, Sitatārā, Vajragāndhārī, Vajrāmṛta, Vajraśṛṅkhalā, Vaśya-Tārā.

Lit.: BBh. 55 a.pl. 33-34; G 18, 32; GBM 79; H 32; HAHI pl. 2A; IC 2:589; KiSB 43; WHW 1:160.

āmra(phala) "fruit from the mango-tree" (attr.), cp. *phala, modaka.* Char. of Bāla-Gaṇapati, Skanda in Somāskanda.

amṛta (*amrita*) "nectar, ambrosia" and *amṛtaghaṭa* (*-kalaśa*) "vessel, jar containing *amṛta*" (attr.). The *a.* was extracted at the churning of the ocean of milk (see Kūrmāvatāra) and brought to the gods by Dhanvantari. Char. of: Amitaprabha, Dhanvantari, Garuḍa, Lakṣmī (in different forms), Viṣṇu. – As regards a jar with *a.*, see also *kalaśa, kamaṇḍalu.* – *a.* is also a symbolic n. of the number "4", see *saṅkhyā.*

Lit.: B 373; G XXVII; GT 28; HAHI 8; HIS 44; R 1:285, 374; WHW 2:131; WM 38.

amṛtaghaṭa, see *amṛta.*

Amṛtāharaṇa ("taking away the nectar, stealing the nectar"), epithet both of Garuḍa, who brought the nectar from heaven to the *nāgas*, and of Indra, who fetched it back from the *nāgas*. A. is also regarded as an *avatāra* of Viṣṇu.

Lit.: B 529; MW 82.

amṛtakalaśa ("nectar-vessel"; attr.), see *amṛta.* Also n. of a crest ornament in architecture.

Lit.: DKI 43; MEIA 242.

amṛtamanthana "nectar-churning", see *kṣirodamanthana.*

Lit.: SSIP 97.

Amṛtaprabha ("light of nectar"; Buddh.), see Amitaprabha.

Lit.: BBh. 90.

Amṛtaprabha-Lokeśvara (Buddh.), n. of a variety of Avalokiteśvara. Char.: att.: *padmāsana*; Vāh.: *padma*; attr.: *kamaṇḍalu, padma, viśvavajra.*

Lit.: BBh. 398 a.pl. 41(A).

Amṛteśvarī ("lady of nectar"), epithet of Vāruṇī.

Lit.: SSI 220.

Amvikā, see Ambikā.

Lit.: IIM 92.

anāgāmin "not coming, not returning" Buddh.), n. given to a Buddhist who will not be reborn into this world (but into a higher one, in which he will attain *nirvāṇa*). – Cp. *sakadāgāmin.*

Lit.: BRI 49; IC 2:554.

Āṉaimukavar (Tam. "elephant-headed") see Gajānana.

Lit.: JDI 40.

Anala ("fire"), n. of one of the *vasus.* Attr.: *akṣamālā, kapāla, śakti, sruva.* – For *anala* as a symbolic n. of the number "3", see *saṅkhyā.*

Lit.: R 2:553.

Analārka ("flash of fire"?), another n. of Vighnāntaka.

Lit.: BBh. 254.

Ānanda ("joy, happiness").

1. (Hind.) Epithet of Śiva and Balarāma.

Lit.: D 14.

2. (Buddh.) NP of the foremost pupil (and half-brother or cousin) of the Buddha, often regarded as a saint; sometimes spoken of as an emanation of the Buddha or said to be the *mānuṣibodhisattva* corresponding to the Buddha. Attr.: *kāṣāya, pātra.*

Lit.: BBh. 79; BRI 16; G 104; GBM 80; IIM 128; KiSB 16.

Ānandādi-Lokeśvara ("L. of Ānanda and others"; Buddh.), n. of a variety of Avalokiteśvara. Char.: att.: *samapādasthānaka*; Mu.: *varadamudrā*; attr.: *padma.*

Lit.: BBh. 395 a.pl. 7(A).

ānanda-tāṇḍava "joy-dance", n. of a kind of *nṛttamūrti*, char. of Śiva Naṭarāja. Esp. connected with the South Indian bronze representations of Naṭarāja, belonging to the Cola school of art; when Naṭarāja is mentioned, this form of Śiva is usually meant. Śiva in this dance is performing the *pañcakriyā.* – In this form he has four arms and the following char.: Vāh.: Apasmāra (represented under Śiva's right foot); att.: *nāṭyasthāna, kuñcitapāda* (? the left leg); Mu.: *abhaya-* (right front hand), *ardhacandrahasta-* (left hind hand), *gajahastamudrā* (left front hand); attr.: *agni* (in the left hind hand), *ḍamaru* (in the right hind

hand), *dhattūra*-flowers, *jaṭābandha*, *prabhāmaṇḍala*. – Another n.: *bhujaṅgatrāsita*.
Lit.: HAHI 27 a.pl. 16B, 19, 88; R 2:223, 252 a.pl. 56-59; SB passim (many ill.); Th. pl. 52-53; ZA 122 a.pl. 411-414; ZM 168 a.pl. 38-40.

Anaṅga ("bodiless"), epithet of Kāma. For having disturbed Śiva's life of austerity by filling him with love for Pārvatī he was made bodiless by a flashing glance from the third eye of Śiva. – Cp. Pradyumna.
Lit.: GH 113; Mw 24.

Ananta ("endless, infinite").
1. (Hind.) N. of a form of Viṣṇu; also n. of a *dikpāla* (of the nadir). Char.: Vāh.: *kūrma*; attr.: *caturmukha*; 12 arms.
Lit.: DHP 131; Gt 31; R 1:257.
2. (Hind.; Vāh.) NP of the world snake (cp. *nāga*) upon which Viṣṇu reposes in his aspect as Ādimūrti (and Vaikuṇṭha). Hence A. may be regarded as a Vāh., but is also considered to be a partial incarnation (*aṅśa*) of Viṣṇu. A. symbolizes eternity and the cosmic ocean; cp. *nāga* as a symbol of water (cp. also *jala*), the element out of which the new world is born, and hence also of fertility. A. is further the king of *nāga*s and the lord of the *pātāla*. He is also mentioned in the group *mahānāga*s. Char.: colour: purple; attr.: *hala*, *musala*. – Epithets: Ādiśeṣa, Śeṣa.
Lit.: D 14; DHP 162; GT 31; IIM 108; MEIA 199; ZA 23; ZM 45, 69.
3. (Jain.) NP of the 14th *tīrthaṅkara*. Symbol: *śyena* or *ṛkṣa*.
Lit.: GJ 278; KiSH 142.

Anantamati ("of endless thought"; Jain.), NP of a *śāsanadevatā* attending on the 14th *tīrthaṅkara*.
Lit.: GJ 362 a.pl. 26:14; KiJ 12 a.pl. 29:14.

Anantamukhī "having the face of Ananta"; Buddh.), NP of a *dhāriṇī*. Char.: colour: green; attr.: *kamaṇḍalu* (with treasures), *viśvavajra*.
Lit.: BBh. 220, 340.

anantāsana ("eternal seat"; Vāh.), n. of a triangular *pīṭha* (*āsana*).
Lit.: B 273; R 1:19.

Anantāśāyana (or -śayana, -śāyin, -śāyi-Nārāyaṇa; "lying upon Ananta"), n. of a representation of Viṣṇu reposing upon the world snake Ananta. This composite representation shows Viṣṇu as the great god, combining the threefold cosmic functions of creator, preserver and destroyer of the universe, as he reclines upon the cosmic ocean (the snake), relaxing between two such world-periods. In this image, as a subordinate deity, Brahmā is represented sitting on a lotus, which grows out of the navel of Viṣṇu (cp. Kamalāsana), this symbolizing the creation of the world, which consequently emanates from Viṣṇu. The *abhayamudrā*, performed with the right hand, is symbolic of the preservation of the world, and the attr. *gadā* (often in the form of a *gadādevī*) of the world's destruction. Lakṣmī is sometimes shown sitting close to the feet of Viṣṇu, caressing his leg. – Epithets and varieties: *bhogaśayana-(mūrti)*, Śeṣāśayana, Śeṣāśāyin, *yogaśayana(murti)*. – Cp. Vaṭapattrāśāyin.
Lit.: BP 140 a.pl. 17-18; H pl.. 6:52; KiH 12 a.pl. 22-23; KiSH 34; KrA pl. 51, 52, 62, 84; MG 105 a.pl. facing p. 99; SSI 50; Th. pl. 9A; ZA 166 a.pl. 111, 286, 597; ZM 43, 68.

Ananteśa ("lord of Ananta"), n. of one of the *vidyeśvara*s.
Lit.: R 2:397.

Anāthapiṇḍada (or -piṇḍika; "giver of cakes or food to the poor"; Buddh.), NP of a rich merchant, an adherent of the Buddha, who presented to him the grove Jetavana.
Lit.: BRI 17; FBKI pl. 17; MW 27.

añcita(hasta)mudrā "bent, cupped hand" (Mu.), n. of a handpose "in which the fingers are kept separated and all turned towards the palm". Char. of Śiva Naṭarāja in the *caturatāṇḍava*-dance. – Another n.: *alapallava*.
Lit.: R 2:267; WM 94.

aṇḍa "egg" (Buddh.), in architecture n. of "the central bulk, the hemispherical dome of a *stūpa*". The *a.* reflects the conception of the cosmos as an egg. – Cp. *garbha*.

Lit.: BRI 113; DKI 13; KiK 7; RAAI 271; SB 23; SeKB 101; ZA 233.

Andhaka-ripu ("enemy of A."), epithet of Śiva killing the demon Andhaka.
Lit.: D 15; Gt 32; WHW 1:90.

Andhakāsuravadhamūrti (also Andhakāsura-saṁhāramūrti, Andhakāntaka, "representation [of Śiva] killing the demon Andhaka"), n. of an *ugra*-representation of Śiva. Char.: Mu.: *tarjanīmudrā*; attr.: *ḍamaru, ghaṇṭā, kaṅkāladaṇḍa, kapāla, khaḍga*.
Lit.: B 486; BP 220 a.pl. 24; GT 32; R 2:192 a.pl. 45:2, 46-47; SSIP 115 a.fig. 58.

Āndhra, n. of a country in Central India with Amarāvatī as its capital, and of a period in art-history (3rd c. B.C. - 3rd c. A.D.).
Lit.: Gz 51; RAAI 62, 123; SeKB 31; WHW 1:40.

andolakamahotsava "the great festival of the rope-swings", n. of a spring festival in honour of Kāma, at which the images are swung.
Lit.: IC 1:590.

aṅga ("limb, member"), n. given to a *bhakta* regarded as a "limb" of the deity which he adores.
Lit.: R 2:473.

aṅgabhāva "body-state" (att.), see *aṅgika*.
Lit.: WHW 1:45.

aṅgada "highly finished ornamental band on the upper arm" (attr.).
Lit.: B 292; R 2:67.

aṅgahāra "gesticulation", n. of the expression of emotion, such as drunkenness, lust, or meditation, which is expressed in pantomime by a dancer; also n. of the body-gyrations in a dance-pose.
Lit.: SIB 61, 67; WHW 1:264.

Aṅgaja ("produced from the body"; Buddh.), n. of a Lamaist *arhat*. Attr.: *dhūpadāna*.
Lit.: G 104.

aṅgaluhana (N.Ind.), n. of three cloths with which an image is wiped after the be-sprinkling with *pañcāmṛta* (attr.; Jain.).
Lit.: GJ 429.

aṅganyāsa "the ceremony of touching certain parts of the body", see esp. *nyāsa*.
Lit.: DiIP 76; MW 7.

aṅgapūjā "body-worship" (Jain.), n. of the act of worship consisting in the bathing, anointing and adorning of a Jain image.
Lit.: GJ 366.

Aṅgāraka ("charcoal"), epithet of the planet Mars, see Maṅgala.
Lit.: MW 8.

aṅgika "bodily (position)" (att.), a common n. of all sorts of attitudes of the body, esp. *āsana-, sthānaka-, śayana*-postures. See the index of att. – Another n.: *aṅgabhāva*.
Lit.: WHW 1:45.

Aṅgiras ("fiery"? but see WM), NP of a *ṛṣi* or a *prajāpati*. Wife: Lajjā or Svadhā; son: Bṛhaspati (Agni).
Lit.: D 16; DHP 317, 319, 321; GH 96; GT 34; WHW 1:45; WM 39.

aṅgula "finger, finger's breadth", n. of a measure used in iconometry.

aṅgulīya "finger-ring" (attr.). Char. of, e.g., Gaṇeśa.
Lit.: R 1:59.

aṅgulīyamudrā "finger-ring-seal" (attr.), n. given to a ring engraved with the name of its wearer and used for making a print with ink on paper, i.e. a kind of signet-ring.
Lit.: Gt Suppl. 6.

Anila ("wind"), n. of one of the *vasus*. Attr.: *akṣamālā, aṅkuśa, śakti, upavīta*. – For *anila* as a symbolic n. of the number "49", see *saṅkhyā*.
Lit.: Gt 35; R 2:553.

Aniruddha ("unopposed"), n. of an aspect of Viṣṇu, see *caturviṁśatimūrti*, or of a manifestation of him as Varāha, see *caturvyūha, caturmūrti*. Śakti: Rati; attr.: *khaḍga, kheṭaka*; furthermore like Viṣṇu.
Lit.: D 17; GT 35; KiSH 39; MEIA 21; R 1:230; WM 40.

añjali(hasta)mudrā (*añjali* is properly "two handfuls", "the open hands placed side by side and slightly hollowed" (MW), e.g. as a measure; Mu.), n. of a handpose of respectful salutation and adoration. It is described thus: "... both hands are clasped together, palms touching, and held near the chest just as in salutation" (Th.; cp. *saṅhatalamudrā*). This coincides with the common interpretation of this Mu., and it is in this sense that it is cited in this dictionary. In this form, too, this Mu. is seen on a faience seal from the Indus Valley civilization (ZA); hence it is perhaps the oldest of all Indian *mudrās*. Since, however, it is well-known also in Mesopotamia and in the Mediterranean countries it is not possible to be definite as to its place of origin. Together with this handpose certain attributes may be held in or between the hands, such as an *akṣamālā* or a *puṣpa*, or else a *dhanus*, a *paraśu* or a *tridaṇḍa*, held under an arm. This form of *a.* is named *sāñjalimudrā*.

A. is, however also interpreted in several other ways, e.g.: "Die Hände hohl an einander legen und dieselben zur Stirn führen ist ein Zeichen der Ehrerbietung und Unterwürfigkeit" (pw; similarly MW); or again: "les mains ouvertes avec les paumes légèrement creusées, mises côte à côte, comme les mains du *bhikṣu* qui attend l'aumône" (IC; cp. WHW); or: "both arms stretched upward above head. Palms are turned up and fingers extended" (G; this description may perhaps best be applied to the Lamaist images, but here no such distinction can be made. Together with a handpose of this kind an image of a *dhyānibuddha* may be held in the hands. This form of *a.* is esp. char. of Avalokiteśvara, and it should rather be labelled as *sampuṭāñjalimudrā*).

Since this Mu. symbolizes worship and adoration, the gods, properly speaking, do not perform it, unless they wish to pay homage to a superior deity. Consequently, this Mu. is char. of the attendants of the gods, *bhaktas*, *riṣis* etc.; further of: Amoghapāśa, Apasmāra, Appar, Avalokiteśvara (in different forms), Brahmā, Caṇḍīkeśvara, Dharma, Garuḍa, Goḷaka-maharṣi, Hanumān, Kāliya, Kṛṣṇa, Mahābala, Mārkaṇḍeya, *nakṣatras*, Nāmasaṅgīti, Nandīśvara, Ṣaḍakṣarī, Sarvarājendramudrā, Siṅhanāda, Yama.

Other n. and varieties: *kṛtāñjali-*, *saṅhatala-*, *vandanī-mudrā*; cp. also *praṇām*, *namaskāra-*, *puṣpapuṭa-*, *sampuṭāñjali-*, *vajra-añjalikarma-mudrā*.

Lit.: B 251; BBh. 432; G 20 (with ill.); H pl. 5:42A; IC 1:570; KiSB 57; KiSH 92; MH 7; MW 11; pw 1:18; R 1:16; SB 78; SM 76; Th. 28 (with ill.); WHW 2:88; WM 98 a.fig. 16; ZA pl. 1b.

añjana "collyrium, the black pigment applied to the eyelashes or to the inner coat of the eyelids; black" (attr.). — Other n.: *kajjala*, *koḥl*.

Lit.: MEIA 258, 340; MW 11; STP 1:211.

Añjana ("anointed, black"), NP of the *diggaja* which accompanies Varuṇa as a *dikpāla*. His wife is Añjanavatī.

Lit.: D 17, 180.

āñjanī (*-ī*) "box filled with *añjana*" (attr.). Char. of: Lalitā, Rājarājeśvarī, Tripurasundarī.

Lit.: MEIA 258; SSI 220.

aṅka "figure, symbol", see *rūpa*. Also a symbolic n. of the numbers "1" and "9", see *saṅkhyā*.

Aṅkāḷammaṉ (or -ai, Tam., "Streitmann-mutter", KiSH), NP of a goddess in South India who shows a graceful aspect, warding off evil and expelling demons, and who belongs to the group *navaśakti*. She is connected with Śiva, and in TL she is said to represent Kālī in her terrible form. Attr.: *ḍamaru* (entwined by a *nāga*), *kapāla*, *khaḍga*, *pāśa*. – Another n.: Aṅkamma(?).

Lit.: DiCh. 32; Gt Suppl. 7; KiH 24 a.pl. 79; KiSH 51; SSR 153; TL 1:21.

Aṅkamma (sic! probably = Aṅkāḷammaṉ), NP of a popular goddess (a sister of Māriyammaṉ), the deity of house and family, worshipped in the district of Nellore (north of Madras).

Lit.: GoRI 2:6.

aṅkuśa "hook, goad, ankus", esp. an elephant-driver's hook (attr.). Symbolizes the activity of a deity. In South India, an emblem of royalty and a *maṅgala* (see *aṣṭamaṅgala*). The Buddhist form of the *a.* is often crowned by one or more *vajras*, cp. also *vajrāṅkuśa*. – It is esp. char. of: Gaṇeśa (Gaṇapati), Indra, Skanda, Śiva, Annapūrṇā, Agni; further of: Aghora, Agni-Durgā, Ahirbudhnya, Aja, Anila, Āpa, Aparājita, Aparājitā, Āryavajravārāhī, Aṣṭabhuja-Kurukullā, Avalokiteśvara (some Lokeśvara forms), Bahurūpa, Bālā-Śakti, Bhairavī, Bhuvaneśvarī, Brahmā, Cāmuṇḍā, Caṇḍā, Cundā, Devī, Dhanada-Tārā, Dharmadhātuvāgīśvara, Durgottāriṇī-Tārā, Ekajaṭā, Gaurī (Buddh.), mGon-dkar, Hara, Hevajra, Īśāna, Jambhala, Jayanta, Kālacakra, Kālajambhala, Kālī, Kārttikeya, Kubera, Kurukullā, Lalitā, kLu-dbaṅ, Mahādeva, Mahākāla, Mahākālī, Mahāpratyaṅgirā, Mahāsāhasrapramardanī, Mahāsarasvatī, Maheśamūrti, Mahiṣāsuramardinī, Mārīcī (in different forms), Māyājālakrama-Kurukullā, Murukaṉ, Nandā, *navadurgās*, Prabhāsa, Prasannatārā, Pratyūṣa, Rājarājeśvarī, Rambhā, Revata, Sadāśiva, Ṣaṇmukha, Śarabha, Sarasvatī, Sarvakāmika, Sarvāpāyañjaha, Senānī, Sitātapatrā, Soma, Sureśvara, Tārakāri, Trailokyavaśaṅkaralokeśvara, Trailokyavijaya, Tripura, Tripurasundarī, Tryambaka, Vajradhara, Vajragāndhārī, Vajrahūṅkāra, Vajrāmṛta, Vajrāṅkuśī, Vajratārā, Vajravārāhī, Vajravetālī, Vajravidāraṇī, *vasus*, Vāyu, Vibhava, Vidyujjvālākarālī, Vighnāntaka, Virūpākṣa, Viśvarūpa, Vyāghrapāda.

Other n.: *gajāṅkuśa*, *kuṭāri*, *sṛṇi*, *tōṭṭi*, *tottra*.

Lit.: AuOW 70; B 301, 358; BBh. 432; G 12 (ill.); H pl. 6:57a; MD 2:130; MH coloured pl. 24; R 1:8 a.pl. 3:3-4; Th. 41; WM 107 a.fig. 62; ZM 226.

Aṅkuśā (Jain.), NP of a *śāsanadevatā* attending on the 14th *tīrthaṅkara*.

Lit.: GJ 362.

aṅkuśabīja "the syllable of *aṅkuśa*", a *bīja* with the form *KROṀ* (attr.).

Lit.: IC 1:567.

aṅkuśamudrā "ankus-*mudrā*" (Mu.), n. of a handpose, the form of which is not described. While performing it a *mudrādaṇḍa* is used.

Lit.: DiIP 106.

annaprāśana "giving of food", n. of a *saṅskāra*-rite, the placing of rice in a child's mouth for the first time (at the age of six months).

Lit.: DiIP 180, 184; GH 334; GJ 411; MW 45; WHW 2:316.

Annapūrṇā ("filled with food", "die Nahrungsfülle"; according to WHW originally Ammāpūrṇā "mother of plenty"), n. of a beneficent aspect of Pārvatī. Char.: Mu.: *abhaya-*, *varada-mudrā*; attr.: *aṅkuśa*, *candra*, *hāra*, *pāśa*, *pātra* (with honey or food or jewels), *sruk* (this may also contain food etc.).

Lit.: GH 142; GI pl. 76; GoRI 2:210; MSHP 91; R 1:370 a.pl. 108:2; SSI 218; Th. 107; W 265; WHW 1:398; ZM 236.

aṅśa "part, share", n. of a partial incarnation of the activity of a deity (esp. of Viṣṇu); thus e.g. the manifestation in an embodied form of the weapons or other attr. of a deity (*āyudhapuruṣa*), sometimes also of a Vāh. (see Ananta). *a.* is however, often used as an equivalent of *avatāra**, since all incarnations are supposed to be contemporaneous with their prototypes. – Cp. also *āveśa*.

Lit.: GH 131; R 1:119.

Aṅśa ("the share of the gods"), NP of an Āditya.

Lit.: DHP 122.

antarabhitti "inner wall" of a temple.

Lit.: BECA 1:260.

antarāla (in architecture) "intermediate space" in a temple.

Lit.: DKI 41; ZA 269.

antarīya "lower garment" (attr.). Not necessarily char. of either sex but may be worn by both men and women. Cp. antarvāsaka.

Lit.: SB 125.

antarvāsaka "under, lower garment, which comes down to the feet" (attr.; Buddh.),

n. of one of the three garments (*tricīvara*) of a Buddhist monk. Cp. *antarīya*.
Lit.: B 294; HIS 42; HSIT 9 a.pl. 12.

antyasaṅskāra "the last sacrament" (esp. Jain.), n. of the funeral ceremony. Cp. *saṅskāra*. – Another n.: *antyeṣṭi*.
Lit.: GJ 417.

antyeṣṭi "funeral sacrifice", see *antyasaṅskāra*.
Lit.: IC 1:365.

anugrahamūrti (also *anugrahaṇa-*) "pacific, boon-bestowing manifestation" of Śiva, in which he is usually represented seated with his wife (because his Śakti is generally accustomed to keep Śiva in a pacific frame of mind). – Forms of *a.* are: Caṇḍeśānugraha-, Kirātārjuna-, Nandīśānugraha-, Rāvaṇānugraha-, Vighneśvarānugraha-, and Viṣṇvanugraha-mūrti.
Lit.: B 466; IC 1:513; R 2:205; WM 167.

Anurādhā(s) ("causing welfare"), n. of a *nakṣatra*. Its influence is good.
Lit.: BBh. 382; IC 2:730.

Anurādhapura, n. of an ancient capital in Sri Lanka with many *dāgabas* or *stūpas*, i.e. relic chambers and, from the 3rd c. B.C. and onwards, numerous Buddhist cave-monastries.
Lit.: DCSS passim; ZA pl. 456.

anuvyañjana "secondary mark" (attr.; Buddh.), n. of the 80 lesser marks of the Buddha, see *lakṣaṇa*. These marks are referred to in abstract terms, such as: *citrakeśatā* "the having beautiful hair", *citratrāṅgulitā* "the having beautiful fingers", *tīkṣṇadaṅṣṭratā* "the having sharp eye-teeth", *madhuracā-umañjusvaratā* "the having a sweet and agreeable and pleasant voice", *mṛdugātratā* "the having soft limbs", *mṛdujihvatā* "the having a soft tongue", *viśuddhanetratā* "the having the eyes bright", *vyapagatatilakagātratā* "the having limbs free from freckles", etc. – Another n.: *upalakṣaṇa*.
Lit.: BBh. 436; BRI 52; Gw 138; MW s.v.

Āpa, NP of one of the *vasus*. Attr.: *aṅkuśa*, *hala*, *śakti*.
Lit.: DHP 86 N.; R 2:552.

Apabharaṇīs ("taking away"), n. of a *nakṣatra*, see Bharaṇīs.

Aparājita ("unconquered").
1. (Hind.) NP of one of the *ekādaśarudras*. Char.: Mu.: *tarjanīmudrā*; attr.: *akṣamālā*, *aṅkuśa*, *cakra*, *ḍamaru*, *gadā*, *ghaṇṭā*, *khaḍga*, *kheṭaka*, *nāga*, *padma*, *pātra*, *paṭṭiśa*, *śakti*, *tomara*, *triśūla*.
Lit.: R 2:390.
2. (Buddh.) NP of an inferior Mahāyāna god.
Lit.: KiSB 78, 98.
3. (Vāh.) On A., lying, Bhūtaḍāmara treads.
Lit.: KiSB 78.

Aparājitā ("unconquered"; fem.).
1. (Hind.) N. of a form of Durgā. Char.: Vāh.: *siṅha*; attr.: *khaḍga*, *kheṭaka*, *nāga*, Pināka, *śara*, Vāsuki. – Also n. of a female *dvārapālaka* of Gaurī.
Lit.: R 1:362, 369.
2. (Buddh.) NP of a Mahāyāna goddess. Char.: colour: yellow; att.: *ālīḍhāsana*; Vāh.: she treads on the Hindu god Gaṇeśa; Mu.: *capeṭamudrā*; attr.: *aṅkuśa*, *daṇḍa*, *ghaṇṭā*, *(tarjanī)pāśa*, *Ratnasambhavabimba* on the crown.
Lit.: BBh. 151, 245 a.pl. 189; KiDG 64; KiSB 97, 106.
3. (Jain.) NP of a *śāsanadevatā* attending on the 19th *tīrthaṅkara*.
Lit.: GJ 362 a.pl. 26:19.

Apasmāra(puruṣa) (interpreted as "forgetfulness"; Vāh. or attr.), n. of the demon of oblivion. He is "evil personified" (B), "the dark cloud of materialism in the Eternal Ether (*ākāśa*), which disappears in the sunshine of the Divine spirit" (MH). Represented as a prostrate dwarf (*vāmana*) upon whose back esp. Śiva Naṭarāja (in different dancing modes, see esp. *ānandatāṇḍava*, but also in other forms, such as Tripurāntaka and *adharottara*) dances. As an attr. he appears together with Śiva Candraśekhara. – Mu.: *nāga-* (or *vyāla-mudrā*?), *añjalimudrā*. – Another n.: Muyalakaṉ; cp. also *rākṣasa*.
Lit.: B 472; MH 11; R 2:225; ZA pl. 305, 412, a.p. 122; ZM 171.

Apāyañjaha ("remover of miseries"), see Sarvāpāyañjaha.

Appar(svāmikaḷ) (*-gaḷ*; Tam.), NP of a *śaiva-bhakta* who lived in the 7th c. A.D. Char.: Mu.: *añjalimudrā*; attr.: *cetukki*, also knots of hair.
Lit.: CBC 11 a.fig. 21, 22; GJ 62; JDI 54; R 2:480 a.pl. 137; SB 333, 347 a.fig. 268B (?), 308; Th. 120.

apsarās (plur. *apsarasas*; "going in the waters"; also interpreted as "the Essences", DHP), n. of a kind of female semidivinity, originally possibly "water-nymphs". They inhabit the sky, are represented dancing and playing music, and are regarded as "wives" of the *gandharva*s. According to later tradition they came forth at the churning of the ocean of milk (see Kūrmāvatāra). – In Buddhism they are regarded as "angels". – Char.: att.: *samapādasthānaka*; Vāh.: *bhadrapīṭha*.
Lit.: B 351; D 19; DHP 167, 301, 304 a.pl. 31; G 38, 103; GH 107; GT 40; H pl. 8; HIS 26; IC 1:328, 529; KrA pl. 143; MEIA 204; R 2:561 a.pl. 158:2; RAAI pl. 162; Th. 117; WM 41.

Ara (or Aranātha; "spoke of a wheel"; Jain.), NP of the 18th *tīrthaṅkara*. Symbol: *nandyāvarta* or *matsya(-yugma)*.
Lit.: GJ 280; KiJ pl. 45; KiSH 143.

ārādhana "worship, adoration" of deities.
Lit.: DiIP 85; MW 150.

arahant (Pāli), see *arhat*.

arālamudrā "crooked (hand)" (Mu.), n. of a variety of the *patākāmudrā**, distinguished from the latter by the forefinger being bent. Symbolizes a bird, blame, the drinking of poison.
Lit.: MEIA 217; WHW 2:86.

araṇi "piece of *aśvattha* wood, used for kindling of fire by friction" (attr.). Char. of Gāṅgeya-Subrahmaṇya. Cp. *śamī*.
Lit.: R 2:442; RV 19.

Arapacana (Buddh.), originally n. of a *dhāraṇī* of Mañjuśrī which, deified, became a variety of this god. Properly a mystical collective n. of the five *buddha*s, each being represented by a letter (IC, MW). According to BBh., A. is accompanied by the four divinities Keśinī, Upakeśinī, Candraprabha and Sūryaprabha, and since this group of five originates from the five syllables *A*, *R P*, *C* and *N*, the principal god is named A-ra-pa-ca-na. – Char.: colour: yellow or red; att.: *padmāsana*; attr.: *khaḍga*, *pañcacīra*, *pustaka*. – Epithets and varieties: Kālamañjuśrī, Prajñācakra, Sadyonubhava-Arapacana, Sadyonubhava-Mañjuśrī.
Lit.: BBh. 120 a.pl. 89-92; G 68; IC 2:589; KiSB 55; MW 87; ZA 199.

ārati(pūjā), see *ārtī* and *ārtīpūjā*.

ārātrika "lamp" (attr.). According to KiH *ā.* signifies an oil-lamp (but cp. the usual term for "lamp": *dīpa*), but as interpreted by MW (and IC) it is a lamp or light which is waved before an image; in this case it may signify a lamp with a handle (and having one or more wicks). *ā.* is also used as a term for the tray provided with several wicks which is fixed with pegs to the hands of a *dīpagopī*. – Cp. *ārtā*, *ārtī*.
Lit.: GH 345, 483; IC 1:570; KiH pl. 137:3-4; MW 150.

arcā(bera) (also *arccā*; lit. "worshipping"; attr.), n. of an image of a deity. An *a.* is a cult-image intended for worship, and is regarded as the embodiment of a god; it has a propitious significance, and is the sacramental cult object. – Another n.: *śrīvigraha*; cp. *pratimā*.
Lit.: GH 58, 346; Gz 113; GoRI 1:336; HIS 19; MW 90; WM 88.

arcana "homage paid to deities and to superiors".
Lit.: MW 90.

arcanabhoga "pleasure of honouring", cp. *arcana*.
Lit.: BECA 1:45.

Arciṣmatī ("brilliant"; Buddh.), NP of a *bhūmi*. Char.: colour: green; attr.: *nīlotpala*, *vajra*.
Lit.: BBh. 334.

ardhacakrakṛpāṇa "scimitar" (attr.). Char. of Chinnamastā. – Cp. *khaḍga*.
Lit.: WM 56.

ardhacandra "half-moon" (attr.). Char. of Rāhu; symbol of Candraprabha. – The

picture of an *a.* with a dot over it symbolizes in Jainism salvation. – See further *candra* (in this dictionary used as the common term for "moon" as an attr. of all kinds).
Lit.: GJ 383; KiSH 63; MEIA 269.

ardhacandra(hasta)mudrā "half-moon-pose" (Mu.), n. of a handpose. Form: the palm of the hand, curved like a crescent is turned upwards. – Also regarded as a variety of the *patākāmudrā** and is said to signify a spear, prayer, greeting, half-moon, battle-axe. – This Mu. (together with the attr. *agni*) is char. of Śiva Naṭarāja (in several dancing modes). – Cp. *ardhavarodyata-mudrā.*
Lit.: H pl. 7:67; SB 188; Th. 30; WHW 2:86; WM 101 a.fig. 27; ZA 122; ZM 170.

ardhacandrākāra ("having the form of a half-moon"; attr.), n. of the half-moon-shaped top of a *liṅga*, see *śirovarttana.*
Lit.: R 2:93.

ardhacandrapāṣāṇa "half-moon-stone", in architecture n. of the half-moon-shaped stone step at the foot of the steps of a temple, esp. in Sri Lanka. Cp. *candrakhaṇḍapā-ṣāṇa.*
Lit.: C. E. Godakumbara, *Moonstones.* Archaeological department (Colombo); MBPC 40.

ardhacandrāsana "half-moon seat" (Vāh.), n. of a *pīṭha*, char. of Agni.
Lit.: R 2:524.

ardhamaṇḍapa (*ardhi-*) "half-pavillion; front porch", n. of a kind of temple intermediary hall or narrow passage connecting the *garbhagṛha* and the *mukhamaṇḍapa.* – Cp. *maṇḍapa.*
Lit.: BECA 1:260; DKI 56; SSI 2; SSIP 71.

Ardhanārī(śvara) ("the Lord being half woman"), n. of a representation of Śiva combined with his Śakti as one person, half man half woman. This embodies a syncretism of the Śiva- and the *śākta*-cults (GoRI: "Die Vorstellung ihrer äonenlangen Begattung entwickelte sich zu der eines zweigeschlechtigen Schöpfergottes"). – Usually the right side of the icon is represented as male and supplied with male attributes (cp. *dakṣiṇa*), while the left side is female and has female attributes (cp. *vāma*).
Char.: Vāh.: *vṛṣan*; Mu.: *abhaya-*, *kaṭaka-* (in order to hold a flower), *varada-mudrā*; attr. (the right side): *ajina, candra, kapāla, khaḍga, musala, nīlotpala, ṭaṅka, triśūla, vīṇā*; (the left side:) *akṣamālā, darpaṇa, dukūla, kuṇḍala, padma, paraśu, pāśa,* a female *stana, tilaka, triśūla, (nāga)yajñopa-vīta*; further *triśiras* (?), *ūrdhvaliṅga.* Sometimes A. has 3 arms, 2 on the right side and one on the left side and at other times usually 2 or 4 arms; the male side may also show the att. which is char. of Vṛṣavāhana-mūrti. – Other n.: Ammaiappaṉ, Naranārī, Parāṅgada; cp. also Harihara(mūrti), Ardhanārīnaṭeśvara, Lakṣmī-Nārāyaṇa.
Lit.: B 465, 475, 552 a.pl. 38:4, 39:4; BECA 1:pl. 2b; DHP 203 a.pl. 20; GoRI 1:257; HAHI pl. 10B; HIS 23; HSIT 13 a.pl. 30; JDI 36; KiH 21 a.pl. 62-63; KiSH 27; KrG pl. 12; R 2:321 a.pl. 94-98; SB 212 a.fig. 131; SSI 120; Th. pl. 57b; WHW 1:43; ZA pl. 139, 256, 258. – NB! KiDG 16 a.pl. 10: this ill. shows a 3-headed god, identified as A. To me this identification seems doubtful.

Ardhanārīnaṭeśvara, an appellation in *devanāgarī* characters under a picture in MG facing p. 97, referring to Śiva, represented both as Ardhanārī and as Naṭeśvara (see Naṭarāja). However, the author (MG) identifies the idol as Harihara. This correction is uncalled-for.
Lit.: see above.

ardhāñjalimudrā "half-*añjalimudrā*" (Mu.), n. of a handpose which is described thus: "one hand is held up against the chest" (like one hand in the *añjalimudrā*). Char. of Caṇḍikeśvara.
Lit.: SB 278.

ardhaparyaṅkāsana (*-aṅka*) "half-*paryaṅkāsana*" (att.), n. of an *āsana* which is usually described thus: one leg is bent upon the seat, the knee resting on the *pīṭha*, the other leg hangs loosely from the *pīṭha* or is slightly supported. According to B (and MEIA) the form of *a.* is identical with that of *lalitāsana* or of *lalitākṣepa*, but according to BBh. (cp. BECA and RN) it is identical with that of *mahārājalīlāsana*. Comparing *a.* with the *paryaṅkāsana*, I would interpret this att. thus: here one leg hangs straight down, while in the *lalitāsana* one leg hangs a little to one side and is slightly supported against the side of the *pīṭha*. This att. is symbolic for serenity.

In G it is, however, said that this att. shows two forms, one being similar to that of *rājalīlāsana*, the other being a *sthānaka* interpreted thus: "dancing attitude; standing on one foot. Other lifted. Position of *ḍākinīs*, Padmanarteśvara." (For this form of att., see *ardhasamapādasthānaka*). This form of *a.* is said to symbolize horror, anger, etc. – In SB a sitting posture which resembles the *vīrāsana* is mentioned as *a.* – In this dictionary the term *a.* is confined to to the first att. described above.

Lit.: B 272 a.pl. 43:1; BBh. 44, 432; BECA 1:260; G 24 (a. note 2); KiSB 57, 59; MEIA 219; RN 31; SB 165 a.fig. 101; WM 92.

ardhapatākāmudrā "half-flag" (Mu.), n. of a variety of the *patākāmudrā* in which the ring-finger and the little finger are bent; it signifies dagger, temple, tower, and other things.

Lit.: WHW 2:86.

ardhasama(pāda)sthānaka "half-straight standing posture" (att.), n. of a *sthānaka*-posture in which one foot is firmly planted while the other foot and leg indicate a movement. According to Th., this att. signifies both the dancing posture (*nṛttamūrti* or *nāṭyasthāna*) of Naṭarāja and Kṛṣṇa (cp. also that of the *ḍākinīs*, Gaṇapatihṛdayā, Gaṇeśa, Nairātmā, Padmanarteśvara, Vajracarcikā and others) and the indolent standing posture of Kṛṣṇa Veṇugopāla (as to this att., see *pādasvastika*). – Other n.: *ekasamapāda*, *asama(pāda)*; cp. *ardhaparyaṅkāsana*.

Lit.: B 268; Th. 34.

ardhavarodyatamudrā (Mu.), n. of a handpose as yet not fully described; in MEIA translated thus: "élevant un demi-cercle" (?). According to this scholar it is perhaps synonymous to *ardhacandramudrā*.

Lit.: MEIA 217.

ardhayogapaṭṭa "half *yogapaṭṭa*" (att.), n. of a cloth or band around one bent leg of a person in meditative pose. Char. of, e.g., Śāstā. Cp. *ardhayogāsana*.

Lit.: SIB 61, 68 a.pl. 21.

ardhayogāsana "half *yogāsana*" (att.), n. of a meditative sitting position like the *yogāsana* (see *sopāśrayāsana*) but in which only one leg is supported by a *yogapaṭṭa* (cp. also *ardhayogapaṭṭa*).

Lit.: SIB 68.

ardhimaṇḍapa, see *ardhamaṇḍapa*.

ardhoraka (*ardoruka*) "short undergarment" (attr.).

Lit.: BECA 1:260.

Ārdrā ("wet, soft"), n. of a *nakṣatra*. Its influence is bad.

Lit.: BBh. 381; IC 2:729.

argha "worth, value", n. of a rite, a respectful reception of a guest (by the offering of rice, flowers, milk, or sometimes only of water), or of a gift of fruit, flowers, milk or honey, offered to an image. Cp. *arghya*.

Lit.: Gt 43; MW 89.

arghā (Hi.) "chalice" (attr.). With an *a.* libations are made; it also symbolizes the *yoni*. – Another n.: *piyālā*. Cp. also *jalaharī*.

Lit.: DHP 231; P 41.

arghya ("valuable"; attr.).

1. The female principle, see *yoni*.

Lit.: B 456.

2. N. of an accessory to the *pūjā* (rice and water). "A respectful offering to the gods" (DiIP), i.e. the water offered for the washing of hands, see *pūjā*. Also n. of the ceremony itself: "réception des hôtes" (IC).

Lit.: DiIP 71, 90; IC 1:362; KiH 36; WHW 1:127.

arghyapātra "sacrificial bowl" (attr.), meant for rice and water, cp. *arghya*.

Lit.: GH 345; IC 1:570; KiH pl. 137:5, 139:7.

arhat (*arhant*, *arhan*; Pāli: *arahant*; "venerable").

1. (Buddh.) N. of a wise man, a saint (who attains *nirvāṇa* in this human existence); the highest rank in the Buddhist hierarchy

(next to a *buddha*). In Lamaism the *as* numbered 16 (see G). – Attr. (often): *pustaka*. – Other n.: *kevalin*, *sthavira* (*thera*).
Lit.: G 38; GRI 231; IC 2:554; MW 93; WHW 1:437.
2. (Jain.) N. of a saint. This term is mostly used as the equivalent of *tīrthaṅkara*.
Lit.: GJ 247; MW 93.

arin "wheel" ("having spokes"; attr.), see *cakra*.
Lit.: MEIA 252.

Ariṣṭanemi ("the felly of whose wheel is unhurt" (MW); Jain.), NP of the 22nd *tīrthaṅkara*. Symbol: *śaṅkha*. – Another n.: Nemi.
Lit.: GJ 290 a.pl. 20B, a.passim; KiSH 143; MW 88.

Arjuna ("white"), NP of the third of the Pāṇḍu-princes, the chief hero in the epic Mahābhārata. He is regarded as the spiritual son (or an *avatāra*) of Indra. Wife (besides Draupadī): Subhadrā. Attr.: Pāśupatāstra (Gāṇḍīva).
Lit.: D 21; GH 93; Gt 43; HIS 68 a.pl. 33-35; SB 77 a.fig. 46; WHW 1:62; WM 41; ZA pl. 111; ZM 71 a.pl. 3.

arka ("ray"), n. of a kind of flower (Calotropis gigantea Br.; attr.), sometimes used in solar cult. Char. of Śiva. – *a.* "sun" is also a symbolic n. of the number "12", see *saṅkhyā*.
Lit.: IC 1:538; MW 89; R 2:225.

arkapuṣpa "ray-flower" (attr.), n. of a jewel worn on the right side of Śiva's crown. Char. of Rudramūrti.
Lit.: SSI 76.

ārṣaliṅga (derivative of *ṛṣi*, *riṣi*), n. of a kind of *acalaliṅga*, spheroidal in shape, which is supposed to have been set up by a *riṣi*.
Lit.: R 2:86.

ārtā (Hi., < Skt *ārātrika*), n. of a wedding ceremony in which a lamp with five wicks (see *ārtī*) forms the chief constituent part.
Lit.: P 38.

Arthapratisaṃvit ("analysis"; Buddh.), n. of a *pratisaṃvit*. Char.: colour: green; attr.: *cintāmaṇi*, *pāśa*.
Lit.: BBh. 343.

ārtī (also *āratī*; Hi., cp. *ārtā*; Tam. *āratti*; attr.) and *ārtīpūjā* "worship with *ārtī*". According to P., *ārtī* signifies a "ceremony performed in adoration of a god by moving circularly around the head of the idol a platter containing a five-wicked burning lamp, flour and incense". In South India this rite is also performed before a married couple when entering their house for the first time (in P. too, *ārtā* is similarly described as a ceremony offered to the bridegroom when he first comes to the house of the bride). In Gt it is described as a ceremony on the birth of a Brāhman child, and its intention is said to be to avert "fascination by the eye". – According to KiH, however, *ārtī* is the lamp itself (a five-wicked lamp, or a lamp with more than one bowl, with a handle; it may also signify a hanging-lamp). The ceremony should therefore be designated by the word *ārtīpūjā*; this remark applies also in the case of GJ.
Lit.: BhIM 35; DiIP 62, 176; GJ 429; Gt 42; KiH pl. 139:1; MEIA 241; P 39; TL 1:241.

Āṟumukaṉ (Tam. "six-headed"), see Ṣaṇmukha.
Lit.: JDI pl. 30.

Aruṇa ("red, reddish brown; dawn"), n. of the *sūta* of *Sūrya*; in South India mostly n. of Sūrya himself. He was a son of Kāśyapa and Vinatā and the elder brother of Garuḍa. – Another n.: Ciṉṉa Aruṇaṉ.
Lit.: DHP 95; IC 1:489; ZA pl. 373.

Arundhatī ("faithfulness"), NP of a goddess, a personification of the morning star, a little star (Alcor) belonging to the Great Bear. She is regarded as the wife either of all *riṣi*s or esp. of the *riṣi* Vasiṣṭha. Attr.: *pattras*.
Lit.: DHP 317; IC 1:491; MW 88; R 1:369.

arūpadhātu "seat of non-form; Welt der Nicht-Form" (Buddh.).
Lit.: SeKB 240.

aruvāḷ (Tam.) "chopping-knife, chopper" (attr.). Char. of Karuppaṉ.
Lit.: SSR 127.

Ārya ("respectable, honourable"), see above, under the Tamil word-form Aiyaṉār which is a corrupt form of this word.
Lit.: GoRI 2:14; R 2:485.

Āryā ("honourable").
1. (Hind.) Epithet of Sarasvatī.
Lit.: DHP 260.
2. (Buddh.) NP of a *yakṣiṇī*.
Lit.: KiSB 74.

Ārya-Cundā ("the honourable C."; Buddh.), see Cundā.
Lit.: KiSB 101.

Ārya-Jāṅgulī(tārā) ("the honourable J."; Buddh.), in Lamaism n. of a variety of Sitatārā. Char.: Mu.: *abhayamudrā*; attr.: *nāga, vīṇā*.
Lit.: G 16, 18, 75.

Aryaman (-mā; "companion; chivalry"), NP of an Āditya. Attr.: *cakra, gadā Kaumodakī*, 2 *padmas*.
Lit.: DHP 116; R 1:309

Ārya-Mārīcī ("the honourable M."; Buddh.), n. of a variety of Mārīcī. Attr.: *sūci, sūtra*.
Lit.: BBh. 210; KiDG 64; KiSB 82.

āryasamāj(a) "assembly of the faithful", n. of a religious society founded in the 19th c. by Dayānand Sarasvatī, which aims at the restoration of the religion of old times.
Lit.: GH 446; GRI 351.

Ārya-Sarasvatī ("the honourable S."; Buddh.), n. of a variety of Sarasvatī. Char.: colour: white; attr.: *padma* with *pustaka*.
Lit.: BBh. 351 a.pl. 234; KiSB 106.

Ārya-Tārā ("the honourable T."; Buddh.), n. of a *dhyānibuddhaśakti*, the Śakti of Amoghasiddhi. She originates from the *bīja TĀṀ*. Char.: colour: green; att.: *lalitāsana*; Mu.: *varada-* and *vyākhyānamudrā*; attr.: *padma* (green) with *viśvavajra*. – Epithet: often called Tārā for short (BBh.); also Vaśyatārā.
Lit.: BBh. 56, 307 a.pl. 35; G 52, 77; GBB 250; KiSB 46.

Ārya-Vajravārāhī ("the honourable V."; Buddh.), n. of a variety of Vajravārāhī. Char.: att.: *ālīḍhāsana*; Vāh.: she treads upon a *mṛtaka*; attr.: *aṅkuśa, kapāla khaṭvāṅga, tarjanīpāśa, trinayana, vajra, varāhamukha* (like Vajravārāhī).
Lit.: BBh. 219; KiSB 87.

Āryāvalokiteśvara ("the honourable Avalokiteśvara"; Buddh.), n. of a variety of Avalokiteśvara (in Lamaism) with 11 heads (arranged, as usual with A., in a pyramid) and 22 arms. Char.: att.: *sthānaka*; Mu.: *añjali-, dharmacakra-, varada-mudrā*; attr.: *akṣamālā, cakra, dhanus, ghaṇṭā, kamaṇḍalu, padma, śara, vajra*.
Lit.: G 44 (ill.), 67.

Āryavarta ("the land of the Āryas"), n. of of Northern and Central India.

āṣāḍha (derived from *aṣāḍha* "invincible"), n. of a month (June-July): its god is Ṣaṇmukha.
Lit.: BBh. 382; IC 2:732.

āṣāḍhādi "beginning with (the month) *āṣāḍha*", referring to the year, see *saṃvatsara*.

asama(pāda) "uneven feet" (att.), see *ardhasamasthānaka*.

asaṃyuta(hasta) or *asaṃyukta* "unconnected (hands)" (Mu.), n. of a simple handpose, performed with only one hand, e.g. *abhaya-, varada-mudrā*. – Cp. *saṃyutahasta*.
Lit.: B 278; SIB 61; WHW 2:85.

āsana "seat, throne".
1. (Hind.) *ā.* is used in the same sense as *pīṭha*, and sometimes also as *vāhana*.
Lit.: BBh. 433; KiH 36 a.pl. 137:2; MEIA 222; R 1:19; SB 23.
2. (Attr.; Buddh.) An empty throne symbolizing the Buddha; cp. *pallaṅka, pīṭha*.
Lit.: CEBI 46; GBB pl. 26; see also H pl. 3:32; ill. (this ill. is also found in CEBI pl. 2:6, but is here designated "Pillar of Fire"); SeKB 161.
3. (Att.) *ā.* in the sense of "sitting (posture)", see *āsanamūrti*.
Lit.: BBh. 433.

āsana(mūrti) "sitting posture" (att.), also n. of a representation of a god in a certain sitting position. The term *ā.* is further often, esp. in meditative Yogic exercises, also used as a common term for standing, lying and dancing attitudes, cp. *ālīḍhāsana, nāṭyāsana*, and see esp. *aṅgika*. – The different modes of *ā.* are listed in the index of att.

In KiH a great number of *ā.* are mentioned and illustrated; most of these are not iconographic but belong to Yoga practice. Even in the cases in which there is a common n. for an iconographic and a Yogic *ā.*, there are differences in the performance.

In the Jaipur Museum collections we also find very many Yogic attitudes illustrated by small figures or sculptures. Among those not given in KiH may here be mentioned: *ardhadhanurāsana* "half-bow-posture" (cp. *dhanurāsana*), *ardhagaruḍa-bheda* "half-Garuḍa-breaking(-posture)", *ardhagomukha* "half-cow-face(-posture"; cp. *gomukhāsana*), *ardhajānvāsana* "half-knee-posture", *ardhakapālī* "half-skull-wearer(-posture"; cp. *kapālika*), *ardhamu-khāsana* "half-face-posture", *baddhāsana* "bound posture", *ekavaiṣṇavapūjāmagna* "solely immersed in Vaiṣṇavite worship", *gorakhāsana* (probably = *gorakṣāsana**), *jānvāsana* "knee-posture" (cp. above *ardha-jānvāsana*), *javāsana* "swift posture", *jhūlā-sana* (?), *kapyāsana* "monkey-posture", *kubaḍī āsana* (?), *matsyāsana* "fish-pos-ture)", *muktapadma* "liberated lotus(-pos-ture", *paścimāsana* "back-posture" (cp. *paścimottāsana*), *sahajāsana* "posture of being born together", *utthānodara* (!) "(posture of) rising the belly" (or, perhaps, *uttānodara* "outstretched belly-posture"?), *viparītakaraṇī* "reversed action-posture" (cp. *karaṇa*, MW 254), *viparītakarṇī* "re-versed ear-posture", *viparītordhvapadma* "reversed raised lotus(-posture)". Many of these terms are illustrated by figures showing several different forms of attitude.

Lit.: B 269; BBh. 135, 433; GoRI 1:339; KiH pl. 151 ff.; R 1:78; SM 121; WHW 1:45, 73; WM 90.

Asaṅga ("free from ties, having no attachment to the objects"; Buddh.), NP of a reformer within the Mahāyāna school, who probably lived in the 5th c. A.D.

Lit.: BRI 162; G 4; WHW 1:77.

aśani "thunderbolt".

1. (Attr.) See *vajra*.

Lit.: MEIA 250.

2. Aśani, epithet of Śiva.

Lit.: DHP 206.

āścaryamudrā "gesture of surprise" (Mu.), see *vismayamudrā*.

asi "sword" (attr.), see *khaḍga*.

Lit.: R 1:293; WHW 2:591.

Asitāṅga ("having a dark-coloured body"), n. of a form of Śiva Bhairava.

Lit.: B 466; MW 120.

Āśleṣā(s) ("contact, adherence; les envelop-pantes"), n. of a *nakṣatra*. Its influence is bad.

Lit.: BBh. 381; IC 2:729.

aśoka ("absence of sorrow").

1. (Attr., esp. Buddh.) N. of a tree and of the (red) flower of that tree. "It is believed that kicks at the tree by chaste women cause it to blossom" (BBh.), but it is also regarded as a symbol of love. Char. of: Kurukullā, Mārīcī (in different forms M. wears a yellow *a.* or a twig or a leaf of an *a.*, *aśokavṛkṣaśākhā*); furthermore, a flower of *a.*, the colour of which is not mentioned, is char. of: Parṇaśavarī, Vadālī, Vajrā-naṅga, Varāhamukhī, Varālī, Vartālī. An *aśoka*-tree is a symbol of Mahāmāyūrī.

Lit.: BBh. 433; CHIIA 233 a.fig. 82; G 12 (ill.); IC 1:538; KiSB 112; STP 8:7.

2. (Jain.) N. of a tree, symbol of Nami.

Lit.: H pl. 16, 82; KiSH 143.

3. Aśoka, NP of the mightiest ruler of ancient India. A. belonged to the Maurya dynasty and ruled about 273-232 (or 236) B.C. An ardent Buddhist, he spread Buddhism all over India. Esp. well-known are the "Aśoka-pillars", which were erected during his reign, the lion-capitals of which form the emblem of modern India.

Lit.: D 26; DKI 3; Gz 40, 44; WHW 1:81; ZA pl. 4.

Aśokā (Jain.), NP of a *śāsanadevatā* attending on the 10th *tīrthaṅkara*.

Lit.: GJ 362.

Aśokakāntā ("the beautiful one with an *aśoka*" or "dear to Aśoka"?; Buddh.), n. of a one-headed, two-armed variety of Mārīcī, sometimes attending on Khadiravaṇī-Tārā. Char.: colour: yellow or golden; Vāh.: *sūkara*; att.: *sthānaka* (*līlayordhvasthita*); Mu.: *varadamudrā*; attr.: *aśoka*-twig (*aśokavṛkṣaśākhā*), *Vairocanabimba* on the crown.
Lit.: BBh. 209; G 74; KiDG 64; KiSB 82.

Aśokottamaśrī ("the highest beauty of *aśoka*"; Buddh.), NP of a medicine-*buddha* in Lamaism, see Bhaiṣajyaguru. Char.: colour: bright red; Mu.: *dhyānamudrā*.
Lit.: G 56.

aspṛśya "untouchable; outcast", n. of the lowest caste or stratum of the population of India. – Cp. *harijan*, *varṇa*.
Lit.: GH 325; GRI 316.

āśrama "hermitage, abode of ascetics". Also n. of a period or stage of religious life of a Brāhman, of which there are four, see *brāhmaṇa*.
Lit.: IC 1:600; MKVI 1:68; WHW 1:84.

asṛkkapāla "bowl filled with blood" (attr.; Buddh.), cp. *raktapātra* and see *kapāla*.
Lit.: BBh. 435.

aṣṭabandhana ("eight ties"; attr.) "is a kind of cement used for fixing the idol to its base and consists of eight ingredients". It consequently belongs to the *sthāpana* ceremony.
Lit.: DiIP 96.

Aṣṭabhuja-Kurukullā ("the eight-armed K."; Buddh.), n. of a form of Kurukullā. Char.: colour: red; att.: *padmāsana*; Mu.: *trailokyavijaya-* and *varada-mudrā*; attr.: *aṅkuśa*, *dhanus*, *nīlotpala*, *pāśa*, *śara*.
Lit.: BBh. 150; KiDG 64; KiSB 97.

Aṣṭabhuja(pīta)-Mārīcī ("the eight-armed [yellow] M."; Buddh.), n. of a variety of Mārīcī, esp. as a sub-form of Mārīcīpicuvā. Char.: colour: golden; att.: *ālīḍhāsana*; Vāh.: *ratha* drawn by 7 *sūkaras* (upon Rāhu); Mu.: *tarjanīmudrā*; attr.: *aṅkuśa*, *aśoka*-leaf, *dhanus*, *(tarjanī)pāśa*, *śara*, *sūcī*, *sūtra*, *triśiras*, *vajra*, *Vairocana-bimba* on the crown. – Epithet: Saṅkṣipta-Mārīcī.
Lit.: BBh. 211 a.pl. 152-154; KiDG 65 a.pl. 17:48 f.; KiSB 97.

Aṣṭabhuja-Vīralakṣmī ("the eight-armed V."), n. of a goddess of the group *aṣṭamahālakṣmī*.
Lit.: SSI 189.

aṣṭadhātu "eight parts", n. of an alloy consisting of eight metals, formerly used in North India for the casting of bronze images. These eights metals are: gold, silver, copper, tin, iron, lead, quicksilver, zinc (or brass, or steel). – Cp. *pañcaloha*, *lohaja*.
Lit.: KIM 29; MH 5; WHW 2:65.

aṣṭadikpāla "the eight regents or guardians of the regions or quarters of the sky", see *dikpāla*.
Lit.: B 519; JDI 106; MEIA 124.

Aṣṭakarṇa ("eight-eared"), epithet of Brahmā in his four-headed form.
Lit.: DHP 237.

aṣṭākṣara ("the Thought-Form of Eight-Syllables of Viṣṇu"; attr.), n. of a *mantra* uttered with the purpose of obtaining liberation.
Lit.: DHP 348.

Aṣṭamahābhaya-Tārā ("T. of eight great perils"; Buddh.), n. of a Tārā of white colour.
Lit.: BBh. 308.

aṣṭamahālakṣmī ("eight Mahālakṣmīs"), n. of a group of 8 Lakṣmī-goddesses, among whom may be mentioned: Gaja-, Indra-, Mahā-, Sāmānya-, Vīra-Lakṣmī and Kollāpura-Mahālakṣmī, Aṣṭabhuja-Vīralakṣmī.
Lit.: SSI 187.

aṣṭamaṅgala "collection of eight auspicious things (for certain great occasions, such as coronation etc.)". Such auspicious things were also early used as motifs in the Indian arts; e.g. in Kuṣāna arts, and of the conventional Indian motifs the following are notable here: *pūrṇakumbha* (see *pūrṇakalaśa*), *vajrāsana*, *svastika*, *mīnamithuna* (see *matsyayugma*), *śarāva*-

sampuṭa, *ratnapātra* (see *kamaṇḍalu*), *triratna*, *nandyāvarta*, *pañcāṅgulitala*, etc.
Lit.: JMS 17, 51.

In the later Indian religions the following things are regarded as *a.* :

1. (Hind.) The *a.* are: *siṅha* (lion), *vṛṣan* (bull), *gaja* (elephant), *kamaṇḍalu* (water-jar or vessel of gems), *cāmara* (fan), *dhvaja* (flag), *tūrī* (trumpet), *dīpa* (lamp). There are also other lists, for instance: a Brāhman, a cow, fire, gold, ghee, the sun, water, and a king (MW); in South India (Skt terms): *cāmara* (fan), *pūrṇakalaśa* (full vase), *darpaṇa* (mirror), *aṅkuśa* (goad), *muraja* (drum), *dīpa* (lamp), *dhvaja* (flag) and *matsyayugma* (couple of fishes).
Lit.: MD 1:45; MW 116; TL 1:40.

2. (Buddh.) In Lamaism the *a.* are: *sitātapatra* (white umbrella), *matsyayugma* (pair of fishes), *śaṅkha* (conch), *padma* (lotus), *dhvaja* (flag), *kalaśa* (jar), *cakra* (wheel), *granthi* (endless knot).
Lit.: G 8.

3. (Jain.) The *a.* are: *svastika* (Fylfot-cross), *śrīvatsa* (curl of hair), *nandyāvarta* (curl), *vardhamānaka* (vase), *bhadrāsana* (throne), *kalaśa* (jar), *matsyayugma* (pair of fishes), *darpaṇa* (mirror).
Lit.: GJ 384 a.pl. 20c; KiSH 153.

aṣṭamātaras (or *-mātṛkās*) "eight mothers", n. of a group of eight *mātaras* or Śaktis. In Hinduism the *a.* are: Indrāṇī, Vaiṣṇavī, Śāntā (or Cāmuṇḍā), Brahmāṇī, Kaumārī, Nārasiṅhī (or Cāṇḍikā), Vārāhī, Māheśvarī. The *a.* (or *ambāṣṭaka*) are sometimes regarded as eight hypostasies of Cāmuṇḍā (for these see MEIA). The *saptamātaras* and in addition Mahā-Lakṣmī are occasionally also counted as the *a.* (SSI). – In Lamaism the *a.* are: Lāsyā, Mālā, Gītā, Nṛtyā, Puṣpā, Dhūpā, Dīpā, Gandhā. – In Jainism they are: Brahmāṇī, Māheśvarī, Kaumārī, Vaiṣṇavī, Vārāhī, Indrāṇī, Cāmuṇḍā, Tripurā. – Another n.: *ambāṣṭaka*.
Lit.: B 561; G 36, 82; GJ 411; KiSH 53; MEIA 153; MW 1044; R 1:381; SSI 190.

aṣṭamūrti "eight representations (of Śiva)", see *mūrtyaṣṭaka*.
Lit.: SSI 77.

Aṣṭāracakravat ("having a wheel with eight spokes"; Buddh.), epithet of Mañjuśrī (cp. *cakra*).
Lit.: MW 117.

aṣṭasvasāras "eight sisters", a term which includes eight aspects of Śiva's Śakti. They are divided into two groups of four, the first containing the gracious aspects Pārvatī, Umā, Gaurī and Jagadambī, the second containing the cruel aspects Kālī, Durgā, Cāmuṇḍā and Māheśvarī. Of these aspects Kālī is said to be the chief.

aṣṭavadana "eight-faced" (attr.), Char. of Prasannatārā.
Lit.: BBh. 249.

aṣṭāvaraṇa "eight shields" (attr.), n. of a group of characteristics, regarded as chief elements of the faith of the Liṅgāyats. They are: *guru*, *liṅga*, *jaṅgama*, *pādodaka*, *prasāda*, *vibhūti*, *rudrākṣa*, and the *mantra* "*namaḥ Śivāya*".
Lit.: GoRI 2:249.

asthi "bone" (attr.). As an attr., held in a hand, char. of Śiva in some representations, such as Aghora, further of Cāmuṇḍā, Durgā, Śrīvidyādevī. Another n.: *trika*.
Lit.: MEIA 215; R 2:199.

asthimañjūṣā "bone-basket" (attr.), n. of a bowl-shaped relic-basket.

astiratēvar (Tam. < Skt. *astra+deva*) "the weapon as god"; *a.* is the deified weapon of a deity; it has the form of a trident (*triśūla*), which is conceived as having the iconographic features of Śiva. Cp. *āyudhapuruṣa*.
Lit.: DiIP 70.

aṣṭottaraśata-liṅga ("108 miniature *liṅgas*"), n. of a kind of *mānuṣaliṅga*.
Lit.: R 2:95 a.pl. 7:2.

astra, properly "missile, arrow", used in the meaning of "weapon", see *āyudha*. – Astra, the personified weapon of Śiva, see Pāśupatāstra.
Lit.: DiIP 70; MEIA 71.

astramantra (Tam.: *astira-*) "weapon-*mantra*" (attr.), n. of a *mantra* which is uttered when worshipping the deified weapons (see *āyudhapuruṣa*).
Lit.: DiIP 71.

astramudrā "missile-*mudrā*" (Mu.), n. of one among the *pañcamudrā*. The form of this Mu. is not stated.
Lit.: DiIP 105.

asura ("spiritual, divine"), originally n. of a certain class of gods (to whom e.g. Varuṇa belonged; cp. *deva*). Also n. of a kind of demons (because of a later wrong etymology *a-sura*, interpreted as "not-god", a new word *sura** "god" came into existence). As demons the *asuras* are conceived as the descendants of Kāśyapa and Diti (cp. *daitya*). Different kinds of *a.* are: *daityas*, *dānavas*, *dasyus*, *kālakañjas*, *kāleyas*, *khalins*, *nāgas*, *nivāta-kavacas*, *paulomas*, *piśācas*, *rākṣasas*.
Lit.: D 27; DHP 140; GH 105; GoRI 1:322; Gt 55; IC 1:525; IIM 111; KiK 45; R 2:559; STP 1:197; Th. 118; WHW 1:90; WM 58.

asurakumāra ("demon prince"; Jain.), n. of a kind of *bhuvanavāsī*.
Lit.: GJ 236.

asuramāyā "the magic power of a demon".
Lit.: R 1:381.

aśva "horse" (Vāh., attr.). The Vāh., esp., of Aiyaṉār (black horse), further of: Aśvarūḍhadevī, Beg-tse, Bhāskara, Brahmā (Buddh.), Kāladūtī, Kubera, Ratnasambhava, Revanta, Śukra, Tha-'og-chos; a white *a.* is Vāh. of Kalkin, Mallāri-Śiva, Sitabrahmā, Ṭhakur Deo; the horse Uccaiḥśravas is the Vāh. of Indra; see also *ratha* drawn by horses. As Attr., an *a.* is swallowed by Kālī, Mahālakṣmī. – An *a.* is also a symbol of Sambhava, and an *a.* (*aśvaratna* "horse-treasure"), meaning a charger, symbolic of military strength, is a *lakṣaṇa* of a *cakravartin*, see *saptaratna*. – *a.* is also a symbolic n. of the number "7", see *saṅkhyā*. Another n.: *vājin*.
Lit.: GH 69; GJ 257 a.pl. 22:3; KiJ pl. 45; W 205; WHW 1:551.

Aśvaghoṣa ("having the sound of a horse"; Buddh.), NP of a celebrated author who lived about A.D. 100. He is regarded by some as the founder of Mahāyāna Buddhism and worshipped as a saint. Attr.: *kāṣāya*.
Lit.: BRI 122; G 38, 105.

aśvakeśara "(having) horse-mane" (attr.). Char. of Hayagrīva, Saptaśatika-Hayagrīva.

aśvamastaka "(having a) horse-head" (attr.). Char. of Hayagrīva (who, in different forms has a horse-head or (more often) one or more small horse-heads in his hair), Hayāsyā, Mārīcī, Paramāśva, Tumpuruvar and sometimes also Kalkin. – Another n.: *aśvamukha*.
Lit.: R 1:223; Th. 74.

aśvamedha "sacrifice of a horse", n. of the greatest sacrificial festival in Vedic age.
Lit.: D 28; GH 69; GoRI 1:168; KT 71; RAAI 271; RV 23; STP 4:14; WHW 1:49, 458.

aśvamukha, see *aśvamastaka*.

Aśvarūḍhadevī ("the goddess on horseback"), n. of a goddess. Vāh.: *aśva*; attr.: *trinayana*.
Lit.: R 1:371.

Aśvaśiras ("horse-headed"), see *Hayaśiras*.
Lit.: MEIA 39.

aśvatara "mule" (Vāh.). Char. of: kLu-dbaṅ, Śrīdevī (Buddh.), Vasantadevī.
Lit.: G 26, 82.

aśvattha (< *aśva-stha* "horse-stand", i.e. "under which horses stand", MW) "Ficus religiosa", n. of the sacred fig-tree which is dedicated to both Viṣṇu and the Buddha. At the foot of an *a.*-tree the Buddha attained Enlightenment. The worship of the *a.* as a sacred tree dates back as early as the Indus Valley civilization; see further *vṛkṣa* and cp. *pippala*.
Lit.: CEBI 9; GH 64; GoRI 1:319; HIS 13; IC 1:537; MW 115; R 1:15; WHW 1:358; ZA 25 a.pl. 2e.

Aśvayujau ("harnessing horses; les deux atteleurs de cheveaux"), n. of a *nakṣatra*. Its influence is beneficent. – Other n.: *Aśvinī*, *Aśvinyau*.
Lit.: IC 2:730.

āśvina, n. of a month (September-October). Its god is Śakra.
Lit.: BBh. 382; IC 2:732.

āśvinādi "beginning with (the month) *āśvina*", referring to the year, see *samvatsara*.

Aśvinī, Aśvinyau, n. of a *nakṣatra*, see Aśvayujau.
Lit.: BBh. 381; IC 2:730.

Aśvins, Aśvinīdevatās ("possessed of horses"), n. of two divine physicians and twin gods, sons of Vivasvān and Saraṇyū. Char.: *ratha* (drawn by horses or birds); attr.: *kamaṇḍalu, oṣadhipātra, pustaka*. For *aśvin* as a symbolic n. of the number "2", see *saṅkhyā*.
Lit.: D 29; DHP 128; GoRI 1:92; IC 1:322; IIM 22, 95; MG 68; R 2:541; Th. 115; WHW 1:93.

ātapatra "large umbrella" (attr.), see *chattra*; cp. also *sitātapatra*.
Lit.: G 12 (ill.), 67.

Āṭavallār (Tam.: "the Dancer par excellence"), epithet of Śiva, see Naṭarāja.
Lit.: SB 218.

atibhaṅga "exceeding bend" (att.), n. of a *sthānaka*, an emphatic variety of *tribhaṅga*.
Lit.: B 266; MH 6; WM 89.

Aticaṇḍikā ("the exceedingly great Caṇḍikā" or "surpassing C."), n. of one of the *navadurgās*.
Lit.: R 1:357.

Atiraktāṅga-Bhairava ("the exceedingly red-bodied Bh."), n. of a form of Bhairava.
Lit.: R 2: pl. 43.

Atiśa ("the exceedingly great lord" or "surpassing the Lord"; Buddh.), n. of a Hindu priest who founded the *bKa'-gdams-pa* sect in Tibet in A.D. 1040; he died in 1058. He is worshipped as a saint. Char.: Mu.: *dharmacakramudrā*; attr.: *stūpa*.
Lit.: G 5, 38, 106.

Āti Śeṣan (Drav. form for Ādi Śeṣa), in Sri Lanka n. of Viṣṇu's servant; see Ananta.
Lit.: CBC.

Atri ("eater, devourer"), NP of a *riṣi* or *prajāpati*. Wife: Anasūyā (daughter of Dakṣa). Sometimes A. is regarded as the father of Viṣṇu, see Dattātreya and Hari-Hara-Pitāmaha.
Lit.: D 32; DHP 317, 323; WHW 1:97; WM 44.

aṭṭa(ka) "tower" (in a miniature form; attr.), see *stūpa*. – Cp. *caitya*.
Lit.: KiDG 81.

AUṀ, see *OṀ*.

aupāsana "worship of the consecrated fire both morning and evening, a duty enjoined on a married Brāhman".
Lit.: DiIP 138; TL s.v.

autsavabera, see *utsavabera*.
Lit.: WM 88.

āvāhana "invocation" of a god. This ceremony forms part of the *pūjā*.
Lit.: DiIP 90; RV 30.

āvāhanamudrā "invocation handpose" (Mu.): "joining both hands keeping them outspread and showing them with both the thumbs joining the lowest knuckles of the ringfingers" (Diehl).
Lit.: Diehl; DiIP 109, 112.

avakrānti "descending (into a womb), conception" (Buddh.); the term used in connection with the descent of the Buddha into his mother's womb (in her dream) in the form of an elephant.
Lit.: HSIT 21; MW 97.

Avalokita-Łokeśvara ("the seen, watchful L." (see Avalokiteśvara); Buddh.), n. of a variety of Avalokiteśvara. **Char.:** att.: *padmāsana*; Vāh.: *padma*; **attr.:** *khaḍga, padma*.
Lit.: BBh. 399 a.pl. 44(A).

Avalokiteśvara (the n. is interpreted in many different ways: "the merciful Lord; the watchful Lord; With pitying look; der herabsehende Herr; der Herr der voll Mitleid (auf die Leiden der Welt) hinabblickt; der Herr des Leuchtens"; Buddh.), n. of a *bodhisattva* who is esp. well-known as the tutelary deity of Tibet and is one of the most popular gods in the Mahāyāna pantheon. Besides the Buddha, he is the Buddhist counterpart, in particular, of the Hindu Viṣṇu, and is mostly identified with Padmapāṇi (who is regarded as a form of A.); he is the spiritual son of the *dhyānibuddha* Amitābha, and in the cosmic process he is responsible for creation.

A. is met with in very many varieties or forms, which are provided with one up to 11 heads (in the eleven-headed form, these are arranged like a pyramid, in rows of 3+3+3+1+1). His Śakti is Pāṇḍarā (properly the Śakti of Amitābha). The chief char. are: colour: white (or red?); Vāh.: *siṅha*; Mu.: *varadamudrā*; attr.: *akṣamālā, kamaṇḍalu, khaḍga*, (*pāśa*) and esp. *padma* or *nīlotpala*, and *Amitābhabimba* on the crown (where the 11 heads are arranged in pyramidal form, the top head is that of Amitābha). Other attributes are listed under the separate varieties mentioned below.

Many different lists of varieties of A. are given in reference-works, some of which may be mentioned here. In G 19 forms are recorded: 1. Early form (Char.: att.: *padmāsana* or *sthānaka*; Mu.: *añjali-, vyākhyāna-* or *varada-mudrā*; attr.: high *uṣṇīṣa*, sometimes *Amitābhabimba* in the hair). – 2. Padmapāṇi. – 3. Siṅhanāda. – 4. As the Buddha. – 5. Trailokyavaśaṅkaralokeśvara. – 6. Nīlakaṇṭhāryāvalokiteśvara. – 7. Ṣaḍakṣarī. – 8. Harihariharivāhanodbhava. – 9. Amoghapāśa. – 10. Nāmasaṅgīti. – 11. Padmanarteśvara. – 12. Amoghapāśa (! cp. no. 9 above). – 13 Hālāhalalokeśvara. – 14. Tantric A. (Char.: Mu.: *añjali-, dhyāna-mudrā*; attr.: *cakra, caturmukha, padma, pustaka, bimba*s of the Buddha and Amitābha, the latter showing *añjalimudrā*). – 15. Māyājālakramāryāvalokiteśvara. – 16. "Merciful Lord" (with 11 heads, arranged in a pyramid, see above; other char.: Mu.: *añjali-* and *varada-mudrā*; attr.: *akṣamālā, cakra, dhanus, kamaṇḍalu, padma, śara*). – 17. Sitātapatra. – 18 and 19: Two forms of Āryāvalokiteśvara.

In BBh. we find the following list of 15 varieties: 1. Ṣaḍakṣarī(-Lokeśvara). – 2. Siṅhanāda. – 3. Khasarpaṇa. – 4. Lokanātha. – 5. Hālāhala. – 6. Padmanartteśvara. – 7. Hariharivāhana. – 8. Trailokyavaśaṅkara. – 9. Raktalokeśvara. – 10. Māyājālakrama. – 11. Nīlakaṇṭha. – 12. Sugatisandarśana. – 13. Pretasantarpita. – 14. Sukhāvatī(-Lokeśvara). – 15. Vajradharma. In KiDG and KiSB a similar group of 15 varieties is also given, but other lists occur: in the Mahāyāna Buddhism of Nepal as many as 108 forms of A. occurred, which were linked together through the term Lokeśvara (the complete enumeration of these 108 forms is given in BBh.; the three-headed forms among them are registered in KiDG). It is possible that many of these forms were originally other Buddhist deities which later became connected with A. – Cp. further Cintāmaṇi-Avalokiteśvara; see also *trimūrti*. – Other n.: Saṅgharatna. Outside India and Tibet A. is also represented in a female form, e.g., in China in the form Kuan-Yin, cp. the Japanese Kwannon.

Lit.: AuOW 28 pl. 14; B 558; BBh. 49, 88, 124, 394 a.pl. 57 and passim; BRI 148; DIA pl. 17; FK 140; G passim; GBB 246 a.pl. 32; GBM 33, 87; H 32: HAHI pl. 7A, 8A; HAA pl. 100; HSIT 15 a.pl. 39; IA 11; IC 2:573; JSV 17 a.pl. 41, 65, 68, 96; KIM pl. 4; KiDG 45, 51 a.pl. 26-37; KiSB 48, 56; KrG pl. 40; SS pl. 28:124; SB 287, 349 a.pl. 191, 325; SeKB passim; SIB pl. 20 f.; Th. pl. 33; ZA pl. 108a, 187, 378, 600.

āvaraṇa "precinct of a temple". – Other n.: *prākāra*.
Lit.: DiIP 112.

āvaraṇadevatā "precinct deity", n. of a tutelary deity placed in the precincts of the shrine.
Lit.: R 1:247.

āvaraṇapūjā "precinct worship", n. of the worship of gods housed in the cloisters (precincts) surrounding the central shrine
Lit.: DiIP 119.

āvartana ("turning round"; Mu., Jain.), n. of a handpose which is interpreted thus: "mit den Händen wird vor dem Gesicht ein Halbkreis vom linken Ohr zum rechten beschrieben, was als ein Ausdruck der den *tīrthaṅkaras* oder *gurus* erwiesenen Verehrung betrachtet wird".
Lit.: GJ 373.

āvasathya "domestic (fire)" (attr.), n. of one of the householder's fires, less important than the *gārhapatya*. See *agni*.
Lit.: WHW 1:359.

āvaśyaka ("necessary"; Jain.), n. of the six necessary duties which a Jain layman should perform every day. These are: 1. *sāmāyika*; 2. *caturviṅśatijinastuti*; 3. *vandanā*; 4. *pratikramaṇa*; 5. *kāyotsarga*; 6. *pratyākhyāna* (q.q.v.).
Lit.: GJ 408; IC 2:638; SchRI 235.

āvaṭaiyār (Tam.) "pedestal" (Vāh.), see *pīṭha*.
Lit.: JDI 11.

avataṅsa "garland, ear-ornament" (attr.), defined in AIP as a flower placed behind the ear.
Lit.: AIP 76; MW 98.

avatāra "descent", n. of a divine incarnation, the birth into the world, in order to save the world from a peril and to restore the system of the world, of a divine being. *a.* generally refers to an incarnation of Viṣṇu, but sometimes also the (28) aspects (see *mūrti*) of Śiva are designated by this term.
a. signifies above all a complete incarnation (*mukhyāvatāra**, e.g. as Rāma or Kṛṣṇa (cp. Bhagavadgītā 4:5-8); as to less complete incarnations, see *aṅśa*, *āveṣa*). The number of the *a.* of Viṣṇu varies; according to the most frequent list there are 10 (see *daśāvatāra*), but other numbers are also mentioned, e.g. 7, 8, 16, 22, 23, 24, or 39. Here, for instance, is a list of 22 incarnations (taken from the Bhāgavatapurāṇa): 1. Puruṣa; 2. Varāha; 3. Nārada; 4. Nara and Nārāyaṇa; 5. Kapila; 6. Dattātreya; 7. Yajña; 8. Ṛṣabha; 9. Pṛthu; 10. Matsya; 11. Kūrma; 12-13. Dhanvantari; 14. Narasiṅha; 15. Vāmana; 16. Paraśurāma; 17. Vedavyāsa; 18. Rāma; 19. Balarāma; 20. Kṛṣṇa; 21. Buddha; 22. Kalkin. – Another n.: *vibhava*; cp. also *prādurbhāva* and *vyūha*.
Lit.: B 388; D 33; DHP 164; GoRI 1:236, 249, 2:122; Gt 66; IC 1:503, 2:750; R 1:119 a.pl. 35; WM 44.

āveṇikadharma "peculiar property" (Buddh.). A kind of mental characteristic: 18 *ā.* characterise a *mānuṣibuddha*.
Lit.: BBh. 76; IC 2:536.

āveśa "entrance, taking possession, or being possessed of", n. of a less complete degree of incarnation of a god (esp. of Viṣṇu) for a certain occasion; the incarnation of Paraśurāma is e.g. so regarded, as is the incarnation of Viṣṇu as the Buddha. – Cp. *aṅśa*, *avatāra*.
Lit.: GH 131; R 1:119.

avyakta "not manifest" (attr.), n. of a cult object without a man-made form, which may represent a god, as, e.g., the *śālagrāma* for Viṣṇu, or the *bāṇaliṅga* for Śiva. Cp. *gṛhadevatā*.
Lit.: R 1:18.

avyaṅga (< Avestan *aiwyåṅhana* "girdle"), n. of a girdle of sun-icons (attr.; North India). Its origin is the woollen thread a Zoroastrian wears round the waist. Char. of Sūrya (his *a.* is named *yāvīyāṅga*). – Cp. *ahyaṅga*.
Lit.: B 292, 437; R 1:314.

āyāgapaṭa (or *-paṭṭa*) "votive tablet" (attr.; esp. Jain.), n. given to a votive tablet with symbolic pictures: images of *jina*-figures in the centre, and of *aṣṭamaṅgala*s at the borders.
Lit.: CEBI pl. 4:14, 16; CHIIA 232 a.fig. 71, 72; JMS 22; KiJ 21 a.pl. 65-66; ZA 253.

ayaḥśūla "iron lance" (attr.). Char. of Śiva-worshippers. Hence a devotee who carries such a lance, is called *āyaḥśūlika*.
Lit.: B 449; HIS 21.

āyaka(stambha) "votive pillar", in architecture a "term applied to pillars placed on platforms attached to *stūpa*s and sometimes to these altar-projections themselves" (RAAI).
Lit.: RAAI 271; SeKB 104.

ayata "unrestrained" (att.), n. of a posture, referring to the legs of a dancer engaged in a dance of calm, with crossed legs and bent knees.
Lit.: KrA 208 a.pl. 117.

āyatana "temple, resting-place, the place of the sacred fire", n. of the domestic hearth, as used for domestic sacrifices. – Another n.: *devāyatana*. See also *devāgāra*.
Lit.: IC 1:576; MW 148; WHW 1:30.

Ayenār or Ayiyanār, see Aiyaṉār.

Ayonijā ("not born from the womb"), epithet of Sītā who, according to legend, was born from a plough-furrow.

āyudha "weapon" (attr.), n. given to the different weapons which the gods hold in their hands (see also *āyudhapuruṣa*), and also (at least in South India), to all kinds of tools. – Another n. : *astra*.
Lit.: WHW 2:590.

āyudhapūjā (Tam. *āyutapūcai*) "worship of the tools", n. of a festival during which all tools are made the object of worship. In South India this festival is connected with the *navarātrī*. – Cp. *pañcamī*.
Lit.: DiCH. 51, 66; DiIP 29, 170; SSR 199.

āyudhapuruṣa "weapon-man", n. of the little human figure which, in some images, stands at the side of the deity carrying its weapon; *ā.* is thus an anthropomorphic personification of the weapon and may be regarded as an *anśa** or a partial incarnation of the activity of a god. *ā.* is a common n. for such personifications, but each specific weapon may, by a particular n., be signified as a personification; thus to the names of the weapons which are either masculine or neuter, is added, as the last member of the compound-name, the word *puruṣa* "man", e.g. *cakrapuruṣa*. (The anthropomorphic forms of the weapons with neuter names are represented as eunuchs). Feminine weapon-names receive in the same manner, as the last member, the word *devī* "goddess", e.g. *gadādevī*. – Cp. also *astiratēvar*.
Lit.: B 537; R 1:105, 287; SB 322 a.fig. 248; SIB pl. 2; Th. 119; WM 105.

Āyurvaśitā ("control of life"; Buddh.), n. of a *vaśitā*. Char. : colour : whitish red; Mu. : *dhyānamudrā*; attr. : *Amitāyur(-Buddha)-bimba, cintāmaṇi* (*Padmarāga*).
Lit.: BBh. 329.

āyutapucai (Tam.), see *āyudhapūjā*.

Ayyanār, see Aiyaṉār.

Ayyappaṉ (or Aiy-), NP of a god of growth; reputation in Kerala esp. connected with Śabarimalai. Sometimes said to be identical with, or a form of Aiyaṉār (cp. ACA : "Doublet d'Aiyaṉār en Kerala"), but this connection is now disputed and, at least by priests, totally denied.
Lit.: ACA 93; DIEHL.

B

Bādāmi, n. of a village in West India, with cave temples.
Lit.: ZA pl. 124 ff.

baddhapadmāsana "bound or joined *padmāsana*" (att.), n. of an *āsana*-posture similar to the *padmāsana*.
Lit.: B 272.

badi, abbreviated form (for *bahula-dina* "*bahula*-day"?) of *bahulapakṣa** or *vadyapakṣa**, see *kṛṣṇapakṣa*.
Lit.: IC 2:722; MW 916.

Bādi Mātā (N.Ind.), NP of one of the *saptamātaras**. She attacks children between seven and fifteen years of age.
Lit.: GH 136.

Bag(a)lā (Hi., "crane", interpreted as "the Deceitful, the Power of Cruelty"), n. of a female personification with a crane's head. She belongs to the group *mahāvidyā** and is then represented by Vīrarātrī.
Lit.: DHP 283.

Bāhubalin (*-ī*, "strong in arms"; Jain.), see Gommaṭa.
Lit.: GJ 392.

bahulapakṣa "the dark half of a month", with the abbreviated forms *badi*, *vadi*, *vati*, see *kṛṣṇapakṣa*.
Lit.: IC 2:722.

Bahurūpa ("multiform"), n. of one of the *ekādaśarudras**. Char. : Mu. : *tarjanīmudrā*;

attr.: *akṣamālā, aṅkuśa, cakra, candra, ḍamaru, dhanus, ghaṇṭā, kamaṇḍalu, kapāla, khaṭvāṅga, nāga, paraśu, paṭṭiśa, triśūla.*
Lit.: R 2:389.

Bahurūpiṇī ("multiform"; Jain.), NP of a *śāsanadevatā* attending on the 20th *tīrthaṅkara.*
Lit.: GJ 362 a.pl. 26:20; KiJ 12 a.pl. 29:20.

bāhuvalaya "armlet" (attr.), see *valaya.*
Lit.: SB 137.

bāhyabhitti "outer wall" of a temple (term in architecture).
Lit.: BECA 1:260.

bairāgi (Hi.) "separated from passion or worldly attachments", n. given to a member of an order founded by Rāmānuja.
Lit.: GH 365; P 208.

baisakhi, see *vaiśākhī.*

bajibandha "ornament (a string of beads) encircling the arm at the elbow" (attr.).
Lit.: BECA 1:260.

baka "heron" (Vāh.), a bird symbolizing hypocrisy and treachery.
Lit.: WHW 1:155.

bakāsuravadha "the killing of Bakāsura", n. given to the heroic deed performed by Kṛṣṇa when he killed a demon in the shape of a crane.
Lit.: JDI 90; W 172.

Bakula (n. of a tree; Buddh.), NP of a Lamaist *arhat.* Attr.: *nakula* (vomiting jewels).
Lit.: G 16, 104.

bala "force" (Buddh.): *b.* is a kind of mental characteristic, and 10 *b.* (*daśabala*) belong to a *mānuṣibuddha.*
Lit.: BBh. 76; BRI 52; Gt 157; IC 2:537.

Balā ("powerful"; Jain.), NP of a *śāsanadevatā* attending on the 17th *tīrthaṅkara.*
Lit.: GJ 362.

bāla "child" (attr.). Carried in the arms or in other ways char. of mother goddesses, such as Ambā, Ambikā, Diti, Durgā, Hāritī, Issakī (*bāla amastaka*), Ṣaṣṭhī, Siṅhavāhinī, Yaśodā(-Kṛṣṇa).

Bālā ("girl, young woman"), NP of a goddess. Char.: Vāh.: *padmapīṭha*; Mu.: *abhaya-, varada-mudrā*; attr.: *akṣamālā, pustaka.*
Lit.: R 1:372.

Balabhadra ("whose strength is good").
1. (Hind.) Epithet of Balarāma, esp. as companion of Kṛṣṇa in his aspect as Jagannātha.
Lit.: D 40; MG 151; R 1:95.
2. (Buddh.) N. given to the Hindu god Balarāma in the Buddhist pantheon. Char.: colour: white; Vāh.: *gaja*; attr.: *hala, khaḍga.*
Lit.: BBh. 378.

Baladeva ("the god of strength"), epithet of Balarāma. – In Jainism B. (with the same attr. as Balarāma), is n. of a group of 9 demi-gods.
Lit.: AI 118; GJ 258, 261.

Bāla-Gaṇapati ("the child-G."), epithet and aspect of Gaṇeśa as a child. Attr.: *āmra, ikṣu, kadala, kapittha, panasa.*
Lit.: R 1:52; Th. 96.

Bālagopāla ("the child-cowherd"), epithet of Kṛṣṇa as a youthful cowherd.

Bālāji (or Ballaji, probably "the dear child", cp. Hi. *bālā* "child"), in North India epithet of Veṅkateśa.
Lit.: R 1:270.

Bāla-Kṛṣṇa ("the child-K."), epithet of Kṛṣṇa, esp. in his forms as Dāmodara, Makkhañcor, Navanītanṛtta-Kṛṣṇa, Santānagopāla, Vāṭapattrāśāyin. See also Kṛṣṇa.
Lit.: KIM pl. 56; R 1:215 a.pl. 67:1-2; SB 348 a.fig. 314; Th. 68 a.pl. 18.

Balapāramitā ("perfection of strength"; Buddh.), n. of a *pāramitā**. Char.: colour: red; attr.: *cintāmaṇidhvaja, pustaka.*
Lit.: BBh. 327.

Balapramathanī ("destroying power"), NP of a goddess (a form of Durgā, MW), the Śakti of one of the *vidyeśvaras**.
Lit.: MW 722; R 1:364, 2:403.

Balarāma ("Rāma of strength"), NP of the elder brother of Kṛṣṇa; he was the son of Vasudeva and Devakī, together with Rohiṇī (as a result of the transfer of the embryo in the womb of Devakī to that of Rohiṇī, B. had two mothers; cp. the story of Mahāvīra); wife: Revatī(devī); sons: Niśatha, Ulmuka.

B. is often regarded as a particular *avatāra* of Viṣṇu, or else (as an *aṅśa*) of Ananta, who himself was a partial incarnation (*aṅśa*) of Viṣṇu. Originally B. may have been an agricultural deity (cp. his attr.). He is, however, seldom worshipped alone, but usually as a companion of Kṛṣṇa, and, in the role of elder brother, he stands on the right-hand side of Kṛṣṇa. – In Jainism he is usually named Baladeva. – Char.: colour: as distinct from the black Kṛṣṇa he is white; attr.: esp. *hala* and *musala*, also *cakra*, *gadā* Saunanda, *khaḍga*, *kheṭaka* (see this word, possibly another n. of his *gadā*), *kuṇḍala*, *madhupātra*, *padma*, *pānapātra*, *śaṅkha*, *tāladhvaja*. – Epithets: Balabhadra, Baladeva, Halabhṛt, Halāyudha, Musalin, Saṅkarṣaṇa(-Baladeva).
Lit.: B 306, 391, 423 a.pl. 22:4, 26:1; D 40; DHP 165, 179; GH 127; GJ 258; Gt 72; HIS 45, 62 a.pl. 21-23; JDI 85; MEIA 35; R 1:123, 195; SIB pl. 8; WHW 1:114; WM 46.

Bālā-Śakti ("the girl-Śakti"), n. of a goddess in South India who is supposed to preside over 6 *cakras*; the *bālāyantra* in particular is sacred to her. Attr.: *akṣamālā*, *aṅkuśa*, *pāśa*, *pustaka*.
Lit.: SSI 222.

Bāla-Subrahmaṇya ("the child-S."), n. of a form of Skanda as a child. Char.: Att.: *nāṭyasthāna*, *samapādasthānaka*; Mu.: *varadamudrā*; attr.: *padma*. The representation of B. dancing resembles the Navanītanṛtta-Kṛṣṇa, with the exception that the left leg is lifted.

Bāla-Svāmin (-mī; "the child-Lord"), n. of a form of Skanda as a child standing beside his parents (cp. Somāskanda). Char.: Mu.: *kaṭimudrā*; attr.: *padma*.
Lit.: R 2:439.

Bālā-Tripurasundarī ("the girl-T."), n. of a mild form of the Śakti, see Tripurasundarī.
Lit.: SSI 218.

Balavikaraṇī ("she who augments strength"), NP of the Śakti of one of the *vidyeśvaras*.
Lit.: R 1:399, 2:403.

Balavikarṇikā ("she who is deaf to power"), NP of a peace-giving goddess, an aspect of Durgā. Attr.: *akṣamālā*, *kapāla*.
Lit.: MW 723; R 1:363.

bālāyantra ("the girl-*yantra*"; attr.), n. of a *yantra* sacred to Bālā-Śakti. For the form of this *yantra*, see SSI.
Lit.: SSI 222.

bali (or *śrībali*) "offering, gift, sacrifice". This sacrifice forms part of the *pūjā**. In South India *b.* was often a bloody sacrifice. – See also *bhūtayajña*.
Lit.: B 521; DiIP 90, 137, 178; GBM 132; Gt Suppl. 17; IC 1:585; MKVI 2:62.

Bali, NP of a demon, the son of Virocana. He was a *daitya**-king, and was dethroned from the dominion over the world by Viṣṇu in his *avatāra* as Vāmana.
Lit.: D 42; GoRI 1:322; Gt 73; IIM 108; R 1:161; WHW 1:452; WM 46.

balibera "offering-icon" (attr.), n. of an icon which is used at the daily *pūjā* within the temple and is then worshipped with *balis*. It is sometimes equivalent to *utsavamūrti* (see *utsavabera*).
Lit.: R 1:17; WM 88.

baliharaṇa "presentation of offerings, oblations", a presentation of cooked rice to various gods, made at different places within and outside the house.
Lit.: GH 330.

balipīṭha "dispensing seat" (Vāh.), n. given to a stone altar in the form of a lotus blossom set up at the main entrance of a temple, on which temple priests place balls of rice.
Lit.: ACA 85; ZA 287.

Ballaji (Mar.), see Bālāji, epithet of Veṅkateśa.

bāṇa "reed-shaft, a short stick" (attr.). Char. of Kaṅkālamūrti. – This term is, however, very often used in the sense of "arrow", for which see *śara*.
Lit.: AIP 74 a.pl. 53 (319); BBh. 433; R 1:6 a.pl. 2:5.

bāṇaliṅga, n. given to white stone of a kind found in the river Narmadā and worshipped as the lithomorphic form (*liṅga**, cp. *avyakta*) of Śiva. A *b.* is egg-shaped and made of quartz. It is sometimes represented

by a five-headed *liṅga*, and is classed as an *acalaliṅga*. – The term *b.* can also signify the five arrows of Kāma, since *bāṇa* also has the sense of "arrow" (see above).
Lit.: B 458; DHP 229; KiH 35; KiSH 77; R 1:12; WM 87.

bāṇāsana "arrow-discharger, i.e. bow" (attr.), see *dhanus*.
Lit.: ACA 33.

bandha "binding"; a term used esp. to refer to the head-dress, cp. *keśabandha*. Another n.: *bhāra*.
Lit.: SB 300.

bandhana "cord" (attr.), see *pāśa*.
Lit.: MEIA 336.

bandya (= Skt *vandya*) "venerable" (Buddh.), in Nepal n. given to a priest.
Lit.: GBM 135.

baṅgālī san "the Bengalī year", n. of an era, beginning in A.D. 593 and used in Bengal and regions nearby. This era is indicated by *san* or sometimes by *sāl* (or by *san*... figures... *sāl*). The year is *vartamāna*, *meṣādi* (solar); the given year of this era + 593 = the year A.D.
Lit.: IC 2:737.

bara deul (N.Ind., "towered temple"), in Orissa and in North India, n. given to of a kind of temple consisting of a *garbhagṛha* and a *śikhara*. – Cp. *vimāna*.
Lit.: DKI 41, 104; P 560.

bārhaspatyasaṃvatsara "year of Bṛhaspati", n. of a solar year according to the *bṛhaspatisaṃvatsaracakra**.
Lit.: IC 2:726.

Barhi-dhvaja, *-ketu* ("having a peacock as banner, symbolized by a peacock"), epithet of Skanda.
Lit.: B 364.

barhin "peacock" (Vāh.), see *mayūra*. – Cp. Barhidhvaja.
Lit.: KiSH 88.

Baṭuka Bhairava (Vaṭuka Bh., "the young Bh."), n. of a form of Bhairava, represented as naked and with protruding teeth. Char.: Vāh.: *śvan*; Mu.: *abhayamudrā*; attr.: *agni*, *ḍamaru*, *dantas*, *kapāla*, *khaḍga*, *khaṭvāṅga*, *nāga*, *nagna*, *pāśa*, *triśūla*.
Lit.: B 466 a.pl. 35:1; DiIP 143; R 2:177.

bauddha "adherent of the Buddha".

Beg-tse (Tib.; G translates this as "brother-sister", but this meaning refers rather to another n. of this god: lCam-sriṅ; B. means rather: "a hidden shirt of mail"; Buddh.); in Lamaism NP of a *dharmapāla* worshipped as a god of war. Char.: Vāh.: *aśva+nara* (or *nārī*; B. has one foot on the *aśva* and the other on the *nara*); attr.: esp. *khaḍga*, further also *agni*, *ajina*, *dhvaja*, *trinayana*.
Lit.: G passim; JT 149, 370.

bel, *bīl* (Hi.; attr.), see *bilva*.

bera (probably from Skt *vera* "body, figure"), n. of an icon; it is as the second member included in many words, such as *arcā-*, *bali-*, *dhruva-*, *kautuka-*, *mūla-*, *snapana-* and *utsava-bera*.
Lit.: R 1:17.

bhaddāsana (Pāli), see *bhadrāsana*.

Bhadra ("auspicious, good"; Buddh.), NP of a Lamaist *arhat*. Char.: Mu.: *dhyāna-*, *vyākhyāna-mudrā*; attr.: *pustaka*.
Lit.: G 104.

Bhadrā ("auspicious"), NP of a goddess, probably belonging to the circle of Śiva. Char.: Vāh.: *bhadrāsana*; attr.: *akṣamālā*, *nīlotpala*, *phala*, *triśūla*.
Lit.: R 1:368.

bhadraghaṭa "vase of fortune" (attr.), see *kamaṇḍalu*. – In architecture *bh.* indicates a bunch of lotuses in a vase, symbolizing the birth of the Buddha.
Lit.: KiDG 67; KiSB 84; MS 44.

Bhadra-Kālī ("the auspicious K."), n. of a form of Śiva's Śakti, partly identical with Mahākālī; see also Kālī and Durgā. Char.: Vāh.: *siṅha*, or *ratha* drawn by 4 *siṅha*s; att.: *ālīḍhāsana*; Mu.: *abhayamudrā*; attr.: 12 or 18 arms, *agni*, *akṣamālā*, *candra*, *daṇḍa*, *dhanus*, *jaṭāmukuṭa*, *kamaṇḍalu*, *khaḍga*, *kṛṣṇājina*, *padma*, *śakti*, *śaṅkha*, *śara*, *sruk*, *sruva*, *trinayana*, *triśūla*. – Another n.: Pattira Kāḷiyammaṉ.
Lit.: R 1:357; SSI 197.

bhādrapada, n. of a month (August-September). Its god is Gaṇeśa.
Lit.: BBh. 382; IC 2:733.

Bhadrapāla ("auspicious protector"; Buddh.), NP of a *bodhisattva*. Char.: colour: red or white; Mu.: *varadamudrā*; attr.: *cintāmaṇi*.
Lit.: BBh. 83, 96 a.pl. 69.

bhadrapīṭha "good, auspicious seat" (Vāh.), n. of a quadrangular (or round) *pīṭha* (cp. *bhadrāsana*). This term refers to the lower part of a throne which can be combined with an upper layer in the form of a *padmapīṭha*. The *bh.* is often made in a separate piece (even when combined with a *padmapīṭha*). – A *bh.* is the Vāh. (i.e. seat) of many gods.
Lit.: B 273, 299; R 1:20, 2:101 a.pl. 12; SSI pl. 1:13.

bhadrāsana (Pāli *bhaddāsana*) "good, auspicious seat or sitting posture".
1. (Vāh.) N. of a mostly rectangular seat or throne (cp. *bhadrapīṭha*). Also n. of a throne as *maṅgala* (Jain.), see *aṣṭamaṅgala*.
Lit.: GJ 384; JMS 77; KiJ 21; KiSH 154; RN 30; SB 63 a.passim.
2, (Att.) N. of an *āsana*-posture which is described thus: "the heels of the legs which cross each other are placed under the testes and the two big toes of the feet are held by the hands" (B), but it is also declared to be "unsere übliche Sitzweise" (KiSB), cp. BBh.: "both the legs are pendant" (as to the latter form of att., see *paryaṅkāsana*). The symbolic meaning of this att. is said to be that it brings material wealth. – It is char. of Vaśya-Tārā.
Lit.: B 270; BBh. 432; G 24; KiH pl. 151; KiSB 99; R 1:18; SM 130; WHW 1:74.

Bhaga ("the Inherited Share; Dispenser; gracious lord"), n. of an Āditya (also epithet of several gods). Wife: Siddhi. Attr.: *cakra*, 2 *padma*s, *triśūla*.
Lit.: DHP 117; R 1:309; WM 49.

Bhagavān (-va(n)t; N.Ind. often Bhagwān, "the Lord"), epithet of Viṣṇu and Kṛṣṇa (cp. Bhagavadgītā "the song of the Lord", referring to Kṛṣṇa), sometimes also of Śiva. Bh. as an appellation for a god ranks higher than *deva*. – With the Bhīls and other tribes Bh. is n. of the highest god. – Cp. Īśvara.
Lit.: FHRI 252; GoRI 1:243, 2:18; KBh. 273.

bhāgavata, n. of an adherent of Bhagavān, i.e. of Kṛṣṇa, and of a sect. The n. is esp. connected with the most popular of the Purāṇas, the Bhāgavatapurāṇa. – Cp. *pañcarātrin*.
Lit.: GoRI 1:243; HIS 18; IC 1:641.

Bhagavatī ("the Lady"), n. of a gracious aspect of Pārvatī.
Lit.: KiH 22 a.pl. 75; KiSH 47.

Bhagīratha "having a golden chariot" MW; the word might be better interpreted as: "the chariot of Bhagī", in which Bhagī (possibly "Lady"; cp. that Bhaga is often used in the meaning of "Lord") could be an epithet of Gaṅgā, see below), NP of a *bhakta* of Śiva who often accompanies this god in the Gaṅgādharamūrti*. (Bh. was an ancient king who caused the holy river Gaṅgā to come down from heaven to earth, and hence was the instrument of her descent). – Mu.: *añjalimudrā*.
Lit.: CHIIA 243 a.fig. 206; MW 744; R 2:315.

Bhagwān (N.Ind.), see Bhagavān.

Bhairava ("terrible, frightful").
1. (Hind.) N. of an *ugra**-aspect of Śiva, said to have been born from the blood of Śiva. Bh. is found in several varieties, such as Baṭuka-Bhairava, Svarṇākarṣaṇa-Bhairava, and also in a group of 64 different Bhairavas, companions of Rudra (i.e. of Śiva). – Char.: Vāh.: *vṛka* or *śvan*, *nara* (*mṛtaka*); Mu.: *kaṭakamudrā*; attr.: esp. *kapāla*, *khaṭvāṅga*, *valaya*, further *agni*, *ajina* (tiger- or elephant-skin), *bhindipāla*, *candra*, *ḍamaru*, (several) *danta*s, *gadā*, *khaḍga*, *kheṭaka*, *kuṇḍa*, *muṇḍamālā*, *nāga*s, *nagna*, *paraśu*, *pāśa*, *śakti*, *triśūla*, and, in general, the attr. of Śiva. – Bh. is also regarded as a servant of Śiva (cp. Bhairon). – Varieties: Govinda-, Kāla-, Pañcavaktra-, and Saṅhāra-Bhairava. – Another n.: Vayiravaṉ.
Lit.: AuOW 59; B 465, 481 a.pl. 35:3-4; D 45; DHP 196, 311 a.pl. 18; DiIP 68; GoRI 1:255; HAHI pl. 12; IIM 43; JDI 25; KiSH 29; KrA pl. 72; R 2:115, 177 a.pl. 41-43; SS pl. 30:134; SB 211, 345 a.fig. 130, 295, a. passim; SSI 151; WM 49.

2. (Buddh.) In Lamaism n. of a variety of Yamāntaka. Char.: colour: blue; attr.: *vṛṣamastaka, kapāla, karttṛkā.*
Lit.: G 90 (ill.).
3. (Vāh.; Buddh.) Upon the prostrate Hindu god Bh. tread the Buddhist deities: Samvara, Vajrahuṅkāra, Vajravārāhī.
Lit.: BBh. 162; KiSB 78.
4. (Plur.; Jain.) N. of a group of deities.
Lit.: B 561.

Bhairavī ("terrible"), n. of a *mātā*, a form of Durgā. She belongs to the group *mahāvidyā* and is then represented by Kālarātrī. Bh. is also n. of a group of maid-servants (demons) of Śiva and Durgā. Attr.: *aṅkuśa, pāśa.*
Lit.: DHP 281, 288; IC 1:528; R 1:366.

Bhairon (Hi., related to Skt Bhairava), n. of a deity developed from Bhairava (regarded as a *dvārapāla* of Śiva); also n. of a hero. Bh. is connected with cult of dogs. Char.: Vāh.: *śvan*; attr.: *ḍamaru, gadā, kapāla.*
Lit.: DiIP 143; GH 111 a.pl. 4; MG 272 a.pl. facing p. 203.

Bhaiṣajyaguru ("Supreme Physician"; Buddh.), esp. in Lamaism n. of a *buddha* who, on one hand, is mentioned as the fifth in one series of *buddhas* (see *mānuṣibuddha*); on the other hand Bh. is the first in a series of "medicine-*buddhas*" for whom the Tibetan term is sMan-bla*. This series lists the following names: 1. Bhaiṣajyaguru; 2. Siṅhanāda; 3. Suparikīrtitanāmaśrī; 4. Svaraghoṣarāja; 5. Survarṇabhadravimalaratnaprabhāsa; 6. Aśokottamaśrī; 7. Dharmakīrtisāgaraghoṣa; 8. Abhijñārāja; 9. Śikhin. These *buddhas* have usually as common attr.: *ūrṇā, uṣṇīṣa* and elongated earlobes. – Bh. as a particular *buddha* has the char.: colour: blue (indigo) or golden; Mu.: *dhyānamudrā* (left hand); attr.: *āmalaka*, sometimes *(bhikṣā)pātra.*
Lit.: G 32, 54, 56; GRI 259; IC 2:570.

Bhājā, n. of a village in West India, with a Buddhist cave temple dating from about B.C. 50.
Lit.: FBKI 45; RAAI 70; ZA pl. 39 ff.

bhājana "vessel (containing water from the Ganges)" (attr.), see *kamaṇḍalu.*

bhakta "devotee", n. given to an ardent worshipper of a god. Images of *bhaktas* are set up for worship in the temples. Lists of *śaivabhaktas* and *vaiṣṇavabhaktas** in South India are given in R. – Cp. also *āḷvār, aṅga, sādhu.*
Lit.: GoRI 1:244, 271; IC 1:664; R 2:473 a.pl. 134-138.

bhaktapūjā "worship of a *bhakta*", esp. of Sundara(mūrti)*.
Lit.: DiIP 142.

bhakti "devotion", (esp. Hind.) n. of a mystical religious doctrine of faith, according to which the *bhakta*, through an ardent love of God, or an uncompromising devotion, attains the union with God. *bh.* may be connected with either Śiva or Viṣṇu (Rāma) or other gods. Esp. well-known is the form of *bh.* connected with Kṛṣṇa and Rādhā.
Lit.: GoRI 1:244, 270; Gt Suppl 18; IC 1:661; KT 155; WHW 1:138; ZA 60.

Bhakti-Vighneśvara, n. of a form of Gaṇeśa. Char.: colour: white; attr.: *āmra, kapāla* with *pāyasa, nārikela, ikṣukāṇḍa.*
Lit.: R 1:52.

Bhālacandra ("having the moon on his forehead"), n. of a form of Gaṇeśa.
Lit.: R 1:59.

bhāmaṇḍala "aureole, circle of light" (attr.). This term may be identical in meaning with *prabhāmaṇḍala.*
Lit.: SB 211; SIB 69.

bhandāra "alms-box" in the temple (attr.; Jain.).
Lit.: GJ 401.

bhaṅg (or *bhāṅg* "hemp", Hi. < Skt *bhaṅga*), n. of an intoxicating beverage made of the leaves of hemp, i.e. Cannabis indica (attr.). Mixed with water and milk, *bh.* is used for bathing the great *liṅga* in the Liṅgarāj-temple at Bhubaneswar.
Lit.: P 180.

bhaṅga (*vaṅga, -u*) "bend(ing), bowing" (att.). This term refers to the posture of the body, seen esp. in *sthānaka*-postures. Cp. *ābhaṅga, atibhaṅga, samabhaṅga (samapāda), tribhaṅga*; see also *dvibhaṅga.*
Lit.: B 264; WHW 1:45, 139.

Bhānu ("light, ray of light"), epithet of Sūrya.

bhāra ("burden, bulk"; attr.). This term esp. refers to the headdress, cp. *jaṭābhāra*; see further *bandha*.
Lit.: WM 753.

bharan (-*t*; Hi.) "metallic alloy of brass and zinc (brass and copper)".
Lit.: BhIM 34.

Bharaṇī(s) (-*yas*; "bearing"), n. of a *nakṣatra*. Its influence is bad. – Another n.: Apabharaṇīs.
Lit.: BBh. 381; IC 2:730.

Bharata ("to be or being maintained"), n. of many heroes. 1. NP of one of the ancestors in the *candravaṅśa**, cp. Bhārata. – 2. NP of a half-brother of Rāma, sometimes regarded as an *aṅśa**, representing the weapon *cakra* of Rāma. Attr.: *dhanus, khaḍga, kheṭaka, śara*.
Lit.: D 47; Gt 89; MW 747; R 1:191 a.pl. 57; WHW 1:141; WM 50.

Bhārata (patronymic of Bharata). This n. forms part of the n. of the epic Mahābhārata and is also identical with the modern n. of India (Bhārata).

bharatanāṭya "the dance of Bharata", n. of a school or style of dancing, which was forged into a tradition by Bharata, an ancient sage supposed to be the author of a manual of dramatic art.
Lit.: MW 747; Sh. 29, 35, 102 a.pl. 2, 6-9; WHW 1:144.

Bhāratī, epithet of Sarasvatī. Bh. is also regarded as the wife of Gaṇeśa.
Lit.: B 358.

Bhārgava (patronymic of Bhṛgu), epithet of Śukra.
Lit.: KiK 141.

Bhārgava-Rāma, epithet of Paraśurāma as the offspring of Bhṛgu.
Lit.: B 390.

Bhārhūt, n. of a town near Allāhābād, famous for a *stūpa* built under the Śuṅga dynasty, and now removed to the Indian Museum at Calcutta.
Lit.: Gz 48; SeKB passim; ZA pl. 31 ff.

Bhāskara ("making light"), n. of a form of Sūrya. Char.: Vāh.: *aśva* (of which he rides astride) or *ratha* drawn by 7 *aśvas*.
Lit.: MEIA 221, 228, 234.

bhasma(n) "ashes" (attr.; esp. Buddh.). In Buddhism it forms part of the *ṣaṇmudrās*. Cp. *vibhūti*.
Lit.: BBh. 438; R 2:276; WHW 1:80.

bhasmasnāna "ash-bath", n. of a ceremony reputed to be a remedy of all ills. The first *bh.* was taken by Śiva in the ashes of Kāma.
Lit.: WHW 1:81.

Bhauma (patronymic of Bhūmī), epithet of Maṅgala.
Lit.: R 1:319 a.pl. 96.

bhaumavāsara (-*vāra*) "Tuesday", see *maṅgalavāra*.

Bhava ("existence, the Existent"), epithet of Śiva (Rudra), esp. in the form in which he married Satī, a daughter of Dakṣa. Bh. is one of the *mūrtyaṣṭaka*-forms. For *bhava* as a symbolic n. of the number "11", see *saṅkhyā*.
Lit.: B 448, 462; DHP 204; R 2:403.

bhavacakra(mudrā) "the wheel of life, existence" (attr.; Buddh.), n. of a symbol of the *saṅsāra*, represented by a wheel (*cakra*). In Tibet this symbol is also made quadrangular. *bh.* is furthermore personified as a three-eyed demon who carries before him a round or quadrangular tray. In Tibet *bh.* is also the subject of paintings.
Lit.: G 27 (ill.); GBM 103; KiSB 38.

bhavanavāsī (-*ín*; "dwelling in places"; Jain.), n. of a species of deities. They have the appearance of young men and are arranged in 10 classes, signified by the word -*kumāra*: 1. *asura*-; 2. *nāga*-; 3. *suparṇa*-; 4. *vāyu*-; 5. *dvīpa*-; 6. *udadhi*-; 7. *dik*-; 8. *vidyut*-; 9. *stanita*-; 10. *agni-kumāra*.
Lit.: GJ 235.

Bhavānī (or Bhowāni, Tam. Pavāṉiyammaṉ; related to Bhava), as "the wife of Bhava", epithet of Pārvatī. She is said to be the Śakti of Rudra. – Cp. Tulajā-Bhavānī.
Lit.: DiCh. 25; DiIP 136; GoRI 1:259; MSHP 23; MW 749.

bhāvapūjā ("worship through the disposition of mind"; Jain.), n. of a form of worship which consists in meditating on and singing the praises of a *tīrthaṅkara*.
Lit.: GJ 365.

Bhavodbhava ("originating from Bhava"), n. of one among the group *ekādaśarudra*.
Lit.: R 2:386.

bheka "frog", see *maṇḍūka*.

Bhela ("timid"), NP of a physician who is mentioned as a *riṣi* and the leader of a certain group of *riṣis*, the *paramaharṣis*.
Lit.: R 2:566.

bherī "drum" (attr.), n. of "un tambour de forme cylindrique (de plus grand diamètre que le *mṛdaṅgam*), légérement renflé au milieu et garni d'un treillis de lanières de cuir fortement tendues".
Lit.: ACA 83.

bhikkhu and *bhikkhunī* (Pāli), see *bhikṣu* and *bhikṣuṇī*.

bhikṣāpātra "alms dish, a mendicant's bowl" (attr.), n. of a round bowl. As an attr. it should properly signify some gods in their mendicant aspects (as Brahmā, Śiva Bhikṣāṭana, Gaṇeśa, and others), but, iconographically, mostly confused with the originally elliptical *kapāla*. In this dictionary *kapāla* is therefore usually taken as being synonymous with *bh*. In Buddhist iconography, however, the difference between *bh*. and *kapāla* is more considerable, and therefore *bh*., or the shorter term *pātra**, is better adapted to indicate the bowl of the Buddha (or *buddhas*) and other Buddhist saints. – Another n.: *kuṇḍī*.
Lit.: G 16; JMS 11; W 86; ZM 192.

Bhikṣāṭana(mūrti) ("wandering about for alms"), n. of a representation of Śiva as a wandering mendicant monk. He is then escorted by a *mṛga*. In the neighbourhood of a Bh. image a *riṣipatnī* is often found. Char.: att.: *kuñcitapāda*; Mu.: *kaṭaka-*, *varada-mudrā*; attr.: *bhriṅgipāda*, *ḍamaru*, *kapāla*, *keśamaṇḍala*, *mayūrapattra*, *nagna*, *pādarakṣa*, *paṭṭa*, *tripuṇḍra*, *yajñopavīta*. – This representation is very much like that of Śiva as Kaṅkālamūrti.
Lit.: B 466, 483 a.pl. 38:2; JDI 30; R 2:306 a.pl. 86-89; SB 170 a.fig. 104, p. 268 a.fig. 175; SIB pl. 49; SSI 97; Th. 89 a.pl. 49B; ZM 140.

bhikṣu and *bhikṣuṇī* (Pāli: *bhikkhu*, *bhikkhunī*) "almsman, mendicant monk" and "nun", respectively; a member of the *saṅgha* (Buddh., Jain.).
Lit.: BRI 55; IC 2:604; SchRI 234; WHW 1:437.

Bhīma or Bhīmasena ("terrible", "having a formidable army").
1. NP of the second of the Pāṇḍu-princes, a hero in the epic Mahābhārata. He is regarded as the spiritual son of Vāyu and worshipped as a hero of terrible strength. Attr.: *gadā*.
Lit.: GH 93; Gt 95, 768; WHW 1:148; WM 50; ZA pl. 111; ZM 71 a.pl. 3.
2. Bh. is sometimes an epithet of Śiva; also mentioned as one of the *ekādaśarudras* or *mūrtyaṣṭaka*-forms. Wife: Diśā; son: Sarga.
Lit.: DHP 195, 205; GoRI 1:254; R 2:386; WM 50.

Bhīmā ("terrible"; Buddh.), NP of a minor Mahāyāna goddess attending on *Buddhakapāla*.
Lit.: BBh. 160.

Bhīmadarśanā ("frightful in appearance"; Buddh.), NP of a minor Mahāyāna goddess attending on Buddhakapāla.
Lit.: BBh. 160; MW 758.

bhindipāla "short javelin or arrow thrown from the hand or shot through a tube" (attr.; it is perhaps not always possible to distinguish this attr. from the *śakti*, which however is of larger size). Char. of: Bhairava, Cundā, Nandīśvara, Nirṛti, Ubhayavarāhānana-Mārīcī, Vidyujjvālākarālī.
Lit.: B 466; MW 757.

Bhīṣaṇa ("frightening"), epithet of Śiva Bhairava.
Lit.: B 466.

bhoga ("enjoyment, possession, wealth"), n. given to a class of icons which are worshipped with a view to obtaining wealth

and prosperity. This is the class of icons most frequently met-with. See also sub *dhruva*.
Lit.: B 399; R 1:18, 79.

bhogamūrti, see *bhoga* and *cala*.

Bhogaśakti (cp. *bhoga*), n. of the Śakti of Śiva in his *Sadāśiva*-aspect.
Lit.: DiIP 123; TL s.v.

bhogāsanamūrti ("sitting representation [of Viṣṇu] of *bhoga**-character"), n. of a form of Viṣṇu sitting with Lakṣmī and Bhūmi. Char.: Vāh.: *siṅhāsana*; att.: *lalitāsana*; Mu.: *abhaya-*, *varada-mudrā*; attr.: *cakra*, *śaṅkha* (*gadā*, *padma*).
Lit.: R 1:87 a.pl. 25-29:1.

bhogaśayanamūrti ("lying representation [of Viṣṇu] of *bhoga**-character), n. of a form of Viṣṇu recumbent, with Lakṣmī sitting close to his feet. See further Anantāśāyana.
Lit.: B 407 a.pl. 22:2; R 1:92 a.pl. 32, 34.

bhogasthānakamūrti ("standing representation [of Viṣṇu] of *bhoga**-character), n. of a form of Viṣṇu standing, four-handed. Char.: Mu.: *abhaya-*, *kaṭaka-* or *kaṭi-*, *varada-mudrā*; attr.: *cakra*, *śaṅkha*.
Lit.: R 1:81 a.pl. 18-20, 22-23.

bhoj patra (also *bhoj pattar*; Hi.) lit. "birch-bark", of which amulet receptacles (cp. *yantrapātra*) and accessories to *hukkā* are made (attr.).
Lit.: P 195.

Bhowāni (N.Ind. "witch, sorceress", probably identical with Bhavānī), among the Bhīls n. of Durgā (or Kālī),
Lit.: KBh. 175.

bhramara "bee" (attr.), see *madhukara*.

bhramaraka "ringlet of hair" (attr.).
Lit.: BECA 1:260.

bhramaramudrā "bee-handpose" (Mu.), n. of a subvariety of the *haṅsamudrā** with the difference that the forefinger is bent so that its tip touches the first joint of the thumb. It denotes silence, bath, parrot, sexual union.
Lit.: WHW 2:87.

bhrātṛdvitīya "(festival dedicated) to brothers, on the second day (in the light half of the month *kārttika*)". On this day (in Bengal) brothers and sisters exchange gifts.
Lit.: GH 356; MW 770.

Bhṛgu or Bhrigu ("Crack-of-Fire"), NP of a *riṣi* or *prajāpati*, the ancestor of Paraśurāma.
Lit.: D 54; DHP 322; MG 301; WHW 1:151; WM 51.

bhṛguvāsara (*-vāra*) "Friday", see *śukravāra*.

bhriṅgipāda (attr.): according to the descriptions this term ought to be translated as "having a *bhriṅgi*, i.e. a bell, on the leg", but such a meaning of *bhriṅgi* or *bhṛṅgi* is not recorded in the dictionaries. In AIP this term is translated as "a garter with bells", and this attr. is worn round the right leg by Śiva in some Naṭarāja- and Bhikṣāṭana-representations. Cp. *kiṅkiṇī-(sūtra)*.
Lit.: AIP 72, 76; MEIA 69; SSI 100 a.pl. II:3.

Bhṛkuṭi ("frowning"; Jain.), NP of a *yakṣa*, an attendant of the 21st *tīrthaṅkara*.
Lit.: GJ 362 a.pl. 26:21.

Bhṛkuṭī(-Tārā) (Bhrikuṭī; "she who frowns").
1. (Buddh.) In Lamaism NP of a (cruel) form of Tārā, regarded as the "yellow Tārā", notwithstanding the fact that she is an emanation of Amitābha (and not of Ratnasambhava who is signified by his colour yellow). Bh. is further said to be a female *bodhisattva*. – Char.: colour: yellow; att.: *sthānaka* (also with crossed legs); Mu.: *abhaya-* or *varada-mudrā*; attr.: *akṣamālā*, *Amitābhabimba* on the crown, *daṇḍa* or *tridaṇḍa*, *kamaṇḍalu*, *padma*, *trinayana*, *triśūla*. Varieties: Jāṅgulī, Vajratārā, sometimes also Khadiravaṇī.
Lit.: BBh. 152, 309 a.pl. 123; G 34, 75; GBM 81; HuGT 17; IP pl. 20; KiDG 64; KiSB 98.
2. (Jain.) NP of a *śāsanadevatā* attending on the 8th *tīrthaṅkara*.
Lit.: GJ 362; pw 4:281.

bhṛṅgāra "vase" (attr.), see *kamaṇḍalu*.
Lit.: B 501; JMS 11.

Bhṛṅgin (-i or ī, -īśa, "the Wanderer", DHP).
1. (Hind.) NP of a *riṣi* attending on Śiva. Sometimes he is represented standing (or dancing) at the side of Śiva Naṭarāja or

Umā-Maheśvara. Char. : att. : *nāṭyasthāna*; attr. : *tripādaka*. – Bh. is also an epithet of Nandīśvara.
Lit.: DHP 220; JDI 53 a.fig. 14; KrA pl. 124 a.p. 209; SSR pl. facing p. 105; SSI 165.

2. (Buddh.) Bh. is also found in Buddhism. Char. : colour : blue; attr. : *akṣamālā* (blue), *kamaṇḍalu*.
Lit.: BBh. 365.

BHRŪṀ, a mystic syllable (*bīja*), signifying the forehead, see *śānti*.
Lit.: GJ 369.

Bhū "earth", see Bhūmi. It is also a symbolic n. given to the number "1", see *saṅkhyā*.

bhūḥ, bhuvaḥ, svaḥ, see *vyāhṛti*.

bhujaṅga "snake", see *nāga*.
Lit.: MEIA 216; R 2:372.

bhujaṅgāsana "snake-sitting" (att.), n. of a posture in which one lies on the stomach with palms placed on the ground near the shoulders.
Lit.: WHW 1:74.

bhujaṅgatrās(it)a(karaṇa) "snake-fright", the technical n. of the best-known dancing-orm (popularly named: *ānanda-tāṇḍava*) of the South Indian type of Śiva Naṭarāja; so called, "since the dancer 'suddenly lifts up his leg as though he had discovered a snake very near him and appears to be of unsteady gait'" (WHW). This att. is also found in a reversed form. See also *nṛtta-mūrti*.
Lit.: R 2:227 a.pl. 56-58; SB 100, 188; SIB pl. 47; SSIP 75; WHW 1:264.

bhujaṅgavalaya "armlet, wrist-ring" (attr.), having the form of a coiling serpent. Char. of Śiva. – Other n. : *sarpavalaya, nāga-valaya*; see further *valaya*.
Lit.: BECA 1:260; R 1:23.

bhujasūtra "armlet string" (attr.).
Lit.: SSIP 150.

bhūmi "earth, floor" = the ground on which all things are founded.

1. (Buddh.) N. of a group of 12 deities. "In Buddhism the *bhūmi*s are recognised as different spiritual spheres through which a *bodhisattva* moves in his quest for Buddhahood and omniscience" (BBh.). They were deified in Vajrayāna Buddhism as 12 goddesses with the names: Adhimuktacaryā, Pramuditā, Vimalā, Prabhākarī, Arciṣmatī, Sudurjayā, Abhimukhī, Dūraṅgamā, Acalā, Sādhumatī, Dharmameghā, Samantaprabhā. Common feature : *vajra*.
Lit.: BBh. 333; GRI 255.

2. In architecture n. of the successive planes or divisions of a Dravidian temple or of the horizontal courses of a *śikhara*.
Lit.: IC 1:576; RAAI 271.

Bhūmi(devī) (or Bhū[devī] "the Earth-goddess"). NP of the second wife of Viṣṇu (or Kṛṣṇa). She is usually represented standing (sitting) to the left of Viṣṇu when he is accompanied by two wives. Bh. is the usual n. of this goddess in South India (cp. in North India Puṣṭi). Son : Naraka. Char. : Vāh. : *padmapīṭha*; Mu. : *abhayamudrā*; attr. : according to R *kucabandha* is her chief attr.; according to JDI, however, her breasts are quite naked, but she wears a *yajñopavīta* (while Lakṣmī, on the other side of Viṣṇu, wears a *channavīra*); other attr. : *dāḍimaphala, kamaṇḍalu, nīlotpala* or *padma, oṣadhipātra, sasyapātra, viṇā* (?). – Bh. (Bhūmi Devatā) is also worshipped as a vegetative fertility deity by many primitive agricultural tribes. – Other n. : Mahī, Pṛthivī, Satyabhāmā, Vasudhārā, Vasundharā, Zami-Mātā.
Lit.: B 398; FHRI 256; GoRI 1:237; JDI 63; KrI pl. 53; R 1:375; SB passim; Th. pl. 64 f.; WM 52.

bhūmisparśa(mudrā) (also : *-sparśana-, bhū-sparśa-*) "touching the earth" (esp. Buddh.). 1. (Mu.) N of a handpose in which the image, sitting in the *padmāsana*-att., touches the earth or ground with the fingertips of the right hand, the palm turned inward, and the hand usually resting on the right knee (at the same time the left hand is held in the lap in the *dhyānamudrā*). The symbolism of this Mu. is explained in several ways : that it reminds of the Buddha who, in Bodh Gayā, calls the earth as a witness of his decision to renounce the world, and of his *buddha*-position, and to witness his right to take his seat beneath the Tree of Wisdom, or as a witness of his having resisted the temptation of Māra*. – This Mu. is also char. of other *buddhas*, both *dhyāni-* and *mānuṣi-buddhas*, in Mahāyānism, esp. of Akṣobhya; further of Vajroṣṇīṣa. – In Hinduism this Mu. is displayed by Śiva in a Vyākhyāna-dakṣiṇā-mūrti.

Lit.: AIM 273; B 262; G 20 (ill.); GBM 97; H pl. 4:41; HIS 43; JMS 59; KiSB 45; RAAI 271; SM 80; WHW 1:74; WM 97; ZA 175 a.pl. 380-381.

2. Bhūmisparśa is also epithet of the Buddha in the att. just described.

Lit.: GI pl. 93; ZA pl. 380-381.

Bhūmiya ("guardian of the fields"), in North India NP of a god of fertility, worshipped in the form of a rough stone idol. In later times he is regarded as a manifestation of Viṣṇu.

Lit.: GH 111.

bhūta.

1. "Spirit, demon, hobgoblin", n. of the ghost of a deceased person who died as a result of an act of violence. The *bhūtas* are supposed to injure men and to destroy them mysteriously. In KiH a number of *bhūtas* is illustrated by South Indian dancers. *bh.* also forms part of compounds, such as Bhūtamātā, Bhūtanātha, and others. – In Jainism *bh.* signifies a species of *vyantaradevatā*.

Lit.: BBh. 433; DHP 311; GH 107; GJ 237, 405; IC 1:528; KiH 27 a.pl. 98-105; KiSH 73; MG 287; WM 52.

2. "Any living being". In this sense *bh.* forms part of the compounds Bhūteśvara, Bhūtapati, and others.

3. "Element", of which there are 5, see *pañcabhūta*; hence, *bh.* is a symbolic n. of the number "5", see *saṅkhyā*.

bhūtabali "offering to the demons (or to all created beings)", a *pūjā* involving the laying down of vegetables, cakes etc. in all quarters as an introduction to a ceremony (Jain.).

Lit.: GJ 431.

bhūtaḍāmara(mudrā) (lit. "causing tumult of demons"), n. of a frightening Mu.: the hands are held in front of the breast and the fingers are intertwined. – Char. of Bhūtaḍāmara(-Vajrapāṇi).

Lit.: G 20 (ill.).

Bhūtaḍāmara(-Vajrapāṇi) ("V. causing tumult of demons"; Buddh.), NP of a Mahāyāna god. Char.: att.: *ālīḍhāsana*; Vāh.: Aparājita (recumbent); Mu.: *bhūtaḍāmara-*, *tarjanī-mudrā*; attr.: *nāgas* in the hair, *trinayana*, *vajra* in a hand or in the hair.

Lit.: BBh. 182; G 20; KiSB 78.

bhūtagaṇa "demon-flock, multitude of ghosts", in architecture used as a decorative motif on a temple frieze displaying a multitude of dwarf figures.

Lit.: BECA 1: pl. 12 b.

Bhūtamātā (-tṛ, -tar, "mother of goblins"), n. of a terrible form of Pārvatī (cp. Śiva as Bhūtapati). Char.: Vāh.: *siṅha* or *siṅhāsana*; attr.: *khaḍga*, *kheṭaka*, *liṅga* (on the head, not held in a hand).

Lit.: R 1:362; SSI 216.

bhūtamātotsava "the festival of Bhūtamātā", n. of a festival.

Lit.: IC 1:591.

Bhūtanātha (Tam. Pūtanātaṉ; probably both "Lord of all beings" and esp. "Lord of goblins"), epithet of Śiva; cp. Bhūtapati, Paśupati. It is also a n. of Ayyappaṉ.

Lit.: TL 5:2833.

Bhūtapati (probably both "Lord of all beings" and "Lord of spirits or goblins"), epithet of Śiva, cp. Bhūtanātha. Śiva is the lord of the ghosts with whom he usually dances at night on battlefields and in burial grounds.

Lit.: B 446; DHP 196.

Bhūtattāḻvār (mixed Tam.-Skt), see Pūtattāḻvār.

bhūtayajña "offering of food to all created beings", n. of one of the 5 *mahāyajñas*. – Another n.: *bali*.

Lit.: IC 1:585; MW 762.

Bhūteś(var)a. 1. Epithet of Viṣṇu or Kṛṣṇa as "Lord of all beings" (*bhūta*). – 2. Epithet

of Śiva either as "Lord of all beings" or as "Lord of spirits" (cp. Bhūtapati).
Lit.: D 56; DHP 210.

Bhuvaneśa-Gaṇapati ("G., Lord of the world"), n. of a form of Gaṇeśa, 8-armed. Attr.: *aṅkuśa, danta, dhanus, pāśa, śaṅkha, śara* of flowers.
Lit.: R 1:58.

Bhuvaneśvara (now Bhubaneswar), n. of the capital of Orissa, with several temples from the period A.D. 750-1100.
Lit.: FES 41; ZA pl. 327 ff.

Bhuvaneśvarī ("Lady of the Spheres, Power of Knowledge"), epithet of several goddesses; also NP of a particular goddess. She belongs to the group *mahāvidyā* and is represented by Siddharātrī. She is symbolized by the *bījamantra māyābīja*. Attr.: *aṅkuśa, pāśa*.
Lit.: DHP 279; R 1:371.

Bhūvarāha ("the Earth and the Boar"), n. of a form of the Varāhāvatāra of Viṣṇu who, in the shape of a boar, lifted up the earth (the Earth-goddess Bhūmi) from the depth of the ocean. Attr.: *cakra, śaṅkha, (padma)*. – Another n.: Nṛvarāha.
Lit.: R 1:132 a.pl. 37.

Bi-har (Tib.; Buddh.), in Lamaism NP of one of the *mahārāja*s. Char.: colour: white; Vāh.: *siṅha* (white); attr.: *churī, daṇḍa, dhanus, gadā, khaḍga, śara, trinayana, triśiras*. He is 6-armed.
Lit.: G 93.

bīja "seed, semen", n. of a mystic syllable (letter) which forms the essential part of a *mantra* (see *bījamantra*). In this sense *b.* belongs to all Indian religions, esp. in their Tantric forms. A *b.* is uttered in ceremonies and also written and drawn as a *yantra*. – *b.* also signifies the reliquiae in a *stūpa*. – Other n.: *akṣara, bījākṣara*; cp. also *HRĪṀ, OṀ*.
Lit.: BBh. 433; DHP 226; DilP 71 and passim; GBM 18; GoRI 2:47; IC 1:567; SM 23; WHW 2:103; ZA 233.

Bīja-Gaṇapati, n. of a form of Gaṇeśa, eating *jambhīra* (= *bījapūra*). Another n.: Vijaya-Gaṇapati (?).
Lit.: SSI 176.

Bījagarbha ("Womb-of-the-Seed"), epithet of Sarasvatī.
Lit.: DHP 260.

bījākṣara "seed syllable", see *bījā*.
Lit.: GBM 91.

bījamaṇḍala "seed circle" (attr.), n. of a *maṇḍala* which represents in visual form "das Darzustellende durch die Keimsilben in Sanskrit-Schrift". Cp. *bīja*.
Lit.: GBM 108.

bījamantra "seed *mantra*, basic thought-form" (attr.), n. of a kind of syllabic (*bīja*) utterance (*mantra*) which symbolizes a sort of manifestation of a deity. Forms of such *mantra*s are: 1. *brahma-bīja* (or *brahma-vidyāmantra*); 2. *vāg-*; 3. *māyā-* (or *śakti-*); 4. *lakṣmī-*; 5. *kāma-*; 6. *ādya-* or *kālī-bīja*. Other *bījamantra*s are also found.
Lit.: DHP 332, 335, 338; DilP passim; GJ 369; GoRI 2:35.

bījapūra ("seed-filled") "citron" (attr.), see *jambhīra*.
Lit.: MEIA 264; BBh. 433.

bilva(vṛkṣa) (Hi. *bel, bīl*; attr.), n. of a sacred tree "wood-apple tree, Aegle marmelos", which is dédicated to Śiva. The fruit (*srīphala*) of this tree is adored as an *avyakta**-form of Śiva and may be coordinated with a *liṅga*. – See *vṛkṣa*.
Lit.: GH 64; KiSH 81; MG 240.

Bilvadaṇḍa, -daṇḍin ("having a staff of *bilva*-wood"), epithet of Śiva.

bilvaphala "fruit of the *bilva*-tree" (attr.), see *śrīphala*.
Lit.: MEIA 264; R 1:374.

bimba "image" (attr.; esp. Buddh.). In this dictionary *b.* is esp. used in composition with the n. of a *dhyānibuddha* (*Amitābha-bimba* etc.), indicating a little image on the crown or on the head or in one hand of a Mahāyāna god. In such compounds it signifies this god as an emanation of the

dhyānibuddha in question. – Other n.: *mukuṭa*, *śekhara*.
Lit.: BBh. passim.

Bimbisāra, NP of a king of Magadha, a contemporary of the Buddha. He is said to have been one of the first converts to Buddhism.
Lit.: BRI 13; HSIT pl. 11; KiSB 15.

bīn (Hi.), see *vīṇā*.

bindu "drop, dot", n. of a *yantra* which represents the centre of the universe. It is also believed to be the visible form of *śūnya*. – See also *OṀ*. For *b.* as a symbolic n. of zero, see *saṅkhyā*.
Lit.: DHP 19, 229, 351; DiIP 116; GH 54, 56; GoRI 2:29; HAHI 12; IC 1:566; WHW 1:152, 2:103.

Bișṇ-pad (Hi.) "the footmark of Viṣṇu", n. of a symbol in the temple of Gayā. – Cp. *Viṣṇupāda* and see *pādukā*.
Lit.: KiH 29; KiSH 91.

bla-ma (Tib.), see *lama*.

BLŪṀ, a mystic syllable which (in Jainism) refers to the feet. See *śānti*.
Lit.: GJ 369.

Bo-tree, see *bodhivṛkṣa*.

bodhaśrīmudrā (or *bodhi-*) "handpose of wisdom" (Mu.), a Skt name-reconstruction for a Japanese n. of a Mu.; see *vajramudrā*.
Lit.: SM 102 and N. 3.

Bodh-Gayā, n. of a place near Gayā, the holy place of Buddhism since it is here that the Buddha is believed to have attained Enlightenment. There is a famous temple (*stūpa*) dating from the 7th-8th cc. A.D. at B.-G.
Lit.: SeKB passim; ZA pl. 99 ff.

bodhi "perfect knowledge or wisdom, enlightenment", by which a man becomes a *buddha* or a *jina* (*tīrthaṅkara*); the illuminated or enlightened intellect (Buddh.; Jain.). See *bodhivṛkṣa*. Other n.: *sambodhi*.
Lit.: IC 2:546.

bodhicitta "Will to Enlightenment is that state of Mind which has already acquired the potentiality of dissolving itself in *śūnya*" (BBh.; Buddh.). In esoteric Mahāyāna Buddhism *b.* is also n. for the sperm.
Lit.: BBh. 393; GBM 160; IC 2:593.

bodhidruma "tree of Enlightenment", see *bodhivṛkṣa*.

bodhighara (Pāli) "temple (of the tree) of Enlightenment" (Buddh.), n. of a temple which was built up round a sacred tree (see *bodhivṛkṣa*). Such temples are known from the 2nd and 1st cc. B.C.
Lit.: FBKI 22; MBPC 51.

bodhimaṇḍa "seat of Enlightenment" (attr.; Buddh.), a tree as symbol of the *bodhivṛkṣa** under which one the Buddha gained Enlightenment.
Lit.: ZA 61.

bodhipākṣika "talent for Enlightenment", n. of a group of 37 special mental gifts char. of a *buddha*.
Lit.: BRI 52.

bodhirukkha (Pāli), see *bodhivṛkṣa*.

bodhisattva (Pāli: *bodhisatta*) "one whose essence is perfect knowledge" (MW), "Buddha-elect or Buddha-designate" (AIP). Other interpretations: "Erleuchtungswesen" or "ein nach der Erleuchtung und Buddhaschaft strebender Heilbringer" (GBM), "ein zur Erleuchtung bestimmtes Wesen" (HIS), "einer dessen Wesen die Erkenntnis (oder Erleuchtung) ist" (SeKB). A. *b.* therefore means an earlier stage of a future *buddha**, e.g., all the former existences or births (*jātaka*) of Gautama Buddha. A *b.* is a kind of saviour who postpones voluntarily his own salvation, his entrance into *nirvāṇa*, in order to help other beings to gain salvation.
The earliest *b.* concept belongs to Mahāyāna Buddhism, where it was fitted into a system according to which each *buddha* corresponds to a *b.* Each *b.* cannot always be reliably identified iconographically; consequently this n. often occurs without a specific identification in iconographic terms. By way of distinction from the *buddha*s the *b.* wears princely ornaments

and garments and a crown (*bodhisattvābharaṇa*). Usual char.: Mu.: *abhaya-* or *dhyāna-mudrā*. A *b.* represents the *śānta*-aspect.

The most important among the *bodhisattvas* are Avalokiteśvara, Maitreya and Mañjuśrī who are widely popular also in Tibet, China and Japan. 3 lists of *b.*, each containing 16, are given in BBh., and 25 *b.* are described in this source: Samantabhadra, Akṣayamati, Kṣitigarbha, Ākāśagarbha, Gaganagañja, Ratnapāṇi, Sāgaramati, Vajragarbha, Avalokiteśvara, Mahāsthāmaprāpta, Candraprabha, Jālinīprabha, Amitaprabha, Pratibhānakūṭa, Sarvaśokatamonirghātamati, Sarvanivaraṇaviṣkambhin, Maitreya, Mañjuśrī, Gandhahastin, Jñānaketu, Bhadrapāla, Sarvāpāyañjaha, Amoghadarśin, Suraṅgama and Vajrapāṇi.

There are in addition, in the Lamaist pantheon 9 female *b.*: Parṇaśavarī, Uṣṇīṣavijayā, Sitātapatrā, Mahāmāyūrī, Sarasvatī, Cundā, Vasudhārā, Mārīcī, Prajñāpāramitā. – See further *dhyānibodhisattva* and *trikāya*.

Lit.: AIP 273; AuOW 21 (ill.); AuT 218; BBh. 27, 82; BRI 145; CHIIA passim; DIA pl. 13 a. passim; G passim; GBB pl. 28; GBM 12, 79; Gw. 164; H 32; HAHI pl. 14B; HIS 13, 43, 56 a.pl. 12-14; HSIT 16 a.pl. 40; IC 2:534, 555, 570; KiDG 44; KiSB 43; KrA pl. 38; RAAI 271 a.pl. 61; SS pl. 11:53; SeKB 213 a. passim; WHW 1:159.

bodhisattvābharaṇa "princely ornaments and garments" (attr.; Buddh.), worn by the gracious manifestations of some deities, esp. by the *bodhisattvas*. This garb serves above all to distinguish a *bodhisattva* from a *buddha* who only wears *tricīvara* and no ornaments. – Cp. *mukuṭadhārin*. Another n.: *kumārābharaṇa*.
Lit.: G 39.

Bodhisattva-Lokeśvara, epithet of Avalokiteśvara (Padmapāṇi).
Lit.: B 547.

bodhitaru "tree of wisdom", see *bodhivṛkṣa*.

bodhivṛkṣa (Pāli: *bodhirukkha*) "the tree of wisdom or Enlightenment" (attr.; Buddh.), primarily n. of the fig-tree (*pippala* or *aśvattha* "Ficus religiosa") under which Gautama Buddha at Bodh-Gayā attained Enlightenment. A branch of the original *b.* was in the 3rd c. B.C. brought to Anurādhapura in Sri Lanka and planted there, and this tree still survives. In 1931 a branch from this tree was planted in Sārnāth, this tree now being regarded as a *b.* in the third generation from the original one.

b. is represented in plastic arts, and is then regarded as a representation of the Buddha or a *mānuṣibuddha* in general. In some representations the *b.* is seen sprouting from the *uṣṇīṣa* of the Buddha. In early Buddhist art an empty throne at the foot of a fig-tree indicates the Enlightenment of the Buddha (see *pallaṅka*). This tree is also dedicated to Mahāpratisarā.

b. is also an attr., held in a hand by Jñānapāramitā. – Other n.: *Bo*-tree, *bodhidruma*, *bodhitaru*, *duminda*, Mahābodhivṛkṣa. See also *bodhimaṇḍa*.

In the Mahāyāna system, however, whose followers believe in several *buddhas*, they ascribe different trees to the different *buddhas*. As *b.* serve, besides, e.g. the *pippala*, also the *uḍumbara*, *vaṭa*, *pāṭali*, *śāla*, *śirīṣa*, *nāgapuṣpa*. – For earlier tree-worship, see *vṛkṣa*.

Lit.: BBh. 31, 328; CEBI pl. 3:11; CHIIA 231 a.fig. 41, 46; FBKI 22; HIS 63 a.pl. 24; IP pl. 4; KiSB 13, 34, 111; MS 58; RIS 64; Th. 2; ZA 25 a.pl. 17.

bodhyaṅgīmudrā ("teaching handpose"), probably another n. of *vyākhyānamudrā*.
Lit.: BBh. 47.

BOṀ, form of a *bīja* representing Kāma.
Lit.: WHW 2:104.

Bombay kā Mayan (N.Ind.), n. of a disease-goddess worshipped under this n. at Gayā.
Lit.: GH 137.

bon (Tib., pronounced *pön*), n. of the original, native animistic religion in Tibet which has given many features to Buddhist Lamaism.
Lit.: G 5; HM and HRT passim; HuGT 8.

Brahmā (-an). The n. is a personification of the neuter noun *brahman*, the oldest sense of which was something like (in German): "Formung, Gestaltung, Formulierung" (THIEME). Earlier it was interpreted as "expansion, development" or "Immense-Being" (being connected with *bṛh-* "grow great").

1. (Hind.) B. is the god of sacrifice and worship and symbolizes the yearning for god. Therefore B. is said to be "ein Produkt der Spekulation". In later times, however, B. is esp. regarded as the god of creation and has gained the position of one of the three chief gods of the Hindu triad. His nature has always been vague and nowadays B. receives no special worship (except at Puṣkara). However, B. is sometimes worshipped as a *dikpāla* of the direction zenith, and he is the god of the month *kārttika*. – His residence is believed to be the capital Brahmavṛndā. Wives: Aditi, Sarasvatī (Brāhmī, Śatarūpā, Sāvitrī) and Gāyatrī; children: Dakṣa, Sandhyā.

The chief char. of B. is that he is always represented as having four heads (*caturmukha*), according to different explanations, symbolizing the four Vedas, the four *varṇas* ("colours, castes"), the four *yugas* ("ages of the world"), or the four cardinal points (*diś*); B. is sometimes represented with only three heads, but in these cases his fourth head is supposed to be turned to the wall and not visible to the spectator. According to legend he had once five heads but lost one of them through the action of Śiva (see Brahmaśiraśchedakamūrti). As far as I know, he is never represented with five heads (but see a talc drawing in IIM).

Other char.: colour: usually red, sometimes also yellow or golden; Vāh.: *haṅsa* (milk-white) or *ratha* drawn by 7 *haṅsas* or *padma(pīṭha)*, *lambakūrcāsana*; Mu.: *abhaya-*, *añjali-*, *varada-mudrā*; attr.: esp. *akṣamālā*, *bhikṣāpātra* (or *kapāla*), *jaṭāmukuṭa*, *kamaṇḍalu*, *lekhanī*, *maṣībhājana*, *padma*, *pustaka* (Veda), *sruk*, *sruva*, further: *ājyapātra*, *aṅkuśa*, *cakra*, *daṇḍa*, *dhanus* Parivīta, *gadā*, *jaṭā*, *kaṭibandha*, *kūrca* (*kuśa*), *pāśa*, *ratnakuṇḍalas*, *yajñopavīta*. – B. is also represented by the *bījamantra brahmabīja*. – Other n., epithets and varieties: Abjaja, Abjayoni, Aṣṭakarṇa, Bṛhaspati, Caturānana, Caturmukha, Haṅsavāhana, Hiraṇyagarbha, Kamalāsana, Kamalayoni, Kañja, Kañjaja, Nābhija, Nārāyaṇa (sometimes), Prajāpati, Sarojin, Svayambhū, Vāgīśvara. – In older tradition also the Kūrma-, Matsya- and Varāha-*avatāras* were regarded as manifestations of B.

Lit.: AIP pl. 32 (217); B 510 a.pl. 45:2; BBh. 382; CEBI 17 a.fig. B; DHP 131, 165, 232 a.pl. 28; GBB 128 a.pl. 6; GH 117 a.pl. 19; GoRI 1:263, 2:64; Gt 102; H pl. 6:48; IC 1:499; IIM 41; JDI 23, 103; KIM pl. 3; KiH 11 a.pl. 19-21; KiSH 40; KrA pl. 63; KrG pl. 6; MEIA 119; MG 85; R 2:501 a.pl. 142-149; RIS 63; SIB pl. 5; SSI 10; Th. 48 a.pl. 4A; THIEME, ZDMG 102:91, 102; W 84; WHW 1:164; WM 53; ZA 156, 168, 371 a.pl. 509a, 562a.

2. (Buddh.) The Hindu god B. is also met with in Buddhism; in Lamaism B. is NP of a *dharmapāla*, see Sitabrahmā. Char.: colour: yellow; Vāh.: *haṅsa*; Mu.: *añjali-mudrā*; attr.: *akṣamālā*, *caturmukha*, *daṇḍa*, *kamaṇḍalu*, *padma*.

Lit.: BBh. 363; CTLP pl. 156; G 36.

3. (Vāh.; Buddh.) Upon the Hindu god B. tread: Hevajra, Mārīcī (in different forms), Prasannatārā, Vidyujjvālākarālī; cp. Māra.

Lit.: BBh. 194.

4. (Jain.) B. is NP of a *yakṣa* attending on the 10th *tīrthaṅkara* (Śītalanātha). Naturally B. is influenced here by the Hindu god. Attr.: *caturmukha*, *ājyapātra*, *gadā*, *jambhīra*, *pāśa*.

Lit.: B 562; GJ 362.

brāhma ("related to Brahmā"), n. of a sect the members of which worship Brahmā.

Lit.: GH 398; IC 1:623.

brahmabīja "Seed-of-the-Immensity" or *brahmavidyābīja* "Thought-form-of-the-Knowl-

edge-of-the-Immensity" (DHP), n. of a *bījamantra*. Form: *AUṀ* (= *OṀ*). According to the usual Hindu interpretation here *A* symbolizes Brahmā, *U* = Viṣṇu, *Ṁ* = Śiva (in older Brahmanism there are many other interpretations of this *bīja*).
Lit.: DHP 338; GoRI 1:336, 2:47; KiJ 12 a.pl. 30.

brahmacārin (*-ī*; "observing chastity"), n. given to a young Brāhman who practices sacred study in the first period of his life (before marriage). See *brāhmaṇa*.
Lit.: GH 335; GJ 422; Gt 105; IC 1:600; WHW 1:85.

Brahmacāriṇī ("observing chasity"), n. of a a variety of Durgā. Attr.: *akṣamālā, kamaṇḍalu*.
Lit.: SSI 202.

Brahmacāri-Subrahmaṇya ("S. the *brahmacārin*"), n. of a form of Skanda. Char.: Vāh.: *padmapīṭha*; attr.: *daṇḍa, kaupīna, mauñji, vajra, yajñopavita*.
Lit.: R 2:442.

Brahmadaṇḍa-Lokeśvara ("L. [holding] the staff of Brahmā"; Buddh.), n. of a variety of Avalokiteśvara; he is accompanied by his Śakti. Char.: att.: *lalitāsana*; Vāh.: *padma*; Mu.: *karaṇa*(?)-, *varada-mudrā*; attr.: *kamaṇḍalu, tridaṇḍa*.
Lit.: BBh. 397 a.pl. 27(A).

brahmadeya "gift to Brāhmans", n. of a kind of donation.

brahmagāyatrī ("the *gāyatrī* of Brahmā"; attr.), n. of a *mantra* which has the purpose: "The attainment of realization by all".
Lit.: DHP 345.

brahmakapāla "the (severed) head of Brahmā" (attr.; Buddh.). It has four faces with grey beards and, held in a hand by Buddhist gods, it expresses aversion towards the Hindus and Hindu gods. Char. of: Kālacakra, Prasannatārā, Samantabhadra, Vajradhātvīśvarī, Vidyujjvālākarālī. – Another n.: *brahmaśiras*. Cp. also *muṇḍa*.
Lit.: BBh. 434.

brahmamantra, n. of a *mantra* which has the purpose "to remove all signs of death, to prevent the withering of the body".
Lit.: DHP 346.

brahmamukha "the head of Brahmā" (attr.; Buddh.). This is the four-faced head of Brahmā superimposed on another head (note the difference from *brahmakapāla* and *muṇḍa*). Char. of Paramāśva.
Lit.: BBh. 433.

brahma(n) (neuter) "the supreme soul of the universe, self-existent"; originally "die 'heilige Macht' im Zauberwort des Veda" (GRI). The personification of this concept is Brahman, see Brahmā.
Lit.: D 56; GRI 35; IC 1:499.

brāhmaṇa (*brāhmin*, derived from *brahman*) "Brāhman", a member of the first caste in India, the sacerdotal class. The religious life of an orthodox *b.* is divided into four successive periods (*āśrama*), i.e. the stages of *brahmacārin, gṛhastha, vānaprastha* and *saṅnyāsin* (or *parivrājaka*).
Lit.: D 59; GH 358; Gt 107; IC 1:600; MKVI 2:80; WHW 1:168.

Brahmaṇaspati ("the priestly-lord"), see Bṛhaspati.
Lit.: DHP 325.

brahmāṇḍa "Brahmā-egg", n. of the colossal shell from which Brahmā was born. Out of this egg Mahākapāla drank. – *b.* is also n. of the innumerable worlds in the universe. – Cp. Hiraṇyagarbha.
Lit.: Gt 203; KiK 55; R 2:201; WHW 1:253.

Brahmāṇī (or Brāhmī, "[the Śakti] of Brahmā"), epithet of a goddess as the wife of Brahmā, see Sarasvatī. Under the n. of B. she is counted among the *saptamātaras* (see also *aṣṭamātaras, navaśakti*) and symbolizes then *mada* "pride". Char.: Vāh.: *haṅsa*; att.: *lalitāsana*; Mu.: *abhaya-, varada-mudrā*; attr.: *akṣamālā, caturmukha, kamaṇḍalu, pītāmbara, pustaka, sruva, triśūla*.
Lit.: B 505 a.pl. 43:1; BECA 1: pl. 14a; KiSH 53; R 1:381, 383 a.pl. 118 f.; Th. 108.

brahmarṣi "*ṛṣi* of the Brāhman caste", n. of a group of *ṛṣis* the leader of whom was Vasiṣṭha.
Lit.: D 62; R 2:566.

brāhmasamāj ("assembly of the faithful, the pious"), n. of a sect, instituted by Rām

Mohan Rai in the 19th. c., which has the aim to establish (or re-establish), on the basis of the Vedas, a monotheistic religion in which all the great religions (including Islam and Christianity) are united.
Lit.: GH 448; GRI 350.

Brahmaśāstā (-ṛ, -ar; Brahmā's commander"), n. of a form of Śāstā. Char.: Mu.: *abhaya-*, *kaṭi-*, *varada-mudrā*; attr.: *akṣamālā*, *kamaṇḍalu*, *śakti*, *vajra*.
Lit.: ACA 73, 105; R 2:439; SB 128 a.fig. 72.

brahmaśiras (attr.), see *brahmakapāla*.
Lit.: BBh. 433.

Brahmaśiraśchedakamūrti ("representation [of Śiva] cutting off the head of Brahmā"), n. of an *ugra*-form (*saṅhāramūrti*) of Śiva who, in this form, cut off the (originally) fifth head of Brahmā. Attr.: *ajina*, *kuṇḍalas*, *paraśu*, *trinayana*, *triśūla*, *vajra*.
Lit.: IIM 41; R 2:174.

Brahmasūtra ("thread of Brahmā"; attr.), n. given to lines of a distinctive sort which are carved on a certain part of a *mānuṣaliṅga*.
Lit.: R 2:87, 94.

brahmavidyābīja, see sub *brahmabīja*.

Brahmavṛndā ("Immense-Grove"), n. of the capital of Brahmā.
Lit.: DHP 237.

brahmayajña "sacrifice to the holy scripture" which consists of the recitation of Vedic words and belongs to the *sandhyā* ceremony. It is one of the 5 *mahāyajñas*.
Lit.: GH 330; IC 1:585; WHW 1:360.

Brahmayakṣa, see Brahmeśvara.
Lit.: GJ pl. 27.

Brahmeru ("coming from, or sent by Brahmā[?]"), n. of a *bhūta* (Jain.).
Lit.: KiSH 74.

Brahmeśvara ("the lord Brahmā"; Jain.), n. of a *yakṣa*, an attendant of the 10th *tīrthaṅkara*. Char.: *padma*. – Another n.: Brahmayakṣa.
Lit.: GJ pl. 25:10; KiJ 11 a.pl. 28:10, 30.

Brāhmī (or Brahmī; "[the Śakti] of Brahmā"), epithet of Sarasvatī as the wife of Brahmā. See Brahmāṇī.
Lit.: DHP 260.

Bram-zei gzugs-can ("substance of *brāhmaṇa*"; Tib.; Buddh.), in Lamaism, n. of a variety of Mahākāla. Char.: Vāh.: *nara*; attr.: *kapāla*, *muṇḍamālā*.
Lit.: G 90.

Bṛhaspati ("Lord of prayer"; also interpreted as "the Great Master"), originally a personification of the activity of the pious towards the gods. He is the son of Aṅgiras and the *guru* of the gods. B. is closely connected (or identical) with Brahmā. He is sometimes associated with the Hittite god of thunder (WHW), which could explain that he is esp. known as the deity of the planet Jupiter.

1. (Hind.) In later Hinduism B. is the planet-god (Jupiter). Wife: Tārā; son: Kaca. Char.: colour: yellow or golden; Vāh.: a golden *ratha* (Nītighoṣa) drawn by 8 tawny horses, or *padmapīṭha* (in a *sthānaka*-att.); Mu.: *abhaya-*, *varada-mudrā*; attr.: *akṣamālā*, *daṇḍa*, *dhanus*, *kamaṇḍalu*, *paraśu* (golden), *pustaka*, *śara*. Epithets: Brahmaṇaspati, Devapurohita, Gaṇapati, Jyeṣṭharāja, Sadasaspati.
Lit.: D 64; DHP 324; GH 96; KiH 7; KiK 141; KiSH 62, 88; R 1:320 a.pl. 96; Th. 114; WHW 1:177; WM 54.

2. (Buddh.) The planet-god (Jupiter). Char.: colour: white; Vāh.: *maṇḍūka* or *kapāla*; attr.: *akṣamālā*, *kamaṇḍalu*.
Lit.: BBh. 368.

bṛhaspati(samvatsara)cakra "cycle (of the years) of Bṛhaspati", n. of a cycle of 60 years, recurrent in the calendar. These years are somewhat shorter (361 days) than the usual solar year. Cp. *bārhaspatyasamvatsara*.
Lit.: IC 2:726.

bṛhaspativāra (or *-vāsara*) "Thursday". – Another n.: *guruvāra*.

bṛhatkukṣi "big-bellied" (attr.), see *tundila*.
Lit.: ACA 41.

bsTan-'gyur (Tib.), see sub initial T-: (bs)Tan-'gyur.

budbudasadṛśa "bubble-like", n. given to the bubble-like top of a *liṅga*, see *śirovarttana*.
Lit.: R 2:93.

buddha "enlightened, awakened" (Buddh.), n. of a kind of World Saviour. A *buddha* is a being who, in certain ways, has attained the highest enlightenment. Esp. according to Mahāyāna Buddhism it is believed, on one hand that the *buddhas* have a threefold nature (see *trikāya*), on the other hand that there are many *b*. The number mentioned varies; early the number 7 was mentioned, later among others the number 25 is found, but in practice all beings can, after endless rebirths, attain to buddhahood. In Mahāyāna Buddhism the usual classification of *buddhas* counts one primeval *b*. (Ādibuddha), 5 *dhyānibuddhas*, 5 *(dhyāni)bodhisattvas* and 5 *mānuṣibuddhas* of whom the historic Buddha was the fourth. In Lamaism there is a further series of *b*. which is closely connected with the *mānuṣibuddhas*, and, in addition, a series of medicine *b*., see Bhaiṣajyaguru. In this form of Buddhism there are also other lists of *buddhas* with different numbers. – In Hīnayāna Buddhism the number of *b*. is very restricted; usually only the historic Buddha is mentioned here. – Cp. *tathāgata*. See also *pratyeka*- and *śrāvaka-buddha*.

Lit.: BBh. passim; BRI 53; G 30, 54; GBB 248; GBM 79; GRI 245; H 32; IC 2:538; KiDG 44; KiSB 31.

Buddha (Gautama, Siddhārta), the historic Buddha.

1. (Buddh.) This n. is properly a title ("enlightened") of the founder of Buddhism, his personal worldly names being Gautama (clan-name) and (?) Siddhārta. The dates of his birth and death, as mentioned in the hand-books, vary considerably; he was probably born at Kapilavastu (near Gorakhpur) in 566 (?) B.C. and he died at Kuśinagara in 486 (?) B.C. (KiSB; but the date of his death is also given (among others) as 543 B.C., this year being basis of an era, see sub *nirvāṇa*). His father was Śuddhodana of the Śākya tribe (therefore B. is named Śākyamuni), and his mother was Māyā(devī). Wife: Yaśodharā; son: Rāhula; his favourite horse was called Kanthaka.

In many respects the B. is the counterpart both of the Hindu Viṣṇu (esp. as a sun genius) and Śiva ("as the master both of the *vajra* and of the animal throne").

For the different representations of the B. see G. Many other *buddhas* and *bodhisattvas* may casually be represented in the form of B., e.g. Avalokiteśvara. B. is usually shown with shaven head or with the hair cut short (cp. Cūḍākaraṇa; the curls of his hair show usually the turning to the right, cp. *dakṣiṇa*), but sometimes he may also wear a crown ("crowned Buddha", *mukuṭadhārin*). Other char.: colour: golden; att. usually: *padmāsana*, but also *sthānaka*- and *śayana*-postures; Vāh.: *padmapīṭha* or *vajrāsana* (sometimes carried by *nāgas*); Mu.: *āhūyavarada*-, *bhūmiparśa*-, *dharmacakravartana*-, *dhyāna*-, *uttarabodhi*-, *varada*- and *vyākhyāna-mudrā*; attr.: *agni* (? on the head), *anuvyañjana*, *(bhikṣā)pātra*, *cakra*, *cintāmaṇi* (upon, or instead of the *uṣṇīṣa*), *cūḍā*, *mahāpuruṣalakṣaṇa*, *nāga*, *nimīlita* (referring to the eyes), *pādajāla*, *śrīvatsa*, *svastika*, *tilaka* (*ūrṇā*), *tricīvara*, *trivali*, *uṣṇīṣa*. In his left hand he often holds an edge of his *saṅghāṭi*. – Also, among other things, the *chattra*, *gaja*, *pāduka* and *pallaṅka* serve as symbols of B., and *mṛga* is emblematic of his first sermon.

Epithets and varieties: Bhūmisparśa, Cūḍākaraṇa, Dharmacakravartin, Durgatipariśodhana, Mahāparinirvāṇamūrti, Mucalinda, Śākyamuni, Śākyasiṅha, Vajrāsana, and many others.

Lit.: AuOW 36; B 391; BBh. 77 and passim; BRI; CEBI pl. 7:29; CHIIA passim; DCSS pl. passim; FBKI passim; G 3, 54; GI pl. 93; Gt 110; Gw. 141, 155 pl. 86; HAHI passim; HIS 12, 41 a.pl. 9-10, 40-41; HAA pl. 96; HSIT passim; IIM 128; IP pl. 12-14, 21; JMS pl. passim; KiSB 8, 34; KrG pl. 21; KrI pl. 20; KT 118; MBPC pl. 98 ff.; MG 143; RN passim; SS pl. 21:94, 33:151; SB passim; SIB pl. 9-10; Th. 69; WAA 25:168 a.fig. 3-9; WHW 1:178; ZA 27 a.pl. passim.

2. *Buddhabimba* (attr.; Buddh.) A little

image of B. is said to be held in the hands, or to be carried in the hair or on the crown of the head by some images, e.g. Uṣṇīṣavijayā. This is stated *passim* in G, but in most cases the image may refer to the *dhyānibuddha* of whom the god in question is an emanation. – Another n. : Padmastha-Buddha.

Lit. : G passim.

3. (Hind.) With an eye to the syncretistic absorbtion of Buddhism, B. was inserted in the Hindu system and regarded as the 9th *avatāra* of Viṣṇu under the pretext that Viṣṇu took this shape in order to abolish the bloody sacrifices, or else that Viṣṇu in this form enticed the heretics to apostatize from the Vedas for the purpose of destroying them. Char. : colour : red; Mu. : *abhaya-*, *dhyāna-*, *varada-mudrā*; attr. : *kāṣāya*.

Lit. : DHP 165, 180; GH 129; GoRI 1:253; KiSH 37; MEIA 36; R 1:216; WM 55.

Buddhabodhiprabhāvaśitā ("control of the light of the knowledge of the Buddha"; Buddh.), n. of a *vaśitā*. Char. : colour : yellow; attr. : *cakra* on a *cintāmaṇidhvaja*.

Lit. : BBh. 332.

Buddhaḍākinī (Buddh.), in Lamaism n. of a *ḍākinī*, the Śakti of Mahāmāya. Char. : colour : white; attr. : *cakra*, *kapāla*, *khaṭvāṅga*.

Lit. : G 34, 80, 84; KiSB 67.

Buddhaheruka (Buddh.), n. of Vairocana as a *herukabuddha*.

Lit. : G 87.

Buddhakapāla ("the Buddha's bowl (skull-cap)"; Buddh.), n. of a Mahāyāna god, an emanation of Akṣobhya and perhaps a form of Heruka. Śakti : Citrasenā. Char. : colour : blue-black; att. : *nāṭyasthāna* with *yab-yum*; attr. : *Akṣobhyabimba* on the crown, *ḍamaru*, *kapāla*, *karttṛkā*, *khaṭvāṅga*.

Lit. : BBh. 159 a.pl. 126, 127; KiSB 65.

Buddhalocanā ("the Buddha's eye"; Buddh.), n. of a *vidyārājñī* or *dhyānibuddhaśakti*; in Shingon Buddhism she is regarded as a female *buddha* or *bodhisattva*. – See also Locanā.

Lit. : G 34; GBM 81, 156, 188 a.pl. facing p. 32.

Buddhapāda "foot-mark of the Buddha", as a symbol of the Buddha. see *pāduka*.

Lit. : AuA pl. 3:26.

buddhapātramudrā (?) "handpose of the Buddha's alms bowl" (Mu.), n. of a gesture which indicates the holding of a bowl and which is probably used only in the Far East.

Lit. : SM 113.

buddhaśakti "Śakti of a *buddha*", see further *dhyānibuddhaśakti*, *mānuṣibuddhaśakti*.

Lit. : G 14.

buddhaśramaṇa(mudrā) "gesture (of salutation) of a Buddhist monk" (Mu.; Buddh.), n. of a handpose. In G (with ill.) it is described thus : "right hand is level with he head, all fingers extending outward. Palm is up". This description corresponds to that which is given in KiSH for *namaskāramudrā*. – This Mu. is char. of Uṣṇīṣavijayā and Vasudhārā.

Lit. : G 20 (with ill.); KiSH 91.

Buddhi ("knowledge, perception"). 1. (Hind.) NP of a goddess who is sometimes said to be the wife of Gaṇeśa.

Lit. : B 358.

2. (Jain.) NP of a goddess.

Lit. : GJ 363.

Budha ("awaking").

1. (Hind.) N. of a planet god (Mercury). He is the son of Soma (= Candra) and Tārā or Rohiṇī. Char. : colour : yellow (or green); Vāh. : *ratha* (of an airy, fiery substance) drawn by 8 redbrown *aśvas*, or *ratha* drawn by *siṅhas* or by one *siṅha*; Mu. : *abhaya-*, *varada-mudrā*; attr. : *akṣamālā*, *gadā*, *dhanus*, *khaḍga*, *kheṭaka*. – Other n. : Candraja, Candrasuta.

Lit. : D 64; Gt 119; KiH 6; KiK 141; KiSH 62; MEIA 234; R 1:320 a.pl. 96; SSI 239; Th. 114; WM 56.

2. (Buddh.) The planet god (Mercury). Char. : colour : yellow; Vāh. : *padma*; attr. : *dhanus*, *śara*.

Lit. : BBh. 368.

budhavāsara (*-vāra*) "Wednesday". – Another n. : *saumyavāra*.

C

caddar (Hi., cp. Pers. *cādar*) "sheet" (attr.), n. of a cloth thrown over the shoulder. Char. of Viṣṇu.

Lit.: KrI 96 a.pl. 7; P 427.

Caitanya ("consciousness'), NP of a *vaiṣṇavabhakta* who lived in A.D. 1486-1533. By his sect he was regarded as an *avatāra* of Viṣṇu or Kṛṣṇa, and he is adored esp. at Nadiya, Bengal, as a beggar god. He is represented as an almost naked man painted yellow. – The word *caitanya* is also used to indicate the divine power present in an image (Diehl).

Lit.: W. Eidlitz, Kṛṣṇa-Caitanya. Sein Leben und seine Lehre (Stockholm 1968); GH 388; IC 1:645; MG 161; WHW 1:214.

caitra (related to the *nakṣatra* Citrā), n. of the second month of spring (March-April, beginning c. March 21). The god of this month is Nirṛti.

Lit.: BBh. 382; IC 2:732; KiK 131.

caitrādi "beginning with (the month) *caitra*", referring to the beginning of the year, see *samvatsara*. A year indicated in this way is solar, see also *meṣādi*.

Lit.: IC 2:724.

caitya, prop. "funeral monument", also reliquary" (Buddh.), in architecture n. of a prayer hall, and a temple hall in which a *stūpa* is placed. In the sense of "reliquary" it also often serves as a term for an attr., a miniature *stūpa* or temple, used as a votive gift or carried in the hands, for which, however, the term *stūpa* is more frequently used. – *c.* represents the Buddhist universe, but partakes also of the symbolism of the large *stūpa*. Cp. *aṭṭa(ka)*, *stūpika*.

Lit.: AuOW 37; BBh. 434; BRI 111; CHIIA 28, 230 a.fig. 29 ff.; DKI 26; FBKI 44; G 12 (ill.); GBM 131; HIS 15; IC 2:319; KiSB 61; SeKB passim; WHW 1:59, 210; ZA 246, 270.

caityaśālā ("reliquary hall, *caitya*-hall"), n. of the hall of assembly in a *vihāra*.

Lit.: SeKB passim.

cakkavattin (Pāli), see *cakravartin*.

cakora "the Greek partridge". It is supposed to subsist on moon-beams.

Lit.: IC 1:537; WHW 1:155.

cakra "wheel, disk, discus" (attr.).

1. (Hind.) *c.* is a warrior, power, or sun symbol; it is also regarded as a "symbol of absolute completeness" (AIP) and "the emblem of protection" (R), and "symbolizes the Creator's mind, or the first thought of the Supreme Being when the desire of Creation moved Him to manifest Himself" (HAHI). In another sense *c.* is "a round, cutting, orbicular weapon, which cuts everything it hits right through" (AI). It is represented either as an attr. in a hand of an idol, or as an independent cult symbol.

The *c.* is, above all, char. of Viṣṇu (Kṛṣṇa) whose *c.* with 6 spokes is named Vajranābha or Sudarśana, and who is probably, by means of this symbol, signified as a sun genius. As a symbol, this 6-spoked wheel may be of great antiquity, since such a sign is found on many seals from the Indus Valley civilization. The *c.* may also have 8 spokes alluding to the 8 points of direction (see *dikpāla*) and signifying universal supremacy. The *c.* is further "represented as a circle of fire with four projecting points of flame" (HAHI) named *cuṭar*. It is also a sign (*maṅgala*) which may be engraved on a foot; further a "mystical centre of orientation", hence, also a mystical diagram connected with the *śākta* worship (cp. also Bālā-Śakti); and it is used as a term equivalent to *yantra*. – Cp. *śiraścakra*. (For other bearers of *c.*, see below).

Lit.: AI 114; AIP 273; B passim a.pl. 26:4; BPR passim; DHP 155; DiIP 275; GJ 256; H pl. 6:54; HAHI 12 a.pl. 7; HIS 42; JDI 60; R 1:4, 236 a.pl. 1:4-5; RAAI 271; SSI 185; Th. 39; WHW 2:597; WM 105 a.fig. 46-47.

2. (Buddh., Jain.) *c.* symbolizes in Buddhism and Jainism the *dharmacakra* "the wheel of the Law", "word-wheel (and World-wheel)". It is here (usually) a stylized representation of a wheel with 8 or 12 (or some other number) of spokes, and is a symbol of *dharma*, referring to the Buddha's first sermon at Sārnāth when he "das Rad des Gesetzes (*dharmacakra*) in Bewegung setzte" (BRI), cp. *dharmacakrapravartanamudrā*. It is also said that *c.* "leads to perfection, its eight spokes symbolizing the eight-fold path" (G), and it is "intended to suggest domination of all by the Buddha's Law, as the sun dominates all space and time". – As an attr. it signifies its bearer as a *buddha* or a *tīrthaṅkara*. It is also a *maṅgala*, see *aṣṭamaṅgala*. See further *bhavacakra*, *kusumacakra*, *padmasthāṣṭāracakra*.

Lit.: BRI 117; CEBI passim a.fig. C, E, F a.pl. 1:2-3, 5:18, 6:25; CHIIA 231 a.fig. 45; G 8 (ill.), 12; GBM 101, 122; Gz 53; H pl. 3:24, 28-30; HuGT pl. 81; JMS pl. 9; KiSB 38; RAAI 271; SeKB 277 fig. 66; SM 96; WM 98 a.fig. 19; ZA 60.

c. 1-2 is char. of: Aghora, Agni-Durgā, Ahirbudhnya, Aja, Akṣobhya, Amoghapāśa, Aparājita, Aryaman, (Aṣṭāracakravat), Avalokiteśvara (in different forms), Bahurūpa, Balarāma, Brahmā, Buddhabodhiprabhāvaśitā, Buddhaḍākinī, Cāmuṇḍī, Caṇḍā, Caturbhujatārā, Cundā, Dattātreya, Devī, Dhruva, Dhvajāgrakeyūra, Ekapādamūrti, Gaṇeśa, Hari-Hara, Hayagrīva, Hevajra, Indra, Jagadgaurī, Jaya-Durgā, Jayanta, Kālacakra, Kalkin, Kapila, Kārttikeya, Krodhahayagrīva, Kṛṣṇa-Yamāri, Lakṣmī, Locanā, Mahākālī, Mahāmantrānusāriṇī, Mahāmāyūrī, Mahāpratisarā, Mahāsāhasrapramardanī, Mahiṣāsuramardinī, Maitreya, Mañjunātha, Mārīcī, Mārttaṇḍa-Bhairava, Mṛtyuvañcana-Tārā, Nandā, *navadurgās*, Padmāntaka, Pāṇḍarā, Phyi-sgrub, Rājagopāla, Revata, Rudra, Rudrāṅśa-Durgā, Samantabhadra, Saṅ-dui, Ṣaṇmukha, Śarabha, Sarasvatī, Savitar, Senānī, Sitabrahmā, Sitātapatra, Sitātapatrā, Skanda, Śrīnivāsa, Sureśvara, Sūrya, Tārakāri, Trailokyavijaya, Trikaṇṭakīdevī, Tripurāntaka, Tryambaka, Uṣṇīṣa, Uṣṇīṣasitātapatrā, Uṣṇīṣavijayā, Vaikuṇṭha, Vairocana, Vajracarcikā, Vajradhātu, Vajradhātvīśvarī, Vajragāndhārī, Vajrajvālānalārka, Vajrāmṛta, Vajrasarasvatī, Vana-Durgā, Varadarāja, Varuṇa, Vāyu, Veṇugopāla, Vidyujjvālākarālī, Vindhyavāsi-Durgā, Vīrabhadra, Virūpākṣa, Viṣṇu-Kubera, Viṣṇu-Lokeśvara, Viṣṇvanugrahamūrti, Viṣvaksena, Viśvarūpa, Yajñamūrti, Yama, Yamāntaka. – A *c.* is further a *lakṣaṇa* of a *cakravartin*, see *saptaratna*.

Cakradānamūrti ("representation of the giving of the *cakra*"), see Viṣṇvanugrahamūrti.

cakradaṇḍa "wheel-staff" (attr.). "Ce mot désigne-t-il le manche d'un disque ou un bâton arrondi au bout?"

Lit.: ACA 41.

Cakrapāṇi ("holding the wheel in the hand"), epithet of Viṣṇu; see also Samantabhadra.

Lit.: WHW 1:160.

Cakra-Perumāḷ ("Wheel-Viṣṇu", mixed Skt-Tam.), n. of a *cakrapuruṣa*, see Sandarśana.

Lit.: SSI 66.

cakrapūjā "circle worship", i.e. worship within a circle of people, n. of an occult rite within the *śākta* sect. This worship is performed through the *pañcamakāras*. – This n. is sometimes also used for *carkh-pūjā*.

Lit.: GBB 158; GRI 182; H. Glasenapp, Indische Geisteswelt (Baden-Baden), I:127; IC 1:596; SSI 226; WHW 1:220.

cakrapuruṣa ("wheel-man"), n. of an anthropomorphic form (*aṅśa*) of the weapon (*cakra*) of Viṣṇu; see also *āyudhapuruṣa*.

Lit.: B 400, 538; HIS 77; SB 322.

cakrastambha ("wheel-pillar"), n. of a pillar which bears a *cakra* as symbol.

Lit.: AuT pl. 10.

Cakrasvāmin ("owner of the *cakra*"), epithet of Viṣṇu and n. of an image at Taneshar.

Lit.: AI 117.

Cakrattāḻvār (mixed Skt-Tam.), see Sudarśana.

cakravāka "a kind of bird (Anas casarca)". "The couples are supposed to be separated and to mourn during the night" (MW). The *c.* is therefore held up as symbolizing the ideal of conjugal fidelity.

Lit.: Gt Suppl. 26; IC 1:537; MKVI 1:252; MW 381; TSP 6:71; WHW 1:155.

Cakravāla ("circle"; Buddh.), n. of the Buddhist universe, displaying three separate planes: the plane around Mount Meru and the planes above and below this mountain. The lower plane contains 136 hells for different kinds of sinners, the middle plane contains the world of men, animals and ghosts, and around the peak of Meru 26 heavens are located, one on top of the other.

Lit.: IIM 135.

cakravartin (-ī; Pāli: *cakkavattin*) "world sovereign", lit. "turning the wheel, swinging the disk", referring to the *cakra* as a warrior symbol and hence n. of a universal monarch (but cp. MW: "a ruler the wheels of whose chariot roll everywhere without obstruction, emperor"). *c.* is also translated as "he who has the movement or puts into movement" (SM) and then alludes perhaps to the solar disk as a royal emblem (cp. *sūryavaṅśa*). – As specially char. of a *c.* it is said that he is the owner of *saptaratna.* In Jainism *c.* is n. of a group of 12 great men who are subordinate to the *tīrthaṅkaras*. – Cp. *dharmacakravartin.*

Lit.: CEBI pl. 5:19-20; GBM 102; GJ 255; Gz 39; IC 2:533; KiSH 123; MW 381; SM 96; ZA 78.

Cakreśvarī ("lady of the *cakra*"; Jain.), NP of a *śāsanadevatā* attending on the first *tīrthaṅkara*; also n. of a *vidyādevī.*

Lit.: GJ 322 a.pl. 24:1; KiJ 11 a.pl. 27:1.

cala "moving, movable", n. of an image carried in processions. Bronze images also belong to this category. Other n.: *bhogamūrti, calamūrti, jaṅgama, utsavabera, utsavamūrti.* Cp. *acala.*

Lit.: R 1:17; SSI fig. 4; ZA 111.

calaliṅga "moving *liṅga*", n. of a *liṅga* of stone or other materials used in processions (see *cala*). There are *c.* of several kinds: *mṛnmaya-, lohaja-, ratnaja-, dāruja-, śailaja-* and *kṣaṇika-liṅga.* – Another n.: *jaṅgama liṅga.*

Lit.: R 2:75.

calamūrti "moving image", see *cala.*

Calendra, see Carendra.

cāḷukya, n. of a dynasty that ruled in the Deccan, and of a school or period of arts flourishing between the 5th and 7th cc. A.D. Also n. of an era beginning in A.D. 1075 and fallen into disuse after 1162. The year of this era is *gata*, and the months have conformed to those of the *śākakāla.* The given year + 1076 = the year A.D.

Lit.: Enc. Brit. 5:721; Gz 129, 133; IC 2:738; WHW 1:221; ZA 84.

camara "Yak" (Vāh.; Buddh.). A blue *c.* is the Vāh. of Grīṣmadevī.

Lit.: G 82.

cāmara (and *-ī*, Hi. *caurī*) "fly-whisk, chowrie, fan" (attr.), the bushy tail of a Yak (*camara*) employed as a "chowrie" or long brush for whisking off insects, flies etc., or as a fan; one of the insignia of royalty (see *rājakakuda*). The *c.* is met with in all Indian religions. In Buddhism it symbolizes the compassion of the divinity, "for by its use he avoids hurting even the smallest and most insignificant of creatures" (SM), but with regard to the historic Buddha it is a symbol of his royalty (cp. above). – Char. of: Avalokiteśvara (some Lokeśvara-forms), Gaṅgā, Mahābala, Mahākāla, Mahāmāyūrī, Mārīcī, Sāvitrī, Svarṇākarṣaṇa(-Bhairava), Totalā, Vajrīputra, Vanavāsi, Viṣṇu (whose *c.* is "eternal law (*dharma*)" DHP), Yamadūtī, Yamunā, and of (female) attendants of gods. – *c.* is also a *maṅgala*, see *aṣṭamaṅgala.* – Another n.: *vālavyajana.*

Lit.: B passim; BBh. 434; DHP 159; G 12 (ill.); HIS 77; HSIT pl. 2; MEIA 261; SM 152; STP 3:84.

cāmaradhāriṇī "fly-whisk-bearer", n. given to the female attendant of a deity who holds a *cāmara.*

Lit.: SIB 70 a.pl. 6.

campa, n. of a certain kind of white flower (attr.; Buddh.), Char. of Maitreya.
Lit.: G 12 (ill.).

campaka(vṛkṣa), n. of a tree (Michelia Champaka Linn.) which is sacred to Mahāśītavatī.
Lit.: IC 1:538; KiSB 112.

lCam-sriṅ ("brother-sister"; Tib.), see Beg-tse.
Lit.: G 36.

Cāmuṇḍā (or -ī).
1. (Hind.) N. of a form of Durgā. She is found in 8 variants (see below). The n. of C. is said to originate in a contraction of two words, Caṇḍa and Muṇḍa (NP of two demons killed by C.). – C. is also one of the *saptamātaras* (or *aṣṭamātaras* or *navaśakti*s, respectively) symbolizing either *moha* ("delusion") or *paiśunya* ("malignity"). In South India she also seems to have adopted the function of Mahiṣāsuramardinī. – Char.: Vāh.: *ulūka, mṛtaka, siṅha*; att.: *lalitāsana, nāṭyasthāna*; attr.: *ajina* (tiger- or elephantskin), *aṅkuśa, asthi, cakra, churikā, ḍamaru, daṇḍa, danta, dhanus, ghaṇṭā, kapāla, kavaca, keśamaṇḍala, khaḍga, khaṭvāṅga, kheṭaka, kuṇḍala*s, *muṇḍa, muṇḍamālā, musala, nāga, paraśu, pāśa, śakti, śaṅkha, śara, śavamālā, trinayana, triśūla, vajra*. Her sacred tree is *vaṭa*. – Variants: Rudra-Carcikā, Rudra-Cāmuṇḍā, Mahālakṣmī, Siddha-Cāmuṇḍā, Siddha-Yogeśvarī, Rūpavidyā, Kṣamā, Danturā. Other epithets and variants: Karālī, Kṛśodarī, Rakta-Cāmuṇḍā; see also Vāruṇī-Cāmuṇḍā. See also Caṇḍikā, Mahākālī, Mahiṣāsuramardinī.
Lit.: B 505, 507 a.pl. 44:5; BECA 1: pl. 17a; DHP 286; JDI 39; KiH 33 a.pl. 78; KiSH 50, 53; KrA pl. 120; MEIA 150, 153; R 1:381, 386; RIS 10; SSI 197; Th. 108.
2. (Buddh.) The Hindu goddess is also met with in Buddhism. Char.: colour: red; Vāh.: *mṛtaka*; Mu.: *añjalimudrā*; attr.: *kapāla, karttṛkā*.
Lit.: BBh. 365.
3. (Jain.) The name-form Cāmuṇḍī is NP of a *śāsanadevatā* attending on the 21st *tīrthaṅkara*.
Lit.: GJ 362 a.pl. 26:21; KiJ 12 a.pl. 29:21.

Cañcalā ("unsteady, the Fickle-One") epithet of Lakṣmī.
Lit.: DHP 262.

caṇḍa "white *dūrvā*-grass" (attr.). Char. of Caṇḍeśvarī. Cp. *dūrvā*.
Lit.: KiSB 77.

Caṇḍa ("fierce, violent").
1. N. of a form of Śiva Bhairava or of a minor deity, an attendant of Śiva, not to be distinguished from Caṇḍeśvara.
2. NP of a demon who was killed by Cāmuṇḍā.
Lit.: B 466; DHP 195; MEIA 65.

Caṇḍā (or -ī; "fierce, violent").
1. (Hind.) N. of a form of Mahiṣāsuramardinī. C. may be identical with Cundā; she is also mentioned as one of the *navadurgā*s. Char.: Mu.: *abhayamudrā*; attr.: *aṅkuśa, cakra, ḍamaru, darpaṇa, ḍhakkā, dhanus, dhvaja, gadā, ghaṇṭā, khaḍga, kheṭaka, mudgara, (nāga)pāśa, paṇava, paraśu, śakti, śalākā, śaṅkha, śara, triśūla, vajra*.
Lit.: BBh. 220; D 66; GH 142; KiSH 49; KrI pl. 22 f.; MEIA 143; R 1:357.
2. (Jain.) NP of a *śāsanadevatā* attending on the 12th *tīrthaṅkara*.
Lit.: GJ 362.

Caṇḍakhaṇḍā, n. of a variety of Durgā. Vāh.: *śyena*.
Lit.: SSI 202.

Caṇḍālī (lit.: "out-cast woman"), in Tibetan Lamaism n. of one of the *gaurī-* or *kerimas*-goddesses. Char.: colour: red or blue; attr.: *agni*.
Lit.: BBh. 312; G 101 (ill.).

candana "sandal" (attr.), n. of a tree of which incense (*dhūpa*) is produced. A paste made with sandalwood is very much used in worship.
Lit.: IC 1:538; WHW 2:218.

candanapūjā "sandal worship" (Jain.), n. of image-worship which consists in the smearing of an image with sandalwood-paste. See *pūjā*.
Lit.: GJ 396; STP 7:105.

Caṇḍanāyikā ("mistress of the Fierce"), n. of one of the *navadurgās*.
Lit.: R 1:357.

Caṇḍaroṣaṇa ("fierce, angry"; Buddh.), NP of a Mahāyāna god, an emanation of Akṣobhya. Char.: colour: yellow; attr.: *Akṣobhyabimba* on the crown, *ajina*, *khaḍga*, *tarjanīpāśa*. – Epithets: Acala, Mahācaṇḍaroṣaṇa.
Lit.: KiSB 64.

Caṇḍarūpā ("of a fierce shape"), n. of one of the *navadurgās*.
Lit.: R 1:357.

caṇḍātaka "petticoat, drawers" (attr.). Cp. *dhotī*.
Lit.: AIP 70 a.pl. 49 (307).

Caṇḍa-Vajrapāṇi ("the fierce V."; Buddh.), in Lamaism n. of a form of Vajrapāṇi. Char.: Mu.: *karaṇamudrā* (G, with ?); attr.: *vajra*.
Lit.: G 63.

Caṇḍavatī ("fierce"), n. of one of the *navadurgās*.
Lit.: R 1:357.

Caṇḍeśānugraha(ṇa)-mūrti (or Caṇḍeśvarānugraha-), n. of a gracious representation (*anugraha*) of Śiva together with his *bhakta* or *dūta* Caṇḍeś(var)a. Śiva's Śakti sometimes sits besides him. – Char.: of Śiva: Mu.: *varadamudrā*; attr.: *mṛga*, *paraśu*. See further Caṇḍeśvara.
Lit.: B 484 a.pl. 35:5; R 2:205 a.pl. 49-50; RIS 53; SSI 143.

Caṇḍeś(var)a ("the lord of Caṇḍā" or "the fierce lord"), n. of a minor deity, an attendant (*dūta*) of Śiva. He is said to have been a young Brāhman cowherd and devotee (*bhakta*) of Śiva. But C. is also regarded as a boon-conferring aspect (*anugrahamūrti*) of Śiva himself. – Char.: att.: *vīrāsana*, *utkuṭikāsana* etc., or *sthānaka*; Vāh.: *padmapīṭha*; Mu.: *abhaya-*, *añjali-*, *varada-mudrā*; attr.: *akṣamālā*, *dhanus* (Pināka), *gadā*, *jaṭāmukuṭa*, *kamaṇḍalu*, *nāgayajñopavīta*, *paraśu*, *pāśa*, *śara* (Amogha), *ṭaṅka*, *triśūla*. – See also Caṇḍeśānugrahamūrti, Caṇḍikeśvara.
Lit.: AIP 273; CBC 12 a.fig. 18; MEIA 65 a.pl. 4a; R 2:205, 463 a.pl. 49 f., 133; SSI 161.

Caṇḍeśvarī ("the fierce lady"; Buddh.), NP of a Mahāyāna goddess. Char.: colour: yellow; att.: *ālīḍhāsana*; Vāh.: *mṛtaka*; attr.: *caṇḍa*, *mṛga*.
Lit.: KiSB 77.

Caṇḍī, see Caṇḍā.

Caṇḍikā ("fierce"), NP of a goddess who is sometimes counted among the *saptamātaras* (*aṣṭamātaras*). She symbolizes *kāma* "desire", and she is sometimes identified with Cāmuṇḍā.
Lit.: KiSH 53; MW 1044 (sub *śakti*); SSI 196.

Caṇḍikeśvara ("lord of Caṇḍikā"), probably n. of a *sādhu* (saint) or *śaivabhakta*, also identified with Caṇḍeśvara. Char.: att.: *utkuṭikāsana*; Mu.: *añjali-*, *ardhāñjali-mudrā*; attr.: *paraśu*, *trinayana*.
Lit.: AIP 273 a.pl. 59 (316); DIA pl. 27; SB 140 a.fig. 84f., p. 180 a.fig. 112, and passim; SIB pl. 35.

Caṇḍogrā ("fierce and terrible"), n. of one of the *navadurgās*.
Lit.: R 1:357.

candra(maṇḍala) or *candrabimba* "moon (sickle), disk of the moon" (attr.). The *c.* as a symbol may be a later transformation of the bull-horns which are seen on many seals from the Indus Valley. As an attr. it is usually seen on the head but may also be held in a hand. Char. of: esp. Śiva in different forms, also of Annapūrṇā, Ardhanārīśvara, Bahurūpa, Bhadrakālī, Candra, Daśabhujasita-Mārīcī, *ekādaśarudra*, Ekapādamūrti, Gaṇeśa, Hālāhalalokeśvara, Mahāmāyūrī, Maṅgala, Nīlakaṇṭhāryāvalokiteśvara, Rāhu, Rājamātaṅgī, Ratnapāṇi, Ratnapāramitā, Ṛddhivaśitā, Śailaputrī, Samvara, Saptākṣara, Sarvanivaraṇaviṣkambhin, Siṅhanādāvalokiteśvara, Sitatārā, Śrīdevī, Ucchuṣma, Vajraśāradā, Vindhyavāsi-Durgā. Besides, *c.* is the symbol of Candraprabha. – As a *yantra*, *c.* (the moon sickle) symbolizes the element air. – *candra* is further a symbolic n. of the number "1", see *saṅkhyā*. – Cp. *ardhacandra*, *indu*, *kaumudī*.
Lit.: BBh. 87, 90; BKI 28 a.pl. 14; DHP 215; G 12 (ill.); GJ pl. 22:8; KiJ pl. 45; KiSH 20.

Candra(mās) ("the moon as a personification, the planet god").

1. (Hind.) C., the planet-god, is regarded as a *dikpāla* of the northerly direction. Wives: Kaumudī, Tārā, the 27 *nakṣatras* (among whom Rohiṇī may be mentioned); Son: Budha. Char.: colour: white; Vāh.: a 2- or 3-wheeled *ratha* drawn by 10 lean white *aśvas*; Mu.: *varadamudrā*; attr.: *gadā*, *kumuda*, *padma*, large *śiraścakra*, *yajñopavīta*. His *bīja* is *DRĀṀ*. Epithets and varieties: Indu, Soma, Śaśin.

Lit.: DHP 98; GBB 129; GHS 48; GoRI 1:231; Gt Suppl. 27; IC 1:490, 567; KiH 6 a.pl. 11; KiK 30; KiSH 60, 88; MSHP pl. 49; R 1:318 a.pl. 96; SSI 239; Th. 113; WM 56.

2. (Buddh.) The planet-god. Char.: colour: white; Vāh.: *haṅsa*; attr.: in both hands *candramaṇḍala* on *padma*.

Lit.: BBh. 367.

candrabimba "moon-image", see sub *candra*.

Candragupta ("moon-protected", NP of the first ruler (B.C. 322-298) of the Maurya-dynasty.

Lit.: Gz 38.

Candraja ("moon-born"), see Budha.

Lit.: KiK 141.

candrakāla "moon-time(-handpose)" (Mu.), n. of a variety of the *muṣṭimudrā** with the difference that the thumb and forefinger are out. Represents Śiva, eyebrows, boar-tusks, crescent of the moon.

Lit.: WHW 2:87.

candrakānta "moonstone", n. of a precious stone, sometimes included among the *navaratna**.

candrakhaṇḍapāṣāṇa "moon-piece-stone", n. given to the stone that forms the bottom step of the flight of steps of a temple, esp. in Sri Lanka. Cp. *ardhacandrapāṣāṇa*.

Lit.: MBPC 44.

candramāsa "lunar month", consisting of 30 lunar days, see *tithi*. Since the Indian chronology was earlier and, in religious relations, is still of the lunisolar type, and since this month does not coincide with but gets displaced in relation to the solar month (*māsa**), periodic adjustments must be made in order to make them agree. Thus it happens that two lunar months may begin during the same solar month. Then both these lunar months receive the same name, the first being regarded as intercalary (*adhika* "additional"), the second as "natural" (*nija*), and the latter is the starting point of adjustment between these months. If, as happens less frequently, two solar *saṅkrāntis** occur in the same lunar month, there will be a lack of one lunar month corresponding to the second *saṅkrānti* (*kṣayamāsa* "one month suppressed"). See also *samvatsara*. The lunar month is divided into two halves, *śuklapakṣa* from the new moon to the full moon, and *kṛṣṇapakṣa* from the full moon to the new moon. The month usually begins with the new moon (*amānta*), but in some parts of India is reckoned as beginning with the full moon (*pūrṇimānta*). – As to the names of the months, see *māsa*. – See also *tithi*.

Lit.: Enc. Brit. 4:622; IC 2:722, 725.

candrapīṭha "moon-seat" (Vāh.), n. of a kind of *pīṭha*.

Lit.: R 2:101.

Candraprabha ("moonlight").

1. (Buddh.) NP of a *bodhisattva*. Char.: colour: white; Mu.: *varadamudrā*; attr.: *candra* on a *padma*, *vajracakra*. – C. is also n. of a deity who accompanies Arapacana.

Lit.: BBh. passim a.pl. 59.

2. (Jain.) NP of the 8th *tīrthaṅkara*. Symbol: *(ardha)candra*.

Lit.: GJ 273 a.pl. 12; KiSH 142; NLEM 349.

Candraprabha-Lokeśvara (Buddh.), n. of a variety of Avalokiteśvara. Char.: att.: *padmāsana*; Vāh.: *padma*; Mu.: *vyākhyānamudrā*; attr.: *padma*.

Lit.: BBh. 398 a.pl. 43(A).

candraprabhāmaṇḍala "halo of the moon" (attr.). Char. of Mahāmāyūrī, Mahāsāhasrapramardanī.

Lit.: BBh. 303.

candrāsana "moon as seat" (Vāh.), n. of a seat. Char. of: Dhanadā, Mahāśrī-Tārā.

Lit.: BBh. 127; R 1:368.

Candraśekhara(mūrti) ("moon-crested, having the moon in the hair or on the crown"), n. of a certain *sthānakamūrti* of Śiva. The (sickle of the) moon may symbolize the horns of a bull. – Char.: Mu.: *abhaya-*, *varada-mudrā*; attr.: *ajina*, Apasmārapuruṣa, *candra*, *ḍamaru*, *dhattūra*-flowers, *hāra*, *jaṭāmukuṭa*, *keyūra*, *khaḍga*, *kheṭaka*, *(kṛṣṇa)mṛga*, *kuṇḍala*, *paraśu*, *triśūla*, *yajñopavīta*. — Sub-forms of C. are: Kevalamūrti, Umāsahitamūrti and Āliṅganamūrti. – Another n.: Śaśāṅkaśekhara.
Lit.: B 464, 466 a.pl. 32:1; DHP 191; HSIT 13 a.pl. 29; KiSH 20; R 2:113 a.pl. 15ff.; SB 289 a.fig. 192, a.passim; SSI 114; Th. 79; ZM 140.

Candrasuta ("moon-born"), see Budha.

candravaṅśa "the lunar race (of kings)", n. of a family of kings, the progenitor of which was Candra (Soma "moon"). Among others Purūravas belonged to this family. It is divided into two sub-branches, on one hand the Yādavas, among whom Kṛṣṇa and Balarāma were counted, on the other the Pauravas, among whom Duṣyanta, Bharata and the Mahābhārata heroes (Yudhiṣṭhira, Bhīma, Arjuna etc.) are found. – Cp. *sūryavaṅśa*.
Lit.: D 68 (with a genealogy); IC: 532.

Caṅkilikkaruppan (Tam., "the black man of the chain"; *caṅkili* = Skt *śṛṅkhalā*), n. of a local god in South India.
Lit.: SB 358 a.pl. 361; TL 3:1227.

Caṅkili(nācciyār) (Saṅgili-; Tam., "the lady of the chain"), NP of the wife of Sundaramūrti-Nāyaṉār.
Lit.: SB 346 a.fig.299.

caṅkrama "the walking-about", performed by a Buddhist monk (originally referring to the first walking-tour of the Buddha after his Enlightenment).
Lit.: Gz 51; HIS 15.

cāpa(ka) "bow", see *dhanus*.
Lit.: ACA 37; B 301; BBh. 434; G 12 (ill.).

capeṭa(hasta)mudrā, *capeṭadānamudrā* "slap-hand; Ohrfeigenhand" (Mu.), n. of a hand-pose, "the right hand is menacingly extended upwards, just as is done in dealing a slap" (BBh.). Properly speaking, a variety of the *patākāmudrā**; signifies "strife, anger". Char. of Aparājitā.
Lit.: BBh. 432; KiSB 106; KiSH 92; WHW 2:86.

carak-pūjā, see *carkh-pūjā*.

caraṇa "foot mark" (attr.), see *pāduka* and *cihna*.

cāraṇa ("wanderer"), n. of a group of heavenly panegyrists and dancers.
Lit.: DHP 306.

caraṇāmṛta "foot-nectar" (attr.), "the water in which the feet of a Brāhman or spiritual guide have been washed" (MW), drunk by the pious adherents. Cp. *pādodaka*.
Lit.: GG p. CVII; MW 389.

Carcikā ("repetition of a word in reciting"; personification; Buddh.), n. of a Mahāyāna goddess. Char.: colour: red; attr.: *kapāla*, *karttṛkā*.
Lit.: KiSB 76.

Carendra ("the Indra, or king among the retinue deities"; Buddh.), n. of a king of *yakṣa*s. Another n.: Calendra.
Lit.: KiSB 74.

cāri (Tam.; attr.), see *sāri*.
Lit.: TL 3:1387.

carkh-pūjā (Pers.-Hi.) "wheel-worship", n. of a ceremony "observed by the lower orders of Hindūs on the day when the sun enters Aries, for the expiation of their sins (they are suspended, by an iron hook thrust through the flesh of the back, to one end of a lever which is raised on the top of a high pole, and whirled round by means of a rope attached to the other end; this penance is often performed by proxy for those who are rich enough to pay for it)" (P). – In South India this ceremony is known to have been performed in honour of Māriyammaṉ. It is there called *ceṭil* (Tam.), *siḍi* (Tel., Kann.) "iron hook, hook machine". It is difficult to say whether it is still in use in India, but in Sri Lanka it occurs even today. – Among the Bhīls the "hook god" is called Gal Bāpsi. – Other name-forms: *carak-pūjā* or *cakra-pūjā*.
Lit.: DED No. 2272; Diehl; GH 356; KBh. 153; MD 1:567; P 429; TL 3:1584; WHW 2:470.

carma(n) (lit. "skin"; attr.), sometimes used as another n. for either *kheṭaka* ("shield") or *ajina* ("skin").
Lit.: B 301; BBh. 205; DHP 464 (No. 505); GJ 256; MEIA 254.

carmāmbara "animal hide serving as cloth" (attr.), see *ajina*.
Lit.: SB 272.

caṣaka "cup, wine-glass' (attr.). Char. of: Hevajra, Jayakara, Kollāpura-Mahālakṣmī, Kubera, Kūṣmāṇḍa-Durgā, Laghuśyāmalā, Madhukara, Surapriyā, Vāruṇī, Vasanta, Vidyujjvālākarālī.
Lit.: BBh. 434.

cātaka "a bird, Cucculus melanoleucus", which is believed to subsist on rain-drops.
Lit.: IC 1:537; WHW 1:155.

Cāttā (Cāttaṉ, Tam. < Skt Śāstā), see Śāstā and Aiyaṉār.
Lit.: ACA 11.

catuḥśālā "four-hall", in architecture n. of a building consisting of a square court surrounded by cells on all four sides.
Lit.: MS 129.

caṭulātilakamaṇi "forehead jewel" (attr.), a circular jewel, together with a jewelled strip along the combed hair, running over the parting of the hair to rest on the forehead.
Lit.: SSIP 40, 159.

catura(hasta)mudrā "quick-hand-handpose" (Mu.), n. of a gesture "in which the little finger is kept vertical, the three others stretched at right angles to the little finger, while the thumb is placed in the middle of the three fingers" (R). Also mentioned as a variety of the *mukulamudrā* (with the little finger raised), and signifies a jackal, a cunning enemy, a pander. Char. of Śiva Naṭarāja in the *catura-tāṇḍava*-dance.
Lit.: R 2:267; WHW 2:87.

catura(tāṇḍava) "dexterous (dancer)" or "charming, beautiful", n. of a certain dance-att.: "Both the legs are bent deeply at the knee but more in the right leg than in the left, with the result that the heel is lifted up high, the toes alone touching the pedestal" (SB). Char. of: Śiva Naṭarāja, Kṛṣṇa Kāliyadamana, Skanda (in the Somāskanda-representation). – N.B. that Śiva Naṭarāja often stands (att. *kuṭṭita*) on the head of Apasmāra; Mu.: *abhaya-*, *añcita-*, *catura-*, *gaja-mudrā*; attr.: *agni*, *ḍamaru*, *nāga*, *paraśu*, *triśūla*.
Lit.: KrG pl. 10; R 2:267 a.pl. 66-67; SB 82 a.pl. 48, p. 139 a.pl. 82 f., a.passim; SIB pl. 42; Th.90 a.pl. 54; WM 94 a.fig. 10.

Caturānana ("four-faced"), epithet of Brahmā; cp. *caturmukha*.
Lit.: DHP 237.

caturbhuja "four-armed" (attr.). Any god may be four-armed, these arms symbolizing the superhuman and consequently the divine character. It is also said that the four arms signify the four quarters and therefore absolute dominion. C. as epithet is above all char. of Viṣṇu.
Lit.: B 403; DHP 152.

Caturbhuja-Tārā ("the four-armed Tārā"; Buddh.), in Lamaism n. of a variety of Ekajaṭā or also of a Tārā of white colour. Char.: att.: *ālīḍhāsana*; Mu.: *utpala-*, *varada-*, *vyākhyāna-mudrā*; attr.: *bodhisattvābharaṇa*, *cakra*, *kapāla*, *khaḍga*, *padma*, *trinayana*.
Lit.: BBh. 308; G 76.

caturmahārāja (*-rājika*) "the four great kings" (Buddh.), see *dikpāla*.
Lit.: B 522.

cāturmahārājika (Buddh.), the *caturmahārājas* as a group.
Lit.: IC 1:492; KiSB 25.

caturmahāvyūha "the great group of four manifestations", see Caturvyūha.

caturmudrā "four auspicious symbols" (attr.), see *ṣaṇmudrā*.

caturmukha "four-faced" (in the four directions; attr.). Esp. char. of Brahmā; in Hinduism Viṣṇu is also found with four faces in the form Caturmūrti. See also: Aghora, Ananta, Brāhmāṇī, Hari-Hara-Pitāmaha, Tatpuruṣa, Vaikuṇṭhanātha, Varuṇa. – In Mahāyāna Buddism several gods are represented with four faces: Acalavajrapāṇi, Avalokiteśvara (some Lokeśvara- and Tantric forms), *ḍākinī*s, Dharmadhātuvāgīśvara, Dhvajāgrakeyūra, Kālacakra, Kun-rig, Mahākāla, Mahāmāya, Mahāmāyūrī, Mahāpratisarā, Mahāsāhasrapramardanī, Mañjughoṣa, Nanda, Paramāśva, Parṇaśavarī, Samvara, Saurabheya-Subrahmaṇya, Sitabrahmā, Trailokyamohana, Trailokyavijaya, Vajradhātu, Vajrajvālānalārka, Vajratārā. – Caturmukha is also an epithet of Brahmā. *c.* is also a term of temples with four doors.

Lit.: DHP 237; G 63 a.passim; GJ 400; KiDG 12.

caturmukha-liṅga, n. of a form of *liṅga* with four faces, representing four aspects of Śiva (the *liṅga* itself being the fifth aspect) on the sides of the pillar.

Lit.: KrA pl. 108.

Caturmūrti ("the four-fold representation").

1. N. of a form of Viṣṇu with four faces (*caturmukha*): one *nara-* (Vāsudeva), one *rākṣasa-* (Pradyumna), one *siṅha-* (Saṅkarṣaṇa), one *varāha-mukha* (Anirudha). See also *caturvyūha*.

Lit.: B 408 a.pl. 22:5; SIB pl. 2.

2. N. of a syncretistic representation of Brahmā + Viṣṇu + Śiva (cp. *trimūrti*) + Sūrya.

Lit.: KiH 20 a.pl. 60.

caturmūrtidāna, n. of a group of four icons which, as votive gifts, are placed in a temple. See also *devadāna*.

Lit.: ZA 111.

caturviṅśatijinastuti (*caturviṅśatīya*) "praising of the 24 *tīrthaṅkara*s" (Jain.), see *āvaśyaka*.

Lit.: GJ 408; IC 2:638.

caturviṅśatimūrti "24 forms (or aspects) of Viṣṇu". The conception of these 24 forms is founded on the fact that the four chief attributes (*cakra, gadā, padma, śaṅkha*) of Viṣṇu in his four hands can be arranged in 24 different ways, each of them being regarded as a particular "aspect" of Viṣṇu and named as follows: 1. Keśava; 2. Nārāyaṇa; 3. Mādhava; 4. Govinda; 5. Viṣṇu; 6. Madhusūdana; 7. Trivikrama; 8. Vāmana; 9. Śrīdhara; 10. Hṛṣīkeśa; 11. Padmanābha; 12. Dāmodara; 13. Saṅkarṣaṇa; 14. Vāsudeva; 15. Pradyumna; 16. Aniruddha; 17. Puruṣottama; 18. Adhokṣaja; 19. Narasiṅha; 20. Acyuta; 21. Janārdana; 22. Upendra; 23. Hari; 24. Śrī-Kṛṣṇa. (Concerning the arrangement of the attributes according to these 24 aspects, see Lit.) All these aspects are represented in *sthānakamūrti*s with four-armed icons.

Lit.: B 388, 410; DHP 153; GoRI 2:116; MEIA 22; R 1:225; SSI 55.

caturviṅśatipaṭṭa (Hi. *cauvisīpaṭṭa*) "plate with the 24" (attr.; Jain.), n. of a representation in bronze of a *tīrthaṅkara* as the centrepiece of the image, surrounded on the back-piece behind the idol, by the 23 other *tīrthaṅkara*s.

caturviṅśatīya (Jain.), see *caturviṅśatijinastuti*.

Caturvyūha ("four kinds of appearance"), either n. of a form of Viṣṇu, see Caturmūrti, or n. of a group of four manifestations (*vyūha*) of Viṣṇu, representing his four aspects as Vāsudeva, Saṅkarṣaṇa, Pradyumna and Aniruddha. Another n. *caturmahāvyūha*.

Lit.: GoRI 2:116; MEIA 15; SIB 5, 69.

catuṣkoṇa "quadrangle" (attr.), n. of a *yantra* symbolizing the earth. A *yantra* with two squares (one inscribed in the other) symbolizes heaven and earth.

Lit.: DHP 352; GH 56.

caugharā (Hi.) properly "four-pot", or *caugharī* "four-fold", n. of a spice box with four or more partitions (with covers) for holding spices such as cloves, cardamom, betel-leaves and areca-nuts, used for betel-chewing; *caugharī* also indicates four betel leaves, folded with spices, contained in a leaf. Cp. also *pāndān*.

caula(karma), see *cūḍākaraṇa*.

Lit.: DHP 185; IC 1:363.

caurī (also *cauṅrī*; Hi. < Skt *cāmara*+*ikā*), see *cāmara*.

Lit.: B passim; P 454.

Caurī (personification of *caurī*; Buddh.), NP of a goddess of the *gaurī*-group. Char.: colour: yellow; attr.: *pāśa*.

Lit.: BBh. 310.

cauvīsīpaṭṭa (Hi.), see *caturviṅśatipaṭṭa*.

cavukku (Tam.) "whip" (attr.). The object in the ill. (see Lit.) is identical with the attr. which in this dictionary is named *ceṇṭu**. Cp. *koṟaṭā*.
Lit.: JDI 114 a.fig. 36.

cāy-pātra "ceremonial tea-urn" (attr.).

cedi(kāla) ("the era of Cedi"), n. given to an era beginning in A.D. 248 and used in the central provinces until the 13th c. The year of this era is *vartamāna*, *āśvinādi*, *amānta* (see *samvatsara*). The given year + 247 or 248 = the year A.D. – Another n. : *kalacūri*.
Lit.: IC 2 :737.

cellukhepa (Pāli; Mu.), n. of a handpose in which one hand waves a cloth, and expressing great joy on the part of the wover.
Lit.: B 262 a.pl. 2 :21.

Ceṅkaḻaṉiyammāḷ (Tam., "lady of the red paddyfield"), in South India NP of a goddess.
Lit.: DiCh. 18.

ceṅkōl (Tam.) "sceptre" (attr.), a symbol of sovereignty, see *ceṇṭu*.
Lit.: SSR 143; TL 3 :1581.

Cennakeśava, see Keśava.
Lit.: R 1 :229 a.pl. C and 69.

ceṇṭu (Tam.) properly "horse-whip" (attr.). Under this term several objects are included which, iconographically, show a considerable degree of resemblance and, therefore, are confused, such as "crooked stick" (R; but ACA : "ce qui est difficilement acceptable"; she translates : "balle à jouer..., bouquet"), "sceptre". Char. of : Aiyaṉār, Vṛṣavāhana. Other n. : *cavukku*, *ceṅkōl*, *koṟaṭā*, *vajradaṇḍa*, *vakradaṇḍāyudha*; cp. also *kaṣā*, *kuṇil*.
Lit.: ACA 12, 49; JDI 114 a.fig. 36; R 2 :486 a.pl. 140 :1; TL 3 :1585.

ceṭī "female servant", n. of a companion of a goddess.
Lit.: SB 322.

ceṭil (Tam.) "hook machine", see *carkẖ pūjā*.

cetukki (Tam.) "hoe" (as used in weeding the gardens of temples; attr.). Char. of Appar.
Lit.: SSR pl. facing p. 176.

Cevvēḷ (Tam., "red-hued'), epithet of Skanda (Gajavāhana).
Lit.: BECA 1 :5, 8; MD 1 :577.

Cēyōṉ (Tam., "rubicund, red-hued; youth, son"), epithet of Skanda in his form as Gajavāhana.
Lit.: BECA 1 :4; MD 1 :581; TL 3 :1632 (sub *cēy*).

chāga "goat" (Vāh.), see *aja*.
Lit.: BBh. 362.

chāgavaktra (*chāgamukha*) "goat-faced" (attr.), see *ajamastaka*.
Lit.: B 363, 562.

Chandaka ("charming"; Buddh.), NP of the Buddha's charioteer.
Lit.: IIM 129.

Chanhu-Dāro, n. of a village in the Indus Valley, with remnants from the Indus civilization.
Lit.: WIC 44.

channavīra is either "a kind of flat ornament, a kind of jewelled disk, meant to be tied on the *makuṭa* or hung round the neck by a string so as to lie over the chest" (R, B, dubiously), or "a crossband" intended to hold other attributes, e.g. a quiver behind the shoulders (SB); it is also interpreted as "cross-belt" (attr.). Worn by women the string hangs down between the breasts and then goes round the waist. When Viṣṇu is flanked by two wives, this attr. is esp. char. of Lakṣmī on his right-hand side (while Bhūmidevī, on his left-hand side, wears instead a *yajñopavīta*). It is also char. of other goddesses and gods, e.g. Kṛṣṇa. Worn by Lakṣmaṇa it is said to be a symbol of his warlike qualities.
Lit.: B 291, 376; BECA 1 :260; R 1 :31; SB 89 a.passim; SIB 69 a.pl. 33.

chattra (or *chatra*) "parasol, umbrella" (attr.), n. given to an ensign of royal or delegated power. The *ch.* is an emblem of royalty or imperial power of ancient date (see *rājakakuda*). As an attr. it is both held in

the hands of an image and occurs as a detail in architecture. The *ch.* is also a screen or roof on a *hti.* – It is above all char. of Varuṇa (whose *ch.* is named *ābhoga*), and in addition of Chattroṣṇīṣa, Jalandharavadhamūrti, Mahāpratisarā, Pañcarakṣā, Revanta, Sitātapatra, Sitātapatrā, Sūrya, Vāmanāvatāra, Vasudhārā, Viṣṇu. – In Buddhist arts an umbrella surmounting a riderless horse represents the Great Departure of the Buddha from his palace. – Another n.: *ātapatra.*
Lit.: B 433, 442; DHP 160; DIA 18; G 12 (ill.), 67; GJ 256; MEIA 261; STP 2:263; WIA 156 a.pl. 40; ZA 234.

chattrākāra "having the form of a parasol", n. of the umbrella-shaped form of the top of a *liṅga*, see *śirovarttana.*
Lit.: R 2:93.

chattrāvala (or *-ī*), n. given to the umbrella-like roof of a *stūpa.*
Lit.: AuT 219; JMS 11.

chattrikā, see *śalākā.*
Lit.: MEIA 144.

Chattroṣṇīṣa (Chatr-, "*uṣṇiṣa* with an umbrella"; Buddh.), n. of an *uṣṇīṣa*-deity. Colour: white; direction: north-east; attr.: *chattra.*
Lit.: BBh. 302.

Chāyā ("shadow"; personification), NP of a goddess who is the reflection of Sañjñā. She is the wife of Sūrya and the mother of the planet Śani.
Lit.: Gt 134; MW 406; WM 56.

Chi-dup (Tib.), see Phyi-sgrub.

Chinnamastakā (or -mastā, "decapitated"), n. of a headless form of Durgā. Ch. stands on Niśumbha, a demon whom she killed whilst in this form. She also belongs to the group *mahāvidyā*, and is then represented by Vīrarātrī. Ch. shows the iconographic influence of the Buddhist Vajrayoginī. Attr.: *ardhacakrakṛpāṇa*, *muṇḍa* (she often holds her own head in a hand), *muṇḍamālā.*
Lit.: BBh. 1; DHP 280; W 264; WM 56.

mChod-rten (Tib., pronounced Chorten; Buddh.), n. given to a sacred pyramidal building, "originally sepulchres containing the relics of departed saints" (JT). May be compared with *stūpa* (and *caitya*).
Lit.: HuGT 16 and passim; pl. 70; JSV passim with ill.; JT 167; RAAI 271.

chos-'khor-lo (Tib.) "prayer wheel" (attr.), see *ma-ṇi chos 'khor.*

Chos-skyoṅ (Tib., pronounced: Chö-cyoṅ; "protector, defender of religion"; Buddh.), in Lamaism n. of a *dharmapāla*, and also of one of the *mahāpañcarājas*. Char.: colour: blue; Vāh.: *gaja* (white); attr.: *churī, pāśa.*
Lit.: G 36, 93; JT 31.

choṭikā: according to BBh.: "whip" (cp. *kaṣā*), but to MW: "snapping the thumb and fore-finger". If MW is correct, *ch.* should signify a *mudrā*, and this seems to be the case in fig. 62 in BBh. – Char. of Pratibhānakūṭa.
Lit.: BBh. 91; MW 407.

chowrie (Engl.), see *cāmara* (*caurī*).

churel, see *curail.*

churī, *churikā* "knife, dagger" (attr.). Char. of: Bi-har, Cāmuṇḍā, Chos-skyoṅ, Durgā, Kālī, Mahācīnatārā, Vajradhātvīśvarī, Viśvarūpa. – Other n.: *kartṛ, kaṭṭāra, kṣurikā*; and cp. esp. *karttṛkā.*
Lit.: G 14 (ill.); MEIA 247.

cihna (orig. "mark, sign"), according to GBM "Wappen". A generic term for a "symbol" signifying one or other of the deities; see also *caraṇa, rūpa, rūpabheda.* – *c.* is also a mark consisting of the male and female signs. Char. of Mahālakṣmī.
Lit.: GBM 105; GJ 39 a.pl. 23; R 1:336; WHW 2:472.

cīnācāra "Chinese behaviour, Chinese practice", another n. of *tantra**. The n. refers to Mahācīna "Great China", i.e. Tibet.
Lit.: GoRI 2:46; GRI 176.

cinmudrā "reflection-, realization-handpose" (Mu.), n. of a variety of the *mukulamudrā*. *c.* resembles the *varadamudrā*, but the tips of the thumb and the index are pressed against each other, forming a ring. "This

suggests realization of the absolute" (Th.). Cp. *vyākhyānamudrā*.
Lit.: B 254; R 1:16; Th. 30; WHW 2:87; WM 98.

Cinna Aruṇan (Tam. "the little Aruṇa"), see Aruṇa.
Lit.: DiCh. 19.

cintāmaṇi (orig. "thought-gem, a jewel which grants all wishes" (attr., esp. Buddh.), n. of a pearl surrounded with flames. The *c.* represents in Buddhism the *manas* or the 6th sense, and it also stands for *triratna.* This attr. is often not distinguishable from the simpler form *ratna* ("pearl"), and in this dictionary (as far as Buddhist icons are concerned) *c.* is used as a common n. for *c.* and *ratna.* Some *buddha*-forms have, instead of an *uṣṇīṣa*, a high hair-crown, which has a *c.* on its top. In South India this attr. is explained as a flame, cp. *agni.* – In Hinduism *c.* is a "gem supposed to yield its possessor all desires" (MW). – This attr. may be held in a hand or worn on the body.
Char. of: Acala, Ākāśagarbha, Akṣobhya, Amitābha, Arthapratisamvit, Buddha, Devadevatā-Lokeśvara, Gaganagañja, Gaṇeśa, mGon-dkar, Heruka, Hevajra, Jambhala, Kālacakra, Kālajambhala, Kṛṣṇa-Yamāri, Kṣitigarbha, Mahābala, Mahākāla, Mahāmantrānusāriṇī, Mahāmāyūrī, Mahāpratisarā, Māmakī, Maṇidhara, Mañjunātha, Māyājālakramakrodha-Lokeśvara, Māyājālakramāryāvalokiteśvara, Nīladaṇḍa, Nīlakanthāryāvalokiteśvara, Padmāntaka, Prajñāntaka, Pramuditā, Pretasantarpita-Lokeśvara, Ratnaḍākinī, Ratnapāṇi, Ratnasambhava, Ratnolkā, Ṣaḍakṣarī, Ṣaḍakṣarī-Mahāvidyā, Samantabhadra, Samvara, Saṅ-dui, gSaṅ-sgrub, Sarasvatī, Sarvanivaraṇaviṣkambhin, Siṅhanātha-Lokeśvara, Sitatārā, Sumbharāja, Ṭakkirāja, Uṣṇīṣa, Uṣṇīṣavijayā, Vajracarcikā, Vajradhātvīśvarī, Vajrasarasvatī, Vidyujjvālākarālī, Vighnāntaka, Virūpākṣa, Yamāntaka. – **A *c.* is further a *lakṣaṇa* of a *cakravartin*, see *saptaratna.*** – Cp. also *maṇi.* – Other n.: *ratna, ratnacchaṭā, sajvālaratna.*
Lit.: BBh. 434; G 14 (ill.), 49; GH 44; Gt 135; IC 1:539; MW 398; SB 107, 240; WHW 1:385; ZM 225.

Cintāmaṇicakra-Avalokiteśvara ("A. with a thought-gem-wheel" or "with *cintāmaṇi* and *cakra*"; Buddh.), n. of a form of Avalokiteśvara.
Lit.: SeKB 222, 231 (ill.).

cintāmaṇidhvaja "banner marked with a jewel, jewel-banner" (attr.; Buddh.). Char. of: Buddhabodhiprabhāvaśitā, Cundā, Dhvajoṣṇīṣa, Jñānaketu, Mahāśītavatī, the *pāramitā*-group, Pariṣkāravaśitā, Ratnolkā.
Lit.: BBh. 96, 329.

Cintāmaṇi-Lokeśvara ("L. of the thought-gem"; Buddh.), n. of a variety of Avalokiteśvara. Char.: att.: *samapādasthānaka*; Vāh.: *padma*; attr.: *stūpa.*
Lit.: BBh. 430 a.pl. 94(A).

cīra(ka), *cīratraya* "strip (a long scarf resembling a stole); the three rags of a mendicant" (attr.; Buddh.). Char. of Mañjukumāra. – Cp. *pañcacīraka, tricīvara.*
Lit.: BBh. 120; KiSB 55.

Cirālan (Tam.), NP of a *nāyan(m)ār* (*śaivabhakta*).
Lit.: R 2:475 a.pl. 135.

Ciruttoṇṭar (Tam.), n. of a *nāyan(m)ār* (*śaivabhakta*).
Lit.: R 2:475 a.pl. 135.

Citipati ("lord of the funeral pile"; Buddh.), in Lamaism n. of a skeleton-genius, who is a companion of Yama. Attr.: *kamaṇḍalu, kapāla.*
Lit.: G 37, 95.

citra ("clear, bright, distinguished"), n. given to an image "in the round with all limbs completely worked out and shown". – Cp. also *vyakta.*
Lit.: R 1:18.

Citrā ("bright"), n. of a *nakṣatra.* Its influence is bad.
Lit.: BBh. 382; IC 2:729.

citrabhāsa ("painted impression"), n. of an image, painted on walls and/or pieces of cloth. Another n.: *citrajā.*
Lit.: R 1:18.

Citragupta ("Manifold-Secret", DHP), NP of the scribe of Yama.
Lit.: DHP 134; Gt 135; R 2:527.

citrajā (scil. *devatā*: "painted deity"), see *citrabhāsa*.
Lit.: B 208.

Citrakālī (Buddh.), NP of a *yakṣiṇī*.
Lit.: KiSB 74.

citrārdha, n. of an image in "half-relief".
Lit.: R 1:18.

citraśālā "room ornamented with pictures; gallery of mural paintings".
Lit.: HAHI 65; MW 397.

Citrasenā ("having a bright spear"; Buddh.), NP of a Mahāyāna goddess, the Śakti of Buddhakapāla.
Lit.: KiSB 65.

citravastra "embroidered clothes" (attr.). Char. of Śrīkaṇṭha.
Lit.: R 2:391.

citrayajñopavīta "*yajñopavīta* of superior workmanship" (attr.). Char. of Śrīkaṇṭha.
Lit.: R 2:391.

Cittadhātu-Lokeśvara ("L. of the world of thought"; Buddh.), n. of a variety of Avalokiteśvara. Char.: att.: *samapādasthānaka*; Vāh.: *padma*; Mu.: *abhayamudrā*; attr.: *Amitābhabimba* held in a hand.
Lit.: BBh. 430 a.pl. 93(A).

Cittavaśitā ("control of thinking"; Buddh.), n. of a *vaśitā*. Char.: colour: white; attr.: *vajra*.
Lit.: BBh. 329.

cīvara "dress or rags of a religious monk" (esp. of a Buddhist or Jain monk; attr.), see *tricīvara*.
Lit.: MW 399.

Civikuṇḍalin (or -ī) see Vicitrakuṇḍalin.

cod-pan (Tib., pronounced *cö-pen*) "tiara, crown" (attr.; Buddh.), n. of a five-leaved crown used by monks in special services for Amitāyus.
Lit.: G 10.

Cola (Tam. Cōḷa), n. of an ancient South Indian Tamil dynasty, and of a period or school of arts flourishing between the 9th-14th cc. A.D.
Lit.: K. A. Nilakanta Sastri, The Cōḷas (Madras 1955); id., A history of South India (London 1955), 444; WHW 1:235.

cūḍā "a single lock or tuft left on the crown of the head after tonsure" (attr., esp. Buddh.), also n. of the tonsure-ceremony (see *cūḍākaraṇa*). Char. of the Buddha, Amitābha.
Lit.: MW 401; WHW 1:433; ZM 178 a.pl. 44.

cūḍākaraṇa "tonsure, forming the crest", n of a *saṅskāra*-rite, a ceremony performed in a child's first or third year; the first visit to a barber. Particularly famous in Indian tradition is the *c.* of the Buddha, which he performed himself with a single cut as a prelude to his departure from home (*mahābhiniṣkramaṇa*). – Other n.: *caulakarma*, *cūḍākarma*.
Lit.: DiIP 180; GH 334; GJ 412.

Cūḍākaraṇa, epithet of the Buddha performing the tonsure.
Lit.: ZA pl. 471a.

cūḍākarma(n), see *cūḍākaraṇa*.
Lit.: IC 1:363.

cūḍāmaṇi (also *cūḷā-*) "lock-jewel" (attr.), n. given to a jewel, worn by men and women on top of the head. Cp. *cintāmaṇi*.
Lit.: MW 401; SB 268.

Cūḍāpanthaka ("having tonsure and knowing the way"; Buddh.), n. of a Lamaist *arhat*.
Lit.: G 104.

cūḍopanayana "tonsure and initiation" (Buddh.), n. of a rite referring to monks.
Lit.: MW 401.

Cūlakokā devatā, n. of a *vṛkṣadevatā*.
Lit.: IP pl. 2; ZA pl. 33b.

cūḷāmaṇi, see *cūḍāmaṇi*.

Cundā (Buddh.), NP of a goddess worshipped in eastern Bengal and in Tibet. C. is an emanation of Vajrasattva or Vairocana and is also regarded as a female *bodhisattva*. She belongs also to the *dhāriṇī*-group and her *mantra* is: *Oṁ Cale Cule Cunde Svāhā*. Char.: colour: white or green; att.: *yogāsana* on the back of a prostrate man (*nara*), or *padmāsana*; Vāh.: *nara*; Mu.: *abhaya-*, *dharmacakra-*, *dhyāna-*, *tarjanī-*, *tripatākā-*, *varada-mudrā*; attr.: *akṣamālā*, *aṅkuśa, bhindipāla, cakra, cintāmaṇidhvaja, ḍamaru, daṇḍa, dhanus, dharmapālābharaṇa, dhvaja, gadā, ghaṇṭā, jambhīra, kamaṇḍalu, karttṛkā, khaḍga, mudgara, padma, paraśu, pāśa, pātra, pustaka* (on a *padma*), *ratnadāma*, (*śakti*), *śaṅkha, śara, triśūla, vajra* (or *viśvavajra*), *Vajrasattvabimba* on the crown. – Another n. : Āryacundā; see also Caṇḍā.

Lit.: BBh. 151, 219 a.pl. 161-164; CBC 21 a.pl. 27:178f.; G 14, 33, 73; Gz 144; KiDG 64; KiSB 97, 101.

Cuntarar (Cundarar, Tam.), see Sundara.

cuṛail (also written *churel*; Hi), n. given to a kind of female ghost, or a semi-divine witch, perhaps belonging to the *mātaras*. *c.* is the "spirit of any woman who dies unpurified within fifteen days of childbirth. She becomes a demon... and is always on the watch to attack other young mothers" (MG). According to Crooke, she also attacks or, in the disguise of a beautiful girl, seduces young men. She may be recognised by the fact that her feet are attached back-to-front (i.e. with the heels facing forwards).

Lit.: W. Crooke, The popular religion and folk-lore of Northern India. 1 (Westminster 1896), 269; MG 252; P 433.

cuṭar (Tam.) "splendour, flame" (attr.), n. of the four flames which issue from the rim of the *cakra*. – See also *agni*.

Lit.: JDI 8; MD 1:542.

D

dāḍima(phala) "fruit of the pomegranate tree" (attr.). In the Orient the pomegranate is generally looked upon as a fertility symbol on account of the multiplicity of seeds contained in the fruit. Char. esp. of Gaṇeśa (in different forms); also of Bhūmidevī, Dhūmorṇā, Kubera. Cp. *phala*.

Lit.: R 1:54; 2:527.

dāgaba (*-oba*, < Singh. *dāgäba* < Pāli *dhātugabbha*, Skt *dhātugarbha**), esp. in Sri Lanka n. given to a *stūpa* "reliquary shrine", but also elsewhere in India used to signify temples which resemble *pagodas**. – *d.* also occurs in a miniature form as a votive gift.

Lit.: CBC 8 a.figs. 71, 189; DCSS 45; W. Geiger, A grammar of the Sinhalese language (Colombo 1938), §86; Gt 143; Gz 41; KiJ 19; KiSH 148; MBPC 14; RAAI 210.

daitya "son or descendant of Diti", n. of a member of a species of demons. Cp. *asura*.

Lit.: DHP 143, 301, 307; GH 106.

daiva "divine", in a special sense, "the art or knowledge of divination or portents".

Lit.: IC 1:615.

daivata "image" of a deity, see *pratimā*.

Lit.: CHIIA 42.

daivikaliṅga (*daivataliṅga* "divine *liṅga*"), n. of a kind of *acalaliṅga*. It has a characteristic shape, like a flame or resembling a pair of hands held in the *añjalimudrā*.

Lit.: R 2:83.

ḍākinī "female imp, witch".

1. Ḍākinī (Hind.), NP of a witch attending on Kālī (feeding on human flesh). She is also counted among a group of 6 Śaktis of Tantric gods, her counterpart being Ḍāmeśvaranātha (see MEIA).

Lit.: DHP 288 a.pl. 25; IC 1:528; MEIA 205.

2. (Buddh.; corresponding to Tib. *mKha'-'gro-ma* "ether wanderer"), esp. in Tibet n. of a kind of women of supernatural powers, sometimes represented as angels, at other times as fairies or witches. *ḍ.* represents a cruel form of the Śakti; a *ḍ.* is also said to have been an abbess who had attained perfection (*siddhi*) and had become a deified woman. – There are many forms of *ḍ.* in Lamaism : Buddha-, Ratna-, Padma-, Viśva-, Karma-, Vajra-, Sarvabuddha-ḍākinī; further Siṅhavaktrā, Makaravaktrā, Vajravārāhī, Ṛkṣavaktrā, Vyā-

ghravaktrā. Among the *ḍ.* also belong the four goddesses of the four seasons: Vasanta-, Grīṣma-, Śarad-, Hemanta-devī, further 17 minor goddesses (not listed here, and having only Tibetan names), and the Lamaist *aṣṭamātaras*. In BBh. four *ḍ.* are enumerated: Ḍākinī, Lāmā, Khaṇḍarohā, Rūpiṇī. – Common char.: att.: *ālīḍhāsana* or *ardhasamapādasthānaka* (*nāṭyasthāna*); attr.: *caturmukha, kapāla, karttṛkā, khaṭvāṅga, ṣaṇmudrā.*

Lit.: BBh. 321, 434 a.pl. 217; G 14, 34; HuET 74; JSV pl. 79; JT 54; ZA 200 a.pl. 602a.

Dakṣa(-Prajāpati) ("able, fit, skilled", as a personification interpreted as "Ritual-Skill"), n. of a *riṣi* who was an Āditya and counted among the 10 *prajāpatis* the leader of whom he was. He was therefore a demiurge or a sun genius. – D. was the son of Brahmā; Aditi is sometimes mentioned as his mother (elsewhere she is said to be the daughter of D.). Wife: Prasūti. According to different traditions he had 16, 25, 50, or 60 daughters, 13 of whom were married to Dharma or Kāśyapa (Aditi, Diti, Kadrū, Vinatā, Kṣamā, Danu, Khasā, Viśvā and others), one (Svāhā) to Agni, one (Svadhā) to the *pitaras* (see *pitā*) or Aṅgiras, and one (Satī) to Śiva (Bhava); among his other daughters also the 27 *nakṣatras*, married to Candra, are counted. – D. quarrelled on one occasion with his son-in-law Śiva and gave him no share in a ritual sacrifice that he offered to all the other gods. He was punished and killed by Śiva in the form of Vīrabhadra, but afterwards restored to life with a goat's head. He is sometimes represented lying prostrate with Vīrabhadra dancing upon his corpse. – Attr.: *ajamastaka.*

Lit.: B 428; D 76; DHP passim; GH 95; GoRI 1:256; Gt 146; IIM 118; KiSH 29; MG 300; R 2:182 a.pl. 45:1; SSR 152 a.pl.; W 222 a.esp. 309; WHW 1:259; WM 57.

Dakṣajā ("born of Dakṣa"), epithet of Pārvatī, esp. in her aspect as Satī.

dakṣiṇa "southern, right (hand); gift, donation to a temple". – Common to all Indian religions is the belief that the right side is the honoured side. People therefore turn their right side to a person or a thing to be honoured; worshippers for that reason move in a clockwise direction when circumambulating a cult object (see *pradakṣiṇa*). Among brothers the elder one is placed to the right (cp. Balarāma and Kṛṣṇa). "Right" is further typical of the male principle (since women are always placed to left of the men, cp. *vāma*), and "male" symbols, such as *liṅga, vajra* etc., are carried in the right hand. The right-hand side is also the auspicious side; the left-hand side is consequently regarded as inauspicious and bad (for men, but not for women). Turning to the right (i.e. clockwise) is accordingly also held to be auspicious, and the locks of the Buddha, for instance, are shown as curling in this direction. Among the gods, esp. Viṣṇu, the Buddha and the *tīrthaṅkaras* are regarded as right-hand divinities; this possibly due to the fact that esp. the *abhayamudrā*, always performed with the right hand, is particularly characteristic of them. Cp. also *dakṣiṇācāra, vāma*, and the "right-handed" *svastika.*

Lit.: GOSA VI.

dakṣiṇācāra "right-hand practice", *dakṣiṇācārin* "follower of the right-hand ritual", n. of a certain form of Tantrism (*tantra*), which, in Hinduism, applies to the worship of the Śakti, though in a more moderate form (in contrast to the more extreme form named "left-hand practice", *vāmācāra*). In Buddhism, however, the *d.* is concentrated on the devotion to male divinities (cp. *dakṣiṇa*), and it is said that the right-hand represents the world of the *buddhas*, the Diamond world. Hence the *vajra*, symbolic of this world, is held in the right hand.

Lit.: BPR 60; GoRI 2:36; SM 17, 33.

dakṣiṇāgni "southern fire" (attr.), n. of one of the domestic sacred fires (see *agni*), used for offerings to the *pitaras* and demons. It is kindled in the southerly direction.
Lit.: WHW 1:359.

dakṣiṇāmūrti (R: "south-representation"), n. of a manifestation of Śiva as the master of knowledge and a teacher of *yoga*, music and other sciences. In this representation Śiva is never accompanied by his wife. *d.* is found in four forms: Vyākhyāna-, Jñāna-, Yoga- and Vīṇādhara-dakṣiṇāmūrti. A feature common to all these forms is the *vyākhyānamudrā*, a handpose performed with one right hand, or sometimes *abhaya-mudrā*, also a right-hand-gesture. R explains his interpretation, referred to above, thus: "because Śiva was seated facing south when he taught the sages *yoga* and *jñāna* he came to be known as *dakṣiṇāmūrti*" (in DHP, p. 281, *d.* is translated as "Southern-Image" and explained thus: "The aspect of Rudra representing the divinity of death is the southern aspect"). It seems to me more probable, however, that *d.* ought to be explained as "right-hand representation" (cp. *dakṣiṇa*), on account of the "teaching gesture" which is emblematic of it, and in this direction also points the remark in JDI that *d.* recalls to mind representations of the first sermon of the Buddha to his five disciples.
Lit.: AIP pl. 36: (289) a.pl. 63; B 464, 470; BECA 1: pl. 25 a.passim; DHP 207, 281; HAHI pl. 6B; JDI 32 a.pl. 15f.; R 2:273 a.pl. 71-81; SB 223; SSI 89; WM 165.

dakṣiṇāyana "southward course", a term used in dating, signifying the southward movement of the sun from summer solstice. Hence, it refers to the period from about June 22 to December 23.

daladā "the Buddha's tooth" (attr.), see *danta-dhātu*.
Lit.: Gt 148.

Dalai Lama (Tib. *ta-lai bla-ma*; the first element is orig. Mong., meaning "ocean, sea"; for *bla-ma*, see *la-ma*). The first D. was originally the abbot of a monastery ('Bras-spuṅs, pronounced D(r)e-puṅ) on the outskirts of Lhasa. He then became the ecclesiastic and political leader of Tibet, the n. D. being the title of the highest dignitary of Tibet. The Dalai Lamas are regarded as reincarnations of Avalokiteś-vara, esp. in his form as Ṣaḍakṣarī(-Lokeś-vara).
Lit.: G passim; CTLP pl. 31; GRI 296; HRT 168; JT 103, 383.

Da-lha (Tib.), see sub initial G-: dGra-lha.

damanamahotsava "the great festival of subduing", n. of a festival in the month *phālguna* in honour of Kāma.
Lit.: IC 1:590.

ḍamaru(ka) (cp. Drav. **ḍamāra* "double drum"), n. given to a small drum or tambourine shaped like an hour-glass (attr.). The *ḍ.* is used by dancers. It represents "the primary creative force and the intervals of the beat of time-process" (MH). Therefore, *ḍ.* signifies "den Ton, das Fahrzeug der Rede ... der Ton wird in Indien mit dem Äther assoziiert ... Ton und Äther zusammen bedeuten darum den ersten, wahrheitsschwangeren Augenblick der Schöpfung, die produktive Energie des Absoluten in ihrer Anfang setzenden kosmogenetischen Kraft" (ZM). This attr., which is above all char. of Śiva, is a symbol of non-Aryan origin (and is found already as a pictogram in the Indus Valley script), and signifies Śiva as a shamanistic ascetic.
Because of its form resembling two triangles (joined at the apex, thus producing on an hour-glass shape), it also symbolizes the male and female principles (cp. *trikoṇa*). – In Lamaism the *ḍ.* serves as a cult symbol. The Lamaist *d.* is made of two human skulls and used to mark the intervals in religious services; it is therefore a "symbol of Tantric manifestations". It is also a common attr. of gods.
The *ḍ.* is char. esp. of Śiva as Naṭarāja

(in different forms), Aghora, Andhakāsuravadhamūrti, (Baṭuka-)Bhairava, Candraśekharamūrti, Bhikṣāṭanamūrti, Maheśamūrti, Mārttanda-Bhairava and Sadāśivamūrti. It is further char. of: Ahirbudhnya, Aja, Aṅkālammaṉ, Aparājita, Bahurūpa, Bhairon, Buddhakapāla, Cāmuṇḍā, Caṇḍā, Cundā, Daśabhuja-Aghoramūrti, Ekapādamūrti, Gajāsurasaṅhāramūrti, mGon-dkar, mGon-po nag-po, Hara, Harasiddhi, Īśāna, Jayanta, Kālī, Kalyānasundaramūrti, *kṣetrapālas*, Mahākāla, Mahāmāyā, Māheśvarī, Mallāri-Śiva, Māriyammaṉ, Māyājālakramāryāvalokiteśvara, Nandīśvara, *navadurgās*, Pratyaṅgirā, Rakṣoghnamūrti, Samvara, Sarasvatī, Sarvabuddhaḍākinī, Śivā, Sureśvara, Svasthāveśinī, Tailopa, Tryambaka, Vajrabhairava, Vajravārāhī, Vidyujjvālākarālī, Vighnāntaka, Virūpākṣa, Vighnāntaka, Viśvaḍākinī, Yogeśvarī. Other n.: *huḍukka*, *uṭukku*. – Cp. *ḍhakkā*, *paṇava*.

Lit.: B 303; DED No. 2406b; DHP 219; G 10 (ill.), 14; H pl. 7:66; KiSH 22; MH 11; R 1:9 a.pl. 3:12-13; SMII 75; Th. 43; ZM 170.

ḍamaruhastamudrā "handpose of holding a drum in the hand" (Mu.), n. of a gesture in which the drum *ḍamaru* is held between the index and the little finger. It is said to be a variety of the *siṅhamukhamudrā*. Char. esp. of Śiva, particularly as Naṭarāja. Another n.: *karaṇaḍamarumudrā*.

Lit.: H pl. 7:66; Th. 29 (ill.); WHW 2:87; WM 100 a.fig. 26.

Dam-can (rDo-rje legs-pa) (Tib., pronounced: Dam-cen dor-je le-pa, or shortly Dor-le; Buddh.), in Lamaism NP of a king of demons. Char.: Vāh.: *siṅha* (white); attr.: *kapāla*, *vajra*.

Lit.: G 37, 94 (ill.), 95.

Dāmodara ("having a rope round the waist"), epithet of Kṛṣṇa as Bālakṛṣṇa (as a baby tethered with a rope to a big mortar so that he might not run away). Later this epithet is explained as "the Self-restrained". – D. is also n. of an aspect of Viṣṇu (see *caturviṅśatimūrti*); Śakti: Lajjā. Attr.: *udarabandha*. – Another n.: Kaṭṭuṇṭa-Kaṇṇaṉ.

Lit.: D 80; DHP 154; GoRI 1:241; KiSH 39; R 1:229; SSI fig. 24; WHW 1:561.

dampati (or *-ī*) "husband and wife", n. given to erotic temple-sculptures, symbolizing the auspicious state of married bliss. See further *maithuna*.

Lit.: KrA pl. 27; WHW 2:375.

dānamudrā "handpose of giving", another n. of *varadamudrā*.

Lit.: SB 203.

Dānapāramitā ("perfection of giving"; Buddh.), n. of a *pāramitā*. Char.: colour: whitish red; attr.: *cintāmaṇidhvaja*, *kaṇiśa*.

Lit.: BBh. 324.

dānava ("descendant of Danu"), n. of a member of a class of demons (*asuras*) or genii.

Lit.: DHP 143, 307; GH 106; WM 59.

dānavīra ("hero in giving"; Jain.), n. of a donator.

Lit.: GJ 335.

daṇḍa "staff, rod, club".

1. (Attr.) *d.* is not always distinguishable from the *gadā*; in this dictionary, however, it is used in the sense of "staff". It is sometimes mentioned as "the rod of Death or Punishment", and "signifies chastisement, coercion, and the rule of force, and symbolizes the fearsome majesty of sovereign power" (WHW). – In Tibetan Lamaism the *d.* is surmounted by a *vajra* (see *vajradaṇḍa*) or by a skeleton. – *d.* is esp. char. of Yama, Brahmā and Śiva (whose *d.* is named Pināka); further of: Aghora, Aparājitā, Bhadrakālī, Bhṛkuṭī, Bi-har, Brahmacāri-Subrahmaṇya, Bṛhaspati, Cāmuṇḍā, Cundā, Ekajaṭā, Gaṇeśa, Harihariharivāhana, Hayagrīva, Jyeṣṭhā, Kālacakra, Kapila, Kaumārī, Khen-pa, Kṛṣṇa-Yamāri, Kuliśeśvarī, Madhva, Mahābala, Mahākāla, Mahāmāyūrī, Mahiṣāsuramardinī, Nīladaṇḍa, Nirṛti, Paramāśva, Phyi-sgrub, Prabhāsa, Prasannatārā, Priyodbhava, Rati, Sadharma, Sani, Śaṅkarācārya, Ṣaṇmukha, Saptaśatika-Hayagrīva, Śarabha, Śaravaṇa-

bhava, Sarvakāmika, Sarvaśokatamonirghātamati, Satya, Senānī, Skanda, Śrīdevī, Śukra, Surapriyā, Ṭakkirāja, Totalā, Trivikrama, Vārāhī, Vāyu, Vibhava, Vijaya, Viśvarūpa, Yajña, Yajñabhadra, Yamāntaka (Yamāri); further also esp. Śiva-worshippers (see *daṇḍin*, *ekadaṇḍin*, *tridaṇḍin*).

d. is also the weapon of the southerly direction. A *d.* (as sign) between two dots symbolizes the *liṅga*. – Another n.: *yamadaṇḍa;* cp. also *kāvaḍi*, *sitadaṇḍa*, *yogadaṇḍa*, *laguḍa*.

Lit.: B 300, 449; BBh. 434; G 14 (ill.); GH 56; GJ 256; HIS 21; MEIA 244; WHW 1:267.

2. Daṇḍa (personification), n. of a form of Yama.

Lit.: GoRI 1:228.

daṇḍahasta(mudrā) "staff-hand-gesture".

1. (Mu.) N. of a handpose which is almost identical with *gajahasta*.

Lit.: ACA 32; B 258; R 1:16; SB 313.

2. (Attr.) *daṇḍahasta* "holding a staff in the hand".

Lit.: B 247.

daṇḍamukhāsana "rod-mouth-sitting" (att.), n. of a Yogic posture.

Lit.: WHW 1:74.

Daṇḍapāṇi ("holding a staff in the hand"; Buddh.), n. of the father-in-law of the Buddha.

Lit.: IIM 129; KiSB 10.

daṇḍāsana "staff-seat".

1. (Vāh.) N. of a certain form of *pīṭha*.

Lit.: R 1:369.

2. (Att.) "Sitting like a staff", n. of an *āsana*-posture, i.e. a certain *yoga*-att.

Lit.: B 270.

daṇḍin (-*ī*) "carrying a stick", n. given to a religious mendicant, a Brāhman in the fourth stage of his life (*saṁnyāsin*). Attr.: *daṇḍa* (small stick) with "a piece of cloth dyed with red ochre (*rakta*), in which the Brahmanical cord is supposed to be enshrined, attached to it" (Gt). This term seems to allude to both *ekadaṇḍin**, and *tridaṇḍin**.

Lit.: Gt 154; WHW 1:437.

daṁṣṭra "large tooth, fang" (attr.), see *danta*.

Lit.: MEIA 267.

danta "tooth, fang, an elephant's tusk" (attr.). *d.* refers both to protruding teeth and a tooth or tusk carried in one hand. Esp. char. of Gaṇeśa, who carries one of his own tusks (which is cut off) in one hand (*dantabhagna*). There are many legends about the incident in which he lost his tusk; according to one, it was lost in a fight with Paraśurāma. – Many (more than one, protruding). *d.* are char. of: (Baṭuka-) Bhairava, Cāmuṇḍā, Dhūmrāvatī, Heruka, Kubera, Nirṛti, Rakṣoghnamūrti, Śatruvidhvaṁsinī, Śrīvidyādevī, Trikaṇṭakīdevī, Viśvarūpa, and also of Agni (4 *d.*) and Airāvata (4 *d.*); 2 or more *d.* are also char. of *dvārapālaka*s and demons. – *d.* is also a symbolic n. of the number of "32", see *saṅkhyā*. – Another n.: *daṁṣṭra*. Cp. *svadanta*, Ekadaṁṣṭra, Ekadanta; for the Buddha's tooth, see *dantadhātu*.

Lit.: DHP 295; KiSH 31; MEIA 267.

dantadhātu "tooth-relic" (attr.). The Buddha's left canine tooth was (according to legend) brought to Sri Lanka at the time of King Sirimeghavanna (A.D. 301-328). It is believed to be the only portion of him that remains, and is kept in a reliquary in the temple of the tooth at Kandy. The Portuguese assert that it was destroyed in 1560, but the Ceylonese affirm that it was only a fake which was spoiled and that the real tooth at this time was concealed in a village. The relic is still worshipped at Kandy with great reverence by all Buddhists. – Another n.: *daladā*.

Lit.: Gt 148; MBPC 16.

Danturā ("having protruding teeth"), n. of a variety of Cāmuṇḍā, symbolizing the plague.

Lit.: KiH 23 a.pl. 81; KiSH 50.

Danu, NP of a daughter of Dakṣa married to Kāśyapa and mother of the *dānavas*.

dappaṇā (M.Ind.), see *darpaṇa*.

dara "rattle" (attr.). A fakir's "alarm-wand", consisting of a metallic staff with many rings attached to it, and intended to be shaken. Cp. *khakkhara*.
Lit.: SMII 45.

darbha, n. of a kind of grass (Saccharum cylindricum Lambk.), often confused with the *kuśa*-grass. It is the most sacred of the grasses, and it is said to have been formed of the hair of Viṣṇu. *d.* or *kuśa* is frequently attached to the flagstaff at festivals in most temples in South India.
Lit.: DiIP passim; GH 65; IC 1:538; STP 1:55; WHW 1:405.

darpaṇa "mirror" (attr.), n. of an object esp. belonging to women and therefore carried by goddesses, e.g. Ambikā, Caṇḍā, Lalitā, Lāsyā, Maṅgalā, Mahiṣāsuramardinī, *navadurgās*, Pārvatī, Rājarājeśvarī, Tripurasundarī, and others; it is further char. of the female aspect in composed and syncretistic representations such as Ardhanārīśvara, Harihara, Mahādeva, Sadāśiva; rarely of male gods, as Kālacakra, Vajrānaṅga. – *d.* as a cult symbol is used in services in the following way: the reflection of an icon in a mirror is moistened with water, and the image is thereby considered, in a sense, to be bathed; cp. *pratibimba*. – As regards the symbolism of *d.*, in Buddhism it is said that it "symbolizes the image of void, for it reflects all the factors of the phenomenal world but deprives them of substance" (SM). – It is also a *maṅgala*, see *aṣṭamaṅgala*. – Other n.: *ādarśa*, *dappaṇā*.
Lit.: B 304, 467; G 8; GBM 105; GH 345; GJ 384; IC 1:570; KiJ 21; KiSH 155; MEIA 258; R 1:12 a.pl. 4:7; SM 165; WM 110.

darśapūrṇamāsa "new and full moon month", n. given to minor festivals held at the new and full moon.
Lit.: Gt 156.

dāruja ("wooden, made of wood"), n. given to certain icons, as *dāruja liṅga*; see *calaliṅga*.
Lit.: R 2:77.

Dāruṇarātrī ("Night-of-Frustration"), n. of an aspect of *mahāvidyā* representing Dhūmavatī.
Lit.: DHP 282.

darvī (or *-i*) "ladle" of a certain form (attr.). Char. of Yajñamūrti. – Cp. *juhū*, *sruk*, *sruva*.
Lit.: DHP 76; RV 74.

daryā-sevak (Hi.) "river-worshipper"; river-worship is found esp. in Punjab, but all over India rivers are considered as goddesses and worshipped. See also *nadīdevatā*.
Lit.: GH 45.

daśabala "ten forces", see *bala*.
Lit.: Gt 157; IC 2:537.

daśabhuja "ten-armed" (attr.). The 10 arms represent the 10 quarters of the sky (see sub *dikpāla*) and therefore symbolize universal dominion. Char. of several gods, e.g., Durgā, Śiva.
Lit.: DHP 216.

Daśabhujā ("ten-armed"), epithet of Durgā.

Daśabhuja-Aghoramūrti, n. of a certain ten-armed form of Aghoramūrti. Char.: Mu.: *abhaya-*, *varada-mudrā*; attr.: *ḍamaru*, *dhanus*, *ghaṇṭā*, *kapāla*, *khaḍga*, *kheṭaka*, *paraśu*, *pāśa*, *triśūla*.
Lit.: R 2:200.

Daśabhujasita-Mārīcī ("the ten-armed white M."; Buddh.), n. of a form of Mārīcī. Char.: colour: white; Vāh.: *ratha* drawn by 10 *sūkaras*, D. is represented trampling upon the four Hindu deities Brahmā, Viṣṇu, Śiva and Indra; attr.: *aṅkuśa*, *aśoka*-branch, *candra*, *daśabhuja*, *dhanus*, *pañcaśiras*, *śara*, *sūci*, *sūrya*, *sūtra*, *tarjanīpāśa*, *triśikhā*, *Vairocanabimba* on the crown, *vajra*, *varāhamukha*.
Lit.: BBh. 213 a.pl. 155; KiDG 64; KiSB 84.

daśabhūmika ("consisting of the ten spiritual spheres"; also, with a last word-member, *-sūtra*; attr.; Buddh.), n. of a book and therefore as attr. the equivalent of *pustaka*. Char. of Vajragarbha.
Lit.: BBh. 28, 88.

daśaharā ("taking away the ten (sins)"), another n. of the *navarātrī* festival (GH). Since this term is identical with the Hi. *dasahrā** it is evident that these festivals were originally one and the same.
Lit.: GH 355; MW 472.

dasahrā (Hi., < Skt *daśa* + *hara* + *ka*: "the taker away of ten sins"; in English spelt *dassera* or *dussehra*), n. of a festival in the month *āśvina* (September-October) dedicated to Durgā or Gaṅgā. Kālī is also sometimes mentioned as the patroness of this festival. Cp. *daśaharā* and *navarātrī*.
Lit.: EGI 234; P 517.

Daśakaṇṭha, Daśakandhara ("ten-necked"), epithet of Rāvaṇa.

Daśānana ("ten-faced"), epithet of Rāvaṇa.
Lit.: WHW 2:291.

Dāśarathī Rāma, epithet of Rāma(candra) as the son of Daśaratha.
Lit.: B 390.

daśāvatāra "ten *avatāras*", i.e. the ten usually recognized reincarnations of Viṣṇu. These are: 1. Matsya; 2. Kūrma; 3. Varāha; 4. Narasiṅha; 5. Vāmana (including Trivikrama); 6. Paraśurāma; 7. Rāma(candra); 8. Kṛṣṇa; 9. either the Buddha or Balarāma; 10. Kalkin. Of these the *avatāras* No. 3, 4, 5, 7 and 8 are represented for worship in the temples, the others generally not being worshipped as chief deities. – See the names mentioned above, which are also composed with *-avatāra*.
Lit.: D 33; IIM 48; MEIA 27; R 1:117; SSI 22.

dassera, see *dasahrā*.

dasyu ("barbarian"), n. of a kind of *asura* or demon.
Lit.: DHP 143; Gt Suppl. 30; WM 59.

Dattā ("given"; Buddh.), n. of a *yakṣiṇī*.
Lit.: KiSB 74.

Dattātreya ("Son of Atri").

1. Originally D. was a teacher of the antigods, later identified with Viṣṇu; hence D. is an epithet of Viṣṇu as the son of Atri and Anasūyā (sometimes he is said to be the son of Kauśika). D. is sometimes mentioned as a separate *avatāra* of Viṣṇu, and is said to have created the *soma*-plant. Śakti: Lakṣmī; attr.: *akṣamālā, cakra, kamaṇḍalu, śaṅkha, triśūla*.
Lit.: B 391; D 84; DHP 165, 183; R 1:123, 251 a.pl. 72-73; Th. 57.

2. D. was also worshipped as a representation of the triad, a common incarnation of the three chief gods Brahmā, Viṣṇu, Śiva, see Hari-Hara-Pitāmaha.

dātura, see *dhattūra*.

Dayā ("compassion"), NP of the Śakti of Acyuta.
Lit.: R 1:233.

dehrā (Hi., < Skt *deva* + *gṛha* + *ka*) "idol temple" (Hind., Jain.).
Lit.: P 561.

dehrāvāsī "who sojourns in temples" (Hi.; Jain.), n. of a Jain sect, the members of which are adherents of an image cult.
Lit.: GJ 386.

Deśika-Subrahmaṇya ("S. the teacher"), n. of a form of Skanda. Char.: Vāh.: *mayūra*; Mu.: *abhaya-, varada-, vyākhyāna-mudrā*; attr.: *akṣamālā, śakti*. Cp. Śiṣyabhāvamūrti.
Lit.: R 2:443.

deul (Pkt < Skt *devakula*), see sub *devāgāra*.

deva "god, deity".

1. (Hind.) *d.* was originally n. of a certain species of gods (cp. *asura*). The number of the *d.* was early said to be 33 (Ṛgveda 1, 139, 11), but the even number of 30 is also mentioned (Ṛgveda 9, 92, 24; see MW sub *tridaśa*). The 33 were divided into three groups, i.e. 11 in each of the 3 worlds. Later the groups were distributed in the following way: 8 Vasus + 12 Ādityas + 11 Rudras + 2 Aśvins, and these words, as well as *deva*, are also used as symbolic names of the numbers "8, 12, 11, 2, and 33', respectively, see *saṅkhyā*. In later Hinduism the number of *d.* is often said to be 330 millions: this number is in the Indian manner written thus: 33, 00, 00, 000 = 33 *koṭis* (Skt) or *kroṛs* (Hi.), this number being best explained as a hyperbolism of the Vedic number of 33. Other numbers of

d. are also given, e.g. 3339. – In later Hinduism the n. *deva* usually refers to the minor gods (Indra etc.) and not to the chief deities of the Hindu triad, for whom other words are used, such as Bhagavān or Īśvara or Mahādeva.

2. (Buddh., Jain.) The Hindu gods are recognized as *deva*s also in Buddhism and Jainism, the n. *d.* here signifying minor gods, much inferior to such deities as *buddha*s, *bodhisattva*s, *tīrthaṅkara*s etc.

Lit.: DHP 79, 143; GBM 80; GH 148; GJ 234; GoRI 1:44, 48; GRI 70; IC 2:530; MW 458; SchRI 239; WHW 1:393; WM 60.

devabhoga "pleasure of gods", obviously n. of an endowment to a deity, belonging to a temple.

Lit.: BECA 1:66.

devadāna "gift to the god" (attr.), n. of a gift to a temple, often consisting of a bronze icon which (as a votive offering) is placed in a temple. Another n.: *mūrtidāna*; cp. also *caturmūrtidāna*, *trimūrtidāna*.

Lit.: ZA 111.

devadāsī "slave girl or female servant of a god", n. given to a temple maid-servant whose duties were divided between the entertainment of the god and sacral prostitution. This system is now officially prohibited.

Lit.: GH 348; GoRI 2:50; STP 1:231; WHW 2:246; ZA 35.

Devadatta ("god-given").

1. (Hind.) N. of a *śaṅkha*, char. of Indra.

Lit.: DHP 110.

2. (Buddh.) NP of a cousin of the Buddha. To begin with, he was an adherent of the doctrine of the Buddha, but later he showed himself to be a traitor and an antagonist, and even tried to kill him.

Lit.: BRI 15; IIM 119; KiSB 15; KT 122.

Devadeva ("god of gods"), n. of one of the *ekādaśarudra*s.

Lit.: R 2:386.

Devadevatā-Lokeśvara ("L. the deity of the gods"; Buddh.), n. of a variety of Avalokiteśvara. Char.: att.: *samapādasthānaka*; Vāh.: *padma*; attr.: *caturmukha*, *cintāmaṇi* (?), *dhanus*, *ghaṇṭā*, *khaḍga*, *pāśa*, *śara*, *triśūla*, *vajra*.

Lit.: BBh. 428 a.pl. 72(A).

devadundubhi "celestial drummer" on top of a *chattravālā*; an architectural term.

Lit.: JMS 11.

devāgāra, *devagṛha* "house of gods temple" Other n.: *devakula* (> Pkt *deul*), *devālaya*.

Lit.: B 55, 69; HIS 19; KiH 48 a.pl. 178.

Devakī ("divine"), NP of a daughter of Devaka, Ugrasena's brother. D. was married to Vasudeva and became the mother of Kṛṣṇa and Balarāma. She was a cousin of Kaṅsa.

Lit.: D 84; Gt 163.

Devakīputra, Devakīsūnu ("son of Devakī"), epithet of Kṛṣṇa.

devakoṣṭha "niche for subordinate deities" in the outer wall of a temple.

Lit.: BECA 1:260 a.pl. 37a.

devakula, *devālaya*, see sub *devāgāra*.

devalaka "attendant on an image", n. of an artisan who makes images, or of those who carry about images; see *pratimākāra*.

Lit.: CHIIA 42.

devaloka "world or heaven of the gods", 13 in number, ranging from the paradise of Indra to the highest heaven of Brahmā.

Lit.: RAAI 271.

devamātā (*-tṛ*, *-tar*) "mother of gods". This n. usually refers to Aditi.

Lit.: MW 494.

Devānandā ("delight of gods"; Jain.), NP of the mother of Mahāvīra. See also Triśalā.

Lit.: KiJ 13; KiSH 121.

Devapurohita ("the domestic priest of the gods"), epithet of the planet-god Jupiter, see Bṛhaspati.

Lit.: KiK 141.

devarāja "king of gods"; this n. usually signifies Indra.

Lit.: MW 494.

devarṣi ("divine *riṣi*"), n. of one among a group of *riṣi*s the leader of whom was Kaṇva.

Lit.: R 2:566.

devarūpa "figure of a god", n. given to an image which serves as a *kuladevatā* on the altar in a household chapel.
Lit.: ZA 370.

Devasenā ("host of celestials", personification), n. of one of the wives of Skanda. This n. usually signifies the wife who stands to the left of Skanda. Attr.: *padma* (in the left hand).
Lit.: R 2: pl. 122; Th. 99.

Devasenāpati, n. of a form of Skanda (as "husband of Devasenā"). Char.: Mu.: 2 hands in *kaṭakamudrā* (signifying the missing attr. *dhanus* and *śara*); attr.: *śakti* (?, thus SB; to the present author it would seem to be *mayūrapattra* or *śikhidhvaja*), *vajra*.
Lit.: SB 171 a.pl. 106; p. 347 a.pl. 304.

devatā "deity, divinity, godling", a term often applied to minor gods or semigods.
Lit.: RAAI 271; WHW 1:397.

devatāpratimā "image of a deity", see *pratimā*.
Lit.: CHIIA 42.

devayajña "sacrifice to the gods", n. of one of the five *mahāyajñas*.
Lit.: IC 1:585; WHW 1:360.

devāyatana "abode of gods, temple", see *āyatana*.
Lit.: IC 1:576.

devī (Tam. *tēvi*) "goddess".
1. (Hind.) Common n. of a female deity, the wife of a god, corresponding to *deva*.
2. (Hind.) *-devī* as the last member of a compound in which the first member is a n. of a weapon (attr.). Signifies a personification of that weapon, cp. *gadādevī*; see further *āyudhapuruṣa*.
3. (Buddh., Jain.) *d.* signifies a minor female deity.
Lit.: GBM 81; WM 62.

Devī ("the Goddess").
1. (Hind.) According to R both Lakṣmī, Pārvatī and Sarasvatī may have this epithet, and in R "Devī" is also the heading of a separate chapter, concerned with the conception of Śakti. Usually, however, this n. refers esp. to Pārvatī as the Śakti of Śiva, in particular in her forms as Durgā or Kālī. – General features of D. (as the Universal Goddess or Śiva's Śakti): Mu.: *abhaya-*, *varada-mudrā*; attr.: *aṅkuśa*, *cakra*, *pāśa*, *śaṅkha*, *triśūla*. – D. in the sense of "Universal Goddess" may also be represented by the *yantra Śrīcakra*. – Cp. Mahārājñī, Mahāśakti.
Lit.: D 86; HAHI 18; HIS 21; IIM 91; MEIA 138; R 1:327, 378; RAAI 271; WM 62; ZM 210.
2. (Buddh.) NP of a *yakṣiṇī*.
Lit.: KiSB 74.

ḍhakkā "(large) drum" (attr.; in SSI this word is translated as "kettle-drum", this term being indifferently used both for *ḍhakkā* and *ḍamaru*. However, it seems likely that in SSI, where the term *ḍhakkā* occurs, the Tam. *ṭakkai* is meant; this is an hour-glass drum, somewhat larger than the *ḍamaru*, from which it is not differentiated. In other works and, at least in North India, *ḍh.* appears to signify a much larger drum (cp. MW: "a large drum"). – Char. of: Aghora, Caṇḍā, Īśāna, Kaṅkāla- and Rudra-mūrti. – Cp. also *paṇava*.
Lit.: IC 1:514; MEIA 256; MW 431; R 2:304, 378; SSI 76 a.pl. III:12.

dhammilla "a woman's hair, braided and ornamented, and worn wound round the head" (attr.).
Lit.: B 286; MW 510; R 1:30, 2:328; SB 156; WHW 1:434.

Dhanada ("wealth-giving"), epithet of Kubera, also (Buddh.) NP of a king of *yakṣas*.
Lit.: BBh. 380; KiSB 73; R 2:533.

Dhanadā or Dhanada-Tārā (Buddh.), NP of a Mahāyāna goddess, an emanation of Amoghasiddhi. Dh. is a variety of Śyāmatārā. Char.: colour: green; Vāh.: *candrāsana*, *sattva*; Mu.: *varada-*, *vyākhyānamudrā*; attr.: *akṣamālā*, *Amoghasiddhibimba* on the crown, *aṅkuśa*, *nīlotpala*, *pāśa*, *pustaka*.
Lit.: BBh. 231 a.pl. 172, p. 307; G 75; KiDG 64; KiSB 99.

Dhaneśvarī ("Divinity-of-Wealth"), epithet of Sarasvatī.
Lit.: DHP 260.

Dhaniṣṭhā(s) ("very rich"), another n. of the *nakṣatra* Śraviṣṭhā(s) or the 24th lunar mansion. Its influence is bad.
Lit.: BBh. 382; IC 2:730; MW 509.

Dhanu(s) (lit. "bow"), n. of a *rāśi*, the zodiacal sign of the Sagittarius "the Archer".
Lit.: BBh. 383; GH 50; IC 2:731.

dhanurāsana "bow-sitting" (att.), in Yogic practice n. of a posture in which "one lies on the belly, raises the head and feet to form a 'bow'" (WHW).
Lit.: KiH pl. 151 row 4:1, WHW 1:75.

dhanus, *dhanvan* "bow" (attr.). This weapon belongs to the symbols of royalty. It is explained as "the destructive-aspect-of-the-notion-of-individual-existence" (DHP). Together with *śara* it symbolizes strength of will; it also signifies "den Geist, der die fünf Pfeile (*pañcaśara*), nämlich die fünf Sinne entsendet..." (ZM). In Buddhism the bow and the arrow symbolize the chasing away of forgetfulness and neglect (of the Law). – *dh.* as an attr. has often a proper n.: 1. Ajagava (or Pināka): char. of Śiva (in different forms, e.g. as Aghora, Daśabhuja-Aghoramūrti, Gajāsurasaṅhāramūrti, Liṅgodbhavamūrti, Tripurāntaka), Skanda, Durgā (Mahiṣāsuramardinī), Caṇḍeśvara, Nandā. – 2. Śārṅga: char. of Viṣṇu, Kṛṣṇa, Rāma(candra). – 3. Puṣpadhanvan (together with *pañcaśara*): char. of Kāma. – 4. Parivīta: char. of Brahmā. – 5. Vijaya: char. of Indra. – 6. Pāśupatāstra: char. of Arjuna, Śiva. – 7. Gāṇḍīva: char. of Arjuna. – 8. *dh.* without any proper n.: char. of Aiyaṉār, Aṣṭabhuja-Kurukullā, Avalokiteśvara (in different forms), Bahurūpa, Bhadrakālī, Bharata, Bi-har, Bṛhaspati, Budha, Cāmuṇḍā, Caṇḍā, Cundā, Dharmadhātuvāgīśvara, Ekajaṭā, Ekapādamūrti, Gaṇeśa (Gaṇapati), Grahamātṛkā, Hanumān, Hayagrīva, Hevajra, Jambhala, Jāṅgulī, Jayakara, Jayanta, Kālacakra, Kālī, Kaumārī, Kirātārjunīyamūrti, Krauñcabhettar, *kṣetrapāla*s, Kurukullā, Lakṣmaṇa, Madhukara, Mahācīnatārā, Mahāmantrānusāriṇī, Mahāmāya, Mahāmāyūrī, Mahāpratisarā, Mahāsāhasrapramardanī, Mahāśītavatī, Māheśvarī, Maṅgalā, Mañjughoṣa, Mañjukumāra, Mañjuśrī, Mañjuvajra, Mārīcī (in different forms), Māyājālakrama-Kurukullā, Mūla-Durgā, *navadurgā*s, Padmaḍākinī, Paramāśva, Paraśurāma, Parṇaśavarī, Prasannatārā, Rāhu, Revata, Ṣaḍbhuja-Sitatārā, Śani, Ṣaṇmukha, Śarabha, Śaravaṇabhava, Sarasvatī, Saurabheya-Subrahmaṇya, Senāpati, Sitatārā, Śrīkaṇṭha, Sureśvara, Tārodbhava-Kurukullā, Trailokyavijaya, Tryambaka, Uṣṇīṣavijayā, Vaikuṇṭha, Vajradhātu, Vajradhātvīśvarī, Vajragāndhārā, Vajrajvālānalārka, Vajraśṛṅkhalā, Vajratārā, Vajravidāraṇī, Vana-Durgā, Varāhamukhī, Vārāhī, Vasanta, Vidyujjvālākarālī, Viśvarūpa, Yogāmbara.
dh. as a sign on the forehead signifies a worshipper of Rāma(candra). – Other n.: *bāṇāsana*, *cāpa* (*pūrṇacāpa*), *iṣvāsa*, *kārmuka* (*adhijyakārmuka*), *kodaṇḍa*, *śarāsana*; for a bow made of sugar-cane, see *ikṣukodaṇḍa*.
Lit.: B 301; DHP 156; G 12; KiSH 94; MEIA 254; R 1:5 a.pl. 2:2-4; SM 148; ZM 226.

Dhanvantari ("moving in a curve" or "arrow-moving"), orig. NP of the physician of the gods; he was a sun deity and was produced at the churning of the ocean of milk (see Kūrmāvatāra) with a cup of *amṛta* in his hands; later he was regarded as an *avatāra* of Viṣṇu. Attr.: 2 *pātra*s containing *amṛta*.
Lit.: B 391; D 88; DHP passim; GoRI 1:231; R 1:123; Th. 57; WHW 1:274; WM 192.

dhānyamañjarī "ears of corn", see *kaṇiśa*.
Lit.: BBh. 202.

Dhara ("bearing, supporting"), n. of one of the *vasu*s. Attr.: *akṣamālā*, *hala*, *padma*, *śakti*.
Lit.: R 2:553.

dhārāliṅga ("stream-*liṅga*"), n. of a form of *mānuṣaliṅga* with vertical fluting on the cylindrical shaft (serving the purpose of

draining-off the water poured over the top of the *liṅga*).
Lit.: B 459; R 2:96 a.pl. 10:3.

Dharaṇapriyā ("friend of supporting"; Jain.), NP of a *śāsanadevatā* attending on the 19th *tīrthaṅkara*.
Lit.: GJ 362.

Dharaṇendra ("the Indra of supporting"; Jain.), NP of a *yakṣa* attending on the 23rd *tīrthaṅkara*. Symbol: *kūrma*. – Another n.: Pārśvayakṣa.
Lit.: GJ 362 a.pl. 27:23; KiJ 11 a.pl. 30:23.

dhāraṇī (also *dhāriṇī*; prob. with the original meaning: "the act of holding, bearing, maintaining") a mystical verse or charm, a meaningless conglomeration of syllables, used as a charm or prayer (in particular in Buddhism). Hence (Buddh.) *dh.* also indicates a group of 12 deities who are deifications of a peculiar kind of Buddhist literature (short works mostly composed of meaningless syllables, which are supposed to generate great mystic power). These deities are: Sumati, Ratnolkā, Uṣṇīṣavijayā, Mārī, Parṇaśavarī, Jāṅgulī, Anantamukhī, Cundā, Prajñāvardhanī, Sarvakarmāvaraṇaviśodhanī, Akṣayajñānakarmaṇḍā, Sarvabuddhadharma-Koṣavatī.
Common attr.: *viśvavajra*. – Cp. *mantra*.
Lit.: BBh. 220, 337, 434; BRI 176; GBM 19; IC 2:608; KT 139; MW 515; RAAI 271; SM 18.

Dhāraṇī ("earth"), NP of the wife of Paraśurāma; Dh. is a personification of the earth and regarded as an *avatāra* of Lakṣmī.
Lit.: DHP 261.

Dhāriṇī ("earth"; Jain.), NP of a *śāsanadevatā* attending on the 18th *tīrthaṅkara*. – For *dhāriṇī*, see sub *dhāraṇī*.
Lit.: GJ 362.

Dharma ("law, usage, practice, right, justice, religion", i.e. all that which is established or firm).

1. (Hind.) The god of law or justice (personification), originally a primeval *riṣi* and creative god, who married 13 of the daughters of Dakṣa. As the god of justice he is also regarded as the spiritual father of Yudhiṣṭhira. – Dh. is furthermore said to be an *avatāra* of Viṣṇu, and in this form, according to some statements, he is the father of Kāma whose mother is either Lakṣmī or Śraddhā. – He is sometimes mentioned as a *dikpāla* of the southerly direction.
Lit.: D 88; IIM 88; JDI 106; R 1:265; WM 62.

2. (Buddh.) *dharma* ("the Law") is the n. given to the Buddhist religion. It forms part of *triratna** and is also conceived as a deity and worshipped in an anthropomorphic form. Char.: att.: *padmāsana*; Mu.: *añjalimudrā*; attr.: *akṣamālā*, *padma*.
Lit.: BBh. 32 a.fig. 9.

3. (Jain.) NP of the 15th *tīrthaṅkara*. Symbol: *vajra* (or *gadā*?, see sub *vajra*).
Lit.: GJ 278 a.pl. 22:15; KiSH 142.

dharmacakra "Law-wheel, wheel of the law", see *cakra* 2.

Dharmacakra-Lokeśvara ("L. of the Law-wheel"; Buddh.), n. of a variety of Avalokiteśvara. Char.: att.: *samapādasthānaka*; Vāh.: *padma*; attr.: *paraśu*, *pāśa*.
Lit.: BBh. 499 a.pl. 81(A).

Dharmacakra-Mañjuśrī ("M., the Law-wheel"; Buddh.), in Lamaism n. of a form of Mañjusrī. Char.. att.: *padmāsana*; Mu.: *dharmacakramudrā*; attr.: *khaḍga*, *padma*, *pustaka*.
Lit.: G 68.

dharmacakramudrā (or *dharmacakra(pra)vartanamudrā*) "gesture of setting in motion the wheel of the Law" (Mu.; esp. Buddh.), n. of a preacher's handpose alluding to the first sermon of the Buddha in Sārnāth near Vārāṇasī. This Mu. is a kind of combined handpose, the right hand showing the *vyākhyānamudrā* and the left hand showing the *jñānamudrā*, both hands, in so doing, touching each other ("The right hand is held before the chest with the tips of the thumb and index finger joined to touch one of the fingers of the left hand, which is turned palm inwards"). This Mu. evidently originally hinted at the solar disk, and its solar character is manifest in early Buddhist representations; cp. *cakravartin*. – However, in BBh. *dh.* is said to be identical with the *vyākhyānamudrā*. – Char. of: Atīśa, the Buddha, Dharmadhātuvāgīśvara, Dharmakīrtisāgaraghoṣa, Digambarā, Dīpaṅkara, Durgatipariśodhana, Grahamātṛkā, Mahāsthāmaprāpta, Maitreya, Saṅgha, Suvarṇabhadravimalaratnaprabhāsa, Vairocana, Vajradhātu; besides also the Hindu Lakulīśa. – Cp. *vyākhyānamudrā, cakra.*

Lit.: B 256 a.pl. 3:4; BBh. 434; BRI 14; G 20 (ill.); GBM 97; H pl. 4:38B, 39; HIS 43; MH 7; RAAI 272; SM 94; WHW 1:75, 181; WM 97.

Dharmacakravartin ("turning the Law-wheel"; Buddh.), epithet of the Buddha displaying the *dharmacakramudrā*. – Cp. *cakravartin*.

Lit.: ZA pl. 177, 470.

Dharmadhara ("Law-supporter"; Buddh.), n. of a *mānuṣibodhisattva*.

Lit.: BBh. 79.

dharmadhātu "Law-world, cosmos, the element of law or of existence" (Buddh.).

Lit.: MW 511.

Dharmadhātu-Lokeśvara ("L. of the Law-world"; Buddh.), n. of a variety of Avalokiteśvara. Char.: att.: *samapādasthānaka*; Vāh.: *padma*; attr.: *kamaṇḍalu*.

Lit.: BBh. 430 a.pl. 90(A).

Dharmadhātuvāgīśvara(-Mañjuśrī) ("M., the lord of speech of the Law-world"; Buddh.), n. of a variety of Mañjuśrī who is an emanation of Amitābha. Char.: colour: reddish white; att.: *lalitāsana*; Mu.: *dharmacakramudrā*; attr.: *Amitābhabimba* on the crown, *aṅkuśa, caturmukha, dhanus, ghaṇṭā, kamaṇḍalu, khaḍga, pāśa, pustaka, śara, vajra.*

Lit.: BBh. 103; G 69; KiSB 53.

dharmagañja ("treasure of the Law"; attr.; Buddh.), probably n. of a symbol held on a *padma* (not described; perhaps a book (*pustaka*); note that *dh.* also is a n. given to a library consisting of sacred books). – Char. of Gaganagañja.

Lit.: BBh. 87; MW 511.

dharmakāya "Law-body", "der Körper des abstrakten Seins" (Buddh.), n. of the abstract body in which a *dhyānibuddha* lives in *nirvāṇa*. – Cp. *trikāya*.

Lit.: BRI 150; G 30; IC 2:566; KiSB 41; MW 510; RAAI 272; WHW 2:15.

Dharmakīrtisāgaraghoṣa ("the sound of the ocean of the glory of the Law"; Buddh.), in Lamaism n. of a medicine *buddha*. Char.: colour: red; Mu.: *dharmacakramudrā*. Cp. Bhaiṣajyaguru.

Lit.: G 56.

Dharmameghā ("cloud of the Law"; Buddh.), n. of a *bhūmi*. Char.: colour: blue; attr.: *pustaka, vajra*.

Lit.: BBh. 336.

dharmapāla "guardian of the Law"; (Buddh.; Tib. n.: *chos-skyoṅ*). Esp. in Lamaism n. given to tutelary deities of terrible appearance, representing the *krodha*-aspect, but with royal ornaments and garments (*dharmapālābharaṇa*), and derived from the Mahāyāna *vidyārājas*. To these *dh.* belong the following 8 gods: Beg-tse, Brahmā (or Sitabrahmā), Hayagrīva, Kubera, Mahākāla, Śrīdevī, Yama, Yamāntaka. Common char.: attr.: *kapāla, karttṛkā, nāga, paraśu*.

Lit.: G passim; GBM 80; HAHI pl. 16A; IC 2:591.

dharmapālābharaṇa "garments of a *dharmapāla*" (attr.; Buddh.), n. of the royal ornaments and garments worn by the terrible manifestations of some deities. They have a terrific appearance. Char. of *dharmapālas*, and e.g., *Kurukullā*.

Lit.: G 39.

Dharmapratisamvit ("nature-analysis"; Buddh.), n. of a *pratisamvit*. Char.: colour: whitish red; attr.: *pāśa, vajrāṅkuśa*.

Lit.: BBh. 342.

Dharmarāja ("Law-king").

1. (Hind.) Epithet of Yama as the judge of the dead. Also epithet of Yudhiṣṭhira.

Lit.: DilP 257; KiH 10.

2. (Buddh.) See Sroṅ-btsan-sgam-po.

Lit.: G 107.

dharmaśaṅkha "Law-conch" (attr.; Buddh.), a term used to emphasize the meaning of the *śaṅkha** as a Buddhist attr.
Lit.: SM 150.

Dharmaśaṅkhasamādhi-Mañjuśrī ("M. with Law-conch [and] meditation (handpose?)"; Buddh.), in Lamaism n. of a form of Mañjuśrī. Char.: colour: white; Mu.: *dhyānamudrā*. – Another n.: Vāc.
Lit.: G 68.

dharmaśarīra "Law-relic" (attr.), n. of small sacred texts which are attached to other relics.
Lit.: IC 2:322.

dharmastambha "Pillar of Righteousness and Cosmic Law and Order" (KrA; Buddh.).
Lit.: KrA 198.

Dharmatala ("Law-base"; Buddh.), NP of a (historically known) teacher of Hīnayāna Buddhism. Char.: Vāh.: *śārdūla*; attr.: *chattra*, *dhūpadāna*.
Lit.: G 104.

Dharmavajra ("Law-*vajra*"; Buddh.), in Lamaism n. of a variety of Vajradhara. Char.: attr.: *ghaṇṭā*, *viśvavajra*.
Lit.: G 50.

Dharmavaśitā ("Law-control"; Buddh.), n. of a *vaśitā*. Char.: colour: white; attr.: *kamaṇḍalu* on a red *padma*.
Lit.: BBh. 332.

dharmin ("one who has done good acts"), n. of a kind of attendant of gods.
Lit.: R 2:526.

Dhartī Mātā (Hi., or Dhartri Mai, N.Ind., cp. Gondī: Darti Awwal; "Mother Earth"), n. of a later deity corresponding to Pṛthivī or Bhūmidevī. She is often said to be the wife of Ṭhākur Deo.
Lit.: FHRI 260, 267; MG 247; P 541.

Dhātar (or -tṛ, -tā, -trī; "creator, supporter"), n. of an Āditya. Attr.: *kamaṇḍalu*, 2 *padmas*, *padmamālā*.
Lit.: B 550; R 1:309; WM 63.

dhātrī "the tree Emblic Myrobalan", see *āmalaka*.
Lit.: IC 1:537; MW 514.

Dhātrī-Sūrya, n. of a syncretistic representation of Dhātrī (Dhātar) and Sūrya.
Lit.: B 550 a.pl. 47:3.

dhattūra (*dhatūra*, *dātura*) "thornapple, Datura alba" (attr.), n. of a flower of the white thorn-apple, usually worn at one side of the head. Char. of Śiva in different forms, as: Candraśekhara-, *dakṣiṇā*-, Gajāsura-saṅhāra-, Kaṅkāla-mūrti and Naṭarāja. – Other n.: *durdhura*, *dhurdhura*.
Lit.: MW 508; P 540; R passim; SB 58.

dhātu "relics", cp. *dantadhātu*, *dhātugarbha*. It has also the meaning of "world, element".

dhātugarbha (also *dhātukaraṇḍaka*) "receptacle for ashes or relics" of a bell-shaped type (attr.). See further *dāgaba*.
Lit.: Gz 93; JMS 11; MW 513.

dhavalaśaṅkha "white shell" (attr.), n. of a horn, made of a shell (usually the Turbinella rapa, but also, e.g., the Charonia Tritonis; cp *śaṅkha* 2) fitted with a mouth-piece, and capable of producing several tones.

dhenu "cow", see *gaus*.

Dhenuka (this n. is in some way connected with *dhenu* "cow"), NP of a demon, who had the shape of an ass. Dh. was killed by Balarāma.
Lit.: DHP 179.

dhenumudrā "cow-gesture" (Mu.), n. of one among the *pañcamudrā*. Form: the fingers are put together in such a way as to imitate the udder of a cow. Cp. *surabhimudrā*.
Lit.: DiIP 105; IC 1:569.

ḍholaka, n. of a kind of drum, similar to the *mṛdaṅga*. It has not the shape of an hour-glass (as said in WM).
Lit.: SMII 72; WM 49 a.passim.

dhotī (Hi., prob. < Skt *adho* + *vastra* + *ikā*) "cloth worn round the waist, passing between the legs and tucked in behind" (attr.). Char. of both men and women. It also forms part of the traditional garb of the Jains. Cp. *caṇḍātaka*, *jaṅghikā*, *kaccha*.
Lit.: B 293; HIS 40 a.pl. 5; P 550; SchRI 235; WHW 1:305.

Dhṛtarāṣṭra (Pāli: Dhattaraṭṭha; "whose empire is firm").
1. NP of a king in the epic Mahābhārata.
Lit.: D 91; Gt 172; MW 519.
2. (Buddh.) NP of a *dikpāla* of the easterly direction. He is regarded as the king of *gandharvas*. Char.: colour: white; attr.: *vīṇā*.
Lit.: B 521; G 18, 37, 92; KiSB 25; ZA 329.

Dhṛti ("firmness"; Jain.), NP of a goddess.
Lit.: GJ 363.

dhruva(bera) "fixed idol", n. of an immovable image (not used in processions). According to the worship dedicated to it, the *dh.* is divided into four kinds: *yoga*, *bhoga*, *vīra* and *abhicārika*; in addition, according to the number of the inferior deities who occur together with the main god, these species are divided into *uttama-*, *madhyama-* and *adhama*-forms. The n. *dhruvabera* is esp. used of the earliest type of Viṣṇu images. – Other n.: *dhruvamūrti*, *mūlamūrti*, *mūlavigraha*.
Lit.: B passim; R 1:17, 79; WM 87; ZA 111.

Dhruva ("immovable"), n. of the (present) pole-star. As a personification Dh. is regarded as the son of Uttānapāda (= the star β in the constellation Ursa Minor; this star was the pole-star in the last millenium B.C.) and (with the n. Dhruva-Nārāyaṇa) as a form or *avatāra* of Viṣṇu. Dh. is also one of the *vasus*. Attr.: *akṣamālā*, *cakra*, *kamaṇḍalu*, *śakti*.
Lit.: DHP 186; Gt 173; G. Liebert, Orientalia Suecana 17 (1968), 155; R 2:553; WHW 1:275; WM 63, 190.

dhruvā, n. of the largest of the three sacrificial ladles; see *sruk*.
Lit.: MW 521; RV 82.

dhruvamūrti, see *dhruvabera*.

dhūmaketu "smoke-banner" (attr.). Char. of Agni.
Lit.: R 2:524.

Dhūmāvatī ("smoky"), n. of a personification, belonging to the group *mahāvidyā*, represented by Dāruṇarātrī.
Lit.: DHP 282.

Dhūmorṇā (Or Dhūmrorṇā, "smoke-wool"), NP of the wife of Yama. Attr.: *dāḍima*.
Lit.: R 2:526.

dhūmra "grey, smoke-coloured, purple, dark-red", a colour.
Lit.: MEIA 238.

Dhūmrāvatī (or Dhūmra-Kālī, "the grey K."), n. of a terrible goddess. Attr.: *dantas*, *kapāla*, *khaḍga*, *muṇḍamālā*.
Lit.: SSI 213.

dhūpa "incense, perfume" (attr.). Char. of Dhūpatārā. *dh.* also forms part of the *pūjā*, cp. *dhūpadīpa*. See also *dhūpadāna*.
Lit.: BBh. 435; JDI 15.

Dhūpā ("incense", personification; Buddh.), n. of one of the Lamaist *aṣṭamātaras*. Char.: colour: yellow; attr.: *dhūpadāna*.
Lit.: BBh. 331; G 36, 82.

dhūpadāna (Hi.: *dhūpdān[ī]*) "incense-pot, censer, box for keeping incense" (attr.). Char. of: Aṅgaja, Dharmatala, Dhūpā. Another n.: *dhūpapātra*.
Lit.: BhIM 35; GH 345; GJ 427; HSIT 19 a.pl. 50; IC 1:570; KiH pl. 137:7, 139:5, 140:1; MH 37 a.pl. 7:1, 23; P 550.

dhūpadīpa (Hi.: *dhūpdīp*) "(offering of) incense and light (to an image)". This act forms part of the *pūjā*.
Lit.: DiIP 90; P 550.

dhūpapātra, see *dhūpadāna*.

dhūpapūjā "incense-worship, worship of an image, consisting of the burning of incense". See *pūjā*.
Lit.: GJ 396, 429

Dhūpatārā ("incense-Tārā"; Buddh.), NP of a minor Mahāyāna goddess. Char.: colour: black; attr.: *dhūpa*.
Lit.: BBh. 241; KiSB 102

dhurdhura, see *dhattūra*.

Dhūrjaṭi ("loaded with matted hair"), epithet of Śiva. It is also n. of a manifestation of Śiva in which his body is smeared with ashes.
Lit.: DHP 202; IC 1:513; R 2:47.

dhvaja "banner, flag, standard, pole, votive column" (attr., all Indian religions). Both as a flag and as a pole it bears the image of the Vāh. of the god. – Its significance is obscure. Generally, *dh.* is the same as *patākā*, but a small difference may on occasion be proved, as e.g., when it is said about Ḍombī that she wears *mahādhvajapatākā*, translated as "the high flag and banner" (BBh.). – In Buddhism *dh.* is often the "standard (victorious) banner erected on summit of Mt. Meru, center of Buddhist universe" (G). – *dh.* is char. of: Beg-tse, Caṇḍā, Cundā, Ḍombī, Hayagrīva, Kāma, Kanakabhāradvāja, Kaumārī, Kubera, *lalāṭatilaka*, Mahākāla, Mahāmantrānusāriṇī, Mahāmāyūrī, Mahāpaṭala-Lokeśvara, Mahāpratisarā, Mahāśītavatī, Mahāviśvaśuddha-Lokeśvara, Mahiṣāsuramardinī, *navadurgās*, Rāhu, Ratnaḍākinī, Ratnolkā, Śarabha, Śiva, Skanda (in different forms; his banner is named: *vaijayantī patākā*), Śukra, Sūrya, Vaiṣravaṇa, Vajrajvālānalārka, Vajravidāraṇī, Vāyu, Vidyujjvālākarālī, Viṣṇu, Viśvarūpa. – *dh.* is the weapon of the north-west direction; it is also a *maṅgala*, see *aṣṭamaṅgala*. – Other n.: *ketu*, *patākā*; cp. *pālidhvaja*.

Lit.: ACA 83; B 103; BBh. 312; DHP 160, 219; G 8, 14; GJ 432; GoRI 1:338; MEIA 244; WHW 1:360.

Dhvaja-Gaṇapati, n. of a form of Gaṇeśa, 4-armed. Attr.: *akṣamālā*, *daṇḍa*, *kamaṇḍalu*, *pustaka*.

Lit.: R 1:58.

Dhvajāgrakeyūra ("ring on the top of a standard"; personification; Buddh.), n. of a Mahāyāna goddess, an emanation of Akṣobhya. She is met with in a blue (black) and a yellow form. Char.: att.: *ālīḍhāsana*; Vāh.: *sūryāsana*; attr.: *ajina* (tigerskin), *Akṣobhyabimba* on the crown, *cakra*, *caturmukha*, *khaḍga*, *khaṭvāṅga*, *musala*, *(tarjanī)pāśa*, *trinayana*, *triśiras*, *triśūla*, *tundila*, *vajra*.

Lit.: BBh. 201 a.pl. 147; KiDG 64, 70 a.pl. 56-57; KiSB 93; MW 522.

dhvajāropaṇa "pole-planting", n. of a rite of great antiquity, performed in the month *caitra* (March-April). In this rite a pole, a tall slender tree, was decorated with garlands of leaves, flowers and flags.

Lit.: WHW 2:222.

dhvajastambha "flagstaff", made of stone, wood or metal, planted upon a platform in a temple (attr.).

Lit.: GJ 400; SSI 3; ZA 288.

Dhvajoṣṇīṣa ("Uṣṇīṣa of the *dhvaja*"; Buddh.), n. of an *uṣṇīṣa*-deity. Char.: direction: south-west; colour: reddish blue; attr.: *cintāmaṇidhvaja*.

Lit.: BBh. 301.

dhyāna "meditation".

dhyānabuddha, see *dhyānibuddha*.

Lit.: RAAI 272.

dhyāna(hasta)mudrā (or *dhyāni-*) "meditation handpose" (Mu.), n. of a gesture of a person in a sitting attitude having, usually, both hands lying in his lap, right hand on left hand, with palms up and all fingers extended; *dh.* may also indicate one hand lying in the lap in this way, the other hand being, at the same time, in e.g. *bhūmisparśamudrā*. This Mu. which is esp. frequent in Buddhism and Jainism and which symbolizes "the complete absorption of thought by intense contemplation of a single object of meditation" (SM) is above all char. not only of the Buddha, Amitābha and Amitāyus, but also of most of the *buddhas*, *bodhisattvas* and *tīrthaṅkaras* of all kinds. – Other n.: *padmāsana-*, *yoga-*, *samādhi-mudrā*. – Cp. *jñānamudrā*.

Lit.: B 252; BBh. 435; G 20 (ill.); GBM 97; GoRI 1:338; H pl. 4:38a; HIS 43; KIM pl. 33-34; MH 7; R 1:17 a.pl. 5:17; RAAI 272; SM 85; Th. 30; WM 100 a.fig. 20.

Dhyānapāramitā ("perfection of meditation"; Buddh.), n. of a *pāramitā*. Char.: colour: sky-dark; attr.: *cintāmaṇidhvaja*, *padma* (white).

Lit.: BBh. 326.

dhyānāsana "meditation sitting" (att.), n. of an *āsana*-posture. This n. is used of different kinds of sitting: in KiDG, KiSB and SIB it is said to be equivalent to *vajraparyaṅkāsana*, *vajrāsana* and *paryaṅkāsana*; in G

it is used of the *āsana* which, in this dictionary, is named *padmāsana*. Probably this use of the term is due to the fact that the last-named *āsana* is connected with *dhyānamudrā*. Cp. also *yogamudrāsana*.
Lit.: BBh. 435; G 24; KiDG 49; KiSB 53; SIB 68.

dhyānaśloka "contemplative hymn intended to help the devotee mentally picture the iconography of the deity".
Lit.: SIB 70.

dhyānibodhisattva "meditation-*bodhisattva*" (Buddh.), n. of a spiritual *bodhisattva* who is an emanation of a *dhyānibuddha*. Usually no distinction is made between the terms *dh.* and *bodhisattva*. In Mahāyāna Buddhism five *dh.* are generally named: Samantabhadra, Vajrapāṇi, Ratnapāṇi, Padmapāṇi (= Avalokiteśvara) and Viśvapāṇi, who have created the perishable universe. We now live in Avalokiteśvara's period the saviour of which is the historic Buddha. – In Lamaism there is, besides this series, one more series with eight or ten *dh.*, which contains: Samantabhadra, Vajrapāṇi, Avalokiteśvara, Mañjuśrī, Maitreya (regarded also, even in Lamaism, as a *mānuṣibuddha*), Ākāśagarbha, Kṣitigarbha, Sarvanivaraṇaviṣkambhin, Mahāsthāmaprāpta and Trailokyavijaya. – The *dh.* usually wear *bodhisattvābharaṇa* and have on the head or crown an image (*bimba*) of the *dhyānibuddha* from whom the *dh.* in question has emanated. – See also *trikāya*.
Lit.: G 30, 59; GBB 248; GBM 86; HAHI 12 a.pl. 5A, 6A; KiSB 45; KT 137.

dhyānibuddha (also *dhyāna-*) "meditation-*buddha*" (Buddh.).

1. Term for a spiritual *buddha* who is an emanation of the Ādibuddha. According to GBM *dh.* is an incorrect name, which is not met with in the original Buddhist literature, the correct term being *tathāgata*; however, the n. *dh.* has won a place in scientific literature and is much more commonly used than *tathāgata*. A *dh.* is, according to the *trikāya*-system, the mystic spiritual counterpart of a human *buddha*. Usually a series of five *dh.* (who are introduced into Vajrayāna Buddhism as embodiments of the five *skandha*s or cosmic elements) is named, consisting of: Vairocana, Akṣobhya, Ratnasambhava, Amitābha, Amoghasiddhi; sometimes a sixth *dh.* is added: Vajrasattva (but this one is also associated with Ādibuddha). – Between the *dh*s distinction is made considering colours, directions, *mudrās* and attributes, but it is not always possible to identify a particular *dh.* Common features are the attr.: *kāṣāya*, *ūrṇā*, *uṣṇīṣa* and absence of ornaments; but sometimes a *dh.* may wear *bodhisattvābharaṇa* with a crown, and he is then said to be "a crowned *buddha*" (*mukuṭadhārin*); he is seated on a full blown *padma*. - In Lamaism a *dh.* may also be represented in the *yab-yum*-att., then belonging to the *yi-dam*-group; in this form he generally has as attr.: *ghaṇṭā* and *vajra* or *vajraghaṇṭā*.
As symbols of the five *dh.* as a group are used: a *vajra* vertically placed in a *padma*, and *tathāgatamaṇḍala*.
Lit.: BBh. 11, 32, 42; CEBI 43, 45 a.fig. G, H: G 30, 36, 51; GBB 248 a.pl. 31; GBM 79, 82, 86; HAHI 12; HuET 47; IC 2:588; KiDG 40; KiSB 43; KT 137; R 1:219 a.pl. 68.

2. *dhyānibuddhabimba* (attr.). The *(dhyāni)-bodhisattva*s usually bear an image (*bimba*) on the head or crown of the *dh.* from whom the said *dhyānibodhisattva* has emanated. This image is often said to be either Ādibuddha or Amitābha. Concerning those who bear such images, see sub the respective *dhyānibuddha*s. There are however also images of this kind, referring to the group of five *dh.* and signifying the god in question as an emanation of all these *dh.* Such images are char. of: Mahākāla, Māyājālakrama-Kurukullā, Prajñāpāramitā, Vajradharma-Lokeśvara, Vajratārā.

(dhyāni)buddhaśakti "Śakti of a *dhyānibuddha*" (Buddh.), n. of a series of female deities

who are regarded as the Śaktis of the *(dhyāni)buddhas*. These are closely associated with the *vidyārājñīs* and *mahārakṣās*. Five *dh.* are generally mentioned: Vajradhātvīśvarī, Buddhalocanā (or Locanā), Māmakī, Pāṇḍarā, Tārā. Common char.: att.: *lalitāsana*; attr.: *kapāla, karttṛkā*.
Lit.: G 34, 77.

Didi Thakrun (N. Ind.), NP of a cholera goddess worshipped at Bardvan (! thus GH).
Lit.: GH 135.

digadhīśa "lord of direction", see *dikpāla*.

digambara "clothed in the sky, clad in space, naked, mit den Himmelsgegenden bekleidet", i.e. "naked" (attr.; Jain.), n. of an adherent of a certain sect within Jainism. Nowadays, however, the *d.* do not go naked, but wear coloured garments. – Cp. *nagna*.
Lit.: GJ passim; Gt 176; HIS 17; IC 2:632; KiSH 119; KT 114; WHW 1:494; Za 56.

Digambarā ("clothed in the sky, naked").
1. (Hind.) Epithet of Kālī.
Lit.: DHP 273.
2. (Buddh.) In Lamaism NP of the Śakti of Yogāmbara. Char.: Mu.: *dhyānamudrā*; attr.: *pātra*.
Lit.: G 50.

diggaja "elephant of a quarter of the sky", n. given to an elephant accompanying a *dikpāla*. There are eight *d.*, their n. being: Airāvata, Puṇḍarīka, Vāmana, Kumuda, Añjana, Puṣpadanta, Sārvabhauma, Supratīka. Images of these *d.* are placed in temples, and are often accompanied by female elephants. – Other n.: *diṅnāga, lokapāla*.
Lit.: D 180; GoRI 1:316; ZA 160 a.pl. 241.

dignātha "lord of direction", see *dikpāla*.
Lit.: WM 131.

dikkumāra "youth or prince of direction" (Jain.), n. of a kind of *bhavanavāsīs*.
Lit.: GJ 236; MW 479.

dikpāla(ka) "regent or guardian of a quarter of the sky, regent of (a) direction", n. of a tutelary deity who protects the world against the demons. In shrines the *d.* is placed facing a certain direction.

1. (Hind., Jain.) The number of *d.* is usually said to be eight (*aṣṭadikpālas*): Kubera (north), Īśāna (or Candra, Soma, Pṛthivī; north-east), Indra (east), Agni (south-east), Yama (or Dharma; south), Nirṛti (or Sūrya; south-west), Varuṇa (west), Vāyu (or Marut; north-west). Sometimes two more are added (bringing the number up to ten): Brahmā (zenith) and Ananta (nadir). The chief of the *d.* is Nirṛta or Indra. Occasionally also the number of *d.* is said to be four or sixteen. – Each *d.* is accompanied by an elephant (*diggaja*) or by two elephants (counting the *diggajas*' mates). – Other n.: *digadhīśa, lokapāla*.
Lit.: B 519; CBC 8 a.pl. 23; DHP 131; GH 114; GJ 363; GoRI 1:227; HIS 17, 25; IC 1:492; JDI 106; MEIA 124; R 2:515; SSI 241; Th. 109; WHW 1:282.

2. (Buddh.) The number of *d.* is usually said to be four: Dhṛtarāṣṭra (east), Virūḍhaka (south), Virūpākṣa (west), Vaiśravaṇa (north). This group is also known as the *caturmahārājas*. The eight Hindu *d.* are also found in Buddhism. Another list of ten *d.* is as follows: Yamāntaka, Prajñāntaka, Padmāntaka, Vighnāntaka, Ṭakkirāja, Nīladaṇḍa, Mahābala, Acala, Uṣṇīṣa, Sumbharāja. This series consists of only three-headed gods; cp. also *uṣṇīṣa* 3. In later Buddhism the number of 14 *d.* is also given (MW). There is further a list of six female *d.*: Vajrāṅkuśī, Vajrapāśī, Vajrasphoṭā, Vajraghaṇṭā, Uṣṇīṣavijayā, Sumbhā (these six goddesses are one-faced), sometimes with the addition of: Puṣpā, Dhūpā, Dīpā, Gandhā. – Other n.: *lokapāla, mahārāja, dignātha, dikpati*; cp. also *sataravaram deviyo*.
Lit.: B 521; BBh. 251, 352; CBC 8, 23; G 37, 92; WM 131.

dikpati "lord of direction", see *dikpāla* 2.
Lit.: GOSA 13.

dīkṣā (Tam. *tīṭcai*) "initiation", n. of a Tantric rite; also, esp., the initiation of disciples (by a *guru*) into the mysteries of the Śaivite religion.
Lit.: IC 1:597; RV 76; TL 4:1937; WHW 1:485.

Dīkṣā ("initiation"), as a personification n. of the wife of Ugra and the mother of Santāna.
Lit.: DHP 206; GJ 422; GoRI 2:37, 47.

Ḍimbha ("child, infant"; Buddh.), another n. of Ucchuṣma-Jambhala.
Lit.: BBh. 179.

diṅnāga "elephant of direction", see *diggaja*.
Lit.: IC 1:492.

dīpa (also *dīpak*, Hi.; Tam. *tipam*) "light, lamp, oil-lamp" (attr.). As an attr. *d.* is esp. char. of: Lakṣmī (the Genius of lamps), Dīpā, Ketu, Trikaṇṭakīdevī (2 *d.*). As cult objects *dīpa*s are made in many forms and with provision for different numbers of wicks. Here may be mentioned: *d.* for one wick, held in the hands by Lakṣmī, see *dīpalakṣmī*; the round *d.* (niche-lamp) with a back-piece like a *prabhāvalī* and figures in relief of Lakṣmī (in particular Gajalakṣmī); the *d.* with many wicks (often five) in the form of a (separate) plate carried in the hands by a *gopī*, see *dīpagopī*; see also *ārātrika*, *ārtī*, *dīpastambha*, *dīpavṛkṣa*, *duvatti*, *haṅsadīpa*, *maṅgaladīpa*, *māviḷakku*, *mayūr dīpak*, *merudīpa*, *nakṣatradīpa*, *pañcavartī*, *taṭṭutīpam*. In Tamil lamp-ritual oblong lamps with double stands are used, upon which, behind the lamp bowl within a *prabhātoraṇa*, figures of different kinds are reproduced; according to the nature of these, the lamps are named horse-, elephant-, ram-, bull-, swan-, or trident-lamp. There is also an anthropomorphic lamp; this shows a *riṣi*, represented as a human figure with a buck's hind-quarters and a tail. – Lamps, with five wicks or stands for five lamps, are used in particular in the *śivapūjā* because the number of "5" is sacred to Śiva. – The custom of lighting lamps, dispelling the darkness, serves also the purpose of protection against evil spirits. – *d.* is also a *maṅgala*, see *aṣṭamaṅgala*. – Another n.: *viḷakku*.
Lit.: BBh. 435; MEIA 241; MH pl. 7; MSHP 48; SSI fig. 5.

Dīpā (personification of the lamp; Buddh.), n. of a light goddess who in Lamaism belongs among the *aṣṭamātaras*. Char.: colour: blue or red; attr.: *dīpa*.
Lit.: BBh. 318 a.pl. 213; G 36, 82.

dīpagopī "lamp-shepherdess" (attr.), n. of a lamp-stand with the form of a standing *gopī* having the hands streched out; in these she carries a separate plate with provision for many (often five or seven) wicks (*ārātrika*). This plate is fastened to the hands with plugs. – A *d.* is usually made of bronze and is often provided with a handle, by means of which it can be moved (swung) around the head of an icon.
Lit.: GH 483 a.pl. 33; SIB pl. 27.

dīpalakṣmī (attr.), n. of a lamp consisting of a tray for one wick, carried in the hands by Lakṣmī, the Genius of lamps (standing). Char.: att.: *samapādasthānaka*; attr.: *śuka* (on one shoulder of Lakṣmī). – This *d.* is cast in bronze in one piece. A *d.* is often placed in shrines as a votive gift. – Cp. *kāmāṭci-viḷakku*.
Lit.: FK pl. 118; KrA pl. 154; MH 37 a.pl. 6, 7:4-6; SB 336 a.fig. 274.

dīpālī(kotsava) "lamp festival", see *dīvālī*.

Dīpaṅkara ("light-causer"; Buddh.), in Lamaism n. of a *buddha* in a particular series of *buddha*s (see sub *mānuṣibuddha*). Char.: colour: yellow; att.: *padmāsana*, also *sthānaka*; Mu.: *abhaya-*, *dharmacakra-mudrā*; no particular attr.
Lit.: G 20, 32, 54.

dīpapūjā "lamp-worship" (Jain.), n. of a ceremony in which a lamp or lamps are swung-about before an image. – See *pūjā*.
Lit.: GJ 396.

dīpastambha "lamp-stand" (attr.), n. of a lamp-stand with many lamp bowls or with one or more plates for many wicks.
Lit.: KiH pl. 138.

Dīpa-Tārā ("lamp-Tārā"; Buddh.), n. of a minor Mahāyāna goddess. Char.: colour: yellow; attr.: *dīpayaṣṭi*.
Lit.: BBh. 241; KiSB 102.

dīpāvalī "lamp festival", see *dīvālī*.

dīpavṛkṣa "lamp-tree" (attr.), n. of a stand (resembling a tree) for lamps or plates for many wicks; a kind of multiple candlestick.
Lit.: P 555.

dīpayaṣṭi "torch" (attr.). Char. of Dīpa-Tārā.
Lit.: BBh. 241.

dīp-dān (Hi.) "giving of a lamp", the offering of a lamp to an image; also n. of a ceremony observed for ten days after the decease of a relative.
Lit.: P 555.

Dīpti ("brightness, light"), NP of a goddess.
Lit.: R 1:368.

Dīrghadevī ("long goddess"), NP of a wife of Nirṛti.
Lit.: JDI 108.

diś "quarter of the sky, direction", see sub *dikpāla.* As to *d.* as a symbolic n. of the number "10", see *saṅkhyā.*

Diśā ("the ten-directions-of space", personification), NP of a goddess who is the wife of Śiva Bhīma and the mother of Sarga.
Lit.: DHP 205.

Diti ("boundness"), n. of a goddess (corresponding to Aditi), daughter of Dakṣa and one of the wives of Kāśyapa and by him the mother of a demon race (*daitya*; cp. also *asura*) and of the *maruts*. Attr.: *bāla, nīlotpala, phala.*
Lit.: D 93; Gt 181; IIM 96; R 1:369; WHW 1:283; WM 63.

dīvālī (or *divālī, dīwālī*; Hi., < Skt *dīpa* + *ālikā* "row of lamps"), n. of a light-festival which is chiefly dedicated to Lakṣmī (Divālī-Mātā), the Genius of lamps (according to P: to Kārttikeya, i.e. Skanda; in the eastern part of India, esp. Bengal, this festival is dedicated to Kālī and is celebrated as *kālīpūjā*; in South India it celebrates the victory of Viṣṇu as Vāmana over the *daitya* king Bali). *d.* is a new moon festival, occurring in the month *kārttika* (October-November). Lakṣmī is worshipped at night with an illumination by rows of lamps (*dīpā*); the lights are interpreted as leading the spirits of the deceased to heaven or to Yama's hell (DiCh.). – Other n.: *dīpālikotsava, dīpāvalī, tīpāvaḷi.*
Lit.: DiCh. 62; EGI 210; GH 355; GJ 435; Gt 180; IC 1:591; KBh. 191; P 531; H. Rydh, Indisk ökenby (Stockholm 1956) 116; WHW 1:352.

Divālī-Mātā ("mother of the *divālī*"), epithet of Lakṣmī as patroness of the *divālī*-festival.
Lit.: KBh. 190.

divyakumārī "celestial maiden" (Buddh.).
Lit.: KiSB 99.

divyamaṇḍapa "divine hall", a temple hall supported by between 108 and 1008 pillars.
Lit.: BECA 1:260.

Divyarātri ("the Divine-Night"), n. of an aspect of *mahāvidyā* representing Ṣoḍaśī.
Lit.: DHP 278.

dolahastamudrā "swinging-arm-gesture" (Mu.), see *gajahastamudrā.*
Lit.: B 472; R 2:228.

dolāyātrā (or *dolay-*) "swing-festival, -procession", n. of a festival in honour of Kṛṣṇa, see *holī.*
Lit.: GH 354; IC 1:590; KBh. 144; WHW 1:354, 2:470.

Dolma (Tib., written sGrol-ma), see Tārā.

Ḍombī (Buddh.), n. of a goddess of the *gaurī*-group. Char.: colour: mixed; attr.: *dhvaja.*
Lit.: BBh. 312 a.pl. 205.

rDo-rje (Tib., pronounced *dorje*; attr.; Buddh.), the Tibetan n. for *vajra. D.* is also n. of a smaller ritual dagger with a *vajra*-handle. Cp. *phur-bu.*
Lit.: GBM 21; HRT pl. 8-9; JT 287.

DRĀṀ, a *bīja* symbolizing Candra.
Lit.: IC 1:567.

Draupadī (patronymic: "daughter of Drupada"), the usual n. (the proper n. being Kṛṣṇā) of the common wife of the five Pāṇḍu-princes (Yudhiṣṭhira etc.) in the epic Mahābhārata. She is regarded as the spiritual daughter (or *avatāra*) of Indrāṇī.
Lit.: DiIP 257; SSI 227; WHW 1:298; ZA pl. 111; ZM 71 a.pl. 3.

drāviḍa (lit. "Dravidian", n. of the people in South India; also n. of a certain style of arts) in architecture n. of an octagonal temple.
Lit.: DKI 41; WHW 1:58.

drāviḍaliṅga ("Dravidian *liṅga*"), n. of a kind of *mānuṣaliṅga*.
Lit.: R 2:92.

(droṇa)kāka "raven", Vāh. of Śani.

dukūla, n. of very fine cloth worn by women (attr.). Char. of the female side of Ardhanārīśvara.
Lit.: HSIT 13; SB 63; SSI 120.

Dulhā Deo (or Dev, Hi.; *dulhā* means "bridegroom"), n. of the god of the bridegroom. Attr.: *paraśu* (hanging from a tree).
Lit.: MG 272.

DUṀ, a *bīja* symbolizing Durgā.
Lit.: DHP 343; IC 1:567.

duminda (Pāli, < Skt *drumendra*) "prince of trees", see *bodhivṛkṣa*.
Lit.: CEBI 39.

Dūraṅgama ("going far away"; Buddh.), n. of a *bhūmi*. Char.: colour: green; attr.: *viśvavajra* on a *mahāmbuja*.
Lit.: BBh. 335.

durdhura, see *dhattūra*.

Durga ("impassable"), n. of an *asura* supposed to have been conquered by Durgā, from which event she is said to have received her name.
Lit.: IIM 93.

Durgā(devī) (Tam. Turkkai; the n. is translated by "difficult of access, impassable, unattainable", referring to D. as the daughter of a mountain god, cp. Pārvatī; but it is also interpreted as "the Unassailable, Unconquerable One"), n. of a terrific (sometimes mentioned as a half-terrific) aspect of the Śakti of Śiva. She is, however, also worshipped as an unmarried maid (Kumārī). D. is generally represented as a beautiful woman and is met with in many manifestations (see the epithets and varieties below; the best-known of them is Mahiṣāsuramardinī). Besides Pārvatī, Ambikā and Kālī she forms the central personality of the *śākta*-cult. It should be noted that D. like Kālī, but unlike to Pārvatī, takes up an independent position towards Śiva. D. is also counted among the group *navaśakti*.
Char.: Vāh.: *siṁha, śārdūla, yāḷi* or *padmapīṭha*; she is also surrounded by several *gṛdhras*; attr.: *ajina, asthi, cakra, churikā, daśabhuja, dhanus* Ajagava, *gadā, ghaṇṭā, javā, khaḍga, khaṭvāṅga, kheṭaka, muṇḍamālā, pāśa, śakti, śaṅkha, śara, śavamālā, śrīphala, śuka, triśūla, vajra*. – According to an Indian text (see R 1:202) D. may be found standing between Kṛṣṇa and Balarāma (it may be questioned whether this goddess is not rather Subhadrā, cp. Jagannātha). – D. is further represented by the *bījamantra DUṀ*.
Epithets and varieties: Agni-Durgā, Aparājitā, Balavikarṇikā, Bhadrakālī, Bhairavī, Bhowāni, Brahmacāriṇī, Cāmuṇḍā or -ī, Caṇḍā or -ī, Caṇḍakhaṇḍā, Chinnamastakā, Daśabhujā, Harasiddhi, Jagaddhātrī, Jaya-Durgā, Jayantī, Kālarātrī, Kālikā, Kāmākṣī, Kātyāyanī, Kṣamā, Kṣemaṅkarī, Kumārī, Kuṣmaṇḍī (or other name-forms), Mahā-Gaurī, Mahāmārī, Mahiṣāsuramardinī, Māyā, Mīnākṣī, Muktakeśī, Mūla-Durgā, Nīlakaṇṭhī, Niśumbhasūdanī, Ripumārī-Durgā, Rudrāṇī, Rudrāṅśa-Durgā, Śailaputrī, Śāradā(devī), Sarvabhūtadamanī, Siddha-Cāmuṇḍā, Siddha-Yogeśvarī, Siddhidāyinī, Siṅharathī, Siṅhavāhanī, Śivadūtī, Skandamātā, Ṣoḍaśabhujā-Durgā, Tārā, Vāmā, Vana-Durgā, Vindhyavāsi-Durgā; see also Kālarātrī, *sṛgāla*.
Lit.: B 491; GBB 129; GH 142 a.pl. 16; GoRI 1:258; Gt 192; IC 1:522, 567; KiSH 48; MG 182; R 1:202, 341 a.pl. 99; SB 325 a.fig. 254; SSI 196; Th. 106; WHW 1:509; WM 63; ZA 90.

durgāmahotsava "the great festival in honour of Durgā" or *durgāpūjā* "worship of Durgā", n. of a festival in the month *aśvina* (September-October).
Lit.: Gt 160; IC 1:591.

Durgatipariśodhana ("purification by misfortune"; Buddh.), epithet or n. of a form of the Buddha. Char.: colour: yellow; Mu.: *dharmacakramudrā*.
Lit.: BBh. 78.

Durgottāriṇī-Tārā ("T. surpassing [or rescuing?] Durgā"; Buddh.), n. of a Tārā of

green colour. Mu.: *varadamudrā*; attr.: *aṅkuśa, padma, pāśa*.
Lit.: BBh. 307.

Duritāri ("enemy of sin"; Jain.), n. of a *śāsanadevatā* attending on the third *tīrthaṅkara*.
Lit.: GJ 362; MW 485.

Durjayā ("unconquerable"; Budd.), n. of a minor Mahāyāna goddess attending on Buddhakapāla.
Lit.: BBh. 160.

dūrvā "bent grass, panic grass" (attr.), cp. *caṇḍa, darbha, kuśa*.
Lit.: MW 490; WHW 1:406.

dussehrā, see *dasahrā*.

dūta "messenger", n. of an attendant of a god, a minor male deity, e.g. Śivadūta.

dūtī "female messenger", n. of a female attendant of a god (goddess).

duvatti (so MSHP; to be interpreted as N. Ind. **duvartī*? cp. *pañcavartī*), n. of a lamp (*dīpa*) with a handle.
Lit.: MSHP 48.

dvāra "door, temple gateway" (cp. *gopura*). Different kinds of *d.* are *śobha-, śālā-, prāsāda-, harmya-dvāra, mahāgopura*; cp. also *ghanadvāra*.
Lit.: BECA 1:260.

Dvārakā ("many-gated"), n. of a capital founded by Kṛṣṇa.
Lit.: D 101; GoRI 1:240; WM 69.

dvādaśākṣara "consisting of twelve syllables", n. of a kind of *mantra*, e.g., the Vaiṣṇavite *oṁ namo bhagavate Vāsudevāya* "Oṁ, Salutation to the Worshipful Lord Viṣṇu".
Lit.: WHW 2:27.

dvārapāla(ka) "door-keeper".

1. (Hind.) N. of a figure which, because of its power of protecting against thieves etc., is placed next to a door or a gateway in shrines (*dvārapālakarūpa* "door-keeper-figure"). Two such figures are placed on either side of the temple entrance, and at temples of goddesses they may be females. They are not considered as gods. Attr.: *dantas*.
Lit.: BECA 1:261 a.pl. 11; Gz 91; H pl. 8:77; JDI 111; R 1:361, 2:449, 507 a.pl. 130, 158:1; SB 353 a.fig. 344; SSI 251 a.fig. 155-156; SSR facing p. 80; WHW 1:400; ZA 23, 87, 288 a.pl. 140, 250, 262.

2. (Buddh.) In Buddhism there are four female *d.*: Tālikā, Kuñcī, Kapaṭā, Paṭadhāriṇī. Common char.: fearful appearance; att.: *ālīḍhāsana*. According to some accounts (G) they may have animal heads.
Lit.: BBh. 316; G 101.

dvārapūjā "worship of the door".
Lit.: ACA 90; DiIP 114.

dvibhaṅga "twofold bend" (att.), n. of a slightly bent, graceful pose. This att. does not belong among the ordinary bent poses (see *bhaṅga*).
Lit.: B 366.

dvimukha (*dviśiras*) "two-headed" (attr.). Char. of: Agni, Agnijāta-Subrahmaṇya, Śarabha, Yajñamūrti.
Lit.: MG facing p. 33.

dvīpakumāra ("island-prince"; Jain.), n. of a kind of *bhavanavāsī*.
Lit.: GJ 236.

dviśiras "two-headed", see *dvimukha*.

Dyaus(pitā) (-pitar, -pitṛ; "sky father"), n. of the god of the sky, generally regarded as the "father", corresponding to Pṛthivī(mātā) "mother Earth", his wife. These personifications are of Indo-European origin.
Lit.: D 102; DHP 92; GoRI 1:95; Gt 200; MG 25; WHW 1:316; WM 69.

E

ekadaṇḍin (-ī; *ēkataṇṭi*) "carrying a single stick (staff, *daṇḍa*)". This n. seems to be applied to both a Vaiṣṇavite mendicant (WHW; the attr. then probably alluding to the *gadā* of Viṣṇu), and, in South India, to a Śaivite ascetic as opposed to a *tridaṇḍin**. The

prototype of the Śaivite *e.* may be Śiva in his form as Bhikṣāṭanamūrti. See also *daṇḍin*.
Lit.: TL 1:552; WHW 1:437.

Ekadaṅṣṭra or Ekadanta ("one-toothed"), epithets of Gaṇeśa (Gaṇapati), who had lost one of his teeth (or tusks), see also *danta* and cp. *ekaviṣāṇa*.
Lit.: DiIP 113; R 1:39, 60.

ekādaśarudra "the (group of) eleven Rudras" (cp. Rudra). There are several lists of this group, e.g., Mahādeva, Śiva, Śaṅkara, Nīlalohita, Īśāna, Vijaya, Bhīma, Devadeva, Bhavodbhava, Rudra and Kapālīśa; or Aja, Ekapāda, Ahirbudhnya, Virūpākṣa, Revata, Hara, Bahurūpa, Tryambaka, Sureśvara, Jayanta and Aparājita; or Tatpuruṣa, Aghora, Īśāna, Vāmadeva, Sadyojāta, Mṛtyuñjaya, Kiraṇākṣa, Śrīkaṇṭha, Ahirbudhnya, Virūpākṣa, Bahurūpa, and an additional twelfth Tryambaka. They are often represented as having 16 arms. Common char.: *ajina* (tigerskin), *candra*, *paraśu*.
Lit.: R 2:386; SSI 77.

Ekajaṭā ("she who has but one chignon"; Buddh.), NP of a Vajrayāna goddess who removes the obstacles and grants happiness. Sometimes she attends on Khadiravaṇī-Tārā. E. is regarded as a form of Tārā, viz. "the blue Tārā", and is an emanation of Akṣobhya. She is represented as one- or twelve-headed. Char.: colour: blue; att.: *rājalīlāsana* or *ālīḍhāsana*; Vāh.: *mṛtaka*; Mu.: *karaṇamudrā*; attr.: *ajina* (tigerskin), *akṣamālā*, *Akṣobhya-* or *Amitābha-bimba* on the crown, *aṅkuśa*, *bodhisattvābharaṇa*, *daṇḍa*, *dhanus*, *ghaṇṭā*, *kapāla*, *karttṛkā*, *khaḍga*, *muṇḍa*, *muṇḍamālā*, *nīlotpala*, *paraśu*, *pāśa*, *śaṅkha*, *ṣaṇmudrā*, *śara*, *trinayana*, *tundila*, *vajra*. – Varieties: Caturbhujatārā, Mahācīnatārā, Ugratārā, Vidyujjvālākarālī.
Lit.: BBh. 151, 193, 309 a.pl. 138; G passim; KiDG 64; KiSB 89, 98.

Ekānaṅśā ("the single portionless one"), n. of a form of Pārvatī (or Durgā) who is closely associated with the Viṣṇu-Kṛṣṇa-cult. She has 2, 4 or 8 arms. Attr.: *darpaṇa*, *padma*.
Lit.: B 502; MW 136.

ekanayana "one-eyed" (attr.),. Char. of Kubera.
Lit.: DHP 136.

Ekanetra ("one-eyed"), n. of one of the *vidyeśvaras*. Char.: Mu.: *abhaya-*, *varada-mudrā*; attr.: *ṭaṅka*, *triśūla*. – Ekarudra resembles in all respects E.
Lit.: R 2:397, 402.

ekapādāsana "one-foot-posture" (att.), n. of some varieties of standing postures (in contradistinction to the ordinary *samapādasthānaka*).
Lit.: WHW 1:75.

Ekapādaśiva ("Śiva on a single foot"; allied to Ekapādamūrti), n. of a Śaivite *trimūrti* in which each god (Śiva, Viṣṇu, Brahmā) has but one leg and in which the whole composition stands on the single leg of the central figure (Śiva).
Lit.: KiDG 24 a.pl. 11 (the same sculpture is in R 1: pl. F mentioned as a *trimūrti*).

Ekapāda(tri)mūrti ("representation or trinity on a single foot"), n. of a Śaivite *trimūrti* (with Śiva as the central figure) with only one leg, standing on Nandin (Vāh.). Char.: Mu.: *abhaya-*, *tarjanī-*, *varada-mudrā*; attr.: *akṣamālā*, *cakra*, *candra*, *ḍamaru*, *dhanus*, *ghaṇṭā*, *ghaṭa*, *kapāla*, *khaṭvāṅga*, *mṛga*, *mudgara*, *paraśu*, *śara*, *ṭaṅka*, *triśūla*. – Cp. Ekapādaśiva.
Lit.: R 2:388, 400 a.pl. 119:1; SSI 97 a.fig. 59-60.

Ekarudra ("the single Rudra"), n. of one of the *vidyeśvaras*. He resembles Ekanetra.
Lit.: R 2:397, 403.

ekasamapāda "one foot even (or firmly) planted" (att.), see *ardhasama(pāda)-sthānaka*, and cp. *ekapādāsana*.
Lit.: B 268.

ekaśṛṅga "unicorn" (Vāh.). The conception of the unicorn originates in the Indus Valley

culture. – *e.* is a symbol of Śreyāṅsa (Jain.). For an anthropomorphic form of Ekaśṛṅga, see AuOW. – Another n. : *khaḍga*.
Lit.: AuOW 38; GJ pl. 23:1; KiJ 11 a.pl. 45; ZA 25 a.pl. 2.

ekāvalī "a single string of pearls, beads or flowers" (attr.).
Lit.: HIS 61, 63 a.passim.

ekaveṇī (or *-i*) "a single braid of hair" (attr.). Worn by women this attr. is a sign of mourning, adopted when their husbands are dead or absent for a long period. Char. of Sītā.
Lit.: MW 229; SB 157.

ekaviṣāṇa "having but one tusk" (attr.). Char. of Gaṇeśa (cp. Ekadaṅṣṭra).
Lit.: B 357.

Elephanta, n. of a small island near Bombay with famous cave temples from the 8th c. A.D.
Lit.: FES 31; Gt 208; RAAI 187; ZA pl. 248 ff.

eli (Tam.) "rat" (Vāh.), see *ākhu*.
Lit.: JDI 42.

Ellamaṉ or Ellaiyammaṉ "lady of the boundary" (Tam.), n. of a goddess of the boundary and of the village fields (South India). She is one among the group *navaśakti*.
Lit.: DiCh. 25; GoRI 2:7; Gt 209.

ēḻu-ammaṉmār (Tam.) "seven mothers", see *saptamātaras*.
Lit.: SSR 147.

Elūrā (Ellora), n. of a place near Aurangabad with cave temples from the 6th-9th cc.
Lit.: AuOW 52; FES 31; Gt 209; SeKB passim; WHW 1:329; ZA pl. 187 ff.

EṀ, form of a *bīja* representing the *yoni*.
Lit.: WHW 2:104.

F

faṣlī (sāl) (or *phaṣlī*; Arab. "belonging to the harvest season"), n. of an era instituted by the Emperor Akbar. It is little used, and in different parts of India reckoned from different years; in Bengal and North-Western India f. begins in A.D. 592, and the year is *vartamāna*, lunisolar, *āśvinādi* and *pūrṇimānta*; in the Deccan it starts from 593, and the year is *vartamāna*, solar, the months being brought into line with the Muslim months; in Madras it begins in 590, the years are *vartamāna*, solar, and the months again conform to the Muslim reckoning. – Cp. *sūrsan*.
Lit.: IC 2:737; P. 781.

G

gadā "mace, club" (attr.). It is called "the emblem of destruction", thus esp. in the representation of Anantāśāyana, and it is generally to be taken as a symbol of strength and power. Sometimes it is also, though probably incorrectly, said to be a (phallic) symbol of fertility. In Buddhism it is mentioned as a "symbol of Tantric manifestations". – There are *gadās* with particular proper names: 1. Kaumodakī: char. of Viṣṇu, Kṛṣṇa, sometimes of Aryaman, Lakṣmī, Mahālakṣmī. 2. Saunanda: char. of Balarāma (see also *kheṭaka*?). 3. *khaṭvāṅga* (see separately) or ordinary *g.*: char. of Śiva (Bhairava), Cāmuṇḍā, Durgā, Gajāsurasaṅhāramūrti, Gaṇeśa (Gaṇapati), Skanda. 4. A *g.* without a proper n.: char. of Aghora, Ahirbudhnya, Aja, Aparājita, Bhairon, Bhīma(sena), Bi-har, Brahmā, Budha, Caṇḍā, Caṇḍeśa, Cundā, mGon-po, Gur-gyi, Hanumān, Hara, Harihara-mūrti, Hayagrīva, Heruka, Jagadgaurī, Jayanta, Ketu, Kollāpura-Mahālakṣmī, *kṣetrapālas*, Kubera, Lakulīśa, kLu-dbaṅ, Mahākāla, Mahākālī, Mahāvajrapāṇi-Lokeśvara, Mahiṣāsuramardinī, Maṅgalā, Maṇibhadra, Nandā, Nandīśvara, Revata, Śāmba, Ṣaṇmukha, Śarabha, Sarasvatī, Senānī, Senāpati, Soma (Candra), Śrīdevī, Sūrya, Tryambaka, Vaikuṇṭha, Vaiṣṇavī, Vidyujjvālākarālī, Vijaya, Vīrabhadra, Virūpākṣa, Viṣṇucakra-Lokeśvara, Viṣṇu-Lokeśvara, Viṣvaksena, Viśvarūpa, Yajñabhadra, Yama, Yamāri. – For *g.* as a possible symbol of Dharma, see *vajra.* – Other n.: *lakuṭa*, *parigha*, and cp. *daṇḍa*.

Lit.: B 300, 373, 469; DHP 156; G 14; MEIA 245; R 1:4, 236 a.pl. 1:6-8; Th. 39; WHW 2:592; WM 106 a.fig. 51-52.

gadādevī ("mace goddess"), n. of an anthropomorphic form of *gadā*, the weapon of Viṣṇu; see further sub *āyudhapuruṣa*.

Lit.: B 400, 537; HIS 77; SB 322.

Gaganagañja ("treasury of ether"; Buddh.), n. of a *bodhisattva*. Char.: colour: yellow, red or golden; Mu.: *varadamudrā*; attr.: *cintāmaṇi*, *dharmagañja*, *kalpavṛkṣa* (in a jar), *nīlotpala*, *padma*.

Lit.: BBh. 86 a.pl. 53; MW 341.

Gaganagañja-Lokeśvara (Buddh.), n. of a variety of Avalokiteśvara. Char.: att.: *padmāsana*; Vāh.: *padma*; Mu.: *vyākhyānamudrā*; attr.: *pustaka*.

Lit.: BBh. 399 a.pl. 48(A).

gaja "elephant" (Vāh.; attr.), a symbol of strength, virility and wisdom. – As Vāh.: 1. (Hind.) *g.* with the proper n. Airāvaṇa or Airāvata is Vāh. of Indra and Indrāṇī. – 2. *g.* (without a proper n.) is Vāh. of: Balabhadra, Śani, Śāstā (= Aiyaṉār), Skanda (see Gajavāhana, Tārakāri), Vārāhī; a white *g.* is Vāh. of Chos-skyoṅ, Mahā-Gaurī; 2 *g.* are Vāh. of Akṣobhya; one or more *g.* support the throne of Samantabhadra; a *g.* is furthermore a symbol of the Śātavāhana-dynasty. It should also be noticed that Gaṇeśa is *gajamukha* and that 2 *g.* sprinkle water on Lakṣmī, see Gajalakṣmī. *g.* is further a *maṅgala*, see *aṣṭamaṅgala*. – 3. (Buddh.) *g.* is a symbol of the Buddha. The white *g.* which, according to legend, penetrated into the side of the mother (Māyā) of the Buddha (in the dream of Māyā), foreshowing the birth of Buddha, has been regarded as a symbol of the male principle to be compared with the *liṅga* or the *vajra* (HuET). – 4. (Jain.) *g.* is a symbol of Ajita, Mahāyakṣa. – 5. As attr.: A *g.* is swallowed by Garuḍa, Kālī, Mahālakṣmī. – *g.* is also a symbolic n. of the number "8", see *saṅkhyā*. Other n.: *hastin*, *ibha*, *kuñjara*.

Lit.: GJ pl. 22:2; GoRI 1:316; H pl. 3:22; HuET 47; IC 1:536; KiJ pl. 45; KiSB 34; MEIA 235, 266; WM 70.

gajacarma(n) "elephant-hide" (attr.), see *ajina*.

Lit.: BBh. 346.

Gajādhipa ("lord of elephants"), epithet of Gaṇeśa.

Lit.: DHP 292.

Gajahāmūrti ("representation as elephant-killer"), see Gajāsurasaṅhāramūrti.

Lit.: R 1:19, 2:150; SSI 125.

gajahastamudrā "elephant-arm-handpose" (Mu.), n. of a dancing gesture in which one arm is thrown in front of the breast (across the chest) in imitation of an elephant's trunk. *g.* is also mentioned as a variety of the *patākāmudrā*. Char. of, above all, Śiva Naṭarāja (in different dancing-modes) and Gaṇeśa. – Other n.: *daṇḍahasta-*, *dolahasta-*, *karihasta-mudrā*, *vīciyakaram*. – Cp. *vaināyakīmudrā*.

Lit.: B 258; H pl. 7:61; R 1:16 a.pl. 5:12; Th. 27; WHW 2:86; WM 101 a.fig. 30; ZA 122.

Gaja-Lakṣmī ("elephant-Lakṣmī"), n. of a form, usually four-handed, of Lakṣmī (one of the group *aṣṭamahālakṣmī*), in which two elephants sprinkle water over the goddess. This probably signifies Lakṣmī as a mother-goddess and a goddess of fertility (cp. the fact that in Buddhism one or two elephants together with a woman symbolize the birth of the Buddha; H). It may also be noticed that G., in relief,

is very often represented on *dīpas* (especially on the back-piece of niche-lamps). Attr.: *amṛtaghaṭa*, *padma*, *śaṅkha*, *śrīphala*.
Lit.: B 374 a.pl. 18: 2; GoRI 2:117; Gw 40; H pl. 3:22; JDI 100 a.pl. 62; R 1:374 a.pl. 111 (here, however, the idol is called Śrīdevī); SSI 187; Th. 105; ZA pl. 280b; ZM 104.

gajamukha (and *gajamastaka*) "elephant-headed" (attr.). Char. of: Gaṇeśa (Gaṇapati, Vināyaka), Pārvatī. – Another n.: *karivaktra*.
Lit.: B 357.

Gajamukhāsura ("elephant-headed demon"), n. of an elephant-headed *asura* who was defeated in combat by Gaṇeśa (Piḷḷaiyār); he then transformed himself into a rat (*ākhu*) which became the Vāh. of Gaṇeśa.
Lit.: JDI 41.

Gajānana ("elephant-faced"), epithet of Gaṇeśa. Another n.: Āṉaimukavar.
Lit.: DHP 292; R 1:39.

gajāṅkuśa "elephant-goad" (attr.), see *aṅkuśa*.
Lit.: ACA 36.

Gajasaṅhāra(mūrti), see Gajāsurasaṅhāra-mūrti.
Lit.: ZA pl. 408; ZM 140.

gajasiṅha "elephant-lion", n. of a mythical being, half-elephant, half-lion.
Lit.: KrI pl. 58; MBPC pl. 33; RAAI 272.

gajasiṅhāsana "elephant-lion-throne" (Vāh.), n. of a throne with elephant figures carved on the supports, a symbol of sovereignty and wisdom. Cp. *siṅhāsana*.
Lit.: MH 44; SM 131.

Gajāsura(saṅhāra)mūrti ("representation [of Śiva] destroying the elephant demon (Gajāsura)"), n. of an *ugra*-aspect of Śiva. The god is here usually represented dancing (cp. *gajatāṇḍava*). Char.: Mu.: *vismaya-mudrā*; attr.: esp. *ajina* (elephant-hide held in one or several hands or surrounding Śiva like a *prabhāmaṇḍala*), *danta*, *pāśa*, further *akṣamālā*, *aṅkuśa*, *ḍamaru*, *daṇḍa*, *dhanus*, *dhattūra*-flowers, *gadā*, *ghaṇṭā*, *kapāla*, *khaḍga*, *khaṭvāṅga*, *kheṭaka*, *mṛga*, *nāga*, *śakti*, *śara*, *ṭaṅka*, *triśūla*, *vajra*. – Other n.: Gajahā-, Gajasaṅhāra-mūrti.
Lit.: AIP pl. 56 (324); B 486 a.pl. 33:2; BP 209 a.pl. 23; JDI 30; KrG pl. 5; R 1:19, 2:115, 150 a.pl. 30ff.; Th. 84 a.pl. 56A; ZA 359 a.pl. 408, 445b; ZM 140.

gaja-tāṇḍava ("elephant-*t*."), n. of a certain form of the *tāṇḍava*-dance performed by Śiva Naṭarāja. In this form he plants his foot on an elephant-head instead of the customary demon (Apasmāra); this dance-form therefore alludes to the Gajāsura-mūrti.
Lit.: Sh. pl. 5.

Gajavāhana ("having an elephant as *vāhana*"), n. of a form, esp. South Indian, of Skanda in which this god has a *gaja* as Vāh. Char.: Mu.: *abhaya-*, *varada-mudrā*; attr.: *kukkuṭa*, *śakti*. – Other n.: Cēyōṉ, Cevvēḷ.
Lit.: BECA 1:4; MD 1:581; R 2:435.

Gajavaktra ("elephant-faced"), epithet of Gaṇeśa.
Lit.: DiIP 113.

Gajendra ("elephant king"), n. of a king who, by means of a curse, was changed into an elephant. When he was once seized by a crocodile while bathing, he was rescued by Viṣṇu. – G. also refers to the *avatāra* of Viṣṇu in which he rescued the king mentioned above.
Lit.: DHP 186 a.pl. 13; WM 191.

Gajendramokṣa ("deliverance of the king of elephants"), see Karivarada.
Lit.: SSI 55.

galaka "fish" (attr.), see *matsya*.
Lit.: MEIA 266.

galantī (or *-ikā*), lit. "dropping", n. given to a kind of water-jar (attr.). This jar has a hole in its bottom from which water drops on to a Śaivite *liṅga* or a Vaiṣṇavite *tulasī* plant. This symbol is rarely represented and is sometimes attributed to Gaurī.
Lit.: MEIA 243; MW 350.

Gal Bāpsi (Bhīlī: "the hook god"), see *carkh pūjā*.
Lit.: KBh. 154.

GAṀ or *GĀṀ*, a bījamantra symbolizing Gaṇeśa.
Lit.: DHP 343.

gaṇa (or *gaṇadevatās*) "flock, body of attendants or followers" of Śiva, usually

represented as obese dwarfs; also a group of godlings ruled by Gaṇeśa; *gaṇa* is also n. of a single individual of these groups. Attr.: *ghaṭa*.
Lit.: D 104; DCSS pl. 59 ff.; DHP 291, 301; H pl. 19; IIM 118; MEIA 70; RAAI 272; SB 308; WHW 1:397.

gaṇadhara "supporting the flocks" (Jain.), n. of a group of 11 disciples of Mahāvīra.
Lit.: IC 2:631.

Gaṇādhipa(ti) ("chief of troups"), epithet of Gaṇeśa.
Lit.: DiIP 113; MW 343.

Gānagopāla ("the singing shepherd, cowherd"), epithet of Kṛṣṇa, esp. in his form as Veṇugopāla.
Lit.: R 1:207 1.pl. 61-62.

Gaṇapati ("lord of *gaṇas*").
1. (Hind.) Esp. in West India the usual n. of Gaṇeśa. – G. is also an epithet of Bṛhaspati.
Lit.: DHP 291; MG 193; R 1:35.
2. (Buddh.) In Mahāyāna Buddhism G. is the usual n. of a god influenced by the Hindu god Gaṇeśa. Char.: att.: *nāṭyasthāna*; Vāh.: *ākhu*; attr.: *aṅkuśa*, *dhanus*, *ekadanta*, *gadā* (*khaṭvāṅga*), *gajamukha*, *kapāla*, *khaḍga*, *modaka*, *mūlaka*, *musala*, *paraśu*, *phaṭka*, *śakti*, *śara*, *trinayana*, *triśūla*, *tundila*, *vajra*. – See also Vighnāntaka, Vināyaka.
Lit.: BBh. 348, 365 a.pl. 227f., 241; G 102; KiSB 77.

Gaṇapatihṛdayā ("the heart, i.e. secrecy, of Gaṇapati", personification; Buddh.), n. of a Mahāyāna goddess, probably to be regarded as the Śakti of Gaṇapati. Char.: att.: *ardhasamapādasthānaka*; Mu.: *abhaya-*, *varada-mudrā*.
Lit.: BBh. 349 a.pl. 229; KiDG 64; KiSB 108.

gaṇapatiyantra, n. of a *yantra* which represents Gaṇeśa.
Lit.: DHP 360.

gāṇapatya "adherent of Gaṇapati", i.e. of Gaṇeśa; n. of a sect.
Lit.: GH 399; GoRI 2:62; Gt 217; IC 1:624.

gāṇapa(tya)liṅga, n. of a kind of *acalaliṅga* which is believed to have been set up by *gaṇas*. It has the shape of a fruit, e.g. a cucumber. citron etc.
Lit.: R 2:86.

gaṇapūjā "offering to the terrific deities" (Buddh.).
Lit.: GBM 142.

gaṇḍabheruṇḍa ("having terrible cheeks"), n. of a fabulous (elephant-devouring) bird-vehicle, used in processions of images.
Lit.: SSI 278 a.ill. p. 268.

Gandhā ("smell, odour", personification; Buddh.), n. of one of the Lamaist *mātaras*. Char.: colour: green; attr.: *gandhaśaṅkha*.
Lit.: G 36, 82.

Gandhahastin (-ī; "odour-elephant"; Buddh.), n. of a *bodhisattva*. Char.: colour: (whitish) green; Mu.; *varadamudrā*; attr.: *gandhaśaṅkha*, *hastikara* on a *padma*.
Lit.: BBh. 95 a.pl. 67.

Gandhāra, n. of a people (in the present Pakistan); also n. of a period in art-history above all famous for its sculptures which are deeply influenced by the Iranian and Greek or Roman cultures. This school flourished in the 1st-6th cc. A.D.
Lit.: FBKI 61; Gz 69; RAAI 75; SeKB 10; WHW 1:369; ZA pl. 63 ff.

Gāndhārī ("coming from Gandhāra"; Jain.), n. of a *śāsanadevatā*, attendant of either the 12th or the 21st *tīrthaṅkara*. – *G.* is also mentioned as n. of a *vidyādevī*.
Lit.: GJ 362 a.pl. 25:12; KiJ 12 a.pl. 28:12.

gandharva(s) (interpreted as "the Fragrances", DHP; etymology uncertain), n. of a kind of semi-divine beings, living in the sky. *g.* are known from the Ṛgveda and were there a sort of physicians; later they are regarded as the musicians of the gods, and are represented as playing different kinds of musical instruments. They are described as having human upper bodies with wings, with the face of Garuḍa, and with the hind quarters of a horse or an ass. The *apsarasas* are regarded as being their wives. The *g.* are known to all Indian religions; in Buddhism their king is named Pañcaśikha; in Jainism *g.* is n. of a kind of *vyantaradevatā*.

Lit.: B 351 a.pl. 16 :1; BBh. 381; DHP 301, 305 a.pl. 30; GH 107; GJ 237; GoRI 1 :101; Gt 218; H pl. 8; HIS 26; IC 1 :528; JDI 28; MEIA 200; MW 346; R 2 :568; Th. 118; WHW 1 :371; ZA pl. 118 f.

Gandharva (Jain.), NP of a *yakṣa* attending on the 17th *tīrthaṅkara*. Symbol : *mṛga*.

Lit.: GJ 362 a.pl. 26 :17; KiJ 11 a.pl. 29 :17.

gandhaśaṅkha "conch containing sandal paste" (attr.). Char. of : Gandhā, Gandhahastin, Gandhatārā.

Lit.: BBh. 95.

Gandha-Tārā ("fragrance-Tārā"; Buddh.), NP of a minor Mahāyāna goddess. Char. : colour : red; attr. : *gandhaśaṅkha*.

Lit.: BBh. 241; KiSB 102.

Gāṇḍīva (or -iva), n. of the bow (*dhanus*) of Arjuna which was given to him by Agni.

According to MAYRHOFER, EWA 1 :333, *g.* may be derived from *gāṇḍī* as n. of a plant (the material of the bow). But, according to MW 353, *gāṇḍī* is "a rhinoceros". Therefore, *g.* may rather be supposed to have been made of the horn of a rhinoceros; cp. that Śārṅga, the bow of Viṣṇu and Kṛṣṇa, and Ajagava, the bow of Śiva, are also made of a horn.

Gaṇeśa (Tam. Kaṇēcaṉ; "lord of the *gaṇa*s"). 1. (Hind.) NP of one of the most popular gods, noted for his elephant-head. G. is the son of Śiva and Pārvatī (it is sometimes said that he is the son of Pārvatī before her marriage with Śiva). In later Hinduism he is regarded as the god of wisdom and art (? see Gt), and as the remover of obstacles (Vighneśvara*); hence he is worshipped before starting a new undertaking or a journey. But originally he was probably a god of fertility, *viz.* of agriculture, as many of his symbols prove, and evidently he was primarily a *yakṣa*, as is seen from his big belly (*tundila*). – He is also the god of the month *bhādrapada*.

Wives : Riddhi and Siddhi; as his wives are sometimes also mentioned : Bhāratī, Śrī (= Lakṣmī), Puṣṭi, Vighneśvarī, Buddhi, Kubuddhi. – Char. : colour : pink or yellow (or green?); Vāh. : *ākhu*, sometimes *siṅha*, and *padmapīṭha*; att. : usually *āsana*, but also *sthānaka* (and *nāṭyasthāna*); Mu. : *abhaya-*, *varada-mudrā*; attr. : *akṣamālā*, *āmra*, *aṅgulīya*, *aṅkuśa*, *cakra*, *candra*, *dāḍima*, *daṇḍa*, *danta*, *dhanus*, *dhvaja*, *ekaviṣāṇa*, *gadā* (*khaṭvāṅga*), *gajamukha*, *ikṣu(kāṇḍa)*, *jambu*, *kalpakalatā*, *kamaṇḍalu*, *kaṇiśa*, *kapāla*, *kapittha*, *kevaṛā*, *kuṇḍa*, *māndāra*, *modaka*, *mudgara*, *mūlaka-(kanda)*, *nāga*, *nīlotpala*, *padma*, *paraśu*, *pāśa*, (*phala*), *ratnapaṭṭa*, *śakti*, *śaṅkha*, *śara*, *sarpakuṇḍala*, *ṭaṅka*, *triśūla*, *tuṇḍaka*, *tundila*, *udarabandha*, *ūrdhvaliṅga* (sometimes), *vetāla*, *vīṇā*, *vyālayajñopavītin*. – Usually G. has only one head, but sometimes he has five heads (Heramba) or four heads (in Siam). – G. is also represented by the *bījamantra*s *OṀ* (= *AUṀ*), *GAṀ* (*GĀṂ*), *GLAUṀ*, by the *yantra gaṇapatiyantra* and the symbol *svastika* in the clockwise form.

Epithets and manifestations : Ākhuratha, Bāla-Gaṇapati, Bhakti-Vighneśvara, Bhālacandra, Bīja-Gaṇapati, Ekadaṅṣṭra, Ekadanta, Gajādhipa, Gajānana, Gajavaktra, Gaṇādhipa(ti), Gaṇapati, Jyeṣṭharāja, Mahākarṇa, Mahākāya, Mahodara, Pañcamukha-Vināyaka, Piḷḷaiyār, Śūrpakarṇa, Suvarṇabhadra, Valampura-Gaṇeśa, Vighneśvara, Vināyaka, Vīra-Vighneśa, and several epithets with a last member -Gaṇapati, such as : Bhuvaneśa-, Dhvaja-, Haridrā-, Heramba-, Kevala-, Lakṣmī-, Mahā-, Nṛtta- or Nṛtya-, Rātri-, Śuddha-, Taruṇa-, Ucchiṣṭa-, Unmatta-ucchiṣṭa-, Ūrdhva-, Vighnarāja-Gaṇapati.

Lit.: B 356 a.pl. 15 :1-3; BBh. 382; D 106; DHP 291 a.pl. 27; DiIP passim; GBB 128 a.pl. 14; GH 116, 477 a.pl. 2; GI pl. 79; GoRI 1 :261, 2 :62; Gt 220; HAHI pl. 17B, 21; HIS 21; IC 1 :498; IIM 100; JDI 40; KiH 18 a.pl. 52 f.; KiSH 31; KrI pl. 30; MEIA 108; MG 190; MH pl. 6; R 1 :35 a.pl. 10 ff.; SB passim (many ill.); SSI 165; Th. 95 a.pl. 58; WHW 1 :376; WM 73; ZA 177 a.pl. passim.

2. (Attr.) G. as a little image (Genius of fertility) is held in one hand or lies as a child in the bosom of Gaurī, Pārvatī. Cp. Gaṇeśajananī.

Lit.: KiH 22 a.pl. 69; KiSH 45; MEIA 271.

3. (Vāh.; Hind. and Buddh.) On the lying G. tread: Aparājitā, Vighnāntaka, Parṇaśavarī.
Lit.: KiSH 106.

4. (Buddh.) In Lamaism G. is regarded as a local god (of riches); He thus in general corresponds to the Hindu G. and has the same attr. (i.e. *akṣamālā, aṅkuśa, cakra, cintāmaṇi, dhanus, kapāla, karttṛkā, mūlaka, paraśu, phur-bu, śara, vajra*). Sometimes, under the n. of Vinayaka, he is regarded as a demon. But else he is usually known under the n. of Gaṇapati. – Cp. also Vighnāntaka.
Lit.: G 102.

5. (Jain.) The Hindu G. is also worshipped as a god by the Jains.
Lit.: B 561.

gaṇeśacaturthī, n. of a festival dedicated to Gaṇeśa in the month *bhādrapada* (August-September).
Lit.: GH 355; GJ 435; WHW 1:353.

Gaṇeśajananī ("mother of Gaṇeśa"), epithet of Pārvatī. Attr.: Gaṇeśa (as an image held in one hand or as a child lying in the bosom).
Lit.: W 266.

gaṇeśapūjā "worship of Gaṇeśa", n. of a cult ritual.
Lit.: DiIP 113.

Gaṅgā (Mā Gaṅgā: "mother Ganges"), n. of a river goddess. G. was originally a heavenly river which (by Bhagīratha) was brought down from heaven and, in order to spare the earth the shock of her fall, was caught by Śiva in his hair; therefore G. is often represented seated in Śiva's hair, and she is also regarded as his second wife. In mythology she is the elder daughter of Himavān and Menā and sister of Pārvatī. She was first married to Viṣṇu, then also to Agni, and as the wife of Śiva (or Agni) she is sometimes regarded as the mother of Skanda. – G. is said to be an "emblem of purity, white as milk" and "represents the causal waters". Together with Yamunā she is symbolized by two *matsyas*. – Char.: colour: white; Vāh.: *makara, matsya*; attr.: *cāmara, kamaṇḍalu, padma*.
Lit.: B pl. 15:4, 17:3; CHIIA 242 a.fig. 177; D 108; DHP 213, 215; DIA pl. 19; GoRI 1:255; Gt 222; IIM 109; KiH 25 a.pl. 85-86; KiSH 72; KrG pl. 20; MG 213; R 2:530 a.pl. 155:1; WHW 1:378; WM 75; ZA 125 a.pl. 105c, 227, 385.

Gaṅgādhara(mūrti) ("representation [of Śiva] bearing Gaṅgā"), n. of a form of Śiva with Gaṅgā (often seated in his hair), and sometimes also with Pārvatī. Char. of Śiva: Mu.: *abhaya-, varada-mudrā*; attr.: *mṛga, paraśu, trinayana*. Another n.: Gaṅgāvisarjanamūrti.
Lit.: B 486 a.pl. 40:2; DHP 191; R 2:313 a.pl. 90-93; SSI 129; Th. 90.

Gaṅgāputra ("son of Gaṅgā"), epithet of Skanda.
Lit.: DHP 299.

Gaṅgāvisarjanamūrti ("representation [of Śiva] giving up Gaṅgā"), n. of a form of Śiva consoling his wife Pārvatī and abandoning his second wife Gaṅgā who is seen seated in his hair; see further Gaṅgādhara.
Lit.: SSI 129.

Gāṅgeya-Subrahmaṇya ("S., son of Gaṅgā"), n. of a form of Skanda. Char.: Vāh.: *makara*; attr.: *araṇi, dhvaja, kukkuṭa, nīlotpala, paraśu, pūrṇakalaśa*.
Lit.: R 2:441.

garbha ("womb"), n. of the inner apartment of a temple or a *stūpa*. Another n.: *mūla*. Cp. *aṇḍa, garbhagṛha*.
Lit.: IC 1:576; SeKB 101; ZA 233.

garbhādhāna "impregnation", n. of a *saṅskāra*-rite, "a ceremony performed before conception or after menstruation to ensure conception" (MW).
Lit.: DiIP 180; GH 332; GJ 409; IC 1:363; MW 350; STP 2:166; WHW 2:238.

garbhadhātu ("womb or embryo of the world, the Matrix World"; Buddh.), n. of a certain *maṇḍala*.
Lit.: GBM 110; SeKB 191, 210.

garbhagṛha "inner, central apartment of a temple" in which the chief image is placed. – Another n.: *mūlasthāna*; cp. *garbha*.
Lit.: BSA 34; DKI 41; GJ 399; GoRI 1:329; R 2:105; RAAI 272; ZA 111, 269.

gardabha "ass" (Vāh.). The symbolical meaning of *g.* is explained thus: "bête lubrique, servant dans le rituel à expier les fautes sexuelles" (IC). Char. of: Alakṣmī, Jyeṣṭhā, Kālarātrī, Nirṛti, Śītalā. Another n.: *khara.*
Lit.: IC 1:536; KiSH 83; MKVI 1:221.

gārhapatya "householder's (fire)" (attr.), n. of one of the five sacred domestic fires (see *agni*); the perpetual fire of the domestic hearth, kindled when the housholder establishes his own household, and from then onwards always kept alive. From this fire all the other domestic fires are kindled.
Lit.: WHW 1:359.

Garuḍa (interpreted as "devourer").
1. (Hind.; Vāh.). NP of a mythical being, originally regarded as a kind of bird, later as half-vulture, half-man. He is a sun symbol (thought of as "the all-consuming fire of the sun's rays") and is perhaps the prototype of the conception of the bird Phoenix. In Hindu mythology he is said to be the son of Kāśyapa and Vinatā, and to have been born from an egg. He is the sworn enemy of the *nāga*s which constitute his chief food. This antagonism may reflect an early pattern, cp. the Sumerian combination of eagle and snake (ZA) and the combination of the bird of heaven and the snake of earth.
G. is the Vāh. esp. of Viṣṇu (and Viśvarūpa) but also of Lakṣmī (Vaiṣṇavī). Wife: Unnati. Char.: Mu.: *añjalimudrā*, often also a pose (both arms stretched out, the palms turned upwards) signifying the supporting of Viṣṇu or humility and devotion to Viṣṇu (see *mudrā* 1[d]); attr.: *amṛtaghaṭa, gaja, kūrma, nāga*; but he may also have the emblems of Viṣṇu: *cakra, gadā, padma, śaṅkha.* – Epithets: Amṛtaharaṇa, Garutmān, Suparṇa, Tārkṣya, Vihaṅgama. Cp. *haṅsa.*
2. (Buddh.; Vāh.) In Buddhism G. is esp. the Vāh. of Vajrapāṇi. Two *g.* are the Vāh. or a symbol of Amoghasiddhi. In Lamaism G. is n. of a group of bird-genii, and he has esp. been adopted as a symbol of the "Red hat" sect. Furthermore, certain gods (provided with wings), in particular Vajrapāṇi, may be represented in a particular "Garuḍa-form": this stands on a *rākṣasa* or a *nāga*; Mu.: *añjalimudrā*; attr.: *kamaṇḍalu, karttṛkā.* – Hayagrīva has also a Garuḍa-form: att.: (sometimes) *yab-yum*; Mu.: *añjalimudrā*; attr.: *ajina, aśvamastaka* (in the hair), *pāśa, puṣpa, trinayana, triśiras, vajra.*
3. (Jain.) In Jainism G. is a symbol of Śreyāṅsa. G. is also NP of a *yakṣa* attending on the 16th *tīrthaṅkara.*
Lit.: 1-3: B 529 a.pl. 26:3; BBh. 435; D 109; DHP 160; G passim; GH 72; GoRI 1:318; Gt 224; H pl. 10; HM pl. 1; HuGT 9, 20; IIM 101; JMS pl. 57; KiH 13 a.pl. 26; KiSH 36; MEIA 48, 232; MG 228 a.pl. facing p. 227; MH pl. 8; R 1:283 a.pl. 84-85:1; SB 352 a.fig. 335; STP 1:103; Th. pl. 12; WHW 1:381; WM 76; ZA 49, 157 a.pl. 425, 523.

garuḍadhvaja "banner (or pillar) with the bird Garuḍa as the sign, or staff surmounted by an image of G." (attr.). Char. of Viṣṇu.
Lit.: DKI 12; HIS 19; SIB pl. 15.

Garuḍa-Nārāyaṇa, n. of a form of Viṣṇu (Nārāyaṇa) riding on Garuḍa and carrying the chief attr. of Viṣṇu.
Lit.: SSI 55.

garuḍāsana.
1. "Garuḍa-sitting" (att.), n. of a Yogic posture.
Lit.: KiH pl. 152 row 4:2.
2. "Garuḍa-throne" (Vāh.), n. of a *pīṭha* supported by Garuḍa.
Lit.: MH 44.

Garuḍāsana-Viṣṇu ("V. having Garuḍa as seat"), epithet of Viṣṇu riding on his Vāh. Garuḍa.
Lit.: B 405.

Garuḍāsyā ("Garuḍa-faced"; Buddh.), n. of a minor goddess.
Lit.: BBh. 319.

Garutmān (-mant, -mat) ("winged"? or "big bird"), probably an epithet of Garuḍa; cp. also Suparṇa.
Lit.: BBh. 529; MW 348.

gata "elapsed", in dating referring to the year, see *samvatsara.*

gati "going; six paths or conditions of existence, metempsychosis" (Buddh.). – In dance (*nāṭya*) *g.* is a generic term for all movements of the feet.
Lit.: N 78; WHW 1:263.

gau (Tib.) "amulet" (attr.; Buddh.). A *g.* is made of sheet-metal and usually bears a representation of a *yantra.*
Lit.: G 11 (ill. facing p. 108).

gaumedha, see *gomedha.*

Gaurī ("white, yellowish, reddish; shining, brilliant").
1. (Hind.) NP of the wife of Varuṇa; see also Vāruṇī. – G. is more often an epithet of Pārvatī esp. in her gracious aspect as a corn goddess. She is said to be the Śakti of Maheśvara. Char.: *siṅha* (sometimes), *vṛka* or *sūkara*; Mu.: *abhaya-*, *varada-mudrā*; attr.: *akṣamālā, darpaṇa, galantī,* Gaṇeśa, *kamaṇḍalu, matsya, padma, trinayana, triśūla, vanamālā.*
Lit.: DiIP 136; GoRI 2:210, 258; KiH 23 a.pl. 74; KiSH 45; MEIA 138, 165; R 1:360; WHW 1:48.
2. (Buddh.) *gaurī* is n. of a group of eight goddesses of fearful appearances: Gaurī, Caurī, Vetālī, Ghasmarī, Pukkasī, Śavarī, Caṇḍālī, Ḍombī. Common char.: att.: *ālīḍhāsana*; Mu.: *tarjanīmudrā*; attr.: *muṇḍamālā.* Cp. *kerimas.* – As may be seen from the list above, Gaurī is also n. of the first mentioned deity of the *gaurī*-group. Char.: colour: white; attr.: *aṅkuśa.*
Lit. BBh. 309.
3. (Vāh.; Buddh.) On the lying G. Trailokyavijayā treads.
Lit.: KiSB 79.
4. (Jain.) NP of a *śāsanadevatā* attending on the 11th *tīrthaṅkara.* G. is also NP of a *vidyādevī.*
Lit.: GJ 362 a.pl. 25:11; Kij 12 a.pl. 28:11.

gaurītāṇḍava ("[Śiva in] a *tāṇḍava*-dance together with Gaurī"), n. of a dance-form of Śiva similar to the *ānandatāṇḍava*; in *g.* Śiva has a *nāga* in one of his left hands. Nandin stands on his right side and Gaurī on his left. See also Naṭarāja.
Lit.: SSI 84.

Gaurī-Tārā ("the yellowish T."; Buddh.), NP of a minor Mahāyāna goddess.
Lit.: BBh. 151; KiSB 97.

gaus "cow, ox", the most sacred animal in Hinduism, to a large extent an object of worship. The cult of *g.* has its beginnings in Indus Valley religion and continues in undiminished degree even at present. The worship cannot here be described in short (see Lit.). – The widespread use of *pañcagavya* is attributed to the Hindu attitude to *g.* – *g.* is also a symbolic n. of the number "9", see *saṅkhyā.* – Other n.: *dhenu, kapilā.* See also Kāmadhenu, Nandin.
Lit.: DiIP 137, 153; GH 67; GoRI 1:315; MKVI 1:231; STP 2:240; WHW 1:255.

Gautama (patronymic from Gotama), clan-name of the historic Buddha, and n. of Indrabhūti.

gavākṣa "bull's eye", in architecture n. of an air-hole, a round (blind) window in a temple.
Lit.: Gz 92, 97; JMS 41; RAAI 272.

Gāyatrī (originally "a hymn composed in a *gāyatrī* metre", or n. of this metre; G. is also n. of a certain hymn, Ṛgveda 3, 62, 10; the best-known of all Hindu hymns, the prayer, dedicated to the sun, with which a Hindu begins the day). As a personification of the hymn mentioned above G. is the (second?) wife of Brahmā, and is perhaps identical with Sarasvatī, the first wife of Brahmā. Attr.: (sometimes) *pañcaśiras.* – The Ṛgveda hymn is further used as a *mantra,* "the Protector of the Vital Energies" (DHP), and since it consists of 24 (later often arranged in 2 lines of 12, instead of the Vedic triplet of 8) syllables, it is regarded as a solar *mantra* (the number "12" being symbolic of the sun, see *saṅkhyā* 12). – See also Sāvitrī.
Lit.: D 111; DHP 345; DiIP 81; GH 55, 140; MG 93 a.pl. facing p. 96; Th. 105; WHW 1:384; WM 77.

gehapati "house-lord", i.e. a chamberlain who conducted the palace affairs, is a *lakṣaṇa* of a *cakravartin*, see *saptaratna*.
Lit.: WHW 1:552.

dGe-lugs-pa (also dGe-ldan-pa) "the virtuous" (Tib.; Buddh.), n. of a sect usually known as "the Yellow Hats" after the colour of the hats worn by members of the sect on solemn occasions. The sect was revitalised and reformed in the 14th c. by Tsoṅ-kha-pa from the older sect bKa'-gdams-pa.
Lit.: Enc. Brit. 22:188 A; GRI 294; JT 86.

ghana.
1. "Solid", n. of a method of casting bronze images (see *madhūcchiṣṭavidhāna*) by which the image is solid throughout. This method is mostly used for making small icons. Cp. *suṣira*.
Lit.: SIB 3.
2. "Cymbal" (attr.), see *tala*.

ghanadvāra "solid, compact door", i.e. a false door of a temple adorned with *toraṇas*.
Lit.: BECA 1:261.

ghaṇṭā "bell, prayer bell" held in one hand (attr.). *gh.* is an independent cult object and as such one of the most ancient of the attributes. It is used at the service in all Indian religions. The *gh.* has been used throughout history to warn away demons, to call the worshippers to cult ceremonies, or to call the attention of the gods the fact that somebody is worshipping. It is also a very common votive offering. – In Buddhism it is either a "Symbol der Erscheinungswelt" (GBM), since it stands for impermanence or represents *prajñā* "wisdom", (the sounds of which travel far and wide); because it "versinnbildlicht das weibliche Prinzip" (GBM) it fills a role in Vajrayāna and Lamaist symbolic conceptions equivalent to *padma* and *yoni* (cp. also Prajñā); *gh.* is then carried in the left hand (cp. *vāma*; see also *vajrahūṅkāramudrā*). – The handle of the Hindu *gh.* usually consists of an image of Hanumān or Garuḍa; among the Buddhists the handle often takes the form of a *vajra* (cp. *vajraghaṇṭā*).
As an attr. *gh.* is carried by many deities and is char. of: Aghora, Aja, Amoghapāśa, Andhakāsuravadhamūrti, Aparājita, Aparājitā, Āryāvalokiteśvara, Bahurūpa, Cāmuṇḍā, Caṇḍā, Daśabhuja-Aghoramūrti, Dharmadhātuvagīśvara, Dharmavajra, Durgā, Ekajaṭā, Ekapādamūrti, Gajāsurasaṅhāramūrti, Ghaṇṭākarṇī, Ghaṇṭāpāṇi, Hevajra, Jñānaḍākinī, Kālacakra, Kamaṇḍalu-Lokeśvara, Kaumārī, Kṛṣṇa-Yamāri, *kṣetrapālas*, Mahādeva, Mahākāla, Mahāmantrānusāriṇī, Mahāmāyūrī, Maheśamūrti, Māheśvarī, Mahiṣāsuramardinī, Mañjughoṣa, Nandā, *navadurgās*, Nīlāmbaravajrapāṇi, Pārvatī, Revata, Sadāśiva, Samantabhadra, Samvara, Ṣaṇmukha, Saptakṣara, Sarasvatī, Śaravaṇabhava, Senāpati, Sureśvara, Śiva, Skanda, Trailokyavijaya, Tripurāntaka, Vajraḍākinī, Vajradhara, Vajrahuṅkāra, Vajrajvālānalārka, Vajrāmṛta, Vajrasattva, Vidyujjvālākarālī, Virūpākṣa, Yamāntaka, *yidam*, Yogeśvarī. – Another n.: *jayaghaṇṭā*.
Lit.: B 303, 364; BBh. 43, 435; G 8 a.pl. facing p. 10, 14; GBM 104; GH 345; IC 1:570; KiH 35 a.pl. 139:2; KiSH 26; MEIA 255; R 1:10 a.pl. 4:1-2; SM 146; SMII 40; ZM pl. 47.

Ghaṇṭākarṇa ("bell-eared"), NP of a god, attendant of Śiva who is "supposed to preside over cutaneous complaints, and worshipped for exemption from them" (MW). Attr.: *ghaṇṭāmālā*, *mudgara*.
Lit.: GH 111; MW 375; MEIA 60.

Ghaṇṭākarṇī ("bell-eared"), NP of a goddess. Attr.: *ghaṇṭā*, *triśūla*.
Lit.: R 1:368.

ghaṇṭāmālā "garland of bells" (attr.). Char. of Ghaṇṭākarṇa.
Lit.: MEIA 215.

Ghaṇṭāpāṇi ("having a bell in the hand"; Buddh.), NP of a *dhyānibodhisattva*, an emanation of Vajrasattva. Char.: colour: white; attr.: *ghaṇṭā*.
Lit.: BBh. 76; GBB 248.

ghaṇṭāvali "line of bells", in architecture n. of a border with bell motifs.
Lit.: JMS 17.

Ghasmarī ("voracious"; Buddh.), n. of a goddess of the *gaurī*-group. Char.: colour: green; attr.: *vajraghaṇṭā*.
Lit.: BBh. 311 a.pl. 203.

ghāṭ (Hi. < Skt *ghaṭṭa*) "landingplace, quay, a flight of stone steps or an incline leading to water", hence also "a (sacred) bathing-place" from which Hindus plunge into the water in order to be cleansed from their sins.
Lit.: GH 340; P 928; RAAI 272.

ghaṭa "pot-drum, a drum in the shape of a jar" (attr.). Char. of: Ahirbudhnya, Ekapādamūrti, *gaṇas*, Hara, Tryambaka, Virūpākṣa. – Another n.: *kuṭamuḷā*. – *ghaṭa*, also "jar", see *kamaṇḍalu*.
Lit.: SB 309.

Ghentu (N. Ind.), n. of a god who sends the itch.
Lit.: GH 111.

ghī (Hi.) "ghee", see *ghṛta*.

Ghora ("terrific, frightful", also interpreted "triumphant"), n. of a terrific aspect of Śiva. Gh. is often used without distinction like Aghora. See also *ugra*, *raudra*.
Lit.: B 464, 477; DHP 195; ZA 359; ZM 205.

ghṛta (Hi.: *ghī*) "ghee" (attr.), clarified butter ("which has been boiled gently and strained and allowed to cool", P). It is much used by the Hindus both as food and for religious rites. For *gh*. as an attr. the term *ājyapātra* is more frequently used. – Another n.: *ājya*.
Lit.: GoRI 1:332; P 940.

Girija-Narasiṁha ("the mountain-born N."), n. of a form of Narasiṁha showing the man-lion coming out from a mountain cave. He is represented without a Śakti. Char.: att.: *utkuṭikāsana*; attr.: *cakra*, *gadā*, *padma*, *śaṅkha*. – Varieties: Kevala-, Yoga-Narasiṁha.
Lit.: R 1:149 a.pl. 42-43.

Girīśa ("mountain-lord"), epithet of Śiva.
Lit.: DHP 191.

Gītā ("song"; Buddh.), n. of a goddess of the *lāsyā*-group, or of one of the Lamaist *aṣṭamātaras*. Char.: colour: red; attr.: *kaṅsī*, *viṇā*.
Lit.: BBh. 313; G 36, 82.

GLAUṀ, a *bījamantra* symbolizing Gaṇeśa.
Lit.: DHP 343.

godhā, *godhikā* "a kind of lizard or alligator" (attr.). It may be held in one hand or be placed beside an image. Char. of: Mahiṣāsuramardinī, Pārvatī. It is also connected with Śrī (for Śrī as a variety of Gaurī, see B.). – Cp. *saraṭa*.
Lit.: B 498, 501 a.pl. 41:4; WHW 1:48.

Goḷakamaharṣi, n. of a *śaivabhakta* (South India), "the founder of a well-known line of Śaiva Ācāryas". – Mu.: *añjalimudrā*.
Lit.: SB 182 a.pl. 114.

Goloka ("world of cows"), n. of the heaven of Kṛṣṇa.
Lit.: WM 80.

gomastaka "cow-head" (attr.). It is held in one hand by Kāladūtī. Cp. *vṛṣamastaka*.
Lit.: KiSB 76.

Gomateśvara ("lord Gomata"; Jain.) = Gommaṭa.
Lit.: Th. pl. 37; SIB pl. 24.

gomeda(ka) (Tam. *kōmētakam*), n. of a precious stone, one of the *navaratna**, sometimes said to be unidentified, but TL: "Sardonyx from the Himalayas and the Indus".
Lit.: MW 366; TL 2:1190.

gomedha (or *gaumedha*) "cattle sacrifice".

Gomedha ("cow-sacrifice"; Jain.), NP of a *yakṣa* attending on the 22nd *tīrthaṅkara* (Nemi of the *śvetāmbara*-sect). Śakti: Ambikā; symbol: *stūpa*; another attr.: *triśiras*.
Lit.: B 563; GJ 362; KiDG 81.

Gommaṭa (Jain.), NP of a saint, the son of Ṛṣabha(nātha); regarded by the *digambara*-sect as a *tīrthaṅkara*. He is represented entwined with a creeper. Epithets: Bāhubalin, Gomateśvara.
Lit.: GJ 268, 392 a.pl. 11; KiJ 15 a.pl. 45; ZA 297 a.pl. 245.

gomukha "cow-face", in architecture n. given to a kind of gargoyle.
Lit.: BECA 1:261.

Gomukha ("cow-headed"; Jain.), NP of a *yakṣa* attending on Ṛṣabha(nātha). He is influenced by the Hindu Śiva. Char.: Vāh.: *vṛṣan*; attr.: *paraśu*, *pāśa*, *vṛṣamastaka*.
Lit.: B 562; GJ 362 a.pl. 24:1; KiJ 11 a.pl. 27:1.

gomukhāsana "cow-face (gargoyle) sitting" (att.), n. of a Yogic posture.
Lit.: KiH pl. 151 row 3:3.

gonasa "snake" (attr.), see *nāga*.
Lit.: MEIA 216.

mGon-dkar ("the white protector"; Tib., pronounced Gon-kar; Buddh.), in Lamaism n. of a variety of Mahākāla. Char.: colour: white; Vāh.: 2 Vināyakas; attr.: *aṅkuśa*, *bodhisattvābharaṇa*, *cintāmaṇi*, *ḍamaru*, *kapāla*, *karttṛkā*, *trinayana*, *triśūla*. He has a fearful appearance.
Lit.: G 90; JT 92.

mGon-po nag-po ("the black protector"; Tib., pronounced Gom-po; Buddh.), in Lamaism n. of a variety of Mahākāla (six-armed). Char.: colour: blue; Vāh.: Vināyaka (who has the attr.: *ākhu*, *kapāla*, *puṣpa*); attr.: *ḍamaru*, *kapāla*, *karttṛkā*, *muṇḍamālā*, *pāśa*, *triśūla*.
Lit.: G 90; JT 92.

Gopaka (Buddh.), NP of a Lamaist *arhat*. Attr.: *pustaka*.
Lit.: G 104.

Gopāla ("cow-herd"), epithet of Kṛṣṇa.

gopī "cowherdess, cowherd's wife". The *g.* signifies primarily the cowherdesses or milkmaids who were the companions of Kṛṣṇa, and the principal of whom was Rādhā; the *gopī*s have therefore in some contexts been regarded as a multiple form of the Śakti. Attr.: *gopīyantra*. – *g.* is also the n. given to a female figure which serves as a lamp-stand, see *dīpagopī*.
Lit.: B 422; GI pl. 69; IC 1:521; RAAI 272; WHW 1:400.

Gopī ("shepherdess"; Buddh.), another n. of the wife of the Buddha, see Yaśodharā.
Lit.: KiSB 10.

gopīcandana "cowherdess-sandal" (attr.), n. of a kind of sandalpaste, or white or yellow clay, used esp. by worshippers of Viṣṇu for making a secterial mark, see *tilaka*.
Lit.: GH 44; IC 1:571; SSI 259.

gopikāvastrāpaharaṇa (or *-haraka*) "the theft of the milkmaids' clothes" (committed by Kṛṣṇa).
Lit.: JDI 93; SSI 47.

gopīyantra "instrument of a cowherdess" (attr.), n. of a musical instrument, a kind of drum, with a string that is pulled ("Zupftrommel"). It is supposed to have been used by the *gopī*s of Kṛṣṇa.
Lit.: SMII 79.

gopura(m) "ornamented, pyramidal gateway of a temple", cp. *dvāra*.
Lit.: DKI 41; RAAI 272; SSI fig. 1; WHW 1:58; ZA 278

gorajī, n. of a kind of *śvetāmbara*-monk (Jain.).
Lit.: GJ 341.

Gorakhnāth, n. of an *avatāra* of Śiva, worshipped in Nepal, and founder of the sect *gorakhnāthī* (the ascetics of this sect are named *kāṇphaṭayogin*s). The n. G. is often rendered as Gorakṣanātha ("the protectors of the cow-keepers (the inhabitants of Nepal, i.e. Gorkhās), or cow-eaters [?]"); hence his sect also as *gorakṣanāthī*; the latter name-form is probably due to an incorrect hypersanskritism.
Lit.: IC 1:630; WHW 1:402.

gorakṣāsana "the position of a *gorakṣa*" (att.), n. of a Yogic posture.
Lit.: KiH pl. 152 row 1:3.

gorocanā "bright yellow orpiment prepared from the bile of cattle" (used for marking the *tilaka*; attr.).
Lit.: IC 1:571; MW 366.

Gośāla ("cow-stall, born in a cow-stall"; M.Ind. Gosāla), see Maskarin Gośāla.

gowar (N.Ind.), n. of a festival (at Suratgarh). During this festival the women knead clay images of Pārvatī and Śiva and other deities and crown them with wreaths of flowers. (The n. may perhaps be identical with Hi. *gobar* "cow-dung", cp. Hi. *gobar-gaṇeś* "thick", lit. "an image of Gaṇeśa in cow--dung").

Lit.: P 921; H. RYDH, Indisk ökenby (Stockholm 1956) 80.

Govardhana ("cow-prosperity"), n. of a famous hill near Mathurā, which was lifted up and supported by Kṛṣṇa for seven days upon one finger or with one hand to give shelter (like an umbrella) to the cowherds from a rain-storm sent by Indra.

Lit.: JMS 69 a.pl. 90; Gt 233; MG pl. facing p. 142; P 921; WM 81; ZA 221 a.pl. 76a.

Govardhana-Kṛṣṇa (or -dhara "Kṛṣṇa supporting Mount Govardhana"), epithet of Kṛṣṇa holding up Mount Govardhana with his right hand.

Lit.: JDI 94; R 1:214 a.pl. 65-66; SSI 43.

Govinda (lit. "finding cows", also interpreted as "the Rescuer of the Earth", DHP), epithet of Kṛṣṇa; also n. of an aspect of Viṣṇu, see *caturviṅśatimūrti*.

Lit.: DHP 154; GoRI 1:241; Gt 233; KiSH 39; R 1:229 a.pl. 70.

Govinda-Bhairava, n. of a form of Bhairava.

Lit.: SSI 151.

graha ("seizing"), n. given to a planet (magically seizing human beings). The number of *g*. is said to be either 5 (Maṅgala, Budha, Bṛhaspati, Śukra, Śani) or 7 (in addition Rāhu, Ketu) or 9 (in addition Sūrya and Candra, see *navagraha*; alluding to this number, *g*. is also a symbolic n. of the number "9", see *saṅkhyā*). Certain *avatāras* of Viṣṇu are also manifested as *g*., and this n. is in addition given to of a kind of evil demons or spirits. – Cp. *nakṣatra*, *rāśi*.

Lit.: DHP 166; KiH 6; IC 1:491; KiK 33; MKVI 1:243; R 1:318.

Grahamātṛkā ("demon mother"; Buddh.), NP of a Mahāyāna goddess, an emanation of Vairocana. Char.: att.: *padmāsana*; Mu.: *dharmacakramudrā*; attr.: *dhanus*, *padma*, *śara*, *triśiras*, *vajra*.

Lit.: BBh. 224 a.pl. 165; KiDG 64, 75 a.pl. 66; KiSB 108.

grahī ("seizing"), n. of a group of witches who kill new-born children.

Lit.: DHP 288; IC 1:528.

graiveya(ka) "jewelled necklace" (attr.), n. of an ornament. Char. of *yakṣas*. Cp. *hāra*.

Lit.: B 290; BECA 1:261.

dGra-lha ("enemy-god", Tib., pronounced Da-lha; Buddh.), in Lamaism n. of one of the *mahāpañcarājas*. Char.: colour: blue; Vāh.: *siṅha* (blue); attr.: *khakkhara*, *vajra*.

Lit.: G 93; JT 88.

grāmadevatā (Tam. *kirāmatēvatai*) "village deity, the tutelar deity of a village". This n. is not quite adequate, because these gods are not restricted to villages but are also found in the large towns and cities of India. "They are qualified first by as a rule not being served by Brāhman priests..." (DiIP). Different forms of deity and esp. of goddesses, e.g. Kālī, Durgā, Cāmuṇḍā, and others (see SSI) figure as *g*. Male village gods are not so numerous (e.g. Aiyaṉār). See also *grāmakālī*, Mātā(ji), and cp. *iṣṭadevatā*, *kuladevatā*.

Lit.: DHP 301, 307; DiIP 172; FKR 110; GH 110; GoRI 2:7; Gt 233; IC 1:486; SB 359 a.pl. 369-372; SSI 223; WHW 1:398; WM 81.

grāmakālī "village-Kālī", common n. of a village deity, see *grāmadevatā*.

Lit.: DHP 301, 307.

Grāmaṇī ("leader of troups"), n. of a *yakṣa* attending on Śiva.

Lit.: MW 373.

granthi "knot, tie" (Buddh.). In Lamaism a *yantra* representing an endless knot symbolizing "the endless cycle of rebirths". A design apparently representing an endless knot is found also on some Indus Valley seals. – See *aṣṭamaṅgala*.

Lit.: G 8 (ill.).

gṛdhra "vulture" (Vāh.). Char. of: Ketu, Śani. Several *g*. are char. of: Tripurā, Durgā.

Lit.: MEIA 236; WHW 1:155.

gṛdhramastaka "vulture-headed" (attr.). Char. of Garuḍa.

Gṛdhrāsyā ("vulture-faced"; Buddh.), n. of a minor goddess.

Lit.: BBh. 319.

gṛhadevatā "houshold deity" (attr.), n. of the tutelary deity of the house. This deity (like

the *kuladevatā)* seldom bears any distinct appellation, but is rather the *avyakta* form of a deity, represented e.g. by a *śālagrāma*, a *bāṇaliṅga*, a *tulasī*-plant, a basket with some rice, a water-jar, etc. The *g.* is also sometimes represented by a small image of a god. Cp. *kuladevatā*.
Lit.: Gt Suppl. 47.

gṛhastha "householder", n. of the second stage of the religious life of a *brāhmaṇa* (performing the duties of the father of a family).
Lit.: Gt 234; IC 1:601; WHW 1:85.

gṛhyaguru "house-priest" (see *guru*).
Lit.: GJ 416.

grīṣma "the hot season, summer" from the middle of May to the middle of July.
Lit.: IC 2:723, 732.

Grīṣmadevī ("summer-goddess"; Buddh.), in Lamaism n. of one of the seasonal deities, a *ḍākinī* who accompanies Śrīdevī. Char.: colour: red; Vāh.: *camara* (blue); attr.: *kapāla, paraśu*.
Lit.: G 35.

grīva "neck", in architecture n. of the narrower part of a *stūpa*.
Lit.: BECA 1:272; SB 23; ZA 270.

sGrol-ma ("saviouress", Tib., pronounced Dol-ma), see Tārā.
Lit.: JT 123.

guhā "cave", see *lenā*.
Lit.: IC 2:320.

Guha ("the secret one"), epithet of Skanda (hidden in the thicket of reeds on the Ganges). Cp. Guha-Subrahmanya.
Lit.: DHP 299.

Guha-Subrahmaṇya (see Guha), n. of a form of Skanda. Char.: Mu.: *abhaya-, varada-mudrā*; attr.: *trinayana, triśūla, vajra*.
Lit.: R 2:442.

guhya "penis" (attr.), see *liṅga*.
Lit.: STP 1:13.

guhyaka ("hidden, concealed"), n. of a class of demigods (attendants of Kubera, 11 in number) who often are identified with the *yakṣas*. Their chief is Revanta. – *g.* is also a symbolic n. of the number "11", see *saṅkhyā*.
Lit.: BPR 28; GH 107; WHW 1:398; WM 82.

gulābdān(ī) (Hi., properly Pers.) "vessel used for sprinkling rose-water at religious ceremonies" (attr.).
Lit.: MH 37.

gūlar (Hi., Skt *guḍa+ra* or *-la*) "wild fig", see *udumbara*.
Lit.: GH 64; P 926.

Gulsiliā Mātā (N. Ind.), n. of one of the *saptamātaras*. She plagues children of every age.
Lit.: GH 136.

gumphā "cave" (with cave pictures), see *lenā*.
Lit.: Gz 54.

guñjamālā "garland made of seeds of the plant Abrus precatorius" (attr.). Char. of Tvaritā.
Lit.: MW 356; SSI 212.

Gupta ("protected"), n. of an empire and dynasty in Magadha, and of a period in art-history from the 4th-6th cc. A.D.
Lit.: Gz 88; RAAI 129; WHW 1:417.

Guptā ("protected"; Buddh.), NP of a *yakṣiṇī*.
Lit.: KiSB 74.

guptakāla "the era of Gupta". n. of an era, beginning in A.D. 319 and used in Central India and Nepal until the 13th c. The year of this era is *vartamāna, caitrādi* and *pūrṇimānta* (see *samvatsara* and *candramāsa*); the year + 318 or 319 = the year A.D. – Cp. *valabhī*.
Lit.: Enc.Brit. 5:721; IC 2:737; WHW 1:334.

guptāsana "secret sitting" (att.), n. of a kind of *āsana*-posture which resembles the *vīrāsana*, but in which the feet are kept hidden under the *dhotī*.
Lit.: KiH pl. 152; row 1:1.

Gur-gyi mGon-po (Tib., pronounced Gur-gyi Gom-po; Buddh.), in Lamaism n. of a variety of Mahākāla. He is the patron of tents. Char.: colour: blue; Vāh.: *nara*; attr.: *gadā, kapāla, karttṛkā*.
Lit.: G 14, 90.

guru ("venerable") "spiritual father or preceptor", a title given to the teacher. For the *liṅgāyats* the *g.* is the first object of adoration and is here included among the *aṣṭāvaraṇa*. *g.* is further esp. the title given

to the ten "preceptors" or patriarchs of the Sikh sect, from Nānak (†A.D. 1539) to Gobind Singh (†A.D. 1708). – Cp. *sādhu*.
Lit.: GH 78; GJ 373; GoRI 2:249; Gt 236; RAAI 272; WHW 1:419, 2:396.

gurudvārā (or *gurdwārā*, Hi.) "residence of a *guru*", n. given to a Sikh temple.

Guru-Granth "the scripture of the *gurus*", n. of the Sikh canon. It is composed of the writings and sayings of the *gurus* and other saints. Another n.: Ādi-Granth.
Lit.: WHW 2:398.

guruvāra (or *-vāsara*) "the teacher's day, Thursday", see *bṛhaspativāra*.

rGyal-mtsan (Tib., pronounced *gyal-tsen*) "trophy, a kind of banner or decoration of cloth, cylindrical in shape, erected upon a flag-staff or carried on a pole" (attr.).
Lit.: HuGT pl. 81 f.; JT 109.

H

HAḤ (Jain.), a mystical *bīia* signifying the navel, see *śānti*.
Lit.: GJ 369.

haima "golden", n. of a colour, see further *pīta*.
Lit.: MEIA 238.

Haimavatī "daughter of Himavān", epithet of Pārvatī.
Lit.: MW 1304.

hala "plough" (attr.), a symbol of agriculture. Char. esp. of Balarāma (particularly as Saṅkarṣaṇa-Baladeva), further of: Ananta, Āpa, Balabhadra, Dhara, Kapila, Ṣaṇmukha, Śarabha, Sarasvatī, Trivikrama, Vārāhī, Viśvarūpa. – Other n.: *lāṅgala*, *sīra*.
Lit.: B 300, 423; MEIA 245, 270; MKVI 2:451; R 1:7 a.pl. 2:8; Th. 39; WM 108 a.fig. 66.

Halabhṛt ("carrying a plough"), epithet of Balarāma.
Lit.: D 116.

hālāhala, n. of a kind of poison, see *kālakūṭa*.
Lit.: DHP 167.

Hālāhala(-Lokeśvara) ("L. [lord] of poison"; Buddh.), n. of a variety of Avalokiteśvara. Char.: colour: white; att.: *lalitāsana* upon a red *padma* (the Śakti upon the left knee); Mu.: *varadamudrā*; attr.: *ajina* (tigerskin), *akṣamālā*, *Amitābhabimba* on the crown, *candra*, *dhanus*, *kapāla*, *padma*, *śara*, *trinayana*, *triśiras*, *triśūla*.
Lit.: BBh. 132, 394 a.pl. 109, 3(A); G 66; KiDG 52 a.pl. 24, 26; KiSB 58, 61.

halāsana "plough-sitting" (att.), n. of a Yogic posture in which "one lies on the back, hands flat alongside body, palms on floor"
Lit.: WHW 1:75.

Halāyudha ("having a plough as weapon, tool"), epithet of Balarāma.
Lit.: D 116; GoRI 1:241.

Halebīd, n. of a village in Mysore state, South India, with temples from the 13th c. A.D.
Lit.: ZA pl. 428 ff.

HAṀ, a *bījamantra*, dedicated to Śiva and symbolizing the element of water.
Lit.: DHP 344; GH 55.

hammiya (Pāli), see *harmikā*.

Hammu Mātā (also Hamu; "mother Hammu", Bhīlī), n. of a mother goddess who is worshipped by the Bhīls.
Lit.: KBh. 160.

haṅsa "(wild) goose, swan" (Vāh.). A variation of the sun bird (esp. the golden *h.*; cp. also Garuḍa), as may be evident from the legend of the Liṅgodbhavamūrti*; *h.* is perhaps "identifié au soleil ou au dieu suprême" (MEIA). It is also said to symbolize the wandering soul and the senses. – In Buddhism *h.* symbolizes the propagation of Buddhist doctrine to all realms. – Char. esp. of Brahmā, also of: Amitābha, Brāhmī, Brahmāṇī, Candra, Sarasvatī, Varuṇa.
Lit.: B 379; GH 71; GoRI 1:318; H pl. 15:159; HAHI 8; HuGT 20; IC 1:536; KiSH 88; KrA pl. 67; MEIA 230; RAAI 272; Th. 43; WHW 1:155; WM 82; ZA 156.

Haṅsa ("goose"), n. of a deity, sometimes regarded as an *avatāra* of Viṣṇu.
Lit.: B 390; WM 191.

haṅsabandhana "swan frieze", in architecture n. of a frieze of a temple building.
Lit.: BECA 1:261.

haṅsadīpa "goose lamp" (attr.), n. of a kind of *dīpa* which has a stand or handle in the shape of a goose. Cp. *mayūr dīpak*.
Lit.: MH 37 a.pl. 7:2.

haṅsamantra "goose *mantra*" ("the Thought-Form of the Swan of Knowledge"), n. of a *mantra* which serves the purpose: "To attain the four objects-of-human-life (*puruṣārtha*): righteousness, pleasure, prosperity, and liberation". As to the form, see DHP.
Lit.: DHP 348.

haṅsamudrā "swan-handpose" (Mu.), n. of a variety of the *mukulamudrā*, with the difference: the thumb, forefinger and middle finger are joined, the others outstretched. It signifies tying the marriage thread, initiation, the wedding night, a drop of water, painting a picture, rubbing, holding a garland. – Subvariety: *bhramaramudrā*.
Lit.: WHW 2:87.

haṅsasiṅhāsana "goose-lion-throne" (Vāh.), n. of a seat with goose-figures carved on the supports. – Cp. *siṅhāsana*.
Lit.: MH 44.

Haṅsavāhana ("having a goose as Vāh."), epithet of Brahmā.
Lit.: DHP 237.

Hanumān (also -mat, -mant, Hanū-; "having [large] jaws"), n. of a very popular god in the shape of a monkey, the son of Pavana (Vāyu) and Añjanā. In the epic Rāmāyaṇa he appears as a companion and doughty supporter of Rāma. He is usually worshipped as a minor god attending on Viṣṇu (Rāma), and upon the altar-stands he stands on the same level as Garuḍa; but he is also worshipped as an independent deity. He is represented as a monkey with a long and powerful tail. Char.: colour: red; att.: (often) *ālīḍhāsana* (treading on the goddess of Laṅkā, the chief town of Sri Lanka), *sampīḍita* (?); Mu.; *abhaya-*, *añjali-*, *varada-mudrā*;; attr.: (esp.) *gadā*, further *dhanus*, *keśa*, *pañcaśiras* (sometimes), *śaila* Mahodaya, *vajra*; also other weapons.
Lit.: B 527; D 116; DHP pl. 15; GH pl. 8; GI pl. 78; GoRI 1:316; Gt 239 a.Suppl. 48; IA 7; IIM 102; JDI 82; MEIA 50; MG 225; R 1:186 a.pl. 54-57; SB 348 a.pl. 319; SSI 64; Th. pl. 17; WHW 1:425; WM 82.

Hara ("remover, seizer, destroyer"), epithet of Śiva; also n. of one among the group *ekādaśarudra*. Char.: Mu.: *tarjanīmudrā*; attr.: *akṣamālā*, *aṅkuśa*, *ḍamaru*, *gadā*, *ghaṭa*, *khaṭvāṅga*, *mudgara*, *nāga*, *paraśu*, *paṭṭikā* (?), *paṭṭiśa*, *śakti*, *tomara*, *triśūla*.
Lit.: DHP 196; GoRI 1:255; R 2:389; ZA 146.

hāra "garland of pearls, necklace" (attr.). Char. of goddesses, e.g. Mahāsarasvatī, also of gods, e.g. Śiva (Candraśekharamūrti), Sūrya, Viṣṇu. – Cp. *graiveyaka*.
Lit.: B 290; R 1:23; SB 61 a.passim; WHW 2:161.

Hara-Pārvatī, n. of a composite representation of Hara (i e. Śiva) and Pārvatī. Char: attr.: (Śiva) *ūrdhvaliṅga*, (Śakti) *darpaṇa*, *nīlotpala*.
Lit.: B 467 a.pl. 38:2, 39:2.

Haṛappā, n. of a village in the Indus Valley (Pakistan), one of the sites of the so-called Indus Valley civilization. Remnants have been excavated there of a culture dating from about B.C. 2500-1800.
Lit.: Gz 23; RAAI 11; WIA 100; WIC 18.

Harasiddhi ("accomplishment of seizing"), n. of a form of Durgā (four-armed). Attr.: *ḍamaru*, *kamaṇḍalu*, *khaḍga*.
Lit.: R 1:343.

Hardaul (or Hardaur; N.Ind.), n. of a cholera god (also wedding god) worshipped in Bundelkhand. H. is in fact based on a historic person (who died in A.D. 1627).
Lit.: MG 256.

Hari ("yellow, reddish brown"; the etymology of this word is ambiguous and it is also, but hardly correctly, interpreted as "the Remover of Sorrow", DHP), epithet used

of several gods, e.g. Indra, Yama, Śiva; but Viṣṇu in particular is known by this n. H. is also regarded as a certain aspect of Viṣṇu, see *caturviṅśatimūrti*.
Lit.: DHP 154; KiSH 39; R 1:230 a.pl. 71; ZA 146.

Hari-ardha(mūrti) (or Haryardha), see Hari-Hara(mūrti).
Lit.: B 465; R 2:332.

haricandana (a sort of sandal tree), n. of one of the five trees of paradise (see *vṛkṣa*).
Lit.: GH 65; MW 1290.

Haridrā-Gaṇapati ("Hari-sleep-G."), n. of a form of Gaṇeśa (four-armed); cp. also Rātri-Gaṇapati ("Night-G."). Both names clearly refer to the sleep of Viṣṇu (Hari) reposing on the serpent Ananta (see Anantāśāyana), and to a festival celebrated on the 11th day of the month *āṣāḍha*, regarded as the night of the gods. – Attr.: *aṅkuśa*, *danta*, *modaka*, *pāśa*.
Lit.: MW 876; R 1:59.

Hari-Hara(mūrti) ("representation of Hari and Hara"), n. of a syncretistic icon, half Viṣṇu (Hari), half Śiva (Hara). This image symbolizes a syncretism between the Viṣṇu and the Śiva cults, and it is mythologically sometimes explained thus: H. is said to be the son of Śiva and Viṣṇu (Mohinī) born by their sexual union (WHW concerning an androgynous form of H., cp. below). Each half of this icon shows the features char. of both gods concerned. Usually the right half (as in Ardhanārī) is endowed with the attr. of Śiva, and the left half has the attr. of Viṣṇu. Often this left half representing Viṣṇu is made in a female shape (as the Śakti of Śiva), probably signifying Mohinī as the female aspect of Viṣṇu, but it may also be pointed out that both Umā, Durgā and Devī are sometimes regarded as the female aspect of Viṣṇu (R). It should also be noted that in the cosmical progress Śiva represents the male principle, and Viṣṇu the female principle. When H. is found in this form (half male, half female), the difference between H. and the similar Ardhanārī may be hard to prove. – Char.: colour: blue; Mu.: *abhayamudrā*; attr.: (Viṣṇu) *cakra*, *gadā*, *padma*, *śaṅkha*; (Śiva) *akṣamālā*, *paraśu*, *triśūla*, (sometimes) *ūrdhvaliṅga*. – Other n.: Hari-ardha-(mūrti), Hari-Śaṅkara, Śaṅkara-Nārāyaṇa, Śiva-Nārāyaṇa.
Lit.: B 465, 546 a.pl. 46:3 (both halves male); HIS 23; IC 1:518; JDI 26; KiH 21 a.pl. 64-65; KiSH 29; MEIA 46; MG 196 (for the pl. facing p. 97, see Ardhanārīnaṭeśvara); R 2:332 a.pl. 99-100; SSI 125; Th. 91; WHW 1:43; WM 83; ZA 147 a.pl. 515.

Harihara-Lokeśvara (Buddh.), n. of a variety of Avalokiteśvara. Char.: att.: *samapādasthānaka*; Vāh.: *padma*; Mu.: *vyākhyānamudrā*.
Lit.: BBh. 429 a.pl. 84(A).

Hari-Hara-Pitāmaha, n. of a *trimūrti*, a composite of Viṣṇu (Hari), Śiva (Hara), and Brahmā (Pitāmaha). This triple person is regarded as the son of Atri and Anasūyā, or of Kauśika and his wife (name unknown). H. may also be represented with four (!) heads and six arms. Dattātreya is mentioned as a common incarnation of these three gods. – Attr.: (Viṣṇu) *cakra*, *gadā*; (Śiva) *khaṭvāṅga*, *triśūla*; (Brahmā) *akṣamālā*, *kamaṇḍalu*; furthermore: *caturmukha* or *triśiras*.
Lit.: R 1:251 a.pl. 72:1, 74.

Hari-Hara-putra ("son of Hari and Hara"), epithet of Aiyaṉār, regarded as the son of Hari (i.e. Viṣṇu, here in his female aspect as Mohinī) and Hara (i.e. Śiva).
Lit.: ACA 10; GoRI 2:14; R 2:485.

Hari-Hara-Sūrya-Buddha, n. of a syncretistic representation of Hari (Viṣṇu) + Hara (Śiva) + Sūrya + the Buddha.
Lit.: B 547 a.pl. 48:1.

Hariharihari-vāhana(-Lokeśvara) (or -vāhanodbhava-; "manifestation of L. having three Haris as Vāh."; Buddh.), n. of a variety of Avalokiteśvara (six-armed). Char.: colour: white; Vāh.: Viṣṇu upon Garuḍa upon a *siṅha* (the 3 Haris in the n. refer to these 3 Vāh.); Mu.: *varada*-,

vyākhyāna-mudrā; attr.: *ajina* (deerskin), *akṣamālā*, *daṇḍa*, *kamaṇḍalu*, *khaṭvāṅga*, *trinayana*, *triśūla*.
Lit.: BBh. 136, 394 a.pl. 113, 4(A); G 65; KiSB 59.

harijan (Hi.) "the people of God (Hari)", modern euphemism created by Gandhi referring to "the untouchables" (cp. *aspṛśya*).

hārin "gazelle" (Vāh.), see *mṛga*.
Lit.: MEIA 230.

Hariṇegamesi (or -in, "Hari, i.e. Indra, as Ṇegamesi"; Jain.), n. of a god who serves as a kind of common Devarāja Indra*. See Naigameṣa.
Lit.: B 562.

Hari-Śaṅkara, another n. of Hari-Hara(mūrti).
Lit.: MEIA 46.

harita "green", n. of a colour. As to other n. of this colour, see MEIA.
Lit.: MEIA 238.

Haritatārā ("the green Tārā"), see Śyāmatārā.

Hārītī (or Haritī; "stealing" or "green").
1. (Hind.) NP of a mother-goddess (*mātā*, see *mātaras*); according to HIS she is the patroness of children; she is perhaps identical with Vṛddhi and may therefore be regarded as the wife of Kubera. Evidently she is a goddess who "steels (and devours?) children" and has much in common with Jarā; she is also identified with Nandā. She is worshipped in the north and the north-west of India. Husband: Pāñcika; attr.: *bāla* (usually sitting on her hip; sometimes being devoured).
Lit.: AIP 274; B 381; FKR 148; HIS 44, 58 a.pl. 16; IC 1:487; KiH 11; ZA 135 a.pl. 64b, 154-155, 473.
2. (Buddh.) NP of a smallpox goddess; also n. of a deity attending on the Buddha. H. is sometimes said to be the Buddhist goddess of fertility.
Lit.: B 383, 639; FKR 148; HIS 44.

Harivāhana-Lokeśvara ("L. having Hari [i.e. Viṣṇu] as vehicle, – or having the vehicle of Hari [?]"; Buddh.), n. of a variety of Avalokiteśvara. Char.: att.: *samapādasthānaka*; Vāh.: *padma*; attr.: *cāmara*, *kamaṇḍalu*.
Lit.: BBh. 429 a.pl. 82(A).

harmikā (Pāli: *hammiya*) "pavilion, the quadrangular housing or terrace that crowns a *stūpa*", an architectural term.
Lit.: BRI 113; DKI 13; FBKI passim; RAAI 272; SB 23; ZA 233.

harmya "large house, palace; courtyard of a palace".
Lit.: DKI 80.

harmyadvāra "palace door", n. of a kind of temple gateway (cp. *gopura*) with five to seven storeys.
Lit.: BECA 1:260.

Harṣā ("joy, desire"), NP of the Śakti of Hṛṣīkeśa.
Lit.: R 1:233.

harṣakāla "the era of Harṣa", instituted by Harṣavardhana and used during the Harṣa empire esp. in Nepal. It begins in A.D. 606 and is indicated by the word *samvat*. The (*vartamāna*) year of this era + 605 or 606 = the year A.D.
Lit.: Enc.Brit. 5:721; IC 2:737; WHW 1:334.

Haryardhamūrti = Hari-ardhamūrti, see Hari-Hara(mūrti).

hasta ("hand") may, on one hand, be interpreted as a Mu. and then refers to a kind of handposes in which the whole hand and arm take part, cp. *abhayahasta(mudrā)*, which properly means: "a gesture in which the hand shows or grants fearlessness"; cp. *gajahasta* in which the whole arm participates in the pose (the word-member *-hasta-* is, however, very often omitted in the terms). On the other hand, *h.* can be connected with a certain attr., and the word then signifies this attr. when held in the hand, cp. *padmahasta* "holding a lotus in the hand". In this case *h.* is to be regarded as an attr. – As to the further differentiation of *hasta* and *mudrā*, see the latter headword.
Lit.: B 246; HAHI 16; SIB 61; Th. 27; WHW 1:422.

Hastā (or Hasta), n. of a *nakṣatra*. Its influence is good.
Lit.: BBh. 382; IC 2:729.

hastanişadana "the sitting down on the hands(?)" (att.), n. of an *āsana*-posture, a *yoga*-att., mentioned, but not described.
Lit.: B 271.

hastapūjāvidhi "the rite of worship on the hand", in esoteric Buddhism n. of a rite connected with the conception that the devotee is able mentally to reconstruct on his left hand a *maṇḍala* of three concentric zones, and with the worship due to this *maṇḍala*.
Lit.: SM 25.

hastasvastika "hand-cross" (Mu.), n. of a handpose (of the *samyukta*-type) in which the hands are crossed. This pose suggests devotion.
Lit.: SIB 61.

hastikara "elephant's trunk" (attr.; Buddh.). The trunk held in one hand, char. of Gandhahastin.
Lit.: BBh. 95.

hastin "elephant" (Vāh.), see *gaja*. A *h.* (*hastiratna* "elephant-treasure"), a mighty war elephant, is a *lakṣaṇa* of a *cakravartin*, see *saptaratna*.
Lit.: MEIA 235; WHW 1:551.

hastisaundika "mode of wearing the lower garment to suggest the contour of the elephant's trunk".
Lit.: SIB 68.

hāth levā (Hi.; lit. "one who takes the hand"), a term alluding to the rite of the "hand-taking" forming part of the *vivāha*-ceremonies, see *pāṇigrahaṇa*.
Lit.: J. G. HITREC, Son of the moon (word-list).

Hatthi (N.Ind.), n. of a cholera goddess who is worshipped in the northwest provinces of India.
Lit.: GH 135.

HAUṀ, a *bījamantra*, representing Śiva.
Lit.: DHP 343.

Hayagrīva ("Horse-neck"), originally probably n. of a horse deity worshipped by a horse-breeding tribe. Later H. was regarded as the "Protector of the Scripture".

1. (Hind.) N. of Viṣṇu in a certain *avatāra* in which he has a horse-head (*aśvamastaka*). Further char.: Mu.: *jñānamudrā*; attr.: *akṣamālā*, *aśvakeśara*, *pustaka* (Veda) and the attr. of Viṣṇu, esp. *cakra*, *kirīṭamukuṭa*, *śaṅkha*. Epithets and varieties: Hayaśiras, Hayaśīrṣa. Cp. Kalkin. – H. is also NP of a demon killed by Viṣṇu in his Matsyāvatāra (?). On account of this, Viṣṇu has also the epithet Hayagrīvaripu "the (victorious) enemy of Hayagrīva".
Lit.: D 120; DHP 185; KiDG 57; KiSB 68; KiSH 37; R 1:260 a.pl. 77; SSI 55; Th. 57 a.pl. 38; WM 84.

2. (Buddh.) NP of a *dharmapāla*, the patron of the horses. H. is an emanation of either Amitābha or Akṣobhya, and is the Buddhist counterpart of the Hindu Hayagrīva. – Śakti: Mārīcī. Char.: colour: red; att.: *lalitāsana*; Vāh.: *nāgas* or *rākṣasas* or *naras*; Mu.: *karaṇa-*, *tarjani-*, *svakucagraha-mūdrā*; attr.: esp. one or more *aśvamastakas* in the hair, *Amitābha-* or *Akṣobhya-bimba* on the crown, *daṇḍa*, *triśiras* (usually), *vajra*, furthermore: *agni*, *ajina* (tigerskin), *cakra*, *dhanus*, *dhvaja*, *gadā*, *khaḍga*, *nāgas*, *padma*, *paraśu*, *pāśa*, *puṣpa*, *śara*, *trinayana*, *triśūla*. – H. is also represented in a Garuḍa-form and is, besides, the deity that is often found on the shaft or handle of the *phur-bu*. – Epithets or varieties: Krodha-, Saptaśatika-Hayagrīva.
Lit.: B 559; BBh. 165 a.pl. 128f.; G 14, 36, 90; KiDG 57; KiSB 68, 74; R. H. van GULIK, Hayagrīva. The Mantrayānic aspect of horse-cult in China and Japan (Leiden 1935. Internationales Archiv für Ethnographie. Bd 33 Suppl.), 9.

Hayagrīva-Lokeśvara ("L. as Hayagrīva"; Buddh.), n. of a variety of Avalokiteśvara. Char.: att.: *padmāsana*; Mu.: *vyākhyānamudrā*; attr.: *akṣamālā*, *padma*.
Lit.: BBh. 394 a.pl. 1(A).

Hayagrīvaripu, see sub Hayagrīva 1.

haya-siṅhāsana "horse-lion-throne" (Vāh.), n. of a seat with horse-figures carved on the supports. – Cp. *siṅhāsana*.
Lit.: MH 44.

Hayaśiras, -śīrṣa ("horse-headed"), perhaps n. of two different aspects or *avatāra*s of Viṣṇu, but usually regarded as identical with Hayagrīva. Char.: Vāh.: *kūrma*. Other n.: Aśvaśiras, Hayāsya.
Lit.: DHP 185; WM 191.

Hayāsya ("horse-faced"), see Hayaśiras.
Lit.: MEIA 39.

Hayāsyā ("horse-faced"; Buddh.), n. of a minor goddess. Attr.: *aśvamastaka*.
Lit.: BBh. 319.

Hemacandra ("golden moon'), n. of a celebrated Jain author (A.D. 1088-1172). He belonged to the *śvetāmbara*-sect.
Lit.: GJ 108 a.passim; MW 1304.

hemagarbha "containing gold in the interior", n. of a kind of gift to a temple.
Lit.: MW 1304.

hemanta "winter, the cold season" from the middle of November to the middle of January.
Lit.: IC 2:723, 733.

Hemantadevī ("winter-goddess"; Buddh.), in Lamaism n. of a seasonal deity, a *ḍākinī* attending on Śrīdevī. Char.: colour: blue; Vāh.: *uṣṭra*; attr.: *kapāla*, *mudgara*.
Lit.: G 35, 82.

hemavaddha (Pāli, < Skt *hemavardhra*) "golden carrying-strap" (attr.: Buddh.), n. of a band worn by monks over the left shoulder and used for carrying the *bhikṣāpātra*.
Lit.: MBPC 78.

Heramba(-Gaṇapati), n. of an eight-armed form of Gaṇeśa which is particularly popular in Nepal but also worshipped in South India. Char.: Vāh.: *siṅha* or *ākhu*; attr.: *akṣamālā*, *danta*, *modaka*, *mudgara* (with 3 heads), *pañcaśiras*, *paraśu*, *pāśa*.
Lit.: KiSH 32; R 1:57 a.pl. 13-14; SSI 173 a.fig. 112; Th. 96.

Heruka (orig. a n. of Gaṇeśa or of an attendant of Śiva; later esp. Buddh.), n. of a Mahāyāna god who is an emanation of Akṣobhya and related with Vajraḍāka. He is one of the most popular deities of the Buddhist pantheon. H. is influenced by the Hindu Śiva and is worshipped in East India. He is regarded as a personification of *karuṇā* ("compassion"). In his Tantric form he is known as Hevajra. Śakti: Nairātmā ("knowledge"). Their union (*yoga*) "leads to a realization of the nothingness of existence, which results in *nirvāṇa*, or *mahāsukha*, eternal bliss" (G.). – Char.: att.: *yab-yum*; Vāh.: *mṛtaka*; attr.: *Akṣobhyabimba*, *cintāmaṇi*, *danta*s, *gadā*, *kapāla*, *karttṛkā*, *khaḍga*, *khaṭvāṅga*, *muṇḍamālā* (50 severed heads), *naracarma*, *pañcakapālaka*, *vajra*. See also *herukabuddha*.
Lit.: B 559; BBh. 155 a.pl. 125; G 87; KiDG 56; KiSB 64; MW 1305.

herukabuddha (Buddh.), n. of a group of Lamaist *yi-dam*-deities who are regarded as forms of Heruka. They are particular forms of the *dhyānibuddha*s who are united with their Śaktis. Att.: *ālīḍhāsana*, *yab-yum*. The names of the *h.* are: Buddha-, Vajra-, Ratna-, Padma-, Karma-heruka.
Lit.: G 36, 87.

Herukī (Buddh.), n. of an inferior Mahāyāna goddess.
Lit.: KiSB 66.

Hevajra (Buddh.), n. of a Tantric *bodhisattva* or *yi-dam* who is an emanation of Akṣobhya and is the Tantric form of Heruka. He is 8-headed and has 2, 4, 6 or 16 arms and 2 or 4 legs. He is represented dancing and is the Buddhist counterpart of the Hindu Śiva Naṭarāja. – Śakti: Nairātmā or Vajravārāhī or Vajraśṛṅkhalā; Char.: colour: blue; att.: *ālīḍhāsana* on animals or genies, *yab-yum*; Vāh.: 4 *māra*s; attr.: *Akṣobhyabimba*, *aṅkuśa*, *bodhisattvābharaṇa* or *dharmapālābharaṇa*, *cakra*, *caṣaka*, *cintāmaṇi*, *dhanus*, *ghaṇṭā*, *kapāla* (in all his hands), *khaḍga*, *khaṭvāṅga*, *padma*, *śara*, *tarjanīpāśa*, *trinayana*, *triśiras*, *triśūla*, *vajra*, *vajraghaṇṭā*. – His Śakti has one head and two arms; attr.: *karttṛkā*.
Lit.: BBh. 157; G 36, 84; GrH 200; ZA 372 a.pl. 563.

hijrat (Arab.-Pers. "departure", i.e. the flight of Muhammad from Mecca to Medina), n.

of the Moslem era, beginning in A.D. 622 (Hijra). The year of this era is lunar, and conversion to the year A.D. must be made according to special tables.
Lit.: IC 2:737; P 1221.

Himavān (-vat, -vant; "snowy, frosty, icy"), n. of the North Indian chain of snowy mountains, the Himālayas. As personification H. is regarded as the father of Pārvatī (cp. Haimavatī) and Gaṅgā (the n. Durgā may also suggest the same origin). The wife of H. is Menā.
Lit.: IIM 109; MW 1299; WM 84.

hīnayāna "lesser, minor vehicle" (Buddh.), a n. of the earliest system of the Buddhist doctrine created by the Mahāyāna Buddhists, the South-Indian branch of Buddhism which spread to Sri Lanka, Indonesia and Indo-China. – Another n.: *theravāda.*
Lit.: BRI 69; GBM 12; HIS 12; IC 2:516; KiSB 42.

Hiṅglāj(-Mātā) (N.Ind.), esp. in Baluchistan NP of a mother goddess.
Lit.: KBh. 186 N.; P 1238.

Hīrā ("diamond"), epithet of Lakṣmī.
Lit.: DHP 262.

Hiraṇyagarbha ("the Golden Embryo", a golden cosmic egg from which the universe is developed), epithet esp. of Brahmā. Cp. *brahmāṇḍa.*
Lit.: DHP 233, 237; GH 117; GRI 94; KiSH 40; WHW 1:252; WM 84.

Hiraṇyakaśipu ("having a golden seat or cushion"), NP of a demon (a brother of Hiraṇyākṣa) who was killed by Viṣṇu in his Narasiṁhāvatāra. H. was an incarnation of Rāvaṇa, but he is also said to be incarnated of Jaya.
Lit.: B 415; DHP 168; Gt 257; HAHI 24; IIM 112; WHW 1:451; WM 84.

Hiraṇyākṣa ("golden-eyed"), NP of a demon (a brother of Hiraṇyakaśipu) killed by Viṣṇu in his Varāhāvatāra. H. is sometimes said to be an incarnation of Vijaya.
Lit.: DHP 168; Gt 257, 680; WHW 1:451.

holī (Hi., < Skt *holikā*), n. of a new year and spring festival in the month *phālguna* (February-March). This is a fertility festival, during which people in the streets throw yellow or red powder, water and confetti at the passers-by. The patroness of the festival is said to be Holkā Mātā, who, however, may rather be regarded as a demon (see Holikā). This festival is usually said to be dedicated to Kṛṣṇa (playing with the *gopīs*), whose image is swung during the ceremonies. – Older n.: *phālgunotsava.* Another n.: *dolāyātrā.*
Lit.: AIM pl. 91; DIA pl. 45; GH 354; GJ 436; GoRI 1:340, 2:19; Gt Suppl. 34, 50; IC 1:590; KBh. 143; J. J. Meyer, Trilogie altindischer Mächte und Feste der Vegetation (Zürich 1937); MSHP 138; P 1242; WHW 1:354.

Holikā (Skt; Hi. Holkā Mātā), the patroness of the *holī*-festival; may originally have been a *rākṣasī* or a female demon. During the *holī* festival she is represented as a straw puppet which is chased by the children and finally burnt in fire.
Lit.: GH 354; IC 1:590; KBh. 149.

homa "oblation by fire", n. of a part of the *pūjā*, but originally connected with the *yajña.*
Lit.: DilP 90; GoRI 1:333; Gt 258; RV 176.

homajakalika (meaning not known; attr.). Char. of Tvaṣṭar.
Lit.: R 1:310.

horā (orig. Greek) "the art of horoscopy" Other n.: *jātaka, sroṅ-ta.*
Lit.: IC 1:619; WHW 1:285.

HRAḤ, a *bījamantra.*
Lit.: GJ 369.

HRĀṀ, a *bījamantra.*
Lit.: GJ 369.

Hrī ("shame, modesty"; Jain.), n. of goddess.
Lit.: GJ 363.

HRĪḤ, a *bījamantra.*

HRĪṀ or *HRIṀ*, *hrīṁ-kāra*, a *bījamantra*, named *māyābīja* or *śaktibīja*, of mystical sense, dedicated to Māyā. It is explained thus: *H* = Śiva, *R* = his nature, *Ī* = Transcendent-Illusion (*mahāmāyā*); the sound (cp. *nāda*) = progenitor of universe, the nasalization = the removing of sorrow. – It is found among the Tantric forms of all the Indian religions. In Jainism it particularly signifies the ears, the throat,

the eyes and the eyebrows, see *śānti*. – See also *yantrarāja*.
Lit.: DHP 342; GH 55; GJ 369, 385 a.pl. 27; IC 1:567; KiJ 12 a.pl. 30; KiSH 151; WHW 2:104.

Hṛṣīkeśa ("Lord of the Senses" [DHP]; probably more correct: "dem das Haupthaar zu Berge steht"), n. of an aspect of Viṣṇu, see *caturviṁśatimūrti*. Śakti: Harṣā.
Lit.: DHP 154; KiSH 39; R 1:229; SIB pl. 14; THUMB-HAUSCHILD, Handbuch des Sanskrit. T. 2 (Heidelberg 1953), 351.

HRŪṀ, a *bījamantra* which (in Jainism) signifies the heart, see *śānti*.
Lit.: GJ 369.

htī (Burmese), a term commonly used in architecture, signifying a reliquary placed at the top of a *stūpa* and covered by one or more *chattras*.
Lit.: CHIIA 81; DKI 13, 95 (ill.).

huḍukka (Tam. *uṭukku*; attr.), see *ḍamaru*.
Lit.: SMII 75.

hukkā (*huqqa*; Hi., orig. Pers.-Arab.) "casket, small box; water pipe (hookah)" (attr.). Char. of, e.g., Agastya.
Lit.: KiH 45; P 479.

Hulkā Devī (N.Ind.), as a personification of the act of vomiting H. is a cholera goddess.
Lit.: GH 135; MG 256.

HUṀ, a *bījamantra* which "protects from anger and demons".
Lit.: DHP 343.

HŪṀ.
1. (Hind.) Form of a *bījamantra* named *kūrcabīja*, representing Śiva.
Lit.: IC 1:567; WHW 2:104.
2. (Buddh.) A *bīja* which is included in the *mantra*: "*oṁ maṇi padme hūṁ*". *HŪṀ* is a blue (black) syllable; from it Akṣobhya and Vajrasattva, originate and it is meant to dispel demons.
Lit.: BBh. 51, 75; GBM 94.

HVĀṀ, a *bījamantra* which (in Jainism) signifies the male organ, see *śānti*.
Lit.: GJ 369.

Hva-saṅ (Tib.; Buddh.), NP of a (historically known) teacher in Mahāyāna Buddhism. Attr.: *akṣamālā*, *śaṅkha*.
Lit.: G 104.

I

i, abbreviation of *iṅlandīya vatsara*, indicating an era, see *khristābda*.

ī, abbreviation of *isvī* or *īsvābda*, indicating an era, see *khristābda*.

ibha "elephant" (Vāh.), see *gaja*.
Lit.: MEIA 235.

ihāmṛga (?), n. of a hybrid animal, often used as a decorative motif, esp. in the art-work of the Mathurā school. Cp. *gaṇḍabheruṇḍa*, *makara*, *śarabha*, *timiṅgala*. (N.B. that the term is dubious, the word-form **ardhamṛga* being what the experienced linguist might expect. It is possibly due to a hypersanskritism of some M.Indian wordform).
Lit.: JSM 17, 21 (ill.).

ikṣu(kāṇḍa) "sugar-cane" (attr.). As a symbol of agricultural fertility char. of Gaṇeśa (in different forms).
Lit.: R 1:54.

ikṣukārmuka "sugar-cane bow" (attr.), see *ikṣukodaṇḍa*.
Lit.: ACA 34, 36.

ikṣukodaṇḍa "sugar-cane bow" (attr.), n. of a variety of *dhanus*; it is connected with *pañcaśara*, and its bow-string is a row of bees (see *madhukara*). Esp. char. of Kāmadeva, but also of Lalitā, Rājarājeśvarī, Tripurasundarī, Ūrdhva-Gaṇapati, Veṇugopāla, and some forms of Aiyaṉār, Skanda. – Another n.: *ikṣu-kārmuka*.
Lit.: GH 113; R 1:210.

Ikṣvāku, n. of the ancestor of the *sūryavaṅśa* in Ayodhyā.
Lit.: D 310; DHP 96; Gt 259; KiSB 8.

iṅ, abbreviation of *iṅlandīya vatsara*, indicating an era, see *khristābda*.

Indirā ("the Powerful-One"), epithet of Lakṣmī.
Lit.: DHP 262.

Indra (strictly speaking the meaning of the n. is unknown; it is sometimes understood as meaning "strong, mighty", derived from *ind-* "equipping with great power" or *inv-* "advance").

1. NP of a Vedic weather god (or sun god) and fertility genius. In the Ṛgveda he is very often named "the bull" (*vṛṣan*, *vṛṣabha*), a fact which is very often forgotten in the descriptions of this god. However from this bull-character of his both his function as a weather god (cp., e.g., the Hittite weather gods, WM) and as a warrior can be explained. In Vedic mythology I. was the king of gods, and his chief weapon was the *vajra*. Sometimes he is said to be the son of Kāśyapa and Aditi (but he is not counted among the usual Ādityas); in the later Vedas he is, however, regarded as the son of Dyauṣ Pitā and Pṛthivī.

In the later stages of the Indian religions he is worshipped as the *dikpāla* of the east direction; his *diggaja* is Airāvata. In Hinduism he is also regarded as an aspect of Śiva. Even in Buddhism and Jainism he is (except as a *dikpāla*) comprehended as a god, though of an inferior rank; in Jainism there is in every heaven one king of gods named Indra. – Wife: Indrāṇī (also named Aindrī, Śacī); sometimes also Sītā and Saraṇyu are mentioned as his wives; sons: Jayanta, Nīlāmbara, Ṛṣabha, Mīḍhuṣa and the Ṛbhus. – Char.: Vāh.: *gaja* Airāvata (Airāvaṇa), or *ratha* Puṣpaka, or the white *aśva* Uccaiḥśravas, (in the Ṛgveda a pair of bays, *harī*, with *ratha* serve as Vāh.), or *siṁhāsana*; Mu.: *varadamudrā*; attr.: *akṣamālā*, *aṅkuśa*, *dhanus* Vijaya (= the rainbow Indradhanus), *jāla* Indrajāla, *kamaṇḍalu*, *khaḍga* Parañjaya, *kirīṭamukuṭa*, *nīlotpala*, *padma*, *pāśa*, *sahasranayana*, *śakti*, *śaṅkha* Devadatta, *śiraścakra*, *trinayana*, *vajra*, *yajñopavīta*. – In Buddhism, I. as a *dikpāla* has the characteristics: colour: yellow; Vāh.: *gaja* Airāvata; attr.: *vajra*. Epithet: Karivāhana.

Lit.: B 552; BBh. 352 a.pl. 236; DHP 106; GBB 128; GI pl. 71; GJ 363; GoRI 1:53, 228; Gt 263; IC 1:319, 492; IIM 15; JSM pl. 59; KiH 10; KiSH 55, 88; Mayrhofer, EWA 1:88; MEIA 125; MG 46; SSI 241; Th. 109; WHW 1:480; WM 1:1, 208, 1:2,112; ZA pl. 242; ZM pl. 2.

2. (Vāh.; Buddh.) Mārīcī (in different forms), Hevajra, Prasannatārā, Vidyujjvālākarālī are shown trampling upon the Hindu god I. Cp. Māra.

Lit.: BBh. 194.

Indrabhūti ("might of Indra"), Gautama I. (Jain.), n of the first pupil of Mahāvīra.

Lit.: GJ 32; IC 2:631; KiJ 15 a.pl. 44; SchRI 222.

Indradhanus "Indra's bow", n. of the rainbow which belongs to Indra and is identical with his *dhanus* Vijaya. Another n.: Śakradhanus.

Lit.: DHP 110.

Indrajāla "Indra's net" (attr.), see *jāla*

Lit.: WHW 1:480.

Indraketu "Indra's banner", n. of a banner which is erected during a spring festival and dedicated to Indra.

Lit.: GoRI 1:340.

Indrākṣī ("Indra's eye"), n. of a goddess (= Indrāṇī?). Attr.: *vajra*.

Lit.: R 1:370.

Indra-Lakṣmī, n. of a two-handed form among the group *aṣṭamahālakṣmī*, very similar to the Gaja-Lakṣmī.

Lit.: SSI 187.

indramahotsava "great festival in honour of Indra", n. of a festival at the end of the rainy period.

Lit.: IC 1:591.

Indrāṇī ("[Śakti] of Indra"), n. of the wife of Indra, daughter of the demon Puloman, who was destroyed by his son-in-law, Indra.

1. (Hind.) I. is also one of the *sapta-* (*aṣṭa-*) *mātaras* or *navaśakti* and symbolizes then *mātsarya* "envy, jealousy" or "fault-finding". She is then often named Aindrī. – Char.: Vāh.: *gaja*, or (when I. is a *mātā*) *siṁha*; att.: *lalitāsana*; attr.: *akṣamālā*, *aṅkuśa*, *kamaṇḍalu*, *sahasranayana*, *santānamañjarī*, *vajra*. Her sacred tree is *kalpa-*

druma. Epithets: Aindrī, Māhendrī, Paulomī, Śacī, Sujātā, Indrākṣī (?).

2. (Vāh.; Buddh.) Upon I. Paramāśva treads.

Lit.: B pl. 44:4; BECA 1: pl. 16a; DHP 287; Gt 266; KiSH 53; MEIA 150; R 1:381, 385, 2:520; Th. 108; WM 114; ZA pl. 243, 246.

indu "moon" (attr.), see *candra(maṇḍala)*; Indu is also another n. of Candra. It is furter a symbolic n. of the number "1", see *saṅkhyā*.

Lit.: MEIA 213.

Indukarī, NP of the wife of Śāmba (Sāmba). Attr.: *kheṭaka*.

Lit.: R 1:241.

Indus Valley (civilization), n. of a culture, which dates back to about 2500-1800 B.C. The two chief sites of this civilization are Harappā and Mohenjo-Dāṛo. Many remnants of this high culture have been excavated, comprising copper and bronze weapons, pottery, sculptures of terracotta and bronze, and, above all, steatite seals with reliefs and inscriptions in a script not yet deciphered.

Lit.: Gz 22; GRI 46; WHW 1:482; WIA; WIC; ZA pl. 1 ff.

induvāra (or *-vāsara*) "Monday", see *somavāra*.

Iṅlandīya vatsara "English year", sometimes abbreviated to *i* or *iṅ*, indicating the Christian era, see *khristābda*.

iṅrājī indicating the Christian era, see *khristābda*.

Īśa or Īśāna ("ruler, master, lord").

1. (Hind.) N. of a form or an aspect of Śiva ("he who is the soul of universe"). Ī. "is ontologically the first face of 'the coming into manifestation' of the transcendental Śiva" (KrA). With the head turned upwards he is included in the Sadāśiva-composition; cp. also Pañcabrahmā. He is further a *dikpāla* of the north-east direction; his *diggaja* is named Supratīka. – Ī. is furthermore mentioned as one of the *ekādaśarudras* and one of the *mūrtyaṣṭaka*-forms of Śiva. – Wife: Śivā. Char. as independent deity: colour: white; Vāh.: *ajā* or *vṛṣan*; Mu.: *abhaya-*, *varada-mudrā*; attr.: *akṣamālā*, *aṅkuśa*, *ḍamaru*, *ḍhakkā*, *jambhīra*, *kapāla*, *pañcaśiras*, *paraśu*, *pāśa*, *ṭaṅka*, *trinayana*, *triśūla*, *vīṇā*. – For *īśa* as a symbolic n. of the number "11", see *saṅkhyā*.

Lit.: B 447, 529; DHP 205, 211; KiSH 55, 57; KrA 207 a.pl. 108; MEIA 136; R 2:736, 403, 537; Th. 111.

2. (Buddh.) As a *dikpāla*: char.: colour: white; Vāh.: *vṛṣan*; attr.: *candra*, *kapāla*, *triśūla*.

Lit.: BBh. 361.

Īśānādayas ("Īśāna and the others"), see Pañcabrahmā.

Lit.: R 2:375.

Issaki, NP of a goddess (Kerala). Attr.: *bāla amastaka* (a headless child).

iṣṭa(mudrā) ("desire"), n. of a Mu., see *varadamudrā*.

Lit.: R 2:378.

iṣṭadevatā (also: *sveṣṭadevatā* = *sva-iṣṭadevatā*) "deity chosen (by the worshipper himself)", "a god chosen by an individual as the object of his special pious attention, from whom he expects help, be it spiritually or materially" (DiIP). Hence *i.* is also a n. given to an icon in the house of the worshipper. Often the *i.* includes three gods (*tri-sveṣṭa-devatā*), namely the *grāmadevatā*, the *kuladevatā* and the worshipper's own favourite deity.

Lit.: DHP 9; DiIP 174; GoRI 1:268, 334; GRI 150, 320; HAHI 17.

iṣṭapradā(mudrā) "gesture of granting wishes" (Mu.), see *varadamudrā*.

Lit.: MEIA 58.

iṣu "arrow" (attr.), see *śara*. Also a symbolic n. of the number "5", see *saṅkhyā*.

Lit.: MEIA 254.

īsvābda "the year of Jesus, the Christian era" (abbreviated: *ī*), indicating an era, see *khristābda*.

iṣvāsa (or *iśvāsa*) "bow" ("throwing arrows"; attr.), see *dhanus*.

Lit.: ACA 31; MEIA 254.

īsvī (or *īsavī*) "the year) of Jesus" (abbreviated *ī.*), indicating the Christian era, see *khristābda.*
Lit.: IC 2:736; P 767.

Īśvara ("Lord, the supreme Lord who rules the universe").
1. (Hind.) Epithet of Śiva. –
2. (Jain.) NP of a *yakṣa* attending on the 11th *tīrthaṅkara.* He is influenced by the Hindu god Śiva and has similar attr. Symbol: *vṛṣan.* Cp. Bhagavān. – For *īśvara* as a symbolic n. of the number "11", see *saṅkhyā.*
Lit.: B 562; GJ 362 a.pl. 25:11; GoRI 1:266, 2:85; KiJ 11 a.pl. 28:11; WM 117.

J

Jagadambā (or -ī: "mother of the world"), epithet of Pārvatī emphasizing her aspect as "the great mother". Another n.: Jaganmātā. See also *aṣṭasvasāras.*
Lit.: B 493; KiSH 13.

Jagaddhātrī ("world-nurse"), epithet of Durgā (sometimes of Sarasvatī). She has four arms. Vāh.: *siṅha.*
Lit.: D 129; GoRI 1:274.

Jagadgaurī ("world-Gaurī"), epithet of Pārvatī or of Manasā. She is four-armed. Attr.: *cakra, gadā, padma, śaṅkha* (N.B. however that these attr. seem rather to display a connection with the Vaiṣṇavite circle of deities).
Lit.: W 254.

jagamohan(a): "In Orissan architecture an enclosed porch proceeding the sanctuary, used as an assembly hall" (RAAI).
Lit.: GOSA passim; RAAI 272.

Jaganmātā (or -mātṛ, -mātar; "world-mother"), see Jagadambā.
Lit.: B 493; KiSH 13.

Jagannāth(a) (N.Ind.: Jaggernaut, Engl.: Juggernaut; "Lord of the world"), n. of a form of Kṛṣṇa (or Viṣṇu, black in colour) which is worshipped in Bengal and Orissa and esp. at Puri. He is there accompanied by his sister Subhadrā and his brother Balabhadra (= Balarāma; he is white). The wooden icons (without arms or legs) of these three deities in the temple of Puri are well-known. Two festivals, the *rathayātrā* and the *snānayātrā*, are esp. dedicated to these deities.
Lit.: D 129; GH 341, 483 a.pl. 31, 34; Gt 270; MG 151; WHW 1:490; WM 117 a.pl. 11; ZA pl. 16c and e.

jagatī "basement moulding" of a temple. *j.* (n. of a metre) is also a symbolic n. of the number "48", see *saṅkhyā.*
Lit.: BECA 1:261.

Jaimini (patronymic of Jeman), n. of a celebrated *ṛiṣi*, the leader of a certain group of *ṛiṣis*, the *kāṇḍarṣis.*
Lit.: R 2:566.

jaina ("relating to, or worshipper of the *jinas*"), Jainism, n. of a religious doctrine which ideologically is related to Buddhism, but which in its social and cultural way of life is more closely related to Hinduism. The founder of this religion was Mahāvīra. The two most important sects are the *śvetāmbaras* and the *digambaras.* – *j.* is also n. of an adherent of this doctrine.
Lit.: GJ; Gt 273; IC 2:609; KiSH 119; KT 114; SchRI 219; WHW 1:492.

jakhin (N.Ind.), see *yakṣiṇī.*

jala "water" (attr.). In ritual worship, water is regarded as having a purifying and life-preserving power. It is also emblematic of fertility and signifies the element from which the world and life have arisen (it should be noted that in Sumer also water was a symbol of fertility). Cp. Ananta, *nāga.*
Lit.: GH 44.

jāla "net" (attr.). Char. of: Indra (*Indrajāla*), Yama. – *j.* can also signify the network of which a *kirīṭa* is made.
Lit.: GoRI 1:226; SB 176.

Jaladhijā ("ocean-daughter"), epithet of Lakṣmī.
Lit.: DHP 262.

jalah(a)rī (Hi., < Skt *jala-dhara+ ikā*) "small pit for water (such as that into which the water in which an idol has been bathed flows)" (attr.). This *j.* can also symbolize the *yoni*. Cp. *arghā*.
Lit.: DHP 231; P 387.

Jalamūrti ("Whose-Form-is-Water"), epithet of Śiva.
Lit.: DHP 191.

Jalandhara-vadhamūrti (or -hāramūrti: "representation [of Śiva] killing, – or seizing – J."), n. of an *ugra*-aspect of Śiva killing the demon Jalandhara. Char. of Śiva: colour: red; attr.: *chattra, hāras, kamaṇḍalu, kuṇḍalas*. Jalandhara shows *añjalimudrā*.
Lit.: R 2:188.

jālāṅguli "net-finger" (attr.) said of fingers which are "delicate and slender suggesting smoothness at once gentle and smoothening".
Lit.: RN 44.

jalapūjā "water-worship" (Jain.), n. of worship which consits in the sprinkling and washing with water. See also *pūjā*.
Lit.: GJ 396.

Jalāśāyin (also Jalaśāya, -śāyana, -śāyya: "lying on the water"), n of a form of Viṣṇu which is closely connected with his representation as Anantāśāyana. Attr.: *santānamañjarī*.
Lit: B 275; MEIA 38; R 1:263 a.pl. 79; SSI 52; ZA pl. 597.

Jālinikumāra ("son of the sun"; Buddh.), another n. of Sūryaprabha as a deity accompanying Arapacana.
Lit.: BBh. 121.

Jāliniprabha ("light of the sun"; Budd.), n. of a *bodhisattva*. Char.: colour: red; Mu.: *varadamudrā*; attr.: *khaḍga, sūrya, vajrapañjara*. Another n.: Sūryaprabha.
Lit.: BBh. 90 a.pl. 60.

Jāliniprabha-Lokeśvara ("L. as J."; Buddh.), n. of a variety of Avalokiteśvara. Char.: att.: *padmāsana*; Vāh.: *padma*; attr.: *khaḍga, padma*.
Lit.: BBh. 398 a.pl. 42(A).

jāmaiṣaṣṭhī, n. of a festival celebrated in May (in Bengal) and dedicated to sons-in-law. At this festival the parents-in-law pay homage to their sons-in-law.
Lit.: GJ 356.

Jāmbavān (or -vat, -vant), NP of a king of bears who aided Rāma in his battle against Rāvaṇa. He was the son of Viṣṇu, and was later killed by Kṛṣṇa.
Lit.: IIM 105.

Jambhala ("having (large) teeth" or devouring"; Buddh.), NP of a Mahāyāna god, an emanation of either Akṣobhya, Vajrasattva, Ratnasambhava or of the five *dhyānibuddhas* as a group. He is attended by *yakṣas* and *yakṣiṇīs*, and is the *yi-dam*-form of Kubera, and hence the Buddhist counterpart of the Hindu Kubera. – Śakti: Vasudhārā. – Char.: colour: blue or white; Vāh.: *nara* or two half-human beings (Padmamuṇḍa and Śaṅkhamuṇḍa) or *śaṅkha*; att.: inter alia *padmāsana* and (sometimes) *yab-yum*; attr.: *Akṣobhyabimba* in the hair, *aṅkuśa, cintāmaṇi, dhanus, jambhīra, kapāla, khaḍga, nakula, navāṅśa, nidhi, pāśa, śara, triśiras, triśūla, tundila, vajra*. – Varieties: Sita-, Kāla-jambhala, Ucchuṣma.
Lit.: B 559 a.pl. 47:2; BBh. 178, 237 a.pl. 176-179; G passim; KiDG 62 a.pl. 46; KiSB 72, 75, 77; RN pl. 10; SB 286 a.fig. 190.

jambhīra(phala) (or *jambhara, jambīra*) "citron" (attr.). Char. of: Brahmā, Cundā, Īśāna, Jambhala, Kubera, Lakṣmī, Mahālakṣmī, Maheśamūrti, Pārvatī, Sadāśiva, Tatpuruṣa, Viśvarūpa, the *yakṣas*. – Other n.: *bījapūra, mātuluṅga*.
Lit.: B 373, 496; G 14 (ill.); KrA text to pl. 100; R 2:135.

jambu (or -*ū*) "rose apple tree" (Eugenia Jambolana or another species).
1. N. of a *sthalavṛkṣa* connected with the temple of Jambukeśvara, Tiruvānaikkā at Tiruchirappalli in South India.

2. (Attr.) The fruit of the *jambu* tree (rose apple). Char. of Taruṇa-Gaṇapati.
Lit.: R 1:52.

3. (Jain.) N. of the *jambu* tree relating to the Jain world-conception.
Lit.: KiJ 6 a.pl. 16.

Jambudvīpa ("the rose-apple island"), n. of the Indian continent according to the ancient Indian world conception. J. is the central continent of the seven that surround Mount Meru, and it is so named either on account of the *jambu* trees abounding in it or because of an enormous *jambu* tree on the top of Meru which is visible throughout the continent.
Lit.: GJ 225; GoRI 1:331; IC 2:649; KiH 4 a.pl. 1; KiJ 5 a.pl. 6; KiK.

janamsakhi (Panj.) "birth-story", in Sikhism n. of stories, collected into four cycles, giving account of Nānak Dev. Cp. *jātaka*.
Lit.: HS 15, 25.

Janārdana ("exciting or agitating men, Giver of rewards"), n. of an aspect of Viṣṇu, see *caturviṅśatimūrti*; also epithet of Kṛṣṇa.
Lit.: B 411; GoRI 1:238; KiH 14 a.pl. 34; KiSH 39; R 2:230.

janeū (Hi., also written *janeo*, *janivāra*), see *yajñopavīta*.
Lit.: Gt Suppl. 57; P 393.

jaṅgama "moving, movable" (attr.), n. of a kind of image, e.g. *jaṅgama liṅga*, see *cala*. – *j.* as a "(predigender) Reisende" (GoRI) is also n. of a priest within the sect of the *liṅgāyat*s, and is here included among the *aṣṭāvaraṇa*.
Lit.: GoRI 2:249; Gt 286; R 2:76.

jaṅghikā "loin-cloth" (attr.), see *dhotī*.
Lit.: BECA 1:261.

Jāṅgulī ("knowledge of poisons"; Buddh.), NP of a Mahāyāna goddess who cures and prevents snake bites. She is an emanation of Akṣobhya, and also belongs to the *dhāriṇī*-group. She is represented in two or three forms, and has one or three heads. Char.: colour: white, green or yellow; Vāh.: *nāga* or *sattva*; Mu.: *abhaya-*, *varada-mudrā*; attr.: *Akṣobhyabimba* on the crown, *dhanus*, *khaḍga*, *kumārīlakṣaṇa*, *mayūrapattra*, *nāga* (white), *nīlotpala*, *viṣa-puṣpa*, *śara*, *tarjanīpāśa*, *trinayana*, *triśiras*, *triśūla*, *vajra* (*viśvavajra*), *vīṇā*.
Lit.: BBh. 191, 220, 307 a.pl. 137; G 75; KiDG 64, 68; KiSB 88.

janmapattra "nativity-paper, horoscope" (attr.), n. of a paper or scroll on which the date of birth, the relative position of the planets (at the birth), etc., are recorded. Cp. *jātaka*, *jyotiṣa*.
Lit.: GH 333; MW 411.

jaṇṭha, n. of a certain kind of drum (attr.).
Lit.: R 2:153.

japa "muttering, repetition" of *mantra*s and prayers.
Lit.: DHP 379; WHW 2:27; ZA 112.

japā "China rose" (attr.), see *javā*.

japamālā (or *japyamālā*) "muttering chaplet, rosary" (attr.), see *akṣamālā*.

Jarā ("growing old"), n. of a female monster, a demon who steals children. She is associated with Hārītī, and is perhaps also connected with Jarāsandha, an enemy of Kṛṣṇa.
Lit.: B 380.

jaṭā "knot of matted hair" (attr.). It is esp. char. of Śiva (but also of Brahmā), and it "represents the lord of wind, Vāyu, who is the subtle form of *soma*, the flow of offering" (DHP). It is also said to symbolize Gaṅgā. – Another n.: *śikhā*.
Lit.: DHP 215; IC 1:515; MEIA 212; SB passim.

jaṭābandha, n. of a certain kind of head-dress (*bandha*), consisting of *jaṭā*s, arranged like a basket round the head (attr.). Char. of: Aiyaṉār, *bhakta*s and *sādhu*s. A form of *j.* is worn by Śiva Naṭarāja. – Other n.: *jaṭābhāra**, *jaṭāvalaya*.
Lit.: B 286; KIM pl. 37, 48; R 1: pl. 9:1-3; SSI pl. II:7; Th. 33 (with ill.).

jaṭābhāra "mass of braided hair" (attr.), see *jaṭābandha*. These two terms signify, however, according to SSI, different head-dresses.
Lit.: SB 304; SSI pl. II:9; WM 102.

Jaṭādhara ("wearing matted hair"), epithet of Śiva.
Lit.: DHP 191.

jātaka "birth-story" (Buddh.), in Buddhist scripture n. of a story of a previous incarnation of Gautama Buddha (as a *bodhisattva*). According to the Sanskrit work Jātakamālā, the number of these former incarnations was 34, but in the Pāli canon 547 *jātakas* are mentioned. One of the best-known *j*. is that in which the Buddha was incarnated as a monkey (see Mahākapi). The *j*. are very often illustrated on friezes and reliefs in the Buddhist temples and *stūpas*. — Cp. also *janamsakhi*.

j. as "nativity" (Hind. etc.) is also another n. for *horā* "horoscopy", cp. also *janmapattra*.
Lit.: AuOW 30; BRI 26; HAHI 20; FBKI 31; IC 1:619; JMS 50 a.pl. passim; KrA pl. passim; WHW 1:499; ZA 242 a.pl. passim.

jātakarma(n) "birth-ceremony", n. of *saṅskāra*-rite, consisting in touching a new-born baby's tongue thrice with ghee after appropriate prayers.
Lit.: DiIP 180; IC 1:363; WHW 2:241.

Jaṭāmakuṭa-Lokeśvara ("L. with a crown of matted hair"; Buddh.), n. of a variety of Avalokiteśvara. Char.: Mu.: *varadamudrā*; attr.: *akṣamālā, kamaṇḍalu (kuṇḍikā), puṣpa (padma)*.
Lit.: BBh. 395 a.pl. 12(A); SB 233 a.pl. 146.

jaṭāmukuṭa (*-makuṭa*) "crown of matted hair" (attr.), n. of a head-dress: a crown of *jaṭās* (often with ornaments). Char. of: esp. Śiva (in different forms) and his Śakti; also of: Brahmā, Caṇḍeśvara, Manonmanī, Rudra. A *j*., surrounded with flames, is char. of Pāśupatamūrti. Cp. also *kaparda*.
Lit.: B 282; HIS 40 a.pl. 44, 45; KiSH 25; R 1:27 a.pl. 7:1-3; SSI pl. 1:8; Th. 32 (with ill.); WM 102 a.fig. 40.

jatara (Drav.), a kind of bloody offering by means of which a popular god, e.g. Poleramma, is appeased.
Lit.: GoRI 2:6.

jaṭāvalaya "circle of matted hair" (attr.), see *jaṭābandha*.

Jaṭāyu(s), n. of a vulture (the king of vultures; the meaning of the n. is not clear, but seems to be connected with *jaṭā* "tuft"), who was the son either of Garuḍa (he is also said to be an *avatāra* of Garuḍa), or of Aruṇa and Śyenī. He was an ally of Rāma.
Lit.: D 134; Gt 287; HM 58; W 379.

jāti "caste", see *varṇa*.
Lit.: WM 123.

jātrā (Hi.), see *yātrā*.

javā (or *japā*) "China rose" (attr.) is the flower of Durgā, Kālarātrī.
Lit.: GoRI 2:47; GRI 176; MW 412.

Jaya ("conquering"), NP of a gate-keeper of Viṣṇu. Hiraṇyakaśipu is regarded as a later incarnation of J.
Lit.: Gt 680; WHW 1:91.

Jayā ("conquering").

1. (Hind.) NP of the Śakti of Ṣaṇmukha; also n. of a female *dvārapālaka* of Gaurī.
Lit.: R 1:361, 2:437.

2. (Budd.) NP of a minor Mahāyāna goddess attending on Buddhakapāla.
Lit.: BBh. 160.

3. (Jain.) See Vijayā.

Jayadurgā ("victorious Durgā"), n. of a four-armed form of Durgā. Attr.: *cakra, khaḍga, śaṅkha, trinayana, triśūla*.
Lit.: R 1:344.

jayaghaṇṭā "victory-bell" (attr.; Jain.), another n. of *ghaṇṭā*.
Lit.: GJ 428.

Jayakara ("victorious"; Buddh.), NP of an (orig. Hindu?) god. Char.: colour: white; Vāh.: *ratha* drawn by *kokilas*; attr.: *caṣaka, dhanus, śara, vanamālā*.
Lit.: BBh. 378.

Jayanta ("victorious"), n. of one of the *ekādaśarudras*. Char.: Mu.: *tarjanīmudrā*; attr.: *akṣamālā, aṅkuśa, cakra, ḍamaru, dhanus, gadā, kamaṇḍalu, kapāla, khaṭvāṅga, mudgara, nāga, paraśu, śakti, śara, triśūla*. Also n. of a son of Indra.
Lit.: R 2:390.

Jayantī ("victorious"), n. of a goddess probably epithet of Durgā). Attr.: *khaḍga, kheṭaka, kunta* (probably = *śakti*), *triśūla*.
Lit.: R 1:369.

Jayatārā ("victorious Tārā"; Buddh.), n. of an inferior Mahāyāna goddess.
Lit.: BBh. 151; KiSB 97.

Jayā-Vijayā ("Victory-Victory"), n. of a pair of twin goddesses (forms of Durgā?). Vāh.: *siṅha*.
Lit.: R 1:368.

Jetavana "Jetṛ's grove" (Buddh.), n. of a grove near Śrāvasti, given to the Buddha by a rich merchant (Anāthapiṇḍika or Anāthapiṇḍada). The Buddha often stayed there.
Lit.: FBKI pl. 17; MW 424.

jhārī (also *zhārī*; Hi) "ceremonial ewer" (attr.), n. of a pitcher with a long neck and a spout, used in ceremonies. Another n.: *pavitrajhārī*.
Lit.: P 400.

jihvā "tongue" (attr.). 3 or 7 *j.* (of fire, cp. *agni*) are char. of Agni. An outstretched tongue is char. of Kālī (either alone or dancing upon the prostrate form of her husband Śiva). In regard to Kālī *j.* is said to symbolize her thirst for blood. When she is shown dancing on Śiva, however, *j.* may indicate civility, because, in several parts of India, Burma and Tibet, the outstretched tongue is regarded as a polite salutation.
Lit.: MW 422

JĪṀ (Buddh.), a *bījamantra* from which Mahāśitavatī has emanated.
Lit.: KiSB 98.

Jīmūtaketu ("having a cloud as banner"), epithet of Śiva.
Lit.: JDI 22.

jina "victorious", also understood as "saviour".

1. (esp. Jain.) *j.* is another n. for *tīrthaṅkara*. For the "death of *jina*" indicating an era, see *vīrasamvat*, and concerning *j.* as a symbolic n. of the number "24", see *saṅkhyā*.
Lit.: GJ 247; HIS 55, 60 a.pl. 11, 19; IC 2:736.

2. (Buddh.) *j.* is sometimes used like *buddha*.
Lit.: GBM 79; IC 2:588.

jineśvara "lord of *jinas*" (Jain.), see *tīrthaṅkara*.
Lit.: GRI 186.

jñānabhāṇḍa "receptacle of knowledge" (attr.). This is symbolized by means of a *kamaṇḍalu* or a *kuṇḍikā*. Char. of Sarasvatī (Lakṣmī).
Lit.: B 379.

Jñānaḍākinī ("*ḍākinī* of knowledge"; Buddh.), n. of a Mahāyāna goddess who is an emanation of Akṣobhya, and is the Śakti of Yogāmbara. Char.: colour: blue; attr.: *ghaṇṭā, kapāla, khaḍga, khaṭvāṅga, paraśu, vajra*.
Lit.: BBh. 186, 204.

Jñāna-dakṣiṇāmūrti, n. of a manifestation of Śiva as a teacher of *jñāna* ("knowledge"), see further *dakṣiṇāmūrti*. Char.: Mu.: *abhaya-, gajahasta-, jñāna-, vyākhyāna-mudrā*; attr.: *akṣamālā, nīlotpala*.
Lit.: B 465, 471; BP 195 a.pl. 22; NLEM 375; R 2:284 a.pl. 71-75; SSI 90.

Jñānadhātu-Lokeśvara ("L. of the world of knowledge"; Buddh.), n. of a variety of Avalokiteśvara. Char.: att.: *samapādasthānaka*; Vāh.: *padma*; Mu.: *añjali-, kṣepana-mudrā*; attr.: *akṣamālā, pāśa, pustaka, tridaṇḍa*.
Lit.: BBh. 398 a.pl. 36(A).

Jñānaketu ("having knowledge as a sign or banner"; Buddh.), n. of a *bodhisattva*. Char.: colour: yellow or blue; Mu.: *varadamudrā*; attr.: *cintāmaṇidhvaja*.
Lit.: BBh. 83, 96 a.pl. 68.

jñānamudrā "gesture of knowledge" (Mu.), n. of a handpose in which the palm of the hand, the tips of the thumb and the index or middle finger touching each other, is held against the bosom near the heart. Sometimes *j.* is identified with the *dhyāna-mudrā* and the *vajramudrā*. *j.* also forms part of the combined (*samyuta*) handpose *dharmacakramudrā*. – Char. of: Hayagrīva, Jñānadakṣiṇāmūrti, Śiṣyabhāvamūrti, Tatpuruṣa, Vyākhyānadakṣiṇāmūrti. – Another n.: *vidyāmudrā*.

Lit.: B 254 a.pl. 3:2; R 1:17 a.pl. 5:16; SM N. 1 to p. 85; WM 98 a.fig. 18.

jñānanetra "eye of knowledge" (attr.), n. of the third eye of Śiva. Cp. *trinayana*.
Lit.: GoRI 1:261; KiSH 23.

Jñānapāramitā ("perfection of knowledge"; Buddh.), n. of a *pāramitā*. Char.: colour: white; attr.: *bodhivṛkṣa* (held in one hand), *cintāmaṇidhvaja*.
Lit.: BBh. 328.

Jñānasambandha ("friend of knowledge"), NP of a *śaivabhakta* (in South India, 7th c. A.D.; author of a part of the Tēvāram, a collection of Śaivite hymns), J. is usually represented as a child. Char.: Mu.: *sūci-mudrā*; attr.: *kapāla*.
Lit.: KIM pl. 51; SB 184, 200 a.pl. 125, a.passim; TL 3:1902.

Jñānavaśitā ("control of knowledge"; Buddh.), n. of a *vaśitā*. Char.: colour: whitish blue; attr.: *khaḍga* on *nilotpala*.
Lit.: BBh. 331.

jñātidevī ("goddess of the relatives"; Jain.), n. of the patroness of a caste.
Lit.: GJ 363.

Juggernaut (Engl. word-form), see Jagannātha.

juhū "offering ladle" (attr.), n. of a ladle made of *palāśa* (*kiṅśuka*) wood. As an independent cult object *j.* is used for pouring *ghṛta* (ghee) into the fire. As attr., held in one hand, char. of Yajñamūrti. Cp. *sruk*, *sruva*, *darvī*.
Lit.: MW 424; R 1:250; RV 69.

juli (N.Ind.; attr.), according to MSHP a kind of bag carried by Śiva under his arm and containing *vibhūti*, i.e. the ashes of dried cow-dung. *j.* probably signifies a bag like that shown in the frontispiece to MSHP (under the left arm of Śiva) or (in MG) under the right arm. – The word is perhaps related to Hi. *jūṛī**, or to Panj. *jūṛī* "bundle of jute or tobacco leaves" (TDIL).
Lit.: GoRI 1:260; MG pl. facing p. 81; MSHP 38; TDIL No. 5258.

Jumādi, n. of a *bhūta*.
Lit.: KiH 27 a.pl. 100, 105.

Jumna, see Yamunā.

jūṛī (Hi., < Skt *juṭ+ikā* or *juḍ+ikā*), n. of "a necklace of small cakes of dried cow-dung strung together (which is cast into fire during the *holī*)"; also n. of a small bundle of sugar-cane (likewise burnt during the *holī*-festival; attr.) – Cp. *juli*.
Lit.: P 397.

jvāla "flame" (attr.), see *agni*.

jvālamālā (or *jvālā-*) "elliptical aureole of flames" (attr.), see *prabhāmaṇḍala*.
Lit.: AIP 71.

Jvālāmālinī ("flame-garlanded"; Jain.), n. of a *śāsanadevatā* attending on the 8th *tīrthaṅkara*.
Lit.: GJ 362 a.pl. 25:8; Kij 12 a.pl. 28:8.

jvalitaśikhā "flaming hair" (attr.), see *keśamaṇḍala*.
Lit.: MEIA 212.

Jvaradeva ("god of fever"), n. of a demigod in the retinue of Śiva. Attr.: *trinayana* (each head), *tripādaka*, *triśiras*.
Lit.: SSI 165.

Jvaraharīśvara ("lord of febrifuge"), n. of a malaria-god in Bengal.
Lit.: GH 111.

jyaiṣṭha (related to the *nakṣatra* Jyeṣṭhā), n. of a month (May-June). Its god is Agni.
Lit.: BBh. 382; IC 2:732.

Jyeṣṭhā(devī) (or Jyeṣṭhā-Lakṣmī, orig. "the most excellent, chief, eldest; the first or eldest wife").
1. J. is regarded as the elder sister of Lakṣmī, and she is the Śakti of one of the *vidyeśvaras*. She is the goddess of ill-luck, a personification of sloth, poverty and misfortune. Earlier (until the 10th c.A.D.) she was worshipped in South India and is represented with two arms, a long nose and a big belly. She is related to Śītalā. Char.: Vāh.: *gardabha* or *bhadrapīṭha*; Mu.: *abhaya-*, *sūci-mudrā*; attr.: *daṇḍa*, *kāka(dhvaja)*, *kapāla*, *lambastana*, *padma* (*nīlotpala*), *śara*, *tundila*, *vāsikābandha*. – She has several epithets (not listed here, see B.).
Lit.: B 382; BECA 1: pl. 23b; R 1:363, 390, 403 a.pl. 121 ff.; SIB 62; SSI 216; Th. 108.

2. N. of a *nakṣatra*. Its influence is bad.
Lit.: BBh. 382; IC 2:730.

Jyeṣṭharāja ("king-of-the-elders"), epithet of Gaṇeśa, sometimes also of Bṛhaspati.
Lit.: DHP 292, 325.

jyotiṣa "astrologer; astrology, astronomy". – As the events of life are supposed to be controlled by the stars, the *j.* is very important since he calculates the auspicious moments and periods of life. – Cp. *horā*, *janmapattra*, *jāṭaka*.
Lit.: DiCh. 139; DiIP 198; Gt 291; IC 2:720; WHW 1:87, 284.

jyotiṣka(s) "luminaries" regarded as a class of deities (arranged under five heads, viz. sun, moon, the planets, fixed stars and lunar mansions; Jain.).
Lit.: MW 427; GJ 235.

K

Ka, n. of several deities, e.g. Brahmā, Dakṣa, Garuḍa, Prajāpati, Viṣṇu, Yama.
Lit.: Gt 295; MW 240.

Kabīr(dās) (A.D. 1440-1518), n. of a sectarian who tried to unite the Hindu and Islamic religions into a single monotheistic faith.
Lit.: GRI 344; IC 1:656; F.E. Keay, Kabīr and his followers (London 1931).

kabīrpanthin (or *-ī*; "one who follows the way of Kabīr"), n. of a follower of the sect founded by Kabīr.
Lit.: IC 1:657.

kaccha (or *kuccha*, Hi. *kācchā*) "loin-cloth; the hem or end of a lower garment (tucked into the girdle or waistband); shorts; a cloth worn round the hips, passing between the legs and tucked in behind" (attr.). The *k.* seems, on the whole, to be identical with the *dhotī*. It is also one of the five essentials of the Sikhs (see *pañcakakāra*), symbolic of activity in service.
Lit.: AIP 71; GG p. CLVII; P 799; SB 208.

Kacchapa ("tortoise", M.Ind. word-form, also used in Skt), see *Kāśyapa*. – As to *kacchapa* as n. of a Vāh., see *kūrma*.
Lit.: BBh. 377.

Kacchapeśvara ("Lord of the Tortoise"), epithet of Śiva; cp. in this connection a representation on a *liṅga* in which Śiva is worshipped by Viṣṇu in the form of a tortoise. This shows an attempt on the part of the adherents of Śiva to give prominence to him at the expense of Viṣṇu (manifested as Kūrmāvatāra).
Lit.: R 1:42 a.pl.D.

kaccu (Tam.) "breast-band" (attr.), see *kucabandha*.
Lit.: JDI 63.

kadala (or *-īphala*) "banana" (attr.). Char. of Bāla-Gaṇapati.

kadamba (n. of a tree, Anthocephalus cadamba), n. of a *sthalavṛkṣa* related to the Mīnākṣī-Sundareśvara-temple at Madurai. At Mathurā the *k.* is also sacred to Kṛṣṇa.
Lit.: R 1:15.

Kadrū ("reddish brown"), NP of a daughter of Dakṣa who became the wife of Kāśyapa and the mother of the *nāgas*, inter alia of Śeṣa (or Ananta) and Manasā.
Lit.: DHP 163; IIM 97.

bKa'-gdams-pa ("precept giving"; Tib. pronounced: *Ka-dam-pa*; Buddh.), n. of a Lamaist sect which later, reformed, appears as *dGe-lugs-pa* (see sub initial *Ge-*).
Lit.: Enc.Brit. 22:188A; G 5; JT 13.

bKa'-'gyur ("the translated word", i.e. the word of the Buddha as translated from Skt; Tib., pronounced: *Kan-jur*; Buddh.), n. of the Tibetan Lamaist canon corresponding to the Buddhist Tipiṭaka. This canon consists of 108 books.
Lit.: G 5; GRI 296; IC 2:391; JT 13, 97.

Kailāsa, n. of a mythical mountain (supposed to be placed in the Himālaya range), the

residence of Kubera and Śiva. It is conceived as resembling a *liṅga*.
Lit.: Gt 297; MW 311; WM 119.

kairava "white lotus" (attr.), see *puṇḍarīka*.
Lit.: IC 1:538.

kaivalya "perfect isolation, supreme knowledge" (Jain.); the supreme state to be strived for by the Jains (corresponding to the Buddhist *bodhi* "enlightenment"). One who has achieved this state is named *kaivalin*.

kajjala "collyrium" (attr.), see *añjana*.
Lit.: MEIA 340.

kāka "crow" (Vāh., attr.). This bird is popularly regarded as being related to the soul of a deceased person. Vāh. of Śani; attr. of Jyeṣṭhādevī. Cp. *droṇakāka*.
Lit.: GH 71.

kākadhvaja "crow-banner" (attr.). Char. of Jyeṣṭhādevī.
Lit.: B 383.

kākapakṣa "crow's wing" (attr.), n. of "sidelocks of hair on the temples", a mode of dressing the hair of children.
Lit.: MW 267; SIB 69 a.pl. 20(A).

Kākāsyā ("crow-faced"; Buddh.), n. of an inferior goddess.
Lit.: BBh. 319.

kākinī (orig. "the shell Cypraea moneta"; attr.), see *śaṅkha*.
Lit.: GJ 257; KiSH 146.

kakuda "peak, emblem of royalty", see *rājakakuda*.
Lit.: MW 241.

Kakudvatī ("humpback"; Buddh.), n. of a *mānuṣibuddhaśakti*.
Lit.: BBh. 79.

Kakusandha (Pāli, corresponding to Skt Krakusunda or Krakucchanda), NP of a *mānuṣibuddha*.
Lit.: KiSB 32.

Kalā, see Kāmakalā. For *kalā* as a symbolic n. of the number "16", see *saṅkhyā*.

kāla "time, age, era; black"; *kālakaraṇa* or *kālanirṇaya* "fixing a time". – As regards the meaning of "age, period of world", see *yuga*.

We shall confine ourselves to considering this complex word in its sense of "era". For general guidance concerning the dating on figures and manuscripts, see IC. – The eras most commonly used in India are: *kaliyuga*, *saptarṣikāla*, *nirvāṇa* of the Buddha, *vīrasamvat*, *vikramakāla*, *khristābda*, *śakakāla*, *licchavi*, *cedi*, *guptakāla*, *valabhi*, *baṅgālī san*, *vilāyatī*, *phaslī*, *thākuri*, *sūrsan*, *harṣakāla*, *hijrat*, *māgisan*, *kollam*, *naipālasamvat*, *cāḷukya*, *siṅhasamvat*, *lakṣmaṇa*, *tārikh-i Ilāhī*, *rājābhiṣekaśaka*. The most usual of these are *vikrama-* and *śaka-kāla*.
Lit.: Enc. Brit. 5:720; IC 1:551, 2:720, 727, 736; WHW 2:502.

Kāla ("time" = "the All-Destroyer", hence = "death"), epithet of Yama, sometimes also of Śiva. K. is also the n. of an attendant of Yama. Attr.: *pāśa*.
Lit.: B 487; D 140; DHP 200; GoRI 1:255; R 2:527.

Kāla-Bhadrā ("Death-Bh."), n. of a form of Śiva's Śakti; the worship is conducted in burial-grounds. Another n.: Karāla-Bhadrā.
Lit.: SSI 197.

Kāla-Bhairava ("Death-Bh."), either n. of a form of Bhairava or another n. of a *bhūta*, otherwise named Mudader.
Lit.: KiH 27 a.pl. 102; SSI 151.

Kālacakra ("time-wheel", i.e. time considered as a rotating wheel).

1. (Buddh.) As personification NP of a Mahāyāna god who, in Lamaism, appears as a *yi-dam*. Char.: colour: blue; att.: *ālīḍhāsana*, *yab-yum*; Vāh.: Kāma (Anaṅga) and Rudra; Mu.: *vajrahuṅkāramudrā*; attr.: K. has 12 or 24 hands, *agni*, *ajina* (tigerskin), *aṅkuśa*, *bodhisattvābharaṇa*, *brahmakapāla*, *cakra*, *caturmukha* (so usually, rarely one-headed), *cintāmaṇi*, *daṇḍa*, *darpaṇa*, *dhanus*, *kapāla*, *karttṛkā*, *khaḍga*, *khaṭvāṅga*, *muṇḍamālā*, *pāśa*, *puṇḍarīka*, *śakti*, *śara*, *trinayana*, *triśūla*, *vajra*, *vajra+ghaṇṭā* (in *vajrahuṅkāramudrā*), *vajraghaṇṭā*, *vajraśṛṅkhalā*. – The Śakti has 2 or 4 heads and 8 hands; attr.: *kapāla*, *karttṛkā*, *trinayana*.
Lit.: G 24, 36, 84 (with ill.).

2. (Jain.) "Time-wheel", picture of the periodicity of the world.
Lit.: GJ 245.

kalacūri(kāla) ("(the era) of Kalacūri, see *cedi.*
Lit.: IC 2:737; WHW 1:334.

Kāladūtī ("messenger of death"; Buddh.), n. of a Mahāyāna goddess. Char.: colour: red; att.: *ālīḍhāsana*; Vāh.: *aśva*; attr.: *gomastaka, kapāla, mudgara, triśūla.*
Lit.: B 487; KiSB 76.

Kālāgni-Rudra ("R. of the death-fire"), n. of an *ugra*-form of Śiva (identical with Kāla-Rudra?). Attr.: *dhanus, khaḍga, kheṭaka, śara.*
Lit.: SSI 155.

Kālahā or Kālahara(mūrti), see Kālasaṅhāra-mūrti.

Kāla-Jambhala ("black J."; Buddh.), in Lamaism n. of a form of Jambhala. Char.: Vāh.: *rākṣasa* or Kubera; attr.: *aṅkuśa, cintāmaṇi, kapāla, nakula, pāśa, triśiras* (also one-headed).
Lit.: G 85.

Kālakāla Mūrtti Cuvāmi (Tamilized Skt), see Kālārimūrti.
Lit.: DiCh. 17.

Kālakañja or Kālakeya ("born of Kālakā 'the Black-One'"), n. of a race of *asuras*, the sons of Kāśyapa and Kālakā; a kind of star-genii.
Lit.: D 140; DHP 143.

kālakūṭa "the black or death substance" (attr.), n. of poison which was produced at the churning of the ocean of milk and swallowed by Śiva (see Nīlakaṇṭha) in order to preserve the world. *k.* is the "gestaltgewordene Todeswunsch der Geschöpfe, das tödliche Prinzip des Naturlebens" (GoRI). – Another n.: *hālāhala.*
Lit.: GoRI 1:255; ZA 228.

Kāla-Mañjuśrī ("the black M."; Buddh.), n. of a sub-form of Arapacana who is a variety of Mañjuśrī. He is represented kneeling on the left knee. Char.: colour, black; attr.: *khaḍga, nīlotpala, trinayana.*
Lit.: G 68.

kālamukha "face of the god of death" (attr.), see *kīrttimukha.*
Lit.: BSA 36.

Kālāntakamūrti ("representation [of Śiva] killing Kāla"), n. of a form of Śiva (Maheśa). – Cp. Kālāri.
Lit.: R 2:369.

Kālarātri (or -ī; the n. is derived either from *kāla* "black" and interpreted as "the black night", or from *kāla* "time" and regarded as "the night of horror", "the night of all-destroying time, night of destruction at the end of the world" (MW).
1. (Hind.) K. as a personification is regarded as a form of either Kālī or Durgā. The Vāh. of K. may hint, however, that she is rather connected with Jyeṣṭhādevī or Śītalā. She is also an aspect of *mahāvidyā* and then represents Bhairavī. – Char.: Vāh.: *gardabha*; attr.: *javā*-flowers, *kuṇḍalas, muṇḍamālā, nagna, vīṇā.*
Lit.: DHP 281; KiSH 49; MW 298; R 1:359.
2. (Buddh.; Vāh.) In Buddhist images K. (as a personification of "the black night"?) is the Vāh. of Samvara, Saptākṣara, Vajravārāhī trampling upon her.
Lit.: KiSB 66, 87.

Kālāri(mūrti) ("representation [of Śiva] as the enemy of Kāla"), n. of an *ugra*-representation of Śiva, showing him punishing Kāla, the god of death (= Yama). Śiva is then often represented dancing upon Kāla. Char.: Mu.: *kaṭaka-, sūci-, varada-* or *vismaya-mudrā*; attr.: *kapāla, khaḍga, kheṭaka, mṛga, paraśu, (nāga)pāśa, triśūla, vajra.* – Kāla shows *añjalimudrā.* – Other n.: Kāla(saṅ)hāramūrti, Kālakāla Mūrtti Cuvāmi. Cp. also Kāmāntakamūrti.
Lit.: B 486 a.pl. 33; R 2:151 a.pl. 34-35; SB 175, 347 a.pl. 305. – N.B. the ill. in FK 116f. undoubtedly shows the same form of Śiva. Note also the bronze image in R 2: pl. 36:2, showing Śiva emanating from a *liṅga.*

Kālarudra ("death-Rudra"), Rudra regarded as the fire that is to destroy the world (identical with Kālāgni-Rudra?). Epithet of Śiva.
Lit.: KiSH 43; MW 278; SSI 155.

kalaśa (M.Ind. *kalasa*) "water-pot, pitcher, jar, vase, a pot filled with sacred water".

1. (Attr. and cult object) *k.* contains *amṛta-* and symbolizes *avadhi*-knowledge (KiSH); in Buddhism it is said that *k.* signifies "the treasure of all desires". *k.* is also the n. given to a bowl filled with water, used in the *pūjā*. – The Jains sprinkle the *pañcāmṛta* over an image from a *k.* – In this dictionary the term *kamaṇḍalu* is used as a synonym for *k.* as an attr. (see this word regarding the gods who use *k.* as an attr.); properly, however, *k.* is a larger jar than the *kamaṇḍalu*. – Cp. *amṛta(ghaṭa)*. *k.* is further in architecture the n. given to a rain-vase on a Hindu temple (in this meaning also the term *kumbha* is used) and of a part of the temple pillar; see also *pūrṇakalaśa*.

Lit.: BBh. 435; BECA 1:272; G 8 (ill.), 14; KiJ 21; KiSH 155; MEIA 242; SM 192; ZA 234, 270.

2. (Budd., Jain.) *k.* "jar" is n. of a *maṅgala*, see *aṣṭamaṅgala*.

Lit.: GBM 102; GJ 384.

Kāla(saṅ)hāramūrti (or Kālahā, Kālahara; "representation as destroyer of Kāla"), n. of an *ugra*-form of Śiva, see Kālārimūrti.

Lit.: SSI 132; Th. 82 a.pl. 50A.

Kalavikaraṇī ("free of limbs, i.e. undivided"), n. of a Śakti of one of the *vidyeśvaras*. (Identical (?) with Kalavikarṇī as epithet of Durgā, as to whom see MW).

Lit.: MW 260; R 1:399, 2:403.

Kalavikarṇikā (etymologically related to Kalavikaraṇī?), n. of a febrifugal and propitious goddess. Attr.: *kapāla, śakti*.

Lit.: R 1:363.

kāleya(s) (derived from Kāla, "demons of Time"), n. of a race of *asuras*.

Lit.: DHP 143.

kalhāra (or *kahlāra*) "the white esculent water-lily" (attr.). Char. of Ūrdhva-Gaṇapati.

Lit.: MW 266; R 1:56.

Kali (originally n. of the die or the losing side of the die), n. of a personification as the spirit of evil. The last and worst of the four *yugas* or world-ages is also connected with K., see *kaliyuga*.

Kali is further a symbolic n. of the number "1", see *saṅkhyā*.

Lit.: D 141; MG 285; MW 261; STP 4:240.

Kālī (or Kālī Mā; Tam. Kāḷi, Kāḷi(y)ammaṉ; the n. is interpreted either as "the Power-of-Time, the Destroyer-of-Time" (DHP), or probably less correctly, as "the Black-One").

1. (Hind.) K. is epithet of several goddesses; usually, however, K. signifies a terrific aspect of Śiva's Śakti. She is then often confused with Durgā (and said to be a form of Durgā), but generally she is regarded as a particular form of the Śakti, and along with Pārvatī, Ambikā and Durgā constitutes the central figure of the *śākta* cult. K. forms the aspect of the natural force of destruction but is also a personification of the Supreme Power. – At many places (esp. in South India) Kālī Devī is regarded and worshipped as a cholera goddess. She also belongs to the group *mahāvidyā* and then represents the Mahārātrī. – K. is also mentioned as the Śakti of one of the *vidyeśvaras*.

K. is usually represented as an ugly woman. She has usually no particular Vāh., but in a certain manifestation she appears dancing (or standing) on Śiva prostrate on his back (or Śiva-Śava). Char.: colour: black; Vāh.: (sometimes): *yāḷi*; attr.: *aṅkuśa, churikā, ḍamaru, dhanus, jihvā, kapāla, keśamaṇḍala* (*agni*), *muṇḍamālā, nagna, pāśa, rākṣasamuṇḍa* (in one hand), *tālas*(?), *triśūla, vibhūti, vikarṇi*; she swallows *aśva, gaja, mahiṣa, nara*. – K. is also represented by the *bijamantra ādyabīja* (*KRĪṀ*) and a "lefthanded" form of the *svastika*. – Epithets and varieties: Bhadra-Kālī, Kalka-Mātā, Kaṅkālinī-Kālī, Karālī, Mahā-Kālī, Śyāmā, Vīramakaḷ-Kāḷi. Cp. also Kālarātrī. The smallpox demonesses Māriyammaṉ, Śītalā and others are also regarded as being forms of K.

Lit.: B 491, 504; ChI 577; DHP 263, 268 a.pl. 24; DiCh. 32; GBB pl. 9; GH 142 a.pl. 9; GoRI 1:258; Gt 303; HAHI 18; KiH 22 a.pl. 70; KiSH 48; MG

185, 255; NLEM 332; SB 319 a.pl. 241; Th. 107 a.pl. 69-70; WHW 1:509; WM 119; ZA 117 a.pl. 422 (in KrA, pl. 150 a.p. 212, the same figure is said to represent an attendant of Kālī), 424 (cp. a drawing of the same icon MSHP pl. 16); ZM 224 a.pl. 68, 69; C.G. Hartman, Aspects de la déesse Kālī dans son culte et dans la littérature indienne (Helsinki 1969).

2. (Jain.) K. is NP of a *śāsanadevatā* attending on the 7th *tīrthaṅkara*; also n. of a *vidyādevī*.

Lit.: GJ 362 a.pl. 25:7; KiJ 12 a.pl. 28:7.

Kāḷiammaṉ (Tam.), see Kālī.

kālībija ("Kālī's *bīja*", interpreted as "the Seed-of-the-Power-of-Time"), see *ādya-bīja*.

Lit.: DHP 343.

Kālīcī (derived from *kāla* "time"?), n. of the palace or law-court of Yama.

Lit.: IIM 77.

Kālika (derived from *kāla* "time" or "black"; Buddh.), NP of a Lamaist *arhat*.

Lit.: G 104.

Kālikā (probably derived from *kāla* "black").

1. (Hind.) Epithet of *Durgā*. K. is also mentioned as the wife of Nirṛti (Nairṛta).

Lit.: MW 277.

2. (Buddh.) NP of a Mahāyāna goddess. Char.: colour: blue (black); att.: *ālīḍhāsana*; Vāh.: *mṛtaka*; attr.: *kapāla, karttṛkā*.

Lit.: KiSB 76.

3. (Jain.) NP of a *śāsanadevatā* attending on the 4th *tīrthaṅkara*.

Lit.: GJ 362.

kālikātāṇḍava, n. of a dance-form of Śiva, see Naṭarāja. When portrayed in this form Śiva has 8 arms. Char.: Mu.: *abhaya-, gajahasta-mudrā*; attr.: *agni, ḍamaru, ghaṇṭā, kapāla, pāśa, triśūla*. No wife stands besides him. According to Tamil tradition, this is the "creating" dance, the first of five or seven (Diehl).

Lit.: SSI 84 a.fig. 53.

Kālindī (the n. should be connected either with *kālinda* "water-melon" or with *kālindī* as a kind of vessel), epithet of Yamunā.

Lit.: MEIA 203.

Kalinga, n. of the country along the Coromandel coast, north of Madras; also n. of a school or period in the arts, flourishing from the 1st c.B.C. – 1st c.A.D.

Lit.: D 144; Gz 62.

kālīpūjā ("worship of Kālī"), n. of a festival celebrated in Bengal in the month *kārttika* (October-November). Kālī is celebrated in this festival on the same night as, in the rest of India, Lakṣmī is worshipped (see *dīvālī*).

kalisaṃvat "the year of Kali", see *kaliyuga*.

Lit.: IC 2:736.

Kāliya (derived from *kāla* "black"), n. of a (five-headed) serpent-demon who was tamed by Kṛṣṇa (Kāliyadamana). He is a *nāga* of evil nature, inhabiting a deep pool of the river Yamunā. Mu.: *añjali-mudrā*.

Lit.: D 144; Gt 307; HIS 26; SB 114; WHW 2:389.

Kāliya-damana (or -mardaka, Kāliyāhi-mardaka; "taming, or crushing the serpent Kāliyā"), n. of a form of Kṛṣṇa dancing upon the head of Kāliya. Char.: dancing-form: *catura*; Mu.: *abhayamudrā*; Kāliya shows *añjalimudrā*. Another n.: Kāliya-Kṛṣṇa.

Lit.: D 144; KrA pl. 110; JDI 91; JMS 69 a.pl. 89; KrG pl. 4; MG pl. facing p. 142; R 1:212 a.pl. 64; SB 114, 343 a.pl. 64, 287 a.passim; SSI 38; Th. 68 a.pl. 20A; WM 96 a.fig. 11; ZA 357 a.pl. 423.

Kāliya-Kṛṣṇa, see Kāliyadamana.

Lit.: SB 114.

Kāḷiyammaṉ (Tam.), see Kālī.

kaliyuga "the Kali age", on one hand n. of an age of the world, see sub *yuga*, on the other hand n. of an era beginning in B.C. 3102, indicated by the word *kalisaṃvat*. The year of this era is *gata* (sometimes *vartamāna*) and either *meṣādi* (solar) or *caitrādi* (lunisolar), see *saṃvatsara*. The number of 3102 – the given year of *k.* = the year B.C.; and the given year of *k.* -3101 = the year A.D. General use.

Lit.: IC 2:736.

Kalka-Mātā (N.Ind.), epithet of Kālī.

Lit.: KBh. 199 N.

Kalkin (-ī or -i, Kalky-avatāra; interpreted as "the Fulfiller" (DHP), but more probably an *l*-form of *Karkin "having a white horse *(karka)*", see MAYRHOFER); n. of a future world-saviour, regarded as the 10th *avatāra* of Viṣṇu who is supposed to return at the end of *kaliyuga* in this shape (see below) in order to punish the evil and reward the good. K. is therefore the counterpart of the Buddhist Maitreya. Char.: Vāh.: *aśva* (white; N.B. K. is conceived of as being either a horse himself, or (MEIA) as riding astride a horse; as to the colour of the coming saviour's mount, cp. Revelations 19,11, where the Messiah, returning, rides on a white horse!); attr.: *aśvamastaka* (sometimes, but cp. Hayagrīva), *cakra*, *khadga*, *kheṭaka*, *śaṅkha*, *śara*. Another n.: Viṣṇuyaśas.

Lit.: B 390, 425; ChI 591; DHP 165, 181; GH 130; GI pl. 73, 80 (K. with Śakti); GoRI 1:253; Gt 308; JDI 99; MAYRHOFER, EWA 1:183; MEIA 37, 221; R 1:221 a pl. 35; Th. 74; WHW 1:512; WM 121. (N.B. According to Th., there should not exist any bronze icons of K., but see GI.)

Kalkuti, n. of a *bhūta*.

Lit.: KiH 27; KiSH 74.

kaḻḻu (Tam.) "wine, palm juice" (attr.). The sellers of *k*., i.e. "toddy", drink it while worshipping the image of Maturaivīrappaṉ, regarded as the god of wine.

Lit.: JDI 116; MD 1:335.

kālmāṟi-āḍiya-tāṇḍava (mixed Tam.-Skt) "dancing with the leg reversed", n. of a certain dance-form performed by Śiva Naṭarāja, and typical of the Madurai district. This representation differs from the usual *ānandatāṇḍava* in these respects: the god carries the *agni* in his right rear hand and the *ḍamaru* in his left rear hand (the *mudrās* of his fore hands remain unchanged), and is treading with his left foot on Apasmāra whilst his right leg is raised. Of this type is also Marukal-Naṭeśa.

Lit.: SB 94 a fig. 54.

kalpa ("practicable").

1. "World-period, a fabulous period of time", said to be equal to 1.000 *yugas* (= one day of Brahmā) = 4.320 millions of years of mortals.

Lit.: GRI 156; Gt 309; IC 1:548, 2:650; MW 262; RAI 272.

2. (Jain.) "Sacred precept, law, rule", hence also n. of a monastic rule or vow.

Lit.: IC 2:637; MW 262.

kalpadruma "tree of a world-period"; regarded as a wishing-tree, the giver of riches and blessings to mankind. It is sacred to Indrāṇī. In an earlier world-period the world was adorned with 10 *k*. Cp. *vṛkṣa*, *kalpavṛkṣa*.

Lit.: GJ 263; MS 48; SSI 196; WHW 2:218.

kalpakalatā "flowers from the *kalpaka*-creeper (a kind of Curcuma)" (attr.). Char. of Gaṇeśa (in different forms).

Lit.: R 1:53, 56.

kalpalatā "creeper of a world-period, wishing-creeper" (attr.), n. of a fabulous winding plant which grants all wishes expressed to it.

Lit.: Gz 91; HIS 39; MS 48.

kalpavṛkṣa (*kalpataru*; Pāli *kapparukkha*) "tree of a world period, wishing-tree" (attr.), n. given to the five magnificent trees of the gods which grant wishes (see also *vṛkṣa* and *kalpadruma*). A *k*. is often depicted on top of the *prabhātoraṇa*. In Buddhism *k*. is a symbol esp. of the Buddha, but also (held in one hand) char. of Gaganagañja and Kṣitigarbha.

Lit.: CEBI 10 a pl. 1:1; CHIIA 229 a fig. 10; GH 65; IC 1:538; STP 1:144; WHW 2:218.

kalyāṇa (lit.:) "auspicious deed, happiness, prosperity". With reference to South Indian representations this word is esp. used in the meaning of "marriage", see Kalyāṇasundaramūrti, *pārvatikalyāṇa*, *tirukalyāṇa*, Vallīkalyāṇasundara.

Lit.: JDI 35; MW 263.

kalyāṇamaṇḍapa "wedding-hall", n. of a "hall for the celebration of the divine wedding-festival".

Lit.: BECA 1:261.

Kalyāṇasundara(mūrti) ("representation of the wedding of the Charming One"), esp. in

South India n. of a representation of Śiva (four-handed) together with Pārvatī (two-handed) with the theme of their marriage. Sometimes they are accompanied by Viṣṇu (as her brother! At Madurai he is depicted celebrating the marriage by pouring water from a pitcher over the hands of Śiva and Pārvatī) and Lakṣmī, and occasionally also by Brahmā. Char.: att.: *sthānaka*; Mu.: esp. *pāṇigrahaṇa*, further *abhaya-* and *varada-mudrā*; attr.: *ḍamaru*, *jaṭāmukuṭa*, *kuṇḍalas*, *mṛga*, *nāgas* (as *kaṭibandha*, *udarabandha* etc.), *nīlotpala*, *paraśu*, *trinayana*, *triśūla*. Another n.: *vaivāhikamūrti*; cp. also *pārvatīkalyāṇa*, *tirukalyāṇa*. In spite of the fact that the bride during the *pāṇigrahaṇa*-ceremony in reality always stands to the left of the bridegroom (see, e.g., SSI fig. 66), it is noteworthy that in the South Indian sculptures of this kind Pārvatī is very often represented standing to the right of Śiva (this probably for artistic reasons).

Lit.: B 485 a.pl. 38:1 a.passim; DIA pl. 21; JDI 35; R 2:337 a.pl. 101-107; SB 203 a.pl. 126 a.passim; SIB pl. 44; SSI 103; Th. 90 a.pl. 40, 44; WM 168.

Kāma(deva) ("love, desire", esp. "sexual love").

1. (Hind.) NP of the god of love. Usually he is said to be the son of Kṛṣṇa and Rukmiṇī (see also Pradyumna), but as his parents are also mentioned Dharma and Śraddhā or Lakṣmī, as his father also Brahmā. K. is supposed to be bodiless (Anaṅga) in consequence of the anger of Śiva, who burnt him with his third eye, because K. disturbed his meditation (see Kāmāntakamūrti). K. is also regarded as the tempter and the Genius of evil, and in this character he is the Hindu counterpart of the Buddhist Māra. – K. (as Manmatha and esp. as Pradyumna) is further reckoned as a form or aspect of Viṣṇu (see *caturviṅśatimūrti*).

K. is mostly represented as two- or eight-armed. Wives: Rati (Revā), Prīti (Madaśakti and Ujjvalā are probably epithets of one or both of his wives). Char.: Vāh.: *śuka*, sometimes also *mayūra*; possibly also *makara* (but this may rather be regarded as an attr., see below); attr.: *dhanus* Puṣpadhanvan (or *ikṣukodaṇḍa*) + *pañcaśara*, *makaradhvaja*, *padma*, *śaṅkha*. – *bījas* representing K. are *BOṀ* and *KLĪṀ*. Epithets (not mentioned above): Kāmeśvara, Kandarpa, Madana; cp. also Madhukara, Māra, Madhusūdana.

Lit.: B 301; D 145; DHP 312; GBB 129; GH pl. 13; GI pl. 68; GoRI 1:325, 2:48; Gt 310; IC 1:496; IIM 88; JDI 101 a.fig. 31; KiH 26 a.pl. 91; KiSH 71; MG 157; R 1:276 a.pl. 82-83; SSI 62; Th. 56; WHW 1:514; WM 122; ZA pl. 129.

2. (Vāh.; Buddh.) Kālacakra is represented as treading upon K. (as Anaṅga); K. with wife upon Rāhu is Vāh. of Tārodbhava-Kurukullā.

Lit.: BBh. 149.

kāmabīja "Seed-of-Lust" or "Seed-of-Desire" (Hind.), n. of a *bījamantra* with the form *KLĪṀ**, dedicated to Kāma, and representing "the form of joy, of pleasure, the procreative aspect of the power of Śiva in the form of his consort, the Transcendent-Goddess (Maheśvarī)" (DHP). It has the purpose of gaining transcendent knowledge and also pleasure, victory, and royal power.

Lit.: DHP 313, 342; IC 1:567.

Kāmadahanamūrti ("representation (of Śiva) burning Kāma"), see Kāmāntakamūrti.

Lit.: B 486; R 2:369.

kāmadhātu "the region (world) of wishes; die Welt der alle möglichen Missetaten und Qualen verursachenden Begierden" (Buddh.).

Lit.: SeKB 127, 240.

Kāmadhenu (or Kāmaduh; "wishing-cow"), epithet of Sarasvatī and of Surabhi.

Lit.: D 147; DHP 260; GH 69; IC 1:535; WHW 1:515; WM 122.

Kāmakalā, n. of a symbolical union of Kāma (Kāmeśvara) with Kalā (Kāmeśvarī), i.e. of Śiva and Lalitā. This union is symbolized by the sound *-ĪṀ* in the *bījamantra KLĪṀ**,

and also by the *śrīcakra yantra*. K. may also be represented by erotic sculptures.
Lit.: GoRI 2:48; M. R. ANAND, Kama Kala. Über die philosophischen Grundlagen der Erotik in der hinduistischen Skulptur (Genf-Paris 1958).

Kāmākṣī ("whose looks are amorous"; Tam. Kāmāṭci), n. of a goddess who is regarded as a form of Śiva's Śakti (at Kanchipuram), but she is also worshipped as an individual goddess in other places in South India.
Lit.: GoRI 2:14; JDI 37; WM 122.

kamala "(red) lotus" (attr.), see *padma*. – In the terminology of architecture *k*. is also n. of part of a capital of a column.
Lit.: BECA 1:272.

Kamalā ("lotus(born)"), esp. in South India epithet of Lakṣmī. K. also belongs to the group *mahāvidyā* representing Mahārātrī. – Cp. Padmā.
Lit.: DHP 261, 284; GoRI 1:319; Gw 37; MG pl. facing p. 177; ZA 158.

Kamalacandra-Lokeśvara ("L., the lotus-moon"; Buddh.), n. of a variety of Avalokiteśvara. Char.: att.: *samapādasthānaka*; Vāh.: *padma*; Mu.: *vyākhyānamudrā*.
Lit.: BBh. 429 a.pl. 77(A).

kamalākṣa(mālā) ("garland of lotus-eyes"; attr.), n. of a certain kind of rosary of beads. Char. of: Brahmā, Dhara, Sarasvatī, Śiva. See further *akṣamālā*.
Lit.: B 304; R 1:13; 2:553.

kamalanayana "lotus-eyed", i.e. having horizontally elongated eyes, shaped like the petals of lotus-flowers (attr.).
Lit.: JMS 39.

kamalāsana "lotus-sitting" or "lotus-seat" (att. and Vāh.), n. of an *āsana*-posture, mentioned, but not described in B; according to other statements *k*. is identical with *padmāsana*, but should be combined with a Mu. similar to *jñānamudrā*. – *k*. is further another n. of *padmapīṭha*.
Lit.: B 271; MEIA 222; R 2:441.

Kamalāsana ("having a lotus as seat").
1. (Hind.) Epithet of Brahmā, who is represented sitting on a lotus sprouting from the navel of Viṣṇu. This representation is often combined with Viṣṇu Anantāśāyana. – Other n.: Kamalayoni, Padmāsana.
Lit.: CEBI 17 a.pl. B; ZA pl. 111; ZM 70.
2. (Buddh.) Epithet of the Buddha
Lit.: CEBI 48.

Kamalayoni ("born from a lotus"), epithet of Brahmā, see Kamalāsana.
Lit.: MSHP 8.

kamaṇḍalu "vessel, water-jar", esp. "the water-jar of an ascetic" (attr.). *k*. is described either as a jar with a narrow neck or as a pot or pitcher with a pipe. In this dictionary *k*. is used as a common term of jars of all kinds, in spite of the differences in construction – which are in any case often not clearly visible in the representations (see the other names below).
k. is thought of as filled with *amṛta** or with (sacred) water from the Ganges, often also with gems (this esp. in Buddhism). It symbolizes "the receptacle of knowledge" (see *jñānabhāṇḍa*, *kalaśa*); it is possible that *k*. is also a symbol of fertility (cp. *jala*). – *k*. is esp. char. of: Brahmā, Sarasvatī, Śiva, Agni, Varuṇa, Gaṅgā, Yamunā, Amitābha, Amitāyus, Avalokiteśvara (in different forms); further of: Aghora, Aja, Akṣayamati, Ambā, Amitaprabha, Amoghapāśa, Aśvinīdevatās, Bahurūpa, Bhadra-Kālī, Bhṛṅgin, Bhṛkuṭī, Bhūmidevī, Brahmacāriṇī, Brahmāṇī, Brahmaśāstā, Bṛhaspati, Caṇḍeśvara, Citipati, Cundā, Dattātreya, Dharmadhātuvāgīśvara, Dharmavaśitā, Dhātā, Dhruva, Gaurī, Harasiddhi, Indra, Indrāṇī, Jalandharavadhamūrti, Jayanta, Kapila, Kaumārī, Kīrti, Kṛṣṇa, Kṣitigarbha, Kubera, Lakṣmī, Madhva, Mahā-Kālī, Mahāmantrānusāriṇī, Mahāmāyūrī, Mahiṣāsuramardinī, Maitreya, Manasā, sMan-bla, Maṇibhadra, Māyājālakrama-Kurukullā, Mṛtyuñjaya, *nāga(devas)*, Nāgasena, Nāmasaṅgīti, Nīlakaṇṭha, Padmapāṇi, Pārvatī, Prasannatārā, Pukkasī, Rambhā, *ṛṣis*, Sadāśiva, Śaṅkarācārya, Sarvamaṅgalā, Saubhāgya-

Bhuvaneśvarī, Sitabrahmā, Śītalā, Sitasamvara, Skanda, Śukra, Surabhi, Sūrya, Svāhā, Svarṇākarṣaṇa-Bhairava, Trimūrti, Uṣṇīṣavijayā, Vajrapāṇi (in the Garuḍa-form), Vallīkalyāṇasundara, Vāmanāvatāra, Vasudhārā, Vāyu, Vyākhyānadakṣiṇāmūrti, Yogadakṣiṇāmūrti. – *k.* (often named *kalaśa*) is also symbol of Malli. It is further a *maṅgala*, see *aṣṭamaṅgala*. Other n. : esp. *kalaśa*, further *bhadraghaṭa, bhājana, bhṛṅgāra, ghaṭa, kuṇḍā* (*-ī* or *-ikā*), *ratnacchaṭāvarṣighaṭa, ratnakalaśa, ratnapātra*. These names may often signify different forms of jars. – Cp. also *galantī, jhārī, karaṇḍa, oṣadhipātra, pātra, pūrṇakalaśa, pūrṇapātra.*

Lit.: B 303; BBh. 435; G 14; GJ pl. 22:19; KiJ pl. 45; MEIA 243; R 1:11 a. pl. 4:3-6, 2: pl. 5:3; SM 192; WM 109 a.fig. 71-72.

Kamaṇḍalu-Lokeśvara ("L., (the genius) of the *kamaṇḍalu*"; Buddh.), n. of a variety of Avalokiteśvara. Char. : att. : *samapādasthānaka*; attr. : *cakra, dhanus, ghaṇṭā, kamaṇḍalu, vajra.*

Lit.: BBh. 395 a.pl. 10(A).

Kāmāntakamūrti ("representation [of Śiva] killing Kāma"), n. of an *ugra*-aspect of Śiva, showing him destroying Kāma with the fire from his third eye, because Kāma had disturbed his meditation in order to make him enamoured of Pārvatī. – Char. : Mu. : *patākā-, sūci-mudrā*; attr. : *akṣamālā, nāga, trinayana*. – Another n. : Kāmadahanamūrti.

Lit.: B 488 a.pl. 33:1; D 146; R 1:19, 2:147; Th. 83.

kāmāṭciviḷakku (Tam.; also *kāmākṣi-*) "Kāmākṣi-lamp", n. of a brass lamp in the form of a woman (representing Kāmākṣi or another lady), holding a lamp-bowl (*dīpa*, for one wick) with both her hands. In South India it is much used at weddings.

Lit.: TL 2:873.

kambu "conch, shell" (attr.), see *śaṅkha.*

kambugrīva "shell-neck" (attr.), cp. *kambugrīvā* "shell-like neck (i.e. one marked with three lines)", *kambukaṇṭha* "having folds on the neck like a spiral shell", see *trivali.*

Lit.: MW 253; SB 30.

Kāmeśvara ("lord Kāma"), see Kāmakalā.

Lit.: DHP 208.

Kāmeśvarī ("lady of Kāma"), see Kāmakalā.

Kāminī ("loving woman"; Buddh.), n. of an inferior Mahāyāna goddess, attending on Buddhakapāla.

Lit.: BBh. 160.

kanaka "gold", n. of a precious thing, sometimes included among the *pañcaratna**.

Kanaka-Bhāradvāja ("golden Bh."; Buddh.), n. of a Lamaist *arhat*. Char. : Mu. : *dhyānamudrā*; attr. : *dhvaja.*

Lit.: G 104.

Kanakamuni (Pāli : Konāgamana; "the golden *muni*"), n. of a *mānuṣibuddha*. Char. : att. : *padmāsana*; Mu. : *abhaya-, dhyāna-mudrā*; no attr. His *bodhivṛkṣa* is the *vaṭa.*

Lit.: G 32; H 32; KiDG 44; KiSB 32.

Kanaka-Prajñāpāramitā ("the golden P."; Buddh.), n. of a variety of Prajñāpāramitā. Char. : colour : golden; Mu. : *dharmacakramudrā*; attr. : 2 *padma*s.

Lit.: BBh. 199 a.pl. 142.

Kanakarāja (the golden king"; Buddh.), n. of a *mānuṣibodhisattva.*

Lit.: BBh. 79.

Kanakavatsa ("the golden calf, child"; Buddh.), n. of a Lamaist *arhat*. Attr. : *pāśa* (with jewels).

Lit.: G 104.

kañcakam (Tam.) "breast-band" (attr.), see *kucabandha.*

Lit.: JDI 63.

kāñcidāma "girdle furnished with small tinkling bells, held in place by rows of chains" (attr.).

Lit.: B 292.

kāṇḍapaṭa "curtain" (attr., held in the hands). Char. of Paṭadhāriṇī.

Lit.: BBh. 317.

Kandarpa ("satisfier, the Inflamer-of-the-Creator"), epithet of Kāma.

Lit.: DHP 314.

Kandarpā (Jain.), see Pannagā.

Lit.: GJ 362.

kāṇḍarṣi ("*riṣi* of certain *kāṇḍas* or portions of the Veda"), n. of a group of *riṣis* the leader of whom was Jaimini.
Lit.: R 2:566; WHW 1:438.

Kaṇēcaṉ (Tam.), see Gaṇeśa.

kaṅghā (Hi.) "comb" (attr.), n. of one of the five essentials of the Sikhs (see *pañcakakāra*). It is symbolic of discipline and order.
Lit.: GG p. CLVII.

Kaṇha (M.Ind.), see Kṛṣṇa.

kaṇiśa "ear of rice" (attr.), held in one hand char. of: Dānapāramitā, Gaṇeśa (in different forms), Vasudhārā. Another n.: *dhānyamañjarī*.

Kaniṣka, n. of a king of the Kuṣāna empire of Mathurā in the 2nd c.A.D. K. is also n. of an era, but the date of its beginning is uncertain (A.D. 78, 128-129, 144 etc. have all been suggested).
Lit.: D 148; Enc.Brit. 5:721; Gz 69; IC 2:737; RĄAI 76; ZA pl. 61.

Kañja ("produced from water, i.e. lotus"), epithet of Brahmā.
Lit.: DHP 235.

Kañjaja ("lotus-born"), epithet of Brahmā.
Lit.: DHP 235.

Kanjur (Tib.), see bKa'-'gyur sub initial Ka'...

kaṅkāla "skeleton" or "necklace of skeletons" (attr.). A skeleton is carried in one hand by Śrīdevī; a necklace of skeletons is char. of Kaṅkālamūrti.
Lit.: G 89; SSI 103.

Kaṅkāla(mūrti) ("representation together with a skeleton"), n. of an *ugra*-representation of Śiva who killed Viṣvaksena, the doorkeeper of Viṣṇu, because of Viṣvaksena's having refused him permission to enter into the presence of Viṣṇu. This representation is very similar to the Bhikṣāṭanamūrti. Char.: Śiva is accompanied by a *mṛga*; Mu.: *kaṭaka-mudrā*; attr.: *ajina* (tigerskin), *bāṇa, candra, ḍhakkā, dhattūra*-flowers, *kaṅkāla* or *kaṅkāladaṇḍa, mayūrapattra* on a *daṇḍa, nāga, yajñopavīta*.
Lit.: B 466; KIM pl. 45; R 2:295 a.pl. 82-85; SB 342 a.pl. 281 a.passim; SSI 103; Th. 85.

kaṅkāladaṇḍa "staff, stick with skeletons" (attr.), n. of a staff or a *triśūla*, on the point of which there is a skeleton of a human sacrificial victim or of demon such as Andhaka, Viṣvaksena. Char. of Śiva as Andhakāsuravadhamūrti, Kaṅkālamūrti. Yama (Buddh.) also carries a sceptre or staff with a skeleton.
Lit.: R 2:304.

kaṅkālī "having a fleshless skeleton body" (fem.; attr.), char. of some of the *mātaras*, Kṛśodarī.
Lit.: B 274.

Kaṅkālinī-Kālī ("skeleton-Kālī"), epithet of Kālī in a very emaciated shape.
Lit.: GH 479 a.pl. 9.

kaṅkana "wrist ornament, bracelet, ring" (attr.).
Lit.: B 292; R 1:23; Th. 46 a.pl. 9.

Kaṅkar Mātā (N.Ind.), n. of one of the *saptamātaras* who send diseases.
Lit.: GH 136.

Kaṇṇaṉ (Tam., < Pkt Kaṇha < Skt Kṛṣṇa, TL; wrongly MD: "celui qui a des yeux, – qui voit tout"), n. of Kṛṣṇa in South India.
Lit.: MD 1:304; TL 2:693.

Kaṇṇappa-nāyaṉār (Tam., interpreted as "He who gave his eye to the god"), n. of a *śaivabhakta*, who is known as a hunter. Char.: Mu.: *añjalimudrā*; attr.: *akṣamālā, dhanus, khaḍga* (at the girdle), *vṛttakuṇḍalas*.
Lit.: AIP pl. 59 (315); R 2:479 a.pl. 133; JDI 16; SB 271, 338 a.pl. 180, 277.

kaṉṉimār (Tam. "virgins"), see *navaśakti*.
Lit.: DiCh. 33.

kāṇphaṭayogin (N.Ind.) "les *yogin* aux oreilles fendues", n. of ascetics of the sect *gorakhnātī*.
Lit.: IC 1:630.

Kaṅsa, n. of a tyrannical king of Mathurā, son of Ugrasena and cousin of Devakī, the mother of Kṛṣṇa, by whom K. was killed. – As the foe of a deity K. is identified with the Asura Kālanemi.
Lit.: D 149; DHP 176; GoRI 1:239; IC 1:509; WHW 1:520; WM 123.

kāṅsā (or *-a*; Hi., < Skt *kaṅsa* or *kaṅsya*) "bronze, bell-metal, an alloy of copper and zinc" (P). Other sources mention it as an alloy of lead and brass. – Cp. *phūl*.
Lit.: BhIM 34; MH 36; P 807; WHW 2:67.

kaṅsī "Indian gong" (attr.). Char. of Gītā.
Lit.: BBh. 313.

Kanthaka (or Kaṇṭhaka; "neck-ornament"; Buddh.), n. of the Buddha's favourite horse, riding upon which he left his royal home and went off to seek enlightenment (see *mahābhiniṣkramaṇa*).
Lit.: KiSB 12.

Kaṇṭhamālinī ("having a garland round the neck"; Buddh.), n. of a *mānuṣibuddha-śakti*.
Lit.: BBh. 79.

kaṇṭhī (or *-ikā*) "necklace, collar, torque" (attr.). *kaṇṭhikā* is also n. of one of the symbols of *ṣaṇmudrā*.
Lit.: BBh. 438; SB passim; SIB 69.

Kānti ("desire, wish"), n. of the Śakti of Nārāyaṇa.
Lit.: R 1:233.

Kaṇva (perhaps "sounding, praising"), n. of a *riṣi* (author of several hymns of the Ṛgveda), also leader of a certain group of *riṣi*s, the *devarṣi*.
Lit.: R 2:566; WHW 1:526.

Kanyā ("virgin"), epithet of Pārvatī. This n. refers to Pārvatī before her marriage with Śiva. – K. is also n. of the "Virgo" sign (see *rāśi*) of the Zodiac.
Lit.: BBh. 383; IC 2:731; GH 50.

kanyā-dān (Skt-Hi.) "the giving of a girl (in marriage)", n. of a rite included among the *vivāha*-ceremonies.
Lit.: P 857.

kanyādi "beginning with (the *rāśi*) *kanyā*", a term used in dating.

kanyā-pāṇi-grahaṇ (Skt-Hi.) "the (bride-groom's) taking the hand of the bride", see *pāṇigrahaṇa*.
Lit.: P 857.

kapāla "cup, dish, alms-bowl of a beggar, skull(-cup)" (attr.) *k.* was originally a cup made of the top part of a skull and therefore oval in shape; in later forms it is round and it is often not distinguishable from the round *bhikṣāpātra*. These two terms are therefore mixed up in literature, and in this dictionary *k.* is used as a common term for both. The *k.* is thought of as containing libations or blood (when carried by idols in cruel representations). As a cult object it is used for bringing libations to the gods. – In Buddhism *k.* is regarded as a symbol "des Sieges über die Dämonen" (GBM); in Lamaism *k.*, as an independent cult object, is a real skull-cap, encased in a metal stand and richly ornamented. – *k.* may also be combined in composite terms with a name indicating the contents, e.g. *pāyasa*. – According to BBh., *k.* may also signify the severed head of a man (see *muṇḍa*, here used as a term in this sense) and, carried by Śiva in some forms, *k.* may therefore represent the skull of Brahmā's fifth head (which was cut off by Śiva; cp. also *brahmakapāla*).
k. is very frequently used as an attr. It is esp. char. of Śiva in many forms and Kālī; further of: Acalavajrapāṇi, Ādidharmā, Ahirbudhnya, Aja, Anala, Andhakāsuravadhamūrti, Aṅkālammaṉ, Ardhanārīśvara, Āryavajravārāhī, Bahurūpa, Balapramāthanī, Balavikarṇikā, Baṭuka Bhairava, Bhairon, Brahmā, Bram-zei gzugs-can, Buddhakapāla, Cāmuṇḍā, Carcikā, Caturbhujatārā, Citipati, *ḍākinī*s, Dam-can, Daśabhuja-Aghoramūrti, Dhūmrāvatī, Ekajaṭā, Ekapādamūrti, Gajāsurasaṅhāramūrti, Gaṇeśa, mGon-dkar, mGon-po nag-po, Gur-gyi mGon-po, Hālāhala, Heruka, Hevajra, Īśāna, Jambhala, Jayanta, Jñānaḍākinī, Jñānasambandha, Jyeṣṭhā-(devī), Kālacakra and his Śakti, Kāladūtī, Kālajambhala, Kālārimūrti, Kalavikarṇikā, Kālikā, Krodhahayagrīva, *kṣetrapālas*, Kubera, Lakulīśa, Locanā, Luipa, Mahācakravajrapāṇi's Śakti, Mahācīnatārā, Mahākāla, Mahālakṣmī, Mahāmāya, Ma-

hāmāyā, Maheśa, Māmakī, Manonmanī, Māriyamman, Mar-pa, Mārttaṇḍa-Bhairava, Māyājālakramakrodha-Lokeśvara, Māyājālakramāryāvalokiteśvara, Mṛtyuñjaya, Nairātmā, Naṅ-sgrub, Nāropa, Naṭarāja (in different forms), *navadurgās*, Nīlakaṇṭhāryāvalokiteśvara, Padmapāṇi, Pāṇḍarā, Pāśupatamūrti, Piṭāri, Prabhāsa, Prajñāpāramitā, Prasannatārā, Pratyaṅgirā, Rakṣoghnamūrti (*k.* with *agni*), Raudrapāśupatamūrti, Ṣaḍakṣarī, Sadāśiva, Samantabhadra, Samvara and his Śakti, gSaṅ-sgrub, Saptakṣara, *saptamātaras*, Śarabha, Sarasvatī, Sarvabhūtadamanī, Sarvanivaraṇaviṣkambhin, Śivadūtī, Śiva-Lokeśvara, Śrīdevī, Śrīvidyādevī, Tailopa, Ubhayavarāhānana-Mārīcī, Ucchuṣma, Ugra-Tārā, Utnauti-Lokeśvara, Vajrabhairava, Vajracarcikā, Vajradhara, Vajradhātvīśvarī, Vajrahūṅkāra, Vajrasarasvatī, Vajrasattvātmikā, Vajraśṛṅkhalā, Vajrayoginī, Vāmā, Vārāhī, Vidyujvālākarālī, Vighnāntaka, Virūpākṣa, Yamadūtī, Yamāntaka, Yamāri, Yamī.

Other n.: *karpara*, *karoṭa*, *mahākapāla*; sometimes *muṇḍa*; see also esp. *asṛkkapāla*, *māṅsakapāla*, *raktapātra*.

Lit.: B 304, 480; BBh. 435; G 8 with ill. facing p. 10, 14 (ill.); GBM 105; H pl. 7:65; MEIA 267; R 1:13 a.pl. 4:8; Th. 40.

Kapāla, n. of a form of Śiva Bhairava.
Lit.: B 466.

kapālamālā ("skull-garland"; attr.), see *muṇḍamālā*.
Lit.: BBh. 182.

Kapālamālin (or -ī; "wearing a skull-garland"), epithet of Śiva.
Lit.: DHP 191; JDI 20.

Kapālī(śa) ("wearing skulls" or "the lord who wears skulls"), n. of one among the group *ekādaśarudra*.
Lit.: R 2:386.

kāpālika "skull-carrier", n. of a Śaivite sect the members of which drank out of *kapālas* (i.e. out of skull-caps).
Lit.: GoRI 1:260; GRI 329; IC 1:629; WHW 1:526.

Kapālinī ("carrying a cup"; Buddh.), n. of an inferior Mahāyāna goddess attending on Buddhakapāla.
Lit.: BBh. 160.

kaparda (or *-rdda*; "small shell"), n. of a certain form of *jaṭāmukuṭa* in which the "matted locks wave spirally upward like the top of a shell" (B; attr.). Char. of Śiva (Kapardin).
Lit.: B 286 a.pl. 3:5; MKVI 1:135; WHW 1:433.

Kapardin (or -ī), epithet of Śiva(-Rudra) wearing a *kaparda*.
Lit.: B 286, 447; D 150; DHP 259.

kapāṭa "door, the leaf or panel of a door, planks" (attr.). Char. of Kapāṭā.
Lit.: BBh. 317.

Kapāṭā (Buddh.), n. of a female *dvārapāla*, a deification of the door. Char.: colour: red; attr.: *kapāṭa*.
Lit.: BBh. 317.

kapila "reddish yellow", n. of a colour.
Lit.: MEIA 238.

Kapila ("monkey-coloured, brown"), n. of a celebrated *riṣi* who is said to be the founder of the Sāṅkhya-philosophy. He is sometimes regarded as an *avatāra* of Viṣṇu (Kṛṣṇa or Agni), and is represented as 8-armed. Char.: Mu.: *abhaya-*, *kaṭi-mudrā*; attr.: *cakra*, *daṇḍa*, *hala*, *kamaṇḍalu*, *khaḍga*, *pāśa*, *śaṅkha*. – K. is also n. of a people.
Lit.: B 391; D 150; DHP 165, 182; Gt 316; KiH 46 a.pl. 167; R 1:123, 247; SSI 254; WM 190.

kāpila, a term used for *rākṣasa*.
Lit.: MEIA 21.

kapilā "cow", see *gaus*.
Lit.: DiIP 137.

Kapilavastu ("seat of the Kapilas"), n. of the capital of the Śākya-clan, the family of the Buddha.
Lit.: IC 2:469.

kapiśīrṣa "ape's head", in architecture n. of a battlement, the upper part of a wall.
Lit.: JMS 17.

kapittha "wood-apple, the fruit of Feronia elephantum" (attr.). Char. of Bāla-Gaṇapati and other forms of Gaṇeśa.
Lit.: B 358.

kapitthamudrā "wood-apple-handpose" (Mu.), n. of a variety of the *muṣṭimudrā** with the difference: the forefinger is bent over the top of the straight thumb so that the thumb sticks out between forefinger and middle finger. It denotes Lakṣmī, Sarasvatī, milking a cow, holding a veil, the end of a robe, offering incense, amorous dalliance, sexual intercourse.
Lit.: WHW 2:87.

kapota "dove, pigeon" (attr.). In the Vedic period *k.* is sometimes mentioned (together with *ulūka*) as a messenger of Nirṛti ("dissolution, misfortune") and was hence comprehended as a bird of evil omen. – In Buddhism *k.* symbolizes (esp. sexual) passion, "desire". – In architecture *k.* is n. of part of the basement.
Lit.: BECA 1:272; GBM 103; MKVI 1:137.

kapparukkha (Pāli), see *kalpavṛkṣa*.

kāppu (Tam.) "protection" (attr.), n. of a bandage tied round the arm during certain ceremonies and serving as an amulet.
Lit.: DiIP 147, 252.

karā (Hi.) "iron ring worn on the wrists or ankles, bangle" (attr.). A (steel) *k.* is one of the five essentials of the Sikhs (see *pañcakakāra*), symbolic of self-control in action.
Lit.: GG p. CLVII; P 831.

karacham "Topftragen" ("pot-carrying"), mentioned in GoRI as n. of a ceremony in South India which is connected with Māriyammaṉ. This term is identical with *karaka**.
Lit.: GoRI 2:6.

karah praṣad (or *k. prashad*; Panj.; *karah* means "pudding", and *praṣad* is said to mean "blessing", hence "blessed pudding"; *praṣad*, however, may originate from Skt *prasāda** and is therefore a kind of sacred food; attr.; Sikhism). *k.* is a kind of pudding made of wheat flour, clarified butter (*ghī*), sugar and water. It is an abridged, symbolical form of *langar**, a sacrament which, at services in the Sikh temple, is distributed to all present, both Sikhs and non-Sikhs. It is received in both hands held out together like a cup. After receiving it, a Sikh bows his head in gratitude and thanks.
Lit.: GG p. CLVI; HS 192; PRAKASH SINGH, The Sikh Gurus and the Temple of Bread (Amritsar 1964).

Kāraikkāl Ammaiyār (or Kārikal-ammai, Tam. "the mother deity of Kārikal (a town near Negapatam)"), n. of a female *śaiva-bhakta* and ascetic worshipped in South India. She is represented in an emaciated shape. Attr.: *tāla*s (she is portrayed as playing cymbals while regarding the dance of Śiva Naṭarāja). – Cp. Punītavatī.
Lit.: J. FILLIOZAT, Indien. Völker und Traditionen (Osnabrück), 116 (ill.); MD 1:355; SB 348, 351 a.pl. 317(A), 332; SSI fig. 162; TL 2:889.

karaka (or *karagam*) "water-vessel" (attr.). "This is a pot filled with water and decorated with mango leaves" (DiIP). It is also described as "lamps of ghee, or earthen pots with blazing fire in them" (SSI); this represents the deity at certain festivals and is carried on the head in processions dedicated to the *grāmadevatās*. – Cp. *karacham*.
Lit.: DiIP 176; MW 254; SSI 227.

Karāla-Bhadrā ("the dreadful Bh."), another n. of Kāla-Bhadrā.
Lit.: SSI 197.

Karālī ("dreadful, terrible"), originally (in Vedic times) n. of one of the seven tongues (cp. Saptajihva) of Agni, later an epithet of Kālī or Cāmuṇḍā.
Lit.: B 491; D 150; SSI 197.

karaṇa ("calculation"), n. of a division of a month in 60 parts, each day (*tithi*) consisting of two *k.*
Lit.: IC 2:722.

karaṇaḍamaru(mudrā) "the handpose of 'doing', i.e. holding the drum" (Mu.), n. of a handpose (in dance) for which see *ḍamaruhasta*.
Lit.: WHW 2:87.

karaṇa(hasta)mudrā ("skilful hand"), n. of a dance-Mu. A hand showing this handpose is outstretched with the index and

the little fingers erect, while the thumb presses the two remaining fingers against the palm of the hand. The hand is held horizontally. Char. of: Avalokiteśvara (in different forms), Caṇḍavajrapāṇi, Ekajaṭā, Hayagrīva, Yama. – *k.* also refers to the dance poses of Śiva Naṭarāja, the number of which is sometimes given as 108.
Lit: B 280; BBh. 435; G 20 (ill.); KiDG pl. 38; KiSB 69; SIB 61; J.M. Somasundaram Pillai, The great temple at Tanjore (2. ed. Tanjore 1958).

karaṇḍa "basket" (filled with jewels: *ratnakaraṇḍa*; attr.). This should be compared with *kamaṇḍalu.* – Char. of: Akṣayajñānakaraṇḍā, Sarvabuddhadharma-Koṣavatī. – Another n.: *peṭaka.*
Lit.: BBh. 341; WHW 1:434.

karaṇḍamukuṭa (or *-makuṭa*; lit. "basket-crown"), n. of a head-dress, shaped like a conical basket with the narrow end turned upwards; a crown decorated with series of flattened pots (attr.). Char. of goddesses and minor deities, also of Skanda as a boy (in Somāskanda).
Lit.: B 287; R 1:29 a.pl. 8:2; SIB 69; Th. 32 (ill.); WM 102 a.fig. 39.

Kāraṇḍavyūha-Lokeśvara ("L. with the basket-array"; Buddh.), n. of a variety of Avalokiteśvara. Char.: att.: *padmāsana*; Vāh.: *padma*; attr.: *pustaka, vajra.*
Lit.: BBh. 398 a.pl. 37(A).

karañja "the tree Pongamia Glabra", a tree sacred to Vārāhī.
Lit.: SSI 196.

karaṅkamālā "skull garland" (attr.), see *muṇḍamālā.*
Lit.: MEIA 215.

karanyāsa "assignment of the fingers of the hand severally to different deities..." (TL), see esp. *nyāsa.*
Lit.: DiIP 76; TL 2:743.

karatāla "cymbal" (attr.), see *tāla.*
Lit.: B 303.

Kar-gyu-pa (Tib.), n. of a Lamaist sect which was founded by Mar-pa and whose first apostle was Mi-la-ras-pa.
Lit.: G 5.

karihasta "elephant-hand" (Mu.), n. of an arm-pose which seems to be identical with *gajahastamudrā.*
Lit.: SB 151.

Kārikal-ammai, see Kāraikkāl Ammaiyār.
Lit.: JDI 53.

Kāriṇī ("doing, acting"; Buddh.), n. of an inferior Mahāyāna goddess attending on Buddhakapāla.
Lit.: BBh. 160.

Karivāhana ("having an elephant as vehicle"), epithet of Indra.
Lit.: JDI 106.

karivaktra "elephant-faced" (attr.), see *gajamukha.*
Lit.: BBh. 365.

Karivarada ("conferring a boon on the elephant"), n. of a representation of Viṣṇu showing him rescuing Gajendra, the king of elephants, from the mortal grasp of a water-monster. – Cp. Varadarāja, Gajendramokṣa.
Lit.: B 426 a.pl. 27:1; R 1:266 a.pl. 80:2.

karka(ṭa), *karkin* (or *-ī, -i*) "crab, the sign Cancer", n. of a symbol of Suvidhi or Puṣpadanta; also n. of a *rāśi* ("Cancer"). – *k.* also has the sense of "white horse", see Kalkin.
Lit.: BBh. 383; GH 50; IC 2:731; KiSH 142.

Kārkoṭa(ka) (or Karka), n. of a *nāga(deva).* Char.: colour: black; attr.: *akṣamālā, kamaṇḍalu, trinayana.*
Lit.: Gt Suppl. 62; MW 275; R 2:557.

Kārlī, n. of a Buddhist cave temple in West India.
Lit: FBKI 47; Gt 317; RAAI 71; ZA pl. 78 ff.

karma(n) "act, action, performance; any religious act or rite, esp. a deed originating in the hope of future recompense (in a future life)".
Lit.: Gt 319; IC 1:555; MW 258; RAAI 272; WHW 1:529.

karma-abhiṣeka "consecrating by 'acts, rites', i.e. by the use of water and objects (instruments) with a symbolical meaning" (Buddh.).
Lit.: GBM 126.

Karmaḍākinī ("*ḍākinī* through *karman*"; Buddh.), in Lamaism n. of a certain *ḍākinī*. Char. : colour : green ; attr. : *kapāla*, *khaḍga*, *khaṭvāṅga*.
Lit.: G 14, 34.

Karmaheruka ("*heruka* through or of *karman*"; Buddh.), n. of Amoghasiddhi as a *heruka-buddha*. Char. : colour, green.
Lit.: G 87.

karmamaṇḍala ("the *m.* of *karman*"; Buddh.), n. of a *maṇḍala* which shows "die Aktivität der verschiedenen Wesenheiten durch ihre Gesten oder durch Symbole ihrer Tätigkeit".
Lit.: GBM 109.

karmāra "blacksmith, metal worker", n. of an artisan occupied in casting bronze images.
Lit.: SIB 4, 70.

karmavajra ("the *v.* of *karman*"), n. of a double *vajra* (i.e. one with points in four directions; attr.; Buddh.), see further *viśvavajra*.
Lit.: CEBI pl. 6:28 (ill. of a *k.* used in Shingon ritual).

Karmavajra (Buddh.), in Lamaism n. of a variety of Vajradhara. Char. : Mu. : *vyākhyānamudrā*; attr. : *padma*.
Lit.: G 50.

Karmavaśitā ("control of *karman*"; Buddh.), n. of a *vaśitā*. Char. : colour : green; attr. : *viśvavajra*.
Lit.: BBh. 330.

kārmuka "bow" (attr.), see *dhanus*.
Lit.: BBh. 192.

Karṇa ("ear"), n. of a hero in the epic Mahābhārata. He was regarded as an illegitimate son of Sūrya and Kuntī (the mother of the Pāṇḍavas); hence he was a half-brother of Yudhiṣṭhira and his brothers.
Lit.: D 150; DHP 96; Gt 320; WHW 1:530.

karṇapatra "ear-rings" (attr.), see *pattra-kuṇḍala*.
Lit.: ACA 28.

Karṇa-Tārā ("ear-Tārā"; Buddh.), n. of an inferior Mahāyāna goddess.
Lit.: BBh. 151; KiSB 97.

karṇavedha "the ear-piercing", n. of a *saṅskāra*-rite performed in the third or fifth year of a child.
Lit.: DiIP 181; GJ 412; MW 257; WHW 2:316.

karṇaveṣṭana "ear-ornament" (attr.).
Lit.: BECA 1:261.

karṇika "ear-rings" (attr.), "lourds anneaux portés dans le lobe fendu des oreilles"
Lit.: ACA 28.

karṇikā.
1. "Pericarp of a lotus-flower", n. of a small *pīṭha* which is combined with a larger *pīṭha* (usually a *padmapīṭha*): an image seated (mostly in *lalitāsana*) on a *padma-pīṭha* has often one foot (or both feet) gracefully resting on a *karṇikā*. This is hence a form of *pādapīṭha*.
Lit.: B 299.
2. "Arrow" (? so MEIA; cp. MW : *karṇikam* "a kind of arrow"); for this sense, see *śara*.
Lit.: MEIA 254, 326; MW 257.

karṇikāra "fleur de l'arbre Pterospermum acerifolium" (attr.), n. of an ear-ornament.
Lit.: ACA 40.

karoṭa "skull-cap (or cup)" (attr.), see *kapāla*.
Lit.: BBh. 194.

karpara "cup, bowl" (attr.), see *kapāla*.
Lit.: BBh. 436.

karpūra "camphor" (attr.), used in ritual.
Lit.: R 1:368.

karpūradānī (Hi.) "camphor-burner" (attr.), n. of a pot for burning camphor-oil.

kaṟṟaḷi (Tam.) "stone temple", an architectural term.
Lit.: BECA 1 : passim; MD 1:338.

kartarī(mukhahasta)mudrā (or *kartari-*; "hand-(pose) suggesting a mouth, i.e. an open pair of scissors"; Mu.), n. of a handpose in which three fingers (index, long and little fingers) are stretched upwards, holding an attr. between the index and middle fingers (forming a V); the thumb presses the ring-finger against the palm of the hand. *k.* is also mentioned as a variety of the *muṣṭimudrā*, and it signifies separation,

lightning, death, hypocrisy, opposition, disagreement. – Cp. *tripatākāhasta*.
Lit.: H pl. 6:56b; MH 7; SIB 61; Th. pl. 40-41; WHW 2:88.

kartṛ "knife" (attr.), see either *churī* or *karttṛkā*.
Lit.: B 507; KiDG 75.

kartrī "saw-knife" (attr.), see *karttṛkā*.
Lit.: DHP 464 (No. 505); KiSB 47.

kārttika (derived from Kṛttikās, n. of a *nakṣatra*), n. of a month (October-November). Its god is Brahmā.
Lit.: BBh. 382; IC 2:733.

kārttikādi "beginning with (the month) *kārttika*", a term referring to the year, see *saṃvatsara*.

Kārttikeya ("related to Kṛttikās").
1. (Hind.) Epithet and n. of a form of Skanda who was fostered by the six Kṛttikās (Pleiades) and therefore is often represented as six-headed (see Ṣaṇmukha). – Śakti: Kārttikī. Char.: Vāh.: *mayūra*; Mu.: *abhaya-*, *varada-mudrā*; attr.: *aṅkuśa*, *cakra*, *khaḍga*, *kheṭaka*, *pāśa*, *śakti*, *śaṅkha*, *śrīphala*, *vajra*. – Another n.: Kataragama Deviyo.
Lit.: D 152; DHP 298; Gt 322; HIS 21; KiH 18; MG 194; R 2:436; RIS 49; WHW 1:531.
2. (Buddh.) K. (as the Hindu god Skanda) is also found in Mahāyāna Buddhism. Char.: colour: red; Vāh.: *mayūra*; Mu.: *añjalimudrā*; attr.: *kukkuṭa*, *śakti*, *vajra*.
Lit.: BBh. 364.

kārttikeyāsana "Kārttikeya-seat" (Vāh.), n. of a throne supported by a peacock (*mayūra*), the vehicle of Kārttikeya (= Skanda).
Lit.: MH 44.

Kārttikī ("the [Śakti] of Kārttikeya"), n. of one among the group *navaśakti*.
Lit.: MW 275, 1044.

karttṛkā (or *kart[t]rikā*, *kartrī*, *kartṛ*, *kart[t]arī*) knife, saw-knife" (attr., esp. Buddh., but also Hind.). The difference between *k.* and *churī* is not clear, but a *k.* is probably more similar to a saw, and *churī* to a dagger. – *k.* is a symbol "des Sieges über die Dämonen" (GBM). – When surmounted with a *vajra* it is named *vajrakartṛ**. – Char. of: Acāta-Lokeśvara, Ādidharmā, Bhairava, Buddhakapāla, *buddhaśaktis*, Cāmuṇḍā, Carcikā, Cundā, *ḍākinīs*, *dharmapālas*, Ekajaṭā, Gaṇeśa, mGon-dkar, mGon-po nag-po, Gur-gyi mGon-po, Hevajra's Śakti, Kālacakra and his Śakti, Kālikā, Mahācakravajrapāṇi's Śakti, Mahācīnatārā, Mahākāla, Mahāmāyā, Maṅgala, Makaravaktrā, Māmakī, Nairātmā, Naṅ-sgrub, Pāṇḍarā, Prajñāpāramitā, Prasannatārā, Ṣaḍakṣarī, Saṃvara and his Śakti, gSaṅ-sgrub, Śaraddevī, Sarasvatī, Sarvanivaraṇaviṣkambhin, Siṅhavaktrā, Tārā, Ubhayavarāhānana-Mārīcī, Vajrabhairava, Vajrapāṇi (the Garuḍa-form), Vajrasarasvatī, Vajrasattvātmikā, Vajravārāhī, Vajrayoginī, Vidyujjvālākarālī, Vighnāntaka, Yamadūtī, Yamāntaka.
Lit.: G 14 (ill.); GBM 105.

kaṟuppaṉ(an), (or -acāmi, Karuppaṇṇasvāmi; Tam. "the Black One"), n. of a popular god who is esp. worshipped by the Kaḷḷar-caste in South India. Attr.: *aruvāḷ*, *śakti*.
Lit.: DiCh. 32; SB 358 a.pl. 362; SSI 230.

kaśā (or *kaṣā*) "whip" (attr.). Char. of: Mahāratnakīrti-Lokeśvara, Revanta. – Cp. *ceṇṭu*, *choṭikā*.
Lit.: B 424.

kāṣāya "the brown-red garment of a beggar monk" (attr.; Buddh.). Char. of: the Buddha, the *dhyānibuddhas*, also monks as Ānanda, Kāśyapa, Maudgalyāyana, Śāriputra, Upāli, and others. – Cp. *tricīvara*.
Lit.: AuT 220; R 1:219.

Kāśī ("the Resplendent City"), n. of a city, now Benares (cp. Vārāṇasī), in which Śiva, in particular, is worshipped.
Lit.: DHP 220.

kasiṇa (Pāli; Buddh.), n. of a kind of aid to mystic meditation, akin to the *maṇḍala*. – There is also a *kasiṇamaṇḍala*, a board or stone "divided by depressions to be used as a mechanical aid" (RhDS) to meditation.
Lit.: GRI 267; RhDS sub *kasiṇa*.

kastūrī "musk" (attr.).
Lit.: R 1:368.

Kāśyapa (also Kaśyapa; Pāli Kassapa, M.Ind. Kacchapa). The Skt n. K. is possibly a hypersanskritism, originating from the M.Ind. *kacchapa* "tortoise" and reflecting the Sino-Tibetan conception of cosmos as a tortoise (cp. Kūrmāvatāra). It has also been connected with the word *kaśipu* "pillow, seat" (in Hiraṇyakaśipu).
1. (Hind.) NP of a Vedic sage (*ṛṣi*), a divine primeval father and demiurge. By his different wives (their number was 13 and they are mentioned as *mātaras*) he became the primeval father of *deva*s, *asura*s, *nāga*s, mankind and all kinds of living beings. – K. is also a n. of the pole-star (MG). – Wives: Aditi, Diti, Surabhi, Vāc, Kadrū, Vinatā, Khasā, and other daughters of Dakṣa. – Another n.: Prajāpati.
Lit.: D 153; DHP 324; GH 96; GoRI 1:263; Gt 324; IC 1:531; KiSH 55; MG 228; WHW 1:535; WM 124.
2. (Buddh.) NP of a *mānuṣibuddha*. Char.: colour: yellow; Vāh.: *padma* on a *siṅha*; att.: *padmāsana* or *sthānaka*; Mu.: *varada-*, *vyākhyāna-mudrā*; no attr. – K. is also n. of a monk and pupil of the Buddha: attr.: *kāṣāya*, *pātra*.
Lit.: G 32, 53, 104; H 32; KiDG 44; KiSB 32.

kaśyapamudrā (or *kacchapa-*) "tortoise-hand-pose" (Mu.), n. of "a variety of joined hand-*mudrās* with fingers intertwining, all of them representing the *liṅga* within the *yoni*". – Cp. *kūrmamudrā*.
Lit.: WHW 2:88.

kaṭaka(hasta)mudrā "ring hand-gesture" (Mu.), n. of a handpose wherein "the tips of the fingers are loosely applied to the thumb so as to form a ring" (R, B). This Mu. indicates the holding of a flower. Char. esp. of Lakṣmī, Pārvatī and other goddesses, but also of gods, e.g. some representations of Śiva, Rāma etc. (here this Mu. may also indicate a hand that holds a fictive bow or that has just released the bowstring; for this see *siṅhakarṇa-mudrā*). – Another n.: *sarpakaramudrā*.
Lit.: B 258; H pl. 6:35b; MH 7; R 1:15 a.pl. 5:7-8; SIB 61; SSI pl. IV:4a; Th. 29; WM 100 a.fig. 24.

Kataragama Deviyo (Singh., a popularized word-form of *Kajara-gama* < Skt *Kārttikeya-grāma* "the village of K.") "the god of Kataragama", see Kārttikeya and Skanda. In Sri Lanka he is a *dikpāla* of the east direction. Kataragama (in Tamil Katirkāmam) is n. of a famous Skanda shrine in South Sri Lanka, also visited by many pilgrims from the Tamil territory.
Lit.: CBC 8, 12 a.pl. 14:34; DIEHL.

kathakaḷi (Mal., < Skt *kathā* + Mal. *kaḷi*) "story-play", n. of a dance-form or dance-tradition which is a speciality of Kerala.
Lit.: Sh. 29 a.pl. 3-4; WHW 1:538.

kaṭibandha (or *-sūtra*) "waistband" (attr.). It may be furnished with a *siṅhamukha* in front, sometimes consisting of a *nāga*. Char. of: Brahmā, Śiva (in different forms), Śrīnivāsa, and others. – Cp. *kāyabandhana*, *mekhalā*.
Lit.: B 292; KrG pl. 6; R 1:23; WHW 2:162.

kaṭi(hasta)mudrā (or *kaṭiga-*, *kaṭistha-*, *kaṭisaṅsthita-*, *kaṭyavalambitahasta-*) "hand resting upon the loin" (Mu.), n of an arm-pose in which "the arm is let down so as to hang by the side of the body, and the hand is made to rest on the loin, indicating thus a posture of ease" (R); in another interpretation "the hand is usually bent a little at the elbow and placed on the upper part of the waist" (B). It is possible that the explanation of R corresponds more closely to the term *kaṭyavalambitahasta*, but the iconographers do not seem to differentiate between these terms. – This Mu. is also mentioned as a variety of the *padmamudrā*. Char. of: Viṣṇu (Śrīnivāsa), Lakṣmī, Skanda, and others. – Another n.: *ūrusaṅsthita*.
Lit.: B 256, 374; BBh. 90; H 37 a.pl. 7:59; R 1:16 a.pl. 5:11; SSI pl. IV:6; Th. 27; WHW 2:87; WM 101 a.fig. 29.

kaṭisama ("having even, equal hips"), n. of a certain dance-form performed by Śiva Naṭarāja (in North India). Char.: att.: *svastikāpasṛta* (or *vaiṣṇavasthāna*), *udvāhita*; Mu.: *ardhacandra-*, *kaṭaka-*, *tripatākā-mudrā*; attr.: *ajina*, *ḍamaru*, *kaṭibandha*, *udarabandha*, *yajñopavīta*.
Lit.: R 2:259 a.pl. 62; WM 94.

kaṭisūtra "waist-band" (attr.), see *kaṭibandha*.
Lit.: SB 31.

kaṭisūtragranthi "knot on the waist-band" (attr.), probably a form of *siṅhamukha* on the *kaṭibandha*.
Lit.: SB 55.

kaṭorā (or *-a*) "vessel for flower-offering" (attr.).
Lit.: KiH pl. 140:4.

kaṭṭāra (or *-ārika*) "dagger, cutting-implement" (attr.), see *churī*.
Lit.: BBh. 368; MEIA 247.

Kaṭṭuṇṭa-Kaṇṇaṉ (Tam. "Kṛṣṇa tied"), epithet of Kṛṣṇa, see Dāmodara, and cp. Kaṇṇaṉ.
Lit.: JDI 88.

kaṭyavalambitahastamudrā (Mu.), see *kaṭihastamudrā*.
Lit.: SB 41; WM 101.

Kātyāyanī ("descendant of Kati [a sage]"), n. of a form of Durgā which is almost identical with Mahiṣāsuramardinī. Vāh.: *siṅha* or *śārdūla*.
Lit.: R 1:347 a.pl. 102 ff.; SSI 202.

kaumāra "adherent of Kumāra, or the religion of the *kaumāras*", n. of a sect which holds Skanda as the Supreme Being and is exclusively devoted to his worship; a sect nowadays very important in South India.
Lit.: TL 2:1206.

Kaumārī ("the [Śakti] of Kumāra"), n. of a wife of Skanda. In this form she is one of the *sapta-* (or *aṣṭa-)mātaras* and symbolizes either *anasūya* "absence of ill-will or envy" or *moha* "delusion, folly". Char.: Vāh.: *mayūra*; att.: *lalitāsana*; Mu.: *abhaya-*, *varada-mudrā*; attr.: *daṇḍa*, *dhanus*, *dhvaja*, *ghaṇṭā*, *kamaṇḍalu*, *kukkuṭa*, *padma*, *paraśu*, *pustaka*, *śakti*, *śara*. Her sacred tree is *uḍumbara*. Another n.: Senā.
Lit.: B 506 a.pl. 43:3; BECA 1: pl. 15a; KiSH 53; R 1:381, 387; SIB pl. 16; Th. 108.

Kaumodakī (or Kaumodī; according to MW perhaps derived from Kumodaka, a n. of Viṣṇu), n. of the *gadā* of Viṣṇu (Kṛṣṇa), given to him by Varuṇa; also n. of the *gadādevī*.
Lit.: B 301; HIS 74; MW 286, 316; SB 322 a.pl. 248.

Kaumudī ("moon-light"), personified as the wife of Candra.
Lit.: MW 316; R 2:388.

kaupīna "small piece of cloth worn over the privities by poor persons, loin-cloth" (attr.). Chr. of: Brahmacāri-Subrahmaṇya, Vāmanāvatāra.
Lit.: MW 316; R 1:163.

Kaustubha, n. of a celebrated jewel (*ratna**), worn by Viṣṇu (Kṛṣṇa) in some forms (attr.). It was obtained at the churning of the ocean of milk (cp. Kūrmāvatāra). K. "represents consciousness, which manifests itself in all that shines: the sun, the moon, fire and speech" (DHP). – Cp. Syamantaka.
Lit.: B 290; DHP 157, 167; GoRI 1:226; Gt 328; HIS 45; WHW 1:385; WM 104.

kautukabera "festival icon" (attr.), n. of an icon meant for the *arcana*.
Lit.: R 1:17 a.passim.

Kauverī (evidently derived from Kuvera; Buddh.), n. of an inferior Mahāyāna goddess attending on Buddhakapāla.
Lit.: BBh. 160.

kavaca (lit. "armour"; attr.).
1. "Metal container (amulet box") in which a *yantra* (with a mystical syllable, *bīja*) of paper, bark, skin or metal is kept and which is worn on a chain round the neck. Char. of: Sūrya, Viṣṇu, Yajña. – Other n.: *rakṣ(ik)ā*, *yantrapātra*.
2. "War-drum, kettledrum". Char. of: Ahirbudhnya, Cāmuṇḍā.
3. "Shield", see *kheṭaka*.
Lit.: AI 114; GH 57; IC 1:570; MW 264; R 1:386, 2:389.

kāvaṭi (*kāvaḍi*, Tam.; attr.), n. of an ornamental staff or pole of wood surmounted with an arch and carried on the shoulders in processions (along with offerings) by devotees of Skanda (Kārttikeya, Murukan̲).
Lit.: TL 2:900; WHW 1:437.

kāya "body" (Buddh.), see *trikāya*.

kāyabandhana "knotted waist-band" with beautiful tassels in front (attr.), see *kaṭibandha*.
Lit.: JMS 29.

kāyotsarga "loosening, setting free, suspending of the body" (to be interpreted both as an att. and a Mu.; esp. Jain.). Most iconographers describe *k*. as a standing att., a variety of *samapādasthānaka*, in which the hands hang straight down by the sides without showing the least bend. Char. of. Jain images and *tīrthaṅkaras*. – According to GJ, however, *k*. can also signify a meditative sitting att., interpreted thus: "Gewöhnlich besteht sie darin, dass der Kontemplierende sich mit gekreuzten Beinen niedersetzt und die lose herabhängenden Arme in den Schoss legt". – *k*., as a duty, is enjoined upon the *āvaśyakas*.
Lit.: B 41, 264; GJ 372, 408; HIS 17; IC 2:638; WHW 1:75; WM 100 a.fig. 25; ZA 133.

Kelimālin (-ī; "wearing a pleasure-garland"; Buddh.), n. of a king of the *yakṣas*.
Lit: BBh. 380; KiSB 74.

Kendra ("centre of a circle"; Jain.), n. of a *yakṣa* attending on the 18th *tīrthaṅkara*. Symbol: *mayūra*.
Lit.: GJ 362 a.pl. 26:18; KiJ 11 a.pl. 29:18.

kerimas (pl., Tib., properly: *keu-ri-ma*; Buddh.), in Lamaism n. of a group of eight burial-ground goddesses, who are perhaps related to the *gaurī*-group. Among the *k*. the red Pukkasī and the yellowish-white Caṇḍālī are mentioned.
Lit.: G 101; JT 5.

keśa (Hi.: *keś*; Skt also *keśara*, *kesara*) "long hair, mane" (attr.). As mane of a lion char. of Narasiṅha; as long hair char. of: Hanumān, Vajraśṛṅkhalā. – *keś* ("long hair") is also one of the five "essentials" of the Sikhs, see *pañcakakāra*, and is symbolic of the saintly devotee. – Another n.: *saṭā*.
Lit.: GG p. CLVII; MEIA 213.

keśabandha "hair-band" (attr.), n. of a mode of dressing the hair with a knot at the back of the head. Char. of some goddesses, e.g. Pārvatī, Sarasvatī, Sāvitrī, further of *pitaras* etc.
Lit.: B 286; R 1:30 a.pl. 4:22; SB 125; Th. 33 (ill.); WHW 2:161; WM 102.

keśabhāra "hair-burden" (attr.), n. of a mode of dressing the hair. Sometimes *k*. has a round form, similar to a nimbus.
Lit.: SB 185, 268, 280.

keśamaṇḍala "hair-disk, -ring, -halo" (attr.), n. of a mode of dressing the hair, in which the hair is worn standing erect, also described as "flaming hair" (*agni*). Char. of: Agni, Cāmuṇḍā, Kālī (Mahākālī), Pratyaṅgirā, Śiva in some forms (as Bhikṣāṭanamūrti, etc.). – Other n.: *jvalitaśikhā*, *ujjvalakeśa(ka)*; *ūrdhvakeśa*.
Lit.: SB 319.

keśamukuṭa (-*makuṭa*) "hair-crown" (attr.), n. of a mode of dressing the hair.
Lit.: SB 145, 317.

keśānta "the cutting-off of the hair", n. of a *saṅskāra*-rite, performed upon Brāhmans at 16 years of age.
Lit.: DilP 180; MW 310.

keśara (*kesara*, "hair"), see *keśa*.

Keśava ("long-haired"), n. of an aspect of Viṣṇu, see *caturviṅśatimūrti*. Śakti: Kīrti. – K. is also epithet of Kṛṣṇa. Another n.: Cenna-Keśava.
Lit.: GoRI 1:238; KiSH 39; R 1:229 a.pl. C and 69.

Keśin (or -ī; "having a mane or hair"), n. of a horse demon, killed by Kṛṣṇa.
Lit.: D 156; Gt 330; JMS pl. 64; WHW 1:91.

Keśinī ("hairy"; Buddh.), n. of a goddess attending on Arapacana.
Lit.: BBh. 120.

ketaka, n. of the tree Pandanus odoratissimus (attr.).
Lit.: IC 1:538.

ketu "banner, flag, sign" (attr.), see *dhvaja*.

Ketu ("brightness" [?]; but cp. also Drav., Tam. *keṭu* "to perish", *kēṭu* "evil, misfortune, ruin").

1. (Hind.) K. is said to represent the descending node which, in the handbooks, is usually connected with the moon's orbit ("Absteigender Knoten der Mondbahn", KiK, cp. B, Th.; Enc.Brit.). He is therefore associated with the planets (see *graha, navagraha*). As a personification he is sometimes said to be the son of Rudra. As "the dragon's tail" he is regarded as the body of a demon which was severed from the head (see Rāhu) by Viṣṇu at the churning of the ocean of milk (see Kūrmāvatāra). – Char.: colour: black or purple; Vāh.: *ratha* drawn by 8 or 10 grey or dark red horses (*aśva*), or *gṛdhra*, or *maṇḍūka*; Mu.: *añjali-*, *varada-mudrā*; attr.: *dīpa, gadā, sarpamastaka*.

Lit.: B 429; DED No. 1614; Enc.Brit. 15:778; Gt 331; IIM 115; KiH 7; KiK 142; KiSH 63, 88; MW 309; R 1:322 a.pl. 96; SSI 239; Th. 115, 125; TL 2:1094.

2. (Buddh.) N. of a planet. Char.: colour: blue or black; attr.: *khaḍga, nāgapāśa*.

Lit.: BBh. 378.

Kevala(candraśekhara)mūrti ("representation [of Śiva] alone", i.e. without Śakti), n. of a sub-form of Candraśekharamūrti of Śiva. Char.: Mu.: *abhaya-*, *āhūya-*, *kartarī-*, *kaṭaka-*, *kaṭi-*, *varada-mudrā*; attr. *mṛga, paraśu, ṭaṅka*.

Lit.: B 466; R 2:117 a.pl. 15; SB 217 a.pl. 136; Th. 80.

Kevala-Gaṇapati ("G. alone", i.e. without Śakti), n. of a form of Gaṇeśa (seated; esp. n. of Gaṇeśa in ivory carvings from Trivandram).

Lit.: R 1:49 a.pl. 10:2.

Kevala-Narasiṅha ("N. alone"), see Girija-Narasiṅha.

Lit.: R 1:150 a.pl. 42-43.

kevalin (*-ī*) "alone, an ascetic", another n. of *arhat*. Cp. *śrutakevalin*.

Lit.: GJ 32; pw 2:99.

kevaṛā (Hi.), n. of the flower of the plant Pandanus odoratissimus (attr.). Char. of Gaṇeśa.

Lit.: P 890.

keyūra "bracelet worn on the upper arm" (attr.). This may sometimes be composed of *nāgas*. Char. of Śiva (in different forms, e.g. in Candraśekharamūrti). – Cp. *valaya*.

Lit.: B 292; R 1:23; SB 30; Th. pl. 40.

KHA, form of a *bījamantra*; purpose: "kills". As to *kha* as a symbolic n. of a number, see *saṅkhyā* 9.

Lit.: DHP 343.

khaḍga "(long) sword" (attr.). This is a symbol very frequently used in all Indian religions. In the first place it is of course a weapon and signifies therefore "the power of destruction". But it also symbolizes "pure knowledge (*jñāna*), whose substance is wisdom (*vidyā*)" (DHP). In Buddhism it symbolizes the protection of the Doctrine, but it is moreover "ein Sinnbild der sieghaften Vernichtung des Irrtums durch die Erkenntnis" (GBM); in this sense the *kh.* is used against demons. Carried by Mañjuśrī it is called "the sword of insight (*prajñākhaḍga*)". — *kh.* is also a symbol of royalty (see *rājakakuda*).

A *kh.* may have a certain proper name: 1. Nandaka, char. of: Viṣṇu, Kṛṣṇa. – 2. Nistriṅśa, char. of the wife (Prīti?) of Pradyumna. – 3. Parañjaya, char. of Indra. – 4. *kh.* without a particular proper name, char. of: Acala, Acalavajrapāṇi, Aghora, Agni-Durgā, Agnijāta-Subrahmaṇya, Ahirbudhnya, Aiyaṉār, Akṣayamati, Akṣobhya, Ambikā, Amoghasiddhi, Andhakāsuravadhamūrti, Aṅkālammaṉ, Aparājita, Aparājitā, Ardhanārīśvara, Avalokiteśvara (in different forms), Balabhadra, Balarāma, (Baṭuka-)Bhairava, Beg-tse, Bhadra-Kālī, Bharata, Bhūtamātā, Bi-har, Budha, Cāmuṇḍā, Caṇḍā, Caṇḍaroṣaṇa, Candraśekhara, Caturbhujatārā, Cundā, Daśabhuja-Aghoramūrti, Dhūmrāvatī, Dhvajāgrakeyūrā, Durgā, Ekajaṭā, Gaṇapati,

Harasiddhi, Hayagrīva, Heruka, Hevajra, Jālinīprabha, Jambhala, Jāṅgulī, Jaya-Durgā, Jayantī, Jñānaḍākinī, Jñānavaśitā, Kālacakra, Kālāgni-Rudra, Kālamañjuśrī, Kālārimūrti, Kalkin, Kaṇṇappanāyaṉār, Kapila, Karmaḍākinī, Kārttikeya, Ketu, Kirātārjunamūrti, Krauñcabhettar, Krodhahayagrīva, Kṛṣṇa-Yamāri, Kṛśodarī, *kṣetrapāla*s, Kumāra, Mahābala, Mahācīnatārā, Mahādeva, Mahākāla, Mahākālī, Mahāmāyūrī, Mahāpratisarā, Mahāpratyaṅgirā, Mahāsāhasrapramardanī, Mahāśītavatī, Mahāsthāmaprāpta, Maheśa, Mahiṣāsuramardinī, Mallāri-Śiva, Maṅgalā, Mañjuśrī (in different forms), Manonmanī, Mārīcī, Māriyammaṉ, Maturaivīraṉ, Muktakeśī, Nāmasaṅgīti, Nandā, *navadurgā*s, Nīladaṇḍa, Nirṛti, Padmāntaka, Padmapāṇi, Paramāśva, Paraśurāma, Pāśupatamūrti, Pradyumna (?), Prajñāntaka, Prajñāvardhanī, Praṇidhānapāramitā, Pratibhānakūṭa, Pratyūṣa. Rāhu, Rakta-Cāmuṇḍā, Raudrapāśupatamūrti, Revata, Rudrāṅśa-Durgā, Sādhumatī, Samantabhadra, Saṅ-dui, Ṣaṇmukha, Śarabha, Sarasvatī, Śaravaṇabhava, Śarva, Sarvanivaraṇaviṣkambhin, Sātyakī, Senānī, Śikhaṇḍī, Sitabrahmā, Sitātapatra, Śiva, Śivadūtī, Skanda, Śrīdevī, Śrīkaṇṭha, Suraṅgama, Ṭakkirāja, Tārā, Tārakāri, Tīkṣṇoṣṇīṣa, Trailokyavijaya, Tripurāntaka, Trivikrama, Tsoṅ-kha-pa, Ubhayavarāhānana-Mārīcī, Uṣṇīṣa, Vaikuṇṭha, Vajrabhairava, Vajracarcikā, Vajradhara, Vajradhātvīśvarī, Vajragāndhārī, Vajrajvālānalārka, Vajrāmṛta, Vajrānaṅga, Vajrasarasvatī, Vajratīkṣṇā, Vajravidāraṇī, Vāmadeva, Vana-Durgā, Vārāhī, Vasanta, Vasantadevī, Vidyujjvālākarālī, Vighnāntaka, Vīrabhadra, Virūḍhaka, Virūpākṣa, Viśvaḍākinī, Viśvarūpa, Yama, Yamāntaka, Yogeśvarī. – It is further the weapon of the north direction. – *kh.* is also another n. of *ekaśṛṅga*.

Other n.: *asi*, *kṛpāṇa*; see also *śakti* 2 (?). Cp. *ardhacakrakṛpāṇa*, *vajrakhaḍga*.

Lit.: B 301; DHP 160, 272; G 11, 14 (ill.); GBM 105; GJ 256; JMS 11; KT 137; R 1:5 a.pl. 1:9-10; SM 182; Th. 39 (ill.); WM 108 a.fig. 65.

khaḍgamālā "garland composed of short daggers (despite the sense of *khaḍga* given above)", (attr.). Char. of Aghora.

Lit.: R 2:199.

Khadiravaṇī(-Tārā) (the n. is perhaps connected with a locality, cp. Khadiravaṇa, MW; Buddh.), n. of a Mahāyāna goddess, an emanation of Amoghasiddhi, who should be regarded as a variety of Śyāmatārā. Sometimes she is also said to be a sub-form of Bhṛkuṭī. Char.: colour: green; att.: *lalitāsana* (but there is no *karṇikā* below the lower foot); Mu.: *(ratnasamyukta-) varada-* and *vyākhyāna-mudrā*; attr.: *Amoghasiddhibimba* on the crown, *nīlotpala*, *padma*. – She is connected with the *bījamantra TAṀ*. – Cp. Vaśyatārā.

Lit.: BBh. 226, 307, 441 a.pl. 166 f.; G 75; KiDG 64; KiSB 99; MW 336; RN pl. 11; SB 296 a.fig. 200.

Khagarbha ("ether-womb"; Buddh.), see Ākāśagarbha.

Khajurāho, n. of a town with famous temples (e.g. Kandārya-Mahādeva) from c. A.D. 1000.

Lit.: FES 66; Gz 164; LCD; RAAI 173 See lit. s.v. Kāmakalā.

khakkhara "beggar's staff, alarm-staff, sistrum" (attr.; Buddh.), n. of an object (probably of Central Asian origin) with a long wooden handle, surmouted by a metal finial with 4, 6, or 12 loosely-attached metal rings. When the instrument is shaken, these rings strike each other and produce a resounding noise. Originally this noise was meant to announce the presence of the begging monk; later it is supposed to warn animals, insects or birds of the approach of the monk who, in this way, may avoid inadvertently killing them. – Char. of: dGra-lha, Kṣiti-garbha, Maudgalyāyana, Nāgasena, Śāriputra. – Cp. *dara*.

Lit.: G 14 (ill.), 104; SM 179; SMII 45.

khalin ("thresher"), n. of a kind of *asura*.
Lit.: DHP 143.

KHAṀ (Buddh.), form of a "green" *bīja* from which Amoghasiddhi is said to originate.
Lit.: BBh. 56.

Khaṇḍagiri-Udayagiri, n. of mountains with cave-temples in Orissa.
Lit.: FBKI 55; ZA pl. 46 f.

Khaṇḍarohā ("whose rising, growth is broken"; Buddh.), n. of a *ḍākinī*.
Lit.: BBh. 321.

khañjana "wagtail" (attr.), n. of a bird sacred to Viṣṇu.
Lit.: GH 71.

khara "ass" (Vāh.), see *gardabha*.
Lit.: MEIA 228.

Khasā ("itch, scab"?), n. of a daughter of Dakṣa, the wife of Kāśyapa and mother of the *rākṣasas* and *yakṣas*.
Lit.: MW 338; WM 124.

Khasarpaṇa(-Lokeśvara) ("L. gliding through the air"; Buddh.), n. of a variety of Avalokiteśvara. Char.: att.: *lalitāsana*; Mu.: *varadamudrā*; attr.: *Amitābhabimba* on the crown, *padma*.
Lit.: BBh. 128 a.pl. 103; 396 a.pl. 21(A); KrI 81 a.pl. 12; KiSB 57.

khaṭvāṅga (or *khaṭṭāṅga*) "club or staff with a skull at the top and with a handle made of a shin or cubital bone" (attr.). In Hinduism, however, the *kh.* is not always distinguished from the *gadā*; here there are also other forms, e.g., a staff surmounted with a figure of Nandin (SSI). It is here regarded as a magic wand. In Buddhism it is a white staff, surmounted with a *vajra*, and in Lamaism a "ritual wand, with *vajra*-top, two heads and *triśūla* above" (G). This is a symbol of the victory over demons.
kh. is char. of: Aghora, Aja, Āryavajravārāhī, Bahurūpa, Baṭuka-Bhairava, Buddhakapāla, Cāmuṇḍā, *ḍākinīs*, Dhvajāgrakeyūra, Ekapādamūrti, Gaṇapati, Hara, Harihariharivāhanodbhava, Heruka, Hevajra, Jayanta, Jñānaḍākinī, Kālacakra, *kṣetrapālas*, Mahākāla, Mahāmāya, Maheśa, Mārttaṇḍa-Bhairava, Māyājālakramāryāvalokiteśvara, Nairātmā, Nāmasaṅgīti, Prasannatārā, Ṣaḍakṣarī, Sadāśiva, Śākyabuddha-Lokeśvara, Samvara, Saptakṣara, Śarabha, Śiva-Bhairava, Śivadūtī, Śrīdevī, Sureśvara, Trailokyavijaya, Tryambaka, Vajragāndhārī, Vajrahūṅkāra, Vajrajvālānalārka, Vajrayoginī, Vidyujjvālākarālī, Virūpākṣa, Yogeśvarī.
Other n.: *khiṅkhira*, *pāṅsula*; see further *gadā*.
Lit.: BBh. 436; D 157; DHP 217; G 16 (ill.); MEIA 101, 245; SSI pl. III:11; STP 9:68; WM 106 a.fig. 57-58.

khecarībīja, a *mantra*: "Flying through the Void"; form: *HA SA KHA PREṀ*; purpose: moving through space.
Lit.: DHP 345.

Khen-ma (Tib.; Buddh.), in Lamaism n. of a female genius who controls the demons of the earth. Char.: Vāh.: *meṣa*; attr.: *pāśa* (golden).
Lit.: G 102.

Khen-pa (Tib.; Buddh.), in Lamaism n. of a male genius who controls the demons of heaven. Char.: Vāh.: *śvan* (white); attr.: *daṇḍa* (crystal).
Lit.: G 102.

kheṭaka (*kheṭa*) "shield (round, oblong or rectangular)" (attr.). This is usually carried together with other weapons, such as *khaḍga* etc. (In BBh., however, it is translated as "stick" (?); as an attr. carried by Balarāma, it should signify a club, thus according to MW (with a question-mark), but in this connexion see *gadā* and Saunanda).
kh. is esp. char. of Skanda, also of: Aghora, Agni-Durgā, Agnijāta-Subrahmaṇya, Aiyaṇār, Ambikā, Aparājita, Aparājitā, Bhairava, Bharata, Bhūtamātā, Budha, Cāmuṇḍā, Caṇḍā, Candraśekhara, Daśabhuja-Aghoramūrti, Durgā, Indukarī, Jayantī, Kālāgni-Rudra, Kālārimūrti, Kalkin, Kārttikeya, Krauñcabhettar, *kṣetrapālas*, Kumāra, Lakṣmī (in different forms), Mahādeva, Mahālakṣmī, Mahiṣāsuramardinī,

Maheśa, Maṅgalā, Maturaivīraṉ, Māyājālakramakrodha-Lokeśvara, *navadurgās*, Nīlakaṇṭhī, Nirṛti, Paraśurāma, Pratyūṣa, Rāhu, Revata, Sadāśiva, Ṣaṇmukha, Śaravaṇabhava, Śarva, Senāpati, Śikhaṇḍī, Śiva, Śrīkaṇṭha, Sūrya, Tārakāri, Tripurāntaka, Trivikrama, Vaikuṇṭha, Vajravidāraṇī, Vāmadeva, Vana-Durgā, Vārāhī, Vijaya, Vīrabhadra, Virūpākṣa, Viśvarūpa, Yama, Yogeśvarī.

Other n.: *carma*, *kavaca*.

Lit.: B 301, 373, 401; BBh. 362; KiSH 26; MEIA 254; MW 340; R 1:5 a.pl. 1:11-12; Th. 39.

khiṅkhira, see *khaṭvāṅga*.

KHRĀṀ (Jain.), form of a *bijamantra*, referring to the arms, see *śānti*.

Lit.: GJ 369.

khristābda "the Christian era". This era is indicated by this word or by *isvī* or *īsvābda* (abbreviated *ī*), or *san*...(figures)...*īsvī*, or also by *iṅlandīya vatsara* (abbreviated *iṅ* or *i*), or by *iṅrājī*.

Lit.: IC 2:736.

kīcaka, n. of a demon-dwarf, see *kumbhāṇḍa*.

Lit.: MS 138.

kīlā "drumstick" (attr.).

Lit.: ACA 83.

kīlaka "pin, wedge" (attr.), n. of "un pieu ou un poteau (*stambha*) auquel on attache un animal ou autre. Par le *kīlaka* le *mantra* est fiché dans le cœur où il se tiendra avec son 'énergie'."

Lit.: ACA 98.

kīlakamudrā "wedge-handpose" (Mu.), n. of a gesture in which "the fists are closed and little fingers intertwined, signifying the union of love, or the conversation of lovers".

Lit.: WHW 2:88.

kiḷi (Tam.) "parrot") (attr.), see *śuka*.

killotaya (Singh.) "lime-box" (attr.), an accessory to the chewing of *tāmbūla*.

Lit.: CBC pl. 19:70.

kimpuruṣa (lit. "what sort of man?"). In the Brāhmaṇas this term designated the "ape", considered as a mimic man. The term then became the n. of a kind of semi-divine beings, see *kinnara*. In Jainism it is n. of a kind of *vyantaradevatā*.

Lit.: GJ 237; MKVI 1:157.

Kimpuruṣa (Jain.), NP of a *yakṣa* attending on the 16th *tīrthaṅkara*. Symbol: *vṛṣan*.

Lit.: GH 107; GJ 362 a.pl. 26:16; KiJ 11 a.pl. 29:16.

kiñjalka "filament (of lotus) or seed-vessel" (attr.), n. of an adornment on the *padmapīṭha*.

Lit.: SIB 70 a.pl. 20f.

kiṅkiṇī "small bell" (attr.). *k.* are attached to *pādasuras* and *kiṅkinisūtras*, adorning the feet of the dancers and marking the rhythm. Char. of Śani. – Cp. *bhriṅgipāda*.

Lit.: MEIA 255; SB 81.

kiṅkiṇīsūtra (or *-jāla*) "thread, chain with small bells" (attr.). Char. of Śani.

Lit.: BECA 1:261; MEIA 255; KiSH 63.

kinnara (*kiṁnara*; also fem. *kinnarī*; lit.: "what sort of man?"), n. of a kind of semi-divine being, originally having human figure and a horse's head (perhaps some kind of monkey). Later the *k.* is represented with a bird's figure (the lower part of the body). *k.* are the singers and musicians of the gods and are counted among the *gandharvas*, but they belong esp. among the retinue of Kubera. They are met with in all Indian religions. In Jainism *k.* signifies a kind of *vyantaradevatā*. – Attr.: *vīṇā*. – Another n.: *kimpuruṣa*.

Lit.: B 351; BBh. 380; DHP 301, 307; G 38, 103; GJ 237; H pl. 9; HIS 26; MEIA 200; SSI 251; WM 125; ZM 135.

Kinnara (Jain.), NP of a *yakṣa* attending on the 15th *tīrthaṅkara*. Symbol: *matsya*; attr.: *triśiras*.

Lit.: GH 107; GJ 362 a.pl. 26:15; KiDG 81 a.pl. 72; KiJ 11 a.pl. 29:15.

kinnarī "zither" ("having two steelstrings"; attr.), esp. in South India n. of a kind of lute (see *vīṇā*) with three or four calabash resonance-boxes.

Lit.: SMII 90.

kiṅśuka, n. of a tree, Batea frondosa, sacred to Soma (attr.). It is used at religious and magic ceremonies. – Another n.: *palāśa*.

Lit.: IC 1:538; MW 282; STP 8:7.

kirāmatēvatai (Tamilized wordform), see *grāmadevatā*.

Kiraṇākṣa ("eye of the sun"), n. of one among the group *ekādaśarudra*. Char.: Mu.: *abhayamudrā*; attr.: *akṣamālā*, *pustaka*, *śuklapāda*, *trinayana*.
Lit.: R 2:391.

Kirātamūrti, n. of a representation of Śiva as a hunter (*kirāta* is n. of a mountain-tribe, living by hunting and having become *śūdra*s by their neglect of all prescribed religious rites). Char.: Mu.: *kaṭakamudrā* (meaning to hold bow and arrows; these attr. are usually missing). – Cp. Kirātārjunamūrti.
Lit.: MW 283; SB 71 a.fig. 44 a.passim; Th. pl. 43; WHW 1:555.

Kirātārjunamūrti ("representation of the *kirāta* [i.e. Śiva as a hunter, see Kirātamūrti] and Arjuna"), n. of a gracious aspect of Śiva who gives his bow (*pāśupatāstra*) to Arjuna. Char. of Śiva: att.: *samapādasthānaka*; attr.: *dhanus*, *khaḍga*, *mṛga*, *mudgara*, *paraśu*, *śakti*, *śaṅkha*, *śara*; of Arjuna: Mu.: *añjalimudrā*. – Another n.: *Pāśupatāstradānamūrti*.
Lit.: R 2:214 a.pl. 52; SSI 141; Th. 82; WHW 1:555.

kirīṭa(mukuṭa) (or *-makuṭa*) "diadem, crest, jewelled crown" (attr.), n. given to a certain crown which consists of a conical cup sometimes ending in an ornamental top bearing a central pointed knob. Symbolism: "The crown is the Unknowable reality" (DHP). – Char. esp. of Viṣṇu (Kṛṣṇa, Nārāyaṇa) and Lakṣmī, further of: Hayagrīva, Indra, Kubera, Pārvatī, Sūrya. – *k.* is also a symbol of royalty (see *rājakakuda*).
Lit.: B 286 a.pl. 4:8; DHP 158; HIS 40 a.pl. 34 (46); MEIA 213; R 1:29 a.pl. 4:20-21; SB 31; SSI pl. 1:7; SSIP 119; Th. 31 (ill.); WHW 1:434; WM 102; a.fig. 33-38.

Kirīṭin (-ī), epithet of Indra wearing a *kirīṭamukuṭa*.

kirpān (Hi.) "small steel dagger, sword, scimitar, sacrificial knife" (attr.). A *k.* is one of the five essentials of the Sikhs (see *pañcakakāra*), symbolic of courage and self-respect.
Lit.: GG p. CLVII; P 823.

Kīrti ("fame, renown, glory").
1. (Hind.) NP of the Śakti of Keśava (or Viṣṇu). Attr.: *kamaṇḍalu*.
Lit.: R 1:233, 366; SSI 189.
2. (Jain.) NP of a goddess.
Lit.: GJ 363.

kīrttimukha (or *kīrti-*) "halo-face" (attr.), n. given to a face of a terrific shape or to a lion's face (*yāḷi*) which is seen on top of a *prabhātoraṇa* or a *prabhāvalī* and which also crowns the arches of the doorways and niches of the temples and is sometimes also found on the back of idols. It is meant to terrify unbelievers and the demons, and to protect the believers who are familiar with it. – *k.* is also used as a term of a face-like clasp of, e.g. a girdle. – Other n.: *kāla-*, *siṅha-mukha*.
Lit.: AIP 75; BSA 36; JDI 130; JMS 41; ZM 155, 195 a.pl. 34, 51, 54.

kīrttistambha "pillar of fame", n. of a certain Jain tower at Chitor in Mewar.
Lit.: ZA 268 a.pl. 394.

KLĪṀ.
1. (Hind.) Form of a *bījamantra* named *kāmabīja**. It is interpreted in different ways: *K* stands for either Water, or Kāma, or Kṛṣṇa, the incarnation of divine lust; *L* means Earth, or the Lord of heaven, Indra; *Ī* means Lust, or satisfaction; *Ṁ* is the Moon, or the giver of both pleasure and pain. The sound *-ĪṀ* is also said to symbolize the union of Śiva (*K*) and Lalitā (*L*).
Lit.: DHP 313, 342; GoRI 2:48; IC 1:567.
2. (Jain.) Form of a *bījamantra* which refers to the belly, see *śānti*.
Lit.: GJ 369.

kLu-dbaṅ, see sub initial Lu...

kodaṇḍa "bow" (attr.), n. of the *dhanus** of Rāma.
Lit.: SSI 35.

Kodaṇḍa-Rāma, epithet of Rāma carrying the bow (*kodaṇḍa*).
Lit.: SSI 35.

kodikkarukku and *kodungai*, see *koṭikkarukku* and *koṭuṅkai*, respectively.

koḥl (Arab.) "collyrium" (attr.), see *añjana*.
Lit.: STP 1:211.

kokila "Indian cuckoo" (Vāh.). Its cry is supposed to inspire love. – See *ratha* (drawn by *kokilas*).
Lit.: BBh. 378; IC 1:537.

kollam (āṇḍu) "occidental year", n. of an era beginning in A.D. 825 and of limited use in Malabar and Mangalore. The year of this era is *vartamāna* and *kanyādi* or *siṅhādi*; the given year + 824 or 825 = the year A.D. – Another n.: *paraśurāma(kāla)*.
Lit.: IC 2:737.

Kollāpura-Mahālakṣmī (also Kolā-; Kollāpura is n. of a town), n. of a six-armed form of a goddess belonging to the group *aṣṭama-hālakṣmī*. Attr.: *caṣaka, gadā, kheṭaka*.
Lit.: SSI 189.

Konāgamana (Pāli; Buddh.), see Kanakamuni.

Koṇārak (Koṇārka, "sun in the corner"), n. of a town in Orissa with a famous temple, the central shrine of which, named "the black pagoda", is dedicated to Sūrya and contains famous erotic reliefs from the 13th c. A.D.
Lit.: FES 50; Gz 161; GOSA 14 a.passim; LCD; WHW 1:156; ZA pl. 348 ff.: see lit. s.v. Kāmakalā.

koṟaṭā (also *kōlṭā*; Tam., < Port. *corda*) "little whip" (attr.), see *ceṇṭu* and cp. *cavukku*.
Lit.: JDI 114; MD 1:433, 441.

koṣa "purse, case wherein money or treasures are kept" (attr.). Char. of: Kubera, Maṇibhadra, Śukra, Viṣṇu-Kubera.

koṣṭha "niche" in a temple. A *koṣṭhapañjara* is a "niche with cage-motif decoration".
Lit.: BECA 1:261.

koṭikkarukku (*kodi-*; Tam.) "foliage-decoration (esp. over the edges of the *śikhara* or *koṭuṅkai*".
Lit.: BECA 1:261.

Koṭiśrī (lit. "the prosperity of 10 millions", also interpreted as "the mother of 7.000 Buddhas"; Buddh.), n. of a female deity.
Lit.: WAA 25:178 a.fig. 37.

Koṭpuli-nāyaṉār (Tam.), n. of a *śaivabhakta*. Mu.: *añjalimudrā*.
Lit.: SB 321 a.pl. 243.

koṭuṅkai (*kodungai*, Tam.) "cornice, moulded projection over a *tala*".
Lit.: BECA 1:261.

Krakucchanda (Buddh.), n. of a *mānuṣibuddha*. Char.: att.: *padmāsana*; Mu.: *dhyāna-mudrā* (both hands); no attr. His *bodhivṛkṣa* is the *śirīṣavṛkṣa*. – Cp. also Krakusunda.
Lit.: G 32, 53; H 32; KiDG 44.

Krakusunda (the n. is connected with Krakucchanda and Pāli Kakusandha and probably signifies the same person), n. of a *mānuṣi-buddha*.
Lit.: KiSB 32, 47.

bKra-śis bla-ma (Tib., the first word means "happiness"), see Tashi Lama.
Lit.: JT 14.

Kratu ("inspiration"), n. of a *riṣi* or *prajāpati*. Wife: Sannati.
Lit.: DHP 317, 323; WM 125.

krauñca "curlew".
1. (Jain.) Symbol of the 5th *tīrthaṅkara* Sumati.
Lit.: GJ pl. 23:5; KiJ pl. 45.
2. (Hind.) N. of a mountain, said to have been split by Skanda.
Lit.: MKVI 1:200; MW 323.

Krauñcabhettar (-ā, -ṛ; "splitting the mountain Krauñca"), epithet or n. of a form of Skanda. Char.: Mu.: *abhaya-, varada-mudrā*; attr.: *dhanus, khaḍga, kheṭaka, śakti, śara, trinayana*.
Lit.: R 2:438.

krauñcaniṣadana ("sitting like a curlew"; att.), n. of an *āsana*-posture, a *yoga*-att., mentioned but not described.
Lit.: B 271.

KRĪṀ, form of a *bijamantra* named *ādyabija* or *kālībija*. It is interpreted thus: *K* = Kālī, *R* = *brahman*, *Ī* = the transcendent power or illusion; the sound is the "Mother of the universe", the nasalization is the dispelling of sorrow. – This *mantra* is used in the worship of Kālī. Purpose: gaining detachment, power over death, transcendent knowledge.
Lit.: DHP 343; GH 54; GRI 2:35.

Kṛishna, see *Kṛṣṇa*.

Kriyā ("action, performance"), n. of a Śakti of Vāmana (in his form as an aspect of Viṣṇu).
Lit.: R 1:233.

krodha "anger, wrath" (Buddh.), n. of a wrathful aspect of the *vidyārājas* (= *dharmapālas*), as opposed to the *śānta*-aspect.
Lit.: SeKB 232.

Krodha ("wrath"), n. of a form of Śiva Bhairava.
Lit.: B 466.

Krodha-Hayagrīva ("H. of wrath"; Buddh.), in Lamaism n. of a variety of Hayagrīva. Char.: *Vāh.: naras*; att.: *yab-yum* with the Śakti; attr.: *aśvamastaka* in the hair, *cakra, kapāla, khaḍga, paraśu, pāśa, puṣpa*.
Lit.: G 90.

Krodharāja ("king of wrath"; Buddh.), n. of a *vidyārāja*.
Lit.: GBM 80.

Krodharātrī ("Night-of-Anger"), as personification an aspect of the *mahāvidyā*, representing Tārā.
Lit.: DHP 274.

krodhaśānti ("Calming-of-Anger"), n. of a *mantra* which has the purpose of "calming the anger of man or the elements".
Lit.: DHP 347.

KROṀ, form of a *bījamantra* named *aṅkuśabija*, representing Śiva.
Lit.: IC 1:567; WHW 2:104.

kṛpāṇa "sword, dagger" (attr.), see *khaḍga*.
Lit.: ACA 36; BBh. 44.

kṛṣṇa "black", the "black" colour. Usually no distinction is made between "black" and "blue" (*nīla*), both these Skt words being used in the same sense. In, e.g., BBh. the term *kṛṣṇa* is usually translated as "blue". It should be noted that the god Kṛṣṇa (properly "black"), in miniatures, is always blue. – Another n.: *śyāma*; as to other n. of this colour, see MEIA.
Lit.: BBh., e.g. 378; MEIA 237; MKVI 2:246.

Kṛṣṇa ("the Black-One, Dark-One"; M.Ind. Kaṇha, Tam. Kaṇṇaṉ), n. of a very popular god, esp. worshipped in the vicinity of Mathurā, his birth-place. He was born by Vasudeva and Devakī, fostered by Nanda and Yaśodā. Originally he was probably a local (pastoral) god, but later he was identified with the hero Kṛṣṇa in the epic Mahābhārata and finally with Viṣṇu and regarded as an *avatāra* (the 8th) of Viṣṇu or as an aspect of him (see *caturviṅśatimūrti*). He is supposed to have been incarnated in Mathurā in order to save the world from the tyranny of the demon king Kaṅsa (his mother's cousin). He restored his uncle Ugrasena to the throne of Mathurā; later he founded a new city, Dvārakā.
K. is sometimes regarded as a vegetation god; some scholars see in him some reflections of the Christian ideal; others look upon K. as a relict from the Indus Valley culture, seeing in the name of Mathurā a transformation of a Dravidian town name, cp. the South Indian Madurai (PARPOLA; n.b. that the Tam. word-form Maturai is used both of Madurai and Mathurā, MD, TL).
K. is esp. worshipped in the form of a little baby (Bālakṛṣṇa) or a young shepherd (he was fostered in a cattle-breeding community; see, e.g., Veṇugopāla, and other epithets and forms below). He is also much loved in the form of a young shepherd together with the shepherdess Rādhā, the pair forming the principal object of a very widespread *bhakti*-cult; he is similarly popular in his form as the Supreme Lord, under which name he is met with in Bhagavadgītā "the song of the Lord" (forming part of the epic Mahābhārata). When K. is represented as the Supreme Lord, it is difficult to differentiate him from Viṣṇu. – K. is also regarded as a manifestation of the planet Candra (but, according to PARPOLA etc., his "black" colour would seem rather to hint at a connection with the black planet Śani = Saturn).
Wives: Rukmiṇī (as an *avatāra* of Lakṣmī;

a son of theirs is Kāmadeva), Satyabhāmā (= Bhūmī) and others (according to legend he had 10.000 or 16.008 wives). Sometimes the object of his youth's tender passion, Rādhā (see above,), is also said to be an *avatāra* of Lakṣmī. – Char.: The n. of the god indicates that his colour is "black", but he is generally portrayed dark-blue, *nīla*; Vāh.: (sometimes) Garuḍa; attr.: (esp. of K.) *channavīra*, Govardhana, *kuṇil*, *veṇu*; (further the usual attr. of Viṣṇu) *cakra* Vajranābha, *dhanus* Śārṅga, *gadā* Kaumodakī, *khaḍga* Nandaka, *śaṅkha* Pañcajanya, *śrīvatsa*. – Epithets and varieties: Bālagopāla, Bālakṛṣṇa, Bhagavān, Dāmodara, Devakī-putra or -sunu, Gānagopāla, Gopāla, Govardhanadhara-Kṛṣṇa, Govinda, Janārdana, Kāliyadamana, Kāliya-Kṛṣṇa, Kāliyamardaka, Kaṭṭuṇṭa-Kaṇṇaṉ, Keśava, Madhusūdana, Makkhañcor, Makkhanlāl, Muralīdhara, Murāri, Murukaṉ, Nara-Nārāyaṇa, Navanītanṛtta-Kṛṣṇa, Nṛtya-Gopāla, Pārthasārathi, Rājagopāla, Rājamannār, Śārṅgin, Tirumāl, Vāsudeva, Vāṭapattrāśāyin, Veṅkaṭeśa, Veṅkaṭeśvara, Veṇugopāla. – As to other epithets of K., see WHW.

Lit.: AIM passim; B 390, 421 a.pl. 26:1-2; D 160; DHP 165, 175; GBB pl. 5; GH 127; GI pl. 81; GoRI 1:237; Gt 341; IIM 61; JDI 85; KiH 14 a.pl. 35-37; MD 2:425; MG 130; MSHP 123 a.pl. 35ff.; R 1:195 a.pl. 58-59; RIS 61; SSI 37; Th. 34, 65; TL 5:3062; WHW 1:559; WM 125; A. Parpola etc., Progress in the decipherment of the Proto-Dravidian Indus script (Copenhagen 1969) 20.

Kṛṣṇā ("the Black-One"), n. of a goddess, represented as four-handed. Char.: Mu.: *añjalimudrā*; attr.: *akṣamālā*, *kamaṇḍalu*. – K. is also NP of the wife of the Pāṇḍu-princes, but she is usually known by her patronymic Draupadī.

Lit.: R 1:370.

Kṛṣṇa-Bhagavān (-vant, -vat), the deity of the *bhāgavata* sect.

Lit.: GoRI 1:268.

kṛṣṇādi "beginning with the dark (half of the month, *kṛṣṇapakṣa**)", see *pūrṇimānta* sub *candramāsa*.

kṛṣṇajanmāṣṭamī ("the eighth [day] after the birth of Kṛṣṇa"), n. of a birthday festival of Kṛṣṇa. This day is celebrated on different days in different parts of India.

Lit.: GH 354.

kṛṣṇājina "skin of the black antelope" (attr.). References are found as early as in the Vedic scriptures to the ritual use of *k*. Char. of: Bhadrakālī, Nīlakaṇṭha-Avalokiteśvara, Śiva. – Cp. *ajina*.

Lit.: GoRI 1:258; MKVI 1:185; R 1:358; RV 58.

kṛṣṇājinayajñopavīta, n. of a certain form of a *yajñopavīta* (made of the skin of a black antelope) which is described thus: a "*yajñopavīta* with three deep curves in it is seen on the body. Added to the curves, an elongated head of an animal with a pair of long wavy horns is seen just in the place where usually the knot is present."

Lit.: SB 169 a.pl. 103.

kṛṣṇamṛga "black antelope", a certain kind of *mṛga* (attr.). Char. of Candraśekharamūrti.

Lit.: R 2:113.

kṛṣṇapakṣa "the dark half" of a lunar month, the 15 lunar days (*tithi*) from full moon to new moon. – Other n.: *bahula-*, *vadya-pakṣa*, with the abbreviated forms *badi*, *vadi*, *vati*. See also *candramāsa*.

Lit.: IC 2:722; MW 306.

kṛṣṇavajra "blue or black *vajra*" (attr.); in this dictionary this is not distinguished from the ordinary *vajra*.

Lit.: BBh. 252.

Kṛṣṇa-Yamāri ("the black Y."; Buddh.), n. of a variety of Yamāri and consequently of Yamāntaka. Śakti: Prajñā. Char.: colour: blue; Vāh.: *mahiṣa*; att.: *ālīḍhāsana*, sometimes together with *yab-yum*; attr.: *ajina* (tigerskin), *Akṣobhyabimba* on the crown, *cakra*, *cintāmaṇi*, *daṇḍa*, *ghaṇṭā*, *khaḍga*, *mudgara*, *musala*, *padma*, *ṣaṇmukha*, *tarjanīpāśa*, *triśiras*, *vajra*, *vajrapāśa*.

Lit.: BBh 167; KiSB 64, 70.

Kṛśodarī ("thin-waisted"), epithet or n. of a variety of Cāmuṇḍā. She has a skeleton-like figure (*kaṅkālī*) and symbolizes famine.

Char.: Vāh.: *mṛtaka*; attr.: *ajina* (tiger or leopard hide), *khaḍga*, *muṇḍa*, *paṭṭiśa*, *triśūla*.
Lit.: KiH 24 a.pl. 76; KiSH 50.

Kṛtāñjali-Lokeśvara ("L. performing *añjali*"; Buddh.), n. of a variety of Avalokiteśvara. Char.: att.: *samapādasthānaka*; Vāh.: *padma*; Mu.: *añjalimudrā*.
Lit.: BBh. 430 a.pl. 98(A).

kṛtāñjalimudrā "handpose with joined hands" (Mu.), another n. of *añjalimudrā* used in supplication.
Lit.: WHW 2:88.

kṛtti "skin, hide" (esp. of a tiger; attr.). Char. of Śiva Kṛttivāsa(s). See further *ajina* which, in this dictionary, is used as a common n. for this kind of attr.
Lit.: SSR 167.

kṛttikā (properly "razor, knife").
1. N. of a festival in the month *kārttika* (October-November), dedicated to Śiva who manifested himself in the form of a pillar of fire (see Liṅgodbhavamūrti).
Lit.: GH 355; MW 304.
2. N. of a *nakṣatra*, see Kṛttikās.
Lit.: BBh. 381.

Kṛttikās (plur. "les tressées or les coupantes" (? IC)), n. of a constellation (*nakṣatra*), the Pleiades, who are six in number and who, personified as nymphs, the wives of the *riṣis*, became the nurses of Skanda, cp. Kārttikeya. – The constellation is sometimes represented as a flame or as a kind of razor or knife. Its influence is very bad.
Lit.: DHP 298; IC 1:491, 2:729; IIM 118; KiSH 30; MW 304; ZA 137.

Kṛttivāsa(s), epithet of Śiva wearing an *ajina* (= *kṛtti*), i.e. the hide of an animal, either a tiger or an elephant.
Lit.: B 447, 487.

KṢAḤ, form of a *bījamantra* (Jain.).
Lit.: GJ 369.

Kṣamā ("patience") as a personification is the daughter of Dakṣa. K. is also n. of a variety or hypostasis of Durgā, but she should perhaps rather be regarded as an independent goddess. Char.: Vāh.: she is surrounded by several *sṛgālas*; Mu.: *varadamudrā*; attr.: *triśūla*.
Lit.: KiSH 50; MEIA 234; MW 326; R 1:367.

kṣaṇika ("momentary"), n. of an icon made for a certain occasion, e.g. a contemporary Bengalī clay icon. A *k*. can also be made of rice or butter. The word can further be combined with other names in composites, e.g. *kṣaṇika-liṅga* "an occasional *liṅga* (of clay)". – See also *calaliṅga* and *lepaja*.
Lit.: R 2:77.

Kṣāntipāramitā ("perfection of patience"; Buddh.), n. of a *pāramitā*. Char.: colour: yellow; attr.: *cintāmaṇidhvaja*, *padma* (white).
Lit.: BBh. 325.

kṣatrapa "(Scythian) governor or satrap". Symbol: *siṅha*.
Lit.: Gz 51, 57.

kṣatriya "member of the military or reigning order" (which in later times constituted the second *varṇa*).
Lit.: Gt 347; IC 1:606; MKVI 1:202; WHW 1:567.

Kṣemaṅkarī ("conferring peace"), n. of a four-handed form of Durgā who grants health. Char.: Mu.: *varadamudrā*; attr.: *padma*, *triśūla*.
Lit.: R 1:342.

kṣepaṇa(hasta)mudrā "gesture of sprinkling (nectar, *amṛta*)" (Mu.). Description: "Hands are joined palm to palm, with tips of index fingers touching and turned down into *kalaśa* containing *amṛta* (nectar)" (G). Char. of: Jñānadhātu-Lokeśvara, Nāmasaṅgīti. Cp. *abhiṣekanamudrā*.
Lit.: BBh. 436; G 22 (ill.); KiSB 80; WHW 2:88.

kṣetrapāla "lord of the field or region".
1. (Hind.) N. of a tutelary (male) deity of a certain area, found in Śaivite temples. There are some differences, depending on whether the idols are regarded as being *rājasa*, *sāttvika* or *tāmasa* in character (see R.). Char.: att.: *samapādasthānaka*; Vāh.: *padmapīṭha*; Mu.: *abhaya-*, *varadamudrā*; attr.: *agni*, *ḍamaru*, *dhanus*, *gadā*, *ghaṇṭā*, *kapāla*, *khaḍga*, *khaṭvāṅga*, *kheṭaka*, *(nāga)pāśa*, *nāgayajñopavīta*, *śara*, *ṭaṅka*,

tomara, triśūla. -- Kṣetrapāla is also n. of an aspect of Śiva Bhairava.
Lit.: DIlP 143, 173; MEIA 68; R 2:495 a.pl. 141; SSI 159.
2. (Jain.) N. of a tutelar deity.
Lit.: B 561.

kṣīrabhājana "milk jar" (attr.). Char. of Kṛṣṇa Makkhañcor.

kṣīrāśana "eating, drinking of milk" (Jain.), n. of a birth ceremony. Cp. *jātakarma.*
Lit.: GJ 411.

kṣīrodamathana "the churning of the ocean of milk" (undertaken by the *deva*s and *asura*s to obtain the *amṛta* etc.). See further Kūrmāvatāra. – Another n.: *amṛtamanthana.*
Lit.: DHP 167; MW 330; WM 135.

Kṣitigarbha ("matrix of the earth" or "Earth Womb" or "Der die Erde als Gebärmutter hat", BRI); Buddh.), n. of a Mahāyāna *(dhyāni)bodhisattva* who is often worshipped also in China and Japan. Char.: colour: yellow or green; att.: *padmāsana* or *sthānaka*; Mu.: *abhaya-, bhūmisparśa-, varada-, vyākhyāna-mudrā*; attr.: *cintāmaṇi, khakkhara* or *kamaṇḍalu* or *pustaka, kalpavṛkṣa* (in a hand), *pātra.*
Lit.: BBh. 83 a.pl. 81; BRI 149; CTLP pl. 9; G 14, 22, 61; GBB 247; GBM 80; GRI 257; KeSB 238 (ill.).

Kṣitigarbha-Lokeśvara ("L., matrix of the earth"; Buddh.), n. of a variety of Avalokiteśvara. Char.: att.: *padmāsana*; Vāh.: *padma*; Mu.: *varadamudrā*; attr.: *kamaṇḍalu* (*ratnapātra*).
Lit.: BBh. 399 a.pl. 50(A).

KŚRAUṀ, form of a *bījamantra* symbolizing Narasiṅha.
Lit.: DHP 343.

kṣudramaṇḍapa "little hall", n. of a temple hall supported by between 4 and 28 pillars.
Lit.: BECA 1:262.

kṣullaka "little, small" (Jain.), n. of a certain stage of monkhood.
Lit.: GJ 422.

kṣurikā "knife, dagger" (attr.), see *churī.*
Lit.: ACA passim.

Kuan-yin (or Kwan-yin, Chin.; K(w)annon, Jap.), n. of a form of Avalokiteśvara which, in China, is often manifested in a female form. K. is there regarded as the goddess of mercy.
Lit.: GBM 33; GRI 256; SeKB passim; ZA pl. 614.

Kubera (or Kuvera; the word may, perhaps, be analysed as *ku-bera* "the ill-shaped one"). 1. (Hind.) K. was originally the chief of the evil beings or the spirits of darkness (*yakṣa*s), but later he became the god of riches and treasure and of power or productivity. He is also a *dikpāla* of the northerly direction (sometimes sharing this position with Soma); his *diggaja* is named Sārvabhauma. K. is further the god of the month *pauṣa.* – He is the son of Pulastya and Iḍāviḍā. Since he was originally a *yakṣa* himself, he is represented in a white, dwarfish shape. He resides in a palace on Mount Kailāsa and also in the city of Alakā. Wives: Yakṣī (Carvī) or Vasudhārā or Vibhavā and Vṛddhi (Hārītī), Lakṣmī. Daughter: Mīnākṣī. Char.: colour: white; Vāh.: esp. *nara* (a Brāhman), or *ratha* Puṣpaka drawn by *nara*s, or *aja* (*meṣa*) or *aśva*, *padmapīṭha*; Mu.: *abhaya-, varadamudrā*; attr.: esp. *koṣa*, further: *āpīcyaveṣa, caṣaka, dāḍima, danta, ekanayana, gadā, jambhīra, kamaṇḍalu, kirīṭa, kuṇḍala, nakula, nidhi* (*padma-* and *śaṅkha-nidhi* or 9 *nidhi*s), *śakti, tripādaka, triśiras, tundila.* – Epithets: Naravāhana, Vaiśravaṇa (see also the Buddhist epithets below). – As to other epithets, see WHW.
Lit.: B 528; BBh. 382; DHP 135; GBB 129; GoRI 1:324; Gt 355; HAHI pl. 40A; HIS 44, 65 a.pl. 26-27; HSIT 14 a.pl. 36-37; IC 1:495; IIM 84; JMS pl. 46, 69; KiH 11 a.pl. 15-18; KiSH 55, 57, 87; KrI pl. 32; MEIA 134; MG 293; R 2:533; SS pl. 22:100; Th. 111; WHW 1:569; WM 128; ZA pl. 34a; ZM 80.
2. (Buddh.) K. is the god of riches, but also (esp. with the n. Vaiśravaṇa) the *dikpāla* of the northerly direction. He is further a *dharmapāla* (probably as a variety of *dikpāla*). Char.: colour: yellow (or red);

Vāh.: *siṅha* or *ratha*, also *nara*; Mu.: *varadamudrā*; attr.: esp. *nakula* (vomiting jewels), further *aṅkuśa*, *bodhisattvābharaṇa*, *dhvaja*, *gadā*, *kamaṇḍalu* (with jewels), *kapāla*, *paraśu*, *pāśa*, *stūpa*, *triśiras* (sometimes), *triśūla*. – Epithets and varieties: Dhanada, Jambhala (= the *yi-dam*-form of K.), Pāñcika, Vaiśravaṇa (Vessa-, Vessā-, Vassā-vaṇa).

Lit.: BBh. 361; G passim.

3. (Vāh.; Buddh.) Upon K. tread: Kālajambhala, Ucchuṣma.

Lit.: G 85; KiSB 73.

4. (Jain.) K. is the god of riches and the *dikpāla* of the northerly direction. K. is furthermore n. of a *yakṣa* attending on the 19th *tīrthaṅkara*. Symbol: *gaja*.

Lit.: B 562; GJ 362 a.pl. 26:19; KiJ 11 a.pl. 29:19.

Kubjikā ("hump-backed"), NP of a Tantric goddess who personifies the 32 syllables.

Lit.: MEIA 159.

kubjikāmaṇḍala, n. of a *maṇḍala* representing Kubjikā surrounded by the *aṣṭamātaras* and six minor deities (Ḍākinī and others).

Lit.: MEIA 206 a.fig. 2.

Kubuddhi (properly "stupid"), NP of a goddess who is mentioned as one of the wives of Gaṇeśa.

Lit.: B 358.

Kuca, epithet of the planet "Mars", see Maṅgala. (N.B. Skt *kuca* means "the female breast, teat"; if this sense has anything to do with the planet it could mean that the "red" planet Maṅgala was regarded as a "teat of heaven".)

kucabandha "breast-band" (attr.), n. of a flat band, used to keep the breasts in position. Char. of female deities. – R says that when a deity like Viṣṇu (Kṛṣṇa) or Skanda is represented with two consorts, one on either side, the one to the right wears a *k.*, i.e. Bhūmidevī (other scholars state that this goddess is Śrīdevī, i.e. Lakṣmī) and Vallī (also Riddhi), respectively. In fact, *k.* may be char. of any of these flanking goddesses and is therefore no sure distinguishing mark. – Another n.: *stanabandha*; cp. also *sarpakucabandha*.

Lit.: B 291; R 1:23, 101, 378; SB 161; WHW 2:161.

kuḍāri (= Tam. *kuṭāri*), see *aṅkuśa*.

kudu, see *kūṭu*.

kukkuṭa "cock" (attr.). It is said to symbolize the rising sun and also stands for discrimination. Char. of: Skanda (in different forms) and Kaumārī; a *k.* in the *dhvaja* is char. of Aiyaṉār.

Lit.: B 106, 304, 364; DHP 298; MEIA 265; R 1:11; WHW 1:155.

kukkuṭāṇḍakāra "having the form of a cock's testicles (or a bird's egg)", n. of the egg-shaped top of a *liṅga*, see *śirovarttana*.

Lit.: R 2:93.

kukkuṭāsana "the sitting like a cock" (att.), n. of an *āsana*-posture which is a variety of *padmāsana* "where the whole weight of the body rests on two arms placed on the ground on both sides, the body thus hanging in the air" (B).

Lit.: B 270; KiH pl. 152: row 2:4.

kuladevatā "family god, household divinity". This is "a god chosen by a family who will assemble for worship at his temple once a year or when occasion arises" (DiIP). – Another n.: *kulanāyaka*. Cp. *grāmadevatā*, *gṛhadevatā*, *iṣṭadevatā*.

Lit.: DiIP 174; Gt 349; R 1:9; ZA 370.

kuladevī "family goddess" (Jain.), cp. *kuladevatā*.

Lit.: GJ 363.

kulanāyaka "family leader", another n. of *kuladevatā*.

Lit.: BECA 1:24.

Kulaśekharāḻvār (mixed Tam.-Skt: "crown of the family"), n. of a *vaiṣṇavabhakta*.

Lit.: R 2:479 a.pl. 136; Th. pl. 77B.

Kulika ("of good family"), n. of a *nāgadeva*. Attr.: *akṣamālā*, *kamaṇḍalu*, *trinayana*.

Lit.: D 170; R 2:557.

kuliśa "axe, thunderbolt" (attr.), see *vajra*.

Lit.: BBh. 92; MW 296.

Kuliśāṅkuśā ("having an axe and a goad"?; Jain.), n. of *vidyādevī*.

Lit.: GJ 362.

Kuliśeśvarī ("lady of the axe or *vajra*"; Buddh.), n. of a Mahāyāna goddess. Char.: colour: white; att. *ālīḍhāsana*; Vāh.: *mṛtaka*; attr.: *daṇḍa*, *vajra*.
Lit.: KiSB 77.

Kumāra ("son, adolescent, youth").

1. (Hind.) N. of "the everlasting young son of Śiva", i.e. a form (or epithet) of Skanda. The n. K. may signify the god as a virile young man, but it is also said to characterize him as a bachelor who dislikes women. Char.: Mu.: *abhaya-*, *varada-mudrā*; attr.: *khaḍga*, *kheṭaka*, *kukkuṭa*, *śakti*. – K. is also regarded as an *avatāra* of Viṣṇu. – Another n.: Sanatkumāra.
Lit.: DHP 165, 297; GH 116; HIS 21; IIM 84; pw 7:197; R 2:437 a.pl. 121:2.

2. (Jain.) N. of a *yakṣa* attending on the 12th *tīrthaṅkara*. Symbol: *mayūra*; attr.: *triśiras*. – Another n.: Surakumāra.
Lit.: B 562; GJ 362 a.pl. 25:12; KiDG 81 a.pl. 70; KiJ 11 a.pl. 28:12.

kumārābharaṇa "princely garments and ornaments" (attr.), see *bodhisattvābharaṇa*.
Lit.: BBh. 116.

Kumārī ("virgin, unmarried girl"), epithet of Durgā. Cape Comorin, at the southernmost point of the Indian peninsula, is named from one of her most famous temples. And at Kathmandu in Nepal a little living girl, during a certain period before the age of puberty, is worshipped as a human incarnation of K.
Lit.: AFN passim; Å. SPARRING, Nepal – landet under jordens tak (Stockholm 1956), 24.

kumārīlakṣaṇa "auspicious marks of a virgin" (attr.; Buddh.). Char. of Jāṅgulī.
Lit.: BBh. 192.

kumbha "vase, jar" (attr.). *k.* as a term is generally used like *kamaṇḍalu* (in this dictionary used as a common n.); *k.* is also n. of a rain-vase on a Hindu temple and of part of the temple pillar, see *kalaśa*. It is also n. of the *rāśi* "Aquarius".
Lit.: BECA 1:272; BBh. 383 a.pl. 247; GH 50; IC 2:731.

Kumbhakarṇa ("pot-eared"), n. of a *rākṣasa*, a brother of Rāvaṇa. He was conquered by Rāma.
Lit.: Gt 349; IIM 117; WHW 1:572.

kumbhāṇḍa ("having testicles shaped like jugs"), n. of a class of demon dwarfs, hostile to mankind, the king of whom was Virūḍhaka. Another n.: *kīcaka*.
Lit.: STP 1:197; ZA 329.

kumbhapañjara "vase-cage", a niche adorned with a vase and foliage.
Lit.: BECA 1:262.

kumbh melā (or *kumbh-kā melā*, Hi.) "pot-fair", n. of a "fair held by Hindū *faqīrs* every twelfth years at Hardwār and Allahabad" (P). In the middle of this period a smaller fair is also held (*ardh kumbh melā* "half pot-fair"). During this festival people bathe in the Ganges in order to wash away sins. The name arises from a legend which tells how, during a battle between the gods, nectar fell down here from heaven out of an overturned pot.
Lit.: P 847.

Kumbhodara ("pot-bellied"; Vāh.), n. of a *siṅha* upon which Śiva first sets his foot when mounting his Vāh. Nandin. This pot-bellied lion is said to symbolize greed for food.
Lit.: DHP 220.

kumuda "white water-lily (Nymphaea alba Roxb.)" (attr.). Iconographically *k.* may be identical with the white lotus *puṇḍarīka*. Char. of Candra. – *k.* evidently also signifies part of the *pīṭha*, but it is not quite clear which part is meant.
Lit.: SB 67; R 1:319.

Kumuda, n. of the *diggaja* which accompanies Nirṛti (Sūrya) as *dikpāla*. His wife is named Anupamā.
Lit.: D 180.

Kuñcī (personification of "key"; Buddh.), n. of a female *dvārapāla*. Char.: colour: yellow; attr.: *kuñcikā*.
Lit.: BBh. 316.

kuñcikā "key" (attr.). Char. of Kuñcī.
Lit.: BBh. 316.

kuñcitapāda "bent, curved foot (leg)" (att.). In SSI *k*. is described only as a leg "slightly bent" in standing positions (with both feet on the ground); at the same time the other, straight leg is said to be *svastika* or *lambita* (?). Thus it should be char. of Bhikṣāṭana, Pārvatī, *dvārapāla*s and others. – But *k*. is also described as the raised leg in the dancing att. which is char. of Śiva Naṭarāja, see esp. *ānandatāṇḍava*.
Lit.: AIP 71 a.pl. 51 (310); SSI 100, 190, 251.

kunda, n. of a plant, the Jasmine flower (Jasminum pubescens; attr.). Char. of Māyājālakrama-Kurukullā. As to *k*. as a symbolic n. of the number "9", see *saṅkhyā*.
Lit.: KiSB 103.

kuṇḍa "pitcher, pot, bowl-shaped vessel" (attr.). *k*. is used (in the *pūjā*) for melted butter or for oil to the *dīpa*s; *k*. is also a receptacle for fire. *k*. is often furnished with an oil-lamp (cp. *dīpak* sub *dīpa*). As attr. char. of: Aghora, Bhairava. – Cp. *kuṇḍikā*.
Lit.: GI pl. 86-87; MH pl. 23; R 2:197.

kuṇḍā "water-jar", cp. *kuṇḍikā* and see *kamaṇḍalu*.
Lit.: MEIA 243.

kuṇḍala(maṇḍala) "ear-ring, ornament for the ear" (attr.). There are several forms of *k*., cp. *makara-*, *pattra-*, *ratna-*, *śaṅkhapattra-*, *sapta-*, *siṅha-*, *vṛtta-kuṇḍala*, *vāḷi(ka)*. *k*. is char. of all kinds of deities, e.g. Balarāma, Kālarātrī, Kubera, Śiva etc. – Another n.: *toṭu*.
Lit.: B 289; R 1:24, 2: pl. 4:2; WHW 2:161; WM 104.

kuṇḍalinī ("consisting of circles", "symboliquement, serpent-femme que l'anatomie hindoue représente lové à la base de la colonne vertébrale", Le Yoga), n. of a rite which is connected with the antique conception of cosmos.
Lit.: IC 1:598; WHW 1:574; Le Yoga (La collection Marabout. Paris 1962).

Kuṇḍalinī ("coiled" see above), n. of a form of the Śakti of Śiva.
Lit.: DHP 254, 286.

kuṇḍikā (or *kuṇḍā*, *-ī*; attr.): *k*. means both "(mendicant) bowl", for which see *bhikṣāpātra*, and "pot, wash-pot, small pitcher, water-jar", for which see *kamaṇḍalu*. When furnished with a *dīpa*, the difference between *k*. and *pūjādīpa* is insignificant; cp. also *kuṇḍa*. As to the symbolism, see *jñānabhāṇḍa*.
Lit.: B 373; BBh. 436.

kuṇil (Tam.) "shepherd staff" (attr.). Char. of Kṛṣṇa. – Cp. *ceṇṭu*.
Lit.: R 1:205.

kuñjara "elephant" (Vāh.), see *gaja*. It is also a symbolic n. of the number "8", see *saṅkhyā*.
Lit.: BBh. 378.

kuṅkuma "saffron" or "turmeric" (used "as a substitute for saffron and other yellow dyes", STP; attr.). *k*. is a red powder which, in the *cakra* ritual, is thrown over the *cakra*s; a *tilaka* of *k*. is worn on the forehead by married women, and, at weddings, they smear their bodies with *k*. Many gods are also said to have the colour of *k*.
Lit.: R 2:437; SSI 220; STP 8:18.

Kun-rig ("all-knowing, all-knowledge"; Tib.; Buddh.), n. of a four-headed form of Vairocana. Char.: Mu.: *dhyānamudrā*; attr.: *cakra*, *caturmukha*.
Lit.: G 51 (ill.), 52.

kunta(ka) "spear, lance" (attr.). *k*. may be identified with *śakti* 2. In BBh., however, it is translated as "knife". – *k*. is said to be the weapon of the south-west direction.
Lit.: BBh. 222; MEIA 253; R 1:369; SM 157.

kuntala "lock of hair" (attr.), n. of a particular head-dress. Char. of Lakṣmī.
Lit.: B 286; R 1:30 a.pl. 4:23-24.

Kunthu ("Juwelenhaufen", GJ; Jain.), n. of the 17th *tīrthaṅkara*. Symbol: *aja*.
Lit.: GJ 280; KiSH 143.

Kuntī (derived from *kunti*, n. of a people), NP of a queen, married to Pāṇḍu and mother of Yudhiṣṭhira, Bhīma, Arjuna, the three eldest of the Pāṇḍava-princes and heroes

of the epic Mahābhārata, and also of Karṇa, another hero in the same epic.
Lit.: D 171; Gt 351; MW 291.

kūrca "bundle of *kuśa*-grass" (attr.). Char. of: Brahmā, Śiva (in some forms).
Lit.: R 2:504; RV 58.

kūrcabīja ("seed of *kūrca*"), n. of a *bījamantra* with the form *HŪṀ*.
Lit.: IC 1:567.

kūrma "tortoise".

1. (Vāh., attr.) Vāh. of: Ananta, Hayaśiras, Rāhu, Yamunā; symbol of Munisuvrata. – *k.* may also (rarely) be held in the hands as an attr. by a deity; it is also shown being swallowed by Garuḍa.
Lit.: B 556; GH 73; GJ pl. 22:20; KiJ pl. 45; KiSH 89; MEIA 232, 266.

2. "Having the form of a tortoise" (attr.). Char. of Viṣṇu Kūrmāvatāra.

kūrmamudrā "tortoise-handpose" (Mu.). "Just as a tortoise contracts its head and limbs, hiding them within its shell, so the fingers are contracted and closed around the flowers that contain the force of the devotee's life-breath". *k.* is the pose of a hand in which the flowers are held during the *pūjā*. – Cp. *kaśyapamudrā*.
Lit.: ZA 319.

kūrmāsana.

1. "Tortoise-seat" (Vāh.), n. of a *pīṭha*, made of wood and of oval shape, upon which the face and the feet of a tortoise should be shown.
Lit.: B 274; R 1:17 a.pl. 6:3-4; SM 131.

2. "Tortoise-sitting" (att.), n. of an *āsana*-posture in which "the legs are crossed so as to make the heels come under the gluteals" (B).
Lit.: B 270; KiH pl. 152: row 3:1; R 1:18.

Kūrmāvatāra "the tortoise incarnation", n. of the second *avatāra* of Viṣṇu in which, in the shape of a tortoise, he served as the basis at the churning of the ocean of milk (cp. *kṣīrodamathana*). This manifestation of Viṣṇu seems to reflect the Sino-Tibetan conception of cosmos as a tortoise (cp. Kāśyapa). – In mythology Viṣṇu is said to have appeared in this form in order to recover some of the things of value lost in the deluge (cp. Matsyāvatāra). According to this tradition the *devas* and the *asuras* assembled and began to churn the ocean of milk, using Vāsuki as a rope which passed around Mount Mandara which served as the churn-staff. From the churning came forth: *amṛta*, Dhanvantari, Lakṣmī, Vāruṇī, *soma*, the *apsarasas*, Uccaiḥśravas, Kaustubha, Pārijāta, Surabhi, Airāvata, Pāñcajanya, Śārṅga, *hālāhala* (or *kālakūṭa*). In this manifestation Viṣṇu is represented as having a human upper-body with four arms and with the lower part of the body shaped like a tortoise. Char.: Mu.: *abhaya-*, *varada-mudrā*; attr.: esp. *cakra*, *śaṅkha*, but also *gadā*, *padma*. – In older tradition K. is sometimes regarded as a manifestation of Prajāpati or Brahmā; later also of the planet Śani.
Lit.: B 390; DHP 165, 167; GH 120; GoRI 1:250; Gt 351; IIM 41; JDI 72; KiH 5, 13 a.pl. 4; KiK 6; KiSH 36, 143; MEIA 28; MG 111 a.pl. facing p. 110; R 1:127 a.pl. 35; Th. 59; W 119; WHW 2:132; WM 128.

kūrpara "elbow" (att.). This term refers to the posture of Śiva (in South-Indian representations) in which he stands leaning against Nandin, having placed his elbow on the back or the head of the bull, or adopts the same attitude even if the bull is absent. Char. of Vṛṣavāhana, Nandīśa, Rājamannār; also Madanagopāla.
Lit.: SSI 114, 267 a.pl. III:9.

Kurukullā (the n. is sometimes analysed as **Kuru-kulyā* "belonging to the Kuru race" [?]; it is also interpreted as "goddess of wealth").

1. (Hind.) NP of a Tantric goddess of boats and wine, riding on a boat of gems.
Lit.: SSI 220.

2. (Buddh.) K. is esp. NP of a popular Mahāyāna goddess, an emanation of Amitābha. Usually she is identified with the "red Tārā" (rarely is she white), and is regarded as the Śakti of Amitābha. She

has a terrific appearance, one head, and 4, 6 or 8 arms. Char. : att. : *ālīḍhāsana* (or *nāṭyasthāna*) on demons; Mu. : *tarpaṇa-mudrā*; attr. : *akṣamālā, aṅkuśa, aśoka, dhanus, dharmapālābharaṇa, pāśa, śara, trinayana*. – Varieties : Aṣṭabhuja-, Māyā-jālakrama-, Śukla-, Tārodbhava-, Uḍḍi-yāna-Kurukullā.
Lit.: BBh. 147, 308; G 12, 34, 76; GBB pl. 33; KiDG 64; KiSB 96; MW 294.

kuśa "a grass (Poa cynosoroides Retz.)" (attr.). It is a sacred grass used at certain religious ceremonies (*pūjā*). Char. of Brahmā (held in a hand). Cp. *darbha, kūrca*.
Lit.: GH 65; IC 1:538; R 2:504; RV 57; Th. 51; W 392; WHW 1:405.

Kuṣāṇa, n. of a nomadic nation and of a centre of arts from about the 1st-3rd cc. A.D.
Lit.: FBKI 73; Gz 66; RAAI 92; SeKB 10; ZA passim.

kusi "a kind of spoon" (attr.), see *ācamanī*.
Lit.: BhIM 35; MH 37.

Kuṣmāṇḍās ("gourds"), n. of a class of demons causing diseases.
Lit.: B 563; Gt 355.

Kuṣmaṇḍī (or -ā, Kūṣmāṇḍa-Durgā, "gourd"), epithet and variety of Durgā. Attr. : *caṣaka*.
Lit.: B 563; MW 298; SSI 202.

Kuṣmāṇḍinī (Jain.), n. of a *śāsanadevatā* attending on the 22nd *tīrthaṅkara*.
Lit.: B 563; GJ 362 a.pl. 27:22; KiJ 12 a.pl. 30:22.

Kusuma ("flower"; Jain.), n. of a *yakṣa* attending on the 6th *tīrthaṅkara*. Symbol : *vṛṣan*.
Lit.: GJ 362 a.pl. 24:6; KiJ 11 a.pl. 27:6.

kusumacakra "flowery discus" (attr.). *k*. is a variety of *cakra*. Char. of Śīlapāramitā.
Lit.: BBh. 325.

kusumamālā "garland of flowers" (attr.), see *vanamālā*.
Lit.: BBh. 381.

kūṭa "hall", n. of a square ornamental pavilion on the storeys of *vimānas*.
Lit.: BECA 1:262.

kūṭāgāra "pleasure-house", n. of an apartment at top of a house.
Lit.: IC 2:319; KiSB 97.

kuṭamuḻā (Tam.) "pot-drum" (attr.), see *ghaṭa*.
Lit.: SB 309.

kuṭāri (*kuḍāri*; Tam.) "goad, hook" (attr.), see *aṅkuśa*.
Lit.: MD 1:377.

kuṭhāra "a sort of axe" (attr.). *k*. may be identified with either *ṭaṅka* or (usually) *paraśu*. Char. of: Aghoramūrti, Gaṇeśa, Tatpuruṣa.
Lit.: AI 120; B 357; MEIA 248; R 1:59, 2:378.

kuṭi (-*ī*, "hut, cottage"), n. of a small dwelling resembling the cottage of an ascetic.
Lit.: DKI 41.

kuṭila "twisted" (att.), n. of an inadequately described bodily posture.
Lit.: WHW 1:45.

kuṭila-kuntala "curl of hair" (attr.).
Lit.: SB 158.

kuṭṭita (or *nikuṭṭita*; "bruised, pounded, flattened"; att.), n. of a posture of the legs, described thus : "one leg rests firmly on the ground and the other, resting upon the toe, strikes the ground with the heel". Char. of Śiva Naṭarāja in the *lalita-* and *catura-tāṇḍava*-dances.
Lit.: R 2:263.

kūṭu (*kudu*, Tam., properly : "bird-cage, bird's-nest"), n. of a decorative motif, a "*caitya*-window motif (horse-shoe-shaped decorative element on the facade of a monument)".
Lit.: BECA 1:262.

Kuvera, see Kubera.

K(w)annon (Jap.), see Kuan-yin.

L

laḍḍu(ka) "a kind of sweetmeat" (attr.), see *modaka*. (Char. of some forms of Gaṇeśa).
Lit.: B 361; GJ 435; KiSH 31; MEIA 108, 269; R 1:55.

laghupātra "light, small bowl" (attr.), n. of a small metal bowl used for holding sandalwood.
Lit.: KiH pl. 140:2.

Laghuśyāmalā ("lightly dark-coloured"), NP of a goddess. Attr.: *caṣaka, viṇā*.
Lit.: SSI 220.

lagna "zodiacal sign", see *rāśi*.
Lit.: IC 1:491.

laguḍa (also *lakuṭa*) "club" (attr.), see *gadā* and Lakulīśa. In MEIA this term is equivalent to *daṇḍa*.
Lit.: MEIA 244; WAA 25:175.

Lajjā ("shame"), as a personification n. of the Śakti of Dāmodara.
Lit.: R 1:233.

lakṣaṇa "mark, sign, symbol, token", also "attribute" in a general sense (attr.). This is esp. "auspicious marks of a *buddha*"; the historical Buddha had 32 great marks (*mahāpuruṣalakṣaṇa*) and 80 lesser marks (*anuvyañjana*). The pecularities which characterize a *cakravartin* may also be labelled as *l.*, see *saptaratna*. Cp. also *bodhipākṣika*.
Lit.: BBh. 76, 436; BRI 51; G XXVIII; IC 2:535; Gw. 138; RAAI 272; RN 28; SM 141.

Lakṣmaṇa ("endowed with auspicious marks"), n. of a younger brother of Rāma. He was the son of Daśaratha and Sumitrā. In group-representations L. is usually the one standing to the left of Rāma. Wife: Ūrmitā (sister of Sītā). Char.: colour: pale gold; attr.: *channavīra, dhanus*.
Lit.: D 175; GI pl. 68; R 1:186 a.pl. 54, 55, 57; SB 145 a.pl. 90; SIB pl. 33; Th. pl. 16; WHW 1:583.

lakṣmaṇa, n. of an era founded by King Lakṣmaṇasena of Bengal and beginning in A.D. 1118. Its use is limited to the region of Mithilā. The year of this era is *gata, kārttikādi* and *amānta*; the given year + 1119 = the year A.D.
Lit.: Enc. Brit. 5:721; IC 2:738; WHW 1:334.

Lakṣmī ("mark, sign, a good or a bad sign"). 1. (Hind.) L. is originally a mother and fertility goddess and is regarded as a personification of the earth; in later times she is said to be the goddess of fortune, riches and beauty. According to the most common legend she sprang from the froth of the ocean at the churning of the ocean of milk (see Kūrmāvatāra), but she is also mentioned as the daughter of Prajāpati or of Bhṛgu and Khyāti. She is also adored as the protectress of the door of the Vaiṣṇavite temple. As to L. as the Genius of lamp, see sub *dīpa*.
L. is said, in different existences, to have been the wife or Śakti of several gods, e.g. of Varuṇa, Gaṇeśa, Kubera, Sūrya, Prajāpati, Dharma and many forms or aspects of Viṣṇu, as Nārāyaṇa, Dattātreya, Vāsudeva. But she is esp. known as the chief consort of Viṣṇu himself, and when he appears in different incarnations (see *avatāra*), his wife, in each *avatāra*, is said to be an *avatāra* of L.; thus Rukmiṇī (or Rādhā), the wife of Kṛṣṇa, or Sītā, the wife of Rāma, or Dharaṇī, the wife of Paraśurāma, or Padmā, the wife of Vāmana. – L. is represented with four or, more usually, two arms. Char.: colour: (dress) white; Vāh.: *padma* or Garuḍa or *ulūka*; Mu.: *abhaya-, kaṭaka-, lolahasta-, varada-mudrā*; attr. esp. *padma*, further: *amṛta-ghaṭa* (or *kamaṇḍalu*), *cakra, channavīra, gadā* Kaumodakī, *jambhīra, kheṭaka, kirī-ṭamukuṭa, kucabandha, nakrakuṇḍala, nidhi* (*padma-* and *śaṅkha-nidhi*), *śaṅkha, śrīphala*. L. is also represented by the *bījamantra lakṣmībīja* (*ŚRĪṀ*).
Epithets and varieties: esp. Śrī, further *aṣṭamahālakṣmī*, Cañcalā, Divālī-Mātā, Gaja-Lakṣmī, Hīrā, Indirā, Jaladhijā, Kamalā, Lokamātā, Łolā, Mahā-Lakṣmī, Padmā, Tiru, Tirumakaḷ, Trailokyamo-

hanī-Lakṣmī, Tulsī. – For L. as one of the *saptamātaras*, see Vaiṣṇavī.
Lit.: B 370; D 176; DHP 261 a.pl. 16; GBB 129; GH 140; GoRI 1:232; Gt 358; HIS 23; IC 1:521; IIM 90; JDI 63; KiSH 36; MEIA 183; MG 103 a.pl. facing p. 99; MW 892; R 1:88, 233, 372 a.pl. 109ff.; SSI 187; Th. 104 a.pl. 63; WHW 1:584; WM 129; ZA 158 a.pl. 564b.

2. (Jain.) NP of a goddess.
Lit.: B 561; GJ 363.

lakṣmībīja ("Seed-of-Existence or Seed-of-Fortune"), n. of a *bījamantra* with the form: *ŚRĪṀ*. "This *mantra* represents the goddess of fortune and multiplicity, Lakṣmī, the consort of Viṣṇu" (DHP).
Lit.: DHP 342; IC 1:567.

Lakṣmī-Gaṇapati, n. of a representation of Gaṇeśa (8-armed) together with his Śakti (see Lakṣmī); also a form of Gaṇeśa with two Śaktis has this n. Attr.: *aṅkuśa, cakra, danta, kalpakalatā, kamaṇḍalu, kapittha, padma, pāśa.*
Lit.: R 1:53 a.pl. 11:1; SSI 173.

Lakṣmī-Narasiṅha, n. of a composite representation of Viṣṇu as Narasiṅha (sitting) together with Lakṣmī. This represents N. in a state of serenity, his wrath (cp. Ugra-Narasiṅha) having subsided through the influence of the prayers of Prahlāda.
Lit.: R 1:160 a.pl. 41:1, 3; SSI 26.

Lakṣmī-Nārāyaṇa, n. of a composite representation of Viṣṇu (Nārāyaṇa), sitting, with Lakṣmī on his left knee, upon the Vāh. Garuḍa (this representation may also be identical with Lakṣmīpati). – L. is also n. of a representation (met with esp. in Nepal) of Viṣṇu and Lakṣmī in one body, half-man and half-woman, a form clearly influenced by the Śaivite Ardhanārī. As usual the right side has male attr. and the left side female attr. In the right hands: *cakra, gadā, padma, śaṅkha*; in the left hands: *amṛta-ghaṭa, darpaṇa, padma, pustaka.*
Lit.: R 1:258 a.pl. 76; SIB pl. 19; SSI 52.

Lakṣmīndralokeśvara, n. of a syncretistic figure composed of two Hindu constituents, Lakṣmī and Indra, and one Buddhist constituent, Lokeśvara. This representation is found in Indo-China.
Lit.: SeKB 48.

Lakṣmīpati ("husband [lord] of Lakṣmī"), n. of a composite representation of Viṣṇu, sitting, with Lakṣmī on his left knee. Cp. Lakṣmī-Nārāyaṇa. – Another n.: Tiruppati.

Lakulin (or -ī; "having a club"), see Lakulīśa.
Lit.: GoRI 1:260; HIS 21.

Lakulīśa (Lakulin; "the lord with the club", derived from *lakuṭa* or *laguḍa* "club"), n. of a reformer of the *pāśupata* cult who, by his adherents, was regarded as an *avatāra* (the 28th) of Śiva. He is esp. worshipped in the Kathiāwar peninsula. Char.: Mu.: *dharmacakramudrā*; attr.: *akṣamālā, gadā, kapāla, triśūla, ūrdhvaliṅga.* – Other n.: Lakuṭapāṇīśa, Nakulin.
Lit.: B 450, 465, 480 a.pl. 39:1, 40:4; GoRI 1:260; GRI 170; HIS 21; JMS pl. 87; WAA 25:175 a.fig. 29; WHW 2:193.

lakuṭa (*laguḍa*) "club" (attr.), see *gadā*.
Lit.: B 481.

Lakuṭapāṇīśa ("the lord with the club in his hand"), epithet of Lakulīśa.
Lit.: B 481.

lalāṭatilaka(-karaṇa) ("making a mark on the forehead"), n. of a certain dance-form performed by Śiva Naṭarāja. Char.: att.: *vṛścika*; Mu.: *abhaya-, patākā-mudrā*; attr.: Apasmāra, *ḍamaru, dhvaja, kapāla, nāga, triśūla, valaya.* – Another n.: *ūrdhva-tāṇḍava.*
Lit.: R 2:264 a.pl. 64-65; SB 94; SSI 82; Th. 89 a.pl. 56B; WM 94 a.fig. 9.

lalita ("played, lovely, charming"), n. either of a handpose (Mu.) or of a dance-form performed by Śiva Naṭarāja. – *l.* as dance: char. of Śiva: att.: *kuṭṭita*; Mu.: *gaja-hasta-, pravartita-, sūci-, tarjanī-, tripatākā-mudrā*; attr.: *ḍamaru, hāra, nāga* as *kaṭi-bandha, paraśu, udarabandha.*
Lit.: MW 897; R 2:262 a.pl. 73; WM 94.

Lalitā(devī) ("lovely, charming"), n. of a four-armed form of Pārvatī. Attr.: *āñjanī, aṅkuśa, darpaṇa, ikṣukodaṇḍa, padma, pañ-*

caśara, *pāśa*, *phala*, *śaṅkha*. – See also Kāmakalā, and cp. Rājarājeśvarī, Tripurasundarī.
Lit.: MEIA pl. 7; R 1:359; SSI 220.

lalitākṣepa (att.), see *lalitāsana*.
Lit.: B 272 a.pl. 33:1, 42:4.

lalitāsana "posture of relaxation" (att.), n. of an *āsana*-posture, "in which one leg, usually the left, is tucked upon the seat (*pīṭha*), while the right one dangles down along it" (B). This (right) foot then often rests upon a *karṇikā*. This att. symbolizes the gracious presence of the god, or, according to RN, serenity. Char. of many gods, e.g. Ādimūrti, *dhyānibuddhaśaktis*, Hālāhala-Lokeśvara, Khasarpaṇa, Lokeśvara, Mañjuśrī (in different forms), Padmapāṇi, Pāṇḍarā, *saptamātaras*, Siṅhanāda, Śyāmatārā, Vajrasattva, Vasudhārā. – Other n.: *lalitākṣepa*, *līlākṣepa*, *sukhāsana*; cp. *ardhaparyaṅkāsana*.
Lit.: B 272; BBh. 432; G 24; Gz 101; H pl. 5:45; KIM pl. 50; MEIA 219; RN 31; SM 127; Th. 36; WHW 1:75; WM 92 a.fig. 8.

LAṀ, form of a *bījamantra* dedicated to Indra. It is also symbolic of the element of earth.
Lit.: DHP 343; GH 55.

Lāmā (Buddh.), n. of a *ḍākinī*.
Lit.: BBh. 321 a.pl. 218.

bla-ma (Tib., pronounced: *lama*; Buddh.) "the superior", title of the spiritual teacher, priest, Lama, the superior of a cloister. – Cp. Dalai Lama, Tashi Lama.
Lit.: G 5; JT 383.

lambakūrcāsana "seat (or mat) made of long grass" (Vāh.). Char. of Brahmā.
Lit.: R 2:503.

lambapattra "long leaf" (attr.), n. of a kind of woman's ear-ornament. It is also worn by Śiva (in Rudramūrti and some other forms) in his left ear (cp. *vāma*).
Lit.: SSI 76.

Lambastanā ("having long, flaccid breasts"), epithet of Jyeṣṭhadevī.

lambita ("hanging"; att.), a term (hardly correctly) used of the straight leg, placed on the pedestal in a certain standing att., while the other leg, slightly bent, is said to be *kuñcitapāda**, cp. *svastika*.
Lit.: SSI 190.

lambodara "having a large, protuberant belly, pot-bellied" (attr.), see *tundila*.
Lit.: MW 897.

Lambodara ("pot-bellied"), epithet of Gaṇeśa.
Lit.: R 1:47, 50; SB 154.

lāñchana "mark, sign, token" (attr.). This term is used to refer to a totemistic emblem and may denote, e.g., a sign of Nandin, or the symbol of a Jain deity, or all kinds of emblems.
Lit.: R 1:389, 2:289; SB 337.

lāṅgala "a kind of plough" (attr.), see *hala*.
Lit.: B 556.

lāṅgalaka "plough-shaped" (att.), n. of a kind of flying att., char. of *gandharvas* and *vidyādharas* in the early plastic arts (Sāñcī etc.).
Lit.: WM 96 a.fig. 12-13.

langar (Panj., said to originate from Skt *analagraha*) "free kitchen; that which is cooked, food" (Sikhism). – *l.* signifies a community meal, and in particular the institution of the Sikhs whereby free food is distributed to everybody who asks for it; thus *l.* symbolizes brotherhood, equality and humility. A symbolical form of this meal is *karah praṣad**.
Lit.: GG p. LX; HS 180.

laṅgūlamudrā "tail-handpose" (Mu.), n. of a variety of the *padmamudrā** with the difference that the ring-finger is stretched out. It symbolizes the water lily, picking a flower, virgin experience.
Lit.: WHW 2:87.

Laṅkā, n. of the island of Ceylon, the modern Sri Lanka, and of the mythical chief town of this island. It is esp. known as the capital of the demon-king Rāvaṇa who was killed by Rāma.
Lit.: MW 894; WM 129.

Laṅkādāhin ("burner of Laṅkā"), epithet of Hanumān who, when participating in Rāmā's war against Rāvaṇa, the demon-

king of Sri Lanka, burnt his capital, the city of Laṅkā.
Lit.: D 116, 177; MW 894.

lāsya "dancing", a kind of dance which is performed in many forms by women. It is considered to be very erotic.
Lit.: MW 899; Sh. 92; WHW 1:265.

Lāsyā ("dancing girl"; Buddh.).
1. NP of one of the Lamaist *aṣṭamātaras*. Char.: colour: white; attr.: *darpaṇa*. – Also n. of the first goddess of the *lāsyā*-group (see below). Char.: colour: red; att.: dancing the *lāsya*-dance.
Lit.: BBh. 313 a.pl. 206; G 36, 82.
2. N. of a group of four goddesses, headed by Lāsyā (see above). The others are: Mālā, Gītā, and Nṛtyā. Common features: att.: *ālīḍhāsana*; Mu.: *tarjanīmudrā*; attr.: *muṇḍamālā*.
Lit.: BBh. 312.

latā "creeper" (attr.). As attr., held in one hand, char. of Upapattivaśitā.
Lit.: BBh. 330.

latāmadhyā (said about a woman) "creeper-like or -waisted" (attr.).
Lit.: SB 109.

lāṭh (Hi., < Pkt *laṭṭhī*, Skt *yaṣṭi*) "pillar, column", see *stambha*.
Lit.: DKI 11.

laukika-devatās "popular deities", a term used of folk-gods as contrasted with the Vedic deities.
Lit.: B 338, 362, 522; GI 67.

laukikāgni "worldly fire", in the modern Brāhman ritual n. of the "domestic fires" (see *agni*), contrary to other fires (not listed here).
Lit.: STP 2:256, 3:160.

laukikakāla "the popular era", see *saptarṣi-kāla*.

laukikasamvat "the year of *laukikakāla*", see sub *saptarṣikāla*.

lekhanī "instrument for writing, reed-pen, pencil" (attr.). This symbol is used together with *maṣībhājana*. Char. of: Agni, Brahmā, Piṅgala-Gaṇapati.
Lit.: MEIA 269.

lenā (Pāli, < Skt *layana*) "cave; lieu de coucher (IC)" (with cave pictures), cp. *gumphā*.
Lit.: Gz 54; IC 2:320.

lepajā (scil. *devatā*), n. of an image, made of clay. – Cp. *kṣaṇika*.
Lit.: B 208.

Lha-mo ("the Goddess"; Tib.; Buddh.), in Lamaism the usual n. of Śrīdevī, a female *dharmapāla*.
Lit.: G 88; JT 599.

licchavi(kāla) "(the era of) L.", n. of an era beginning in A.D. 110, used in Ancient Nepal.
Lit.: IC 2:737.

līlā (properly "play, sport"; att.), a short word-form for *rājalīlāsana**. It is also interpreted thus: "A semblance or illusion as in a play or dance" (RAAI).
Lit.: KiSB 57; RAAI 272.

līlākṣepa "playful sideways-movement (i.e. of the leg)" (att.), see *lalitāsana*.

līlāmūrti "playful representation", n. of different postures and forms, displaying a mystical meaning, of esp. Śiva and Kṛṣṇa.
Lit.: B 267; R 2:369; SSI 89; ZA 359.

līlayāsthita "playfully performed; Pose der Anmut" (KiSB; Mu.); this term signifies a handpose (not described). Char. of Vāgīśvara.
Lit.: KiSB 54.

līlayordhvasthita "standing sportively erect" (att.), n. of an inadequately described *sthānaka*-posture. Char. of Aśokakāntā.
Lit.: BBh. 209.

liṅga(m) ("sign, the sign of gender or sex") "phallus, male organ", a symbol of the male principle.
1. (Hind.) The *l.* as a fertility symbol appears already in the Indus Valley civilization. It was suppressed by the Indo-Aryans for a long time, but eventually reappeared and is esp. connected with Śiva (*bījavān* "Giver-of-Seed") as his chief symbol, and a *l.* made of stone may be regarded as a lithomorphic form of Śiva. Both in the temples and at home a *l.* of

stone or metal is worshipped as a symbol of Śiva, and it is now also interpreted as "a symbol of the Eternal Unity, or of the 'formless god'" (HAHI). – In large representations the *l.* is supplied with flutings running down the sides, cp. *dhārāliṅga*, *mānuṣaliṅga*, *mukhaliṅga*. In both small and in large representations the *l.* is often placed in a *yoni* thus forming a composite representation (in a kind of coitus; this *yoni* serves as a *piṇḍikā*); with bronze *liṅga*s this is always the case. In these compositions the *yoni* is often made of bronze and a *l.* of quartz is placed in it, cp. *bāṇaliṅga*. In the large forms the *yoni* is shaped in such a manner that it draws off the water which is poured over the *l.* Many Hindus therefore deny that it is a *yoni*-symbol and assert that it is only an outflow receptacle. However, it is undeniable that this object really signifies a *yoni*. – The *l.* may also be entwined with a *nāga* (which is also a fertility symbol). It should in addition be mentioned that, at festivals, phallic cakes are made and eaten. As an attr. a *l.* (in a *yoni*) is held in one hand by Pārvatī and carried on the head by Mahālakṣmī and Bhūtamātā. A *l.* is also char. of the Liṅgāyats who, however, regard the *l.* as a god, not as a male organ.

In *yantra*s the *l.* is symbolized by a triangle with the point upwards, likewise by a staff (*daṇḍa*) between two dots; a hexagon (= two triangles upon each other) symbolizes the composition of a *l.* placed in a *yoni*; see further *trikoṇa*. – Another n.: *guhya*. See also *śivaliṅga*, *śūla*, *sphaṭikaliṅga* and under *galantī*.

Lit.: B 496; CHIIA 232 a.fig. 66, 68; D 177; DHP 213, 217, 222 a.pl. 19; FES 9; GH 42, 343 a.pl. 7; GoRI 1:255; Gt 361; HAHI 21; IC 1:516, 571; JDI 11; KiH 30 a.pl. 69, 108-116; KiSH 45; KrA pl. 46; R 1:375 a.pl. 112; 2:58, 73 a.pl. 1 ff.; RIS 22; SSI 72; WHW 1:594; WM 130; ZA 22 a.pl. A8.

2. (Buddh.) The *l.* as n. of the male principle seems to be restricted to Hinduism, Buddhism having substituted for this word the term *vajra*, and also *maṇi* and *gaja*. In the *yantra*s the *l.* is symbolized by a triangle.

Lit.: G 11; HuET 47.

Liṅga, n. of the representation of Śiva as a phallus (*liṅga*).

Lit.: B 454 a.pl. 31:3-4; GH pl. 7; HIS 21; KiSH 18; MG 169; SS pl. 8:42; ZA pl. 289, 566.

liṅgamudrā, n. of one among the group *pañcamudrā*. This Mu. "is obviously involving a reference to the *liṅga*" (further details are not given).

Lit.: DiIP 70, 105.

liṅgapūjā, n. of worship or cult dedicated to the *liṅga*. Cp. *pūjā*.

Lit.: GBB pl. 3; JMS pl. 10; MSHP pl. 12.

liṅgāyat (Hi.; Skt *liṅgavant* "wearing a *liṅga*"), n. of a Śaivite sect, fairly numerous in the Deccan. The members of this sect are named thus because they wear a *liṅga* in a small box or reliquary suspended on a chain hung about the neck. Char. of the faith of the *l.* is further *aṣṭāvaraṇa*. – Another n.: *vīraśaiva*.

Lit.: GH 393; GoRI 2:243; GRI 331; IC 1:638; JDI 12; P 965; WHW 1:597.

Liṅgodbhavamūrti ("representation of the origin of *liṅga*"), n. of a kind of image of *liṅga*-type, in which Śiva is represented as having "appeared in the form of a blazing pillar of immeasurable size to quell the pride of Brahmā and Viṣṇu". Here Brahmā, in the shape of a *haṅsa*, is seen flying up in the air in order to investigate the height of the *liṅga*, and Viṣṇu, in the shape of a *varāha*, is seen diving into the sea in order to investigate its depth. This representation is also interpreted as the Śiva who emanated from the *liṅga* for the sake of his devotee Mārkaṇḍeya. Śiva, in an anthropomorphic form with four arms, is carved in a hollow of the *liṅga*-pillar with the char.: Mu.: *abhaya-*, *kaṭi-*, *varada-*

mudrā; attr.: *ajina* (elephantskin), *dhanus* Pināka, *mṛga*, *paraśu*, *triśūla*, *yajñopavīta*.
Lit.: B 462 a.pl. 31:4; HSIT 11 a.pl. 23; R 2:103 a.pl. 13ff.; SSI 93; Th. 78; ZM 143.

Lipidevī ("goddess of writing, alphabet"), epithet of Sarasvatī, as the goddess of learning.
Lit.: MEIA 190.

Locanā ("eye"; Buddh.), in Mahāyāna Buddhism n. of a *dhyānibuddhaśakti*, the Śakti of Akṣobhya or Vairocana. Char.: colour: blue or white; att.: *lalitāsana*; Mu.: *varada-*, *vyākhyāna-mudrā*; attr.: *kapāla*, *padmas* with one or two *vajras*. She is also found in *yab-yum*-att. (with Akṣobhya). Attr.: *cakra*, *kapāla*, *vajra*. – Cp. also Buddhalocanā, with whom L. may be identical.
Lit.: BBh. 54 a.pl. 31; G 52, 77, 86; GBM 156; KiSB 45.

lohaja "made of metal", n. of a kind of image, e.g. *lohaja liṅga* (see *calaliṅga*). The technique of casting such metal icons (and other metal articles) was earlier usually – and is even now in many places – the "lost wax" process (see *madhūcchiṣṭavidāna* and MH). The material used was either a pure metal such as copper (*tāṅbā*) or even gold and silver, but might also be alloys of different kinds, cp. *pañcaloha*, *aṣṭadhātu*, and in particular various bronze and brass alloys (see the index of architectural and artistic terms).
Lit.: KIM 28; MH 5; R 2:76; Th. 25.

loka "world", in the cosmological system esp. n. of the spheres or paradises of the gods above the earth, the number of which is said to be either 3, or 7, or even 14. *l.* is therefore also a symbolic n. of the number "7", see *saṅkhyā*.
Lit.: Gt 362; MW 906; WHW 1:253.

lokakāla "world era", see *saptarṣikala*.
Lit.: IC 2:736.

Lokamātā ("world mother"), epithet of Lakṣmī.
Lit.: DHP 262.

Lokanātha ("world protector").
1. (Hind.) N. of a form of Viṣṇu, sometimes regarded as an *avatāra* of him.
Lit.: B 392; Th. pl. 35.
2. (Buddh.) L. (or Lokanātha-Raktāryāvalokiteśvara) is n. of a variety of Avalokiteśvara. Char.: colour: white; att.: *lalitāsana*; Mu.; *varadamudrā*; attr.: *Amitābhabimba* on the crown, *padma*.
Lit.: BBh. 130 a.pl. 105-108; KiSB 58; SB 169 a.pl. 103.

lokapāla, properly: "world protector", usually used in the sense of "regent of a direction or quarter of the world", see *dikpāla*. – *l.* is also another n. for *diggaja*.
Lit.: B 519; D 180; DHP 301; G 37, 92; HIS 25; IC 1:492, 2:591; KiH 10 a.pl. 7-8; KiSH 55; Th. 109; WM 131.

Lokeśvara ("lord of the world") is firstly n. of a group of deities whose forms have arisen out of a syncretistic confusion of Hindu and Buddhist ideas. These deities are above all signified by a little figure (in *padmāsana*-att.) on the head of the icon, and this little figure is usually said to be Ādibuddha or Amitābha. Such images are Śiva-, Sūrya-, Viṣṇu-, Lakṣmīndra-Lokeśvara and others. These are Hindu deities, which through Buddhist influence are regarded as emanations of a primeval father in the same manner as most Buddhist deities are said to be emanations of the different *dhyānibuddhas* or Ādibuddha, signified by a similar figure (*bimba*) on the head. – Secondly, in a restricted sense, L. is a group-name of varieties of Avalokiteśvara, among others of the group of 108 forms of this Buddhist god, enumerated in BBh. (It should be noted that the number 108 is a frequently used number of beads in the *akṣamālā*).
Lit.: B 540, 547; BBh. 394 a.pl. 1-108(A); KiDG 51 a.pl. 26-37; RAAI pl. 155.

Lolā ("the Fickle-One"), epithet of Lakṣmī.
Lit.: DHP 262.

lolahastamudrā "the pose of moving, restless hand" (Mu.), n. of a gesture in which

(on images) the arm and the hand hang down loosely, the hand being at right angles to the wrist in an attempt to convey the to-and-fro movement of the hand in walking. It is also described as the arm hanging down loose "like the tail of a cow" (SSI). This Mu. is also mentioned as a variety of the *patākāmudrā*. Char. of many goddesses, such as Pārvatī, Lakṣmī.
Lit.: SSI 190; Th. 27; WHW 2:86; WM 101.

loṭā (Hi.) "water-bottle" (attr.). A small, round metal pot, used by Brāhmans.
Lit.: P 967; RAAI 272.

kLu-dbaṅ ("serpent-power"; Tib., pronounced: Lu-vaṅ; Buddh.), in Lamaism n. of one of the *mahāpañcarājas*. Char.: colour: red; Vāh.: *aśvatara* (blue); attr.: *aṅkuśa*, *gadā*.
Lit.: G 93.

Lui-pa (Tib.; Buddh.), in Lamaism n. of one of the *mahāsiddhas*. He lived about A.D. 669. – Attr.: *kapāla*.
Lit.: G 94.

rLuṅ-rta (Tib., pronounced: *Luṅ-ta*; Buddh.) "airy horse, carrying the flaming pearl" (*cintāmaṇi*). This symbol is represented on *dhvajas*.
Lit.: G 16 (ill.); JT 538.

M

maccha "fish" (M.Ind.), see *matsya*.

Madana ("love, the Seducer-of-the-Mind"), epithet of Kāma.
Lit.: DHP 219.

Madanā ("love"), n. of the wife of Aiyaṉār.
Lit.: ACA 3; R 2:489.

Madanagopāla ("herdsman of love"), n. of a form of Veṇugopāla (Kṛṣṇa), often represented leaning against a cow. Att.: *kūrpara*, *pādasvastika*.
Lit.: R 1:210 a.pl. 63; SSI 43 a.fig. 28.

madanotsava "festival of Madana (Kāma)", n. of a spring festival in the month *caitra* (March-April). – Another n.: *vasantotsava*.
Lit.: IC 590.

Mādhava ("descendant of Madhu, the lord of knowledge"), n. of an aspect of Viṣṇu, see *caturviṅśatimūrti*. Śakti: Tuṣṭi. M. is also an epithet of Kṛṣṇa.
Lit.: DHP 154; KiSH 39; R 1:229 a.pl. 70; SSI 41.

madhūcchiṣṭa-vidāna (or *-vidhāna*) "wax-model, wax-method", n. of the model which is used for the production of bronze icons, or of the method of casting bronze images, known as "the lost-wax method" ("cire perdue"). There are two modes of casting icons, by which they are made either solid (*ghana*) or hollow (*suṣira*). – Cp. *lohaja*.
Lit. MH 5; SIB 3, 65; ZA 110.

madhukara "bee (honey-maker)" (attr.). A row of *m.* form the bow-string of *ikṣu-kodaṇḍa*. Char. of Kāma. Another n.: *bhramara*.
Lit.: GH 113.

Madhukara ("bee"; Buddh.), n. of an (originally Hindu?) god, perhaps identical with Kāma. Char.: colour: white; Vāh.: *ratha* drawn by *śukas*; attr.: *caṣaka*, *dhanus*, *makaradhvaja*, *śara*.
Lit.: BBh. 379.

madhupātra (originally) "honey-vessel", n. of a chaliced (i.e. flower-shaped) drinking vessel for intoxicating drinks (attr.). Char. of Balarāma.
Lit.: HIS 62 a.pl. 22; MW 780.

Madhusūdana ("destroyer of Madhu"), epithet of Kṛṣṇa as the slayer of the demon Madhu ("honey"); also n. of an aspect of Viṣṇu, see *caturviṅśatimūrti*. There is a theory, put forward by PARPOLA, that the n. Madhu, being a curious name of a demon, may be due to an erroneous translation into Sanskrit of a Dravidian name, since in

Dravidian languages there is a word *tī* "evil", homophonous with **tī* "honey" (cp. Tam. *tī* "evil", *tīm* "sweet", *tēṉ* "honey"), and from a Dravidian idea of Viṣṇu-Kṛṣṇa as "the annihilator of evil" hence, through a misunderstanding, the conception of a demon "Honey" (Skt Madhu), conquered by him, might have arisen. Cp. Kāma, often regarded as the Genius of evil, who has attributes belonging to the idea of sweetness and honey; see also Madhukara.

Lit.: D 182; DED No. 2673 f.; DHP 154; KiSH 39; A. PARPOLA, JTS 2:93; R 1:299 a.pl. 70; W 106.

Madhva (or Madhvācārya), n. of a *vaiṣṇavabhakta*, who lived in the 13th c. A.D. (1197-1276). He is represented as a *saṁnyāsin*. Char.: Mu.: *cinmudrā*; attr.: *daṇḍa, kamaṇḍalu, pustaka, ūrdhvapuṇḍra*.

Lit.: GH 386; IC 1:642; SSI 259; WHW 2:1.

mādhva, n. of a sect founded by Madhva.

Lit.: IC 1:642.

madhyama ("middle"), see sub *dhruva(bera)*.

mādhyamika(-vāda) "adherent of the middle doctrine", n. of a variety of Buddhist doctrine.

Lit.: GRI 263; IC 2:577.

Madurai (-a, Maturai), n. of an old South Indian town, the centre of later Dravidian arts (from the 17th c. A.D. to the present time).

Lit.: JDI 7.

Maduraivīraṉ, see Maturaivīraṉ.

madya "intoxicant, wine" (attr.), see *pañcamakāra*.

Lit.: WHW 1:221.

Mā Gaṅgā "mother G.", see Gaṅgā.

Maghā(s) (*magha* "gift, reward"; "les généreuses", IC), n. of a *nakṣatra*. Its influence is good.

Lit.: BBh. 381; IC 2:729.

māgha ("relating to the *nakṣatra* Maghā"), n. of a month (January-February). Its god is Viṣṇu.

Lit.: BBh. 382; IC 2:733; MW 805.

māgisan, n. of an era beginning in A.D. 638. Limited use in the district of Chittagong.

Lit.: IC 2:737.

Mahābala ("exceedingly strong"; Buddh.), n. of a Mahāyāna god, a fierce emanation of Amitābha. He is also regarded as a *dikpāla* of the north-west direction. Char.: colour: red; att.: *ālīḍhāsana*; Mu.: *añjali-, tarjanīmudrā*; attr.: *ajina* (tigerskin), *Amitābhabimba* on the crown, *cāmara* (white), *cintāmaṇi, daṇḍa* (white), *khaḍga, nāga*s, *padma, triśiras, triśūla*. – Other n.: Mahākāla, Paramāśva.

Lit.: BBh. 145, 255; KiSB 74.

Mahābalipuram, see Māmallapuram.

Mahābhayakarī-Lokeśvara (Mahā-abhaya-; "the great fearlessness-causing L."; Buddh.), n. of a variety of Avalokiteśvara. Char.: att.: *samapādasthānaka*; Vāh.: *padma*; attr.: *akṣamālā, Amitābhabimba* on the head, *ghaṇṭā, pustaka, tridaṇḍa, triśiras, vajra*.

Lit.: BBh. 400 a.pl. 64(A); KiDG 55 a.pl. 35.

Mahābhayaphalada-Lokeśvara (Mahā-abhaya-; "the great L., giving the fruit of fearlessness"; Buddh.), n. of a variety of Avalokiteśvara. Char.: att.: *samapādasthānaka*; Vāh.: *padma*; attr.: *Amitābhabimba* on the head, 2 *ghaṇṭā*s, *khaḍga, nīlotpala, pustaka, triśiras, vajra*.

Lit.: BBh. 400 a.pl. 63(A); KiDG 55 a.pl. 34.

mahābhiniṣkramaṇa "the great departure" (Buddh.), term indicating the Buddha's abandonment of his own family, from which he departed riding away his horse Kanthaka.

Lit.: MW 798.

Mahābja ("great lotus"), n. of a *mahānāga*, obviously identical with Mahāpadma.

Lit.: MEIA 196.

Mahābodhivṛkṣa ("the great tree of Enlightenment"), see *bodhivṛkṣa*.

Lit.: CEBI 39.

mahācakra "great wheel", n. of the mystic circle or assembly in the *śākta* ceremonial.

Lit.: MW 795.

Mahācakra-Vajrapāṇi ("V. of the great wheel"; Buddh.), in Lamaism n. of a variety of Vajrapāṇi. Char.: att.: *sthānaka* and *yab-yum* with the Śakti; Vāh.: 2 *nara*s (or

mṛtakas), on whom he treads; attr.: *dharmapālābharaṇa*, *nāgas*, *trinayana*, *triśiras*, *vajra*; the Śakti carries: *kapāla*, *karttṛkā*.
Lit.: G 63.

Mahācaṇḍaroṣaṇa ("the great C."), see Caṇḍaroṣaṇa.
Lit.: BBh. 154.

Mahācandrabimba-Lokeśvara ("L. of the great moon-disk"; Buddh.), n. of a variety of Avalokiteśvara. Char.: att.: *samapādasthānaka*; Vāh.: *padma*; attr.: *Amitābhabimba* on the head, *cakra*, *dhanus*, *nīlotpala*, *phala*, *śara*, *triśiras*, *vajra*.
Lit.: BBh. 400 a.pl. 61(A); KiDG 54 a.pl. 32.

Mahācīnatārā ("Tārā of Great China, i.e. of Tibet"; Buddh.), n. of a Mahāyāna goddess, an emanation of Akṣobhya. In Lamaism M. is n. of a fierce variety of Ekajaṭā. She appears in three forms: one-headed with 4 hands, one-headed with 8 hands, and 12-headed with 24 hands. Char.: att.: *ālīḍhāsana*; Vāh.: *mṛtaka*(s) (sometimes perhaps gods); attr.: *ajina* (tigerskin), *Akṣobhyabimba* on the crown, *churī* or *karttṛkā*, *dhanus*, *kapāla*, *khaḍga*, *muṇḍa*, *muṇḍamālā*, *nāgāṣṭaka*, *nīlotpala*, *pañcamudrā*, *paraśu*, *śara*, *trinayana*, *tundila*, *vajra*. – Another n.: Ugratārā.
Lit.: BBh. 189, 309 a.pl. 135f.; G 76; KiDG 64.

Mahādeva (N.Ind.: Mahādeo; "the Great God"), epithet of Śiva as the Supreme god, but esp. n. of a representation of Śiva with three heads, two male and one female, which signify three aspects of Śiva, as Aghora (or Ghora, Aghora-Bhairava, the face on the right side), as Saumya (Tatpuruṣa, the central face), and as Śakti (Vāmadeva-Umā, the face on the left side). Attr.: *aṅkuśa*, *darpaṇa*, *ghaṇṭā*, *khaḍga*, *kheṭaka*, *paraśu*, *pāśa*, *triśūla*, *vajra*. – M. is also mentioned as one of the *mūrtyaṣṭaka*-manifestations of Śiva and as one of the *ekādaśarudra*. – Other n.: Maheśa(mūrti), Maheśvara.
Lit.: B 446, 476 a.pl. 39:3, 40:1; DHP 198, 206; GoRI 1:255; HIS 20; KrA pl. 100-102 a.p. 207; MG pl. facing p. 81; R 2:47, 379 a.pl. 114:1, 116-118; ZA pl. 253-255.

Mahādevī ("the great Goddess"), epithet of Pārvatī.
Lit.: KiSH 13.

Mahā-Gaṇapati ("the great G."), n. of a form of Gaṇeśa together with his Śakti. Attr.: *dāḍima*, *danta*, *gadā*, *ikṣu*, *kamaṇḍalu*, *kaṇiśa*, *kapittha*, *padma*, *pāśa*.
Lit.: R 1:55; SSI 173; Th. 97.

Mahā-Gaurī ("the great G."), n. of a variety of Durgā. Vāh.: *gaja* (white).
Lit.: SSI 202.

mahāgopura "large *gopura*", n. given to a lofty temple-gateway, comprising 7 to 16 storeys. Another n.: *mahāmaryādā*.
Lit.: BECA 1:260.

mahājyaiṣṭhī "the night of full-moon in the month *jyaiṣṭha*", n. of a festival with a procession in honour of Puruṣottama.
Lit.: IC 1:592.

Mahākailāsa ("the great (lord of) Kailāsa"), n. of a form of Śiva, see Mahā-Sadāśiva.
Lit.: SSI 77.

Mahākāla (either "the Great Time = the Great Death or Destroyer" or "the Great Black-One").

1. (Hind.) N. of an *ugra*-manifestation of Śiva together with his Śakti Mahākālī. Char.: colour: black; Vāh.: *siṁhāsana*; Mu.: *āliṅgahastamudrā*; attr.: *ajina* (tiger-skin), *brahmāṇḍa*, *daṇḍa*, *gadā*, *kapāla*, *khaṭvāṅga*, *muṇḍamālā*, *pañcaśiras*, *paraśu*, *trinayana*, *triśūla*.
Lit.: R 2:201; SSI 151; Th. 84; ZA 94.

2. (Buddh.) N. of a Lamaist god (originally the Hindu god Śiva), an emanation of the five *dhyānibuddhas*. He is a *dharmapāla* and the protector of tents and of science, also the lord of riches. Char.: colour: black, blue or white; att.: *yab-yum* with the Śakti; Vāh.: he treads on Vināyaka (the latter having the attr.: *ākhu*, *kapāla*, *puṣpa*) or on 2 elephant-headed *naras*, or sits on a *nara* (or *mṛtaka*); attr.: esp. *cintāmaṇi*, *triśūla*, further (e.g. as the protector of science) *ajina* (elephantskin),

akṣamālā, *aṅkuśa*, *bimba* of the 5 *dhyānibuddhas*, *cāmara*, *caturmukha* (sometimes; he may also have 8 or 16 heads), *ḍamaru*, *daṇḍa*, *dhvaja*, *ghaṇṭā*, *kapāla*, *karttṛkā*, *khaḍga*, *khaṭvāṅga*, *mudgara*, *muṇḍa*, *muṇḍamālā*, *nāgas*, *pañcakapāla*, *śakti*, *trinayana*, *triśūla*, *vajra*, *vajrapāśa*. – Particular varieties : Bram-zei gzugs-can, mGon-dkar, mGon-po nag-po, Gur-gyi mGon-po. – M. is also another n. of Mahābala.

Lit.: BBh. 255, 344, 366 a.pl. 226; G passim; JSV pl. 78; KiSB 75.

Mahākālī (probably "the Great Black-One", but cp. Kālī).

1. (Hind.) N. of a form of Kālī or Cāmuṇḍā, with 4 or 8 hands. She also appears as the Śakti of Mahākāla. Attr. : *aṅkuśa*, *cakra*, *churī*, *gadā*, *kamaṇḍalu*, *kapāla*, *keśamaṇḍala* (*agni*), *khaḍga*, *kheṭaka*, *muṇḍamālā*, *musala*, *pāśa*, *śaṅkha*, *vajra*. – Concerning several epithets, not listed here, see B.

Lit.: B 496; KiSH 48; R 1:358 a.pl. 107; SB pl. 241; SSI 197; Th. 107 a.pl. 69A.

2. (Jain.) N. of a *vidyādevī* and of a *śāsanadevatā* attending on the 5th *tīrthaṅkara*. See also Ajitā.

Lit.: B 496; GJ 362 a.pl. 25:9.

mahākapāla "large skull-cap" (or cup)" (attr.), probably a variety of *kapāla*. Char. of Ubhayavarāhānana-Mārīcī.

Lit.: KiDG 67.

Mahākapi ("the great Ape"; Buddh.), epithet of the Buddha as a *bodhisattva* in one of his earlier incarnations, in which he was re-born as an ape. The story of M. is related in two of the best-known *jātakas*.

Lit.: FBKI 31 a.pl. 16; MS 78; ZA 242 a.pl. 31b.

Mahākarṇa ("having large ears"), epithet of Gaṇeśa.

Lit.: DiIP 113.

Mahākāya ("large-bodied"), epithet of Gaṇeśa.

Lit.: DiIP 113.

Mahā-Lakṣmī ("the great L."), epithet and n. of a particular representation of Lakṣmī as the Supreme goddess, the Great Divine Mother. In this sense she may be the Śakti of Śiva and Brahmā as well as of Viṣṇu, and she may be regarded as a form of either Pārvatī (Durgā) or Sarasvatī or Lakṣmī. M. is also mentioned as a form of the group *aṣṭamahālakṣmī*, and sometimes she is also counted among the *aṣṭamātaras*. Attr. : *cihna*, *gadā* Kaumodakī, *jambhīra*, *kapāla*, *kheṭaka*, *liṅga* on the head, *pātra*, *śrīphala*, *trinayana*, *triśūla*. She is also represented as swallowing *aśva*, *gaja*, *mahiṣa*, *nara*.

Lit.: B 496; BP 60 a.pl. 4-6; DHP 262; GI pl. 77; KiK 103; KiSH 50; MEIA 266; MW 800; R 1:335, 375 a.pl. 112; SSI 189; Th. 106.

Mahā Māi ("the great mother"), see Mātā(ji).

Mahāmānasī ("great-minded"; Jain.), n. of a *śāsanadevatā* attending on the 16th *tīrthaṅkara*.

Lit.: GJ 362 a.pl. 26:16; KiJ 12 a.pl. 29:16.

Mahāmānasikā ("great-minded"; Jain.), n. of a *vidyādevī*.

Lit.: GJ 362; MW 798.

mahāmaṇḍala "great *circle*" (attr.; Buddh.), n. of a form of *maṇḍala* on which pictorial representations of saints and sacred objects are made.

Lit.: GBM 108.

mahāmaṇḍapa "great hall", n. of a big pavilion in a temple.

Lit.: SSI 2.

Mahāmañjubhūta-Lokeśvara ("L., the great lovely being" or "son of Mañju"; Buddh.), n. of a variety of Avalokiteśvara. Char. : att. : *samapādasthānaka*; Vāh. : *padma*; attr. : *akṣamālā*, *Amitābhabimba* on the head, *ghaṇṭā*, *kamaṇḍalu*, *khaḍga*, *nīlotpala*, *triśiras*, *vajra*.

Lit.: BBh. 428 a.pl. 65(A); KiDG 55 a.pl. 36.

Mahāmañjudatta-Lokeśvara ("L., the great son of Mañju[?]"; Buddh.), n. of a variety of Avalokiteśvara. Char. : att. : *samapādasthānaka*; Vāh. : *padma*; attr. : *ghaṇṭā*, *khaḍga*, *nīlotpala*, *ratnadāma*, *triśiras*, *vajra*.

Lit.: BBh. 400 a.pl. 60(A); KiDG 54 a.pl. 31.

Mahāmantrānusāriṇī ("following the great sacred text"; Buddh.), n. of a Mahāyāna goddess, one of the *mahārakṣās*. She is an

emanation of Akṣobhya, and she is a regent of either the west (so KiDG) or south (so BBh.) or east (so G) direction. Char.: colour: blue or black or white or green or (according to KiSB: properly) red; Mu.: *abhaya-*, *dharmacakra-*, *dhyāna-*, *varada-mudrā*; attr.: esp. *pāśa*, *vajra*, further: *Akṣobhyabimba*, *cakra*, *cintāmaṇi*, *dhanus*, *dhvaja*, *ghaṇṭā*, *kamaṇḍalu* (marked with a lotus), *padma*, *paraśu*, *śara*, *sūrya-prabhāmaṇḍala*, (*tarjanīpāśa*, cp. *pāśa* above), sometimes *triśiras*; she has 4, 6 or 12 arms.
Lit.: BBh. 200, 304 a.pl. 198; G 34, 78; KiDG 64, 74 a.pl. 63; KiSB 92, 112; MW 798.

Mahāmārī ("great death, the great destroying goddess"), n. of a personification of cholera, supposed to be a form of Durgā.
Lit.: IC 1:487; MW 799.

mahāmaryādā ("having large limits"), see *mahāgopura*.
Lit.: BECA 1:260.

mahāmātaras "great mothers", n. of a class of personifications of the Śakti or female energy of Śiva. – See also *mātaras*.
Lit.: MW 798.

Mahāmati ("great-minded"; Buddh.), n. of a *mānuṣibodhisattva*.
Lit.: BBh. 79.

Mahāmāyā ("great illusion").

1. (Hind.) N. of a form (a mother-aspect) of *Pārvatī*.
Lit.: B 493, 508 a.pl. 45:2.

2. (Buddh.) M. is now used as an epithet of Māyā ("the great Māyā"), the mother of the Buddha, now as a n. of a Mahāyāna goddess (identical with Māyā?). Char.: colour: blue; att.: *ālīḍhāsana*; Vāh.: *siṅha*; attr.: *ḍamaru*, *kapāla*, *karttṛkā*, *mudgara*.
Lit.: CEBI 73 N. 48; KiSB 76.

3. Mahāmāyā or -māya (Buddh.). Mentioned by G only as n. of a Lamaist *yi-dam*, but otherwise regarded as a variety of the Mahāyāna god Vajraḍāka or Hevajra (Heruka). His Śakti is known as Buddhaḍākinī. Char.: colour: blue; att.: (sitting, standing or dancing the *tāṇḍava*-dance), *yab-yum* with the Śakti; Mu.: *vajrahuṅkāramudrā*; attr.: *caturmukha*, *dhanus*, *dharmapālābharaṇa*, 1 or 2 *kapāla*s, *khaṭvāṅga*, *naracarma*, *śara*, *trinayana*. – N.B. Though n. of a male god M. is, in BBh. and G., generally written with a long final vowel -ā, which may bring about an erroneous identification with the goddess mentioned above as No. 2.
Lit.: BBh. 163; G. 36, 83 (ill.), 84; KiSB 65.

Mahāmāyūrī ("the great peacock-daughter"; Buddh.), n. of a very popular Mahāyāna goddess. She is regarded either as a female *bodhisattva* or as a *mahārakṣā* (or *vidyārājñī*), and as an emanation of Amoghasiddhi. She is the regent of the south (or north: so G) direction. Char.: colour: green (or yellow or red); att.: *rājalīlāsana* or *lalitāsana* or *padmāsana*; Mu.: *dharmacakra-*, *varada-mudrā*; attr.: besides being one-headed, she is sometimes *caturmukha* or *triśiras*, *Amoghasiddhibimba* on the crown, *bhikṣāpātra*, *cakra*, *cāmara*, *candraprabhāmaṇḍala*, *cintāmaṇi*, *dhanus*, *dhvaja*, *kamaṇḍalu* (with jewels), *khaḍga*, *mayūrapattra*, *pātropari bhikṣu*, *śara*, *trinayana*; as a *mahārakṣā*, M. has esp. the attr. *mayūrapattra*, and beside the above mentioned attr. further: *candra*, *daṇḍa*, *ghaṇṭā*, *padma*, *pāśa*, *pātra*, *pustaka*, *triśūla*, *viśvavajra*.
Lit.: BBh. 234, 305 a.pl. 200; G passim; GBM 81; KiDG 64, 72 a.pl. 60-61; KiSB 100, 104, 111; MW 799.

mahāmbuja ("great lotus"; attr., Vāh.), n. both of a "double lotus" (as attr. char. of: Amitaprabha, Dūraṅgamā, Padmanarteśvara, Paramāśva, Prabhākarī) and of a *pīṭha* with two rows of lotus petals, i.e. the lotus of the *pīṭha* has two superimposed tiers of petals. Such a *pīṭha* is char. of Brahmā and esp. of Buddhist icons. – Another n.: *viśvapadma*.
Lit.: B 299, 519; R 2:101.

mahāmudrā "the great Mu.", n. of one among the group *pañcamudrā*. The form of this Mu. is not described. In Vajrayāna Buddhism

m. indicates a mode of attaining *nirvāṇa* while performing the *yab-yum*-rite (cp. *mudrā*).
Lit.: DilP 105; S. CHANDRA DAS, A Tibetan-English dictionary (rev.ed., Delhi etc. 1973), 831.

mahānāga "great serpent", n. of a group of seven snake gods (Ananta, Takṣaka, Karka, Padma, Mahābja, Śaṅkha, Kulika), most of whom are identical with a group of seven *nāgadevas* (see *nāga* 2).
Lit.: MEIA 196.

mahānirvāṇa "the great *nirvāṇa*", "total extinction of individual existence" (MW) (Buddh.), a term often used about the *nirvāṇa* of the Buddha.
Lit.: GoRI 2:31; MW 797.

mahānubhava (N.Ind. *manbhau*, "high-minded"), n. of a Vaiṣṇavite sect in the Mahratta region.
Lit.: IC 1:655.

Mahāpadma ("the great lotus"), n. of a *nāga(deva)* or of a *diggaja*. Attr.: *akṣamālā*, *kamaṇḍalu*, *trinayana*, mark of a *triśūla* on the hood. Cp. Mahābja.
Lit.: Gt Suppl. 73; R 2:557.

mahāpañcarāja "five great kings" (Buddh.), in Lamaism n. of a group of five inferior gods, protectors of cloisters and oracles. They have only Tibetan proper names: 1. Bi-har; 2. Chos-skyoṅ; . dGra-lha (see sub initial Gra-); 4. kLu-dbaṅ (see sub Lu-); 5. Tha-'og-chos.
Lit.: G 37, 92.

mahāparinirvāṇa "the great, complete *nirvāṇa*", see *parinirvāṇa*.
Lit.: MS 46.

Mahāparinirvāṇamūrti ("representation of the great, complete *nirvāṇa*"; Buddh.), n. of a representation of the Buddha lying (in *nirvāṇa*). Another n.: Nirvāṇabuddha.
Lit.: B 275; CBC pl. 15:40; G 55; IC 2:490; JMS 66 a.pl. 85; MBPC 93 a.pl. 143 ff.

Mahāpaṭala-Lokeśvara ("L. of the great veil [or mass, retinue]" [if the spelling -*paṭala*- is reliable]; Buddh.), n. of a variety of Avalokiteśvara. Char.: att.: *samapādasthānaka*; Vāh.: *padma*; attr.: *dhvaja*, *ghaṇṭā*, *kamaṇḍalu*, *nīlotpala*, *triśiras*, *vajra*, *viśvavajra*.
Lit.: 400 a.pl. 59(A); KiDG 54 a.pl. 30.

mahāpīṭha "great pedestal" (Vāh.), n. of a seat which is shadowed by a *kalpavṛkṣa* (instead of a *prabhāvalī*). Char. of Śiva.
Lit.: SSI 76.

Mahāpratisarā (or Pratisarā, "the great protectress"; Buddh.), n. of a *mahārakṣā*, an emanation of Ratnasambhava. She is the regent of the central (or south: thus G) direction. Char.: colour: yellow (or white); att.: *lalitāsana*; Mu.: *varadamudrā*; attr.: esp. *cakra*, *caturmukha*, *cintāmaṇi*, further: *chattra*, *dhanus*, *dhvaja*, *khaḍga*, *paraśu*, *pāśa*, *Ratnasambhavabimba* on the crown, *śaṅkha*, *śara*, *stūpa* (on the crown), (*tarjanīpāśa*), *trinayana*, *triśiras*, *triśūla*, *vajra*.
Lit.: BBh. 243 a.pl. 184 f.; G 34, 78; KiDG 64, 71 a.pl. 58; KiSB 94, 111.

Mahāpratyaṅgirā ("the great [goddess] whose speech is directed westwards" [? probably indicating that she comes from the East, as her origin suggests]; Buddh.), n. of a Mahāyāna goddess, an emanation of Akṣobhya (whose direction is the East). Char.: colour: blue; Mu.: *varadamudrā*; attr.: *Akṣobhyabimba* on the crown, *aṅkuśa*, *khaḍga*, *padma* (red), *tarjanīpāśa*, *triśūla*.
Lit.: BBh. 200, 303 a.pl. 144-146, 196; KiDG 64; KiSB 92.

mahāpreta "giant" (Vāh.), see *mṛtaka*.
Lit.: MEIA 227.

mahāpuruṣalakṣaṇa "(auspicious) mark, sign (on the body indicating) a great man" (attr.; Buddh.), n. of 32 special great marks of the Buddha. To this group belong *abhinīla*, *ūrṇā*, *uṣṇīṣa*; also other attributes, and some *mudrās* and attitudes. – See *lakṣaṇa*, *sāmudrika*.
Lit.: Gw. 138; HIS 16; IC 2:535; KiSB 35.

mahārāja ("great king"; Buddh.), another n. of a *dikpāla*.
Lit.: B 521; KiSB 25.

Mahārājalīla-Mañjuśrī ("M. in the att. *mahārājalīlā*"; Buddh.), in Lamaism n. of a variety of Mañjuśrī. Char.: colour: yellow;

Vāh.: *siṅha* or *siṅhāsana*; att.: *rājalīlāsana* or *lalitāsana*; Mu.: *dharmacakramudrā*; attr.: *nīlotpala*, *puṣpa*.
Lit.: G 68.

mahārājalīlā(sana), as n. of an att., see *rājalīlāsana*.
Lit.: BBh. 432.

mahārājika ("great king"), n. of one among a class of inferior deities, 236 or 220 in number. Also with the Buddhists (as *mahārājikadeva*) n. of a class of gods, inhabitants of the lowest heaven.
Lit.: D 193; MW 799.

Mahārājñī ("the great queen"), see Mahāśakti and Devī.
Lit.: HAHI 18.

mahārakṣā ("great protectress" or "granting great protection"; Buddh.), n. of a group of five protectresses, probably all personifications of amulets or *mantras*: 1. Mahāpratisarā; 2. Mahāmāyūrī; 3. Mahāsāhasrapramardanī; 4. Mahāśītavatī; 5. Mahāmantrānusāriṇī. Common attr.: *chattra*. – Another n.: *pañcarakṣā*. – Cp. also *vidyārājñī* which is perhaps another n. of the same conception. The *buddhaśakti*s may also be related to *m.*
Lit.: BBh. 302; G 34, 78; KiSB 110; MW 799.

Mahāratnakīrti-Lokeśvara ("L. of the great gem-glory"; Buddh.), n. of a variety of Avalokiteśvara. Char.: att.: *samapādasthānaka*; Vāh.: *padma*; attr.: *dhanus*, *kaṣā*, *nīlotpala*, *phala*, *śaṅkha*, *triśiras*.
Lit.: BBh. 399 a.pl. 55(A); KiDG 54 a.pl. 27.

Mahāratnakula-Lokeśvara ("L. of the great gem-family"; Buddh.), n. of a variety of Avalokiteśvara. Char.: att.: *samapādasthānaka*; Vāh.: *padma*; attr.: *akṣamālā*, *Amitābhabimba* on the head, *khaḍga*, *nīlotpala*, *padma*, *pustaka*, *triśiras*. – Cp. *ratnakula*.
Lit.: BBh. 400 a.pl. 58(A); KiDG 54 a.pl. 29.

Mahārātrī ("the great night"), n. of a goddess. As "the Night-of-Eternity" she is connected with Kālī, and as "the Night-of-Splendor" with Kamalā.
Lit.: DHP 268, 284.

maharṣi ("great *riṣi*"), n. of one among a group of *riṣi*s, the leader of whom was Vyāsa.
Lit.: R 2:566.

Mahārudra ("the great Rudra"), epithet of Śiva.

Maha-Sadāśiva(mūrti) ("the great S."), n. of a variety of Sadāśivamūrti with 25 heads and 50 hands. Char.: attr.: *ajina* (tigerskin), *muṇḍamālā*. – Another n.: Mahākailāsa.
Lit.: R 2:373 a.pl. 114:2; SSI 77.

Mahāsahasrabhuja-Lokeśvara ("the great thousand-armed L."; Buddh.), n. of a variety of Avalokiteśvara. Char.: att.: *padmāsana*; Vāh.: *padma*; Mu.: *varadamudrā*; attr.: *khaḍga*.
Lit.: BBh. 399 a.pl. 54(A).

Mahāsāhasrapramardanī (or -inī; personification of a *sūtra*: "the great thousand-fold destroying"; Buddh.), n. of a *mahārakṣā*, an emanation of Vairocana. She is the regent of the east (or central: so G) direction. Char.: colour: white; att.: *lalitāsana*; Vāh.: *padmacandrāsana*; Mu.: *varadamudrā*; attr.: esp. *cakra*, *caturmukha* (but she is also one-headed), *khaḍga*, *pāśa*, further: *aṅkuśa*, *candraprabhāmaṇḍala*, *dhanus*, *dharmapālābharaṇa*, *padma*, *paraśu*, *śara*, *tarjanīpāśa*, *triśūla*, *Vairocanabimba* on the crown, *(viśva)vajra*.
Lit.: BBh. 216, 303 a.pl. 197; G passim; HAA pl. 99; KiDG 64; KiSB 86, 111; MW 801.

Mahāsahasrasūrya-Lokeśvara ("the great L. of a thousand suns"; Buddh.), n. of a variety of Avalokiteśvara with 11 faces. Char.: att.: *samapādasthānaka*; Vāh.: *padma*; Mu.: *abhaya-*, *varada-mudrā*; attr.: *akṣamālā*, *cakra*, *dhanus*, *kamaṇḍalu*, *nīlotpala*, *śara*.
Lit.: BBh. 400 a.pl. 57(A).

Mahāśakti ("the great Śakti"), n. of Devī as a Mother aspect, worshipped by the *śākta*s. – Another n.: Mahārājñī.
Lit.: HAHI 18.

Mahāśaṅkhanātha-Lokeśvara ("L., the great conch-protector"; Buddh.), n. of a variety of Avalokiteśvara. Char.: att.: *samapā-*

dasthānaka; Vāh. : *padma*; Mu. : *buddhaśramaṇamudrā*; attr. : *ghaṇṭā, pāśa, śara*, 2 *vajras*.

Lit.: BBh. 400 a.pl. 56(A); KiDG 54 a.pl. 28.

Mahā-Sarasvatī ("the great S.").

1. (Hind.) N. of a goddess, an emanation of Mahālakṣmī. Attr. : *akṣamālā, aṅkuśa, pustaka, viṇā*.

Lit.: B 496.

2. (Buddh.) N. of a variety of Sarasvatī. Char. : colour : white; Vāh. : *padma*; Mu. : *varadamudrā*; attr. : *hāra, padma* (white).

Lit.: BBh. 349 a.pl. 230; KiDG 64; KiSB 105.

Mahā-Śāstā ("the great Ś."), epithet of Aiyaṉār.

Lit.: SSI 229.

mahāsattva "great being, having a great essence", another term for a *bodhisattva*.

Lit.: KiSB 43.

Mahāsena ("the Great Captain or Great General"), epithet of Skanda.

Lit.: DHP 299.

mahāsiddha ("very perfect, powerful"; Buddh.), in Lamaism n. of a group of 84 magicians who were originally historical persons and authors of Tantric treatises. In G some of them are specifically mentioned; e.g. Saraha, Lui-pa, Tailopa, Nāropa.

Lit.: G 37, 94; HuGT 25.

Mahāśītavatī (or -sitavatī, -śetavatī; "the great cold one"; Buddh.), n. of a *mahārakṣā*, an emanation of Amitābha and of the syllable *JĪṀ*. She is the regent of the north (or west, so G) direction. Char. : colour : red (also yellow or green); Mu. : *abhaya-, varadamudrā*; attr. : she is one-headed or *triśiras*, *Amitābhabimba* on the crown, *(cintāmaṇi)-dhvaja, dhanus, khaḍga, mayūrapattra, padma, paraśu, pāśa, pātra, pustaka* (her chief attr.), *śara, sūryaprabhāmaṇḍala, tarjanīpāśa, trinayana, vajra* or *viśvavajra, vajrāṅkuśa*.

Lit.: BBh. 153, 305 a.pl. 199; G 34, 79; KiDG 64, 75 a.pl. 64; KiSB 98, 112; MW 801.

Mahāśrī-Tārā ("T. of great beauty"; Buddh.), n. of a Mahāyāna goddess, an emanation of Amoghasiddhi. Char. : colour : green; Vāh. : *candrāsana*; Mu. : *vyākhyānamudrā*; attr. : *Amoghasiddhibimba* on the crown, 2 *padmas* at her sides.

Lit.: BBh. 227 a.pl. 169.

Mahāsthāma(prāpta) ("he who has attained great strength", also translated as "greatstance" [WHW]; Buddh.), n. of a Mahāyāna *(dhyāni)bodhisattva*, the embodiment of wisdom. Char. : colour : white or yellow; Mu. : *dharmacakra-, varada-, vyākhyānamudrā*; attr. : *khaḍga* or *padma* or 6 *padmas*; or no attr.

Lit.: BBh. 89 a.pl. 58; BRI 149; EB; G 33, 59, 61; GBM 80; GRI 257; WHW 1:160.

Mahāsthāmaprāpta-Lokeśvara (cp. above; Buddh.), n. of a variety of Avalokiteśvara which is identical with the Padmapāṇi-Lokeśvara-variety.

Lit.: BBh. 431 a.pl. 106(A).

Mahāsūryabimba-Lokeśvara ("L. [of] the great sun-disk"; Buddh.), n. of a variety of Avalokiteśvara. Char. : att. : *samapādasthānaka*; Vāh. : *padma*; attr. : *Amitābhabimba* on the head, *cakra, kamaṇḍalu*, 2 *nīlotpalas, triśiras*, 2 *vajras*.

Lit.: BBh. 400 a.pl. 62(A); KiDG 54 a.pl. 33.

mahātmā 'great soul", an honorific title given to men of great character; M. K. Gandhi is a modern instance of the title being applied to a person in his lifetime.

Mahattarī-Tārā ("the very great T."; Buddh.), n. of a Tārā of green colour.

Lit.: BBh. 307 a.pl. 201.

Mahā-Vairocana ("the great V."; Buddh.), epithet of Vairocana as an "All-*buddha*"

Lit.: GBM 85.

Mahāvajradhātu-Lokeśvara ("L. [of] the great Vajradhātu"; Buddh.), n. of a variety of Avalokiteśvara. Char. : att. : *samapādasthānaka*; Vāh. : *padma*; attr. : *caturmukha, dhanus, ghaṇṭā, kamaṇḍalu, khaḍga, pāśa, śara, triśūla, vajra*.

Lit.: BBh. 428 a.pl. 67(A).

Mahāvajradhṛk-Lokeśvara ("L. the great carrier of the *vajra*"; Buddh.), n. of a variety of Avalokiteśvara. Char. : att. : *samapādasthā-*

naka; Vāh.: *padma*; attr.: *aṅkuśa, caturmukha, dhanus, ghaṇṭā, khaḍga, nīlotpala, pāśa, śara, vajra.*
Lit.: BBh. 428 a.pl. 68(A).

Mahāvajranātha-Lokeśvara ("L., the great protector of the *vajra*"; Buddh.), n. of a variety of Avalokiteśvara. Char.: att.: *samapādasthānaka*; Vāh.: *padma*; Mu.: *abhaya-, varada-mudrā*; attr.: *akṣamālā, padma, pāśa, pustaka, tridaṇḍa, triśiras.*
Lit.: BBh. 428 a.pl. 70(A); KiDG 55 a.pl. 37.

Mahāvajrapāṇi-Lokeśvara ("L., the great Vajrapāṇi"; Buddh.), n. of a variety of Avalokiteśvara. Char.: attr.: *akṣamālā, aṅkuśa, cakra, caturmukha, gadā, khaḍga, nīlotpala, pāśa, pustaka.*
Lit.: BBh. 428 a.pl. 69(A).

mahāvajrapīṭha "the great *vajra*-seat" (Vāh.), n. of a kind of *pīṭha.*
Lit.: R 2:101.

Mahāvajrasattva-Lokeśvara ("L., the great Vajrasattva"; Buddh.), n. of a variety of Avalokiteśvara. Char.: att.: *padmāsana*; Vāh.: *padma*; Mu.: *abhayamudrā*; attr.: *akṣamālā, cakra, kamaṇḍalu, khaḍga, pāśa, śaṅkha, tridaṇḍa.*
Lit.: BBh. 397 a.pl. 29(A).

Mahā-Valli ("the great V."), see Valli.

Mahāvaṇī ("the great voice, Transcendent Word"), epithet of Sarasvatī.
Lit.: DHP 260; R 1:335.

mahāvedi "great altar" (attr.), n. of a sacrificial altar in Vedic religion.
Lit.: IC 1:350; RV 124.

mahāvidyā ("great knowledge, the [ten-objects-of-] Transcendent-Knowledge"), n. of a group of 10 personifications of the Śakti as the female Energy of Śiva. These are: 1. Kālī (Mahārātrī); 2. Tārā (Krodharātrī); 3. Ṣoḍaśī (Divyarātrī); 4. Bhuvaneśvarī (Siddharātrī); 5. Chinnamastā (Vīrarātrī); 6. Bhairavī (Kālarātrī); 7. Dhūmāvatī (Dāruṇarātrī); 8. Bagatā (Vīrarātrī); 9. Mātaṅgī (Moharātrī); 10. Kamalā (Mahārātrī).
Lit.: DHP 268; GH 148; MW 800; (R 1:335).

Mahāvidyā ("Transcendent-Knowledge"), epithet of Sarasvatī or Mahāsarasvatī.
Lit.: B 496; DHP 260.

Mahāvīra ("the great hero"; Jain.), the well-known epithet of the 24th *tīrthaṅkara* (with the NP Vardhamāna), which was given to him when finally becoming an *arhat*. He was the son of the Brāhman Ṛṣabhadatta and Devānandā. According to legend, the embryo of the future M. was transferred from the womb of his mother Devānandā to that of Triśalā (the wife of the *kṣatriya* Siddhārta; cp. the similar episode in the story of Balarāma), and he lived about B.C. 540(?)-477; he died at Pāvā (now Pāvapurī near Patna). He is regarded as the founder of Jainism (but cp. also Pārśvanātha). – Wife: Yaśodā; daughter: Anavadyā; symbol: *siṅha.* – Epithet: Nigaṇṭha Naṭṭaputta. – Since the Jains suppose that the death of M. occurred in B.C. 527, this date constitutes for them the beginning of an era (see *vīrasamvat*).
Lit.: GBB 160; GJ 23, 296 a.passim, a.pl. 16; Gt 372; HIS 16; IC 2:629, 736; IIM 136; KiJ 11 a.pl. 25, 31, 39-43; KiSH 119; KrA pl. 54h; SB 330 a.pl. 266, 276; SchRI 220; WHW 1:493, 2:13.

Mahā-Viṣṇu ("the great V."), in South India n. of a form of Viṣṇu accompanied by two wives. Char.: att.: *lalitāsana*; Mu.: *abhaya-, varada-mudrā*; attr.: *cakra, śaṅkha.* – M. is also a n. of Viṣṇu when worshipped by Buddhists.
Lit.: MW 800.

Mahāviśvaśuddha-Lokeśvara ("the great, wholly-pure L."; Buddh.), n. of a variety of Avalokiteśvara. Char.: att.: *samapādasthānaka*; Vāh.: *padma*; attr.: *samapādasthānaka*; Vāh.: *padma*; attr.: *aṅkuśa, caturmukha, dhvaja, ghaṇṭā, khaḍga, padma, nīlotpala, śaṅkha, vajra.*
Lit.: BBh. 428 a.pl. 66(A).

mahāyajña "great sacrifice", n. of five principal offerings, obligatory for all twice-born Hindus, viz. *bhūta-, brahma-, deva-, manuṣya-* and *pitṛ-yajña* (see these words).
Lit.: IC 1:585; MW 799; WHW 1:360.

Mahāyakṣa ("the great *yakṣa*"; Jain.), n. of a *yakṣa* attending on the 2nd *tīrthaṅkara*. Symbol : *gaja*.
Lit.: GJ 362 a.pl. 24:2; KiJ 11 a.pl. 27:2.

mahāyāna "great vehicle" (Buddh.), n. of the North Indian form of Buddhism (as opposed to *hīnayāna*) which (partly in its secondary, Tantric form, see *vajrayāna*) spread to Tibet, China, Japan, etc. The religious ideal of *m.* is the *bodhisattva*, and its aim is that every human being, and not only the *saṅgha*, the monks, may (after many rebirths) attain to this stage of a *bodhisattva* and thence to *nirvāṇa*.
Lit.: BBh.; G 4; BRI 120; GBM 12; GRI 253; HIS 12; IC 2:564; KiSB 42; WHW 2:14.

Mahāyaśā ("very glorious"; Buddh.), n. of an inferior Mahāyāna goddess attending on Buddhakapāla.
Lit.: BBh. 160.

Mahāyogin (-ī, "the great *yogin*, ascetic"), n. of a form of Śiva. In this form he is represented as naked (*nagna*) and besmeared with ashes (*vibhūti*).
Lit.: DHP 202; H pl. 7:58.

Māhendrī ("the great Indrī"), another n. of Indrāṇī as one of the *saptamātaras*.
Lit.: SSI 190.

Maheśa(mūrti) (or Maheśvara, "the great Lord").

1. (Hind.) N. of a representation of Śiva as the Supreme Lord, usually named Mahādeva. A variety of M. may be the representation of Śiva together with his Śakti. Char. : Mu. : *abhaya-*, *varada-mudrā*; attr. : *aṅkuśa*, *ḍamaru*, *ghaṇṭā*, *jambhīra*, *kapāla*, *khaḍga*, *khaṭvāṅga*, *kheṭaka*, *paraśu*, *pāśa*, *triśūla*, *vajra*, *yajñopavīta* (white). The Śakti has the same Mu. and the attr. : 2 *nīlotpalas*. – M. is also (rarely) an epithet of Kṛṣṇa and of the *dikpālas*, esp. of Indra, Agni, Yama and Varuṇa. – The Śakti of M. is named : Gaurī.
Lit.: B 465; DHP 198; DiIP 136; HIS 20; MW 802; R 2:47, 379 a.pl. 114:1, 116-118; ZM 140.

2. (Buddh.) The Hindu god Śiva is to be found under the n. M. in the pantheon of Mahāyāna Buddhism. Char. : colour : white; Vāh. : *vṛṣan*; Mu. : *añjalimudrā*; attr. : *kapāla*, *triśūla*.
Lit.: BBh. 364.

3. (Vāh., Buddh.) On the lying M. Trailokyavijaya treads.
Lit.: KiSB 79.

Māheśvarī ("the [Śakti] of Maheśvara"), n. of one of the *saptamātaras* (or *aṣṭamātaras* or *navaśakti*). She symbolizes *lobha* ("avarice, desire") or *krodha* ("anger"). In this form she is a female counterpart of Śiva (cp. Maheśvara). She is also represented by the *bījamantra kāmabīja*. Char. : Vāh. : Nandin; Mu. : *abhaya-* (*āhūya-*), *varada-mudrā*; attr. : *akṣamālā*, *ḍamaru*, *dhanus*, *ghaṇṭā*, *mṛga*, *paraśu*, *śara*, *triśūla*, *vajra*. – Another n. : Śaṅkarī.
Lit.: B 186, 506 a.pl. 43:5; BECA 1: pl. 14b; GoRI 1:258; KiSH 53; MEIA 150; R 1:381, 387; SB 184 a.pl. 116; Th. 108.

Mahī ("Earth"), another n. of Bhūmidevī. For *mahī* as a symbolic n. of the number "1", see *saṅkhyā*.
Lit.: SSI 17, 187.

Mahīdharā ("supporting the earth"; Buddh.), n. of a *mānuṣibuddhaśakti*.
Lit.: BBh. 79.

mahiṣa "buffalo" (Vāh., attr.), as Vāh. char. of : Yama (in different forms; the NP of this *m.* is Ugra), Yamadūtī, Yamāri (in different forms), Vārāhī. It is a symbol of Vāsupūjya, Hayagrīva. As attr. : a *m.* is swallowed by Kālī, Mahālakṣmī.
Lit.: GJ pl. 23:12; KiDG pl. 43; KiJ pl. 45; KiSH 87; MEIA 229, 266.

Mahiṣāsuramardinī (or -anī, Mahiṣamardinī; "slayer of the buffalo demon"), n. of one of the principal forms of Durgā, under which she subdued the buffalo-demon (Mahiṣa, Mahiṣāsura). In this form she received from all the gods their special weapons which she carries in her hands. She is usually 8- or 10-armed, and is often depicted treading with one foot upon her Vāh. and with the other foot upon the subdued buffalo-demon. The demon has usually a human head or human upper body, his buffalo head lying severed on the ground beside him. – Char.: Vāh.: *siṅha* (or *śārdūla*); attr.: *aṅkuśa, cakra, daṇḍa, darpaṇa, dhanus, dhvaja, gadā, ghaṇṭā, godhā, kamaṇḍalu, khaḍga, kheṭaka, mudgara, paraśu, pāśa, śakti, śaṅkha, trinayana, triśūla, vajra.* – Other n. or epithets: Caṇḍī, Caṇḍā; cp. also Cāmuṇḍā, Kātyāyanī.

Lit.: B 497 a.pl. 41-42; BP 230 a.pl. 25; DHP 288 a.pl. 26; GOSA pl. 2; HAHI 23 a.pl. 14A; HIS 23, 46, 78 a.pl. 47; IIM 93; KiH 22 a.pl. 71, 73; KiSH 49; KrA 49, 86; MH pl. 61; R 1:345 a.pl. 102 ff.; SB 279; SIB pl. 17; SSI 202; Th. 106; WHW 1:91; ZA 91 a.pl. passim; ZM 213 a.pl. 58-59.

Mahodadhi ("the great ocean"; Buddh.), n. of an inferior Mahāyāna goddess attending on Buddhakapāla.

Lit.: BBh. 160.

Mahodara ("big-bellied"), epithet of Gaṇeśa.

Lit.: DilP 113.

Mahodaya ("great prosperity"; attr.), n. of a mountain. On its summit there grew the herbs which could cure Rāma and his warriors who were wounded in a battle. Hanumān, who was not able to discern the proper herbs, broke off the whole top with all the herbs and brought it to Rāma. After Rāma was cured, Hanumān restored the summit to its place. – As an attr. the top of M. (*śaila*) is carried in one hand by Hanumān.

Lit.: GH 479 a.pl. 8; IIM 104.

mahoraga "great serpent", n. of a snake deity (see *nāga*). In Jainism n. of a kind of *vyantaradevatā*.

Lit.: GJ 237; WHW 2:388.

mahotsava "great festival", cp. *utsava*.

Māi (Māī, Hi.), see Mātā.

MAIṀ (Buddh.), form of a yellow *bīja* from which Maitreya originates.

Lit.: BBh. 81.

maithuna (or *mithuna*) "paired, coupled; copulation", n. of a composite representation of a man and a woman, a loving couple, often engaged in sexual intercourse; often found in the temples as a symbol of fortune. Hence *m.* is a term both for a representation of a man together with a woman, and of the erotic representations, e.g., of Koṇārak and Khajurāho. *m.* does not however properly appear to be the term for religious sculptures showing a god in sexual union with his Śakti, which is esp. connected with the Vajrayāna Tantric form of Buddhism (see *yab-yum*). *m.* is interpreted as "the union of Supreme Man and Nature" (DHP). – *m.* as sexual intercourse also belongs to the *pañcamakāra*. – Other n.: *dampati, yuga(naddha), yugma.*

Lit.: A; DHP 224; FES; LCD; SeKB 214; WHW 1:221, 2:375, 392; ZA pl. passim.

Maitreya (Pāli: Metteyya, "friendly, benevolent, Loving One"; Buddh.), NP of a future human *buddha* (*mānuṣibuddha*); M. is therefore often (and more correctly) regarded as a *bodhisattva.* He originates from the yellow *bīja MAIṀ* and lives in the Tuṣita heaven, and he is worshipped alike by the Hīnayānists and the Mahāyānists. Thus M. is the Buddhist counterpart of the Hindu Kalkin. – He is represented as a rubicund, laughing figure, dispensing salvation to all men. Char.: colour: yellow or golden; att.: esp. *paryaṅkāsana*, also *sthānaka*; Vāh.: *siṅha*; Mu.: *dharmacakra-, varada-, vyākhyāna-mudrā*; attr.: *cakra, campa*, the 5 *dhyānibuddhas* (on the *prabhāvalī*), *kamaṇḍalu* (*kalaśa*), *nāgakeśara*-flower, *stūpa* (in the hair or on the crown), *trinayana, triśiras* (in Tantric forms). His *bodhivṛkṣa* is *nāgapuṣpa* (?). Since he is thought of as not yet having appeared, he has no Śakti.

Lit.: BBh. 80, 93 a.pl. 47, 65; BRI 148; FK 127; G 26, 32, 53; GBB 247 a.pl. 27; Gw. 163; H 32; HAHI pl. 15B; HIS 23; HRT pl. 6; HuGT pl. 31 f.; IC 2:573; JSV pl. 62, 76; KiDG 44, 48 a.pl. 20; KiSB 32, 52; MBPC pl. 157; RN passim; SB 46 a.pl. passim; SIB pl. 31; Th. pl. 36; WHW 1:161; ZA pl. 179.

makara (Vāh.: attr.), n. of a kind of mythological sea-monster, often confounded with the crocodile although represented with a fish's tail and (often) an elephant's trunk; the term is often translated as "dolphin", and some scholars have derived *m.* as a symbol from the dolphin of Aphrodite. It is an emblem of water. – *m.* is the Vāh. of Gaṅgā, Gāṅgeya-Subrahmaṇya, Varuṇa, perhaps also of Kāma (but as a symbol of Kāma it may be better characterized as an attr., cp. *makaradhvaja*). Further it is a symbol of Suvidhi (in a rather *matsya*-like form) and Puṣpadanta. – *m.* is also n. of the *rāśi* "Capricornus". – In the older plastic arts *m.* is used very much as an ornament.

Lit.: BBh. 383; DCSS pl. 44ff.; GH 50, 74; GJ pl. 22:9; Gt 377; H pl. 11; HuGT 12; IC 2:731; KiSH 71, 89; KrA pl. 19; MEIA 233; MW 771; RAAI 273; WHW 1:48; ZA 71.

makara-dhvaja (*-ketana*) "banner marked with a *makara*" (attr.). Char. of: Kāma, Madhukara.

Lit.: B 104.

Makaradhvaja (-ketana; "having a *makara* upon his banner"), epithet of Kāma.

makarakuṇḍala "ear-ring in the shape of a *makara*" (attr.), n. of an ear-ornament made of thin leaves of metal, ivory or wood, in the shape of a crocodile. This is esp. a man's ornament. Two such *m.* "represent the two methods of knowledge, intellectual-knowledge (*sāṅkhya*) and intuitive-perception (*yoga*)" (DHP). – Char. of: Viṣṇu, and Śiva (Rudramūrti), worn in his right ear. – Another n.: *nakrakuṇḍala*.

Lit.: B 289; DHP 158; R 1:24 a.pl. 4:18; SSI 76; WM 104 a.fig. 44.

makaramukha "mouth of a *makara*", n. of a motif in the plastic arts, representing, e.g., a *prabhāvalī* arising from the mouth of a *makara*.

Lit.: SB 75.

makarāsana.

1. "Having a *makara* as seat" (Vāh. or epithet) signifies an image depicted as sitting or standing upon a *makara*, e.g. Gaṅgā (Makarāsanā). Also n. of a *pīṭha* supported by a *makara*.

Lit.: R 1:17 a.pl. 6:2; SM 131.

2. "Dolphin-sitting" (att.), n. of a Yogic posture.

Lit.: KiH pl. 153 row 1:3.

makarasaṅkrānti ("the passage [of the sun] into the [*rāśi*] Capricornus"), n. of a festival of the new year, which marks the beginning of the sun's northern course (*uttarāyana*, about January 12). – Cp. *poṅkal*.

Lit.: GH 353; IC 1:593; MW 771; STP 8:19; WHW 1:355.

makaratoraṇa "portal (adorned) with *makara* motifs". This ornamentation is found on *toraṇa*s and *prabhāvalī*s (cp. *makaramukha*) and often esp. on top of the *siṅhāsana*-pedestal, char. of Jain images.

Lit.: CBC 6 a.pl. 15:39; SSI 265.

Makaravaktrā ("Dolphin Headed"; Buddh.), in Lamaism n. of a *ḍākinī*. Char.: colour, green; att.: *sthānaka*; attr.: *dharmapālābharaṇa, kapāla, karttṛkā, khaṭvāṅga.* She has the head of a *makara* and accompanies Śrīdevī.

Lit.: G 35, 81.

Makkhali Gosāla (or Makkhaliputta; M.Ind.), see Maskarin Gośāla.

makkhan (also *mākhan*, Hi., < Skt *mrakṣaṇa*) "butter" (attr.). A lump of butter is carried in one hand by Bālakṛṣṇa Makkhañcor and Navanītanṛttamūrti.

Lit.: P 1060.

Makkhañcor ("butter-thief"; Hi.), epithet or n. of a form of Bālakṛṣṇa, represented crawling. Attr.: *kṣīrabhājana, makkhan*, perhaps also some kind of rattle. Icons of M., esp. in bronze, are very popular and recall to worshippers the story of how Kṛṣṇa, as a baby, stole butter from the shepherdesses. - Another n.: Makkhanlāl.

Lit.: CBC 17 a.fig. 98f.; FK 120; GI pl. 69; P 1060; R 1:215 a.pl. 67:1-2.

Makkhanlāl ("the darling, infant boy, with the butter"; Hi.), epithet of Bālakṛṣṇa, see Makkhañcor.

Lit.: P 946, 1060.

makuṭa (Pāli), see *mukuṭa.*

Māl ("greatness, great man"; Tam.), epithet of Viṣṇu.
Lit.: TL 5:3175.

mala "dirt, impurity" (attr.) which fetters or restricts the soul in its function. In this sense *m.* is another n. of *pāśa.*
Lit.: GRI 330.

mālā "wreath, garland; a string of beads, rosary" (attr.). This term is used as an abbreviated n. for either *akṣamālā* or *vanamālā.*
Lit.: BBh. 432; G 10 with ill., 16; R 1:310.

Mālā (or Mālyā, "garland"; Buddh.), n. of one of the Lamaist *aṣṭamātaras*, or of a goddess of the *lāsyā*-group. Char.: colour: yellow or red; attr.: *vanamālā* or *ratnadāma.*
Lit.: BBh. 313; G 36, 82.

mālābaddha "binding garland", n. of a kind of ornament in architecture.
Lit.: ZA 270.

Malagiri ("the mountain of impurity" [in JMS named Nālāgiri]; Buddh.), n. of a drunken elephant that was provoked by Devadatta to attack the Buddha as he was begging alms. Overcome by the Buddha's spiritual power M. faltered and laid its head on the ground before him. – Cp. *abhayamudrā.*
Lit.: IIM 134; JMS 64.

mālava(kāla) "the era of Mālava" (the country of Malwa); see *vikramakāla.*

Malhāl Mātā, n. of one of the Bengal *saptamātaras*: she sends diseases.
Lit.: GH 136.

Mallāri-Śiva ("Śiva, the enemy of [the *asura*] Malla"), n. of an *ugra*-form of Śiva. Char.: Vāh.: *aśva* (white) surrounded by 7 dogs (*śvan*); attr.: *ḍamaru, khaḍga.*
Lit.: R 2:191.

Malli ("the act of holding"; Jain.), n. of the 19th *tīrthaṅkara*; according to the *digambaras** M. was a male, but according to the *śvetāmbaras*, a female *tīrthaṅkara.* Symbol: *kamaṇḍalu.*
Lit.: GJ 283; KiSH 143.

maḻu (Tam.) "axe" (attr.), see *paraśu.*
Lit.: JDI 20.

Mālyā, see Mālā.

Māmakī ("mine" or "selfish, greedy"; Buddh.), n. of a female *bodhisattva* or a *(dhyāni)buddhaśakti.* She originates from the blue *bīja MĀṀ* and is regarded as the Śakti of Ratnasambhava (or Akṣobhya: BBh.). – Char.: colour: yellow or blue; att.: *lalitāsana, yab-yum* (sometimes); Mu.: *varada-, vyākhyāna-mudrā*; attr.: *cintāmaṇi, kapāla, karttṛkā, puṣpas* with 3 *mayūrapattras, vajra.*
Lit.: BBh. 52 a.pl. 24; G passim; GBM 81, 156; KiSB 46.

Māmallapuram (now: Mahābalipuram), n. of a place not far from Madras also called "Seven pagodas", with famous rockcut and cave temples from the Pallava era, 7th-8th cc. A.D.
Lit.: AuOW 51; FES 18; ZA pl. 266 ff.

māṉ (Tam.) "antelope" (attr.), see *mṛga.*
Lit.: JDI 20.

Manasā(devī) ("heartful, spiritual"), n. of a snake goddess, "the destroyer of poison", "eine alte Vertreterin destruktiver und zugleich regenerativer Macht" (GoRI). She is said to be the daughter of Kāśyapa and Kadrū or of Śiva, and is the sister of the snake king Vāsuki (or Śeṣa), and the wife of the *riṣi* Jaratkāru. M. represents a gracious, generative aspect of Pārvatī (cp. *nāga*), but she is influenced by the Buddhist goddess Jāṅgulī. In Laṅkeśvara she is flanked by a *liṅga* and a Gaṇeśa. – She is worshipped esp. in Bihar, Bengal and Assam. – Char.: Vāh.: *nāga* (she is shaded by a 7-headed *nāga*); attr.: *kamaṇḍalu, nāga.* – Other n.: Jagadgaurī, Padmāvatī, Pātālakumārī, Viṣaharī.
Lit.: BBh. 1; D 106; GH 137; GoRI 2:20; IIM 97; KiH 23 a.pl. 77; KiSH 47; MG 258; NLEM 363; RIS 21; W 395; WHW 1:399, 2:388.

Mānasa(rovara) ("the most excellent Lake of the Mind"), n. of a lake in the Himālayas, regarded as a heavenly lake, which is a symbol of fertility and from which the four world rivers (which water the four continents) originate.
Lit.: D 106; Gt Suppl. 78; HAHI 8; WM 132.

Mānasī ("mental, spiritual"; Jain.), n. of a *śāsanadevatā* attending on the 15th *tīrthaṅkara*. M. is also a *vidyādevī*.
Lit.: GJ 362 a.pl. 26:15; KiJ 12 a.pl. 29:15.

m̄ānastambha ("house-pillar"; Jain.), n. of a pillar, made of a huge monolith, standing in front of a temple.
Lit.: GJ 400.

Mānavī ("descended from Manu"; Jain.), n. of a *śāsanadevatā* attending on the 10th *tīrthaṅkara*. M. is also a *vidyādevī*. – See also Śrīvatsa.
Lit.: GJ 362 a.pl. 25:10; KiJ 12 a.pl. 28:10.

manbhau (N.Ind.), see *mahānubhava*.

sMan-bla ("physician general"; Tib., pronounced: Man-la; abbreviated form for sMan-gyi-bla bai-duryai 'od-kyi rgyal-po; Buddh.), n. of a medicine *buddha* who is worshipped to a great extent in Tibet. There are two groups of such *buddha*s, one containing 9 *buddha*s (headed by Bhaiṣajyaguru), one containing 8 *buddhas*. This variety of *buddha* may show in its conception influence from an Iranian light-religion. – Char.: Mu.: *dhyāna-*, *varada-mudrā*; attr.: *āmalaka*, *kamaṇḍalu* (*pātra*).
Lit.: G passim; HuGT 21 and passim; IC 2:570; JT 426.

Manda ("slow"), epithet of the planet Saturn, see Śani.

maṇḍala "magic circle" (attr.), n. of a kind of *yantra*. The circle is, in itself, of magic nature, and a *m.* is a picture, containing a geometric disposition of mystic figures and diagrams of symbolic attributes, germ syllables (*bija*) and figures of gods and goddesses; a *m.* signifies water, and cosmos, and this device is used in all Indian religions and held in all to be endowed with magic power. A *m.* can be produced in different ways; it can be drawn on a paper or a thin metal leaf, or be delineated with rice grains on the ground. Such a rice *m.*, a "symbolic offering of the universe" (G), is, e.g., made every day by Buddhists and offered to the gods. It is also used as a mechanical aid to meditation. – *m.* is further a geometrical diagram of the temple, the plan according to which it is constructed. – *m.* is further used as n. of the ringlike arrangement of the *jaṭābandha*. – Cp. *kasiṇa*.
Lit.: BBh. 436; BSA 25; CEBI 31, fig. D., a.pl. 8:30, 9:31, 10:32-33; DHP 352; G 8, 27; GBM 30, 107 a.pl. facing p. 112; GRI 267; IC 1:568, 2:608; SeKB 279; SIB pl. 49; SM 24; STP 3:201; WHW 2:21; ZA 212 a.pl. 608.

maṇḍapa "hall for the worshippers", n. of a hall with pillars in a temple. *m.* often indicates a pavilion to which the idol is brought on special occasions. Cp. *ardha-*, *mukha-*, *nṛtta-*, *sabhā-*, *snapana-maṇḍapa*.
Lit.: DKI 41; GJ 399; IC 2:319; ZA 269, 272.

Mandara ("slow"), n. of the mountain which was used as a churn-staff at the churning of the ocean of milk (see Kūrmāvatāra).
Lit.: D 197; DHP 167; GoRI 1:250; WM 132.

mandāra "the coral tree, Erythrina Indica" (attr.), n. of one of the five heavenly trees, see *vṛkṣa*.
Lit.: GH 65; MW 788; WHW 2:218.

māndāra leaves of the coral tree (*mandāra*)" (attr.). Char. of Gaṇeśa.

mandavāra (or *-vāsara*) "Saturday", see *śanivāra*.

Māndhātā (-tṛ, -tar; "thoughtful[?]"), NP of a universal lord; also n. of an *avatāra* of Viṣṇu.
Lit.: B 391, 427 a.pl. 8:8; D 197; Gt 378; WHW 2:22.

mandir (Hi., < Skt *mandira*) "temple, pagoda; palace".
Lit.: WHW 2:490.

maṇḍūka "frog" (Vāh.) Char. of: Bṛhaspati, Ketu. – Another n.: *bheka*.
Lit.: KiSH 63, 89.

maṇḍūkāsana "frog-sitting" (att.), n. of a Yogic posture.
Lit.: KiH pl. 152 row 3:3.

maṅgala "auspicious sign" (attr.). Usually eight *m.* are mentioned, which differ in the three Indian religions, see *aṣṭamaṅgala*.
Lit.: GBM 102; GJ 384; KiSH 153.

Maṅgala ("auspicious"), n. of the planet Mars.

1. (Hind.) The planet god. Char. : colour : red; Vāh. : (a golden) *ratha* drawn by 8 ruby-red fire-born horses (*aśva*), or *aja*, or *siṁhāsana*; Mu. : *abhaya-*, *varada-mudrā*; attr. : *gadā*, *padma*, *śakti*, *triśūla*. – Other n. : Aṅgāraka, Bhauma, Kuca. – N.B. The planet Mars should, according to some scholars, properly be represented by Śiva, as its "red" colour might indicate. Since the red colour is symbolic of terror and cruelty, the n. "auspicious" could be meant euphemistically in the same way as the n. Śiva is traditionally interpreted; it should, however, be noticed that, in Tamil, the n. of this planet is Cevvāy "the red one". The "euphemistic" n. Maṅgala could therefore suggest a reflection of an older, now forgotten, identification of Śiva as the god of the planet Mars (PARPOLA).

Lit. : D 198; KiH 7; KiK 141; KiSH 62, 88; R 1:319 a.pl. 96; Th. 114; A. PARPOLA etc., Progress in the decipherment of the Proto-Dravidian script (Copenhagen 1969) 15.

2. (Buddh.) The planet god. Char. : colour : red; Vāh. : *aja*; attr. : *karttṛkā*, *muṇḍa*.

Lit. : BBh. 368.

Maṅgalā ("auspicious"), n. of a form of Pārvatī. Char. : Vāh. : *siṁhāsana*; attr. : she is often 10-armed, *akṣamālā*, *candra*, *darpaṇa*, *khaḍga*, *kheṭaka*, *śara*, *triśūla*. – M. is also n. of a female *dvārapālaka* of Gaurī. – Cp. Sarvamaṅgalā.

Lit. : R 1:359, 362.

maṅgaladīpa "auspicious lamp" (attr.), n. of a type of oil-lamp which is swung to-and-fro before an icon.

Lit. : GJ 429.

maṅgalavāra (or *-vāsara*) "Tuesday". -- another n. : *bhaumavāra*.

māṅgalyasūtra, n. of a kind of necklace (attr.). Here *māṅgalya* seems to signify the *tāli*. – Another n. : *tāliccaraṭu*.

Lit. : SB 62, 19 a.passim.

maṇi "jewel" (Skt; cp. Tib. *ma-ṇi* or *ma-ni*; attr.). *m.* is a symbol which grants victory and cures wounds. From early times onwards it was used as an amulet against all kinds of evil. For the Hindu symbol, see *ratna*. In Buddhism *m.* may be regarded as an abbreviated word-form of *cintāmaṇi* which, in this dictionnary, is used as a common term. – In the Lamaist *mantra* : *oṁ ma-ṇi pad-me hūṁ*, the word *ma-ṇi* may, according to the usual meaning, signify the Buddha or Avalokiteśvara. Other scholars declare that *m.* is here equivalent to *liṅga*; in this sense *m.* is also compared with *vajra* (Tib. *rDo-rje*).

Lit. : BBh. 436; G 65; GJ 257; HuET 47; IC 2:593; KT 148; MKVI 2:119; SM 154.

Maṇibhadra (also Māṇi-; "the excellent one with jewels").

1. (Hind.) N. of a king of *yakṣas* and brother of Kubera. M. is the patron of travellers and merchants. Attr. : *gadā*, *kamaṇḍalu*, *koṣa*, *ratna*.

Lit. : GoRI 1:324; MW 775.

2. (Buddh.) N. of a king of *yakṣas*.

Lit. : BBh. 380; KiSB 74.

ma-ṇi chos 'khor (Tib., pronounced : *ma-ni chö khor*) "prayer-wheel, praying-cylinder" (attr.; Buddh.). *m.* is a cylinder rotating about an axis, and contains one or more strips inscribed with prayers or *mantras* (most commonly the *mantra* : *oṁ ma-ṇi pad-me hūṁ*), which may be repeated hundreds of times on the strips. At every turn of the cylinder all the prayers written on the strips are considered as having been prayed. – There are many kinds of *m.* Most common is the hand-*m.*, which belongs among the equipment of every Lamaist monk. It is made of copper or bronze and has a wooden handle. On the outside of the cylinder the above mentioned *mantra* is often engraved or beaten out in relief (often in Indian *lantsa*-characters; GBM). A larger type of *m.* is placed on a table, and still larger types are found in the temples. They are placed outside, in a row round the *garbhagṛha*, and are set in motion by the monks walking round the *garbhagṛha*. Some forms of temple *m.* can be very large (several metres high) and may contain whole scriptures, such as bKa'-'gyur or bsTan-'gyur. – According to HuGT, a common hand-*m.* should be named *ma-ni 'khor-lo*, while a larger *m.* should be labelled as *chos-'khor-lo.* – Another n. : *mantracakra*.

Lit.: G 8, 10 (with ill.); GBM 94, 101; GRI 297; HuGT 75, 107; JSV 98, 102; JT 58, 409; D. MacIntyre, Hindu-Koh (1891), 230, 254; R. Pischel, Leben und Lehre des Buddha. 2. Aufl. (1910), 119.

Maṇidhara ("holding a jewel"; Buddh.), n. of an inferior Mahāyāna god, attending on Ṣaḍakṣarī. Attr. : *cintāmaṇi, padma*.

Lit.: BBh. 125; KiSB 57.

ma-ni-'khor-lo "prayer wheel", see *ma-ṇi chos 'khor*.

Māṇikkavācakar (or *-vāśagar*, "ruby-worded"; Tam.), n. of a *śaivabhakta* who lived about A.D. 900. Char. : Mu. : *vyākhyānamudrā*; attr. : *pustaka*.

Lit.: CBC 11 a.fig. 19; GJ 62; JDI 55; R 2:480 a.pl. 137f.; SB 347 a.pl. 310; Th. 120 a.pl. 71B; WHW 2:24.

māṇikya (Tam. *māṇikkam*) "ruby, carbuncle", n. of a precious stone included both among the *navaratna** and the *pañcaratna**.

Lit.: TL 5:3153.

māṇikyapātra "ruby-bowl" (attr.).

Lit.: ACA 35, 36

maṇimālā "string of beads" (attr.), see *akṣamālā*.

Lit.: BECA 1:262.

Maṇipadma-Lokeśvara ("L. (of) the jewel-lotus"; Buddh.), n. of a variety of Avalokiteśvara. Char. : att. : *padmāsana*; Vāh. : *padma*; Mu. : *añjalimudrā*; attr. : *akṣamālā, padma*. Cp. Ṣaḍakṣarī-Lokeśvara.

Lit.: BBh. 396 a.pl. 22(A).

mañjā (or *mañji*, Panj.; properly "couch") "diocese" (Sikhism). The Sikh brotherhood was divided into 22 *m.*, each under the care of a pious Sikh. These *m.* were "couches" on which the *gurus* sat issuing instructions to their audiences and organising the Sikh *sangats* (see *saṅgha*).

Lit.: GG p. LXV

mañjīra "foot-ornament, an elliptical ornament worn on the upper surface of the foot" (attr.).

Lit.: B 292; MW 774.

Mañjughoṣa ("whose sound is sweet"; Buddh.), n. of a variety of Mañjuśrī. He is an emanation of Akṣobhya. Char. : colour : white or golden yellow; att. : *padmāsana* or *lalitāsana* or *sthānaka*; Vāh. : *siṅha*; Mu. : *dharmacakra-, varada-, vyākhyānamudrā*; attr. : *Akṣobhyabimba, caturmukha, dhanus, ghaṇṭā, khaḍga, nīlotpala, pustaka, śara, vajra*.

Lit.: BBh. 95; BRI 149; G 68; KiSB 53.

Mañjukumāra ("the charming son or youth"; Buddh.), n. of a variety of Mañjuśrī. Char. : att. : *padmāsana*; Mu. : *varadamudrā*; attr. : *cīratraya, dhanus, khaḍga, nīlotpala, pustaka, śara, triśiras, vajra*.

Lit.: BBh. 104, 119 a.pl. 88; KiDG pl. 22; KiSB 55.

Mañjunātha ("the charming protector"; Buddh.), n. of a variety of Mañjuśrī. Char. : Mu. : *varadamudrā*; attr. : *cakra, cintāmaṇi, khaḍga, padma, triśiras, vajra*.

Lit.: G 66; KiSB 56.

Mañjunātha-Lokeśvara ("L. as M."; Buddh.), n. of a variety of Avalokiteśvara. Char. : att. : *samapādasthānaka*; Vāh. : *padma*; attr. : *akṣamālā, pustaka*.

Lit.: BBh. 430 a.pl. 96(A).

Mañjuśrī (translated in different ways: "Pleasing splendor; sagesse transcendentale; die milde Heiligkeit or Herrlichkeit"; personification as the god of wisdom; Buddh.), NP of a very popular and celebrated *(dhyāni)bodhisattva* who is the Buddhist counterpart of the Hindu Brahmā. He is worshipped in all Buddhist countries, and he is made an offspring of either Amitābha or Akṣobhya. Closely connected with M. is Prajñāpāramitā who, however, is not regarded as his Śakti, but rather as a personification of the scripture (*pustaka*) which he usually carries in one hand. The usual type of M. is represented thus : colour : black or yellow (golden), or white or red; att. : *padmāsana* or *rājalīlāsana* or *lalitāsana*; Vāh.: *śārdūla* (or *siṁha*); Mu.: *dharmacakra-*, *dhyāna-*, *varada-*, *vyākhyānamudrā*; attr.: esp. *khaḍga* (*prajñākhaḍga*), *pustaka*, further: *dhanus*, *nīlotpala*, *śara*, *triśiras*.

M. is met with in many varieties; KiSB mentions 14: Vāc, Dharmadhātuvāgīśvara, Mañjughoṣa, Siddhaikavīra, Vajrānaṅga, Nāmasaṅgītimañjuśrī, Vāgīśvara, Mañjuvara, Mañjuvajra, Mañjukumāra, Arapacana, Sthiracakra, Vādirāṭ, Mañjunātha (see separately). – G. lists 12 forms: 1. The usual type (see above); 2. Dharmacakramañjuśrī; 3. Mañjughoṣa; 4. Mahārājalīlamañjuśrī; 5. Dharmaśaṅkhasamādhimañjuśrī (Vāc); 6. Siddhaikavīra; 7. Arapacana; 8. Vajrānaṅgamañjughoṣa; 9. Mañjuvajra; 10. Dharmadhātuvāgīśvaramañjuśrī; 11. "Archaic Mañjuśrī" (5-headed, 8-armed, with Śakti; attr.: 4 *pustaka*s, 4 *khaḍga*s); 12. Yamāntaka. – BBh. describes 13 forms: Vajrarāga, Dharmadhātuvāgīśvara, Mañjughoṣa, Siddhaikavīra, Vajrānaṅga, Nāmasaṅgītimañjuśrī, Vāgīśvara, Mañjuvara, Mañjuvajra, Mañjukumāra, Arapacana, Sthiracakra, Vādirāṭ. – Other epithets: Aṣṭāracakravat, Śārdūlavāhana. See also *trimūrti*.

Lit.: B 558; BBh. 94, 100 a.pl. 66; BRI 149; CEBI pl. 13:39; G passim; GBB 247; GBM 80; GRI 256; Gw. 175; H 33; HAHI 22 a.pl. 11B; HSIT 17 a.pl. 44; HuGT pl. 22; IC 2:574; KiDG 45, 49 a.pl. 21-22; KiSB 48, 52; KT 137; NLEM 357; Th. 72 a.pl. 34.

Mañjuvajra ("the charming *vajra*"; Buddh.), n. of a variety of Mañjuśrī. Char.: colour: red; att.: *padmāsana*, *yab-yum* with the Śakti; Mu.: *varadamudrā*; attr.: *dhanus*, *khaḍga*, *padma* (*nīlotpala*), *śara*, *triśiras*, 2 *vajra*s. The Śakti is *triśiras* and bears, in the same manner, the corresponding attr.

Lit.: BBh. 118 a.pl. 87; G 69; KiSB 55.

Mañjuvara ("the charming selected"; Buddh.), n. of a variety of Mañjuśrī. Char.: colour: golden yellow; att.: *lalitāsana*; Vāh.: *siṁha*; Mu.: *dharmacakramudrā*; attr.: *nīlotpala*, *pustaka*.

Lit.: BBh. 117 a.pl. 83-86; KiSB 54.

Maṅkhaliputta (M.Ind.), see Maskarin Gośāla.

Manmatha ("sexual love", also translated as "the Churner-of-the-heart", DHP), epithet of Kāma.

Lit.: B 301; DHP 314; JDI 100; R 1:276 a.pl. 82-83; Th. 56.

Manogupti ("preserving, restraint of mind"), see Manovegā.

Manonmanī ("excited in mind [?]"), n. of a form of Durgā, also said to be the Śakti of Śiva in his aspect as Sadāśiva. Attr.: *kapāla*, *khaḍga*.

Lit.: DiIP 136; MW 785; R 1:364.

Manovegā ("speed or velocity of thought"; Jain.), n. of a *śāsanadevatā* attending on the 6th *tīrthaṅkara*. – Another n.: Manogupti.

Lit.: GJ 362 a.pl. 24:6; KiJ 12 a.pl. 27:6; MW 785.

māṁsa "flesh, meat" (attr.). A piece of (cooked) *m.* is char. of Śivadūtī, Vāruṇī. – *m.* also belongs among the *pañcamakāra*.

Lit.: R 1:365; WHW 1:221.

māṁsakapāla "(skull-)bowl filled with (human) flesh" (attr.).

Lit.: : BBh. 435.

māntirīkam (Tam., derived from Skt *mantra*) "magic, art of exercising supernatural powers (attr.). Many forms of *m.* are described in DiIP. Cp. *mantraśāstra*.

Lit.: DiIP 268; TL 5:3160.

mantra (Tam. *mantirikam*) "thought-form, magic formula, mystic syllable(s)" (attr.). A *m.* consists of a sequence of syllables, with or without intelligible sense. It is shorter than a *dhāraṇī* and is believed to be a contracted form of a *dhāraṇī*; often a *m.* is found within a *dhāraṇī* (at the beginning or the end and sometimes in the middle of it), and it is intended as a means whereby the mass may obtain salvation, simply by muttering it. A *m.* may be either *kaṇṭhika* "throated" (i.e. voiced, uttered aloud) or *ajapa* "non-uttered" (i.e. not spoken but repeated internally). – *m.* is used in all Indian religions, and as an example of a (Buddhist) *m.* may be mentioned: *oṁ ma-ṇi pad-me hūṁ**. –

A special type of the *m.* is the *bījamantra.* – A written *m.* may also, as a charm, be put into a hollow image which, by this *m.*, receives the quality of being a manifestation of the deity (so esp. in the Nepalese and Tibetan images). – As particular *m.* see, e.g.; *agniprajvālana, agnistambhana, aṣṭākṣara, brahmagāyatrī, brahmamantra, dvādaśākṣara, gāyatrī, haṅsamantra, khecarībīja, krodhaśānti, mantrarāja, nidrāstambhana, pañcādaśī, pañcākṣara, parāśakti, parameṣṭhīmantra, rudramantra, ṣaḍakṣara.*

Lit.: BBh. 29, 436; DHP 334; DilP passim; GBM 18, 93; GH 54; GJ 366; GoRI 2:28; GRI 182; Gt 380; IC 1:565; RV 122; SM 18; TL 5:3068; WHW 2:25; ZA 112 a.pl. 610.

mantracakra "prayer wheel", (attr.), better known under the Tibetan term *ma-ṇi chos 'khor.*

mantrarāja "king of *mantras*" (attr.), n. of a *mantra*, attributed to Kṛṣṇa, with the form: *ŚRĪṀ, HRĪṀ, KLĪṀ Kṛṣṇāya Svāhā*: "*Śrīṁ, Hrīṁ, Klīṁ*, oblation to Kṛṣṇa". Purpose: To inspire divine love and lead to liberation.

Lit.: DHP 346.

mantraśāstra "magic science": "eine Art okkulter Sprachwissenschaft, welche den geheimen Sinn von Formeln usw. studiert, um über die sich in denselben manifestierenden Potenzen Gewalt zu haben".

Lit.: GoRI 1:248.

mantravādin "reciter of *mantras*", see *māntrika.*

mantrayāna ("magic vehicle"), see *vajrayāna.*

Lit.: SM 18; WHW 2:25.

māntrika (or *mantravādin*) "reciter of spells (*mantras*), enchanter, sorcerer".

Lit.: MW 810.

Manu ("man, mankind"), n. of a mythological primeval father or progenitor of mankind. Properly there are 14 Manus, mythological progenitors and rulers of the earth at different mythic periods (*manu* is consequently also a symbolic n. of the number "14", see *saṅkhyā*). By the n. M. the seventh of these is usually understood; this M. is said to be the son of Vivasvān (Sūrya; hence he has the epithet Vaivasvata) or of Brahmā (Svayambhū). Another epithet: Satyavrata.

Lit.: D 199; DHP 326; GH 91; GoRI 1:235; Gt 380; IC 1:533; IIM 118; WHW 2:27, 29; WM 133.

Manuja ("born of Manu"; Jain.), n. of a *yakṣa* attending on the 11th *tīrthaṅkara.*

Lit.: GJ 362.

mānuṣa "man" (Vāh.), see *nara.*

Lit.: MEIA 227.

mānuṣaliṅga ("*liṅga* belonging to mankind"), n. of a class of *acalaliṅga* which comprises those *liṅgas* which are set up by human hand (in contrast to, e.g., *svāyambhuvaliṅga*). On a certain part of these certain lines (*brahmasūtras*) are carved, and the top may have a different characteristic shape (see *śirovarttana*). – Different classes of *m.* are: *sārvadeśika-, sarvasama-* (or *sarvatobhadra-*), *vardhamāna-, śaivādhika-, svastika-, trairāśika-* (or *traibhāgika-*), *āḍhya-, nāgara-, drāviḍa-, vesara-, aṣṭottara-, śata-, sahasra-, dhāra-, śaiveṣṭya-, mukha-liṅga.* – Of these, the *mukhaliṅga* has one or more human faces carved on its sides; see also Liṅgodbhavamūrti.

Lit.: B 458; R 2:86.

mānuṣamuṇḍa "human head" (attr.), see *muṇḍa.*

Lit.: BBh. 368.

Mānuṣa-Vāsudeva ("the human V."), epithet of Kṛṣṇa (the son of Vasudeva), which characterizes him as a human *avatāra* of Viṣṇu. Attr.: *cakra, śaṅkha.*

Lit.: R 1:239.

mānuṣibodhisattva "human (mortal) *bodhisattva*" (Buddh.), a little-used term probably originating in a hyper-systematization: whilst a series of five *dhyānibuddhas*, five *mānuṣibuddhas*, and five *dhyānibodhisattvas*, is usually posited, a series of five (or seven) *mānuṣibodhisattvas* is sometimes added. – This series (of seven) consists of: Mahāmati, Ratnadhara, Ākāśagañja, Śakamaṅgala, Kanakarāja, Dharmadhara, Ānanda. – See further *trikāya.*

Lit.: GBB 248.

mānuṣibuddha "human (or mortal) *buddha*" (Buddh.), n. of a kind of saviour working on earth, contrasting to a *dhyānibuddha* (see further *trikāya*). The concept is closely associated with Mahāyāna Buddhism, but the Hīnayānists also believe in *m.* and recognise 24 *m.* Among the Mahāyānists 32 names have been recorded (they give several lists of *m.*). Generally a series of 5 *m.* is mentioned, namely: 1. Krakucchanda; 2. Kanakamuni; 3. Kāśyapa; 4. Śākyamuni (= the historical Buddha); 5. Maitreya (a future *buddha*). In the older tradition, however, they counted 7 *m.*: 1. Vipaśyin; 2. Śikhin; 3. Viśvabhuj; 4. Krakusunda (probably = Krakucchanda); 5. Kanakamuni; 6. Kāśyapa; 7. Śākyamuni; and as a future and 8th *m.* they sometimes added Maitreya. Other series of *m.* also occur; in Lamaism, e.g., the following: 1. Dīpaṅkara; 2. Kāśyapa; 3. Gautama (= Śākyamuni); 4. Maitreya; 5. Bhaiṣajyaguru.

A *m.* is distinguished by three kinds of mental characteristic: 10 *bala*s, 18 *āveṇika dharma*s, and 4 *vaiśaradya*s. Further common char.: att.: *padmāsana*; Mu.: *bhūmisparśamudrā*; attr.: *bodhivṛkṣa*, *ūrṇā*, *uṣṇīṣa*, and long ears.

Lit.: BBh. 76 a.pl. 45; G 30, 53; GBB 248, 250; H 32; IC 2:588; KiDG 44; KiSB 31.

mānuṣibuddhaśakti "Śakti of a *mānuṣibuddha*". There is a series of 7 *m.*: Vipaśyantī, Śikhimālinī, Viśvadharā, Kakudvatī, Kaṇṭhamālinī, Mahīdharā and Yaśodharā.

Lit.: BBh. 79.

manuṣyakautuka "festival of human beings" or "human wonder", n. of an intricate device of varied human figures or bodies interwoven together in architectural decoration.

Lit.: GOSA 18 a.pl. 7.

manuṣyaloka "the human world" (according to the Jain cosmic system).

Lit.: KiJ 5 a.pl. 5, 7.

manuṣyayajña "man-offering", the honouring of guests; one of the five *mahāyajña*s. Another n.: *narayajña*.

Lit.: IC 1:585; MW 784; WHW 1:360.

Māra ("killing; death; Destroyer, Tempter").
1. (Hind.) Epithet of Kāma.

Lit.: DHP 314.

2. (Buddh.); god and Vāh.) M. as "the Tempter", "der Tod, der Böse" (GoRI), is "die symbolische Verköperung des Bösen" (KiSB), the Evil-One, who created several hindrances in the way of the Buddha and who corresponds to Kāma in Hindu mythology. Attr.: *mīnadhvaja*. The four Hindu gods Brahmā, Viṣṇu, Śiva and Indra are, in Buddhism, regarded as four *māra*s (i.e. 4 forms of M.), and some Buddhist deities are depicted treading them underfoot, e.g. Hevajra, Vidyujjvālākarālī.

Lit.: B 301; BBh. 159, 195; GoRI 1:228; IC 2:475; JMS 51; KiSB 13.

marakata(maṇi) "emerald" (attr.). Held in one hand, char. of Sudurjayā. It is further a precious stone included both among the *navaratna** and the *pañcaratna**.

Lit.: BBh. 335; TL 5:3083.

mārgaṇa "arrow" (attr.), see *śara*. For *m.* as a symbolic n. of the number 5, see *saṅkhyā*.

Lit.: MEIA 148.

mārgaśīrṣa (relating to the *nakṣatra* Mṛgaśiras), n. of a month (November-December). Its god is Rudra.

Lit.: BBh. 382; IC 2:733.

Mārī ("killing"; Buddh.), n. of a *dhāraṇī* (personification). Char.: colour: reddish white; attr.: *sūci*, *sūtra*, *viśvavajra*.

Lit.: BBh. 220, 339.

Marīci (light, ray of light"), n. of a demiurge or *prajāpati*, who was born of Brahmā. He was the father of Kāśyapa. Sometimes he is counted among the *ṛṣi*s. Wife: Sambhūti.

Lit.: DHP 317, 324; GoRI 1:263; WHW 2:38; WM 133.

Mārīcī ("shining", derived from *marīci* "light"; Buddh.), NP of a Mahāyāna goddess of

the aurora, who is a distant counterpart to the Hinduist Sūrya. She is regarded as a female *bodhisattva* and as an emanation from and the Śakti of Vairocana. Sometimes she is also mentioned as the mother of Śākyamuni. In her three-headed form (*triśiras*) she passes for the Śakti of Hayagrīva. In this instance her left face is that of a swine (*varāhamukha*). – Char. : colour : yellow, red or white; att. : *lalitāsana, sthānaka*; Vāh. : *ratha* drawn by 7 *sūkaras* (the charioteer is either a goddess without legs, or Rāhu, a head without a body), or *padma*, also drawn by *sūkaras*; Mu. : *tarjanī-, varada-, vyākhyāna-mudrā*; attr. : she is one-headed, or *triśiras* or *ṣaṇmukha*; *aśoka* (yellow), *aśvamastaka* (a little horse-head image in the hair), *cakra, cāmara, dhanus, dharmapālābharaṇa, khaḍga, pāśa, śara, sūci, sūrya, sūtra, trinayana, vajra, varāhamukha*. – Varieties: Āryamārīcī, Aśokakāntā, Daśabhujasitamārīcī, Mārīcīpicuvā, Ubhayavarāhānanamārīcī, Vajradhātvīśvarī.
Lit.: BBh. 207; G 12, 33, 74; KiDG 25, 64 a.pl. 47 ff.; KiSB 81, 104.

Mārīcīpicuvā (Buddh.), n. of a variety of Mārīcī. Char. : colour : golden; Vāh. : Prajñā and Upāya; attr. : *aṅkuśa, aśoka*-leaf, *dhanus, pāśa, śara, sūci, sūtra, trinayana, triśiras, vajra*. – Varieties : Aṣṭabhujamārīcī (Saṅkṣiptamārīcī).
Lit.: KiDG 64, 65; KiSB 82.

Mārī Māī(yā) (or Mārī Māī; Hi., < Skt *mārī[ka]*, "Mother Death, Mother Plague"), n. of a cholera goddess, who is regarded as the sister of Śītalā. See also Māriyammaṉ.
Lit.: GH 135; MG 256.

Māriṇī ("killing"; Buddh.), n. of an inferior Mahāyāna goddess, attending on Buddhakapāla.
Lit.: BBh. 160.

Māriyammaṉ (Māriyammai, Māri Amma "death, smallpox mother", Tam. and other Drav. word-forms for Mārī Māī), n. of a frightful South Indian goddess, the smallpox deity (cp. Śītalā), who is regarded as one among the group *navaśakti* or as a *grāmadevatā*, and also identified with Kālī. In honour of M. the ceremony *carkh pūjā* is performed. – Attr. : *ḍamaru* (entwined by a *nāga*), *kapāla, khaḍga, pāśa, śuka, triśūla*. – Cp. Mātā(ji), Ammaṉ, Muttālammaṉ. – Another n. : Māriyāttāḷ.
Lit.: DiCh. 20, 33; FKR 109; GH 136, 356; GoRI 2:6, 13; IC 1:487; KiH 24 a.pl. 80; KiSH 51; MG 253; SSR 134, 147.

Māriyāttāḷ (-yattāḷ, "death mother"; Tam.), see Māriyammaṉ.
Lit.: JDI 114.

mārjāra "cat" (Vāh.). Char. of Sastī (Ṣaṣṭhī).

Mārkaṇḍeya (or -kaṇḍa), NP of a *śaivabhakta*, blessed by his lord with the boon of eternally remaining a youth of sixteen years. Char. : Mu. : *añjalimudrā*; attr. : *puṣpa*.
Lit.: B 486; JDI 18; SB 183 a.fig. 115; TL 5:3169; WHW 1:607.

Mar-pa (Tib.; Buddh.), NP of a pupil of Atīśa who lived in the 11th c. A.D. He founded the Lamaist *Kar-gyu-pa*-sect and was the teacher of Mi-la-ras-pa. Attr. : *kapāla, pustaka*.
Lit.: G 38, 106; JT 412.

Mārtāṇḍa (or Mārt(t)aṇḍa, "sun", also interpreted as "the bird in the heavens" = the sun), n. of an aspect of the sun-god (Sūrya).
Lit.: B 428, 550.

Mārttaṇḍa-Bhairava, n. of a syncretistic representation of Sūrya and Śiva Bhairava. Char. : colour : red; attr. : *akṣamālā, cakra, ḍamaru, kapāla, khaṭvāṅga, nāga, nīlotpala* or *padma* (red), *pāśa, śakti, triśiras, triśūla*.
Lit.: B 549; MEIA 8, 95.

Marukal-Naṭeśa ("Naṭeśa of [the town of] Marukal"), n. of a form of Śiva Naṭarāja, in the Madras museum, belonging to the type of *kālmāṟi-āḍiya-tāṇḍava**.

marutgaṇa, *maruts*, n. of a class of storm-gods who, in the Vedic religion, are friends and allies of Indra. They are said to be the sons of Rudra or of Kāśyapa and Diti.
Lit.: D 204; DHP 103; GoRI 1:61; Gt 386; IC 1:321; IIM 96; MG 72; R 2:569; WM 133.

māsa "month". This word usually denotes a solar month; for the lunar month, see *candramāsa* (see also at that point details of the periodic adjustments between the solar and the lunar months, in accordance with which *māsa* may be regarded as "lunisolar"). In this dictionary only the 12 usual Hindu months are listed (*caitra, vaiśākha, jyaiṣṭha, āṣāḍha, śrāvaṇa, bhādrapada, āśvina, kārttika, mārgaśirṣa, pauṣa, māgha, phālguna*) but not the Vedic or other Indian names of months (see further IC, MKVI). The Indian month generally begins about the 21st of the corresponding European month; hence, e.g., *caitra* corresponds to the period about March 21-April 20, and here therefore *caitra* is interpreted as "March-April". – For the year, see *saṃvatsara*, and concerning *m.* as a symbolic n. of the number "12", see *saṅkhyā*.
Lit.: Enc. Brit. 4:622; IC 2:732; MKVI 2:156.

maṣībhājana (or *maṣi-*, *masī-*) "ink-stand" (attr.). This symbol is used together with *lekhanī*. Char. of: Agni, Brahmā, Piṅgala-Gaṇapati.
Lit.: MEIA 269.

Maskarin Gośāla ("one who carries a bamboo cane, and one who was born in a cow-stall"), n. of the founder of the *ājīvika* sect. He lived at the same time as the Buddha and Mahāvīra, i.e. about B.C. 500, and, according to Jain tradition, was at first the pupil of Mahāvīra, but later apostatized from him. – Other name-forms: Maskariputra, Makkhali Gosāla, Maṅkhaliputta.
Lit.: GJ 28; GoRI 1:286; GRI 134; SchRI 227; WHW 1:21.

Maskariputra, see Maskarin Gośāla.

mastaka "head, skull" (attr.), see *muṇḍa*. It also forms part of compound words, signifying certain animal heads, e.g. *aśvamastaka* "horse-headed".

Mātā(ji) (or Māi, Māī, Hi., < Skt *mātā, mātṛ* "mother"), as n. of a goddess may originally reflect the "Great Mother", the Primeval Mother of all living beings. It should be noted that the wives of the demiurge Kāśyapa are called *mātaras*. In North India M. is, in every village, the n. given to the tutelary deity (cp. also *grāmadevatā*), which in South India is named Ammā (Ammaṉ). – M., also called Mahā Māi, is also regarded as a smallpox goddess.
Lit.: DIA pl. 1; P 977; ZA 68.

Mātali, n. of the charioteer (*sūta*) of Indra.
Lit.: DHP 110; Gt 387.

Mātaṅga ("elephant"; Jain.), n. of a *yakṣa* attending on the 7th and the 24th *tīrthaṅkaras*. Symbol: *gaja*.
Lit.: GJ 362 a.pl. 27:24; KiJ 11 a.pl. 30:24.

Mātaṅgī ("female elephant" or "elephant power, the Power of Domination"), n. of the mythical mother of an elephant tribe; also regarded as epithet of Kālī (or Durgā, Pārvatī). M. also belongs to the group *mahāvidyā* and is represented there by Moharātrī.
Lit.: AIP 74 a.pl. 55 (317); DHP 283; FKR 110; MG ill. facing p. 177; MW 806; SSR 149.

mātaras (or *mātṛs, mātṛkās*) "mothers", collective n. of the Divine mothers, a species of tutelary deity. This n. also refers to the wives of the demiurge Kāśyapa, and these seem therefore originally to have been Mother goddesses. The *m.* are also called Śaktis, and they are consequently personifications of the energy of certain gods (e.g. Indrāṇī of Indra, Brahmāṇī of Brahmā, Vaiṣṇavī of Viṣṇu, Kaumārī of Kumāra, Māheśvarī of Maheśvara, etc.). Their number differs; mostly they are said to be seven (*saptamātaras**) or eight (*aṣṭamātaras** or *ambāṣṭaka**), sometimes also nine (*navaśakti*), but other numbers are also given (e.g. 16, or even 50; see lists in B, KiSH, MW). – The images of the *m.* are usually made of stone; in bronze only three of them are said to occur, Brahmāṇī, Kaumārī, Vaiṣṇavī. They are usually represented in a terrific shape, sitting (*lalitāsana* or *ardhaparyaṅkāsana*, the respective Vāh.

under the *pīṭha*), sometimes on corpses (*pretāsana*, see also *mṛtaka*). Mu.: *vyākhyā-namudrā*; attr.: (sometimes) *bālā*, *kaṅkālī*. *mātṛkā* is also n. of the sign or letter (*bīja*) which is written in a meditational diagram (*yantra*). – Cp. Mahāmātaras, *śakti*; see also Mātāji.

Lit.: B 503 a.pl. 43-44; BECA 1: pl. 14-17a; D 206; GH 135; GoRI 2:42; HIS 17; KiSH 53; MEIA 150; MW 1044; SSR 145 (with ill.); WM 137.

maṭha "cloister, college (for young Brāhmans)".

Lit.: GoRI 2:83.

Mathurā (Engl. Muttra), n. of the birth-town of Kṛṣṇa, situated on the shore of the River Yamunā; also n. of a centre of activity in the arts from the 1st-10th cc. A.D.

Lit.: D 206; FBKI 144; RAAI 92; SeKB passim; WHW 2:47; ZA pl. 59 ff.

Mathurakaviyāḻvār (or Matura-; Tam.), n. of a *vaiṣṇavabhakta* (South India).

Lit.: R 2:480 a.pl. 136.

Mati ("thought, mind, perception"; personification; Buddh.), n. of an inferior Mahāyāna goddess.

Lit.: KiSB 105.

Mātṛ(s), see Mātāji, *mātaras*.

mātṛkā(s), see *mātaras*. – For *m.* as n. of a type of *yantra* consisting of a written letter, see *bīja* and *bījamaṇḍala*.

Lit.: GRI 177.

matsya "fish" (Vāh. and attr.), as Vāh. char. of: Varuṇa, Gaṅgā; symbol of: Ara, Kinnara; as an attr. (held in one hand) char. of: Gaurī, Śivadūtī, Vārāhī. Two *matsyas* are symbols of the Rivers Gaṅgā and Yamunā. In Buddhism and Jainism two *m.* (*matsyayugma*) are "symbols of happiness and utility" and also form a *maṅgala* (see *aṣṭamaṅgala*); they signify "increase", since fish themselves increase very rapidly. – *m.* also belongs among the *pañcamakāra*. – Other n.: *galaka*, *rohitamatsya*, *sāmiṣa*; and cp. *mīna*.

Lit.: BBh. 364; G 8 (ill.); GBM 102; GH 74; GJ 384; KiJ 21 a.pl. 45; KiSH 155; R 2:530; WHW 1:221.

Matsya, Matsyāvatāra ("fish-incarnation"), n. of the first *avatāra* of Viṣṇu, in which, in the shape of a huge fish, he saved Manu, the Primeval man, from a great deluge. This story has a certain likeness to the Sumerian and biblical stories of the Deluge. Comparisons have also been made with some forms of fish-gods in Assyria and with the Philistine god Dagon, which perhaps (together with this M.) point to a common Sumero-Dravidian deluge-legend. In this connection it should also be noted that, according to some scholars, the fish-sign in the Indus script signifies a god. – In the older Indian tradition M. was regarded as a manifestation of Prajāpati or Brahmā; later also as a manifestation of the planet Ketu. – In this form Viṣṇu is often represented with the lower-body of a fish and a human upper-body with 4 arms. Char.: Mu.: *abhaya-*, *varada-mudrā*; attr.: *cakra*, *śaṅkha*. – Another n.: Mīna.

Lit.: B 390, 413; ChI 593; D 206; DHP 165; GH 120; GoRI 1:250; Gt 389; JDI 70; KiH 13 a.pl. 97; KiSH 36, 38, 40; KrI pl. 48; MEIA 28; MG 109; R 1:124 a.pl. 35; Th. 59; W 113; WM 134.

matsyayugma "pair of fishes" (attr.), see sub *matsya*. Another n.: *mīnamithuna*.

Lit.: GJ 384.

matsyendrāsana "the posture of Matsyendra" (att.), n. of a Yogic posture (Matsyendra is n. of a teacher of *yoga*).

Lit.: KiH pl. 152 row 1:4 f.

mattaḷam (Tam. < Skt *mardala*; SMII: Tam. *maṭaḷam*) "drum" (attr.), n. of a kind of long drum which is beaten with the hands. Char. of Nandīśvara.

Lit.: JDI 54 a.fig. 14; MD 2:425; SMII 73.

Māttāṅkī (Tam.), see Mātaṅgī.

mātuluṅga(phala) "citron, sweet lime; pomegranate" (attr.), see *jambhīra*.

Lit.: R 1:336, 2:135, 372; WM 106.

Maturaivīraṉ (or -vīrappaṉ, Madurai-; "the hero of Madurai"), n. of a fierce deity of lower rank, worshipped in South India (the deification of a police officer who lived in the 17th c. A.D. He eloped with the king's daughter and was killed.). He is regarded as the god of wine (*kaḷḷu**), and he attends on Aiyaṉār. Attr.: *khaḍga*, *kheṭaka*.

Lit.: DiIP 237; GH 91; JDI 115; SSR 123, 144; SB 358 a.fig. 360; L. DUMONT, Une sous-caste de l'Inde du Sud (Paris 1957) 139.

Maudgalyāyana (Pāli Mogallāna; patronymic of Maudgalya; Buddh.), n. of one of the first pupils of the Buddha. Attr.: *kāṣāya*, *khakkhara*.

Lit.: BRI 16; G 14, 104; KiSB 15.

mauktikajālaka "pearl-festoons" (attr.).

Lit.: BECA 1:262.

mauli "head, top of anything", a common n. of ornaments relating to the head, such as crown, diadem etc. – Cp. *mukuṭa*.

Lit.: B 286; R 1:26.

maulimaṇi "crest gem, jewel worn in a diadem" (attr.).

Lit.: MW 837; SIB pl. 18.

maulin "crowned", see *mukuṭin*.

Lit.: BBh. 165.

Maunavratin (-ī; "performing a vow of silence"), n. of a form of Viṣṇu. He displays a certain form of Mu., for which see sub *mudra* 1 b).

Lit.: B 406 a.pl. 24.

mauñji "girdle of *muñja*-grass" (attr.). Char. of Brahmacāri-Subrahmaṇya.

Lit.: DiIP 186; R 2:443.

Maurya, n. of a dynasty (323-187 B.C.), the first member of which was Candragupta; the best-known emperor of this dynasty was Aśoka. Under this dynasty the first notable manifestations of Indian arts (after the Indus Valley culture) occurred. – The badge of this dynasty was the *mayūra*.

Lit.: D 207; Gz 38; RAAI 39.

māviḷakku (Tam.) "flour lamp", "lamp made of sugared dough with cotton wick, fed with ghee and placed in the presence of a deity" (TL; attr.).

Lit.: DiIP 140, 176; MD 2:461; TL 5:3180.

Maya ("artificer, measurer"), n. of "the-Architect-of-the-Antigods" (*asuras*; DHP).

Lit.: DHP 315; MW 789; WHW 1:91.

Māyā(devī) ("illusion, Power-of-Illusion", regarded as the source of cosmos or the visible universe; personification).

1. (Hind.) M. is epithet of Durgā as a mother aspect of Pārvatī. – Māyādevī is n. of the wife of Pradyumna.

Lit.: B 493; D 207; DHP 28; Gt 391; STP 6:34; WHW 2:53; WM 134.

2. (Buddh.) Māyā(devī) is n. of the mother of the Buddha. M. is regarded in this conception as the Buddhist counterpart of the Hindu Lakṣmī as a manifestation of the World-Lotus (cp. Padmā); from this World-Lotus the Buddha was born. – Sometimes M., as the mother of the Buddha, has the epithet Tārā.

Lit.: BBh. 31; CEBI 22, 73 N.48; KiSB 8; ZA 333 a.pl. 31d a.passim.

māyābīja ("Seed-of-Illusion"), n. of a *bīja-mantra*. Form: *HRĪṀ*. "This *mantra* represents *māyā*, the power of Illusion" (DHP). It is attributed to Bhuvaneśvarī. – Another n.: *śaktibīja*.

Lit.: DHP 342; IC 1:567.

Māyājālakrama(-Avalokiteśvara) (or -Lokeśvara, Māyājālakramāryāvalokiteśvara; "the [honourable] A. who has his going or course in the net of illusion"; Buddh.), n. of a form of Avalokiteśvara. Char.: colour: blue; att.: *ālīḍhāsana*; Mu.: *tarjanīmudrā*; attr.: he is 12-armed, *Amitābhabimba* on the crown, *aṅkuśa*, *cakra*, *cintāmaṇi*, *ḍamaru*, *dhanus*, *dharmapālābharaṇa*, *kapāla*, *khaṭvāṅga*, *nāga*, *padma* (red), *pañcaśiras*, *pāśa*, *śara*, *trinayana*, *vajra*.

Lit.: BBh. 139, 394 a.pl. 5(A); G 12, 67; KiDG 52; KiSB 60.

Māyājālakramakrodha-Lokeśvara ("L. of wrath owing to his going in the net of illusion"; Buddh.), n. of a variety of Avalokiteśvara. Char.: att.: *ālīḍhāsana*; attr.: *ajina* (both tiger- and deerskin), *aṅkuśa*, *cakra*, *cintāmaṇi*, *kapāla*, *khaḍga*, *kheṭaka*, *pañcaśiras*, *pāśa* and *tarjanipāśa*, *śara*, *triśūla*, *vajra*.

Lit.: BBh. 395 a.pl. 15(A).

Māyājālakrama-Kurukullā ("K. who has her going or course in the net of illusion"; Buddh.), n. of a Mahāyāna goddess who is an emanation of all *dhyānibuddhas*. Char.: colour: red; att.: *padmāsana*; Vāh.: Takṣaka; Mu.: *abhaya-*, *trailokya-vijaya-mudrā*; attr.: *akṣamālā*, *aṅkuśa*, *bimba* of the 5 *dhyānibuddhas* on the crown, *dhanus*, *kamaṇḍalu*, *kunda*-sprout, *padma* (red), *śara*.
Lit.: BBh. 151; KiDG 64; KiSB 103.

mayil "peacock" (Tam.), see *mayūra*.

mayūra (M.Ind. *mora*, Hi. *mor*) "peacock" (Vāh.). In the Ṛgveda and Atharvaveda *m.* is mentioned with reference to its efficacy against poison, this very likely having to do with the bird's function as a snake-killer. It is later also regarded as the bird of immortality (KrA) and as a variety of the sun-bird (cp. Garuḍa; for the further symbolism of *m.* see Skanda). As a Vāh. char. of esp. Skanda (or Kārttikeya, in different forms; the NP of his *m.* is Paravāṇi), further of: Kaumārī, Mahāmāyūrī, Vajradharma-Lokeśvara; 2 *m.* are Vāh. of Amitābha; a *m.* is also sometimes found standing next to Sarasvatī. *m.* is a symbol of Kendra, Kumāra. It was also the emblem of the Maurya dynasty. – Other n.: *barhin*, *mayil*, *śikhin*.
Lit.: DHP 298, 300; GH 71; H pl. 15:158, 161; HuGT 20; IIM 86 (ill.); KiSH 88; KrA 200; MEIA 230; MKVI 2:134; Th. 52, 103 a.pl. 4b; WHW 1:155.

mayūramudrā "peacock-handpose" (Mu.), n. of a variety of the *mukulamudrā*, with the difference that the tips of the thumb and the ring-finger are touching, the little and fore-finger upright and back, the middle finger straight but slightly forward. It symbolizes beak, creaper, wiping away tears, discussion.
Lit.: WHW 2:87.

mayūrapattra "peacock-feather", a bundle of the tail-feathers of a peacock (attr.). Char. of: esp. Skanda, further Bhikṣāṭanamūrti, Jāṅgulī, Kaṅkālamūrti, Mahāmāyūrī (the yellow form), Mahāśītavatī, Māmakī (3 *m.*), Parṇaśavarī, Ṣaṇmukha, Śaraddevī, Śiva in *sandhyātāṇḍava*, Śrīdevī. – A *m.*, as a cult-object, is used for dusting-off images. – Other n.: *mayūrapiccha*, *śikhidhvaja*, *śikhipiñcha*.
Lit.: G 16; GJ 429; Th. 99.

mayūrapiccha (or *-puccha*) "bundle of the tail-feathers of a peacock", see *mayūrapattra*.
Lit.: BBh. 436; G 8, 16 (ill.).

mayūrāsana "peacock-sitting" (att.), n. of a Yogic posture in which "the legs are crossed as in *padmāsana*, the body is made to lean forward so that the weight rests on the flat of the palms placed on the floor; the body is then raised and balanced on the hands" (WHW).
Lit.: KiH pl. 152 row 2:3; WHW 1:75.

mayūr dīpak (Hi.) "peacock-lamp" (attr.), n. of a kind of *dīpa* which has a stand in the shape of a peacock. – Cp. *haṅsadīpa*.
Lit.: MH 7:3.

Medhā ("wisdom, intelligence"; Buddh.), n. of an inferior Mahāyāna goddess, who is the Śakti of Śrīdhara.
Lit.: KiSB 105; R 1:233.

medhi "base of a *stūpa*" (Buddh., architectural term). A *m.* may be either round or quadrangular in shape and made up of one or more terraces.
Lit.: CHIIA 30; DKI 14; ZA 233.

Meghanāda ("Roar-of-the Cloud"), n. of the son of Rāvaṇa who once got the better of Indra and therefore received the epithet Indrajit ("Indra-conqueror").
Lit.: DHP 110; IIM 76.

mekhalā "girdle" (attr.). Char. of goddesses. – *m.* also forms part of the *ṣaṇmudrā*. Cp. *kaṭibandha*, *ratnamekhalā*.
Lit.: B 292; BBh. 438; SB 337; WHW 2:161.

Menā or Menakā, NP of an *apsarās* or a mountain goddess, the wife of Himavān and the mother of Gaṅgā and Pārvatī.
Lit.: D 208; MW 833; WM 134.

Meru.

1. N. of a mythical mountain in the Himālaya range which, according to the cosmic system, is situated in the middle of

the continent Jambudvīpa (= India). M. is the Olympos of the Hindus, and upon it the heaven of Indra is located (*svarga*). – An epithet of M., Sumeru, has a special sense among the Buddhists.

Lit.: D 208; GJ 237; Gt 392; IC 1:547; IIM 109; KiH 5 a.pl. 2; KiJ 5 a.pl. 6, 11-14; KiK; WHW 1:254; WM 134.

2. (Attr.) An image of M., held in one hand, char. of Śavarī. (This should not be confused with the *śaila* Mahodaya as attr.).

Lit.: BBh. 311.

merudīpa (Tam. *māruttipam*) "Meru-lamp" (attr.), n. of a quadrangular plate (with a handle) upon which is a 'mountain' made up of many small oil-lamp bowls, arranged in tiers or 'terraces' and provided with wicks. It is waved before images of the gods. Cp. *nakṣatradīpa.*

Lit.: TL 6:3354.

meṣa "ram" (Vāh.). Char. of: Agni, Kubera, Khen-ma; a ram is also said to be the sacred animal of Varuṇa, see *uraṇa.* – *m.* is further n. of the *rāśi* "Aries".

Lit.: BBh. 383; GH 50; IC 2:731; KiSH 87.

meṣādi "beginning with (the *rāśi*) *meṣa*"; this refers to the year (*samvatsara**) beginning with the month (*caitra*) which is connected with the *rāśi meṣa.* Hence it is partly another term for *caitrādi.*

Metteya (Pāli), see Maitreya.

miga (Pāli), see *mṛga.*

Mi-la-ras-pa ("dressed in cotton"; Tib., pronounced Mi-la-re-pa; Buddh.), NP of a Buddhist reformer in Tibet who lived in the 11th-12th cc. A.D. and was a pupil of Mar-pa. He belonged to the *Kar-gyu-pa*-sect. Attr.: *kāṣāya, pātra.*

Lit.: G 5, 38, 106; JT 413; Ras-chun, Tibet's great yogi, Milarepa, ed. with introd. and annot. by W. Y. Evans-Wentz (2nd ed. Oxford 1951).

mīna (from Tam. *mīṉ*; cp. Mīnākṣī) "fish", as n. of a Vāh., see *matsya*; *m.* is also n. of the *rāśi* "Pisces". – Mīna is further used as another n. for Matsya (Matsyāvatāra).

Lit.: BBh. 383 a.pl. 248; GH 50; IC 2:731; WM 134.

mīnadhvaja "fish standard" (attr.), char. of Māra.

Lit.: JMS 59.

Mīnākṣī (Tam. Mīṉākṣi; "fish-eyed"), n. of a fish-eyed goddess in South India, who is very likely a local deity (since she has a big temple at Madurai), but who is also regarded as the Śakti of Śiva, equivalent to Durgā, and as the daughter of Kubera. Son: Ugra.

Lit.: DiCh. 27; GoRI 2:14; MW 818; WHW 2:71; WM 136; ZA 115.

mīnamithuna "pair of fishes" (attr.), see *matsyayugma.*

mithuna "(loving) pair", see *maithuna.* – *m.* is also "the act of love". – *m.* in the sense of "a pair of twins" is further n. of the *rāśi* "Gemini".

Lit.: BBh. 383; FES 9; GH 50; GOSA passim IC 2:731.

Mitra ("friend" or "friendship"), n. of an Āditya. In the Vedic religion M. was connected with Varuṇa. Attr.: 2 *padma*s, *soma, triśūla.*

Lit.: D 209; DHP 115; GoRI 1:230; IC 1:318; R 1:309; WM 136.

mleccha "foreigner, barbarian", n. given to non-Hindu groups of population, such as Muslims and Christians who are regarded by he Hindus as unclean. – It is possible that the term *m.* originally indicated a pre-Indo-Aryan population (cp. Sum. *Meluḫḫa*, Pāli *milakkha*; Parpola and others).

Lit.: GRI 317; Gt 400; MW 837; A. Parpola etc., Decipherment of the Proto-Dravidian inscriptions of the Indus civilization (Copenhagen 1969), 3.

modaka(bhāṇḍa) "sweets, a kind of sweetmeat" (attr.). *m.* esp. signifies a rice-cake or rice-puff, but it is also used as a common term of several closely allied attributes which are all fruits (*phala*) and symbols of agricultural fertility, such as *āmra, dāḍima, ikṣu, jambhīra, jambū, kadala, kaṇiśa, kapittha, mūlaka, panasaphala.* – *m.* is esp. char. of Gaṇeśa (in different

forms); it is held in one hand or in the trunk. – Another n.: *laḍḍu(ka)*.
Lit.: B 358; R 1:50, 56.

Mogallāna (Pāli), see Maudgalyāyana.

Moharātrī ("the Night-of-Illusion"), n. of an aspect of *mahāvidyā*, representing Mātaṅgī.
Lit.: DHP 283.

Mohenjo-Dāṛo (or Moenjo-; "the town of the dead"), n. of a village in the Indus Valley, one of the sites of the so-called Indus (Valley) civilization. Excavations there have revealed remains of a culture dating from about B.C. 2500-1800.
Lit.: Gz 23; RAAI 11; WIA 94; WIC 27.

Mohinī ("the Illusive" or "Illusion"), n. of a female representation (or *avatāra*) of Viṣṇu in which form he/she became the mother of Aiyaṉār (with Śiva as the father). And in this shape Viṣṇu is thought of as forming part of the composite deity Hariharamūrti. M. is therefore pertinent to the endeavours to bring about a syncretistic fusion between Vaiṣṇavism and Śaivism. – For the symbolism of M., see also *yoni* and *trikona*. – M. is further n. of a female *dvārapālaka* of Gaurī.
Lit.: B 391; DHP 165, 186 a.pl. 14; KrA pl. 130; R 1:362; SSI fig. 61; Th. 57; WHW 1:43; WM 192.

Mojaghāñjabala-Lokeśvara (meaning doubtful; Buddh.), n. of a variety of Avalokiteśvara. Char.: att.: *samapādasthānaka*; Vāh.: *padma*; Mu.: *abhayamudrā*; attr.: *pāśa*.
Lit.: BBh. 394 a.pl. 2(A).

mom(a)battī-dānī (Hi.; *mom* perhaps < Skt *madhu-mala* "bees-wax") "holder of a candle-stick" (attr.).
Lit.: P 1094.

mora (M.Ind.; Hi. *mor*) "peacock", see *mayūra*.

mṛdaṅga "a kind of drum, barrel-shaped and two-headed" (attr.). Char. of companions of the gods. Cp. *ḍholaka*.
Lit.: B 303; MW 830; SMII 71; WM 110.

mṛga (Pāli *miga*) "gazelle, antelope, deer; ram, buck". *m.* as a symbol, signifying the principal deity as the Lord of animals or of all living beings, may be traced back to the Indus Valley civilization. In Buddhism *m.* symbolizes the first sermon of the Buddha.

1. (Vāh.). Char. of: Vāyu, Śaraddevī; a white *m.* draws the *ratha* of Candra; *m.* is further a symbol of Śānti. For *m.* connected with some forms of Śiva, see below. – Other n.: *hārin*, *mṛgāṅka*; variety: *sūtraharin*; cp. also *kṛṣṇamṛga*.
Lit.: GJ pl. 23:16; KiJ pl. 45; KiSH 88.

2. (Attr.) *m.* as a little image is represented as held (in one hand) by the hind legs, either with the head hanging down (like ram), or as a buck, in the pose of "bucking up". It is esp. char. of Śiva and it is said that the deer is held by Śiva "as a trophy of the occasion when he destroyed the sacrifice of his father-in-law Dakṣa" (SSI). *m.* is met with in many representations of Śiva, esp. as Paśupati, but also as Candraśekhara-, Ekapāda-, Kalyāṇasundara-, Kevala-, Liṅgodbhava-, Mṛtyuñjaya-, Śiṣyabhāva-, Somāskanda-, Sukhāsana-, Vīṇādhara-, Viṣapraharaṇa-, Vṛṣavāhana-mūrti, further as Vṛṣārūḍha, Śarabha, *mūrtyaṣṭakas* and yet other forms of Śiva, further of Caṇḍeśvarī, Māheśvarī, Nandīśvara. A free *m.* accompanies Śiva in some forms, as Aghora, Bikṣāṭana- and Kaṅkāla-mūrti. – See also *paśu*.
Lit.: B 463; H pl. 3:28; R 1:11 a.pl. 3:15-16; SSI 267 a.pl. IV:17; Th. 42.

Mṛgadāva ("deer-park"), n. of a place in Sārnāth (near Vārāṇasī) where the Buddha preached his first sermon. – As part of the celebrations of a visit of the Dalai Lama in 1956 a small enclosure for gazelles was made here in commemoration of this deer-park.

mṛgāṅka "deer-marked, *mṛga* as symbol" (attr.), see *mṛga*
Lit.: B 549.

mṛgasiṅhāsana "antelope-(lion-)seat" (Vāh.), n. of a kind of *pīṭha* with antelope figures carved on the supports. – Cp. *siṅhāsana*.
Lit.: MH 44.

Mṛgaśiras (or -ā, -śīrṣa; "head of a gazelle"), n. of a *nakṣatra*. Its influence is good.
Lit.: BBh. 381; IC 2:729.

mṛnmaya "made of (baked or unbaked) clay" (attr.), n. of a kind of icons, e.g. *mṛn-maya liṅga*. See also *calaliṅga*.
Lit.: R 2:76.

mṛtaka or *mṛtakāsana* "corpse" or "having a corpse as seat" (Vāh. or attr.). A deity may sit or tread upon a *m*. Char. of: Āryavajravārāhī, Cāmuṇḍā, Caṇḍeśvarī, Ekajaṭā, Kālikā, Kṛśodarī, Kuliśeśvarī, Mahācīnatārā, *mātaras*, Nairātmā, Nirṛti, Oḍḍiyāna-Kurukullā, Ugra-Tārā, Vajracarcikā, Vajrayoginī, Vāsya-Vajravārāhī. – Other n.: *preta*, *pretāsana*, *śava*; see also *nara*, *rākṣasa*.
Lit.: BBh. 199, 438.

Mṛtyuñjaya ("conquering death"), epithet of Śiva and n. of one among the group *ekādaśarudra*. Char.: Mu.: *dhyāna-*, *jñānamudrā*; attr.: *ajina*, *akṣamālā*, *kamaṇḍalu*, *kapāla*, *mṛga*, *muṇḍamālā*, *pāśa*, *triśūla*.
Lit.: MEIA 53; R 3:391; WM 137.

Mṛtyuvañcana-Tārā ("T., the death-cheater"; Buddh.), n. of a white Tārā. Attr.: *cakra*.
Lit.: BBh. 308; MW 828.

Mucalinda (or Mucilinda; Buddh.), n. of a king of *nāgas*, the tutelary deity of a lake near Bodh Gayā, who sheltered the Buddha from a violent storm (after his Enlightenment) by coiling himself around him. – Cp. *nāga*.
Lit.: KiSB 14; MS 69; ZA 64.

Mucalinda-Buddha (or Mucilinda-), epithet of the Buddha as sheltered by the *nāga* king Mucalinda. Sculptural representations of this form of Buddha are rare in India itself, but are more often found in Ceylon, Indo-China and Java. – Iconographically M. displays a connection with the Jain Pārśvanātha, since he is represented sitting, sheltered by a *nāga* which spreads out its many-headed hood behind the head of the Buddha. Attr.: *saṅghāṭi*.
Lit.: CBC pl. 15:38; IIM 130; MBPC 78 a.pl. 114, 116; ZA 63 a.pl. 557-559.

Mudader (Drav.), n. of a *bhūta* in South India.
Lit.: KiH 27 a.pl. 102.

muddā (Pāli), see *mudrā*.

Mudgala, n. of a Vedic *ṛṣi*.
Lit.: D 210; Gt 403.

mudgara "hammer" (attr.). Esp. in Buddhism the term *m*. is sometimes used synonymously with either *daṇḍa* or *gadā*. Char. of: Aghora, Ahirbudhnya, Aja, Caṇḍā, Cundā, Ekapādamūrti, Gaṇeśa (in different forms), Ghaṇṭākarṇa, Hara, Hemantadevī, Jayanta, Kāladūtī, Kirātārjunamūrti, Kṛṣṇayamāri, Mahākāla, Mahāmāyā, Mahiṣāsuramardinī, *navadurgās*, Śarabha, Sureśvara, Tryambaka, Viśvarūpa, Vidyujjvālākarālī, Yamāntaka.
Lit.: BBh. 436; MEIA 246; R 1:52.

mudrā (or sometimes *mudrikā*; Pāli *muddā*; Tam. *muttirai*) "seal, sign, token" (e.g. a mark of divine attributes impressed upon the body).

1. *m*. is sometimes conceived as a bodily att. and as one of the component parts of *aṅgika*, but it is above all n. of a certain position or intertwining of fingers or a pose of hands which is practised in religious worship (it is in this sense that the abbreviated form "Mu." is used in this dictionary). It is possible that some traces of *m*. are already to be found in the Indus Valley civilization (cp. *añjalimudrā*), but thereafter *mudrās* seem to have been first met with in the Buddhist Gandhāran plastic arts, from where they spread to the other religions. Originally the *m*. (disregarding the *añjalimudrā* above-mentioned) had perhaps no precise iconographic meaning; in the times of Gandhāran arts the number of symbolic handposes seems to have been small, but their number later increased greatly. *Mudrās* in this later period became gestures that "assume metaphysical meanings", and "with the development of Esotericism, they become endowed with magico-religious values" (SM).

In the term for a Mu. the word-member *-hasta-* is very often included or substituted for *-mudrā*. It is said that if the whole hand or arm participates in the pose, the word *-hasta-* should be included, but that it should be left out if only one or some of the fingers are involved. However, this rule is not strictly followed; thus, e.g., the name-forms *abhayamudrā*, *abhayahasta* and *abhayahastamudrā* are used promiscuously. Another rule (even that not regularly followed) lays down that *-hasta* should signify an attribute held in a hand, but *-mudrā* should indicate a finger pose : thus, *kapālahasta* should mean "a cup held in the hand", but *kapālamudrā* "a finger pose suggesting a cup"; from this it would seem to follow that the former meaning should rather be labelled as an attribute than a Mu. – Some authors say that *hasta* is the common n. of a handpose, the term *mudrā* being used when the gesture has some religious significance. Others stress the fact that the term *-mudrā* is esp. used in Buddhist works, and the term *-hasta* in Brāhmanic works.

The *mudrās* are either *asamyukta* (*asamyuta*) "uncombined" (i.e. performed with one hand) or *samyukta* (*samyuta*) "combined" (performed with two hands). It is said that there are 32 'major' handposes, 12 hand movements and 24 combined handposes, but many minor variations are also found (see the index of Mu., which includes a selection of hand-positions). *Mudrās* may further be performed either by gods or by worshippers (as well as in dancing); in this dictionary however we are chiefly concerned with *m.* of the first kind; note that the second kind of *m.* can be performed by inferior gods and attendants of gods.

m. also belongs among the *pañcamakāra*.

Lit.: B 246; BBh. 437; DiIP 69; GBM 96; GJ 373; GoRI 1:338; GRI 266; HIS 42; IC 1:569, 2:593; KM; SIB 61; SM; SeKB 163 fig. 53; Th. 26; WHW 2:85; WM 96.

There are also some *mudrās* which are unnamed in iconographic literature, or of which the Sanskrit names are unknown to me. These "unnamed" *mudrās* include:

(a) A "handpose where two fingers (index and thumb) are put inside the mouth in order to produce some whistling sound".

Lit.: B 262 a.pl. 2:21.

(b) The clenched (right) hand is raised towards the mouth with the index finger placed on the chin or on a corner of the lower lip. This pose is a token of silence. Char. of Maunavratin.

Lit.: B 261 a.pl. 3:6-7, 24.

(c) The hand (with the palm inwards) is placed upon the mouth. This pose indicates the attitude of silent respect and ungrudging obedience of the devoted follower. Char. of Hanumān.

Lit.: B 261; KIM pl. 29-30; R 1 : pl. 54.

(d) Both hands are stretched forwards, the palms turned up. This pose depicts humility and devotion (so Th.). However, according to IIM, the bronze statuette of Hanumān here referred to originally held a lamp in its hands. The same pose is also, in bronze statuettes, found performed by Garuḍa who is not normally a lamp-holder.

Lit.: IIM 102; Th. 64 a.pl. 17A.

(e) Both hands, one-on-another, the palms downwards, are held under the chin. This pose depicts contemplation.

Lit.: SIB pl. 18.

2. Esp. in Vajrayāna esoteric mysticism *m.* is used as a term for "die konsekrierte Frau", the female consort, giving the original meaning of "manifestation of magical efficacy". Cp. *mahāmudrā*.

Lit.: GBM 160; SM 7.

3. In Yogic practice *m.* is also n. of several forms of breathing exercises which are not given detailed consideration in this dictionary.

Lit.: KiH pl. 155f.

mudrādaṇḍa "*mudrā*-staff" (attr.), n. of a sort of staff which is used while performing the *aṅkuśamudrā*.

Lit.: DiIP 106 with ill.

mudrikā "little seal", as a term for handposes sometimes used instead of the usual term *mudrā*.
Lit.: WHW 2:85.

Mūkāmbikā ("the dumb mother"), epithet of Vindhyavāsi-Durgā.
Lit.: SSI 220.

mukhaliṅga "face-*liṅga*" (attr.), n. of a kind of *mānuṣaliṅga*, on the outside of which one or more faces, representing different aspects of Śiva, are carved. Cp. Pañcamukhaliṅga.
Lit.: B 460; R 1:18, 2:97 a.pl. 7:3, 9 ff.; ZA 209 a.pl. 566.

mukhamaṇḍapa "front-hall", n. of a temple-hall situated in front of the *ardhamaṇḍapa*.
Lit.: BECA 1:262; SSI 2.

mukhayāma "facade" of a temple.
Lit.: BECA 1:262.

Mukhendra ("the chief Indra", i.e. "the chief king"; Buddh.), n. of a king of *yakṣas*. – Another n.: Sukhendra.
Lit.: BBh. 380; KiSB 74.

mukhyāvatāra "chief, principal incarnation", n. of a complete *avatāra* of Viṣṇu, e.g. as Kṛṣṇa, Rāma, etc.
Lit.: GH 131.

mukkuṭai (Tam.) "umbrella of three tiers, peculiar to an *arhat*".
Lit.: TL 6:3219.

muktā (Skt; Tam. *muttu*) "pearl" (attr.). It is also included among the *navaratna** and the *pañcaratna**.
Lit.: MEIA 214; MW 820; TL 6:3255.

Muktakeśī ("loose-haired", having the hair dishevelled or hanging down), n. of a form of Durgā. Char.: Mu.: *abhaya-*, *varada-mudrā*; attr.: *khaḍga*.
Lit.: MW 821.

muktāsana "liberated sitting" (att.), n. of a Yogic posture in which "both ankles are placed against the *yoni*-place, soles of the feet flat up against each other, with knees outspread" (WHW).
Lit.: KiH pl. 151 row 2:1; WHW 1:75.

muktā-yajñopavīta "sacred thread composed of pearls" (attr.), see further *yajñopavīta*.
Lit.: JMS 40; SIB 6, 69; SSIP 76.

mukti "liberation", n. of a *yantra* which is constructed round the *bīja HRĪṀ*. "It shows the different principles which the living being has to overcome in his effort to attain liberation".
Lit.: DHP 358.

mukulamudrā "bud-handpose" (Mu.), n. of a 'major' handpose, in which "the tips of the fingers and the thumb are brought together. It signifies a bud, virgin, delicacy, littleness, an offering, the *yoni*, the god of love, a monkey, eating, contempt". Varieties: *tāmracūḍā-*, *catura-*, *siṅha-mukha-*, *karaṇaḍamaru-*, *haṅsa-*, *bhramara-*, *mayūra-*, *cin-mudrā*.
Lit.: WHW 2:87.

mukunda "a kind of drum, kettle-drum" (attr.). Char. of Mukundā.
Lit.: BBh. 315.

Mukunda (explained as "giver of liberation" [?]), a n. of Viṣṇu.
Lit.: DiIP 144; MW 819.

Mukundā (Buddh.), personification of the musical instrument *mukunda*. Char.: colour: white; attr.: *mukunda*.
Lit.: BBh. 315 a.pl. 210.

mukuṭa (Pāli *makuṭa*) "crown, diadem, tiara" (attr.). There are several forms of *m.*, see *jaṭā-*, *kirīṭa-mukuṭa*. – In Buddhism the *m.* indicates its bearer as a future *buddha*, and therefore whilst *bodhisattvas* wear a *m.*, the *buddhas* usually do not (with the exception of a *mukuṭadhārin* "a crowned *buddha*"). The *m.* has here generally five leaves, and in the East-Asian esoteric mysticism (if not elsewhere) these leaves symbolize the five *dhyānibuddhas* (*tathāgatas*). – In Buddhism the term *m.* is also used like *bimba* (if the image of a *dhyānibuddha* is found on the crown). – Another n.: *mauli*.
Lit.: B passim; BBh. 156; GBM 105, 122; WHW 1:434.

mukuṭadhārin "crowned (*buddha*)", n. of a *buddha* who wears a crown and princely ornaments (cp. *bodhisattvābharaṇa*).

mukuṭin (*-ī*) "crowned, wearing a diadem" (attr.; Buddh.). This term is often used together with the n. of a *dhyānibuddha*, whose effigy (*bimba*) is found on the crown of a god, e.g. *Akṣobhya-mukuṭin*. – Another n.: *maulin*.
Lit.: BBh. 155; MW 819.

mūla- as the first member of many of the following word-compounds has the sense of "root" and refers in architectural terminology to the inner part of the shrine; in this usage equivalent to *garbha*.

Mūla (abbreviated form of Mūlabarhaṇī "celle qui déracine", IC), n. of a *nakṣatra*. – Its influence is very bad. – Another n.: Vicṛtau.
Lit.: BBh. 382; IC 2:730.

mūlabera "root-idol; la statue du sanctuaire" (attr.), cp. *acala*.
Lit.: ACA 87.

mūladevī "root-goddess', i.e. the goddess of the central shrine (*garbhagṛha*).
Lit.: DiIP 136.

Mūla-Durgā ("shrine-D."), n. of a form of Durgā. Attr.: *dhanus*, *śara*.
Lit.: SSI 199.

mūlaka(kanda) "radish" (attr.). Char. of Gaṇeśa (in different forms). – Cp. *modaka*.
Lit.: B 357.

mūlaliṅga "*liṅga* in the *garbhagṛha* or the central shrine", which is never moved.
Lit.: DiIP 110; JDI 12.

mūlamantra "root-*mantra*", n. of a *mantra* which is uttered while performing the *tarpaṇa*.
Lit.: DiIP 73.

mūlamūrti "fixed idol, root idol", see *dhruva(bera)*.
Lit.: DiIP 135.

mūlanāyaka "leader, the chief person of a shrine" (Jain.), another n. of *tīrthaṅkara*.
Lit.: GJ 392, 401.

mūlasaṅgha "root-congregation" (esp. Jain.), n. of a sect or society.
Lit.: MW 826.

mūlasthāna, see *garbhasthāna*.
Lit.: ZA 288.

mūlatrikoṇa "root-triangle", see *trikoṇa*.
Lit.: DHP 231.

mūlavigraha "fundamental form", as e.g., the *liṅga* which represents Śiva. – See *dhruvabera*.
Lit.: R 1:17; ZA 359.

mūlayantra "root diagram", n. of a kind of elementary graphic figure, which may serve to represent a deity.
Lit.: DHP 332.

muṇḍa "head, skull, a severed head" (attr.). Held in a hand char. of: Cāmuṇḍā, Chinnamastakā, Ekajaṭā, Kālī, Kṛśodarī, Mahācīnatārā, Mahākāla, Maṅgala, *navadurgās*, Saṃvara, Siṅhavaktrā, Śiva, Tārā, Vajrayoginī. – Other n.: *mānuṣamuṇḍa*, *mastaka*, *naraśiras*, *śiras*; cp. also *brahmakapāla*. *m.* is sometimes also used equivalently to *kapāla*.
Lit.: B 507; MEIA 267.

Muṇḍa, n. of a demon killed by Cāmuṇḍā who therefore wears the attr. *muṇḍa*.

muṇḍamālā "skull garland, garland composed of skulls" (attr.). Regarded as being probably a vestige of a skull cult. Char. of: Bhairava, Bram-zei gzugs-can, Cāmuṇḍā, Chinnamastakā, Dhūmrāvatī, Durgā, Ekajaṭā, the *gaurī*-group, mGon-po nag-po, Heruka, Kālacakra, Kālarātrī, Kālī, the *lāsyā*-group, Mahācīnatārā, Mahākāla, Mahā-Sadāśiva, Mṛtyuñjaya, Prasannatārā, Saṃvara, Saptaśatika-Hayagrīva, Sarvanivaraṇaviṣkambhin (in *yi-dam*-form), Śiva, Śivadūtī, Tripurā-Bhairavī, Uḍḍiyāna-Kurukullā, Vajracarcikā, Vajravārāhī, Vīrabhadra. – Other n.: *kapālamālā*, *karaṅkamālā*, *naraśiromālā*.
Lit.: DHP 218, 272; GoRI 1:258; KiSH 22.

muni "saint, sage, seer", see further *riṣi*. *m.* is also a symbolic n. of the number "7", see *saṅkhyā*.

Munisuvrata ("who fulfils all good vows of the *munis*"; Jain.), n. of the 20th *tīrthaṅkara*. Symbol: *kūrma*.
Lit.: GJ 284; HSIT 14 a.pl. 35; KiSH 143.

Munīśvara ("the *muni*-lord"; Tam. Muṉicāmi = Skt Munisvāmin), n. of a deification of a *muni* worshipped in South India. Men and women are given names related to M., because they are supposed to be born as the result of appeasing M. – In the Tamil territory there are also other cognate names, e.g. Muṉiyāṇṭi, Muṉiyappaṉ, Munīcuraṉ, referring to a low-rank deity whose shrines are situated, for instance, at the beginning of a mountain path. This may perhaps have to do with the "raging" or "wild" character of *muni* (Diehl).

muñja "a species of rush- or sedge-like grass, Saccharum Sara or Munja" (attr.). *m.* is held to have a purifying action and is used in worship. See also *mauñji*.
Lit.: DilP 186; MKVI 2:165; MW 821.

muraja (Tam. *muracam*) "(large) drum, tambourine" (Vāh. and attr.). As a Vāh. it is char. of Nandīśvara, as an attr. char. of Murajā, Nandīśvara. It is also an emblem of royalty and a *maṅgala*, see *aṣṭamaṅgala*.
Lit.: BBh. 315, 366.

Murajā (Buddh.), n. of a goddess who is the deified musical instrument (*muraja*). Char.: colour: smoky; attr.: *muraja*.
Lit.: BBh. 315.

muralī "flute" (attr.), see *veṇu*. The n. forms part of the n. Kṛṣṇa Muralīdhara.
Lit.: B 303; R 1:10; SMII 148; Th. 43.

Muralīdhara ("flute-bearer"), epithet of Kṛṣṇa, generally called Veṇugopāla.
Lit.: MW 823.

Murāri ("enemy of Mura"), epithet of Kṛṣṇa who killed the demon Mura (or Muru).
Lit.: D 212.

mūrdhnyuṣṇīṣa "cranial protuberance" (attr.; Buddh.), see *uṣṇīṣa*.
Lit.: RN 29.

mūrti "manifestation, embodiment, personification, the (anthropomorphic) representation of a god"; also "image, idol, statue" (see *pratimā*). This term is mostly used to signify the different aspects, personifications or representations of the gods; the different forms of Śiva (which are often said to be 28 in number) in particular are indicated by this term, cp. Ādimūrti, Aghoramūrti etc.; see also *trimūrti*. – Cp. *avatāra*.
Lit.: CHIIA 42; DHP 4, 362; MW 824.

mūrtidāna "gift of an icon"; as n. of an icon, see *devadāna*.
Lit.: ZA 111.

mūrtyaṣṭaka, n. of a group of "eight manifestations" of Śiva comprising: Bhava, Śarva, Īśāna, Paśupati, Ugra, Rudra, Bhīma, Mahādeva. – Common features: they have usually 4 hands. Char.: Mu.: *abhaya-*, *varada-mudrā*; attr.: *jaṭāmukuṭa*, *mṛga*, *ṭaṅka*.
Lit.: R 2:403; SSI 77.

Murukaṉ (Murugan; Tam. "young man"), n. of a divine youth in old Tamil tradition. According to GoRI he was originally probably a local snake god (a view rejected by Diehl), and later identified with either Kṛṣṇa (?) or Skanda (Kumāra); in present-day Tamil religious life he has received great importance, being to many the chief god and taking the place of Subrahmaṇya. Attr.: *aṅkuśa* and other attr. of Skanda.
Lit.: Diehl and DilP 135; GoRI 2:15.

mūṣa(ka) "rat, mouse" (Vāh.), see *ākhu*.
Lit.: DHP 296.

musala (also *muśala*, *muṣala*, exceptionally *mūṣala*) "(wooden) pestle" (attr.). The *m.* is emblematic of agriculture. Char. of esp. Balarāma (see also Saṅkarṣaṇa), further of: Ananta, Ardhanārīśvara, Cāmuṇḍā, Dhvajāgrakeyūrā, Gaṇapati, Kṛṣṇa-Yamāri, Mahākālī, Rakta-Cāmuṇḍā, Sadāśiva, Ṣaṇmukha, Śarabha, Śiva (Vīrabhadra), Skanda, Tārakāri, Vajradhātvīśvarī, Vidyujjvālākarālī, Viśvarūpa, Yamāntaka.
Lit.: B 302, 423; BBh. 177; Gt 407; MEIA 245; R 1:5 a.pl. 2:1; WM 108 a.fig. 67.

Musalin (-ī; "having a pestle"), epithet of Balarāma.

mūṣika "mouse" (Vāh.), see *ākhu*.
Lit.: BBh. 348.

muṣṭi(mudrā) "clenched hand, fist, fist-hand-pose" (Mu.). *muṣṭi* (not fully described)

is said to be char. of Śarabha. – *m.* is further n. of a 'major' handpose in which the thumb is bent over the closed palm. It symbolizes strength, holding a weapon, wrestling. Some varieties : *śikhara-*, *candrakāla-*, *kapittha-*, *sūci-*, *kartari-*, *tarjanī-mudrās*.
Lit.: MEIA 217; WHW 2:87.

muṣṭika, see *muṣṭimudrā*. – Muṣṭika (derived from *muṣṭi* "fist") is NP of a wrestler killed by Balarāma.
Lit.: Gt 407.

Muttālammaṉ (Tam., cp. Tel. Mutyālamma; "Pearl-Mother"), n. of a plague-goddess. M. may preside over smallpox (as a variety of Māriyammaṉ) or over cholera.
Lit.: DiCh. 33; KiSH 51; SSI fig. 138.

muttirai (Tam.), see *mudrā*.

Muttra (= Mattra), see Mathurā.

Mutyālamma (Tel.), see Muttālammaṉ.

Muyalakaṉ (Tam., also written Mūyaḷaka, B), see Apasmāra.
Lit.: B 472; HAHI 28; TL 6:3274; ZA 122.

N

Nābhija ("navel-born"), epithet of Brahmā, who was born from the navel of Viṣṇu. This event is iconographically represented esp. in the Anantāśāyana-composition.
Lit.: CEBI 17 a.pl. B; DHP 235; MSHP pl. 3.

nābhisūtra ("navel-thread") = *udarabandha* (?).
Lit.: R 2:118, 167, 225.

nāc (Hi., < Skt *nṛtya*) "dance", performed by a *devadāsī*.
Lit.: GH 348.

nāda "resonance", symbolically represented by a stroke (–), is said to be a "fifth sound", included in the *bījamantra OṀ*.
Lit.: GH 54, 56; IC 1:566.

nādānta "ending with a sound (or resonance)", n. of a certain dance performed by Śiva Naṭarāja. (Here *nāda* "sound" or "resonance" may be symbolized by the *ḍamaru*, the attr. carried by the god.) In this dance Śiva represents "the kinetic aspect of the Deity, or the Spiral Force of Yoga, regarded as the elemental force through which the universe is created, maintained, and eventually destroyed" (HAHI).
Lit.: HAHI 27; R 2:234; SSR 166.

nadīdevatā "river deity", e.g. Gaṅgā, Kāverī, Sarasvatī, Yamunā, etc. Rivers are considered as goddesses and worshipped, and images are found along their banks. Cp. *daryāsevak*.
Lit.: KiH 25; KiSH 71; WM 71.

nāga "snake" (rarely "elephant").
1. (Vāh. and attr.) *n.* is a symbol of fertility and water (the snake reproduced as a wavy line may symbolize water), cp. *jala*. In Buddhism the *n.* symbolizes hatred. It is not always easy to make a distinction between this symbol used as a Vāh. and its use as an attr. As a Vāh. however it should be regarded as char. of Manasā, Jāṅgulī, Viśvamātā (a white *n.*), Hayagrīva (more than one *n.*), and the Garuḍa-form of Vajrapāṇi; sometimes the *pīṭha* of the Buddha is carried by *nāgas*. Cp. also Ananta (Śeṣa), the World Snake upon which Viṣṇu is reposing. It is also a symbol of Pārśvanātha.
As an attr. *n.* may either be carried in one of the hands (e.g. by Śiva) or worn on different parts of the body, either upon the head, behind the ears or round the belly (see *udarabandha* etc.); the hood of a *n.* may also be seen spread-out behind the head of an image. Ornaments can be made in the shape of a *n.*, attributes may be formed of a *n.* (see e.g., *nāgapāśa*, *sarpakucabandha*, etc.), and a *n.* may be entwined round an attr., such as a *ḍamaru*

or a *liṅga*. – *n.* (in different forms) is char. of: Aja, Amoghasiddhi, Aparājita, Aparājitā, Āryajāṅgulītārā, Bahurūpa, Bhūtaḍāmara(vajrapāṇi), Buddha, Cāmuṇḍā, *dharmapāla*s, Gaṇeśa, Garuḍa, Hara, Hayagrīva, Jāṅgulī, Jayanta, Kālī, Kāmāntakamūrti, Mahābala, Mahācakravajrapāṇi, Mahācīnatārā, Mahākāla, Mahālakṣmī, Manasā, Mārttaṇḍa-Bhairava, Māyājālakrama-Avalokiteśvara, Mucalinda-Buddha (snake-hood behind the head), Nāgārjuna, Nīlakaṇṭha, Paṭṭinī Devī (snake-hood behind the head), Pārśvanātha (snake-hood behind the head), Revata, Sadāśiva, Saptaśatika-Hayagrīva, Siṅhanāda, Śiva (in different forms), Śivadūtī, Śrīdevī, Tārā, Trimūrti, Tryambaka, Ucchuṣma, Ugratārā, Varuṇa, Vidyujjvālākarālī, Virūpākṣa, Viśvavajra-Lokeśvara, Yamāntaka. – Other n.: *ahi*, *bhujaṅga*, *gonasa*, *sarpa*, *uraga*.

Lit.: B 358; DHP 217; GBM 103; GH 72; GoRI 1:316; MEIA 236; WM 159; ZM 45.

2. *nāga(deva)* (fem. *nāginī*), n. of a snake deity, snake spirit. *nāga*s were worshipped as deities as early as in the Indus Valley civilization and since then in all Indian religions. It is also possible that the cult of *n.* has aboriginal tribal connections. – In Hinduism the *nāga*s are said to be descendants of Kāśyapa and Kadrū and are regarded as the chief enemies of Garuḍa and as a kind of *asura*s. There are seven great *nāgadeva*s (*nāgarāja*s, *mahoraga*s): Vāsuki, Takṣaka, Karkoṭaka (Karka), Padma (Puṇḍarīka), Mahāpadma (Mahābja), Śaṅkhapāla, Kulika. Sometimes their number is said to be eight; hence, *nāga* is also a symbolic n. of the numbers "7" and "8", see *saṅkhyā*. – Other n. may also be mentioned, e.g. Śeṣa, or Ananta, the king of the *nāga*s which inhabit *pātāla*, Kāliya, Manasā. Cp. *mahānāga*. Common char.: colour: red; Vāh.: *padmapīṭha*; Mu.: *abhaya-*, *varada-mudrā*; attr.: *akṣamālā*, *kamaṇḍalu*, *trinayana*. They are also often represented with more than one head; a five-headed *n.* sometimes represents Gaṇeśa. – In Buddhism the *nāga*s are regarded as water-spirits and often represented as anthropomorphic persons or as human beings with snake hoods growing out of the shoulders. They can be of good or evil nature; see, e.g., Mucalinda, and Nanda mentioned as king of *nāga*s. They have the power to bring or withhold rains. – Cp. Ananta.

Lit.: B 344 a.pl. 14:3; BBh. 437; DHP 143, 301, 308 a.pl. 29; G 16 (ill.), 35, 95; GoRI 2:8; Gt 409; H pl. 3:34, 10; HAHI pl. 11A; HIS 26; IC 1:525; IIM 108; JMS pl. 1; KiSH 72; MBPC 28, 32; R 2:554 a.pl. 157; RIS 19; SSI 248; STP 3:142; Th. 117; WAA 25:174 a.fig. 23; WHW 2:387; WM 139; ZA 26, 329 a.pl. A16a, 1b; ZM pl. 4-5.

nāgabandha "frieze of *nāga*s" on a temple. It is also another n. of an *udarabandha** consisting of a snake.

Lit.: BECA 1:262.

nāgakal (or *nākakkal*, mixed Skt-Tam.) "serpent-stone", in South India n. of a kind of stone table with engraved snake-motives. The n. is regarded as a fertility symbol, the snakes perhaps being conceived as imbuing the *n.* with a "soul".

Lit.: DiIP 159, 254; GoRI 2:8; JDI 111; KiH 26 a.pl. 92-96; KiSH 72; SSI 248; TL 4:2195; WHW 2:73; ZM pl. 8.

nāgakesara "snake or elephant hair" (attr.; Buddh.), n. of a tree (Mesua ferrea). As an attr. a twig of this tree is carried by Maitreya. – Cp. *nāgapuṣpa*.

Lit.: KiDG 49; KiSB 52.

nāgakucabandha, see *sarpakucabandha*.

Lit.: SB 280.

nāgakumāra "snake-prince" (Jain.), n. of a kind of *bhavanavāsī*.

Lit.: GJ 236.

nāgakuṇḍala, see *sarpakuṇḍala*.

Lit.: JDI 19.

nāgamudrā "snake-handpose" (Mu.), n. of a gesture in which ail the fingers are held in a cupped attitude, resembling the hood of a snake. Char. of Apasmārapuruṣa. – Another n.: *vyālamudrā*(?).

Lit.: R 2:225.

nāgapañcamī "the (festival held) on the fifth day (of the month *śrāvaṇa* in honour) of the *nāgas*", n. of a festival.
Lit.: IC 1:592; WHW 1:355.

nāgapāśa "snake-noose" (attr.), n. of a *pāśa* consisting of a snake. Char. of: Caṇḍā, Ketu, *kṣetrapālas*, Pratyṅgirā, Śiva (in different forms), Sumbhā, Varuṇa.
Lit.: B 301; MEIA 252; R 2:496.

nāgapuṣpa ("snake-flower"; attr.), n. of a tree (Michelia Champaka), as a *bodhivṛkṣa* ascribed to Maitreya. It is however probable that this attr. is identical with the *nāgakesara*.
Lit.: MS 76.

nāgara ("town"), n. of the northern or Indo-Aryan type of temple, characterized by the *śikhara* tower. It has a quadrangular form.
Lit.: DKI 41; RAAI 273.

nāgarāja "snake-king", n. of a snake deity (identical with *mahoraga* or *nāgadeva*) see *nāga* 2.
Lit.: CHIIA 34 a.fig. 172; MBPC passim; WHW 2:388.

nāgaraliṅga "town-*liṅga*", n. of a kind of *mānuṣaliṅga*.
Lit.: R 2:91.

Nāgārjuna ("serpent-white"; Buddh.), n. of a reformer of the Mahāyāna sect of Buddhism and saint who lived in the 2nd c. A.D. Attr.: *kāṣāya, nāga, stūpa, ūrṇā, uṣṇīṣa*.
Lit.: BRI 122; G passim; GBM 50; GRI 262; SeKB 31, WHW 2:110.

Nāgasena ("having an army of snakes"; Buddh.), n. of a Lamaist arhat. Attr.: *kamaṇḍalu, khakkhara*.
Lit.: G 104.

nāgāṣṭaka "eight ornaments of snakes" (attr.). Char. of Mahācīnatārā. Cp. *sarpābharaṇa*.
Lit.: BBh. 190.

nāgavalaya, see *bhujaṅgavalaya*.
Lit.: SB 61.

nāgayajñopavīta "*yajñopavīta* consisting of a snake" (attr.). Char. of: Caṇḍeśvara, *kṣetrapālas*, Vīrabhadra. – Another n.: *sarpayajñopavīta*.
Lit.: R 2:497.

Nag-dup (Tib.), see Naṅ-sgrub.

nāginī "snake-goddess", represented as a "mermaid" with a human body and serpentine tail; see further *nāga* 2. Attr.: *sarpakucabandha*.
Lit.: B 344, 350; H pl. 10; KrG pl. 24; RAAI pl. 273; ZA pl. 105b.

Nāginī (Jain.), n. of a goddess, the counterpart of the Hindu Manasā.

nagna (fem. *nagnā*) "naked" (attr.). Char. esp. of Kālī and many Jain *tīrthaṅkaras* (Pārśvanātha etc.), further, e.g., of: (Baṭuka) Bhairava, Bhikṣāṭanamūrti, Kālarātrī, Mahāyogin, Pāṇḍurāṅga, Śatruvidhvaṅsinī, Śītalā, Yogāmbara; rarely also other gods and goddesses. – Cp. *digambara*.
Lit.: Gt 410; HAHI 18.

Naigameṣa (the *n.* includes the member *meṣa* "ram"; in the older religion [Atharvaveda] there was a demon with the head of a ram, also named Nejameṣa, which was supposed to seize or injure children; the first member of this word may allude to *nija* "own"), n. of a god (cp. Naigameya). Attr.: *ajamastaka*. Wife: Revatī (she is also *ajamastaka*). Another n.: Hariṇegamesi.
Lit.: B 562; JMS 24; MW 568, 570.

Naigameya (in a way connected with Naigameṣa), n. of a god who was either the son, or the brother of Skanda, or an aspect of Skanda himself. Attr.: *ajamastaka*.
Lit.: B 146, 363, 367.

naipālasamvat "Nepalese year", n. of an era beginning in A.D. 878 and used in Nepal. The year of this era is *gata, kārttikādi* and *amānta*. The given year + 879 or 880 = the year A.D.
Lit.: IC 2:738.

Nairātmā ("no-soul", said to be another word for *śūnya*; personification; Buddh.), n. of a Mahāyāna goddess, an emanation of Akṣobhya. She is also regarded as a personification of *prajñā* "knowledge" (so G), and as the Śakti of Heruka (Hevajra). N. also belongs among the retinue of Buddhakapāla. Char.: colour: blue or black; att.: *nāṭyasthāna*; Vāh.: *mṛtaka*;

attr.: *Akṣobhyabimba* on the crown, *kapāla*, *karttṛkā*, *khaṭvāṅga*, *pañca-* or *ṣaṇ-mudrā*, *trinayana*.
Lit.: BBh. 157, 160, 203 a.pl. 148-149; G 87; KiDG 64; KiSB 94.

Nairṛta or Nairṛti, see Nirṛti.
Lit.: BBh. 362; MEIA 129.

naivedya "offering of (cooked) food for an image". This rite forms part of the *pūjā*. – Another n.: *nivedya*.
Lit.: B 299, 501; DiIP 122; GBM 132; JDI 15; SSI 7.

naivedyapātra "vessel with food for the *naivedya*" (attr.).

naivedyapūjā (Jain.), n. of the act of worship of an image which consists in the offering of sweetmeats. – See *pūjā*.
Lit.: GJ 396.

nakrakuṇḍala (attr.), n. of a certain ear-ornament, see *makarakuṇḍala*.
Lit.: B 289; R 1:24; WM 104.

nakṣatra (or *-ttra*) "star, constellation (through which the moon passes), lunar mansion", a common n. of the stars including the fixed stars and the sun and moon. The n. *graha** (see also *navagraha*) is, however, more generally used for the planets (including sun and moon). *n.* is hence esp. used for the 27 (or, according to some statements, 28) lunar mansions into which the ecliptic is divided. They are not all equal in size, some consisting of only one or two stars. In deified form the *nakṣatras* appear as goddesses and as daughters of Dakṣa and wives of Candra (Soma). Here one list of *n.* in Hinduism may be given: Aśvinī, Bharaṇī, Kṛttikā, Rohiṇī, Mṛgaśiras, Ārdrā, Punarvasu, Puṣyā, Āśleṣā, Maghā, Pūrvaphalgunī, Uttaraphalgunī, Hastā, Citrā, Svātī, Viśākhā, Anurādhā, Jyeṣṭhā, Mūlā, Pūrvāṣāḍhā, Uttarāṣāḍhā, Śravaṇā, Dhaniṣṭhā, Śatabhiṣā, Pūrvabhādrapadā, Uttarabhādrapadā, Revatī, Abhijit (IC; other lists, see in KiK and MKVI). They are supposed to have a great influence, either good or bad, on mankind during the whole course of life. – Another n.: *ṛkṣa*. Cp. *rāśi*.
Lit.: BBh. 381; DHP 97; GH 50; GJ 404; GoRI 1:231; Gt 411 a.Suppl. 88; IC 1:491, 2:721, 734; KiH 6; KiJ 8 a.pl. 19; KiK 33, 138, 280; KiSH 65; MKVI 1:409; M. M. UNDERHILL, The Hindu religious year (Calcutta 1921), 17; WHW 1:196; WM 78.

nakula (fem. *nakulī*) "ichneumon, mongoose" (attr.). This animal is esp. famous as a snake-killer. It is also believed to be a receptacle of all gems, and a *n.*, vomiting jewels, is esp. char. of Jambhala, further of: Bakula, Kālajambhala, Kubera, Sitajambhala, Śrīdevī, Ucchuṣma, Vaiśravaṇa, *yakṣas*.
Lit.: B 560; G 16 (ill.); STP 3:115.

Nakula, in the epic Mahābhārata n. of a twin brother of Sahadeva (and half-brother of Yudhiṣṭhira etc.). Like his twin brother he is regarded as an *avatāra* of the Aśvins.
Lit.: ZA pl. 111; ZM 71 a.pl. 3.

Nakulin (for Lakulin) see Lakulīśa.
Lit.: GRI 170.

nāla "tube", n. of a tubular projection on the *pīṭhikā* of a *liṅga*, through which the water which is poured on to the *liṅga* is projected.
Lit.: B 460; R 2:101.

Nālāgiri, see Malagiri.

Nālandā, n. of a Buddhist monastery and university in Bihar, flourishing in the 7th-9th cc. A.D.
Lit.: AuOW 41; SeKB passim; WHW 2:114; ZA pl.376 ff.

nālikera "cocoa-nut", see *nārikela*.

namaḥ Śivāya "hail to Śiva", a *mantra* included among the *aṣṭāvaraṇa*.
Lit.: GoRI 2:249.

nāma(dheya)karaṇa "name-giving", n. of a *saṁskāra*-rite, the ceremony of naming a child after its birth.
Lit.: DiIP 180, 184; GH 333; GJ 411; IC 1:363; MW 536.

nāmaṁ (Hi., < Skt *nāma* "name") "mark" (attr.), n. of the mark made on the forehead, see *tilaka*. *n.* sometimes refers esp. to the *tiryakpuṇḍra*. – Cp. *tirunāmam*.
Lit.: Gt 413; P 1118; WHW 1:208.

namas (with the sentence-forms: *namaḥ*, *namo*) "obeisance, bowing, adoration, salutation, hail (to)". Together with a dative form of a name (e.g. *namaḥ Śivāya*, *namo Gaṇeśāya* "salutation to Śiva" and "Gaṇeśa" respectively) it forms part of many short *mantras*.
Lit.: IC 1:565; MW 528; P 1154.

Nāmasaṅgīti ("the singing together of the Name"; Buddh.), n. both of a form of Avalokiteśvara and of an independent god who is an emanation of Vairocana. Like Prajñāpāramitā N. is a personification of a scripture, *viz.* the *nāmasaṅgīti* literature and seems to be regarded as a *bodhisattva*. – Char.: colour: white; att.: *padmāsana*; Vāh.: *padma*; Mu.: *abhaya-* (also with two hands), *añjali-* (either in the usual or in the esp. Buddhist form), *dhyāna-*, *kṣepaṇa-*, *tarpaṇa-*, *uttarabodhi-mudrā*; attr.: *bodhisattvābharaṇa*, *kamaṇḍalu*, *khaḍga*, *khaṭvāṅga*, *padma*, half a *vajra* in the *uṣṇīṣa*, *viśvavajra*.
Lit.: BBh. 206 a.pl. 151; G 22, 66; KiSB 79.

Nāmasaṅgīti-Mañjuśrī ("M. of N."; Buddh.), n. of a form of Mañjuśrī. Char.: att.: *padmāsana*; attr.: *Akṣobhyabimba*, *dhanus*, *khaḍga*, *pustaka* (= the *nāmasaṅgīti*-scripture?), *śara*, *triśiras*.
Lit.: BBh. 115 a.pl. 79-80; KiDG pl. 21; KiSB 54.

namaskāramudrā "the gesture of making salutation" (Mu.), n. of a handpose of adoration or salutation. It is described in different ways: (a) According to BBh.: "The hand, slightly bent, is raised above in a line with the shoulder with fingers outstretched or slightly bent with the palm turned upwards" (cp. FK, ill.). This form of the Mu. corresponds to the *buddhaśramaṇamudrā*. – (b) According to B, this Mu. is identical with the *añjalimudrā* (or *vandanamudrā*), but in addition he declares that it "denotes also the action of touching the forehead with folded hands" (cp. Gt; in this case it might be combined with a prostration at the feet of the person saluted, cp. KiH). – (c) According to G: "Hands are at breast in attitude of prayer". This form is identical with that which was preferred for *añjalimudrā**. – (d) In a novel (*Durbar*, by D. Kincaid) it is stated that *n.* is performed with the hands folded under the chin. – For the purposes of this dictionary the description of B is to be preferred if made more precise in the following way: The hands are clasped together (as in *añjalimudrā*) and touch the forehead, possibly combined with a prostration.
Lit.: B 251, 342 a.pl. 13:1; BBh. 437; FK 137 (ill.); G 22; Gt Suppl. 90; JMS pl. 56; KiDG 54 a.pl. 27; KiH 36; KiSB 74; KiSH 91.

nameru, n. of a tree (Elaeocarpus ganitrus Roxb.), sacred to Śiva (attr.).
Lit.: IC 1:538.

namghar (N.Ind.) "adoration house", n. of a little shrine erected in a village.
Lit.: GH 339.

Nammāḻvār (Tam.), n. of a *vaiṣṇavabhakta*.
Lit.: R 2:480 a.pl. 136.

namo, see *namas*.

Nānak Dev, named Guru Nānak (A.D. 1469-1539), n. of the founder of the Sikh sect.
Lit.: GoRI 2:108; GG; GRI 346, HS; IC 1:658; WHW 2:121.

Nanda ("joy, delight" or "son").
1. (Hind.) NP of the foster-father of Kṛṣṇa. Wife: Yaśodā.
Lit.: B pl. 26:1; D 217; Gt 414.
2. (Buddh.) NP of the king of *nāgas*. Attr.: *caturmukha*, *dhanus*. He has a snake's body.
Lit.: G 95.

Nandā ("joy"), n. of a form of Pārvatī, with 4 or 8 arms. Char.: Mu.: *abhaya-*, *varada-mudrā*; attr.: *aṅkuśa*, *cakra*, *dhanus* Ajagava, *gadā*, *ghaṇṭā*, *khaḍga*, *padma*, *pāśa*, *śaṅkha*, *śara*. – Cp. Hārītī.
Lit.: AIP 274; R 1:355; Th. 107.

Nandaka ("joy"; attr.), n. of the *khaḍga* of Viṣṇu (Kṛṣṇa).
Lit.: B 301; DHP 160.

Nandikeśvara, see Nandīśvara.
Lit.: DHP 220; R 2:455; Th. 100 a.pl. 72.

Nandin (or -ī; "rejoicing, gladdening"), NP of the Vāh. (*vṛṣan*, a white bull) of Śiva, Pārvatī, Māheśvarī and other Śaktis of Śiva. N. is regarded as a theriomorphic form of Śiva, and he can therefore receive adoration like an independent idol. In the temples N. is represented lying in an outer room, facing the door of the *garbhagṛha* where the chief icon of Śiva (or the *liṅga*) is situated, whereas in bronze representations a N. is found before a bowl, in which a *liṅga* or a *bāṇaliṅga* is placed.

Lit.: B 534; DHP 219; GoRI 1:257; Gt 414; H pl. 7:62; HIS 21; KiH pl. 49, 139:3; KiSH 87; R 2:460 a.pl. 132; SB 315 a.fig. 233; WM 140.

nandipada "foot-print of Nandin" (attr.), cp. *pāduka*. There is perhaps a connection between *n.* and the *triśūla* and the Buddhist *triratna*.

Lit.: AuT 221; CEBI 15 a.pl. A; HSIT 6 a.pl. 4.

Nandīśa or Nandīśvara, Nandikeśvara ("the lord Nandin" or "the lord of Nandin").

1. (Hind.) N. is usually n. of a companion of Śiva (Śivadūta), who is regarded as an anthropomorphic form of Nandin. But sometimes N. is also used as n. of a form of Śiva himself. Char.: att.: (sometimes) *kūrpara*; Mu.: *añjali-*, *tarjanī-mudrā*; attr.: *akṣamālā, bhindipāla, ḍamaru, gadā, mattaḷam, mṛga, ṭaṅka, trinayana, triśūla, vajra,* (sometimes) *vṛṣamastaka*. – Other n.: Adhikāranandin, Bhṛṅgin; see also Nandīśānugrahamūrti.

Lit.: AIP 274; B 534; BKI 30; D 218; JDI 54 a.fig. 14; KIM pl. 44; MEIA 66; R 2:212, 217, 455 a.pl. 131; SB 351 a.pl. 331; SSI 162; Th. 100 a.pl. 72.

2. (Buddh.) Nandīśvara (or Nandikeśvara), originally a Hindu god, is also found in Buddhism. Char. colour: blue; Vāh.: (sitting on a) *muraja*; attr.: *muraja*.

Lit.: BBh. 366.

Nandīśānugrahamūrti ("gracious representation [of Śiva] together with Nandīśa"), n. of a form of Śiva being worshipped by Nandin (Nandīśa).

Lit.: R 2:212.

Nandivāhana(mūrti) ("representation [of Śiva] having Nandin as a Vāh."), see Vṛṣavāhanamūrti.

nandyāvarta (M.Ind. *nandyāvatta*; "curl, whirl of happiness" or "of Nandin?"; attr.), n. of a kind of diagram or sign which resembles a hooked cross; it is also a *maṅgala* (see *aṣṭamaṅgala*) which is found both in Buddhism and in Jainism. It is a symbol of Ara.

Lit.: GBM 102; GJ 383 a.pl. 23:18; KiJ pl. 45; KiSH 143, 154.

Naṅ-sgrub (Tib., pronounced Nag-dup [sic G]; note however that if this is the case, the meaning of the word is far from clear, the element *naṅ* meaning "interior, space, heart"; if however the form Nag-sgrub is connected with *nag-po* "black", it might, as "the Black One", be a counterpart of Kāla*, the god of death, in the meaning of "the Black One" [and not of "Time, All-Destroyer"]; Buddh.), in Lamaism n. of a variety of Yama. Char.: colour: dark blue; Vāh.: *nara*; attr.: *kapāla, karttṛkā*. – N. is sometimes accompanied by Yamī and others.

Lit.: G 91, 126; JT 300.

nara (or *nṛ*) "man".

1. N. of a manifestation (*vyūha*) of Viṣṇu as Vāsudeva.

2. (Vāh. or attr.) N. esp. of the Vāh. of Kubera (Naravāhana; this Vāh. was properly a Brāhman) and Nirṛti. In Buddhism *n.* may signify a man, upon whom a deity stands, or who bears a god. It is not easy to distinguish between *n.* and *mṛtaka* or *rākṣasa*. A Vāh. of this type is char. of: Beg-tse, Bhairava, Bram-zei gzugs-can, Gur-gyi mGon-po, Hayagrīva, Jambhala, Krodha-Hayagrīva, Mahācakravajrapāṇi, Mahākāla, Naṅ-sgrub, Nirṛti, Samvara, Sarvanivaraṇaviṣkambhin (in *yi-dam*-form), Siṅhavaktrā, Vajravārāhī, Yama. – As an attr. a *n.* is swallowed by Kālī, Mahālakṣmī. – Another n.: *mānuṣa*.

Lit.: MEIA 227.

naracarma(n) "flayed human skin" (attr.), either held in one hand (the hands) or worn on the body. Char. of: Heruka, Mahāmāya, Saptākṣara.
Lit.: BBh. 156, 162.

Nārada (sometimes interpreted as "Giver-of-Advice", DHP), n. of a *riṣi* or *prajāpati.* He was the son of Kāśyapa, and he is esp. connected with music and said to be the inventor of the *viṇā* (which he holds as an attr.); for this reason N. was the chief of the *gandharvas* or heavenly musicians. N. is also regarded as an *avatāra* of Viṣṇu.
Lit.: B 391; D 218; DHP 165, 187, 323; GH 96; Gt 415; MG 302; R 1:123; Th. pl. 79B; WHW 2:123; WM 190.

Naradattā ("daughter of Nara"; Jain.), n. of a *śāsanadevatā* of the 20th *tīrthaṅkara.* She is also a *vidyādevī.*
Lit.: GJ 362.

naraka "hell" and *nāraka* "inhabitant of hell". A place of torture to which the souls of the wicked are sent. There are a great number of different hells (see KiK). – *n.* as NP Naraka (or Narakāsura) is n. of a demon who was the son of Viṣṇu and Bhūmidevī, but who was killed by Kṛṣṇa. – Cp. *pātāla.*
Lit.: D 219; GJ 232; Gt 416; IC 1:547; KiK 49, 147, 199; MW 529; WHW 1:253, 434.

naramukha (or *naramastaka*) "(having a) human head" (attr.), n. of one of the heads or faces in many-headed representations, in which the other heads show animal or demon faces. See, e.g., *caturmūrti*, Vaikuṇṭhanātha.

Nara-Nārāyaṇa, n. of a composite image, of which the *Nara* element is identified with Arjuna, and Nārāyaṇa with Kṛṣṇa. N. are also mentioned as two ancient *riṣis* or saints and are further regarded as *avatāras* of Viṣṇu.
Lit.: D 220; DHP 165, 182 a.pl. 12; GoRI 1:247; R 1:274; SS pl. 27:120; WM 190.

Naranārī "man-woman", see Ardhanārīśvara.

Narasiṅha (or -siṅhāvatāra, Nṛsiṅha; "the Man-Lion", half-man, half-lion).
1. N. given to the fourth *avatāra* of Viṣṇu as a man-lion, in which shape he rescued the world from the tyranny of the demon Hiraṇyakaśipu. N. signifies in this case an *ugra*-aspect of Viṣṇu; see also *caturmūrti* and *caturviṅśatimūrti.* In this manifestation he is also named Saṅkarṣaṇa. He has the usual char. of Viṣṇu, and his chief attr. are: *siṅhamukha, keśa.* N. is represented in three forms: Girija-, Sthauna- and Yānaka-Narasiṅha. N. is also symbolized by the *bījamantra KŚRAUṀ* and is further regarded as a manifestation of the planet Maṅgala. – Cp. Vaikuṇṭhanātha, Ugra-Narasiṅha.
Lit.: B 390, 415 a.pl. 23:3; BP 53 a.pl. 3; ChI 595; DHP 165, 168 a.pl. 10; GH 121; GoRI 1:251; Gt 418; HAHI pl. 13; JDI 76; KiH 13 a.pl. 29; KiSH 36; MEIA 31 a.pl. 3a; MG 112 a.pl. facing p. 110; R 1:19, 145 with pl.; SIB pl. 18; SSI 24; Th. 60 a.pl. 14; W 124; WHW 1:452; WM 140; ZA pl. 445a.
2. (N. as Vāh. or attr.). Śiva is depicted as trampling, in the form of a mythological animal, upon the prostrate N., see Śarabha.

Narasiṅha-munaiyataraiyar (Tam.), n. of a king or, perhaps, a form of Rāma; South India.
Lit.: SB 269 a.fig. 178.

Narasiṅhī (as the female counterpart or potency or Śakti of Narasiṅha) is sometimes mentioned as one of the *sapta-* or *aṣṭa-mātaras* or *navaśakti.*
Lit.: B 508 a.pl. 44:2; MW 1044.

naraśiras "head of a man" (attr.), see *muṇḍa.*
Lit.: BBh. 346.

naraśiromālā "garland of human heads, skulls" (attr.), see *muṇḍamālā.*
Lit.: BBh. 199.

Naravāhana ("having a man as Vāh."), epithet of Kubera.

narayajña "man-worship", see *manuṣyayajña.*
Lit.: WHW 1:360.

Nārāyaṇa (this n. is interpreted in different ways: "the son of Nara, the original, eternal man", or "abode of man", "the Universal Abode", and "moving on the waters" (DHP), "Sohn des Urmenschen" (WM), "der seinen Gang im Wasser hat", from *nāra* "waters" being the first *ayana* or place of motion of Brahmā). N. in this sense may be primarily regarded as a cosmical god or giant (the son of Dharma), and is esp. met with in the *Brāhmaṇa*-texts.

1. N. is commonly identified with Viṣṇu and regarded as an *avatāra* or aspect of him, cp. *caturviṅśatimūrti*. He can therefore also pass for a form of Kṛṣṇa (see Nara-Nārāyaṇa) and also for Vāṭapattrāśāyin. Śakti: Kānti (or Lakṣmī).
Lit.: B 391; DHP 151, 154, 165; GoRI 1:246; HIS 19; JDI 65; KiSH 35, 39; MG pl. facing p. 33; R 1:229; WHW 2:123; WM 141.

2. N. is also an epithet of Brahmā.
Lit.: D 220; DHP 234; KiSH 35.

3. N. is also an epithet of Śiva. Cp. Sūrya-Nārāyaṇa.
Lit.: KiH 13 a.pl. 24; KiSH 35.

Narbada, see Narmadā.

nārī "woman" (Vāh. or attr.). A *n.* is the customary Vāh. of Samvara, upon which he stands; Beg-tse is also shown treading with one foot on a *n.*; Yama in the form Phyi-sgrub stands on a *mahiṣa* (or *vṛṣan*), while the latter stands on a *n.*
Lit.: G 25, 91.

nārikela (or *nārī-*, *nārikera*, *nālikera*) "cocoanut" (attr.). It is symbolic of fertility. Char. of: Lakṣmī, Bhakti-Vighneśvara. Cp. *śrīphala*, *modaka*.
Lit.: GH 65; MW 537; WHW 1:243.

Narmadā (N.Ind. Narbada, Engl. Nerbudda), n. of a holy river in Middle India, which in sacredness is almost equal to Gaṅgā. As a personification N. is regarded as the wife of Purukutsa.
Lit.: D 221; MG 218.

narmadeśvara ("lord of Narmadā"), n. of a stone found on the River Narmadā and sacred to Śiva.
Lit.: IC 1:539.

Na-ro mkha'-spyod-ma ("Na-ro, enjoyment of heaven"; Tib., pronounced: Na-ro kha-cö-ma; Buddh.), see Sarvabuddhaḍākinī.
Lit.: G 34, 81.

Nā-ro-pa (Tib.; Buddh.), n. of one of the Lamaist *mahāsiddhas*. He lived about A.D. 990. Attr.: *kapāla*, *pātra*.
Lit.: G 94; JT 300.

nartana "dancing" as a rite forms part of the *pūjā*.
Lit.: DiIP 90.

nāstika "denier", one who says "there is not" (*nāsti*), a term, generally used for "atheist", is also n. of some unorthodox sects.
Lit.: WHW 2:125.

naṭamandira "dancing hall", n. of a hall in a temple, in which dancing is performed. Other n.: *nāṭya-*, *nṛttamaṇḍapa*.
Lit.: GOSA p. VIII.

Naṭarāja (or Naṭeśa, Naṭeśvara, Nṛteśvara; "King-of-dance", "Lord-of-dance"), a common n. of Śiva in many manifestations as a cosmical dancer (cp. *nāṭyasthāna*, *nṛttamūrti*). Such dance-forms are esp. the *tāṇḍava*-dances: *ānanda-* (or *bhujaṅgatrāsita*), *catura-*, *gaja-*, *gaurī-*, *kālmāṛi-āḍiya-*, *kālikā-*, *sandhyā-*, *saṅhāra-*, *tripura-*, *umā-*, *ūrdhva-tāṇḍava*, further *kaṭisama*, *lalāṭatilaka*, *lalita*, *nādānta*, *talasaṅsphotita*. But Śiva is also represented dancing in other manifestations (such as Kālārimūrti) which are not strictly regarded as *nṛttamūrtis*. – Śiva has in these dance-forms between 4 and 16 arms, and usually dances upon Apasmāra or other demon-figures; rarely he has Nandin as a Vāh.
The best-known of these dance-forms is the South-Indian bronze-representation of *ānandatāṇḍava*, which is the one usually meant by the n. N. and which shows Śiva performing the *pañcakriyā*. – Other n.: Āṭavallār, Sabhāpati. See also *adharottara*.
Lit.: B 465, 472 a.pl. 34:4, 36-37; BP 157 a.pl. 19-21; CBC passim; DIA pl. 24, 26; GI pl. 70, 83; H pl. 7:60-61; HAHI 27 a.pl. 16B, 19, 88; HSIT 11 a.pl. 24; IA 8; IP pl. 34-35; KrA pl. 124; KrI pl. 57; MH pl. 3-5; R 2:223 a.pl. 55ff.; SB 58 a.passim; SIB pl. 42, 46f.; SSI 77; Th. pl. 52-53; WM 93, 167; ZA 122 a.pl. 231f., 411-414; ZM 168 a.pl. 38-40.

Naṭeśa ("lord of dance"), see Naṭarāja.
Lit.: SB passim; SIB pl. 29.

nātha "lord", n. of a Yogic cult esp. in northern India. Cp. *siddha*.
Lit.: WHW 2:128.

nāṭya "dance". To the *n*. belong many forms of bodily postures (*aṅgikas*), handposes (*mudrās*) etc., which, however, are not listed here.
Lit.: R 2:269; WHW 1:261.

nāṭyamaṇḍapa "dancing hall", see *naṭamandira*.
Lit.: SSIP 106.

nāṭyāsana "dancing attitude" (att.), a term used in BBh. as a variety of *ardhaparyaṅkāsana* (see this word in its sense of a dancing att.) and in WHW as a dance posture like that of the dancing Śiva (Naṭarāja). See *nāṭyasthāna*.
Lit.: BBh. 433; WHW 1:74.

nāṭyasthāna "dance-standing or stance" (att.), n. of a representation of a deity in a dancing pose, esp. of Śiva (Naṭarāja) and Kṛṣṇa, but also of Bhṛṅgin, Cāmuṇḍā, Gaṇeśa (Gaṇapati), Kurukullā, Nairātmā, Padmanarteśvara, Siṅhavaktrā, Skanda (Bāla-Subrahmaṇya), Uḍḍiyāna-Kurukullā, Vajracarcikā, Vajrahuntika-Lokeśvara, Vajrapāṇi-Lokeśvara, Vajravārāhī, Vāsya-Vajravārāhī. Other n.: *nāṭyāsana*, *nṛtya*.
Lit.: SIB 61.

navadurgā ("nine Durgās"), n. of a group of nine deities which may represent different forms of Durgā. These are: Rudracaṇḍā, Pracaṇḍā, Caṇḍogrā, Caṇḍanāyikā, Caṇḍā, Caṇḍavatī, Caṇḍarūpā, Aticaṇḍikā, Ugracaṇḍikā. This last one is the principal of the group. Common char.: att.: *ālīḍhāsana*; Vāh.: *rathas* shaped like *padmas*; Mu.: *tarjanīmudrā*; attr. (may be carried by any one of the 9): *aṅkuśa*, *cakra*, *ḍamaru*, *darpaṇa*, *dhanus*, *dhvaja*, *ghaṇṭā*, *kapāla*, *khaḍga*, *kheṭaka*, *mudgara*, *muṇḍa*, *padma*, *pāśa*, *śakti*, *śalākā*, *śaṅkha*, *śara*, *triśūla*, *vajra*.
Lit.: MEIA 147; R 1:356.

navagraha (*navagṛha*) "nine planets, the nine planet deities". Their names are: Ravi (or Sūrya "sun"), Candra ("moon"), Maṅgala ("Mars"), Budha ("Mercury"), Bṛhaspati ("Jupiter"), Śukra ("Venus"), Śani ("Saturn"), Rāhu ("ascending node"), Ketu ("descending node"); other name-forms also occur. The names are alike in Hinduism and Jainism. See also *graha*, *nakṣatra*, *rāśi*.
Lit.: B 429; HIS 17; KiH 6 a.pl. 5-6; MEIA 81; MW 531; R 1:299, 318 a.pl. 96; RAAI 273; SSI 235; Th. 112.

navagrahaśānti "propitiation rite to appease the nine planet-deities".
Lit.: A. Parpola etc., Progress in the decipherment of the Proto-Dravidian Indus script (1969), 14.

navakaṉṉikaḷ (*-mār*, Tam., from Skt *navakanyā* "nine virgins"), see *navaśakti*.
Lit.: SSR 143, 147.

navamaṇi "nine gems", see *navaratna*.
Lit.: TL 4:2178.

Navanītanṛtta-Kṛṣṇa (or -nṛtya-, Navanītanṛtta-mūrti; "butter-dance-Kṛṣṇa"), n. of a representation of Bālakṛṣṇa (Nṛtya-Gopāla) dancing. In this form Kṛṣṇa usually stands on the left foot, lifting the right foot. For the significance of the butter, cp. Makkhañcor. – Char.: *nāṭyasthāna*; Mu.: *abhayamudrā* or a dance handpose; attr.: *makkhan*.
Lit.: CBC 18 a.fig. 25; JDI 89; R 1:206 a.pl. 60; Th. 68 a.pl. 19; WM 94.

navāṅśa "nine-parted emerald" (attr.), held in one hand, char. of Jambhala.
Lit.: KiSB 73.

navaratha "having nine chariots or parts", n. of a form of the *pīṭha* which, however, is not adequately described.
Lit.: B 403.

navaratna "nine gems", n. of a collection of precious stones which are closely connected with and represent the planets (see *navagraha*). They are: *muktā* "pearl" (full-moon), *māṇikya* or *padmarāga* "ruby" (sun), *puṣparāga* "topaz" (Jupiter), *vajra* "diamond" (Venus), *marakata* "emerald" (Mercury), *pravāla* or *vidruma* "coral" (Mars), *nīla* "sapphire" (Saturn), *vaiḍūrya** "cat's eye" (or, possibly, *vaidūrya*? "lapis lazuli"?, or *candrakānta* "moonstone", the

waxing moon?, = Rāhu), and *gomeda** "sardonyx"? (or *vaiḍūrya* "cat's eye", the waning moon?, = Ketu). – *n.* is also metaphorically used as n. of a group of nine men of high merit in the sphere of literature and the arts, mentioned as the protégés of Vikramāditya (see D, WHW). – Cp. *pañcaratna*.
Lit.: D 221; MW 864; WHW 2:569.

navarātrī ("lasting for nine nights"), n. of a festival which originally lasted for nine days and which takes place in the month *āśvina* (October). The patroness of this festival is, in Bengal, Durgā, in other places, Lakṣmī or Sarasvatī. In South India this feast is connected with the *āyudhapūjā*, the day when all tools are made the object of worship. – Another n.: *daśaharā*.
Lit.: DiCh. 51, 66; DiIP 170; GH 355; WHW 1:355.

navaśakti "nine Śaktis", n. of a group of nine *mātaras* or Śaktis. These are: Vaiṣṇavī, Brahmāṇī, Raudrī, Māheśvarī, Narasiṁhī, Vārāhī, Indrāṇī, Kārttikī, Pradhanā. In other lists Māriyammaṉ is mentioned. – In South India the *n.* form a group of nine virgins (*navakaṉṉikaḷ*) who are held in higher esteem than the *saptamātaras*. At the head of them are placed Pūraṇai and Puṭkalai, the wives of Aiyaṉār; further belong to this group: Māriyammaṉ, Kāliyammaṉ, Ellamaṉ, Aṅkālammaṉ, Piṭāri, Cāmuṇḍi (Cāmuṇḍā), Durgā.
Lit.: FKR 110; MW 1044; SSR 143.

nāyaka "guide, leader" (KiDG, KiSB; Buddh.). This term seems to refer to the particular *buddha* from which a certain deity emanates; cp. *kulanāyaka*, *nāyaṉ(m)ār*. *n.* is also a term for "lover" and for the hero of a drama, cp. *nāyikā*.
Lit.: Gt Suppl. 93; KiDG 68; KiSB 86; WHW 2:19.

Nāyaṉār (Tam.), see Aiyaṉār.

nāyaṉ(m)ār (Tam. "guide, leader"), another n. of a *śaivabhakta**, see *bhakta*.
Lit.: B 302; SSI 259.

nāyikā "mistress, courtezan; a class of female representations representing illicit sexual love", n. of a female sculptural figure, also n. of a heroine of a drama.
Lit.: GOSA passim; Gt Suppl. 93; MW 536.

Negameṣa, see Naigameṣa.
Lit.: JMS 24.

Nemi(nātha) ("protector of the felly of the wheel"; Jain.), esp. among the *digambaras* n. of the 22nd *tīrthaṅkara*. Symbol: *śaṅkha*. – See Ariṣṭanemi.
Lit.: JMS pl. 66; KIM pl. 18; KiSH 143.

Nerbudda (Engl.), see Narmadā.

netramudrā "eye-gesture" (Mu.), n. of a "hand-pose in which the thumb and the little finger are linked together and the other three fingers are held erect in front of the eyes".
Lit.: DiIP 112.

nibbāna (Pāli), see *nirvāṇa*.

nidhi "treasure" (attr.). As an attr. this is represented as a jar filled with gems. *n.* is esp. char. of Kubera who is said to have 9 *n.*: *padma-*, *mahāpadma-*, *śaṅkha-*, *makara-*, *kacchapa-*, *mukunda-* (or *kunda-*), *nanda-*, *nīla-* and *kharva-nidhi*. Of these *padma-* and *śaṅkha-nidhi* are those most frequently mentioned, and all of them may be represented in personified forms as attendants of Kubera. – *n.* is further char. of Jambhala and Śukra. – In Jainism a *cakravartin* is said to be supplied with 9 *n.*
Lit.: B 344 a.pl. 14:2; D 221; GJ 257; MW 548; WHW 1:385.

nidrāstambhana "prevention of sleep", n. of a *mantra* with the purpose: "to suppress sleep".
Lit.: DHP 347.

nidrātahastamudrā "sleeping hand" (Mu.), n. of a handpose in which the hand rests upon the *pīṭha*, supporting the weight of that side of the body.
Lit.: Th. 28 (ill.); WM 101 a.fig. 31.

Nigaṇṭha Nāṭṭaputta (M.Ind.; Jain.), epithet of Mahāvīra.
Lit.: KiDG 79.

nija(māsa) "natural month", see sub *candramāsa*.

nikuṭṭita "pounded, flattened" (att.), see *kuṭṭita*.
Lit.: R 2:263.

nīla "dark blue", the blue colour; see further *kṛṣṇa*. – *n.* is also "sapphire", a precious stone included among the *navaratna** and the *pañcaratna**.
Lit.: MEIA 238; MKVI 2:246; TL 4:2313.

nīlābja "blue lotus" (attr.), see *nīlotpala*.
Lit.: MEIA 262.

nīladaṇḍa "blue staff" (attr.), in this dictionary not distinguished from the *daṇḍa*.
Lit.: BBh. 254.

Nīladaṇḍa (Buddh.), n. of a *dikpāla* of the south-west direction. Char.: colour: blue (black); attr.: *cintāmaṇi*, *daṇḍa*, *khaḍga*, *padma*, *triśiras*. – Other n.: Herukavajra, Vajrakāla.
Lit.: BBh. 254.

Nīladevī ("the blue or black goddess"), n. of a goddess who is sometimes mentioned as the third wife of Viṣṇu (besides Lakṣmī and Bhūmidevī).

Nīlakaṇṭha ("blue-necked"), epithet of Śiva. The n. recalls the occasion on which Śiva's throat turned blue, when, in order to save the world, he drank the poison (*kālakūṭa*) which was produced at the churning of the ocean of milk (see Kūrmāvatāra). Attr. (in one hand): Vāsuki. – N. is also n. of a blue-necked heron which is sacred to Śiva. – Cp. Śrīkaṇṭha, Sitakaṇṭha, Viṣapraharamūrti.
Lit.: B 315; DHP 191; GH 71; GoRI 1:255; MEIA 54; R 2:48; SSI 137; ZA 228.

Nīlakaṇṭha(-Avalokiteśvara, -Lokeśvara, -kaṇṭhāryāvalokiteśvara; "the [honourable] blue-necked A. or L."; Buddh.), n. of a variety of Avalokiteśvara. Char.: colour: yellow; att.: *padmāsana*; Mu.: *dhyānamudrā*; attr.: *ajina*, *Amitābhabimba* on the crown, *candra*, *kamaṇḍalu* (with jewels), *kapāla*, *kṛṣṇājina*, *nāgas*, *nirbhūṣaṇa* (sometimes), *ratnas*.
Lit.: BBh. 140, 396 a.pl. 116, 17(A); G 12, 65; KiSB 60.

Nīlakaṇṭhī ("blue-necked"), n. of a form of Durgā said to grant fortune. Char.: Mu.: *varadamudrā*; attr.: *kheṭaka*, *triśūla*.
Lit.: R 1:342.

Nīlalohita ("dark-blue and red, purple"), n. of one among the group *ekādaśarudra*.
Lit.: Gt 421; R 2:386.

Nīlāmbara ("dressed in a blue garment"), n. of a son of Indra.
Lit.: GH 144.

Nīlāmbara(-Vajrapāṇi) ("V., dressed in a blue garment"; Buddh.), n. of a variety of Vajrapāṇi. Char.: att.: *āliḍhāsana*; attr.: *dharmapālābharaṇa*, *ghaṇṭā*, *nāgas*, *trinayana*, *vajra*.
Lit.: G 62, 64 (ill.).

nīlanalina "blue lotus" (attr.), see *nīlotpala*.
Lit.: DHP 464 (No. 505).

nīlotpala "blue lotus" (a fairly long water lily, Nymphaea stellata or coerulea Willd.; attr.). As attr. *n.* is often confused with the *padma*, but when stress is laid on the colour of the flower, it frequently is used in order to distinguish an image carrying this attr. from one carrying a lotus of another colour. Thus it is said that when Viṣṇu (in South Indian representations) is supplied with two wives, the wife on his right holds a *padma* (Lakṣmī), and the wife on his left a *nīlotpala* (Bhūmidevī). – *n.* may also be made into a garland. – This blue lotus is char. of many deities: Arciṣmatī, Ardhanārīśvara, Aṣṭabhuja-Kurukullā, Avalokiteśvara (in different forms), Bhadrā, Bhūmidevī, Dhanadā, Diti, Ekajaṭā, Gaganagañja, Gaṇeśa, Gāṅgeya-Subrahmaṇya, Hara-Pārvatī, Indra, Jāṅgulī, Jñānadakṣiṇāmūrti, Jñānavaśitā, Kālamañjuśrī, Kalyāṇasundaramūrti, Khadiravaṇī, Mahācīnatārā, Mahārājalīlamañjuśrī, Mañjughoṣa, Mañjukumāra, Mañjuvara, Mārttaṇḍa-Bhairava, Pāṇḍarā, Prajñāpāramitā, Prajñāvardhanī, Praṇidhānapāramitā, Praṇidhānavaśitā, Prasannatārā Rājamātaṅgī, Sadāśiva, Ṣaḍbhuja-Sitatārā, Sādhumatī, Siddhaikavīra, Sitatārā, Śukla-Kurukullā, Śyāmatārā, Tārā, Tulasīdevī,

Vajragarbha, Vajrāṅkuśī, Vajratārā, Vidyujjvālākarālī, Vīryapāramitā, Viśvarūpa, Vyākhyānadakṣiṇāmūrti, Yamunā. – A blue lotus with 5 leaves is a symbol of Nami. – Other attr., such as *khaḍga* or *pustaka* etc., may also be combined with (placed in or on) a *n*. – Other n. or n. of other blue lotuses : *abja* (*nīlābja*), *nīlanalina*, *puṣkara*, *utpala*, *viṣapuṣpa*. See also esp. *padma* and *rājīva*.

Lit.: B 304, 468; G 18 (ill.); MEIA 262; R 1:14 a.pl. 4:14; Th. 42.

nīm (Hi., < Skt *nimba*[*vṛkṣa*]; attr.), n. of a tree (Melia azadirachta or Azadirachta Indica) with bitter fruits, and the leaves of which are chewed at funeral ceremonies. This tree is worshipped together with Śītalā.

Lit.: IC 1:538; P 1169.

Nimbārka (Nimbāditya), n. of a *vaiṣṇavabhakta*, who lived in the 12th c. A.D., the founder of the *nimandi* sect (also called *nimāvats*).

Lit.: GH 387; WHW 2:133.

nimīlita "closed, slightly downcast" (attr.), a term used of the eyes of an image. As a *lakṣaṇa* char. of the Buddha.

Lit.: AIP 78.

rÑiṅ-ma-pa ("the old, ancient order"; Tib.; Buddh.), n. of a (non-reformed) Lamaist sect, known as the "Red hats" (after the colour of the hats which are worn at solemn ceremonies).

Lit.: Enc.Brit. 22:188A; G 5; JT 195.

nirājana "lustration of arms", n. of a ceremony performed by *kṣatriyas* in the month *āśvina* or *kārttika*.

Lit.: IC 1:570; MW 566.

nirbhūṣaṇa "not adorned, having no ornaments" (attr.). Char. of Jain images and Nīlakaṇṭha-Avalokiteśvara, Siṅhanāda-Lokeśvara.

Lit.: B 284.

nirmāṇakāya "body of transformations, or of creation", "Körper der magischen Schöpfung" (BRI; Buddh.), n. of the mortal and ascetic body in which a *mānuṣibuddha*, according to the *trikāya*-system, lives on the earth.

Lit.: BRI 150; G 30; KiSB 41; MW 556; RAAI 273; WHW 2:15.

Nirṛta (or Nirrita; "dissolved; Misery"), n. of the son of Kāśyapa and Surabhi. N. is sometimes counted among the *ekādaśarudra*, sometimes mentioned as a *dikpāla* of the south-west direction (cp. Nirṛti), and even said to be the "Lord-of-the-directions".

Lit.: DHP 137; IIM 32.

Nirṛti (or Nirruti, Nirriti, Nairṛta, Nairṛti; "dissolution, misery, destruction"; originally possibly "disorder, *ṛta*-lessness"). N. was at first NP of a goddess as a personification of misery, but later regarded as a male deity (sometimes, however, also as the wife of Nirṛta), the Genius of death and dissolution. As a messenger of N. *kapota* is mentioned.

1. (Hind.) In Hinduism he is a tutelar god and the *dikpāla* of the south-west direction (cp. Nirṛta). His *diggaja* is Kumuda. He is also the god of the month *caitra*. Usually he is represented as having a terrific appearance which may vary in different images. Wives: Devī (Dīrghādevī), Kālikā, Kṛṣṇāṅgī, Kṛṣṇāvadanā, Kṛṣṇapāśā. Char. : colour : blue or black; Vāh. : *siṅha* or *nara* (or *mṛtaka*) or *gardabha* or *śvan* or *bhadrapīṭha*; attr. : *bhindipāla*, *daṇḍa*, *dantas*, *khaḍga*, *kheṭaka*.

Lit.: B 526; BBh. 382; DHP 138; GoRI 1:98; IIM 33; JDI 108; KiH 10; KiSH 55, 57; MEIA 129; R 2:527 a.pl. 154:2; SSI 243; Th. 110; WM 142.

2. (Buddh.) As a *dikpāla*: Char. : colour : blue; Vāh. : *mṛtaka*; attr. : *khaḍga*, *kheṭaka*.

Lit.: BBh. 362.

Niruktipratisamvit ("etymological analysis"; personification; Buddh.), n. of a *pratisamvit*. Char. : colour : red; attr. : *padma*, *śṛṅkhalā*.

Lit.: BBh. 343 a.pl. 224.

nirvāṇa (Pāli : *nibbāna*). This word is, esp. in Buddhism, but also in the other Indian religions, n. of a state occuring after death which is equivalent to the end of the *saṅsāra*; *n.* is the aim to be striven for by all, but which will be reached only by a few, e.g. by a *buddha* or a *tīrthaṅkara*, who has received perfect enlightenment. Etymologically the word may be interpreted, either as *nirvā-ṇa* "extinction" or annihilation (*śūnya*) of individual existence, the total extinction of all desires or passions, and therefore of all such qualities as cause rebirth (or, with the Hindus, final emancipation and re-union with the Supreme Spirit), or, on the other hand, as *nir-vāṇa* "the windless (state)", this meaning an eternal state in which the deceased cannot be moved or reached by any impression or disturbance from the material world, just as a light, in total calm, neither flickers nor is moved by any puff of wind (which is to be compared with a disturbance from the material world). This corresponds to the view of L. DE LA VALLÉE POUSSIN (see WELBON) that *n.* originally probably signified "un séjour inébranlable". But in spite of the fact that the first explanation does not properly signify a state (but rather the end of a state), this interpretation is the one generally adopted. – See Mahāparinirvāṇamūrti, a representation of the Buddha lying in *nirvāṇa*. – The *nirvāṇa* of the Buddha is also n. of an era beginning in B.C. 543 (B.C. 544, Enc. Brit.), the year in which the Buddha, according to the Buddhists, is believed to have died. This era is used in Sri Lanka and Indo-China. – Another n.: *siddhi*; see also *parinirvāṇa*.

Lit.: J. CHARPENTIER, Buddha, hans liv och lära (Stockholm 1926), 118; Enc.Brit. 5:721; GRI 194, 233, 259; Gt 424; IC 2:546, 736; N 135; ZA 63; G.R. WELBON, The Buddhist Nirvāṇa and its western interpreters (Chicago and London 1968), 299.

Nirvāṇabuddha ("the Buddha [lying] in *nirvāṇa*"; Buddh.), a term used, esp. in Sri Lanka, for Mahāparinirvāṇamūrti.

Lit.: MBPC 93.

Nirvāṇī ("the [goddess] of *nirvāṇa*"; Jain.), n. of a *śāsanadevatā* attending on the 16th *tīrthaṅkara*.

Lit.: GJ 362.

niścalāsana "immovable sitting" (att.), n. of the posture of a bowman: "Left knee straight, right foot back, with knee bent" (cp. *ālīḍhāsana*).

Lit.: WHW 1:76.

niṣka "neck-ornament, necklace, torque" (attr.).

Lit.: B 289

niṣkramaṇa "carrying out", n. of a *saṅskāra*-rite, the ceremony in which a child is for the first time taken out of the house, in the fourth month after birth, to see the sun.

Lit.: DilP 180; MW 562; WHW 2:315.

Niṣpannatārā ("the completed Tārā"; Buddh.), n. of an inferior Mahāyāna goddess.

Lit.: BBh. 151; KiSB 97.

Nistriṅśa ("merciless, terrific"; attr.), n. of the *khaḍga* of the wife (Prīti?) of Pradyumna, and of the *khaḍga* of Ṣaṇmukha and Śāstā.

Lit.: ACA 33; B 301; pw 3:229.

Niṣṭyā ("external"), another n. of a certain *nakṣatra*, see Svātī.

Lit.: IC 2:730.

Niśumbhasūdanī ("destroying the demon Niśumbha"), n. of a form of Durgā. Attr. like Durgā.

Lit: BECA 1: pl. 8; SB 279, 342 a.fig. 284.

nityadevatā ("eternal deity"), n. of minor deities or genies.

Lit.: DHP 301.

nityahoma "perpetual sacrifice", n. of a rite

Lit.: DilP 124; MW 547.

Nityanātha-Lokeśvara ("L., the eternal protector"; Buddh.), n. of a variety of Avalokiteśvara. Char.: att.: *samapādasthānaka*; Vāh.: *padma*; attr.: *akṣamālā, pustaka*.

Lit.: BBh. 431 a.pl. 103(A).

nityotsava "daily festivals", which form part of the *pūjā*.

Lit.: DilP 90, 130, 158.

nivātakavaca ("bearer of impenetrable armor"), n. of a kind of *asura*.
Lit.: D 224; DHP 143.

nivedya ("to be presented, delivered"), see *naivedya*.

nivibandha "knot of lower garment" (attr.), worn by women.
Lit.: SIB 68 a.pl. 37.

niyama "restraining, controlling", in Yogic practice n. of some kinds of observances which are not dealt with in this dictionary.
Lit.: KiH pl. 153.

nṛ "man", see *nara*.

Nṛsiṁhāvatāra (or Nṛsiṁha), see Narasiṁha.
Lit.: DHP 168; GH 121; KiSH 39.

Nṛteśvara (Naṭeśvara, "lord of dance"), see Naṭarāja.

Nṛtta-Gaṇapati (or Nṛtya-; "the dance-G."), n. of a dance-manifestation of Gaṇeśa (8-armed). Attr.: *aṅgulīya, aṅkuśa, danta, kuṭhāra, modaka, pāśa, valaya.*
Lit.: B pl. 15:2; R 1:59 a.pl. 16; SB 349 a.fig. 322; Th. 96; WM 96.

nṛttamaṇḍapa "dance-hall", see *naṭamandira.*
Lit.: BECA 1:262.

nṛttamūrti (or *nṛtya-*), n. of a "dance-manifestation" (*līlā*) of a god, esp. of Śiva, but also of Kṛṣṇa. A *n.* may be represented in many forms; best-known is that of Śiva as *Naṭarāja* (with varieties). Cp. *nāṭyasthāna.*
Lit.: B 277, 464, 472; HSIT 11 a.pl. 24; R 2:223 a.pl. 56ff.; WM 92, 167; ZM 140.

nṛtya "dance" (att.), n. of a dancing posture, see *nāṭyasthāna*, and cp. *nāṭyāsana.*
Lit.: MEIA 218.

Nṛtyā ("dance"; personification; Buddh.), n. of a goddess of the *lāsyā*-group or of one of the Lamaist *aṣṭamātaras*. Char.: colour: green or mixed; att.: *nāṭyasthāna*; attr.: *vajra.*
Lit.: BBh. 314 a.pl. 208; G 36, 82.

nṛtyābhinaya "exhibiting a dancing pose" (Mu.), see *nṛtyahastamudrā.*
Lit.: BBh. 135.

Nṛtya-Gaṇapati (or -Gaṇeśa), see Nṛtta-Gaṇapati.

Nṛtya-Gopāla ("the dancing cow-herd"), epithet of Kṛṣṇa in a dancing att., esp. Navanītanṛtta-Kṛṣṇa.

nṛtyahastamudrā "dance-hand-gesture" (Mu.), n. of a handpose of dancing. Such a pose can be either *asamyuta* (simple, not combined) or *saṃyuta* (combined). Many such poses are mentioned in B, but they are not listed here. – Another n.: *nṛtyābhinaya.*
Lit.: B 278.

nṛtyamūrti, see *nṛttamūrti.*

Nṛvarāha ("man-boar; half-man, half-boar"), n. of Viṣṇu in his Varāhāvatāra. As a representation, see Bhūvarāha.
Lit.: R 1:132.

nūpura "anklet" with small bells attached to it; when the leg moves, it tinkles melodiously (attr.). Char. of: Śiva, Viṣṇu. – Cp. *taṇṭai, valaya.*
Lit.: BBh. 437; SB 115; Th. 46 a.pl. 47; WHW 2:162.

nyagrodha ("down-growing", n. of a tree, Ficus Bengalensis; attr.), see *vaṭa.*
Lit.: GH 63.

nyāsa (properly: "putting down, fixing"), n. of a ceremony, the "assignment of the various gods to the parts of the body" (DiIP). The *n.* means "that gods and divine powers are made to occupy a place. It may be a part of the worshipper's body or parts of an idol". When performing this ceremony a *mantra* is uttered (see esp. DiIP). – Cp. *aṅganyāsa, karanyāsa,* and other forms of *n.*
Lit.: DiIP 75, 100; GRI 172; Gt Suppl. 95; IC 1:569.

O

Oḍḍiyāna-Kurukullā, see Uḍḍiyāna-Kurukullā.
Lit.: KiDG 64; KiSB 97.

Oḍiyāna-Mārīcī, see Uḍḍiyāna-Mārīcī.

ojaḥ sahaḥ saha ojaḥ "might, power, power, might", form of a certain *mantra*.
Lit.: WHW 2:27.

Ola Bībī (Beng.), n. of a cholera goddess in Bengal.
Lit.: GH 135.

ōlai (Tam.), see *pātrakuṇḍala*.
Lit.: R 1:25.

OṀ, *oṁ-kāra* (also given in the analysed form: *AUṀ*) "the syllable *OṀ*", n. of a *bījamantra* named *brahmabīja* or *brahmavidyāmantra*. This is the most celebrated of all *bīja*s. In the Vedic age it was explained in many different ways; in Hinduism it is usually analysed thus: *A* represents Brahmā (and, at the same time, "creation"), *U* represents Viṣṇu (and "maintenance"). *M* represents Śiva (and "destruction"), together symbolizing the Trimūrti. Sometimes it is said that *OṀ* consists of 5 sounds: *A*+*U*+*M*+*bindu* (the point, signifying the *anusvāra* = nasal *m*, sometimes said to symbolize Sadāśiva) + *nāda* (here in the sense of a kind of echo, sometimes said to symbolize Īśvara).
This syllable is used at the beginning of all rituals and all books. Thus it represents, besides Brahmā, Viṣṇu and Śiva, also Gaṇeśa. Its purpose is that it "leads to realization, to liberation from bondage, to the attainment of Supreme Reality" (DHP).
In Buddhism (where its symbolical sense coincides with *triratna*) and in Jainism this *bījamantra* plays an equally essential role. From this *bīja* Vairocana originates.
Lit.: BBh. 53; BPR 17; D 244; DHP 295, 338; GBM 94; GH 54; GJ 367, 384 a.pl. 27; GoRI 1:336, 2:47; Gt 430; IC 1:566; KiJ 12 a.pl. 30; MW 235; WHW 2:104; ZA 103.

OṀ AḤ HUṀ, form of a *mantra* used by both Hindus and Buddhists and interpreted as "Creation, Preservation, Destruction" (also other meanings).
Lit.: WHW 2:27.

oṁ bhūr bhuvas suvaḥ (the last word means *svar*), a frequently used *mantra* or *vyāhṛti* representing the three worlds: earth, space, sky; the words *bhūr bhuvas svar* are also called "the great *vyāhṛti*s". This *mantra* is used "by every Brāhman in commencing his daily prayers" (MW).
Lit.: DHP 248; DiIP 87; MW 1039; WHW 2:27.

oṁ Gaṇeśāya "hail to Gaṇeśa", a *mantra* frequently used at the beginning of a writing, such as e.g. a book, *esp.* a sacred book. – Cp. Piḷḷaiyār.

oṁ maṇi padme hūṁ (Hybrid Skt; Tib. *oṁ-ma-ni-pad-me-hūṁ*; Buddh.), a Lamaist *mantra* or *dhāraṇī* which is esp. connected with Avalokiteśvara, the chief patron of Tibet (whose chief attr. is *padma*) and Dalai Lama as an incarnation of this god. It is generally interpreted in about the following way: "Hail, the Jewel in the Lotus" (CEBI), and here *maṇi*, the jewel, would seem to signify the Buddha, and *padma*, the lotus, should signify the world (the Matrix-World). Connected with Avalokiteśvara it could also allude to his birth from a *padma*. – However, in this *mantra* the word *maṇipadme* is also comprehended as a vocative of a feminine name and translated thus: "O Thou, in whose lotus the jewel stands", which is taken to be an invocation to Avalokiteśvara's Śakti (female potency) with the esoteric meaning: "Thou (Tārā, the Śakti) in whose *yoni* (womb) stands the *liṅga* (the male genital member)", and thus the formula is an expression of the union between Avalokiteśvara and his Śakti (KT). This explanation (of Maṇipadmā as a fem. proper n.) may, however, be doubted. But it is

nevertheless very probable that *maṇi*, like *vajra*, is a term of the male principle (or male genital member; the word *liṅga* is generally not used in Buddhism), and *padma* is a term of the female principle (cp. *yoni*); cp. HuET: "... das *ma-ni*, das Kleinod, dabei den Phallus als Attribut des Mannes und *pad-ma(me)*, die Lotusblüte, den Eingang zum empfangenden Mutterschoss bedeutet...". But it is, on the other hand, also possible that this explanation is founded on a later conception of the *vajra/maṇi* idea. – Every syllable of this *mantra* is identified with a colour: *oṁ* "white", *ma* "blue", *ṇi* "yellow", *pad* "green", *me* "red", *hūṁ* "black".
This *mantra* is, in Tibet and Nepal, repeated on all kinds of banners and banderols, on prayer-strips (in the prayer-wheels, see *ma-ṇi chos 'khor*), etc. – Cp. also *ṣaḍakṣara*.

Lit.: CEBI 86; A. David-Neel, Magic and mystery in Tibet (1965), 259; GBM 94, 101; GRI 297; HuET 47; IC 2:594; JT 607; KT 148; SM 23, 160; WHW 2:27.

ompatu-ammanmār (Tam. "the nine mothers"), see *navaśakti*.
Lit.: SSR 143.

oṁ sac cid ekam brahma "*Oṁ*, das Seiende, das Bewusstsein, das Eine, Brahman", a *mantra* which is connected with a regulation of the breathing in a Tantric text.
Lit.: GoRI 2:50.

oṁ sarvatathāgatasiddhivajrasamaya tiṣṭha eṣas tvāṁ dhārayāmi vajrasattva hi hi hi hum iti (Buddh.), form of a *mantra*, associated with a certain *mudrā* (unnamed), the right hand holding a *vajra*, and the left hand holding a *ghaṇṭā*. It expresses the invocation of the success attained by all *tathāgatas*.
Lit.: B 263 a.pl. 5:7.

oṁ sarvavid vajradhūpe trāṁ (Buddh.), form of a *mantra*, associated with a certain *mudrā* (unnamed), an incense-burner (*dhūpa*) held in the right hand, and the left hand placed below.
Lit.: B 263 a.pl. 5:8.

oṁ tat sat "*Oṁ* That reality", a *mantra* found in Bhagavadgītā and often used by the Hindus.
Lit.: WHW 2:27.

oṁ vajradvī(dī)pe svāhā (Buddh.), form of a *mantra*, associated with a certain *mudrā* (unnamed), and, in some mystic way, connected with a *dīpa*.
Lit.: B 263 a.pl. 5:4.

oṁ vajra guru padma siddhi huṁ "*Oṁ*, most excellent powerful *guru* Padma, miracle worker, *huṁ*" (Buddh.), a Lamaist *dhāraṇī* or *mantra*, which is often repeated by the followers of the Red cap sect (see *rÑiṅ-ma-pa* sub initial *Ñiṅ-*). It is a mantra of praise in honour of their founder Padmasambhava.
Lit.: A. David-Neel, Magic and mystery in Tibet (1965), 262.

oṁ vajranaivedya svāhā (Buddh.), form of a *mantra*, associated with a certain *mudrā* (unnamed), and connected with the *naivedya*.
Lit.: B 263 a.pl. 5:6.

oṁ vajrānalahandaha-pathamabhañjana huṁ (Buddh.), form of a *mantra*, associated with a certain *mudrā* (unnamed), the hands displaying the waving of flames of fire (*anala*).
Lit.: B 263 a.pl. 5:1.

oṁ vajrāṅkuśa ja (Buddh.), form of a *mantra*, associated with a certain *mudrā* (unnamed), the hands imitating the form of an *aṅkuśa*.
Lit.: B 263 a.pl. 5:5.

oṁ vajrapāśa hrīṁ (Buddh.), form of a *mantra*, associated with a certain *mudrā* (unnamed), showing the hands tied by a *pāśa*.
Lit.: B 263 a.pl. 5:2.

oṁ vajrapuṣpe svāhā (Buddh.), form of a *mantra*, associated with a certain *mudrā* (unnamed), the hands indicating the offering of a palmful of flowers.
Lit.: B 263 a.pl. 5:3.

oṁ vajra sattva "*Oṁ*, most excellent (diamond) being" (Buddh.), a Lamaist *dhāraṇī*. The excellent-one indicates the Buddha.
Lit.: A. David-Neel, Magic and mystery in Tibet (1965), 262.

ōri (Tam.) "jackal" (Vāh.), see *sṛgāla.*

oṣadhipātra "vessel containing medicinal herbs" (attr.). Char. of: Aśvinīdevatās, Bhūmidevī.
Lit.: R 1:376.

Ostārakī (Hybrid Skt: "covering, slaying down" (?); Buddh.), n. of a minor Mahāyāna goddess attending on Buddhakapāla.
Lit.: BBh. 160; EB 160.

P

paccekabuddha (Pāli), see *pratyekabuddha.*

pādacihna (or *pada-*) "foot-mark, -print" (attr.), see *pāduka.*

pādajāla "foot-net" (attr.), perhaps a kind of anklet (cp. *pādajālaka*). Char. of the Buddha.
Lit.: MBPC 81.

pādajālaka "anklet" (attr.), see *pādasara.*
Lit.: AIP passim.

pādamudrā "foot-seal" (attr.), see *pāduka.*
Lit.: WHW 1:362.

Padañjeli (Tam. more correctly: Patañcali), see Patañjali.
Lit.: HSIT 13 a.pl. 32.

pādapīṭha "footstool" (Vāh.), n. of a small *pīṭha*, on which the image, while sitting on a larger *pīṭha*, rests one foot or both feet. A special kind of *p.* is the *karṇikā*. Cp. also Kumbhodara.
Lit.: BECA 1:262; Th. pl. 13.

pādarakṣa "foot-guard" (attr.), n. of a kind of wooden sandals. Char. of Bhikṣāṭanamūrti and devotees.
Lit.: JDI 31.

pādasara (Th.: *-sura*) "short chain used as an anklet" (attr.). – Another n.: *pādajālaka.*
Lit.: SB 31, 37, 59; SIB 69; Th. 46 a.pl. 46.

pādasvastika "foot-cross, crossed legs" (att.), n. of a standing posture in which one leg crosses the other leg which is firmly planted. Char. of: Madanagopāla, Veṇugopāla, Vṛṣavāhana. – Another n.: *vidgala*(?)
Lit.: SIB 61; SSI 43.

padma "lotus (Nelumbium speciosum Willd.)" is one of the most important symbols of Indian iconography. It is "the emblem of creation" (R) and a "Repräsentant fleckenloser Reinheit und Schönheit" (HIS), and it symbolizes the "purity of descent" (BBh.), "la naissance miraculeuse" (H), i.e. "divine birth"; but it is "also the Tree of Life and of Good Fortune" (MS); and "represents the Universe" (DHP); for *p.* as "Earth-Lotus", see CEBI. – A full-blown *p.* (*vikasitapadma*) may principally be regarded as a sun symbol; cp. that the sun-god Sūrya carries two such *padmas*; also the *p.*, held by Viṣṇu in one of his hands, should, according to KiSH, characterize him as a sun Genius, but it may be noticed that the *p.* of Viṣṇu usually has the form of a lotus-bud, and this may rather be interpreted as a creative or fertility symbol. – In Buddhism *p.* is a "pledge of salvation and symbol of divine origin" (G). "The lotus flower, by reproducing from its own matrix, rather than in the soil, is a symbol of spontaneous generation. And the lotus which serves as a throne for the Buddhas indicates, therefore, divine birth" (SM). It is here also a symbol of the Matrix-World, and in the esoteric Vajrayāna Buddhism it signifies the female principle or the female genitals (as a substitute for the Hindu *yoni*).

As pointed out above a *p.* is represented both in its full-blown form and as a bud, these forms eventually being connected with different symbolic meanings. The *p.*, though properly indicating a lotus of red colour, may be regarded as a common n. for lotus-flowers whatever their colour (cp. *kamala* "red lotus", *puṇḍarīka* and *kumuda* "white lotus", *nīlotpala* and other names for the "blue lotus"; cp. also *puṣpa* "flower", sometimes used like *p.*), but the *nilotpala* is in particular usually differentiated from the other *padmas*. – Other n.: *abja*, *ambhoja*, *mahāmbuja*, *paṅkaja*, *puṣpābja*, *saroja*, *viśvapadma*.

The symbolic functions of *p.* may be classified as follows:

1. (Vāh.) *p.* corresponds to a Vāh., when an image is represented sitting or standing on or in a *p.* Char. esp. of: Lakṣmī, Brahmā, Sarasvatī (in different forms), the Buddha, Avalokiteśvara (in different forms); further of: Budha, Nāmasaṅgīti, Prajñāpāramitā, Rājamātaṅgī, Śākyamuni Śani, Śītalā, Śrīvidyādevī, Śukra, Sūrya(?), Tārodbhava-Kurukullā, Tulasīdevī, Vajraprastāriṇī, Vajraśāradā, Vajratārā, Vindhyavāsi-Durgā, Viṣṇu. A *p.* drawn by *sūkaras* is the Vāh. of Mārīcī.

2. (Attr.) *p.* as an attr. may be carried in one hand or worn on other parts of the body, or may in other ways be connected with an image; it may also be combined with other attributes so that e.g. a *pustaka*, a *vajra*, a *viśvavajra* is placed within a *p.*; in this dictionary this combination of attr. is referred to thus: "*padma* with *pustaka*" etc.

Char. of: esp. Viṣṇu (red *p.*), Lakṣmī (in different forms), Sūrya (2 *vikasita-padmas*), Sarasvatī, Amitābha, Avalokiteśvara (in different forms, esp. as Padmapāṇi); further of: Acala, Acalā, Adhimuktacaryā (red *p.*), the 12 Ādityas (2 or more *p.*), Aghora, Ākāśagarbha, Akṣobhya, Aparājita, Ardhanārīśvara, Āryasarasvatī, Āryatārā, Balarāma, Bhṛkuṭī, Bhūmidevī, Brahmā, Caturbhuja-Tārā, Cundā, Devasenā, Dhara, Dharma, Dharmavaśitā, Dhyānapāramitā (white *p.*), Durgottāriṇī-Tārā, Gaganagañja, Gaṇeśa, Gaṅgā, Grahamātṛkā, Hari-Hara, Hayagrīva, Hevajra, Indra, Jagadgaurī, Jyeṣṭhā, Kāma, Karmavajra, Khadiravaṇī, Kṣāntipāramitā (white *p.*), Kṣemaṅkarī, Lalitā, Locanā, Lokanātha, Mahābala, Mahāmantrānusāriṇī, Mahāmāyūrī, Mahāpratyaṅgirā, Mahāsāhasrapramardanī, Mahāsarasvatī, Mahāśītavatī, Mahāsthāmaprāpta, Maṅgala, Maṇidhara, Mañjuśrī (in different forms), Mārttaṇḍa-Bhairava (red *p.*), Māyājālakrama-Kurukullā (red *p.*), *navadurgās*, Nīladaṇḍa, Nirukti-Pratisamvit, Padmaḍākinī, Padmāntaka (red *p.*), Pāṇḍarā, Paramāśva, the *pāramitā*-group (*p.* of different colours), Paṭṭinī Devī, Prajñāntaka, Prajñāpāramitā (red *p.*), Priyodbhava, Rājarājeśvarī, Raktalokeśvara (red *p.*), Riddhi, Ṣaḍbhuja-Sitatārā, Sadharma, Samantabhadra, Saṅ-dui, Ṣaṇmukha, *saptamātaras*, Śarabha, Śaravaṇabhava, Satya, Saubhāgya-Bhuvaneśvarī (red *p.*), Saurabheya-Subrahmaṇya, Senānī, Siṅhanāda, Sita-Prajñāpāramitā (red *p.*), Sitatārā (white *p.*), Skanda, Skandamātā, Soma (Candra), Sukhāvatī, Sumbharāja, Sureśvara, Sūrya-Lokeśvara, Sūrya-Nārāyaṇa, Ṭakkirāja, Tārodbhava-Kurukullā (red *p.*), Trimūrti, Tripurasundarī, Tsoṅ-kha-pa, Tulasīdevī, Uḍḍiyāna-Kurukullā (red *p.*), Uṣṇīṣa, Vaikuṇṭha, Vajracarcikā, Vajradhātvīśvarī, Vajrānaṅga, Vajraśāradā, Vajrasarasvatī, Vallī, Varuṇa, Vāruṇī, Vasudharā, Veṇugopāla, Vibhava, Vighnāntaka, Vimalā (white *p.*), Viṣṇu-Lokeśvara, Viśvamātā (white *p.*), Viśvarūpa, Vyākhyānadakṣiṇāmūrti, Yamadūtī, Yamāntaka; also other deities not mentioned here.

A red *p.* with 7 leaves is a symbol of Padmaprabha. – It may be noticed that a Hindu two-armed goddess who carries a *p.*, may very often be identified as a Lakṣmī (or Bhūmidevī, Riddhi), but that a two-armed goddess without any attr. in the hands may be regarded as Pārvatī.

p. is also n. of a Hindu *yantra* and a Buddhist *maṅgala* ("ein Symbol der Vollkommenheit" GBM; see *aṣṭamaṅgala*). – In architecture *p.* is n. of part of the basement or foundation.

Lit.: B 304, 436; BECA 1:272; CEBI 17; DHP 156,

354; G 8, io (ill.); GBM 102, 160; GH 65; GJ pl. 22:21, 23:6; H 20 a.pl. 5:46a-b, 16; HIS 38; HuET 47; IC 2:593; KiJ pl. 45; KiSH 35; MEIA 263; MS 48; R 1:13, 236 a.pl. 4:11-13; SM 159; Th. 39; WM 110; ZA 168; ZM 110.

Padma ("lotus"), NP of a *nāgadeva*. Attr.: *akṣamālā, kamaṇḍalu, trinayana*. Another n.: Puṇḍarīka.
Lit.: R 2:557.

Padmā (personification of the lotus or of a goddess as emanated from a lotus), NP of the wife of Viṣṇu Vāmanāvatāra (as an incarnation of Lakṣmī). It is also said that P. symbolizes Lakṣmī as the "Earth-lotus". – Another n.: Kamalā; see also Padmāvatī.
Lit.: CEBI 22; DHP 261; GoRI 1:319; MG 103; R 1:373; ZA 22, 158.

padmabandha "lotus-frieze", n. of a section of a pillar of a temple.
Lit.: BECA 1:262, 272.

padmacandrāsana "moon as a seat upon a *padma*" (Vāh.). Char. of Mahāsāhasrapramardanī.
Lit.: BBh. 216.

Padmaḍākinī (Buddh.), n. of a *ḍākinī*; she is also found attending on Mahāmāya. Char.: colour: red; attr.: *caturmukha, dhanus, kapāla, khaṭvāṅga, padma, śara.*
Lit.: BBh. 164; G 16, 34, 80; KiSB 67.

padmahasta "holding a lotus in the hand" (attr.), see *padma*.

Padmaheruka ("lotus-Heruka"; Buddh.), n. of Amitābha as a *herukabuddha*. Colour: red.
Lit.: G 7.

Padmaja (or -jāta; "born from a lotus"), epithet of Brahmā.
Lit.: ZA 168.

padmāka "having the form of a lotus leaf", in architecture n. of a kind of village-plan.
Lit.: DKI 79.

padmamālā "lotus-garland" (attr.). Char. of Dhātā.
Lit.: R 1:310.

padmamudrā "lotus-pose", or *padmakośamudrā* "lotus-bud-pose" (Mu.), n. of a 'major *mudrā*': "the palm is gently hollowed, fingers separated and a little bent as if holding a round object. It signifies the female breast, a fruit, a bud, the hole of a snake, an egg". (WHW). As varieties thereof are mentioned: *saurapadma-, alapadma-, laṅgūla-, sandaṅśa-* and *kaṭihasta-mudrās*. – *p.* is also mentioned as belonging to the *pañcamudrā*.
Lit.: DiIP 105; WHW 2:87.

Padmamuṇḍa ("lotus-head"; Vāh.; Buddh.), n. of a human being upon which Jambhala treads.
Lit.: KiSB 75.

Padmanābha ("he who has a lotus navel" or "he whose navel is the World lotus"), epithet of Viṣṇu alluding to his manifestation as Anantāśāyana, in which Brahmā was born from the lotus growing up from the navel of Viṣṇu. P. is an aspect of Viṣṇu, see *caturviṅśatimūrti*. Śakti: Śraddhā.
Lit.: CEBI 17 a.pl. B; DHP 154; Gt 432; KiSH 39; R 1:229; SSI 50.

Padmanarteśvara (or -nartteśvara; "lord of the lotus dance"; Buddh.), n. of a variety of Avalokiteśvara. Char.: colour: red; att.: *nāṭyasthāna* together with the Śakti, also *āsana*; Mu.: *nṛtyahasta-, sūci-mudrā*; attr.: *Amitābhabimba* on the crown, *padmas, mahāmbujas, trinayana*; he is 18-armed.
Lit.: BBh. 133 a.pl. 110-112; G 66; KiSB 58.

padmanidhi "lotus-treasure" (attr.), n. of a form of *nidhi*. Char. of: Kubera, Lakṣmī. As a personification Padmanidhi is an attendant of Kubera; P. is further n. of an elephant in the retinue of Lakṣmī.
Lit.: B 344, 374, 376; R 2:536.

Padmāntaka ("destructive to the lotus"; Buddh.), n. of a *dikpāla* of the west direction. Char.: colour: red; attr.: *cakra, cintāmaṇi, khaḍga, padma* (red), *triśiras*. – Another n.: Vajroṣṇīṣa.
Lit.: BBh. 253.

Padmapāṇi ("having a lotus in the hand"; Buddh.), n. of a *bodhisattva* who usually is regarded as a form of Avalokiteśvara. Char.: colour: white or red; att.: *lalitāsana, rājalīlāsana* or *sthānaka*; Mu.: *abhaya-, varada-, vyākhyāna-mudrā*; attr.:

akṣamālā, *Amitābhabimba* in the hair, *jaṭā-mukuṭa*, *kamaṇḍalu*, *padma*, *pustaka*, *trinayana*, *triśūla*.
Lit.: AIP 78 a.pl. 60 (334); BBh. 49, 51 a.pl. 21; CEBI pl. 15:44; G 14, 64; HAHI pl. 3B; IP pl. 36; KiDG 36; KiSB 46; KrA pl. 109; RAAI pl. 98; WAA 25:172 a.fig. 19-20; ZA 181.

Padmapāṇi-Lokeśvara ("L. as P."; Buddh.), n. of a variety of Avalokiteśvara. Char.: att.: *samapādasthānaka*; Vāh.: *padma*; Mu.: *varadamudrā*; attr.: *padma*.
Lit.: BBh. 431 a.pl. 104(A).

padmapīṭha "lotus-throne, -seat" (Vāh.), n. of a kind of *pīṭha* upon which a deity sits or stands. This seat is round and adorned with either a single or a double row of lotus leaves round the basal layer, which may be round or quadrangular. The seat may also consist of the pericarp of a lotus. The *p.* is often equipped with a *karṇikā* as a footstool and often has a *prabhāvalī*. Char. of (among others): Brahmā, Bṛhaspati (standing), the Buddha, Caṇḍeśvara, Rudramūrti, Sarasvatī, and many other deities. – Other n.: *pīṭhapadma*, *kamalāsana*, *padmāsana*.
Lit.: B 273; MEIA 222; R 1: pl. 6:1; 2:101, 503 a.pl. 12; SSI pl. I:12.

Padmaprabha ("lotus-splendour"; Jain.), n. of the 6th *tīrthaṅkara*. Symbol: red *padma* with 7 leaves.
Lit.: GJ 273 a.pl. 24:6; KiJ 11 a.pl. 27:6; KiSH 142.

Padmarāga ("lotus-hued"; attr.), n. of the *cintāmaṇi* (possibly a "ruby", see *navaratna*) worn by Āyurvaśitā.
Lit.: BBh. 329; MW 584.

Padmasambhava ("born in or from a lotus"; Buddh.), n. of a Tibetan Tantric learned man and saint in the 8th c. A.D., who is regarded as the founder of Lamaism. He is esp. worshipped by the *rÑiṅ-ma-pa*-sect. Char.: att.: *padmāsana* on a *padmapīṭha*; attr.: *khaṭvāṅga*, *pātra*, *vajra*.
Lit.: G passim; GBM 67; HSIT 16 a.pl. 41; HuGT 22.

padmāsana "lotus sitting attitude; lotus seat". 1. (Att.) Popular n. of the sitting posture, esp. of the Buddha and many Buddhist images, many *tīrthaṅkaras* and also many Hindu deities. It is described thus: "both legs are crossed and the feet are brought to rest on the opposite thighs" (Th.), cp. GH: "man lege den rechten Fuss auf den linken Schenkel und den linken Fuss auf den rechten Schenkel und ergreife mit beiden Händen fest die grossen Zehen" (as to the last part of the description, cp. *bhadrāsana*). R gives an explanation similar to that of Th., but in the ill., to which he refers, the feet are not resting upon the thighs but on the knee-joints.
In this dictionary the term *p.* is used according to the explanation of Th. and the posture illustrated in ZA pl. 62a. In Buddhist icons a little *vajra*, sometimes shown upon the seat beside the idol, indicates the meditative att., cp. *vajrāsana*. – Other n. (or n. of slightly varying forms): *baddhapadmāsana*, *dhyānāsana*, *kamalāsana*, *vajraparyaṅkāsana*, *vajrāsana*; another variety is *kukkuṭāsana*; sometimes also *paryaṅkāsana* and *yogāsana* are identified with *p.*
Lit.: B 270; BBh. 433; GH 292; GJ 390; KiH pl. 151 row 1:4; MH 7; R 1:18 a.pl. 5:17; SM 122; Th. 36; WHW 1:76; WM 90 a.fig. 2; ZA pl. 62a.
2. (Vāh.) *p.* is also n. of a *pīṭha*, a (usually round) "lotus-seat", which however, is generally named *padmapīṭha*.
Lit.: BBh. 433; G 24; R 1:17, 19; SB 23 a.fig. 14.

padmāsanamudrā "the handpose in the *padmāsana*-attitude" (Mu.), see *dhyānamudrā*.
Lit.: SM N.1 on p. 85.

Padmāsana ("having a lotus as seat"), epithet of Brahmā sitting upon the pericarp of a lotus which is growing up from the navel of Viṣṇu (Anantāśāyana). – P. is also an epithet of the Buddha. – See also Kamalāsana.
Lit.: CEBI 17 a.pl. B, a.p. 48.

padmasiṅhāsana "lotus-lion-throne", n. of a seat with supports carved in the form of a lotus. – Cp. *siṅhāsana*.
Lit.: MH 44.

Padmastha-Buddha ("the Buddha on a *padma*"; attr.; Buddh.), another n. of *Buddhabimba* (see sub Buddha), usually carried on the crown or in one of the hands of an image.
Lit.: BBh. 214.

padmasthāṣṭāracakra "the eight-spoked wheel of a lotus" (as a variety of *cakra*, alluding to the eight-fold path; attr.; Buddh.). Char. of Mahāsāhasrapramardanī.
Lit.: BBh. 303.

Padmatārā ("lotus-Tārā"; Buddh.), n. of an inferior Mahāyāna goddess.
Lit.: KiSB 61.

Padmāvatī ("having a lotus").
1. (Hind.) As Padmā or Padmāvatī epithet of Manasā.
Lit.: B 563; GoRI 2:21.
2. (Jain.) NP of a *śāsanadevatā* attending on the 23rd *tīrthaṅkara*. She is connected with the *nāgas* and a Jain counterpart of the Hindu Manasā.
Lit.: B 563; GJ 362 a.pl. 27:23; KiJ 12 a.pl. 30:23.

Padmoṣṇīṣa ("lotus-*uṣṇīṣa*"; Buddh.), n. of an *uṣṇīṣa*-deity. Char.: colour: red; Mu.: *dhyānamudrā*; direction: west.
Lit.: BBh. 300.

pādodaka "foot-water" (attr.), n. given to the water used for washing the feet (of a *guru* and others, cp. *caraṇāmṛta*), and then used by the Liṅgāyats in the adoration of the *liṅga*. It is included among the *aṣṭāvaraṇa*. Cp. *pādya*.
Lit.: GoRI 2:249.

pāduka (or *-kā*, plur. *pādukā*, Hybrid Skt) "foot-mark, -print", also "shoes, slippers" (attr.), used as the symbol of a god. The Buddha was early worshipped by the adoration of his *pādukā* (together with *pallaṅka* under the *bodhivṛkṣa*). Later Hindu gods are also symbolized by *p.*, esp. Viṣṇu. In his incarnation as Rāma, his sandals were installed on his throne as a symbol of his ruling power during his exile; hence, *p.* is also a symbol of royalty (see *rājakakuda*). The *p.* of Gaurī is also worshipped. – The *p.* is usually adorned with pictures, e.g. of *cakra* (*dharmacakra*), *svastika* and other *maṅgalas*. – Other n.: *caraṇa*, *pādacihna*, *pādamudrā*, *śrīpatula*; cp. also Biṣṇ-pad, Buddhapāda, Nandipāda, Viṣṇupāda.
Lit.: BKI 84; BBh. 36 (fig. 4); CBC 20 a.pl. 21:108; CEBI 17 a.pl. 4:13; 4:15; CHIIA 31; H pl. 3:26; KiH 29 a.pl. 108, 111; KiSB 150; KiSH 90; WHW 1:361.

pādya "water for the washing of feat" (attr.), see *pūjā*.
Lit.: DiIP 90.

pagod(a) (N.Ind., cp. Port. *pagode*, < Pkt *bhagodī* < Skt *bhagavatī*, or, according to another explanation, derived by a kind of metathesis from *dāgaba**, *dagoba*; a third etymology refers *p.* to Pers. *butkada* "idol temple"), n. of a sacral building, similar to a *stūpa*, in East Asia.
Lit.: Gz 41; F. Kluge, Etymologisches Wörterbuch der deutschen Sprache (18. Aufl. 1960), 527; The Oxford dictionary of English etymology, ed. by C.T. Onions... (1966); SeKB 99.

pākajā (scil. *devatā*: "made by cooking, melting"), n. of an icon made of metal, a cast icon.
Lit.: B 208.

pakṣa (properly "wing") "half a lunar month, i.e. 15 days (*tithis**) of a month". The n. originates in the *pūrṇimānta*-reckoning of the month (beginning with the full-moon), in which the dark fortnight (*kṛṣṇapakṣa*) and the bright fortnight (*śuklapakṣa*) are regarded as "wings" on either side of the new moon. – *p.* is also a symbolic n. of the number "2", see *saṅkhyā*. –
Lit.: IC 2:722; MW 573.

Paḻaṉiyāṇṭavaṉ (Tam., a god of Palni), n. of a South Indian god who is a form of either Skanda or Murukaṉ.
Lit.: DiCh. 34.

palāśa, n. of a tree, see *kiṅśuka*.
Lit.: IC 1:538.

Pāla-Sena, n. of two dynasties in Bengal, and of a centre of arts in the 8th-12th cc. A.D.
Lit.: Gz 141; RAAI 152.

pālidhvaja "row of flags" (attr.; Jain.); see *dhvaja*.
Lit.: GJ 432.

pālikā "earthen pot, in which nine different seeds are sown and allowed to sprout. It is carried in procession by women..." (attr.). This forms an important part of the ritual at the weddings in South India.
Lit.: DiIP 176; SSR 51.

Palinātar (or Palināyakar; Tam. from Skt *bali* + *nātha* and *nāyaka* respectively; "lord of sacrifice"), in South India n. of an aspect of Śiva, represented at the daily festivals and processions. – Another n.: Śrīpalinātar.
Lit.: DiIP 129, 151 with ill.

Palināyaki (Tam., fem. to Palināyakar, see Palinātar; "lady of sacrifice"), n. of an aspect of Pārvatī as Śakti of Palinātar.
Lit.: DiIP 129, 151 with ill.

pāliyā (!), a so-called *satī*-memorial, set up in memory of a woman who has burned herself with her husband's corpse. Cp. *virakkallu.*
Lit.: KiH 33 a.pl. 127a-e.

pallaṅka (Pāli, < Skt *paryaṅka*) "throne, seat" (esp. Buddh.), n. of an empty throne at the foot of the *bodhivṛkṣa*, symbolizing the Buddha, or, more correctly, it "suggests the moment when he at last attained Spiritual Enlightenment" (DIA). – See further *āsana, pīṭha.*
Lit.: CEBI 39, 49; DIA 18 a.pl. 11.

pallava "sprout, shoot, spray; tender leaves of plants" (attr.). When held in one hand char. of Aiyaṉār.
Lit.: R 2:489.

Pallava, n. of South Indian dynasty who ruled at Kānchipuram, and of an epoch of arts flourishing between the 5th-9th cc. A.D., leaving monuments of fine arts still existent.
Lit.: Gz 121; K.A. NILAKANTA SASTRI, A history of South India (London 1955), 437; RAAI 180; WHW 2:169.

paḷḷi (Tam.) "town, castle; temple, almshouse, habitation of ascetics". This word is included in many South Indian local names (e.g. Tirucchirapalli). In South Indian inscriptions the term is esp. used to signify Jain temples.
Lit.: MD 2:274; SB 103; TL 4:2552.

PĀṀ, form of a red *bīja* from which Pāṇḍarā originates (Buddh.).
Lit.: BBh. 50.

pān (Hi., < Skt *parṇa*) "leaf, betel-leaf" (attr.), n. of an accessory to the betel-chewing, see *tāmbūla.*

pānāpātra "drinking-vessel, cup" (attr.). Char. of Balarāma.
Lit.: B 306.

panasa(phala) "(fruit of) the breadfruit or Jaka tree, Artocarpus Integrifolia" (attr.). Char. of Bāla-Gaṇapati.

paṇava "small drum or cymbal" (attr.). Char. of Caṇḍā.
Lit.: MEIA 257; MW 580.

pañca "five". That this is a number of magical and mystical significance may be seen from the many following articles in which *pañca* is included as the first word-member. In STP it is explained as follows, "It consists of 2+3, the first even and first odd numbers – i.e. if unity is God alone, 2 = diversity, while 3 = 1+2 = unity and diversity. Thus the two principles of nature are represented". This number is, above all, characteristic of Śiva. – Cp. also *smarahara.*
Lit.: STP 1:255, 5:175, 8:247; WHW 2:137.

pañcabhūta "the five elements" (earth, air, fire, water and ether). See also *bhūta, pañcaratna.*
Lit.: MW 576.

Pañcabrahmā ("the five Brahmās"), collective n. of the five aspects of Śiva as Īśāna, Tatpuruṣa, Aghora, Vāmadeva and Sadyojāta. – Another n.: Īśānādayas; see also Sadāśivamūrti, Pañcānana.
Lit.: R 2:375.

pañcacīra(ka) "the five pieces of monkish garments" (attr.). Char. of: Vāc, Arapacana. – Cp. *tricīvara.*
Lit.: BBh. 103.

pañcadaśī "the Thought-form of Fifteen-Syllables of the First goddess"), a *mantra*, representing the power of the Self, the power of the world's enchantment, and

with the purpose of attaining all desires and liberation.
Lit.: DHP 349.

Pañcadehamūrti ("representation [of Śiva] with five bodies"), n. of a form of Śiva consisting of five images, four of which stand in the four directions, the fifth is placed in the middle with its head higher than the others. This concept is also symbolized by the Pañcamukhaliṅga.
Lit.: SSI 77.

pañcagavya "the five products of the cow (*viz.* milk, coagulated or sour milk, butter, urine and dung)" (attr.), which are regarded as beneficial means of purification.
Lit.: DiIP 108; GH 68; IC 1:535; MW 575; WHW 1:257.

pañcāgni "five fires" (attr.), n. of the five domestic fires, see sub *agni*; also another n. for *pañcatapas*.
Lit.: MW 577.

Pāñcajanya (derived from Pañcajana; attr.), NP of the conch (*śaṅkha*), carried by Viṣṇu and Kṛṣṇa. According to usual tradition, this attr. was taken from the demon Pañcajana who was slain by Kṛṣṇa. The n. is also interpreted as "Born-of-Five" (DHP), and it is also said that P. came forth at the churning of the ocean of milk, see Kūrmāvatāra.
Lit.: B 300; D 226; DHP 155; MW 614; WHW 1:47; WM 105.

pañca-ka-kāra (or *pañca-kakka*) "the five *ka*-things" (attr.), n. of a group of five essentials of the Sikhs (named by words beginning with the letter *k*). This group is evidently made up as a counterpart of the *pañca-ma-kāra*, and it is said that the Sikhs wear the five *k*s, viz. *keś* "long hair", *kaṅghā* "comb", *kācchā* (or *kuccha*) "loin cloth", *kaṛā* "iron bangle" and *kirpān* "dagger".
Lit.: GG p. CLVII; R. SEGAL, The crisis of India (London 1965), 85; WHW 2:399.

pañcakapāla(ka) "(wearing) five skulls (on the head, *śiras*)" (attr.). Char. of: Heruka, Mahākāla.
Lit.: BBh. 156.

pañcakoṇa "pentagon (star)", n. of a *yantra* which symbolizes "love and lust as well as the power of disintegration"; the number of "five" is esp. associated with Śiva, the Progenitor and the source of life.
Lit.: DHP 353.

pañcakriyā "five activities", n. of the "embodiment and manifestation of the eternal energy (of Śiva as Naṭarāja, esp. in the *ānandatāṇḍava*-dance) in five activities" (ZA): 1. *sṛṣṭi* (creation); 2. *sthiti* (maintenance); 3. *saṅhāra* (destruction or taking back); 4. *tirobhāva* (concealing, hiding the transcendental essence behind the garb of apparitions); 5. *anugraha* (favouring, bestowing grace through a manifestation that accepts the devotee).
Lit.: Sh. 100; ZA 122 a.pl. 411-414; ZM 168.

pañcākṣara "consisting of five syllables", n. of a *mantra* composed of five syllables. Best-known is the *p.* dedicated to Śiva and having the form: *(Oṁ) Śi-vā-ya-na-ma* or *na-ma-Śi-vā-ya* "praise to Śiva". It may be noticed that the number "five" is esp. connected with Śiva, and this *mantra* plays an important part in Śaivite symbolism and has as its aim "Spiritual realization as well as worldly achievement and warding off danger and fear" (DHP). – There is, however, also a *p.* dedicated to Viṣṇu with the form: *(Oṁ) na-mo-Vi-ṣṇa-ve* "praise to Viṣṇu".
Lit.: DHP 348; DiIP 286; R 2:246; WHW 2:27.

pañcaloha (or *-lauha*) "five metals" or "consisting of five metals" (*viz.* copper, brass, tin, lead, iron), a term, signifying a bronze icon made of an alloy containing the above mentioned metals. This kind of alloy was used in earlier times, esp. in South India. – Cp. *aṣṭadhātu, lohaja.*
Lit.: GJ 390; KIM 29; MH 5; MW 577; WHW 2:66; ZA 111.

pañca-ma-kāra "the five *m*s"; the five essentials of the left-hand Tantra ritual, named by words beginning with the letter *m.*, viz. *madya* "wine", *māṅsa* "meat", *matsya*

"fish", *mudrā* "intertwining of the fingers", and *maithuna* "sexual union". "In the higher yogic practice these become 'drinking of the wine which flows from the center-of-the-thousand-petals at the summit of the head; killing lust, anger, greed, delusion, and other evil beasts; cooking the fish of deceit, calumny, envy, etc.; showing the gestures of hope, desire, and contempt; and enjoying the lustful beauties found along the spinal cord. These five actions lead man to inner perfection'" (DHP). The *p.* belong to the *cakrapūjā* rite. – See also *pañcatattva*.
Lit.: BPR 73; DHP 383; GRI 183; IC 1:594; MW 576; WHW 1:221.

pañcamī ("the fifth"), n. of a spring festival about the vernal equinox, at which the tools are made the object of worship. – Cp. *āyudhapūjā*.
Lit.: GH 51.

pañcāmṛta "five-nectar-drink" (attr.), n. of a drink consisting of milk, coagulated or sour milk, *ghī*, honey (or water), sugar. This mixture is put in a *kalaśa* and then poured over an icon during the *pūjā*.
Lit.: DiIP 109; GJ 429.

pañcamudrā.
1. (Mu.) "Five handposes" to be made when presenting offers to an image. These are: *dhenu-*, *padma-*, *liṅga-*, *astra-* and *mahā-mudrā*.
Lit.: DiIP 105; MW 577.
2. (Attr.) "Five auspicious symbols" (Buddh.). These symbols should properly be six in number, and they are mentioned sub *ṣaṇmudrā*; if one of those symbols is missing, the remaining five symbols are called *p.* – Char. of: Mahācīnatārā, Vajracarcikā.
Lit.: BBh. 190.

pañcamukha "five-headed" (attr.), see *pañcaśiras*.

Pañcamukhaliṅga ("five-faced *liṅga*"), n. of a *liṅga* with the heads of four Śiva-images figured on the four sides, the *liṅga* itself being the fifth face. It symbolizes the Pañcadehamūrti.
Lit.: SSI 77.

Pañcamukha-Pātradeva ("the five-headed bowl-god"; Buddh.), n. of a god. Char.: att.: *nāṭyasthāna*; attr.: *bhikṣāpātra* (in each of his 16 hands), *pañcaśiras*.

Pañcamukha-Vināyaka ("the five-headed V."), n. of a form of Gaṇeśa.
Lit.: SSI 176.

Pañcamukhin ("five-headed"), epithet of Śiva, see Pañcānana.
Lit.: KiH 17 a.pl. 47.

pañcamūrdhan "five-headed" (attr.), see *pañcaśiras*.

Pañcānana ("five-faced"), n. of a form of Śiva. Attr. (esp.): *pañcaśiras*, *ūrdhvaliṅga*. – The heads may be arranged in a ring round the neck (with one head directed towards the zenith) or in a row upon the shoulders. Of these five heads three belong to Śiva, see Mahādeva, and the other two are said to signify Brahmā and Viṣṇu. See, however, also Pañcabrahmā and Sadāśivamūrti. – Another n.: Pañcamukhin.
Lit.: D 298; DHP 191, 210; JDI 18; KiH pl. 47; KiSH 25; MG 168; W 236; see also FK 112 f. (the ill. is here wrongly said to signify Brahmā).

pañcāṅga "five-limbed", n. of the calendar, almanac. This calendar treats five things, viz. *vāra*, *tithi*, *nakṣatra*, *yoga* and *karaṇa*. The term is derived from *p.* meaning the five limbs of the body, i.e. head, arms and legs.
Lit.: GT 437; IC 2:727; MW 578; WHW 1:195.

pañcāṅgulitala "handprint" (attr.), n. of a decorative motif, used as a *maṅgala*, see *aṣṭamaṅgala*.
Lit.: JMS 17.

pañcaparameṣṭhin "five chief gods" (Jain.), n. of a group of five idols, worshipped in the daily worship at home or in *maṭhas*.
Lit.: SSI 265.

pañcapātra "five cups or vessels" (attr.), n. of a small vessel from which water is poured over the image in the course of worship.
Lit.: P 271.

pañcapaṭṭikā "five bands", in architecture n. of five mouldings on a temple, of diminishing size placed one over the other.
Lit.: JMS 17.

pañcapradīpa "five-lamp" (attr.), n. of a type of lamp used in temples. This term probably means a lamp with five wicks.
Lit.: MH 37.

pañcarakṣā "five-fold protection" (Buddh.), collective n. of a group of five tutelary deities ("spell goddesses"), see *mahārakṣā*.
Lit.: BBh. 153; G 12, 78; KiSB 110.

pañcaratha "five-car" (Vāh.), n. of a kind of *pīṭha*, rather summarily described by B. as a "pedestal in three tiers".
Lit.: B 402, 555.

pañcaratna "collection of five gems or precious things" (attr.). These gems are: *muktā* "pearl", *māṇikya* "ruby", *nīla* "sapphire", *vajra* "diamond", *marakata* "emerald", or *kanaka* (or *svarṇa*) "gold"; *rajata* (or *raupya*) "silver" may also be included in this collection. These gems are said to signify the five elements (*pañcabhūta*); cp. also *navaratna*. The *p.* is used for the making of the *vaijayantīmālā*.
Lit.: MEIA 214; MW 577.

pañcarātra(ka) "period of, or lasting for five days (nights)", n. of a number of sacred books belonging to one of the two main Vaiṣṇavite systems, the *pañcarātrin*s.
Lit.: GoRI 2:119, 125; GRI 323; IC 1:647; MW 577; WHW 2:176.

pañcarātrin (derived from *pañcarātra*), n. of a Viṣṇu-worshipper and of a certain Vaiṣṇavite sect. Cp. also *bhāgavata*.
Lit.: GoRI 1:247; GRI 323; HIS 19; IC 1:647.

pañcaśara "five arrows (in a sheaf)" (attr.). These arrows are flowers of *padma*, *aśoka*, *āmra*, *kunda*, *nīlotpala* and have the PN: Lambinī, Tāpinī, Drāviṇī, Māriṇī, Vedinī (or according to another list: Tāpanī, Dāhanī [or Dāhinī], Viśvamohinī [or Sarvamohinī], Viśvamardinī, Mādinī or Māraṇī). They are connected with the *ikṣukodaṇḍa* and are char. of: Kāma, Lalitā, Rājarājeśvarī, Tripurasundarī.
Lit.: B 301; R 2:148; SSI 62.

Pāñcaśikha ("five-crested, having five tufts of hair on the head (as an ascetic)"; Buddh.), n. of the king of *gandharva*s. Attr.: *vīṇā*.
Lit.: BBh. 381.

pañcaśiras "five-headed" (attr.). Char. of: Śiva Pañcānana or Sadāśiva (Pañcabrahmās) or Maheśamūrti, Daśabhujasita-Mārīcī, Gāyatrī, Hanumān, Heramba(-Gaṇapati), Mahākāla, Māyājālakramakrodha-Lokeśvara, Māyājālakramāvalokiteśvara, Pañcamukha-Pātradeva, Pañcamukha-Vināyaka, Vajravidāraṇī; sometimes (perhaps) Brahmā). – Other n.: *pañcamukha*, *pañcamūrdhan*.
Lit.: MG facing p. 96.

pañcaskandha "the five cosmic elements", see *skandha*.
Lit.: SM 33.

pañcasūcika(kuliśa) "*vajra* with five prongs" (attr.; Buddh.). Char. of Sarvaśokatamonirghātamati.
Lit.: BBh. 92.

pañcatapas "five fires". This term indicates the practice of ascetics of exposing themselves, as a form of self-mortification, to four fires in the four quarters, sitting amidst them, and to the sun overhead as a fifth fire. – Another n.: *pañcāgni*.
Lit.: MW 576.

pañcatathāgatamukuṭa (or *-ī*) "having images of the five *dhyānibuddha*s (*tathāgata*s) on the crown" (attr.). Char. of Sitatārā.
Lit.: BBh. 232.

pañcatattva "five essentials", n. of a Tantric rite which is performed by means of the *pañcamakāra*s.
Lit.: IC 1:594; MW 576.

pañcatīrthī (*-ikā*) "group of five *tīrthaṅkara*s" (attr.; Jain.), n. of a representation (in bronze) of a *tīrthaṅkara* as the chief idol surrounded by four other *tīrthaṅkara*s.

pañcavaktra "five faces (manifestations, of Śiva)", see Sadāśiva.
Lit.: GRI 170.

Pañcavaktra-Bhairava, n. of a five-faced form of Bhairava.
Lit.: SSI 151.

pañcavartī (or *-i*) "lamp with five wicks" (attr.). This term is here made on *pancha-vatti* (thus MSHP); cp. also MW sub *varti*.
Lit.: MSHP 48; MW 925.

pañcavaṭī "the five fig-trees", viz. *aśvattha*, *bilva*, *āmalaka* (*dhātrī*), *aśoka* and *vaṭa-(vṛkṣa)*.
Lit.: IC 1:537; MW 577.

pañcāyatana (properly "five supports, abodes, altars", or n. of a round open metal dish on which are placed the five stones listed below; attr.), n. of the group of five idols (representing the five chief sects of Hinduism), worshipped in their lithomorphic forms (i.e. as stone-symbols). These are: for Viṣṇu the *śālagrāma**-stone, for Śiva the *liṅga* (*bāṇaliṅga**), for Durgā (Pārvatī) the *svarṇarekhā**, for Sūrya the *sūrya-kānta**, and for Gaṇeśa the *svarṇabhadra**-stone. – Cp. *pañcāyatana-pūjā*. – *p.* is also n. of a type of temple with four shrines grouped round a fifth main sanctuary and attached to it by cloisters.
Lit.: B 541; GH 330; KiSH 77, 109; RAAI 273; WHW 1:395.

Pañcāyatana-liṅga, n. of a certain kind of *caturmukha-liṅga* on the four sides of which images of Gaṇeśa, Viṣṇu, Pārvatī and Sūrya are carved, the *liṅga* itself representing Śiva. Hence the five chief sects of Hinduism are symbolized on this P.
Lit.: B 545 a.pl. 46:2.

pañcāyatana-pūjā "worship of *p.*", n. of a ceremony "in which the principal deities of the five approved Brāhmanical Hindu cults were the objects of veneration" (B). They are worshipped in their aniconic forms (see *pañcāyatana*), and before them sacred *mantras* are murmured and incense, rice-grains and flowers are offered to them. – Nowadays the number of these sects is, in South India, increased to six to give room for *kaumāra**, this sect there now being the most important.
Lit.: B 541; Diehl; GH 330.

Pañcāyudha ("armed with five weapons"), epithet of Viṣṇu.

panchavatti, see *pañcavartī*.

Paṇ-chen Rin-po-che (Tib. "great and precious sage"; also named Pan-chen Lama), see Tashi Lama.
Lit.: G 6, 107; JT 323, 529.

Pāñcika (derived from *pañca* "five"), epithet of Kubera (Buddh.), and n. of the husband of Hārītī (Hind.).
Lit.: HIS 25, 44, 59 a.pl. 17; ZA 135 a.pl. 64b.

paṇḍā (or *pāṇḍā*, Hi.), n. of a Brāhman priest who officiates at the temple of an idol, though, in some places (e.g. at Vārāṇasī) only on special occasions, the duties of the daily worship then being performed by subordinate priests (*pujārī*).
Lit.: P 273; WHW 1:438.

pāndān (Hi., < Skt *parṇa*+*dāna*; attr.) "box in which betel and its apparatus are kept" (attr.). Cp. *caugharā*.
Lit.: MH 34 a.passim; P 219.

Pāṇḍarā (also Pāṇḍurā, "yellowish white"; Buddh.), n. of a female *bodhisattva* or a *dhyānibuddhaśakti*, who originates from the *bīja PĀṀ*. She is the Śakti or spiritual consort of Amitābha (or Avalokiteśvara). Char.: colour: rose; att.: *lalitāsana*; also *yab-yum* with her consort; Mu.: *varada-*, *vyākhyāna-mudrā*; attr.: *nīlotpala* (*padma*); in the *yab-yum*-form: *cakra*, *kapāla*, *karttṛkā*. Images and paintings of P. are rare. – Another n.: Pāṇḍaravāsinī.
Lit.: BBh. 50 a.pl. 20; EB s.v.; G 16, 52, 77, 86; KiSB 46.

paṇḍāram, see *paṇṭāram*.

Pāṇḍaravāsinī ("dressed in white"; Buddh.), see Pāṇḍarā. – P. is also used as a n. of the Śakti of Padmanarteśvara.
Lit.: BBh. 134; EB s.v.; GBM 156.

Pāṇḍava, patronymic n. of the five "sons of Pāṇḍu", i.e. Yudhiṣṭhira, Bhīma, Arjuna, Nakula and Sahadeva, the five chief heroes in the great epic Mahābhārata.
Lit.: Gt 439; WHW 2:178.

Paṇḍharinātha ("protector of the town Paṇ-ḍhari (= modern Pandharpur in Western

India)", epithet of Viṭṭhala, who is a form of Viṣṇu.
Lit.: R 1:271.

Pāṇḍurā, see Paṇḍarā.

Pāṇḍurāṅga ("white-limbed"), n. of a two-armed form of Viṣṇu. Char.: Mu.: *kaṭi-mudrā*; attr.: *nagna, śaṅkha.*
Lit.: SSI 55 a.fig. 39-40.

Pāṇḍya, n. of an ancient South Indian Tamil kingdom and its rulers having Madurai as their capital, and of an epoch of arts flourishing between the 12th-14th cc. A.D.
Lit.: Gz 183 a.passim; JDI 7; K.A. Nilakanta Sastri, A history of South India (London 1955), 453; WHW 2:180.

pāṇigrahaṇa "hand-taking", n. of a ceremony, the essential rite at the *vivāha* (in older times this rite was also named *hastagraha*); n. of a Mu.: in this ceremony the bride stands to the left of the bride-groom, and they grasp each other's right hands. Char. of the composition Kalyāṇasundaramūrti, Vallīkalyāṇasundaramūrti. – Other n.: *hāth levā, kaṇyā-pāṇi-grahaṇ.*
Lit.: B 485; SB 205.

pañjara "cage", n. of a small pavilion-like cage, used as a decorative motif in architecture.
Lit.: BECA 1:262.

Pañjarli, n. of a *bhūta.*
Lit.: KiH 27 a.pl. 101.

paṅkaja "lotus" (attr.), see *padma.*
Lit.: MEIA 222.

Pannagā (a kind of female snake demon; Jain.), n. of a *śāsanadevatā* attending on the 15th *tīrthaṅkara.* Epithet: Kandarpā.
Lit.: GJ 362.

Pānsāhi Mātā (N.Ind.), n. of one of the *saptamātaras*; she attacks children under seven years.
Lit.: GH 136.

pāṅsula (properly "dusty"; attr.), see *khaṭvāṅga.*
Lit.: D 157; MW 613.

paṇṭāram (or *paṇḍāram*, Tam.), n. of a sacrificial priest of inferior rank and belonging to a lower caste (e.g. a *śūdra*). In South India he takes an active part in the Śaivite cult and performs the bloody sacrifices which no Brāhman priest would perform.
Lit.: DiIP 181; SSR 144.

Panthaka ("knowing the way"; Buddh.), n. of a Lamaist *arhat.* Attr.: *pustaka.*
Lit.: G 104.

pāpakṣepaṇābhinayin "(act of) removing all sins", n. of a Mu., which is performed with both hands but which is not fully described. Char. of Sarvāpāyañjaha.
Lit.: BBh. 97.

paramaharṣi ("excellent *riṣi*"), n. of one among a group of *riṣis*, the leader of whom was Bhela.
Lit.: R 2:566.

Paramaśiva ("the highest Śiva"), epithet of Śiva causing the *vidyeśvaras* to create the universe.
Lit.: R 2:392, 403.

Paramāśva ("great horse, the highest horse"; Buddh.), n. of a Mahāyāna god who is possibly a form of Hayagrīva. Char. colour: red; Vāh.: he is shown trampling on 4 female Hindu deities: Indrāṇī, Śrī, Rati, Prīti; att.: *ālīḍhāsana*; Mu.: *tripatākā-mudrā*; attr.: *aśvamastaka, brahmamukha, caturmukha, daṇḍa, dhanus, khaḍga, mahāmbuja, padma, śakti, śara, trinayana, viśvavajra*; he has 4 legs. – P. is also another n. of Mahābala as a *dikpāla.*
Lit.: BBh. 185 a.pl. 132; KiSB 79.

parameṣṭhi (or *-in*) "superior or chief god"; Jain.). Cp. *pañcaparameṣṭhin.*
Lit.: MW 588.

parameṣṭhimantra ("teacher-*mantra*"; Jain.), n. of a *mantra*, written in Prākrit, which is repeated daily: *namo Arihantānaṁ, namo Siddhānaṁ, namo Āyariyānaṁ, namo Uvajjhāyānaṁ, namo loe savvā-Sāhūnaṁ* "hail to the *arhats*, hail to the perfect-ones, hail to the masters, hail to the teachers, hail to all monks of the world".
Lit.: GJ 367.

pāramitā ("perfection"; Buddh.), n. of one among a group of 12 philosophical deities: Ratna-, Dāna-, Śīla-, Kṣānti-, Vīrya-, Dhyāna-, Prajñā-, Upāya-, Praṇidhāna-,

Bala-, Jñāna- and Vajrakarma-pāramitā. "These are certain cardinal human virtues carried to perfection in one birth" (BBh.). Their spiritual father is Ratnasambhava. Common features: attr.: *cintāmaṇidhvaja*; also *padma* (of variable colours). – A group of 6 *p.* is also mentioned, who are not adequately described.
Lit.: BBh. 323, 438; GRI 255.

paramudrā "supreme posture" (att.) is "a purposive arrangement of the limbs and organs of the human body into certain mystical poses, for obtaining the maximum concentration of psychic power. It is the ultimate expression of *aṅgika*...". It is said that there are 88 different varieties of *p.*, but since these have no close relation to iconography, they are not dealt with in this dictionary.
Lit.: WHW 2:187.

Parāṅgada ("giving form to another [scil. to Durgā with whom he forms one body, or to Kāmadeva whose body he restored after reducing it to ashes]"), n. of a form of Śiva, see Ardhanārīśvara.
Lit.: MW 587.

Parañja(ya) ("conquering the foes"; attr.), n. of the *khaḍga* of Indra. According to WHW, it is n. of Indra's lance.
Lit.: DHP 110; WHW 1:480.

parāśakti "supreme energy", n. of a *mantra* with the form: *AUṀ KRĪṀ KRĪṀ KRĪṀ HŪṀ HŪṀ HRĪṀ HRĪṀ SVĀHĀ*. Its purpose is "To acquire all attainments"
Lit.: DHP 345.

paraśu "axe, hatchet" (attr.). This object was originally shaped like a real axe, but later on the blade was made smaller, and the object was often confused with the *ṭaṅka*. R therefore describes it in its earlier forms as a battle axe and in its later forms as "a heavy club, closely resembling the *gadā*, into which the head of the *paraśu* is fitted. The blade is disproportionately small in these later forms". Consequently, the iconographers make no strict difference between *p.* and *ṭaṅka*, and in MEIA these symbols are equivalent. – In Buddhism the *p.* takes the form of an axe, usually crowned by a *vajra*, this object being said to symbolize the act of building or developing the Doctrine, or else the idea of protection. The divinities carrying it "use it to cut out all Evil which menaces the Law" (SM).
This attr. is char. esp. of Śiva and Skanda in different forms, further of: Ahirbudhnya, Aiyaṇār, Aja, Bahurūpa, Bṛhaspati, Cāmuṇḍā, Caṇḍā, Caṇḍeśvara, Caṇḍikeśvara, Cundā, Dharmacakra-Lokeśvara, *dharmapālas*, Dulhā Deo, *ekādaśarudra*, Ekajaṭā, Ekapādamūrti, Gaṇeśa, Gomukha, Grīṣmadevī, Hariharamūrti, Hayagrīva, Jayanta, Jñānaḍākinī, Kaumārī, Krodhahayagrīva, Kubera, Mahācīnatārā, Mahākāla, Mahāmantrānusāriṇī, Mahāpratisarā, Mahāsāhasrapramardanī, Mahāśītavatī, Māheśvarī, Mahiṣāsuramardinī, Mārīcī (in different forms), Nandīśvara, Paraśurāma, Parṇaśavarī, Rakṣoghnamūrti, Revata, Saṃvara, Sitātapatra, Sureśvara, Tha-'og-chos, Tryambaka, Vajragāndhārā, Vāmadeva, Veṇugopāla, Vidyujjvālākarālī, Virūpākṣa, Viśvarūpa, Yamāntaka. – Other n.: *kuṭhāra*, *maḷu*.
Lit.: B 301, 357, 463; DHP 217; G 16 (ill.); JDI 20; MEIA 248; R 1:6 a.pl. 2:6-7, 2: pl. 5:2; SM 145; Th. 40; WM 106 a.fig. 55-56.

Paraśurāma (or Paraśurāmāvatāra; "Rāma with the battle-axe"), n. of the sixth *avatāra* (or, in this case, *āveśa*) of Viṣṇu, in which he saved the world from the tyranny of the *kṣatriyas*, the aristocracy of warriors. P. is thus an *ugra*-aspect of Viṣṇu. P. is said to be the son of Jamadagni (descendant of Bhṛgu) and Reṇukā. Wife: Dharaṇī (= an *avatāra* of Lakṣmī). Char.: Mu.: *sūcimudrā*; attr.: esp. *paraśu*, further: *ajina*, *dhanus*, *khaḍga*, *kheṭaka*, *śara*. P. has usually 2 or 4 arms. – P. is also regarded as a manifestation of the planet Śukra. – Epithet: Bhārgava-Rāma.
Lit.: B 390, 420; ChI 597; D 230; DHP 165, 170; FKR 111; GH 122; GoRI 1:252; Gt 500; JDI 80;

KiSH 37; MEIA 35; MG 114 a.pl. facing p. 110; R 1:19, 181; WHW 2:189; WM 142; ZA 16.

paraśurāmakāla "the era of Paraśurāma", see *kollam*.
Lit.: IC 2:737.

Paravai(nāchiyār), n. of a wife of Sundaramūrti-nāyaṉār.
Lit.: SB 346 a.fig. 299A.

Paravāṇi (probably: "whose voice carries far"; Vāh.), n. of a *mayūra*, the Vāh. of Skanda.
Lit.: DHP 298.

Para-Vāsudeva ("the highest V."), epithet of Vāsudeva (= Kṛṣṇa or Viṣṇu) as the highest god in whom, or through whom the universe exists.
Lit.: R 1:239.

pardā (Hi.-Pers., often written *purdah*) "screen, curtain", hence also "seclusion, concealment". This word is used as a term signifying the life of women in seclusion. – Another n.: *zanāna*.
Lit.: P 246; STP 2:163; WHW 1:429.

paribhogika (Pāli) "object of use" (attr.; Buddh.), n. of objects of adoration, such as begging bowls, belts, bathing robes, drinking vessels, seats, etc.
Lit.: SeKB 99; ZA 233.

parigha "a kind of club" (attr.), see *gadā*.
Lit.: R 2:181.

pārijāta ("coral-tree"; attr.), n. of a mythical tree, one of the five trees of paradise (see *vṛkṣa*). It was produced at the churning of the ocean of milk (see Kūrmāvatāra) and came into the possession of Indra. Later on it was stolen by Kṛṣṇa and planted in the town of Dvārakā. After the death of Kṛṣṇa it was brought back to the heaven of Indra. – Flowers of *p.* adorn Vāruṇī.
Lit.: D 231; DHP 167: GH 65; Gt 449; WHW 2:218.

pariṇāyaka "guide", meaning a general or a commander-in-chief, n. of a *lakṣaṇa* of a *cakravartin*; see *saptaratna*.
Lit.: WHW 1:551.

parinirvāṇa "the complete *nirvāṇa*", a term signifying the Buddha's death or departure from this life. It is symbolized by a *stūpa*. As NP, Parinirvāṇa, this n. signifies an image of the Buddha lying recumbent, see further Mahāparinirvāṇamūrti.
Lit.: G 55 (with ill.); GRI 234; H pl. 3:25; HIS 15; IC 2:321; IIM 134; ZA 61 a.pl. 10, 184, 467.

Pariṣkāravaśitā ("control of purification"; Buddh.), n. of a *vaśitā*. Char.: colour: yellow; attr.: *cintāmaṇidhvaja*.
Lit.: BBh. 329.

parivāradevatā (or *parivāramūrti*) "deity of the retinue", n. of an icon which is not placed in the *garbhagṛha* or inner room of a temple, but in the surrounding circuits or corridors. The place of the different deities of this kind is shown in R.
Lit.: BECA 1: pl. 38; HSIT 123; R 1: App. A, 2:464.

parivārālaya (also *parivāradevatāgṛha*) "shrine (of a deity) of the retinue", signifies "one of the subshrines round the main shrine, housing subordinate deities".
Lit.: BECA 1:263.

parivārapūjā "worship of the retinue (deities)", cp. *parivāradevatā*.
Lit.: HSIT 124.

Parivīta ("veiled, covered"; attr.), n. of the *dhanus* of Brahmā.
Lit.: MW 602.

parivrājaka "wandering religious mendicant", n. given to a *brāhmaṇa* at the fourth stage of his religious life. Attr.: *daṇḍa*, *tridaṇḍa*. – Cp. *saṅnyāsin*.
Lit.: B 232; MW 602; WHW 1:438.

Parjanya ("rain-cloud, or rain-giver"), n. of a Vedic god of rain, who in later Hinduism was replaced by Indra. He is sometimes mentioned as an Āditya.
Lit.: D 232; DHP 111, 126; Gt 450; WM 143.

parṇapicchikā "garment or cluster of leaves" (attr.; Buddh.). Char. of Parṇa-Śavarī. – Another n.: *patracchaṭā*.
Lit.: BBh. 196.

Parṇa-Śavarī (or -Śabarī; "the Śavarī [-woman dressed] in leaves"; Buddh.), n. of a Mahāyāna goddess (a female *bodhisattva*) who is an emanation either of Akṣobhya or of Amoghasiddhi. She also belongs to the *dhāraṇī*-group, and her native country is the north-west of India. Char.: colour: yellow or green; Vāh.: *vighnas*, Gaṇeśa; att.: *ālīḍhāsana*; Mu.: *tarjanīmudrā*; attr.: *ajina*, *Akṣobhyabimba* or *Amoghasiddhibimba* on the crown, *aśoka*-flower, *caturmukha* (sometimes, she has then, 8 arms), *dhanus*, *mayūrapattra*, *paraśu*, *parṇapicchikā*, *(tarjanī)pāśa*, *śara*, *trinayana*, *triśiras* (sometimes, she has then, 6 arms), *vajra* (*viśvavajra*).

Lit.: B 492; BBh. passim a.pl. 140, 173f.; G 18, 33, 72; KiDG 64, 68 a.pl. 18:52-54; KiSB 90, 100.

Pārśva(nātha) (the original sense of the n. probably alludes to *pārśva* "region of the ribs, side, flank", because P. is originally represented with a (many-headed) snakehood growing from his shoulders behind his head (like a *nāgadevatā*); but on later representations this hood belongs to a separate snake; Jain.), n. of the 23rd *tīrthaṅkara* (possibly a historic person living in the 8th c. B.C. [or about 600 B.C.; FBKI] and the true founder of Jainism). Char.: att.: *vīrāsana* (also *padmāsana*); Mu.: *dhyānamudrā*; attr.: *nagna*; symbol: *nāga* (as to the snake hood, see above).

P. bears a close resemblance to the Buddhist Mucalinda-Buddha; the chief difference between them being that P. is naked, but the Buddhist image has the attr. *saṅghāṭi*. – It may be asked whether the name P. might possibly be a later transformation of an original word **pārśvanāga* meaning "shoulder-snake".

Lit.: CHIIA 234 a.fig. 86; FBKI 13; GI pl. 89; GJ 19, 293 a.passim, a.pl. 27:23, 28; GRI 187; HIS 16, 26; IC 2:629; KIM pl. 17; KiJ 11 a.pl. 30:23; KiSH 143; SB 336 a.fig. 273; SchRI 220; WHW 2:191; ZA 56, 297 a.pl. B2b-c, a.pl. 247.

pārśvadevatā "side-deity" (attr.), n. of the image of a deity placed in a niche (*koṣṭha*) of a temple.

Lit.: GOSA 12.

Pārśvayakṣa ("the *yakṣa* of Pārśva"; Jain.), epithet of a *yakṣa*, see Dharaṇendra.

Lit.: GJ 362.

Pārthasārathi ("the charioteer of Pārtha", i.e. the son of Pṛthā (another n. of Kuntī); the n. Pārtha is esp. used for Arjuna), n. of a form of Kṛṣṇa, who, in the epic Mahābhārata (and in Bhagavadgītā), acted as the charioteer of Arjuna. Char.: Mu.: *varada-*, *vyākhyāna-mudrā*; attr.: *śaṅkha*.

Lit.: R 2:210; SSI 47 a.fig. 31.

Pārvatī ("the mountain-daughter"), the usual n. of the chief wife of Śiva. Her n. shows her original connection with mongoloid mountain tribes of the Himālaya. As such she is regarded as the daughter of Himavān and Menā and younger sister of Gaṅgā. In South India, however, she is said to be the sister of Viṣṇu. – P. is the gracious, friendly aspect ("a permanent, peaceful, all-pervading, spatial aspect", DHP) of Śiva's Śakti (for the cruel aspects, cp. esp. Durgā and Kālī; see also *śākta*, *aṣṭasvasāras*), and she may generally be looked upon as a fertility and mother deity, as is shown by Gaṇeśa in the form of an attr. of hers (as image or baby). – Sons: Gaṇeśa, Skanda. Char.: Vāh.: in her gracious aspects she shares the Vāh. *vṛṣan* Nandin with Śiva, but sometimes she is also represented with the *siṅha*, properly the Vāh. of Durgā; att.: often *kuñcitapāda*; Mu.: *abhaya-*, *kaṭaka-*, *lola-*, *varada-mudrā*; attr.: she has usually two arms when accompanying Śiva, but four arms when represented independently; *akṣamālā*, *darpaṇa*, *gajamukha* (sometimes, South India), Gaṇeśa (as a baby or statuette) *ghaṇṭā*, *jambhīra*, *jaṭā-* or *karaṇḍa-* or *kirīṭa-mukuṭa* or *keśabandha*, *kamaṇḍalu*, *liṅga*, *padma* (rarely), *paṭṭabandha*, *śaṅkha*, *yajñopavīta*. – The aniconic, lithomorphic form of P. is *suvarṇarekhā*.

Varieties and epithets: Āhlādinī-Śakti, Ajā, Ambā, Ambikā, Annapūrṇā, Bhagavatī, Bhavānī, Bhūtamātā, Dakṣajā, Devī, Ekānaṅśā, Gaṇeśajananī, Gaurī, Haimavatī, Jagadambā, Jagadgaurī, Jaganmātā, Kanyā, Kuṇḍalinī, Lalitā, Mahādevi, Manasā,

Maṅgalā, Mīnākṣī, Nandā, Rājarājeśvarī, Rambhā, Sarvamaṅgalā, Śivakāmī, Svayamvarā, Tripurasundarī, Umā, Vajraprastāriṇī(?), Vāmadeva-Umā, Vicālāṭciyammaṉ. – As to other epithets see DHP.
Lit.: B 489, 502 a.pl. 43:2; DHP 263, 266 a.pl. 23; GḤ 141; GI pl. 72; GoRI 1:257; IA 6; JDI 37; KiH pl. 69; KiSH 22; KrA pl. 114; MG 181; R 1:360 a.pl. 108, 2:409 a.pl. 120; SB 109, 203 a.fig. 59 a.passim; SIB pl. 22; SSI 190; Th. 104 a.pl. 61; WHW 2:192; WM 143; ZA 115 a.pl. 259, 415-421.

pārvatīkalyāṇa "the happiness (marriage) of Pārvatī", commemorated in the representation Kalyāṇasundaramūrti.
Lit.: JDI 35.

paryaṅka (Vāh.) "couch, seat, tḥrone", see *pallaṅka*. – (Att.) *p.* is an abbreviated word-form for *paryaṅkāsana*. – (Attr.) "Cloth girt round the back, loins, and knees (by a person) when sitting on his hams" (ASED), see *yogapaṭṭa*.
Lit.: ASED 2:993; CEBI 49, 54; MW 607; SM 126 and N. 24, 51; ZA 25.

paryaṅkabandhana "the act of sitting with the legs bent and binding a cloth round the back and loins and knees" (MW; att.). See *soprāśrayāsana* (*yogāsana*).
Lit.: MW 607; SM 126.

paryaṅkagranthibandha "ascetic's band of cloth around the legs" (attr.), see *yogapaṭṭa*.
Lit.: SSIP 82, 84.

paryaṅkāsana (or *paryaṅka*) "sitting on a throne, seat" (att.), n. of a posture which is described in many different ways, either as "seated in a European fashion" with the legs dangling from the seat (B, WM; char. of esp. Maitreya, and also Siṅhanātha-Lokeśvara; for this form of att., cp. *pralambapadāsana* (*pīṭhāsana*) and *ardhaparyaṅkāsana*, see also *bhadrāsana*), or = *padmāsana* (so MH), or = *dhyānāsana*, *vajraparyaṅkāsana*, *vajrāsana* (so KiDG). According to MW, *p.* should signify a way of sitting, with a cloth wound round the back and loins and knees (for which see *sopāśrayāsana*).
Lit.: B 272; KiDG 49; KiSB 52; MH 7; MW 607; SM 129; WHW 1:76; WM 92 a.fig. 7; ZA 25.

paryuṣaṇa "spending the rainy season" (Buddh., Jain.), n. of a festival in the rainy season.
Lit.: GJ 433; MW 601; pw 4:53.

pāśa (Tam. *pācam*) "noose, fetter" (attr.), n. of a cord-snare carried in one hand (for a more detailed description, see MEIA). This is a weapon by means of which enemies (in Buddhism Māra and other wicked beings) are caught and bound. In its spiritual meaning it symbolizes "the love of the Buddha and Bodhisattva for all Sentient Beings, whom they catch and lead to salvation with the help of the rope" (SM, Buddh.), and it also signifies "anything that binds or fetters the soul, i.e. the outer world, nature" (Jain.; see also *śaivasiddhānta*) and the fetters of ignorance and "das Wissen, die Meisterkraft des Intellektes, welche die Gegenstände erfasst und mit festem Griff hält" (ZM, Hind.). – In modern iconography *p.* is ornamented with three flames (*cuṭar*). In Tantrism it is, as a symbol, always found together with the *aṅkuśa*. – It is also represented by the *bījamantra AṀ*.

p. is esp. char. of Yama, Śiva, Varuṇa, Gaṇeśa; further of: Aghora, Agni, Agni-Durgā, Ambā, Amoghapāśa, Aṅkālammaṉ, Annapūrṇā, Aparājitā, Ardhanārīśvara, Arthapratisamvit, Aṣṭabhuja-Kurukullā, Avalokiteśvara (in different forms), Balapramathanī, Bālā-Śakti, (Baṭuka-)Bhairava, Bhairavī, Bhuvaneśvarī, Brahmā, Cāmuṇḍā, Caṇḍā, Caṇḍeśvara, Caurī, Chos-skyoṅ, Cundā, Daśabhuja-Aghoramūrti, Devī, Dhanada-Tārā, Dharmadhātuvāgīśvara, Dharmapratisamvit, Dhvajāgrakeyūrā, Durgā (esp. as Mahiṣāsuramardinī), Durgottāriṇī-Tārā, Ekajaṭā, Gajāsurasaṅhāramūrti, Gomukha, mGon-po nag-po, Hayagrīva (also in the Garuḍa-form), Īśāna, Jambhala, Kāla, Kālacakra, Kālajambhala, Kālārimūrti, Kālī, Kanakavatsa, Kapila, Kārttikeya, Khen-ma (a golden *p.*), Krodhahayagrīva, Kubera, Kurukullā, Lalitā, Mahādeva, Mahākālī,

Mahāmantrānusāriṇī, Mahāmāyūrī, Mahāpratisarā, Mahāsāhasrapramardanī, Mahāśītavatī, Maheśamūrti, Mārīcī (in different forms), Māriyammaṉ, Mārttaṇḍa-Bhairava, Mṛtyuñjaya, Nandā, Naṭarāja (in different forms), *navadurgās*, Parṇa-Śavarī, Phyi-sgrub, Piṭāri, Puraṁdara, Rājarājeśvarī, Rāhu, Sadāśiva, Śaraṇabhava, Sarvakāmika, Sitātapatrā, Śivottama, Skanda, Sūrya-Lokeśvara, Tārakāri, Trailokyavijaya, Tripura, Tripurasundarī, Trivikrama, Vadālī, Vajradhara, Vajragāndhārī, Vajrahūṅkāra, Vajrajvālānalārka, Vajrāmṛta, Vajrapāṇi (in different forms), Vajraśṛṅkhalā, Vajratārā, Vajravārāhī, Vajravetālī, Vajravidāraṇī, Vārāhī, Varālī, Vartālī, Veṇugopāla, Vibhava, Vidyujjvālākarālī, Viśvaḍākinī, Viśvarūpa, Yamāntaka, Yamāri. – *p.* is also the weapon of the westerly direction.

Another n.: *bandhana*; as to particular forms of *p.*, see *nāgapāśa* and *vajrapāśa*; cp. also *tarjanīpāśa* and *mala*.

Lit.: B 301, 358; BBh. 437; DHP 218; G 16; GRI 330; H pl. 6:57b; JDI 22; MEIA 251; MKVI 1:523; R 1:8 a.pl. 5-6; SM 172; Th. 41; WM 107 a.fig. 63-64; ZM 226.

pāsāda (Pāli), see *prāsāda*.

pāśatarjanī "noose and threatening finger" (combined Mu. and attr.), see *tarjanīpāśa*.

Lit.: KiSB 86.

paścimottānāsana "sitting with the back upwards" (att.), n. of a Yogic posture.

Lit.: KiH pl. 152 row 1:2.

paśu (Tam. *pacu*) "cattle; any animal", in Śaivite doctrine symbolizing "the individual soul" (as distinct from the divine soul of the universe) see *śaivasiddhānta*. Symbollically *p.* is often represented by a *mṛga*. Cp. Paśupati.

Lit.: IC 1:634; RV 97.

paśubandha "animal-binding", a term including all kinds of animal sacrifices in Vedic times.

Lit.: WHW 1:49.

pāśupata ("relating to Paśupati"), n. of a Śaivite sect and doctrine of faith (reformed by Lakulīśa), according to which Paśupati, who is supplied with unsurpassed powers and active force, creates, maintains and destroys the universe. Here *paśu* "the cattle", i.e. the individual souls, are dependent on him, like a creature which is tied to the post. – *p.* is also n. of an adherent of this sect.

According to JDI, *p.* is also n. of a small sort of trident (*triśūla*), char. of Śiva (attr.).

Lit.: GH 390; GoRI 1:260; IC 1:628; JDI 22; WHW 2:193.

Pāśupatamūrti, n. of a *sthānakamūrti* and *ugra*-form of Śiva with four arms. Char.: att.: *samapādasthānaka*; Mu.: *abhaya-*, *varada-mudrā*; attr.: *akṣamālā*, *jaṭāmukuṭa* (surrounded with flames), *kapāla*, *khaḍga*, *nāga*, *ṭaṅka*, *trinayana*, *triśūla*. – Cp. Paśupati.

Lit.: R 2:125; Th. 80.

Pāśupatāstra ("weapon originating from Paśupati"; attr.), n. of either a *dhanus* or a *śakti*, a weapon given to Arjuna by Śiva (Paśupati). It is also mentioned as n. of the trident (*triśūla*) of Śiva and also found in personificated form (cp. *astra*).

Lit.: DHP 217; MEIA 71; R 2:216.

Pāśupatāstradānamūrti ("representation of the giving of the weapon Pāśupatāstra"), n. of a gracious representation of Śiva, who as Paśupati grants the *dhanus* to Arjuna. See Kirātārjunamūrti.

Lit.: R 2:216 a.pl. 52:2.

Paśupati ("Lord of the wild animals or cattle"), n. of a form of Śiva as *yogin*. This form may be regarded as a reflection of a pre-Indo-Aryan god who was worshipped in the Indus Valley civilization and was there represented on seals as a horned, three-faced, sitting god, surrounded by several animals (the "Proto-Śiva"). Later P. may also be interpreted as "Lord of the individual souls" (see *paśu*). – P. is further

mentioned as one of the *mūrtyaṣṭaka*-forms of Śiva. Wife: Svāhā; son: Ṣaṇmukha. Attr.: esp. *mṛga*, in other respects like Śiva. – Cp. Pāśupatamūrti, Bhūtanātha and Bhūtapati.
Lit.: B 446; DHP 205, 208; GoRI 1:260; GRI 170; HIS 10, 20; KiSH 21; R 2:403; WM 143; ZA 27 a.pl. 2a; ZM 140.

paṭa(citra) "woven cloth" (attr.; Buddh.), n. of a painted, quadrangular cotton cloth, on which a person from the pantheon is represented. It is used in Buddhist ritual worship.
Lit.: GBM 100, 144; WHW 1:304.

Paṭadhāriṇī ("bearing a cloth"; Buddh.), n. of a female *dvārapāla* who is a deification of the curtain. Char.: colour: blue; attr.: *kāṇḍapaṭa*.
Lit.: BBh. 317.

patākā (or *-a*) "flag, banner" (attr.), see *dhvaja*.
Lit.: BBh. 195.

patākā(hasta)mudrā "streamer-hand-gesture" (Mu.), a term meaning either a hand, carrying a flag or standard, or a handpose, in which a hand is kept stretched horizontally (like a streamer) away from the shoulder. In this case "the open palm is upright, usually facing the spectator, fingers close together and pointing upward, thumb slightly bent inwards to touch the lower side of the forefinger" (WHW). It symbolizes (in dancing) assurance, meditation, a flower, cloud, forest, night, river, horse; it is also said to convey power. – Char. of Śiva in different forms, Vāyu, Viśvarūpa. – *p.* is further said to be a 'major' Mu., and as varieties are then regarded: *ardhapatākā-*, *capeṭa-*, *tripatākā-*, *vajrapatākā-*, *śukatuṇḍa-*, *triśūla-*, *arāla-*, *lola-*, *gaja-*, *varada-*, *abhaya-*, and *ardhacandra-mudrās*.
Lit.: MEIA 217; R 1:213, 2:264, 533; WHW 2:86.

pātāla(loka) "(hell;) the lowest of the seven regions under the earth". The lord of *p.* is Ananta (Śeṣa). – Cp. *naraka*.
Lit.: DHP 163; GRI 155; Gt 451; IC 1:547; KiK 143; WM 144.

Pātāla (personification: "lord of hell"; Jain.), n. of a *yakṣa* attending on the 14th *tīrthaṅkara*. Symbol: *makara*; attr.: *triśiras*.
Lit.: GJ 362 a.pl. 26:14; KiDG 81 a.pl. 71; KiJ 11 a.pl. 29:14.

Pātālakumārī ("maid from the lower regions, hell"), epithet of Manasā.
Lit.: GoRI 2:21.

pāṭali "the Trumpet-flower-tree (Bignonia suaveolens), n. of a tree, as *bodhivṛkṣa* ascribed to Vipaśyin.

Pāṭaliputra ("the Trumpet-flower-tree-town"), n. of the capital (now Patna) of Magadha, which above all developed under the Maurya dynasty.
Lit.: D 233; Gz 39; RAAI 47; WHW 2:194.

Patañjali (Tam. Patañcali; meaning obscure), n. of a philosopher (of the *yoga* philosophy), who lived some time between 200 B.C.-500 A.D. (if not identical with the grammarian P. who lived in the 2nd c. B.C.). He is regarded as a *riṣi* and attendant of Śiva; he is then represented as having a fish-tail. Mu.: *añjalimudrā*.
Lit.: JDI 51; MD 2:240; SSI fig. 51; WHW 2:195.

pāṭhaka "reciter, reader", n. of a kind of teacher or monk. *Lit.:* GJ 350.

pati "lord; Supreme Being", one of the principles of *śaivasiddhānta**.

pātra "drinking-vessel, bowl, cup, alms-bowl", sometimes also "a jar with water from the Ganges" (attr.). *p.* is esp. used as n. of the begging-bowl (made of wood, ceramics or metal) of the Buddha and of the different *buddhas* and *bodhisattvas* and of monks, also of Aparājita, Revata, Sureśvara, Tryambaka and others; cp. further *bhikṣāpātra*, *piṇḍapātra*. Otherwise *p.* is also used as a term equivalent to either *kamaṇḍalu* or *kapāla*.
Lit.: B 208; BBh. 437; BRI 59; G 16 (ill.); IC 1:570; RV 98; SM 143.

patracchaṭā, see *pattracchaṭā*.

patrakuṇḍala, see *pattrakuṇḍala*.

pātropari bhikṣu "mendicant on bowl" (attr.), n. of an image of a man placed in a cup, held in one hand. Char. of Mahāmāyūrī.
Lit.: BBh. 305.

paṭṭa(bandha) "ornamented band" (attr.), n. of a band with painted or engraved figures of gods, demons, *maṇḍalas*, etc., which is worn round the head on the forehead. – Another n.: *phālapaṭṭa*; cp. *ratnapaṭṭa*. – *paṭṭa* is also a shorter term for *yogapaṭṭa*.
Lit.: R 2:275, 306; SB 58 a.passim; WHW 2:196.

Paṭṭadakal, n. of a *tīrtha* near Bādāmī in South India.
Lit.: Gz 134; RAAI 168; ZA pl. 299.

paṭṭar (Tam., < Skt *bhaṭṭa* < *bhartṛ*), n. of an officiating priest.
Lit.: DiIP 28.

patteyabuddha (Pkt), see *pratyekabuddha*.

paṭṭi (properly some kind of cloth?), n. of a part of the *pīṭha* (not fully described).
Lit.: MW 579; SB 67.

paṭṭikā "band(age), ribbon" (attr.). Char. of Hara. – Also n. of a moulding on a temple. Cp. *pañcapaṭṭikā*.
Lit.: R 2:389; ZA 270.

Paṭṭinī Devī (properly Paṭṭiṉi, "Queen goddess", Tam. fem. from Skt *bhaṭṭa*, *bhartṛ*), n. of a South Indian or esp. Singhalese goddess who is said to be an apotheosis of Kaṇṇaki, the wife of Kōvalaṉ. They came to Madurai to sell her anklet which a goldsmith took and showed to the king in place of another anklet which he had stolen from the queen. Thereafter, Kaṇṇaki was wrongfully accused of the theft, but after death she was canonized (the story is from the Tamil epic Cilappatikāram). – She is the goddess of chastity, and controller of diseases such as smallpox, measles, and cattle-murrain. Attr.: the hood of a *nāga* behind the head, *padma*.
Lit.: BECA 1:11; CBC 12 a.fig. 42f., 171, 184; RAAI pl. 145A; TL 2:691, 4:2426; ZA 114 a.pl. 462bf.

Pattira Kāḷiyammaṉ (Tam.), see Bhadrakālī.
Lit.: DiCh. 15.

paṭṭiśa "sharp-edged iron rod, or a weapon with three points" (attr.). In MEIA this symbol is equivalent to the *vajra*. Char. of: Ahirbudhnya, Aja, Aparājita, Bahurūpa, Cāmuṇḍā, Hara, Kṛśodarī, Revata, Sureśvara, Tryambaka, Viśvarūpa. – Cp. also *triśūla*.
Lit.: KiH 24; KiSH 51; MEIA 250; R 2:388.

pattracchaṭā (or *patra-*) "cluster of leaves" (attr.), see *parṇapicchikā*.
Lit.: BBh. 233.

pattrakuṇḍala (or *patra-*) "ear-rings, ear-ornaments made of bands or of thin golden leaves" (attr.). – Other n.: *karṇapatra*, *ōlai*.
Lit.: B 289; R 1:24 a.pl. 4:15; SB passim; WM 104 a.fig. 41.

pattras (pl.) "leaves" (attr., held in one hand). Char. of Arundhatī.
Lit.: R 1:369.

pauloma ("related to Puloman" or "son of the sage Smooth-Hair, Pulastya"), n. of a kind of *asuras*.
Lit.: D 234; DHP 143.

Paulomī ("daughter of Puloman"), see Indrāṇī,
Lit.: DHP 287; IC 1:520.

pauṣa, n. of a month (December-January). Its god is Kubera.
Lit.: BBh. 382; IC 2:733.

pauṣṭika "rite of nourishing", n. of a rite (Buddh.).
Lit.: BBh. 166.

Pāvaka ("Son of the Purifier" or "Son of the Fire"), epithet of Skanda (as the son of Agni). – (In Vedic lit. P. is also epithet of Agni and other gods). – For *pāvaka* as a symbolic n. of the number "3", see *saṅkhyā*.
Lit.: DHP 299.

Pavana ("purifier"), n. of the god of the winds, Vāyu, esp. as the father of Hanumān. Wife: Añjanā. – For *pavana* as a symbolic n. of the number "5", see *saṅkhyā*.

Pavāṉiyammaṉ (Tam.), see Bhavānī.
Lit.: DiCh. 25.

pavin (= *pavi* "thunderbolt"?; attr.), another n. of *vajra*.
Lit.: MEIA 329.

pavitra ("means of purification"; attr.), n. of a thread or ring around the arm which is made of *kuśa*-grass. It serves as a self-protector for a Brāhman while performing ceremonies and rituals, and it also marks

him off for a special service of devotion; he is "bound" by it. Char. of: Aiyaṉār, Vāmanāvatāra.
Lit.: DilP 88, 94; R 1:163, 2:490; RV 96.

pavitra-jhārī "ritual ewer" (attr.), see *jhārī.*

pavitra-vajra "sacred, ritual *vajra*" (attr.), see *vajra.*

pāyasa "a sweet preparation of milk and rice" (attr.). This term is used together with *kapāla* or another word for bowl. Char. of Bhakti-Vighneśvara.
Lit.: R 1:52.

pecaka "owl" (Vāh.), see *ulūka.*
Lit.: BBh. 364.

Pēraṉtalu (Tam.), n. given to the mother of a family who has died before her husband and then receives adoration as a goddess.
Lit.: GoRI 2:8.

Periyāḻvār (Tam.), n. of a *vaiṣṇavabhakta.*
Lit.: R 2:480 a.pl. 136.

Perumāḷ (Tam. "distinguished, illustrious"), epithet of Viṣṇu in South India. Cp. Cakra-Perumāḷ.
Lit.: DilP 147.

peṭaka "little basket" (attr.), see *karaṇḍa.*
Lit.: BBh. 342.

pēy (Tam.) "demon", possibly a goblin, vampire (cp. *vetāla*). Cp. *piśāca.*
Lit.: JDI 111; SSR 122.

Pēyāḻvār (Tam.), n. of a *vaiṣṇavabhakta.*
Lit.: R 2:480 a.pl. 136.

phala "fruit" (not precisely described; this term is used of, e.g., *dāḍima, jambhīra,* etc.; attr.). It symbolizes agricultural fertility (sometimes combined with *pallava,* ACA). Char. of: Aiyaṉār, Bhadrā, Diti, Gaṇeśa (but in this case the fruit is mostly mentioned), Lalitā, Mahācandrabimba-Lokeśvara, Mahāratnakīrti-Lokeśvara, Yama, Yamadaṇḍa-Lokeśvara. – Cp. *modaka.*
Lit.: ACA 41; MEIA 264; R 1:359.

phalakahāra "slab-garland" (attr.), a necklace "composed of short strands of pearls and gem-set slabs at intervals".
Lit.: SSIP 159.

phālapaṭṭa "band or ornament on the forehead" (attr.), see *paṭṭabandha.*
Lit.: SSI 190.

phalapūjā ("worship with fruits"; Jain.), n. of worship of an idol which consists in presenting fruits, as bananas, almonds, etc. – Cp. *pūjā.*
Lit.: GJ 396.

phālguna (related to the *nakṣatra* Phalgunī), n. of a month (February-March). Its god is Yama.
Lit.: BBh. 382; IC 2:733.

phālgunotsava ("the *phālguna*-festival"), a festival in the month *phālguna,* see *holī.*

phaṇin (*-ī*) "hooded, snake" (attr.), see *nāga.*
Lit.: ACA 34.

phaṣlī, see *faṣlī.*

PHAṬ, form of a *bījamantra* symbolizing "the weapon which can destroy anything".
Lit.: DHP 343.

phaṭka (meaning unknown; possibly the symbol of *PHAṬ* [?]; attr.; Buddh.). Char. of Gaṇapati.
Lit.: KiSB 78.

phūl (kāṅsā) (Hi., < Skt *phulla-*) "white metal". According to MH, in Northern India *phūl* is n. of a metal alloy identical with *kāṅsā,* but according to BhIM it is an alloy of pewter, copper and silver.
Lit.: BhIM 34; MH 36.

phuldān(ī) (also *phūl[a]dānī;* Hi.) "vase" (attr.).

Phul Mātā (N.Ind.), n. of one of the *saptamātaras.* She attacks children under seven years.
Lit.: GH 136.

phur-bu (Tib.; attr.; Buddh.), n. of a kind of symbolic ritual dagger, used against demons. The *ph.* has often a bulb or shaft formed as a figure, *viz.* Hayagrīva, who may then be represented in his Garuḍa-form (*triśiras,* with wings and sometimes in the *yab-yum*-att. with the Śakti). *ph.* is either an independent cult object or is, as an attr., carried by Gaṇeśa. – Cp. *rDo-rje* (see sub initial *do-*); *phur-bu* is mostly

a larger object than the *rDo-rje*. – Another n.: *vajrakīla*.
Lit.: G 11, 16 (ill.), 90, 102; HuGT 7 a.pl. 112; JSV 45 a.pl. 100; JT 344.

PHUT, form of a *bījamantra* with a mystical meaning.
Lit.: GJ 369.

Phyi-sgrub ("the External-One"; Tib., pronounced Chi-dup; Buddh.), in Lamaism n. of a variety of Yama. Char.: colour: blue, yellow or white; Vāh.: *mahiṣa* or *vṛṣan* upon a *nārī*; attr.: *cakra*, *daṇḍa* (crowned by a skeleton), *pāśa*, *vṛṣamastaka*.
Lit.: G 91.

Piḍāri, see Piṭāri.

Piḷḷaiyār (or Pulliyār; Tam. "the honourable child"), in South India the usual epithet of Gaṇeśa. P. is also included in the n. of a sign, *piḷḷaiyārcuḻi*, which a Śaivite adherent places at the beginning of a writing; it may therefore be equivalent to the *mantra*: *oṁ Gaṇeśāya*.
Lit.: DiCh. 34; GH 56, 116; IC 1:571; JDI 40; KiH 18; TL 5:2714.

Pināka ("staff or mace"; attr.), n. either of the *triśūla* or the *dhanus* or of the *daṇḍa* which is carried esp. by Śiva. Also char. of: Aparājitā, Caṇḍeśvara, Rudra-Śiva.
Lit.: B 301; DHP 217.

Pinākin ("bearing the *Pināka*"), epithet of Śiva.

piṇḍa "lump, ball" (attr.), n. esp. of the lump of boiled rice, sesamum seeds, honey and butter (also other ingredients) which is offered to the *pitaras* in the worship of the manes. See *śrāddha*.
Lit.: Gt 454; MG 279; MKVI 1:524; RV 99; WHW 1:39.

piṇḍapātra "alms-dish" (attr.), see *pātra*.
Lit.: BBh. 428.

Piṇḍapātra-Lokeśvara ("L. with the alms-dish"; Buddh.), n. of a variety of Avalokiteśvara. Char.: att.: *samapādasthānaka*; Vāh.: *padma*; attr.: *piṇḍapātra* (or *pātra*).
Lit.: BBh. 428 a.pl. 73(A).

piṇḍikā "base or pedestal (sometimes made of a ball of rice or of meat) for the image of a deity or for a *liṅga*" (Vāh.). Cp. *pīṭha*.
Lit.: MEIA 271; MW 625; R 2:56, 99.

Piṇḍolabhāradvāja ("Bhāradvāja with the lumps of food or leavings of the meal"; Buddh.), n. of a Lamaist *arhat*. Attr.: *pātra*, *pustaka*.
Lit.: G 104.

piṅgala "reddish-brown, tawny, yellow", n. of a colour.

Piṅgala-Gaṇapati ("the yellow G."), n. of a form of Gaṇeśa, six-armed, together with his Śakti. Attr.: *āmra*, *ikṣu*, *kalpakalatā*, *lekhanī*, *maṣībhājana*, *modaka*, *paraśu*, *tila*.
Lit.: MEIA 269; R 1:56; Th. 97.

pippala (N.Ind. *pīpal*) "the sacred fig-tree (Ficus religiosa)" (attr.). This is another frequently used term for *aśvattha**, which is worshipped as a representation of both Viṣṇu (hence also Vaiṣṇavī, Kṛṣṇa), Brahmā, Śiva, Ṭhakur Deo, and the Buddha. See also *bodhivṛkṣa*.
Lit.: CHIIA 229 a.fig. 6; GH 64; IC 1:537; KiSH 81; MG 235; Th. 2; WHW 1:357.

piśāca (real meaning uncertain; often explained as "eater of raw flesh"), n. of a kind of demons (*asuras*); a *p.* is esp. believed to be the spirit of a murderer or of a criminal and is represented as lean-bodied. – According to SSR *p.* is identical with *pēy*. – In Jainism *p.* is a kind of *vyantaradevatā*.
Lit.: D 234; DHP 143, 310; GH 107; GJ 237; MEIA 201; MG 287; MKVI 1:533; R 2:562; SSR 122.

piśitāśanā "eating carcasses, feeding on carrion", epithet of a *mātā* (see *mātaras*). Attr.: *kaṅkālī*, *khaṭvāṅga*.
Lit.: B 274.

pitā (*pitṛ*, *pitar*, pl. *pitaras* or *pitṛs*) "father", in pl. "manes, deceased ancestors". As their wife Svāhā is mentioned. *pitṛgaṇas* should also be mentioned here; the word means "groups of *pitaras*" and refers to groups of sons of certain *ṛṣis* who constitute the *pitaras* (see R). Common attr.: *keśabandha*, *vibhūti*, *yajñopavīta*.

Lit.: D 235; DHP 307, 321; IIM 118; MG 279; MKVI 1:526; R 2:562; WHW 1:39; WM 144.

pīta "yellow"; as to other n. of this colour, see MEIA.

Lit.: MEIA 238.

piṭaka "basket", see Tipiṭaka.

Pitāmaha ("grandfather"), epithet of Brahmā as father (creator) of the universe.

Lit.: D 235; GoRI 1:263.

pītāmbara "yellow garment" (attr.). This is said to represent the Vedas. Char. of: Brahmāṇī, Vaiṣṇavī, Viṣṇu. It also seems to signify an elaborate sort of undergarment worn by many Buddhist *bodhisattvas* and *(dhyāni)buddhas*.

Lit.: DHP 158; RN 32; SB 37 a.passim.

Pīta-Prajñāpāramitā ("the yellow P.": Buddh.), n. of a variety of Prajñāpāramitā. Char.: colour: yellow; Mu.: *vyākhyānamudrā*; attr.: *pustaka* on a *padma*.

Lit.: BBh. 198 a.pl. 141; G 74; KiDG 64; KiSB 91.

pitar(as), see *pitā*.

Piṭāri (or Piḍāri; Tam. "snake-catcher"), n. of one of the *navaśaktis*. She is adored as a *grāmadevatā*. According to DiCh., she has no special iconographic characteristics and is usually represented by a stone; according to SSR, she has the attr.: *agni*, *kapāla*, *pāśa*, *triśūla*.

Lit.: BECA 1:1; DiCh. 33; SSR 155.

pīṭha (*pīṭhikā*) "seat, throne" (Vāh.), n. of a pedestal of an image or a *liṅga*. *p.* is used as a term for the pedestal of all kinds of sculptures. At the back of the *p.* there is often a *prabhāvalī*. In the older bronze representations the idol, the *p.* and the *prabhāvalī* are usually cast all in one piece, but later the pieces are separate. There are also *pīṭhas*, with or without *prabhāvalīs*, which are not intended for particular idols but which, in the sense of "a small altar", may be used for any icon at the *pūjā*. – The *p.* of the Buddha is sometimes carried by *nāgas*. An empty *p.* symbolizes, in the older Buddhist representations, the Buddha, see *pallaṅka*. – Certain forms of *p.* are: *bhadra-*, *candra-*, *mahāmbuja-*, *mahāvajra-*, *padma-*, *saumyaka-*, *śrīkāmya-*, *śrīkara-*, *vajra-* and *vikara-pīṭha*; cp. also *pañcaratha*, *piṇḍikā*. – Other n.: *āsana*, *āvaṭaiyār*.

p. is also n. of a mystical geometrical figure or *yantra* connected with Śakti worship.

Lit.: B 298, 460; H pl. 3:32; JDI 11; R 1:19, 332, 2:99 a.pl. 12; SSI 185, 220; ZA 368.

pīṭhapadma, see *padmapīṭha*.

pīṭhāsana "throne-sitting" (att.), see *pralambapadāsana*.

Lit.: WHW 1:75.

pīṭhikā, see *pīṭha*.

pitṛgaṇa "flock, body of manes", see *pitā*.

Lit.: R 2:562.

pitṛloka "the world of the deceased ancestors" (*pitaras*, see *pitā*).

Lit.: GRI 84; MW 626.

pitṛyajña "sacrifice to the manes", n. of one of the five *mahāyajñas*. See also *tarpaṇa*.

Lit.: IC 1:585; WHW 1:360.

piṭṭutiruviḻā (Tam. "cake-festival"), n. of a festival (in August at Madurai) celebrated in memory of Śiva who once, in disguise, helped an old woman and was paid by her with cakes.

Lit.: SSR 200; TL 5:2651.

piyālā (Hi., orig. Pers.) "cup, chalice" (attr.), see *arghā*.

plavaṅga "monkey" (Vāh.), see *vānara*.

Lit.: BBh. 379.

Poleramma (Tel.), n. of a smallpox goddess who is also responsible for other maladies. She is worshipped with bloody offerings (*jatara*).

Lit.: GoRI 2:5.

poṅkal (*poṅgal*, Tam., properly: "boiling over") "rice-meal prepared as an offering to the gods and eaten as sacred food"; also n. of a Tamil harvest- and cattle-festival (in January, in South India coinciding with the *makara-saṅkrānti*). During this festival the married women cook rice

meals, which are eaten in the manner described above. A kind of bracelet (Hi. *rākhī*) is also worn as an amulet during this feast.
Lit.: ACA 85; DiCh. 57; DiIP 169, 176; Gt 457; IC 1:593; SSR 134, 196; TL 5:2911.

poṉṉēr kaṭṭutal (Tam.) "the first ploughing of the season on an auspicious day with appropriate ceremonies"
Lit.: DiCh. 67.

poṣadha (Ved. *upavasatha*, Pāli *uposatha*) "fasting day" (Buddh.), n. of the chief Buddhist festival celebrated by the monks on the 15th day of the lunar half-month.
Lit.: BRI 56; RhDS 151.

Po-ta-la (Tib.; Buddh.), n. of an immense castle, once the chief residence of Dalai Lama at Lhasa.
Lit.: JSV pl. 11 f., 14 ff.; JT 325.

Potapāda-Lokeśvara ("L., the vessel-footed" or "having the feet of a young animal"; Buddh.), n. of a form of Avalokiteśvara. Char.: att.: *padmāsana*; Mu.: *añjalimudrā*; attr.: *akṣamālā*, *pāśa*.
Lit.: BBh. 395 a.pl. 9(A).

Poykaiyāḻvār (Tam.), n. of a *vaiṣṇavabhakta*.
Lit.: R 2:480 a.pl. 136.

prabhā(maṇḍala) "circle of rays" (attr.), n. of a great halo, glory, esp. a circle of flames which surrounds Śiva Naṭarāja and others; it is then said to symbolize the dance of nature. A *p.* as a decorative motif (in art-works of the Mathurā school) is a symbol of the Buddha. – Other n.: *bhāmaṇḍala*, *jvālamālā*, *tiruvāṭci*; cp. also *prabhātoraṇa* and *-valī*, and see esp. *toraṇa*. – The word *prabhā* is sometimes also used for *prabhātoraṇa*. – Sometimes *prabhāmaṇḍala* is made the equivalent of the *śiraścakra* (see in B).
Lit.: B 296; HIS 42; JMS 11, 13; R 1:32; SIB pl. 23; ZA 122; ZM 171.

Prabhākarī ("light-maker"; Buddh.), n. of a *bhūmi*, probably representing the sun. Char.: colour: red; attr.: *sūrya* on a *mahāmbuja*, *vajra*.
Lit.: BBh. 334.

Prabhāsa ("shining dawn"), n. of one of the *vasus*, representing the sky. Attr.: *aṅkuśa*, *daṇḍa*, *kapāla*, *śakti*.
Lit.: DHP 86; Gt 459; R 2:553.

prabhātoraṇa (sometimes also *prabhā*) "arch of rays" (attr.), n. of an arched doorway or portal. This term is often used like *prabhāvalī*, but as an attr. of images it means rather a portal of rays in the middle of which the idol is placed, while *prabhāvalī* signifies a halo behind the idol. At the top of the *p.* there is usually a *kīrttimukha*, and the aureole is sometimes crowned by a *kalpavṛkṣa* as a decorative motif. – In later bronze representations the *p.* is usually made in a separate piece which is attached to the *pīṭha* with pegs. – Cp. *prabhāmaṇḍala*.
Lit.: SIB pl. 23; ZM 203.

prabhāvalī "glory, halo" (attr.), n. of an ornamental decoration similar to the *prabhātoraṇa* (see this word for the difference between these kinds of decorations; on other points they agree in the essentials). Cp. *prabhāmaṇḍala*.
Lit.: B 297; R 1:32.

Prabhūtaratna ("the appeared, manifest jewel" [or possibly "the jewel that waxes powerful"]; Buddh.) is sometimes said to be a n. of a *buddha* (of a far-off age) or of a *bodhisattva*.
Lit.: MW 684.

Pracaṇḍā ("excessively violent, furious"), n. of one of the *navadurgās*.
Lit.: R 1:357.

Pracetas ("wise"), n. of a *riṣi* or *prajāpati* who, at least in the latter function, may be equivalent to Dakṣa. Also n. of a deity presiding over the tongue.
Lit.: D 237; Gt 460.

pradakṣiṇa (or *-ā*) "moving to the right", n. given to the clockwise movement round a person or a cult object (imitating the rotation of the sun round the earth) and turning the right side towards the object

of worship as a sign of honour or reverence. Cp. *dakṣiṇa* and *prasavya*.
Lit.: BRI 66; DiIP 100; GBM 124, 129; GrH 237; SeKB 100; STP 1:190.

pradakṣiṇā(patha) "circumambulatory" of a temple, a passage around the *garbhagṛha*, which makes it possible for the devotee to perform the *pradakṣiṇa* round the idol-shrine.
Lit.: DKI 13; RAAI 273; ZA 269.

Pradhānā ("the principal, most important"), n. of one of the *navaśaktis*.
Lit.: MW 1044.

Pradīpatārā ("light-Tārā"; Buddh.), n. of an inferior Mahāyāna goddess.
Lit.: BBh. 151; KiSB 97.

Pradoṣamūrti ("evening representation"), n. of a *sthānakamūrti* of Śiva together with Pārvatī. This can probably be regarded as a form of the Āliṅganamūrti. Char.: Mu.: *āliṅgahastamudrā*; attr.: *mṛga, paraśu*.
Lit.: SB 306 a.fig. 214 a.passim.

prādurbhāva "manifestation" of a god in which he remains transcendental in his true form. Cp. *avatāra*.
Lit.: GoRI 1:249.

Pradyumna ("wealthiest, the pre-eminently mighty one", the god of love).
1. N. of an aspect of Viṣṇu, see *caturviṅśatimūrti* and *caturvyūha*; P. represents the *rākṣasa*-manifestation of Viṣṇu; see also *caturmūrti*. Śakti: Prīti.
Lit.: DHP 154; KiSH 39; R 1:229.
2. In most cases P. (as the god of love) is regarded as the son of Kṛṣṇa and Rukmiṇī and as Kāma summoned back to life (for Kāma's being killed by Śiva, see Anaṅga). Sometimes he is also said to be the son of Viṣṇu. Wives: Māyādevī, Kakudmatī. Attr.: *khaḍga*.
Lit.: B 301; D 237; GoRI 1:240; Gt 461; MEIA 47; R 1:199, 239; SSI 62; WHW 2:231.

Prahlāda ("joyful excitement, happiness"), n. of a *daitya* who was the son of Hiraṇyakaśipu. P. was an ardent worshipper of Viṣṇu and was hence pained by his father, who was the enemey of Viṣṇu. In the Narasiṅhāvatāra Viṣṇu helped him and killed his father.
Lit.: D 238; Gt 463; HAHI 24; R 1:146; WHW 1:451; WM 145.

Prajāpati ("lord of creatures, beings"); *prajāpati* is often a general n. of a demiurge or a creative genius, often combined with Brahmā, and esp. with a group of 10 *riṣis*: Marīci, Atri, Aṅgiras, Pulastya, Pulaha, Kratu, Vasiṣṭha, Pracetas (or Dakṣa), Bhṛgu and Nārada, or with the group *saptarṣi*. P. is also an epithet of other gods, e.g. Kāśyapa, Indra. – As the wife of P. Lakṣmī, among others, is mentioned. – The number of 17 is char. of P. – See also Kūrma-, Matsya- and Varāhāvatāra.
Lit.: BPR 14; D 239; DHP 238, 301; GH 117; GoRI 1:187; GRI 93; Gt 464; IIM 118; KiSH 40; WHW 2:232; WM 145.

prajñā ("wisdom, the delivering knowledge"; Buddh.), n. of a passive aspect, the female principle, manifested in a woman who, as a "konsekrierte Frau", may be united with a man (see *upāya, yab-yum*). Hence *p.* is related to Śakti, *vidyā*.
Lit.: GRI 273.

Prajñā ("wisdom, transcendental knowledge"; Buddh.), n. of a personification, regarded as a goddess. She is sometimes said to be the Śakti of Ādibuddha and is then combined with Prajñāpāramitā (also attending on Sthiracakra), and sometimes regarded as the Śakti of several Mahāyāna gods. In this case P. is a term, alternating with Śakti, for the female counterpart of a god, see *prajñā*. – P. is also the Vāh. of Mārīcīpicuvā.
Lit.: BBh. 211, 438; GBB 250; GBM 157, 162; IC 2:593; KiSB 63, 105.

Prajñācakra ("wheel of intelligence"; Buddh.), n. of a form of Arapacana, who is shown sitting upon an animal.
Lit.: BBh. 120.

prajñākhaḍga "sword of wisdom" (attr.), n. of the *khaḍga* that is carried by Mañjuśrī and "is believed to destroy the darkness

of ignorance by the luminous rays issuing out of it".
Lit.: BBh. 436.

Prajñāntaka ("making an end of *prajñā*"; Buddh.), n. of a *dikpāla* of the south direction. Char.: colour: white; attr.: *cintāmaṇi, khaḍga, padma, sitadaṇḍa, triśiras*. – Cp. Yama. – Another n.: Vajrakuṇḍalin.
Lit.: BBh. 253.

prajñāpāramitā ("perfection of knowledge"; attr.: Buddh.), n. of a scripture containing the 10 "perfections of realisation" constituting Mahāyāna Buddhist philosophy and possibly originating in South India. These 10 perfections are: *dāna* (liberality), *śila* (good life), *kśānti* (patience), *vīrya* (energy), *dhyāna* (meditation), *prajñā* (perfection), *upāyakauśalya* (skilled application of the means of the salvation of living beings), *praṇidhāna* (resoluteness), *bala* (transcendant faculties) and *jñāna* (knowledge). – This attr. has the form of a book (e.g. a manuscript of palm leaves), and this term may therefore often be substituted for the common n. for "book", *pustaka*. – Char. of Mañjuśrī (in different forms).
Lit.: BRI 122; KISB 54; KT 137.

Prajñāpāramitā (Buddh.), n. of the personification of the scripture *prajñāpāramitā*, regarded as a goddess. She is said to be an emanation of Akṣobhya or of all *dhyānibuddhas* and is conceived as a female *bodhisattva*, and she is then regarded as the Śakti of Vajradhara (Ādibuddha); in this capacity she is "die lebenspendende Tugend *aller* Erlöser" (ZM, or represents *karuṇa* "compassion"). She is then apprehended as the mother of all *buddhas*. Furthermore she is closely connected with Mañjuśrī, though not as his Śakti. She also belongs to the *pāramitā*-group and is then the embodiment of transcendental intuition. In a general sense she may be regarded as the Buddhist counterpart of the Hindu Lakṣmī. – Char.: colour: white (*sita-*) or reddish white, or yellow (*pīta-*), or golden (*kanaka-*); Vāh.: *padma*; att.: *padmāsana*; Mu.: *abhaya-*, *dharmacakra-*, *vyākhyāna-mudrā*; attr.: *akṣamālā, bimbas* of the 5 *dhyānibuddhas* on the crown, *cintāmaṇidhvaja, kapāla, karttṛkā, nīlotpala, padma* (red), *pustaka, ūrṇā*. – Varieties: Sita-, Pīta- and Kanaka-Prajñāpāramitā; cp. also Prajñā.
Lit.: BBh. 43, 197, 326; G 16, 33, 74; GBB pl. 30; GBM 34, 81, 156; H 33; HAHI 17 a.pl. 9; KIM pl. 8; KiDG 64; KiSB 47, 91, 103; KT 137; SeKB 230, 234; ZA 140, 184 a.pl. 499-501; ZM 110 a.pl. 20.

Prajñapti ("teaching, information"; Jain.), n. of a *śāsanadevatā* attending on the 3rd *tīrthaṅkara*. She is also a *vidyādevī*.
Lit.: GJ pl. 24:3; KiJ 11 a.pl. 27:3.

Prajñāvardhanī ("growth of wisdom" or "jar of wisdom", cp. *vardhanī*; Buddh.), n. of a *dhāriṇī*. Char.: colour: white; attr.: *khaḍga* on a *nīlotpala, viśvavajra*.
Lit.: BBh. 220, 341.

prākāra "bounding wall" of a temple, see *āvaraṇa*. There are generally five *p.*, but seven *p.* may also be found.
Lit.: BECA 1:263; ZA 269.

Pralamba ("hanging down"), n. of a demon killed by Bālakṛṣṇa or Balarāma.
Lit.: D 240.

pralambapadāsana "sitting posture with the legs hanging down" (att.), n. of an *āsana*-posture which is also known as the "European sitting posture". It symbolizes authority. – Another n.: *pīṭhāsana*; cp. also *paryṅkāsana*.
Lit.: CHIIA 76; Gz 101; KIM 18; MH 7.

Pralayavarāha ("boar of destruction"), n. of a form of the Varāhāvatāra of Viṣṇu. Here Varāha sits on a *siṅhāsana* with his Śakti Bhūmidevī. Char.: att.: *lalitāsana*; attr.: *cakra, śaṅkha*.
Lit.: R 1:136.

Pramuditā ("delighted"; Buddh.), n. of a *bhūmi*. Char.: colour: red; attr.: *cintāmaṇi, vajra*.
Lit.: BBh. 333.

praṇām (Hi., < Skt *praṇāma*; Mu. or att.) "bending, bowing; a bow; respectful salu-

tation, prostration, obeisance (esp. to a Brāhman or to a deity)". This form of salutation is connected with *añjalimudrā*, and therefore this term is sometimes used for *añjalimudrā*.
Lit.: P 254; SM N. 4 to p. 76.

prāṇapratiṣṭhā "consecration through breathing", n. of a ceremony connected with the consecration of an image.
Lit.: IC 1:575; WHW 1:470.

Prāṇaśakti ("presiding over the centres of physical life"), n. of a terrific goddess. Char.: Vāh.: *padma*; attr.: *kapāla* with blood.
Lit.: SSI 212.

prāṇayāma "breath control", a term applied to the practice of breathing techniques used in Hindu occultism and meditative exercises (*yoga*).
Lit.: Gt 466; S. Lindquist, Die Methoden des Yoga (Lund 1932), 39; WHW 1:174.

praṇava "the mystical or sacred syllable *OṀ*", the technical n. of this syllable.
Lit.: BPR 18; R 2:295; RV 107.

Praṇidhānapāramitā ("perfection of abstract contemplation"; Buddh.), n. of a *pāramitā*. Char.: colour: blue; attr.: *cintāmaṇi*, *khaḍga* on a *nīlotpala*.
Lit.: BBh. 327.

Praṇidhānavaśitā ("control of abstract contemplation"; Buddh.), n. of a *vaśitā*. Char.: colour: yellow; attr.: *cintāmaṇidhvaja*, *nīlotpala*.
Lit.: BBh. 331.

prasāda "favour" ("Gunst", GoRI; attr.). This term also signifies "the food presented to an idol, or the remnants of food left by a spiritual teacher (which anyone may freely appropriate to his own use)" (MW). In this sense it is included among the *aṣṭāvaraṇa* and used by the *liṅgāyats* and may also be identical with Panj. *praṣad* in the term *karah praṣad*.
Lit.: GoRI 2:249; MW 697.

prāsāda (Pāli *pāsāda*) "palace", n. of a type of temple building in the shape of a terraced pyramid, generally char. of South Indian or Dravidian architecture.
Lit.: BECA 1:263; IC 2:319; RAAI 273; WHW 1:59.

prāsādadvāra "palace door", n. of a kind of temple gateway (*gopura*) with three to five storeys.
Lit.: BECA 1:260.

prasādamudrā "gesture of favour, graciousness" (Mu.), a term probably equivalent to *varadamudrā*.
Lit.: MEIA 58; WM 169.

Prasanna-Gaṇapati ("the gracious G."), n. of a *sthānaka*-representation of Gaṇeśa. Char.: Mu.: *abhaya-*, *varada-mudrā*; attr.: *aṅkuśa*, *danta*, *karaṇḍamukuṭa*, *modaka*, *pāśa*.
Lit.: R 1:57 a.pl. 15:1-2; Th. 96.

Prasannatārā ("the gracious Tārā"; Buddh.), n. of an inferior Mahāyāna goddess. She is an emanation of Ratnasambhava. Char.: colour: yellow; att.: *ālīḍhāsana*; Vāh.: she is depicted trampling underfoot 4 Hindu gods: Brahmā, Indra, Rudra, Upendra; Mu.: *abhaya-*, *tarjanī-mudrā*; attr.: *aṅkuśa*, *aṣṭavadana*, *brahmakapāla*, *daṇḍa*, *dhanus*, *kamaṇḍalu* (*ratnapātra*), *kapāla*, *karttṛkā*, *khaṭvāṅga*, *muṇḍamālā*, *nīlotpala*, *śara*, (*tarjanī*)*pāśa*, *trinayana*, *vajra*.
Lit.: BBh. 151, 249 a.pl. 192; KiSB 97.

prasāritahasta(mudrā) "(gesture) extended hand(?)" (Mu.), n. of a handpose not fully explained. Char. of Skanda.
Lit.: R 2:427.

prasavya "turned (or turning) to the left", n. of the counter-clockwise movement, considered to be unlucky and ill-omened (cp. *vāma*, *dakṣina*, *pradakṣiṇa*).
Lit.: STP 1:192.

Prasūti ("procreation, generation"), n. of the daughter of Svāyambhuva Manu, one of the wives of Dakṣa.
Lit.: DHP 321.

Pratibhānakūṭa ("of excellent intelligence, summit of brilliancy"; Buddh.), n. of a *bodhisattva*. Char. colour: yellow or red; Mu. or attr.: *choṭikā*; attr.: *khaḍga* on a *padma*.
Lit.: BBh. 82, 91 a.pl. 62.

Pratibhānakūṭa-Lokeśvara ("P. as L."; Buddh.), n. of a variety of Avalokiteśvara. Char.: att.: *padmāsana*; Vāh.: *padma*; attr.: *kamaṇḍalu, pāśa*.
Lit.: BBh. 398 a.pl. 40(A).

Pratibhānapratisamvit ("context-analysis"; Buddh.), n. of a *pratisamvit*. Char.: colour: green; attr.: *vajraghaṇṭā* (of which the *vajra* has 3 prongs).
Lit.: BBh. 343 a.pl. 225.

pratibimba "reflected, mirrored"; "Representation. Reflexion or counterpart of real forms. In Indian art the term describes the mirroring or reconstruction of the imagined shape of the cosmos or celestial regions in architectural form". – Cp. *darpaṇa*.
Lit.: RAAI 273.

pratīka "outward form or shape, image, iconographic symbol" (attr.), another term for *rūpa*.
Lit.: MW 675; SM 10.

pratikramaṇa ("going to confession"; Buddh.; Jain.), see *āvaśyaka*.
Lit.: GJ 408; IC 2:638; MW 664.

pratikṛti "(likeness) image" of a deity (attr.), see *pratimā*.
Lit.: CHIIA 42.

pratimā, properly "reflected image"; "image, idol, icon, statue, figure" (attr.). Such an image should therefore not be regarded as the real god (a common misunderstanding) but as a "symbolical reflection of the deity", and, hence, the worship dedicated to it is reflected or redirected to the real deity. If an image is damaged it is usually no longer fit to be worshipped, and is then removed, thrown into the water and replaced by a new image. – Other n.: *daivata, devatāpratimā, pratikṛti, mūrti*.
Lit.: B 37; CHIIA 42; Gz 113; IC 1:571: JMS 73; WHW 1:470; ZA 319.

pratimākāra "image-maker", n. of the guild that comprises the artisans who make representations of gods (images), sculptors etc. – Another n.: *devalaka*.
Lit.: WHW 1:424.

pratisamvit ("analytical science"; Buddh.). In Buddhism four *p.* are acknowledged as the branches of logical analysis, and in Vajrayāna Buddhism they are personified as female goddesses. These are: Dharma-, Artha-, Nirukti and Pratibhāna-pratisamvit.
Lit.: BBh. 342.

Pratisarā, see Mahāpratisarā.

pratiṣṭhā "consecration or dedication of an idol to a temple etc.". Cp. *sthāpana*.
Lit.: ACA 9 a.passim; GJ 430; IC 1:572.

pratiṣṭhāguru, n. of a priest or teacher (*guru*) who performs the ceremony of the consecration of an idol etc. (Jain.).
Lit.: GJ 431.

prativāsudeva "anti-Vāsudeva" (Jain.), n. of a group of nine cruel rulers.
Lit.: GJ 258, 261.

pratyākhyāna ("rejection, refusal"; Jain.), i.e. assuming a vow to give up certain enjoyments; see also *āvaśyaka*.
Lit.: GJ 408; IC 2:638.

pratyālīḍha(pada) (or *pratyālīḍhāsana*; att.). MW: "a particular attitude in shooting (the left foot advanced and right drawn back)". It is also described as "standing as in violent fight" (RN). Thus it is n. of a *sthānaka*-posture and is said to symbolize destruction and loathsomeness. It seems (at least according to some interpretations) to constitute the opposite-handed form of *ālīḍhāsana*, which in this dictionary is used as a common term for both att., since the descriptions of these att. in iconographic literature are somewhat vague and confusing. See *ālīḍhāsana* for further details.
Lit.: B 266; BBh. 432; G 24· KiDG 61; MW 677; RN 31.

Pratyaṅgirā ("whose speech is averted, or turned westward"), n. of a terrible goddess. Char.: Vāh.: *siṅha*; attr.: *ḍamaru, kapāla, keśamaṇḍala, nāgapāśa, triśūla*.
Lit.: SSI 213.

pratyekabuddha (Pāli *paççeka-*, Pkt *patteya-buddha*; "*buddha* for one, i.e. for himself";

Buddh., Jain.), n. of a kind of *buddha* who lives in seclusion and obtains emancipation for himself only (as distinguished from the *buddhas* who also liberate others).
Lit.: BBh. 8; BRI 48, 51; SchRI 234.

Pratyūṣa ("scorching, daybreak"), n. of one of the *vasus*. Attr.: *aṅkuśa*, *khaḍga*, *kheṭaka*, *śakti*.
Lit.: R 2:553.

pravāla (or *pravāḍa*; Tam. *pavaḷam*) "(red) coral", n. of a precious stone included among the *navaratna**.
Lit.: TL 4:2541.

pravartitahasta(mudrā) (Mu.), n. of a hand-pose, meaning simply "uplifted arm" Char. of Śiva Naṭarāja in the *lalita*-dance.
Lit.: R 2:263.

prāyaścitta "expiation", n. of a purification ceremony performed before death and on certain other occasions.
Lit.: Gt Suppl. 109; IC 1:606; RV 116; WHW 2:258.

PREṀ, form of a *bījamantra* that "is used for enchantments and magic".
Lit.: DHP 343.

preta ("dead, departed"), n. of a kind of ghost, the evil-disposed, disturbed spirit of a cripple, haunting cemeteries and other places. *pretas* are described as meagre-bodied and pot-bellied. – For *p.* as Vāh., see further *mṛtaka*.
Lit.: BBh. 438; D 242; DHP 301, 311; GBM 114; GoRI 1:323; MEIA 201, 227; MG 279, 287; WM 146.

pretāsana.

1. (Att.) "The sitting of, or like a corpse", n. of a Yogic *āsana*-posture "in which the whole body lies rigid and motionless like a corpse" (B).
2. (Vāh.) "Having a corpse as seat", a term alluding to an idol shown as seated on a corpse, see *mṛtaka*. Char., e.g., of *mātaras*.

Lit.: B 274; R 1:21; WM 90.

Pretasantarpita(-Lokeśvara) ("L. who is satiated with corpses"; Buddh.), n. of a variety of Avalokiteśvara. Char.: colour: white; Mu.: *varadamudrā*; attr.: *akṣamālā*, *cintāmaṇi*, *pustaka*, *triśūla* (*tridaṇḍa*).
Lit.: BBh. 141, 395 a.pl. 118, 14(A); KiSB 61.

Prīti ("pleasure, joy, love").

1. Personification, regarded as the daughter of Dakṣa and wife of Kāma (also said to be the Śakti of Pradyumna or Viṣṇu).
Lit.: R 1:233.
2. (Vāh.; Buddh.) Upon P. Paramāśva treads.
Lit.: BBh. 186.

Priyadarśanā ("pleasant to the sight"; Buddh.), n. of an inferior Mahāyāna goddess attending on Buddhakapāla.
Lit.: BBh. 160.

priyaṅgukusumamañjarī "bud of a *priyaṅgu*-flower (panic-seed)" (attr.; Buddh.). Char. of Adhimuktavaśitā.
Lit.: BBh. 331.

Priyodbhava ("of pleasant origin"), n. of a *dvārapālaka* of Brahmā. Attr.: *akṣamālā*, *daṇḍa*, *pustaka* (*āgama*).
Lit.: R 2:507.

prokṣaṇī(pātra) "vessel for holy water" (attr.). This is used for sprinkling water on the offerings at the *pūjā*. Held in one hand char. of Agni.
Lit.: GH 345; IC 1:570; SSI 243.

pṛṣṭhasvastika "backward cross" (att.), a kind of dance pose, with the legs crossed and the face turned to look back.
Lit.: SSIP 85 a.fig. 39.

Pṛthivī(mātā) (or Pri-, Pṛthvī; "Earth-mother"), identical with Bhūmidevī. Under the n. of P. (as a personal aspect) she is regarded as the wife of Dyauṣ(pitā). – P. is sometimes met with as n. of the *dikpāla* of the north-east direction.
Lit.: D 243; DHP 86; GoRI 1:95; Gt 470; IC 1:492; IIM 95; MG 25; SSI 187; WM 147.

Pṛthu (or Pri-; "broad, wide"), n. of a primeval king of the solar race, who instituted agriculture. He is also mentioned as an (unusual) *avatāra* of Viṣṇu.
Lit.: B 391; D 242; DHP 165, 185, 326; Gt 470; IC 1:533; IIM 96; R 1:123.

pūcai (Tam.), see *pūjā*.

pūcāri (Tam.), see *pūjāri*.

Pudgalā, see Puṭkalai.

pūjā (Tam. *pūcai*) "honour, worship, adoration of the gods", n. of Hindu and Jain worship. The Hindu *p*. is described in detail in DiIP. It is said to be 16-fold: 1. *āvāhana*; 2. *sthāpana*; 3. *pādya*; 4. *ācamana*; 5. *arghya*; 6. *abhiṣeka*; 7. *vastropavīta*; 8. offering of flowers (cp. *puṣpāñjali*); 9. *dhūpadīpa*; 10. *naivedya*; 11. *bali*; 12. *homa*; 13. *nityotsava*; 14. *vādya*; 15. *nartana*; 16. *udvāsana*. – Jain worship is found in three forms: *bhāva-*, *aṅga-* and *agra-pūjā*. It is 8-fold: 1. *jala-*; 2. *candana-*; 3. *puṣpa-*; 4. *dhūpa-*; 5. *dīpa-*; 6. *akṣata-*; 7. *naivedya-*; 8. *phala-pūjā*. – Cp. also *liṅga-*, *Śiva-* and *Viṣṇu-pūjā*.
Lit.: B 59; DHP 366; DiIP 66, 90; GH 344; GJ 365, 395; GoRI 1:332, 334, 2:16; IC 1:573; KiH 35; WHW 1:50; 2:252.

pūjādīpa "ritual lamp" (attr.), n. of a kind of oil-lamp attached to a pot, which is used in worship. The difference between a *p*. and a *kuṇḍī* is often insignificant.

pūjārī (or *pujārī*, *pujari*, Hi. (and common N.Ind.) < Skt *pūjā*+*kārī*; Tam. *pūcāri*) "worshipper; priest" (of a popular or tribal god) who officiates at smaller shrines and lives upon the offerings made to the idol. This service is held to be degrading and is not performed by higher-class Brāhmans. Most of the *p*. are illiterate.
Lit.: DiCh. 133; DiIP 31; FHRI 258; GH 359; GJ 401; GoRI 2:4, 8; P 229, 277; WHW 1:438.

pūjopakaraṇa "requisites for the ritual worship of a god", e.g. *dīpa*, *ghaṇṭā*, *naivedya* etc.
Lit.: B 299; SSI fig. 5.

Pukkasī (Tib.; Buddh.), in Vajrayāna Buddhism and Lamaism n. of one of the *gaurī-* and *kerimas*-goddesses. Char.: colour: yellowish white or blue; attr.: *kamaṇḍalu*.
Lit.: BBh. 311 a.pl. 204; G 101 (with ill.).

Pulaha ("bridger of space"), n. of a *riṣi* or *prajāpati*. Wife: Kṣamā.
Lit.: D 244; DHP 317.

Pulastya ("wearing the hair straight or smooth"), n. of an ancient *riṣi* (one of the *prajāpati*s or mind-born sons of Brahmā). Wife: Prīti.
Lit.: D 244; DHP 317; Gt 473; WHW 2:253.

Pulli(y)ār, see Piḷḷaiyār.
Lit.: JDI passim; MG 190.

Punarvasū (or -u; "restoring goods"), n. of a *nakṣatra*. Its influence is good.
Lit.: BBh. 381; IC 2:729.

puṇḍarīka "white lotus" (Vāh.; attr.). As Vāh. char. of Sita-Prajñāpāramitā; as attr. char. of: Candra, Kālacakra, Sarasvatī. – Other n.: *kairava*, *kumuda*, *sitāmbuja*, *śvetāmbhoruha*, *śvetapaṅkaja*. See also *padma* (where many cases in which deities carry white lotuses are listed). –
Puṇḍarīka is NP of the *diggaja* which accompanies Agni as a *dikpāla*. His wife is Kapilā. P. is also another n. of a *nāgadeva*, see Padma.
Lit.: B 377; D 180; Gt 474.

puṇḍra "sectarian mark made on the forehead with ashes or colouring matter" (attr.), see *tilaka*, *tiryakpuṇḍra*, *ūrdhvapuṇḍra*.
Lit.: MW 632; WHW 1:208.

Punītavatī ("purified"), n. of an inferior goddess, worshipped at Kāraikkāl (near Negapatam, whence also named Kāraikkāl Ammaiyār). She is a deification of the wife of a Brāhman merchant.
Lit.: JDI 53.

puṇṇaghaṭa (Pali, < Skt *pūrṇaghaṭa*) "full pitcher" (as an offering on festive days to the monks; attr.), n. of a symbol of abundance. Cp. *pūrṇakalaśa*.
Lit.: CHIIA 65.

puṁsavana(vrata) "(vow of) male-production", n. of a *saṁskāra*-rite performed in the third or the eighth month of gestation and before the period of quickening; the aim is to secure a male child.
Lit.: DiIP 180; GH 332; GJ 410; IC 1:363; MW 630; WHW 2:239.

pūṇūl (Tam.), see *yajñopavīta*.
Lit.: JDI 125.

puṇyaśālā "alms-house", "a holy hall or place of worship for the laity".
Lit.: ZA 326.

Pupala-Lokeśvara (Buddh.), n. of a variety of Avalokiteśvara. Char.: att.: *padmāsana*; Vāh.: *padma*; Mu.: *abhaya-*, *karaṇa(?)-mudrā*; attr.: *akṣamālā*, *pustaka*.
Lit.: BBh. 396 a.pl. 24(A).

Puraiyar (Tam.; meaning uncertain), n. of a form of Skanda in South India.
Lit.: DiCh. 18.

Puraṁdara ("destroyer of strongholds"; Buddh.), probably epithet of Indra. Attr.: *pāśa*, *vajra*.
Lit.: KiSB 84.

Purāṇa ("old"), n. of ancient tales or legends, old traditional history. A P. is chiefly concerned with legends of gods, hence it is n. of a class of sacred works, dedicated to certain gods.
Lit.: D 245; Gt 475; WHW 2:253; WM 148.

Pūraṇai (Tam.; < Skt *pūrṇā* "fullness"), n. of one of the wives of Aiyaṉār. She belongs to the group *navaśakti*.
Lit.: ACA passim; SSR 143; TL 5:2846.

purdah (Pers.), see *pardā*.

Puri, n. of a town in Orissa with a Jagannāth-temple from about A.D. 1150.
Lit.: FES 38; ZA pl. 324 ff.

Pūrṇā ("full, fullness"), see Pūraṇai.
Lit.: ACA passim.

Pūrṇabhadra ("abundant good"; Buddh.), n. of a king of *yakṣas*.
Lit.: BBh. 380; KiSB 74.

pūrṇacāpa "full bow, i.e. a strung bow" (attr.), see *dhanus*.
Lit.: MEIA 145.

pūrṇaghaṭa "full vase" (attr.), see *pūrṇakalaśa*.
Lit.: JMS 77.

pūrṇakalaśa "full vase" (attr.), a vase of flowers as a decorative motif in relief. It is a symbol of fertility. Char. of Gāṅgeya-Subrahmaṇya. *p.* is also a *maṅgala*, see *aṣṭamaṅgala*. – Other n.: *pūrṇakumbha*, *pūrṇaghaṭa*. Cp. also *puṇṇaghaṭa*.
Lit.: Gz 53; JMS 17 a.pl. 29.

pūrṇakumbha "vessel filled (with water)" (attr.), see *pūrṇakalaśa*.
Lit.: R 2:441.

pūrṇapātra "vessel full (of water)" (attr.), see *kamaṇḍalu*.
Lit.: SSI 243.

pūrṇimānta "ending with the day of the full moon", referring to the month, see sub *candramāsa*. Another n.: *kṛṣṇādi*.

purohita ("appointed, commissioned"), n. of the class of private priests or chaplains in the service of a prince.
Lit.: GoRI 2:17; Gt 484; MKVI 2:5; RV 103; WHW 1:438.

-puruṣa ("man"), as the second member of a compound word in which the first member is the n. of a weapon, *p.* signifies a personification of the weapon. Fundamental to this principle is *āyudhapuruṣa*; cp. further *cakrapuruṣa*.
Lit.: B 537.

Puruṣa is the primeval man, the original individual from which Macrocosm developed (cp. Ṛgveda 10, 90). Then P. is regarded as the male counterpart of the great Mother, see Mātā. – P. is sometimes said to be an *avatāra* of Viṣṇu.
Lit.: B 391; DHP 44; GoRI 1:269, 303; KiSH 14; MKVI 2:1; R 1:123, 247; WHW 2:263; WM 149.

Puruṣadattā ("daughter of Puruṣa"; Jain.), n. of a *śāsanadevatā* attending on the 5th *tīrthaṅkara*.
Lit.: GJ 362 a.pl. 24:5; KiJ 12 a.pl. 27:5.

puruṣamedha "human sacrifice".
Lit.: STP 4:64; WHW 1:463.

Puruṣottama ("the best of men", the supreme person, the highest Puruṣa).
1. (Hind.) N. of a Tantric form or aspect of Viṣṇu as the supreme god (see *caturviṁśatimūrti*).
Lit.: DHP 154; KiSH 39; MEIA 43; R 1:230.
2. (Buddh.) Epithet of the Buddha.
Lit.: CEBI 47.

Pūrvabhādrapadā(s) (or -bhadrapada; "'aux pieds auspicieux' antérieure", IC), another n. of a *nakṣatra*, see Pūrvaproṣṭhapadās.
Lit.: BBh. 382; IC 2:730.

Pūrvāphālgunī (or Pūrvaphalgunī; "the first Phālgunī; la grise antérieure", IC), n. of a *nakṣatra*. Its influence is medium.
Lit.: BBh. 382; IC 2:729.

Pūrvaproṣṭhapadās ("'aux pieds de banc [?]' antérieure", IC), n. of a *nakṣatra*. – Another n.: *Pūrvabhādrapadās*. Its influence is medium.
Lit.: IC 2:730.

Pūrvāṣāḍhā(s) ("the first *āṣāḍhās*; 'les invincibles' antérieure", IC), n. of a *nakṣatra*. Its influence is medium.
Lit.: BBh. 382; IC 2:730.

Pūṣan ("Nourisher"), n. of a Vedic god, originally connected with the sun. He belongs to the Ādityas. Attr.: 4 *padmas*.
Lit.: DHP 123; Gt 490; IC 1:323; R 1:309; WHW 2:263; WM 149.

Puṣkalā ("abundant"), see Puṭkalai.
Lit.: ACA passim.

puṣkara "blue lotus" (attr.), see *nīlotpala*.
Lit.: MKVI 2:9.

puṣpa "flower" (attr.). Char. of Ākāśagarbha, Hayagrīva, Jaṭāmukuṭa-Lokeśvara, Krodhahayagrīva, Mahārājalīlamañjuśrī, Māmakī, Mārkaṇḍeya, Puṣpā, Satyabhāmā, Skanda in Somāskanda. – *p.* is sometimes also used equivalently to *padma*.
Lit.: R 1:204.

Puṣpā ("flower"; Buddh.), NP of one of the Lamaist *aṣṭamātaras*. Char.: colour: white; attr.: *puṣpa*.
Lit.: G 36, 38.

puṣpābja "lotus" (attr.), see *padma*.
Lit.: ACA 31.

puṣpadaṇḍa "tige de fleur" (attr.).
Lit.: ACA 32.

Puṣpadanta ("flower-toothed").
1. (Hind.) N. of a *diggaja* which accompanies Vāyu as a *dikpāla*. P:s wife is Śubhadantī.
Lit.: D 180.
2. (Jain.) NP of the 9th *tīrthaṅkara*. Symbol: *makara* or *karkī*. – See Suvidhi.
Lit.: GJ 273; KiSH 142.

Puṣpadhanvan ("bow of flowers", or "armed with a bow of flowers", respectively).
1. (Attr.) N. of a certain *dhanus*, char. of Kāma, Uḍḍiyāna-Kurukullā, Vajrānaṅga.
2. Epithet of Kāma.
Lit.: B 301; MW 639.

Puṣpaka ("made of flowers"; Vāh.), n. of a *ratha*, char. of Rāma; also a *ratha* drawn by fallow horses (*aśvas*) and steered by Mātalī, char. of Indra or Kubera; a *ratha* drawn by lions (*siṅhas*), char. of Budha.
Lit.: D 251; IIM 84; KiSH 56, 57, 62.

puṣpāñjali (or *-ī*) "the presentation of flowers or a nosegay with both hands open and hollow" (cp. *añjalimudrā*). This forms part of the *pūjā* and is the ordinary oblation to the gods (being comparable to the honouring of a guest with flowers).
Lit.: DiIP 90, 112; P 263; ZA 72, 276, 319.

puṣpamālā "garland of flowers" (attr.), see *vanamālā*.
Lit.: BBh. 378.

puṣpapātra "vessel for holding flowers and other offerings during ceremonies" (attr.).
Lit.: MH 37.

puṣpapūjā "worship with flowers" (Jain.), n. of the worship of an image which consists in the crowning or covering of the icon with flowers. See *pūjā*.
Lit.: GJ 396, 429.

puṣpapuṭamudrā "flower-basket-gesture" (Mu.), n. of a handpose in which "the hands are slightly curved, joined at the sides, palms up as though to receive water in them. It denotes a water or flower offering". Cp. *sampuṭāñjalimudrā*.
Lit.: WHW 2:88.

puṣparāga (Tam. *puruṭarākam*) "topaz", n. of a precious stone included among the *navaratna**.
Lit.: MW 640; TL 5:2775.

puṣpaśara "flower-arrow" (attr.). Char. of Śāstā. Cp. *śara* and *pañcaśara*.
Lit.: ACA 34.

Puṣpatārā ("flower-Tārā"; Buddh.), n. of a minor Mahāyāna goddess. Char.: colour: white; attr.: *vanamālā*.
Lit.: BBh. 241 a.pl. 183; KiSB 102.

pustaka (also *pusta*) "manuscript, book" (attr.). A book in this sense usually takes the form of a manuscript of palm leaves. In the case of Hindu images this *p.* generally signifies a Veda or an *āgama*; in the hands of Buddhist images it usually means the *prajñāpāramitā*-scripture, or possibly the Tipiṭaka. Other books that may be signified by *p.* are: *daśabhūmika*, *dharmagañja* and *nāmasaṅgīti*. – With Buddhist icons this attr. is sometimes carried on a *padma*. – Char. esp. of: Brahmā, Prajñāpāramitā, Sarasvatī; further of: Abhimukhī, Aghora, Ākāśagarbha, Amoghapāśa, *arhat*s, Āryasarasvatī, Aśvins, Avalokiteśvara (in different forms), Bālā, Balapāramitā, Bālā-Śakti, Bhadra, Brahmāṇī, Bṛhaspati, Cundā, Dhanadā, Dharmameghā, Gaṇeśa, Gopaka, Hayagrīva, Kaumārī (?), Kiraṇākṣa, Kṣitigarbha, Madhva, Mahāmāyūrī, Mahāsarasvatī, Maṇikkavācakar, Mañjuśrī (in different forms), Mañjuvara, Mar-pa, Piṇḍolabhāradvāja, Pretasantarpita-Lokeśvara, Priyodbhava, *riṣi*s, Ṣaḍakṣarī, Sadharma, Sadyojāta, Saṅgha, Śaṅkarācārya, Śarabha, Sarvanivaraṇaviṣkambhin, Satya, Sāvitrī, Skanda (in Somāskanda), Śukra, Tatpuruṣa, Tīkṣṇoṣṇīṣa, Tripurā, Tsoṅ-kha-pa, Vajragarbha, Vajraśāradā, Vajratīkṣṇa, Vāmanāvatāra, Vasudhārā, Viṣṇu, Yajña. – Cp. *vidyā*.

Lit.: B 304, 377; G 16 (ill.); H pl. 5:46d; MEIA 244; R 1:13 a.pl. 4:9; SM 178; SSI pl. IV:5; WM 109 a.fig. 70.

Puṣṭi ("growth, increase"), as personification n. of a goddess. In North India P. is the usual n. of the second wife of Viṣṇu (in South India she is named Bhūmidevī). Sometimes she is also associated with Sarasvatī; therefore the n. Puṣṭi-Sarasvatī is also occasionally met with. P. is sometimes also mentioned as the wife of Gaṇeśa.

Lit.: B 368, 377, 398; WHW 1:377.

Puṣṭi-Sarasvatī, see sub Puṣṭi.

Puṣyā (or -a; "nourishment"), n. of a *nakṣatra*. Its influence is good.

Lit.: BBh. 381; IC 2:729.

Pūtanā ("putrid"), n. of a female demon, a *ḍākinī* that is said to cause a particular disease in children and unsuccessfully tried on one occasion to kill Bālakṛṣṇa by suckling him with her poisoned breast. P. is also n. of a group of female demons. – P. is furthermore n. either of the calamitous weapon of the smallpox goddess Śītalā or of Śītalā herself.

Lit.: D 251; DHP 288; FKR 114; IC 1:528; MW 641.

Pūtattāḻvār (Tam.), n. of a *vaiṣṇavabhakta*.

Lit.: R 2:480 a.pl. 136.

Puṭkalai (or -ā, Tam., < Skt *puṣkalā* "abundant; fullness"; also, probably wrongly, regarded as a Hybrid Skt word connected with Skt *puruṣa*), NP of one of the wives of Aiyaṉār. She belongs to the group *navaśakti*.

Lit.: ACA passim; EB 347; SSR 143; TL 5:2748.

R

Rādhā (Rādhikā; "prosperity, succes"; as to this interpretation, cp. Śrī), NP of the chief among the *gopī*s who was the favourite mistress of the young Kṛṣṇa. R. is sometimes regarded as an *avatāra* of Lakṣmī, hence also as the chief consort of Kṛṣṇa, but according to the usual legends she was not married to Kṛṣṇa (but to a cowherd). In the *bhakti*-cult of Kṛṣṇa she is a central personage, symbolizing the yearning for the salvation of mankind or the human soul, drawn to the ineffable god, Kṛṣṇa. – Attr.: *padma*. – Cp. *sakhībhāva*. – As to R. as n. of a *nakṣatra*, see Viśākhā.

Lit.: AIM (passim); D 251; DHP 177, 263; GI pl. 81; IC 1:521, 2:730; IP pl. 38; KT 160; R 1:376; RIS 61; WM 150.

rāga "love; tint, a particular basic musical mode", of which 6 or 7 or 26 are mentioned. 5 secondary *rāgiṇī*s correspond to each *r*.

Lit.: HAHI 16; SKh. 13; WHW 2:266.

Rāgarāja ("king of passion"; Buddh.), n. of a *vidyārāja* in the east Asiatic esoteric doctrine.

Lit.: GBM 92.

Rāgavidyārāja ("king of passion and knowledge"; Buddh.), n. of a *vidyārāja*.

Lit.: GBM 80.

Rāghava(-Rāma), epithet of Rāma as a descendant of Raghu.

Lit.: R 1:186; WHW 2:270.

rāgiṇī "a secondary modification of the musical mode *rāga**".

RAḤ, a syllable (*bīja*) with a mystical meaning.

Lit.: GJ 369.

Rāhu ("seizer").

1. (Hind.) In astronomy R. is the cause of eclipses, and the n. is used to signify the eclipse. Mythologically R. is supposed to seize the sun and the moon and to swallow them, thus bringing about the eclipse. He is counted among the planets and in this role represents the ascending node (connected with the moon's orbit, cp. Ketu). He is regarded as the son of Kāśyapa or Rudra or Vipracitti and Siṅhikā and is represented with four hands, his lower part ending in a tail. In other instances he is represented as a mere head without a body (i.e. the head having been cut off from his body by Viṣṇu; the body is then known as Ketu). Char.: colour: dark-blue or black; Vāh.: *siṅha* (blue-black) or *ulūka* or *kūrma* or *siṅhāsana* or *ratha* drawn by 8 black horses; Mu.: *añjali-*, *varada-mudrā*; attr.: *amastaka*, *ardhacandra*, *khaḍga*, *kheṭaka*, *triśūla*.

Lit.: B 429; BBh. 149; ChIMS pl. facing p. 80; D 252; DHP 315; Gt 496; IIM 115; KiH 7; KiK 141; R 1:321 a.pl. 96; SSI 239; STP 2:81; Th. 115, 125; WHW 2:272.

2. (Buddh.) In Lamaism R. is regarded as a demon and represented with 9 heads (with the head of a crow upon the 9th head) and a dragon's body; besides, R., in the form of a head without a body (see above), appears as the charioteer of Mārīcī. He is also, as in Hinduism, a planet god. – R., together with Kāma and his wife (these riding upon R.), is also the Vāh. of Tārodbhava-Kurukullā. – Char.: colour: reddish blue; attr.: *candra*, *sūrya*.

Lit.: BBh. 149, 377 a.pl. 242; G 37, 96.

Rāhula ("seizer"; Buddh.), NP of the son of Gautama Buddha and Yaśodharā. He probably died before his father, and he is worshipped as an *arhat*.

Lit.: BRI 16; CTLP pl. 28; G 3, 104; KiSB 12; SeKB 148 (ill.).

rājadaṇḍa "sceptre" (attr.), a symbol of royalty (see *rājakakuda*) shown lying on the throne.

Lit.: WHW 1:552.

Rājagopāla ("the royal cowherd"), n. of a form of Kṛṣṇa. He is then often represented with two wives. Attr.: *cakra*, *śaṅkha*, *veṇu*.

Lit.: Th. 69.

rājakakuda (*kakuda*) "ensign, symbol of royalty", of which there are five: *khaḍga* "sword", *sitātapatra* (*chattra*) "white umbrella", *kirīṭa* "crown", *pādukas* "shoes, slippers" (rested on the *pādapīṭha* "footstool"), *cāmara* "chowrie". Others add *siṅhāsana* "lion's seat, throne" and *rājadaṇḍa* (see above). Cp. also *saptaratna*.

Lit.: STP 5:175; WHW 1:552.

rājalīlā(sana) "the sitting posture 'royal ease'" (att.), n. of an *āsana*-posture which may be described as follows: both legs are bent and placed upon the *pīṭha*, the feet close beside each other; one knee (usually the right one) is raised, the other rests flat on the *pīṭha*; one arm rests on the raised knee, the body is leant a little awry backwards and is supported by the other arm which is propped up against the *pīṭha*. This att. is char. of: Avalokiteśvara, Ekajaṭā, Mahāmāyūrī, Mañjuśrī (in different forms), Padmapāṇi, Siṅhanāda and other *bodhisattvas*. – Other n.: *līlā*, *mahārājalīlā-(sana)*.

Lit.: BBh. 432; G 24; MH 7; SM 128; WHW 1:75; ZA 183, a.pl. 321.

Rājamannār, in South India epithet of Kṛṣṇa (corresponding to Rājagopāla?). Att.: *kūrpara.*
Lit.: SB 267 a.fig. 173.

Rājamātaṅgī, n. of a goddess (connected with Mātaṅgī?). Char.: Vāh.: *padma*; attr.: *candra, nīlotpala(mālā), śuka, tilaka, viṇā.*
Lit.: R 1:372; SSI 220.

Rājarājeśvarī ("royal lady"), n. of a form of Pārvatī. Attr.: *āñjanī, aṅkuśa, darpaṇa, ikṣukodaṇḍa, padma, pañcaśara, pāśa, phala.* Cp. Lalitā, Tripurasundarī.
Lit.: SSI 220.

rājarṣi "royal *riṣi* or saint", e.g. Viśvāmitra. *rājarṣi*s form a group of *riṣi*s the leader of whom was Ṛtuparṇa.
Lit.: D 253; R 2:566.

rājāsana "royal seat, throne" (Vāh.), n. of a *pīṭha.* Cp. *siṅhāsana.*
Lit.: MH 44.

rājasabhā "king's hall", n. of a hall of coronation in a temple.
Lit.: BECA 1:25.

rājasika ("belonging to the quality *rajas* 'passion'", n. given to the image of a deity sitting upon the Vāh. and characterized by the Mu. *varadamudrā*, by weapons and other ornaments.
Lit.: MH 7; R 2:495.

rajata "silver", n. of a precious thing, sometimes included among the *pañcaratna**.

Raji, n. of a leader of the *daitya*s who temporarily got the better of the gods and ousted Indra from his heaven. Later on Indra was reinstated in his heaven by means of a ruse.
Lit.: IIM 76.

rājīva "lotus" (attr.). According to MW this is a blue lotus-flower; it might therefore be analogous to *nīlotpala.*
Lit.: BBh. 168; MW 875.

rājopacāra "the paying of royal honours", n. of a ritual observed in the temples of Śiva and Viṣṇu.
Lit.: SSI 3.

rājyābhiṣekaśaka ("the era of the coronation"), n. of a Mahratta era founded by Śivajī in A.D. 1673. Out of use.
Lit.: Enc.Brit. 5:721; IC 2:738.

rākhī (Hi., < *rakṣikā*) "piece of thread or silk bound round the wrist as an amulet a certain festival" (attr.). The festival in question is named *rākhī bandhan* or *rakṣābandhapūrṇimā, rākhīpūrṇimā.* – Another n.: *rakṣā* (*bandhan*). Cp. also *poṅkal.*
Lit.: Gt 498; KBh. 168; P 582.

rākhīpūrṇimā (Hi.), see *rakṣābandhapūrṇimā.*

Rakhumāī (N.Ind), see Rukmābāyi.

rakṣā (*-ikā*; lit. "protection"), n. of an amulet. As to a general term for "amulet", see *kavaca.* – *rakṣā bandhan* (Hi.) "amulet", see *rākhī.*
Lit.: IC 1:571; KBh. 168; P 596; SSR 115.

rakṣābandhapūrṇimā "the full moon festival of the binding of amulets (*rakṣā*)", n. of a festival in the month *śrāvaṇa.* Another n.: *rākhīpūrṇimā.* Cp. *rākhī* (*bandhan*).
Lit.: IC 1:591.

rākṣasa (fem. *-ī*) "a kind of demon" (*asura*, goblin or evil spirit), a descendant of Kāśyapa and Khasā. The chief of the evil *r.* was Rāvaṇa. *r.* may often be regarded as a Vāh., inasmuch as a god is represented treading or dancing upon one or more *r.*: thus Hayagrīva, Kālajambhala, Acalavajrapāṇi, Śiva Naṭarāja (on a *r.* named Apasmāra), Vajrapāṇi (in the Garuḍa-form); cp. also *mṛtaka, nara.* - *r.* (as attr.) sometimes further signifies one of the faces of Viṣṇu (see *rākṣasamuṇḍa*). It is also n. of a manifestation of Viṣṇu (see *caturvyūha*). – In Jainism *r.* is n. of a kind of *vyantaradevatā.* – Another n.: *kāpila.*
Lit.: D 254; DHP 143, 301, 309; GH 107; GJ 237; GoRI 1:322; Gt 499 a.Suppl. 112; IIM 114; R 2:559; WHW 2:277; WM 151.

rākṣasa-muṇḍa (or *-mukha, -mastaka*) "head, skull of a demon" (attr.), also "having a demon head" (attr.). *r.* is carried in one hand by Kālī, Tārā (this attr. usually being named *muṇḍa*). The head (or, in polyheaded representations, one head) of an idol may be *rākṣasamukha*, one face of Viṣṇu in the composition Caturmūrti being a notable instance.

Rakṣoghnamūrti ("representation [of Śiva] destroying Rakṣas [this being another n. for Yama]"), n. of an *ugra*-form of Śiva feasting on corpses in the burning-ground. Char.: attr.: *ḍamaru*, *dantas*, *kapāla* (with *agni*), *paraśu*, *triśūla* (piercing Yama).
Lit.: SSI 148.

rakta "blood" (attr.), believed to be a magical substance and, when poured out on the ground, to have a fertility-character; it forms an important part of the *pūjā*. Instead of *r.* red ochre or vermilion dye is often used, and with that the idol is daubed and the body of the sacrificer is marked. – *r.* is also the n. of the colour red. For the many other n. of this colour, see MEIA.
Lit.: FHRI 288; MEIA 238; WHW 1:157.

Rakta-Cāmuṇḍā ("the red C." or "the blood-C."), n. of a form of Cāmuṇḍā. Attr.: *khaḍga*, *musala*. – Variety: Yogeśvarī.
Lit.: R 1:364.

raktakaroṭaka "*kapāla* full of blood" (attr.), see *kapāla*.
Lit.: BBh. 156.

Raktalokeśvara ("the red Lord"; Buddh.), n. of a variety of Ṣaḍakṣarī(-Lokeśvara) who, on the other hand, is a variety of Avalokiteśvara. Char.: colour: red; he is shown sitting under an *aśoka*-tree with red flowers; attr.: *Amitābhabimba*, *aṅkuśa*, *dhanus*, *padma* (red), *pāśa*, *śara*.
Lit.: BBh. 138 a.pl. 115; G 12, 65; KiSB 60.

raktapadma "red lotus" (attr.), see *padma*.
Lit.: BBh. passim.

raktapaṅkaja "red lotus" (attr.), see *padma*.
Lit.: MEIA 263.

raktapātra "vessel filled with blood" (attr.), see *kapāla*. (Char. of Śivadūtī). – Cp. *asṛkkapāla*.
Lit.: R 1:365.

Rakta-Yamāri ("the red Y."; Buddh.), n. of a variety of Yamāri and consequently of Yamāntaka. He is an emanation of Akṣobhya. Char.: colour: red; att.: *ālīḍhāsana* and *yab-yum* with the Śakti; see further Yamāntaka.
Lit.: BBh. 166; KiSB 64, 70.

RAṀ (or *RAṄ*), form of a *bījamantra* symbolizing the element "fire" (Agni).
Lit.: DHP 344; GJ 369; GH 55; GoRI 2:35.

RĀṀ, form of a *bījamantra* symbolizing Rāma, see Rāma 2.
Lit.: WHW 2:104.

Rāma (also Rāmacandra; the n. is of unknown origin; it is, however, often interpreted as either "black" or "pleasing, charming").

1. NP of a king in Ayodhyā, who is regarded as the 7th *avatāra* of Viṣṇu (representing the sun-aspect of Viṣṇu; he is also said to be a manifestation of the planet Sūrya), who made his appearance in the world in order to save it from the tyranny of the demon Rāvaṇa (the story is the grand subject of the epic Rāmāyaṇa). In this person he is one of the most beloved gods of India. He was the son of Daśaratha and Kauśalyā. Wife: Sītā (regarded as an *avatāra* of Lakṣmī). Char.: colour: dark (black); Vāh.: *ratha* Puṣpaka; att.: (sometimes) *ālīḍhāsana*; Mu.: *kaṭaka-* (or *siṅhakarṇa-*)*mudrā*; attr.: esp. *dhanus* Śārṅga, further: *kaustubha*, *śara*, *śrīvatsa*. He is usually two-armed. Epithets: Dāśarathi-Rāma, Kodaṇḍa-Rāma, Narasiṅha-munaiyataraiyar, Rāghava-Rāma.
Lit.: B 419; D 256; DHP 165, 172; GH 123; GI pl. 68; GoRI 1:252; Gt 501; IA 9; IIM 54; JDI 81; KiSH 37; MG 118; R 1:186 a.pl. 54-57; SB 145 a.fig. 90 a.passim; SIB pl. 33; SSI 35; Th. 62 a.pl. 15; WHW 2:278; WM 151.

2. *Rāma* (N.Ind. *RĀṀ*), a form of a *bījamantra* representing the god Rāma. This is considered one of the basic *mantras* "through which can be expressed all that words can express". Many Hindus die uttering this *mantra* as their last word.
Lit.: DHP 174.

3. Rāma, see Paraśurāma.

4. Rāma, see Balarāma.

5. *rāma*, a symbolic n. of the number "3", see *saṅkhyā*.

rāmalīlā "Rāma-play", n. of a festival dedicated to Rāma. On this occasion parts of the epic Rāmāyaṇa are recited, and episodes

from it are performed in mime. – Cp. also *yātrā*.
Lit.: GH 355.

rāmānandī (or *-in*; "having delight in Rāma"), n. of a Vaiṣṇavite sect which has esp. concentrated its devotion upon Rāma.
Lit.: IC 1:654.

Rāmānuja (or -ācārya), n. of a *vaiṣṇavabhakta* (who lived A.D. 1050-1137). He was the creator of the Viśiṣṭādvaita philosophical system, and the main seat of his activity was Srirangam near Tiruchirapalli. Char.: Mu.: *añjali-* (i.e. *sāñjali-)mudrā*; attr.: *tridaṇḍa, ūrdhvapuṇḍra*.
Lit.: GH 385; GJ 64; IC 1:652; R 2:480 a.pl. 136; SSI 251.

Rambhā ("the plantain, Musa sapientum"), n. of a gracious aspect of Pārvatī, who grants all the desires of her votaries. She is four-armed. Attr.: *agni, akṣamālā, aṅkuśa, kamaṇḍalu, vajra*.
Lit.: R 1:361.

Rāmeśvara (Rāmeśwaram; "lord of Rāma"), n. of a great *liṅga* and of a village and a temple dedicated to Śiva. This temple is situated on an island between India and Sri Lanka. Rāma is supposed to have set up the *liṅga* when crossing to Sri Lanka in his search of his wife Sītā.
Lit.: D 263; WHW 2:289.

RAṄ, see *RAṀ*.

raṅga "assembly hall" of a temple.
Lit.: SSI 50.

Raṅganātha ("lord of the *raṅga*"), n. of a *śayana*-representation of Viṣṇu in South India. Char.: Mu.: left hand in *kaṭimudrā*, right arm bent upwards, the hand under the head; R. lies on a bed (not on Ananta).
Lit.: GoRI 2:117; JDI 64; R 1:269; SIB 62; SSI 50.

rasa (lit.: "fluid") "love, emotion, passion", n. of 10 emotional sentiments which are expressed in the face when dancing. – *r.* also signifies "taste, flavour", of which there are 6 kinds; hence, *r.* is a symbolic n. of the number "6", see *saṅkhyā*.
Lit.: Gt 505; P 591.

rasayātrā "passion procession", n. of a festival celebrated, in some parts of India, in the month *kārttika* by nocturnal dances and representations of the sports of Kṛṣṇa.
Lit.: Gt 505.

rāśi "zodiacal sign". The *rāśi*s appear in deified forms and are 12 in number: Meṣa, Vṛṣan (Vṛṣabha), Mithuna, Karkī, Siṅha, Kanyā, Tulā, Vṛścika, Dhanu(s), Makara, Kumbha, Mīna. – Another n.: *lagna*.
Lit.: BBh. 383; IC 1:491, 2:721; KiSH 67; WHW 1:196.

rāslīlā "passion-sport, folk-dance". The term refers esp. to the dance of Kṛṣṇa and Rādhā, surrounded by their companions, the cowgirls (*gopī*s) and cowherds.
Lit.: Gt 505; Th. 66; WHW 1:266.

raśmi "rein" (attr.). Char. of Revanta.

Rāṣṭrakūṭa, n. of a people and of an epoch of arts, 8th-10th cc. A.D.
Lit.: Gz 173.

ratanchūḍa (Beng.), n. of an ornament (attr.): "small round discs are held in the inside centre of the palm with two chains crossing at its back, and the fingers are adorned with rings".
Lit.: B 293.

ratha (*rath*) "chariot, car" (Vāh.). **As Vāh.** of gods *r.* is differentiated **by the following** kinds of draught animals: *r.* **drawn by** *aśva*s **(no fixed number) is char. of Agni,** Tripurāntaka and the Aśvins. – *r.* **with 7** *aśva*s, char. of Sūrya, Bhāskara, Varuṇa. – *r.* with 8 *aśva*s, char. of the planets: Bṛhaspati, Budha, Ketu, Rāhu, Śani, Śukra. – *r.* with 10 *aśva*s, char. of Candra (Soma). – *r.* with fallow *aśva*s or *siṅha*s, see further Puṣpaka, char. of Budha, Indra, Kubera. – *r.* with 7 *gaus* (or *aśva*s), char. of Uṣas. – *r.* with 7 *haṅsa*s, char. of Brahmā. – *r.* with *kokila*s, char. of Jayakara. – *r.* with 4 *siṅha*s, char. of Bhadrakālī. – *r.* with *śuka*s, char. of Madhukara. – *r.* with 4 *śuka*s, char. of Agni. – *r.* with 7 *sūkara*s, char. of Mārīcī (in different forms). – *ratha*s shaped like *padma*s, char. of the *navadurgās*. – The term *ratha* is sometimes used synonymously with Vāh. (of other kinds of *vāhanas* than cars).

r. is also n. of a processional car, in which an idol is drawn at festivals (cp. *rathayātrā*). Such cars are often very large (up to 15 metres high). Since the processional car often is made to look like a shrine, the term *r.* is also used as a popular n. esp. of Pallava shrines; cp. also *vimāna* and *triratha*.

There are also wooden or metal miniature forms of such processional cars, sometimes as votive gifts placed in shrines.

Lit.: BBh. 378; BECA 1:13; DKI passim; KiDG 65; KiH 47 a.pl. 172; MEIA 233; RAAI 273; Th. 114; ZA 3 with pl. A2.

rathāṅga "disk" ("chariot-wheel"; attr.), see *cakra*.

Lit.: MEIA 252.

rathamahotsava, see sub *rathayātrā*.

rathayātrā (Hi. *rath-yātrā* or *-jātrā*; N.Ind. also *rath jattra*) "car-procession" (cp. also *rathamahotsava* "great car-festival, a solemn procession of an idol on a car"). This term refers esp. to the car-procession of Jagannāth(a) at Purī which occurs in the month *āṣāḍha* (June-July). Similar processions are also made elsewhere.

Lit.: D 129; GH 344; GJ 432; IC 1:574, 590; JDI 130; KiH 47 a.pl. 172f.; MG 153 a.pl. facing p. 150; P 587; ZA 3 with pl. A2.

rath jattra, see sub *rathayātrā*.

Rati ("love, desire, sexual lust or union"; personification).

1. NP of one of the wives of Kāma (Manmatha). She is the daughter of Dakṣa, or, according to some statements, of Śiva. Attr.: *khaḍga* named Nistriṅśa. – Epithet: Revā.

Lit.: B 301; D 263; IIM 96; R 1:276 a.pl. 82-83; WHW 1:515; ZA pl. 129, 508.

2. NP of the Śakti of Aniruddha.

Lit.: R 1:233.

3. NP of a goddess (no further details available). Attr.: *akṣamālā, daṇḍa, karpūra, kastūrī, vīṇā*.

Lit.: R 1:368.

4. (Vāh.; Buddh.) The god Paramāśva is represented trampling R. underfoot.

Lit.: BBh. 186.

Rati-Manmatha, n. of a form of Kāma (Manmatha) together with his wife Rati.

Lit.: SSI fig. 41.

ratna (*ratnacchaṭ*) "jewel, gem, treasure" (attr.). The term *r.* signifies jewels and precious stones which are worn on the body by gods and goddesses, e.g., by Aghora, *vidyādharas*. *ratnas* with particular names are Kaustubha and Syamantaka, char. of Viṣṇu (Kṛṣṇa). – For *r.* as a Buddhist symbol, see *cintāmaṇi*, which is used as a common term in this dictionary (although the *r.* has properly speaking a rather simpler form than the *cintāmaṇi* which is represented as encircled by flames). – Certain jewels further form special collections, thus a collection of 5 gems, see *pañcaratna*, and a collection of 9 gems, see *navaratna*; on account of the last group, *r.* is also a symbolic n. of the number "9", see *saṅkhyā*. – *r.* forms further part of the *ṣaṇmudrā**, and it is also, sometimes, n. of a special jewel, "ruby"(?), see sub *ratnaja*. – Cp. *maṇi, triratna*.

Lit.: BBh. 195, 438; G 16 (ill.); WHW 1:385.

ratnacchaṭā "jewel, lump of jewel" (attr.), see *cintāmaṇi*.

Lit.: BBh. 74.

ratnacchaṭāvarṣighaṭa "jar showering jewels" (attr.), see *kamaṇḍalu*.

Lit.: BBh. 305.

Ratnaḍākinī ("the jewel-*ḍākinī*"; Buddh.), n. of a Mahāyāna *ḍākinī*. She is also found attending on Mahāmāya. Char.: colour: yellow; attr.: *caturmukha, cintāmaṇi, dhvaja, kapāla, khaṭvāṅga, sṛgāla*.

Lit.: BBh. 164; G 34, 80; KiSB 67.

Ratnadala-Lokeśvara ("the jewel-leaf-L."; Buddh.), n. of a variety of Avalokiteśvara. Char.: att.: *samapādasthānaka*; Vāh.: *padma*; Mu.: *varadamudrā*.

Lit.: BBh. 429 a.pl. 75(A).

ratnadāma(n) "garland of jewels" (attr., worn on the body or carried in the hands). This term includes here some other forms and names of this attr., the *ratnamālā*, *ratnamañjari*, *ratnapallava*. Char. of: Cundā, Mahāmañjudatta-Lokeśvara, Tathatāvaśitā.
Lit.: BBh. 222.

Ratnadhara ("wearing jewels"; Buddh.), n. of a *mānuṣibodhisattva*.
Lit.: BBh. 79.

Ratnaheruka ("the jewel-Heruka, Heruka of the *ratnakula*"; Buddh.), epithet of Ratnasambhava as a *herukabuddha*. Colour: yellow.
Lit.: G 87.

ratnaja "born of (i.e. carved in) precious stone" (attr.), n. of a kind of icon. Icons of this sort are made of such stones as: *sphaṭika* ("crystal"), *padmarāga* (B: "lapis lazuli" [?]; the usual meaning of *p.* is "ruby"), *vaiḍūrya* ("cat's-eye"), *vidruma* ("coral"), *puṣya* [?] and *ratna* (B: "ruby" [?], the usual words for "ruby" being *māṇikya* or *padmarāga*). Cp., e.g., *ratnaja liṅga*, see *calaliṅga*.
Lit.: B 223; R 2:76.

ratnakalaśa "vessel of gems" (attr.), see *kamaṇḍalu*.
Lit.: BBh. 249.

Ratnaketu ("jewel banner"; Buddh.), n. of a deity. Mu.: *varadamudrā*.
Lit.: BBh. 45.

ratnakula "jewel family" (Buddh.), n. of a group of deities with the jewel (*ratna* or *cintāmaṇi*) as a family symbol, the head of whom is Ratnasambhava.
Lit.: BBh. 239.

ratnakuṇḍala "ear-ring with jewels" (attr.). Char. of Brahmā.
Lit.: B 289; R 1:24 a.pl. 4:17; WM 104 a.fig. 45.

ratnamakuṭa (*-mukuṭa*) "jewel diadem" (attr.). Char. of: Tripurabhairavī, Ucchiṣṭa-Gaṇapati.
Lit.: R 1:54, 366.

ratnamālā "garland of jewels" (attr.), see *ratnadāma*.
Lit.: BBh. 332.

ratnamañjarī "branch of jewels" (attr.), see *ratnadāma*.
Lit.: BBh. 332.

ratnamekhalā "gem-set girdle" (attr.).
Lit.: SB 125.

ratnamukuṭa, see *ratnamakuṭa*.

ratnapallava "sprout of jewels" (attr.), see *ratnadāma*.
Lit.: BBh. 400.

Ratnapāṇi ("bearing a jewel in the hand"; Buddh.), n. of a *(dhyāni)bodhisattva* who belongs to the *ratnakula* and is an emanation of Ratnasambhava. Char.: colour: yellow or green; att.: *padmāsana* or *sthānaka*; Mu.: *dhyāna-*, *varada-mudrā*; attr.: *candra*, *cintāmaṇi*.
Lit.: BBh. 74 a.pl. 40, p. 87 a.pl. 54; G 14; H 32; KiDG 44; KiSB 46.

Ratnapāṇi-Lokeśvara ("L. as R."; Buddh.), n. of a variety of Avalokiteśvara. Char.: att.: *padmāsana*; Vāh.: *padma*; Mu.: *varadamudrā*; attr.: *khaḍga*.
Lit.: BBh. 399 a.pl. 47(A).

Ratnapāramitā ("the jewel-*pāramitā*"; Buddh.), n. of a *pāramitā*. Char.: colour: red; attr.: *candra(maṇḍala)* on a *padma*, *cintāmaṇidhvaja*.
Lit.: BBh. 324.

ratnapātra "vessel of gems" (attr.), see *kamaṇḍalu*.
Lit.: R 1:376, 2:524.

ratnapaṭṭa, evidently a "band of jewels" (attr.), worn round the head, cp. *paṭṭa*. Char. of Gaṇeśa and others.
Lit.: SB 154.

Ratnasambhava ("jewel-born"; Buddh.).

1. NP of a *dhyānibuddha*, the chief of the *ratnakula*, who originates from the yellow *bīja TRĀṀ* and represents the *skandha vedanā*. Śakti: Māmakī (or Vajradhātvīśvarī, BBh.). Char.: colour: yellow; direction: south; Vāh.: 2 *siṅhas* or *aśva*; att.: *padmāsana*; Mu.: *varada-* and (left hand:) *dhyāna-mudrā*; attr.: *cintāmaṇi* (*ratna*, in the hand which shows the *dhyānamudrā*), *tricīvara*. – In the *yi-dam*-form: att.: *padmāsana* with *yab-yum*; attr.: *cintāmaṇi*, *ghaṇṭā*. – As a *herukabuddha* he has the

n. Ratnaheruka. – Emanations from R. are the *(dhyāni)bodhisattva* Ratnapāṇi, further: Aparājitā, Jambhala (Ucchuṣma-Jambhala), Mahāpratisarā, the 12 *pāramitās*, Prasannatārā, Vajratārā, Vajrayoginī, Vasudhārā.
Lit.: BBh. 73, 237 a.pl. 37-38; G 14, 32, 52 (with ill.); GBM 79; H 32; IC 2:589; KiSB 43, 64.
2. *Ratnasambhavabimba* (attr.). An image of R. (usually worn on the crown) is char. of: Aparājitā, Mahāpratisarā, Vasudhārā (and other emanations).

ratnasamyukta-varadamudrā (Mu.), n. of a form of the *varadamudrā*, in which a jewel is seen stamped on the hand showing the Mu., which is "the gift-bestowing attitude (more correctly: gesture) together with a jewel" (BBh.). Char. of: Ākāśagarbha, Khadiravaṇī. – Another n.: *sarvaratnavarṣin*.
Lit.: BBh. 441.

ratnatraya "the three jewels", see *triratna*.
Lit.: CEBI 13.

Ratnolkā ("jewel-meteor"; Buddh.), n. of a Light-goddess or *dhāriṇī*. Char.: colour: yellow; attr.: *cintāmaṇidhvaja*. – Another n.: Ulkādharā.
Lit.: BBh. 220, 318, 338.

Ratnoṣṇīṣa ("the jewel-*uṣṇīṣa*"; Buddh.), n. of an *uṣṇīṣa*-deity. Char.: colour: blue; direction: south; Mu.: *varadamudrā*.
Lit.: BBh. 300.

Rātri-Gaṇapati (Night-G."), see Haridrā-Gaṇapati.
Lit.: R 1:59.

raudra "terrific", as n. of a terrific aspect of a god, see *ugra* and *ghora*.
Lit.: R 1:19; SB 211.

raudra-cum-saumya, n. of an aspect (of Durgā) which is both *ugra* ("terrific") and *saumya* ("gracious").
Lit.: SB 280.

Raudra-Pāśupata(mūrti) ("the terrific P."), n. of an *ugra*-aspect of Śiva, a variety of the Pāśupatamūrti. Attr.: *kapāla, khaḍga, ṭaṅka, triśūla*.
Lit.: B 465; R 2:125; Th. 80.

Raudrī ("terrific"), n. of one among the group *navaśakti* and of the Śakti of one of the *vidyeśvaras*. According to MW and pw, R. is an epithet of Gaurī, and R. may therefore be identical with the terrific aspect of Pārvatī (as Durgā or Kālī).
Lit.: MEIA 167; MW 891; pw 5:208; R 1:363, 403.

RAUṀ, form of a syllable (*bīja*) with a mystical meaning.
Lit.: GJ 369.

raupya "silver" (attr.); see also *pañcaratna*.
Lit.: MEIA 214.

Rāvaṇa ("roaring" or "causing to cry"), n. of the pincipal of *rākṣasas* or demons. He was a younger brother of Kubera and ruled over Sri Lanka. R. has three incarnations: First as Hiraṅyakaśipu*. In his second incarnation he is one of the chief persons of the epic Rāmāyaṇa. The subduing of R. is the main topic of this epic. He carried off Sītā, the wife of Rāma, and was then killed by that hero. His third incarnation was Śiśupāla*. – He symbolizes lust or rut, and he is represented as 10-headed. Son: Meghanāda. – Epithets: Daśānana, Daśakaṇṭha, Daśakandhara.
Lit.: D 264; DHP pl. 17; FKR esp. 159; GoRI 1:322; Gt 507; HAHI pl. 18; IIM 58, 76, 116; MG 289; MSHP pl. 31; NLEM 336; WHW 2:290; WM 153; ZA pl. 211.

Rāvaṇānugrahaṇamūrti (or -grahamūrti; "manifestation [of Śiva] showing favour, together with Rāvaṇa"), n. of a gracious representation (see *anugrahamūrti*) of Śiva, who is seated, with his wife Pārvatī, on Mount Kailāsa, below which Rāvaṇa is held captive. This demon is seen in a kneeling attitude trying to lift up the mountain.
Lit.: B 484 a.pl. 36:1; JDI 34; JMS 70 a.pl. 83; R 2:217 a.pl. 53-54; RAAI pl. 161A; SSR pl. facing p. 104.

Ravi ("sun", as a planet), n. of a form of Sūrya. Wives: Uṣā, Chāyā. – *ravi* is also a symbolical n. of the number of "12". see *saṅkhyā*. – Another n.: Āditya.
Lit.: Th. 113.

ravivāra (or *-vāsara*) "Sunday". – Another n. : *ādi(tya)vā(sa)ra*.

Ṛbhu (*ṛbhus*, *ribhus*; "clever, skilful; the Skilful-Craftsmen"), n. of three semi-divine beings, Ṛbhu (Ribhu), Vāja and Vibhu (Vibhvan), a kind of solar deities and artisan elves. They are said to be the sons of Indra and Saraṇyu.
Lit.: D 267; DHP 304; Gt 510; IC 1:328; IIM 18; WM 153.

Ṛddhi, see Riddhi.

Ṛddhivaśitā ("control of prosperity"; Buddh.), n. of a *vaśitā*. Char. : colour : green; attr. : *sūrya* and *candra-maṇḍala*.
Lit.: BBh. 330.

rDo-rje, see sub initial *do-*.

rekhā ("streak, stripe, outline"), in Orissan architecture n. of the *śikhara*-type of temple.
Lit.: RAAI 273.

Revā (Revati).
1. Epithet of Rati. – 2. Epithet of the River Narmadā.
Lit.: D 266.

Revanta ("rich"), n. of a son of Sūrya and Sañjñā. He is the chief of *guhyakas* and a huntsman, and he saves mankind from the dangers of the forest. He is worshipped in East India and in Gujarat. He is rarely represented in the arts. Char. : *aśva*; attr. : *chattra*, *kaśā* (in the right hand), *raśmis* (in the left hand).
Lit.: AI 119; B 425, 437, 442; HIS passim a.pl. 36.

Revata ("wealthy"), n. of one among the group *ekādaśarudra* who grants all the goods of the world to his worshippers. Char. : Mu. : *tarjanīmudrā*; attr. : *akṣamālā*, *aṅkuśa*, *cakra*, *dhanus*, *gadā*, *ghaṇṭā*, *khaḍga*, *khaṭvāṅga*, *kheṭaka*, *nāga*, *paraśu*, *pātra*, *paṭṭiśa*, *triśūla*.
Lit.: R 2:389.

Revatī ("rich").
1. N. of a *nakṣatra*. Its influence is good.
Lit.: BBh. 382; IC 2:730.
2. Revatī(devī), NP of the daughter of Raivata. She was one of the wives of Balarāma. Attr. : *padma*.
Lit.: D 266; DHP 179; R 1:202.
3. (Jain.) N. of the wife of Naigameṣa. Attr. : *ajamastaka*.
Lit.: JMS 24.

Ṛgveda or Rigveda, see Veda.

Ribhu, see Ṛbhu.
Lit.: IIM 18.

Riddhi (Ṛddhi; "Abundance, Prosperity"), n. of one of the wives of Gaṇeśa. Attr. : *kucabandha*, *padma*. – N.B. When she does not accompany her husband, it is difficult to distinguish this goddess from Lakṣmī and Puṣṭi (Bhūmidevī), the wives of Viṣṇu, who have all the same attr.; cp. also that Lakṣmī (under the n. Śrī) also is mentioned as the wife of Gaṇeśa.
Lit.: DHP 292; GH 117; GI pl. 74; R 1:367.

RĪṀ, a syllable (*bīja*) with a mystical meaning.
Lit.: GJ 369.

Ripumāri-Durgā ("D. killing enemies"), n. of a form of Durgā. Char. : Mu. : *tarjanīmudrā*; attr. : *triśūla*.
Lit.: R 1:345.

Riṣabha, see Ṛṣabha(nātha).

riṣi (*ṛṣi*) "inspired poet or sage"; *riṣis* is n. of a group of inspired sons of Brahmā. The number of *r.* is given as 7 (*saptarṣis*) or 8, 9, 10 or 12; the group of 7 *r.* contains : Gautama, Bharadvāja, Viśvāmitra, Jamadagni, Vasiṣṭha, Kāśyapa and Atri (collectively forming the constellation of the Great Bear). Elsewhere also Agastya, Aṅgiras, Bhṛgu, Dakṣa, Kratu, Kutsa, Marīci, Mudgala, Nārada, Pracetas, Pulaha, Pulastya, and others are counted among the *r.* One group of 10 *r.* is named *prajāpatis**. Sometimes the *r.* are divided into 7 groups : *maharṣis*, *paramaharṣis*, *devarṣis*, *brahmarṣis*, *śrutarṣis*, *rājarṣis* and *kāṇḍarṣis*. – Common char. : Mu. : *añjalimudrā*; attr. : *akṣamālā*, *kamaṇḍalu*, *pustaka*. They are also often, esp. in bronze sculptures, represented as "anthropomorphical", i.e. as human figures with the hind-legs of a buck and tails. – Another n. : *muni*. – See suppl.
Lit.: D 268; DHP 316 a.pl. 32; GH 95; GoRI 1:235; Gt 515; IC 1:531; KiSH 59; KrA pl. 64-65; MKVI 1:115; R 2:564; Th. 118 a.pl. 79A; WM 154.

riṣipatnī "wife of a *riṣi*". Images of *r.* are often placed in shrines in the neighbourhood of the image of Śiva, esp. in his form as Bhikṣāṭana, because the *riṣipatnīs* had once become enamoured of Śiva.
Lit.: SB 300 a.fig. 204.

ṛjulekhā "straight line", n. of a *yantra.* "The straight line is taken to represent unhindered movement, that is, the principle of all development".
Lit.: DHP 351.

ṛjvāyata "straight stretched" (att.), see *samapādasthānaka.*
Lit.: B 397.

ṛkṣa "bear" (Jain.), symbol of Ananta. It is also an appellative for "star, lunar mansion", see *nakṣatra.*

Ṛkṣavaktrā ("bear-headed"; Buddh.), n. of a *ḍākinī* with a black bear-head. Char.: colour: yellow. She is a companion of Siṅhavaktrā.
Lit.: G passim.

rLuṅ-rta, see sub initial *Luṅ-.*

Rohiṇī ("red").

1. N. of a *nakṣatra* or lunar asterism and of the lunar day belonging to it. Its influence is good. As personification also n. of a daughter of Dakṣa. She is the wife of Candra (Soma) and mother of Budha.
Lit.: BBh. 381; GoRI 1:231; 2:729.

2. (Jain.) N. of a *śāsanadevatā* attending on the second *tīrthaṅkara.* She is also a *vidyādevī.*
Lit.: GJ 362 a.pl. 24:2; KiJ 11 a.pl. 27:2.

rohitamatsya "red fish" (attr.), see *matsya.*
Lit.: MEIA 266.

ṛṣabha (= *vṛṣabha*) "bull", see *vṛṣan.*

Ṛṣabha ("bull"), n. of an unusual *avatāra* of Viṣṇu. He is said to be identical with the Jain Ṛṣabhanātha, and this may show a Hindu attempt to absorb the Jain religion.
Lit.: B 391; DHP 165, 184; R 1:123; WHW 2:297; WM 191.

Ṛṣabha(nātha) (Riṣabha; Jain.), NP of the first *tīrthaṅkara.* Symbol: *vṛṣan* (*vṛṣabha*). – Cp. Ṛṣabha.
Lit.: GJ 10, 266 a.passim, a.pl. 1, 24:1; KiJ 11 a.pl. 24, 27:1; KiSH 142; ZA 55 a.pl. 389.

Ṛṣabhadatta ("son of Ṛṣabha"; Jain.), n. of the father of Mahāvīra.
Lit.: GJ 297; KiSH 121.

ṛṣi, see *riṣi.*

ṛṣṭi "spear" (attr.), perhaps a javelin, but in this dictionary the term is not distinguished in sense from *śakti.*
Lit.: MEIA 253.

Ṛtuparṇa ("leaf of the season"), n. of a king and leader of a certain group of *riṣis,* the *rājarṣis.*
Lit.: R 2:566.

ṛtvij "sacrificial priest", n. of all the different kinds of priests employed at sacrifices in the Vedic period.
Lit.: MKVI 2:566.

rucaka "bracelet" forming part of the *ṣaṇmudrā* (attr.; Buddh.).
Lit.: BBh. 438.

Rudra (meaning obscure; the Hindus interpret it as meaning "howler, crier", but it possibly has the sense of "der Wilde, Rohe" (MAYRHOFER), and a relation to the Pāli *ludda, rudda* "frightful" is also supposed; among other explanations should be mentioned that of PISCHEL and others, according to which the n. means "the Red One", in which case it could be an importation into the Indo-Aryan language of an aboriginal word with the sense of "red", possibly signifying the "Proto-Śiva" of the Indus Valley culture, regarded by many scholars as the prototype of R. (the word-form *-dra,* instead of the *-dhra* expected, like Indra); but note that this explanation is rejected in GoRI).

1. N. of a Vedic storm god and terrific deity who, as Rudramūrti, was soon identified with Śiva (esp. in his terrific aspects; hence the n. Rudra-Śiva). R. was later regarded as an Āditya, and as such a deity he has the attr.: *akṣamālā, cakra,* 2 *padmas.* The n. Rudramūrti is often used

as a common n. of Śiva represented in the form of an image. Char. : Vāh. : *padma-* or *mahā-pīṭha*; Mu. : *abhaya-*, *varada-mudrā*; attr. : *arkapuṣpa*, *ḍhakkā*, *lambapattra*, *makarakuṇḍala*; he has usually 4 arms. – Rudra is further mentioned as one of the *mūrtyaṣṭaka*-forms of Śiva. There is also a group of 11 *rudras*, the *ekādaśarudra*; hence, *rudra* is a symbolic n. of the number "11", see *saṅkhyā*. R. is also the god of the month *mārgaśīrṣa*. – Śakti : Bhavānī (or Svadhā).

Lit. : B 446; BBh. 382; D 269; DHP 102, 188, 192; DilP 136; GoRI 1:85; Gt 519; IC 1:321; IIM 36 (ill.); KiSH 16; MAYRHOFER, EWA 3:66; NLEM 341; R. PISCHEL, Vedische Studien 1:55; R 1:309, 2:47, 386; WHW 2:313, 406; WM 156.

2. (Vāh.; Buddh.) Kālacakra and Prasannatārā are portrayed treading upon R.

Lit. : BBh. 187.

Rudra-Cāmuṇḍā, n. of a variety of Durgā.

Lit. : KiSH 50.

Rudracaṇḍā, n. of one of the *navadurgās*.

Lit. : R 1:357.

Rudra-Carcikā, n. of one of the *aṣṭamātaras* or of a variety of Durgā.

Lit. : KiSH 50; MEIA 154.

rudrākṣa(mālā) "a kind of rosary" (attr.). This is properly n. of a tree (Eleocarpus ganitrus) the berries of which are used for such rosaries. These rosaries are made of either bigger or smaller kinds of berries (both kinds nowadays mostly faked). Char. of : esp. Śiva (in some forms), Brahmā, Śaṅkarācārya, Sarasvatī; it is also included among the *aṣṭāvaraṇa*; see further *akṣamālā* (in this dictionary used as a common term for all kinds of rosaries). – *r.* is also worn as a necklace.

Lit. : B 303; MEIA 242; R 1:13, 2:275; SB 84, 151; WM 108.

rudramantra, n. of a *mantra* which has the purpose, "to remove all the signs of death, to prevent the withering of the body".

Lit. : DHP 346.

Rudramūrti "representation (of Śiva) as Rudra", see Rudra 1.

Rudrāṇī ("the (wife) of Rudra"), epithet of Durgā (Pārvatī), and n. of a girl, 11 years of age (in whom menstruation has not yet commenced), who represents Durgā at the Durgā festival.

Lit. : MW 884.

Rudrāṅśa-Durgā ("D. as an *aṅśa** of Rudra, i.e. of Śiva"), n. of a form of Durgā; four-armed. Char. : Vāh. : *siṅha*; attr. : *cakra*, *khaḍga*, *śaṅkha*, *triśūla*.

Lit. : R 1:343.

Rudra-Śiva, epithet of Śiva, supposed to be derived from the Vedic Rudra.

Lit. : DHP 204; GoRI 1:254; KiSH 16.

Rudrasūnu ("son of Rudra, i.e. of Śiva"), epithet of Skanda.

Lit. : DHP 299.

rukkha (Pāli), see *vṛkṣa*.

Rukmābāyi (N.Ind.; "mère protectrice", IC), n. of the wife of Viṭṭhala. She is identical with Rukmiṇī. – Another n. : Rakhumāī.

Lit. : IC 1:521; R 1:271.

Rukmiṇī ("wearing golden ornaments"), NP of the first wife of Kṛṣṇa; she is represented standing at his right (when he is accompanied by two wives). She was the daughter of Bhīṣmaka and had by Kṛṣṇa the son Kāma (Pradyumna); R. is regarded as an *avatāra* of Lakṣmī. – Attr. : *padma*. – Cp. Rukmābāyi.

Lit. : D 270; DHP 262; GoRI 1:240; IC 1:521; R 1:203, 376 a.pl. 58-59; SB 340 a.fig. 279; Th. 106; WHW 2:314.

rūpa "form, figure, sign, symbol" (attr.). The term *r.* refers to the forms and the symbols (attributes) of the gods and the icons; cp. *aṅka*, *cihna*, *pratīka*. – As regards *r.* as a cosmic element, see *skandha*, and as a symbolic n. of the number "1", see *saṅkhyā*.

Lit. : BBh. 42; CHIIA 43, 290.

rūpabheda (lit. : "diversity or variety of forms and manifestations"), a term for "iconography".

Lit. : CEBI 3.

rūpadhātu "the element of form, seat of form; Welt der reinen Form" (Buddh.).

Lit. : MW 886; SeKB 240.

rūpakāya "form-body", n. of a manifest or visible shape of a divinity or *buddha*.
Lit.: RAAI 273.

Rūpavidyā ("knowledge of form"), n. of a variety of Durgā.
Lit.: KiSH 50.

Rūpiṇī ("having a particular form, embodied"; Buddh.), n. of a *ḍākinī* and a minor Mahāyāna goddess attending on Buddhakapāla.
Lit.: BBh. 160, 321.

Ruru ("a kind of antelope or wild animal"), n. of a form of Śiva Bhairava.
Lit.: B 466.

S

Śabarī, see Śavarī.

sabhā(maṇḍapa) "assembly-hall" in a temple.
Lit.: GJ 399; MKVI 2:426; RV 159.

Sabhāpati ("lord of the assembly"), n. of a form of Śiva, identical with Naṭarāja.
Lit.: SSI 77.

sabhya "(fire of) the assembly-hall" (attr.), n. of one of the five domestic fires (see sub *agni*) which is lighted at assemblies.
Lit.: WHW 1:359.

Śacī ("powerful; mighty help"; personification), epithet of Indrāṇī.

ṣaḍakṣara "consisting of six letters (or syllables)". In South India *ṣ.* signifies a *mantra* consisting of the six letters (in Tamil characters:) *ca-ra-va-ṇa-pa-va* (see Skt Śaravaṇabhava) "(praise to) Śaravaṇabhava", relating to the god Subrahmaṇya, i.e. Skanda. – A six-syllable-formula alluding to Viṣṇu is: *na-mo-Nā-rā-ya-ṇa* (see Nārāyaṇa) "praise to Nārāyaṇa". – In Buddhism *ṣ.* refers to the *mantra*: *oṁ maṇi padme hūṁ*, see Ṣaḍakṣarī-Mahāvidyā.
Lit.: DiIP 284, 290; WHW 2:27.

Ṣaḍakṣarī(-Lokeśvara) (also -Avalokiteśvara: "lord of the six-syllable[-formula]"; Buddh.), n. of a variety of Avalokiteśvara. This is the particular form of Avalokiteśvara that is incarnated in the Dalai Lamas. – Char.: colour: white; att.: *padmāsana* or *sthānaka* (also together with *yab-yum* with the Śakti); Mu.: *añjali-*, *dhyāna-mudrā*; attr.: *akṣamālā*, *bodhisattvābharaṇa*, *cintāmaṇi*, *padma*, *pustaka*, *śaṅkha*, *uṣṇīṣa* (with *cintāmaṇi*); in the Tantric form also: *kapāla*, *karttṛkā*, *khaṭvāṅga*. – For the meaning of Ṣ., see *ṣaḍakṣara* and Ṣaḍakṣarī-Mahāvidyā. – A variety is Raktalokeśvara; cp. also Maṇipadma-Lokeśvara.
Lit.: BBh. 125, 395 a.pl. 94-97, 6(A); G 46 (ill.), 65 (with ill.); KiSB 57; RN pl. 9; SB 294 a.fig. 197f.

Ṣaḍakṣarī-Mahāvidyā (because *vidyā*, properly "knowledge, science", can also mean "spell, magic formula", this n. may be translated thus: "the great formula of the six-syllable-verse"; see further *vidyā*. At all events the word *ṣaḍakṣarī* refers to the *mantra*: *oṁ maṇi padme hūṁ*. – The Ṣ. is, of course, a personification; Buddh.), n. of a Mahāyāna deity attending on Ṣaḍakṣarī-Lokeśvara. Attr.: *cintāmaṇi*. — Cp. *ṣaḍakṣara*.
Lit.: BBh. 125 a.pl. 98; KiSB 57; KT 148.

ṣaḍakṣarī vidyā "the six-syllable-formula", see Ṣaḍakṣarī-Mahāvidyā.
Lit.: KT 148.

Ṣaḍānana(-Subrahmaṇya) (("the six-faced S."), epithet or form of Skanda.
Lit.: DHP 299; R 2:429; SSI 178.

Sadasaspati ("lord of the assemblies"), epithet of Bṛhaspati.
Lit.: DHP 325.

Sadāśiva(mūrti) ("representation as the Ever-lasting-Śiva"), n. of a manifestation of Śiva with five aspects, concentrated in one form. He is therefore represented with five heads or faces, of which four are arranged in a ring round the neck and the fifth head. The face directed to the east represents Tatpuruṣa, the face to the south is Aghora,

the face to the west is Sadyojāta, the face to the north is Vāmadeva, the fifth head, directed to the zenith, is Īśāna. – The Śakti of S. is Bhogaśakti or Manonmanī; sometimes however he is said to have nine Śaktis. Char.: colour: white; Mu.: *abhaya-*, *varada-mudrā*; attr.: he has 10 arms, *akṣamālā*, *candra*, *ḍamaru*, *darpaṇa*, *ghaṇṭā*, *jambhīra*, *kamaṇḍalu*, *kapāla*, *khaṭvāṅga*, *kheṭaka*, *musala*, *nāga*, *nīlotpala*, *pañcaśiras*, *paraśu*, *pāśa*, *śakti*, *ṭaṅka*, *triśūla*. – Variety: Mahāsadāśivamūrti; cp. Pañcānana, Pañcabrahmā; *pañcavaktra*.
Lit.: B 465, 478 a.pl. 40:3; DHP 211; 284; GRI 170; KiDG 14; KiSH 25; MEIA 54; R 2:361 a.pl. 113, 115; WM 169.

Ṣaḍbhuja-Sitatārā (or -Śuklatārā; "the six-armed white Tārā"; Buddh.), n. of a variety of Sitatārā, an emanation of Amoghasiddhi. Char.: colour: white; Mu.: *varadamudrā*; attr.: *akṣamālā*, *Amoghasiddhibimba* on the crown, *dhanus*, *nīlotpala*, *padma*, *śara*, *triśiras*.
Lit.: BBh. 230, 308 a.pl. 171; KiDG 64, 72 a.pl. 59; KiSB 99.

sādhaka (may mean: "adapted to the purpose, coming to the goal; a Tantric worshipper", also "effecting by magic, possessed of magic power"), in both Buddhist and Hindu Tantrism and Śaktism n. of an adept who is just on the point of being united with a *vidyā*.Cp. *upāya*.
Lit.: BPR 46; GBM 161; GoRI 2:34.

sādhana ("leading to the goal"), in both Buddhist and Hindu Tantrism and Śaktism n. of a practice by means of which the result that is wished for is obtained ("die praktische Realisation", GoRI); *s.* also signifies a procedure of worship for invocation of gods; in Buddhism also n. of a class of ritual-iconographical handbooks.
Lit.: BBh. 438; GoRI 2:39; IC 1:610; SeKB 234.

Sadharma ("having the same nature or qualities"), n. of a *dvārapālaka* of Brahmā. Attr.: *daṇḍa*, *padma*, *pustaka*, *sruk*.
Lit.: R 2:507.

sādhu ("coming, leading straight to the goal, i.e. one who has attained certain [magical] powers").
1. (Hind.) N. of a teacher or a saint.
2. (Jain.) N. of an *arhat*, i.e. = *tīrthaṅkara*. – Cp. *bhakta*, *guru*.
Lit.: GH 362; KrA pl. 141; MG 265; pw 7:112; WHW 2:322.

Sādhumatī ("good"; Buddh.), n. of a *bhūmi*. Char.: colour: white; attr.: *khaḍga* on a *nīlotpala*, *vajra*.
Lit.: BBh. 336.

sādhya ("means-of-realization", or, according to an Indian source, "ray of light"; personification), n. of a class of semi-divine beings, the number of which is 12 or 17. Attr.: *akṣamālā*, *kamaṇḍalu*.
Lit.: D 271; DHP 303; R 2:558.

Sadyojāta ("newly born"), n. of an aspect of Śiva which, in the composite representation Sadāśivamūrti, is represented by the face that is directed to the west, and also n. of one among the group *ekādaśarudra*. Char.: Mu.: *abhaya-*, *varada-mudrā*; attr.: *akṣamālā*, *pustaka*, *trinayana*. – See also Pañcabrahmā.
Lit.: B 478; DHP 212; KiSH 25; R 2:371, 388.

Sadyonubhava-Arapacana (and -Mañjuśrī; "the A., [or M.] of a quickly-made perception"; Buddh.), see Arapacana.
Lit.: BBh. 121.

Sāgaramati ("ocean-mind"; Buddh.), n. of a *bodhisattva*. Char.: colour: white; Mu.: *taraṅgābhinayin*; attr.: *śaṅkha*, *vajra-khaḍga*.
Lit.: BBh. 87 a.pl. 55.

Sāgaramati-Lokeśvara ("L. as S."; Buddh.), n. of a variety of Avalokiteśvara. Char.: att.: *padmāsana*; Vāh.: *padma*; attr.: *padma*, *viśvavajra*.
Lit.: BBh. 399 a.pl. 46(A).

Sahadeva ("together with the gods"), n. of the youngest of the Pāṇḍu-princes, the twin brother of Nakula and half-brother of Arjuna (in the epic Mahābhārata). S. and his twin brother are regarded as incarnations of the twin gods, the Aśvins.
Lit.: D 272; ZA pl. 111; ZM 71 a.pl. 3.

sahagamana "the act of going with", esp. of a woman's going with (her husband), i.e. burning herself together with the body of her deceased husband on the funeral pyre. Such a woman is called a *satī*.
Lit.: MW 1193.

Sahasrākṣa ("thousand-eyed"), epithet of Indra.
Lit.: D 273.

sahasraliṅga ("thousand-fold *liṅga*"), n. of a kind of *mānuṣaliṅga*, or of a *liṅga* having 25 facets, each of them bearing miniature representations of 40 *liṅga*s (amounting to the number of 1.000).
Lit.: R 2:96; SSI 74.

sahasranayana "thousand-eyed" (attr.), epithet and attr. of Indra and Indrāṇī, who have 1.000 eyes, distributed over the bodies.

śaila "rock" (attr.). As a symbol of Hanumān; see Mahodaya. Cp. also Meru as an attr. As to *ś.* as a symbolic n. of the number "7", see *saṅkhyā*.
Lit.: MEIA 270.

śailaja "made of stone", n. of a type of icon, e.g. *śailaja liṅga*, see *calaliṅga*.
Lit.: R 2:77.

Śailaputrī ("mountain-daughter"), n. of a variety of Durgā. Char.: Vāh.: Nandin; attr.: *candra, triśūla*.
Lit.: SSI 202.

śailasthāpana "installation of a stone idol", n. of a rite.
Lit.: ACA 67.

śaivabhakta "ardent worshipper of Śiva", also "one belonging to the Śaivite sect". There are 63 canonized Śaivite saints, and the most famous of these are Appar, Sundara(-Nāyaṉār), Māṇikkavācakar, Tirujñānasambandha. – Cp. *bhakta, nāyaṉmār*.
Lit.: GH 390; HIS 17, 20; R 2:475 (with a list of *ś.*).

śaiva-siddhānta "the Śaivite settled opinion or doctrine", n. of a doctrinal system in South India, according to which Śiva is the everlasting absolute subject of all understanding or perception and the effective cause of all that is happening. This system is characterized by three fundamental principles: *pati* ("the Supreme Being"), *pacu* (= Skt *paśu*, "Individual soul, spirit, as bound by *pācam*"), *pācam* (= Skt *pāśa*, "Bond, or the obstructive principle which hinders the soul from finding release in union with Śiva"; TL).
Lit.: GH 392; GRI 330; IC 1:632; TL 4:2348, 2473, 5:2584; WHW 2:328.

śaiveṣṭyaliṅga "a Śaivite sacrifice-*liṅga*", n. of a kind of *mānuṣaliṅga*.
Lit.: R 2:95.

sajvālaratna (also written *sajj-*) "glistening jewel" (attr.), see *cintāmaṇi*.
Lit.: BBh. 96.

saka(?), n. of an era, beginning from the Saka invasion, about B.C. 90-80, or 84.
Lit.: IC 2:736.

śākābda "the year of Śāka", a term indicating an era, see *śākakāla*.

sakadāgāmin (Pāli, Skt *sakṛdāgāmin*) "one who is to return only once", i.e. a convert, who will not be reborn more than once in this world. – Cp. *anāgāmin*.
Lit.: BRI 49; IC 2:554.

śākakāla (or *śaka-*) "the era of Śāka", n. of the era most used in India (and in parts of Indo-China), instituted by a celebrated prince and beginning in A.D. 78. It is indicated by *śaka* (*śake, śākābda*). The year is usually *gata, meṣādi* or *caitrādi* and *pūrṇimānta* (in North India) or *amānta* (in South India). The given year of this era + 78 or 79 (and 77 or 78, respectively, if the year is *vartamāna*) = the year A.D. – Regarding the use of this era in modern India, see Enc.Brit. – Another n.: *śālivāhanakāla*.
Lit.: Enc.Brit. 5:721; IC 2:737; P 718; WHW 1:334.

Śakamaṅgala ("having cow-dung as an auspicious mark"; Buddh.), n. of a *mānuṣibodhisattva*.
Lit.: BBh. 79.

sakhībhāva ("the state of being a girl-friend"), n. of an 'androgynous' or 'transvestite' sect of the *bhakti*-type. Male members of this sect dress like women, playing the

part of the girl-friends of Rādhā, the *gopīs*.
Lit.: KT 160; WHW 1:44.

śākinī ("able one"), n. of a kind of witch attending on Durgā.
Lit.: DHP 213, 288; IC 1:528.

Śakra (Pāli Sakka, "strong, mighty"), epithet of Indra, esp. in Buddhism. He is also the god of the month *āśvina*. For *śakra* as a symbolic n. of the number "14", see *saṅkhyā*.
Lit.: B 523; BBh. 382; DHP 108; GoRI 1:225.

Śakradhanus "the bow of Śakra", see Indradhanus.
Lit.: WHW 1:480.

sakṛdāgāmin (Buddh.), see *sakadāgāmin*.

śākta ("relating to the Śakti or divine energy under its female personification, Śaktism"), n. of a sect and cult which is related to the Śakti of Śiva in her different aspects. The chief persons of this sect are Ambikā, Durgā, Kālī and Umā (= Pārvatī); see also Mahāśakti. Among the major rites in the *śākta* cult are *cakrapūjā* and *strīpūjā*. – The n. *śākta* also signifies a worshipper of this Śakti.
Lit.: B 491; GH 395; GoRI 2:26; Gt 538; HAHI 18; IC 1:624; MW 1062.

śakti.

1. *ś.*, in this dictionary rendered as "Śakti", is derived from the verb *śaknoti* "to be strong or powerful", and consequently means "energy, effective power", also "the All-pervading Energy". Hence it signifies the energy of a god in its personified form and is in this sense comprehended as the female counterpart (without particular proper name) of any god, in Buddhism esp. of the *bodhisattvas*, but also of the *buddhas*. *ś.* is therefore the creative force in its feminine aspect. We may thus speak of the Śakti of any god related to all the religions that are dealt with in this dictionary.

In a restricted sense Śakti refers to the personification of the energy of Śiva in his different aspects, and Śakti is therefore the chief person of the *śākta* cult (cp. Devī); but Śakti most commonly alludes to the *ugra*-forms, such as Durgā, Kālī. Śakti may also, as the female aspect, be included in poly-headed representations of Śiva or Viṣṇu, such as Mahādeva (Vāmadeva-Umā), Vaikuṇṭhanātha. – The Śakti has often the same characteristics as the principal god.

ś. may furthermore signify the female organ worshipped by the *śākta*-sect, cp. *yoni*. Śakti worship is also associated with the use of mystical charms or geometrical figures, called *cakras*, *pīṭhas* and *yantras*. Other n.: *mudrā*, *prajñā*, *vidyā*, *svābhā*, *svābhā-prajñā*, *svābhā-vidyā*. – See also *navaśakti*.
Lit.: B 489; BBh. 438; DHP 253; DilP 136 a.passim; GBM 38; GH 140; GoRI 1:259; GRI 174; HIS 23, 25; IC 1:519, 2:590; KiH 21; KiSH 12, 45; MG 179; MW 1044; R 1:338; RAAI 273; SSI 184; ZM 152; C.G. Hartman, Śakti et Šes rab (Helsinki 1973).

2. *śakti*, *śaktyāyudha* "(the weapon) spear, lance"; in this sense *ś.* is etymologically probably not related to *śakti 1*; attr.). *ś.* is usually represented as a kind of lance, and it is not always distinguishable from *bhindipāla*. However, it is also described in this way: "a weapon like a double-edged sword which has in the middle a pestle like that of a mortar" (AI). And in SSI, a very small weapon (like the *ṭaṅka* illustrated in Th.) is illustrated as *ś.* (*vēl*). – Symbolically the *ś.* of Skanda is said to manifest the *icchā*, *jñāna* and *kriyā śaktis* "the spears of desire, knowledge and performance". Otherwise it is, of course, a warrior emblem. – *ś.* is esp. char. of Skanda (Kārttikeya) in different forms and of Durgā Mahiṣāsuramardinī; further of: Aghora, Agni, Ahirbudhnya, Aja, Aparājita, Bhadra-Kālī, Bhairava, Brahmaśāstā, Cāmuṇḍā, Caṇḍā, Cundā, Devasenāpati(?), Gaṇeśa (Gaṇapati), Hara, Indra, Jayanta, Jayantī, Kālacakra, Kalavikarṇikā, Karuppaṉ, Kaumārī, Kirātārjunamūrti, Kubera, Mahākāla, Maṅgala,

Mārttaṇḍa-Bhairava, *navadurgās*, Paramāśva, Prabhāsa, Sadāśiva, Śarabha, Sarasvatī, Sarvaśokatamonirghātamati, Śiva, Vārāhī, *vasus*, Vidyujjvālākarālī, Virūpākṣa, Viśvarūpa, Yogeśvarī. – It is also the weapon of the south-east direction. – Other n.: *kunta, ṛṣṭi, śūla, tomara, vēl*; see also Pāśupatāstra, *bhindipāla*.

Lit.: AI 118; B 301; MEIA 249; R 1:8 a.pl. 3:8-9, 2:430; SSI pl. III:2; Th. 41; WM 108.

śaktibīja ("Seed-of-Energy"), see *māyābījā*.

Śaktidhara ("holding a spear"), n. of a form of Skanda. It is an embodiment of *jñānaśakti* "the spear of knowledge". Char.: Mu.: *abhayamudrā*; attr.: *kukkuṭa, śakti, vajra*.

Lit.: DHP 299; R 2:433.

Śakti-Gaṇeśa, n. of a group of icons, representing a composition of Gaṇeśa with his Śakti. These are: Lakṣmī-, Ucchiṣṭa-, Mahā-, Piṅgala- and Ūrdhva-Gaṇapati.

Lit.: R 1:53.

śaktikā (attr.), see *śalākā*.

Lit.: MEIA 144.

śaktyāyudha "the weapon spear" (attr.), see *śakti* 2.

Lit.: R 2:425.

śākya "mendicant" (Buddh.).

Lit.: GRI 280.

Śākya, n. of the family or clan to which the Buddha and his father Śuddhodana belonged. Cp. Śākyamuni.

Lit.: IC 2:468; WHW 2:340.

Śākyabuddha-Lokeśvara ("L., the *buddha* of the Śākya clan"; Buddh.), n. of a variety of Avalokiteśvara (in BBh. this n. is twice mentioned as forms of Avalokiteśvara, both as No. 31 and No. 92, belonging to the 108 forms of Avalokiteśvara). Char.: att.: *sthānaka*; Vāh.: *padma*; Mu.: *tarjanīmudrā*; attr.: *dhanus, khaṭvāṅga, śara, vajra*.

Lit.: BBh. 397, 430 a.pl. 31(A), 92(A).

Śākyamuni (Pāli Sakyamuni) "the wise (sage) of the Śākya-family", a n., used esp. in Tibet, of the historical Buddha or of a form of *buddha*. Char.: colour: golden; Vāh.: *padma*; Mu.: *vyākhyāna-* and *varada-* or *dharmacakra-*, or *bhūmisparśa-* and *dhyāna-mudrās*; attr.: *pātra*. – See also *mānuṣibuddha*. – Another n.: *Śākyasiṅha*.

Lit.: BBh. 76; G 32, 53; H 32; HIS 54 a.pl. 9; HRT pl. 3; KiDG 44; KiSB 32.

Śākyasiṅha ("the lion of the Śākya family"), see Śākyamuni.

Lit.: BBh. 76.

sāl (Pers.) "year" sometimes indicates the era *baṅgālī san*. See also *faṣlī sāl*.

Lit.: IC 2:737.

śāla (attr.), n. of a tree (Vatica robusta) which, as a *bodhivṛkṣa*, is ascribed to Viśvabhuj. – *śāla* with the meaning of "enclosure, fence" is n. of a rectangular ornamental *pañjara* with a waggon-roof on the storeys of *vimānas*.

Lit.: BECA 1:263.

śālabhañjikā (also *śālā-, s-, śālabhañjakāsana*; lit.:) "breaking a branch of a *śāla*-tree" (att.), n. of a *sthānaka*-posture of a woman, standing close to a tree, "a classic attitude of tree-goddesses in Indian art" (ZA); by linguistic transference it is also n. of the tree-nymph itself and later also of a figure made of *śāla*-wood. – The att. is char. of *vṛkṣadevatās*.

Lit.: AuOW 16; GOSA 17 a.pl. 6; JMS 74 a.pl. 99; MW 745, 1067; WHW 1:76; ZA 80 a.pl. 33 f.

śalabhāsana "grashopper-sitting" (att.), n. of a Yogic posture.

Lit.: KiH pl. 153 row 1:2.

śālādvāra "hall door", n. of a kind of temple gateway (*gopura*) with two to four storeys.

Lit.: BECA 1:260.

śālagrāma (or *śāli-*, "the village with *śāla*-trees", properly n. of a village situated on the River Gaṇḍakī in Nepal), n. of a sacred stone, an ammonite found in the river above mentioned (attr.). The *ś.* is a black stone with a form resembling the *cakra* of Viṣṇu, and therefore it is regarded as a lithomorphic form of this god. Certain other black stones from Gaṇḍakī, not actually having the form of a *cakra*, but in which there are small marks or holes resembling the *cakra*, are also regarded

as *śālagrāmas*. It is believed that Viṣṇu, assuming the form of a *vajrakīṭa*, has bored those holes with his mouth. – The above mentioned village is sacred to Viṣṇu.
Lit.: D 275; GH 42, 330; Gt 541; IC 1:539; KiH 35; KiSH 77; MG 241; MW 1067; R 1:8 a.pl. A; SSI 70; WM 87.

śalākā, a little instrument, described either as "eye-opener (Augenöffner, GBM)" or "bâtonnet à fard" (MEIA), or as a painter's brush; a thin bamboo rod with a small copper pin stuck into it and a small feather attached, used for drawing the final fine lines for "opening" the eyes of the figure (SSIP; attr.). It is used together with the *darpaṇa*. In Buddhism it symbolizes "dass dem Eingeweihten das Auge für die Heilswahrheit aufgetan wurde" (GBM). Char. of Caṇḍā, *navadurgās*, and some Buddhist idols. – Other n.: *chattrikā*, *śaktikā*, *tūlikā*.
Lit.: GBM 105, 122; MEIA 144, 258, 330; SSIP 23.

śālivāhanakāla "the era of Śālivāhana", as n. of an era, instituted by Śālivāhana, see *śākakāla*.
Lit.: IC 2:737; P 718.

sam, abbreviated form of *samvat* (*samvatsara*).
Lit.: IC 2:736.

samabhaṅga (lit.: "equal bend"), n. of a *sthānaka*-posture, see *samapādasthānaka*.
Lit.: B 264; MH 6; WM 89.

samādhi "meditation, concentration of the thoughts, intense contemplation", the final stage of *yoga*.

samādhimudrā "meditation gesture" (Mu.), n. of a handpose which symbolizes the deepest form of abstract meditation, see *dhyānamudrā*.
Lit.: B 252; BBh. 435, 438; GBM 97; HIS 43.

samaṇa (Pāli), see *śramaṇa*.

Samantabhadra ("wholly auspicious, All-Goodness, Universal-Goodness"; Buddh.), n. of a *(dhyāni)bodhisattva*, an emanation of Vairocana. S. is regarded by the unreformed *rÑiṅ-ma-pa*-sect as the Ādibuddha. Char.: colour: green or white or blue; Vāh.: one or more *gajas* carry his throne; att.: *padmāsana* or *sthānaka* (sometimes together with *yab-yum* with the Śakti); Mu.: *vajrahuṅkāra-*, *varada-*, *vyākhyāna-mudrā*; attr.: *cintāmaṇi*, *ghaṇṭā*, *kapāla* (*brahmakapāla*), *padma* with a *cakra* or a *khaḍga*. – Another n.: Cakrapāṇi.
Lit.: BBh. 55, 83 a.pl. 32, 48; CTLP pl. 9; G 14, 25, 31 (N.B. see also p. 32), 49, 59; GBM 80; KiDG 44; KiSB 45.

Samantabhadra-Lokeśvara ("L. as S."; Buddh.), n. of a variety of Avalokiteśvara. Char.: att.: *padmāsana*; Vāh.: *padma*; Mu.: *varadamudrā*; attr.: *padma*.
Lit.: BBh. 399 a.pl. 53(A).

Samantaprabhā ("possessing universal splendour"; Buddh.), n. of a *bhūmi*. Char.: colour: red; attr.: *Amitābhabimba* (in one hand), *vajra*.
Lit.: BBh. 337.

Sāmānya-Lakṣmī ("universal L."), n. of a form grouped among the *aṣṭamahālakṣmī*, very like Gaja-Lakṣmī, but two-handed.
Lit.: SSI 187.

samapādasthānaka "holding the feet even, standing on even feet" (att.), n. of a *sthānaka*-posture in which the idol is standing symmetrically with straight legs. – Other n.: *ṛjvāyata*, *samabhaṅga*.
Lit.: B 264; KIM pl. 40; MH 6; Th. 34; SSI pl. II:4; WM 89.

samasaṅsthāna ("the even standing"; att.), n. of a *sthānaka*-posture which is mentioned, but not described. Possibly identical with *samapādasthānaka*.
Lit.: B 271; MW 1153.

samāvartana "the return home from the house of the preceptor", n. of a *saṅskāra*-rite, performed at the return home of a Brāhman student.
Lit.: DiIP 180.

samaya "conventional sign" (Buddh.), n. of a symbol or attribute which is characteristic of a deity. – Cp. *uddesika*.
Lit.: GBM 105.

samayamaṇḍala (Buddh.), n. of a *maṇḍala* in which conventional signs (*samaya*) are used to represent e.g. weapons etc. instead of pictures.
Lit.: GBM 108.

sāmāyika ("equanimity"; Jain.), n. of devotion which is performed daily; see *āvaśyaka*.
Lit.: GJ 408; IC 2:638.

Sāmba (or Ś-), n. of the son of Kṛṣṇa and Jāmbavatī (or possibly Rukmiṇī). He is also mentioned as the son of Viṣṇu. Wife: Indukarī; attr.: *gadā*.
Lit.: AI 118; B 301; D 276; MW 1207; R 1:240; WHW 2:343.

Ṣambara (Buddh.), see Samvara.

sambat (N.Ind.) "year", see *samvat*.
Lit.: P 673.

Sambhava ("birth, origin"; Jain.), n. of the 3rd *tīrthaṅkara*. Symbol: *aśva*.
Lit.: GJ 272; KiSH 142.

sambhogakāya "body of enjoyment, splendour; Leib der Seligkeit" (KiSB; Buddh.), according to the *trikāya*-system n. of the body in which a *(dhyāni)bodhisattva* lives in heaven.
Lit.: BRI 150; G 30; KiSB 41; RAAI 273; WHW 2:15.

Śambhu (generally interpreted as "benevolent; the Abode of Joy" (DHP); it has, however, been suggested by A. Parpola that this is a folk-etymological version of an originally Dravidian word, cp. Tam. *cempu*, Kannaḍa *cambu* "copper", and that the meaning is properly: "the Red One"), epithet of Śiva. Among the Gonds there is a god named Sri Shembu Mahadeo (i.e. Śiva; FHRI), and this Gondī NP, Shembu, might correspond to this name.
Lit.: DED 2282; DHP 202; FHRI 264; GoRI 1:255; WHW 2:406.

sambodhi "perfect enlightenment", see *bodhi*.
Lit.: MS 45.

śamī (lit.: "effort"; attr.), n. of a tree Prosopis spicigera or Acacia suma). Its wood is used for kindling the sacred fire. – Cp. *araṇi*.
Lit.: MW 1054; P 734; RV 19.

sāmiṣa, a kind of fish (thus MEIA; MW: "possessed of flesh or prey"; attr.), see *matsya*.
Lit.: MEIA 266; MW 1206.

saṁlekhanā (lit.: "strict abstinence"; Jain.), n. of the voluntary starving to death performed esp. by Jain ascetics.
Lit.: GJ 425.

saṁmārjanī "broom, bunch (i.e. of twigs)" (attr.). Char. of Śītalā.

sampatnī, n. of a large copper bowl which is used for libations (attr.).
Lit.: KiH 140:3.

sampīḍita, lit. "squeezed" (att.), n. of a pose not explained. Char. of Hanumān.
Lit.: MEIA 219.

sampuṭāñjalimudrā "bowl-like *añjalimudrā*" (Mu.), n. of a handpose which is mentioned, but not described in B. It is also compared to the usual *añjalimudrā* (BBh.), but since *sampuṭa* means a "hemispherical bowl" this term may allude to the particular Buddhist form of *añjalimudrā**. This Mu. is said to be char. of some forms of Avalokiteśvara.
Lit.: B 251; BBh. 432.

Samudra (meaning either "ocean" or "sealed, stamped, marked"), n. of the god of the month *śrāvaṇa*. For *samudra* as a symbolic n. of the number "4", see *saṅkhyā*.
Lit.: BBh. 382.

sāmudrika "relating to the bodily marks" is a term for the interpretation of bodily marks, such as *mahāpuruṣalakṣaṇa*, *lakṣaṇa*.
Lit.: STP 2:7.

Samvara (G.: Ś-; BBh.: Saṁbara; "keeping back, shutting out"; Buddh.), n. of a Mahāyāna god who is an emanation of Akṣobhya and who is said to be a form of Hevajra or (one-headed) of Vajraḍāka; in Lamaism he is a four-headed *yi-dam*-god. – Śakti: Vajravārāhī. Char.: colour: blue or black; att. and Vāh.: *ālīḍhāsana* (with *yab-yum*), treading upon one or two 4-armed beings (esp. Kālarātrī and Bhairava); Mu.: *vajrahuṅkāra*; attr.: *ajina*, *Akṣobhyabimba* on the crown, *candra*, *caturmukha*, *cintāmaṇi* (or *viśvavajra*) on the head, *ḍamaru*, *ghaṇṭā*, *kapāla*, *karttṛkā*, *khaṭvāṅga*, *muṇḍa* (= a 4-faced Brahmā-head), *muṇḍamālā*, *paraśu*, *trinayana*, *tri*-

śūla, *vajra* (*vajrapāśa*). The Śakti carries: *kapāla*, *karttṛkā* (or *vajra*). – Variety: Sitasamvara.
Lit.: BBh. 160; G passim (ill. p. 84); KiSB 66.

samvat (abbreviated form of *samvatsara*; together with the Hi. forms: *sam*, *sambat*, *saṅvat*) "year". These word-forms indicate the era *vikramakāla*; see also *harṣakāla*.
Lit.: IC 2:736; MKVI 2:411; P 688.

samvatsara "year". This was, in India, formerly usually measured according to the solar system, but since it was made up of something half-way between lunar and solar months, the civil year consisting of 360 lunar days (see *tithi* and *candramāsa*), periodic adjustements had to be made. This was usually effected by periodical addition of one intercalary month (see *candramāsa*) and also by the periodical addition of days (about every five years), until accordance with the solar year was effected. Thus the year may be called "lunisolar". Usually the lunisolar year begins with the vernal equinox and with the month *caitra* (see *caitrādi*) or *vaiśākha*, but it may also begin with the month *āṣāḍha* (*āṣāḍhādi*) or *āśvina* (*āśvinādi*) or *kārttika* (*kārttikādi*). The dates of the beginning differ according to the lunar month system. – The solar year, beginning with the month *caitra*, is called *meṣādi*. – In dating, the year mentioned is either elapsed (*gata*) or current (*vartamāna*). In converting the date of a given year of an era into the corresponding date of the Christian era, certain numbers must be either added or subtracted in the following way: for those eras which were founded after Christ, the lower of the numbers mentioned under the era in question, must be added concerning the period ending with the day corresponding to Dec. 31, and the higher number concerning a later date; for the eras founded before Christ, where dates after Christ are concerned, the higher of the numbers mentioned under the era in question, must be subtracted regarding dates before Jan. 1, and the lower one regarding later dates. N.B. to convert dates with accuracy certain tables are necessary. – Lastly it must be added that an entirely lunar year is used in India, *viz.* the Moslem era, see *hijrat*.
Lit.: Enc.Brit. 4:621; IC 2:724; L.D.S. PILLAR, Indian chronology (Madras 1911); WHW 1:333.

samyaksambuddha "one who has attained to complete enlightenment" (Buddh.), n. given to a *buddha* who, contrary to the *pratyekabuddha*, wishes to teach the Law to all for their liberation.
Lit.: BRI 52.

samyuta(hasta) (or *samyukta*) "joined" (Mu.), a common n. of a combined handpose, i.e. a pose performed with both hands, *añjalimudrā*, for instance. Cp. *asamyuta-(hasta)*.
Lit.: B 278; SIB 61; WHW 2:85.

san (Hi., < Arab. *sanat*) "year, age", indicating the Christian era (*san*...figures..., or *san*... figures...*īsvī*), see *khristābda*. – *san* also indicates the *baṅgalī san*.
Lit.: IC 2:736; P 679.

Śanaiścara ("walking or moving slowly"), see Śani(ścara).
Lit.: MW 1051.

Sanatkumāra ("eternal youth"), epithet of Kumāra as an *avatāra* of Viṣṇu. S. is also said to be n. of a *riṣi* or sage, the son of Brahmā.
Lit.: DHP 165; MW 1141.

sāñcā (Hi.) "mould, matrice" for the casting of bronze icons.

Sāñcī (Sāñchī), n. of a town, famous for a *stūpa* built under the Maurya and Śuṅga dynasties.
Lit.: FBKI 35; FES 15; Gz 50; RAAI 53; SeKB passim; ZA pl. 6 ff.

sandaṅśamudrā "the biting pose, the pose like a pair of tongs" (Mu.), n. of a variety of the *padmamudrā** with the difference that the fingers are graspingly and passionately bent. It represents the climax of love, the offerings of love's fruits.
Lit.: WHW 2:87.

sandarśanamudrā "gesture of showing, displaying" (Mu.), see *vyākhyānamudrā*.
Lit.: B 255; R 1:7.

sandhyā "junction, juncture", n. esp. of the religious acts performed at the three (four) divisions of the day, morning, noon, evening (or, in addition, midnight). This service consists in sipping water, and in repeating prayers and *mantras*, esp. the *gāyatrī*. – In the dance (*nāṭya*) *sandhyānṛtta* or *sandhyātāṇḍava* ("juncture-dance, morning or evening twilight dance"), *s.* is a term for a pose of balance symbolizing the balance of Creation. This dance-form is char. of Śiva Naṭarāja and Kṛṣṇa. In *s.* the dancer typically stands on his left leg, the knee slightly bent, and the right leg stretched out the heel downwards, toes pointing up, sole of foot turned to the spectator (see further WHW). Char. of Śiva: depicted in *s.* he has four arms; Mu.: *vismayamudrā* (one left hand); attr.: *mayūrapattra* (in one left hand). Apasmāra is absent in this dance.
Lit.: CBC 10 a.pl. 5:8; DiIP 98; GH 330; IC 1:584; MW 1145; SB 334; SSI 84; WHW 1:264.

Sandhyā ("juncture, twilight"). As personification said to be the daughter of Brahmā and the wife of Śiva or other gods. This n. also refers to the three personifications of the rites performed at the three junctures of the day, morning, noon and evening, as homage to the sun.
Lit.: D 277; Gt 547; MEIA 167; MW 1145.

sandhyātāṇḍava (*-nṛtta*) "juncture-dance", see *sandhyā*.

Saṅ-dui (Tib.; Buddh.), n. of a Lamaist *yi-dam* (represented together with the Śakti). Char.: colour: blue; att.: *yab-yum*; Mu.: *vajrahuṅkāra*;; attr.: *bodhisattvābharaṇa*, *cakra*, *cintāmaṇi*, *ghaṇṭā*, *khaḍga*, *padma*, *trinayana*, *triśiras*, *vajra*. He is 6-armed; the Śakti has the same attr.
Lit.: G 12, 83 (ill.), 84; JSV pl. 70.

Saṅ-dup (Tib.), see gSaṅ-sgrub sub initial Saṅ-.

saṅgha (Panj. *sangat*; "assemblage, community"; Buddh., Jain.), n. of the brotherhood of monks (*bhikṣu*; Buddh.) or of the monkish fraternity or sect (Jain.); *sangat* is n. of the Sikh disciples congregation (see also *mañjā*). – *s.* forms part of the *triratna* and is also conceived in a personified form as a deity, and worshipped in an anthropomorphic form. Att.: *padmāsana*; Mu.: *dharmacakramudrā*; attr.: *pustaka*.
Lit.: BBh. 32 a.fig. 11; BRI 55; GG p. LXV; MW 1129; N 200; SchRI 234.

saṅghārāma ("convent, monastery"), n. of a row of *vihāras* in the form of cells.
Lit.: DKI 37.

Saṅgharatna ("jewel of the assemblage"; Buddh.), epithet of Avalokiteśvara.
Lit.: BBh. 124.

saṅghāṭi (or *-ī*) "long garment, a monk's robe, worn over the other garments" (attr.; Buddh.), n. of one of the three garments of a monk (*tricīvara*). Char. of Amitābha, the Buddha and others. – Another n.: *uttarīya*.
Lit.: B 294; HIS 42; HSIT 9 a.pl. 12; RAAI 273; SB 18.

Saṅgili(nācciyār) (Tam.), see Caṅkili(nācciyār).

Saṅgilikkaruppaṉ (Tam.), see Caṅkilikkaruppaṉ.

saṅhāra(mūrti) "terrific, destructive manifestation", n. of a certain kind of *ugra*-representation (usually 10-armed) of Śiva. As *saṅhāramūrtis* are mentioned (R): Andhakāsura-, Brahmaśiraśchedaka-, Gajāsurasaṅhāra-, Jalandhara-, Kāmāntaka-, Kālāri-, Śarabheśa-, Vīrabhadra-mūrti and Tripurāntaka.
Lit.: B 466; IC 1:512; R 2:145; WM 166; ZA 359; ZM 140.

Saṅhāra-Bhairava, n. of a form of Bhairava.
Lit.: SSI 151.

saṅhāratāṇḍava "destruction-dance" (att.), n. of a dance-pose of Śiva Naṭarāja. In this form he has 8 arms and the char.: Vāh.: he stands on Apasmāra; Mu.: *abhaya-*, *gajahasta-*, *vismaya-mudrā*; attr.: *agni*, *ḍamaru*, *kapāla*, *pāśa*, *triśūla*. – Cp. *tāṇḍava*.
Lit.: SSI 84; Th. pl. 55A.

saṅhatalamudrā "joined palms" (Mu.), n. of a handpose described thus (WHW): "when the flattened palms are joined". This coincides with the usual description of the *añjalimudrā*.
Lit.: WHW 2:88.

Śani or Śaniścar(a) (Hi.; Skt:) Śanaiścara ("slow-moving"), n. of the planet Saturn.
1. (Hind.) Ś. as a planet god is the son of Sūrya and Chāyā. Char.: colour: black or blue; Vāh.: *padma* or *ratha* (iron) drawn by 8 (or 10) piebald horses, or a blue *gṛdhra*, or *(droṇa)kāka*, or *gaja*; Mu.: *añjali-*, *varada-mudrā*; attr.: *akṣamālā*, *daṇḍa*, *dhanus*, *kiṅkiṇī(sūtra)*, *śara*, *triśūla*.
Lit.: KiH 7; KiK 141; KiSH 63; R 1:321 a.pl. 96; SSI 239; Th. 114.
2. (Buddh.) Ś. as a planet god: Char.: colour: blue (black); Vāh.: *kūrma*; attr.: *daṇḍa*.
Lit.: BBh. 377.

śanivāra (or *-vāsara*) "Saturday". – Another n.: *mandavāra*.

sāñjalimudrā "together with *añjalimudrā*" (Mu.), n. of the *añjali*-handpose when an attr. is held in or between the hands together with this handpose, see *añjalimudrā*.
Lit.: SSI 259.

sāñjhā (Hi.) "image of cow-dung made by children during the dark half of the month Asin to represent an idol" (attr.).
Lit.: P 628.

Sañjñā ("conscience").
1. (Hind.) NP of the daughter of Tvaṣṭar (or of Viśvakarman). She is one of the wives of Sūrya and, according to some sources, the mother of Yama.
Lit.: B 429; D 278; Gt 550; MG 36.
2. ("Perception"; Buddh.), see *skandha*.
Lit.: BBh. 42.

Śaṅkara ("giver of joy"), epithet of Śiva as one among the group *ekādaśarudra*. See also Hari-Śaṅkara.
Lit.: DHP 202; GoRI 1:254; R 2:386; ZM 141.

Śaṅkarācārya (also Śaṅkara; "Dr. Śaṅkara"), n. of a famous Vedānta philosopher who lived in A.D. 788-830. Ś. is the chief representative of the *advaita* philosophy. He is sometimes regarded as an incarnation of Śiva and is said to be his son by a Brāhman widow; iconographically he is represented as a *saṅnyāsin* with the char.: att.: *padmāsana*; Mu.: *cin-*, *vyākhyāna-mudrā*; attr.: *daṇḍa*, *kamaṇḍalu*, *pustaka*, *rudrākṣamālā*.
Lit.: GH 364; GRI 310; Gt 550; R 1: pl. B; SSI 259; WHW 2:348.

Śaṅkara-Nārāyaṇa (i.e. Śiva and Viṣṇu), another n. for Hari-Haramūrti.
Lit.: SSI 125.

Śāṅkarī ("[the wife] of Śaṅkara"), as n. of one of the *saptamātaras*, see Māheśvarī.
Lit.: MEIA 150.

Saṅkarṣaṇa ("the ploughing, Resorber").
1. N. of an aspect of Viṣṇu, see *caturviṅśatimūrti*, or of a manifestation of Viṣṇu as *siṅha* or *nṛsiṅha*, see *caturvyūha*, *caturmūrti*. Śakti: Sarasvatī.
Lit.: DHP 154; KiSH 39; R 1:229.
2. Epithet of Balarāma (Saṅkarṣaṇa-Baladeva or -Balarāma), the elder brother of Kṛṣṇa. This n. refers esp. to the function of this god as the Genius of agriculture. Char.: *hala*, *musala*.
Lit.: B 300, 302; HIS 18.

saṅkaṭāsana "the contracted sitting (die gefährliche Positur)" (att.), n. of a Yogic posture.
Lit.: KiH pl. 152 row 2:2.

śaṅkha "conch, conch-shell". In Vedic times the *ś.* signified a pearl-shell used as an amulet. Later it is also interpreted thus: "a sea-shell which people blow when riding on elephants" (AI). It has been regarded either as a weapon or as a horn or wind-instrument (trumpet), "... car le son de la conque, qui peut être entendu de très loin, passe pour être terrifiant" (MEIA). However the symbolical meaning of *ś.* is described in several other ways: "the emblem of salvation" or "the origin of existence" (DHP); within Buddhism: "symbol of blessedness of turning to the right" (G). In this instance the bearer of

ś. is regarded as "Verkünder der Heilslehre" (GBM), and *ś.* also symbolizes the universality and the strength of the Law (SM). – A *ś.* of the cowry type may further, because of the longitudinal form of its opening, signify the *yoni* (similarly also in other Eastern cultures), this esp. when carried by Śiva or Pārvatī and when used as an independent cult object (cp. *arghā*).
As the pattern for the *ś.* (leaving aside the cowry type, see above), either the Charonia Tritonis (a larger kind of conch) or the Turbinella pyrum Linn. (a smaller one) has most commonly been used (see WM). Both these conches (like most other such shells) have their spirals turning to the right. In South India the conch of Viṣṇu is usually represented with the spirals turning to the right (cp. also Tel. *valamuri*, lit. "conch whose spirals turn to the right", n. of Viṣṇu's conch, see also DED), but in North India the *ś.* is just as often reproduced with the spirals turning to the left (although this is contrary to the natural form of conch) as to the right. The reason for the frequent appearance in North-Indian iconography of this 'unnatural' form of conch is not known. A possible explanation is that this symbol was transferred from the Dravidian peoples to the Indo-Aryans, and in the course of this transaction this attr. may have lost parts of its original symbolism and pattern, which, in Dravidian South India would seem to have been better preserved. It is also possible that the symbolism of *ś.* originally somehow stressed the meaning of "the right side" (cp. *dakṣiṇa* and the explanation of *ś.* in Buddhism, cited above from G) and that this attr. had a meaning closely related to the right hand gesture *abhayamudrā*; it is noticeable that *ś.* (like *abhayamudrā* and the attr. *trivali* which is intimately connected with *ś.*) is esp. char. of Viṣṇu and the Buddha, the foremost representatives of the so-called "right hand doctrines".

1. (Attr.) The *ś.* is usually carried in one of the left hands, often in a 'hind' hand, with the point upwards; if it is held in a fore hand, its point is usually turned downwards, in the same direction as the finger-tips. It is also often represented with three or four flames (*cuṭar*). (a) A *ś.* with the NP Pāñcajanya is char. of Viṣṇu, Kṛṣṇa, Śrīnivāsa; (b) a *ś.* with the NP Devadatta is char. of Indra; (c) *ś.* without a proper n. is char. of: Balarāma, Bhadrakālī, Cāmuṇḍā, Caṇḍā, Cundā, Dattātreya, (Devī), *dhanus* Indradhanus, Durgā, Ekajaṭā, Gaṇeśa, Hari-Haramūrti, Hayagrīva, Hva-saṅ, Jagadgaurī, Jaya-Durgā, Kalkin, Kāma, Kapila, Kārttikeya, Kirātārjunamūrti, (Gaja-)Lakṣmī, Lalitā, Mahākālī, Mahāpratisarā, Mahāratnakīrti-Lokeśvara, Mahāvajrasattva-Lokeśvara, Mahāviśvaśuddha-Lokeśvara, Mahiṣāsuramardinī, Nandā, *navadurgās*, Pāṇḍurāṅga, Pārthasārathi, Pārvatī, Rājagopāla, Rudrāṅśa-Durgā, Ṣaḍakṣarī, Sāgaramati, Śaṅkhanātha-Lokeśvara, Ṣaṇmukha, Sarasvatī, Sitabrahmā, Śiva, Sūrya, Trikaṇṭakīdevī, Tripurāntaka, Vaikuṇṭha, Vaiṣṇavī, Vajrasattvadhātu-Lokeśvara, Vajratārā, Vana-Durgā, Varuṇa, Veṇugopāla, Vindhyavāsi-Durgā, Vīrabhadra, Viṣvaksena, Viśvarūpa, Yajñamūrti.

Lit.: AI 114; B 300 a.passim; DED 4319; DHP 155, 231; G 8, 18 (ill.); GBM 122; H pl. 6:56 a-b; JDI 61; MEIA 257; R 1:3, 236 a.pl. 1:1-3; SSR 155; SM 150; WHW 1:47; WM 105 a.fig. 48-50; ZA pl. 387.

2. (Attr.) A white *ś.* is also an independent cult object lying on a tripod and containing water for the *pūjā*. – A *ś.* used as a horn, usually made of the white Turbinella rapa, is further blown during the *pūjā* in order to attract the attention of the worshippers of the god. It is also used in temple and funeral processions and in village dances (cp. *dhavalaśaṅkha*). – A *ś.* can also be used

for the keeping up of *añjana*. – In South India *ś*. (= Tam. *caṅku*) is also a vessel, formed like a conch.

Lit.: BBh. 438; DiIP 107; GH 345; IC 1:570; KiH pl. 139:4; SMII 169.

3. (Vāh.; Buddh.) Jambhala sometimes sits on a *ś*.; cp. Śaṅkhamuṇḍa.

Lit.: G 25.

4. (Buddh.) *ś*. is n. of a *maṅgala* symbolizing "den alles durchdringenden Ton (eines Befehls)", cp. *aṣṭamaṅgala*.

Lit.: GBM 102.

5. (Jain.) *ś*. is a symbol of Ariṣṭanemi (or Nemi).

Lit.: GJ pl. 23:22; KiJ pl. 45.

Other n.: *dharmaśaṅkha*, *kākinī*, *kambu*.

Śaṅkha ("conch"), n. of a *mahānāga*, obviously identical with Śaṅkhapāla.

Lit.: MEIA 196.

śaṅkhakaṇṭha "conch-neck" (attr.), n. of a "coquillage ou portion de coquillage servant d'ornement d'oreilles et ordinairement réservé aux hommes, aux rois, aux *saṅnyāsi*, etc.".

Lit.: ACA 40.

Śaṅkhamuṇḍa ("conch head"; Vāh.; Buddh.), n. of a being, half-man, on which Jambhala treads; cp. *śaṅkha* 3.

Lit.: KiSB 75.

Śaṅkhanātha-Lokeśvara ("L., the protector of the conch"; Buddh.), n. of a variety of Avalokiteśvara. Char.: Vāh.: *padma*; attr.: *padma*, *śaṅkha*.

Lit.: BBh. 430 a.pl. 101(A).

śaṅkhanidhi "conch treasure" (attr.), n. of a certain *nidhi*. Char. of: Kubera, Lakṣmī. As a personification n. of an attendant of Kubera and of an elephant in the retinue of Lakṣmī.

Lit.: B passim; R 2:536.

Śaṅkhapāla ("conch protector"), n. of a *nāga-(deva)*. Attr.: *akṣamālā*, *kamaṇḍalu*, *trinayana*. Cp. Śaṅkha.

Lit.: R 2:557.

śaṅkhapattrakuṇḍala (or *-patra-*) "ear-ornament made of leaves of conch shells" (attr.). Char. of Umā (Pārvatī) and others.

Lit.: B 289; R 1:24 a.pl. 4:16; WM 104 a.fig. 42.

śaṅkha-siṅhāsana "conch-lion-throne" (Vāh.), n. of a seat with conch-shell figures carved on the supports. – Cp. *siṅhāsana*.

Lit.: MH 44.

saṅkhyā "number". In arithmetic, astronomy, astrology, and in dating symbolical words corresponding to numerals are often used, i.e. words which are connected in some way with a certain number (*akṣi* "eye" is, for instance, symbolical of the number "2", because men and animals have two eyes), but in which no numeral is expressly included. When, in order to indicate higher numbers, two or more such words are compounded, the order of the words is often reversed. Here a list of symbolical Sanskrit names of numbers may be given (in this article we are neither concerned with the part numbers play in Hindu occultism, nor with the speical potencies which are believed to reside in certain numbers; regarding this, see WHW):

0: *ananta* "endless" (but cp. also below, 1), *bindu* "drop, dot", *śūnya* "empty", *ha*, an arithmetical figure symbolizing "0".

1: *ananta* (cp. also above, 0), *bhū*, *bhūmi*, *dharā*, *kṣam*, *kṣiti*, *mahī*, all having the meaning of "earth", which constitutes one, the first, of the three worlds; – *candra*, *indu*, *niśākara*, *śaśin* "moon" (no unequivocal explanation is given as to why the moon symbolizes the numeral "1"); – *rūpa* "a single specimen or exemplar"; – *kali* "the side of a die marked with one dot"; – *aṅka* "hook", symbolizing both "1" and "9" (possibly because the hook, turned to either one or the other side, has resemblance to the *devanāgarī* figures 1 and 9, respectively).

2: *akṣi*, *netṛ*, *netra* "eye" (on account of the two eyes); – *yamala*, *yuj* "pair, twin", *yama* (the god Yama and his twin sister Yamī), *aśvin* (see Aśvins; see also sub *deva*); – *pakṣa* "wing" (also n. of one half of a lunar month); – *bāhu* "arm" and *kara* "doer, hand, the claws of a crab, the lunar mansion Hasta ('hand')" (but no other word for "hand" symbolizes "2").

3: *agni, anala, dahana, hutāśa, pāvaka, śikhin, vahni* "fire" (on account of the three most sacred fires, see *agni*); – *maheśanetra* "Śiva's eye (or eyes)" (from the third eye, see *jñānanetra*, or the three eyes, of Śiva); – *rāma* (on account of the three celebrated Rāmas: Paraśurāma, Rāmacandra and Balarāma).

4: *abdhi, ambudhi, arṇava, sāgara, samudra, sarit, sindhu, vāridhi*, "ocean" (on account of the four principal cosmic oceans, one for every quarter of the sky, see KiK 17); – *aya, āya* "die" (a die having 4 sides), *kṛta* "the side of a die marked with 4 dots"; – *yuga* "age of the world" (there being 4 such ages); – *veda* (because of the 4 Vedas); – *koṇa* "corner; an intermediate point of the compass; (hence) the number 'four'" (MW); – *ambu, ambhas* "water; a collective n. for gods, men, Manes and Asuras; hence the number 'four'" (MW); *amṛta* ("immortal, nectar, etc."; the meaning of "4" is not explained).

5: *bāṇa, iṣu, mārgaṇa, śara, sāyaka* "arrow" (on account of Kāma's 5 arrows, see also *pañcaśara*); – *indriya, viṣaya* "sense", *artha* "object of senses" (because of the 5 senses); – *bhūta* "element" (from the 5 elements: ether, air, fire, water, earth); – *pavana, samīraṇa* "air" (there are 5 vital airs of the body, see MW); – *akṣa* "die" (probably because of the 5 methods of dice-playing, see MKVI; cp. also *akṣa* "50").

6: *ṛtu* "season" (there are 6 seasons, Spring, Summer, Rains, Autumn, Winter, and Cool season); – *rasa* "taste" (on account of the 6 original kinds of flavour: sweet, sour, salt, pungent, bitter, and astringent); – *aṅga* "limb" (the 6 Vedāṅgas); – *tarka* "doctrine" (there are 6 philosophical systems); – *ūrmi* "wave" (on account of the 6 waves of existence: cold and heat [of the body], greediness and illusion [of the mind], and hunger and thirst [of life]); – *arāti, ari* "enemy" (there are 6 sins or internal enemies: *kāma* "desire", *krodha* "anger", *lobha* "avarice", *harṣa* "lust", *māna* "arrogance", *mada* "intoxication").

7: *adri, bhūbhṛt, bhūdhara, bhūmidhara, naga, parvata, śaila* "mountain" (there are 7 principal mountains, see KiK 59, 61; but see also 8, below); – *aśva, haya, turaga, vājin* "horse" (because of Sūrya's 7 horses); – *muni, ṛṣi* "seer" (on account of the 7 *riṣis**, symbolized by the 7 stars of the Great Bear); – *svara* "tone" (from the heptatonic scale); – *loka* "world" (because of the 7 worlds, also symbolized in the 7 *vyāhṛtis**, see KiK 6, MW 906); – *nāga* "snake" (on account of the 7 snake deities, see *nāga* 2; cp. also *nāga* below, 8); – *pūrva* (= *gajapūrva* "preceeding the number of '8'", hence = 7; cp. *gaja*, below, 8).

8: *gaja, kañjara, kumbhin, sindhura* "elephant" (on account of the 8 elephants of the directions, see *diggaja*); – *ahi, phaṇabhṛt* "snake" (cp. above, 7: *nāga*; the snake deities are sometimes said to be 8 in number; for *phaṇabhṛt*, see also below, 9); – *nāga* may mean either "elephant" or "snake", and *vyāla* also may mean any one of several kinds of animals; it may here be associated with either "elephant" or "snake", see above; – *giri* "mountain" ("there being 8 mountains which surround Mount Meru", MW); – *vasu*, n. of a class of gods, being 8 in number (see *deva*); – *anuṣṭubh*, n. of a metre (and of a class of metres, of 4 × 8 syllables).

9: *graha, khecara* "planet" (the planets being reckoned 9 in number, see *navagraha*); – *ratna* "gem" (there being 9 gems, see *navaratna*); – *chidra, raudhra* "opening" (there are 9 openings of the body: mouth, 2 ears, 2 eyes, 2 nostrils, and the organs of excretion and generation, see MW s.v. *kha*, this word also being n. of a number, though not specified); – *kunda* (also named *mukunda*, n. of one of the 9 treasures of Kubera, see *nidhi*); – *nanda* (n. of a dynasty of 9 successive princes); – *phaṇabhṛt* "snake" (cp. above, 8); – *aṅka* "hook" (see above, 1); – *gaus* "cow" ("the earth [as the milk-cow of kings]; ... [hence] the number 'nine'", thus MW).

10: *ambara*, *diś* "direction, sky" (because of the 10 cardinal points, see *dikpāla*); – *virāj*, n. of a metre (of 4 × 10 syllables).

11: *rudra*, *bharga*, *bhava*, *īśa*, *īśvara*, *madanadahana*, names of the god Rudra (on account of the group of 11 *rudra*s, see *ekādaśarudra* and *deva*; the same number-meaning is also found in Rudrāṇī ["Rudra's wife"], n. of a girl, 11 years of age, representing Durgā at the Durgā festival); – *guhyaka**, n. of 11 attendants of Kubera.

12: *āditya*, *arka*, *ravi*, *sūrya* "the Sun god" (being one of the 12 Ādityas*, see also *deva*, and in allusion to the sun in the 12 signs of the zodiac, or in the 12 months; see also KiK 130); – *māsa* "month" (from the 12 months); *yuga* (cp. also above, 4).

13: *viśva*, *viśvedeva*, n. of a group of 13 minor gods; *ambuvāha* "cloud" (the meaning of "13" is not explained); – 14: *manu* (Manu; this n. is "esp. applied to 14 successive mythical progenitors and sovereigns of the earth", MW); *indra*, *śakra* (the god Indra; the meaning of "14" is not explained); – 15: *tithi* "lunar day" (the half of a month, *pakṣa*, consisting of 15 *tithi*s); – 16: *bhūpa*, *nṛpa*, *rājan* "king" (not explained); *kalā* "a small part of anything"; *aṣṭi*, n. of a metre (of 4 × 16 syllables); – 17: *atyaṣṭi*, n. of a metre (of 4 × 17 syllables); – 18: *smṛti* "remembrance" ("the whole body of codes of law as handed down by tradition, esp. the codes of Manu, Yājñavalkya and the 16 successive inspired lawgivers", MW); *dhṛti*, n. of a class of metres (of 4 × 18 syllables); – 19: *atidhṛti*, n. of a class of metres (of 4 × 19 syllables); – 20: *nakha* "nail" (the 20 finger- and toe-nails); *kṛti*, n. of a metre (of 4 × 20 syllables); – 22: *ākṛti*, n. of a metre (of 4 × 22 syllables); – 24: *jina*, *siddha* (on account of the 24 Jain *jina*s or *tīrthaṅkara*s*); also *tattva*, cp. 25; – 25: *tattva* "truth, principle" (25 in number in the Sāṅkhya philosophical system; but the number of 24 is also given); – 26: *utkṛti*, n. of a metre (of 4 × 26 syllables); – 27: *bha* "star, lunar mansion" (27 in number, see *nakṣatra*); – 32: *danta*, *rada* "tooth" (on account of the 32 teeth of man); – 33: *amara*, *deva*, *sura* "god" (because of the number of the gods, see *deva*); – 36: *bṛhatī*, n. of a class of metres (of 36 syllables); – 48: *jagatī*, n. of a class of metres (of 48 syllables); – 49: *anila* "wind" (there are 49 Anilas or winds); – 50: *akṣa* (as to the meaning of "50", see *akṣamālā*; cp. also above, 5).

Also the following words have a similar symbolical meaning: $^1/_4$: *pāda* "foot" (as one out of the four feet of a quadruped, or as a fourth part of a metre); – $^1/_8$: *śapha* "hoof" (as one out of the eight hoofs of the cow with cloven hoofs). – There are also many names of higher numbers, specified and not specified, which are not listed here. Some of these high numbers are given in KiK 333.

Lit.: KiK passim; MKVI 1:2; MW s.v.; A. WEBER, Indische Studien 8 (1863), 167; WHW 2:136.

saṅkrānti "passage of the sun or of a planet from one zodiacal sign into another", hence, e.g., *meṣa-saṅkrānti* "the passage into the sign of Aries", etc.

Lit.: IC 2:721; MW 1127; WHW 1:196.

Saṅkṣipta-Mārīcī ("the thin or short M."; Buddh.), epithet or another n. of Aṣṭabhuja(pīta)-Mārīcī.

Lit.: BBh. 211; KiDG 65; KiSB 83.

śaṅku "peg, nail" (attr.), n. of an inadequately described symbol.

Lit.: MEIA 246.

Ṣāṇmātura ("born of six mothers"), epithet of Skanda.
Lit.: SSI 177.

ṣaṇmudrā "six *mudrā*s', i.e. "six auspicious ornaments or symbols" (here *mudrā* has a different meaning than the usual one; attr.; Buddh.). *ṣ.* consist of: *bhasma, kaṇṭhikā, mekhalā, ratna, rucaka, sūtraka.* If one of these six symbols is left out, the rest is called *pañcamudrā*, and if two of them are left out, the rest is called *caturmudrā*. They are usually made of human bones. Char. of: *ḍākinī*s, Ekajaṭā, Nairātmā, the 6 *pāramitās*, Vajracarcikā, Vajravārāhī, Vajrayoginī, Vidyujjvālākarālī, Yamāri.
Lit.: BBh. 438; G 10 (with ill.), 16 (ill.).

ṣaṇmukha "six-headed" (attr.). Char. esp. of Skanda in different forms, see esp. Kārttikeya; further of: Kṛṣṇa-Yamāri, Mārīcī, Vajradhātvīśvarī (with varieties), Vajragāndhārī, Yamāntaka.
Lit.: KiSB 70.

Ṣaṇmukha ("six-headed").

1. (Hind.) Ṣ., as a particular form of Skanda, is regarded as the son of Paśupati and Svāhā. He is the god of the month *āṣāḍha*. Śaktis: Jayā, Vijayā. Char.: Vāh.: *mayūra*; Mu.: *abhaya-, kaṭaka-, tarjanī-, varada-mudrā*; attr.: *aṅkuśa, cakra, daṇḍa, dhanus, dhvaja, gadā, ghaṇṭā, hala, khaḍga* (Nistriṅśa), *kheṭaka, kukkuṭa, mayūrapattra, musala, padma, pāśa, śakti, śaṅkha, śara, ṭaṅka, triśūla, vajra.* – Another n.: Āṟumukaṉ.
Lit.: B 364; DHP 205, 299; MEIA 117; R 2:417, 437 a.pl. 127f.; Th. 59.

2. (Jain.) NP of a *yakṣa* attending on the 13th *tīrthaṅkara*. He is influenced by the Hindu Skanda and has therefore similar attr. Symbol: *kukkuṭa*.
Lit.: B 562; GJ 362 a.pl. 25:13; KiJ 11 a.pl. 28:13.

ṣaṇmukhāsana "six-face-sitting" (att.), n. of a Yogic posture.
Lit.: WHW 1:76.

saṅnyāsin (or *-ī*) "abandoning, renouncing", n. given to a Brāhman at the fourth and last stage of his religious life (see *brāhmaṇa*). It is also n. of a kind of religious mendicant, a member of an order, dedicated to Śiva and founded by Śaṅkarācārya. Attr.: *daṇḍa.* – Cp. *daṇḍin, parivrājaka.*
Lit.: D 280; GH 365; Gt 354; IC 1:602; RAAI 273; WHW 1:85.

saṅsāra "course, metempsychosis, the cycle of existences or rebirths".
Lit.: Gt 637; IC 1:558; MW 1119; N 198; ZA 32, 60.

gSaṅ-sgrub (Tib., pronounced: Saṅ-dup; "the Secret, Concealed-One"; Buddh.), in Lamaism n. of a variety of Yama. Char.: colour: red; Vāh.: *vṛṣan*; attr.: *cintāmaṇi* (signifying him as the god of riches), *kapāla, karttṛkā, vṛṣamastaka.*
Lit.: G 91.

saṅskāra "sacrament, a sacred or sanctifying ceremony, one which purifies from the taint of sin contracted in the womb and leading to regeneration" (MW). Usually 12 *s.* are enumerated: *garbhādhāna, puṅsavana, sīmantonnayana, jātakarma, nāmakaraṇa, niṣkramaṇa, annaprāśana, cūḍākarma, upanayana, keśānta, samāvartana, vivāha.* These 12 *s.* are enjoined on the first three castes, and every male member of these castes has to perform them. – Other numbers are also given, e.g. 16; for other *s.*, cp. *karṇavedha, antyasaṅskāra, ṣaṣṭhīsaṅskāra.* One who performs the *s.* is named *yājñika.* – For *s.* as a cosmic element ("conformation"), see *skandha.*
Lit.: BBh. 42; DilP 180; GBM 132; GH 332; GoRI 1:115; Gt 555; IC 1:363; MW 1120; WHW 2:315.

śānta(mūrti) ("the appeased, tranquil representation"), n. of an auspicious aspect of a god, esp. of Śiva. Cp. *saumya. śānta* is also n. of the mild, peaceful aspects of the *bodhisattvas.*
Lit.: B 464; R 1:19, 2:115; SeKB 232.

Śāntā ("appeased").

1. (Hind.) NP of a goddess who is sometimes regarded as a Śakti or is mentioned among the *saptamātaras* or *aṣṭamātaras* (instead of Cāmuṇḍā).
Lit.: MW 1044 s.v. *śakti.*

2. (Jain.) NP of a *śāsanadevatā* attending on the 7th *tīrthaṅkara*.
Lit.: GJ 362.

Śāntamati-Lokeśvara ("L., of appeased mind"; Buddh.), n. of a variety of Avalokiteśvara. Char.: att.: *samapādasthānaka*; Vāh.: *padma*; Mu.: *varadamudrā*; attr.: he holds the bough of a tree.
Lit.: BBh. 430 a.pl. 95(A).

Santāna ("continuous succession, offspring"), as personification n. of the son of Ugra and Dīkṣā. – *S.* is also one of the five trees of paradise, see *vṛkṣa*.
Lit.: DHP 206; GH 65.

Santāna-Gopāla ("offspring-cowherd"), n. of a form of Bālakṛṣṇa who is worshipped when wishing offspring. He is represented as a little boy suckling at the breast of his mother. He is also represented as a baby lying on its back (like Vaṭapattrāśāyin, but not on a fig-leaf).
Lit.: MW 1142; R 1:215; SSI 37.

santānamañjarī (or *-i*; R without translation, probably: "flower or sprig of the *Santāna*-tree"; attr.). Char. of: Indrāṇī, Jalaśāyin.
Lit.: R 1:264, 2:520.

Śāntarakṣita ("protected, free from passions"; Buddh.), n. of a Lamaist abbot (A.D. 705-762). Attr.: *kāṣāya*.
Lit.: G 105.

Śāntāsi-Lokeśvara ("L., of the appeased sword"; Buddh.), n. of a variety of Avalokiteśvara. Char.: att.: *samapādasthānaka*; Vāh.: *padma*; Mu.: *abhaya-*, *dharmacakra-*, *varada-mudrā*; attr.: *akṣamālā*, *pustaka*.
Lit.: BBh. 397 a.pl. 32(A).

śānti ("tranquillity, peace of mind"; with a special meaning, Jain.), n. of a ceremony at which several *bījamantras*, referring to different parts of the body, are uttered.
Lit.: GJ 280, 369.

Śānti ("peace of mind").
1. (Hind.) NP of the wife of Trivikrama (or Viṣṇu).
Lit.: R 1:233.

2. Śānti(nātha), NP of the 16th *tīrthaṅkara*. Symbol: *mṛga*.
Lit.: IIM 139 (ill.); KiSH 143.

śāntidamudrā (also shortly *śānti*) "gesture of the granting of peace, tranquillity" (Mu.), see *abhayamudrā*.
Lit.: B 250; MEIA 18.

śāntikavidhi "rite of pacification" (Buddh.), n. of a rite.
Lit.: BBh. 166.

Sāntschī, see Sāñcī.

saṅvat (Hi.), see *samvat*.

Saptajihva ("seven-tongued"), epithet of Agni. Cp. *jihvā*.
Lit.: MW 1149.

Saptākṣara ("seven-syllabled"; personification of a *mantra* containing seven syllables; Buddh.), n. of a variety of the Mahāyāna god Vajraḍāka or Hevajra. Char.: att.: *ālīḍhāsana*; Vāh.: Kālarātrī; attr.: *Akṣobhyabimba* on the crown, *candra*, *ghaṇṭā*, *kapāla*, *khaṭvāṅga*, *naracarma*, *trinayana*, *triśiras*, *triśūla*, *vajra*, *viśvavajra* on the crown.
Lit.: KiDG 56; KiSB 66.

saptakuṇḍala "seven-fold ear-ring" (attr.), n. of a type of ear-ornament not described.
Lit.: AIP 76.

saptamātaras, *-mātṛkās* "seven mothers", n. of a group of mother deities, the number of whom is usually mentioned as seven (see *mātaras*). These are Śaktis who in later times became generally regarded as evil-disposed goddesses. There are many lists of the *s.*, one of which may be given here: 1. Brahmāṇī (Brāhmī); 2. Māheśvarī (Śāṅkarī); 3. Kaumārī; 4. Vaiṣṇavī (Lakṣmī); 5. Vārāhī; 6. Indrāṇī (Aindrī); 7. Yamī or Cāmuṇḍā. Devī (Durgā), the Śakti of Śiva is regarded as the mother goddess *par excellence*; she has the ability to absorb all *s.* (in fact, so she did in the fight with the demon Mahiṣāsura, see Mahiṣāsuramardinī). – When the *s.* are represented together in a group, this group is often flanked by Sarasvatī (or Vīrabhadra) and

Gaṇeśa(-Vināyaka). – A New Indian list of *s.* may usefully be added here *viz.* from Bengal: 1. Phul Mātā; 2. Pānsāhi M.; 3. Bādi M.; 4. Gulsiliā M.; 5. Malhāl M.; 6. Kankar M.; 7. (the chief of them:) Śītalā. The *s.* attack mankind at different stages of life with sicknesses. – Common char.: colour: red; att.: *lalitāsana*; attr.: *kapāla, padma*. – Another n.: *ēḻu-ammaṉ-mār*; see also *mātaras* and Mātāji.

Lit.: B 482, 505; BECA 1: pl. 14-17a; DHP 287; GH 136; HIS 25; KiH 24 a.pl. 82-83; KiSH 53; MG 252; R 1:379 a.pl. 118f.; SSI 190; SSR 144.

saptaphaṇa "seven-hooded" (referring to snake-hoods; attr.; Buddh.), char. of Varuṇa.

Lit.: BBh. 361.

saptaratna "seven jewels" (attr.), n. of a group of 7 pecularities (*lakṣaṇa*) belonging to, and characterizing a *cakravartin*. These 7 are: *cakraratna* "wheel-treasure", *hastiratna* "elephant-treasure", *aśvaratna* "horse-treasure", *cintāmaṇi* "thought-jewel", *strīratna* "wife-treasure", also named Lakṣmī, *gehapati* "house-lord, i.e. minister", *pariṇāyaka* "guide, i.e. general". Cp. also *rājakakuda*.

Lit.: Gw 135; WHW 1:551.

saptarṣi "seven *riṣi*s", see sub *riṣi*.

saptarṣikāla "the era of the seven *riṣis*", n. of an era beginning in B.C. 3076. It is indicated by *laukikasamvat*. The year is *vartamāṇa, caitrādi, pūrṇimānta* (with some modifications), cp. *samvatsara*. The centuries are mostly not put down. The given year of this era - 3076 = the year A.D. – This era is adopted in Kashmir and adjacent territories. – Other n.: *laukikakāla, lokakāla, śāstrakāla*.

Lit.: IC 2:736.

Saptaśatika-Hayagrīva ("H. of seven hundred"; Buddh.), n. of a Mahāyāna god, a variety of Hayagrīva. Char.: colour: red; attr.: *ajina, Amitābhabimba* on the crown, *aśvakeśara* above the head, *daṇḍa, muṇḍamālā, trinayana, vajra*.

Lit.: B 559; BBh. 146; KiSB 68, 74.

śara "arrow (reed)" (attr.). As to its symbolism, see *dhanus*. A *ś.* with the proper n. Amogha is char. of Caṇḍeśvara; *ś.* without a proper n. char. of: Agni-Durgā, Aiyaṉār, Aparājitā, Avalokiteśvara (in different forms), Bhadrakālī, Bharata, Bi-har, Bṛhaspati, Budha, Cāmuṇḍā, Caṇḍā, Cundā, Dharmadhātuvāgīśvara, Durgā, Ekajaṭā, Ekapādamūrti, Gajāsurasaṅhāramūrti, Gaṇeśa (Gaṇapati), Grahamātṛkā, Hayagrīva, Hevajra, Jambhala, Jāṅgulī, Jayakara, Jayanta, Jyeṣṭhā, Kālacakra, Kālāgni-Rudra, Kalkin, Kaumārī, Kirātārjunamūrti, Krauñcabhettar, *kṣetrapāla*s, Kurukullā (in different forms), Madhukara, Mahācīnatārā, Mahāmantrānusāriṇī, Mahāmāya, Mahāmāyūrī, Mahāpratisarā, Mahāsāhasrapramardanī, Mahāśītavatī, Māheśvarī, Maṅgalā, Mañjughoṣa, Mañjukumāra, Mañjuśrī, Mañjuvajra, Mārīcī (in different forms), Mūla-Durgā, Nandā, *navadurgās*, Padmaḍākinī, Paramāśva, Paraśurāma, Parṇaśavarī, Prasannatārā, Rāhu, Rāma, Ṣaḍbhuja-Sitatārā, Śani, Ṣaṇmukha, Śarabha, Saraha, Sarasvatī, Śaravaṇabhava, Saurabheya-Subrahmaṇya, Sitātapatrā, Sitatārā, Śiva, Skanda, Śrīkaṇṭha, Sureśvara, Trailokyavijaya, Tripūrāntaka, Trivikrama, Tryambaka, Uṣṇīṣasitātapatrā, Uṣṇīṣavijayā, Vaikuṇṭha, Vajradhātu, Vajragāndhārī, Vajrajvālānalārka, Vajrānaṅga, Vajraśṛṅkhalā, Vajratārā, Vajravidāraṇī, Vana-Durgā, Varāhamukhī, Vasanta, Vāyu, Vidyujjvālākarālī, Vīrabhadra, Viṣṇu, Yogāmbara. – Cp. also *pañcaśara* (char. of Kāma). For *ś.* as a symbolic n. of the number "5", see *saṅkhyā*.

Other n.: *bāṇa, iṣu, karṇikā*(?), *mārgaṇa, uccaṇḍāstra, viśikha*.

Lit.: B 301, 401; BBh. 439; G 18 (ill.); MEIA 254; R 1:6 a.pl. 2:5; SM 148.

śarabha "fabulous animal represented as having 8 legs, and as being stronger than the lion or the elephant".

Lit.: AuT 127; D 282; IC 1:534; MW 1057.

Śarabha (see above).

1. N. of an *ugra*-form of Śiva who in the shape of the animal described above defeated Narasiṅha (i.e. Viṣṇu in the *avatāra* named thus). Here Ś. is represented trampling underfoot the prostrate Narasiṅha. This seems to indicate a Śaivite legend rivalling that of the Vaiṣṇavite Narasiṅhāvatāra. Char.: Mu.: *abhaya-*, *muṣṭi-*, *varada-mudrā*; attr.: *agni*, *akṣamālā*, *aṅkuśa*, *cakra*, *daṇḍa*, *dhanus*, *dhvaja*, *dvimukha*, *gadā*, *hala*, *kapāla*, *khaḍga*, *khaṭvāṅga*, *mṛga*, *mudgara*, *musala*, *nāga*, *padma*, *paraśu*, *pāśa*, *pustaka*, *śakti*, *śara*, *siṅhamastaka*, *tripādaka*, *vajra*. – Cp. Śarabheśa.

Lit.: B 486, 488 a.pl. 34:2; R 1:45, 155 a.pl. E; 2:172; SSI 147; Th. 18.

2. N. of a monkey, an ally of Rāma.

Lit.: D 282; MW 1057.

Śarabheśa(mūrti) ("representation of the Lord as Śarabha"), n. of a *saṅhāramūrti* of Śiva, see Śarabha.

Lit.: R 2:172; Th. 83.

Śarabhū ("born in the thicket"), epithet of Skanda.

Lit.: DHP 299.

śarad "autumn", n. of the autumnal season from the middle of September to the middle of November.

Lit.: IC 2:723, 733.

Śāradā(devī) (since *śāradā* is a kind of *vīṇā*, Ś. is "the goddess with the lute"), epithet of Sarasvatī (sometimes also of Durgā).

Lit.: MW 1066; R 1: pl. B a.pl. 117:1.

Śaraddevī ("autumn goddess"; Buddh.), in Lamaism n. of a seasonal goddess, a *ḍākinī* attending on Śrīdevī. Char.: Vāh.: *mṛga*; attr.: *kapāla*, *karttṛkā*, *mayūrapattra*.

Lit.: G 16, 35, 82.

Saraha ("having a secret"; Buddh.), in Lamaism n. of one of the *mahāsiddhas* (A.D. 633). Attr.: *śara*.

Lit.: G 94.

Śarajanman ("born in the thicket of reeds"), epithet of Skanda.

Lit.: R 2:429.

Saramā ("the fleet one"), n. of a dog (bitch), guardian of the herds of Indra.

Lit.: D 282; DHP 134; MW 1182; WHW 1:288.

Saraṇyu ("the fleet runner"), n. of the daughter of Tvaṣṭar, wife of Vivasvān (or of Indra) and the mother of the twins Yama and Yamī and of the Aśvins (respectively of the Ṛbhus).

Lit.: D 283; IIM 18, 95.

sārasa "crane", a bird symbolizing caution.

Lit.: WHW 1:155.

śarāsana "arrow-discharger, i.e. bow" (attr.), see *dhanus*.

Lit.: ACA 31 (and 126, here wrongly translated as "flèche").

Sarasiri(?)-Lokeśvara (Buddh.), n. of a variety of Avalokiteśvara. Char.: att.: *samapādasthānaka*; Vāh.: *padma*; attr.: *padma*, *triśūla*.

Lit.: BBh. 429 a.pl. 83(A).

Sarasvatī ("the Flowing-One").

1. (Hind.) Originally n. of different rivers, e.g. of the Indus and of other holy rivers, S. was later identified with the goddess Vāc and regarded as a manifestation of knowledge, learning and speech, and also of poetry and music. She is usually mentioned as the wife (sometimes as the daughter) of Brahmā, but she is also often said to be a rival of Lakṣmī and hence also to be the wife of Viṣṇu, in which case she is associated with Puṣṭi. This rivalry is interpreted in terms of there being hatred between Lakṣmī and S. "da Reichtum und Beredsamkeit (Gelehrsamkeit) selten Hand in Hand gehen" (pw). – Besides, S. is said to be the Śakti of Saṅkarṣaṇa. – Char.: colour: white; att.: *samapādasthānaka* or *āsana*; Vāh.: *padma* or *haṅsa*, *śuka* or *mayūra*; Mu.: *vyākhyānamudrā*; attr.: esp. *vīṇā*, further: *akṣamālā*, *aṅkuśa*, *cakra*, *ḍamaru*, *dhanus*, *gadā*, *ghaṇṭā*, *hala*, *kamaṇḍalu*, *keśabandha*, *padma (puṇḍarīka)*, *pustaka*, *śakti*, *śaṅkha*, *śara*, *sruk* or *sruva*, *triśiras* (rarely), *yajñopavīta*. She is usually 4-armed. – The *bījamantra*, char. of S., is *vāgbīja*. – Epithets

and varieties: Āryā, Bhāratī, Bījagarbhā, Brahmāṇī, Dhaneśvarī, Jagaddhātrī, Kāmadhenū, Lipidevī, Mahāsarasvatī, Mahāvidyā, Śāradādevī, Śatarūpā, Śrutadevī, Vāc, Vāgīśvarī.

Lit.: B 376 a.passim a.pl. 18:3; D 284; DHP 238, 259; GBB 129; GH 139 a.pl. 20; GoRI 1:96; Gt 559; IIM 41, 89; IP pl. 33; KiH 21 a.pl. 66; KiSH 41, 52; KrA pl. 137; MEIA 189; MG 90 a.pl. facing p. 96; MH pl. 86; MKVI 2:434; MSHP pl. 15; MW 1182; pw. 7:79; R 1:233, 377 a.pl. 113ff.; SIB pl. 7; SSI 185; Th. 103 a.pl. 4B; WHW 1:165; WM 158; ZM 100 a.N. 19.

2. (Buddh.) N. of a Mahāyāna goddess, a female *bodhisattva* who corresponds to the Hindu S. – Char.: colour: white; Mu.: *varadamudrā*; attr.: *cakra*, *cintāmaṇi*, *kapāla*, *karttṛkā*, *khaḍga*, *padma*, *pustaka*, *triśiras* (sometimes), *vīṇā*. – Epithets and varieties: Ārya-Sarasvatī, Mahāsarasvatī, Mahāvāṇī, Vajraśāradā, Vajra-Sarasvatī, Vajravīṇā-Sarasvatī. S. is also n. of a *yakṣiṇī*.

Lit.: BBh. 349; G 33, 73; KiDG 64; KiSB 74, 105.

3. (Jain.) N. of a *vidyādevī* or another kind of goddess.

Lit.: B 561; GJ 362 a.pl. 27; KiJ 12 a.pl. 30.

sarasvatīpūjā "worship of Sarasvatī", n. of a festival for Sarasvatī in September-October, or, in Bengal, in spring. During this festival books are placed around an image of the goddess.

Lit.: DiIP 171.

saraṭa "lizard, chameleon" (attr.), n. of an animal dedicated to Śiva. Cp. *godh(ik)ā*.

Lit.: GH 73.

Śaravaṇabhava ("born in the thicket of reeds"), n. of a form of Skanda. Char.: Mu.: *abhaya-*, *varada-mudrā*; attr.: *daṇḍa*, *dhanus* (sometimes of sugar-cane, *ikṣukodaṇḍa*), *dhvaja*, *ghaṇṭā*, *khaḍga*, *kheṭaka*, *kukkuṭa*, *padma*, *pāśa*, *śakti*, *ṣaṇmukha*, *śara*, *ṭaṅka*, *vajra*. – The six-syllabic form *śa-ra-va-ṇa-bha-va* is also a *mantra* connected with Skanda, see *ṣaḍakṣara*.

Lit.: R 2:436.

śarāva-sampuṭa "cup-bowl", n. of two bowls placed one over the other, used as a decorative motif. It is a *maṅgala*, see *aṣṭamaṅgala*.

Lit.: JMS 17, 51 (ill.).

śārdūla "tiger" (Vāh.). It is a symbol of strength. Char. of: Durgā and varieties, Mañjuśrī (cp. Śārdūlavāhana), Dharmatala, Vādirāṭ. Concerning Durgā it should be noticed that she is often represented with this Vāh.; there is, however, no epithet of Durgā alluding to this Vāh. (her usual Vāh. being *siṅha*, cp. Siṅharathī, Siṅhavāhinī). – Another n.: *vyāghra*.

Lit.: GH 71; MKVI 2:337, 375.

Śārdūlavāhana ("having a tiger as Vāh."), epithet of Mañjuśrī.

Sarga ("creation"), as a personification n. of the son of Śiva Bhīma and Diśā.

Lit.: DHP 205.

sāṛī (or *sāṛhī*, Hi., < Skt *śāṭī*?; Tam. *cāri*) "Sari, a long piece of cloth wrapped round the body and passed over the head (or the left shoulder)" (attr.). Char. of women (being women's usual dress). In SB there is a very special description concerning this word (here written *sāri*): "a lower garment is rendered like a pair of trousers closely covering the legs", this explanation perhaps appertaining to the old meaning of Skt *śāṭī*, which was applied only to the draped lower garment (petticoat or skirt) worn by women.

Lit.: MW 1063; P 625; SB 110; WHW 1:307.

sārikā "mynah", a bird symbolizing secretiveness. As a bird which easily learns to speak very good it is often as a "wife" connected with the *śuka*.

Lit.: WHW 1:155.

Śāriputra ("son of Śāri"; Pāli Sāriputta; Buddh.), n. of one of the first pupils of the Buddha. Attr.: *kāṣāya*, *khakkhara*.

Lit.: BRI 16; G 14, 104; CTLP pl. 30; KiSB 15.

sarīra (*sarīrika*, Pāli; Skt *śarīraka*; etymologically belonging to the Skt word *śarīra* "body") "physical remains" (attr.; Buddh.). Such are the bones, nails, hair, foot-prints of holy men, esp. the Buddha;

these are objects of worship. – Cp. *dharma-śarīra.*
Lit.: IC 2:605; SeKB 99; ZA 233.

Sārnāth, n. of a town and centre of arts near Vārāṇasī, the site where the Buddha preached his first sermon after his Enlightenment. This is also the site of an Aśoka-pillar with a lion-capital (3rd c. B.C.), which is now a national symbol of India.
Lit.: SeKB passim; ZA pl. 4.

Śārṅga ("made of horn?"; attr.), n. of the *dhanus* which is carried by Viṣṇu and Kṛṣṇa. *Ś.* came forth at the churning of the ocean of milk (see Kūrmāvatāra).
Lit.: B 301; DHP 167; WHW 1:55 (etymology untenable).

Śārṅgapāṇi ("holding the *Śārṅga* in one hand"), epithet of Viṣṇu.
Lit.: JDI 59.

Śārṅgin ("carrying the *Śārṅga*"), epithet of Viṣṇu or Kṛṣṇa.

saroja "lotus" (attr.), see *padma.*
Lit.: BBh. 88.

Sarojin (wearing a lotus"), epithet of Brahmā.
Lit.: DHP 235.

sarpa "snake" (Vāh. or attr.), see *nāga.*

sarpabali "offering to the snake", n. of a ceremony.
Lit.: IC 1:362, 535.

sarpābharaṇa "snake ornament" (attr.). Cp. *nāgāṣṭaka.*
Lit.: BBh. 165.

sarpakara "forming a snake" (Mu.), see *kaṭakamudrā.*
Lit.: R 2:290.

sarpakucabandha "breast-band (*kucabandha*) in the shape of a snake" (attr.). Char. of Nāginī and other goddesses. – Another n.: *nāgakucabandha.*
Lit.: B 350 a.pl. 20:4; SB 280.

sarpakuṇḍala "ear-ornament (*kuṇḍala*) in the shape of a snake" (attr.). Char. of Gaṇeśa, Śiva. – Another n.: *nāgakuṇḍala.*
Lit.: B 289; R 1:24 a.pl. 4:19; WM 104 a.fig. 43.

sarpamālā "snake-garland" (attr.). Char. of: Ācāryavajrapāṇi, Śiva.

sarpamastaka "snake-headed" (attr.). Char. of Ketu.

sarpāsana "snake-position" (att.), n. of a Yogic posture.
Lit.: KiH pl. 153 row 2:2.

sarpavalaya "armlet (*valaya*) in the shape of a snake" (attr.), see *bhujaṅgavalaya.*
Lit.: R 2:224.

sarpayajñopavīta "sacred thread (*yajñopavīta*) consisting of a snake" (attr.), see *nāgayajñopavīta.*
Lit.: R 2:465.

Sārthavāha-Lokeśvara ("the merchant-L."; Buddh.), n. of a form of Avalokiteśvara. Char.: att.: *samapādasthānaka*; Vāh.: *padma*; Mu.: *varadamudrā*; attr.: *pātra.*
Lit.: BBh. 428 a.pl. 74(A).

Śarva ("Archer"), n. of one of the *mūrtyaṣṭaka*-forms of Śiva. Char.: colour: white; Vāh.: *padmapīṭha*; Mu.: *abhaya-*, *varada-mudrā*; attr.: *jaṭāmukuṭa* with *candra*, *khaḍga*, *kheṭaka.*
Lit.: DHP 204; GoRI 1:254; R 2:403.

Sārvabhauma ("relating to, ruling over the whole earth"), n. of the *diggaja* which accompanies Kubera as a *dikpāla.*
Lit.: D 180; MW 1210.

Sarvabhūtadamanī ("taming all beings"), n. of a form of Durgā as the Śakti of one of the *vidyeśvaras.* Attr.: *kapāla, vajra.*
Lit.: R 1:364, 2:403.

Sarvabuddhaḍākinī ("demoness of all *buddhas*"; Buddh.), n. of a *ḍākinī*, a gracious aspect of the Śakti, though influenced by the Hindu Kālī. Char.: colour: red; att.: *ālīḍhāsana*; attr.: esp. *kapāla, karttṛkā, khaṭvāṅga*, further *ḍamaru, triśūla, viśvavajra* in the *uṣṇīṣa, dharmapālābharaṇa.* – Another n.: Na-ro mkha'-spyod-ma; cp. also Vajrayoginī.
Lit.: G 34, 81; ZA 200 a.pl. 602b.

Sarvabuddhadharma-Koşavatī ("possessing the treasure of the virtues of all *buddhas*"; Buddh.), n. of *dhāriṇī.* Char.: colour: yellow; attr.: *karaṇḍa* (with jewels), *viśvavajra.*
Lit.: BBh. 220.

sārvadeśikaliṅga ("*liṅga* of all places"), n. of a kind of *mānuṣaliṅga* characterized by certain measurements.
Lit.: R 2:87.

Sarvaguṇanāthasvāmin (-ī; also Sarguṇa-; "Lord of all good qualities"), see Umāsahita.
Lit.: SB 273.

Sarvāhna ("the whole day"; Jain.), n. of a *yakṣa* attending on the 22nd *tīrthaṅkara* (Ariṣṭa-)Nemi (of the *digambara*-sect). Symbol: *stūpa*.
Lit.: GJ 362 a.pl. 27:22; KiDG 81 a.pl. 73; KiJ 11 a.pl. 30:22.

Sarvakāmika ("fulfilling all wishes"), n. of a *dvārapālaka* of Brahmā. Attr.: *akṣamālā, aṅkuśa, daṇḍa, pāśa*.
Lit.: R 2:507.

Sarvakarmāvaraṇaviśodhanī ("washing away the obstruction of all deeds"; Buddh.), n. of a *dhāriṇī*. Char.: colour: green; attr.: *vajra, viśvavajra*.
Lit.: BBh. 220, 341.

Sarvamaṅgalā ("universally auspicious"), n. of a four-armed form of Pārvatī. Char.: Vāh.: *siṅha*; attr.: *akṣamālā, kamaṇḍalu, padma, triśūla*.
Lit.: R 1:359.

sarvāṅgāsana "all-limbs-sitting" (att.), n. of a Yogic posture, in which "one lies on the back, raises the legs to a vertical position so that the body rests on the shoulders".
Lit.: WHW 1:76.

Sarvanivaraṇaviṣkambhī-Lokeśvara ("L., the effacer of all sins"; Buddh.), n. of a variety of Avalokiteśvara. Char.: att.: *padmāsana*; Vāh.: *padma*; attr.: *khaḍga, padma, vajra*.
Lit.: BBh. 398 a.pl. 38(A).

Sarvanivaraṇaviṣkambhin (-ī; "effacer of all stains or sins"; Buddh.), n. of a Mahāyāna *(dhyāni)bodhisattva*. Char.: colour: white or blue; att.: *padmāsana* or *sthānaka*; Mu.: *bhūmisparśa-, varada-, vyākhyāna-mudrā*; attr.: *candra, cintāmaṇi, khaḍga, pustaka, viśvavajrāṅkapatākā*. – The *yi-dam*-form has as Vāh. a *nara*, and the attr.: *kapāla, karttṛkā, muṇḍamālā*.
Lit.: BBh. 92 a.pl. 64; CTLP pl. 7, 11; G passim.

Sarvāpāyañjaha ("remover of all miseries"; Buddh.), n. of a *(dhyāni)bodhisattva*. Char.: colour: white; Mu.: *pāpakṣepaṇābhinayin*; attr.: *aṅkuśa* (in two hands). – Another n.: Apāyañjaha.
Lit.: BBh. 83, 97 a.pl. 70.

sarvarājendramudrā (meaning unclear, but probably: "a gesture which is shown to all kings"; Mu.), see *añjalimudrā*.
Lit.: BBh. 432.

sarvaratnavarṣin ("showering all kinds of jewels"; Mu.), n. of a handpose which is probably identical with *ratnasamyuktavaradamudrā*.
Lit.: BBh. 86.

Sarvārthasiddha ("one who has accomplished all aims"; Buddh.), n. of the king of the *vidyādharas*. Char.: colour: white; attr.: *vanamālā* (in two hands).
Lit.: BBh. 381; MW 1188.

sarvasamaliṅga (*liṅga* having all sides equal"), n. of a kind of *mānuṣaliṅga*. – Another n.: *sarvatobhadraliṅga*.
Lit.: R 2:88 a.pl. 6.

Sarvaśokatamonirghāta-Lokeśvara ("L. who destroys all sorrows and inertia"; Buddh.), n. of a variety of Avalokiteśvara. Char.: att.: *padmāsana*; Vāh.: *padma*; Mu.: *abhayamudrā* (with two hands); attr.: *akṣamālā, nīlotpala*.
Lit.: BBh. 398 a.pl. 39(A).

Sarvaśokatamonirghātamati ("one whose mind is concentrated on the destroying of all sorrows and inertia"; Buddh.), n. of a *(dhyāni)bodhisattva*.
Lit.: BBh. 92 a.pl. 63.

sarvāstivāda, *-vādin* (Buddh.) "the doctrine that all things are real", and an adherent of this doctrine respectively. This doctrine was of great importance for the development of Mahāyāna Buddhism.
Lit.: BRI 92; IC 2:562; MW 1188.

Sarvāstramahājvālā ("the great blaze of all weapons"; Jain.), n. of a *vidyādevī*.
Lit.: GJ 362.

sarvatobhadra ("guarded on all sides"), n. of a *mantra* which "is said to be the instrument of the fulfillment of all wishes, in the

present and the future, in the visible and the invisible world". It consists in its written form of 64 squares (like a chess-board).
Lit.: DHP 355.

sarvatobhadraliṅga, see *sarvasamaliṅga.*
Lit.: R 2:88.

śāsanadevatā "deity of government or order" (Jain.), n. of a female messenger of a *tīrthaṅkara.* Therefore the *ś.* are 24 in number. According to the *śvetāmbaras* these are: 1. Cakreśvarī; 2. Ajitabalā; 3. Duritāri; 4. Kālikā; 5. Mahākālī; 6. Acyutā; 7. Śāntā; 8. Bhṛkuṭī; 9. Sutārakā; 10. Aśokā; 11. Śrīvatsā; 12. Caṇḍā; 13. Vijayā; 14. Aṅkuśā; 15. Pannagā; 16. Nirvāṇī; 17. Balā; 18. Dhāriṇī; 19. Dharaṇapriyā; 20. Naradattā; 21. Gāndhārī; 22. Ambikā; 23. Padmāvatī; 24. Siddhāyikā. – According to the *digambaras*: 1, 23 and 24 as above, otherwise: 2. Rohiṇī; 3. Prajñapti; 4. Vajraśṛṅkhalā; 5. Puruṣadattā; 6. Manovegā; 7. Kālī; 8. Jvālamālinī; 9. Ajitā; 10. Mānavī; 11. Gaurī; 12. Gāndhārī; 13. Vairoṭī; 14. Anantamatī; 15. Mānasī; 16. Mahāmānasī; 17. Vijayā; 18. Ajitā; 19. Aparājitā; 20. Bahurūpiṇī; 21. Cāmuṇḍī; 22. Kuṣmāṇḍinī.
Lit.: GJ 361; MW 1069.

śaśāṅka ("hare-marked", i.e.) "moon" (attr.), see *candra(maṇḍala).*
Lit.: MEIA 213.

Śaśāṅkaśekhara ("moon-crested"), see Candraśekhara.
Lit.: B 467.

śaśin ("containing a hare", i.e.) "moon" (attr.), see *candra(maṇḍala).* – *ś.* is also a symbolic n. of the number "1", see *saṅkhyā.*
Lit.: MEIA 213.

Śāstā (or -a, -ṛ; Tam. Cāttā, -aṉ; "ruler of the country", "celui qui châtie, commande, instruit", ACA), n. of a form of Aiyaṉār worshipped in South India, esp. in Kerala. His function as "celui qui instruit" is often hinted at in South India. There are many subvarieties of Ś. (here not treated separately). Char.: Vāh.: *gaja* (white), or (rarely) *aśva*, or *padmapīṭha* (sometimes on a *gaja* or an *aśva*); attr.: *ikṣukodaṇḍa, jaṭābandha* or *keśabandha, (puṣpa)śara, śikhādaṇḍa, śikhipota, yogapaṭṭa* (sometimes, over the left leg); for the rest like Aiyaṉār.
Lit.: esp. ACA; Diehl; GH 111; GoRI 2:14; R 2:485 a.pl. 139; SS pl. 40:181; TL 3:1360.

sāṣṭāṅga (praṇām) (Skt-Hi.) "(prostration) with eight members" (att.), n. of the "ceremony of touching the ground (in prostration) with eight parts of the body, *viz.* the forehead, breast, shoulders (or knees), hands and feet" (P).
Lit.: Gt Suppl. 123; P 625.

ṣaṣṭhāṅga (?) "the sixth limb" (att.?). In a novel, *Durbar* by D. Kincaid (in the glossary, here written *shashtanga*), we have found this term interpreted as above and explained as the prayer-posture of Brāhmans belonging to the *liṅga* cult. It may, however, be doubted that this is correct since, in the novel, the att. to which this term refers bears a close resemblance to the *sāṣṭāṅga** att. If, on the other hand, such a term is used within the *liṅga* cult, it might refer to the *liṅga* as the sixth limb of the body (cp. *pañcāṅga*).

Ṣaṣṭhī(devī), (Sastī; meaning properly: "the sixth day of a lunar fortnight; the sixth day after the birth of a child"; personification as the goddess who is worshipped on the sixth day after the birth of a child, when the chief danger to mother and child is held to be over), n. of the goddess of the married women. She is of Bengalī origin and is regarded as the protectress of children against evil powers, and an enemy of Śītalā. Ṣ. is sometimes conceived as a form of Durgā or identified with Śrī (Lakṣmī). – Char.: colour: yellow; Vāh.: *mārjāra*; attr.: *bāla.*
Lit.: B 384 N.; GH 137; GoRI 1:97, 2:20; IIM 97; MG 250; WHW 1:399.

ṣaṣṭhīsaṅskāra "ceremony on the sixth day", n. of a *saṅskāra*, a birth ceremony consisting

in worship of the *aṣṭamātaras*; cp. also Ṣaṣṭhī.
Lit.: GJ 411.

śastra "short sabre" (attr.), see *khaḍga*.
Lit.: MEIA 247.

śāstrakāla "the rule era", see *saptarṣikāla*.

śastrotkīrṇā (scil. *devatā*; "carved by metal instruments"), n. of a kind of icon.
Lit.: B 208.

sasyapātra "vessel containing vegetables" (attr.). Char. of Bhūmi.
Lit.: R 1:376.

saṭā "mane" (attr.), see *keśa*.
Lit.: MEIA 213.

Śatabhiṣā (-bhiṣaj; "qui a cent médecins", IC), n. of a *nakṣatra*. Its influence is bad.
Lit.: BBh. 382; IC 2:730.

sātāni, n. of a sect in South India, belonging to the Vaiṣṇavite sphere.
Lit.: IC 1:656.

satara-varam deviyo (Singh.) "gods or regents of the four quarters" (Buddh.), in Sri Lanka n. of the group of 4 *dikpālas*: Dhṛtarāṣṭra, Virūḍhaka, Virūpākṣa, Vaiśravaṇa.
Lit.: CBC 23 a.pl. 23:137-140.

satarjanīpāśa, also *satarjanikāpāśa*, see *tarjanīpāśa*.
Lit.: KiDG 68.

Śatarūpā ("having a hundred forms"), epithet of the wife (and daughter) of Brahmā, see Sarasvatī.
Lit.: IIM 41.

Śātavāhana (also Sāta-), n. of a dynasty (c. B.C. 100 - A.D. 200) in the northern Deccan. It is connected with the Āndhra epoch of arts. Symbol: *gaja*.
Lit.: Gz 51; SeKB 31.

śatavallika (*-valika*) "mode of wearing (a garment) with many folds" (attr.).
Lit.: SIB 69.

Satī ("good, faithful wife" or "truth"), n. of the daughter of Dakṣa who was married to Bhava (i.e. Rudra-Śiva = Śiva). In her affliction at an insult addressed to her husband by her father, she destroyed herself by fire (by the fire of her anger, according to some). She is often regarded as a former incarnation of Pārvatī (Umā). A faithful wife who immolates herself together with her husband's corpse on the funeral pyre (this act, probably an old Indo-European custom, being named *sahagamana*) afterwards came to be called a *satī* (Engl. "suttee" which, however, means the practice, not the woman), and in South India such a woman is often honoured with a memorial stone (*pāliyā*). In this region *satī*-worship also seems (at *grāmadevatā*-ceremonies) to be connected with the fire-walking ceremony which, however, is usually carried out by men.
Lit.: D 494; DHP 263, 321; GH 338; GoRI 2:210; Gt 565, 624; JDI 48; KiSH 29; MG 247; SSI 229; STP 4:255; W 224; WHW 2:357, 461; WM 158; ZA 117.

śāṭī, k. of dress, see *sāṛī*.

ṣaṭkoṇa "hexagon", a *yantra* symbolizing the element "air". – As to a *ṣ*. in the form of two combined triangles, see *trikoṇa*.
Lit.: DHP 352.

satpherī (Hi.) "seven circumambulations" round the wedding-fire, n. of a rite which forms part of the *vivāha* ceremonies.
Lit.: P. 293.

Śatrughna ("foe destroyer"), n. of the twin brother of Lakṣmaṇa and half-brother of Rāma. Ś. is sometimes regarded as an *aṅśa* of Rāma (i.e. Viṣṇu) representing the weapon *śaṅkha*.
Lit.: D 287; R 1:195 a.pl. 57.

śatruvidhvaṅsinī ("destroying enemies"), n. of a terrible goddess. Attr.: *dantas*, *nagnā*, *triśiras*, *tundila*.
Lit.: SSI 213.

sattabhūmakapāsāda (Pāli; "tower with seven platforms"), in architecture n. of a certain kind of palace.
Lit.: DKI 83.

sattva "animal, creature" (also *sattvaparyaṅka* "animal as throne"; Vāh.). Char. of: Dhanadā, Jāṅgulī, Kurukullā (white, Śukla-Kurukullā), Vajrāmṛta.
Lit.: BBh. 148, 226.

sattvāsana ("the true sitting; the sitting att. of the Supreme Being"; att.), n. of an

āsana-posture described thus: "legs loosely locked, soles of feet scarcely visible. Position of some *bodhisattvas*".
Lit.: G 24.

sāttvika (derived from *sattva*, relating to a quality "goodness, purity"), n. of a certain kind of idol, represented in the *yogāsana*-posture and with the *varadamudrā*.
Lit.: MH 7; R 2:495.

Satya ("true, truthful"), n. of a *dvārapālaka* of Brahmā. Attr.: *daṇḍa, padma, pustaka, sruk*.
Lit.: R 2:507.

Satyabhāmā (also -vāmā; "having true lustre", MW), n. of the daughter of Satrājit; S. is, esp. in South India, n. of the second wife of Kṛṣṇa, the one who in images stands to his left; she corresponds to the second wife of Viṣṇu (named Puṣṭi or Bhūmi). Attr.: *puṣpa*.
Lit.: B 422; D 287; Gt 566; KiSH 36; MW 1136; R 1:203, 376; SB 340 a.fig. 279; Th. 106.

Sātyaki (patronymic of Satyaka), n. of a kinsman of Kṛṣṇa, sometimes said to be his younger brother. Char.: Mu.: *varada-mudrā*; attr.: *khaḍga*.
Lit.: D 287; R 1:212.

satyavāda "truth-utterance", n. of a magical truth-act which even the gods cannot resist, and which is considered powerful enough to make miracles occur. It is performed in such a way that the speaker, by referring to a true fact, tries by its magic force to "call forth" another event to become equally true.
Lit.: STP 2:31, 3:179.

Satyavrata ("devoted to a vow of truthfulness"), epithet of Manu.
Lit.: D 288; DHP 166; Gt 570.

Saubhāgya-Bhuvaneśvarī ("Bh. of good fortune"), n. of a mild goddess. Char.: colour: red; attr.: *kamaṇḍalu* (with gems), *padma* (red).
Lit.: SSI 218.

saumya ("auspicious, pleasant, gentle, mild"), n. of a gracious aspect of a god, esp. of Śiva (see further Mahādeva); also n. of the friendly appearance of one among the several faces of a god, cp. Ubhayavarāhānana-Mārīcī. – See also *śānta*.
Lit.: B 464; KiDG 67; R 1:19.

saumyakapīṭha, n. of a kind of *pīṭha* (Vāh.).
Lit.: R 2:101.

saumyavāra (or *-vāsara*) "Wednesday", see *budhavāra*.

Saunanda ("delighting"), n. of the *gadā* (shaped like a pestle) of Balarāma.
Lit.: D 290.

saura (derived from *sūra, sūrya*; "relating to the sun, *sūrya*"), n. given to the member of a sect who worships the sun.
Lit.: GH 399; IC 1:623.

Saurabheya-Subrahmaṇya (the first word-member is derived from Surabhi*), n. of a form of Skanda. Char.: Vāh.: *padma-pīṭha*; Mu.: *abhaya-, varada-mudrā*; attr.: *caturmukha, dhanus (ikṣukodaṇḍa), padma, śakti, śara, triśūla, vajra*.
Lit.: R 2:441.

saurapadmamudrā "sun-lotus, full-blown lotus gesture" (Mu.), n. of a variety of the *padmamudrā* with the difference that the forefinger and middle finger are straightened out. It signifies the yearning for the lover, caressing the breast, the full moon.
Lit.: WHW 2:87.

sauvastika (derived from *svastika*; attr.), n. of a "left-handed" *svastika*, see further this word.

śava "corpse, body". This term is on one hand included in the conception of Śiva-Śava, and is on the other hand another n. of *mṛtaka* (Vāh.).
Lit.: BBh. 438; MEIA 227.

śavamālā "garland of corpses" (attr.). Char. of: Cāmuṇḍā, Durgā.
Lit.: MEIA 215.

Śavarī (this spelling is analogous to Parṇa-Śavarī; also written Śabarī; Buddh.), n. of a goddess of the *gaurī*-group. Char.: colour: white; attr.: Meru.
Lit.: BBh. 311.

śavāsana "corpse-like posture" (att.), n. of a recumbent position, somtimes char. of

Śiva (when Kālī dances upon him). Cp. Śiva-Śava.

Lit.: KiH pl. 151 row 4:2; WHW 1:76.

Savitar (-tā, -tṛ; "generator"; in the Vedas n. of an aspect of Sūrya), n. of an Āditya. Char.: colour: golden; attr.: *cakra*, *gadā*, 2 *padmas*.

Lit.: D 291; DHP 125; GoRI 1:94; R 1:309; WM 159.

Sāvitrī ("belonging to Savitar") originally n. of a hymn dedicated to Savitar, esp. of the Ṛgveda-stanza 3,62,10; later S. is regarded as a personification of this stanza. As such she is mostly identified with Sarasvatī as the wife (and daughter) of Brahmā, but she is also mentioned as an independent goddess at the side of Sarasvatī, and she is sometimes also said to be the wife of Agni. Attr.: *akṣamālā*, *cāmara*, *pustaka*, *triśiras* (this attr. occurs probably because the stanza RV 3,62,10 is composed in the *gāyatrī* metre and consists of 3 metrical lines). – Cp. Gāyatrī.

Lit.: B 518; D 111, 291; GoRI 1:230; KiSH 41; MG pl. facing p. 96.

śayanālayapūjā "rite of the sleeping chamber", n. of a rite in which the priest symbolically awakens Śiva and his Śakti from their sleep with song and music performed by *devadāsīs*.

Lit.: DiIP 106.

śayanamūrti (or *śayanāsana*) "lying posture" (att.), n. of the representation of a god in a recumbent posture. This att. is properly char. only of Viṣṇu and the Buddha; N.B. however, in this connection representations of the recumbent Śiva with Kālī dancing upon him (cp. *śavāsana*). Similarly many deities are found in a recumbent att. serving as Vāh. to other deities who tread or dance upon them (so esp. in Buddhism); but in these images the recumbent deities are regarded as inferior to the standing deities or even as demons defeated by them.

Lit.: B 274; MEIA 220; R 1:78; WHW 1:45, 76; WM 92.

sedukki (Tam.; attr.), see *cetukki*.

śekhara "top, crown"; this term refers not only to an ornament worn on the head (cp., e.g., Candraśekhara "moon-crested"), but also to the little image of a *dhyānibuddha* carried on the head which is usually named *bimba*. Therefore e.g. *Amitābhaśekhara* etc. is used like *Amitābhabimba*.

Lit.: BBh. 128.

Senā ("army"; personification), epithet of Kaumārī.

Senānī ("leader of an army"), n. of a form of Skanda. Char.: Mu.: *abhaya-*, *varada-mudrā*; attr.: *aṅkuśa*, *cakra*, *daṇḍa*, *gadā*, *khaḍga*, *padma*, *śakti*, *triśūla*.

Lit.: R 2:439.

Senāpati (either "husband of Senā" or "lord of armies"), n. of a form of Skanda who (at least as "husband of Senā") is represented with a Śakti. Char.: Mu.: *abhaya-*, *āliṅgahasta-mudrā*; attr.: *dhanus*, *gadā*, *ghaṇṭā*, *kheṭaka*, *kukkuṭa*, *triśūla*, *vajra*.

Lit.: DHP 299; R 2:434 a.pl. 126:3.

śeṇḍu (Tam.; attr.), see *ceṇṭu*.

seṅdūr (Hi., < Skt *sindūra*) "minium, vermilion" (attr.). This is much used for the *tilaka*.

Lit.: P 713.

seṅdūrdān (Hi.) "giving of *seṅdūr*", n. of a rite which forms part of the *vivāha*-ceremonies and signifies that the bridegroom, as a token of his receiving of the bride, places a round mark of *seṅdūr* on her forehead (cp. *tilaka*).

Lit.: J. G. Hitrec, Son of the moon (word-list).

Śeṣa(nāga) ("Remainder"), epithet of the world-snake which is more often named Ananta. Ś. is regarded as the son of Kāśyapa and Kadrū.

Lit.: D 291; DHP 162; Gt 581; MG pl. facing p. 259; WM 161; ZA 23; ZM 71.

Śeṣāśāyin (-ī, -śayana; "recumbent on Śeṣa"), epithet of Viṣṇu, see Anantāśāyana.

Lit.: B 275; Th. pl. 9A.

Shembu (Gondī), see sub Śambhu.

siddha "perfected, accomplished, endowed with supernatural faculties"

1. (Hind.) N. of a group of inferior deities, said to possess the eight supernatural faculties. – *s.* is also n. of a sect in Northern India, partly synonymous with *nātha*.

Lit.: DHP 303; IIM 118; MW 1215; WHW 2:128.

2. (Buddh.) On the one hand n. of a class of saints who have already attained *siddhi* or perfection in a Tantric rite; on the other hand (as an attr.) n. of a kind of *yantra*, a graphical (*devanāgarī*) sign of mystical significance, e.g. *A* representing either Ādibuddha or Amitābha.

Lit.: BBh. 439; GBM 56; GoRI 1:339; SeKB 210, 278 (ill.).

3. (Jain.) In Jainism this term is equivalent to *tīrthaṅkara*. On account of this meaning *s.* is also a symbolic n. of the number "24", see *saṅkhyā*.

Lit.: IIM 137; MW 1215.

siddhacakra "wheel of a *siddha* (*tīrthaṅkara*)" (attr.; Jain.), in Jain doctrine n. of a symbol in the shape of an eight-leaved lotus.

Lit.: GJ 384.

siddhacakrapūjā "worship of the *siddha* wheel (*siddhacakra*)" (Jain.), n. of a festival in the month *caitra* (March-April).

Lit.: GJ 434 a.pl. 21.

Siddha-Cāmuṇḍā ("C. of perfection"), n. of a variety of Durgā.

Lit.: KiSH 50.

Siddhaikavīra ("the unique hero of perfection"; Buddh.), n. of a variety of Mañjuśrī, an emanation of Akṣobhya. Char.: Mu.: *varadamudrā*; attr.: *nīlotpala*.

Lit.: BBh. 113 a.pl. 77; KiSB 54; WAA 25:167 a.fig. 2.

Siddharātrī ("Night-of-Realization"), n. of an aspect of *mahāvidyā*, represented by Bhuvaneśvarī.

Lit.: DHP 279.

Siddhārta ("one who has attained his goal"; Buddh.), the wordly n. of the historical Buddha.

Lit.: HAHI 8; HIS 13; HSIT 19 a.pl. 48; KiSB 9.

siddhāsana "posture of perfection" (att.), n. of an *āsana*-posture, which is described thus: "man lege den linken Fussknöchel über den Penis und über diesen den anderen Fussknöchel" (GH). It is also said that one should fix the sight between the eyebrows and meditate on the syllable *OṂ*. Char. of Jain images.

Lit.: B 271; GH 292; KiH pl. 151 row 1:3; MW 1216; SSI 265; WHW 1:76.

Siddhasena ("Captain-of-the-Realized"), epithet of Skanda.

Lit.: DHP 299.

Siddhāyikā ("prob. for *siddha-dāyikā*" (MW) "giving, causing perfection"; also Siddhāyinī; Jain.), n. of a *śāsanadevatā*, attending on the 24th *tīrthaṅkara*.

Lit.: GJ 362 a.pl. 27:24; KiJ 12 a.pl. 30:24; MW 1216.

Siddha-Yogeśvarī ("Y. of perfection"), n. of a variety of Durgā.

Lit.: KiSH 50.

siddhi "accomplishment, complete attainment (of some object)". This term is on one hand another n. for *nirvāṇa*, on the other hand it also means: "the acquisition of supernatural powers by magical means or the supernatural faculty so acquired" (MW). Usually eight such faculties are enumerated (as to these, see WHW).

Lit.: BBh. 439; GBM 56, 147; GRI 194; Gt 582; MW 1216; WHW 2:394.

Siddhi (for the meaning, see above; also: "success, good luck, fortune"), as personification n. of a goddess who grants wishes. She is usually mentioned as the wife of Gaṇeśa (in older times the wife of Bhaga).

Lit.: DHP 292; GH 117; R 1:367.

Siddhidāyinī ("granting accomplishment"), n. of a variety of Durgā, attended by demigods.

Lit.: SSI 202.

siḍi (Tel., Kann.) "hook (machine)", see *carkhpūjā*.

Lit.: SSI 226.

sigāla (M.Ind.), see *sṛgāla*.

sikh (N.Ind., < Skt *śiṣya* "pupil"), n. of a reformist Hindu sect founded by Guru Nānak (A.D. 1469-1539) and further developed under nine successive *gurus* or pre-

ceptors. Though originally a pacifist sect, it received under the tenth *guru* (Gobind Singh, 1666-1708) a militaristic character. The canon of the *s.* is known as Ādi-Granth (Guru-Granth).
Lit.: GoRI 2:109; IC 1:655; P 665; WHW 2:396.

śikhā "tuft or lock of hair" (attr.), a term probably equivalent to *jaṭā*.
Lit.: MEIA 212.

śikhādaṇḍa "staff with feathers from a peacock's tail" (attr.). Char. of Śāstā.
Lit.: ACA 32.

Śikhaṇḍin (-ī; "wearing a tuft of hair"), n. of one of the *vidyeśvaras*. Char.: Mu.: *abhaya-*, *varada-mudrā*; attr.: *khaḍga*, *kheṭaka*.
Lit.: R 2:397, 402; WHW 2:399.

śikhara "spire, tower", n. of a typical form of temple-tower in Indo-Aryan architecture; this word is therefore used in the term "*śikhara* temple". Such a tower is usually placed above the *garbhagṛha*. Cp. *bara deul*, *vimāna*.
Lit.: BECA 1:263, 271 a.pl. 29; CHIIA 78; DKI 38; Gz 92; IC 1:576; RAAI 273; WHW 1;58; ZA 270.

śikharamudrā "peak-handpose" (Mu.), n. of a variety of the *muṣṭimudrā* with the difference that the thumb is directed upwards. It symbolizes the erect penis, husband, embracing, pillar, tooth, silence.
Lit.: WHW 2:87.

śikhidhvaja "banner made of peacock feathers" (attr.), see *mayūrapattra*. Śikhidhvaja is also an epithet of Skanda.
Lit.: R 2:429.

Śikhimālinī ("having a garland of peacock feathers"; Buddh.), n. of a *mānuṣibuddha-śakti*.
Lit.: BBh. 79.

śikhin (*-ī*) "peacock" (Vāh.), see *mayūra*. *s.* has also the meaning of "fire" and is hence also a symbolic n. of the number "3", see *saṅkhyā*.
Lit.: B 366.

Śikhin (-ī; Pāli: Sikhin; Buddh.), n. of a *mānuṣibuddha*; in Lamaism also n. of a medicine-*buddha* (see Bhaiṣajyaguru). Char.: colour: yellowish red; Mu.: *abhaya-*, *dhyāna-mudrā*.
Lit.: G 57; GRI 246; KiSB 32.

śikhi-piccha, *-piñcha*, *-puccha* "a peacock's tail, feathers from a peacock's tail" (attr.), see *mayūrapattra*.
Lit.: MEIA 268; MW 1071; R 2:308.

śikhipota "young peacock" (attr.), held in a hand, char. of Śāstā.
Lit.: ACA 31.

Śikhivāhana ("having a peacock as Vāh."), n. of a form of Skanda. Char.: Vāh.: *mayūra*; Mu.: *abhaya-*, *varada-mudrā*; attr.: *śakti*, *vajra*.
Lit.: R 2:439 a.pl. 126:2.

Śīlapāramitā ("perfection of character"; Buddh.), n. of a *pāramitā*. Char.: colour: white; attr.: *cintāmaṇidhvaja*, *kusuma-cakra*.
Lit.: BBh. 325.

śilpaśāstra "book or manual on the fine arts or crafts, such as architecture, handicrafts etc.".
Lit.: RAAI 274; SIB 61; WHW 1:66, 2:163; ZA 110, 321.

śilpin (*-ī*) "craftsman".
Lit.: RAAI 274.

sīmantonnayana "hair-parting", n. of a *saṅskāra*-rite performed in the 4th, 6th or 8th month of a woman's first pregnancy.
Lit.: DiIP 180; GBM 332; IC 1:363; WHW 2:240.

siṅha "lion" (Vāh.). This animal as a Vāh. is very often confused with the tiger (*śārdūla*), at least as the Vāh. char. of Durgā and Avalokiteśvara. Thus, *s.* is char. of Durgā and varieties, esp. in the form Siṅhavāhinī or Siṅharathī (and Bhadra-Kālī, Cāmuṇḍā), and of Avalokiteśvara esp. in the form Siṅhanāda(-Lokeśvara); further of: Bi-har (a white *s.*), Bhūta-mātā, Budha, Dam-can (a white *s.*), Gaṇeśa (as Heramba-Gaṇapati), Gaurī, dGra-lha (a blue *s.*), Indrāṇī, Jayā-Vijayā, Kāśyapa, Kubera, Mahāmāyā, Maitreya, Maṅgalā, Mañjuśrī (in different forms), Nirṛti, Pratyaṅgirā, Rāhu (a bluish-black *s.*), Sarvamaṅgalā, Siṅhanāda-Tārā, Śūlinī,

Vāgīśvara, Vairocana; 2 *siṅhas* are Vāh. of Ratnasambhava; a *s.* with the proper n. Kumbhodara* is a kind of Vāh. of Śiva. – *s.* is a symbol of Mahāvīra, and also of the Scythian *kṣatrapas*; *s.* is also a *maṅgala* (see *aṣṭamaṅgala*) and n. of a *rāśi* ("Leo"). – As regards a *s.*, signifying a face or manifestation of Viṣṇu, see Narasiṅha, Caturmūrti and Caturvyūha.

Lit.: DHP 220; GH 50; GJ pl. 23:24; IC 2:731; KiJ pl. 45; KiSH passim; MKVI 2:448; Th. 95, 110.

siṅhādi "beginning with (the *rāśi*) *siṅha*".

siṅhakarṇamudrā "lion-ear-handpose" (Mu.), see *kaṭakamudrā*. In SSI, however, *s.* is illustrated as different from the *kaṭakamudrā*. – *s.* also signifies the handpose of the right hand having just released the bowstring when shooting-off an arrow, this pose being very similar to that of holding a flower (*kaṭakamudrā*).

Lit.: B 258; R 1:15; SSI pl. I:1.

siṅhakuṇḍala "ear-ornament in the shape of a lion-head" (attr.).

Lit.: ACA 39.

siṅha-mukha (or *-mastaka*).

1. *siṅhamukha(mudrā)* "lion-face-handpose" (Mu.), n. of a variety of the *mukulamudrā* with the difference that the little finger and forefinger are raised. It signifies a pearl, lion, salvation, garland. Subvariety: *karaṇaḍamarumudrā*, see *ḍamaruhastamudrā*.

Lit.: WHW 2:87.

2. "Lion-faced, lion-headed" (attr.). Char. of: Viṣṇu as Narasiṅhāvatāra and Caturmūrti, also of a three-headed form of Viṣṇu, and of Siṅhavaktrā. – *siṅhamukha* is also n. of a stud or knot on the *śiraścakra* or in front of the *kaṭibandha* or other bands. It is further n. of "a lion's face" at the top of the *prabhātoraṇa* or *prabhāvalī*, as to which see *kīrttimukha*.

Lit.: HIS 73 a.pl. 42-43; JDI 130; SB 38 a.passim.

Siṅhanāda(-Lokeśvara) (or Siṅhanādāvalokiteśvara; "a lion's roar", also interpreted as "the recital of Buddhist doctrine"; Buddh.).

1. N. of a variety of Avalokiteśvara (often shortly named Siṅhanāda). This representation shows influence from the Hindu Śiva. Char.: colour: white; Vāh.: *siṅha*; att.: *lalitāsana* or *rājalīlāsana* or *sthānaka*; Mu.: *añjali-*, *varada-mudrā*; attr.: *ajina*, *akṣamālā*, *Amitābhabimba* on the crown, *cāmara*, *candra*, *kapāla*, *khaḍga*, *nirbhūṣaṇa*, *padma*, *nāga*, *trinayana*, *triśūla*.

Lit.: B 284, 558; BBh. 127, 429 a.pl. 99-102, 85(A); G 64 a.passim; KiSB 57; SB 83 a.fig. 49; ZA 169 a.pl. 321, 598.

2. S. is n. of a medicine-*buddha* (see Bhaiṣajyaguru). Char.: Mu.: *dhyāna-*, *vyākhyāna-mudrā*; attr.: *pātra*.

Lit.: G 56, 58.

3. S. is n. of a form of Mañjughoṣa.

Lit.: G 68.

Siṅhanāda-Tārā ("T. of the lion's roar"; Buddh.), in Lamaism n. of a variety of Śyāmatārā. Char.: she is one-headed and two-armed; att.: *lalitāsana*; Vāh.: *padmapīṭha* supported by a roaring *siṅha*; Mu.: *varada-*, *vyākhyāna-mudrā*.

Lit.: G 75.

Siṅhanātha-Lokeśvara ("L., the lion-protector"; Buddh.), n. of a variety of Avalokiteśvara. Char.: att.: *paryaṅkāsana*; attr.: *cintāmaṇi*, *khaḍga*, *pāśa*, *pustaka*.

Lit.: BBh. 396 a.pl. 20(A).

Siṅharathī or Siṅhavāhinī, -vāhanī ("having a lion as Vāh."), n. of a form of Durgā. Char.: Vāh.: *siṅha*; attr.: (sometimes) *bāla*.

Lit.: B 500 a.pl. 42:4, 43:4; W 257; ZA pl. 285.

siṅhasamvat "the lion's year", n. of an era beginning in A.D. 1113. The year is *vartamāṇa*, lunisolar and probably *āṣāḍhādi*, *amānta*. In very restricted use in Kathiawar and Gujrat, possibly until the 13th c.

Lit.: IC 2:738.

siṅhāsana.

1. "Lion-sitting-posture" (att.), n. of an *āsana*-posture similar to the *kūrmāsana*, but the palms of the hands, with the fingers kept stretched out, rest on the thighs. The

mouth is kept open and the eyes are fixed on the tip of the nose.

Lit.: B 270; KiH pl. 151 row 3:2; R 1:18; WHW 1:76.

2. "Lion-seat, -throne" (Vāh.), n. of a (usually rectangular) *pīṭha* with 4 (lion-)feet, or of a lotus throne supported by a lion. Char. of many gods, e.g. Avalokiteśvara, Bhūtamātā, Indra, Mahākāla, Maṅgala, Mañjuśrī (Mahārājalīlamañjuśrī), Rāhu, Vāyu, Viṣṇu, Yama. A *s.* with a *makaratoraṇa* on it is esp. char. of Jain images. – A *s.* is further used as a separate idol-throne. – *s.* is further a royal seat, used by kings, the term signifying the practice of carving lion figures on the supports. Because of this usage it has become the common term of a throne or seat, independent of the decoration on the supports, cp. *gaja-, haṅsa-, haya-, mṛga-, padma-, śaṅkha--siṅhāsana.*

Lit.: AuT 109; B 273; BBh. 433; BhIM 35; G 25; JMS pl. 33; MH 44; R 1:19; SM 131.

Siṅhāsyā ("lion-faced"; Buddh.), n. of a minor goddess. Cp. Siṅhavaktrā.

Lit.: BBh. 321 a.pl. 215.

Siṅhavāhanī (-vāhinī), see Siṅharathī.

Siṅhavaktrā ("lion-faced"; Buddh.), in Lamaism n. of a *ḍākinī*. Char.: colour: red or blue; att.: *nāṭyasthāna* on a *nara*; attr.: *dharmapālābharaṇa, kapāla, karttṛkā, khaṭvāṅga, muṇḍa* in the hair, *siṅhamukha*. She is sometimes accompanied by Vyāghravaktrā and Ṛkṣavaktrā, and she herself often attends upon Śrīdevī. – Cp. Siṅhāsyā.

Lit.: G 35, 81; ZA 200 a.pl. 602 a.

sīra "plough" (attr.), see *hala.*

Lit.: B 300.

Śīrāḷan (Tam.), see Cīrāḷaṉ.

śiras "head"; for *ś.* signifying a severed head (attr.), see *muṇḍa.* – *ś.* also forms part of compound words, indicating in such instances animals' heads.

Lit.: KiDG 67.

śiraścakra "head-wheel, halo (larger or smaller) or sun-wheel" behind the head of an image (attr.). *ś.* is thought of as being the survival of an older round form of nimbus which is found e.g. behind the head of Buddha-sculptures from the Gandhāran epoch on. This, in its turn, may originate from Near Eastern or Iranian religion with its light cult. – *ś.* has the form of a wheel, from the nave of which a knot (*siṅhamukha*) often hangs down. Sometimes the *ś.* has the form of a full-blown lotus (*padma*), and occasionally only a little knob or button is left at the back of the head. It is often furnished with 8 spokes (or lotus petals) alluding to the 8 points of direction (see sub *dikpāla*) and signifying the dominion of the world. Sometimes the *ś.* is described as identical with the *prabhāmaṇḍala.* – In South India *ś.* is char. of any deity, but esp. of Candra, Sūrya, Indra. – Cp. *cakra.*

Lit.: B 296; BECA 1:263; CHIIA 41; HIS 42; R 1:31 a.pl. 4:25f. and 9:4f.; SB 135 a.passim; SeKB 160; WHW 1:432.

śirastraka or *śirastrāṇa* "a kind of neatly formed turban" (attr.). Char. of: *yakṣas, nāgas, vidyādharas* of the Śuṅga period.

Lit.: B 287; HIS 39; R 1:30; WM 101 a.fig. 32.

śirīṣa(vṛkṣa), n. of a tree "Albizzia Lebek Benth.", dedicated to Mahāmantrānusāriṇī, and as a *bodhivṛkṣa* ascribed to Krakucchanda.

Lit.: KiSB 112.

Śiriṣarā-Lokeśvara (Śiriṣarā?; Buddh.), n. of a variety of Avalokiteśvara. Char.: att.: *samapādasthānaka*; Vāh.: *padma*; attr.: *khaḍga, pāśa.*

Lit.: BBh. 429 a.pl. 80(A).

sirivaccha (M.Ind.), see *śrīvatsa.*

śirobandha "band on the forehead" (attr.). Char. of Viṣṇu.

Lit.: KrG 96 a.pl. 7.

śirovarttana ("head-spindle"), n. of the top part of a *liṅga* which may be fashioned in different forms, such as *chattrākāra, tripuṣākāra, kukkuṭāṇḍākāra, ardhacandrākāra* and *budbudasadṛśa.*

Lit.: R 2:87, 93.

śīrṣāsana "head-posture" (att.), n. of a Yogic posture in which one stands on one's head.
Lit.: WHW 1:76.

Śiṟuttoṇḍar (Tam.), see Ciṟuttoṇṭar.

śiśira "the cool season" from the middle of January to the middle of March.
Lit.: IC 2:723, 733.

Śiśupāla ("child-protector"), n. of a king, an enemy of Kṛṣṇa, later believed to be an incarnation of Rāvaṇa.
Lit.: Gt 583; NLEM 339.

Śiṣyabhāvamūrti ("representation as a pupil"), n. of a form of Śiva in which he was taught by his son Skanda (see Deśika-Subrahmaṇya) the significance of the sacred syllable *OṀ*. He is accompanied by Pārvatī. Char.: att.: *āsana*; Mu.: *jñānamudrā*; attr.: *mṛga*, *ṭaṅka*.
Lit.: R 2:443.

sita "white, pale", the colour white; cp. *śukla*, *śveta*.

Sītā ("furrow"), n. of the foster-daughter of Janaka, the wife of Rāma (sometimes said to be the wife of Indra) and the heroine of the epic Rāmāyaṇa. She was carried away to Sri Lanka by the demon king Rāvaṇa and was later rescued by her husband Rāma. According to legend she was born from a furrow, and in the Veda she was the personified Furrow and worshipped as the deity presiding over agriculture and fruits. As the wife of Rāma (he being regarded as an *avatāra* of Viṣṇu) she is believed to be an *avatāra* of Lakṣmī. She is usually represented standing to the right of Rāma, his younger brother Lakṣmaṇa at the same time standing to his left. Attr.: *ekaveṇī*, *nīlotpala*. – Epithet: Ayonijā.
Lit.: D 294; DHP 261; GI pl. 68; GoRI 1:252, 319; Gt 585; MG 119; R 1:186, 376 a.pl. 54, 55, 57; SB 145 a.fig. 90 a.passim; SIB pl. 43; WHW 2:404; WM 161.

Sita-Brahmā ("the white B."; Tib. Tshaṅs-pa dkar-po, pronounced Tshaṅ-pa kar-po; Buddh.), in Lamaism n. of a *dharmapāla*. Char.: colour: white; Vāh.: *aśva* (white) or *ahi*; Mu.: *abhayamudrā*; attr.: esp. *khaḍga*, further: *bodhisattvābharaṇa*, *kamaṇḍalu*, *śaṅkha* (on the turban); sometimes also: *cakra*, *caturmukha*.
Lit.: G 88 (with ill.).

sitadaṇḍa "white staff" (attr.; Buddh.). Char. of: Prajñāntaka, Yamāntaka. – Cp. *daṇḍa*.
Lit.: BBh. 167.

Sita-Jambhala ("the white J."; Buddh.), in Lamaism n. of a form of Jambhala. Char.: Vāh.: *ahi*; attr.: *nakula*, *triśūla*.
Lit.: G 84 (with ill.).

Śītala(nātha) ("cold, the cooling protector"; Jain.), n. of the 10th *tīrthaṅkara*. Symbol: *śrīvatsa*.
Lit.: GJ 274; KiSH 142.

Śītalā(-Mātā) (or Śītalādevī, interpreted as "the mother [or goddess] Cold"?, but the word is possibly of Dravidian origin, see MAYRHOFER), n. of the goddess of smallpox. She is one of the *saptamātaras* and is worshipped esp. in Bengal, Orissa, Gujrat and the Panjab. Ś. is related to Jyeṣṭhā and is iconographically akin to the Buddhist Hārītī. She is occasionally identified with Kālī and is an enemy of Ṣaṣṭhī. Her icon is usually a fetish of crude stone with a painted human face. Char.: Vāh.: *padma* or *gardabha*; attr.: *kamaṇḍalu*, *nagnā*, *saṁmārjanī*. – Cp. also Māriyammaṉ, Pūtanā.
Lit.: B 383; FKR 114; GH 136; GJ 436; HSIT 12; IC 1:487; IIM 97; KBh. 199; MAYRHOFER, EWA 3:466; MG 253; SSI 213; W 394; WHW 1:399; WM 161; ZA 137.

sitāmbuja "white lotus" (attr.), see *puṇḍarīka*.
Lit.: MEIA 263.

Sita-Prajñāpāramitā ("the white P."; Buddh.), n. of a variety of Prajñāpāramitā. Char.: colour: white; Vāh.: *puṇḍarīka*; attr.: *Akṣobhyabimba* on the crown, *padma* (red), *pustaka*. – Another n.: Śukla-Prajñāpāramitā.
Lit.: BBh. 197; KiDG 64.

sitār (Pers.-Hi.; prop. "three-stringed") "guitar" (attr.), n. of more recent form of

lute with a single calabash as resonance-box. Cp. *viṇā*.
Lit.: SMII 124.

Sita-Samvara (or -Śamvara; "the white S."; Buddh.), n. of a variety of Samvara. Char.: att.: *āsana* with *yab-yum*; attr.: *kamaṇḍalu*.
Lit.: G 85 (with ill.).

sitātapatra "white umbrella" (attr.), n. of an emblem of royalty (see *rājakakuda*). In Buddhism it is a *maṅgala* (cp. *aṣṭamaṅgala*) which "keeps away the heat of evil desires" (G). – Cp. *chattra*.
Lit.: G 8 (ill.); MW 1214.

Sitātapatra ("having a white umbrella"; Buddh.), n. of an 11-headed, 12-armed variety of Avalokiteśvara. Char.: att.: *padmāsana*; attr.: *chattra*, *khaḍga*, *paraśu* and others.
Lit.: G 67 (here misprinted: Sitātapatrā).

Sitātapatrā (Aparājitā) ("A. having a white umbrella"; Buddh.), n. of a Mahāyāna goddess (a female *bodhisattva*) who is an emanation of Vairocana (N.B. she is different from the other Aparājitā). Char.: colour: white; att.: *padmāsana*; Mu.: *abhayamudrā*; attr.: *aṅkuśa* (one or two), *cakra*, *chattra*, *dhanus*, *(tarjanī)pāśa*, *śara*, sometimes *trinayana*, *triśiras*, *vajra* (white). – Another n.: Uṣṇīṣasitā; cp. Uṣṇīṣasitātapatrā.
Lit.: BBh. 215 a.pl. 158; G 12, 33, 72; KiDG 64, 68; KiSB 86.

Sitatārā ("the white Tārā"; Buddh.), in Lamaism n. of a form of Tārā, an emanation of Vairocana or Amoghasiddhi. She is regarded as a mild manifestation of Tārā and is said to be the incarnation of a Chinese princess who was the wife of the Tibetan king Sroṅ-btsan-sgam-po. Later she came to be conceived as the female manifestation of Avalokiteśvara-Padmapāṇi. – Char.: colour: white; att.: *padmāsana* or *lalitāsana*, also *sthānaka*; Mu.: *utpala-*, *uttarabodhi-*, *varada-*, *vyākhyānamudrā*; attr.: usually one-headed, *akṣamālā*, *Amoghasiddhibimba* on the crown, *candra*, *cintāmaṇi*, *dhanus*, *nīlotpala* or *padma* (white), *pañcatathāgatamukuṭa*, *śara*, *trinayana* (properly *saptanayana* "seven-eyed", as she may also be depicted as having eyes on the palms of the hands and on the soles of the feet), *triśiras*. – Another usual n.: Śuklatārā; see also sub Tārā. – Varieties: Āryajāṅguḷī, Ṣaḍbhuja-Sitatārā, Uṣṇīṣasitātapatrā.
Lit.: BBh. 231; G 16, 75; HAHI pl. 22C; HuGT 26; JSV pl. 57; KIM pl. 10, 12; KiDG 64; KiSB (99), 103; MH pl. 2.

Sitikaṇṭha (probably "dark-necked"; the translation "white-necked, having a white throat" is also suggested, see MW), in the first sense an epithet of Śiva, cp. Nīlakaṇṭha; it should, however, be noticed that white is also char. of Śiva.
Lit.: MW 1214; R 2:49.

Śiva.

1. Ś. is usually included in the Hindu triad (cp. Trimūrti) as the third god and conceived as "the Destroyer, the Annihilator". His n. is mostly connected with the Skt adjective *śiva-* "kind, friendly, auspicious, gracious", regarded as a euphemistic n. of the Vedic god Rudra from whom Ś. is believed to have developed, or as a n. of the god in his gracious aspects. But nowadays most scholars look on Ś. as a pre-Indo-Aryan god (many attr., esp. char. of Ś., are also found on seals from the Indus Valley civilization, esp. that depicting the "Proto-Śiva"), and some are of opinion that the n. of Śiva is derived from the Drav. *ce-*, *cevv-* "red", and that it, therefore, originally, had the sense of "the red one" (cp. Rudra). It has, however, been proved that *c-* in this Drav. word is due to a recent palatalization of an original *k-* and that the *ś-* of Skt *śiva-* is thus not accounted for by this explanation. Nevertheless, red is often char. of Ś., and this colour "hängt mit Tod und allem Schrecklichen zusammen" (thus ZACHARIAE, see GoRI), and it should be noticed that red is also char. of Virūpākṣa, the Buddhist counterpart of Ś. However, red also signi-

fies the creative force and may, in this sense, be symbolic of Ś. in many aspects. White too is esp. char. of Ś., since he smears his body with ashes (*vibhūti*). – As to the origin of Ś., attention has also been drawn to his resemblance to the Sumerian god Ningizzida.

The nature of this god is rather complicated. He is not only the Destroyer, but particularly the Generator, as his theriomorphic (the *vṛṣan*) and lithomorphic (the *liṅga*) forms indicate. The Śaivite sect regards him both as the Creator, the Preserver and the Destroyer. It should, however, be observed that the manifestations of Ś. are either of gracious or of destructive character (see below). The warrior nature of Ś. is proved by his bull character, and his cosmic function is esp. manifested in his many forms as Naṭarāja. In the centre of his forehead there is a third eye (*jñānanetra*) which has a destructive force (representing *agni*, cp. *trinayana*). – His residence is Kailāsa. His principal wife or Śakti is Pārvatī or Devī in her different aspects, corresponding to the different aspects of Ś.; sons: Gaṇeśa, Skanda; daughter: Rati (?). As his second wife is sometimes Gaṅgā regarded (usually represented sitting in his hair); Sandhyā is also mentioned as one of his wives. Ś. had in addition a casual association with Mohinī (the female form of Viṣṇu); the son born of this connection was Aiyaṉār. This legend reflects syncretism between Śaivism and Vaiṣṇavism and also the fact that in terms of the cosmic dualism Ś. represents the male principle and Viṣṇu the female principle (see *trikoṇa*). – Vīrabhadra too is sometimes mentioned as the son of Ś.

Char.: colour: red or white; Vāh.: *vṛṣan* Nandin; (as Bhairava: *vṛka* or *śvan*); further *mahāpīṭha* and *siṅha* Kumbhodara; att.: often *nāṭyasthāna* (see Naṭarāja) but, of course, also many other forms of att.; Mu.: *abhaya-*, *ḍamaruhasta-*, *patākā-* and *tripatākā-*, *varada-mudrā* (and, as an attendant of Viṣṇu in Vaiṣṇavite representations, *añjalimudrā*); his principal attr. are: *ḍamaru*, *dhanus* Ajagava, *gadā* (*khaṭvāṅga*), *pāśa*, *triśūla* Pināka; other attr. (in part belonging to certain manifestations of Ś.): *agni*, *ajina* (deer-, elephant- or tiger-skin), *akṣamālā* Śivamālā or *rudrākṣa*, *aṅkuśa*, *arkapuṣpa*, *bhujaṅgavalaya*, *daṇḍa*, *daśabhuja*, *dhvaja* (provided with the picture of *vṛṣan*), Gaṅgā, *ghaṇṭā*, *jambhīra*, *jaṭā-(mukuṭa)*, *kamaṇḍalu*, *kapāla*, *khaḍga*, *kheṭaka*, *kṛṣṇājina*, *lambapattra* (in the left ear), *makarakuṇḍala* (in the right ear), *muṇḍa*, *muṇḍamālā*, *musala*, *nāga*s, *nūpura*, *pañcaśiras*, *paraśu*, *pāśupatāstra*, *śaṅkha*, *śara*, *sarpakuṇḍala*, *sarpamālā*, *śrīphala*, *ṭaṅka*, *tiryakpuṇḍra*, *trinayana*, *triśiras*, *ūrdhvaliṅga*, *vajra*, Vāsuki, *vibhūti*. – Ś. is also represented by the Mu. *candrakāla* and the *bījamantra*s: *brahmabīja*, *smarahara* and *HAUṀ*, *HŪṀ*, *KROṀ*. The number of "five" (*pañca*) is also char. of Ś. His tree is esp. *bilva*; his stone is *bāṇaliṅga* or Narmadeśvara.

A common n. of the gracious aspects of Ś. is *anugraha(mūrti)*, and *ugra(mūrti)* is the n. of his cruel or destructive aspects, see also *saṅhāramūrti*. – The manifestations, varieties and epithets (of which there exist more than a thousand) which are listed in this dictionary are (many of the following n. may be completed with the word-member -mūrti): Aghora, Āliṅgana, Andhakaripu, Andhakāsuravadha, Ardhanārīśvara, Aśani, (Baṭuka) Bhairava, Bhava, Bhikṣāṭana, Bhīma, Bhūtanātha, Bhūteśvara, Caṇḍa, Caṇḍeśānugrahaṇa, Candraśekhara, *dakṣiṇāmūrti*, Dhūrjaṭi, *ekādaśarudra*, Ekapāda, Ekapādaśiva, Gajasaṅhāra, Gajāsurasaṅhāra, Gaṅgādhara, Ghora, Girīśa, Gorakṣanātha, Hara, Īśāna, Īśvara, Jala, Jalandharavadha, Jaṭādhara, Jīmūtaketu, Kālāntaka, Kālāri, Kālarudra, Kālasaṅhāra, Kalyānasunḍara, Kāmadahana, Kāmāntaka, Kāmeśvara, Kaṅkāla, Kapāla, Kapālamālin, Kapardin, Kevalacandraśekhara, Kirāta, Kṛttivāsas, Kṣetrapāla, Kuṇḍalinī, Lakulīśa, Liṅgodbhava, Lokeśvara, Mahādeva, Mahākāla, Mahārudra, Mahāsadāśiva, Mahāyogin, Maheśvara, Mallāri-Śiva, Mṛtyuñjaya, *mūrtyaṣṭaka*, Nandivāhana, Naranārī, Naṭarāja, Naṭeśa, Nīlakaṇṭha, *nṛtta*, Palinātar, Palināyakar, Pañcabrahmā, Pañcadeha, Pañcānana, Pañcamukhin, Paramaśiva, Pāśupata, Pāśupatāstradāna, Paśupati, Pinākin, Rakṣoghna, Raudra-Pāśupata, Rāvaṇānugrahaṇa, Rudra-Śiva, Sadāśiva, Sadyojāta, Śambhu, Śaṅkara, Śarabha, Śarabheśa, Śarva, Śiṣyabhāva, Sitikaṇṭha, Somāskanda, Śrīkaṇṭha, Sthāṇu, Sukhāsana, Śūladhara, Śūlapāṇin, Śūlin, Sundara, Tāṇḍava, Tatpuruṣa, Trilocana, Trinetra, Tripurāntaka, Tryambaka, Ugra, Umāpati, Umāsahita, Uṣṇīṣin, Vāmadeva, Vibhūṣaṇa, *vidyeśvaras*, Vīrabhadra, Virūpākṣa, Viṣapraharaṇa, Viśvanātha, Viśveśvara, Vṛṣadhvaja, Vṛṣāṅka, Vṛṣarājaketana, Vṛṣārūḍha, Vṛṣavāhana, Yogeśvara.

Lit.: B 446; D 296; DHP 188 a.pl. 1, 21; GBB 128 a.pl. 4; GH 131 a.pl. 19; GoRI 1:85, 254; HIS 20, 46; HSIT 13 a.pl. 31; IC 1:512; IIM 42; IP pl. 24; JDI 11; KiDG 13 a.pl. 2ff.; KiH 14 a.pl. 38ff.; KiSH 17, 20; MEIA 52; MAYRHOFER, EWA 3:344; MG 166; SS pl. 29:127, 30:138; R (esp.) 2:39 (with numerous ill.); RAAI pl. 169B; SSI 72; Th. 75; W 218; WHW 2:406; WM 162; ZA pl. 2, 217 a.passim; ZM 225 a.passim.

2. (Attr. or Vāh.) Ś. is represented as a prostrated man (*śava*, Śiva-Śava) on whom his wife Kālī dances. – In Buddhism some deities are represented treading on Ś.: Hevajra, Mārīcī (in different forms), Vidyujjvālākarālī. – Cp. Māra.

Lit.: BBh. 194; HAHI 18; ZM 239 a.pl. 69.

śivā "jackal" (Vāh.), see *sṛgāla*.

Lit.: MEIA 228.

Śivā (probably a feminine transformation of Śiva or a particular term for the Śakti of Śiva), wife of Īśāna. Char.: Vāh.: *vṛṣan*; attr.: *ḍamaru, trinayana, triśūla*.

Lit.: Gt 587; R 1:366.

śivadūta "Śiva-messenger", term of an inferior deity attending on Śiva.

Śivadūtī (may be interpreted as either "Śiva's messenger" (MW) or "having Śiva as her messenger" (B), n. of a four-armed form of Durgā. Char.: att.: *ālīḍhāsana*; attr.: *aṅkuśa, gadā, kapāla, khaḍga, khaṭvāṅga, kheṭaka, kuṭhāra, māṅsa, matsya, muṇḍamālā, nāgas, padma, pāśa, raktapātra, triśūla*.

Lit.: B 33, 504; MW 1074; R 1:365; SSI 216.

Śiva-Kāmasundarī ("having Śiva as her love-god"), n. of an idol representing Pārvatī. It may be identical with Śivakāmī.

Lit.: MH pl. 5; SB 264, 292 a.fig. 195.

Śivakāmī ("the beloved of Śiva"), epithet of Pārvatī. Under this n. she is often found standing at the side of Śiva as Naṭarāja. Cp. Śiva-Kāmasundarī.

Lit.: SB 222.

śivaliṅga, see *liṅga*.

Lit.: B pl. 31:3 a.passim.

Śiva-Lokeśvara, n. of a syncretistic representation of the Hindu Śiva and the Buddhist Avalokiteśvara. Attr.: *Ādibuddhabimba* or *Amitābhabimba* on the head, *akṣamālā, jaṭāmukuṭa, kamaṇḍalu, kapāla, triśūla, ūrdhvaliṅga*.

Lit.: B 547 a.pl. 46:4; HIS 46, 74 a.pl. 44f.

Śivamālā ("Śiva's chaplet"; attr.), n. of the *akṣamālā* of Śiva.

Śiva-Nārāyaṇa, see Hari-Haramūrti.

śivapūjā "worship of Śiva".

Lit.: JDI 15; MSHP pl. C facing p. 363.

śivarātri ("Śiva's night"), n. of a festival dedicated to Śiva in the month *māgha* (January-February, or else in March) at which the *liṅga* symbol is esp. worshipped.

Lit.: GH 354; Gt Suppl. 127; JDI 15; MW 1075; SSR 197; WHW 1:354.

Śiva-Śava (*śava* means "corpse, dead body"; for the word's symbolic meaning see esp. ZM), n. of a lying "double" man, repre-

senting both the living and a lifeless form of Śiva on whom Kālī dances.
Lit.: DHP 271; ZM 228.

Śiva-Umā, sometimes n. of compound sculptures in which Śiva and Pārvatī (= Umā) are represented together, either sitting or standing.
Lit.: HIS 23.

Śivottama ("the highest Śiva" or "the highest of the *śiva*s (i.e. of manifestations of Śiva)"), n. of one of the *vidyeśvara*s. Char.: att.: *samapādasthānaka*; Vāh.: *padmapīṭha*; Mu.: *abhaya-*, *varada-mudrā*; attr.: *pāśa*, *triśūla*.
Lit.: R 2:397, 402.

Skanda, n. of the war god, the army leader of the gods. The n. was earlier interpreted as "attacker" (MW); nowadays explained by most scholars as "der Spritzer" (GoRI) or "die Ausgiessung" (WM), cp. the meaning of "to emit seminal fluid" of *skand-ati*. Hence the n. would seem first of all to signify the god as a virile young man (cp. Kumāra); note that semen also plays an important rôle in the mythology of S. (cp. below). – However S. may also be interpreted as "one who hops, jumps" (cp. *tṛṇa-skanda* "grasshopper"); on this basis the two particular characteristics of S., the Vāh. *mayūra* "peacock" and the attr. *kukkuṭa* "cock", may be considered. Both these fowl are bellicose and have a characteristic way of jumping when fighting. The way in which young men leap while fighting in single combat is very often compared to that of these fowls (cp. that the cockfighting is a very popular sport in the East and that the att. *ālīḍhāsana* "jumping" also characterizes a warrior). Therefore I think it likely that Skanda ("jumper") illustrates this way of fighting and is a deification of the young warrior. And just as the bull Nandin is regarded as a theriomorphic form of Śiva, the peacock and the cock may be regarded as theriomorphic forms of S.

S. is further the chief of the demons of diseases who befall children, and he is also the patron of thieves. – He is the son of Śiva and Pārvatī (or Gaṅgā), but he is also said to be the son of Agni and Gaṅgā; according to one legend Śiva deposited his seed into the mouth of Agni, and this god put it afterwards into the River Gaṅgā (hence regarded as the mother of S.) or into a thicket of reeds on the Ganges (cp. Guha, Śaravaṇabhava). S. was then brought up by the 6 Kṛttikās (see Kārttikeya). – He is represented either as one-headed or as six-headed (*ṣaṇmukha*) and has 2, 4, 6 or 12 arms. Wives: Kaumārī (or Devasenā) and Vallī; sons (or brothers?): Śākha, Viśākha, Naigameya. Char.: Vāh.: *mayūra* Paravāṇi or *gaja* (esp. in South India, see Gajavāhana); Mu.: *abhaya-*, *kaṭi-*, *prasāritahasta-*, *varada-mudrā*; chief attr.: *dvaja* (*vaijayantī patākā*), *kukkuṭa*, *mayūrapattra*, *śakti*, *ṭaṅka*, *vajra*; further: *akṣamālā*, *aṅkuśa*, *cakra*, *daṇḍa*, *dhanus* Ajagava, *gadā*, *ghaṇṭā*, *kamaṇḍalu*, *khaḍga*, *khaṭvāṅga*, *kheṭaka*, *musala*, *padma*, *parasu*, *pāśa*, *śara*, *triśūla*.
Varieties and epithets: esp. Kumāra, Kārttikeya, Subrahmaṇya, further: Agnijāta-Subrahmaṇya, Bāla-Subrahmaṇya, Bālasvāmin, Barhidhvaja, Barhiketu, Brahmacāri-Subrahmaṇya, Deśika-Subrahmaṇya, Devasenāpati, Gajavāhana, Gaṅgāputra, Gāṅgeya-Subrahmaṇya, Guha(-Subrahmaṇya), Krauñcabhettar, Mahāsena, Murukaṉ, Pāvaka, Puraiyar, Rudrasūnu, Ṣaḍānana, Śaktidhara, Ṣaṇmātura, Ṣaṇmukha, Śarabhū, Śarajanman, Śaravaṇabhava, Saurabheya-Subrahmaṇya, Senānī, Senāpati, Siddhasena, Śikhivāhana, Svāminātha, Tārakajit, Tārakāri, Vallīkalyāṇasundara, Vēlaṉ, Vēlāyudha-Subrahmaṇya. See also Somāskanda.
Lit.: B 146, 361 a.pl. 16:2, 17:2, DHP 279 a.pl. 22; DiIP 135; GBB 128; GH 116; GI pl. 69; GoRI 1:262; Gt 589; H pl. 15:172; HIS 21; KiH 18 a.pl. 50f.; IC 1:497; IIM 84; JDI 44; KiSH 30; KrI pl. 9; MEIA 113; MG 194; R 2:415 a.pl. 121 ff.; SSR pl.

facing p. 80, 81, 168; SS pl. 21:93; 35:159; SB passim (by the n. of Subrahmaṇya); SSI 177; Th. 97; W 276; WM 170; ZA pl. 137.

Skandamātā ("mother of Skanda"), n. of a variety of Durgā. Char.: Vāh.: *siṅha*; attr.: *padma*s.
Lit.: SSI 202.

skandha "branch, aggregate, cosmic element" (Buddh.). The world is, according to Buddhist doctrine, composed of 5 *s.* (*pañca-skandha*), namely: *rūpa* "bodily form", *vedanā* "sensation", *sañjñā* "perception, name", *saṅskāra* "aggregate of formations, conformation", and *vijñāna* "consciousness, or thought-faculty". These *s.* are embodied in the 5 *dhyānibuddha*s in this way: Amitābha from *sañjñā*, Akṣobhya from *vijñāna*, Vairocana from *rūpa*, Amoghasiddhi from *saṅskāra*, and Ratnasambhava from *vedanā*.
Lit.: BBh. 42; BRI 37; MW 1256; SM 33.

smarahara "Remover-of-Desire", n. of a *yantra* which is found in two forms. It consists of five triangles which either form a pentagram or are inscribed within one another. This *yantra* belongs to Śiva, the number "five being the number corresponding to the procreative and destructive principle" (cp. *pañca*).
Lit.: DHP 356.

smārta ("relating to tradition, based on memory"), n. of a sect the members of which are adherents of the pure *advaita* doctrine.
Lit.: GH 400; GRI 320; IC 1:623; MW 1272.

śmaśāna "elevated place for burning dead bodies, cemetery or burial-place for the bones of cremated corpses".
Lit.: MW 1094; RV 150.

Smṛti ("remembrance, tradition"; Buddh.), n. of an inferior Mahāyāna deity. For *smṛti* as a symbolic n. of the number "18", see *saṅkhyā*.
Lit.: KiSB 105.

snāna "religious bathing". As regards the bathing of an image, see *abhiṣeka*.
Lit.: DiIP 90; IC 1:574.

snānajala "water for bathing a deity" (attr.), cp. *abhiṣeka*.
Lit.: B 36.

snānayātrā "bathing-festival", n. of a festival in the month *jyaiṣṭha* (May-June) which is esp. sacred to Jagannātha at Puri.
Lit.: D 129.

snapanabera (also *snāpana-*) "bathing-icon", n. of an icon which is used at the daily *pūjā* and is particularly intended for the bathing ritual (*snapanapūjā*).
Lit.: R 1:17; 52; WM 88.

snapanamaṇḍapa "bathing-hall", n. of a temple hall intended for the ceremonial baths of deities.
Lit.: BECA 1:263.

snapanapūjā "preparation for the sacred bath", worship of an image by bathing or besprinkling it with water.
Lit.: DiIP 109.

śobhadvāra "the bright door", n. of a kind of temple gateway (*gopura*) with one or two storeys.
Lit.: BECA 1:260.

Ṣoḍaśabhuja-Durgā ("the sixteen-armed D."), n. of a variety of Durgā. Attr.: *trinayana*, *triśūla* (in all the hands).

Ṣoḍaśī ("the Girl-of-Sixteen", "the Power-of-Perfection"); as personification Ṣ. belongs to the group *mahāvidyā* and is represented by Divyarātrī.
Lit.: DHP 278.

soma "essence", n. of a sacrificial, yellow beverage which in the oldest Vedic times, was extracted from a certain still-unidentified plant. At the libations it was offered to the gods and drunk by the Brāhmans. This beverage came forth, according to later tradition, at the churning of the ocean of milk (see Kūrmāvatāra). Among the gods Indra and Mitra are esp. connected with this beverage.
Lit.: D 301; DHP 65, 167; GH 65; GoRI 1:62; Gt 591; KT 56; MKVI 2:474; R 1:310; RV 166; WHW 2:418; WM 171.

Soma. As the deification of the beverage *soma* this god was more important in Vedic times

than later. In Hinduism S. is identified with Candra (a bowl with the yellow beverage, resembling the full moon). S. is sometimes also regarded as a *dikpāla* of the northerly direction and is mentioned as one of the *vasus*. Char.: att.: *akṣamālā*, *aṅkuśa*, *padma*, *śakti*. His tree is *kiṅśuka*. See further Candra.
Lit.: D 301; GoRI 1:62; IC 1:325; IIM 19, 81; KiSH 55; MG 54; R 1: pl. 96, 2:563; WHW 2:417; WM 171.

Somāskanda(mūrti) (= sa-Umā-Skanda-, i.e. "representation [of Śiva] together with Umā and Skanda"), n. of a composite form of Śiva (four-armed), Pārvatī and Skanda as a boy. This representation shows Śiva in an *āsana*-posture (as a sub-form of *sukhāsanamūrti*) and belongs esp. to South India during the Pallava and Cola periods. The second son of Śiva, Gaṇeśa, is missing in this family group, owing to the fact that during these periods Gaṇeśa was not generally regarded as the son of Śiva. – Char.: Śiva: Mu.: *abhaya-*, *varada-mudrā*; attr.: *mṛga*, *paraśu*, *ṭaṅka*; Skanda: att.: *sthānaka* (often *nāṭyasthāna*); attr.: *āmra*, *channavīra*, *karaṇḍamukuṭa*, *puṣpa* or *pustaka*, *śrīphala*; Pārvatī: Mu.: *kaṭaka-*, *varada-mudrā*; attr.: *padma*.
Lit.: B 464, 470; DiIP 140; KIM pl. 49 f. (here Skanda is missing); KrI pl. 52; MH pl. 5; R 2:131 a.pl. 22; SB passim; SIB pl. 32, 45; SSI 107; Th. 81 a.pl. 45; ZM 140.

somavāra (or *-vāsara*) "Monday". Another n.: *induvāra*.

sopāna "staircase", a term in architecture.
Lit.: ZA 233.

sopāśrayāsana (or *sopāśraya*; "having a support"; att.), n. of an *āsana*-posture which is sometimes said to be similar to or identical with *yogāsana*. Here the legs are crossed and the raised knees supported by a *yogapaṭṭa*. – Another n.: *paryaṅka bandhana*. Cp. *utkūṭikāsana*.
Lit.: B 271; MH 7; (Th. 36).

sotāpanna (Pāli; Skt *srotāpanna*) "one who has entered the river (leading to *nirvāṇa*), a convert" (Buddh.).
Lit.: BRI 48; IC 2:554.

sotthiya (M.Ind.), see *svastika*.
Lit.: KiJ 21.

sphaṭikaliṅga "*liṅga* of crystal, quartz" (attr.), n. of a form of *liṅga* which is usually worshipped at home.
Lit.: R 1:233.

sphoṭa "chain" (attr.), see *śṛṅkhalā*.
Lit.: BBh. 310.

śrāddha ("faithful"), n. of a kind of funeral rite or a ceremony in honour of dead relatives (manes). This ceremony is performed by the daily offering of water, and on stated occasions by the offering of *piṇḍa*s or balls of rice and meal to three paternal and three maternal forefathers.
Lit.: GH 339; Gt 596; IC 1:367, 583; KBh. 175; MW 1097; P 724; STP 1:56; WHW 2:427.

Śraddhā ("faith", personification), n. of the Śakti of Padmanābha or Dharma.
Lit.: Gt 604; R 1:233.

sragdāma(n) "filet or tie of a garland" (attr.).
Lit.: MEIA 214.

sraj "wreath of flowers, garland" (attr.), see *vanamālā*.
Lit.: MEIA 271.

śramaṇa (Pāli *samaṇa*) "labouring", n. of an ascetic, monk, esp. in Buddhism and Jainism.
Lit.: HIS 13; WHW 1:439.

śrāvaka(buddha) ("hearing, listening to"; Buddh.), properly n. of one who heard the *dharma* from the Buddha's (or a *buddha*'s) own lips, but who had to wait till the advent of another *buddha* for his emancipation. – *ś.* is also n. of a Jain disciple.
Lit.: BBh. 8; IC 2:638; WM 1097.

Śravaṇā ("the lame (cow)"), n. of a *nakṣatra*. Its influence is good. – Another n.: Śroṇā.
Lit.: BBh. 382; IC 2:730.

śrāvaṇa ("relating to the *nakṣatra* Śravaṇā"), n. of a month (July-August). Its god is Samudra.
Lit.: BBh. 382; IC 2:732.

Śrāvasti, n. of the ancient capital of the kingdom of Kosala (north of the Ganges).

Its most famous king, Prasenajit, was an adherent of the Buddha. Here the grove Jetavana was situated.
Lit.: IC 2:482; MW 1098; R. PISCHEL, Leben und Lehre des Buddha (2. Aufl. 1910), 10, 36.

Śraviṣṭhā(s) ("most famous"), n. of a *nakṣatra*. Another n.: Dhaniṣṭhās.
Lit.: IC 2:730.

śreṇi "guild" e.g. of artisans, such as *sthapatis*.
Lit.: SB 24.

Śreyāṅsa ("auspicious, fortunate"; Jain.), n. of the 11th *tīrthaṅkara*. Symbol: *ekaśṛṅga* or Garuḍa.
Lit.: GJ 274; KiSH 142.

sṛgāla (or *śṛgāla*, M.Ind. *sigāla*) "jackal".
1. Durgā, in the shape of a *s.*, aided Kṛṣṇa on the night of his birth by protecting him from the wrath of Kaṅsa.
Lit.: IC 1:536; W 373.
2. (Vāh.). Char. of Kālī. More than one *s.* are char. of Kṣamā. – Another n.: *śivā*.
Lit.: MD 1:284 s.v. *ōri*.
3. (Attr.). Carried in one hand, char. of Ratnaḍākinī.
Lit.: SB 24.

Śrī, Śrīdevī ("Prosperity, Welfare, Good Fortune, Wealth, Beauty"; personification).
1. (Hind.) Śrī was early combined with Lakṣmī, who is also named Śrī-Lakṣmī. Ś. is further found as a variety of Gaurī; see also Gajalakṣmī. – N.B. Śrī is also used (as a prefix) as a first member of word compounds (as a title with a meaning translatable as "reverend, blessed, excellent, etc."), forming names of eminent persons or of sacred objects (e.g. Śrī-Kṛṣṇa, Śrī-liṅga).
Lit.: B 368, 502; GoRI 1:96; Gt 605; MW 1098; R 1:374 a.pl. 109 ff.
2. (Buddh.) In Lamaism Śrī(devī) is a female *dharmapāla*, the protectress esp. of the Dalai Lamas. Siṅhavaktrā, Makaravaktrā and the four season-goddesses (see *ḍākinī*) are among others found in her retinue. She has a frightful appearance. Char.: colour: blue; Vāh.: *aśvatara* (white or blue); attr. esp.: *daṇḍa*, *kapāla*; further: *candra*, *gadā*, *kaṅkāla*, *khaḍga*, *khaṭvāṅga*, *mayūrapattra*, *nāgas*, *nakula*, *trinayana*, *triśiras* (sometimes), *vajra* (a half). – Another n.: Lha-mo.
Lit.: G 80 a.passim; HSIT 18 a.pl. 47.
3. (Vāh.; Buddh.) On Ś. (i.e. the Hindu goddess) Paramāśva treads.
Lit.: BBh. 186.
4. (Jain.) N. of a goddess.
Lit.: GJ 363.

śrībali "the blessed offering" (attr.), see *bali*.
Lit.: BECA 1: passim; SSI 3.

śrīcakra ("Wheel-of-Fortune" or "the blessed Wheel"), n. of a *yantra* "which represents the Universal Goddess" (Devī; DHP). It symbolizes the union of Śiva with Lalitā and is esp. sacred to Lalitā; see also Kāmakalā. – Another n.: *śrīyantra*.
Lit.: DHP 359; GoRI 2:48; R 1:330 a.pl. 97 f.; SSI 222.

Śrīdhara ("Bearer-of-Fortune"), n. of an aspect of Viṣṇu, see *caturviṅśatimūrti*. Śakti: Medhā.
Lit.: B 411; DHP 154; KiH 14 a.pl. 32; KiSH 39; R 1:229.

śrīkāmyapīṭha ("the very desirable seat"), n. of a kind of *pīṭha*.
Lit.: R 2:101.

Śrīkaṇṭha ("the (blessed) Neck; beautiful-throated"), epithet of Śiva referring to his darkish blue neck. Ś. is also n. of one among the group *ekādaśarudra*. Char.: attr.: *citravastra*, *citrayajñopavīta*, *dhanus*, *khaḍga*, *kheṭaka*, *śara*. – Ś. is further n. of one of the *vidyeśvaras*. Char.: Mu.: *abhaya-*, *varada-mudrā*; attr.: *ṭaṅka*, *triśūla*. This form is also said to be identical with Nīlakaṇṭha. – Cp. Viṣapraharamūrti.
Lit.: HIS 21; R 2:391, 397, 402; SSI 137.

śrīkarapīṭha ("the prosperity-causing-seat"), n. of a kind of *pīṭha*.
Lit.: R 101 a.pl. 12.

Śrīkṛṣṇa ("the blessed Kṛṣṇa"), epithet of Kṛṣṇa; also n. of an aspect of Viṣṇu, see *caturviṅśatimūrti*.
Lit.: R 1:230 a.pl. 71.

śrikvā, see *sṛkvan*.

Śrīlakṣmī ("the blessed Lakṣmī"), see Śrī.

ŚRĪṂ, a *bīja* designating the head; also symbolizing Śrī (= Lakṣmī, Mahālakṣmī), see *lakṣmībīja*.
Lit.: DHP 342; GJ 369; IC 1:567; WHW 2:104.

Śrīmadāryāvalokiteśvara ("the glorious, honourable Avalokiteśvara"; Buddh.), n. of a variety of Avalokiteśvara. Char.: att.: *samapādasthānaka*; Vāh.: *padma*; attr.: *padma*, *vajra*.
Lit.: BBh. 431 a.pl. 108(A).

Śrīnivāsa ("Abode of Śrī"), n. of a form of Viṣṇu. Char.: att.: *samapādasthānaka*; Mu.: *abhaya-*, *kaṭi-*, *varada-mudrā*; attr.: *cakra*, *kaṭibandha*, *śaṅkha*. Cp. Veṅkaṭeśvara.
Lit.: SB 30 a.passim (several ill.).

Śrīpalinātar ("the blessed Palinātar"), see Palinātar.

śrīpatula (Singh.) "sacred footprints (of the Buddha)", see *pāduka*.
Lit.: CBC 20 a.pl. 21:108.

śrīphala "the blessed Fruit, i.e. wood-apple" (attr.), n. of the fruit of the *bilva*-tree (thus B, MEIA, MW; according to GH it is = *nārikela* "the coconut"). Char. of: Durgā, (Gaja-)Lakṣmī, Kārttikeya, Mahālakṣmī, Śiva, Skanda in Somāskanda. – Another n.: *bilvaphala*.
Lit.: B 373; GH 65; MEIA 184, 264; MW 1099; SSI passim.

śrīpūjya ("venerable"; Jain.), n. of the head of an order.
Lit.: KiSB 94.

Śrīvasu ("excellent, good"; Buddh.), n. of a minor Mahāyāna goddess.
Lit.: KiSB 94.

Śrīvasumukhī ("excellent-faced"; Buddh.), n. of a minor Mahāyāna goddess, attending on Vasudhārā.
Lit.: BBh. 203; KiSB 94.

Śrīvasundharā ("earth"; Buddh.), n. of a minor Mahāyāna goddess attending on Vasudhārā.
Lit.: BBh. 203.

śrīvatsa ("the Beloved-of-Fortune"), n. of a *maṅgala* (see *aṣṭamaṅgala*; attr.). *ś.*, which originates in the Indus Valley culture, is a triangular mark or curl of hair on the breast of a deity. Esp. in the Gupta period this sign is marked on the breast of an icon. "It represents the source of the natural world, Basic-Nature" (DHP). On the breast of Viṣṇu it is sometimes said to represent Lakṣmī.
Char. of: Viṣṇu (in some forms), Kṛṣṇa, Lakṣmī, the Buddha, *tīrthaṅkaras*. It is also esp. a symbol of Śītalanātha.
Lit.: B 290 N. 2, 376 a.pl. 2:11 f.; D 305; DHP 157; GJ 383 a.pl. 23:10; HIS 17, 45; KiJ pl. 45; KiSH 154; R 1:25; Th. 46 a.pl. 5; WM 104.

Śrīvatsā (personification; Jain.), n. of a *śāsanadevatā* attending on the 11th *tīrthaṅkara*. Epithet: Mānavī.
Lit.: GJ 362.

śrīvatsa-svastika (properly a combination of the two *maṅgalas*: *śrīvatsa* and *svastika*; attr.; Jain.), n. of a particular form of the *śrīvatsa*.
Lit.: GJ 384.

Śrīvidyādevī ("goddess of excellent knowledge"), n. of a terrible goddess. Attr.: *dantas*, necklaces of *asthi*.
Lit.: SSI 212.

śrīvigraha ("individual form, body"), see *arcā*.
Lit.: HIS 19.

śrīyantra "the blessed *yantra*" (attr.), see *śrīcakra*.
Lit.: DHP 387; IC 1:581.

sṛkvan (*-ā*, also written *srikvā*) "corner of the mouth" (attr.), n. of the bold depressions made at the two corners of the lips in order to render the smile more effective.
Lit.: JMS 38 a.pl. 71.

śṛṅga "horn" (carried in one hand; attr.). Char. of: Trailokyamohana, Viśvarūpa, Yajñamūrti. – *ś.* is also n. of the four horns on the two heads of Agni.
Lit.: R 1:257.

śṛṅgī: as n. of an attr. carried in one hand, mentioned in MEIA (without an explanation). Char. of Viśvarūpa; probably identical with *śṛṅga*.
Lit.: MEIA 20.

sṛṇi "elephant-goad" (attr.), see *aṅkuśa*.
Lit.: MEIA 249.

śṛṅkhalā (also *-a*) "chain" (attr.). Carried in one hand., char. of: Niruktipratisamvit, Vetālī. Another n.: *sphoṭa*. See also *vajraśṛṅkhalā*.
Lit.: BBh. 439.

Śroṇā, as n. of a *nakṣatra*, see Śravaṇā.

Sroṅ-btsan-sgam-po ("the mighty and profound one"(?); Tib., pronounced: S(r)oṅ--tsan-gam-po; Buddh.), n. of a Tibetan king (in the 7th c. A.D.) whose two wives, one from China, the other from Nepal, are said to have introduced the Buddhist religion into Tibet (about A.D. 643). These wives are regarded as incarnations of Sitatārā and Śyāmatārā. S., himself, is also named Dharmarāja.
Lit.: G 5, 107; JT 585.

srotāpanna (also *ś-*), see *sotāpanna*.

Sṛṣṭikānta-Lokeśvara ("L., dear to the creation, nature"; Buddh.), n. of a variety of Avalokiteśvara. Char.: att.: *samapādasthānaka*; Vāh.: *padma*; Mu.: *varadamudrā*; attr.: *Amitābhabimba* on the head.
Lit.: BBh. 399 a.pl. 52(A).

sruk (also *sruc*, *śruc*, *śruca*) "a kind of large wooden ladle" (attr.). There are three forms of *s.*: *juhū*, *upabhṛt* and *dhruvā*. It is made of *khadira* or *pālāśa* wood and should be as long as an arm; the receptacle is either round or quadrangular and has a trunk-shaped pipe. As an attr. of an image it refers to the character of the deity as a sacrificer or to his or her generosity (thus Annapūrṇā). Char. of: Agni, Annapūrṇā, Brahmā, Sadharma, Sarasvatī, Satya, Tvaṣṭar, Yajñamūrti. – Cp. also *ācamanī*, *darvī*, *sruva*.
Lit.: B 302; MEIA 243; MKVI 2:491; MW 1275; R 1:12 a.pl. 3:17-19; RV 171; Th. 38; WM 109 a.fig. 69.

sruṅ-ta (Tib.) "horoscope" (attr.) which is printed on paper or silk. Cp. *horā*.
Lit.: G 11.

Śrutadevī ("goddess of learning").
1. (Hind.) Epithet of Sarasvatī.
2. (Jain.) N. of a *vidyādevī*.
Lit.: B 561; MW 1101.

Śrutakevalin (-ī; "wholly devoted to learning, tradition"; Jain.), n. of a kind of patriarch; cp. *kevalin*.
Lit.: GJ 33, 304.

śrutapañcamī ("the fifth day of learning"; Jain.), n. of a festival on the 5th day of the light half of the month *jyeṣṭha* (May-June).
Lit.: GJ 434.

śrutarṣi ("*riṣi* by tradition"), n. of one among a group of *riṣi*s "who did not receive the *śruti* ('revelation') direct, but obtained it at second-hand from the Vedic *riṣi*s" (D). Their leader was Suśruta.
Lit.: D 305; R 2:566.

sruva (also *śruva*) "a small sacrificial wooden ladle" (attr.) "used for pouring clarified melted butter into the large ladle or *sruk*" (MW; or "into the *juhū*", ZA; or "into the sacrificial fire", B). In later times the *s.* is usually made of bronze. With this kind of ladle water is offered to a deity. As an attr. it refers to the character of the deity as a sacrificer. Char. of: Agni, Agnijāta-Subrahmaṇya, Anala, Brahmā, Brahmāṇī, Bhadra-Kālī, Sarasvatī, Tulajā-Bhavānī, Yajñamūrti. – Cp. *ācamanī*, *darvī*, *juhū*, *sruk*.
Lit.: B 302; GH 345; KiH pl. 137:8-10; MEIA 243; MG pl. facing p. 239; MKVI 2:491; MW 1274; RV 171; WM 108 a.fig. 68; ZA 39 with pl. Blc.

stambha "pillar", a term in architecture. The *s.* may be shaped in different forms, after which they are named, and symbols of different kinds (e.g. the Buddhist *dharmacakra*) may be put on them. – Other n.: *lāṭh*, *sthānu*; see also *vedikā*.
Lit.: BECA 1:263; DKI 11; ZA 233, 253, 324.

Stambhinī ("supporting"), n. of a female *dvārapālaka* of Gaurī.
Lit.: R 1:362.

stana "female breast" (attr.). A single *s.* is char. of Ardhanārīśvara.

stanabandha "breast-band" (attr.), see *kucabandha*.

stanahāra "breast-necklet" (attr.), n. of a necklet, which touches the breasts.
Lit.: BECA 1:264.

stanitakumāra ("thundering-prince"; Jain.), n. of a kind of *bhavanavāsī*.
Lit.: GJ 236.

sthalavṛkṣa ("place-tree"), n. of a tree sacred to a temple. It is not uncommon in Śaivite temples (e.g. also Kandaswami, i.e. Skanda, temple) in South India especially.
Lit.: BECA 1:17; R 1:15.

sthālī "a fairly large dish or vessel" (attr.). The *s.* is meant for fruits and sweetmeats, and is used at the offering of such gifts.
Lit.: KiH pl. 140:6.

sthalīdevatā "deity of the soil, place, local deity".
Lit.: D 305.

sthānaka(mūrti) (also short *sthāna*; att.), n. of a representation of a standing deity. The standing posture may be differentiated, cp. *samapādasthānaka*, *ardhasamapādasthānaka*, but the term *s.* is often used without further classification, esp. respecting Viṣṇu. – Cp. also *bhaṅga* and see the index of att.
Lit.: B 264; R 1:78 a.pl. 21; WM 89.

sthānakavāsin (-ī "living in community houses"; Jain.), n. of a Jain sect the members of which are opposed to the worship of icons.
Lit.: GJ 70.

sthaṇḍila "piece of open ground" squared and levelled for large sacrifices, "lit de grains" (ACA).
Lit.: ACA 69, 84; MW 1261; WHW 1:30.

sthāṇu "pillar", see *stambha*.
Lit.: R 2:69.

Sthāṇu ("the Immutable, Pillar"), epithet of Śiva.
Lit.: DHP 191.

sthāpana "fixing", the erecting of an image. This forms part of the *pūjā*. Cp. *pratiṣṭhā*.
Lit.: ACA 9; DiIP 90; MW 1263.

sthāpanamudrā "staying handpose" (Mu.), n. of a gesture.
Lit.: DiIP 105.

sthapati "artisan, architect, artist, metal-sculptor, maker of icons".
Lit.: R 2:309; SB 21 a.passim; SIB 70.

sthāpatya "architecture".
Lit.: WHW 1:56.

Sthauṇa-Narasiṁha ("the Pillar-N."), n. of a certain form of Viṣṇu in his Narasiṁhāvatāra in which the man-lion is represented breaking forth from a pillar. However, S. also refers to an *āsana*-representation of Narasiṁha, and sometimes N. is also represented tearing Hiraṇyakaśipu to pieces. He is usually four-armed. Attr.: *cakra*, *śaṅkha* (*gadā*, *padma*).
Lit.: R 1:151 a.pl. 44-47.

sthāvaraliṅga "stationary *liṅga*", see *acalaliṅga*.
Lit.: R 2:80.

sthavira (Pāli *thera*) "old, ancient" (Buddh.), n. of a saint, "an elder", a term in the main corresponding to *arhat*.
Lit.: G 38; IC 2:557; MW 1265.

Sthiracakra ("whose wheel is firm, fixed"; Buddh.), n. of a variety of Mañjuśrī who is accompanied by Prajñā. Char.: Mu.: *varadamudrā*; attr.: *bodhisattvābharaṇa*, *khaḍga*.
Lit.: BBh. 122 a.pl. 93; KiSB 55.

sthiraliṅga "fixed *liṅga*", see *acalaliṅga*.
Lit.: R 2:80.

sthirasukha "motionless comfortable posture" (att.), n. of an *āsana*-posture(?), a *yoga*-att., mentioned, but not described.
Lit.: B 271; WHW 1:73.

STRAUṀ, a *bījamantra* which is "the giver of lust".
Lit.: DHP 343.

STRĪṀ, a *bījamantra* which "delivers from difficulties".
Lit.: DHP 343.

strīpūjā "woman-worship", n. of a rite in the *śākta* cult which involves the worship of the nude female and the *yoni*.
Lit.: WHW 2:431.

strīratna "wife-treasure", symbolizing a "king's female entourage, which reflected

his wealth and power", is a *lakṣaṇa* of a *cakravartin*, see *saptaratna*.
Lit.: WHW 1:553.

stūpa ("crest, top, summit"; attr. etc.; Buddh., Jain.). This was originally a "top-knot" of hair, designating the upper part of the head, but subsequently became used as an architectural term, indicating a monument of a pyramidal or dome-shaped form over the sacred relics of the Buddha (or other saints). The *s.* is thus a sepulchral monument and is very frequent in Buddhist temples. By a *s.* "deutet man das irdische Ende, das Parinirvāṇa des Buddha an". A *s.* made in a miniature form, is also used as a votive gift, which may further serve as a reliquary (cp. *stūpākāramañjūṣā*), or may be carried in the hands of an image (in sculptures) as an attr., cp. *caitya*; it is then char. of: Abheda, Atīśa, Cintāmaṇi-Lokeśvara, Gomedha, Kubera, Mahāpratisarā, Maitreya, Nāgārjuna, Sarvāhna, Virūpākṣa. – Cp. also *aṭṭaka, dāgaba, pagoda, stūpika.*
Lit.: BBh. 32; BRI 66, 111; CHIIA passim; DKI 13; FBKI 17; G 8 with ill. facing p. 10; GJ 396; HAHI 46; HIS 15 a.pl. 8; HSIT pl. 4f.; IC 2:317; JMS pl. 12; KiJ 19 a.pl. 52-55; KiSB 16; KiSH 147; MKVI 2:483; RN passim; SB 22 a.fig. 13; SeKB 99; SM 166; Th. pl. 22; WHW 2:437; ZA 231 a.passim.

stūpākāramañjūṣā "reliquary formed as a *stūpa*" (attr.), see sub *stūpa*.

stūpi "pinnacle", in architecture n. of the finial on a temple-building, a pot-shaped crowning ornament over the *vimāna* or the *gopura*.
Lit.: BECA 1:264, 271; ZA 270.

stūpika "miniature *stūpa*, a small dome-like structure resembling a *stūpa*", employed as a crowning detail on Dravidian temples. It is also another n. of a votive *stūpa*.
Lit.: RAAI 166, 274; SeKB 108 (ill.), 122.

Subba(rāya), see Subrahmaṇya.

Śubhā ("splendid, beautiful"; Buddh.), n. of a minor Mahāyāna goddess attending on Buddhakapāla.
Lit.: BBh. 160.

Subhadrā ("very splendid").
1. (Hind.) N. of the daughter of Vasudeva, the sister of Kṛṣṇa and wife of Arjuna. S. is represented standing beside Kṛṣṇa (Viṣṇu) in his form as Jagannātha.
Lit.: D 305; Gt 608; MG 151; R 1:376.
2. (Buddh.) N. of a *yakṣiṇī*.
Lit.: KiSB 74.

Subhagā ("very fortunate"), n. of a minor Mahāyāna goddess attending on Buddhakapāla.
Lit.: BBh. 160.

Śubhamekhalā ("having a splendid girdle"; Buddh.), n. of a minor Mahāyāna goddess attending on Buddhakapāla.
Lit.: BBh. 160.

Subhūti ("well-being, welfare"; Buddh.), n. of a saint.
Lit.: GBM 80.

Subrahmaṇya (or Subrahmiṇya; in Dravidian languages sometimes also contracted to 'Subba, Subbarāya' (SSI); "very kind, dear to Brāhmans, very pious"), esp. in South India epithet (and a form) of Skanda. – Cp. Murukan̲.
Lit.: D 306; DHP 299; GH 116; GoRI 2:151; Gt Suppl. 129; JDI 44; KiH 18 a.pl. 51; R 2:415; SB passim; SSI 177; Th. 97 pl. 60.

sūci (or *-ī*) "needle" (attr.). Char. of: Mārī, Mārīcī (in different forms), Vadālī, Varālī, Vartālī. – In the terminology of ornament *s.* signifies the sockets for horizontal interlinking beams.
Lit.: G 74; HIS 51 a.pl. 2; ZA 233.

sūci(hasta)mudrā (or *sūcī-*).
1. (Mu.) "Needle-handpose", n. of a pointing, indicating gesture. It is described in different ways, either: a closed hand with the index-finger pointing downwards; or: the same, but the index-finger pointing upwards (sometimes also the little finger is here stretched upwards); or: all the fingers are stretched with the tips joining at the end, so as to resemble a needle. – *s.* is also mentioned as a variety of the *muṣṭimudrā* (difference: "the forefinger is raised, the other fingers folded in,

encircling the thumb; it denotes a circle, universe, flame, elephant tusks, one hundred, sin, city, astonishment, umbrella" WHW). – Char. of: Jñānasambandha, Kālārimūrti, Kāmāntakamūrti, *lalita*, Padmanarteśvara. – Cp. *kartarīmudrā*.
Lit.: B 259; BBh. 439; H 7 a.pl. 6:53a; KiSB 59; MH 7; SB 200; WHW 2:87; WM 100 a.fig. 21.
2. (Attr.) "Holding a sewing needle in the hand".
Lit.: B 247.

Sūcīmukha ("needle-mouth", probably signifying a protruding, pouting mouth; Buddh.), n. of the none-too-clearly described being that catches the jet of nectar from the hand of Khasarpaṇa-Lokeśvara.
Lit.: KiSB 57.

Sudarśana(cakra) ("of good appearances" or "the good Eye"; attr.), n. of the *cakra* of Viṣṇu or Kṛṣṇa or Aja. It is esp. a n. of the *cakra* as an independent cult emblem, and in South India there are many forms of S., e.g. with a *ṣaṭkoṇa* or a *cakrapuruṣa* (with many hands and weapons, named Cakra-Perumāḷ) or other figures in its centre. – Other n.: Cakrattāḻvār, Vajranābha.
Lit.: B 300; HAHI 12 a.pl. 7B; HIS 74; HSIT 12 a.pl. 27; R 1:287 a.pl. 85:2-85:A; SB 322 a.fig. 249; SSI 66.

Sudattā ("well given, good daughter"; Buddh.), n. of a *yakṣiṇī*.
Lit.: KiSB 74.

Śuddha-Gaṇapati ("the cleansed G.", i.e. "G. as worshipped by those who have cleansed their mouths (from remnants of food)"), n. of a form of Gaṇeśa. – Cp the contrast Ucchiṣṭa-Gaṇapati.
Lit.: MW 1082.

śuddhapakṣa "the light half of a month", see *śuklapakṣa*.
Lit.: IC 2:722.

Śuddhodana ("having pure rice-food"; Buddh.), n. of the father of the Buddha. He was the king of Kapilavastu, of the Śākya tribe. Wife: Māyādevī.
Lit.: KiSB 8; MW 1082.

Sudeva ("the good god" or "having a good god"), n. of an attendant of Skanda.
Lit.: R 2:449.

Sudhāmālinī (lit. "nectar-garlanded"), epithet of Vāruṇī.
Lit.: SSI 220.

Sudhana(ka)kumāra ("the very rich prince"; Buddh.), n. of a minor Mahāyāna god, a companion of Khasarpaṇa.
Lit.: BBh. 128; KiSB 98.

Sudharmā (or -man; "practising justice"; Jain.), n. of a pupil of Mahāvīra.
Lit.: GJ 32.

śudi (or *sudi*, *suti*), abbreviated word-forms from *śukla-dina* "a day of *śuklapakṣa*".
Lit.: IC 2:722; MW 1081.

śūdra "a man of the lowest of the original castes", n. of the fourth caste. The duty of the members of this caste was to serve the three other higher castes. – Cp. *varṇa*.
Lit.: Gt 610; IC 1:606; MKVI 2:388; MW 1085; WHW 2:442.

Sudurjaya ("very difficult to conquer"; Buddh.), n. of a *bhūmi*. Char.: colour: yellow; attr.: *marakatamaṇi*, *vajra*.
Lit.: BBh. 335.

Sugatisandarśana(-Lokeśvara) ("L., manifestation of happiness"; Buddh.), n. of a variety of Avalokiteśvara. Char.: colour: white; Vāh.: *padma*; Mu.: *abhaya-*, *varada-mudrā*; attr.: *akṣamālā*, *kamaṇḍalu*, *padma* (*nīlotpala*), *tridaṇḍa*, *triśūla*.
Lit.: BBh. 141 a.pl. 117, p. 396 a.pl. 16(A); KiSB 60.

Sugrīva ("beautiful, strong neck"), n. of a god in the shape of a monkey. He was the son of the sun-god, and the king of the monkey-army which (with Hanumān as its chief) aided Rāma.
Lit.: D 306; Gt 610; IIM 108; MW 1223; W 326; ZA pl. 497d.

Sujātā ("well-born"; Buddh.), epithet of Indrāṇī.
Lit: IC 1:520.

śuka "parrot".
1. (Vāh.) A *ś.* or a *ratha* drawn by *śuka*s is char. of Agni and Kāma; a *ś.* is also char. of Sarasvatī.
2. (Attr.) A *ś.* carried on the shoulder,

in one hand, perching on the back of the palm, or sitting beside the image on the *pīṭha* is char. of: Durgā, Dīpalakṣmī, Māriyammaṉ, Rājamātaṅgī and other goddesses. – Another n.: *kiḷi*. See also *sārikā*.
Lit.: R 1:11; SSI pl. IV:19; Th. 42.

śukanāsa "parrot's nose", a term in architecture denoting a part of the *śikhara* tower.
Lit.: DKI 43.

sūkara "boar, pig, swine" (Vāh.). In Buddhism *s.* symbolizes the passion of "infatuation". Char. of: Aśokakāntā, Gaurī. A *ratha* drawn by 7 *s.*, or a *padma* supported by *sūkaras*, is char. of Mārīcī (in different forms). Cp. *varāha*.
Lit.: GBM 103; WHW 1:48.

Sūkarāsyā (also Ś-; "sow-faced"; Buddh.), n. of a minor goddess.
Lit.: BBh. 320.

śukatuṇḍa(mudrā) "parrot-beak" (Mu.), n. of a variety of the *patākāmudrā* with the difference: forefinger and ring-finger are bent. It denotes shooting an arrow, dismissal, mystery, ferocity.
Lit.: WHW 2:86.

sukhāsana "comfortable sitting posture" (att.), n. of an *āsana*-posture which is usually identified with the *lalitāsana*. But, according to B, "one leg, generally the left one, rests flat on the seat while the right knee is raised upwards from it and the right arm is stretched out on the raised knee" (this form of att. is very similar to the *rājalīlāsana*; cp. also MEIA). According to BBh., however, *s.* is not used in the technical sense, but may describe any easy att. of sitting and may therefore be either = *paryaṅkāsana*, or = *lalitāsana*, or = *ardhaparyaṅkāsana*.
Lit.: B 271 a.pl. 34:1; BBh. 433; MEIA 220; SB passim; WHW 1:76; WM 90 a.fig. 4 (= *rājalīlāsana*).

Sukhāsana(mūrti) ("representation in a comfortable sitting posture"), n. of a form of Śiva (without Śakti) in a sitting att. Char.: Vāh.: *bhadrapīṭha*; Mu.: *abhaya-*, *kaṭaka-*, *varada-mudrā*; attr.: *ajina* (tiger-skin), *kaṅkanas*, *kuṇḍalas*, *mṛga*, *nāga*, *paraśu*, *yajñopavīta*. – Regarding a form of Śiva and Pārvatī (seated), also named S., see Umāsahita 2.
Lit.: B 464; R 2:129; SSI 110; Th.pl. 39.

Sukhāvatī ("full of joy or pleasure"; Buddh.), n. of the paradise of the westerly direction, over which Amitābha presides.
Lit.: KiSB 46; SeKB passim.

Sukhāvatī-Lokeśvara ("L. of Sukhāvatī"; Buddh.), n. of a variety of Avalokiteśvara. Char.: colour: white; att.: *lalitāsana*; Mu.: *dharmacakra-*, *varada-mudrā*; attr.: *akṣamālā*, *dhanus*, *kamaṇḍalu*, *padma*, *pustaka*, *triśiras*.
Lit.: BBh. 142 a.pl. 119; KiDG 53 a.pl. 25; KiSB 61.

Sukhendra ("Indra of joy"; Buddh.), see Mukhendra.
Lit.: BBh. 380.

śukla "bright, white", the colour of white; cp. also *sita*, *śveta*.

śuklādi "beginning with the light half of the month (*śuklapakṣa*)", another n. of *amānta*, see this word sub *candramāsa*.

Śukla-Kurukullā ("the white K."; Buddh.), n. of a form of Kurukullā. Char.: colour: white; att.: *padmāsana*; Vāh.: *sattva*; attr.: *akṣamālā*, *Amitābhabimba* on the crown, *nīlotpala*.
Lit.: BBh. 148; KiDG 64; KiSB 96.

śuklapāda "white light-rays" (? attr., carried in one hand). Char. of Kiraṇākṣa.
Lit.: R 2:391.

śuklapakṣa "the light half of a month, the 15 lunar days (*tithi*) of the moon's increase". – Another n.: *śuddhapakṣa*; see also *candramāsa* and the abbreviated word-form *śudi* (*sudi*, *suti*).
Lit.: IC 2:722; MW 1080.

Śukla-Prajñāpāramitā ("the white P."; Buddh.), see Sita-Prajñāpāramitā.
Lit.: BBh. 198; KiSB 91.

Śukla-Tārā ("the white T."; Buddh.), n. of a Mahāyāna goddess who, according to some statements, is an emanation of all

dhyānibuddhas. She may, however, be identical with the "white Tārā", see Tārā; see further Sitatārā. Cp. also Ṣaḍbhuja-Sitatārā.
Lit.: G 16, 34; KiSB 99, 103.

Śukra ("bright, clear").
1. (Hind.) N. of the personification of the planet Venus. Ś. was the teacher and priest of the demons (*daitya*). He is sometimes represented as a woman, probably because once, due to a trick of the demons, he was made to swallow his disciple Kaca (the son of Bṛhaspati) and thus had him in his stomach. He was, however, able to restore Kaca to life and, in this way, became the "mother" of Kaca. This story may explain why Ś. is made the counterpart of the "female" planet Venus (Babylonian Ištar). – Char.: colour: white; Vāh.: a golden *ratha* drawn by 8 earth-born *aśvas* or a silvery *ratha* drawn by 10 *aśvas*, or an *uṣṭra*, *aśva*, *ākhu*; Mu.: *abhaya-*, *varada-mudrā*; attr.: *akṣamālā*, *daṇḍa*, *dhvaja*, *kamaṇḍalu*, *koṣa*, *nidhi*, *pustaka*. – Epithets: Bhārgava, Uśanas.
Lit.: ChIMS 153; D 138, 307; DHP 325; Gt 613; IC 1:523; KiH 7; KiK 141; KiSH 62, 88; R 1:320 a.pl. 96; SSI 239; Th. 114; WHW 2:448.
2. (Buddh.) The above-mentioned planet-god. Char.: colour: white; Vāh.: *padma*; attr.: *akṣamālā*, *kamaṇḍalu*.
Lit.: BBh. 377.

śukravāra (or *-vāsara*) "Friday"

Sūkṣma ("small, atomic"), n. of one of the *vidyeśvaras*. Char.: colour: white or blue; Mu.: *abhaya-*, *varada-mudrā*; attr.: *ṭaṅka*, *triśūla*.
Lit.: R 2:397, 401.

śūla(ka) "spear" (attr.). This term is sometimes used for *śakti* 2, and more often, esp. in B and R, for *triśūla* (see these terms). – In Tantrism a *ś*. is a symbol of the erect penis.
Lit.: B 301, 466 a.passim; JDI 20; R 1:7 a.pl. 3:1-2; WHW 1:595.

Śūladhara, Śūlapāṇi (-in, -ī), Śūlin (-ī, -i), epithets of Śiva carrying a *triśūla*.
Lit.: DHP 217; R 2:233.

śūlagava "impaled ox, ox fit for a spit", n. of an offering performed at the beginning of autumn.
Lit.: IC 1:362; MW 1086; WHW 1:50.

Śūlinī ("having a *triśūla*"), n. of a terrible goddess. Char. Vāh.: *siṅha*; attr.: *triśūla*.
Lit.: SSI 213.

Sumālinī ("well-garlanded"; Buddh.), n. of a minor Mahāyāna goddess attending on Buddhakapāla.
Lit.: BBh. 160.

Sumati ("good mind, very wise"; Jain.), n. of the 5th *tīrthaṅkara*. Symbol: *krauñca*.
Lit.: GJ 272; KiSH 142.

Sumatī (-i; "very wise"; Buddh.), n. of a *dhāriṇī*. Char.: colour: yellow; attr.: *kaṇiśa*, *viśvavajra*.
Lit.: BBh. 220, 338.

Sumbhā ("the [goddess] of *sumbha*?"; cp. that *sumbha* or *śumbha* is found as the n. of a people; Buddh.), n. of a female *dikpāla* of the direction nadir. Char.: colour: blue; Mu.: *tarjanīmudrā*; attr.: *nāgapāśa*.
Lit.: BBh. 299.

Sumbharāja ("the king of *sumbha*?"; cp. Sumbhā; Buddh.), n. of a *dikpāla* of the direction nadir. Char.: colour: blue; attr.: *cintāmaṇi*, *khaḍga*, *padma*, *triśiras*, *vajra*. – Another n.: Vajrapātāla.
Lit.: BBh. 256.

Sumeru (probably = Meru; Buddh.), n. of "a mythical mountain, whence the Bodhicitta loses itself in *śūnya*" (BBh.).
Lit.: BBh. 434; HuGT 84.

Sumitra ("good friend" or "having good friends"), n. of an attendant of Skanda.
Lit.: R 2:450.

Sumukha ("good-faced"), n. of an attendant of Skanda.
Lit.: R 2:449.

Sundara(mūrti) (Tamilized Cuntarar; "[representation of] the Charming One").
1. N. of a prosperous, blessed aspect of Śiva.
Lit.: ZM 205.
2. Sundara(mūrti)-Nāyaṉār (or -Svāmi), n. of a *śaivabhakta* in South India who lived in the 8th or 9th c. A.D. Wives: Caṅkili

(nācciyār), Paravai(nācciyār). Mu.: *añjalimudrā*.

Lit.: CBC 11 a.figs. 15-17; DiIP 142; GJ 62; Gt Suppl. 130; JDI 55; R 2:480 a.pl. 137; RAAI pl. 126, 145B; SSR pl. facing p. 176; SB 310 a.fig. 222 a.passim.

Sundarā and Sundarī ("charming"; Buddh.), n. of minor Mahāyāna goddesses attending on Buddhakapāla.

Lit.: BBh. 160.

Śuṅga (orig. n. of an Indian fig-tree), n. of a dynasty (B.C. 187-75) and of an epoch of arts (2nd c. B.C.).

Lit.: Gz 47; RAAI 51; WHW 2:450.

śūnya ("void, zero") and *śūnyatā* ("emptiness, zero-ness") signify a state of mind, neither existence nor non-existence. In Hinduism *ś.* is symbolized by a *bindu*, in Buddhism by a *vajra*. See also *saṅkhyā*.

Lit.: BBh. 10, 439; SeKB 31; WHW 2:103, 452.

supārī (Hi.) "betel-nut" (attr.), see *tāmbūla*.

Suparikīrtitanāmaśrī ("the Lord bearing the very celebrated name"; Buddh.), n. of a medicine-*buddha* (see Bhaiṣajyaguru) in Lamaism. Char.: colour: yellow; Mu.: *abhaya-*, *varada-mudrā*.

Lit.: G 56.

Suparṇa ("having beautiful leaves or wings"), n. of a large mythical bird, a vulture or an eagle; sometimes an epithet of Garuḍa (cp. Garutmān); also epithet of Sūrya or Candra (in that case interpreted as "having beautiful rays").

Lit.: MKVI 2:455; MW 1227.

suparṇakumāra "eagle-prince" (Jain.), n. of a kind of *bhavanavāsī*.

Lit.: GJ 236.

Supārśva(nātha) ("having beautiful sides"; Jain.), n. of the 7th *tīrthaṅkara*. Symbol: *svastika*.

Lit.: GJ 273 a.pl. 25:7; KiJ 11 a.pl. 28:7; KiSH 142.

Supratīka ("handsome, lovely"), n. of the *diggaja* which accompanies Īśāna (Soma) as a *dikpāla*.

Lit.: D 180.

sura, n. of a kind of gods. The word is probably, in consequence of a wrong derivation, abstracted from *asura* (interpreted as *a-sura* "not-god", hence *sura* "god"), but it was earlier supposed to be connected with *svar* "sun" and conceived as n. of a kind of sun-genii. For *s.* as a symbolic n. of the number "33", see *saṅkhyā*.

Lit.: D 309; DHP 139, 143; MW 1234.

Surā ("wine"; personification), n. of a terrible unmarried goddess. Attr.: *trinayana*.

Lit.: SSI 212.

Surabhi (or -ī; "well-flavoured, juicy"), n. of a mythical, wealth-giving cow, originally the daughter of Dakṣa, one of the wives of Kāśyapa and the progenitor of cattle. She was, according to some myths, produced at the churning of the ocean of milk (see Kūrmāvatāra). In later times she is represented as a beautiful woman with a cow-face. Attr.: *kamaṇḍalu*, *tṛṇa*.

Lit.: D 309; DHP 137, 167, 316; R 1:370.

surabhimudrā "cow-gesture" (Mu.; cp. *dhenumudrā*), n. of a handpose "which means arranging the ten fingers so as to form four tips symbolizing the four teats of the cow (Surabhi)".

Lit.: DiIP 70.

Surakṣiṇī ("well guarding or guarded"; Buddh.), n. of a Mahāyāna goddess attending on Buddhakapāla.

Lit.: BBh. 160.

Surakumāra ("the divine prince"; Jain.), see Kumāra.

Lit.: GJ 362.

Suraṅgama ("bright-coloured"; Buddh.), n. of a *bodhisattva*. Char.: colour: white; attr.: *khaḍga*.

Lit.: BBh. 83, 98 a.pl. 73.

Surapriyā ("fond of wine"), n. of a goddess. Attr.: *caṣaka*, *daṇḍa*.

Lit.: SSI 212.

Sureśvara ("lord of the gods"), n. of one among the group *ekādaśarudra*. Char.: Mu.: *tarjanīmudrā*; attr.: *aṅkuśa*, *cakra*, *ḍamaru*, *dhanus*, *ghaṇṭā*, *khaṭvāṅga*, *mudgara*, *padma*, *paraśu*, *pātra*, *paṭṭiśa*, *śara*, *triśūla*.

Lit.: R 2:390.

Śūrpakarṇa (or S-; "having ears like winnowing-fans"), epithet of Gaṇeśa.
Lit.: MW 1086; R 1:60.

sūrsan (*sursanna*, < Arab. *šuhūrsana* "year of months"), n. of a Mahratta era, beginning in A.D. 599.
Lit.: IC 2:737.

Sūrya ("sun").
1. (Hind.) The Sun god. Worship of S. in an anthropomorphic form is perhaps introduced into India from Iran. S. is an Āditya, later regarded as the chief of the Ādityas and, above all, as the representation of the sun (as a planet-god, however, mostly named Ravi); he is sometimes also mentioned as a *dikpāla*. S. is in addition, esp. in Koṇārak (Orissa), identified with Viṣṇu. S. was the son of Dyaus or of Kāśyapa and Aditi, and he is thought of as a *kṣatriya* (sometimes a *brāhmaṇa*). Wives: Sañjñā (children: Yama, Revanta, Yamunā, Manu and others) and Chāyā (Prabhā); Uṣā, Lakṣmī, Rājñī and Svarṇā are sometimes also named as wives. – Char.: Vāh.: *padma* or a 1-wheeled (or 7-wheeled) *ratha* drawn by 7 (or 10 or other numbers) red-brown *aśva*s (the horses are usually yoked 3 and 3, with 1 in the middle), or an *aśva* named Tārkṣya; att.: *sthānaka* (less often: *āsana*); attr.: *ahyaṅga*, *cakra*, *dhvaja* (with a lion), *gadā*, *kavaca*, *kheṭaka*, 2 *padma*s, *śaṅkha*, *trinayana* (sometimes), *triśūla*, *udīcyaveṣa*. – As an Āditya he has the particular attr.: *akṣamālā*, *kamaṇḍalu*, 2 *padma*s. – The mystical diagram *sūryayantra* is connected with the worship of S. For *sūrya* as a symbolic n. of the number "12", see *saṅkhyā*. – Epithets and varieties: Āditya, Bhānu, Bhāskara, Mārtāṇḍa, Ravi, Virocana, Vivasvān. Cp. also Savitar.
Lit.: B 428 a.pl. 30:2-3; D 310; DHP 92 a.pl. 7; GBB 129; GH 48 a.pl. 5; GoRI 1:94, 230, 2:63; Gt 619; HIS 24; HAA pl. 95; IC 1:489; JMS 35; KIH 6 a.pl. 9-10; KiK 18, 130; KiSH 59; KrA pl. 74; KrI 112 a.pl. 24; MEIA 73, 233; MG 35; MKVI 2:465; MSHP pl. 47; NLEM 325; R 1:299 a.pl. 86-94; SS pl. 30:136; SB 305 a.fig. 211; SIB pl. 39; SSI 235; Th. pl. 77; W 25; WHW 2:457; WM 172; ZA 371.
2. (Buddh.) The planet-god is, as an Āditya, also found in Buddhism. Char.: colour: red; Vāh.: *ratha* drawn by 7 *aśva*s; attr.: in both hands: *sūrya(maṇḍala)* on *padma*.
Lit.: BBh. 367; CTLP pl. 178.
3. *sūrya(maṇḍala)* "sun disk" (attr.). It is often held on a *padma*. Char. of: Ākāśagarbha, Jālinīprabha, Mārīcī (in different forms), Prabhākarī, Rāhu, Ṛddhivaśitā, Sūrya, Sūryahastā, Tejoṣṇīṣa. – Cp. *sūryaprabhā(maṇḍala)*.
Lit.: BBh. 90, 439; G 18 (ill.).

Sūrya-Buddha: MSHP denotes by this term a particular seven-headed idol. Char.: att.: *padmāsana*; Mu.: *dhyānamudrā*. This icon is probably a syncretistic representation of Sūrya and the Buddha. Cp. Sūrya-Lokeśvara.
Lit.: MSHP 173 a.pl. 42.

Sūryadharā ("holding the sun") or Sūryahastā ("having the sun in the hand"; Buddh.), n. of a light-goddess. Char.: colour: white; attr.: *sūrya(maṇḍala)*.
Lit.: BBh. 318.

sūryakānta ("sun-beloved"; attr.), n. of the sun-stone, a kind of crystal which is adored as the lithomorphic form of Sūrya. Cp. *pañcāyatana*.
Lit.: D 311; GH 330; IC 1:539; MW 1243; WHW 1:385.

Sūrya-Lokeśvara, n. of a syncretistic representation of Sūrya and Avalokiteśvara. Attr.: *Ādibuddha-* or *Amitābha-bimba* on the head, *padma*, *pāśa*. Cp. Sūrya-Buddha.
Lit.: B 548 a.pl. 48:3.

sūryamaṇḍala, see Sūrya 3.

Sūrya-Nārāyaṇa, n. of a syncretistic representation of Sūrya and Śiva (= Nārāyaṇa). Char.: Mu.: *varadamudrā*; attr.: 2 *padma*s (Sūrya symbols), *mṛgāṅka* (*mṛga*) and *triśūla* (Śiva symbols). Note, however, that S. may also be a representation of Sūrya and Viṣṇu.
Lit.: B 548; SB 305.

Sūryaprabha ("light of the sun"; Buddh.), see *Jālinīprabha*. It is also n. of a deity who accompanies Arapacana. Another n.: Jālinīkumāra.
Lit.: BBh. 90, 120.

sūryaprabhā(maṇḍala) "halo of the sun" (attr.). Char. of: Mahāmantrānusāriṇī, Mahāśītavatī. – Cp. *sūrya(maṇḍala)*.
Lit.: BBh. 304.

sūryapūjā "worship of the sun".
Lit.: DiIP 111.

sūryāsana "sun(-disk) as a seat" (Vāh.; Buddh.). Char. of several Buddhist deities who sit on the *s.*, e.g. Dhvajāgrakeyūra.
Lit.: BBh. 201.

sūryavaṅśa "the solar race", n. of a royal race or dynasty which is descended from Sūrya or from his grand-son Ikṣvāku. Rāma and the Buddha, for instance, belonged to this race.
Lit.: D 310 (with a table); IC 1:533; KiSB 8; MW 1243.

sūryayantra, n. of a *yantra* connected with the worship of Sūrya.
Lit.: SSI 239.

suṣira "hollow", n. of a mode of casting hollow bronze images (see *madhūcchiṣṭavidhāna*). This method is mostly used for large icons. The process is as follows: a raw clay model is covered with wax in which the figure is elaborately modelled out. This figure is then covered with clay, and when a "lost-wax-mode"-casting has been made the resulting figure is hollow.
Lit.: SIB 3.

Suśruta ("very famous"), n. of the leader of a certain group of *riṣi*s, the *śrutarṣi*s. S. was the author of a system of medicine, in the 4th c. A.D.
Lit.: R 2:566.

sūta "charioteer". The profession e.g. of Aruṇa and Mātali. In the battle described in the great epic Mahābhārata, Kṛṣṇa was the *s.* of Arjuna. *s.* is also a term for bards and chroniclers.
Lit.: Gt 622; MW 1241; WHW 1:125.

Sutārakā ("having beautiful stars"; Jain.), n. of a *śāsanadevatā* attending on the 9th *tīrthaṅkara*.
Lit.: GJ 362; MW 1224.

suti, see *śudi*.

sūtra(ka) "thread".
1. (Attr.) As a symbol (used together with *sūci*)) char. of Mārī, Mārīcī. It is also as a term used for "rosary", e.g. in *(akṣa)-sūtra*, another n. for *akṣamālā*. It has further been used for "the sacred thread" (see *yajñopavita*), and in Buddhism it forms part of the *ṣaṇmudrā*.
Lit.; B 303; BBh. 339, 438; KiDG 67; MEIA 262; R 1:384.
2. *sūtra* "short rule, doctrine, and any work consisting of strings of aphoristic rules (like threads, stitches" or "verses strung together in sequence like the beads of a rosary").
Lit.: GBM 24; MW 1241.

sūtradhāra "architect or carpenter"
Lit.: RAAI 274.

sūtraharin "striped gazelle" (Vāh.), see *mṛga* (as char. of Varuṇa).
Lit.: MEIA 133.

suttee (Engl. word-form), see sub Satī.

suvarṇabhadra, see *svarṇabhadra*.

Suvarṇabhadravimalaratnaprabhāsa ("the bright, auspicious, pure jewel-splendour"; Buddh.), n. of a medicine-*buddha* (see Bhaiṣajyaguru) in Lamaism. Char.: colour: yellowish white; Mu.: *dharmacakra-mudrā*.
Lit.: G 56.

suvarṇavaikakṣaka "golden *vaikakṣa*" (attr.), n. of "a golden chain, worn like a cross-belt". See further *vaikakṣa*.
Lit.: SIB 69 a.pl. 37, 51.

Suvidhi ("good rule or ordinance"; Jain.), n. of the 9th *tīrthaṅkara*. Symbol: *makara* (it should perhaps be interpreted as *matsya*) or *karkī*. – Another n.: Puṣpadanta.
Lit.: GJ 273 a.pl. 22:9; KiSH 142.

svābhā ("own light"; Buddh.), another n. for Śakti (see *śakti* 1), being the principal god's own creation.
Lit.: BBh. 438.

svābhā-prajñā, see *śakti* 1.

Svabhāva ("Self-Existent"; Buddh.), epithet of Ādibuddha who has originated from himself.
Lit.: G 49.

svābhā-vidyā, see *śakti* 1.

svadanta "own tooth, tusk" (attr.), see *danta*.

Svadhā (Invocation-at-Offering"), n. of the daughter of Dakṣa and Prasūti, married to the *pitaras* or to Aṅgiras, or to Rudra or Agni.
Lit.: D 314; DHP 321; MW 1278.

Svāhā (properly an exclamation "hail (to)!") often forms the termination or the finishing syllables of *mantras* and *bījamantras*. As a personification S. is regarded as the daughter of Dakṣa and Prasūti and as the wife of Agni or of Rudra (= Śiva) Paśupati. In the last form she is mentioned as the mother of Ṣaṇmukha. – Attr.: *kamaṇḍalu*.
Lit.: D 314; DHP 205; GJ 369; R 2:524; RV 173.

svakucagrahamudrā "gesture of touching one's own breast" (Mu.), n. of a handpose, char. of Hayagrīva.
Lit.: BBh. 165.

svāmin (*-ī*) "master", n. of a spiritual preceptor, a learned Brāhman; also, now, a cultic title of initiates of certain religious orders who have taken the vow of the *saṅnyāsin*.
Lit.: WHW 1:439.

Svāminātha ("Lord-protector"), epithet of Skanda.
Lit.: R 2:429.

śvan (*śvā*) "dog" (Vāh., mostly as an accompanying animal). Char. of: Śiva as Bhairava, Baṭuka Bhairava, Bhairon, Nirṛti, Vīrabhadra; also of Khen-ma. See also Mallāri-Śiva. – Cp. *vṛka*, Śvāśva.
Lit.: GH 70; MKVI 2:405.

Śvānāsyā ("Dog-face"; Buddh.), n. of a minor goddess.
Lit.: BBh. 320.

Svaraghoṣarāja ("king of the sound of the recitation tone»; Buddh.), n. of a medicine-buddha (see Bhaiṣajyaguru) in Lamaism. Char.: colour: yellow red; Mu.: *dhyāna-*, *varada-mudrā*.
Lit.: G 56.

svarga (or *svarloka*) "the heaven = the world of light", n. of the abode of the gods, supposed to be situated on Mount Meru.
Lit.: IC 1:554; KiK 128.

svarṇa "gold" (attr.), sometimes included among the *pañcaratna*.
Lit.: MEIA 214.

svarṇabhadra (*suv-*; "the bright, auspicious (stone)"), n. of a red stone (jasper) which is found in a river at Arrah and forms the lithomorphic form of Gaṇeśa. Cp. *pañcāyatana*.
Lit.: GH 330; IC 1:498; KiH 35; KiSH 78.

Svarṇākarṣaṇa(-Bhairava) ("attraction of gold [by magic formulæ]» personification), n. of a form of Bhairava. Char.: colour: yellow; attr.: *cāmara*, *kamaṇḍalu* (with gold and gems), *tomara*, *trinayana*, *triśūla*.
Lit.: R 2:179.

svarṇarekhā (or *suv-*; "gold streak [on a touchstone]"), n. of a kind of stone (a piece of ore) found in a river in South India and regarded as the lithomorphic form of Devī (Durgā). – Cp. *pañcāyatana*.
Lit.: GH 330; IC 1:539; KiH 55; KiSH 78.

Svasthāveśinī ("entering one's natural state"?), n. of a terrific goddess. Char.: colour: scarlet; attr.: *ḍamaru*, *triśiras*, *triśūla*.
Lit.: SSI 213.

svastika "any lucky or auspicious object, esp. a kind of mystical cross, a swastika".
1. (Attr.) *s.* is a magical, auspicious *maṅgala* (see *aṣṭamaṅgala*), a *yantra* or mark in the form of a "croix cramponnée". A "right-handed" *s.* (i.e. turned clockwise) is always "lucky" and represents the male principle (cp. *dakṣiṇa*), a "left-handed" *s.* (*sauvastika*) represents the female principle (cp. *vāma*). It is believed by some that the *s.* has its origin in the Mediterranean culture, but it is already found in the Indus Valley civilization. This symbol is esp. connected with the snakes (*nāga*) and snake deities, since the "spectacle marks'

on the cobra's hood are thought to constitute half a *s.* The *s.* is further regarded as a sun symbol, constituting the form of the *cakra* (of Viṣṇu). "The *s.* is meant to remind man that the Supreme Reality is not within the reach of the human mind nor within man's control" (DHP). – *s.* is char. of the *pāduka* of the Buddha and other *pādukas*, the hood of Takṣaka, and a clockwise *s.* is a symbol of Gaṇeśa and Supārśva, and also of the reformed Tibetan red-cap sect; an anticlockwise *s.* (fylfot) is sacred to Kālī.

In some parts of India another view appears to be held concerning the meaning of the *s.* in the matter of the direction of its arms, and in GH an anti-clockwise *s.* is illustrated as the auspicious symbol.

Lit.: D 314 (ill.); DHP 295, 353; G 18 (ill.); GBM 101; GH 56; GJ 383 a.pl. 22:7; HuGT 9, 19; KiJ pl. 45; KiSB 35; KiSH 94, 153; KT 22; MW 1283; WHW 2:387, 469.

2. (Att. or Mu.) N. of a pose which can be performed either with the hands (with fingers crossing each other or with the hands in *patākāmudrā* touching each other at the wrists), or with the legs crossing each other. (In SSI *s.* is, however, said to involve the straight leg placed on the pedestal; cp. *lambita*). Char. of Agnijāta-Subrahmaṇya. – Cp. the variety *svastikāpasṛta*.

Lit.: MEIA 217; R 2:260, 441; SSI 190, 251.

svastikaliṅga, n. of a kind of *mānuṣaliṅga*.

Lit.: R 2:89.

svastikāpasṛta ("retracted *svastika*"; att.), n. of a pose performed with the legs crossing each other without touching. Char. of Śiva in the *kaṭisama*-dance. – Cp. *svastika*, *vaiṣṇavasthāna*.

Lit.: R 2:260.

svastikāsana ("*svastika*-sitting"; att.), n. of an *āsana*-posture "practised by Yogins (in which the toes are placed in the inner hollow of the knees)" (MW); in GH it is described thus: "man lege gleichzeitig beide Fuss-sohlen zwischen Knie und Schenkel und sitze mit aufrechtem Körper da." – Char. of Yogadakṣiṇāmūrti.

Lit.: B 270; GH 292; KiH pl. 151 row 3:1; MW 1283; WHW 1:76, 2:469.

Śvāśva ("having a dog as horse [i.e. as a mount]"), epithet of (Śiva) Bhairava.

Svāti (or -ī; meaning doubtful), n. of a *nakṣatra*. Its influence is good. – Another n.: Niṣṭyā.

Lit.: BBh. 382; IC 2:730.

Svayambhū ("self-existing, one who has come into existence of-himself").

1. (Hind.) Epithet of Brahmā; also of Manu.

Lit.: D 314; DHP 234; GoRI 1:263.

2. (Buddh.) "Self-Creative", epithet of Ādibuddha.

Lit.: G 49.

svayambhūliṅga "*liṅga* existing by itself"

Lit.: BPR 48.

svāyambhuvaliṅga (derived from the preceding word), n. of a kind of *liṅga* (see *acalaliṅga*) which is said to have come into existence of-itself.

Lit.: R 2:80.

svayambuddha ("self-enlightened"; Jain.), another n. for *tīrthaṅkara*.

Lit.: GJ 421.

svayampradhāna "of-himself object of worship".

Lit.: R 1:376.

Svayamvarā ("who chooses [her husband] herself"), n. of Pārvatī as a bride.

Lit.: SSI 107.

sveṣṭadevatā (*sva-iṣṭadevatā*) "deity dear to one's self, a favourite deity", see *iṣṭadevatā*.

Lit.: MW 1277.

śveta "white", the colour of white, cp. *sita*, *śukla*. For other n. of this colour, see MEIA.

Lit.: MEIA 237.

Śvetā ("white"), n. of a goddess.

Lit.: R 1:368.

śvetāmbara ("white-dressed"), n. of an adherent of one of the two main *jaina* sects. Cp. *digambara*.

Lit.: GJ passim; HIS 17; IC 2:632; KiSH 119; KT 114; WHW 1:494.

śvetāmbhoruh(a) "white lotus" (attr.), see *puṇḍarīka*.
Lit.: BBh. 198.

śvetapaṅkaja "white lotus" (attr.), see *puṇḍarīka*.
Lit.: MEIA 263.

śyāma "black, dark-grey", see *kṛṣṇa*. Indicating the colour of a Tārā, *ś.* is, however, equivalent to green.
Lit.: MKVI 2:246.

Śyāma ("black"; Jain.), n. of a *yakṣa* attending on the 8th *tīrthaṅkara*. Symbol: *haṅsa*.
Lit.: GJ 362 a.pl. 25:8; KiJ 11 a.pl. 28:8.

Śyāmā ("black").
1. (Hind.) Epithet of Kālī.
2. (Jain.) See Acyutā.
Lit.: GJ 362.

Syamantaka ("sounding"?; attr.), n. of a celebrated jewel (*ratna*), given to Satrājit by the Sun, later in the possession of Kṛṣṇa (Viṣṇu). It yields its owner 8 loads of gold daily and preserves from dangers. Cp. Kaustubha.
Lit.: D 315; DHP 179; Gt 630; MW 1273.

Śyāmatārā (lit. "the black Tārā", usually known as the "green T.", cp. *śyāma*; Buddh.), in Lamaism n. of a gracious form of Tārā, an emanation of Amoghasiddhi. She is regarded as an incarnation of the wife (from Nepal) of Sroṅ-btsan-sgam-po; later also as a female manifestation of Avalokiteśvara (Padmapāṇi). – Char.: colour: black (green); att.: *lalitāsana* (the right foot being supported by a *karṇika*); Mu.: *varada-*, *vyākhyāna-mudrā*; attr.: *nīlotpala*. – Other n. and varieties: Dhanadā, Haritatārā, Jāṅgulī, Khaḍiravaṇī, Siṅhanādā. – See also sub Tārā.
Lit.: G 34, 75; HAHI pl. 10A; HSIT 10 a.pl. 22; HuGT 26; JSV pl. 56; KIM pl. 11; KiSB 99; ZA pl. 382.

śyena "eagle, falcon, hawk, any bird of prey (kite)" (attr.; Jain.), symbol of the 14th *tīrthaṅkara* Ananta. As "kite" char. of Caṇḍakhaṇḍā.
Lit.: GJ pl. 22:14; KiJ pl. 45.

T

tablā (or *ṭ-*; Hi.; attr.), n. of a small kettle-drum.
Lit.: Gt Suppl. 135; SMII 70.

tabu (Polynesian) "taboo, forbidden, prohibited", referring to actions barred by rules of manners. According to A. WEBER, this word is derived from Skt *tābuva* (Atharvaveda: "an antidote against poison" [?]).
Lit.: Enc. Brit. 21:732; GRI 36; MW 442.

Taḍitkarā ("lightning"; Buddh.), n. of a light goddess. Char.: colour: green; attr.: *vidyullatā*. – Another n.: Vidyuddharā.
Lit.: BBh. 318.

Tai-lo-pa (Tib.; Buddh.), in Lamaism n. of a *mahāsiddha* who lived c. A.D. 948. Attr.: *ḍamaru*, *kapāla*.
Lit.: G 94.

ṭakkai (Tam.) "a kind of hour-glass, a small drum" (attr.), see *ḍhakkā*. (There is also another Tam. word corresponding to *ḍhakkā*, viz. *iṭakkai*, translated in TL as "a large double drum".)
Lit.: TL 1:277, 3:1693.

Ṭakkirāja (Buddh.), n. of a *dikpāla* of the south-east direction. Char.: colour: blue; attr.: *cintāmaṇi*, *daṇḍa* (blue), *khaḍga*, *padma*, *triśiras*. – Other n.: Vajrajvālānalārka, Vajrayakṣa.
Lit.: BBh. 254.

Takṣaka ("cutter"), n. of a *nāga* king who also acts as a Vāh. Attr.: *akṣamālā*, *kamaṇḍalu*, *svastika* on the hood, *trinayana*. He is the Vāh. of Māyājālakrama-Kurukullā (sitting).
Lit.: D 316; R 2:557; WHW 2:388.

takṣaṇa "cutter, sculptor" whose chief work was to make images for installation in temples, for processions and for domestic worship.
Lit.: WHW 2:373.

Takṣaśilā, see Taxila.
Lit.: SeKB 23.

tala "place", in the cosmological system n. of the subterranean regions. Cp. *loka*, *naraka*. – In its sense of "surface" *t.* is n. of the first level or lower part or base of a temple.
Lit.: BECA 1:272; WHW 1:253.

tāla (Tam. *tāḷam*) "cymbal" (attr.). There are many different kinds of *t.* which are not listed here. Char. of: Tirujñānasambandha, Kāraikkāl-Ammaiyār, Kālī (? ZA pl. 422, said to be Kālī, can, perhaps, rather be regarded as Kāraikkāl-Ammaiyār). – *T.* are also used in the Buddhist rite. – Other n.: *ghana*, *karatāla*.
Lit.: J. Filliozat. Indien. Völker und Traditionen. (Osnabrück), 116 (ill.); G 10 with ill.; KrA pl. 150; SMII 19; ZA pl. 422.

tāladhvaja "banner of the fan palm" (attr.). Char. of Balarāma.
Lit.: B 104.

talasaṅsphoṭita ("the surface made to burst"), n. of a dance-form, performed by Śiva Naṭarāja. In this dance he stamps vehemently the ground. Mu.: *abhaya-*, *patākā-mudrā* and other dance poses.
Lit.: R 2:268 a.pl. 68 f.; SB 60 N.; WM 94.

tāli (Tam.; attr.), n. of the central piece of a neck ornament (emblematic of the married state) which the bridegroom ties on his bride's neck on the wedding-day and which she afterwards always wears. In South India the tying on of the *t.* (*tālikaṭṭu*) forms the central and decisive part of the *vivāha* ceremony. The *t.* consists of an image of Gaṇeśa. – Char. of goddesses.
Lit.: DiCh. 110; DiIP 189; MSHP 95; TL 3:1848.

tāliccaraṭu (Tam.) "necklet with a *tāli*" (attr.), see *māṅgalyasūtra*.
Lit.: SB 109.

tālika "lock, bolt" (attr.). Char. of Tālikā.
Lit.: BBh. 316.

Tālikā (Buddh.), n. of a female *dvārapāla* as the deification of the lock. Char.: colour: white; attr.: *tālika*.
Lit.: BBh. 316.

tālikaṭṭu (Tam., also written *-kettu*) "the ceremony of the tying on of the *tāli*".
Lit.: J. H. Hutton, Caste in India (1961) 294; MD 2:49; TL 3:1848.

TAṀ (Buddh.), a *bīja* from which Khadiravaṇī has emanated.
Lit.: KiSB 99.

TĀṀ (Buddh.), a (golden green) *bīja* from which Āryatārā originates.
Lit.: BBh. 56.

tāmasa (or *-sika*; from *tamas* "darkness; the quality of ignorance, illusion, lust etc.", hence pertaining to the quality of *tamas*), n. of an aspect of a god in cruel, fighting and demon-destroying representations.
Lit.: MH 7; R 2:495.

tāmbūla "betel; its pungent and aromatic leaf together with the arecanut (*supārī*)" (attr.). *t.* also signifies the box in which the betel is kept. Small pieces of areca-nut are wrapped in a betel-leaf together with a sort of lime and the resultant "packet" is chewed for its own sake or as an aid to digestion. The flavour is sharp but pleasant. Among the accessories may be mentioned: *pāndān*, *killotaya*, and a kind of scissors for cutting the areca nuts. – Another n.: *pān*.
Lit.: MEIA 260; MW 443; P 306; STP 8:237; WHW 1:133.

tāmra "copper". Cp. *tāṅbā* and see *lohaja*.

tāmracūḍāmudrā "red-crest-handpose" (Mu.), n. of a variety of the *mukulamudrā** with the difference that the forefinger is separated and bent to indicate the crest of a cock. It denotes a cock, crane, camel, calf, writing, hook and noose.
Lit.: WHW 2:87.

tāmrakuṇḍa "copper basin for the bathing of images" (attr.).
Lit.: MH 37.

tāṅbā (Hi., < Skt *tāmra*+*ka*) "copper", used for casting metal icons (see *lohaja*) and other metal articles. The so-called "dark

bronzes" of India are made of pure copper, artificially darkened.
Lit.: BhIM 12, 32; MH 5; P 307; WHW 2:66.

taṇḍai, see *tanṭai*.

tāṇḍava (a kind of wild dance; originally a Dravidian word, cp. Tam. *tāṇṭavam* "leaping, jumping") signifies either a dance performed by Śiva in cemeteries and burning-grounds while trampling on a demon, expressing raging and fierce emotion (being emblematic of Śiva's cosmic function of creation and destruction and constituting the *tāmasika* aspect, therefore the Bhairava aspect of Śiva), – or Śiva himself performing this dance. This dance is also char. of Vajradhara. There are many different forms of this dance (see sub Naṭarāja).
Lit.: BBh. 44; GoRI 1:255; JDI 27; KiH pl. 42; MH 11; R 2:234; RAAI 274; Sh. 100; WHW 1:264.

bsTan-'gyur (pronounced *Tan-jur*; Tib., "the translated doctrine"), n. of a commentary on the Lamaist canon *bKa'-'gyur* (see sub initial *K*-). This commentary consists of 225 books.
Lit.: G 5; GRI 296; IC 2:394; JT 225.

taṅka "banner painting" (Tib.; attr.), see *thaṅ-ka*.

ṭaṅka (*ṭaṅkāyudha*) "hatchet, a stone-cutter's chisel; axe" (attr.). This object is described in different ways: according to B it is "a stone-mason's chisel", cp. Th., but it is often lumped together with or considered equivalent to the *paraśu* (see H, MEIA). It may therefore be regarded as a tool with two forms, either as a chisel or as a little axe (both of these being used as stone-cutting tools). In the hand of Śiva it usually has the form of an axe. – Char. of: Aghora, Ardhanārīśvara, Caṇḍeśvara, Ekanetra, Ekapādamūrti, Gajāsurasaṅhāramūrti, Īśāna, *kṣetrapālas*, *mūrtyaṣṭakas*, Nandīśvara, Pāśupatamūrti, Raudrapāśupatamūrti, Sadāśiva, Ṣaṇmukha, Śaravaṇabhava, Śiṣyabhāvamūrti, Śiva, Skanda, Somāskanda, Śrīkaṇṭha, Sūkṣma, Tripurāntaka, Vāmadeva, Viṣṇvanugrahamūrti, Vṛṣārūḍha, Vṛṣavāhana.
Lit.: B 300; H pl. 7:59; JDI 45; MEIA 248; R 1:7 a.pl. 2:11, 2:469 a.pl. 133:2; SSI pl. III:3; Th. 41 (ill.); WM 109 a.fig. 73.

ṭaṅkāyudha "the weapon *ṭaṅka*", see *ṭaṅka*.
Lit.: JDI 45.

bsTan-ma (Tib., pronounced Ten-ma; Buddh.), in Lamaism n. of a group of female devils, controlled by Ekajaṭā.
Lit.: G 96.

taṇṭai (*taṇḍai*, Tam.; attr.), n. of a kind of *nūpura* "probably hollow and rattling" (SB), worn by children.
Lit.: SB 201; TL 3:1736.

tantra (prop. "warp [of a textile]", then "doctrine, rule, ritual, system, Tantrism"), n. of a class of works which do not belong to the Vedas. The *tantras* are mostly of ritualistic character, with sacral, and chiefly magical and mystical contents. Therefore, *t.* may also be interpreted as "a magical formula". This Tantric tendency is char. of all Indian religions.

t. evolved, esp. in Buddhism, into two main currents, known as Left-hand and Right-hand Tantrism. Left-handed Tantrism (see *vāmācāra*) is esp. connected with the development of the adoration of female "saviouresses" (Tārās, see also *vajrayāna*), but Right-handed Tantrism (see *dakṣiṇācāra*) emphasizes the devotion to male divinities. – In Hinduism, Tantrism, on the whole, is connected with the worship of the Śakti (*śākta*), Right-handed Tantrism denoting merely a certain practice within this worship. – Another n.: *cīnācāra*.
Lit.: BPR 39; GH 54; GoRI 2:26; GRI 171; Gt 633; IC 1:593, 2:586; MW 436; pw 3:9; SM 17; WHW 2:482.

tapas "heat; religious austerity, penance, ascetism; Yogic practice".
Lit.: RAAI 274; STP 1:79.

Tārā (Tārakā). This word should prop., regarding its etymology, be interpreted as "star, constellation" and may therefore, as name of a deity, be connected with the

Babylonian Ištar. But since the word may also be associated with the verb *tar-* (caus. *tārayati* "cause to arrive at, lead over or across, rescue, save"), it is generally understood and translated as "saviouress"; thus esp. in Buddhism. – T. is particularly a manifestation of the divine mother.

1. (Hind.) T. is either an epithet or a variety of Durgā who destroyed the demon Śumbha; attr.: *khaḍga, rākṣasamuṇḍa*; – or, as a personification ("Power-of-Hunger", DHP), n. of one of the *mahāvidyā*-group, and is then represented by Krodharātrī; she has been influenced by the conception of the Buddhist Mahācīnatārā. She is supposed to be the wife of Bṛhaspati or Candra (Soma); attr.: *ajina, karttṛkā, khaḍga, muṇḍa, nāgas, nīlotpala, trinayana.*

Lit.: BBh. 1, 189; D 318; DHP 274; GoRI 2:77; Gt 635; MG 180, 252 a.pl. facing p. 177 (the 2nd ill.).

2. (Buddh.) T. is epithet of the mother (Māyā) of the Buddha. In Mahāyāna and Vajrayāna Buddhism T. is n. of a goddess who is usually regarded as a *dhyānibuddhaśakti*, the Śakti of Avalokiteśvara (attr.: *padma*) or of Amoghasiddhi (see also Āryatārā), but often also as the Śakti of Ādibuddha and the different *dhyānibuddhas* (as a group). T. is then characterized by different colours, either corresponding to the colours of the different *dhyānibuddhas* or being of another and independent symbolical character. These Tārās are (see further the separate names): Sitatārā ("white T."; cp. also Śuklatārā), Śyāmatārā ("green T."), Bhṛkuṭī ("she who frowns") is the "yellow T.", Ekajaṭā ("she who has but one chignon") is the "blue T.", and Kurukullā ("Wealth goddess") is the "red T.". Of these the "white" and the "green" Tārās are gracious forms of T.; the others are cruel forms. Besides these principal Tārās there are several goddesses (Tārās) having these colours; they are enumerated in BBh. Attr. (all Tārās): *viśvavajra.* – T. is sometimes also regarded as a female *bodhisattva.* – T. is, in addition, often found as a final member in compound name-forms of inferior Mahāyāna goddesses, such as Pradīpatārā, Prasannatārā, Puṣpatārā and others. – The Tibetan name-form for T. is sGrol-ma (pronounced Dolma).

Lit.: B 492; BBh. 306; G 34, 52, 75; GBB 245, 249; GBM 81, 156; H 33; HAHI pl. 8B; IA 10; IC 2:591; KiDG 72; KiSB 109; SS pl. 31:141, 34:155, 37:166; Th. pl. 31 f.

3. (Jain.) T. is n. of a Śakti.

Lit.: MW 443.

Tāraka ("saving"), n. of a demon which was killed by Skanda. According to some myths T. was an Āditya who was subdued by Indra aided by Skanda. – Cp. Tārakajit, Tārakāri.

Lit.: D 318; KiSH 30; R 2:430; ZA 117.

Tārakā ("saving"), see Tārā.

Tārakajit ("conqueror of Tāraka"), epithet of Skanda.

Lit.: DHP 299.

Tārakāri ("enemy of Tāraka"), n. of a form of Skanda. Char.: Vāh.: *gaja*; Mu.: *abhaya-, kaṭaka-, varada-mudrā*; attr.: *akṣamālā, aṅkuśa, cakra, dhvaja, khaḍga, kheṭaka, musala, pāśa, śakti, trinayana, vajra.*

Lit.: R 2:430, 438 a.pl. 128a.

taraṅga ("wave"; attr.), n. of a kind of fold or pleat in the dress.

Lit.: SB 90.

taraṅgābhinayin (*-ī*; "miming the sea-waves"; Mu.), n. of a handpose which is performed with all the fingers of a hand. Char. of Sāgaramati.

Lit.: BBh. 87.

tārīkh-i ilāhi (Arab. "the divine era"), n. of an era instituted by the Emperor Akbar and beginning in A.D. 1556. Out of use since the time of Shah Jahān.

Lit.: IC 2:738.

tarjanīmudrā (also *tarjana-, -anīkā(hasta)-mudrā*) "threatening finger" (Mu.), n. of a handpose, "the pose of the raised index

finger in a menacing attitude, ... the other fingers locked up in the fist" (BBh.). This Mu., also mentioned as a variety of the *muṣṭimudrā*, is of indicating or threatening character. Char. of: Agni-Durgā, Bhūtaḍāmaravajrapāṇi, *ekādaśarudra*s, Ekapāda, the *gaurī*-group, Hayagrīva, the *lāsyā*-group, Mahābala, Mārīcī (in different forms), Māyājālakramāryāvalokiteśvara, Nandīśvara, *navadurgās*, Parṇaśavarī, Prasannatārā, Ripumāri-Durgā, Śākyabuddha-Lokeśvara. Ṣaṇmukha, Sarasvatī, Sumbhā, Uṣṇīṣavijayā, Vajraghaṇṭā, Vajrāṅkuśa, Vajrapāśī, Vajrasphoṭā, Vajraśṛṅkhalā, Vajratārā, Vana-Durgā, Vanavāsī, Vidyujjvālākarālī, Viṣvaksena. – Cp. *sūcimudrā*.
Lit.: B 259; BBh. 165, 222, 439; G 22 (ill.); Gz 182; R 1:15 a.pl. 5:10; SSI pl. III:18, 26; Th. 29; WHW 2:88.

tarjanīpāśa(hasta) (or *pāśatarjanī*, *satarjanīpāśa*, *satarjanikāpāśa*) "(hand with) raised index finger and a noose" (Mu. + attr.; esp. Buddh.), n. of a combination of the Mu. *tarjanīmudrā* and the attr. *pāśa* in the same hand (the noose round the index finger). Char. of: Aparājitā, Āryavajravārāhī, Caṇḍaroṣaṇa, Dhvajāgrakeyūrā, Hevajra, Jāṅgulī, Kṛṣṇa-Yamāri, Mahāmantrānusāriṇī, Mahāpratisarā, Mahāpratyaṅgirā, Mahāsāhasrapramardanī, Mahāśītavatī, Mārīcī (in different forms), Māyājālakramakrodha-Lokeśvara, Parṇaśavarī, Prasannatārā, Sitātapatrā-Aparājitā, Uṣṇīṣavijayā, Vajragāndhārā, Vajravetālī, Vighnāntaka, Yamāntaka.
Lit.: B 259; BBh. 154, 439; KiDG 67; KiSB 71; WM 100 a.fig. 22.

Tārkṣya (or Tārkṣa), n. of a mythical being, originally described as a horse, later taken to be a bird (MW). T. is therefore regarded as a personification of the sun, and T. is NP of the *aśva*, the Vāh. of Sūrya; at a later date T. is identified with Garuḍa.
Lit.: B 429; D 318; MEIA 40, 232; MW 444.

Tārodbhava-Kurukullā ("K. who is descended from Tārā"; Buddh.), n. of a form of Kurukullā. Char.: colour: red; att.: *padmāsana*; Vāh.: *padma* (red), or Kāmadeva with wife on Rāhu; Mu.: *abhayamudrā*; attr.: *Amitābhabimba* on the crown, *dhanus*, *padma* (red), *śara*.
Lit.: BBh. 149 a.pl. 121; KiDG 64; KiSB 96.

tarpaṇa "libation, offering of water" to the gods, *riṣi*s and manes (*pitaras*, see *pitā*). See also *pitṛyajña*.
Lit.: DiIP 73; GH 330; IC 1:585.

tarpaṇamudrā "libation gesture" (Mu.), n. of a handpose which is performed while paying homage to the departed fathers. This Mu. is described thus: "arm or arms bent and raised on level with the shoulders. Palms are turned in and fingers are slightly bent and pointing toward the shoulders" (G). It is also said to be performed with the hands held before the chest, the palms, with the tips downwards, turned toward the spectator. Char. of: Kurukullā, Nāmasaṅgīti, and others.
Lit.: BBh. 440; G 22 (ill.); JMS 48 a.pl. 91; KiSB 80.

Taruṇa-Gaṇapati ("the young G."), n. of a form of Gaṇeśa. Attr.: *aṅkuśa*, *jambu*, *kapittha*, *pāśa*.
Lit.: R 1:52; Th. 96.

Tashi Lama (Tib.; pronounced so or Trashi-; the n. is written: bKra-śis bla-ma; the first word means "happiness"). T. is, in the West, the usual n. of the highest official in Tibet next only to the Dalai Lama (until 1957). His real n. is Pan-chen Rin-po-che or, outside Tibet, known as Panchen Lama ("Great and Precious Sage"). He is the abbot of the monastery of bKra-śis-lhun-po (Trashi Lhümpo), and he is regarded as a reincarnation of Amitābha.
Lit.: Enc.Brit. 7:3; G 6, 107; GRI 296; JT 14.

Taṣṭar, see Tvaṣṭar.

tāṭaṅka (Tam.) "woman's ear-ornament" (attr.), "ole de palmier ou de cocotier enroulée et enfilée dans le lobe fendu de l'oreille."
Lit.: ACA 29; TL 3:1827.

tathāgata (Buddh.). This word is translated in different ways, e.g. "So-come, So-gone = Who has entered into the Such-ness"

(CEBI), "der So-dahingelangte" (N), "der Sogegangene" (GBM), "he who has arrived at the truth" (MS). It is an epithet of a *buddha* who has attained the highest state of perfection. Statements as to the real sense of this term differ remarkably: according to KiSB, *t.* is a human, mortal *buddha* (*mānuṣibuddha*), and, in fact, by this title the Buddha referred to himself, but according to GBM, *t.* signifies a meditation-*buddha* who more often (though properly wrongly) is named *dhyānibuddha*.
Lit.: BBh. 440; CEBI 4; GBM 47, 79, 82; IC 2:534; KiSB 43; MS 157; N 218.

tathāgatamaṇḍala "the magic circle of the five *dhyānibuddhas*".
Lit.: BBh. 45.

tathāgatī, female form of a *buddha* (corresponding to *tathāgata*) in later Tantrism; e.g. Buddhalocanā.
Lit.: GBM 81.

Tathāvaśitā ("control of the Such-ness"; Buddh.), n. of a *vaśitā*. Char.: colour: white; attr.: *padma* (white).
Lit.: BBh. 332.

Tatpuruṣa ("the Original or Supreme Spirit"), n. of one of the five aspects of Śiva in five-headed representations. In the Sadāśivamūrti T. signifies the head which is directed towards the east; cp. Pañcabrahmā. In the three-headed Mahādeva-composition T. denotes the central figure. T. is also mentioned as one among the group *ekādaśarudra*. – T. as an independent deity has the char.: colour: yellow; Mu.: *abhaya-*, *jñāna-*, *varada-mudrā*; attr.: *akṣamālā*, *caturmukha*, *jambhīra*, *kuṭhāra*, *pustaka*, *trinayana*.
Lit.: B 476; DHP 211; KiSH 25; KrA 207 a.pl. 100; MW 433; R 2:731.

taṭṭutīpam "plate-lamp" (Tam.; cp. *dīpa*), n. of a plate on which are placed small bottle-like objects in the necks of which are wicks. A *t.* may have provision for either 1, 2, 3, 5, 7, or 9 wicks.

tattva "reality, principle". It is a symbolic n. of the numbers "24, 25", see *saṅkhyā*.

tattvārcanā "worship of the 'reals' or elements of existence (*tattva*)". In Sāṅkhya philosophy there are 25 *tattvas*.
Lit.: DiIP 121; MW 432.

Taxila (Greek name-form from Takṣaśilā), n. of an ancient city (near Islamabad) with Gandhāran style temples.
Lit.: FBKI 67; RAAI 86; SeKB 23.

Tejoṣṇīṣa ("*uṣṇīṣa* of sharpness"; Buddh.), n. of an *uṣṇīṣa*-deity. Char.: colour: whitish red; direction: south-east; attr.: *sūrya-(maṇḍala)*.
Lit.: BBh. 301.

Tēvi (Tam.), see Devī.

ṭhag (Hi., < Skt *sthaga*; "thug", "a robber, assassin, cut-throat, one of a gang who strangle or poison travellers"), n. of an originally religious sect which worshipped Durgā, but which developed into an assassin gang. Exterminated since about A.D. 1882.
Lit.: GH 397; P. 363; WHW 2:501.

Ṭhākur Deo (or Ṭhākkur, N.Ind., Hi., Beng. etc., < Skt *ṭhakkura* ("deity, man of rank") + *deva*), n. of a village god (*grāmadevatā*). Wife: Dhartī Mātā. Vāh.: *aśva* (white).
Lit.: FHRI 260; Mayrhofer, EWA 1:458.

thākuri(kāla), n. of an era adopted by the Thākuri dynasty in Nepal and beginning in A.D. 595.
Lit.: Enc.Brit. 5:721; IC 2:737.

thaṅ-ka (*taṅka*; "banner painting"; Buddh.), in Tibet and Nepal n. of a type of painting depicting deities; temple banner; nowadays also painting in a general sense, of landscapes etc.
Lit.: B 2; G 27, 109; HuGT 72 a.pl. 33, 54; JSV (ill. passim); JT 228; ZA 197 a.pl. 606.

Tha-'og-chos (Tib., pronounced: Thok-chö; Buddh.), in Lamaism n. of one of the *mahāpañcarājas*. Char.: colour: green; Vāh.: *aśva* (black); attr.: *paraśu*.
Lit.: G 93.

thera (Pāli), see *sthavira*.

theravāda (Pāli, for Skt *sthaviravāda*) "the speech of the Elders", n. of the southern form of Buddhism, above all the Buddhism of Sri Lanka. Cp. *hīnayāna*.

theravādin (Pāli) "adherent of the *theravāda* school of Buddhism".
Lit.: IC 2:557.

thsa-thsa (*tsa-tsa*; Tib.; attr.), n. of small images of the Buddha and of conical figures, moulded of clay and used at sacrifices.
Lit.: HuGT 16, 76; JSV pl. 52 f.; JT 443.

thug (Eng. word-form), see *ṭhag*.

thūpa (or *thūva*; M.Ind.), see *stūpa*.

ṭīkā (Hi.), see *tilaka*.

ṭiklī (Hi., derived from *tilaka*) "spangle, ornament" (attr.). The *t.* is worn on the forehead by Hindu women of good caste.
Lit.: STP 2:22.

tīkṣṇabāṇa "sharp arrow" (attr.), see *śara*.
Lit.: MEIA 145.

Tīkṣṇoṣṇīṣa ("the sharp, hot *uṣṇīṣa*"; Buddh.), n. of an *uṣṇīṣa*-deity. Char.: colour: sky-green (sic BBh. translates Skt *nabhaḥśyāma*; perhaps better "sky-dark, sky-grey"); direction: north-west; attr.: *khaḍga*, *pustaka*.
Lit.: BBh. 301.

tila "Sesamum Indicum" (plant or seed; attr., held in one hand). Char. of Piṅgala-Gaṇapati.
Lit.: MW 448; R 1:56.

tilaka (Hi. *ṭīkā*) "(round) mark on the forehead (made with coloured earths or unguents)" (attr.). The mark of the Buddha (*ūrṇā*) is said to signify "nobility". The *t.* is also commonly made on many occasions, such as at the ceremony of betrothal, or when a journey is to be undertaken, etc. Women wear a round red mark (made of *kuṅkuma*) on the forehead, signifying that they are married (cp. *seṅdūrdān*). – Char. of: the Buddha, Ardhanārīśvara (the female aspect), Rājamātaṅgī. – *t.* also refers to different secterial and caste marks: the *gāṇapatya*s wear a red mark in the shape of a half-moon, the Jains have a mark in the shape of a heart between the eyebrows; for the Śaivite and Vaiṣṇavite marks, see *tiryakpuṇḍra*, *triphala*, *ūrdhvapuṇḍra*. – Other n.: *nāmaṁ*, *puṇḍra*, *ūrṇā*. See also *ṭiklī*.
Lit.: BRI 23; GH 57, 330, 399; HIS 78; MW 448; P 367; STP 2:22; WHW 1:207.

timiṅgala ("swallower of *timi*"; *timi* is an unknown kind of fish), n. of a sea-monster.
Lit.: IC 1:534; MW 447.

tīpam (Tam.), see *dīpa*.

tīpāvaḷi (Tam.), see *dīvālī*.

Tipiṭaka (Pāli, Skt Tripiṭaka) "three baskets or collections of sacred writings", n. of the Buddhist canon which is written in Pāli.
Lit.: BRI 78; G 4.

tīrtha "bathing-place, stairs for landing and descent into a river, passage", in common language "sacred tank or bathing-place", of which some 4.000 are listed for India. – Bathing in sacred places has a ritual meaning which indubitably originates in the Indus Valley civilization. – In Jainism *t.* has received a transferred sense: "ein Ort, der die Bahn für das Durchschreiten des Stromes der Seelenwanderung öffnet" (GJ). It is noteworthy that *t.* in Jainism does not signify a bathing-place. In Jain contexts *t.* also refers to the four components of the Jain church: the monks, the nuns, the male and the female laity.
Lit.: GJ 32, 436; GoRI 1:320; IC 1:577, 580; RV 70; WM 175.

tīrthaṅkara (originally probably "one who makes or has made a *tīrtha*, ford-finder, ein Furtbereiter", then also interpreted as "Maker of the River crossing"; Jain.). I. The usual n. of the 24 salvation-preachers or chief saints of Jainism of whom the last (Mahāvīra) was a historical person. These 24 *t.* are: 1. Ṛṣabha(nātha); 2. Ajita; 3. Sambhava; 4. Abhinandana; 5. Sumati; 6. Padmaprabha; 7. Supārśva; 8. Candraprabha; 9. Suvidhi; 10. Śītala; 11. Śreyāṅsa; 12. Vāsupūjya; 13. Vimala; 14. Ananta; 15. Dharma; 16. Śānti; 17. Kunthu; 18. Ara; 19. Malli; 20. Munisuvrata; 21. Nami; 22. Ariṣṭanemi; 23. Pārśva; 24. Mahāvīra. – Common char.: att.: *padmāsana* or *vīrāsana*; Mu.: *dhyāna*-

mudrā; attr.: often *nagna*. It is often hard to differentiate between these *t.*, as the divergencies are usually only to be found in their symbols; only Pārśva is esp. distinguished by his cobra hood. – Other n.: *jina*, *jineśvara*, *arhat*, *mūlanāyaka*, *siddha*, *svayambuddha*.

Lit.: GBB 179; GI pl. 89; GJ 274 a.pl. 9; GRI 186; Gt 636; HIS 16; IC 2:628; KiJ 10; KiSH 119; KrA pl. 40; RAAI pl. 81A; SB 329 a.fig. 259; SchRI 234; WHW 2:505; ZA 27, 59.

II. *-bimba* (attr.) A Jain deity (*yakṣa* etc.), attending on a certain *t.*, may wear an image of this *t.* on the hair crown.

Lit.: SB 323.

Tiru (Tam.), corresponding to Skt Śrī, see Lakṣmī. Like Śrī it is also used as the first member of compounds, signifying "reverend, blessed, excellent".

Tirujñānasambandha (-Svāmi or -sampanta, mixed Tam. and Skt; "friend of the highest knowledge"), n. of a *śaivabhakta* who lived in South India in the 7th c. A.D. Attr.: 2 *tāla*s.

Lit.: B 454; CBC 11 a.fig. 20; JDI 55; R 2:480 a.pl. 137; SSR pl.facing p. 176; Th. 120 a.pl. 71A, 78C.

tirukalyāṇa "divine marriage" (mixed Tam.-Skt), n. of a festival in honour of the marriage of Śiva and Pārvatī.

Lit.: Gt Suppl. 137; JDI 35.

tirukuppū (Tam.) "a flower-like ornament in the head-dress" (attr.).

Lit.: SB 299; TL 3:1900.

Tirumakaḷ (-magaḷ; Tam., "the young woman Śrī"), in South India epithet of Lakṣmī.

Lit.: Gw. 37, 41.

Tirumāl (Tam., "the excellent Black one"), epithet of Viṣṇu or esp. Kṛṣṇa.

Tirumaḷicaiyāḻvār (Tam.), n. of a South Indian *vaiṣṇavabhakta*. Cp. *āḻvār*.

Lit.: R 2:480 a.pl. 136.

Tirumaṅkai(yāḻvār) (Tam.), n. of a South Indian *vaiṣṇavabhakta*. Attr.: *khaḍga*, *kheṭaka*. –

Lit.: R 2:480 a.pl. 136; SSR 186; SSI fig. 160e.

tirunāmam (Tam., for Skt **śrīnāma* "the sacred mark", cp. *nāmaṁ*), see *triphala*.

Lit.: JDI 58.

tiruniṟu (Tam.) "sacred ashes" (attr.), identical with *vibhūti*.

Lit.: DiIP 74; JDI 19.

Tiruppāṇāḻvār (Tam.), n. of a South Indian *vaiṣṇavabhakta*.

Lit.: R 2:480 a.pl. 136; SB 345 a.fig. 297.

Tiruppati (mixed Tam.-Skt), see Lakṣmīpati.

tiruvāṭci (or -vāci, Tam., "the excellent fire, ornamental arch over the head of an idol"; attr.), see *prabhāmaṇḍala*.

Lit.: JDI 129; SB 72; TL 3:1917.

tiryakpuṇḍra "horizontal mark" (attr.), n. of a Śaivite secterial mark, consisting of three horizontal streaks, one red and two white, often with a point (= an eye) on the middle one, applied mostly on the forehead, but also on the arms etc. This mark can be made with coloured earths or with (white) *vibhūti*. – Other n.: *nāmaṁ*, *tripuṇḍra*, *vibhūtipuṇḍra*. See also *tilaka*.

Lit.: GH 57, 330; GJ 382; SSR 142; WHW 1:208.

tithi "lunar day", a 30-th part of a lunar month. Since a lunar day (of about 23 hours and a half) does not coincide with a solar day, periodic adjustments, concerning the months, must be made as follows: "When two sunrises occur on the same lunar day, a second day is added with the same date number. When no sunrise occurs during another lunar day, one is omitted". (Enc.Brit.) 15 *t.* constitute the "light half" of the month during the moon's increase (*śuklapakṣa*), and the other 15 *t.* constitute the "dark half" of the month (*kṛṣṇapakṣa*). Each *t.* is divided into 2 *karaṇa*s. – *t.* is also a symbolic n. of the number "15", see *saṅkhyā*.

Lit.: BBh. 382; Enc.Brit. 4:622; IC 2:722, 734; MW 446.

todakenakallu, see sub *tōta-*.

tōḍu, see *tōṭu*.

tomara "iron club, pestle" (so B; MW: "lance"; MEIA: "Le *tomara* serait une massue de fer et un javelot"; attr.). Char. of: Agni, Ahirbudhnya, Aparājita, Hara, *kṣetrapāla*s, Svarṇākarṣaṇa(-Bhairava), Viśvarūpa.

Lit.: B 268; MEIA 253; MW 455; R 2:389.

Toṇṭaraṭippotiyā̱lvār (Tam.), n. of a South Indian *vaiṣṇavabhakta*.
Lit.: R 2:480 a.pl. 136.

toraṇa "arch, arched doorway, portal", also n. of an arch erected at a festivity; in addition n. of the gate of the enclosure of a Buddhist *stūpa*. This n. also refers to the circle of flames in which Śiva Naṭarāja dances and symbolizes then "the Hall of Universe in which Śiva is dancing" (HAHI). – Cp. *prabhāmaṇḍala*, *prabhātoraṇa*, *prabhāvalī*, *makaratoraṇa*.
Lit.: BECA 1: pl. 30; DKI 13; H pl. 1:2; HAHI 28; KiSH 148; MH 11; MW 456; R 1: pl. 95; RAAI 274.

torma "cake or holy food" (attr.; Buddh.).
Lit.: G 8.

tōtakeṇakallu (or *tōda-*; Tam., perhaps from *tōtakam* "deceit, sleight-of-hand", or *tōtakaṉ* "deceiver", + *kal* "stone"; attr.), n. of a stone embellished with magical signs, used as an amulet in order to avert maladies of animals.
Lit.: KiH 32 a.pl. 124; TL 4:2109.

Totalā (Totilā), n. of a four-armed form of Pārvatī (?) who destroys all sins Attr.: *akṣamālā*, *cāmara* (white), *daṇḍa*, *triśūla*.
Lit.: R 1:361.

tōṭṭi (Tam.) "goad" (attr.), see *aṅkuśa*.

tottra "goad" (attr.), see *aṅkuśa*.
Lit.: MEIA 249.

tōṭu (*tōḍu*; Tam.) "ear-ring", see *kuṇḍala*.

traibhāgyaliṅga ("a *liṅga* of the three-fold asterism of Bhaga"), see *trairāśikaliṅga*.

trailokya "pertaining to the three worlds, the divine, the terrestrial and the infernal"
Lit.: BBh. 440.

Trailokyamohana ("confusing the three worlds"), n. of a form of Viṣṇu with 16 arms. Char.: Mu.: *dhyāna-*, *varada-mudrā*; attr.: *aṅkuśa*, *cakra*, *caturmukha*, *dhanus*, *gadā*, *kamaṇḍalu*, *mudgara*, *padma*, *pāśa*, *śakti*, *śaṅkha*, *śara*, *śṛṅga*. This representation is similar to the Vaikuṇṭha.
Lit.: R 1:257.

Trailokyamohanī-Lakṣmī, n. of a form of Lakṣmī, clearly as the Śakti of Trailokyamohana.
Lit.: MEIA 186.

Trailokyavaśaṅkara(-Lokeśvara) ("L., subjugating the three worlds"; Buddh.), n. of a variety of Avalokiteśvara. Char.: colour: red; Vāh.: *padma*; att.: *padmāsana*; attr.: *aṅkuśa*, *trinayana*, *vajrapāśa*.
Lit.: BBh. 137 a.pl. 114; G 65; KiSB 59.

Trailokyavijaya ("conquering the three worlds, Lord of the three worlds"; Buddh.), n. of a Mahāyāna god. Char.: colour: blue; att.: *ālīḍhāsana*; Vāh.: T. is depicted treading upon two figures = Maheśvara and Gaurī; Mu.: *vajrahuṅkāramudrā*; attr.: *aṅkuśa*, *cakra*, *caturmukha*, *dhanus*, *ghaṇṭā*, *khaḍga*, *khaṭvāṅga*, *pāśa*, *śara*, *vajra*. – T. is also another n. of Acala as a *dikpāla*.
Lit.: BBh. 184, 255; G 14, 33, 61; KiSB 79.

trailokyavijayamudrā "handpose of the conquering of the three worlds" (Mu.), according to KiSB "eine nicht näher bekannte Handstellung, die sich auf die Eroberung der Dreiwelt (Himmel, Erde, Unterwelt) bezieht"; note, however, that this Mu. may, according to BBh., be understood as the 'reversed' form of the *vajrahuṅkāramudrā* (see the explanation sub this word). Char. of: Aṣṭabhuja-Kurukullā, Māyājālakrama-Kurukullā.
Lit.: BBh. 440; KiSB 97 N. 43.

trairāśika-liṅga ("*liṅga* relating to three zodiacal signs"), also named *traibhāgyaliṅga*, n. of a *mānuṣaliṅga*.
Lit.: R 2:89 a.pl. 7:1.

TRĀṀ, a (yellow) *bīja* from which Ratnasambhava originates.
Lit.: BBh. 73.

trāyastriṅśa ("the 33"), a collective n. of the gods, the number of whom is considered to be 33; see further *deva*.
Lit.: BRI 35; KiSB 29.

tretā "triad, the three sacred fires" (attr.), see *agni*.
Lit.: MW 462.

tri "three", a sacred and lucky number, exemplified in the equilateral triangle (*trikoṇa*) and, above all, in the number of great gods, the triad Brahmā, Viṣṇu, Śiva, see *trimūrti*. Its mystical significance is proved by its frequent occurrence as the first word-member of many headwords preceding and following this one.
Lit.: WHW 2:137.

tribhaṅga "three bends" (att.), n. of a *sthānaka*-representation in which "the centre line passes through the left (or right) pupil, the middle of the chest, the left (or right) of the navel, down to the heels. The lower limbs, from the hips to the feet, are displayed to the right (or left) of the figure, the trunk between the hips and neck, to the left (or right), while the head leans towards the right (or left)" (A. N. TAGORE in B), also described as "eine Biegung des Körpers, die seine Achse zweimal bricht". (HIS).
Lit.: B 265; HIS 35; MH 6; RAAI 274; SIB pl. 37; WM 89.

tricīvara (Buddh.), n. of the three vestments of a Buddhist monk. These are: *antaravāsa(ka), uttarāsaṅga, saṅghāṭi*. Char. of the Buddha and the *buddhas*, esp. the *dhyānibuddhas*.
Lit.: BBh. 75; BRI 59; HIS 42; RN 32.

tridaṇḍa(ka) (Tam. *tiritaṇṭam*) "the three staves tied together (of a Brāhman who has renounced the world)" (attr.), carried by religious mendicants and ascetics (*parivrājakas*). In North India this attr. seems to be identical with the Śaivite *triśūla** (cp. also *tiryakpuṇḍra*), but in South India it is regarded as a Vaiṣṇavite emblem, though even there expressly mentioned as a "trident-staff" (TL). It is also char. of Buddhist images, e.g.: Avalokiteśvara (in different forms), Bhṛkuṭī, Pretasantarpita, Rāmānuja. (In KiSB and often in BBh. *t.* is given as *tridaṇḍī*).
Lit.: BBh. passim; KiSB 98; MW 458; TL 3:1890; WHW 1:437.

tridaṇḍin (-*ī*; Tam. *tiritaṇṭi*) "carrying a *tridaṇḍa*", n. of a religious mendicant, either a Śaivite, or a Vaiṣṇavite believer (see *tridaṇḍa*; cp. also *ekadaṇḍin*).
Lit.: TL 3:1890; WHW 1:437.

tridaśa "30", referring to the number of the gods, see *deva*.

trika "bone" (?, attr.), see *asthi*.
Lit.: MEIA 246.

trika-doctrine ("threefold-"), n. of a Kashmirī form of Śaivism, characterized by an idealistic-monistic tendency.
Lit.: GH 393.

Trikaṇṭakīdevī ("three-thorn-goddess"), n. of a terrible goddess. Char.: colour: partly black, partly red, partly white; attr.: *cakra, danta*s, 2 *dīpa*s, *śaṅkha*.
Lit.: SSI 213.

trikāya "three bodies" (Buddh.), n. of a doctrine in Mahāyāna Buddhism, according to which the *buddhas* have a three-fold nature. From the unique self-creative Ādibuddha the *dhyānibuddhas* (meditative *buddhas*) first emanated; from these emanated the *(dhyāni)bodhisattvas* (the real creators of the universe in certain world-periods), and from these in turn emanated the *mānuṣibuddhas* (the human, mortal incarnations of the respective *bodhisattvas*) who became the saviours of the respective world-periods. The numbers of these three kinds of *buddhas* (apart from the Ādibuddha) are usually said to be five in each group. These *buddhas* have different kinds of bodies which are: *dharmakāya* in which a *dhyānibuddha* lives in *nirvāṇa*, *sambhogakāya* in which a *bodhisattva* lives in heaven (Tuṣita), and *nirmāṇakāya* in which the *mānuṣibuddha* lives on earth. – The doctrine that the human *buddha* in this way has a mystic counterpart in one of the *dhyāni*-heavens, appears to have been influenced by the Zoroastrian theory that every being has his "Fravashi" which at birth joins the body and after death intercedes for it (Gw.).
Lit.: BRI 150; G 30; GRI 260; Gw. 170; KiSB 41; WHW 2:15.

trikoṇa "equilateral triangle" (attr.). The *t.* is an important *yantra* of manifold meanings. – An upward-pointing *t.* symbolizes *agni* and the *liṅga*, hence also the male principle of the cosmos, as well as Śiva and Śaivism (cp. however GH). – A downward-pointing *t.* symbolizes the *yoni* and the female principle of the cosmos, hence also the Śakti, as well as Viṣṇu (see Mohinī) and Vaiṣṇavism. – 2 *t.*, interpenetrating so as to form a hexagon, symbolize the united male and female principles and therefore also Śāktism; this is also a syncretistic sign of Śaivism and Vaiṣṇavism (but cp. HAHI which sees this combination as "symbolizing respectively the evolutionary and involutionary cosmic powers. This is the mystic symbol of the universe known as King Solomon's Seal.") – A *t.* pointing upwards (= *liṅga*) is also inscribed in a *t.* pointing downwards (= *yoni*) symbolizing the *svayambhūliṅga* situated in the heart of the *yoni*. – A *t.* with a circle either inscribed or circumscribed, represents the *trimūrti*; this combination is further a syncretistic symbol of Śaivism and Vaiṣṇavism. – 2 *t.*, together having the form of a *ḍamaru* (like an hourglass), also represent the *trimūrti*.

In Buddhism a *t.* pointing upwards symbolizes the *triratna*. In addition (or therefore), the *buddhas* represented in the *padmāsana*-att. (*dhyānāsana*) often show the outer form of a triangle (thus esp. in Indo-China and in the Far East). – *t.* as an attr. is char. of Vajradhātvīśvarī. – Another n. (in Tantrism): *mūlatrikoṇa*.

Lit.: BPR 48; DHP 219, 231, 352; G 18 (ill.); GH 56; HAHI 12 a.pl. 7B; KiSH 93; SM 88.

trilocana "three-eyed" (attr.), see *trinayana*. Trilocana is also an epithet of Śiva.

Lit.: DHP 191; KiSH 23.

Trilokasandarśana-Lokeśvara ("L., the manifestation of the three worlds"; Buddh.), n. of a variety of Avalokiteśvara. Char.: Mu.: *jñāna-* (?) and *karaṇa-mudrā*.

Lit.: BBh. 396 a.pl. 19(A).

trimukha "three-headed, three-faced" (attr.), see *triśiras*; Trimukha is also NP of a *yakṣa* attending on the 3rd *tīrthaṅkara* (Jain.). Symbol: *mayūra* or *haṅsa*; attr.: *triśiras*.

Lit.: BBh. 44; GJ 362 a.pl. 24:3; KiDG 81 a.pl. 69; KiJ 11 a.pl. 27:3.

trimūrdhan "three-headed (attr.), see *triśiras*.

Lit.: KiDG 30.

Trimūrti ("triple representation").

1. (Hind.) N. of a three-headed syncretistic composition representing the Hindu triad (as creator, preserver and destroyer) of the gods Brahmā (or Sūrya), Viṣṇu and Śiva. However, some scholars have stressed the fact that it is unbelievable that Brahmā, who is almost always represented with four heads, should form part of this composition with only one head. – A T. is usually built up on a central figure which is that either of Viṣṇu or Śiva, constituting the chief person of the composition, and the salient characteristics of the icon belong then to this chief deity (cp. Ekapādamūrti or Ekapādaśiva), this depending on whether the icon is produced in Vaiṣṇavite or Śaivite circles.

More rarely the term T. refers to an icon representing three aspects of the same god (see GoRI, ZM). In this case the term T. would seem to be wrongly used, cp. the celebrated composition in Elephanta which was earlier named Trimūrti and regarded as representing the triad Śiva, Brahmā and Viṣṇu, but which is nowadays identified as a Mahādeva (Maheśvara or Maheśamūrti). Char.: Vāh.: Garuḍa, *haṅsa*, Nandin (may occur in a combined form as Vāh.); attr.: 1 or 2 *padmas* (representing Viṣṇu or Sūrya, respectively), *nāga*, *triśūla* (signifying Śiva), *akṣamālā*, *kamaṇḍalu* (signifying Brahmā), *triśiras*. – The *yantra trikoṇa* and the syllable *OṀ* may symbolically represent T. – T. is also the n. of one of the *vidyeśvaras*. – See also Hari-Hara-pitāmaha.

Lit.: B 550; D 320; GoRI 1:261; GRI 151; Gt 643; IC 1:518; KiDG 17 a.pl. 14f.; KiH 19 a.pl. 57-59; KiSH 24, 43; MG 82 a.pl. facing p. 81; R 1: pl. F,

2:382, 397; WHW 1:395; WM 176; ZA pl. 253ff.; ZM 150.

2. (Buddh.) N. of a three-headed, six-armed composition, composed of the three gods Mañjuśrī, Avalokiteśvara (Padmapāṇi) and Vajrapāṇi.

Lit.: HAHI 23 a.pl. 17A.

trimūrtidāna ("the giving of a triple representation"; attr.), n. denoting a group of three icons which, as a votive gift, is placed in a temple, or the act of donation itself. – Cp. *devadāna*.

Lit.: ZA 111.

trinayana "three-eyed" (attr.). In Hinduism, Śiva esp. has three eyes representing the sun, the moon and *agni* (fire). This third eye (in the centre of the forehead, and pointing up and down) is also named *jñānanetra*. In Buddhism, esp. Lamaism, three-eyed deities are very frequent, and three-eyed deities are also found in Jainism, but in these religions this attr. is obviously of Śaivite origin.

Char. of: Ācāryavajrapāṇi, Agni, Aśvarūḍhadevī, Beg-tse, Bhadra-Kālī, Bhṛkutī, Bhūtaḍamaravajrapāṇi, Bi-har, Brahmaśiraścchedakamūrti, Cāmuṇḍā, Caṇḍikeśvara, Caturbhujatārā, Dhvajāgrakeyūrā, Ekajaṭā, Gaṇeśa (Gaṇapati), Gaurī, mGon-dkar, Guha-Subrahmaṇya, Hālāhala(-Lokeśvara), Harihariharivāhanodbhava, Hevajra, Indra, Jāṅgulī, Jaya-Durgā, Kālacakra (also the Śakti), Kāla-Mañjuśrī, Kalyāṇasundara, Kāmāntakamūrti, Kiraṇākṣa, Krauñcabhettar, Kurukullā, Mahācakravajrapāṇi, Mahācīnatārā, Mahākāla, Mahākāya, Mahālakṣmī, Mahāmāya, Mahāmāyūrī, Mahāpratisarā, Mahāśītavatī, Maheśamūrti, Mahiṣāsuramardinī, Mārīcī (in different forms), Māyājālakramāryāvalokiteśvara, *nāgadevas*, Nairātmā, Nīlāmbaravajrapāṇi, Padmanarteśvara, Padmapāṇi, Paramāśva, Parṇaśavarī, Pāśupatamūrti, Prasannatārā, Sadyojāta, Saṃvara, Saṅ-dui, Saptakṣara, Saptaśatika-Hayagrīva, Sarvanivaraṇaviṣkambhin (in the *yi-dam*-form), Siṅhanāda, Sitātapatrā, Sitatārā, Śiva, Śivā, Ṣoḍaśabhujā-Durgā, Śrīdevī, Surā, Sūrya, Svarṇākarṣaṇa(-Bhairava), Tārā, Tārakāri, Tatpuruṣa, Trailokyavaśaṅkara(-Lokeśvara), Ucchuṣma, Uṣṇīṣavijayā, Vajracarcikā, Vajraśāradā, Vajrasarasvatī, Vajraśṛṅkhalā, Vajratārā, Vajravārāhī (in different forms), Vajrayoginī, Vāmā, Vāmadeva, Vīrabhadra, Viṣṇvanugrahamūrti, Vyākhyānadakṣiṇāmūrti.

Other n.: *tridṛś*, *trilocana*, *trinetra*, *tryambaka*.

Lit.: DHP 214; KISH 23, 31; W 27.

Trinetra ("three-eyed"), attr. and epithet of Śiva (see *trinayana*).

Lit.: R 2:49.

tripādaka "three-footed" (attr.). Char. of: Agni (sometimes), Bhṛṅgin, Jvaradeva, Kubera, Śarabha, Viṣṇu Vāmanāvatāra, Yajñamūrti.

Lit.: B 525; DHP 136; KiSH 56; W 18, 131 (ill.).

tripāṭakahasta (Mu.). I have seen this term only in WM, where it is (without translation) used in the sense of *tripatākāmudrā* 2, see below. If the term *t.* is in fact linguistically 'sound', it may allude to *pāṭaka* ("splitter, divider") and signify the two fingers 'divided' by the object held between them (cp. *kartarīmudrā*.) But if this is the case, the meaning of *tri* ("3") is obscure.

Lit.: WM 101 a.fig. 28.

tripatākā(hasta)mudrā (or *-patāka-*; lit. "three-flag-hand", cp. *patākā* "flag"; Mu.).

1. This term is explained in R as a pose of the arm: "the upper arm lifted up as high as the shoulder horizontally and the forearm held at right angles to it vertically and the palm of the hand bent at right angles to the forearm and facing upwards", cp. "dreifach gebeugte Haltung" (WM). In this form *t.* would be char. of Śiva in some dance-forms, such as *lalita*, *kaṭisama*. – Cp. *patākāmudrā*.

2. In MW *t.* is interpreted thus: "(the

hand) with 3 fingers stretched out". In this form it seems to form part of or to be identical with the *kartarīmudrā** and to signify the index, the long and little fingers stretched upwards (like three flags and holding an attr. between the index and the long fingers), and it is in this sense that *t.* is most commonly used. In WHW *t.* is described as a variety of the *patākāmudrā* with the difference: the ring-finger is bent forward; it represents coition. – Cp. *tripāṭakahasta.*

Lit.: AIP passim; MW 459; R 2:263; Th. 29 (ill.); WHW 2:86; WM 94.

triphala ("three fruits"; attr.), n. of a Vaiṣṇavite mark on the forehead consisting of three vertical strokes, the middle one being red. – Cp. *ūrdhvapuṇḍra.* – Another n.: *tirunāmam.*

Lit.: IC 1:571; JDI 58.

Tripiṭaka, see Tipiṭaka.

tripuṇḍra "three-mark" (attr.), see *tiryak-puṇḍra.*

Lit.: IC 1:571; KiSH 93; R 2:306.

tripura "three cities" of gold, silver and iron, respectively, which Maya built for the *asuras* (for the three sons of Tāraka), one in heaven, one in the air and one on earth, and which were later destroyed by Śiva in his form as Tripurāntaka. – Tripura as NP is also another (probably abbreviated) n. for Tripurāntaka.

Lit.: MW 459; R 2:164.

Tripurā (probably "Lady of the three cities"), n. of a form of Pārvatī (Devī) as the Śakti of Tripurāntaka. She is regarded by the Jains as one of the *aṣṭamātaras.* – Char.: Vāh.: she is surrounded by several *gṛdhras*; Mu.: *abhaya-, varada-mudrā*; attr.: *akṣamālā, aṅkuśa, pāśa, pustaka.* – Cp. Tripura-Bhairavī, Tripurasundarī.

Lit.: GJ 411; MEIA 164; R 1:361.

Tripurā-Bhairavī ("the frightful Lady of the three cities"), n. of a form of Pārvatī as the Śakti of Tripurāntaka, cp. Tripurā. Char.: Mu.: *abhaya-, varada-mudrā*; attr.: *akṣamālā, muṇḍamālā, vidya* (?).

Lit.: R 1:366; SSI 212.

Tripuradahana ("burning the three cities"), epithet of Tripurāntaka.

Lit.: R 2:115

Tripurāntaka ("Destroyer of the three cities"), n. of an *ugra-* (*saṅhāra-*)representation of Śiva burning the three cities (*tripura,* sometimes conceived as a demon, Tripura). As regards his Śakti, see Tripurā (with other epithets). T. is found in 8 forms; in one of them Śiva is represented standing in a chariot, the driver (*sūta*) of which is Brahmā. Char.: Vāh.: Apasmāra or *ratha* drawn by horses (*aśva*); att.: *ālīḍhāsana*; Mu.: *kartarī-, kaṭaka-* (two forehands may show this Mu., the left hand holding a fictive bow, the right having just released the bow-string), *sūci-, vismaya-mudrā*; attr.: *cakra, dhanus* (sometimes missing, in which case suggested by a Mu.), *gadā, ghaṇṭā, khaḍga, kheṭaka, (kṛṣṇa)mṛga, paraśu, śaṅkha, śara, ṭaṅka, triśūla, vajra.* T. originates probably in a conception rivalling that of the Vaiṣṇavite Trivikrama. – Other n.: Tripuradahana, Tripurasaṅhāra.

Lit.: B 486 a.pl. 32:3; BECA 1: pl. 36b; JDI 31, 103; R 1:19; 2:115, 164 a.pl. 37-40; SB 53 a.fig. 32 a.passim; SIB pl. 28, 50; SSI 140; Th. 83 a.pl. 46; ZA 224 a.pl. 226; ZM 206 a.pl. 55.

Tripurasaṅhāra ("[representation of] the destruction of the three cities"), see Tripurāntaka.

Lit.: JDI 31.

Tripurasundarī ("the beautiful Lady of the three cities or of Tripura"), n. of a form of Pārvatī as the Śakti of Tripurāntaka. Attr.: *āñjanī, aṅkuśa, darpaṇa, ikṣukodaṇḍa, padma, pañcaśara, pāśa, phala.* See Bālā-Tripurasundarī, Tripurā, and cp. Lalitā, Rājarājeśvarī.

Lit.: B 469; SB 225; ZA 91.

Tripuratāṇḍava ("the *tāṇḍava*-dance of Tripura"), n. of a dance-form associated with Śiva Naṭarāja, alluding to Śiva as Tripurāntaka. He has 16 arms with different weapons; Gaurī stands on his left, and Skanda on his right.

Lit.: SSI 84.

tripurotsava "festival (in honour) of Tripura", n. of a festival in the month *kārttika* (October-November).
Lit.: IC 1:592.

tripuṣākāra ("having the shape of the plant Convolvulus turpethum"), n. of the cucumber-shaped apex of a *liṅga*, see *śiro-varttana*.
Lit.: R 2:93.

triratha (lit. "three-chariot"; attr.), a term referring to the layers of the pedestal of a *pīṭha*.
Lit.: B 436, 547 a.pl. 46:4.

triratna "three jewels" (attr.; Buddh., Jain.), n. of a symbol representing, in Buddhism: the Buddha, the *dharma* and the *saṅgha* (of these, *dharma* and *saṅgha* are sometimes, like the Buddha, conceived as deities and worshipped in both symbolic and anthropomorphic forms), cp. *OṀ*. The symbol or sign of *t.* is either a triangle (*trikoṇa*) or a three-pronged sign which is connected with both the *triśūla* and the *vajra* and which probably originates in the Indus Valley civilization; this sign is found esp. on the *stūpa* at Sāñcī. – Among the Jains *t.* symbolizes: right knowledge, right belief, and right conduct, and it is represented by three dots. – *t.* is also a *maṅgala*, see *aṣṭamaṅgala*. – Cp. *cintāmaṇi*.
Lit.: BBh. 32, 438 a.figs. 9-11; CEBI 13 a.pl. 1:1, 2:4, 6:22-23; GJ 383; Gz 53; H pl. 3:29-30; KiSB 34; ZA 27.

Triśalā ("three bristles long"; Jain.), n. of a queen into whose womb the embryo of Mahāvīra was transferred (after having been begotten in the womb of Devānandā), and who is therefore also regarded as the mother of Mahāvīra.
Lit.: GJ 23 a.pl. 20a; KiJ 13 a.pl. 34-37.

triśikha "three-pointed", a hooked staff (attr.), probably identical with the *triśūla*.
Lit.: B 501; MW 460.

triśikhā "three tufts of hair" (attr.). Char. of Daśabhujasita-Mārīcī.
Lit.: KiSB 85.

triśiras (*triśīrṣa[n]*) "three-headed" (attr.). The conception of a three-headed deity should, according to some scholars, originate in Mediterranean culture, although such a deity is, however, already to be found in the Indus Valley civilization. An admixture of such a Mediterranean feature with elements in the Dravidian Śaivite imagination, may account, esp. in Buddhist culture, for the *t.* concept. In Hinduism, Śiva Mahādeva and Trimūrti particularly are represented with three heads; in Buddhism and Jainism three-headed deities and three-headed varieties of (usually) one-headed gods are rather frequent (see KiDG).
Char. of: Acala, Agni, Ardhanārīśvara, Avalokiteśvara (some Lokeśvara-forms), Bi-har, Dhvajāgrakeyūrā, Gomedha, Grahamātṛkā, Hālāhala, Hari-Hara-Pitāmaha, Hayagrīva, Hevajra, Jambhala, Jāṅgulī, Jvaradeva, Kālajambhala, Kinnara, Kṛṣṇa-Yamāri, Kubera, Kumāra, Mahābala, Mahācakravajrapāṇi, Mahādeva, Mahāmantrānusāriṇī, Mahāmāyūrī, Mahāpratisarā (?), Mahāśītavatī, Maitreya, Mañjuśrī (some forms), Mārīcī (in different forms), Mārttaṇḍa-Bhairava, Nīladaṇḍa, Padmāntaka, Parṇaśavarī, Pātala, Prajñāntaka, Ṣaḍbhuja-Sitatārā, Saṅ-Dui and his Śakti, Saptakṣara, Sarasvatī, Sarvāhna, Śatruvidhvaṅsinī, Sāvitrī, Sitātapatrā(-Aparājitā), Sitatārā, Śrīdevī, Sukhāvatī-Lokeśvara, Sumbharāja, Svasthāveśinī, Ṭakkirāja, Trimukha, Trimūrti, Uṣṇīṣa, Uṣṇīṣavijayā, Vajradhara, Vajrasarasvatī, Vajraśṛṅkhalā, Vighnāntaka, Viśvarūpa, Yamāntaka.
Other n.: *trimukha, trimūrdha(n)*.
Lit.: HuGT 6; KiDG 30; KiSH 19, 24; MG ill. facing p. 96.

Triśiras ("three-headed"), epithet of Kubera.

triśīrṣa(n) "three-headed" (attr.), see *triśiras*.

trisūcika "three-pointed" (attr.), see sub *vajra*.

triśūla "trident" (attr.), n. of one of the most important attributes in Indian iconography, used as a symbolic weapon against enemies or Evil. It is a symbol of magical nature, probably originating in the Indus

Valley civilization, a Shamanic emblem, esp. thus when signifying Śiva (whose *t.* is named Pinãka), and it is char. of him in most of his manifestations. It is "the symbol of the three qualities of Nature, the three *guṇa*s, and hence of the three functions of Creator, Preserver, and Destroyer" (DHP); it is further "considered to be in continual motion over the universe to guard and preserve its creatures" (Gt); in Tantrism it is "an exorcising instrument, a magic wand to conjure power over demons" (SM). Some scholars see in *t.* a symbol of fire. In Buddhism there is a symbolical connection between *t.* and *vajra* and *triratna.* – A *t.* is usually carried by images as an attr. in one hand, but it is also worshipped as an independent, aniconic cult emblem; as an emblem it is also carried by Śaivite ascetics and Yogins. Char. of: Aghora, Agni, Ahirbudhnya, Aja, Amoghapāśa, Aparājita, Bahurūpa, Bhadrā, Bhadra-Kālī, Bhaga, Bhṛkuṭī, Brahmāṇī, Cāmuṇḍā, Caṇḍā, Caṇḍeśvara, Cundā, Dattātreya, Devadevatā-Lokeśvara, Devī, Dhvajāgrakeyūrā, Ekanetra, Ekapādamūrti, Gaṇapati, Ghaṇṭākarṇī, Guha-Subrahmaṇya, Hālāhala-Lokeśvara, Hara, Hari-Hara, Harihariharivāhanodbhava, Hayagrīva, Hevajra, Jambhala, Jāṅgulī, Jaya-Durgā, Jayanta, Jayantī, Kālacakra, Kāladūtī, Kālī, Kṛśodarī, Kṣemaṅkarī, *kṣetrapāla*s, Kubera, Lakulīśa, Mahābala, Mahākāla (in different forms), Mahālakṣmī, Mahāmāyūrī, Mahāpratisarā, Mahāpratyaṅgirā, Mahāsāhasrapramardanī, Mahāvajradhātu-Lokeśvara, Maheśamūrti, Maheśvarī, Mahiṣāsuramardinī, Maṅgala, Maṅgalā, Māriyammaṉ, Māyājālakramakrodha-Lokeśvara, Mitra, Mṛtyuñjaya, Nandīśvara, Naṭarāja (in different forms), *navadurgās*, Nīlakaṇṭhī, Padmapāṇi, Pārvatī, Piṭāri, Pratyaṅgirā, Pretasantarpita-Lokeśvara, Rāhu, Rakṣoghnamūrti, Ratnaḍākinī, Revata, Ripumāri-Durgā, Rudrāṅśa-Durgā, Śailaputrī, Samvara, Śani, Ṣaṇmukha, Saptakṣara, Sarasiri-Lokeśvara, Sarvabuddhaḍākinī, Sarvamaṅgalā, Saurabheya-Subrahmaṇya, Senānī, Senāpati, Siṅhanādāvalokiteśvara, Sitajambhala, Śiva (in different forms), Śivā, Śiva-Lokeśvara, Śivottama, Skanda, Ṣoḍaśabhuja-Durgā, Śrīdevī, Sugatisandarśana-Lokeśvara, Sūkṣma, Śūlinī, Sureśvara, Sūrya, Sūrya-Nārāyaṇa, Svasthāveśinī, Totalā, Trimūrti, Tryambaka, Uḍḍiyāna-Kurukullā, Vajradhātvīśvarī, Vajragāndhārī, Vana-Durgā, Vārāhī, Vidyujjvālākarālī, Vighnāntaka, Virūpākṣa, Viśvarūpa, Vivasvān, Yama, Yogeśvarī. *t.* is also the weapon of the north-east direction; it also figures as a mark on the hood of Mahāpadma. – Regarding a *t.* with the body or bones of a killed person or demon, see *kaṅkāladaṇḍa.* – Cp. also *nandipada*, *pāśupata*, *paṭṭiśa*, *tridaṇḍa.* – Another n.: *śūla.*

Lit.: B 301; BBh. 440; CEBI 13, 15 a.pl. 1:1, 2:4, 6:23; DHP 216; G 18 (ill.); Gt Suppl. 142; H pl. 7:64; HSIT 11 a.pl. 26; MEIA 250; R 1:7 a.pl. 3:1-2, 2:193; SB 314 a.fig. 232; SM 157; Th. 40; WM 106 a.fig. 53-54; ZA 27.

triṣveṣṭadevatā "three favourite deities", three deities chosen by the worshipper", see *iṣṭadevatā.*

Trita (Āptya) ("the Third, the water-deity"), in the Ṛgveda n. of a form of Indra.
Lit.: DHP 138; IC 1:322; WM 178.

tritīrthī (*-ikā*) "group of three *tīrthaṅkara*s" (attr.; Jain.), n. of a representation (in bronze) of a *tīrthaṅkara* as the chief idol flanked by two other *tīrthaṅkara*s.

trivali (or *-ī*) "three conventional folds" of beauty, indicative of good fortune, on the neck or the stomach (attr.). Char. of: the Buddha, Viṣṇu. This attr. is, as the other n. *kambugrīva** "shell-neck" shows, derived from the three folds which occur at the opening on many shells (see *śaṅkha*), and which are regarded as a mark of beauty. – Another n.: *kambugrīva.*
Lit.: HIS 65 a.pl. 26; SB 165; SIB 70 a.pl. 54.

Trivikrama ("taking three steps; he who strode over the three worlds in three steps; Conqueror of the three worlds"), epithet of Viṣṇu in the Vāmanāvatāra* and n. of an aspect of Viṣṇu, see *caturviṅśatimūrti*. The n. T. probably originally signified Viṣṇu as a sun-god and referred to the three outer points of the orbit of sun (east, zenith, west); later it was connected with the acquisition of the three worlds, heaven, the atmosphere, and the earth, and then with the three steps of Viṣṇu in his dwarf manifestation, by which he measured the universe, consisting of the three worlds: heaven, earth and the infernal regions. – Śakti: Śānti. Char.: att.: the left leg is usually extended and raised; Mu.: *kaṭaka-*, *sūci-mudrā*; attr.: *cakra*, *daṇḍa*, *dhanus* Śārṅga, *gadā*, *hala*, *khaḍga*, *kheṭaka*, *padma*, *pāśa*, *śaṅkha*, *śara*. Cp. also Virāṭarūpa.
Lit.: B 385, 411; BP 82 a.pl. 7-9; D 322; DHP 154; GoRI 1:251; H pl. 6:50; HIS 18; KiH pl. 31; KiSH 39; KrG pl. 9; R 1:161, 229 a.pl. 48-53; SB 88 a.fig. 53; ZA pl. 125, 388.

tṛṇa "bundle of grass" (held in one hand; attr.). Char. of Surabhi.
Lit.: R 1:370.

Tryambaka ("three-eyed"; for *tryambaka* as an attr., see *trinayana*). – The original sense of T. is possibly "one who has three mothers" (cp. *ambe ambike ambālike*, VS) or "having three wives or sisters". T. is also an epithet of Śiva and n. of one among the group *ekādaśarudra*. In this form he has the char.: Mu.: *tarjanīmudrā*; attr.: *akṣamālā*, *aṅkuśa*, *cakra*, *ḍamaru*, *dhanus*, *gadā*, *ghaṭa*, *khaṭvāṅga*, *mudgara*, *nāga*, *paraśu*, *pātra*, *paṭṭiśa*, *śara*, *triśūla*.
Lit.: D 332; DHP 191; MW 463; R 2:390; W 230; VS = Vājasaneyi-Saṅhitā; ZA 28.

tsa-tsa, see *thsa-thsa*.

Tsoṅ-kha-pa ("the man from Bulb-valley"; Tib.; Buddh.), n. of a Buddhist reformer (A.D. 1357-1419). He was the founder of the *dGe-lugs-pa*-sect. Attr.: *kāṣāya*, *khaḍga*, *padma*s, *pustaka*.
Lit.: CTLP pl. 17; G 5, 38, 107; GRI 294; HSIT 17 a.pl. 43; JSV pl. 58, 69; JT 432.

tulā (*-a*) "weight", n. of the *rāśi* "Libra"
Lit.: BBh. 383 a.pl. 246; GH 50; IC 2:731.

tulābhāra "weight-load", or *tulāpuruṣadāna* "giving of a man's weight", n. of a kind of donation to a temple, consisting of a gift of gold etc. equal to a man's weight.
Lit.: BECA 1:71; MW 451.

Tulajā-Bhavānī ("Bh. born from the *rāśi tulā* (?)"), n. of a goddess. Attr.: *pātra* with food, *sruva*.
Lit.: SSI 220.

tulasī (Hi. *tulsī*), n. of a small shrub, the "holy basil, Ocimum basilicum or sanctum" which is sacred to Viṣṇu; the *akṣamālā* of the Viṣṇu *bhakta*s is made of grains or twigs of this shrub. – Tul(a)sīdevī is a deification of this shrub and probably regarded as identical with Lakṣmī. Char.: Vāh.: *padma(-pīṭha)*; Mu.: *abhaya-*, *varada-mudrā*; attr.: *nīlotpala*, *padma*. – See also sub *galantī*.
Lit.: GH 64; IC 1:538; P. L. Jungblut, Die Missetäterstämme (Mödling bei Wien 1945), 173. MG 237; R 1:15, 371; SSR 184.

tūlikā, a kind of painter's brush (attr.), see *śalākā*.
Lit.: SSIP 23.

Tumbura (Jain.), n. of a *yakṣa* attending on the 5th *tīrthaṅkara*. Symbol: Garuḍa.
Lit.: GJ 362 a.pl. 24:5; KiJ 11 a.pl. 27:5.

Tumpuruvar (Tam. "guitar-player"), n. of an attendant of Viṣṇu or Śiva. Attr.: *aśvamastaka*.
Lit.: JDI 63; MEIA 62.

tūṇa "quiver" (attr.).
Lit.: MEIA 254.

tuṇḍa(ka) "trunk (of an elephant)" (attr.). Char. of Gaṇeśa.
Lit.: DHP 296.

tundila "having a large or protuberant belly, pot-bellied" (attr.). This attr. often seems to indicate *yakṣa* origin or a relation to

these deities. Char. of: Agastya, Dhvajāgrakeyūrā, Ekajaṭā, Gaṇeśa (Gaṇapati), Jambhala, Jyeṣṭhā, Kubera, Mahācīnatārā, Śatruvidhvaṅsinī, Ucchuṣma, Vajragāndhārī, Vajravetālī, Varuṇa, *yakṣas*. – Other n.: *bṛhatkukṣi*, *lambodara*.
Lit.: B 338, 356, 529.

tūri "trumpet" (attr.), n. of a *maṅgala*, see *aṣṭamaṅgala*.

Turkkai (Tam.), see Durgā.

Tuṣita ("satisfied").
1. (Hind.) N. of a class of genii or celestial beings, the sons of Vedaśiras and Tuṣitā.
Lit.: DHP 302.
2. (Buddh.) N. of the heaven in which the *(dhyāni)bodhisattvas*, i.e. the future *buddhas* (e.g. Maitreya), temporarily live. Cp. *trikāya*.
Lit.: G 53; KiSB 26.

Tuṣṭi ("satisfaction"; personification), n. of the Śakti of Mādhava or Viṣṇu.
Lit.: R 1:233; SSI 189.

Tvaritā ("swift"), NP of a Tantric goddess. Attr.: *guñjamālā*.
Lit.: MEIA 160; SSI 212.

Tvaṣṭar (also -ṭā, -tṛ, Taṣṭar, Tvashtri; "carpenter"), n. of a divine builder, the former of men and animals; "Gott der Zeugung". He was an Āditya and the father of Saraṇyū. Attr.: *homajakalika*, 2 *padmas*, *sruk*. – Epithet: Viśvakarman.
Lit.: D 323; DHP 123; GoRI 1:27; GRI 69; Gt 646; IIM 17; R 1:309; WM 178.

U

Ubhayavarāhānana-Mārīcī ("M. having boar-faces on both sides"; Buddh.), n. of a variety of Mārīcī. Char.: colour: red; att.: *ālīḍhāsana*; Vāh.: she tramples underfoot several Hindu deities, e.g. Viṣṇu, Śiva, Brahmā and others; Mu.: *tarjanīmudrā*; attr.: *ajina* (tigerskin), *aṅkuśa*, *aśoka* (flower or bough), *bhindipāla*, *brahmakapāla*, *kamaṇḍalu*, *kapāla*, *karttṛkā*, *khaḍga*, *mahākapāla*, *paraśu*, *sūci*, *sūtra*, *trinayana*, *triśiras* (2 boar-faces, the face between them is *saumya*), *Vairocanabimba* on the crown, *vajradaṇḍa*, *vajrāṅkuśa*, *vajrapāśa*; she is usually 12-armed. – U. is attended by the *dikpālas*.
Lit.: BBh. 212; KiDG 64; KiSB 84.

Uccaiḥśravas (or -ās; "having the ears raised" or "neighing aloud"), n. of a divine horse (*aśva*), the Vāh. of Indra, produced at the churning of the ocean of milk (see Kūrmāvatāra) and fed on ambrosia; the king of horses.
Lit.: D 324; DHP 167; KiSH 88; MW 173; WHW 1:457.

uccaṇḍāstra "terrible arrow" (attr.), see *śara*.
Lit.: ACA 34.

Ucchiṣṭa-Gaṇapati (or -Gaṇeśa; "G. worshipped by the *ucchiṣṭas* [or men who leave the remains of food in their mouth during prayer]", MW), n. of a form of Gaṇeśa together with his Śakti (contrasting to Śuddha-Gaṇapati). Char.: Vāh.: *padmapīṭha*; attr.: *akṣamālā*, *aṅkuśa*, *dāḍima*, *dhanus*, *ikṣukāṇḍa*, *modaka*, *padma*, *ratnamukuṭa*, *pāśa*, *śara*, *trinayana*, *vīṇā*. – Cp. Unmatta-Ucchiṣṭa-Gaṇapati.
Lit.: MW 174; R 1:53 a.pl. 11:2, 12; Th. 97.

Ucchuṣma(-Jambhala) ("one whose crackling becomes manifest"; Buddh.), n. of a form of Jambhala, an emanation of Akṣobhya or Ratnasambhava. Char.: att.: *ālīḍhāsana*; Vāh.: Kubera (lying, vomiting jewels); attr.: *Akṣobhyabimba* in the hair, *candra*, *kapāla*, *nāgas*, *nakula*, *trinayana*, *tundila*, *ūrdhvaliṅga*. – Another n.: Ḍimbha.
Lit.: BBh. 179, 239 a.pl. 130; KiSB 73; MW 174.

udadhikumāra ("ocean-prince"; Jain.), n. of a kind of *bhavanavāsī*.
Lit.: GJ 236.

udarabandha (*-ana*) "band, girdle round the belly" (attr.). Char. of: Dāmodara and other forms of Kṛṣṇa, Gaṇeśa (whose band

is a *nāga*, *nāgabandha*), and others. Cp. *ahyaṅga*.
Lit.: B 291; R 1:23; SSI 10, 50; WHW 2:162; WM 104.

udbhavamudrā "creation-handpose" (Mu.). This handpose "means that the god is created again in the *liṅga*".
Lit.: DiIP 107.

uddesika (Pāli) "significant symbol" (attr.; Buddh.). This term signifies an object of worship, such as *cakra*, *stūpa*, *triratna* etc. – Cp. *samaya*.
Lit.: SeKB 99; ZA 233.

Uḍḍiyāna-Kurukullā (Oḍḍiyāna-; Buddh.), n. of a form of Kurukullā (the word Uḍḍiyāna alludes either to a place or to a certain position of the fingers). Char.: colour: red; att.: *nāṭyasthāna* or *lalitāsana*; Vāh.: *mṛtaka*; attr.: *ajina*, *muṇḍamālā*, *padma* (red), *puṣpadhanvan*, *śara* (of a red *padma*), *triśūla* (of flowers).
Lit.: BBh. 149 a.pl. 122; EB 159; KiDG 64; KiSB 97; MW 175.

Uḍḍiyāna-Mārīcī (Oḍiyāna-; Buddh.), another n. of Vajradhātvīśvarī; regarding Uḍḍiyāna, see Uḍḍiyāna-Kurukullā.
Lit.: BBh. 214.

udīcyaveṣa "the Northerner's dress" (attr.), n. of a dress worn by inhabitants of North India. It consists of trousers, long coat, flat round cap and high boots. Char. of Sūrya.
Lit.: B 437, 439; JMS 35.

uḍukkai, see *uṭukku* and further *ḍamaru*.

uḍumbara (or *ud-*) "Ficus glomerata" (attr.), n. of a wild fig-tree which is said to blossom when a *buddha* has been born. It is sacred to Kaumārī. The fruits of this tree are picked by the gods in the night of the *dīvālī*-festival. – Another n.: *gūlar*.
Lit.: GH 64; IC 1:537; SSI 196; WHW 1:358.

udvāhita ("raised, lifted up"; att.), n. of a pose in which one side of the pelvis is raised and the other lowered proportionately. Char. of Śiva in the *kaṭisama*-dance.
Lit.: R 2:259.

udvāsana "send off", n. of the last part of a *pūjā*.
Lit.: DiIP 90, 100.

udyata-khaṭvāṅga "raised *kh.*" (attr.), n. of a particular form of *khaṭvāṅga*.
Lit.: BBh. 159.

ugra(mūrti) "powerful, violent representation".
1. N. of a punishing or vengeful representation of a god, esp. of Śiva. An *u.* may be of different kinds, see esp. *saṅhāramūrti*; cp. also Ghora, *raudra*. – Ugra is further n. of one of the *mūrtyaṣṭaka*-forms of Śiva and an epithet or n. of a variety of Rudra-Śiva regarded as the son of Mīnākṣi. Wife: Dīkṣā; son: Santāna.
Lit.: B 416, 464; DHP 191; GoRI 1:268; R 1:19, 2:403.
2. Ugra is also NP of a black *mahiṣa*, the Vāh. of Yama.
Lit.: DHP 133.

Ugra-Caṇḍikā (or -Caṇḍā; "the violent C."), n. of one of the *navadurgās*.
Lit.: R 1:357.

Ugra-Narasiṅha ("the violent N."), n. of an *ugra*-representation of Narasiṅha showing him tearing asunder the demon Hiraṇyakaśipu. Attr. like Viṣṇu.
Lit.: SB 349 a.fig. 323; SSI 26.

ugrāsana "the mighty sitting" (att.), n. of a Yogic posture in which "one sits with straightened legs flat out and a little apart, bends down till the forehead touches the knees".
Lit.: WHW 1:76.

Ugra-Tārā ("the violent T.").
1. (Hind.) N. of a terrible goddess. Char.: att.: *ālīḍhāsana*; attr.: *mṛtaka* (carried on her head), *kapāla*.
Lit.: SSI 213.
2. (Buddh.) N. of a form of Mahācīnatārā. Attr.: *nāga*.
Lit.: G 16, 76; KiSB 88.

ujjvalakeśa(ka) "flaming hair" (attr.), see *keśamaṇḍala*.
Lit.: ACA 28.

Ulkādharā ("carrying a meteor"; Buddh.), see Ratnolkā.
Lit.: BBh. 318.

ulūka "owl" (Vāh.). From the Vedic period onwards this animal was looked on as a harbinger of ill-fortune. Char. of: Cāmuṇḍā, Lakṣmī, Rāhu, Vārāhī. – Another n.: *pecaka*.
Lit.: KiSH 88; MKVI 1:102; Sh. 25; WHW 2:540.

Ulūkāsyā ("owl-faced"; Buddh.), n. of a minor goddess.
Lit.: BBh. 319.

Umā, epithet or form of Pārvatī, esp. as the daughter of Dakṣa. Attr.: *akṣamālā, darpaṇa, kamaṇḍalu, padma.* – The real meaning of the n. is not clear. The Hindus interpret it thus: *u mā* "O (child), do not (practice austerities)!" (MW). Another translation is "Light". However, since U. particularly seems to refer to the mother-aspect of Pārvatī, it is possible that the word contains a second member *mā* "mother", as is the case with so many other popular (originally Sino-Tibetan?) goddesses. An attempt has also been made to combine U. with the Sumerian *umu* "mother".
Lit.: D 325; DHP 285; GH 141; GoRI 1:258; Gt 650; HIS 10; KIM pl. 38; Mayrhofer, EWA 1:108; MG 180; MW 217; R 1:360; W 238; WHW 2:530; WM 179; ZA 117 a.pl. 462a.

Umā-Maheśvara(mūrti), n. of a composite representation of Śiva (in an *āsana*-posture) together with Pārvatī, who sits on his left knee. Char.: Śiva: Mu.: *abhayamudrā*; attr.: *ḍamaru, nāgas, triśūla*; Pārvatī: Mu.: *āliṅgahastamudrā*; attr.: *jambhīra.* – This term sometimes refers to a representation of the whole family of Śiva: Śiva (either in anthropomorphic form or represented by a *liṅga*) with his Vāh. Nandin, Pārvatī (sometimes with the Vāh. *siṅha*), Gaṇeśa with the Vāh. *ākhu*, and Skanda with the Vāh. *mayūra*. Sometimes also other attendants, e.g. Bhṛṅgin, Nārada, etc.
Lit.: B 464; GI pl. 75; IP pl. 31; R 2:132 a.pl. 23-29; SSI 113.

Umāpati, epithet of Śiva as the "husband of Umā", i.e. of Pārvatī. In this aspect he is a father god.
Lit.: B 446.

Umāsahita(mūrti) ("representation [of Śiva] together with Umā").

1. N. of a *sthānaka*-representation of Śiva and Pārvatī (a sub-form of Candraśekharamūrti). Char.: Mu.: *abhaya-, āhūyavarada-, varada-mudrā.* – Another n.: Sar(va)guṇanāthasvāmin.
Lit.: B 464, 466; R 2:120 a.pl. 15, 17f.; SB 273, 304 a.fig. 208; Th. 80 a.pl. 41.

2. N. of an *āsana*-representation of Śiva and Pārvatī (sitting beside him). The form of Śiva corresponds to the *sukhāsanamūrti*. Char. of Pārvatī: Mu.: *kaṭaka-, varada-mudrā*; attr.: *nīlotpala.*
Lit.: R 2:130 a.pl. 21; SSI 110.

umā-tāṇḍava "(Śiva in) a *tāṇḍava*-dance together with Umā", n. of a dance-form of Śiva Naṭarāja with Umā (Pārvatī) standing to his left. He has 6 arms. Spec. char. of Śiva are *vismayamudrā* and the attr. *triśūla*; his left foot is placed on Apasmāra. Umā: char.: Vāh.: her left foot is placed on Apasmāra; Mu.: *abhaya-, gaja-, vismaya-mudrā*; attr.: *ḍamaru, kapāla, triśūla.*
Lit.: SSI 84.

Unmatta-Bhairava ("the frantic Bh."), n. of a form of Śiva Bhairava.
Lit.: B 466.

Unmatta-Ucchiṣṭa-Gaṇapati ("the frantic U.-G."), n. of a form of Gaṇeśa, cp. Ucchiṣṭa-Gaṇapati. Char.: attr.: *aṅkuśa, danta, modaka, pāśa.*
Lit.: R 1:49, 58 a.pl. 10:1.

Unnati ("progress"), n. of the wife of Garuḍa.
Lit.: MW 193.

upabhṛt "sacrificial vessel or ladle" made of *aśvattha*-wood (attr.), see *sruk*.
Lit.: MW 203; RV 42.

upacāra "the offering; a vessel, jar" used for libations to the gods (attr.).
Lit.: ACA 90; KiH pl. 139:6.

upadeśamudrā "teaching-gesture" (Mu.), see *vyākhyānamudrā*.
Lit.: RN 31.

upādhyāya "teacher, preceptor".
Lit.: BRI 64; GJ 425; WHW 1:439.

upākaraṇa "the beginning" (of studying the Veda after the initiation), n. of a ceremony.
Lit.: IC 1:364.

Upakeśinī ("beside Keśinī"; Buddh.), n. of a deity who accompanies Arapacana.
Lit.: BBh. 120.

upalakṣaṇa "lesser mark" (of a *buddha*; attr.), see *anuvyañjana*.
Lit.: BRI 52.

Upāli (Buddh.), n. of one of the most prominent of the Buddha's pupils. Attr.: *kāṣāya, pātra.*
Lit.: BRI 16; G 104; MW 214.

upanayana "initiation", n. of a *saṅskāra*-rite "in which a *guru* draws a boy towards himself and initiates him into one of the three twice-born (*dvija*) classes" (MW). The rite is performed in the child's 8th-12th year. This rite is reckoned as the second birth of the "twice-born"; with this rite the boy is invested with the *yajñopavīta* and brought into the stage of a *brahmacārin*. – Cp. *varṇa.*
Lit.: DiIP 180, 186; GBM 136; GH 334; GJ 412; Gt Suppl. 144; IC 1:364; MW 201; STP 7:76.

upanāyikā ("fit for or belonging to an offering"), n. of a class of minor deities, "the minor ruling-powers or fairies".
Lit.: DHP 301; MW 201.

Upapattivaśitā ("control of fitness, accomplishing"; Buddh.), n. of a *vaśitā*. Char.: colour: mixed; attr.: *latā.*
Lit.: BBh. 330.

upapīṭha "sub-basement" of a temple on which the *adhiṣṭhāna* mostly rests.
Lit.: BECA 1:264, 270, 272.

upāsaka (fem.: *upāsikā*) "follower".

1. (Buddh.) N. of a Buddhist lay worshipper and attendant of the Buddha.
Lit.: BRI 55; KiSB 14; MW 215.

2. (Jain.) N. of a minor deity that accompanies, e.g., a *tīrthaṅkara*. See the more frequent term *yakṣa. u.* is also n. of a lay worshipper.
Lit.: B 562; IC 2:638; SchRI 234.

upāśraya ("refuge"; Jain.), n. of a cult centre.
Lit.: GJ 396; GRI 202.

upaveśa "seated (attitude)", see *āsanamūrti.*
Lit.: WHW 1:45.

upavīta ("invested with the sacred thread"; attr.), n. of a certain manner of wearing of the deerskin (*ajina*). Char. of Viṣṇu in some forms (e.g. as Vāmanāvatāra). The term *u.* is also used as another n. for *yajñopavīta* (thus ACA).
Lit.: ACA passim; R 1:22.

upāya ("approach, means"; Buddh.). In Vajrayāna Buddhism this is the male principle, the device by which the truth may be manifest. It corresponds to *prajñā*, and the union of these two principles (means and knowledge) is represented by the sexual union of a man and a woman (see *yabyum*). Cp. also *vajraghaṇṭā, vajrahuṅkāramudrā.* Cp. *sādhaka.*
Lit.: GRI 273; SM 107.

Upāya ("approach"; Vāh.; Buddh.), n. of a man on whom (together with Prajñā) Mārīcīpicuvā treads.
Lit.: BBh. 211; IC 2:593.

Upāyapāramitā ("perfection of the means of success against an enemy"; Buddh.), n. of a *pāramitā*. Char.: colour: green; attr.: *cintāmaṇidhvaja, vajra* on a yellow *padma.*
Lit.: BBh. 327.

Upendra ("beside Indra, the younger brother of Indra").

1. (Hind.) N. of an aspect of Viṣṇu, see *caturviṅśatimūrti.*
Lit.: DHP 154; KiSH 39; R 1:230.

2. (Vāh.; Buddh.) Prasannatārā is depicted treading upon U.
Lit.: BBh. 250.

uposatha (Pāli), see *poṣadha.*

Upulvan (Singh., < Pāli Uppalavaṇṇa, Skt Utpalavarṇa "having the colour of the blue lotus"), in Sri Lanka n. of a popular god who is taken to be identical with Viṣṇu, but whose task was originally to protect the people of Sri Lanka and the religion of the Buddha.
Lit.: S. PARANAVITANA, The shrine of Upulvan at Devundara (Colombo 1953).

uraga "snake" (Vāh. and attr.), see *nāga*.
Lit.: MEIA 236.

uraṇa "ram" (Vāh.), etymologically associated with Varuṇa*. For "ram" as Vāh., see *meṣa*.

uras-sūtra "band round the chest" (attr.). Char. of, e.g., Śiva Naṭarāja.
Lit.: R 2:225.

ūrdhvabāhu "lifted arm" (Mu.), n. of a hand-pose, the arms being lifted above the head.
Lit.: ZA 89 a.pl. 276.

Ūrdhva-Gaṇapati ("the erect G."), n. of a form of Gaṇeśa together with his Śakti. Char.: colour: golden yellow; attr.: *danta, ikṣu-kodaṇḍa, kalhāra*-flowers, *kaṇiśa, śara*.
Lit.: R 1:56; Th. 97.

ūrdhvajānu "raising one knee or the knees high upwards" (att.), n. of a dance-posture, char. of Śiva Naṭarāja.
Lit.: SB 60 a.fig. 34f.; SIB pl. 29.

ūrdhvakeśa (or -*ā*) "erect hair, having the hair erect" (attr.), n. of a head-dress "in a beautiful big bud-like form... and hanging locks of hair with twisted tips" (SB). See *keśamaṇḍala*.
Lit.: MEIA 212; MW 222; SB 212.

ūrdhvaliṅga "having the *liṅga* erect" (attr.), n. of an ithyphallic pose, emblematic of fertility. Char. of: Ardhanārīśvara, Gaṇeśa, Hara-Pārvatī, Lakulīśa, Pañcānana, Śiva, Śiva-Lokeśvara, Ucchuṣma. – Another n.: *ūrdhvameḍhra*.
Lit.: B 359 a.passim a.pl. 15:1, 38:2, 39:1-2, 40:4.

ūrdhvameḍhra "having the *liṅga* erect" (attr.), see *ūrdhvaliṅga*.
Lit.: JMS 33.

ūrdhvapuṇḍra (-*tilaka*) "upright mark on the forehead" (attr.), n. of a Vaiṣṇavite sectarian mark, made on the forehead with white clay and red pigment, in the form of a U or Y with a dot in the middle. Char., e.g., of Rāmānuja, Madhva. – Cp. *tilaka, triphala*.
Lit.: GH 57, 330; GJ 382; KiSH 90; MW 222; SSI 259; WHW 1:208.

ūrdhvāsyapāda "having face and foot (feet) lifted up" (att.), n. of a dancing posture.
Lit.: MEIA 219.

ūrdhvatāṇḍava "the erect *tāṇḍava*-dance", n. of a dancing-form, see *lalāṭatilaka*.
Lit.: SB 94; SSI 82.

ūrṇā, originally a "whorl of hair between the eyebrows" (attr.; Buddh.), n. of a certain form of *tilaka* which later took on the shape of a round mark or protuberance on the forehead. It belongs to the group *mahā-puruṣalakṣaṇa* and is a mark of nobility and illumination. Char. of: the Buddha, *(dhyāni)buddhas* and *bodhisattvas*; also Nāgārjuna, Viṣṇu. – Many forms of *ū*. are illustrated in RN.
Lit.: H pl. 4:37a; HIS 16; JMS 28, 30; KiSB 36; RAAI 274; RN 33 a.pl. 30; SS pl. 31:140; SeKB 160.

ūrudāma(n) "thigh wreath, thigh garland" (attr.), n. of festoons hanging down from the hip girdle along the thighs. – Another n.: *ūrumālai*.
Lit.: AIP 59.

ūrumālai (Tam. for Skt *ūru-mālā*) "festoons hanging down to the thighs from the hip girdle" (attr.), see *ūrudāma*.
Lit.: Th. 45.

ūrusaṅsthita(mudrā) "(hand) resting on the thigh" (Mu.), see *kaṭimudrā*.
Lit.: ACA 40.

uruśṛṅga, n. of "the small turrets clustered on the successive levels of a *śikhara* and duplicating its shape in a miniature"; architectural term.
Lit.: RAAI 274.

Uṣādevī ("dawn goddess"; Jain.), n. of a goddess; see also Uṣas.
Lit.: GJ 363.

Uśanas ("wishing"[?]), epithet of Śukra.
Lit.: MW 219.

Uṣas (or -ās, -ā: "the Dawn", an ancient personification, cp. Latin Aurora), n. of one of the oldest Vedic deities, the daughter of Dyaus and sometimes mentioned as the wife of Sūrya (Ravi). Char.: Vāh.: *ratha* drawn by 7 reddish *gaus* (or *aśvas*), representing the 7 days of the week. – Cp. Uṣādevī.
Lit.: D 327; DHP 97; GoRI 1:91; Gt 661; IC 1:324; IIM 21; MG 67; WHW 2:536; WM 179.

usīra, n. of the fragrant root of the grass "Vetiveria zizanioides Nash. (Andropogon muricatus)" (attr.; Jain.). A brush is made of the roots of this grass and used for the cleaning of the icons (see *vālakuñci*).
Lit.: GJ 429.

uṣṇīṣa, general meaning: "row of small curls of hair fringing the forehead" (R).
1. (Attr.; Hind.) *u.* signifies in older Hindu sculpture a kind of turban or fillet (worn already by the Vedic Indians); cp. Uṣṇīṣin.
Lit.: Bh. 15; MKVI 1:104; R 2:373.
2. (Attr.; Buddh.) *u.*, which originally signified a raised part of the coiffure (cp. above, a kind of turban), was later on regarded as a kind of excrescence or protuberance on the head covered by small short curls, and it is emblematic of the Buddha's more than mortal knowledge and consciousness. It is also said to be the symbol of *nirvāṇa*. Consequently it is char. of the Buddha, further of all kinds of *buddhas* and also of some other images (e.g. Nagārjuna), and belongs to the group *mahāpuruṣalakṣaṇa*.
The *u.* was at the beginning rounded, but later it received a more or less peaked shape, and in Siamese representations it has a very long pointed top which may possibly be explained as originating in a *cintāmaṇi* placed on the *u.* (cp. the frequent appearance of such a feature in Tibetan representations). This pointed top is also conceived as a flame (*agni*), esp. in South India, Indonesia and Sri Lanka. – In ornamental art *u.* signifies a coping or crown of the stone railing; see *vedikā*. – Another n.: *mūrdhnyuṣṇīṣa*.
Lit.: H pl. 4; HIS 16, 50 a.pl. 1-2; HAA pl. 101; KiSB 36; MW 220; RAAI 274; RN 29; SS pl. 30:137, 31:140, 33:152; SeKB 160 (ill.); Th. 72; ZA 233.
3. (Buddh.) *u.* is also n. of a class of 8 deities who have nothing to do with the *u.* as a crown or excrescence, but who are rather connected with the *dikpālas* and seem to be an extension of the *dhyānibuddhas*. They are: Vajroṣṇīṣa, Ratnoṣṇīṣa, Padmoṣṇīṣa, Viśvoṣṇīṣa, Tejoṣṇīṣa, Dhvajoṣṇīṣa, Tīkṣṇoṣṇīṣa, Chatroṣṇīṣa. Cp. also Uṣṇīṣa, below.
Lit.: BBh. 299.

Uṣṇīṣa (cp. *uṣṇīṣa* 3; Buddh.), n. of a *dikpāla* of the zenith direction. Char.: colour: yellow; attr.: *cakra* (yellow), *cintāmaṇi*, *khaḍga*, *padma*, *triśiras*.
Lit.: BBh. 256.

Uṣṇīṣasitā ("the white *uṣṇīṣa*(-goddess)"; Buddh.), see Sitātapatrā.
Lit.: G 12, 72.

Uṣṇīṣasitātapatrā ("Sitātapatrā of the *uṣṇīṣa*"; Buddh.), n. of a variety of the Sitatārā in Lamaism. She is, according to the description, 1000-headed and 1000-armed with eyes in all the hands. Further attr.: *cakra*, *chattra*, *śara* and other Tantric symbols.
Lit.: G 75.

Uṣṇīṣavijayā ("victory, or victorious, by the *uṣṇīṣa*"; Buddh.), n. of a Mahāyāna goddess who is an emanation of Vairocana and is regarded as a female *bodhisattva*, but also as a female *dikpāla* of the zenith direction, and also belongs to the *dhāriṇī*-group. She is very popular, esp. in Tibet. – Char.: colour: white; att.: *padmāsana*; Mu.: *abhaya-*, *buddhaśramaṇa-*, *dhyāna-*, *tarjanī-*, *varada-mudrā*; attr.: *bimba* of the Buddha on a *padma*, or of Vairocana (or Amitābha?) on the crown or in one hand, *cakra*, *cintāmaṇi*, *dhanus*, *kamaṇḍalu* (sometimes with jewels), *śara*, *tarjanīpāśa*, *trinayana*, *triśiras*, *viśvavajra*; she is 8-armed.
Lit.: BBh. 214, 338 a.pl. 156f.; BRI 176; G 33, 72; JSV pl. 77; KiDG 64, 67 a.pl. 50f.

Uṣṇīṣin ("wearing a turban"), epithet of Śiva.
Lit.: MW 220.

uṣṭra "camel" (Vāh.). Char. of: Śukra, Hemantadevī.
Lit.: G 82; KiSH 62, 87.

uṣṭraniṣadana "the sitting of (or like that of) a camel" (att.), n. of a Yogic posture probably identical with *uṣṭrāsana*.
Lit.: B 271.

uṣṭrāsana "camel-sitting" (att.), n. of a Yogic posture; cp. *uṣṭraniṣadana.*
Lit.: KiH pl. 153 row 2:1.

utkaṭāsana "excessive posture" (att.), n. of a Yogic posture; in the Jaipur Museum it is illustrated by a figure standing straight up and down on the head, with the hands performing the *añjalimudrā.*
Lit.: KiH pl. 152 row 2:1.

utkuṭikāsana (or *-kūṭi-*; cp. MW: *utkuṭakāsana* "the sitting upon the hams"; the word is also translated thus: "kauernde Sitzstellung"; att.), n. of an *āsana*-posture, a Yogic att. "where one sits with heels kept close to the bottom and with the back slightly curved and the forearms resting on the knees raised above the seat. In order to keep the knees firm in the position described, a cloth band known as *yogapaṭṭa* is tied round the raised knees." (B, cp. WM). – A quite different att. is described in SB under this term: "the right leg bent and kept somewhat slantingly on the pedestal and the left leg hanging down." (cp. SIB and RN). – *u.* is char. of (among others): Caṇḍikeśvara, Yogadakṣiṇāmūrti. – Cp. *sopāśrayāsana.*
Lit.: B 271; MW 176; pw 1:220; R 1:19; RN 31; SB 140, 149 a.fig. 86, 92 a.passim; SIB 68; WAA 25:176 a.fig. 29; WM 90 a.fig. 5.

Utnauti-Lokeśvara (Utnauti?; Buddh.), n. of a variety of Avalokiteśvara. Char.: att.: *ardhaparyaṅkāsana*; Vāh.: *padma*; Mu.: *abhayamudrā*; attr.: *akṣamālā, kamaṇḍalu, kapāla, pāśa, vajra.*
Lit.: BBh. 397 a.pl. 25(A).

utpala "lily, blue lotus" (attr.), see *nīlotpala.*
Lit.: ACA passim; G 18 (ill.).

utpalamudrā "night-lotus-gesture" (Mu.), n. of a handpose, described thus: it "wird dargestellt, indem man die Hände mit ihren Wurzeln (Gelenken) aneinander legt, sie dann mit gespreizten halbgekrümmten Fingern wieder voneinander entfernt, wobei die beiden Daumen und die kleinen Finger sich mit ihren Spitzen eben berühren, so gleichsam einen Blütenkelch bildend" (KiSB). It symbolizes a temple tower, wrestling, sexual intercourse. – Char. of Sitatārā.
Lit.: KiSB 104 N.44 with further lit., WHW 2:88.

utsava "festival" in the festival calender. Cp. *mahotsava, nityotsava.*
Lit.: DiIP 158.

utsava-bera (and *-mūrti, -vigraha*) "ceremonial image", n. of an icon which is carried in procession at the festivals (*utsava*). Cp. *balibera, cala.*
Lit.: DiIP 135; R 1:17, 2:511; SB 108, 271; WM 88; ZA 111.

uttama ("highest"), see sub *dhruvabera.*

uttānakūrmāsana "outstretched tortoise-sitting" (att.), n. of a Yogic posture.
Lit.: KiH pl. 152 row 3:2.

uttānamaṇḍūkāsana "outstretched frog-sitting" (att.), n. of a Yogic posture.
Lit.: KiH pl. 152 row 3:4.

Uttarabhadrapadā(s) (or Uttarābhādra-; "'aux pieds auspicieux' postérieure" IC), another n. of a *nakṣatra*, see Uttaraproṣṭhapadās.
Lit.: BBh. 382; IC 2:730.

uttarabodhi(hasta)mudrā "gesture of the highest degree of perfection" (Mu.), n. of a handpose: "all fingers are locked, palms together, thumbs and index fingers are touching at tips, with fingers extending upward". Char. of: the Buddha (the Liberator of the *nāgas*), Nāmasaṅgīti, Sitatārā. – Cp. *abhiṣekamudrā.*
Lit.: G 22 (ill.).

Uttaraphālgunī (or Uttarā-; "'la grise(?)' postérieure" IC), n. of a *nakṣatra.* Its influence is medium.
Lit.: BBh. 382; IC 2:729.

Uttaraproṣṭhapadās ("'aux pieds de banc(?)' postérieure" IC), n. of a *nakṣatra.* Its influence is medium. Another n.: Uttarabhadrapadās.
Lit.: IC 2:730.

Uttarāṣāḍhā(s) ("'les invincibles' ultérieures" IC), n. of a *nakṣatra.* Its influence is good.
Lit.: BBh. 382; IC 2:730.

uttarāsaṅga "upper or outer garment" (attr.; Buddh., Jain.), n. of a garment which covers the upper part of the body and

reaches to the knees; one of the three garments (*tricīvara*) of a Buddhist monk. Also, as a "shoulder cloth", n. of the upper garment of a Jain monk.
Lit.: B 294; GJ 402, 428; HIS 42.

uttarāyana "northward course", a term used in dating, meaning that the sun gradually moves northwards from the winter solstice. Hence it refers to the period between c. December 23 to June 22.
Lit.: Enc.Brit. 4:621; Gt Suppl. 146.

uttarīya "upper garment or scarf" (attr.), n. of a cloth, thrown round the neck and reaching to the knees. See *saṅghāṭi*.
Lit.: JMS 28; SB 31; SIB pl. 16; SSI 10.

uttarīyaka-nyāsa "the placing, applying of the upper garment", n. of a ceremony among the *śūdras*.
Lit.: GJ 414.

uṭukku (*-kkai*, *uḍukkai*, Tam.; Skt *huḍukka*; attr.), n. of a drum, see *ḍamaru*.
Lit.: CBC 9; JDI 20; MD 1:199.

V

Vāc (Vāk; "Speech", personification).

1. (Hind.) V. is regarded as the daughter of Dakṣa, the wife of Kāśyapa and the mother of the *gandharvas* and *apsarasas*. Originally V. was a Vedic goddess (Ṛgveda 10, 125) and said to be the daughter of the *riṣi* Ambhṛṇa. She is sometimes identified with Sarasvatī.
Lit.: D 329; DHP 260; GoRI 1:96; WM 180.

2. (Buddh.) In Buddhism V. is regarded as a variety of Mañjuśrī, hence as a male deity, a god who is an emanation of Amitābha. He is not clearly distinguishable from Amitāyus. Char.: att.: *padmāsana*; Mu.: *dhyānamudrā*; attr.: *bodhisattvābharaṇa*, *pañcacīraka*. – See esp. Dharmaśaṅkhasamādhimañjuśrī. – Other n.: Vajrarāga, Amitābha-Mañjuśrī.
Lit: BBh. 102 a.pl. 75 f.; G 68; KiSB 53.

vācaka "speaker, reciter".
Lit.: GJ 425.

Vadālī (Buddh.), n. of a minor Mahāyāna goddess attending on Mārīcīpicuvā. Attr.: *aśoka*-flower, *pāśa*, *sūci*, *vajra*.
Lit.: BBh. 211; KiSB 83.

vādaśālā "hall of disputation" (in a temple).
Lit.: BECA 1:265.

vaddhamānaga (M.Ind.), see *vardhamānaka*.
Lit.: KiJ 21.

vadi, see *badi* (abbreviation of *bahula-dina*).

Vādirāṭ (-rāj; "king among disputants"; Buddh.), n. of a variety of Mañjuśrī. Char.: att.: *lalitāsana* or *rājalīlāsana*; Vāh.: *śārdūla*; Mu.: *vyākhyānamudrā*; attr.: *bodhisattvābharaṇa*.
Lit.: BBh. 122; KiSB 56; MW 940.

vādya "music"; this forms part of the *pūjā*.
Lit.: DiIP 90.

vāgbīja "Seed-of-Consciousness or Seed-of-Speech", n. of a *bījamantra*. Form: *AIṀ*. "It represents the form of consciousness embodied in the goddess Sarasvatī. With it the 'Word' is worshipped".
Lit.: DHP 341.

Vāgīśvara ("Lord of speech").

1. (Hind.) Epithet of Brahmā.
Lit.: SS pl. 34:156.

2. (Buddh.) N. of a variety of Mañjuśrī, an emanation of all five *dhyānibuddhas*. V. is the patron of Nepal, Char.: Vāh.: *siṅha* or *siṅhāsana*(-throne); Mu.: *līlayā-sthita*; attr.: *nīlotpala*.
Lit.: BBh. 116 a.pl. 81; EB s.v.; KiSB 54.

3. (Jain.) N. of a *tīrthaṅkara* (?) or *jina*.

Vāgīśvarī "Lady of speech", epithet of Sarasvatī, esp. represented by the *vāgīśvarī-maṇḍala*.
Lit.: MEIA 192 a.pl. fig. 1; SSI 185.

vāgupaṭṭai (or *vākupaṭṭai*; Tam.), see *yoga-paṭṭa*.

vāhana "vehicle, mount" of a god, in this dictionary rendered by "Vāh.". Vāh. signifies the creature upon which a deity rides or which accompanies the deity;

sometimes the Vāh. is carried as a sign on the banner. The Vāh. represents a theriomorphic form of the quality or character of a deity. – The term Vāh. is here also used respecting other objects on which a deity is placed, such as *padma*, *mṛtaka*, *nara*, *vetālī*, *rākṣasa* and the *pīṭha*s (see further the particular indices of vehicles and seats). – In Jainism the particular "symbol" of a *tīrthaṅkara* is closely connected with the Vāh. – Another n.: *ratha*.

Lit.: BBh. 440; D 330; Gt 667; Sh. 25; Th. 42; WHW 1:46, 2:540.

Vahni ("Conveyer" of oblations to the god = "fire"), epithet of Agni.

Lit.: MW 933; R 1:293.

vahni(kuṇḍa) "fire-pot" (attr.), see *agni*. *vahni* is also a symbolic n. of the number "3", see *saṅkhyā*.

Lit.: BBh. 312.

vaiḍūrya (Tam. *vaiṭuriyam*; in Skt also written *vaidūrya*. There seems to be some confusion concerning the meaning of the word written in these two ways; in MW and pw the latter is listed as an incorrect reading for *vaiḍūrya*, but in ASED the word-forms are translated differently: *vaiḍūrya* as "cat's eye" (thus also MW, pw), and *vaidūrya* as "lapis lazuli". However, the meaning of "cat's eye" seems to be the best-established.) N. of a precious stone, included among the *navaratna**.

Lit.: ASED 3:1502; MW 1021; pw 6:155; TL 6:3852.

Vaijayantīmālā ("a kind of garland prognosticating victory"; attr.), n. of the *vanamālā* of Viṣṇu. It is made of gems, see *pañcaratna*.

Lit.: B 290; HIS 45; MW 1021; R 1:26; Th. 45 a.pl. 10; WM 104.

vaijayantī patākā "banner prognosticating victory" (attr.), see *dhvaja*. Char. of Skanda.

Lit.: B 364.

vaikakṣa "upper garment, mantle"; also a "ring-like *v.* two strands of which go one on each side while the third simply hangs in the middle" (SB; attr.), evidently n. of the strings (of pearls and other ornaments) which hang on the upper body and between the breasts of a woman. – Cp. *suvarṇavaikakṣa*.

Lit.: SB 128, 157, 237 a.fig. 149 f.

vaikhānasa (Tam. *vaikāṉacaṉ*; real meaning uncertain), n. of a Brāhman in the third stage of his religious life (cp. *vānaprastha*), and also of the members of a Vaiṣṇavite sect in South India, regarded as orthodox.

Lit.: GoRI 1:217, 2:125; TL 6:3850.

vaikramābda "the year of Vikrama", term indicating an era, see *vikramakāla*.

Lit.: IC 2:736.

Vaikuṇṭha ("the Land-of-No-Hindrance"), n. of the heaven of Viṣṇu.

Lit.: D 331; DHP 160.

vaikuṇṭha-ekādaśī "(fast-day) on the 11th day (of the light half of the month *mārgaśirṣa*) sacred to Vaikuṇṭha (i.e. Viṣṇu)".

Lit.: GH 357.

Vaikuṇṭha(nātha) ("the Lord of V.", also Vaikuṇṭha-Nārāyaṇa), epithet and n. of a form of Viṣṇu residing in the heaven Vaikuṇṭha. Char.: Vāh.: Garuḍa or Ananta; att.: *āsana*-posture; attr.: *cakra*, sometimes *caturmukha* (the central head is then *nara*; the head to the right: Narasiṅha; the head to the left: Śakti; the head behind: Varāha), *dhanus*, *gadā*, *khaḍga*, *kheṭaka*, *padma*, *śaṅkha*; 8-armed. – Cp. Trailokyamohana.

Lit.: B 401; GoRI 1:249; JDI 65; R 1:256 a.pl. 75; SB 346 a.fig. 303; SSI 52 a.fig. 33.

vaimānika "borne or living in a heavenly car or flying palace (*vimāna*)" (Jain.), n. of a class of gods.

Lit.: GJ 235.

vaināyakīmudrā "handpose (hinting at) Vināyaka", i.e. Gaṇeśa (the elephant-headed god; Mu.), n. of a certain pose of the palm of the hand in the Mu. *gajahastamudrā*.

Lit.: B 258 a.pl. 3:8.

Vairāṭyā, see Vairoṭī.

Vairocana ("coming from or pertaining to the sun"; Buddh.).

1. N. of the oldest and first *dhyānibuddha*

(displaying an originally solar nature), regarded as the *dharmakāya*-aspect of the Buddha. V. originates from the white *bīja OṀ* and represents the *skandha rūpa*. Śakti: Vajradhātvīśvarī (according to BBh.: Locanā). – Char.: colour: white; direction: the zenith, centre (hence he is seated in the inner shrine of a *stūpa*); att.: *padmāsana*; Vāh.: *siṅha* or 2 *ahis*; Mu.: *dharmacakra-*, *vajra-mudrā*; attr.: *cakra*, *tricīvara*. – The *yi-dam*-form of V. has the char.: att.: *padmāsana* and *yab-yum* with the Śakti; attr.: *cakra*, *ghaṇṭā*. – As a *herukabuddha*, he is named Buddhaheruka. – Emanations of V. are: the *(dhyāni)bodhisattva* Samantabhadra, further Cundā, Grahamātṛkā, Mahāsāhasrapramardanī, Mārīcī, Nāmasaṅgīti, Sitātapatrā-Aparājitā, Uṣṇīṣavijayā, Vajravārāhī. – Variant forms: Kun-rig, Mahāvairocana, Vajradhātu.
Lit.: B 262; BBh. 53 a.pl. 28-30, p. 206; G passim; GBM passim; GRI 258; H 32; IC 2:589; KiSB 43; MW 1025; SM 96; WHW 1:160.

2. *-bimba* (attr.), image of V., char. of Vajravārāhī and other emanations (see above).

Vairoṭī (Vairoṭyā, Vairāṭyā; Jain.), n. of a *śāsanadevatā* attending on the 13th *tīrthaṅkara*. Under the n. of Vairoṭyā she is also known as a *vidyādevī*.
Lit.: GJ 362 a.pl. 25:13; KiJ 12 a.pl. 28:13.

vaiśākha ("related to Viśākhā"), n. of a month (April-May). Its god is Vāyu.
Lit.: BBh. 382; IC 2:732; KiK 131.

vaiśākhāsana "the branched sitting" (att.), n. of a posture (of the bowman) in which "one stands on tip-toe, feet apart, thighs flexed. The arms are raised".
Lit.: WHW 1:77.

vaiśākhī, properly the day of full moon in the month *vaiśākha* (April), now n. of the Hindu solar New Year's day, observed throughout Northern India and Madras. *v.* is a religious festival at which the people bathe in rivers. – Among the Sikhs, *v.* is a special festival, since it was on this day in A.D. 1689 that Guru Gobind Singh founded the Sikh community.
Lit.: MW 1026.

vaiśaradya "point of self-confidence or assurance" (Buddh.), *v.* is the n. of a kind of mental characteristic; 4 *v.* characterize a *mānuṣibuddha*.
Lit.: BBh. 76.

vaiṣṇava(bhakta) "devoted worshipper of Viṣṇu", see *bhakta*.
Lit.: GH 384; HIS 17; R 2:478 (with lists of *bhaktas*).

vaiṣṇava-dharma "the Vaiṣṇavite doctrine", also n. of a syncretism of the worship of Viṣṇu and that of Kṛṣṇa (i.e. the *bhāgavata* doctrine).
Lit.: HIS 19.

vaiṣṇavasthāna (lit. "the Viṣṇu-stance"; att.), the technical n. of a pose in which "one leg should be resting firmly on the ground and the other bent and placed across the first". Char. of Śiva in the *kaṭisama*-dance. – Cp. *svastikāpasṛta*.
Lit.: R 2:260.

Vaiṣṇavī ("the [Śakti] of Viṣṇu"), n. of a form of Lakṣmī, esp. representing the Vaiṣṇavite aspect, one of the *sapta-* or *aṣṭa-mātaras* or *navaśakti*. V. represents, in this quality, the passion *mātsarya* "envy" or *lobha* "avarice". Char.: att.: *lalitāsana*; Vāh.: Garuḍa; Mu.: *abhaya-*, *varada-mudrā*; attr.: *bāla*, *cakra*, *gadā*, *padma*, *pītāmbara*, *śaṅkha*. Her sacred tree is the *pippala*.
Lit.: B 506 a.pl. 44:1; BECA 1: pl. 15b; KiH 21 a.pl. 67; KiSH 52; MEIA 150; R 1:381, 384 a.pl. 117; Th. 108.

Vaiśravaṇa (Pāli: Vassāvaṇa; derived from *viśravaṇa* "very famous"; esp. Buddh.), a patronymic epithet of Kubera, esp. in Buddhism. V. is the usual n. for the deity as a *dikpāla* of the north direction. Char.: colour: yellow; attr.: *dhvaja*, *nakula*. – He is regarded as the king of *yakṣas*.
Lit.: BBh. 380; G passim; KiSB 74; ZA 329.

vaiśya ("man who settles on the soil"), n. of (a man of) the third caste; a member of the burgess and peasant caste. – Cp. *varṇa*.
Lit.: IC 1:606; MKVI 2:333; MW 1026; WHW 2:543.

Vaivāhikamūrti "marriage representation", n. of a composite representation of Śiva and Pārvatī, depicting their marriage; see Kalyāṇasundaramūrti.
Lit.: B 485; SIB 62.

Vaivasvata (patronymic), epithet of Yama as the son of Vivasvān; cp. also Manu.
Lit.: GH 91; R 2:525.

vājībandha ("strength-band"; attr.), n. of a kind of band.
Lit.: SB 90 a.passim.

vājin "horse" (as attr.), see *aśva*. The term is also a symbolic n. of the number "7", see *saṅkhyā*.
Lit.: MEIA 266.

vajra (attr.).

1. The *v.* is one of the most important symbols, esp. in Buddhism. Its origin is obscure; some authors derive it from the lightning bolt of Jupiter, but its connection in ancient times with the trident is evident. The trident, both in the single and double form, is found in the Ancient Near East, representing lightning. In Vedic religion, the *v.* was primarily a weapon, a kind of club which was char. esp. of Indra (whose *v.*, according to the myth, was made by Tvaṣṭar of the bones of the *riṣi* Dadhīci). In later Hinduism *v.* is also esp. char. of Śiva and Skanda, and in these contexts it is usually translated as "thunderbolt". The form of the *v.* in later Hinduism is influenced by its Buddhist form (regarding which see below).

In Buddhism the *v.*, despite its form, is generally interpreted as "diamond". As a symbol in Buddhism it has been put to extremely multifarious uses. The magic nature of this symbol is esp. stressed and has given birth to a particular form of the religion, *vajrayāna* Buddhism, which has esp. contributed to the formation of Lamaism. The *v.* is interpreted as "a destroying but indestructible emblem" and symbolizes "the ultimate reality", "das Absolute" (*śūnya*, *śūnyatā*). In Tantric Hinduism and in Vajrayāna esoteric doctrine, the *v.* also signifies the *liṅga* (a term which is rarely used in Buddhism), i.e. the male genitalia (the erect penis), and the male principle of cosmic order (as opposed to *ghaṇṭā*, *padma*; note that the present author has advanced the opinion that *vajra* originally signified the bull's penis, and was from very early times used as a magical symbol).

The *v.* as an iconographic element is usually, at least in Buddhism, carried in one right hand (cp. *dakṣiṇa*). As regards shape, it is a kind of double magical staff having at each end either 3 (*trisūcika*), 5 (*pañcasūcika*), or 9 prongs, united in one point; in the Far East, the *v.* also occurs with 1, 2, 4, 7 and 8 prongs, all of these with different symbolic meanings. There exists a connection between *v.* and the *triśūla* and the *triratna* (the *v.* may also symbolize the *triratna*). Sometimes a small *v.*, indicating the meditative attitude, is placed on the *pīṭha* beside an image. The *v.* as an independent cult emblem is esp. found in Lamaism, and a *v.*, perpendicularly placed in a *padma*, symbolizes the five *dhyānibuddhas*, as well as sexual union (cp. above and see *vajrahuṅkāramudrā*). Half a *v.* often crowns other cult objects, cp. *vajraghaṇṭā* (symbolizing the united male and female principles), *vajrāṅkuśa*, *vajrakhaḍga*, *vajrapāśa*. The *viśvavajra** is a 'double' form of *v.*

Char. of: Acala, Agni, Agnijāta-Subrahmaṇya, Akṣobhya, Amoghapāsa, Āryavajravārāhī, Avalokiteśvara (in different forms), the *bhūmi*-group, Brahmacāri-Subrahmaṇya, Brahmaśāstā, Cāmuṇḍā, Caṇḍā, Cittavaśitā, Cundā, Dam-can, Dharmadhātuvāgīśvara, Dhvajāgrakeyūrā, Durgā, Ekajaṭā, Gajāsurasaṅhāramūrti, Gaṇapati, Gaṇeśa, dGra-lha, Guha-Subrahmaṇya, Hanumān, Hayagrīva, Heruka, Hevajra, Indra, Indrākṣī, Indrāṇī, Jambhala, Jāṅgulī, Jñāṇaḍākinī, Kālacakra, Kālārimūrti,

Kārttikeya, Kṛṣṇa-Yamāri, Kuliśeśvarī, Mahācīnatārā, Mahādeva, Mahākāla, Mahākālī, Mahāmantrānusāriṇī, Mahāpratisarā, Mahāśītavatī, Maheśamūrti, Māheśvarī, Mahiṣāsuramardinī, Māmakī, Mañjughoṣa, Mañjukumāra, Mañjunātha, Mārīcī (in different forms), Nandīśvara, *navadurgās*, Nṛtyā, Padmasambhava, Parṇaśavarī, Prasannatārā, Purandara, Rāhu, Rambhā, Śaktidhara, Samvara, Ṣaṇmukha, Saptakṣara, Saptaśatika-Hayagrīva, Śarabha, Śaravaṇabhava, Sarvabhūtadamanī, Sarvakarmāvaraṇaviśodhanī, Senāpati, Śikhivāhana, Sitātapatrā, Śiva, Skanda, Sumbharāja, Tārakāri, Trailokyavijaya, Tripurāntaka, Upāyapāramitā, Vadālī, Vajracarcikā, Vajraḍākinī, Vajradhara, Vajradhātu, Vajragāndhārī, Vajragarbha, Vajrahuṅkāra, Vajrajvālānalārka, Vajramātṛkā, Vajrāmṛta, Vajrapāṇi (in different forms), Vajrasattva, Vajraśṛṅkhalā, Vajratārā, Vajravārāhī, Vajravidāraṇī, Vajrayoginī, Varāhamukhī, Varālī, Vidyujjvālākarālī, Vighnāntaka, Viśvarūpa, Yamāntaka, *yi-dam*, Yogāmbara. – *v.* is also the weapon of the east direction.

A half-*v.* on the *uṣṇīṣa* characterises: Nāmasaṅgīti, Sarvanivaraṇaviṣkambhin, Śrīdevī. – 2 *v.* carry: Mañjuvajra, Locanā (who may have 1 or 2 *v.*). – A *v.* (?, or possibly a *gadā* – the ill. in GJ shows a *gadā*, but in KiSH it is said to be a "Donnerkeil") is a symbol of Dharma.

Lastly it should be mentioned that *vajra-* is very frequent as the first member in word-compounds; in these cases this first member often retains its full symbolic sense, as outlined above, but just as often probably does little more than emphasize the fact that the term in question refers to the *vajra*-group, i.e. to the Vajrayāna branch of Buddhism.

Other n.: *aśani*, *kuliśa*, *pavin*, *pavitra-vajra*, *vajrāśani*; cp. *paṭṭiśa*.

Lit.: AIP 275; B 301; BBh. passim; CEBI 14 a.pl. 6:26; D 332; DHP 110; G 18 (ill.); GBM 21, 104, 160; GJ pl. 22:15; H pl. 5:46c; HRT pl. 8f.; HuET 47; IC 2:593; KiDG 53; KiJ pl. 45; KiSH 49, 142; KrG 100 a.pl. 11; KT 148; G. Liebert, Or.Suec. 11 (1962), 126; MEIA 250; R 1:8 a.pl. 3:7; RAAI 274; SeKB 278 fig. 68; SM 184; Th. 41; WHW 1:387, 595; WM 106 a.fig. 59-61.

2. *vajra* (Tam. *vayira*) "diamond", n. of a precious stone included among the *navaratna** and the *pañcaratna**.

Lit.: TL 6:3499.

vajra-añjalikarmamudrā "handpose of making a salutation of the *vajra*(-sect)", see *añjalimudrā*.

Lit.: SM 76.

Vajrabhairava ("Bhairava of the *vajra*[-sect]"; Buddh.), in Lamaism n. of a variety of Yamāntaka. Char.: colour: black; att.: *ālīḍhāsana*; Vāh.: different beings (animals, birds, demons, and Hindu deities); attr.: V. is 9-headed (the centre head *vṛṣamastaka*, 3 heads on each side, a red head above the bull-head, and on top of that the head of Mañjuśrī), also *ḍamaru*, *kapāla*, *karttṛkā*, *khaḍga*, and other Tantric symbols. – He is sometimes accompanied by the Śakti (in *yab-yum*-att.).

Lit.: G 91.

Vajrabhīṣaṇa ("Bhīṣaṇa of the *vajra*[-sect]"; Buddh.), another n. of Acala as a *dikpāla*.

Lit.: BBh. 255.

vajracakra "discus (*cakra*) marked with a *vajra*" (attr.; Buddh.). Char. of Candraprabhā.

Lit.: BBh. 89.

Vajracarcikā ("Carcikā of the *vajra*[-sect]"; Buddh.), n. of a Mahāyāna goddess, an emanation of Akṣobhya. Char.: colour: red; att.: *nāṭyasthāna*; Vāh.: *mṛtaka*; attr.: *ajina* (tigerskin), *Akṣobhyabimba* on the crown, *cakra*, *cintāmaṇi*, *kapāla*, *khaḍga*, *muṇḍamālā*, *padma*, *pañca-* or *ṣaṇmudrā*, *trinayana*, *vajra*.

Lit.: BBh. 199 a.pl. 143; KiDG 64; KiSB 92.

Vajraḍāka ("imp of the *vajra*(-sect)"; Buddh.), n. of a kind of Mahāyāna god who is related to Heruka and an emanation of Akṣobhya. In the *yab-yum*-att. he is united

with the *ḍākinī* Vajravārāhī, and he has 1, 3 or 4 heads. – Varieties : Samvara, Saptakṣara, Mahāmāya.
Lit.: KiSB 65.

Vajraḍākinī ("*ḍākinī* of the *vajra*[-sect]"; Buddh.), in Lamaism n. of a *ḍākinī* attending on Mahāmāya. Char. : colour : blue; attr. : *caturmukha*, *ghaṇṭā*, *kapāla*, *khaṭvāṅga*, *vajra*. Concerning the attr. *vajra* (and *ghaṇṭā*), it is said that she wears them "als Zeichen des phallisch fruchtbar Zerstörerischen" (HuGT).
Lit.: BBh. 164; G 34, 80; HuGT 24; KiSB 67.

vajradaṇḍa "*vajra*-staff" (attr.). This term probably on one hand signifies an object identical with the *ceṇṭu** ("Un bâton incrusté de diamant? Mais ne pourrait-on lire ici plutôt "*vakradaṇḍa*" : bâton à bout recourbé...", thus ACA concerning *v.*); on the other hand a staff surmounted by a *vajra* (thus in Buddhism). The latter object is char. of: Padmanartheśvara, Ubhayavarāhānana-Mārīcī.
Lit.: ACA 30; BBh. 252, 434; R 2:490.

Vajradaṇḍa (Buddh.). As a personification of the object mentioned above, epithet or another n. of Yamāntaka as a *dikpāla*.
Lit.: BBh. 252.

Vajradhara ("holding a *vajra*"; Buddh.), n. of an allegorical *buddha* who is the highest "All-*buddha*" and is often (but not always) regarded as a form (or an epithet) of Ādibuddha. V. is esp. popular in Nepal and Tibet. Śakti : Prajñāpāramitā. Char. : att. : *padmāsana* (and sometimes *yab-yum* with the Śakti), also *tāṇḍava*; Mu. : *vajrahuṅkāra*; attr. : *aṅkuśa*, *bodhisattvābharaṇa*, *ghaṇṭā*, *kapāla*, *khaḍga*, *pāśa*, *triśiras*, *vajra*. The Śakti has the attr. : *kapāla*, *karttṛkā*. – Epithet : Vajrasattva; varieties : Dharmavajra, Karmavajra, Yogāmbara.
Lit.: BBh. 42 a.fig. 12-16; G 32, 50; GBM 85 a.pl. facing p. 160; JSV pl. 67; KiDG 43; KiSB 46, RN pl. 22; G. Tucci, Tibet, pl. 70; ZA pl. 610.

Vajradharma ("Dharma of the *vajra*[-sect], or the Law of the *vajra*[-sect]"; Buddh.), epithet of Amitābha.
Lit.: KiSB 58.

Vajradharma(-Lokeśvara) ("L. as V.". Buddh.), n. of a variety of Avalokiteśvara. Char. : colour : reddish white; att. : *padmāsana*; Vāh. : *mayūra* or *padma*; Mu. : *abhayamudrā*; attr. : *bimba* of the 5 *dhyānibuddhas* on the crown, *padma* (*nīlotpala*).
Lit.: BBh. 142, 396 a.pl. 120, 23(A); KiSB 61.

Vajradhātu ("adamantine world" or "world of the *vajra*"; Buddh.).

1. N. of a form of Vairocana. Char. : colour : white; att. : *padmāsana*; Mu. : *dharmacakra-* or *vyākhyāna-* and *dhyānamudrā*; attr. : *akṣamālā*, *cakra*, *caturmukha*, *dhanus*, *śara*, *vajra*; he is 8-armed.
Lit.: BBh. 54 a.pl. 30.

2. *vajradhātu(maṇḍala)*, n. of a *maṇḍala* or *yantra* belonging to V. ("the magic diagram of the Spiritual World").
Lit.: GBM 110 a.pl. facing p. 112; RAAI 274; SeKB 191, 210.

Vajradhātu-Lokeśvara ("L. as V."; Buddh.), n. of a variety of Avalokiteśvara. Char. : att. : *samapādasthānaka*; Vāh. : *padma*; Mu. : *varadamudrā*; attr. : *padma*.
Lit.: BBh. 430 a.pl. 91(A).

Vajradhātvīśvarī(-Mārīcī) ("[M. the] Lady of the adamantine world"; Buddh.), n. of a variety of Mārīcī, usually regarded as a *dhyānibuddhaśakti* and the Śakti of Vairocana (or Ratnasambhava, BBh.). Char. : colour : white or yellow; att. : *lalitāsana* or *ālīḍhāsana*, also *yab-yum*; Mu. : *dharmacakra-*, *varada-*, *vyākhyāna-mudrā*; attr. : *ajina* (tigerskin), *aṅkuśa*, *aśoka*-twig, *Brahmakapāla*, *cintāmaṇi*, *dhanus*, *kapāla*, *khaḍga*, *musala*, *padmas*, *paraśu*, *pāśa*, *ṣaṇmukha*, *śara*, *trikoṇa*, *trinayana*, *triśūla*, *Vairocanabimba* on the crown, *vajra*, *varāhamukha*. As a Śakti in the *yab-yum*-att., she has the attr. : *cakra*, *churī*, *kapāla*. – Varieties : Uḍḍiyāna-Mārīcī, Vajravetālī.
Lit.: BBh. 74 a.pl. 39; G passim; GBM 157; KiDG 64; KiSB 45, 85.

Vajragāndhārī ("Gāndhārī of the *vajra*[-sect]"; Buddh.), n. of an inferior Mahāyāna goddess. Char. : colour : blue or golden; att. : *ālīḍhāsana*; Mu. : *tarjanīmudrā*; attr. : *Amoghasiddhibimba* on the crown, *aṅkuśa*,

cakra, *dhanus*, *ghaṇṭā* (or *vajraghaṇṭā*), *khaḍga*, *khaṭvāṅga*, *paraśu*, *pāśa* (or *tarjanīpāśa*), *ṣaṇmukha*, *śara*, *triśūla*, *tundila*, *vajra*.
Lit.: BBh. 236; KiDG 64; KiSB 98, 107.

Vajragarbha ("Matrix-of-Thunderbolt"; Buddh.), n. of a *bodhisattva*. Char.: colour: blue or bluish white; attr.: *nīlotpala*, *pustaka* (*daśabhūmika*), *vajra*.
Lit.: BBh. 88 a.pl. 56.

Vajragarbha-Lokeśvara (Buddh.), n. of a variety of Avalokiteśvara. Char.: att.: *padmāsana*; Vāh.: *padma*; attr.: *padma*, *vajra*.
Lit.: BBh. 399 a.pl. 45(A).

vajraghaṇṭā "bell (*ghaṇṭā*) crowned or marked with (half) a *vajra*" (attr.). This attr. is held esp. by deities in the *yab-yum*-att.; since *vajra* also signifies the male principle and *ghaṇṭā* the female principle, both attr. together may mean "the united male and female principles" and consequently be a symbolical representation of the same idea which, at the same time, is illustrated in a more obvious form by the *yab-yum*-att. – Char, of: Ghasmarī, Hevajra, Kālacakra, Pratibhānapratisamvit (the *vajra* of her *v.* has 3 prongs), Vajragāndhārī, Vajraghaṇṭā, Vajrasattva, *yi-dam*-deities, Yogāmbara, and others.
Lit.: BBh. 435; HuET 47; KiSB 98; SeKB 278 fig. 69.

Vajraghaṇṭā (personification of *vajraghaṇṭā*; Buddh.), n. of a minor Mahāyāna goddess. She is, among others, regarded as a female *dikpāla* of the north direction. Char.: colour: green or white; Mu.: *tarjanīmudrā*; attr.: *vajraghaṇṭā*.
Lit.: BBh. 242, 298; HuET 47; KiSB 103.

Vajraheruka ("Heruka of the *vajra*[-sect]"; Buddh.), n. of Akṣobhya as a *heruka-buddha*. Colour: blue.
Lit.: G 87.

Vajrahuṅkāra (or *-hūṅ-*; "the syllable *HŪṀ* of the *vajra*[-sect]"; Buddh.), n. given to a personification of the *bīja HŪṀ*. V. is an emanation of Akṣobhya and is sometimes identified with Trailokyavijaya. Char.: att.: *ālīḍhāsana*; Vāh.: Bhairava (lying prostrate); Mu.: *vajrahuṅkāra-mudrā*; attr.: *aṅkuśa*, *ghaṇṭā*, *kapāla*, *khaṭvāṅga*, *pāśa*, *vajra*.
Lit.: BBh. 181; KiSB 78.

vajrahuṅkāramudrā (or *-hūṅ-*) "handpose of the syllable *HŪṀ* of the *vajra*[-sect]"; Mu.; Buddh.), n. of a gesture: the wrists of the hands are crossed over the chest, the right hand holding a *vajra*, the left hand holding a *ghaṇṭā* (rarely other symbols), both of which are turned inwards (N.B., if both symbols and hands are turned outwards, the Mu. is called *trailokyavijaya-mudrā*; BBh.). This Mu. symbolizes the dawn of enlightenment, release from the fetters of passion, and the mystery of sound. It is also said to signify the symbolical marriage between Wisdom (*prajñā**) and Way (probably meaning *upāya**; cp. also *vajraghaṇṭā*). – Char. of: Samantabhadra, Samvara, Trailokyavijaya, Vajradhara, Vajrahuṅkāra, *yi-dam*-deities.
Lit.: BBh. 440 a.fig. 12; G 22 (ill.); KiSB 47; SM 114; G.Tucci, Tibet, pl. 70, 72; WHW 2:88.

Vajrahuntika(?)-Lokeśvara (Buddh.), n. of a variety of Avalokiteśvara. Char.: att.: *nāṭyasthāna*; Vāh.: *padma*; attr.: *nīlotpala* in all 12 hands.
Lit.: BBh. 398 a.pl. 35(A).

Vajrajvālā ("flame of *vajra*"; Buddh.), n. of the grand-daughter of Virocana.
Lit.: MW 913.

Vajrajvālānalārka ("radiating the flames of the *vajra*"; Buddh.), n. of a Mahāyāna god. Char.: colour: blue; att.: *ālīḍhāsana*; Vāh.: he tramples upon Viṣṇu; attr.: *cakra*, *caturmukha*, *dhanus*, *dhvaja*, *ghaṇṭā*, *khaḍga*, *khaṭvāṅga*, *pāśa*, *śara*, *vajra*. – V is also another n. of Ṭakkirāja.
Lit.: BBh. 183, 254; KiSB 78.

Vajrakāla ("Kāla [god of death] of the *vajra*[-sect]"; Buddh.), another n. of Nīladaṇḍa.
Lit.: BBh. 254.

Vajrakarmapāramitā ("perfection of the *vajra* performance"; Buddh.), n. of a *pāramitā*. Char.: colour: variegated; attr.: *cintāmaṇidhvaja*, *viśvavajra* on a *padma*.
Lit.: BBh. 328.

vajrakartṛ (or *trī*) "*karttṛkā* with (half) a *vajra* at the top" (attr.; Buddh.).
Lit.: BBh. 436.

vajrakhaḍga "sword marked with a *vajra*" (attr.). Char. of Sāgaramati. – See also *khaḍga*.
Lit.: BBh. 88.

Vajrakhaṇḍa-Lokeśvara ("L., part of the *vajra*"; Buddh.), n. of a variety of Avalokiteśvara. Char.: att.: *samapādasthānaka*; Vāh.: *padma*; attr.: *padma*, *pustaka*.
Lit.: BBh. 429 a.pl. 78(A).

vajrakīla (a kind of dagger with a *vajra*-shaft), a translation into Sanskrit of the Tibetan *phur-bu*.
Lit.: HuGT 7.

vajrakīṭa "diamond-worm", n. of a kind of insect which bores holes in wood and stone. It is believed that Viṣṇu, in the form of a *v.*, makes *cakra*-holes in *śālagrāma**-stones.
Lit.: MW 913; SSI 70.

Vajrakuṇḍalin (-ī; "decorated with *vajra* earrings"; Buddh.), another n. of Prajñāntaka.
Lit.: BBh. 253.

Vajrāmṛta ("the immortal, or the nectar, of the *vajra*[-sect]"; Buddh.), n. of a Mahāyāna god, an emanation of Amoghasiddhi. Char.: colour: green; Vāh.: *sattva*; attr.: *aṅkuśa*, *cakra*, *ghaṇṭā*, *khaḍga*, *pāśa*, *vajra*.
Lit.: BBh. 226.

vajramudrā "*vajra*-handpose" (Mu.; Buddh.). This term (in SM with a question-mark) indicates a gesture in which the left hand is clenched so as to form a solid fist, the thumb tucked in and grasped by the other fingers, the index finger being raised; this index is inserted into the fist formed by the right hand. The left hand is held on a level with the navel, the right hand thus being placed over the left. – This Mu. is very rare and seems to be char. only of Vairocana. It is said to symbolize the highest knowledge or wisdom (SeKB), the knowledge of Vairocana as the supreme divinity (SM). – In GBM it is said that this Mu. signifies the act of coition and consequently the union of *upāya* and *prajñā* (see *vajrahuṅkāramudrā* and *yab-yum*), but this cannot be true since the male principle in this case should be symbolized by the left hand, and the female principle by the right, which is against the general rule (cp. *dakṣiṇa*, *vāma*). – Other n.: *bodhaśrīmudrā* (?), *jñānamudrā* (?).
Lit.: GBM 34 a.pl. 2; SeKB 163 fig. 53 a.p. 191 (ill.); SM 102.

Vajranābha ("having a hard nave" or "having a thunderbolt as nave"; attr.), n. of the *cakra* of Viṣṇu or Kṛṣṇa.
Lit.: D 333; MW 913.

Vajranāda ("the sound of the *vajra*"; Buddh.), n. of a *bodhisattva*, esp. in the Japanese form of Buddhism.
Lit.: GBM 189 a.pl. facing p. 80.

Vajrānaṅga(-Mañjughoṣa) ("Anaṅga of the *vajra*[-sect]"; Buddh.), in Lamaism n. of a variety of Mañjuśrī, being the Buddhist god of love. He is an emanation of Akṣobhya. Char.: att.: *ālīḍhāsana*; attr.: *Akṣobhyabimba* on the crown, *aśoka*-flower, *darpaṇa*, *dhanus* Puṣpadhanvan, *khaḍga*, *padma*, *śara* with a lotus bud as a point.
Lit.: G 69; GBM 54; KiSB 69.

Vajranātha-Lokeśvara ("L., the protector of the *vajra*[-sect]"; Buddh.), n. of a variety of Avalokiteśvara. Char.: att.: *ardhasamapādasthānaka*; Vāh.: *padma*; attr.: *padma*, *vajra*.
Lit.: BBh. 431 a.pl. 107(A).

vajrāṅkuśa "*aṅkuśa* crowned (or marked) with (half) a *vajra*" (attr.; Buddh.). Char. of: Dharmapratisamvit, Mahāśītavatī, Ubhayavarāhānana-Mārīcī, Vajrāṅkuśī, Vajratārā, Vartālī.
Lit.: BBh. 432; KiSB 83.

Vajrāṅkuśī (personification of *vajrāṅkuśa*; Buddh.), n. of a minor Mahāyāna goddess,

sometimes regarded as a female *dikpāla* of the east direction. Char.: colour: black or white; Mu.: *tarjanīmudrā*; attr.: *aṅkuśa* (*vajrāṅkuśa*), *nīlotpala*.
Lit.: BBh. 131, 242, 297; KiSB 102.

Vajrapāṇi ("having a *vajra* in the hand"; Buddh.), esp. in Tibet n. of a (*dhyāni*)*bodhisattva* who is often regarded as a Buddhist counterpart of the Hindu Indra (this is, however, doubtful). V. is sometimes identified with Ādibuddha, but is more often said to be an emanation of Akṣobhya. Char.: colour: dark blue or white; att.: *padmāsana* or *lalitāsana*, also *sthānaka*; Vāh.: (sometimes) *mayūra*; Mu.: *abhayamudrā*; attr.: *nāga*, *pāśa*, *vajra* (in one hand or on the *pīṭha*). – Varieties: Acalavajrapāṇi, Ācāryavajrapāṇi, Bhūtaḍāmaravajrapāṇi, Caṇḍavajrapāṇi, Garuḍa-form of V., Mahācakravajrapāṇi, Nīlāmbaravajrapāṇi. – See also Trimūrti.
Lit.: AuOW 55; B 558; BBh. 44, 53, 98 a.pl. 25-27; G 16, 59, 62; H 82; HAHI pl. 4; HSIT pl. 1; JSV pl. 83; KiSB 44.

Vajrapāṇi-Lokeśvara (Buddh.), n. of a variety of Avalokiteśvara. Char.: att.: *nāṭyasthāna*; Vāh.: *padma*; attr.: *vajra*.
Lit.: BBh. 431 a.pl. 105(A).

vajrapañjara "*vajra*-marked cage" (attr., held in one hand). Char. of Jālinīprabha.
Lit.: BBh. 90.

vajraparyaṅkāsana "*vajra*-throne-sitting" or "sitting on a throne with a *vajra*" (att.), n. of an *āsana*-posture, identical in most respects with the *padmāsana*; in SIB it is equivalent to *vajrāsana* and *dhyānāsana*. A *vajra*, indicating the meditative att., is sometimes found on the *pīṭha* beside the image.
Lit.: B 272; BBh. 435; HIS 43, 54 a.pl. 9; SS 128; SIB 68; SM 124.

vajrapāśa "noose (*pāśa*) with (half) a *vajra*" (attr.; Buddh.). It refers symbolically to the seizening of the hair of Māra. Char. of: Kṛṣṇa-Yamāri, Mahākāla, Samvara, Trailokyavaśaṅkara-Lokeśvara, Ubhayavarāhānana-Mārīcī, Vajrapāśī, Yamāntaka.
Lit.: BBh. 437; KiDG 61; KiSB 71.

Vajrapāśī (personification of *vajrapāśa*), n. of a minor Mahāyāna goddess who is also regarded as a female *dikpāla* of the southerly direction. Char.: colour: yellow or golden; attr.: (*vajra*)*pāśa*.
Lit.: BBh. 242, 297 a.pl. 193; KiSB 71.

vajrapatākāmudrā "*vajra*-flag-gesture" (Mu.), n. of a variety of the *patākāmudrā** with the difference that the tips of thumb and ring-finger are touching; it represents a thunderbolt (*vajra*), an arrow, a tree.
Lit.: WHW 2:86.

Vajrapātāla ("Pātāla ['lord of the infernal regions'] of the *vajra*[-sect]"; Buddh.), another n. of Sumbharāja.
Lit.: BBh. 256.

vajrapīṭha, n. of a kind of *pīṭha*.
Lit.: R 2:101 a.pl. 12.

Vajraprastāriṇī ("extending the *vajra*"), n. of a form of Pārvatī(?). Vāh.: *padma*.
Lit.: SSI 212.

vajrāsana.

1. (Att.; esp. Buddh.) The word may be translated either as "*vajra*-sitting", the term *vajra* referring to the Vajrayāna sect, or as "having a *vajra* on the seat", the *vajra* here symbolizing the meditative att. (cp. *vajraparyaṅkāsana*). This mode of sitting is very similar to the *padmāsana* (but, according to some authors, at the same time involving the handpose *dhyānamudrā*, and a *vajra* placed on some part of the *pīṭha*), and it is not distinguished from this att. in this dictionary; in WHW the term *v.* is said to signify any posture when made very rigid. – Cp. also *dhyānāsana*. – *v.* is also n. of a *maṅgala*, see *aṣṭamaṅgala*.
Lit.: B 272; BBh. 435; KiDG 49; KiH pl. 151 row 2:3; SM 124; WHW 1:77; WM 90 a.fig. 6.

2. (Vāh.; Buddh.) "Adamantine throne (of the Great Enlightenment)", n. of an oblong lotus-throne (*padmapīṭha*, see also *āsana*) which is adorned with a *vajra* or a *svastika*.

It refers to the seat on which the Buddha sat beneath the *bodhi*-tree.
Lit.: B 272; CEBI 43, 52; G 25; Gw. 14; RAAI 274.

Vajrāsana ("having a seat with a *vajra*" or "having a diamond throne"; Buddh.), n. of a form of Akṣobhya. The n. probably refers to the fact that a *vajra* is often placed beside V. on the seat. – V. is sometimes said to be a variety of Śākyamuni.
Lit.: BBh. 77 a.pl. 46; G 52, 55.

vajrāśani "thunderbolt (of Indra)" (attr.), see *vajra*.
Lit.: MEIA 250.

Vajraśāradā ("Śāradā of the *vajra*[-sect]"; Buddh.), n. of a variety of Sarasvatī. Char.: Vāh.: *padma* (white); attr.: *candra, padma, pustaka, trinayana*.
Lit.: BBh. 351 a.pl. 232; KiSB 106.

Vajrasarasvatī ("Sarasvatī of the *vajra*[-sect]"; Buddh.), n. of a variety of Sarasvatī. Char.: colour: red; att.: *ālīḍhāsana*; attr.: *cakra, cintāmaṇi, kapāla, karttṛkā, khaḍga, padma, trinayana, triśiras*.
Lit.: BBh. 351 a.pl. 235; KiDG 75 a.pl. 65.

Vajrasattva (usually translated as "having an adamantine soul or heart", but should perhaps rather be interpreted: "the Supreme Being of the *vajra*[-sect]"; Buddh.).
1. N. of a Mahāyāna god who is sometimes regarded as a sixth *dhyānibuddha* and the priest of the other five *dhyānibuddhas*. By the Tibetan *rÑiṅ-ma-pa*-sect and also by other North Indian sects he is worshipped as Ādibuddha, and he is sometimes also identified with Vajradhara. V. originates from the *bīja HŪṀ*, his Śakti is Vajrasattvātmikā or Vasudhārā, and from him the *(dhyāni)bodhisattva* Ghaṇṭāpāṇi and the female *bodhisattva* Cundā emanate. – Char.: colour: white; att.: *padmāsana* or *lalitāsana* or *sthānaka*, also with *yab-yum* with the Śakti; attr.: *bodhisattvābharaṇa* (not *tricīvara*), *ghaṇṭā* (*vajraghaṇṭā*), *vajra*.
Lit.: BBh. 47, 74 a.pl. 41-44; G passim; GBB 246; KiSB 77; SeKB 232 (ill.); SM 191.

2. *Vajrasattvabimba* (attr.), an image of V., carried in the hair char. of Cundā.
Lit.: G 73.

Vajrasattvadhātu-Lokeśvara ("L., the world of Vajrasattva"; Buddh.), n. of a variety of Avalokiteśvara. Char.: att.: *samapādasthānaka*; Vāh.: *padma*; attr.: *cakra, śaṅkha*.
Lit.: BBh. 429 a.pl. 88(A).

Vajrasattvātmikā ("having the nature of Vajrasattva"; Buddh.), n. of the Śakti of Vajrasattva. She is generally depicted in the *yab-yum*-att. with her husband. Attr.: *kapāla, karttṛkā*.
Lit.: BBh. 76; GBB 250.

vajrasphoṭa (either a Mu., or an attr., or both?).
1. (Mu.) "Clapping one's hands" ("in die Hände klatschend"?), char. of Vajrasphoṭī (?).
Lit.: KiSB 103.
2. (Attr.) "Chain marked with a *vajra*". Char. of Vajrasphoṭā, Vajrasphoṭī. – See *vajraśṛṅkhalā*.
Lit.: BBh. 242, 297.

Vajrasphoṭā (personification; Buddh.), n. of a female *dikpāla* of the westerly direction. Char.: Mu.: *tarjanīmudrā*; attr.: *vajrasphoṭa*.
Lit.: BBh. 297.

Vajrasphoṭī (personification; Buddh.), n. of an inferior Mahāyāna goddess. Char.: Mu.: *vajrasphoṭa* (? KiSB); attr.: *vajrasphoṭa*.
Lit: BBh. 242; KiSB 103.

vajraśṛṅkhalā "chain (*śṛṅkhalā*) marked with a *vajra*, or having a *vajra* at the top" (attr.; Buddh.). This object is probably identical with *vajrasphoṭa* 2. Char. of: Kālacakra, Vajraśṛṅkhalā, (Vajrasphoṭā, Vajrasphoṭī).
Lit.: BBh. 235, 439.

Vajraśṛṅkhalā (personification).
1. (Buddh.) N. of a Mahāyāna goddess, an emanation of Amoghasiddhi. She is sometimes said to be the Śakti of Hevajra. Char.: colour: green; att.: *lalitāsana*;

Mu.: *abhaya-*, *tarjanī-mudrā*; attr.: *ajina*, *Amoghasiddhibimba* on the crown, *dhanus*, *kapāla*, *keśa*, *pāśa*, *śara*, *trinayana*, *triśiras*, *vajra*, *vajraśṛṅkhalā*.
Lit.: BBh. 235 a.pl. 175; KiDG 64, 73 a.pl. 62; KiSB 101.
2. (Jain.) N. of a *śāsanadevatā* attending on the 4th *tīrthaṅkara*. She is also mentioned as a *vidyādevī*.
Lit.: GJ 362 a.pl. 24:4; KiJ 12 a.pl. 27:4.

Vajrasṛṣṭa-Lokeśvara ("L. created by or from the *vajra*"; Buddh.), n. of a variety of Avalokiteśvara. Char.: att.: *samapādasthānaka*; Vāh.: *padma*; attr.: *cāmara*, *padma*.
Lit.: BBh. 430 a.pl. 100(A).

Vajra-Tāra: in MH n. of an image which is identified in KIM as a Viṣṇu (Tāra is sometimes found as an epithet of Viṣṇu; MW). The statements as to the age of the icon differ considerably in KIM and MH.
Lit.: KIM pl. 9; MH pl. 5; MW 443.

Vajratārā ("Tārā of the *vajra*[-sect]"; Buddh.), n. of a Mahāyāna goddess who is regarded as a common emanation of all *dhyānibuddha*s, or else of Ratnasambhava; she is also said to be a variety of Bhṛkuṭī. Char.: colour: golden; att.: *padmāsana*; Vah.: *padma*; Mu.: *tarjanī-* or *tarjanīpāśahasta-*, *varada-mudrā*; attr.: *aṅkuśa* (or *vajrāṅkuśa*), *caturmukha*, *dhanus*, *nīlotpala*, *pāśa*, *śaṅkha*, *śara*, *trinayana*, *vajra* and *bimba* of the 5 *dhyānibuddha*s on the crown; she is 8-armed.
Lit.: BBh. 240, 308 a.pl. 180-182; G 16, 75; KiDG 64; KiSB 61, 102, 104.

vajratarjanī (or *-ikā*), n. of a combination of a Mu. and an attr.: it "signifies the *vajra* held in the fist, while the index is raised in a menacing attitude". Cp. *tarjanīmudrā*. Char. of Vajravārāhī.
Lit.: BBh. 439.

Vajratīkṣṇa ("diamond-hard" or "Tīkṣṇa of the *vajra*[-sect]"; Buddh.), n. of a Mahāyāna god. Attr.: *khaḍga*, *pustaka*.
Lit.: JSV pl. 75.

vajratriśūla "*triśūla* having a *vajra* at the top" (attr.; Buddh.). Char. of Padmanarteśvara.
Lit.: BBh. 135.

Vajravairocanī ("the solar deity or Virocana-daughter of the *vajra*[-sect]"; Buddh.), n. of a *yoginī*.
Lit.: KiSB 107.

Vajravārāhī (translated as "Diamond Sow" (G), probably meaning "Vārāhī of the *vajra*[-sect]"; Buddh.), n. of a Mahāyāna goddess who is an emanation of Vairocana. She is sometimes said to be the Śakti of Hevajra. In Lamaism she is a *ḍākinī* who appears together with Vajraḍāka (Samvara). – Char.: colour: red; Vāh.: she treads on a *nara* (Bhairava) or on Kālarātrī or on both; att.: *ālīḍhāsana* or *nāṭyasthāna*; attr.: esp. *kapāla*, *karttṛkā*, *khaṭvāṅga*, further *aṅkuśa*, *ḍamaru*, *dharmapālābharaṇa*, *muṇḍamālā*, *pāśa*, *ṣaṇmudrā*, *trinayana*, *triśūla*, *Vairocanabimba* on the crown, *vajratarjanī*, *varāhamukha* (she has either herself a sow-face, or an excrescence near her right ear resembling the face of a sow). – V. is also represented by the *mantra* "*Oṁ Sarva-Buddhaḍākiniye Vajravarṇanīye hūṁ hūṁ phaṭ phaṭ svāhā*", or "*Oṁ Vajravetālī hūṁ phaṭ*". – Varieties: Ārya-Vajravārāhī, Vāsya-Vajravārāhī.
Lit.: BBh. 161, 208, 217 a.pl. 159 f.; G 35, 81; KiDG 64; KiSB 65, 87.

Vajravarṇanī ("Varṇanī of the *vajra*[-sect]"?, cp. the meaning of Varṇanī, or a personification of "the act of painting, explaining of a *vajra*"?; Buddh.), n. of a *yoginī*.
Lit.: KiSB 107.

Vajravetālī ("Vetālī of the *vajra*[-sect]"; Buddh.), n. of a form of Vajradhātvīśvarī. Char.: colour: red; att.: *ālīḍhāsana*; Mu.: *tarjanīmudrā*; attr.: *Akṣobhyabimba* on the crown, *aṅkuśa*, *pāśa*, *tundila*, *vajraghaṇṭā*.
Lit.: BBh. 151, 214; KiSB 98.

Vajravidāraṇī ("Vidāraṇī ['tearing asunder'] of the *vajra*[-sect]"; Buddh.), n. of a Mahāyāna goddess. Char.: att.: *ālīḍhāsana*; Mu.: *abhaya-*, *varada-mudrā*; attr.: *aṅ-*

kuśa, dhanus, dhvaja, khaḍga, kheṭaka, pañcaśiras, pāśa, śara, vajra.
Lit.: BBh. 205 a.pl. 150; KiDG 64; KiSB 108.

Vajravīṇā-Sarasvatī ("S. with the *vīṇā*, of the *vajra*[-sect]"; Buddh.), n. of a variety of Sarasvatī. Char.: colour: white; attr.: *vīṇā*; in other respects similar to Mahāsarasvatī; cp. Vajraśāradā.
Lit.: BBh. 350 a.pl. 231; KiDG 64.

Vajrayakṣa ("*yakṣa* of the *vajra*[-sect]"; Buddh.), another n. of Ṭakkirāja.
Lit.: BBh. 254.

vajrayāna (usually translated as "the diamond vehicle", but "the magic vehicle" seems to be more adequate; Buddh.), n. of a Tantric form of Mahāyāna Buddhism which has esp. contributed to the formation of Lamaism and which is chiefly concerned with magic manifestations. This form of religion which constitutes a left-handed form of Tantrism (see *tantra*), has very much in common with Hindu Śāktism, and since esp. the *vajra* seems to be of phallic nature, the occurance of such specifically sexual manifestations as *yab-yum*, *vajraghaṇṭā* etc. are understandable; cp. KT: "*vajra* (the thunderbolt and also the name of the male genitals) is worn as a symbol of the Buddha's creative power and has given its name to the whole school which is called Vajrayāna". – Most of the word compounds beginning with *vajra-* and often being proper names of deities, may be regarded as expressly signifying conceptions belonging to this form of Buddhism. – Another n.: *mantrayāna*.
Lit.: BBh.; BRI 173; GBM; GRI 218, 265; HIS; HuGT 6; KT 139; G. Liebert, Or.Suec. 11 (1962), 142.

Vajrayoginī ("*yoginī* of the *vajra*[-sect]"; Buddh.), n. of a Mahāyāna goddess. Char.: colour: yellow; att.: *ālīḍhāsana*; Vāh.: *mṛtaka*; attr.: *amastaka* and *muṇḍa* (her head is severed from her body, and she carries it in her hand; she can also, however, have her head intact), *kapāla*, *karttṛkā, khaṭvāṅga, ṣaṇmudrā, trinayana, vajra.* – Another n.: Sarvabuddha-Ḍākinī.
Lit.: BBh. 247; KiDG 64; KiSB 107.

Vajrīputra ("son of Vajrī"; Buddh.), n. of a Lamaist *arhat*. Char.: Mu.: *vyākhyānamudrā*; attr.: *cāmara*.
Lit.: G 12, 104.

Vajroṣṇīṣa ("Uṣṇīṣa of the *vajra*"; Buddh.), n. of an *uṣṇīṣa*-deity, also another n. of Padmāntaka. Char.: colour: white; direction: east; Mu.: *bhūmisparśamudrā*.
Lit.: BBh. 253, 299 a.pl. 195.

Vajroṣṇīṣa-Lokeśvara ("L. as V."; Buddh.), n. of a variety of Avalokiteśvara. Char.: att.: *samapādasthānaka*; Vāh.: *padma*; Mu.: *abhaya-*, *varada-mudrā*; attr.: *akṣamālā, pāśa, pustaka, tridaṇḍa.*
Lit.: BBh. 398 a.pl. 34(A).

Vāk, see Vāc.

Vaka, Vakāsura, see Bakāsura.

vakradaṇḍa or *vakradaṇḍāyudha* "crooked stick" (attr.), see *cenṭu*.
Lit.: ACA 30; R 2:353.

vākupaṭṭai (or *vāgu-*; Tam.), see *yogapaṭṭa*.
Lit.: KiH 45.

valabhī(kāla) "(the era of) V.", n. of an era beginning in A.D. 318 and closely related to the *guptakāla*. The year is *vartamāna*, *kārttikādi* and either *pūrṇimānta* or *amānta* (see *samvatsara, candramāsa*). The given year of this era + 317 or 318 = the year A.D.
Lit.: Enc.Brit. 5:721; IC 2:737.

Vālakhilya, n. of a class of 60.000 *riṣis* characterized by being the size of a thumb, produced from Brahmā's body and surrounding the chariot of the sun.
Lit.: D 333; GH 109; MW 946.

vālakuñci "brush made of the fragrant roots of the *uśīra*-grass" (attr.). This brush is used for cleaning the icons.
Lit.: GJ 429.

Valampura-Gaṇeśa (the first word member is Tam.), n. of a form of Gaṇeśa "with the trunk turning to the right". Attr.: *valampuri*.
Lit.: SB 154.

valampuri (Tam.) "a certain mode of holding the trunk (turning to the right)" (attr.). Char. of Valampura-Gaṇeśa.
Lit.: SB 178.

valamuri (Tel.) "conch (whose spirals turn to the right)" (attr.), see sub *śaṅkha*.

vālavyajana "fly-whisk" (attr.), see *cāmara*.
Lit.: MEIA 261.

valaya "armlet, ring worn on the wrist (by men and women)" (attr.). The *v.* sometimes has the shape of a snake (cp. *bhujaṅgavalaya*, *nāgavalaya*, *sarpavalaya*, Vāsuki). Char. of Śiva Bhairava. – Another n.: *bāhuvalaya*; cp. also *keyūra*, *nūpura*.
Lit.: B 292; SB 366 a.passim.

vāḷi(ka) (Tam.) "ear-ornament" (attr.), see *kuṇḍala*.
Lit.: R 2:325.

Vallabha ("beloved above all, dear"), n. of a *vaiṣṇavabhakta* (A.D. 1479-1531) and after him n. of a religious sect.
Lit.: GH 387; IC 2:644.

Valli (or -ī; Tam. Vaḷḷi; "earth"), n. of the second wife of Skanda, the wife who stands on his right. Attr.: *kucabandha*, *padma*. – N.B. Since V. takes the same place beside Skanda as Bhūmi beside Viṣṇu, it is more probable that the original sense of V. is "earth" (see MW sub *valli*) than "creeper" (see MW sub *vallī*). – Another n.: Mahāvalli.
Lit.: MW 928; R 2: pl. 122; Th. 99.

Vallīkalyāṇasundaramūrti ("representation of the wedding of the Charming One with Vallī"), n. of a composite representation of Skanda together with his wife Valli, depicting their marriage (this evidently being a counterpart of the Śaivite Kalyāṇasundaramūrti). Char.: Mu.: *abhaya-*, *kaṭi-mudrā*; attr.: *akṣamālā*, *kamaṇḍalu*.
Lit.: R 2:440.

Vālmīki ("ant-hill"), n. of the author of the epic Rāmāyaṇa.
Lit.: D 333; GH 97; Gt 676; MW 946; WHW 2:550; WM 180.

VAṀ, a *bījamantra* symbolizing the element "water", dedicated to Varuṇa.
Lit.: DHP 344; GH 55.

vāma "left, the left hand". The original meaning of *v.* is possibly "dear" (cp. Vāmā), but also "left"; later, the left side (as opposed to the right side, *dakṣiṇa**) received a depreciatory sense: "adverse, crooked, unfavourable". Inauspicious and destructive attributes (e.g. *agni*) are therefore, except in some reversed representations, carried in the left hand. But since a woman is always placed to the left of a man or sits on his left knee, it has no depreciatory sense in this use. For a woman the quivering of the left eye or arm, for instance, is a good omen (cp. also the "left-handed" *svastika*, *sauvastika*), for a man, however, an inauspicious omen. Consequently, *v.* indicates the female principle; attributes signifying the female character (*yoni*, *ghaṇṭā* [in Lamaism], etc.) are carried in the left hand or placed on the left side of the deity in question. It should be noticed that when Śiva (in some forms) has a female ear-ring (see *lambapattra*), he wears it in his left ear. In Ardhanārīśvara and (often) in Harihara, the left side is female. *v.* signifies further Śāktism (see *vāmācāra*), but may sometimes also indicate the Vaiṣṇavite sect, since Viṣṇu, as opposed to Śiva, represents the left side (cp. Harihara). Lastly, in the offering dedicated to the *pitaras*, all the rites which are otherwise performed with the right hand, are performed with the left hand; this mode of action is meant to mark out the difference between the world of the living and the world of the dead. – Cp. *prasavya*.
Lit.: MW 941.

Vāmā (either "lovely, dear, beautiful; woman" or "the left one" as a personification of the Śakti according to *vāmācāra* Tantrism), n. of a form of Durgā and also of the Śakti of one of the *vidyeśvaras*. Char.: Mu.: *abhayamudrā*; attr.: *kapāla*, *trinayana*
Lit.: R 1:362, 402.

vāmācāra "left-hand practice" ("das umgekehrte Benehmen", GoRI; cp. *vāma*), *vāmācārin* "follower of left-hand ritual", n. of the left-hand doctrine of *tantra* which involves a certain 'extreme' form of the worship of the Śakti, the female energy personified as the wife of Śiva. To this tradition belongs, e.g., the *pañca-makāra*. – Consequently, *v.* also signifies the Matrix World, and, in Buddhism, *v.* emphasizes the devotion of the Tārās, the "Saviouresses". – Cp. *dakṣiṇācāra*.

Lit.: BPR 60; GoRI 2:36; MW 941; SM 17, 33.

Vāmadeva ("the god to the left"), n. of the head of the Sadāśiva-composition directed to the north (and consequently of the left head); cp. Pañcabrahmā. V. also occurs as an independent deity and is further n. of one among the group *ekādaśarudra*. He has probably nothing in common with the Vedic Vāmadeva. – Char.: colour: red; Mu.: *abhaya-*, *varada-mudrā*; attr.: *akṣamālā*, *candra*, *khaḍga*, *kheṭaka*, *paraśu*, *ṭaṅka*, *trinayana*.

Lit.: B 478; DHP 212; KiSH 25; MKVI 2:286; R 2:371, 388.

Vāmadeva-Umā ("U. as the deity to the left"), n. of Śiva's Śakti who, in the Mahādeva-composition, takes the same place as Vāmadeva in the Sadāśiva-composition (cp. also *vāma*). Her face is "the face of bliss and beauty, the face of the goddess in Śiva".

Lit.: KrA pl. 102 a.p. 207.

Vāmana ("dwarf"; also interpreted as "deserving of praise").

1. N. of the form in which Viṣṇu appears in the Vāmanāvatāra; further, of an aspect of Viṣṇu, see *caturviṅśatimūrti* (Śakti: Kriyā); V. is also regarded as a manifestation of the planet Bṛhaspati; it is in addition n. of the *diggaja* which accompanies Yama as a *dikpāla*; the wife of this *diggaja* is Piṅgalā.

Lit.: DHP 154.

2. (Vāh.) Amoghasiddhi is depicted trampling upon V. Apasmāra, on whom Śiva Naṭarāja dances, is also sometimes named V.

Lit.: G 52.

Vāmanāvatāra ("Dwarf-Incarnation"), n. of the 5th *avatāra* of Viṣṇu in which, in the form of a dwarf, he saved the world from the power of Bali. This form has been fused with the form of Viṣṇu as Trivikrama. V. is the son of Kāśyapa and Aditi. Wife: Padmā (or Kamalā, an *avatāra* of Lakṣmī). Attr.: *chattra*, *kamaṇḍalu*, *kaupīna*, *pavitra*, *pustaka*, *upavīta*, and the chief. attr. of Viṣṇu.

Lit.: B 390, 417 a.pl. 23:1, 4; BP 82 a.pl. 7-9; D 3; DHP 165, 169, 261; GH 121; GoRI 1:251; Gt 677; HIS 18; IIM 50; JDI 78; KiSH 37, 39; MEIA 32 a.pl. 3b; MG 113 a.pl. facing p. 110; R 1:161, 229; SSI 30; Th. 61; W 130; WHW 1:452.

vāṇa (= *bāṇa*; attr.), see *śara*.

Lit.: MEIA 254.

Vana-Durgā ("the forest-Durgā"), n. of a form of Durgā worshipped by foresters. Char.: Mu.: *tarjanī-*, *varada-mudrā*; attr.: *ajina* (elephantskin), *cakra*, *dhanus*, *khaḍga*, *kheṭaka*, *śaṅkha*, *śara*, *triśūla*; she is 8-armed.

Lit.: BECA 1:10; R 1:343.

vanamālā "forest-garland" (attr.), n. of a long garland made of flowers and worn on the body or carried in one hand. Char. of: Gaurī, Jayakara, Mālā, Puṣpatārā, Sarvārthasiddha, Viṣṇu (his *v.*, if composed of gems, is named Vaijayantīmālā, although his *v.* is sometimes said to be made of *tulasī*-flowers), *vidyādharas*, Vivasvān. – Other n.: *kusumamālā*, *mālā*, *puṣpamālā*, *sraj*.

Lit.: B 290; BECA 1:7; DHP 157; HIS 45; WM 104.

vānaprastha "living in the woods, ascetic", n. of a *brāhmaṇa* in the third stage of his religious life. Another n.: *vaikhānasa*.

Lit.: IC 1:601; WHW 1:85.

vānara "monkey". Monkeys are objects of popular worship: Hanumān and Sugrīva furnish particular examples of this cult. – A *v.* is a symbol of Abhinandana, Vasanta. It is also the Vāh. of Vasanta.

Lit.: GH 70; GJ pl. 23:4; GoRI 1:316; KiJ pl. 45.

vanaspati "Lord of the Wilderness", another n. of *vṛkṣa*.

Lit.: CEBI 7; MKVI 2:241; ZA 27.

Vanavāsi ("living in the forest"; Buddh.), n. of a Lamaist *arhat*. Char.: Mu.: *tarjanīmudrā*; attr.: *cāmara*.
Lit.: G 12, 104.

vandana "adoration, reverence (of the *guru*)" (Jain.), see *āvaśyaka*.
Lit.: GJ 408; IC 2:638.

vandanamudrā (*vandanī-*) "gesture of adoration, reverence" (Mu.), n. of a handpose which is equivalent either to *añjalimudrā* or to *namaskāramudrā*. It is sometimes said that this handpose is performed with only one hand (cp. MEIA).
Lit.: B 251; KiSB 74; MEIA 203, 218, 333.

vaṅga and *vaṅgu* (cp. *vaṅgus* "bodily inflexions" HAHI), see *bhaṅga*.
Lit.: HAHI 16.

vaṅki (*vaṅgi*, Tam.) "bracelet" (attr.).
Lit.: JDI 19.

vaṅśa "flute" (attr.), see *veṇu*.
Lit.: BBh. 314.

Vaṅśā (deification of *vaṅśa*; Buddh.), n. of a goddess. Attr.: *veṇu*.
Lit.: BBh. 314.

vāra (*vāsara*) "day" of the seven-day-week, cp. *ravi-* (or *ādi-*, *āditya-*), *soma-* (*indu-*), *maṅgala-* (*bhauma-*), *budha-* (*saumya-*), *bṛhaspati-* (*guru-*), *śukra-* (*bhṛgu-*) and *śani-* (*manda-*)*vāra*. These weekdays, named after the planets, are similar in the Indian and the European calendar; this nomenclature, contrary to other aspects of Indian chronology, is of Western origin.
Lit.: IC 2:734; WHW 1:195.

varadamudrā (or *vara(da)hastamudrā*) "gesture of the granting of wishes" (Mu.), n. of a handpose shown by gods while conferring boons or dispensing favours; it therefore indicates the charity of the god. The hand in this pose hangs loose, the palm outwards with all the fingers outstretched; the hand may also be half closed. This Mu. is also mentioned as a variety of the *patākāmudrā*. Almost any of the deities of all Indian religions may show it, and here only a few of them may be mentioned, as, e.g., Viṣṇu (Śrīnivāsa), the Buddha, Ākāśagarbha, Gaṇeśa, Kāśyapa, Maitreya, sMan-bla, Muktakeśī, Ratnapāṇi, Samantabhadra, Sarvanivaraṇaviṣkambhin, Sitatārā, Śyāmatārā. – Other n.: *dāna-*, *iṣṭa-*, *iṣṭapradā-*, *prasāda-*, *varaprada-mudrā*; cp. also *āhūyavarada-*, *ratnasamyuktavarada-mudrā*.
Lit.: B 251; BBh. 441; DHP 272; G 22 (ill.); GBM 97; H pl. 5:42c; KiSH 91; MH 7; R 1:14 a.pl. 5:4-6; SM 51; Th. 29; WHW 2:86; WM 98 a.fig. 15.

Varadarāja ("king conferring boons, king of giving"), epithet of Viṣṇu, esp. in his form as Karivarada. Char.: Vāh.: Garuḍa; Mu.: *varada-* and *āhūyavarada-mudrā*; attr.: *cakra*, *śaṅkha*.
Lit.: JDI 66; R 1:266 a.pl. 80:1; SB 37, 353 a.fig. 19, 342 (why not here Śrīnivāsa?), 343; Th. 56.

Varada-Tārā ("T. conferring boons"; Buddh.), n. of a green Tārā.
Lit.: BBh. 307.

Varadāyaka-Lokeśvara ("L. granting wishes"; Buddh.), n. of a variety of Avalokiteśvara. Char.: Mu.: *añjali-*, *karaṇa(?)-mudrā*; attr.: *akṣamālā*.
Lit.: BBh. 395 a.pl. 11(A).

varāha "boar" (Vāh.); sometimes char. of Vārāhī; symbol of Vimala. – Cp. *sūkara*.
Lit.: GH 70; GJ pl. 22:13; KiJ pl. 45; KiSH 53.

Varāha, Varāhāvatāra ("Boar-Incarnation"), n. of the 3rd *avatāra* of Viṣṇu in which, in the form of a giant boar, he rescued the Earth, which was immersed in the ocean by the demon Hiraṇyākṣa. As a boar he dived into the deep and brought up the Earth in the shape of a young woman. The boar, which roots in the earth, is symbolic of ploughing and agriculture. – Attr.: *varāhamukha* and the chief attr. of Viṣṇu. – V. is found in three different forms: Bhūvarāha (also Ādi-, Nṛ-varāha), Yajñavarāha and Pralayavarāha. – Varāha also signifies a manifestation of Viṣṇu as Aniruddha. In older tradition V. is sometimes regarded as a manifestation of Prajāpati or Brahmā; later also as a manifestation of Rāhu.
Lit.: B 414 a.pl. 25; BP 107 a.pl. 10-16; DHP 165, 168; GH 121; GoRI 1:251; Gt 680; H pl. 6:49;

IIM 35 (ill.); JDI 75; KiH 13 a.pl. 28; KiSH 36, 40; KrA pl. 47; MEIA 28; MG 112 a.pl. facing p. 110; R 1:128 a.pl. 35f., 38-41; SSI 22; Th. pl. 13; W 121; ZA pl. 109.

varāhamukha (or *-mastaka*) "having a boar's-head" (attr.). Char. esp. of Viṣṇu in the Varāhāvatāra and in poly-headed (3- or 4-headed) forms, such as Caturmūrti, Vaikuṇṭhanātha; further, of Mārīcī (in different forms), Vajravārāhī, Varāhamukhī, Vārāhī, Vartālī.

Lit.: B 408 a.pl. 22:5; HIS 73 a.pl. 42f.

Varāhamukhī ("having a boar's-head"; Buddh.), n. of an inferior Mahāyāna goddess attending on Mārīcīpicuvā. Attr.: *aśoka*-flower, *dhanus*, *śara*, *vajra*, *varāhamukha*.

Lit.: BBh. 211; KiSB 83.

Vārāhī (related to Varāha).

1. (Hind.) N. of one of the *sapta- (aṣṭa-) mātaras* or *navaśakti*, forming the female aspect of Varāhāvatāra. She symbolizes *anásūya* ("absence of envy"). Char.: att.: *lalitāsana*; Vāh.: *mahiṣa* or *varāha* or *gaja*; Mu.: *abhaya-*, *varada-mudrā*; attr.: *daṇḍa*, *dhanus*, *hala*, *kapāla*, *khaḍga*, *kheṭaka*, *nūpuras*, *pāśa*, *śakti*, *triśūla*, *varāhamukha*. Her sacred tree is *karañja*.

Lit.: B 185, 506 a.pl. 44:3; BECA 1: pl. 16b; KiSH 53; R 1:388 a.pl. 117; Th. 108.

2. (Buddh.) V. is found also in Buddhism. Char.: colour: blue; Vāh.: *ulūka*; Mu.: *añjalimudrā*; attr.: *kapāla*, *matsya*.

Lit.: BBh. 364.

Varālī ("whitish"?; Buddh.), n. of an inferior Mahāyāna goddess attending on Mārīcīpicuvā. Attr.: *aśoka*-flower, *pāśa*, *sūci*, *vajra*.

Lit.: BBh. 211; KiSB 83.

Varanandi ("excellent joy"; Jain.), n. of a *yakṣa* attending on the 7th *tīrthaṅkara*. Symbol: *siṅha*.

Lit.: GJ 362 a.pl. 25:7; KiJ 11 a.pl. 28:7.

Vārāṇasī (N.Ind. Banāras, Engl. Benares), n. of a sacred city, see further Kāśī. It is said that the n. is derived from the names of two rivers, Varaṇā and Asī.

Lit.: MW 944; WHW 1:118.

varapradamudrā "gesture of granting wishes" (Mu.), see *varadamudrā*.

Lit.: BBh. 87.

vārapūjāvidhi "weekly worship" which "means a special selection of offerings which are made in the common ritualistic setting on each day of the week or on particular days yielding life, fame, sons and health as result".

Lit.: DiIP 159.

Vardhamāna ("prosperous, increasing"; Jain.), the worldly n. of Mahāvīra as a child and as a beggar monk.

Lit.: GJ 296; KiSH 123.

vardhamāna(ka) (M.Ind. *vaddhamānaga*) "prosperous; succes" (attr.), n. of a *maṅgala* (see also *aṣṭamaṅgala*) which is found in all Indian religions and which, in Buddhism, has the form of a banner of victory, in Jainism, of a vase (or of a powder-box).

Lit.: GBM 102; GJ 384; KiJ 21; KiSH 154.

vardhamānaliṅga "prosperous *liṅga*" (attr.), n. of a kind of *mānuṣaliṅga*.

Lit.: R 2:88.

vardhanī (Tam. *varttaṉi*) "water-jar" (attr.), "a vessel of water in which Umā is invoked and worshipped".

Lit.: DiIP 107, 146.

varṇa "caste" (properly "colour"). There were originally four chief castes in India: *brāhmaṇa*, *kṣatriya*, *vaiśya*, *śūdra*. The first three of these were classed as *dvija* "twice born" (see *upanayana*). Numerous sub-classes or castes have sprung form these four castes, and there are also classes of people which are not reckoned among these castes but are called "outcasts, untouchables" (*aspṛśya*, *harijan*). – Another n.: *jāti*.

Lit.: D 336; Gt 120; MKVI 2:247; MW 924; WHW 1:201; WM 123.

Varṇanī ("leading the caste, tribe"?), n. of a wife of Aiyaṉār.

Lit.: ACA 3; R 2:489.

varṣa "the rainy season", n. of a season of two

months, from the middle of July to the middle of September.
Lit.: IC 2:723, 732.

varṣasthala "rain-vase for receiving dew or rain", in architecture n. of an ornamental vase which is placed on the *chattra* of a *stūpa*.
Lit.: ZA 234.

Vartālī ("having bees, scorpions, as a livelihood[?]"; Buddh.), n. of an inferior Mahāyāna goddess attending on Mārīcīpicuvā. Char.: colour: red; attr.: *aśoka*-flower, *pāśa*, *sūci*, *vajrāṅkuśa*, *varāhamukha*.
Lit.: BBh. 211; KiSB 83.

vartamāna "current", referring, in dating, to the year, see *saṃvatsara*.

Varuṇa (meaning uncertain; interpreted both as "Coverer, Binder" or "All-enveloping. Sky" and as "der [Gott] mit dem Widder, Herr des Widders", in this case the word may be derived from *uraṇa*, see below).
1. (Hind.) N. of one of the chief Vedic gods, probably identical with the Avestan Ahura Mazdā. He was the lord of *asura*s and the waters, and the guardian of the system of the world (*ṛta*). The ram (*uraṇa*) is said to be the sacred animal of V. in the Vedic age (Oldenberg). V. is later regarded as an Āditya and the son of Kardama. Wife: Gaurī (also named Varuṇānī, Vāruṇī), but as the god of waters he is also connected with Gaṅgā and Yamunā; son: Puṣkara. – In later Hinduism he is esp. known as a *dikpāla* of the westerly direction (but, at least in South India, he is still worshipped as a rain-god, though only at times of drought); his *diggaja* is named Añjana. Char.: colour: white; Vāh.: *matsya* or *makara*, *ratna* drawn by 7 *aśva*s (or *haṅsa*s), or one *haṅsa* or *aśva*; Mu.: *abhaya-*, *varada-mudrā*; attr.: *caturmukha*, *chattra* Ābhoga, *kamaṇḍalu* (with gems), *nāga*, *(nāga)pāśa*, *padma*, *śaṅkha*, *triśūla*, *tundila*, *yajñopavīta*. – As an Āditya he has the attr.: *cakra*, 2 *padma*s, *pāśa*.
Lit.: B 526 a.pl. 46:1; D 336; DHP 118 a.pl. 9; GBB 129; GoRI 1:73, 227; Gt 683; IC 1:317, 494; IIM 14, 78; KiH 11 a.pl. 13; KiSH 55, 57; M. Mayrhofer, EWA 3:151; MEIA 131; MG 41; H. Oldenberg, Die Religion des Veda, 189 N. 4, 440; R 1:309, 2:529; Th. 110; WHW 2:552; WM 181.
2. (Buddh.) V. is here a *dikpāla*. Char.: colour: white; Vāh.: *makara*; attr.: *nāgapāśa*, *śaṅkha*, *saptaphana*.
Lit.: BBh. 361.
3. (Jain.) N. of a *yakṣa* attending on the 20th *tīrthaṅkara*. No particular symbol.
Lit.: B 562; GJ 362 a.pl. 26:20; KiJ 11 a.pl. 29:20.

Vāruṇī (derived from Varuṇa), n. of a form of the wife of Varuṇa, see Gaurī. She forms the female aspect of Varuṇa and is sometimes also said to be his daughter. She is generally held to have originated at the churning of the ocean of milk (see Kūrmāvatāra), and she is regarded not only as the "wine-goddess", the deity of spirituous liquor, but also that of boats. She is represented as seated in a boat, ornamented with gems. Attr.: *caṣaka*, *māṅsa*, *padma*, *pārijāta*-flowers. Epithets: Amṛteśvarī, Sudhāmālinī.
Lit.: DHP 167; Gt 687; MW 944; SSI 220.

Vāruṇī-Cāmuṇḍā, n. of a composition of two goddesses. Of these, Vāruṇī has the attr.: *śara*, *triśūla*; Cāmuṇḍā is poly-armed.
Lit.: R 1:364.

vāsa "perfume; a kind of powder" (attr.).
Lit.: GJ 427.

vasanta "spring (season)", n. of a season from the middle of March to the middle of May.
Lit.: IC 2:723, 732.

Vasanta ("spring-god"; Hind. and Buddh.), n. of an (originally Hindu?) god (an attendant of Śiva). Char.: colour: white; Vāh.: *vānara*; attr.: *caṣaka*, *dhanus*, *khaḍga*, *śara*.
Lit.: BBh. 379; R 2:148.

Vasantadevī ("spring-goddess"; Buddh.), in Lamaism n. of a seasonal goddess, a *ḍākinī* in the retinue of Śrīdevī. Char.: Vāh.: *aśvatara*; attr.: *kapāla*, *khaḍga*.
Lit.: G 35, 82.

vasantapañcamī, n. of a spring festival which takes place on the 5th day of the light half of the month *māgha* (January-February) and is dedicated to Sarasvatī. – Another n.: *vasantotsava*; cp. *madanotsava*.
Lit.: GH 353.

vasantotsava "spring festival", see *vasantapañcamī* and *madanotsava*.
Lit.: DiIP 166.

vāsara "day of the week", see *vāra*.

vāsikābandha, n. of a kind of hairdress (named after a plant, Gendarussa vulgaris?) which is peculiar to Jyeṣṭhā.
Lit.: SSI 216, 268 a.fig. pl. I:10.

Vasiṣṭha ("Owner-of-Wealth"), n of a renowned *riṣi* or *prajāpati*, the son of Brahmā and the owner of the famous cow Kāmadhenu. He was also the leader of a certain group of *riṣis*, the *brahmarṣis*. Wife: Arundhatī.
Lit.: D 339; DHP 317, 320; MKVI 2:274; R 2:566; WHW 2:553; WM 183.

vaśitā ("will, control"; Buddh.), n. of a group of 12 goddesses, personifying "the controls or disciplines which lead to the spiritual regeneration of its followers". These are: Āyur-, Citta-, Pariṣkāra-, Karma-, Upapatti-, Ṛddhi-, Adhimukti-, Praṇidhāna-, Jñāna-, Dharma-, Tathatā-, and Buddhabodhiprabhā-vaśitā.
Lit.: BBh. 328.

Vassāvaṇa (Pāli, Sri Lanka, = Vaiśravana). see Kubera.

vastra "cloth(es)" (attr.), n. of a scarf wrapped round the *cakra*.
Lit.: JDI 8.

vastrayajñopavīta "sacred thread made of cloth" (attr.), n. of a kind of *yajñopavīta* furnished with long strips of cloth; the term also refers to a garment worn as a sacred thread.
Lit.: SB 88; SSIP 81.

vastropavīta "dressing and perfuming (an idol)", n. of a rite which forms part of the *pūjā*.
Lit.: DiIP 90.

vāstukhaṇḍa "architectural fragment"

vāstumaṇḍala "house-circle, plan of a building", a term in architecture. The *v.* is "le plan idéal, l'archetype, sur lequel doit s'élever toute construction, maison, temple, ville."
Lit.: ACA 59.

vasu ("excellent, good"), n. of a group of 8 gods or demigods, attendants of Indra. There are several lists of these gods; one of these comprises: Anala, Anila, Āpa, Dhara, Dhruva, Prabhāsa, Pratyūṣa, Soma. Common attr.: *akṣamālā* (not all of them), *śakti* (all). – *v.* is also a symbolic n. of the number "8", see *saṅkhyā*.
Lit.: D 342; DHP 83; R 2:550.

Vasudeva ("god of good (men)" or "god of wealth, property"), n. of a prince, the father of Kṛṣṇa and Balarāma. Wives: Devakī, Rohiṇī, and others
Lit.: D 342; Gt 689.

Vāsudeva (patronymic of Vasudeva), epithet of Kṛṣṇa as the son of Vasudeva; also n. of a manifestation of Viṣṇu as a *nara*, see *caturvyūha*, *caturmūrti*, or of an aspect of Viṣṇu, see *caturviṅśatimūrti* (in this form the n. of V. is also interpreted as "the Indweller") with the Śakti: Lakṣmī. – In Jainism, V. is n. of a demigod (in a group of 9 demigods) whose attributes are equivalent to those of Viṣṇu. – Cp. Mānuṣa-Vāsudeva, Para-Vāsudeva.
Lit.: D 343; DHP 154; GJ 258, 261; Gt 690; KiH 13 a.pl. 25; KiSH 35; MEIA 16, 21; R 1:229; WM 185.

Vāsudeva-Kṛṣṇa, epithet of Kṛṣṇa as the son of Vasudeva. The n. may perhaps allude to a fusion of two mythical characters of Kṛṣṇa: on one hand the god of youth of a shepherd tribe (Kṛṣṇa, the son of Vasudeva), and on the other hand the famous hero Kṛṣṇa in the epic Mahābhārata.
Lit.: HIS 18.

Vāsudeva-Viṣṇu, an epithet indicating the underlying identity of Kṛṣṇa (Vāsudeva) and Viṣṇu (since Kṛṣṇa is regarded as an *avatāra* of Viṣṇu).
Lit.: B 370.

Vasudhārā (Vasundharā; "holding the treasure"), n. of an earth-goddess.

1. (Hind.) NP of the Śakti of Kubera; see also Bhūmi.

Lit.: B 560 a.pl. 48:2.

2. (Buddh.) N. of a female *bodhisattva*. She is either the Śakti of, or at least is connected with Jambhala, or the Śakti of Vajrasattva, and is an emanation of either Akṣobhya or Ratnasambhava. Char.: colour: yellow; att.: *lalitāsana*; Mu.: *añjali-* (?), *buddhaśramaṇa-*, *varada-mudrā*; attr.: *Akṣobhyabimba* on the crown, *chattra*, *cintāmaṇi*, *kamaṇḍalu* (with gems), *kaṇiśa*, *padma*, *pustaka*, *Ratnasambhava-bimba* on the crown.

Lit.: BBh. 202, 244 a.pl. 187f.; G 33, 74; JMS pl. 34; KiDG 64; KiSB 74, 77, 94.

Vāsuki (according to MW, derived from *vasuka* "one who clothes"; a connection with *vasu* may also be possible), n. of a seven-headed *nāga*-king (at times also in the function of an attr.). At the churning of the ocean of milk (see Kūrmāvatāra), he was used as a rope wound round Mount Mandara. – As an attr., he is shown worn round the body by Śiva, or as an armlet by Aparājitā, and he is carried in one hand by Nīlakaṇṭha. – V. is pearl-white. Attr.: *akṣamālā*, *kamaṇḍalu*, *svastika* (on the hood), *trinayana*.

Lit.: D 343; DHP 308; Gt 690; IIM 108; MW 948; WHW 2:388.

Vasumatiśrī ("the beautiful one with the excellent mind"; Buddh.), n. of a minor Mahāyāna goddess attending on Vasudhārā.

Lit.: BBh. 203; KiSB 94.

Vasundharā ("containing wealth"), see Vasudhārā.

Lit.: B 560.

Vāsupūjya (patronymic: "son of Vasupūjya"; Jain.), n. of the 12th *tīrthaṅkara*. Symbol: *mahiṣa*.

Lit.: GJ 276; KiSH 142.

Vasuśrī ("excellent beautiful"; Buddh.), n. of a minor Mahāyāna goddess attending on Vasudhārā.

Lit.: BBh. 203; KiSB 94.

Vaśyādhikāra-Lokeśvara ("L. having authority over the subject ones"; Buddh.), n. of a form of Avalokiteśvara. Char.: att.: *padmāsana*; Mu.: *dhyānamudrā*; attr.: *kamaṇḍalu*.

Lit.: BBh. 395 a.pl. 8(A).

Vaśya-Tārā ("the tamed, subjected T."; Buddh.), n. of a Mahāyāna goddess, an emanation of Amoghasiddhi and properly identical with Khadiravaṇī-Tārā or Ārya-Tārā. Char.: colour: green; att.: *bhadrāsana*; Mu.: *varadamudrā*; attr.: *Amogha-siddhibimba* on the crown, *nīlotpala*.

Lit.: BBh. 229 a.pl. 170; KiDG 64; KiSB 99.

Vāsya-Vajravārāhī (possibly "Vajravārāhī with (or of) the knife", *vāsya* [= *vāśī*?] here indicating the *kartṛ* [*karttṛkā*] which she carries in her right hand instead of a *vajra*), n. of a variety of Vajravārāhī. Char.: Vāh.: *mṛtaka*; att.: *nāṭyasthāna*; attr.: *kapāla*, *karttṛkā*, *khaṭvāṅga*.

Lit.: BBh. 219 a.pl. 159f.; MW 947, 949.

vaśyavidhi "rite of subduing", n. of a rite (Buddh.).

Lit.: BBh. 166, 307.

vaṭa(vṛkṣa) "the Banyan or Indian fig-tree (Ficus Bengalensis)", n. of a tree which symbolizes the cosmos. It is sacred to Viṣṇu (cp. Vaṭapattrāśāyin) and Śiva ("comme arbre phallique?" IC) and Cāmuṇḍā; also to Mahāsāhasrapramardanī, and is, as a *bodhivṛkṣa*, associated with Kanakamuni. The Buddha sat under a *v.* at Sārnāth while fasting before his enlightenment. – Another n.: *nyagrodha*.

Lit.: GH 63; IC 1:537; KiSB 111; MG 236; WHW 1:357.

Vaṭapattrāśāyin (-ī; "lying on a fig-leaf"), n. of Viṣṇu or Kṛṣṇa in the form of a baby lying floundering on its back on a fig-leaf. As a representation in bronze, V. symbolizes the god reposing upon the world ocean after destroying cosmos at the end of a cosmic period (cp. Anantāśāyana).

According to R, this representation forms an *ugra*-aspect of Viṣṇu. – Cp. Santāna-Gopāla. – Another n. : Nārāyaṇa.
Lit.: B 275; FK 108; R 1:19, 215 a.pl. 67:3; SSI 37; Th. 67; ZM 51.

vātapuṭa "empty fold, wind-bag, inflated bladder" (attr., carried in the hands; Buddh.). Char. of Vāyu.
Lit.: BBh. 362.

vati, see *badi*.

Vaṭuka-Bhairava, see Baṭuka-Bhairava.

Vayiravaṉ (Tam.), see Bhairava.

Vāyu ("wind, air")., n. of the god of the wind
1. (Hind.) V. is one of the Vedic gods and celebrated "als das Leben der Welt und die universelle, mit *prāṇa* (dem Lebensatem) identische Seele" (GoRI). In later Hinduism, he is a *dikpāla* of the north-westerly direction; his *diggaja* is named Puṣpadanta. He is also the god of the month *vaiśākha*. V. is also sometimes mentioned as the charioteer of Agni. Char. : colour : dark-blue; Vāh. : *mṛga* or *siṅhāsana*; Mu. : *abhaya-*, *patākā-*, *varada-mudrā*; attr. : *aṅkuśa*, *cakra*, *daṇḍa*, *dhvaja*, *kamaṇḍalu*, *śara*. – Epithet : Pavana.
Lit.: B 527; BBh. 382; D 343; DHP 90; GBB 129; GoRI 1:231; Gt 691; IC 1:324, 494; KiH 11; KiSH 55; MEIA 132; R 2:532 a.pl. 151:2; Th. 111; WM 185.
2. (Buddh.) V. is a *dikpāla* (cp. above). Char. : colour : blue; Vāh. : *mṛga*; attr. : *vātapuṭa*.
Lit.: BBh. 362.

vāyukumāra ("prince of the wind"; Jain.), n. of a kind of *bhavanavāsī*.
Lit. GJ 236.

Veda ("knowledge"; attr.), n. of the sacred books of Vedic religion, also regarded as the canon of later Hinduism. There are four books of V. : Ṛgveda (Rigveda or Hymn-Veda), Yajurveda (the sacrificial Veda), Sāmaveda (the Veda of chants) and Atharvaveda (a Veda belonging to a certain class of priests). Besides these four books, a great mass of religious literature of a Vedic kind has arisen which will not be further mentioned here. – Since the book (*pustaka*) held in one hand or all hands, esp. by Brahmā, and by Viṣṇu, is supposed to contain the Veda, the term V. is sometimes used as a n. of this attr. – For *veda* as a symbolic n. of the number "4", see *saṅkhyā*.
Lit.: D 344; Gt 699; MW 1015; R 2:378; WHW 2:556; WM 185.

vedanā "sensation", see *skandha*.
Lit.: BBh. 42.

Vedānta ("the end of Veda"), n. of a philosophical system, the main stream of Indian thought.
Lit.: GH 455; Gt 695; WHW 2:559.

Vedāntadeśika ("teacher in Vedānta"), n. of a Vaiṣṇavite saint. Char. : att. : *vīrāsana*; Mu. : *vyākhyānamudrā*.
Lit.: SSI 259 a.fig. 160b.

Veda-Vyāsa ("arranger, compilator of Veda"), see Vyāsa.
Lit.: B 390; DHP 165; R 1:123.

vedi (or *-ī*) "elevated piece of ground serving for a sacrificial altar", or a "sacrificial altar" made of clay. *v.* is further an altar-stand, pedestal = *pīṭha*, meant for several idols, and provided with a *prabhāvalī* (attr.).
Lit.: DiIP 97; MW 1017; RV 142; WHW 1:30.

vedikā "railing or fence" of a sacred enclosure, esp. of a *stūpa*. Regarding different parts of *v.*, see *ālambana*, *stambha*, *sūci*, *uṣṇīṣa*.
Lit.: BRI 113; DKI 13 a.passim; HIS 53 a.pl. 8; RAAI 274; SeKB passim; ZA 233.

vedikāsana "railing-seat" (Vāh.), n. of an unadorned *pīṭha* intended for minor deities (e.g. for *abhicārikāsanamūrti*).
Lit.: R 1:90.

vēl (Tam.) "spear" (attr.), see *śakti* and cp. Vēlāyudha-Subrahmaṇya.
Lit.: R 2: pl. 121:1.

Vēlaṉ (Tam. "spear-furnished"), epithet of Skanda.
Lit.: MD 2:651.

Vēlāyudha-Subrahmaṇya (mixed Tam.-Skt, "S. with the spear-weapon"), epithet of Skanda.
Lit.: R 2: pl. 122:1.

Veṅkaṭeśa (or -ṭeśvara, -ṭaramana; "Lord of Veṇkaṭa [a sacred hill in South India]"), n. of a form of Kṛṣṇa or Viṣṇu worshipped at Tirupati (now also called Saptagiri, near Madras). V. is, according to SSI, another n. of Śrīnivāsa. – Other n.: Bālāji (Ballaji), Vyaṅkaṭeśa.
Lit.: JDI 99; KiH 13 a.pl. 30; KiSH 37; Th. 58; R 1:270; SSI 62.

veṇu "flute" (attr.). Char. of: Kṛṣṇa Veṇugopāla, Rājagopāla, Vaṅśā. – Other n.: *muralī, vaṅśa.*
Lit.: B 303; R 1:10 a.pl. 3:14; SMII 148; Th. 43.

Veṇugopāla ("the cowherd with the flute"), n. of a form of Kṛṣṇa, represented playing the flute. Char.: att.: *pādasvastika*; attr.: esp. *veṇu*, further *cakra, dhanus* (or *ikṣukodaṇḍa*), *padma, paraśu, pāśa, śaṅkha.* – Epithets and varieties: Gānagopāla, Madanagopāla, Muralīdhara.
Lit.: B pl. 27:2; H pl. 6:51; HSIT 13 a.pl. 34; KrA pl. 155; R 1:207 a.pl. 61-63; SB 340 a.fig. 279; SIB pl. 26; Th. 68 a.pl. 20B; ZA 357 a.pl. 435.

vesara "ornament on the nose" (attr.). Char. of icons of later times, e.g. Kṛṣṇa, Rādhā. – In architecture, *v.* is n. of a kind of round temple, characteristic, in the form of a Buddhist *caitya*-hall, of Central India.
Lit.: B 289; DKI 41; RAAI 274.

vesaraliṅga, n. of a kind of *māṇuṣaliṅga.*
Lit.: R 2:92.

Vessabhū (Pāli), see Viśvabhuj.

vetāla "demon, ghost, vampire (esp. someone occupying a dead body)" (attr.). N. of a kind of demon "die von toten Körpern Besitz nehmen und sich derselben als Hülle bedienen" (pw). A *v.* is described as having a hideously ugly face. As an attr. a *v.* may be held in one hand. Char. of: Aghora, Vīra-Vighneśa. – Cp. *pēy.*
Lit.: D 355; DHP 310; MW 1014; pw 6:157; R 1:52, 2:199, 562; STP 6:136.

vetālī (fem. of *vetāla*; attr.). Char. of Yamāntaka.
Lit.: KiSB 71.

Vetālī (Buddh.), n. of a goddess of the *gaurī*-group. Char.: colour: red; attr.: *śṛṅkhalā.*
Lit.: BBh. 310 a.pl. 202.

vibhajyavāda (and *-vādin*) "analytical doctrine" (and, respectively, "adherent of this doctrine"), n. of a Buddhist doctrine.
Lit.: GRI 283.

Vibhaktā ("secluded, different, manifold"), n. of a female *dvārapālaka* of Gaurī.
Lit.: R 1:362.

vibhava "manifestation, the act of coming into existence in a special manner" (a term almost equivalent to *avatāra*).
Lit.: B 388; GoRI 2:122; MEIA 15.

Vibhava ("powerful, rich"), n. of a *dvārapālaka* of Brahmā. Attr.: *aṅkuśa, daṇḍa, padma, pāśa.*
Lit.: R 2:507.

Vibhavā ("rich"), n. of the wife of Kubera.
Lit.: R 2:536.

Vibhīṣaṇa ("frightful"), epithet of Śiva. – In Sri Lanka V. is sometimes mentioned as a *dikpāla* of the westerly direction.
Lit.: CBC 8; DHP 195.

vibhūti (Tam. *vipūti*).
1. "Pervading; multiplication, superhuman power", n. of a group of 8 attendants of Viṣṇu.
Lit.: DHP 163; GoRI 1:269.
2. (Attr.) "The ashes of cow-dung (with which Śiva is said to smear his body, and hence used in imitation of him by devotees)" (P). Char. of: Śiva (in different forms), Kālī, *pitaras, śaivabhaktas.* It is also included among the *aṣṭāvaraṇa.* Śiva owes his white colour to *v.*, and it is therefore an appendage of ardent Śiva-worshippers, see *tiryakpuṇḍra.* It is kept in a *juli.* – Another n.: *tiruniṟu*; cp. also *bhasman.*
Lit.: DHP 214, 218; DiIP 74; GoRI 1:260; Gt Suppl. 151; JDI 19; KiH 45; MSHP 38; P 1179; R 2:276; SSR 142; TL 6:3682.

vibhūtipuṇḍra "mark made with cow-dung ashe" (attr.), see *tiryakpuṇḍra.*
Lit.: JDI 19.

Vicālāṭciyammaṉ (or Vicālākṣi-, Tam., from Skt *viśālākṣī*; "the Lady with large eyes"), epithet of Pārvatī.
Lit.: DiCh. 18.

Vicitrakuṇḍalin (or -ī, "wearing a diamond ring"; Buddh.), n. of a *yakṣa* king. – Another n.: Civikuṇḍalin.
Lit.: BBh. 380; KiSB 74.

vīciyakaram (Tam.) "swinging arm" (Mu.), see *gajahastamudrā*.

Vicṛtau ("les deux qui délient"), another n. of a *nakṣatra*, see Mūla.
Lit.: IC 2:730.

Viditā ("known"; Jain.), see Vijayā.
Lit.: GJ 362.

vidgala (?, att.): "does it refer to the manner of showing one leg crossing the other firmly planted leg?" (thus B); cp. *pādasvastika*.
Lit.: B 268.

vidruma "coral", n. of a precious stone included among the *navaratna**.

vidyā "knowledge; wisdom", also "magical knowledge or power". – In Vajrayāna esotericism *v.* is also a term for "die konsekrierte Frau" (GBM), hence it is used almost as an equivalent of Śakti, cp. *prajñā*. – *v.* is sometimes (as a n. of a book of knowledge) used for *pustaka* (as an attr.).
Lit.: BBh. 438; GBM 160; GRI 273; IC 1:610; R 1:366.

vidyādevī ("goddess of knowledge, learning"; Jain.), n. of one belonging to a group of 16 deities headed by Sarasvatī. Several of these coincide with the *śāsanadevatās*. The *v.* comprise: Rohiṇī, Prajñapti, Vajraśṛṅkhalā, Kuliśāṅkuśā, Cakreśvarī, Naradattā, Kālī, Mahākālī, Gaurī, Gāndhārī, Sarvāstramahājvālā, Mānavī, Vairoṭyā, Acchuptā, Mānasī, Mahāmānasikā. – Another n.: *śrutadevī*.
Lit.: AIP pl. 62 (329); B 561; GJ 362; MW 964.

vidyādhara ("bearer-of-wisdom"; here "wisdom" probably alludes to a magical knowledge or power); n. of a kind of mythical beings (in human form) possessing magical knowledge, attendants esp. of Indra, and belonging to air-space (*kha*). They are found in all Indian religions, and their king is named Sarvārthasiddha (thus in Buddhism). *v.*-figures are often found as decorative motif in the temples. Attr.: *ratna*, *vanamālā*. – Vidyādhara is also n. of the *khaḍga* of Viṣṇu.
Lit.: AIP 275; BBh. 381; BECA 1:265; D 356; DHP 304; GH 109; HIS 26; IC 1:529; KrA pl. 68, 77; MEIA 200; WM 187.

Vidyādharā (Buddh.), n. of the Śakti of Yamāntaka.
Lit.: KiSB 71.

vidyāmudrā "gesture of knowledge" (Mu.), see *jñānamudrā*.
Lit.: R 2:378.

Vidyāpati-Lokeśvara ("L., lord of knowledge"; Buddh.), n. of a variety of Avalokiteśvara. Char.: att.: *samapādasthānaka*; Vāh.: *padma*; attr.: *cāmara*, *padma*.
Lit.: BBh. 430 a.pl. 102(A).

vidyārāja ("king of knowledge"; Buddh.), n. of a Mahāyāna tutelary god, see further *dharmapālo*
Lit.: GBM 80.

vidyārājñī "queen of (magical) knowledge" (Buddh.), n. of a class of deities who in part may be personifications of magical formulæ (*dhāraṇī*), e.g. Mahāmāyūrī. Closely related to *v.* are *mahārakṣā*, *dhyānibuddhaśakti*.
Lit.: BRI 176; GBM 81.

vidyeśvara ("lord of knowledge"), n. of one belonging to a group of 8 emancipated beings: Ananteśa, Sūkṣma, Śivottama, Ekanetra, Ekarudra, Trimūrti, Śrīkaṇṭha, Śikhaṇḍin. They are connected with Śiva as aspects of himself. As Śaktis of the *v.* the following are mentioned: Vāmā, Jyeṣṭhā, Raudrī, Kālī, Kalavikaraṇī, Balavikaraṇī, Balapramathanī, Sarvabhūtadamanī.
Lit.: R 2:392, 403.

Vidyuddharā ("holding, bearing the lightning"), see Taḍitkarā.
Lit.: BBh. 319.

Vidyujjvālākarālī ("having tongues of lightning-flames"; Buddh.), n. of a 12-headed form of Ekajaṭā. V. is said to have originated from the sweat of the Buddha.

Char.: colour: blue or black; att.: *ālīḍhāsana* (on white skulls); Vāh.: she is portrayed treading upon the 4 Māras: Indra, Brahmā, Viṣṇu, Śiva; Mu.: *tarjanīmudrā*; attr.: *akṣamālā*, *Akṣobhyabimba* on the crown, *aṅkuśa*, *bhindipāla*, *brahmakapāla*, *cakra*, *caṣaka*, *cintāmaṇi*, *ḍamaru*, *dhanus*, *dhvaja*, *gadā*, *ghaṇṭā*, *kapāla*, *karttṛkā*, *khaḍga*, *khaṭvāṅga*, *mudgara*, *musala*, *nāgas*, *nīlotpala*, *paraśu*, *pāśa*, *śakti*, *ṣaṇmudrā*, *śara*, *triśūla*, *vajra*.
Lit.: BBh. 194; KiSB 89.

vidyullatā "creeperlike lightning" (attr., held in one hand). Char. of Taḍitkarā.
Lit.: BBh. 318.

vidyutkumāra ("lightning-prince"; Jain.), n. of a kind of *bhavanavāsī*.
Lit.: GJ 236.

vighna "obstacle, destroyer" (Vāh.). *vighnas* are "obstacles" in personified form which are removed by the gods, who may be represented treading on *v*. They may therefore be regarded as a kind of Vāh. Char. of, e.g.: Parṇaśavarī, Gaṇeśa. (In Buddhist images *v*. may be regarded as a form of the Hindu Gaṇeśa).
Lit.: BBh. 197; KiSB 91.

Vighnāntaka ("remover of obstacles"; Buddh.), n. of a Mahāyāna god, an emanation of Akṣobhya. He resembles the Hindu Gaṇeśa (Vighneśvara). Char.: colour: blue; att.: *ālīḍhāsana*; Vāh.: Gaṇeśa; attr.: *aṅkuśa*, *ḍamaru*, *kapāla*, *karttṛkā*, *tarjanīpāśa*, *triśūla*, *vajra*. – He is also regarded as a *dikpāla* of the northerly direction. Char.: colour: green; attr.: *cintāmaṇi*, *khaḍga*, *padma*, *triśiras*, *vajra*. – Another n.: Analārka.
Lit.: BBh. 180, 253 a.pl. 131; KiSB 78.

Vighnarāja(-Gaṇapati) ("king of obstacles"), n. of a form of Gaṇeśa. Char.: Vāh.: *ākhu*; attr.: *āmra*, *aṅkuśa*, *pāśa*.
Lit.: DHP 292; R 1:58.

Vighneśvara (Vighneśa; "lord of obstacles"), epithet of Gaṇeśa, the remover of obstacles. Cp. Vighneśvarānugrahamūrti.
Lit.: DiCh. 26; DiIP 113; R 1:35, 49; ZA 46, 315; ZM 204.

Vighneśvarānugrahamūrti, n. of a gracious representation (*anugrahamūrti*) of Śiva together with Pārvatī and Gaṇeśa (Vighneśvara) who, after having been killed by Śiva, was now restored to life and had acquired the head of an elephant. Char.: Śiva: colour: black; Mu.: *abhaya-*, *varadamudrā*; attr.: *mṛga*, *paraśu*; Pārvatī: Mu.: *varadamudrā*; attr.: *nīlotpala*, *trinayana*; Gaṇeśa: Mu.: *añjalimudrā*; attr.: *aṅkuśa*. *pāśa*.
Lit.: R 2:213.

Vighneśvarī, n. of the Śakti of Gaṇeśa as Vighneśvara.
Lit.: B 358.

Vihaṅgama ("moving in the sky"), epithet of Garuḍa. V. is sometimes also regarded as an *avatāra* of Viṣṇu.
Lit.: B 529; MW 1003.

vihāra "monastery" (Buddh.), n. of a certain kind of temple(-cave)-building.
Lit.: BRI 111; DKI 37; FBKI passim; GBM 135; Gz 43; IC 2:319; RAAI 212; SeKB 129; WHW 1:209; ZA 246.

Vijaya ("victory").
1. (Hind.) N. of one among the group *ekādaśarudra*; also n. of a *dvārapālaka* of Brahmā or Viṣṇu. Hiraṇyākṣa is regarded as an incarnation of V., serving as the *dvārapālaka* of Viṣṇu. Attr.: *akṣamālā*, *daṇḍa*, *gadā*, *kheṭaka*. – V. is also n. of the *dhanus* of Indra.
Lit.: DHP 110; R 2:386, 507; WHW 1:91.
2. (Jain.) N. of a *yakṣa* attending on the 8th *tīrthaṅkara*.
Lit.: GJ 362.

Vijayā ("victory"; personification).
1. (Hind.) N.. of the Śakti of Ṣaṇmukha; also n. of a female *dvārapālaka* of Gaurī. See further Jayā-Vijayā.
Lit.: R 2:437.
2. (Jain.) N. of a *śāsanadevatā* attending on either the 13th, or the 17th *tīrthaṅkara*. – Another n.: Viditā.
Lit.: GJ 362 a.pl. 26:17; KiJ 12 a.pl. 29:17.

Vijaya-Gaṇapati ("G. of victory"), possibly another n. of Bīja-Gaṇapati.
Lit.: SSI 176.

Vijayanagara, n. of a city and an empire in Karṇāṭa, and of a centre of arts in the 14th-17th cc. A.D.
Lit.: D 356; Gz 189; RAAI 190; ZA pl. 437 ff.

vijñāna "consciousness", see *skandha*.
Lit.: BBh. 42.

vijñāna-mātra-vāda "only consciousness doctrine; Nur-Bewusstseinslehre" (Buddh.), n. of a Buddhist doctrine.
Lit.: GRI 263.

Vikālarātrī ("night of twilight"; Buddh.), n. of a minor Mahāyāna goddess attending on Buddhakapāla.
Lit.: BBh. 160.

vikarapīṭha ("*pīṭha* like an earth-pit?"), n. of a kind of *pīṭha*.
Lit.: R 2:101.

Vikarṇī (either "having no ears" or "having large, protruding ears"), epithet of Kālī.
Lit.: KiSH 48; MW 950.

vikasitapadma (or *-kās-*) "full-blown lotus" (attr.), see *padma*.
Lit.: BBh. 89.

vikramakāla (*vikramādityakāla*) "the era of Vikrama (Vikramāditya)", n. of an era beginning in B.C. 58. It was instituted by a celebrated king of Ujjayinī. This era, still used in considerable areas of Western and Central India, is indicated by *sam(vat)*, *sambat*, *vikramasamvat* or *vaikramābda*. The year is *gata* and either *caitrādi* and *pūrṇimānta* (in North India), or *kārttikādi* and *amānta* (in South India and Gujrat), or *āṣāḍhādi* and *amānta* (sometimes in Kathiawar and Gujrat), see *samvatsara* and *candramāsa*. The given year of this era – 57 or 56 = the year A.D. – Another n.: *mālavakāla*.
Lit.: Enc.Brit. 5:721; IC 2:736; P 1198; WHW 1:334.

vikramasamvat "the year of Vikrama", a term indicating an era, see *vikramakāla*.

vikṛta "disfigured" (attr.).
Lit.: ACA 41.

viḷakku (Tam.) "lamp", see *dīpa*.

vilāyatī(kāla), n. of an era beginning in A.D. 592 and used in Bengal and Orissa. The year is *vartamāna*, solar and *kanyādi*; the given year of this era + 591 or 592 = the year A.D. – See also *amle Oṛisā*, a closely comparable era used in Orissa.
Lit.: IC 2:737.

Vimala(nātha) ("bright, pure"; Jain.), n. of the 13th *tīrthaṅkara*. Symbol: *varāha*.
Lit.: GJ 277; KiSH 142.

Vimalā ("stainless, bright, pure"; Buddh.), n. of a *bhūmi*. Char.: colour: white; attr.: *padma* (white), *vajra*.
Lit.: BBh. 334.

vimalāsana ("pure seat"), n. of a hexagonal *pīṭha*.
Lit.: B 273; R 1:19.

vimāna (properly "chariot of the gods, a mythical self-moving aerial car"), n. on the one hand of a Vāh. of several gods and also of an aerial palace, on the other of a temple (cp. *ratha*). In the latter sense the term is applied to a temple as a whole, comprising the sanctuary and attached porches. Esp. in South India it is n. of a kind of temple consisting of *garbhagṛha* and *śikhara*. Cp. *bara deul*. *v.* is sometimes also used as a term for "throne", cp. *devavimāna*.
Lit.: BECA 1:265; DKI 41; GJ 235; GRI 240; IC 1:577; KiSB 27; R 1:22; RAAI 274; WHW 2:490; ZA 272.

vimānadevatā "*vimāna* deity" (attr.), n. of an icon which is placed in a niche (*devakoṣṭha*) on the outer wall of a temple.
Lit.: BECA 1:265.

vīṇā (Hi. *bīn*) "lute, staff-zither" (attr.), n. of a popular musical instrument, usually having 7 strings, supposed to have been invented by Nārada. There are many kinds of *v.* the chief of which is the North Indian *mahatī vīṇā* "large zither" with two calabash resonance-boxes. Cp. also *kinnarī*, *sitār*. – As attr. char. of: esp. Sarasvatī, further Ardhanārīśvara, Āryajāṅgulītārā, Dhṛtarāṣṭra, Gaṇeśa, Gītā, Īśāna, Jāṅgulī, Kālarātrī, Kinnara, Laghuśyāmalā, Mahāsarasvatī, Puṣṭi (Bhūmidevī), Pāñcaśikha, Rājamātaṅgī, Rati, Śiva Vīṇādhara(dakṣiṇā)mūrti, Vajraśāradā(?), Vajravīṇā-Saras-

vatī, Vīṇā and, of course, Nārada. – Cp. *śāradā* in the NP vajraśāradā.
Lit.: B 303; Gt Suppl. 152; KiH pl. 137:11; MEIA 257; MKVI 2:316; Th. 79; SMII 91; WM 110.

Vīṇā (Buddh.), n. of a goddess who is a deified musical instrument (*vīṇā*). Char.: colour: yellow; attr.: *vīṇā*.
Lit.: BBh. 315 a.pl. 209.

Vīṇādhara(dakṣiṇā)mūrti ("representation [of Śiva] holding the lute"), n. of a form of Śiva in which he is represented as a great teacher of music (see *dakṣiṇāmūrti*). V. is the tutelary god of the South Indian Brāhmans. Char.: Mu.: *kaṭakamudrā* (one or two hands in order to hold a lute; this attr. is often missing; others say that one hand (the right) should display a playing gesture), also *vyākhyānamudrā*; attr.: *ajina*, *dhattūra*-flower, *mṛga*, *paraśu*, *vīṇā* (sometimes missing, see above).
Lit.: AuOW 60; B 465; BECA 1: pl. 17b; Gz 188 pl.; HSIT 11 a.pl. 25; R 2:289 a.pl. 80f.; SB 68, 104 a.fig. 40, 56 a.passim; SIB pl. 40; SSI 90; Th. 79 a.pl. 47; ZA pl. 410.

Vinatā ("bent, curved"), n. of the mother of Garuḍa and Aruṇa. She was the wife of Kāśyapa, daughter of Dakṣa and sister of Kadrū. She was originally probably a bird deity, since her children were born from eggs.
Lit.: D 337; MW 969.

Vināyaka ("removing"; the n. has the same sense as Vighneśvara).
1. (Hind.) Epithet of Gaṇeśa, in the South very often used as the NP of this god. Also n. of some companions of Gaṇeśa.
Lit.: DHP 292; DiIP 113; WHW 1:398.
2. (Buddh.) N. of an elephant-headed demon, evidently the Buddhist counterpart of Gaṇeśa who is, in fact, also to be found in Lamaism.
Lit.: G 25, 37, 96.
3. (Vāh.) One or two V. form the Vāh. of Mahākāla (e.g., in the forms mGon-dkar and mGon-po nag-po).

vināyakacaturthī "the 4th day of the festival in honour of Gaṇeśa", n. of Gaṇeśa's birthday festival celebrated in August-September.
Lit.: SSR 199.

vināyakaśānti "appeasement of evil spirits of diseases", n. of a certain rite.

Vindhya, n. of a range of hills forming the northern border of the Deccan; also n. of a mountain deity (personification).
Lit.: IIM 109; MW 972.

Vindhyavāsi-Durgā (or Vindhyavāsinī, "D. dwelling in the Vindhyas, on the Vindhya-mountains"), n. of a form of Durgā. Char.: Vāh.: *padma* (golden), or *siṅha*; Mu.: *abhaya-*, *varada-mudrā*; attr.: *aṅgadas*, *cakra*, *candra*, *kuṇḍalas*, *śaṅkha*. – Epithet: Mūkāmbikā.
Lit.: R 1:344; SSI 220.

Vipaśyantī ("perceiving"; Buddh.), n. of a *mānuṣibuddhaśakti*.
Lit.: BBh. 79.

Vipaśyin (-ī; Pāli Vipassin "perceiving"; Buddh.), n. of a *buddha*, see *mānuṣibuddha*. His *bodhivṛkṣa* is *pāṭali*.
Lit.: GRI 245; KiSB 32.

vipūti (Tam.), see *vibhūti*.
Lit.: MSHP 38; TL 6:3682.

vīra ("hero"), n. of an uncommon form of icon which is worshipped by those who desire heroic courage. – See *dhruva*.
Lit.: B 397; R 1:18, 79.

Vīrabhadra ("distinguished hero"), n. of a demigod, an emanation or incarnation of Śiva which, according to different statements, originated either from the sweat or from a lock of hair of Śiva, or came forth from Śiva's mouth, and was created in order to punish Dakṣa. V. is regarded as an *ugra*-aspect, and sometimes also as the son of Śiva. Char.: colour: black; Vāh.: Dakṣa (V. often dances upon him), or *padmapīṭha*, or *śvan*; Mu.: *abhaya-*, *varada-mudrā*; attr.: *cakra*, *dhanus*, *gadā*, *khaḍga*, *kheṭaka*, *muṇḍamālā*, *musala*, *paraśu*, *śaṅkha*, *śara*, *trinayana*, *triśūla*, *(nāga)-yajñopavīta*.
Lit.: B 465, 472, 482 a.pl. 35:2; D 76, 358; GH pl.

37; GI pl. 82; Gt 713; JDI 47; KiH pl. 44; KiSH 29; MEIA 62; MSHP pl. 23; R 2:182 a.pl. 44; SB 352 a.fig. 336; SSI 155; SSR 152; Th. pl. 55B.

vīrakkal(lu) (*vīrkal*; Tam.) "hero-stone" (attr.), in South India n. of a stone set up in memory of a warrior who died gloriously in battle and who is believed to be brought to the heaven of heroes (*vīrasvarga*) by celestial nymphs, hovering round the battle-field. Cp. *pāliyā*.
Lit.: KiH 33; SSI 234.

Vīralakṣmī, n. of a 4-handed form of the group *aṣṭamahālakṣmī*. Char.: Mu.: *abhaya-*, *varada-mudrā*; attr.: 2 *padma*s.
Lit.: SSI 189.

Vīramakaḷ Kāḷi (Tam., the goddess of bravery), n. of a South Indian form of Kālī.
Lit.: DiCh. 15.

Vīrarākavar (Tam., < Skt Vīra + Rāghava), epithet of Viṣṇu in South India. Vāh.: *yāḷi*.
Lit.: DilP 160, 163.

Vīrarātri ("Night-of-Courage"), n. of an aspect of *mahāvidyā* which is represented either by Chinnamastā or by Bagalā.
Lit.: DHP 280, 283.

vīraśaiva ("Śiva worshipper of courage"), n. applied to themselves by the Liṅgāyāts.
Lit.: GJ 63; GoRI 2:243; GRI 331; IC 1:638.

vīrasamvat "year of the hero", a term indicating an era beginning in B.C. 527 (Enc. Brit.: B.C. 528), the supposed date of death of Mahāvīra; this era is, consequently, adopted by Jains.
Lit.: Enc.Brit. 5:721; IC 2:736.

vīrāsana ("hero-sitting"; att.), n. of an *āsana*-posture said to be a variant of the so-called *vajrāsana* and described in B in the following terms: "When the thighs are placed together and the left foot rests upon the right thigh and the left thigh on the right foot it is known as *v*." In other explanations it is not stated that the thighs should be placed together, but that one foot should be placed against the groin, the other leg lying flat under the first one. However, this att. is known as the usual Indian sitting att. – A quite different explanation is given in R: "the right leg should be hanging below the seat while the left one is bent and rested across the right thigh". The author of this dictionary is inclined to believe that the term designates a modified form of the first posture described above. – Cp. also SB where this att. is mentioned as *ardhaparyaṅkāsana*). – Char. of, e.g., Caṇḍeśvara, Pārśva.
Lit.: B 270 a.pl. 20:5; GH 292; KiH pl. 151 row 3:4; MH 7; R 1:18, 2:274; SB 165 a.fig. 101; SIB 68; SM 125; WM 90 a.fig. 3.

Vīrāsanamūrti, n. of a so-called *vīra*-representation of Viṣṇu, sitting, together with Lakṣmī and Bhūmi. Char.: att.: *rājalīlāsana*; Vāh.: *siṅhāsana*; Mu.: *abhaya-*, *kaṭaka-mudrā*; attr.: *cakra*, *śaṅkha*.
Lit.: R 1:89 a.pl. 30.

vīraśayanamūrti, n. of a so-called *vīra*-representation of Viṣṇu, lying, together with Lakṣmī and Bhūmi. Attr.: *cakra*, *śaṅkha*.
Lit.: R 1:94.

vīrasthānakamūrti, n. of a so-called *vīra*-representation of Viṣṇu, standing. Attr.: *cakra*, *śaṅkha*.
Lit.: R 1:83.

Virāṭarūpa ("having the figure of [a] Virāṭa"), n. of Viṣṇu as a colossus, developed out of the dwarf (see Vāmanāvatāra) and being on the point of taking the three steps (see Trivikrama). (Virāṭa is properly n. of a district, perhaps = Berar. Its sense here is hard to understand; it alludes perhaps to the conception of "disguise" [Viṣṇu disguised as a dwarf], since the Pāṇḍavas once lived here in disguise).
Lit.: B 418; WHW 2:570.

Vīra-Vighneśa ("the hero V."), n. of a form of Gaṇeśa. Attr.: *aṅkuśa*, *dhanus*, *dhvaja*, *gadā*, *khaḍga*, *kheṭaka*, *kuṇḍa*, *mudgara*, *paraśu*, *pāśa*, *śakti*, *śara*, *vetāla*; he is 16-armed.
Lit.: R 1:52.

vīrkal (*vīrgal*), see *vīrakkallu* and further, *pāliyā*.

Virocana ("shining, brightening"), n. of the sun or the sun god (Sūrya), sometimes also an epithet of Viṣṇū. V. is also n. of an *asura*, the son of Prahlāda and father of Bali.
Lit.: D 359; MW 983.

Virūḍhaka (Virūḷhaka; "shot out, sprouted; a grain that has begun to sprout"; Buddh.), n. of a *dikpāla* of the southerly direction. Char.: colour: blue or green; attr.: *ajina* (the skin from the head of an elephant), *khaḍga*. – V. is the king of a class of demons, the *kumbhāṇḍas*.
Lit.: B 521; G 37, 92; KiSB 25; ZA 329.

Virūpākṣa ("of-Misinformed-Eyes", thus DHP).
1. (Hind.) Epithet of Śiva and n. of one of the *ekādaśarudras*. Char.: Mu.: *tarjanī-mudrā*; attr.: *akṣamālā, aṅkuśa, cakra, ḍamaru, gadā, ghaṇṭā, ghaṭa, kapāla, khaḍga, khaṭvāṅga, kheṭaka, nāga, paraśu, śakti, triśūla*.
Lit.: B 465, 558; DHP 191; R 2:389.
2. (Buddh.; also the Pāli n.: Virūpakkha), N. of the *dikpāla* of the westerly direction. He is the king of *nāgas* and the Buddhist counterpart of the Hindu Śiva. Char.: colour: red; attr.: *cintāmaṇi, nāga, stūpa*.
Lit.: B 521; G 37, 92; KiSB 25; ZA 329.

Vīryapāramitā ("perfection of energy, strength"; Buddh.), n. of a *pāramitā*. Char.: colour: green; attr.: *cintāmaṇi-dhvaja, nīlotpala*.
Lit.: BBh. 325.

viṣa "poison, venom" (attr.), n. of an object held in one hand. Char. of Viṣaprahara-ṇamūrti (Viṣāpahara).
Lit.: AIP 70 a.pl. 49 (306); WHW 2:221.

Viṣahari ("removing venom"), see Manasā.

viṣakanyā "poison-girl", n. of a (demon-) woman who is supposed to have been brought up on poison and who is believed to kill men by means of intercourse or with a mere kiss or touch.
Lit.: Gt Suppl. 155; STP 2:275.

Viśākhā (or -e; "branched"), n. of a *nakṣatra*. Its influence is bad. – Another n.: Rādhā.
Lit.: BBh. 382; IC 2:730.

Viṣāpahara(mūrti) (also: -haraṇa-; "removing or destroying poison"), see Viṣaprahara-mūrti.
Lit.: AIP 275; R 2:356; SB passim; SIB pl. 30; SSI 140.

Viṣaprahara(ṇa)mūrti ("representation as removing [or destroying] poison"), n. of a gracious representation of Śiva who swallowed the dreadful poison that emerged from the ocean of milk when it was churned (see Kūrmāvatāra) and that threatened the world with destruction. As a consequence of the power of the venom, the throat (neck) of Śiva took on a livid colour (cp. Śrīkaṇṭha, Nīlakaṇṭha). – Char.: Mu.: *varada-mudrā*; attr.: *mṛga, nāga, paraśu, viṣa, vṛścika*. – Another n.: Viṣāpahara.
Lit.: R 2:356; SB passim; Th. 92.

viṣapuṣpa (lit. "poisonous flower"), another n. of *nīlotpala*.
Lit.: BBh. 182, 340.

viśikha "arrow" (attr.), see *śara*.
Lit.: ACA 33.

Viṣkambhin (-ī; Buddh.), abbreviated name-form of Sarvanivaraṇaviṣkambhin.
Lit.: BBh. 93.

vismaya(hasta)mudrā "gesture of astonishment or of praise" (Mu.), n. of a hand-pose "in which the forearm is folded at the elbow with the palm facing the image and fingers pointing upwards" (Th.). Usually one hand, but sometimes both hands, may be raised up in this way. Char. of, e.g., Gajāsuramūrti, Kālāri-mūrti, Naṭarāja (in different forms), Viṣṇvanugrahamūrti. – Another n.: *āścar-yamudrā*.
Lit.: B 260 a.pl. 4:4, 38:3; R 1:16 a.pl. 5:13, 2:211; SSI pl. III:15, 22; Th. 29 (with ill.); MW 100 a.fig. 23.

vismaya-vitarkamudrā "gesture indicating astonishment and reflection" (Mu.), n. of a handpose "with the index and middle fingers placed on the chin"
Lit.: B 260 a.pl. 4:3.

Viṣṇu.

1. (Hind.) V. is generally regarded as the highest god of the Hindu triad, in which he occupies the second place, as the Preserver or Protector of the cosmic system. The meaning of his name is very much in dispute. The Hindus interpret it usually as "Pervader" and connect it either with the root *viś-* "to enter" or with *viṣ-* "to be active, to work". According to THUMB-HAUSCHILD, the n. consists of the prefix *vi-* and the formative *-snu-*, the sense being "ein Durchdringender" (= "Pervader"). Others (BLOOMFIELD, OLDENBERG, MAYRHOFER) emphasize that the chief function of V. in Vedic religion is that of a sun deity, manifested in the three steps (see Trivikrama) which should be considered the three extreme points of the orbit of the sun. The n. should therefore be interpreted as composed of *vi-* + *snu-* (zero grade of *sānu-* "summit, top"), meaning "qui franchit les hauteurs (du ciel)" (IC).

V. was, accordingly, originally a sun god, as moreover, his symbol, the *cakra* (and *padma*?) and his Vāh. Garuḍa (the sun bird) indicate, and the sun god Sūrya is also sometimes regarded as a manifestation of V. His three steps (see above) were later connected with the acquisition of heaven, atmosphere and earth, or heaven, earth and the infernal regions. In later Brāhmanic cult, V. was "das Resultat des Synkretismus der drei Gottkonzeptionen des heroisierten Vāsudeva-Kṛṣṇa, des vedischen Viṣṇu und des kosmischen Gottes Nārāyaṇa der Brāhmaṇa-Texte" (HIS). His function as the preserver of the system of the world is above all manifested in his *avatāra*s in the shape of which he saved the world from demons and perils. The numbers of these *avatāra*s vary, but they are usually mentioned as 10 (see *daśāvatāra* and *avatāra*). In later Vedic literature, V. embodies the chief Brāhmanical ritual of sacrifice (see Yajñamūrti).

In Hinduism V. is often mentioned by his worshippers as the "Right-hand god", a fact which perhaps originates in his right-hand gesture *abhayamudrā*, symbolizing his chief function as preserver; the attr. *śaṅkha** has perhaps a similar meaning. – Furthermore, his 4 principal symbols (*cakra*, *gadā*, *padma*, *śaṅkha*) may be arranged in his 4 hands in 24 different ways, and these are considered to signify 24 different aspects (with particular names) of V., see *caturviṅśatimūrti*. – Regarding the connection or syncretism between V. and Śiva, see Mohinī and Śiva.

Theriomorphic forms of V. are Garuḍa and probably the snake Ananta, cp. also *vajrakīṭa*; a lithomorphic form is the *śālagrāma*. Among the trees, esp. the *aśvattha* (or *vaṭa*, see *vṛkṣa*) is sacred to V. He is further represented by the *bījamantra*s *brahmabīja* and *aṣṭākṣara*, by the *viṣṇupāda* and the *viṣṇuyantra*. He is the god of the month *māgha*. – Atri is sometimes mentioned as the father of V. His wives are: Lakṣmī (Śrī), Bhūmi (Puṣṭi) and, as a third wife, Nīladevī is occasionally added; at other times eight Śaktis are attributed to him: Śrī, Bhū, Sarasvatī, Prīti, Kīrti, Śānti, Tuṣṭi and Puṣṭi. – As the sons of V. Sāmba and Pradyumna are mentioned, although these should rather be considered the sons of Kṛṣṇa; further, Naraka (son of V. and Bhūmi), and Jāmbavān.

Char.: colour: (dress) yellow; att.: both *sthānaka-*, *āsana-* and *śayana-* postures occur in representations of different aspects of V.; Vāh.: Garuḍa (Garuḍāsana), Ananta (Śeṣa), *yāḷi*; Mu.: *abhaya-*, *kaṭi-*, *varada-mudrā*, and (as a *bhakta* of Śiva, see Viṣṇvanugrahamūrti) V. may show the *añjalimudrā*; attr.: *amṛtaghaṭa*, *caddar*, *cakra* named Vajranābha or Sudarśana (usually held in one right hand), *cāmara*, *caturmukha* (V. being poly-headed has one *siṁhamastaka*, one *varāhamastaka*, one *rākṣasamastaka* and, if 4-headed, one human face), *dhanus* Śārṅga, *dhvaja*, *gadā* Kaumodakī, *hara*, *kavaca*, *khaḍga* named Nandaka or Vidyādhara, *kheṭaka*, *kirīṭa-mukuṭa*, *makarakuṇḍalas*, *nūpuras*, *padma* (red), *pītāmbara*, *pustaka* (Veda), *ratna* named Kaustubha or Syamantaka, *śaṅkha* Pāñcajanya (usually held in one left hand), *śara*, *śirobandha*, *śrīvatsa*, *triśiras* (cp. above *caturmukha*), *trivali*, *ūrṇā*, *vanamālā* Vaijayantīmālā (made of gems), *yajñopavīta*; he is mostly 4-handed. – V. is also reckoned among the Ādityas, and in this function he has the attr.: *cakra*, 3 *padmas*.

Epithets and varieties (most of the *avatāra*-names and names of aspects of V. are not listed here; regarding these, see *daśāvatāra*, and *caturviṁśatimūrti*): *abhicārikāsana-*, *abhicārikaśayana-*, *abhicārikasthānaka-mūrtis*, Ādimūrti, Anantāśāyana, *-śāyin*, Ballaji, Bhagavān, *bhogāsana-*, *bhogaśayana-*, *bhogasthānaka-mūrtis*, Cakrapāṇi, Cakrasvāmin, Caturbhuja, Caturmūrti, Dattātreya, Dhanvantarin, Dharma, Hari, Hayagrīva, Hṛṣīkeśa, Jagannātha, Jalāśāyin, Karivarada, Keśava, Kirīṭin, Kṛṣṇa, Lakṣmīpati, Māl, Manmatha, Maunavratin, Mohinī, Mukunda, Nara-Nārāyaṇa, Padmanābha, Pañcāyudha, Paṇḍharinātha, Pāṇḍurāṅga, Perumaḷ, Raṅganatha, (Śarabheśamūrti), Śārṅgapāṇi, Śārṅgin, Śeṣāśāyin, Śrīnivāsa, Tirumāl, Trivikrama, Upulvan, Vaikuṇṭhanātha, Varadarāja, Vāṭapattrāśāyin, Veṅkaṭeśvara, Vīrarākavar, *vīrāsana-*, *vīraśayana-*, *vīrasthānaka-mūrtis*, Virocana, Viṭhobā, Viṭṭhala, Yajñamūrti, Yajñeśvara, Yoga-Narasiṁha, *yogāsana-*, *yogaśayana-*, *yogasthānaka-mūrtis*, Yogāsana-Viṣṇu; Yogeśvara-Viṣṇu.

Lit.: AI 118; B 305, 385 a.pl. 21 ff.; D 360; DHP 126, 149 a.pl. 11; GBB 128; GH 119 a.pl. 19; GoRI 1:89, 236, 250; Gt 716; HIS 18, 44, 73 a.pl. 42; HSIT 13 a.pl. 33; IC 1:323, 500; IIM 46; JDI 57; JMS pl. 38, 88; KiDG pl. 12 ff.; KiH 12 a.pl. 22 ff.; KiSH 33; KrG pl. 7; M. MAYRHOFER, EWA 3:231; MEIA 15; MG 95; MH pl. 2; NLEM 325; H. OLDENBERG, Die Religion des Veda. 2. Aufl. (1917), 228; R 1:73, 309 a.pl. 17; SB passim (many ill.); SIB pl. passim; SS pl. 20:88, 33:150; SSI 17; Th. 53; THUMB-HAUSCHILD, Handbuch des Sanskrit 2:315; WHW 2:574; WM 187; ZA pl. passim.

2. (Buddh.) V. is found as (an inferior) god in Buddhism. Char.: Vāh.: Garuḍa; Mu.: *añjalimudrā*; attr.: *cakra*, *dhanus*, *gadā*, *śaṅkha*.

Lit.: BBh. 363; CTLP pl. 156.

3. (Vāh.; Buddh.) V. (sometimes together with his Vāh. Garuḍa) may in Vajrayāna Buddhism serve, trampled underfoot, as a Vāh. to some Buddhist deities e.g., Harihariharivāhana, Hevajra, Mārīcī (in different forms), Vajrajvālānalārka, Vidyujjvālākarālī; cp. also Māra.

Lit.: BBh. 194.

Viṣṇucakra-Lokeśvara ("L. (with) the wheel of Viṣṇu"; Buddh.), n. of a variety of Avalokiteśvara. Char.: att.: *samapādasthānaka*; Vāh.: *padma*; attr.: *cakra*, *gadā*.

Lit.: BBh. 430 a.pl. 97(A).

Viṣṇukānta-Lokeśvara ("L. who is dear to Viṣṇu"; Buddh.), n. of a variety of Avalokiteśvara. Char.: att.: *samapādasthānaka*; Vāh.: *padma*; Mu.: *varadamudrā*; attr.: *pustaka*.

Lit.: BBh. 430 a.pl. 99(A).

Viṣṇu-Kubera, n. of a rare syncretistic form of Viṣṇu and Kubera. Char.: Mu.: *varadamudrā*; attr.: *cakra*, *koṣa*.

Lit.: HSIT 15 a.pl. 38.

Viṣṇu-Lokeśvara, n. of a syncretistic representation of the Hindu god Viṣṇu and the Buddhist god Avalokiteśvara. Attr.: *Amitābhabimba* on the head or crown, *cakra*, *gadā*, *padma*.

Lit.: B 554 a.pl. 48:4.

viṣṇupāda "footmark of Viṣṇu" (attr.), see *pāduka*.

Lit.: HIS 67 a.pl. 32.

Viṣṇupāṇi-Lokeśvara ("L., the hand of Viṣṇu"; Buddh.), n. of a variety of Avalokiteśvara.

Char.: att.: *samapādasthānaka*; Vāh.: *padma*; attr.: *padma, triśūla.*
Lit.: BBh. 429 a.pl. 76(A).

viṣṇupūjā "worship of, cult dedicated to Viṣṇu".
Lit.: MSHP pl. C facing p. 356.

Viṣṇusvāmin (-ī; "having Viṣṇu as lord"), n. of a South Indian *vaiṣṇavabhakta* who lived about A.D. 1250; after him n. of a sect.
Lit.: GH 387; IC 1:642.

viṣṇuyantra, n. of a *yantra*, dedicated to Viṣṇu which "expresses the all-pervasiveness of *sattva*, the ascending quality".
Lit.: DHP 361 (ill.).

Viṣṇuyaśas ("[having] the fame, glory of Viṣṇu"), epithet of Kalkin; also n. of the father of Kalkin.
Lit.: MW 1000.

Viṣṇv-anugrahamūrti ("representation [of Śiva] showing favour to Viṣṇu"), n. of a gracious representation of Śiva who granted Viṣṇu his *cakra*, *ratna* Kaustubha and *pītāmbara* (thus forming a manifestation of the Śaivite opinion of Śiva's supremacy over Viṣṇu). Char.: Śiva: Mu.: *kaṭaka-, varada-, vismaya-mudrā*; attr.: *cakra, (kṛṣṇa)-mṛga, ṭaṅka, trinayana*; Viṣṇu: Mu.: *añjalimudrā*; attr.: *cakra, śaṅkha.* – Another n.: Cakradānamūrti.
Lit.: R 2:209 a.pl. 51.

viśva(s) or *viśvedeva*(s) ("all-gods, the Universal-Principles"), n. of a group of minor deities, 10 or 12 or 13 in number, the sons of Dakṣa (or Dharma) and Viśvā (the wife or daughter of Dakṣa). – *viśva* is also a symbolic n. of the number "13", see *saṅkhyā.*
Lit.: D 363; DHP 302; Gt 727; MW 992.

viśvābhayamudrā "gesture of (granting) fearlessness to all" (Mu.), see *abhayamudrā.*
Lit.: MEIA 216.

Viśvabhuj (also -bhū, Pāli Vessabhū; "all-enjoying"; Buddh.). n. of a *buddha*, see also *mānuṣibuddha.* His *bodhivṛkṣa* is *śāla.*
Lit.: BBh. 76; GRI 245; KiSB 32.

Viśvabhūta-Lokeśvara ("L. of all beings"; Buddh.), n. of a variety of Avalokiteśvara. Char.: att.: *samapādasthānaka*; Vāh.: *padma*; attr.: *akṣamālā, padma.*
Lit.: BBh. 430 a.pl. 89(A); MW 993.

Viśvaḍākinī ("*ḍākinī* of all [gods]"; Buddh.), n. of a Mahāyāna *ḍākinī* who is also found attending on Mahāmāya. Char.: colour: blue (or green); attr.: *caturmukha, kapāla, khaṭvāṅga, viśvavajra.*
Lit.: BBh. 164; G 18, 34, 80; KiSB 67.

Viśvadharā ("preserving all things"; Buddh.), n. of a *mānuṣibuddhaśakti.*
Lit.: BBh. 79.

Viśvahana-Lokeśvara ("the all-killing L."; Buddh.), n. of a variety of Avalokiteśvara. Char.: att.: *lalitāsana*; Vāh.: *padma*; attr.: *cakra, dhanus, khaḍga, pāśa, śara.*
Lit.: BBh. 397 a.pl. 30(A).

Viśvakarman (-mā; "Architect-of-the-Universe, Omnificient"), n. of the architect or artist of the gods, later sometimes identified with Tvaṣṭar. He is the son of Prabhāsa and Yogasiddhā.
Lit.: D 363; DHP 314; IIM 88; MG 70 a.pl. facing p. 64; MW 994; WHW 2:576; WM 194.

Viṣvaksena ("whose hosts or powers go everywhere, All-Conqueror")
1. NP of the gate-keeper and attendant of Viṣṇu and the leader of his troups. V. represents the "Scriptures of Earthly Wisdom" (DHP). Char.: Mu.: *tarjanīmudrā*; attr.: *cakra, gadā, śaṅkha.*
2. (Attr.) V. was killed by Śiva Bhairava because he once refused Śiva admittance to Viṣṇu's presence. He is therefore, as a skeleton, carried on the prongs of the *triśūla* by Śiva Kaṅkālamūrti.
Lit.: B 466, 484; DHP 163; MEIA 38; MW 998; R 2:296; SSI 62; Th. 58.

Viśvamātā (-tṛ; "All-Mother"; Buddh.), n. of a white Tārā. Char.: Vāh.: *nāga* (white); Mu.: *abhayamudrā*; attr.: *padma* (white).
Lit.: BBh. 308.

Viśvāmitra ("Universal Friend"), n. of a *riṣi* (*rājarṣi*). Born a *kṣatriya*, he raised himself to the *brāhmaṇa* caste through intense austerities and became one of the seven great *ṛṣi*s.

Lit.: D 364; DHP 320; GH 96; Gt 728; MKVI 2:310; WHW 2:578; WM 194.

Viśvanātha ("Lord-of-the-Universe"), epithet of Śiva.

Lit.: DHP 191.

viśvapadma "All-Lotus" (attr.), see *mahāmbuja*.

Lit.: B 299, 375; BBh. 437.

Viśvapāṇi (abbreviated word-form for Viśvavajra-pāṇi [?] "holding a double or crossed *vajra* in the hand"; Buddh.), n. of a *(dhyāni)bodhisattva*, an emanation of Amoghasiddhi. Char.: colour: green; att.: *padmāsana* or *sthānaka*; Mu.: *dhyāna-* and *varada-mudrās*; attr.: *viśvavajra*.

Lit.: BBh. 73 a.pl. 36; G 33, 61; H 32; KiDG 44; KiSB 46.

Viśvarūpa ("having all forms"), n. of an *ugra*-aspect of Viṣṇu or Kṛṣṇa. In the Ṛgveda he is mentioned as the three-headed son of Tvaṣṭar. – Char.: Vāh.: Garuḍa; Mu.: *dhyāna-*, *patākā-*, *varada-mudrā*; attr.: *akṣamālā*, *aṅkuśa*, *cakra*, *churikā*, *daṇḍa*, *danta*, *dhanus*, *dhvaja*, *gadā*, *hala*, *jambhīra*, *khaḍga*, *kheṭaka*, *musala*, *nīlotpala*, *padma*, *paraśu*, *pāśa*, *paṭṭiśa*, *śakti*, *śaṅkha*, *śara*, *śṛṅga*, (*śṛṅgī*), *tomara*, *triśūla*, *vajra*.

Lit.: B 426 a.pl. 26:2; D 368; KiDG 31; MEIA 19; R 1:19, 258.

Viśvatārā ("All-Tārā, Tārā of all (gods)"; Buddh.), n. of a Mahāyāna goddess.

Lit.: KiSB 61.

viśvavajra "all-*vajra*, *vajra* (pointing) in all (directions)" (attr.; Buddh.), n. of a double *vajra*, i.e. two crossed *vajra*s with points in four directions. Char. of: Amoghasiddhi, Amṛtaprabha-Lokeśvara, Āryatārā, the *dhāriṇī*-group, Dharmavajra, Dūraṅgamā, Karmavaśitā, Mahāmāyūrī, Mahāpaṭala-Lokeśvara, Mahāsāhasrapramardanī, Mahāśītavatī, Nāmasaṅgīti, Paramāśva, Sāgaramati-Lokeśvara, Samvara, Saptakṣara, Sarvabuddhaḍākinī, Tārā, Uṣṇīṣavijayā, Vajrakarmapāramitā, Viśvaḍākinī, Viśvapāṇi. – Another n.: *karmavajra*.

Lit.: BBh. 440; G 18 (ill.); KiDG 56; KiSB 46.

Viśvavajra-Lokeśvara ("L. of the *viśvavajra*"; Buddh.), n. of a variety of Avalokiteśvara. Char.: att.: *samapādasthānaka*; Vāh.: *padma*; Mu.: *varadamudrā*; attr.: *nāga*.

Lit.: BBh. 429 a.pl. 86(A).

viśvavajrāṅkapatākā "banner marked with a *viśvavajra*" (attr.; Buddh.), Char. of Sarvanivaraṇaviṣkambhin.

Lit.: BBh. 93.

viśvedeva "all-gods", see *viśva*.

Viśveśvara ("Lord of the Universe"), n. of a form of Śiva which is worshipped esp. at Vārāṇasī.

Lit.: GH 343.

Viśvoṣṇīṣa ("*uṣṇīṣa* of the universe"; Buddh.), n. of an *uṣṇīṣa*-deity. Char.: colour: green; Mu.: *abhayamudrā*; direction: north.

Lit.: BBh. 300.

vitarkamudrā "gesture of argumentation (reasoning), assumed in discussion" (Mu.), n. of a handpose which seems to be (at least almost) identical with the *vyākhyānamudrā*.

Lit.: B 254; BBh. 441; G 22 (ill.); H pl. 5:42d; SM 66.

Viṭhobā (N.Ind.), see Viṭṭhala.

Lit.: R 1:271; SSI 55.

Viṭṭhala (from Mar. *viṭ* "brick" + *ṭhal* [Skt *sthala*] "place, ground", hence "having a brick as ground, standing on a brick"; see further WM), n. of a god who is worshipped at Paṇḍharpūr in West India and regarded as a form of Viṣṇu (or Kṛṣṇa). He is represented as his n. indicates. Wife: Rukmābāyi (Rakhumāī). – Epithets: Viṭhobā, Paṇḍharinātha.

Lit.: GH 342; MW 961; R 1:271 a.pl. 81; WM 196.

vivāha "marriage", n. of a *saṅskāra*-rite. In South India the central part of this rite is the tying of the *tāli*; elsewhere the *pāṇigrahaṇa* forms an essential part.

Lit.: DiIP 180, 187, 204; GH 335; GJ 414; Gt 385; IC 1:364; MW 987; WHW 2:38.

Vivasvān (-vant, -vat; "shining forth, far shining; the rising sun"), epithet of Sūrya; V. is, however, sometimes also mentioned as an independent Āditya. Wife: Saraṇyū. He was the father of Yama, Yamī, Manu and the Aśvins. He is also declared to be

"the Ancestor, the Embodiment of Morality or Ancestral Law". Attr.: 2 *padmas*, *triśūla*, *vanamālā*.
Lit.: B 428; D 368; DHP 124; GoRI 1:93; R 1:309; WM 196.

vrata "solemn vow" which a man may take with the help of an ascetic.
Lit.: GJ 416; IC 1:586; RV 145; WHW 2:581.

vratavisarga "release from a vow", n. of a ceremony signifying release from the position of being a pupil.
Lit.: GJ 413.

Vṛddhi ("growth, increase"; personification), n. of the wife of Kubera. Epithet: Hāritī (?).
Lit.: KiH 11.

vṛka "wolf" (Vāh.). As an accompanying animal, char. of: Śiva Bhairava, Gaurī. – Cp. *śvan*.
Lit.: MEIA 228.

vṛkṣa (Pāli: *rukkha*) "tree; the tree of life" (attr.). Worship of trees as symbolic of fertility, esp. of *aśvattha*, is found already in the Indus Valley civilization, as may be seen from many seals. In Hinduism all the chief gods have particular trees dedicated to them; in Buddhism *v.* is esp. a symbol of the Buddha. – Most important among the trees are the fig-tree, Ficus religiosa (*aśvattha*, *pippala*) and Ficus Bengalensis (the Banyan-tree, *vaṭa*, *nyagrodha*), both being sacred to Viṣṇu and the Buddha; the tree of Śiva is the *bilva* (also the *vaṭa*). – There are also five magnificent trees of paradise: *haricandana-*, *kalpa-*, *mandāra-*, *pārijāta-* and *santāna-vṛkṣa*. – Cp. also: *akṣayavaṭa*, *bodhivṛkṣa*, *kalpadruma*, *vanaspati*.
Lit.: BKI 28 a.pl. 14i; CEBI 7; FBKI 22; MW 1290; WM 47; ZA 25 a.pl. 2e, 17.

vṛkṣadevatā (*vṛkṣakā*) "tree deity", n. of a class of dryads, comparable to the *yakṣiṇīs* (*yakṣīs*). Char.: att.: *śālabhañjikā*.
Lit.: HIS 25; IP pl. 32; ZA 71 a.pl. 322; WHW 2:218; ZM 68.

vṛkṣāsana "tree-posture" (att.), n. of a Yogic posture in which "one stands on one leg, with the sole of the other foot placed high up on the thigh of the straight leg" (WHW).
Lit.: KiH pl. 152 row 4:1; WHW 1:77.

vṛṣabha "bull" (Vāh.), see *vṛṣan*.

Vṛṣabhadhvaja (or Vṛṣa-; "whose banner is the bull"), epithet of Śiva. As an attr. *vṛṣabhadhvaja* is the "bull banner" of Śiva.
Lit.: DHP 29; KiSH 19; SSIP 150.

Vṛṣabhāntikamūrti ("representation [of Śiva] beside the bull"), see Vṛṣavāhanamūrti.
Lit.: SB 121.

Vṛṣabhārūḍhamūrti ("representation [of Śiva] seated on the bull"), see Vṛṣavāhanamūrti.
Lit.: R 2:352; SB 121.

Vṛṣabhavāhana, see Vṛṣavāhanamūrti.
Lit.: SB 121, 209 a.fig. 128.

vṛṣamastaka "bull-headed" (attr.). Char. of: Gomukha, Vajrabhairava, Yama (in different forms), Yamāntaka.

vṛṣan (*-ā*) "bull" (Vāh.). A white *v.* is char. of Śiva (Vṛṣavāhana), see further Nandin; *v.* is also char. of: Gomukha, Īśāna, Yama, (in some forms); *v.* is a symbol of Bhṛkuṭi Kimpuruṣa, Ṛṣabhanātha. *v.* is also n. of a *rāśi* ("Taurus") and of a *maṅgala*, see *aṣṭamaṅgala*. – Other n.: *vṛṣabha*, *ṛṣabha*.
Lit.: B 529; BBh. 383; DHP 219; GH 50; GJ pl. 23:1; KiJ pl. 45.

Vṛṣāṅka ("having *vṛṣan* as his sign, mark"), epithet of Śiva.
Lit.: DHP 219.

Vṛṣāntika(mūrti) ("representation [of Śiva] beside the bull"), see Vṛṣavāhanamūrti.
Lit.: SB 57.

Vṛṣarājaketana ("having the king of bulls as his sign"), epithet of Śiva.
Lit.: KiSH 19.

Vṛṣārūḍha ("mounted on the bull"), n. of a form of Śiva, seated on his Vāh. Nandin, with Skanda on his right and Pārvatī (Gaurī) on his left. Attr.: *mṛga*, *ṭaṅka*.
Lit.: SSI 113.

vṛṣāsana.

1. "Bull-throne" (Vāh.), n. of a kind of *pīṭha*, a throne supported by the *vṛṣan* Nandin. Char. of Śiva.
Lit.: MH 44.

2. "Bull-posture" (att.), n. of a Yogic posture.
Lit.: KiH pl. 153 row 1:1.

Vṛṣavāhana(mūrti) ("representation [of Śiva] together with his *vāhana*, the bull"), n. of a form of Śiva, often represented accompanied by his Śakti, which may therefore, in such cases, be regarded as an *anugraha-mūrti*. Śiva is found here either sitting on, or, more often, standing beside his Vāh. In the latter case the Vāh. may even be missing, its presence being indicated by the att. of Śiva (*kūrpara*; N.B. however that the bull may in fact be lost in these representations). Char.: att.: *kūrpara* (*pādasvastika*); Mu.: *abhaya-*, *kaṭaka-*, *patākā-mudrā*; attr.: *ḍamaru*, *ceṇṭu*, *mṛga*, *paraśu*, *ṭaṅka*, *triśūla*. – Other n.: Vṛṣabhāntika, Vṛṣāntika, Vṛṣabhārūḍha, Vṛṣabhavāhanamūrti.
Lit: B 464 a.pl. 34:3; KiH pl. 48; KiSH 19; KrA pl. 61; R 2:352 a.pl. 108-112; SB 121 a.fig. 67; SIB pl. 48; SSI 114; Th. 91 a.pl. 48; WM 169.

vṛścika "scorpion".
1. (Att.) N. of a posture in which one leg "is lifted up as if going to mark the forehead with its toe with a *tilaka*-mark... (for it then resembles the tail of a scorpion)" (R). Char. of Śiva in the *lalāṭatilaka*-dance.
Lit.: R 2:265; Th. 90; WM 95 fig. 9.
2. (Attr.) N. of a garland composed of scorpions, emblematic of poison. Char. of Śiva Viṣapraharaṇamūrti. *v.* is also n. of a *rāśi* ("Scorpio").
Lit.: BBh. 383; GH 50; IC 2:731; R 2:358, 377.

Vṛṣṇācana(!)-Lokeśvara (Buddh.), n. of a variety of Avalokiteśvara. Char.: att.: *lalitāsana*; Vāh.: *padma*; Mu.: *abhaya-*, *varada-mudrā*; attr.: *dhanus*, *nīlotpala*, *pustaka*, *śara*.
Lit.: BBh. 397 a.pl. 26(A).

vṛṣotsarga "the letting loose of a bull", n. of a kind of offering.
Lit.: IC 1:362; MW 1012.

Vṛtra (lit.: "obstruction"; personification), in Vedic religion n. of a dragon (*ahi*) which created drought and was killed by Indra.
Lit.: D 369; DHP passim; GoRI 1:55; Gt 735; WHW 1:92; WM 197.

vṛttakuṇḍala (or *vritta-*) "round, circular earring" (attr.), n. of a *kuṇḍala* of a ring-like form. Char. of Kaṇṇappanāyaṉār.
Lit.: AIP 73 a.pl. 59 (315).

vyāghra "tiger" (Vāh.), see *śārdūla*.

vyāghracarma(n) or *vyāghrāmbara* "tigerskin" (attr.), see *ajina*.
Lit.: BBh. 127, 155; JMS 44.

Vyāghrapāda ("having tiger-feet"), n. of a *riṣi*, a Brāhman boy-devotee of Śiva. Char.: *añjali-* (*sāñjali-*)*mudrā*; attr.: *akṣamālā*, *aṅkuśa*.
Lit.: CBC 12; HSIT 13 a.pl. 32; JDI 52 a.fig. 14; SSI 52.

Vyāghravaktrā ("tiger-headed"; Buddh.), in Lamaism n. of a *ḍākinī* (tiger-headed) who accompanies Siṅhavaktrā. Colour: red.
Lit.: G 35, 37, 96.

vyāhṛti "utterance, speech". This term refers to groups of three and seven mystical words (names of the seven worlds), respectively: *bhūr*, *bhuvaḥ*, *svar* (= the three great *vyāhṛti*s), and, in addition *mahar*, *janar*, *tapar*, *satya*. These words, esp. the first group of three, are pronounced by the Brāhmans when commencing their daily prayers.
Lit.: D 369; DHP passim; GRI 97; Gt 737; MW 1039; RV 144.

Vyākhyāna-dakṣiṇāmūrti ("representation [of Śiva] explaining"), n. of a manifestation of Śiva as a teacher of *śāstra*s or sciences (see *dakṣiṇāmūrti*). Char.: Vāh.: *padmapīṭha*, Apasmāra; Mu.: *bhūmisparśa-*, *gajahasta-*, *jñāna-*, *varada-*, *vyākhyāna-mudrā*; attr.: *agni*, *ajina* (tigerskin), *akṣamālā*, *kamaṇḍalu*, *kuṇḍala*s, *kūrca*, *nāga*, *nīlotpala*, *padma*, *rudrākṣamālā*, *trinayana*, *udarabandha*, *upavīta*, *vibhūti*, *yajñopavīta* (white).
Lit.: B 465, 470; R 2:274.

vyākhyānamudrā "gesture of explanation, argumentation" (Mu.), n. of a handpose, mostly performed with the right hand. It is similar to the *abhayamudrā* (from which it has probably developed), but the tips of the index-finger and the thumb are pressed together, thus forming a circle, the palm facing outwards towards the spectator, the tips of the fingers upwards. Sometimes this circle may be formed by the thumb and another finger (than the index) and it is sometimes called "the triangular pose" (see SM). In BBh., however, this Mu. is said to be identical with the *dharmacakramudrā*. It is sometimes also named *cinmudrā*, and by this n. it is mentioned as a variety of the *mukulamudrā*; in this case, however, the tips of the fingers point downwards (as in *varadamudrā*). – *v.* is a gesture of explaining or preaching; in the case of the Buddha it represents the exercise of his perfect wisdom and the performance of his vows.

Char. of: Ākāśagarbha, the Buddha, *dakṣiṇāmūrti*s, Karmavajra, Kāśyapa, Kṣitigarbha, Maitreya, Maṇikkavācakar, Pīta-Prajñāpāramitā, Samantabhadra, Siṅhanāda, Tārās (e.g. Sitatārā, Śyāmatārā), Vajradhātu, Viṣṇu, *sādhu*s and *bhakta*s. – Other n.: *bodhyaṅgī-*, *sandarśana-*, *upadeśa-*, *vitarka-mudrā*.

Lit.: B 255 a.pl. 3:3; BBh. 434; H pl. 5:42d; KIM pl. 11 (left hand), 12 (right hand); MH 7; R 1:16 a.pl. 5:15; SM 66; Th. 30; WHW 2:87; WM 98 a.fig. 17; ZM pl. 32.

vyakta "adorned, decorated, manifest" (attr.), n. of an icon which is wholly sculptured and adorned (as opposed to *avyakta*). Cp. *citra*.

Lit.: R 1:18.

vyaktāvyakta ("manifest-and-not-manifest"), n. of an icon which combines the characteristics of an adorned, sculptured form of an idol (*vyakta*) and a form not worked by human agency (as e.g. a *śālagrāma* or a *bāṇaliṅga*; i.e. *avyakta*).

Lit.: R 1:18.

vyālaka "horned lion; Löwenwidder". Such hybrid forms are to be found esp. in Pallava art.

Lit.: AuT 125; H pl. 12:129-132 a.p. 61.

vyālamudrā (mentioned, with a question-mark, in SSI) "snake-handpose" (Mu.). The *v.* is said to be char. of Apasmāra who, with his right hand, points towards a snake seen beside Naṭarāja. It is very probable that *v.* should rather be regarded as another n. of *nāgamudrā*.

Lit.: SSI 79.

vyālayajñopavīta "snake serving as the sacred thread" (attr.). Char. of Gaṇeśa. – Cp. *yajñopavīta* and *nāgayajñopavīta*.

Lit.: B 360.

vyālayakṣa, n. of a human figure with serpent-shaped lower limbs.

Lit.: JMS 80 a.pl. 7.

Vyaṅkaṭeśa, see Veṅkaṭeśa.

Lit.: GH 343.

vyantaradevatās (or *vyantara*s) "deities occupying an intermediate position" (esp. Jain.), n. of some groups of inferior deities, attendants of the principal gods. Though deities of this kind are also found in Hinduism, the term *v.* and the conception arose independently in Jainism. The *v.* are of 8 kinds: *kinnara*, *kimpuruṣa*, *mahoraga*, *gandharva*, *yakṣa*, *rākṣasa*, *bhūta*, *piśāca*.

Lit.: B 335; GJ 231, 235; KiK 276; MW 1028.

Vyāsa (Vedavyāsa; "compiler [of the Vedas]"), originally probably a common n. for authors and compilers, afterwards supposed to be NP of a single person, the mythical compiler or arranger of the Vedas, the epic Mahābhārata, the Purāṇas and Vedānta philosophy. – V. is also regarded as an *avatāra* of Viṣṇu and as a *riṣi* and the leader of a group of *riṣi*s, the *maharṣi*s.

Lit.: B 391; D 370; DHP 165, 185; GH 97; Gt 739; KiH 45 a.pl. 166; R 1:123, 250, 2:566; WHW 2:585; WM 191.

vyatyastarekhādvaya "cross, two crossed lines", a *yantra* which symbolizes "the dominion of power over multiplicity".
Lit.: DHP 353 a.passim (see s.v. cross).

vyūha "manifestation, appearance", n. of a manifestation esp. of Viṣṇu which is not regarded as cultic in the same way as *avatāra*. See also *caturvyūha*.
Lit.: GoRI 2:116, 120; MEIA 15.

Y

yab-yum (Tib. "father-mother"; att.; Buddh.), n. of a posture in which a god and his Śakti are represented in sexual intercourse. This att. may be either an *āsana*- or a *sthānaka*-posture (esp. *ālīḍhāsana*). The attr. *vajraghaṇṭā* (a symbolical representation with the same content, see also *vajrahuṅkāramudrā*) is esp. connected with this att. This form of religious manifestation is above all found in Nepalese and Tibetan Tantric Buddhism. Its esoteric meaning is the union of the male *upāya* ("means; die Methode der Heilsvermittlung") and the female *prajñā* ("knowledge; Erkenntnis", the Śakti, in this case also named *vidyā* or *mudrā*). This way of experiencing the attainment of knowledge is not reserved for the gods only, but may in Vajrayāna esotericism be conferred to any member of the *saṅgha* (see *sādhaka*). – This att. is char. of the Tantric forms of the Buddhist gods, e.g.: Ādibuddha, *bodhisattvas*, *dharmapālas*, *dhyānibuddhas*, Heruka and *herukabuddhas*, Vajradhara, Yamāntaka, *yi-dam*-deities. – A Sanskrit translation of *y.* is *yuga(naddha)*, but this kind of symbolical representation does not (at least not often) occur in Hinduism (cp. here *liṅga* and *yoni*). – Cp. *maithuna*, *dampati*.
Lit.: BBh. 441; G 24; GBB 249; GBM 154; GRI 273; HuET 47; HuGT 6; JSV 74; JT 507; KiSB 46, 70; KiSH 15; KT 139 (with ill.); ZA 195, 230 a.pl. 603, 610f.; ZN pl. 35.

yāga "offering", see *yajña*.
Lit.: R 2:457.

yāgaśālā "offering-hall", an architectural term.
Lit.: ACA 69.

YAḤ, a mystical syllable (*bīja*) which, in the *śānti*-ceremony, refers to the legs.
Lit.: GJ 369.

yajña "sacrifice; oblation, offering". In Vedic religion *y.* was n. of sacrificial worship (as opposed to the *pūjā* in later Hinduism). Later *y.* means "oblation". – Another n.: *yāga*.
Lit.: DHP 67 a.pl. 5; Gt 743; RV 128.

Yajña(mūrti) as a personification of "the sacrifice", NP of a god who is regarded as an *avatāra* of Viṣṇu. He embodies the chief Brāhmanic ritual. Attr.: *ājyapātra*, *cakra*, *darvī*, *dviśiras*, *juhū*, *śaṅkha*, 4 *śṛṅgas*, *sruk*, *sruva*, *tripādaka*, 7 hands. – A Yajña is also mentioned as a *dvārapālaka* of Brahmā; attr.: *daṇḍa*, *kavaca*, *pustaka*, *āgama*, *sruk*. – Another n.: Yajñeśvara.
Lit.: B 390; DHP 76, 165, 183; R 1:123, 248, 2:507; WHW 2:316; WM 192.

Yajñabhadra ("skilful in sacrifice"), n. of a *dvārapālaka* of Brahmā. Attr.: *akṣamālā*, *daṇḍa*, *gadā*.
Lit.: R 2:507.

yajñasūtra "sacred thread" (attr.), see *yajñopavīta*.
Lit.: SSI 10.

Yajñavarāha ("sacrificial boar"), n. of a form of Varāhāvatāra with Varāha together with Lakṣmī (she has the attr. *nilotpala*).
Lit.: R 1:135.

Yajñeśvara (Yajñeśa; "lord of sacrifice"), epithet of Viṣṇu, see Yajñamūrti.
Lit.: R 1:248.

yājñika "belonging to sacrifice", n. of someone who performs the *saṅskāras*.

yajñopavīta (attr.), originally "the investiture with the sacred thread" (see *upanayana*), but the n. refers later to "the sacred thread" itself. This thread is worn by members of the three "twice-born" (*dvija*) castes (see *varṇa*) over the left shoulder and hanging down under the right arm. It usually consists of three cotton strings, which are sometimes worn separately, in such a way that the middle one hangs loosely over the right arm. Thus an unmarried man wears one three-stringed *y.*, but a married man wears a double three-stringed *y.* – Among the Brāhmans, the three strings are said to symbolize the three constituents of the primordial matter: *sattva*, *rajas*, *tamas*, whilst among the Jains, the three strings symbolize the *triratna*. – On icons the *y.* may also consist of a *nāga* (see *nāga-*, *vyāla-yajñopavīta*) and of other materials (see *ajina-*, *kṛṣṇājina-*, *muktā-*, *vastra-yajñopavīta*). – A *y.* may be char. of any idol; cp., e.g., Agni, Bhūmidevī, Brahmacāri-Subrahmaṇya, Pārvatī, Śiva, Viṣṇu. – N.B. Among mortals, only men wear the *y.*, but among the gods, goddesses too may wear the sacred thread. – Other n.: *janeū*, (*janivāra*), *pūṇūl*, *sūtra(ka)*, *yajñasūtra*; cp. also *upavīta*.

Lit.: B 290; GJ 382; Gt Suppl. 57; IC 1:364; JDI 125; MW 840; R 1:22, 2:377; SB 33, 65; WHW 2:500; WM 104.

yakṣa ("ghost; Spukgestalt").

1. (Hind., Buddh.) The *yakṣas* (in mythology born of Kāśyapa and Khasā) were originally regarded as a kind of local deities, genii loci, living in the forests and mountains and being guardian spirits of treasures. They were misshapen dwarfs, esp. characterized by their protuberant bellies (*tundila*). Later they were considered to belong to the retinue of Kubera (who, himself, was originally a *y.*) or Jambhala. In Buddhism 8 *y.* are particularly mentioned: Maṇibhadra, Pūrṇabhadra, Dhanada, Vaiśravaṇa, Kelimālin, Vicitrakuṇḍalin, Mukhendra, Carendra, who are attendants of Kubera (Jambhala). – Common attr.: *jambhīra*, *nakula*, *tundila*. – Another n.: *guhyaka*.

Lit.: B 337; BBh. 238, 380, 441; D 373; DHP 137, 301; DIA pl. 2; G 38, 103; GH 107; GJ 237; GoRI 1:323; H pl. 8; HIS 25, 52 a.pl. 6; IC 1:526; KiH 25 a.pl. 87; KiSB 69, 74; KrA pl. 5; Th. 117; WM 200; ZA pl. 520.

2. (Jain.) N. of a semidivinity (*vyantaradevatā*) who, as a messenger or attendant, stands by the side of a *tīrthaṅkara*, each *tīrthaṅkara* having a particular *y.* Thus the 24 *yakṣas* corresponding to the 24 *tīrthaṅkaras* (according to the *śvetāmbaras*; divergences according to the *digambaras* in brackets) are: 1. Gomukha; 2. Mahāyakṣa; 3. Trimukha; 4. Yakṣeśvara; 5. Tumbura; 6. Kusuma; 7; Mātaṅga (Varanandi); 8. Vijaya (Śyāma); 9. Ajita; 10. Brahmā; 11. Manuja or Īśvara; 12. (Sura-)Kumāra; 13. Ṣaṇmukha; 14. Pātāla; 15. Kinnara; 16. Garuḍa (Kimpuruṣa); 17. Gandharva; 18. Yakṣendra (Kendra); 19. Kubera; 20. Varuṇa; 21. Bhṛkuṭi; 22. Gomedha (Sarvāhna); 23. Dharaṇendra or Pārśvayakṣa; 24. Mātaṅga. – Female counterparts of these *y.* are the *śāsanadevatās*. – Another n.: *upāsaka*.

Lit.: GJ 237; KiDG 80; KiJ 11.

Yakṣendra ("Indra or king of *yakṣas*"; Jain.), n. of a *yakṣa* attending on the 18th *tīrthaṅkara*.

Lit.: GJ 362.

Yakṣeśvara ("lord of *yakṣas*"; Jain.), n. of a *yakṣa* attending on the 4th *tīrthaṅkara*. Symbol: *gaja*.

Lit.: GJ 362 a.pl. 24:4; KiJ 11 a.pl. 27:4.

yakṣī (*yakṣiṇī*).

1. (Hind., Buddh.) N. of the female counterpart of *yakṣa*. The *y.* is a sort of vegetation genius and closely related to the *vṛkṣadevatā*. In Buddhism 8 *y.* are mentioned in the retinue of Vasudhārā

(the Śakti of Kubera or Jambhala): Citrakālī, Dattā, Sudattā, Āryā, Subhadrā, Guptā, Devī, Sarasvatī.
Lit.: AuOW 38; BBh. 238; D 373; DHP 137; DIA pl. 5, 9; G 38, 103; GBB pl. 17; H pl. 8; HAHI 40 a.pl. 23A; HIS 25, 51 a.pl. 3-4; KiH 25 a.pl. 88; KiSB 9, 74; KrA 14, 39; SS pl. 9:47; WM 200; ZA pl. 15, 33a, c.

2. (Jain.) Sometimes n. of the female counterpart of a *yakṣa* (standing by the side of a *tīrthaṅkara*), but this deity is more often named *śāsanadevatā*. – *y.* is here also the n. given to spirits of deceased women, these spirits being dangerous to children.
Lit.: GJ 405; KiDG 80; KiJ 11.

Yakṣī, n. of the wife of Kubera (see further *yakṣī* 1.).
Lit.: D 373.

yāḷi (Tam.) "leogryph, a mythological lion-faced animal" (Vāh.). The *y.* is sometimes char. of Viṣṇu (Vīrarākavar), and also of Kālī or Durgā, but seems in these cases to be confused with the *siṅha*. – The *y.* is often found as a decorative motif on a temple frieze and also on the top of the *kīrttimukha*.
Lit.: BECA 1:265, 270; DiIP 163; MD 2:528; RAAI 274.

YAṀ, a *bījamantra* dedicated to Vāyu and symbolizing the element: air.
Lit.: DHP 343; GH 55.

Yama (the Hindus connect this n. with the root *yam-* and interpret it as "Restrainer, Binder", but its original meaning is "twin", the twin sister of Y. being Yamī), n. of the god of Death.

1. (Hind.) NP of the god and judge of the dead. He is the son of Vivasvān and Saraṇyū, or, according to other myths, of Sūrya and Sañjñā. Wife: Dhūmorṇā (or Yamī who, in fact, is his sister; in some sources Y. and Yamī are regarded as the first human pair and originators of mankind). In later Hinduism Y. is regarded as a *dikpāla* of the southerly direction; his *diggaja* is named Vāmana. He is the god of the month *phālguna*, and his palace is Kālīcī. – Char.: colour: black; Vāh.: a black *mahiṣa* named Ugra, or *siṅhāsana*; Mu.: *abhaya-*, *varada-mudrā*; attr.: esp. *pāśa*, *daṇḍa* (*yamadaṇḍa*), further *akṣamālā*, 2 *dantas* (or horns), *gadā*, *jāla*, *khaḍga*, *kheṭaka*, *phala*, *triśūla*, and a frightful appearance. – Epithets: Daṇḍa, Dharmarāja, Kāla, Vaivasvata. – For *yama* as a symbolic n. of the number "2", see *saṅkhyā*.
Lit.: AI 119; B 525; BBh. 382; D 373; DHP 132 a.pl. 8; GBB 129; Gt 745; IIM 77; JDI 106; GRI 82; KiH 10 a.pl. 14; KiSH 55; MEIA 128; MG 36; R 2:525 a.pl. 153:1; Th. 110; WHW 2:614; WM 201.

2. (Buddh.) N. of a *dharmapāla* or *dikpāla*. Char.: colour: blue, red, white or yellow; Vāh.: *nara* or *mahiṣa* on a *nārī*; Mu.: *añjali-*, *karaṇa-mudrā*; attr.: esp. *(kaṅkāla)daṇḍa*, *pāśa*, further *akṣamālā*, *cakra*, *gadā*, *jāla*, *khaḍga*, *triśūla*, *vṛṣamastaka*; he is often 16-armed. – Varieties: gSaṅ-sgrub (Saṅ-dup), Phyi-sgrub (Chi-dup), Naṅ-sgrub.
Lit.: BBh. 352, 361; G passim; JSV pl. 82; HM 126 a.pl. 7 f.; HRT 48, 54.

yamadaṇḍa "staff of Yama" (attr.), see *daṇḍa*.
Lit.: BBh. 346.

Yamadaṇḍa-Lokeśvara ("L., the staff of Yama"; Buddh.), n. of a variety of Avalokiteśvara. Char.: att.: *lalitāsana*; Vāh.: *padma*; Mu.: *karaṇa(?)-mudrā*; attr.: *kamaṇḍalu*, *khaḍga*, *padma*, *phala*, *vajra*.
Lit.: BBh. 397 a.pl. 33(A).

Yamadūtī ("messenger of Yama"; Buddh.), n. of a Mahāyāna goddess. Char.: colour: blue; att.: *ālīḍhāsana*; Vāh.: *mahiṣa*; attr.: *cāmara*, *kapāla*, *karttṛkā*, *padma*.
Lit.: KiSB 76.

yamaka "twin miracles" of fire and water. There is a representation of the Buddha "accomplissant les miracles jumeaux de l'eau et du feu (*yamaka prātihārya*)".
Lit.: HSIT 8 a.pl. 12.

Yamāntaka ("Destroyer of Yama"; Buddh.), n. of a Lamaist *dharmapāla*, an emanation of Akṣobhya who once put an end to the frantic rage of Yama. He is, esp. in his 9-headed form (as Vajrabhairava), regarded as an *ugra*-representation of Mañjuśrī, who in this form conquered Yama and who may be considered a development of the Hindu Yama. Śakti: Vidyādharā. – Y. is also regarded as a *dikpāla* of the easterly direction. – Char.: colour: black or blue, or white or red; att.: *ālīḍhāsana* and *yab-yum* with the Śakti; Vāh.: he is represented as treading on several beings, sometimes on 8 birds; attr.: as spec. char. of Y. may be mentioned that he has 32 arms and 16 legs; the number of heads varies between 1, 3 (*triśiras*), 6 (*ṣaṇmukha*), and 9 arranged in the form of a pyramid); further attr.: *ajina* (tigerskin), *Akṣobhyabimba* on the crown, *cakra*, *cintāmaṇi*, *daṇḍa* (*sita-daṇḍa*), *dharmapālābharaṇa*, *ghaṇṭā*, *kapāla*, *karttṛkā*, *khaḍga*, *mudgara*, *musala*, *nāgas*, *padma*, *paraśu*, *pāśa* (*tarjanīpāśa*, *vajrapāśa*), *vajra*, *vetālī*, *vṛṣamastaka*. – Varieties: Bhairava, Yamāri, Vajrabhairava, Vajradaṇḍa.

Lit.: BBh. 166, 252; G passim; GBM 80; HM 129 a.pl. 14; HRT 23, 162; HuGT pl. 66; JSV pl. 74; KiDG 60 a.pl. 44f.; KiSB 70; ZA 199 a.pl. 603.

Yamāri ("enemy of Yama"; Buddh.), n. of a Vajrayāna god influenced by the Hindu Kālārimūrti-form of Śiva, but also by Yama, and regarded as a form of Yamāntaka. Char.: colour: red; att.: sometimes *yab-yum* with the Śakti; Vāh.: *mahiṣa* (often on a body); attr.: *ajina*, *daṇḍa*, *gadā* (sometimes with a *vajra* on the top), *kapāla*, *pāśa*, *ṣaṇmudrā*. – Varieties: Kṛṣṇa- and Rakta-Yamāri.

Lit.: B 559; BBh. 166, 168; G 18, 91; KiDG 60; KiSB 70.

Yamī (or Yāmī; "twin", cp. Yama), n. of the twin sister of Yama.

1. (Hind.) Y. is sometimes regarded as the wife of Yama and as one of the *sapta-* or *aṣṭa-mātaras*, in this case symbolizing *paiśunya* ("malignity; Grausamkeit"). She is also identified with the river goddess Yamunā. Char.: att.: *lalitāsana*; attr.: *kapāla*.

Lit.: GRI 83; Gt 748; KiSH 53; MG 60.

2. (Buddh.) N. of a goddess who sometimes attends on Yama (Phyi-sgrub).

Lit.: G 91.

Yamunā (Engl. Jumna), n. of a river, on which the city of Mathurā is situated. As a personification Y. is n. of a river goddess, the daughter of Sūrya and Sañjñā and sister of Yama (in this case identical with Yamī). Char.: colour: blue; Vaḥ.: *kūrma*; attr.: *cāmara*, *kamaṇḍalu*, *nīlotpala*. – Y. together with Gaṅgā is sometimes symbolized by 2 *matsyas*. – Another n.: Kālindī.

Lit.: D 375; IIM 110; KiSH 72; MEIA 203; R 2:530 a.pl. 155:2; ZA 126.

Yānaka-Narasiṁha ("N. having a vehicle"), n. of a form of Narasiṁhāvatāra. Vāh.: Garuḍa or Ādiśeṣa.

Lit.: R 1:154.

yantra "geometrical, 'cabbalistic' diagram" (attr.). A *y.* is made on thin sheet-metal, bark, birch-leaf (cp. Hi. *bhojpatra*), skin or paper, and is often kept as an amulet in a cylinder of gold, silver or bronze (*kavaca*). The various *yantras*, being objects of concentration, "the visual equivalents of the *mantras* or thought-forms" (DHP), may also represent different deities and, when kept in an icon (i.e. placed in it at the *pratiṣṭhā*-ceremony) a *y.* confers magical power upon it (thus esp. in Buddhist icons). There is a close association between *yantras* and Śakti worship. – Among the *yantras* may here be esp. mentioned: *bindu*, *catuṣkoṇa*, *gaṇapatiyantra*, *maṇḍala*, *mukti*, *padma*, *pañcakoṇa*, *ṛjulekhā*, *sarvatobhadra*, *ṣaṭkoṇa*, *smarahara*, *śrīcakra*, *svastika*, *trikoṇa*, *viṣṇuyantra*, *vyatyasta-rekhādvaya*, *yantrarāja*. Cp. also *cakra*. – See further the index.

Lit.: B 489; BPR 67; DHP 295, 350; DiIP 286; GH 57 a.pl. 35; GJ 385; HAHI 12; IC 1:568; KiH 30 a.pl. 117; KiSH 94; R 1:8 a.pl. A, 1:330; SSI 185, 220; Th. 4; ZA 318; ZM 156.

yantrapātra "amulet box" (attr.), see *kavaca* 1.

yantrarāja ("king of *yantras*"), n. of a *yantra* which is built up on the *bīja HRĪṀ*. "The purpose of this *yantra* is to create contacts

with supernatural worlds. With its help, the worshipper can gain all wordly and supranatural powers"
Lit.: DHP 354.

Yaśodā ("conferring fame").
1. (Hind.) NP of the foster-mother of Kṛṣṇa. She was married to Nanda.
Lit.: B pl. 26:1; D 375.
2. (Jain.) NP of the wife of Mahāvīra.
Lit.: GJ 24.

Yaśodā-Kṛṣṇa, n. of a composition of Kṛṣṇa together with his foster-mother Yaśodā. She is sometimes represented holding him as a baby (*bāla*) on her arm.
Lit.: SB 348 a.fig. 315; SIB pl. 41; Th. 67.

Yaśodharā ("preserving glory"; Buddh.), NP of the wife of the Buddha (before he had attained Buddhahood); she is consequently considered to belong to the group *māṇuṣī-buddhaśaktis*. She was the daughter of Daṇḍapāṇi. – Cp. Gopī.
Lit.: G 3; IIM 129; KiSB 11.

yaṣṭi "mast, pole" (Buddh.), in architecture n. of a mast, furnished with umbrellas (*chattra*), on a *stūpa*.
Lit.: BRI 113; CHIIA 30; MEIA 260; RAAI 274.

yathāsukha ("according to ease, comfortably"; att.), n. of an *āsana*-posture, a Yogic att., mentioned, but not described.
Lit.: B 271.

yati "striver", n. of an ascetic, a man who has renounced the world, a holy and wandering mendicant. In Jainism *y.* is another n. for a monk.
Lit.: GJ 341, 350; MW 841.

yātrā (Hi. *jātrā*) "festival train, procession", n. of an open-air performance with stage representations, round-dances, car festivals, processions of idols, etc. The *rāmalīlā* may be counted among this class of festivals. – Cp. *rathayātrā*.
Lit.: GoRI 2:25; IC 1:574; P 369; Sh. 121.

yātu(dhāna) ("receptacle of sorcery"), n. of a kind of evil spirit or demon.
Lit.: D 375; DHP 310; GH 107; IC 1:527; MW 849.

yāvīyāṅga, n. of the girdle of Sūrya, see *avyaṅga*.
Lit.: B 437.

yi-dam(-lha) (Tib.) "tutelar god" (Buddh.), n. of a group of Lamaist tutelary deities, chosen by the worshippers to be their patrons. To this group belong: *dhyāni-buddhas* in the *yab-yum*-att. (these are sometimes known as "crowned Buddhas"), *herukabuddhas*, Hevajra, Jambhala, Kālacakra, Mahāmāya, Samvara, Saṅ-dui. The *yi-dam*-deities are either mild and peaceable or violent and terrible. Char.: att.: *āḷīḍhāsana* and *yab-yum* with the Śakti; Mu.: *vajrahuṅkāra*; attr.: *bodhisattvābharaṇa* (char. of the mild forms) or *dharmapālābharaṇa* (the terrific forms), *ghaṇṭā*, *kapāla*, *vajra*, *vajraghaṇṭā*.
Lit.: G 14, 36, 83; HSIT 19 a.pl. 49; IC 2:591; JT 509.

yoga (properly "the act of yoking, joining; union") "ist die systematische Zusammenfassung der verschiedenen körperlichen und geistigen Übungen zum Zweck der Befreiung der Seele vom Materiellen mit dem Endziel der Gewinnung der Erlösung." (GJ) – *y.* is also n. of a kind of icon which is worshipped by adorers "who desire to attain *yoga* or spiritual self-realisation" (R). The idol may then be represented either in a *yogāsana*- or *yogaśayana*- or *yogasthānaka-mūrti*; see further sub *dhruva*. – In astronomy *y.* is n. of a constellation, corresponding to a *nakṣatra*. There are 27 *y.* (their n. are not listed here, see IC).
Lit.: B 397; GJ 376; IC 2:725, 734; R 1:18, 79; WHW 2:616.

yogācāra "joining-behaviour" (Buddh.), n. of an esoteric doctrine within Vajrayāna Buddhism.
Lit.: G 87.

Yoga-dakṣiṇāmūrti, n. of a representation of Śiva as teacher in *yoga*; see *dakṣiṇāmūrti*. Char.: att.: *svastikāsana*, *utkuṭikāsana*; Mu.: *abhaya-*, *dhyāna-*, *vyākhyāna-mudrā*; attr.: *agni*, *akṣamālā*, *hāra*, *kamaṇḍalu*, *keyūras*, *rudrākṣa*, *triśūla*, *yajñopavīta*, *yogapaṭṭa*.
Lit.: BECA 1: pl. 103b; KISH 21; R 2:284 a.pl. 76-78; SSI 90.

yogadaṇḍa "*yoga* staff" (attr.), n. of a kind of rod or stick, used by ascetics. Char. of Aiyaṉār. – Cp. *daṇḍa*.
Lit.: JDI 114 a.fig. 36.

Yogāmbara ("having a *yoga*-garment"; Buddh.), in Lamaism n. of a variety of Vajradhara, represented naked. Śakti: Digambarā or Jñānaḍākinī. Char.: colour: blue; Mu.: *dharmacakramudrā*; attr.: *abjabhājana, dhanus, nagna, śara, vajra, vajraghaṇṭā*.
Lit.: BBh. 186 a.pl. 133.

yogamudrā (Mu.), see *dhyānamudrā*.
Lit.: B 252; R 1:17.

yogamudrāsana (att.), n. of an *āsana*-posture, probably signifying *yogāsana* (= *padmāsana*) together with *yogamudrā* (= *dhyānamudrā*); cp. *dhyānāsana*.
Lit.: GJ 428.

Yoga-Narasiṁha, n. of a *yoga*-variety of Narasiṁhāvatāra, see Girija-Narasiṁha. Att.: *yogāsana, utkuṭikāsana*.
Lit.: R 1:150; SB 342 a.fig. 283; SSI 26; Th.pl. 14A.

Yoganidrā ("meditation-sleep"), n. of a form of Pārvatī.
Lit.: MW 857; R 1:362.

yogapaṭṭa(ka) (or *paṭṭa*) "cloth or band round the knees encircling the hips" (attr.). This band is intended as a support of the att. during meditation; therefore it is found in some *āsana*-postures, such as *sopāśrayāsana* or *utkuṭikāsana*. Char. of, e.g., Agastya, Narasiṁha. – Other n.: *paryaṅkagranthibandha, vākupaṭṭai*. – Cp. *ardhayogapaṭṭa, paryaṅka*.
Lit.: MW 857; Th. 36 (ill.).

yogāsana ("*yoga*-posture").
1. (Att.) N. of an *āsana*-posture which is described in different ways, either (and most commonly) = *sopāśrayāsana*, or = *padmāsana*. This att. is said to symbolize "transcendence".
Lit.: Gz 101; KIM pl. 18; KiH pl. 153 row 2:3; MH 7; SM 26; Th. 36.
2. (Vāh.) N. of an octagonal *pīṭha*.
Lit.: B 273; R 1:19.

Yogāsana(mūrti)-Viṣṇu.
1. N. of a *yoga*-variety of Viṣṇu seated (cp. Yoga-Narasiṁha). Char.: att.: *yogāsana* = *padmāsana*; Mu.: *yogamudrā* = *dhyānamudrā*; attr.: *cakra, śaṅkha*. – Another n.: Yogeśvara-Viṣṇu.
Lit.: B 405 a.pl. 23:2; R 1:85 a.pl. 14; SSI 55.
2. (Attr.) N. of a little image (*bimba*) on the *kirīṭamukuṭa* of Viṣṇu.
Lit.: B 405.

yogaśayanamūrti, n. of a *yoga*-variety of the reclining Viṣṇu: the body and legs are here held straight. Mu.: *kaṭakamudrā*. Some representations of Anantāśāyana are of this kind.
Lit.: R 1:90 a.pl. 29:2, 31 f.

yogasthānakamūrti, n. of a *yoga*-variety of the standing Viṣṇu. Char.: Mu.: *abhaya-, kaṭi-, varada-mudrā*; attr.: *cakra, śaṅkha*; he is 4-armed.
Lit.: R 1:80 a.pl. 17.

Yogeśvara ("lord of *yoga*"), epithet of Śiva.
Lit.: GoRI 1:258.

Yogeśvara-Viṣṇu, see Yogāsana-Viṣṇu.
Lit.: SSI 55.

Yogeśvarī ("lady of *yoga*"), n. of one of the *sapta-* or *aṣṭa-mātaras*. She symbolizes *kāma*, "desire". Y. is also identified with Rakta-Cāmuṇḍā. Char.: attr.: *ḍamaru, ghaṇṭā, khaḍga, khaṭvāṅga, kheṭaka, śakti, triśūla*.
Lit.: KiSH 53; R 1:380.

yogin (*-ī*), n. of a member of a class of esp. Śaivite monks who practice the meditation exercises (*yoga*) of Patañjali.
Lit.: GH 365.

Yogin ("god of *yoga*"), epithet of Śiva represented practising austerities and, as such, very probably having an origin in the Indus Valley culture.
Lit.: IIM 42.

yoginī ("power-of-realisation"; Hind., Buddh.), n. of a female minor deity or demon (in a group of 8 [or 8 times 8] attendants) in the retinue of Durgā, or of a female adorer. (See esp. MEIA where there is a list of the 64 y.).
Lit.: D 377; DHP 288, 301; IC 1:528; KiSB 59, 107; MEIA 169, 304.

yoni "the female sexual organ, vulva" (attr.), n. of the symbol of the female principle: *yoni*s in the shape of ring-stones, are found in the Indus Valley civilization. Later *y.* is worshipped, esp. by the *śākta*-sect, as a representation of the Śakti, and it is often or perhaps even generally represented in composition with the *liṅga. y.* is further symbolized by a triangle, with the point downwards (see *trikoṇa*; this is perhaps an old symbol; it may be noted that in the old Sumerian script this same sign means both "vulva" and "woman"), and by an *arghā* (or *jalahrī*) which is sometimes made in a form comparable to a *śaṅkha* of the cowry type. The *śaṅkha* may, consequently, sometimes also be regarded as a symbol of *y.* The *bija* of *y.* is *EṀ.* – In Buddhism (Vajrayānism, Lamaism) this term is rarely used, here being replaced by *padma* and *ghaṇṭā*, both of which also symbolize the female principle. – *y.* as a symbol is char. of: Pārvatī, Mahālakṣmī (carried on the head). – Another n.: *arghya.* See also *śakti* 1, *śākta* and *strīpūjā*.

Lit.: B 456, 496; D 377; DHP 223, 230; FES 9; GH 42; HIS 9, 75; HuET 47; MG 169; R 2:58; WHW 2:618; ZA 22 a.pl. A8, 387; ZM 154 a.pl. 34.

yonimudrā (Mu.), n. of a handpose in the *pūjā* of Durgā which includes a reference to the *yoni*: "les doigts sont rapprochés pour circonscrire la figure d'un triangle" (IC). – *y.*, translated as "vulva-posture", is also n. of a certain *paramudrā*.

Lit.: DiIP 69 a.passim; IC 1:569; WHW 2:187.

Yudhiṣṭhira ("firm, steady in battle"), n. of a hero in the epic Mahābhārata, the eldest of the five Pāṇḍava princes. He is regarded as the spiritual son of Dharma. – Epithet: Dharmarāja.

Lit.: D 378; DiIP 257; Gt 754; WHW 2:619; ZA pl. 111; ZM 71 a.pl. 3.

yuga.

1. "Pair, couple", as n. of a loving couple, see *maithuna.* –

2. "Age of the world". There are four *yugas*: Kṛta *y.* (= 1.728.000 years), Tretā *y.* (= 1.296.000 years), Dvāpara *y.* (= 864.000 years) and Kali *y.* (= 432.000 years); these four *y.* (together 4.320.000 years) constitute one *mahāyuga* ("great *y.*"), and 1.000 such *mahāyugas* constitute one *kalpa.* – For *y.* as a symbolic n. of the numbers "4, 12", see *saṅkhyā.* – Cp. *kāla.*

Lit.: D 381; GRI 156; Gt 375, 761; IC 1:550; IIM 24; MKVI 2:192; MW 854; WHW 1:6; WM 199.

yuganaddha ("joined as a pair"), a Sanskrit translation of the Tib. *yab-yum* (cp. also *yuga, maithuna*).

Lit.: BBh. 217.

yugma "pair, couple", see *maithuna.*

yūpa "sacrificial post", n. of a post to which the sacrificial victim is tied. A *y.* may be made of either stone or wood.

Lit.: CHIIA 69; MKVI 2:194; RAAI 274; RV 129; WHW 1:30; 2:621.

Z

Zamī Mātā (Hi., "earth mother"), with the Bhīls n. for Bhūmi.

Lit.: KBh. 280.

zanāna (Pers.-Hi.) "female; women's apartments, harem", see *pardā.*

Lit.: STP 2:162.

zen (Jap.; via Chin. *chan* developed out of Skt *dhyāna* "meditation"), n. of the bestknown Japanese form of Buddhism.

Lit.: GRI 305.

zhārī, see *jhārī.*

INDICES

The indices that follow are meant to facilitate the use of this dictionary as a work of reference. Short explanations or translations are generally given; if a short explanation is not possible, a cross-reference to the appropriate main headword is provided. Terms which are not main headwords, are placed within parentheses.

I. VĀHANAS

1. Vechicles

Index of terms concerning the vehicles or mounts (*vāhanas*) of gods, i.e. living or dead beings on which the gods ride or stand, or by which they are accompanied, in the dictionary referred to as "Vāh.". For the sake of completeness, animals sacred to certain gods, are also included in this index although not properly "vehicles" but rather "attributes", and which in this sense are listed also in other indices.

(Ādiśeṣa), see Ananta
ahi "serpent, dragon"
(Airāvaṇa, -vata), see *gaja*
aja "he-goat, ram"
ajā "she-goat"
ākhu "mouse, rat"
Ananta, NP
Apasmāra, NP, cp. *rākṣasa*
aśva "horse"
aśvatara "mule"
baka "heron"
(*barhin*), see *mayūra*
Bhairava, NP
(*bheka*), see *maṇḍūka*
(*bhujaṅga*), see *nāga*
Brahmā, NP
cakora "Greek partridge"
cakravāka, k. bird
camara "Yak"
cātaka, k. bird
(*chāga*), see *aja*
(*dhenu*), see *gaus*
diggaja "elephant of direction"
droṇakāka "raven"
ekaśṛṅga "unicorn"
(*eli*), see *ākhu*
gaja "elephant"
gajasiṅha "elephant-lion"
gaṇḍabheruṇḍa, k. mythological bird
Gaṇeśa, NP
gardabha "ass"
Garuḍa, NP
Gaurī, NP
gaus "cow"
godh(ik)ā "lizard"
gṛdhra "vulture"
haṅsa "goose"
(*hārin*), see *mṛga*
(*hastin*, *ibha*), see *gaja*
ihāmṛga, k. mythical animal
(*kacchapa*), see *kūrma*
kāka "crow"
Kāma, with wife, on Rāhu, NP
(*kapilā*), see *gaus*
kapota "dove"
karka(ṭa), *karkin* "crab"
(*khaḍga*), see *ekaśṛṅga*
khañjana "wagtail"
(*khara*), see *gardabha*
kokila "Indian cuckoo"
krauñca "curlew"
kṛṣṇamṛga "black antelope"
Kubera, NP
kukkuṭa "cock"
(*kuñjara*), see *gaja*
kūrma "tortoise"
(*maccha*), see *matsya*
madhukara "bee"
(*mahāpreta*), see *mṛtaka*
Maheś(var)a, NP
mahiṣa "buffalo"
makara, k. sea-monster
makarāsana "having a *m*. as seat"
maṇḍūka "frog"
(*mānuṣa*), see *nara*
Māra, NP
mārjāra "cat"
matsya, *matsyayugma* "fish"
mayūra (*mayil*) "peacock"
meṣa "ram"
(*miga*), see *mṛga*
(*mīna*), see *matsya*
(*mora*), see *mayūra*
mṛga "antelope, buck"
mṛtaka "corpse"
(*mūṣaka*, *-ikā*), see *ākhu*
(Muyalakaṉ), see Apasmāra
nāga "snake"
nakula "ichneumon"
(Nandin, NP), see *vṛṣan*
nara "man"
Narasiṅha, NP
nārī "woman"
nīlakaṇṭha "blue-necked heron"
(*ōri*), see *sṛgāla*
(Paravāṇi, NP), see *mayūra*
(*pecaka*), see *ulūka*
(*plavaṅga*), see *vānara*
Prajñā, NP
(*preta*, *pretāsana*), see *mṛtaka*
rākṣasa "demon"
Rati, NP
ṛkṣa "bear"
(*ṛṣabha*), see *vṛṣan*
(*sāmiṣa*), see *matsya*
śarabha, k. fabulous animal
sārasa "crane"
saraṭa "lizard"
śārdūla "tiger"
sārikā "mynah"
(*sarpa*), see *nāga*
sattva (*sattvaparyaṅka*) "animal, creature"
(*śava*), see *mṛtaka*
(*sigāla*), see *sṛgāla*

(*śikhin*), see *mayūra*
siṅha "lion"
Śiva, NP
(*śivā*), see *sṛgāla*
Śiva-Śava, NP
sṛgāla "jackal"
śuka "parrot"
sūkara "boar"
śvan "dog"
śyena "eagle"
timiṅgala, k. sea-monster
ulūka "owl"
(*uraga*), see *nāga*
(*uraṇa*), see *meṣa*
uṣṭra "camel"
vāhana "vechicle"
(*vājin*), see *aśva*
vajrakīṭa "diamond-worm"
Vāmana, NP
vānara "ape"
varāha "boar"
vighna "obstacle"
Vināyaka, NP
Viṣṇu, NP
vṛka "wolf"
vṛṣan (*vṛṣabha*) "bull"
vṛścika "scorpion"
(*vyāghra*), see *śārdūla*
vyālaka "horned lion"
yāḷi "lion-faced animal"

2. Seats

Index of terms concerning seats or thrones (*pīṭhas*) and accessories (in this dictionary often also referred to as "Vāh.).

anantāsana "eternal seat"
ardhacandrāsana "half-moon-seat"
āsana "seat, throne"
(*āvaṭaiyār*), see *pīṭha*
balipīṭha "dispensing seat"
bhadrapīṭha "good seat"
bhadrāsana "good seat"
(*bhāmaṇḍala*), see *prabhāmaṇḍala*
bodhimaṇḍa "seat of enlightenment"
candrapīṭha "moon-seat"
candrāsana "moon as seat"
daṇḍāsana "staff-seat"
gajasiṅhāsana "elephant-lion-throne"
garuḍāsana "Garuḍa-throne"
haṅsasinhāsana "goose-lion-throne"
hayasiṅhāsana "horse-lion-throne"
(*jvālāmālā*), see *prabhāmaṇḍala*
(*kamalāsana*), see *padmapīṭha*
karṇikā, k. foot-stool
kārttikeyāsana "peacock-throne"
kiñjalka "lotus-filament adornment"
kīrttimukha "halo-face"
kumuda, part of a seat
kūrmāsana "tortoise-seat"
lambakūrcāsana "grass-seat"
mahāmbuja, part of a seat
mahāpīṭha "great seat (or throne)"
mahāvajrapīṭha, k. seat
mahāvedi "great altar"
makarāsana "*makara*-seat"
makaratoraṇa, k. portal
mṛgasiṅhāsana "antelope-lion-throne"
muraja "drum"
nāla "tube"
navaratha "having 9 chariots"
pādapīṭha "foot-stool"
padma "lotus"
padmacandrāsana "moon on *padma* as seat"
padmapīṭha (*padmāsana*) "lotus throne"
padmasiṅhāsana "lotus-lion-throne"
pallaṅka "throne, seat"
pañcaratha "pedestal in 3 tiers"
(*paryaṅka*), see *pallaṅka*
paṭṭi, part of the seat
piṇḍikā, k. pedestal
pīṭha, *-ikā* "pedestal, seat, throne"
(*pīṭhapadma*), see *padmapīṭha*
prabhā(maṇḍala) "circle of rays"
prabhātoraṇa "arch of rays"
prabhāvali "halo"
puṇḍarīka "white lotus"
rājāsana "royal seat"
ratha "chariot"
śaṅkha "conch"
śaṅkhasiṅhāsana "conch-lion-throne"
śrīkāmyapīṭha, k. seat
(*siṅhamukha*), see *kīrttimukha*
siṅhāsana "lion-throne"
śrīkāmyapīṭha, k. seat
śrīkarapīṭha, k. seat
sūryāsana "sun as seat"
(*tiruvaṭci*), see *prabhāmaṇḍala*
triratha "having 3 chariots"
vajrapīṭha "*vajra*-seat"
vajrāsana "diamond throne"
vedī "sacrificial altar"
vedikāsana "railing-seat"
vikarapīṭha, k. seat
vimalāsana "pure seat"
vimāna "chariot"
(*viśvapadma*), see *mahāmbuja*
vṛṣāsana "bull-throne"
yogāsana, an octogonal seat

II. ATTITUDES

Index of terms concerning the poses of the body or the legs (*aṅgikas*, see also s.v. *āsanamūrti*; referred to in this dictionary as "att.").

ābhaṅga "bend"
adharottara "upside down"
ālīḍha-cum-*dvibhaṅga*, k. att.
ālīḍhāsana (*ālīḍhapada*), k. standing att.
(*aṅgabhāva*), see *aṅgika*
aṅgahāra "gesticulation"
aṅgika "bodily position"
ardhaparyaṅkāsana "half-*paryaṅkāsana*"
ardhasamasthānaka "half-straight standing att."
ardhayogāsana "half-*yogāsana*"
(*asamapāda*), see *ardhasamasthānaka*
āsana(mūrti) "sitting att."

III. MUDRĀS

Index of terms concerning the poses of arms, hands and fingers referred to in this dictionary by the abbreviation "Mu."; the word *-mudrā* may be found as a terminal element with almost any of the words listed here.

āvāhana "invocation"
āvartana "turning round"
bhramara "bee"
bhūmisparśa "earth touching"
bhūtaḍāmara, a frightening Mu.
(*bodhaśrī*), see *vajra*
(*bodhyaṅgī*), see *vyākhāna*
buddhapātra "handpose of the Buddha's bowl"
buddhaśramaṇa, k. salutation Mu.
candrakāla "moon-time"
capeṭahasta "slap hand"
catura "quick"
cellukhepa "waving a cloth"
choṭikā, k. Mu.
cin "reflection"
ḍamaruhasta "drum-hand"
(*dāna*), see *varada*
(*daṇḍahasta*), see *gajahasta*
dharmacakra(pravartana) "setting in motion the Law wheel"
dhenu "cow"
dhyāna "meditation"
gajahasta (*dolahasta*) "elephant arm"
haṅsa "swan"
hasta "hand-, arm-pose"
hastasvastika "hand-cross"
(*iṣṭa*, *-pradā*), see *varada*
jñāna "knowledge"
kapittha "wood-apple"
(*karaṇaḍamaru*), see *ḍamaruhasta*
karaṇahasta "skilful hand"
(*karihasta*), see *gajahasta*
kartarīmukhahasta "scissor-mouth-hand"
kaśyapa "tortoise"
kaṭakahasta "ring-hand"
kaṭi(saṅsthita)hasta (*kaṭyavalambitahasta*) "hand resting on the loin"
kāyotsarga, k. Mu. and att.
kīlaka "wedge"
kṛtāñjali "with joined hands"
kṣepaṇahasta "sprinkling hand"
kūrma "tortoise"
lalita "charming"
laṅgūla "tail"
līlayāsthita, k. Mu.
liṅga, k. Mu.
lolahasta "moving hand"
mahā "great"
mayūra "peacock"
mudrā (*muddā*, *mudrikā*) "pose of fingers or hands"
mukula "bud"
muṣṭi "fist"
(*muttirai*), see *mudrā*
nāga "snake"
namaskāra "adoration"
netra "eye"
nidrātahasta "sleeping hand"
nṛtyahasta (*nṛtyābhinaya*) "dance-hand"
padma "lotus"
(*padmāsana*), see *dhyāna*
pañcamudrā "5 gestures"
pāṇigrahaṇa "hand-taking"
pāpakṣepaṇābhinayin "removing sins"
(*pāśatarjanī*), see *tarjanīpāśa*
patākāhasta "flag-hand"
(*praṇām*), see *añjali*
(*prasāda*), see *varada*
prasāritahasta, k. Mu.
pravartitahasta "uplifted arm"
puṣpapuṭa "flower-basket"
ratnasamyuktavarada, k. Mu.
(*samādhi*), see *dhyāna*
sampuṭāñjali "bowl-like *añjali*"
samyukta or *samyutahasta* "joined hands"
sandaṅśa "biting"
(*sandarśana*), see *vyākhyāna*
(*saṅhatala*, *sāñjali*), see *añjali*
(*śāntida*), see *abhaya*
(*sarpakara*), see *kaṭakahasta*
(*sarvarājendra*), see *añjali*
(*sarvaratnavarṣin*), see *ratnasamyuktavarada*
(*satarjanīpāśa*), see *tarjanīpāśa*
saurapadma "sun-lotus"
śikhara "peak"
(*siṅhakarṇa*), see *kaṭakahasta*
siṅhamukha "lion-face"
sthāpana "staying"
sūcihasta "needle-hand"
śukatuṇḍa "parrot-beak"
surabhi "cow"
svakucagraha "touching one's own breast"
svastika "cross"
tāmracūḍā "red-crest"
taraṅgābhinayin, k. Mu.
tarjanī "forefinger"
tarjanīpāśa "forefinger and *pāśa*"
tarpaṇa "libation"
trailokyavijaya, see s.v.
tripatākāhasta "3-flag-hand"
tripāṭakahasta, see s.v.
udbhava "creation"
(*upadeśa*), see *vyākhyāna*
ūrdhvabāhu "lifted arm"
(*ūrusaṅsthita*), see *kaṭihasta*
utpala "night-lotus"
uttarabodhi "the best perfection"
vaināyakī, see s.v.
vajra, see s.v.
(*vajra-añjalikarma*), see *añjali*
vajrahuṅkāra, see s.v.
vajrapatākā, see s.v.
vajrasphoṭa, see s.v.
vajratarjanī "*vajra* and forefinger"
vandana, *-ī* "adoration"
varada (*varaprada*) "granting wishes"
(*vīciyakaram*), see *gajahasta*
vidyā "knowledge"
vismaya "astonishment"
vismaya-vitarka "astonishment and reflection"
(*viśvābhaya*), see *abhaya*
(*vitarka*), see *vyākhyāna*
vyākhyāna "explanation"
vyāla "snake"
(*yoga*), see *dhyāna*
yoni, see s.v.

IV. ATTRIBUTES

1. Index of terms concerning attributes, with reference to limbs or parts of the body, including abnormal or unnatural forms of these parts.

abhinīla "intensely blue"
ajamastaka "goat-headed"
amastaka "headless"
anuvyañjana "secondary mark"
aṣṭavadana "8-faced"
aśvakeśara "having horse-mane"
asvamastaka (*-mukha*) "horse-headed"
brahmamukha "the head of Brahmā"

(*bṛhatkukṣi*), see *tundila*
caturbhuja "4-armed"
caturmukha "4-headed"
(*chāgavaktra*, *-mukha*), see *ajamastaka*
danta (*daṅṣṭra*) "tooth"
daśabhuja "10-armed"
dvimukha (*dviśiras*) "2-headed"
ekanayana "one-eyed"
ekaviṣāṇa "having only one tusk"
gajamukha (*-mastaka*) "elephant-headed"
gṛdhramastaka "vulture-headed"
jihvā "tongue"
(*jñānanetra*), see *trinayana*
kamalanayana "lotus-eyed"
(*kambugrīva*), see *trivali*
kaṅkālī "having a skeleton body"
(*karivaktra*), see *gajamukha*
kumārīlakṣaṇa "marks of a virgin"
lakṣaṇa "mark"
(*lambodara*) see *tundila*
latāmadhya "creeper-waisted"
mahāpuruṣalakṣaṇa "mark of a great man"
(*mūrdhnyuṣṇiṣa*), see *uṣṇiṣa*
naramukha (*-mastaka*) "having a human head"
nimīlita "closed"
pañcaśiras (*-mukha*, *-mūrdhan*) "5-headed"
rākṣasamuṇḍa (*-mukha*, *-mastaka*) "demon-head(ed)"
sahasranayana "1000-eyed"
ṣaṇmukha "6-headed"
saptaphana "7-hooded'
sarpamastaka "snake-headed"
siṅhamukha (*-mastaka*) "lion-headed"
sṛkvan (*srikvā*) "corner of the mouth"
stana "female brest"
(*trilocana*), see *trinayana*
(*trimukha*, *-mūrdhan*), see *triśiras*
trinayana "3-eyed"
tripādaka "3-footed"
triśiras (*-śirṣan*) "3-headed"
trivali "3 folds"
tuṇḍa(ka) "trunk"
tundila "pot-bellied"
(*upalakṣaṇa*), see *anuvyañjana*
ūrdhvaliṅga (*-medhra*) "erect *liṅga*"
uṣṇiṣa "excrescense on the head"
valampuri "mode of holding the trunk"
varāhamukha (*-mastaka*) "boar-headed"
vikṛta "disfigured"
vṛṣamastaka "bull-headed"

2. Index of terms concerning attributes carried in one hand or in the hands of an idol, or, if not held in a hand, placed near the idol.

(*ābhoga*), see *chattra*
abjabhājana "lotus bowl"
ācamanī "spoon"
(*ādarśa*), see *darpaṇa*
(*adhijyakārmuka*), see *dhanus*
Ādibuddha, image
(*āgama*), see *pustaka*
agni "fire, flames"
ajina "skin"
ājyapātra (*-sthalī*), see *ājyapātra*
akṣamālā (*-sūtra*) "rosary"
āmalaka, k. fruit
āmra "mango fruit"
amṛta (*-ghaṭa*, *-kalaśa*) "nectar"
āñjanī "box with collyrium"
aṅkuśa "hook, ankus"
araṇi "piece of wood for generating fire"
ārātrika, k. lamp
ardhacakrakṛpāṇa "scimitar"
arghā "chalice"
(*arghya*), see *yoni*
(*arin*), see *cakra*
arka, k. flower
aruvāḷ "chopper"
(*aśani*), see *vajra*
(*asi*), see *khaḍga*
aśoka, k. flower
(*asṛkkapāla*), see *kapāla*
asthi "bone"
(*astra*), see *āyudha*
aśva "horse"
(*ātapatra*), see *chattra*
(*aṭṭa[ka]*), see *stūpa*
āyaḥśūla "iron lance"
āyudha "weapon"
(*bāhuvalaya*), see *valaya*
bāla "child"
bāṇa "short stick", see *śara*
(*bāṇāsana*), see *dhanus*
(*bandhana*), see *pāśa*
(*bhadraghaṭa*, *bhājana*), see *kamaṇḍalu*
bherī, k. drum
bhikṣāpātra "alms-bowl"
bhindipāla "javelin"
(*bhramara*), see *madhukara*
(*bhṛṅgāra*), see *kamaṇḍalu*
(*bhujaṅga*), see *nāga*
bimba "image"
(*bīn*), see *viṇā*
bodhivṛkṣa "tree of wisdom"
brahmakapāla "head of Brahmā"
brahmāṇḍa "Brahmā-egg"
(*brahmaśiras*), see *brahmakapāla*
(*caitya*), see *stūpa*
cakra "wheel"
cakradaṇḍa "wheel-staff"
cāmara "fly-whisk"
caṇḍa, k. grass
candra(maṇḍala, *-bimba*) "moon(-disk)"
(*cāpa*), see *dhanus*
(*carma[n]*), see either *ajina* or *kheṭaka*
caṣaka "wine-glass"
(*caurī*), see *cāmara*
ceṇṭu (*cavukku*, *ceṅkōl*) "horse-whip"
cetukki "hoe"
chattra "parasol"
(*chattrikā*), see *śalākā*
churi, *-ikā* "knife"
cihna "sign"
cintāmaṇi "pearl, jewel"
cintāmaṇidhvaja "banner with a pearl"
cuṭar "flames (on the *cakra*)"
dāḍima(phala) "pomegranate-fruit"
ḍamaru, k. drum
daṇḍa "staff"
danta "tusk, tooth"
(*dappaṇā*), see *darpaṇa*
dara "rattle"
darpaṇa "mirror"
darvī "ladle"
(*daśabhūmika*), see *pustaka*
ḍhakkā "drum"
dhanus (*dhanvan*) "bow"
(*dharmagañja*), see *pustaka*
(*dharmaśaṅkha*), see *śaṅkha*
dhavalaśaṅkha "white shell"
ḍholaka, k. drum
(*dhruvā*), see *sruk*
dhūmaketu "smoke banner"

vajrapāśa "noose with a *vajra*"
(*vajrāśani*), see *vajra*
vajraśṛṅkhalā (*-sphoṭa*) "chain with a *vajra*"
vajratarjanī "*vajra* with *tarjanī*-Mu."
vajratriśūla "trident with a *vajra*"
(*vakradaṇḍa, -āyudha*), see *ceṇṭu*
(*valamuri*), see *śaṅkha*
(*vālavyajana*), see *cāmara*
(*vāṇa*), see *śara*
vanamālā "forest-garland"
(*vaṅśa*), see *veṇu*
vātapuṭa "empty fold"
(*veda*), see *pustaka*
(*vēl*), see *śakti*
veṇu "flute"
vidyullatā "creeper-like lightning"
vikasitapadma "full-blown lotus"
vīṇā "lute"
viṣa "poison"
viśvavajra, k. *vajra*
viśvavajrāṅkapatākā, k. banner
(*vyāghracarma[n]*, *-āmbara*), see *ajina*
(*yamadaṇḍa*), see *daṇḍa*
yogadaṇḍa "*yoga*-staff"
yoni "vulva-image"

3. Index of terms concerning attributes worn on the body or concerning dress, colours, ornaments.

Ādibuddha-bimba "image of Ā."
(*ahi*), see *nāga*
ahyaṅga, k. band
ajina "skin"
ajinayajñopavīta "*yajñopavīta* of deer skin"
akṣamālā "rosary"
Akṣobhya-bimba "image of A."
alakacūḍaka "crest of curls"
Amitābha-bimba "image of A."
Amitāyur-bimba "image of A."
Amoghasiddhi-bimba "image of A."
aṅgada, k. ornamental band
aṅgulīya "finger-ring"
aṅgulīyamudrā "finger-ring-seal"
añjana "black; collyrium"
antarīya "lower garment"
antarvāsaka "lower garment"
ardhacandra "half-moon"
ardhayogapaṭṭa "half *yogapaṭṭa*"
ardhoraka "shorts"
arka, k. flower
arkapuṣpa "ray-flower", k. jewel
aśoka, k. flower
avataṅsa, k. ear-ornament
avyaṅga, k. girdle
(*bāhuvalaya*), see *valaya*
bajibandha "arm-ornament"
bandha "binding (of head-dress)"
bhāra "head-dress"
(*bhasman*), see *vibhūti*
bhramaraka "ringlet of hair"
bhriṅgipāda, see s.v.
bhujaṅgavalaya "armlet"
bhujasūtra "armlet-string"
bimba "image"
bodhisattvābharaṇa "princely ornaments"
Buddha-bimba "image of B."
caddar "sheet"
campa, k. flower
caṇḍātaka "drawers"
candra(maṇḍala, -bimba) "moon-disk"
candraprabhāmaṇḍala "halo of the moon"
(*cāri*), see *sārī*
(*carma[n]*, *carmāmbara*), see *ajina*
caṭulātilakamaṇi "forehead jewel"
(*caturmudrā*), see *ṣaṇmudrā*
channavīra, k. ornament
cihna "mark, sign"
cintāmaṇi "pearl"
cīra(ka, -traya) "strip"
citravastra "embroidered clothes"
citrayajñopavīta, k. sacred thread
cīvara "monk's dress"
cūḍā "lock, tuft"
cūḍāmaṇi (*cūlā-*) "lock-jewel"
dhammilla, k. head-dress
dharmapālābharaṇa "royal ornaments"
dhattūra "the flower Datura alba"
dhotī "waist-cloth"
dhūmra "grey"
dhyānibuddha-bimba "image of a *dh.*"
digambara "naked", cp. *nagna*
dukūla, k. cloth
ekāvalī "string of pearls"
ekaveṇī "single braid of hair"
(*gajacarma[n]*), see *ajina*
ghaṇṭāmālā "garland of bells"
(*gonasa*), see *nāga*
gopīcandana, k. white clay
graiveyaka "necklace"
guñjamālā, k. garland
haima "golden"
hāra "garland of pearls"
harita "green"
hastisaundika, see s.v.
hemavaddha "golden strap"
(*indu*), see *candra*
jālāṅguli "net-finger"
(*janeū*, *janivāra*), see *yajñopavīta*
(*jaṅghikā*), see *dhotī*
jaṭā "knot of hair"
jaṭābandha (*-bhāra*, *-mukuṭa*, *-valaya*), k. head-dress
juli "bag for *vibhūti*"
jūrī, k. necklace
jvalitaśikhā "flaming hair"
kaccha "hem of a garment"
kācchā 'shorts'
(*kaccu*), see *kucabandha*
(*kajjala*), see *añjana*
kākapakṣa "crow's wing"
kalpakalatā, k. flower
(*kamala*), see *padma*
kamaṇḍalu "water-jar"
(*kañcakam*), see *kucabandha*
kāñcidāma(n), k. girdle
kaṅghā "comb"
kaṅkana "wrist ornament"
kaṇṭhī, *-ikā* "necklace"
(*kapālamālā*), see *muṇḍamāla*
kaparda, k. head-dress
kapila "reddish yellow"
kāppu, k. bandage
karā "bangle"
karaṇḍamukuṭa, k. head-dress
(*karaṅkamālā*), see *muṇḍamālā*
(*karṇapatra*), see *pattrakuṇḍala*
karṇaveṣṭana "ear-ornament"
karṇika "ear-rings"
karṇikāra, k. flower
kāṣāya, k. garment
kaṭibandha (*-sūtra*) "waist-band"
kaṭisūtragranthi "knot on the waist-band"
kaupīna "loin-cloth"
kavaca "amulet(-box)"
(*kāyabandha*), see *kaṭibandha*
keś, *keśa(ra)* "mane"
keśabandha, k. head-dress
keśabhāra, k. head-dress
keśamaṇḍala, k. head-dress

4. Index of terms concerning objects of worship, types of icons, sacred stones.

5. Index of terms concerning cult-accessories.

6. Index of terms concerning trees and plants, sacred to certain deities or used in worship.

bodhivṛkṣa (*-druma, -rukkha, -taru, bo*-tree) "tree of enlightenment"
campa, k. flower
campakavṛkṣa, k. tree
caṇḍa, k. grass
candana "sandal"
dāḍima(phala) "pomegranate(fruit)"
darbha, k. grass
(*dātura*), see *dhattūra*
(*dhānyamañjarī*), see *kaṇiśa*
(*dhātrī*), see *āmalaka*
dhattūra (*dhatūra, dhurdhura, durdhura*) "the flower Datura alba"
(*duminda*), see *bodhivṛkṣa*
dūrvā "panic seed"
(*gūlar*), see *udumbara*
haricandana, paradise-tree
ikṣukāṇḍa "sugar-cane"
jambhīra "citron"
jambu "rose-apple tree"
javā (*japā*) "China rose"
kadala (*-īphala*) "banana"
kadamba, k. tree
(*kairava*), see *puṇḍarīka*
kalhāra "white water-lily"
kalpadruma "wishing-tree"
kalpakalatā "flowers from a k. tree"
kalpalatā "wishing-creeper"
kalpavṛkṣa "wishing-tree"
(*kamala*), see *padma*
kaṇiśa "ear of rice"
kapittha "wood-apple"
(*kapparukkha*), see *kalpavṛkṣa*
karañja, k. tree
ketaka, k. tree
kiṅśuka, k. tree
(*kumuda*), see *puṇḍarīka* or *padma*
kunda "Jasminus pubescens"
kuśa, k. grass
latā "creeper"
mahāmbuja "great lotus"
mandāra "coral-tree"
(*mātuluṅga*), see *jambhīra*
mūlaka(kanda) "radish"
muñja, k. grass
nāgakesara "snake-hair"
nāgapuṣpa, k. tree
nameru, k. tree
nārikela (*-kera, nālikera*) "cocoanut"
nīlotpala (*nīlābja, nīlanalina*) "blue lotus"
nīm (*nimba*) "Melia azadirachta"
(*nyagrodha*), see *vaṭa*
padma "lotus"
(*palāśa*), see *kiṅśuka*
panasa "bread-fruit tree"
pañcavaṭī "5 fig-trees"
(*paṅkaja*), see *padma*
pāṭali "trumpet-flower tree"
(*pippala, pīpal*), see *aśvattha*
priyaṅgukusumamañjarī, k. flower
puṇḍarīka "white lotus"
(*puṣkara, rājīva*), see *nīlotpala*
(*rakta-padma, -paṅkaja*), see *padma*
(*rukkha*), see *vṛkṣa*
śāla, k. tree
śamī, k. tree
(*saroja*), see *padma*
śiriṣavṛkṣa, k. tree
(*sitāmbuja*), see *puṇḍarīka*
śrīphala "wood-apple"
sthalavṛkṣa "place-tree"
(*śvetāmbhoruha, śvetapaṅkaja*), see *puṇḍarīka*
tila "Sesamum Indicum"
tul(a)sī "holy basil"
uḍumbara "wild fig-tree"
uśīra "root of Vetiveria zizanioides"
(*utpala*), see *nīlotpala*
(*vanaspati*), see *vṛkṣa*
vaṭa(vṛkṣa) "Banyan-tree"
vikasitapadma "full-blown lotus"
(*viṣapuṣpa*), see *nīlotpala*
(*viśvapadma*), see *mahāmbuja*
vṛkṣa "tree"

7. Index of terms concerning syllabic and geometrical symbols, *maṇḍala*s, *mantra*s, *yantra*s (syllabic and other *mantra*s are given without explanation).

A
ādyabīja
agniprajvālana
agnistambhana
AIṀ
(*akṣara*), see *bīja*
AṀ
aṅkuśabīja, a *bīja*
ardhacandra "half-moon"
aṣṭākṣara "8-syllabic"
astramantra
(*AUṀ*), see *OṀ*
bālāyantra "girl-*yantra*"
BHRŪṀ
(*bhūr, bhuvaḥ, svar*), see *vyāhṛti*
bīja "seed", syllabic *mantra*
bījākṣara "seed-syllable"
bījamaṇḍala "seed-circle"
bījamantra "seed-*mantra*"
bindu "dot", a *yantra*
BLŪṀ
BOṀ
brahmabīja
brahmagāyatrī
brahmamantra
(*brahmavidyābīja*), see *brahmabīja*
catuṣkoṇa "quadrangle"
dhāraṇī (*-iṇī*), k. *mantra*
DRĀṀ
DUṀ
dvādaśākṣara "12-syllabic"
EṀ
GAṀ, GĀṀ
gaṇapatiyantra, a *yantra*
garbhadhātu, a *maṇḍala*
gau, amulet with a *yantra*
GLAUṀ
granthi "knot, tie", a *yantra*
HAḤ
HAṀ
haṅsamantra "goose-*mantra*"
HAUṀ
HRAḤ
HRĀṀ
HRĪḤ
HRĪṀ (*HRIṀ*), *hrīṁ-kāra*, a *bīja*
HRŪṀ
HUṀ
HŪṀ
HVĀṀ
janmapattra "horoscope"
JĪṀ
(*kālībīja*), see *ādyabīja*
kāmabīja "Seed-of-Lust"
karmamaṇḍala, a *maṇḍala*
kasiṇa, see s.v.
KHA
KHAṀ
khecarībīja
KHRĀṀ
KLĪṀ
KRĪṀ
krodhaśānti

V. OTHER TERMS

1. Index of astronomical and chronological terms. For the symbolic names of numbers, see *saṅkhyā*.

2. Index of architectural and artistic terminology.

3. Index of terms concerning types of deities and supernatural beings.

pañcaparameṣṭhin "5 chief gods"
pañcarakṣā, k. tutelary goddess
pañcavaktra "5 faces"
paramaharṣi "excellent *riṣi*"
parameṣṭhi "chief god"
pāramitā, group of deities
parivāradevatā (*-mūrti*) "deity of the retinue"
pārśvadevatā "side-deity"
pati "lord"
(*patteyabuddha*), see *pratyekabuddha*
pauloma, k. demon
pēy, k. demon
piśāca, k. demon
piśitāśanā "eating carcass"
pitā, *-taras* (*pitṛgaṇa*), "father, manes"
prādurbhāva, k. manifestation
prajāpati, k. demiurge
prajñā, see *Śakti*
pratisamvit, k. personification
prativāsudeva, group of rulers
pratyekabuddha, k. *buddha*
preta, k. ghost
rājarṣi "royal *riṣi*"
rājasika, k. aspect
rākṣasa (*-sī*), k. demon
ratnakula, group of deities
(*raudra*), see *ugra* and *ghora*
raudra-cum-*saumya*, k. aspect
ṛbhu, group of deities
riṣi (*ṛṣi*) "sage"
riṣipatnī "wife of a *riṣi*"
(*sādhu*), see *tīrthaṅkara*
sādhya, k. semi-divine being
śākini, k. witch
śakti "Śakti, wife of a deity"
samyaksambuddha, k. *buddha*
saṅhāra(mūrti) "terrific aspect"
śānta(mūrti) "peaceful representation"
saptamātaras "7 mothers"
saptarṣi "7 *riṣis*"
śāsanadevatā, k. attendant goddess
(*sataravaram deviyo*), see *dikpāla*
śatruvidhvaṅsinī "destroying enemies"
saumya "gracious aspect"
siddha, k. deity
śivadūta, k. attendant deity
śrāvaka(buddha), k. *buddha*
śrutarṣi "tradition-*riṣi*"
stanitakumāra, k. deity
sthalīdevatā "local deity"
suparṇakumāra "eagle-prince"
sura, k. god
(*svābhā*, *svābhā-prajñā*, *-vidyā*), see *śakti*
(*svayambuddha*), see *tīrthaṅkara*
(*sveṣṭadevatā*), see *iṣṭadevatā*
tāmas(ik)a, k. aspect
tathāgata, k. *buddha*
tathāgati, k. female *buddha*
tīrthaṅkara, k. saviour
trāyastriṅśa "the 33 (gods)"
tridaśa "the 30 (gods)"
(*triṣveṣṭadevatā*), see *iṣṭadevatā*
udadhikumāra "ocean-prince"
ugra(mūrti), k. cruel aspect
upanāyikā, k. deity
upāsaka, k. attendant of gods
uṣṇīṣa, k. deity
vaimānika, k. deity
vānara "monkey (as god)"
vaśitā, group of deities
vasu, group of deities
vāyukumāra "wind-prince"
vetāla, k. demon
vetālī, female *vetāla*
(*vibhava*), see *avatāra*
vibhūti, group of attendants
vidyādevī, k. deity
vidyādhara, k. deity
(*vidyārāja*), see *dharmapāla*
vidyārājñī, k. deity
vidyeśvara, k. deity
vidyeśvara, k. deity
vidyutkumāra "lightening-prince"
vighna "obstacle" (personification)
viśva, *viśvedeva* "all-gods"
vṛkṣadevatā (*vṛkṣakā*) "tree deity"
vyālayakṣa "snake-*yakṣa*"
vyantaradevatā, k. inferior deity
vyūha "manifestation"
yakṣa, k. semi-deity
yakṣī, *yakṣiṇī*, female *yakṣa*
yātu(dhāna), k. demon
yi-dam, k. tutelary deity
yoginī, k. female deity

4. Index of terms concerning types of human beings, religious officials, sectaries.

ācārya "teacher"
adhvaryu "officiating priest"
ādivāsi "primitive"
ājīvika, k. sect
(*āḻvār*), see *bhakta*
anāgāmin "not returning"
(*aṅga*), see *bhakta*
arhat (*arahant*) "venerable"
āryasamāj, a society
aspṛśya "untouchable"
āyaḥśūlika "wearing an *āyaḥśūla*"
bairāgi, k. sect
bandya, k. priest
bauddha "Buddha-worshipper"
bhāgavata, k. Kṛṣṇa-worshipper
bhakta "devotee"
bhikṣu (*bhikkhu*) "mendicant monk"
bhikṣuṇī (*bhikkhunī*) "nun"
(*bla-ma*), see *lama*
brāhma, k. sect
brahmacārin, Brāhman student
brāhmaṇa "Brāhman"
brāhmasamāj, k. sect
candravaṅśa "the lunar race"
Dalai Lama
dampati "husband and wife"
dānavīra "donator"
daṇḍin (*-ī*) "carrying a stick"
daryā sevak "river-worshipper"
dehravāsī, k. sect
devadāsī "slave-girl of a god"
devalaka "attendant of an image"
digambara, Jain sectary
ekadaṇḍin (*-ī*) "carrying a single stick"
gaṇadhara "porte-groupes"
gāṇapatya "worshipper of Gaṇeśa"
gehapati "house-lord"
dGe-lugs-pa "the Yellow Hats"
gopī "cowherdess"
gorajī, k. monk
gorakhnāthī, k. sect
gṛhastha "house-holder"
gṛhyaguru "chaplain"
guru "teacher"
harijan "the people of God"
jaina "Jain"
(*jāti*), see *varṇa*
jyotiṣa "astrologer"
kabīrpanthī, k. sect
bKa'-gdams-pa "giving precepts"
(*kāṇphaṭayogin*), see s.v. Goraknāth
kāpālika, k. Śaivite sect
kaumāra, a sect
(*kevalin*), see *arhat*

kṣatrapa "governor"
kṣatriya "the warrior caste"
bla-ma, *lama* "Lama"
liṅgāyat, k. Śaivite sect
mādhva, k. sect
mādhyamika, k. Buddhist sect
mahānubhava, k. sect
mahātmā "great soul"
maithuna "coupled"
(*manbhau*), see *mahānubhava*
mañjā "diocese"
māntrika (*mantravādin*) "reciter of spells"
(*mithuna*), see *maithuna*
mleccha "barbarian"
muni "saint"
nāstika "denier"
nātha "lord", k. sect
nāyaka "lover"
(*nāyaṉmār*), see *(śaiva)bhakta*
nāyikā "mistress"
nimandi (*nimāvats*), k. sect
rÑiṅ-ma-pa "the old order, the Red Hats"
pañcarātrin "worshipper of Viṣṇu"
paṇḍā, k. priest
paṇṭāram (*paṇḍāram*), k. priest
pariṇāyaka "guide"
parivrājaka "mendicant monk"
pāśupata, k. Śaivite sectary
pāṭhaka "reciter"
paṭṭar, k. priest
pratiṣṭhāguru, k. priest
pūjārī (*pūcāri*) "worshipper, priest"
purohita "family priest"
rāmānandī, k. sect
ṛtvij "sacrificial priest"
sādhaka "worshipper"
sādhu "teacher"
śaivabhakta "worshipper of Śiva"
sakadāgāmin (*sakṛd-*) "not returning more than once"
sakhibhāva, k. sect
śākta, k. sect
śākya "mendicant"
(*samaṇa*), see *śramaṇa*
saṅnyāsin, k. Brāhman
sarvāstivādin, k. Buddhist school
sātāni, k. sect
saura, k. sect
siddha, k. sect
sikh, k. sect
smārta, k. sect
sotāpanna (*srotā-*) "converted"
śramaṇa "monk"
śrīpūjya "venerable"
sthānakavāsin, k. sect
sthavira "an Elder"
strīratna "wife-treasure"
śūdra "the lowest caste"
sūryavaṅśa "solar race"
sūta "charioteer"
svāmin "master"
śvetāmbara "Jain sectary"
ṭhag "robber"
(*thera*), see *sthavira*
theravādin, k. Buddhist sectary
tridaṇḍin "carrying a *tridaṇḍa*"
upādhyāya "teacher"
upāsaka "lay worshipper"
vācaka "reciter"
vaikhānasa, k. sect
vaiṣṇava(bhakta) "worshipper of Viṣṇu"
vaiśya "the third caste"
vānaprastha, k. Brāhman
varṇa "caste"
vibhajyavāda, k. Buddhist doctrine
vijñānamātravāda, k. Buddhist doctrine
vīraśaiva, k. Śaivite sect
viṣakanyā "poison-girl"
viṣṇusvāmin, k. sect
yājñika "belonging to sacrifice"
yati "striver"
yogin, k. Śaivite monk
(*yuga*, *yugma*), see *maithuna*

5. Index of terms concerning religious ceremonies, rites, festivals, dances and other religious conceptions.

abhiṣeka "consecrating, bathing"
ācamana "sipping of water"
adhyayana "commencement of study"
agnihotra "fire-sacrifice
agrapūjā "chief worship"
āhuti "offering of oblations"
ākarṣaṇa "attraction"
akṣatapūjā, k. rite
(*amṛtamanthana*), see *kṣīrodamanthana*
ānanda-tāṇḍava, k. dance
andolakamahotsava, k. festival
aṅganyāsa "touching the limbs"
aṅgapūjā "bathing an icon"
annaprāśana "food-giving"
antyasaṅskāra (*antyeṣṭi*) "the last sacrament"
ārādhana "worship"
arcana(bhoga) "homage"
argha, *arghya* "reception of guests"
ārtā "wedding ceremony"
ārtī, k. ceremony
ārtīpūjā (*āratī-*), k. ceremony
arūpadhātu "seat of non-form"
āśrama "hermitage, stage of religious life"
asuramāyā "magic power of a demon"
aśvamedha "horse-sacrifice"
aupāsana "worship of fire"
āvāhana "invocation"
avakrānti "conception"
āvaraṇapūjā "precinct worship"
āvaśyaka "necessary (duty)"
āveṇikadharma "peculiar property"
āyudhapūjā (*āyutapūcai*) "worship of tools"
bala "force"
bali "offering"
baliharaṇa "presentation of offerings"
bhaktapūjā "worship of a *bhakta*"
bhakti "devotion"
bharatanāṭya, k. dance
bhasmasnāna "ash-bath"
bhāvapūjā, k. worship
bhrātṛdvitīya, k. festival
bhujaṅgatrāsita, k. dance
bhūtabali "offering to demons"
bhūtamātotsava, k. festival
bhūtayajña "offering to all beings"
bodhi "enlightenment, knowledge"
bodhicitta "will to enlightenment"
bon, the original religion of Tibet
brahmadeya, k. gift
brahmayajña "sacrifice to the scripture"
cakrapūjā "worship of *cakra*"
candanapūjā "sandal worship"
caṅkrama "walking about"
carkẖ-pūjā (*carak-*) "wheel worship"
catura(tāṇḍava), k. dance
caturviṅśatijinastuti "praise of the 24 *tīrthaṅkaras*"
(*ceṭil*), see *carkẖ pūjā*
(*cīnācāra*), see *tantra*
cūḍākaraṇa (*-karma*, *caulakarma*) "tonsure"
cūḍopanayana "tonsure and initiation"

prāṇayāma "breath control"
prasavya "turned to the left"
pratikramaṇa "going to confession"
pratiṣṭhā "consecration"
pratyākhyāna "rejection"
prāyaścitta "expiation"
pūjā (*pūcai*) "worship"
puṁsavana(vrata), k. rite
(*purdah*), see *pardā*
puruṣamedha "human sacrifice"
puṣpāñjali "presentation of flowers"
puṣpapūjā "worship with flowers"
rāga "particular musical mode"
rāgiṇī, modification of a *rāga*
rājopacāra "paying of royal honours"
rākhī bandhan (*rakṣā bandhana*), k. festival
rakṣābandhapūrṇimā (*rākhī pūrṇimā*), k. full-moon festival
rāmalīlā "Rāma-play"
rasa "passion"
rasayātrā "passion procession"
raslīlā "folk-dance"
rathayātrā (*rath jattra*, *ratha-mahotsava*) "car procession"
rūpa "form"
rūpabheda "iconography"
rūpadhātu "seat of form"
rūpakāya "form-body"
sādhana, k. ritual handbook
sahagamana "going with"
śaivasiddhānta "Śaivite doctrine"
śākta "Śakti cult"
samādhi "meditation"
samāvartana "the return home"
sāmāyika "equanimity"
sambhogakāya "body of enjoyment"
(*sambodhi*), see *bodhi*
saṁlekhanā, voluntary death
sāmudrika "relating to the bodily marks"
sandhyā "twilight rite"
sandhyātāṇḍava (*-nṛtta*) "twilight dance"
saṅgha "assemblage, the body of monks"
saṅsāra "metempsychosis"
saṅskāra "rite, sacrament"
śānta "mild aspect"
śānti "tranquillity"
śāntikavidhi "rite of pacification"
sarasvatīpūjā "worship of Sarasvatī"
sarpabali "offering to snakes"
sarvāstivāda, k. Buddhist doctrine
ṣaṣṭhisaṅskāra, k. birth-ceremony
(*satī*), see sub Satī
satpherī "7 circumambulations"
satyavāda "truth utterance"
śayanālayapūjā "sleeping-chamber worship"
seṅdūrdān, wedding-rite
siddhacakrapūjā, k. spring festival
siddhi "fulfilment"
(*siḍi*), see *carkh pūjā*
sīmantonnaya "hair-parting"
śivapūjā "worship of Śiva"
śivarātrī "Śiva's night"
skandha "branch, cosmic element"
(*snāna*), see *abhiṣeka*
snānayātrā "bathing-festival"
snapanapūjā "bathing-worship"
śrāddha, k. funeral rite
(*śrībali*), see *bali*
śrutapañcamī, k. festival
sthāpana "fixing"
strīpūjā "woman-worship"
śūlagava "impaled ox", k. offering
śūnya "void"
śūnyatā "zero-ness"
sūryapūjā "sun worship"
sūtra "doctrine"
(*suttee*), see sub Satī
svarga (*svarloka*) "heaven"
tabu "forbidden"
talasaṅsphoṭita, k. dance-form
tālikaṭṭu, wedding-ceremony
tāṇḍava, k. dance
tantra "doctrine"; k. religious works
tapas "heat, penance"
tarpaṇa "libation"
tattva "reality"
tattvārcana "worship of the 'reals'"
theravāda "the speech of the Elders"
(*tīpāvaḷi*), see *dīvālī*
tīrtha "(sacred) bathing place"
tirukalyāṇa "divine marriage"
trailokya "pertaining to the 3 worlds"
trika, k. Buddhist doctrine
trikāya "3 bodies"
tripura "3 cities"
tripurotsava "Tripura-festival"
tulābhāra, k. gift to a temple
udvāsana, part of the *pūjā*
umātāṇḍava, k. dance
upākaraṇa "beginning"
upanayana "initiation"
upāśraya, cult centre
upāya "means"
(*uposatha*), see *poṣadha*
(*ūrdhvatāṇḍava*), see *lalāṭatilaka*
utsava "festival"
uttarīyakanyāsa, k. ceremony
vādya "music"
vaikuṇṭha-ekādaśī, festival
vaiśākhī, festival
vaiśaradya, k. of mental characteristic
vaiṣṇavadharma "Vaiṣṇavite doctrine"
vajrayāna "the magic vehicle"
vāmācāra "left-hand practice"
(*vandana*), see *āvaśyaka*
vārapūjāvidhi "weekly worship"
vasantapañcamī, spring festival
vasantotsava "spring festival"
vastropavīta "dressing (of an idol)"
vaśyavidhi "rite of subduing"
vedanā "sensation"
vidyā "(magical) knowledge"
vijñāna "consciousness"
vināyakacaturthī, festival
vināyakaśānti, rite
viṣṇupūjā "worship of Viṣṇu"
vivāha "marriage"
vrata "solemn vow"
vratavisarga "release from a vow"
vṛṣotsarga "letting loose of a bull"
vyāhṛti "utterance"
(*yāga*), see *yajña*
yajña "sacrifice"
yātrā "procession"
yoga "joining"; k. doctrine
yogācāra "esoteric doctrine"
yuga "age of the world"
(*zanāna*), see *pardā*
zen, Japanese Buddhism

SUPPLEMENT

P. 240: *riṣi*: The proper transliteration of the Skt word is *ṛṣi*, but it is in this dictionary given as *riṣi*, since most of the readers dealing with iconography are used to meet the word in this form or as *rishi* (cp. MW p. 226: *ṛishi*).

This book has been published under the series which is mentioned on the title page of the book. If you want further nformation for the series as well as for the new titles coming under the series. Please return this card. And mention the series you desire.

Series ....

From :

....

....

....

....

Stamp

To,

Sri Satguru Publications
40/5, Shakti Nagar
Delhi-110 007
India